BP 3193

AUTHOR	CLASS
	914.95

TITLE LET'S go: the budget guide to Greece & Turkey, 1993

ooks by Let's Go, Inc.

et's Go: Europe
et's Go: Britain & Ireland
et's Go: France
et's Go: Germany, Austria & Switzerland
et's Go: Greece & Turkey
et's Go: Israel & Egypt
et's Go: Italy
et's Go: London
et's Go: Paris
et's Go: Rome
et's Go: Spain & Portugal

et's Go: USA
et's Go: California & Hawaii
et's Go: Mexico
et's Go: New York City
et's Go: The Pacific Northwest, Western Canada & Alaska
et's Go: Washington, D.C.

LET'S GO:
GREECE & TURKEY

is the best book for anyone traveling on a budget. Here's w

No other guidebook has as many budget listings.

In Istanbul, we found 11 hotels or hostels for under $15 a night
tryside we found hundreds more. We tell you how to get there t
way, whether by bus, plane, or ferry, and where to get an inexp
satisfying meal once you've arrived. There are hundreds of mo
tips for everyone plus lots of information on student discounts.

LET'S GO researchers have to make it on their own.

Our Harvard-Radcliffe researchers travel on budgets as tight a
no expense accounts, no free hotel rooms.

LET'S GO is completely revised every year.

We don't just update the prices, we go back to the places. If a
café has become an overpriced tourist trap, we'll replace the li
new and better one.

No other budget guidebook includes all this:

Coverage of both the cities and the countryside; directions, ad
phone numbers, and hours to get you there and back; in-depth
on culture, history, and the people; listings on transportation b
within regions and cities; tips on work, study, sights, nightlife, a
splurges, city and regional maps; and much, much more.

**LET'S GO is for anyone who wants to see Greece & Turkey
on a budget.**

LET'S GO:

The Budget Guide to

GREECE & TURKEY

1993

Elijah T. Siegler
Editor

Muneer I. Ahmad
Assistant Editor

Written by
Let's Go, Inc.
a wholly owned subsidiary of
Harvard Student Agencies, Inc.

PAN BOOKS
London, Sydney and Auckland

Helping Let's Go

If you have suggestions or corrections, or just want to share your discoveries, drop us a line. We read every piece of correspondence, whether a 10-page letter, a tacky Elvis postcard, or, as in one case, a collage. All suggestions are passed along to our researcher/writers. Please note that mail received after May 5, 1993 will probably be too late for the 1994 book, but will be retained for the following edition. Address mail to:

> *Let's Go: Greece & Turkey*
> Let's Go, Inc.
> 1 Story Street
> Cambridge, MA 02138

In addition to the invaluable travel advice our readers share with us, many are kind enough to offer their services as researchers or editors. Unfortunately, the charter of Let's Go, Inc. and Harvard Student Agencies, Inc. enables us to employ only currently enrolled Harvard students.

05640183

Published in Great Britain 1993 by Pan Books Ltd
Cavaye Place, London SW10 9PG
9 8 7 6 5 4 3 2 1

Published in the United States of America
by St. Martin's Press, Inc.

LET'S GO: GREECE & TURKEY.
Copyright © 1993 by Let's Go, Inc.,
a wholly owned subsidiary of Harvard Student Agencies, Inc.
Maps by David Lindroth, copyright © 1993, 1992, 1991, 1990, 1989, 1986
by St. Martin's Press, Inc.

ISBN: 0 330 32696 1

Let's Go: Greece & Turkey is written by the Publishing Division of
Let's Go, Inc., 1 Story Street, Cambridge, Mass. 02138

Let's Go® is a registered trademark of Let's Go, Inc.

Printed and bound in the United States of America
on recycled paper with biodegradable soy ink.

About Let's Go

A generation ago, Harvard Student Agencies, a three-year-old non-profit corporation dedicated to providing employment to students, was doing a booming business booking charter flights to Europe. One of the extras offered to passengers on these flights was a 20-page mimeographed pamphlet entitled *1960 European Guide,* a collection of tips on continental travel compiled by the HSA staff. The following year, students traveling to Europe researched the first full-fledged edition of *Let's Go: Europe,* a pocket-sized book with tips on budget accommodations, irreverent write-ups of sights, and a decidedly youthful slant.

Throughout the 60s, the series reflected the times: a section of the 1968 *Let's Go: Europe* was entitled "Street Singing in Europe on No Dollars a Day." During the 70s *Let's Go* evolved into a large-scale operation, adding regional European guides and expanding coverage into North Africa and Asia. In the 80s, we launched coverage of the United States, developed our research to include concerns of travelers of all ages, and finetuned the editorial process that continues to this day. The early 90s saw the introduction of *Let's Go* city guides.

1992 has been a big year for us. We are now Let's Go, Incorporated, a wholly owned subsidiary of Harvard Student Agencies. To celebrate this change, we moved from our dungeonesque Harvard Yard basement to an equally dungeonesque third-floor office in Harvard Square, and we purchased a high-tech computer system that allows us to typeset all of the guides in-house. Now in our 33rd year, *Let's Go* publishes 17 titles, covering more than 40 countries. This year *Let's Go* proudly introduces two new entries in the series: *Let's Go: Paris* and *Let's Go: Rome.*

But these changes haven't altered our tried and true approach to researching and writing travel guides. Each spring 90 Harvard University students are hired as researcher-writers and trained intensively during April and May for their summer tour of duty. Each researcher-writer then hits the road for seven weeks of travel on a shoestring budget, researching six days per week and overcoming countless obstacles in the quest for better bargains.

Back in Cambridge, Massachusetts, an editorial staff of 32, a management team of six, and countless typists and proofreaders—all students—spend more than six months pushing nearly 8000 pages of copy through a rigorous editing process. By the time classes start in September, the typeset guides are off to the printers, and they hit bookstores world-wide in late November. Then, by February, next year's guides are well underway.

A NOTE TO OUR READERS

The information for this book is gathered by Let's Go's researchers during the late spring and summer months. Each listing is derived from the assigned researcher's opinion based upon his or her visit at a particular time. The opinions are expressed in a candid and forthright manner. Other travelers might disagree. Those traveling at a different time may have different experiences since prices, dates, hours, and conditions are always subject to change. You are urged to check beforehand to avoid inconvenience and surprises. Travel always involves a certain degree of risk, especially in low cost areas. When traveling, especially on a budget, you should always take particular care to ensure your safety.

Acknowledgments

I got the phone call one early April evening, when my prospects of finding a summer job were dimming rapidly. "Do you want to edit the Greece and Turkey book," July asked. If my oracular skills had been up to snuff, I could have guessed— I had eaten Turkey covered in Grease for dinner that night. "I know nothing about those countries." "That's okay," she said, "you'll learn."

Well, I learned a few things (like how to spell Istanbul) and there's a few things I still haven't learned (like not to be surprised when I see my tiny pay cheque) but most of all I learned that what makes *Let's Go* so darn special is the people who make it work. My co-editor Muneer basically saved my ass. My personal and professional respect for him can't be communicated with a few injokes or oblique references. If AEs were vocalists, he'd be Nusrat Fateh Ali Khan.

I inherited an amazing bunch of researchers. I wish you could meet them. Richard Foltz, a graduate student in Middle Eastern Studies, has traveled to 52 countries and speaks 10 languages. He's worldly, slightly mysterious and way overqualified for this job.

George "Odysscus" Gavros, a rising senior majoring in Government, had the longest itinerary of anyone at *Let's Go* in recent memory (I could tell you exactly how many days, but then I'd have to kill you). He did the impossible, "running with the devil" all the way.

Sinan Ali Kurmus, a rising sophomore in Social Studies, overhauled the Turkey introduction. The fact that he's an Istanbul native made him a good researcher. The fact that he's a great writer, a conscientious worker and an all-around cultured and witty guy made him a superb one.

Tim Souris, a recent graduate in Romance Languages and Literature, did a thorough job on a mostly lonely, untouristed route, a shame for such a likeable fellow. He endured lower back surgery in Thessaloniki, and worse than that, he missed Fox's Wednesday night lineup.

Finally, Courtney Williams, a recent graduate in Philosophy, sent back, along with her peerless work, letters and marginalia both thought-provoking and hilarious. I feel I've known her for years. I wish I had.

Tim thanks Polyctor Tours in Ithaka, the GNTO in Corfu, the Stavridis family of Cyprus, Anna Stavrakopoulou, and his parents. Courtney thanks Bob and Mike; and Pete Kolovos "for his native advice and swarthy Mediterranean company." George thanks Dimitris Moshovelis.

I wish to thank: My dear eagle-eyed Managing Editor July; our whole ME Group who made the term "working day" an oxymoron (I wish I were as wise as Nell, as hip as David, and married to Kayla); previous editors and researchers who advised; the typists and proofers (especially those of the final hours—what would we do without AEs); people who took me away for the weekend; Charley Bhature; Ruby R; Will S; Melrose P; Steve P; my housemates Jim McI, Jonathan L and Sarah D; and, most of all, my family: we'll always have Wegman's.

This book goes out to you, the readers. Thanks for your mail and your patience. I hope to meet a lot of you as I'm out test-driving this guide this spring. But please: don't tell me how lousy G&T '93 is unless you're buying the *ouzo*.

—Elijah

In the beginning, it was a challenge. In the end, it was a book. And somewhere in between it was more fun, more frustration, and more satisfaction than I could have imagined. Working for *Let's Go* reminded me of the plight of Sisyphus, condemned to push a boulder up a hill only to have it fall back down before reaching the top. Poor Sisyphus—hero or chump, you decide—would start up the hill again, and the boulder tumble down again, and again, and again. This summer would have been just like that, were there not the occasional plateau on which to rest my boulder and dance the night away; were there not an office full of friends managing their own burdens and yet still willing to help me with mine; and were there not five wonderful researchers making my load lighter. Every once in a while, the rock fell down, and every once in a while we let it slip, just for the hell of it. But in the end, we reached the top. I like Sisyphus.

I like my editor Elijah, too. To him I owe countless thanks for his dedication, his humor (off-color though it may be), and his warmth. Oh, and thanks for hiring me, too. Perhaps we'll meet again in Greece or Turkey next year at Niki's or Sammy's—you know the rendezvous.

R/W George Gavros proved rock-solid in his odyssey. He's a dude. My fellow Rhode Islander Courtney Williams impressed us with her thoroughness and had us laughing uncontrollably with her racy marginalia. Forever conscientious, Tim Souris displayed remarkable resilience in his journey. In Turkey, Sinan Kurmus was a star, his meticulous copy punctuated by occasional strokes of genius. And Richard Foltz, confident and resourceful, made travel in Eastern Turkey seem like butter.

Thanks also to Mark Templeton, my term-time roommate and my longtime friend, who was good-hearted and understanding the whole summer long, and still made the computers run on time. I am forever grateful to René Celaya for his unwavering friendship, support, and love. I will miss him dearly in the coming years. July Belber manage-edited with compassion, and the "weird" part of the office—Mike and Al, Kayla and David, and Nell and Jane—made me glad to be a little weird myself. For Gary Bass I have tremendous respect surpassed only by my admiration for him. I look forward to a lasting friendship with him. Ed Owen was always chummy, and Rick Abrams is something more than just a good ol' boy. My Tuesday nights will be empty without Carolyn McKee, my refrigerator will be empty without Rebecca Jeschke, and my trunk will be empty without Peter Keith. Thanks to Liz, Jen, and Cecily for last-minute proofing and summer-long fun. Bart St. Clair and Aida Bekele helped me, amused me, and humored me. They kept the office running and fixed it when it was broke. And then there's the Escort Eight: Nancy, Lorraine, Chuck, the aforementioned René, Pete, Liz, Gary, and myself. Who knew that an American car could be so tough, or so much fun.

Outside of the office, there was a group of people I affectionately labeled Dimik: Ashvin, Maria, John and John. Along with extended Dimik—Jenny and Rocco—they became some of my most important friends.

Finally, thanks to my brother Nadeem for his support and my sister Furhana for her quiet inspiration. I thank my parents for nurturing the travel spirit in me long before I knew it was there, and for realizing that such spirit dies slowly, if ever at all.

—Muneer

CONTENTS

ix

List of Maps

LET'S GO: GREECE & TURKEY

General Introduction

Greece and Turkey are legendary countries. The legends are as old as time itself and as new as tomorrow's bus schedule. Here creation stories, histories of the oldest civilizations and the mightiest empires, the development of architecture, medicine and philosophy, the centuries of foreign domination, and the uneasy leap into the modern world are splayed out for all to see.

Tourism is big business here; for some Greek islands and Turkish resort towns it's the only business. But compared to the hyped-up, repackaged zoos that are the major European destinations, Greece and Turkey are a breath of fresh air—prices are lower, people are friendlier, and happy accidents are all the more possible.

Tales are legion of travelers who came to a town for a day and stayed for a month—or came for a week and stayed forever. Ancient ruins, secluded beaches, or mountain trails may lie just off the beaten path, waiting to delight you. The new mythology of Greece and Turkey is yours to create.

How to Use this Book

Note: The dates in this book are given using BCE (Before Common Era) and CE (Common Era), which are numerically equivalent to BC (Before Christ) and AD (Anno Domini).

This year, our updating of prices and schedules has been particularly rigorous (after a year without researchers things were even more out of date than usual). Turkey is getting more time this year; it's not just a little side trip from the islands. Eastern Turkey is truly one of the last frontiers of the budget traveler and we give you the information you need to make it your own. From here, roads lead north to Georgia and Armenia, south to Syria. And Cyprus—well, let's just say our book wouldn't feel complete without it.

Our book begins with a guide to the maze of tasks that need to be performed before you go. This **General Introduction** gives details about applying for passports, visas, and student IDs; what to pack; how to secure inexpensive tickets; and procedures for sending mail and money overseas. This information applies to travel in Greece, Turkey, or Cyprus (and many other countries as well). The introductions to each country tell you what specifically to expect when you're there: how to eat, sleep, and get around with maximal enjoyment and minimal expenditure. Also, we include travel-sized nuggets on the countries' history and culture. These aren't intended to slake your thirst for background, only to whet your appetite. At the end of the book you'll find a handy **index** and a short **glossary** of pronunciations and useful phrases in Greek and Turkish. The countries themselves are arranged geographically, more or less. Coverage of **Greece** begins with Athens and the Attic plains, moves south down the Peloponnese and then continues north up through Central and Northern Greece. The **island chains,** for lack of a better system, are arranged alphabetically. We cover **Cyprus** south to north until the Green Line; Northern Cyprus is covered separately. **Turkey** is arranged counterclockwise, beginning with İstanbul and Northwest Turkey, moving down the Agean and across the Mediterranean, then up through Central and Eastern Turkey and ending on the Black Sea Coast.

A final word: Like travel itself, guidebooks are inherently imperfect. Greece and Turkey in particular are subject to enormous instabilities in prices and schedules. The

1

summer of 1992 saw simultaneous bus, plane, ferry, mail and phone strikes. Be patient, be flexible, be adventurous. And even though our book may be right, it's not comprehensive. The best discoveries of your trip may be the ones you make on your own.

If *Let's Go* is indeed the bible of the budget traveler, healthy skepticism will serve you better than blind faith.

Planning Your Trip

A Note on Prices

   Throughout the guide, we quote prices effective in the summer of 1992. Since inflation and exchange rates fluctuate considerably, be advised that listed prices could raise prices an additional 10-30%. Because inflation in Turkey generally keeps pace with the devaluation of the *lira*, prices are quoted in U.S. dollars and should be slightly more stable.

Plan ahead to get the most out of your vacation. Tourism in Greece, Turkey, and Cyprus is heavy industry, and an astounding amount of travel information is available. Stop by your local travel agency or library, look over the Useful Organizations and Publications section below, and talk to people who have recently traveled to the places that interest you. A few hours of letter writing and phone calling will yield a deluge of pamphlets and maps.

Also consider drafting an itinerary, if only to give yourself a sense of what you really want to see once you arrive. Inevitably, you'll want to investigate some places further—and leave others behind. Unless you are a do-or-die sightseer bent on seeing every archaeological sight by day and every disco by night, spend a few leisurely days indulging yourself in the countryside or simply strolling through the streets of a town. You may not get to every sight you had originally planned, but you'll discover that soaking up atmosphere is often better than seeing whatever's on the Grand Tour.

Useful Organizations and Publications

   The following organizations and agencies contain a wealth of travel information. If you don't know where to begin, start early, write a few polite letters, and reinforce the bolt on your mailbox before it's bombarded. Read through the materials, write down your specific questions, then send another query. Calling offices directly is always an option and perhaps necessary if you're in a rush. Calling usually works best if your questions are general (i.e. send me stuff on Greece) or reasonably specific (i.e. send me updated ferry routes between Cyprus and Rhodes). Anything in between (i.e. send me info on museums in İstanbul) is likely to drain your informant's patience and joviality. Also remember that if the office you call cannot answer your question specifically, they probably will refer you to someone who can.

Tourist Offices

   Greek National Tourist Organization (GNTO): In U.S., Head Office, Olympic Tower, 645 Fifth Ave., 5th Floor, New York, NY 10022 (tel. (212) 421-5777, fax 826-6940); 168 N. Michigan Ave., Chicago, IL 60601 (tel. (312) 782-1084, fax 782-1091); 611 W. 6th St. #2198, Los Angeles, CA 90017 (tel. (213) 626-6696, fax 489-9744). **In Canada,** Upper Level, 1300 Bay St., Toronto, Ont. M5R 3K8 (tel. (416) 968-2220, fax 968-6533). **In Britain,** 4 Conduit St., London WIR DOJ (tel. (01) 734 59 97). **In Australia,** 51-57 Pitt St., Sydney, NSW 2000 (tel. (02) 241 16 63). Provides general information, including pamphlets on different regions and other tourist literature. Ask for the booklet *General Information About Greece.*

   Turkish Cultural and Information Office: In U.S., 821 United Nations Plaza, New York, NY 10017 (tel. (212) 687-2194), or 1714 Massachusetts Ave. NW, Washington, DC 20036 (tel. (202) 429-9844). **In Great Britain,** 170-173 Piccadilly, London, W1V 9DD (tel. (441) 734 86 81 or -82). Offices are also located in other European nations. Supplies general information about travel in Turkey and will send you a travel guide, several maps, and regional brochures.

Cyprus Tourist Organization, P.O. Box 4535, Limassol Ave. 19, Nicosia, Cyprus (tel. 02 31 57 15); **in the U.S.,** 13 E. 40th St., New York, NY 10016 (tel. (212) 683-5280). Get a copy of the *Cyprus Hotels and Tourist Services Guide;* while it does not list all of the country's cheap hotels (many are unofficial), it does include all government-regulated hotels and pensions.

Greek Press and Information Office: In U.S., 601 Fifth Ave., 3rd floor, New York, NY 10017 (tel. (212) 751-8788); 2211 Massachusetts Ave. NW, Washington, DC 20008 (tel. (202) 332-2727). **In Canada,** 80 MacLaren St., Ottawa, Ont. K2P OK6 (tel. (613) 232-6796). **In Australia,** Stanhill Bldg. #103, 34 Queens Rd., Melbourne 3004 (tel. 267 27 37). Provides information on cultural offerings and political and economic development in Greece.

Consulates and Embassies

Greek Consulates: In U.S., 2441 Gough St., **San Francisco,** CA 94123 (tel. (415) 775-2102); 168 N. Michigan Ave., 6th floor, **Chicago,** IL 60601 (tel. (312) 782-1084); 2318 International Trade Mart Bldg., **New Orleans,** LA 70130 (tel. (504) 523-1167); Park Square Bldg., 31 St. James Ave., **Boston,** MA 02116 (tel. (617) 542-3240); 69 E. 79th St., **New York,** NY 10021 (tel. (212) 988-5500). **In Canada,** 100 University Ave., #902, **Toronto,** Ont. M5G 1V6; 1010 Sherbrooke St. W., #204, **Montréal** PQ, Que. H3A 2R7 (tel. (514) 845-8127); 890 One Bentall Center, 501 Burrard St., **Vancouver,** British Columbia V6Z 2C7 (tel. (604) 681-1381). **In Britain,** 1A Holland Park, London W-11. **In Australia,** 9 Turrana St., Yarralumla, Canberra ACT 2600. **In New Zealand,** 235-237 Willis St., 8th floor, Wellington.

Greek Embassies: In U.S., 2221 Massachusetts Ave. NW, Washington, DC 20008 (tel. (202) 667-3168). **In Canada,** 76-80 MacLaren St., Ottawa, Ont. K2P OK6 (tel. (613) 238-6271, ext. 3). **In Britain,** 1A Holland Park, London W-11. **In Ireland,** One Upper Pembroke St., Dublin 2. **In Australia,** 9 Turrana St. Yarralumla Canberra, ACT 2600.

Turkish Embassy: In U.S., 1714 Massachusetts Ave. NW, Washington, DC 20036 (tel. (202) 659-8200). **In Canada,** 197 Wurtemborg St., Ottawa, Ont. KIN 8L9. **In Great Britain,** 42 Belgrave Sq., London SWIX 8PA. **In Ireland,** 11 Clyde Rd. Ballsbridge, Dublin 4. **In Australia,** 60 Muggaway, Red Hill ACT 2603. **In New Zealand,** Attn: Turkish Honorary Consulate General, P.O. Box 2259, Otahumn, Auckland, 6. Provides useful information and answers specific questions.

Cypriot Embassy: In U.S., 2211 R St. NW, Washington, DC 20008 (tel. (202) 462-5772). **In Great Britain,** 93 Park St., London W1Y 4ET (tel. (71) 499 82 72). **In Australia,** 37 Endeavour St., Canberra (tel. (16) 295 21 20). **In Canada,** Attn: Mr. Michael Paidawssis, Honorary Consul of Cyprus, 2930 Rue Edouard Mont Petit, Ste. PH2, Montreal, PQ H3T 1J7 (tel. (514) 735-7233).

Travel Services

Council on International Educational Exchange (CIEE), 205 E. 42nd St., New York, NY 10017 (tel. (212) 661-1414; for charter flights (800) 800-8222); 1153 N. Dearborn St., Chicago, IL 60610 (tel. (312) 951-0585); 2000 Guadalupe St., Austin, TX 78705 (tel. (512) 472-4931); and 919 Irving St., Los Angeles, CA 94122 (tel. (415) 566-6222). Information on academic, work, voluntary service, and professional opportunities abroad. **Council Travel,** CIEE's budget travel subsidiary, has 38 offices throughout the U.S. and sells Eurail passes, discount travel cards, and the **International Student Identity Card (ISIC).** Write for their biannual *Student Travels,* free from any CIEE office. Also available are *Work, Study, Travel Abroad: The Whole World Handbook* ($12.95, postage $1.50) and *Going Places: The High School Student's Guide to Study, Travel, and Adventure Abroad* ($13.95, postage $1.50).

Educational Travel Centre (ETC), 438 N. Frances St., Madison, WI 53703 (tel. (608) 256-5551). Provides flight information, HI/IYHF cards, and Eurail/BritRail passes. Write or call for a free copy of their travel newspaper, *Taking Off.*

Federation of International Youth Travel Organizations (FIYTO), Islands Brygge 81, DK-2300, Copenhagen S, Denmark (tel. (01) 31 54 60 80). Issues the YIEE (International Youth ID or FIYTO) card to anyone under 26. Free catalogue filled with discount airfares for students with ISICs or International Youth Cards.

Hostelling International/International Youth Hostel Federation (HI/IYHF), 9 Guessens Rd., Welwyn Garden City, Herts AL8 6QW, England (tel. (0707) 33 24 87).

Interexchange Program, 161 Sixth Ave., #902, New York, NY 10013 (tel. (202) 947-9533). Formerly the United States Student Travel Sevice. Write for their catalogues on work abroad and low cost camping tours for students.

International Student Travel Confederation (ISTC), Gothersgade 30, 1123 Copenhagen K, Denmark (tel. 45 33 93 03). In the **U.S.,** CIEE/Council Travel Service (see address above).

Let's Go Travel Services, Harvard Student Agencies, Inc., Thayer Hall-B, Harvard University, Cambridge, MA 02138 (tel. (617) 495-9649). Sells Railpasses, HI/IYHF and AYH memberships (valid at all HI/IYHF youth hostels), International Student and Teacher ID cards, YIEE cards for non-students, travel guides and maps (including the *Let's Go* series), discount airfares, and a complete line of budget travel gear. All items available by mail. Call or write for a catalogue.

STA Travel: In U.S., 17 E. 45th St., New York, NY 10017,(tel. (800) 777-0112 or (212) 986-9470); 7202 Melrose Ave., Los Angeles, CA 90046, (tel. (213) 934-8722); 17 E. 45th St., New York, NY, (tel. (800) 777-0112 or (212) 986-9470). **In Britain,** 74 & 86 Old Brompton Rd., London SW7 3LQ (tel. (071) 937 99 21 for European travel, 937 99 71 for North American Travel, and 937 99 62 for the rest of the world). **In Australia,** 220 Faraday St., Melbourne, Victoria 3053 (tel. (03) 347 69 11). **In New Zealand,** 10 High St., Auckland (tel. (09) 309 99 95). **WST Charters,** Priory House, 6 Wrights Lane., London W8 6TA (tel. (071) 938 43 62; fax (071) 937 71 54), arranges discount flights and tours for Israel, Egypt, and Turkey. Offers ISICs, bargain flights, and travel services.

Travel CUTS (Canadian Universities Travel Service), 187 College St., Toronto, Ont. M5T 1P7 (416-979-2406). Offices throughout Canada. **In Britain,** 295-A Regent St., London W1R 7YA (tel. (071) 637 31 61). Offers discounted transatlantic flights from Canadian cities with special student fares. Sells the ISIC, FIYTO, and HI/IYHF hostel cards, and discount travel passes. Canadian Work Abroad Program for ages 18-25. *The Canadian Student Traveler* is available free at all offices and campuses across Canada.

Publications

Courier Air Travel, c/o Thunderbird Press, 5930-10 W. Greenway Blvd., Ste. 112H, Glendale, AZ 85306 (tel. (800) 345-0096). Publishes *Courier Air Travel Handbook,* which explains step-by-step procedures for traveling as a courier and contains names, telephone numbers, and contact points of courier companies ($10.70).

Forsyth Travel Library, 9154 W. 57th St., P.O. Box 2975, Shawnee Mission, KS 66201 (tel. (913) 384-3440 or (800) 367-7984). Forsyth's mail-order service stocks a wide range of city, area, and country maps, as well as guides for rail and boat travel in Europe. They are the sole North American distributor of the Thomas Cook *European Timetable*, a compilation train schedule that covers all of Europe and Britain ($24.95, postage $4). Write or call for their free newsletter and catalogue.

John Muir Publications, P.O. Box 613, Santa Fe, NM 87504 (tel. (505) 982-4078). Publishes books by veteran traveler Rick Steves, including the helpful *Europe Through The Back Door* ($14.95).

Superintendent of Documents, U.S. Government Printing Office, Washington, DC 20402-9325 (tel. (202) 783-3238). Publishes many useful travel-related booklets, including *Safe Trip Abroad* ($1). List of publications available.

Documents and Formalities

When planning a trip, be sure to file all applications early. Processing may take several weeks, or even months, to complete. Many a trip has been put off because of a bureaucratic snarl at the passport agency. Always carry at least two forms of ID, including at least one photo ID. Many places—banks in particular—require more than one ID before cashing traveler's checks.

Losing your passport can be a nightmare. A replacement may take weeks to be processed and your new passport may be valid for a limited time only. In addition, any visas contained in your old passport will be irretrievably lost. To expedite replacement of your passport if it is lost or stolen, make a photocopy of it showing its number, date, and place of issuance. Keep this information in a location separate from your passport or give it to someone with whom you will be traveling. In the event that your passport is lost or stolen, notify your embassy/consulate and the local police immediately. To replace the passport, you'll need identification and proof of citizenship. The U.S. Passport Office recommends that you carry an *official* birth certificate (not necessarily the one issued at your birth, of course), or an expired passport, in a location apart from your other documents.

Always travel with a friend.

Get the International Student Identity Card, recognized worldwide.

For information call toll-free **1-800-GET-AN-ID**. or contact any Council Travel office. (See inside front cover.)

 Council on International Educational Exchange 205 East 42nd Street, New York, NY 10017

Passports

Citizens of the U.S., Canada, Great Britain, Ireland, Australia, and New Zealand all need valid passports to enter Greece, Turkey, and Cyprus and to re-enter their respective countries. Be advised that some countries won't allow entrance if the holder's passport will expire in less than six months, and returning to the U.S. with an expired passport results in a hefty $80 fine. If you plan on an extended stay, you may want to register your passport with the nearest embassy or consulate; notify them or the local police immediately if your passport is lost or stolen while traveling. Your consulate will be able to issue you a new passport or temporary traveling papers in such an emergency.

If you are a **U.S. citizen,** you may apply for a passport, good for 10 years (5 years if you are under 18), at any office of the **U.S. Passport Agency** (13 nation-wide), or at one of the several thousand federal or state courthouses or post offices authorized to accept passport applications.

All **new passport applications** must be filed in person if you are between 13 and 18 years old, applying for the first time, or replacing a passport that has been lost or stolen or that was issued over 12 years ago. Your passport will be mailed to you. Parents must apply on behalf of children under 13 years of age. You must submit the following with your application: (1) proof of U.S. citizenship (a certified copy of your birth certificate, naturalization papers, or a previous passport); (2) identification bearing your signature and either your photo or your description, such as a driver's license; (3) two identical passport photographs taken not more than six months before the application date; and (4) the passport fee. The application fee is $65 for adults (valid for 10 years), $40 if you are under 18 (valid for 5 years). When paying, keep in mind that post offices and courts don't always accept cash and that passport agencies require applicants to pay in exact change.

To apply by mail requires only a DSP 82 form, your old passport, two new passport photos, and $55 ($40 for those under 18). Write your date of birth on the check and photocopy the data page for your personal records. Normal processing takes about two weeks if you apply in person at the passport agency, often much longer if you apply at a courthouse or post office. If you wish, you may pay for express-mail return of your passport, and urgent service is available if you provide evidence (such as plane tickets) that you are leaving soon. Call **U.S. Passport Information** at (202) 647-0518 for a recorded message with general information, or write the Passport Agency nearest to you.

If you are a **Canadian citizen,** you may apply by mail for a five-year, renewable passport from the **Passport Office,** Department of External Affairs, Ottawa, Ont. KIA OG3, or in person at one of 26 regional offices. Expect a five-day wait if applying in person, three weeks if applying by mail. With your application, you must submit: (1) evidence of Canadian citizenship (an old passport does *not* suffice as proof) and (2) two identical photographs, taken within the past year, both signed on the back by the photographer, with the address of the studio and the date the pictures were taken. Your identity must be certified on your application and photos by a "guarantor," someone who has known you for at least two years and who falls into one of a number of categories listed on the application. Currently, the passport fee is CDN$35. If a passport is lost abroad, Canadians *must* be able to prove citizenship with another document or a new one will not be issued. More complete information can be found in the booklet *Bon Voyage, But...* free from the Passport Office, Dept. of External Affairs, Ottawa, Ont. K1A 0G3.

British citizens may apply for one of two types of passports, only one of which may be held at one time: the British Visitor's Passport and the Full British Passport. The former is valid for one year, requires two passport photos and identification, and costs UK£7.50. The full passport requires an application signed by a guarantor, two photos, an old passport or other accepted form of identification, and a fee of UK£15. It is valid 10 years (5 years for those under 16). Processing takes four to six weeks. **Irish citizens** should pick up an application at a local guard station or request one from one of the two passport offices. If you have never had a passport, you must send your birth certificate, the long application, and two identical pictures to Passport Office, Setanta

Centre, Molesworth St., Dublin 2 (tel. (01) 71 16 33) or Passport Office, 1A South Mall, Cork, County Cork (tel. (021) 27 25 25). To renew, send your old passport, the short form, and the photos. Passports cost IR£45 and are valid for 10 years. Rush service is available.

Australian citizens must pay an application fee of AUS$76 (valid 10 years); AUS$31 for those under 18 (valid 5 yrs.). You must also submit two photographs signed by a guarantor, and proof of citizenship. Expect a two-week wait. **New Zealand's** requirements are the same as those of Australia, and passports are available at travel agencies (fee NZ$56.25 for adults, NZ$25.30 for children under 16).

Visas

Citizens of the U.S., Canada, Great Britain, Ireland, Australia, and New Zealand do not need to obtain a visa ahead of time to visit Greece; a valid passport will allow you to stay for up to three months. Apply to stay longer at the **Aliens Bureau,** 173 Alexandros Ave., Athens 11522 (tel. 646 81 03) or check with the Greek embassy or consulate for information. Citizens of other nations should check regulations at offices of the Greek embassy or consulate in their home country. A **transit visa,** valid for four days, can be obtained from any Greek consulate if you wish to stay in Greece on your way to another country. Similarly, a Cyprus advance visa is required to visit Cyprus. However, both Greece and Cyprus will **deny entry** to anyone bearing a passport that shows evidence of travel to the Turkish Republic of Northern Cyprus.

Citizens of the U.S., Canada, and New Zealand do not need a visa for a visit Turkey up to three months long; for British, Irish, and Australian citizens a visa is required and is obtainable at the port of entry. Citizens of other nations should check regulations at offices of the Turkish embassy or consulate in their home country.

Customs

Upon entering Greece, you must declare certain items, including cameras, typewriters, portable radios, and musical instruments. These may be brought in duty-free as long as they will be taken with you upon departure. You must also register all currency above $500, or you may not take it with you when you leave.

Upon entering Turkey, travelers may bring along: one camera and five rolls of film, prescription drugs (you should bring the prescription, too), one transistor radio, and no more than 400 cigarettes, 50 cigars, 200g tobacco, 1kg coffee, 1.5g instant coffee, 1kg tea, and five 100cc or seven 70cc bottles of spirits. No sharp instruments or firearms of any sort may be brought in, and under *no circumstances* should you bring any illegal drugs into Turkey (see Drugs below).

There is no limit on the amount of foreign currency you may bring into Turkey, but you may not take out more than $5000 worth of Turkish currency. It is also absolutely forbidden to export antiques from Turkey, even though shopkeepers may try to convince you otherwise. Make sure that the curious knickknack or carpet you pick up as a souvenir isn't an antique: customs officials may well require, even as your plane is boarding for departure, that you produce a signed statement from a merchant stating that the item is not an antique. If you intend to purchase anything really old or potentially valuable, have the shopowner draft up a brief, signed statement saying that what you bought can be legally exported.

Upon re-entering your own country, you must declare all articles acquired abroad, and pay a duty on the value of those articles exceeding the allowance established by your country's customs service. Keep receipts for valuable items you intend to reimport, or have a customs agent stamp a list of serial numbers of items you bring on your trip at your point of departure. Keep in mind that anything you buy at duty-free shops abroad is not exempt from duty at your point of return, and must be declared along with other purchases: "Duty-free" means only that you didn't pay taxes in the country of purchase. A Value-Added Tax (VAT) of 18% (a form of sales tax levied in the European Economic Community) is generally included in the price of all Greek goods and services.

U.S. citizens, after at least two days abroad, may bring $400 worth of goods with them duty-free, including gifts; you must then pay 10% tax on the next $1000 worth.

The duty-free goods must be for personal or household use and cannot include more than 100 cigars or 200 cigarettes (1 carton), and one liter of liquor or two liters of wine (you must be 21 or older to bring liquor into the U.S.). If you mail a parcel worth over $50, the Postal Service will collect a duty plus a handling charge from the U.S. recipient upon delivery. Customs occasionally makes spot checks on parcels, so be sure to mark the accurate price and nature of the gift on the package. For more detailed information, get a copy of *Know Before You Go,* available as item 477Y for 50¢ from the Consumer Information Center, Pueblo, CO 81009.

Canadian citizens should, before departing, identify or list serial numbers of all valuables on form Y-38 at the Customs Office or point of departure (these goods can then be reimported duty-free). Once every calendar year, after you have been abroad at least seven days, you may bring in up to CDN$300 worth of duty-free goods. These can include no more than one carton of cigarettes, 50 cigars, two 200g containers of loose tobacco (if you are 16 years old or older), and 1.1 liters of wine or alcohol (if you meet the age requirements of the province of your port of return). Anything above the duty-free allowance is taxed: 20% for goods which accompany you, more for shipped items. You can send gifts up to a value of CDN$40 duty-free, but you may not mail alcohol or tobacco. The Revenue Canada Customs and Excise Department, Communications Branch, MacKenzie Avenue, Ottawa, Ont. K1A OL5 (tel. (613) 957-0275), will send you their pamphlet *I Declare/Je Déclare.* Contact External Affairs, Ottawa, Ontario K1A OG2 (tel. (613) 996-2825) for the pamphlet *Bon Voyage, But...* **British citizens** may take back a maximum of £32 duty-free. For those over 17 this allowance includes 100 cigarettes or cigarillos, 50 cigars, 250g tobacco, 2 liters of still table wine and either 1 liter of alcohol over 44 proof or 2 liters of alcohol under 44 proof. Write Her Majesty's Customs and Excise Office, Custom House, Nettleton Rd., Heathrow Airport North, Hounslow, Middlesex TW6 2LA (tel. (01) 081 750) for more information.

Irish citizens may import a maximum of IR£34 per adult traveler duty-free (IR£17 per traveler under the age of 15). Travelers above the age of 17 may bring in 200 cigarettes or 100 cigarillos or 50 cigars or 250g of tobacco, and one liter of alcohol over 44 proof or two liters of alcohol under 44 proof. You may import as much currency into Ireland as you wish. For more information, write Division 1, Office of the Revenue Commissioners, Dublin Castle, Dublin 1 (tel. 679 27 27).

Australian citizens age 18 or older may import up to AUS$400 worth of duty-free goods; for those under 18, the limit is AUS$200. Duty-free allowances include no more than one liter of alcohol (for those under 18) and one carton of cigarettes. **New Zealand citizens** can bring in NZ$500 of duty-free goods. Those 16 or older are allowed 200 cigarettes, 50 cigars, 250g of tobacco, or a mixture of all three not to exceed 250g; 4.5 liters of beer or wine; and one 1125ml bottle of liquor.

The U.S., Canada, Australia, and New Zealand prohibit or restrict the importation of explosives, firearms, ammunition, fireworks, many plants and animals, lottery tickets, obscene literature and film, and controlled drugs. To avoid problems when carrying prescription drugs, make sure bottles are clearly marked and have a copy of the prescription ready to show the customs officer. In addition, articles made from protected species, such as elephants, many reptiles, cats (the big ones), and whales will be seized.

Student and Youth Identification

Both the **International Student Identity Card (ISIC)** and a school photo ID entitle students to discounts on international flights, museum admissions, local transportation, theater tickets, and other services throughout Europe. In Greece, the ISIC secures discounts on admission to archaeological sites and certain festivals. Cardholders are also eligible for reduced airfares from Athens (but not within the country), up to 40% discount on train fares, and up to 25% discount on ferries from Greece. In Turkey, the card enables students to visit state-run museums for free and obtain 50% off Turkish Air flights to the Middle East or Asia and 60% off flights to Europe. Similar discounts can be found in Cyprus.

The ISIC is issued in Greece, but many budget travel offices and campus travel services in the U.S. also sell the card. When purchased in the U.S., the card includes medical insurance of up to US$3000, and US$100 per day coverage of hospital care for up to two months. To be eligible for an ISIC, you must be a secondary or post-secondary school student over 12 years of age during the school year you apply. When applying, you must supply the following: (1) proof of current student status (a letter on school stationery signed and sealed by the registrar, or a photocopied grade report); (2) a 1½ x 2 inch photo (vending machine-size) with your name printed and signed on the back; (3) proof of your birthdate and nationality; and (4) name and address of beneficiary (for insurance purposes). The fee is US$15, and the card is valid from September 1 of one year to the end of the following year. When you apply, be sure to pick up the *ID Discount Guide,* which lists by country some of the available discounts; you can also write to CIEE for a copy. If you can't find a local agency that issues the ISIC, contact one of the budget travel offices listed in Useful Organizations above.

Because of the proliferation of phony and improperly issued ISIC cards, many airlines and some other services now require double proof of student identity. It's a good idea to have a signed letter from the registrar testifying to your student status (have it stamped with the school seal) or to carry your school ID card with you.

If you are ineligible for the ISIC but are under 26, you can apply for the **International Youth Card,** also known as the **FIYTO Card.** This travel document is good for discounts on sightseeing tours within Greece, train rides from northern Europe, and ferry travel between Greece and Italy, Israel, and Egypt. If purchased in the U.S. the card carries the same insurance coverage described above for the ISIC. Let's Go Travel, CIEE, Travel CUTS, and budget travel agencies all over the world issue the FIYTO card; you must bring your passport, a copy of a valid driver's license, or a copy of your birth certificate, a 1½ x 2 inch photo (with your name printed on the back) and a certified check or money order for US$14 when you apply. For further information, write to FIYTO, Islands Brygge 81, DK-2300, Copenhagen S, Denmark (tel. (01) 31 60 80). Their free annual catalogue lists over 8000 discounts available to cardholders.

Youth Hostel Associations

Greek and Turkish youth hostels are an excellent alternative to hotels. In general, the accommodations are good and the cost is reasonable. Unfortunately, these bastions of budget travelers are relatively scarce; they may turn up in places you'd least expect them and not in places you most need them. At present, Greece has more than 25 youth hostels affiliated with **Hostelling International (HI)** (formerly **International Youth Hostel Federation,** or **HI/IYHF**). Turkey has none. HI membership is available through your own country's youth hostel organization. Hostel membership cards are available while you wait from many budget travel agencies.

U.S.: American Youth Hostels (HI/AYH), P.O. Box 37613, Washington, DC 20013-7613 ((202) 783-6161); also 39 regional offices across the U.S. (call above number for information). HI and ISIC cards, hostel handbooks, student and charter flights, travel equipment, and literature on budget travel. Membership for 1 yr. US$25, under 18 US$10, over 54 US$15, families US$35.

Canada: Hostelling International—Canada (HI-C), National Office, 1600 James Naismith Dr., #608, Gloucester, Ontario, Canada K1B 5N4 (tel. (613) 748-5638).

England and Wales: Youth Hostels Association of England and Wales (YHA), Trevalyn House, 8 St. Stephen's Hill, St. Albans, Hertfordshire AL1 2DY (tel. (0727) 85 52 15, fax (0727) 441 26). Membership for 1 yr. £8.90, ages 16-20 UK£4.70; family UK£17.80.

Ireland: An Óige, 39 Mountjoy Sq., Dublin 1 (tel. (01) 36 31 11, fax (01) 36 58 07). Membership for 1 yr.: IR£7.50, under 18 IR£4; family IR£15.

Australia: Australian Youth Hostels Association (AYHA), Level 3, 10 Mallett St., Camperdown, New South Wales 2050 Australia (tel. (02) 565 16 99). Membership for 1 yr. AUS$40, under 18 AUS$24.

New Zealand: Youth Hostels Association of New Zealand, P.O. Box 436, Christchurch 1 (tel. (03) 79 99 70, fax (03) 654 476). Membership for 1 yr.: NZ$24, ages 15-17 NZ$12.

Other Countries: Hostelling International (HI), Midland Bank Chambers, Howardsgate, Welwyn Garden City, Herts, England (tel. (0707) 33 24 87).

If you arrive in Greece without an HI/IYHF card, you can purchase an International Guest Card from the **Greek Youth Hostel Association,** 4 Dragatsaniou St., Athens 10559 (tel. 323 41 07).

International Driver's License

An **International Driving Permit** is required for driving in Greece. You must be over 18 to apply, although some rental owners quote 23 as a minimum age to rent a car in Greece. The permit is good for one year and is available from any local office of the **American Automobile Association,** or at the main office, AAA Travel Agency Services, 1000 AAA Drive #75, Heathrow, FL 32746-5063 (tel. (407) 444-8008). It is also available from the **American Automobile Touring Alliance (AATA),** 188 The Embarcadero #300, San Francisco, CA 94105 (tel. (415) 777-4000), or the **Canadian Automobile Association (CAA),** Head Office, 60 Commerce Valley Dr. E, Markham, Ont. L3T 7P9 (tel. (416) 771-3170). With your application, you will need two passport-size photos, your valid U.S. or Canadian driver's license (which must always accompany the International Driving Permit), and US$5. To get the license in Greece, you must present your national driver's license, passport, a photograph, and 2000dr to the **Automobile and Touring Club of Greece (ELPA).** Their main office is at 2-4 Messogion St., Athens 11527 (tel. (01) 779 16 15 or 779 74 01). They also provide a 24-hour emergency road service (dial 104) and an information line (dial 174).

If you are going to drive, you will need a "green card" or **International Insurance Certificate** for comprehensive coverage. Most rental agencies include this coverage in their prices; if you buy or lease a car, you can obtain a green card through the dealer from whom you are renting, leasing, or buying, or from some travel agents. (It is no longer available from the AAA.) Check to see that your insurance applies abroad. If not, you can take out short-term policies

Money

Nothing can cause you more anxiety than money—even when you have enough of it. Plan carefully to avoid having to call home in woe and desperation.

Currency and Exchange

Before leaving home, exchange US$50 or so for the currency of the country to which you are headed. Though you will pay a higher exchange rate (and you may have to call your bank well ahead to find *drachmae,* Cypriot *pounds,* or Turkish *lira*), this will save you time and exasperation, especially if when you arrive the banks are closed and you need immediate cash.

Greek *drachmae* are issued in both paper notes (50, 100, 500, 1000dr) and coins (1, 2, 5, 10, 20, and 50dr). If you are carrying more than US$500 in cash when you enter Greece, you must declare it upon entry in order to export it legally (this does not apply to traveler's checks). You can bring up to US$190 worth of *drachmae* into Greece. In addition, no more than US$100 worth of *drachmae* can be changed back into foreign currency at one time after any one visit to Greece. Hotels, restaurants, airports and train stations will generally offer lower rates; your best bet is to stick with banks.

The official currency in Turkey is the Turkish *lira* (TL). Coins are divided into 50 and 100 *lira* pieces, and paper currency comes in denominations of 10, 20, 50, 100, 500, 1000, 5000, and 10,000 *lira* notes. It is hard to get change for bills of 1000TL or more at museum entrances and cheap restaurants.

Once in Turkey, currency can be exchanged almost everywhere, but the best rates can be obtained at banks and exchange bureaus. Look for the signs "change/exchange/wechsel." Turkey has 24-hr. currency exchanges at border crossings, major airports, and train stations; major tourist areas have places to change money on weekends. Hold on to exchange slips when you convert foreign money into Turkish *lira,* since you may have to present them when you're re-converting your cash. If you take gifts out of Turkey, you will have to prove that they were bought with legally-exchanged foreign currency. If you change U.S. dollars into *lira* at Pamukbank, you can only change it back to U.S. dollars at an airport, railway, or frontier post branch of Pamukbank. You must

Don't forget to write.

Now that you've said, "Let's go," it's time to say, "Let's get American Express® Travelers Cheques." Because when you want your travel money to go a long way, it's a good idea to protect it. So before you leave, be sure and write.

have your receipt and the amount must be less than or equal to the amount you originally converted. There is no limit to the amount of foreign currency that can be brought
into Turkey, but no more than US$5000 in *lira* may be brought into or taken out of the
country, and no more than US$5000 can be exchanged for *lira* at any one time. If you
are coming from Greece, exchange your money before arriving. The few banks that accept *drachmae* exchange them at an absurdly high rate.

The main unit of currency in Cyprus is the pound (£), which is divided into 100
cents. Banks are officially open only from 8:30am to noon, but nearly all those in the
major tourist areas provide an afternoon tourist service in summer (usually 4-7pm).

Traveler's Checks

Traveler's checks are the safest and least troublesome means of carrying cash. They
are easy to use and can be replaced if lost or stolen. Traveler's checks are accepted for
exchange at virtually every bank in Greece, Turkey, and Cyprus and as cash for purchases at some stores and restaurants. Banks and agencies all over the world sell traveler's checks, usually charging a commission of about 1.5% or a set fee. You may be
able to purchase them from certain travel agencies.

AAA: Tel. (407) 444-7000 in the U.S. Issues American Express traveler's checks to members
only. No fee.

American Express: Tel. (800) 221-7282; from abroad call the U.K. collect (44) 273 57 16 00.
Commission 1%, but American Express Travel Offices cash their own traveler's checks at no additional cost. A new option allows 2 people traveling together to share 1 set of checks. Send for
their free booklet, *Traveler's Companion,* which lists all travel offices, including those in Greece,
Turkey, and Cyprus, in powerful yet sensitive prose.

Bank of America: Tel. (800) 227-3460 in the U.S.; from Canada and abroad, call Canada collect
(415) 624-5400. Checks are free in CA, about 1% elsewhere (depending on the issuing bank).
Checks only in US$. Free booklet lists over 40,000 refund offices worldwide. Checkholders may
use **Travel Assistance Hotline** tel. (800) 368-7878 from the U.S., from abroad call the U.S. collect (202) 331-1596.

Barclay's: Tel. (800) 221-2426 in the U.S.; from Canada and abroad, call California collect (415)
574-7111. Affiliated with Visa. Checks may be obtained in UK£, US$, CDN$, and DM; for lost
checks call (800) 227-6811, in Europe call the U.K. collect at (071) 937 80 91. Charges a 1-1½%
commission.

Citicorp: Tel. (800) 645-6556 in the U.S. and Canada; from abroad, call the U.S. 24-hr. line collect (813) 623-1709. Checks available in 4 currencies. Commission 1%, checkholders automatically enrolled in Travel Assist Hotline (tel. (800) 523-1199) for 45 days after purchase. Checks in
US$, JP¥, UK£, and DM.

Thomas Cook: Tel. (800) 223-4030 in the U.S and Canada; from abroad, call the U.S. collect
(212) 974-5696. Available in 11 currencies, 1% commission, and refundable at over 170,000 locations worldwide. For lost checks call (800) 223-7373, abroad call collect (609) 987-7300. Connected to Mastercard. They will cash their own checks for no additional fee, but since their checks
must be purchased through an affiliated bank, the seller may levy an extra commission.

Visa: Tel. (800) 227-6811 in the U.S. and Canada; tel. (071) 973 80 91 in London; call New York
collect (212) 858-8500 from elsewhere. Available in 13 currencies.

Buy most of your checks in large denominations to avoid spending too much time in
bank lines, but carry some checks in small denominations to minimize your losses at
times when you need money fast and have to cash a check at a poor rate. To get the best
exchange, purchase traveler's checks in your own national currency rather than foreign
currencies.

All companies give you an emergency telephone number, which you should use if
your checks are lost or stolen. Get a list of refund centers—American Express has over
90,000 worldwide, Bank of America some 40,000—and other companies provide
phone numbers you can call collect (some numbers are listed above). You should expect a fair amount of red tape and delay even under the best circumstances. To expedite
the refund process, separate your check receipts and keep them in a safe place (e.g. take
the checks with you during the day and leave the receipts in your luggage). Record

check numbers as you cash them to help you identify exactly which checks are missing.

Credit Cards

While most low-cost establishments don't honor credit cards, they can prove enormously helpful should a financial emergency arise. Major credit cards, such as American Express, provide instant cash advances from banks throughout Europe in U.S. dollars. Quite often, a cash advance may be your only quick source of funds.

Local **American Express** offices will cash personal checks for green card holders, up to US$1000 in any 21-day period (US$200 in cash and US$800 in traveler's checks). Gold card holders may cash up to US$5000. Offices will cancel and replace lost or stolen cards and arrange temporary ID if you lose your wallet. Cardholders can use American Express offices as mailing addresses free of charge; others must pay a fee (or show AmEx traveler's checks). The card also provides automatic travel insurance. For a US$1.50 service charge per transaction, you can use American Express Automated Teller Machines throughout the U.S. and Europe, where cardholders can get up to US$1000 (US$500 in cash, US$500 in traveler's checks). For more information on their coverage policy get *The Traveler's Companion,* a list of full-service offices throughout the world; write American Express Travel Service, 65 Broadway, New York, NY 10016. **Barclay's Bank** is Britain's largest international bank, with 4000 offices in 70 countries. **Mastercard** (tel. (800) 826-2181) offers cash advances through an affiliated bank; look for the Mastercard logo on the door. **Visa** also has teller machines throughout Europe. Cash advances in *lira* can be obtained from Iktisat Bank, the official Visa Card representative in Turkey. There are Iktisat banks in İstanbul, Ankara, İzmir, Kuşadası, Mersin, Marmaris, Ürgüp, Kayseri, and Antalya. When using your credit card in Greece or Turkey, be sure that the forms are filled in correctly; otherwise you may find a huge surprise on your bill at the end of the month.

Sending Money

The cheapest way to obtain money without a credit card is to have someone **cable** money through the U.S. office of a large foreign bank. Larger national banks will have branches throughout the country that may be able to reach you in remote corners. Bank of America's Global Seller Services (tel. (800) 227-3333) offers worldwide delivery, although money must be sent to a Seller affiliate. Allow three to five working days for delivery and expect to pay a 1% commission, plus a US$15 fee to have money cabled abroad.

Another way to send money is by **cable transfer.** Contact your home bank by telegram and state the amount of money you need, whether it should be in U.S. or other foreign currency, and the name and address of the bank to which it should be cabled. This service takes about 24 hours—a bit longer in smaller cities—and costs about US$25 for amounts under US$1000. Citibank will send money to points in Adana, Ankara, Bursa, Gaziantep, İskenderun, İstanbul, İzmir, Mersin, Samsun, and Trabzon.

Slower than the cable, but still effective, is a **bank draft.** Citicorp (tel. (212) 558-7256) in Athens, or any large commercial bank should be able to connect you with a network of corresponding banks in Greece. The sender must either have an account with the bank or bring cash to one of their branches (some won't cable for non-customers). The bank will charge US$15-20. The money might arrive the same day, the next day, or a week later, depending on when the money is sent and what time zones it must cross. The sender must specify whether the money is to be disbursed in local currency or in U.S. dollars, and must make certain that information, such as the passport number and recipient's bank name and address, is exact; otherwise, expect significant delays. The sender will not receive confirmation of delivery.

Yet another way to get money from home is to bring an **American Express card:** AmEx allows green card holders to draw cash from their checking accounts (checkbook welcomed but not required) at any of its full-fledged offices and many of its representatives' offices, up to US$1000 every 21 days (no service charge, no interest). With someone feeding money into your account back home, you'll be all set. You can also send money through American Express (tel. (800) 543-4080). It costs about as much as sending it through a bank. Normally, the sender must have an AmEx card to use these services, but some offices will waive this requirement for a commission. Money is guaranteed to arrive within 24 to 72 hours at the designated overseas office, where it will be held for 14 days before being returned to the sender. It costs US$15 to send up to US$500, and US$60 to send up to the maximum amount, US$2000. The first US$200 is payable in local currency and the remainder in U.S. dollars traveler's checks.

Western Union offers a convenient, though expensive, service for cabling money abroad. A sender in the U.S. with a MasterCard or Visa can call Western Union (tel. (800) 325-6000) and state their card number and the amount of money they wish to cable. A sender without a card must go in person to a Western Union office with cash, a cashier's check, or AmEx traveler's checks (no money orders accepted). The money will arrive at the central telegram office in the city the sender designates and can be picked up with suitable ID. Offices in Greece are located in Athens, Piraeus, and Thessaloniki. Money will generally arrive between two to five business days, in *drachmae,* and will be held at the office for 14 days, after which time it will be returned to the sender minus the transaction costs. To send US$50 to Europe costs US$13; amounts above US$100 cost about an additional US$5 per US$100.

If you are an American and suddenly find yourself in big trouble, you can have money sent to you via the **State Department's Citizen Emergency Center,** 2201 C St. NW, #4811, Washington, DC 20520 (tel. (202) 647-5225). For a fee, officials will send the money—preferably under US$500—within hours, or sometimes overnight, to the nearest consulate. Finally, if you are stranded without recourse, a consulate will wire home for you and deduct the cost from the money you receive. This is considered an extreme imposition, so use it only in life or death situations. Citizens of other countries might check if their own government provides a similar service.

When to Go

Summer is the high tourist season in Greece; if you visit between late May and early September, expect to meet the usual hordes of travelers almost everywhere you go. Prices increase with the temperature in high season. If you feel stifled by crowds or taxed by the frantic pace of summer travel, consider visiting during the off-season (Sept.-May), when inexpensive airfares are easier to obtain and lodging is cheaper. Some facilities and sights may close down, but locals are often more receptive and the weather more pleasant. Even during the winter months, some areas continue to be mild. (Athens and southern Greece average 73°F in mid-October.) Greece also has winter sports, with ski areas at Parnassos, Mt. Pelion, Metsovo, and elsewhere in northern Greece.

The main tourist season in Turkey runs early April to June, and September to November. Climate varies quite substantially. The Mediterranean and Aegean coasts are known for being extremely hot and dry during July and August; in central and eastern Anatolia, winter cold and summer heat are especially severe. Receiving an average of 140cm of rain per year, the Black Sea coast is quite moderate almost all year round.

Cyprus is most popular from about March to mid-June, and from September to November. Summer, especially in Nicosia, can be enormously hot and dry. Troodos, the rainiest part of the island, usually receives snow between January and March. Because temperatures at higher altitudes can drop quickly at night even during summer, if you plan to do extensive camping, be sure to dress warmly.

Packing

You've heard it again and again, but this time make sure you do it: **Pack lightly.** Lay out everything you want to take with you and then pack half. Take a bit more money and wash your clothes in the sink rather than packing a week's worth of outfits. It's always a good idea to carry your bags around the block a few times. If beads of sweat start trickling down your brow, you've probably packed too much. Try again.

Traveling by foot? Then a backpack is probably your best bet. Your two options are the **internal frame** and the **external frame.** The internal is less cumbersome and won't be broken by brutish baggage handlers, but the external offers you added support and comfort by lifting the pack off your back, allowing for more air flow and better ventilation. External frame packs can also support a sleeping bag lashed to the outside of the pack, saving room. A good pack runs anywhere between US$100-300. Beware of cheap packs—the straps may rip or fray under heavy strain, which you *will* give it.

No matter what kind of luggage you choose, a small daypack is indispensable for carrying things like your camera, plane tickets, passports, jewelry, your well-thumbed copy of Homer or Rumi, and your riveting, reliable *Let's Go.* Protect your money and valuables *at all times* by keeping them in a purse, pouch, or money belt. These are slim, zippered pouches worn under the clothes—you will come to feel naked without it. For an assortment of travel luggage, consult Let's Go Travel (see Travel Services section).

When packing, opt for natural fibers, lightweight cottons, and clothes that can be washed in a sink and won't wrinkle easily. *Good walking shoes are essential,* particularly if you're planning a foray up Nemrut Dağı or Mt. Olympus. Make sure you break them in before your departure. Sprinkling talcum powder on your feet and inside your shoes helps prevent uncomfortable rubs and sores, while moleskin will cushion any pains due to blisters.

Most monasteries and archaeological sites require modest dress, which means no shorts, miniskirts, cropped tops, or bathing suits are allowed. Trousers and shirts are appropriate for men; women should bring at least one comfortable skirt that covers the knees. Long skirts are invaluably versatile travel wear, and can help you downplay your tourist identity.

The standard electrical outlet in Greece produces 220 volts AC using the two-pronged plug used elsewhere in Europe. Although Turkey uses the same European plug, be careful and ask the exact voltage, since both 110 volts and 220 volts are used. In Cyprus, 220 volt outlets require either the two or three-pronged outlets used in Africa and Asia. Because North American appliances are usually designed for 110 volts

AC and the prong won't fit, if you're planning on bringing a beloved electrical appliance, you will need a converter and a three-pronged adapter, both available in department and hardware stores. To order a converter by mail (US$15-18) or to receive their free and enlightening pamphlet, *Foreign Electricity is No Deep Dark Secret,* write to Franzus Company, Murtha Industrial Park, P.O. Box 142, Railroad Ave., Beacon Falls, CT 06403 (tel. (212) 463-9393). Better still, leave the hair dryer at home.

Safety and Security

Common sense and basic precautions should carry you safely through your travels. Large cities, of course, demand extra caution. Crowded youth hostels and overnight trains are vacation opportunities for thieves. Petty robbery is not only costly, but can put a real damper on the rest of your trip. To avoid unwanted attention, leave the Gucci luggage at home and keep your money and valuables on you at all times, even while sleeping—a necklace pouch or money belt is relatively inexpensive. If you're planning on sleeping outside, or simply don't want to carry everything with you, try storing your gear in a locker at a train or bus station. Hotels and hostels often provide daytime luggage storage for a small fee.

Photocopy two sets of all your important documents, including passport, IDs, credit cards, traveler's checks' number slips, plane tickets, and railpasses. Leave one set with someone at home and carry the other with you, *separate from the actual documents themselves.* Be sure to label all your luggage (inside and out) in case the tags rip off. A bright piece of ribbon or twine tied on the handles of your bags will make them easily identifiable amidst the sea of suitcases at baggage claim.

Insurance

Avoid unnecessary insurance coverage. Check whether your homeowner's insurance (or your family's coverage) covers theft during travel. Some policies will reimburse you for the value of stolen documents, such as passport, plane ticket, or railpass, up to US$500. University term-time medical plans often include insurance for summer travel. Students under 23 should check whether their parents have travel insurance for them. Canadians are usually protected under their home province's health insurance plan; check with your Ministry of Health or Health Plan headquarters.

If your insurance policy does not extend overseas, you may want to purchase a short-term policy for your trip. Purchasing an International Student, Youth, or Teacher Identity Card in the U.S. provides you with basic accident and sickness coverage. Also provided is a multi-lingual 24-hour hotline for legal and financial aid as well as oodles of benefits should you suffer through hospitalization, dismemberment, or death. An American Express card also provides some travel insurance automatically.

Always keep receipts—often you must pay emergency expenses on the spot and then file your claim (along with necessary documents and receipts) upon return to your home country. Generally, insurance companies require proof of loss or expenditures before they will honor your claim. In case of theft, you must submit a copy of the police report; in case of medical expenses, you must submit receipts and doctors' statements. For more information on specific insurance policies, contact any of the firms listed below.

Access America, Inc.: 6600 W. Broad St., P.O. Box 90310, Richmond, VA.23230 (tel. (800) 284-8300). Covers trip cancellation/interruption, on the spot hospital admittance costs, emergency medical evacuation, and a 24-hr. hotline.

Travel Assistance International: 1133 15th St. NW, #400, Washington, DC 20005 (tel. (800) 821-2828). Medical and travel insurance, up to US$30,000. Frequent Traveler plan offers US$15,000 coverage for up to 90 days of travel during a single calendar year. Short term plans available.

TravelGuard International: 1145 Clark St., Stevens Point, WI 54481 (tel. (800) 826-1300). Offers comprehensive travel insurance packages which all include a 24-hr. emergency service network.

Wallach and Co. Inc.: 107 W. Federal St., P.O. Box 480, Middleburg, VA 22117 (tel. (800) 237-6615). Insurance and emergency medical assistance services, including a 24-hr. hotline.

Drugs

The horror stories you've heard about travelers getting "busted" abroad are based on fact. Possession of drugs in Greece, Turkey, and Cyprus is considered a serious offense. In Greece and Cyprus, the least you can expect is to be expelled from the country, but remember that your state department is of little assistance in Greek courts. Possessing drugs in Turkey is an *extremely* serious offense: *Midnight Express* was based on a true story. The minimum sentence for possessing even the smallest quantity of illegal drugs in Turkey is 16 months and in most cases, embassies are helpless. Also remember that Turkish law also provides for "guilt by association," which means that even those in the company of the person caught are subject to prosecution.

As far as illegal substances go, the best advice is to *stay away* from drugs while abroad and to *never* bring drugs across international borders. Should you be imprisoned, consular officers are allowed to visit you, provide a list of attorneys, and inform family and friends. Their benevolence ends there. As a U.S. State Department bulletin dourly states, you're virtually "on your own" if you become involved, *however innocently,* in illegal drug trafficking.

Make sure you get a statement and/or prescription from your doctor if you'll be carrying insulin, syringes, or any narcotic drugs abroad. In addition, be aware that **codeine,** a painkiller commonly prescribed by U.S. physicians, is illegal in Greece.

To find out more about drug enforcement policies, send a self-addressed stamped envelope for *Travel Warning on Drugs Abroad* from the Bureau of Consular Affairs, PA Room #5807, Department of State, Washington, DC 20520 (tel. (202) 647-1488).

Health

For **medical emergencies** in Greece, dial 166. In Turkey, dial 077 or call your consulate. In Cyprus, dial 190.

A whirlwind vacation can take its toll on your health. Eating properly and drinking lots of fluids is essential. Although most water in Greece is filtered through mountain rocks (meaning it's about as naturally clean as anywhere in Europe), relying on bottled mineral water, which is relatively inexpensive and readily available, is always a good idea and a necessity in Turkey. Write to IAMAT (see below) for their free and inspiring pamphlets *How to Adjust to the Heat, How to Adapt to Altitude,* and *How to Avoid Traveler's Diarrhea,* a perennial favorite.

Bring a copy of any medical prescriptions you require, and carry an ample supply of all medications—matching your prescription with a foreign equivalent is not always economical, easy, or safe. It's a good idea to distribute medication between carry-on and checked baggage in case one or the other goes astray. Should you find yourself without a necessary prescription drug, carry a dosage schedule from your own pharmacist. Remember that codeine is an illegal substance in Greece (see Drugs above).

Some of the most extensive health services for travelers are furnished by the **International Association for Medical Assistance to Travelers (IAMAT),** 417 Center St., Lewiston, NY 14092 (tel. (716) 754-4883); in Canada, 40 Regal Rd., Guelph, Ont. NIK IB5 (tel. (519) 836-0102). IAMAT provides a worldwide directory of English-speaking physicians whose services are available at fixed and generally reasonable rates. English-speaking doctors can also be found by inquiring at U.S., Canadian, and British embassies and consulates, through American Express and Thomas Cook offices, or at the emergency rooms of university hospitals. Also, many of the first-aid centers listed in *Let's Go* can provide medical care from an English-speaking doctor.

It is always wise to carry a small **first-aid kit** with you on vacation. Include such items as antiseptic soap, multiple vitamins, aspirin, antacid tablets, bandages, tweezers, a Swiss Army knife, sunscreen, a thermometer, an antiseptic ointment such as Bacitracin, medication for motion sickness and diarrhea, and an antihistamine. Even if you have never experienced an allergic reaction before, *to nephos,* the infamous smog around Athens, might provoke a reaction in even the most tranquil of sinus passages.

If you wear glasses or contacts, be sure to take an extra pair, as well as a copy of your prescription. As additional precaution, leave a copy of the prescription with someone at home in case your lenses are lost are stolen. Take along extra saline and cleansing solutions, as availability and price are unpredictable.

Travelers with a medical problem or condition that cannot be easily recognized (e.g. diabetes, allergies to antibiotics, epilepsy, or heart conditions) should obtain a **Medic Alert identification tag,** an internationally recognized emblem that conveys vital information in emergencies. It indicates the nature of the problem, and provides the number of Medic Alert's 24-hr. hotline, through which attending personnel can obtain information about the member's medical history. Lifetime membership is US$25; for the fashion-conscious, silver and gold-plated tags are available at US$38 and US$48, respectively. Write to Medic Alert Foundation International, P.O. Box 1009, Turlock, CA 95381 (tel. (800) 432-5378). Additionally, the **American Diabetes Association,** 1660 Duke St., Alexandria, VA 22314 (tel. (800) 232-3472), provides information and ID cards to travelers. Call or write for details.

Specific Concerns

Wherever possible, *Let's Go* lists emergency, police, and consulate numbers in every large city; consult them if you encounter difficulties.

Women Travelers

Women traveling alone are likely to experience harrassment and must always take extra precautions. Even groups of two or three women may be bothered. But don't despair. Women have traveled on their own, elegantly and adventurously, for years. You can too.

Freelance camping, swimming, or scuba diving in secluded areas and hitching rides can be **extremely** dangerous. Women will be safer and more comfortable enjoying public parks areas in groups. Always look as if you know where you're going, even when you don't. Ask women or couples for directions rather than men and keep spare change handy for telephone calls and emergency bus or taxi fares. Always leave nighttime activities before closing; you don't want to stumble out into the darkness with the rest of the drunks. Conforming to local standards of dress and behavior can reduce the hassles you encounter. Should you find yourself the object of catcalls or strange propositions, your best response is no response. Avoid prolonged eye-contact, except to assert your strength and personhood. To call for help in Greece, hurl "vo-EE-thee-ah!" In Greece and Greek Cyprus, memorize the **emergency police number** (dial 100; in Cyprus, dial 190).

In Turkey, women travelers may find themselves receiving more than the usual number of catcalls and propositions. To silence a particularly vociferous suitor, shout *"Ayıp"* (Ah-YUP), or "Shame!" Use the expletive sparingly, however, since Turks take the term seriously. Should you find yourself in a threatening situation, threaten to call the authorities. Never hitchhike, no matter how hospitable the driver may appear, and invest in secure accommodations, particularly pensions and hotels with the word "aile," or "respectable, family-style" in their names.

Be aware that in Turkey, men and women tend to socialize separately. Especially in the smaller towns, men frequent *çay* shops, while the women stay at home. Although women are on the same legal and political footing as men in Turkey, the past fades slowly: nothing prevents a woman from entering a mosque but unwritten law (of course women can and do enter *some* mosques).

Proper dress is a always a good idea. In Turkey, stay away from revealing tank tops or short shorts. In the east, you should wear long skirts, long-sleeved blouses, and even a head scarf. To avoid offending the locals, particularly in smaller villages, you may wish to cover your knees. *Always* carry a headscarf with you. Shorts may be worn in İstanbul, the four major resorts—Kuşadası, Bodrum, Marmaris, and Kaş, and, of course, around any beach. In Greece, anything goes on the more touristy islands. Athens is more conservative but still cosmopolitan. The less touristed the area, the more skin should be covered.

If sexual activity is part of your itinerary, bring plenty of **contraceptives.** Condoms are easy to find, but it's best just to load up on hefty U.S. Trojans and "come prepared." You can find British Durex at some pharmacies. All other birth control devices are unavailable, if not unheard of.

Men as well as women should consider taking a self-defense course. Community colleges offer basic courses or try private organizations such as **Model Mugging.** Model Mugging offers courses tailored to real-life threatening situations, for both men and women. A three-week, 25-hour course costs around US$500—it's a life skill. Check your phone book for a local branch.

For further tips see *The Handbook for Women Travelers* (£6.95) by Maggie and Gemma Moss. For more information contact Judy Piatkus Publications, 5 Windmill St., London, W1, 1P 1HF, England.

Senior Travelers

Greeks and Turks of all ages have a great deal of respect for their elders, so senior citizens should receive a warm welcome. Senior citizens, like students, are often offered a variety of discounts and special services; **Hostelling International** sells memberships to those over 55 at a reduced rate. Below is a brief list of services that provide additional information:

American Association of Retired People (AARP), Special Sevices Dept., 601 E St., NW, Washington, DC 20049 (tel. (800) 927-0111; in Washington (202) 434-2277). Those 50 years and older can receive benefits from AARP Travel Services and get discounts for hotels, motels, car rentals and sight-seeing companies. Annual membership fee US$8.

Superintendent of Documents, U.S. Government Printing Office, Washington, DC 20402-9325 (tel. (202) 783-3238). Publishes *Travel Tips for Older Americans* (US$1).

Elderhostel, 80 Boylston St., #400, Boston, MA 02116 (tel. (617) 426-7788). Week-long program covering a variety of subjects; US$245-270 fee covers room, board, tuition, and extracur-

ricular activities. Workshops given at over 1500 locations internationally. You must be 60 years or older to participate; companions must be 50.

Pilot Books, 103 Cooper St., Babylon, NY 11702 (tel. (516) 422-2225). Publishes guides for the older traveler, including the *Senior Citizens' Guide to Budget Travel* (US$5.95 post paid) and *The International Health Guide for Senior Citizen Travelers* (US$4.95, postage US$1).

Travelers with Disabilities

Greece, Turkey, and Cyprus are only slowly beginning to respond to the needs of travelers with disabilities. Many cruise ships that sail throughout the Greek islands are equipped to accommodate those with disabilities. Special air transportation is available aboard Olympic Airways, for example, to many of the larger islands. Hotels, train stations, and airports have recently installed facilities for the disabled; however, many of the archaeological sites throughout the region are still not wheelchair-accessible.

When making arrangements with airlines or hotels, inform them of your handicap; some establishments may need time to prepare for your needs. Blind travelers may import seeing-eye dogs, provided they bring a health certificate stating that anti-rabies injections have been administered to the animal within the last year.

Useful publications for travelers with disabilities include *Access to the World,* by Louise Weiss, Facts on File, 460 Park Ave. S., New York, NY 10016 (tel. (800) 829-0500, (212) 683-2244 in AL and HI; US$16.95), and *Travel for the Disabled,* by Helen Heckler, Twin Peaks Press, P.O. Box 129, Vancouver, WA 98666 (tel. (800) 637-2256; US$19.95). The following organizations can provide further information:

American Foundation for the Blind, 15 W. 16th St., New York, NY 10011 (tel. (800) 829-0500 or (212) 620-2147). ID cards (US$10) and information on discounts. Write for a catalogue.

The Society for the Advancement of Travel for the Handicapped (SATH), 347 Fifth Ave., Suite 610, New York, NY 10016 (tel. (212) 447-7284). Provides advice and assistance on trip planning, listings, and several useful booklets (free for members; non-members, US$2). Annual membership US$45; students and seniors, US$25.

Travel Information Service, Moss Rehabilitation Hospital, 1200 W. Tabor Rd., Philadelphia, PA 19141 (tel. (215) 456-9603). Send US$5 for information for travelers with disabilities on tourist sights, accommodations, and transportation.

The following organizations and travel agencies offer special tours or services for those with disabilities:

Flying Wheels Travel, P.O. Box 382, 143 W. Bridge St., Owatonne, MN 55060 (tel. (800) 535-6790; in MN (800) 722-9351). Arranges international trips for groups or individuals.

Evergreen Travel Service, 4114 198th St. SW, Suite 13, Lynnwood, WA 98036 (tel. (800) 435-2288 or (206) 776-1184). Provides travel informatin and plans worldwide tours for travelers with disabilities.

Gay and Lesbian Travelers

Through the centuries, Greeks have had a reasonably tolerant attitude towards homosexuality. In Turkey, on the other hand, social conservatism and religious dictates tend to keep most activity discreet. If problems do arise, plan on authorities to be almost uniformly unsympathetic.

In Greece, Athens in particular offers a variety of gay bars, clubs, and hotels. For further information, contact **AKOE-AMPHI (Gay and Lesbian Liberation Movement),** P.O. Box 26022, 10022 Athens (tel. 771 92 21), which publishes *AMPHI* magazine. The islands of Hydra, Lesbos, Paros, Rhodes, and especially Mykonos also offer gay and lesbian resorts, hotels, bars, and clubs.

The best resources for gay and lesbian travelers are **Gay's the Word,** 66 Marchmont St., London, WC 1AB, England (tel. (071) 278 76 54), **Giovanni's Room,** 345 S. 12th St., Philadelphia, PA 19107, **Renaissance House,** P.O. Box 292, Village Station, New York, NY 10014 (tel. (212) 674-0120), and **Glad Day Books,** 598A Yonge St., Toronto, Ont. M4Y 1Z3 (tel. (416) 961-4161). All bookstores offer mail order service. Useful publications include **Women Going Places** (US$14), a new women's travel and resource guide, emphasizing women-owned and -operated enterprises. Also available is **Are You Two...Together?** a gay and lesbian guide to some of Europe's hottest spots (US$18). In Australia, inquire at **Open Leaves,** 71 Cardigan St., Carlton, Victoria 3053. The **Spartacus Guide for Gay Men** covers virtually every country in the world. It is available for US$27.95 from the above bookstores or UK£15 from Bruno Gmünder, Postfach 30 13 45, D-1000 Berlin 30, Germany (tel. (030) 261 16 46). For a more scholarly look at homosexuality in ancient Greece, pick up a copy of K.J. Dover's *Greek Homosexuality* (Vintage Books). Homosexual intercourse between adult men 17 and older is legal. Condoms are available throughout Western Europe but should be brought from home since local brands may not be necessarily well made.

Traveling with Children

Both Greeks and Turks love small children. Expect a stream of compliments, advice, and candy for your child. Children often receive substantial discounts on transportation throughout Greece and Turkey, but you shouldn't always count on this. Setting up a detailed itinerary can be especially helpful if you are traveling with children; you may want to slow your pace considerably. Avoid hassles by booking rooms in advance and planning some sightseeing stops that your children will enjoy.

A variety of books can prepare you with witty advice. Try *Travel with Children* (US$11 + $1.50), available from Lonely Planet Publications, P.O. Box 617, Hawthorn, Victoria 3122, Australia; in U.S., 155 Filbert #251, Oakland, CA 94607 (tel. (800) 275-8555 or (510) 893-8555). *Sharing Nature With Children* (US$7.95) and *Backpacking With Babies and Small Children* (US$8.95) are available from Wilderness Press, 2440 Bancroft Way, Berkeley, CA 94704 (tel. (800) 443-7227 or (510) 843-8080).

Special Diets

The Jewish Travel Guide, a guide to keeping kosher on the road, can be obtained from the **Sepher-Hermon Press,** 1265 46th St., Brooklyn, NY 11219 (tel. (718) 972-9010; USUS$11.50); in England, **Jewish Chronicle Publications,** 25 Furnival St., London EC4A IJT (US$10.95, postage $1.50).

Mediterranean cuisine includes many tasty **vegetarian** dishes. Though vegetarians on Cyprus may be disappointed by the lack of truly indigenous meatless entrees, in Greece foods such as *fasolia* (beans), *spanakopita* (spinach-filled pastry), and *tyropitakia* (cheese-filled pastry) are readily available. In Turkey, *hummus, fasülye* (beans), and numerous *meze* appetizers are plentiful. During the summer, when fresh produce abounds in the outdoor markets, vegetarians will find an abundance of fresh vegetables, fruits, and interesting cheeses.

For more information, contact the **Vegetarian Society of the U.K.,** Parkdale, Dunham Rd., Altrincham, Cheshire WA14 4QG (tel. (061) 928 07 03), or the **North American Vegetarian Society,** P.O. Box 72, Dolgeville, NY 13329 (tel. (518) 568-7970).

Alternatives to Tourism

Work

Finding work in Greece and Turkey is difficult. Because of extremely high domestic unemployment, job opportunities are scarce and the governments try to restrict employment to citizens and visitors from the European Economic Community (EEC).

For long-term employment in Greece, you must first secure a work permit from your employer; permits are available at the **Ministry of Labor,** 40 Pireos St., Athens 10437 (tel. 523 31 10). Your best bet is to first secure a job with a company from your home country, but this usually requires fluency in the language and some specialized skill. All arrangements and negotiations should be made before you leave home. For a list of U.S. firms, subsidiaries, and affiliates operating in Greece, write the **American Hellenic Chamber of Commerce,** 16 Kanari St., 3rd Floor, 10674 Athens (tel. 361 83 85, fax 361 01 70). The list costs US$150. They can also offer advice about finding temporary or permanent employment in Greece.

For **hotel jobs** (bartending, cleaning, etc.) it is best to arrive in the spring and early summer to search for work. Most night spots don't pay more than 2200dr per day. To find jobs, check the bulletin boards of hostels in Athens and the classified ads in the *Athens News*. Or, contact **Working Holidays** at 11 Nikis St., 1st and 6th floors, Athens 10557 (tel. 322 43 21 or 325 51 68). They will take applications from overseas, but require prepayment of the US$40 registration fee. Another possibility is to work as a farm laborer—the Peloponnese and Crete are good places to look.

The process for obtaining a job in Cyprus is similar. Before you arrive, you must find an employer who can assert that you are particularly suited for your position due to academic interest or experience, and that there are no suitably qualified local employees available in your field. Your employer must then secure written permission of the **Migration Officer,** Ministry of the Interior, Nicosia (tel. (02) 30 28 00; fax (02) 44 92 21).

For information about jobs in Turkey, contact the nearest consulate.

Several organizations sponsor **workcamp opportunities** abroad. **Volunteers for Peace** sponsors international workcamp programs in 37 nations for college students. For their free newsletter or their *International Workcamp Directory* (US$10 ppd) write to 43 Tiffany Rd, Belmont, VT 05730 (tel. (802) 259-2759). In Greece, the American Farm School runs summer work and recreation programs for high school and university students. Write to 1133 Broadway, New York, NY 10010 (tel. (212) 463-8434), or in Greece, P.O. Box 10140, Thessaloniki 54110 (tel. 30 31 47 18 03). **Service Civil International (SCI-USA),** c/o Innisfree Village, Rte. 2 Box 506, Crozet, VA 22932 (tel. (804) 823-1826), sponsors workcamps in over 25 countries; participants do volunteer community work. If you have a technical background, the **International Association for the Exchange of Students for Technical Experience (IAESTE),** 10400 Little Patuxent Parkway, Ste. 250, Columbia, MD 21044-3510 (tel. (410) 997-2200), sponsors programs in several countries, including Greece and Turkey.

Other work opportunities are limited. Check the nearest university library for ideas. The **Council on International Educational Exchange, or CIEE** (see Useful Organizations and Publications above), puts out several publications that may help you on a foreign job search, including *Volunteer! The Comprehensive Guide to Voluntary Service in the U.S. and Abroad* (US$8.95, postage $1.50).

For an extensive list of 50,000 volunteer and paid work opportunities, send for the *1992 Directory of Overseas Summer Jobs* (US$14.95, postage $4.75), or look through *Work Your Way Around the World* (US$16.95, postage $4.75); both publications are available from Peterson's, P.O. Box 2123, Princeton, NJ 08543 (tel. (800) 338-3282), or a CIEE office.

Study

Many U.S. students go abroad on programs run by American universities or organizations, or on independent study projects financed by universities. Talk to a counselor at your college or check your school library for information about studying abroad; many colleges give credit for classes taken at a foreign university.

The **Institute of International Education (IIE),** 809 United Nations Plaza, New York, NY 10017 (tel. (212) 888-8200), is the largest U.S. higher educational exchange agency. While they cannot provide direct assistance by mail or phone, their *Academic Year Abroad* (US$39.95) describes over 1800 semester and year study programs, while their *Vacation Study Abroad* lists 1300 summer and short-term study programs (US$31.95 + $3 shipping).

College Year in Athens runs a two-semester program on Greek civilization for undergraduates (usually juniors), which includes travel to important sites as well as classroom instruction (in English). The program has its own faculty and issues transcripts to home universities. Cost is US$8000 for one semester and US$12,000 for a full year; some scholarship money is available. For more information, contact the American Representative, College Year in Athens, Dept. L, 1910 E. First St., Bloomington, IN 47401-5225 (tel. (812) 336-2841); or the Director, College Year in Athens, P.O. Box 17176, Athens GR-10024 (tel. 721 87 46).

The Aegean Institute, c/o Dr. Paul Stavrolakes, 25 Waterview Dr., Port Jefferson, NY 11777 (tel. (516) 473-7075), organizes a six-week summer program in Poros, Greece, with college-credit courses in Greek art and archaeology, drama, cultural anthropology, Greek mythology, ancient history, and all levels of modern Greek including literature. It also offers guided fieldtrips to museums and ancient sites, including Crete, Argolid, Corinth, Olympia, Delphi, and Athens. **The Athens Centre,** 48 Archimidous St., Athens 11636 (tel. 701 52 42 or 701 22 68) offers programs in Greek language. **Study in Greece,** Neoforos 1, Athens GR-16121 (tel. 723 88 25 or 722 27 89), has semester-long courses taught in English, in addition to Greek language courses and independent 10-day field projects. Other organizations include the **Hellenic American Union,** 22 Massalias St., Athens 10680 (tel. 360 73 05), with courses in modern spoken Greek, studio art, and folk dancing; those interested in agriculture can try the **American Farm School,** 1133 Broadway, New York, NY 10010 (tel. (212) 463-8434) and P.O. Box 10140, Thessaloniki, GR54101, (tel. (011) 30 31 47 18 03); **Delta School of Technical and Business Studies,** 3 Rethumnou St., Museum, Athens 10682 (tel. 822 00 83).

High school students who want to study for a year in Greece or Turkey may write for information from **American Field Service (AFS) Intercultural Programs,** 313 E. 43rd St., New York, NY 10017 (tel. (800) 463-4636, or (212) 949-4242), and the **American Institute for Foreign Study,** 102 Greenwich Ave., Greenwich, CT 06830 (tel. (800) 727-2437 and (203) 869-9090).

More information on educational programs in Greece can be obtained from the Greek Press and Information Office (see Useful Organizations above). Your best bet for information on study in Turkey is to call the education office at the nearest information office (in New York, tel. (212) 687-8395). You may also enroll in one of several small colleges on Cyprus. For more information, contact the Department of Education in Nicosia.

Keeping in Touch

Before leaving, it is best to leave a rough copy of your itinerary with someone at home. Mail delivery and *poste restante* are slow, and plenty of time must be allowed. Though you can make international calls from most anywhere, service is sporadic, lines poor or jammed, and your first minute may cost you more than your last three meals.

One convenient way to keep in touch is to use **EurAide's** Overseas Access Service. Friends and family may dial direct to EurAide's "home base" in Munich to leave short messages for European travelers. The service operates seven days a week and travelers simply phone the office in Munich to check on messages from home. For more information, write P.O. Box 2375, Naperville, IL 60567 (tel. (708) 420-2343). For information on telephone and mail services, see the country introductions.

Getting There

> *Escape may be checked by water and land, but the
> air and sky are free.*

So said Daedalus to his son Icarus as they prepared to flee Crete on a pair of homemade wings. While survival rates and in-flight entertainment have improved greatly since then, airfares have risen accordingly. Take the time to shop around and above all, *plan ahead.*

From North America

Flexibility can save you money, especially when faced with the high cost of regularly scheduled direct flights; an indirect flight through Brussels or Luxembourg may cost considerably less than a flight going directly to Athens. **Off-season** travelers are faced with less competition for inexpensive seats and benefit from the lower fares. **Peak-season** rates begin either on May 15 or June 1 and run through September 15. You can save yourself a bundle by carefully arranging your travel dates. Consult a travel agent to guide you through the labyrinth of travel companies and find out what your options are. Commissions are somewhat smaller on budget flights, and as a result some travel agents are not as eager to help you search for the cheapest fare. Scan the travel section of the Sunday *New York Times* and other major newspapers for cheap, albeit erratic, fares. Student travel organizations such as Let's Go Travel, CIEE, or Travel CUTS (see Useful Organizations above) offer special deals that regular travel agents may not be aware of through ticket consolidators. In the summer of 1992, New York-Athens round-trip flights cost approximately US$750, and New York-İstanbul round-trip flights cost around US$770.

One of the most consistently economical options available is the **charter flight.** These may be booked up to the last minute; however, most flights usually fill up months in advance. A charter flight allows you the flexibility to stay abroad for as long as you wish and often lets you book departures and arrivals out of different cities. Once your reservations are made, no changes may be made. Departure and return dates must be chosen when you book. If you cancel your ticket, you'll lose all or most of your money. Charter companies can also be unreliable: they reserve the right to change the dates of your flight, add fuel surcharges after you have made your final payment, and even cancel the flight (up to 48hr. before departure). They'll do their best to get you on another flight, but the delay could be days, not just hours.

One of the largest U.S. charter operators, **CIEE,** offers service to most major European cities. CIEE's flights are extremely popular, so reserve early (tel. (800) 800-8222). They also offer a variety of flights for students and teachers (tel. (212) 661-1450). The charter companies **Tourlite** (tel. (800) 272-7600; in NY (212) 599-2727) and **Homeric Tours** (tel. (800) 223-5570) offer service to Greece, but not Turkey. When you inquire about charter options, ask about the company's recent record of delays and cancellations.

If you decide to make your transatlantic crossing with a regular airline, you will purchase greater reliability and flexibility. The major airlines offer two options for the budget traveler. The first is to fly **standby** (without a reservation). Some airlines have begun phasing out standby fares and destinations, and standby tickets are not the budget wonders they once were. You can purchase standby tickets in advance, but you are not guaranteed a seat on any particular flight.

The second option is to fly on the **Advanced Purchase Excursion Fare (APEX)**, offered by many major airlines. APEX will provide confirmed reservations and will often allow you to leave and depart from different cities. APEX does have its drawbacks—your excursion has to fit rigid minimum/maximum length requirements, usually seven to 60 days, and you must purchase your ticket two to three weeks in advance. Book APEX fares early—summer flights can fill up as soon as June. Changes in reservations cost US$50 and up; changes in return date or time cost US$100.

If your plans are flexible, take advantage of travel services that sell **last-minute seats.** You usually must give the agency three to five weeks advance notice before the desired departure date and pay a US$35-50 membership fee. Although there are no guarantees that a flight will be found, this option may save you money in the long run. **Last Minute Travel Club** (tel. (800) 527-8646; in MA, (617) 267-9800), has no membership fee and offers club services, including a travelers' hotline. Other agencies include: **Traveler's Advantage** (tel. (800) 548-1116; US$49.95 membership per year), and **Access International** (tel. (800) 825-3633). **Travel Avenue** (tel. (800) 333-3335) discounts international flights 8-25%. A less conventional option is **Air Hitch** (tel. (212) 864-2000), a commercial jet hitchhiking assistance program operating on a region-by-region basis across the Atlantic. During the summer of 1992, Air Hitch advertised a one-way rate of US$169 from the East Coast to Europe; from the West Coast, US$269. Remember to check all flights and departure sites directly with the airline, read *all* the fine print they send you, and don't trust *anything* that's not in writing.

It is also possible to save money by traveling as a **courier. Now Voyager** (tel. (213) 432-1616) and **Halbart Express** (tel. (718) 656-8189) offer the option of traveling to Europe at discounted rates. Only two restrictions apply: only carry-on luggage is permitted (the company uses your baggage space) and the number of possible flights depends on the courier's needs. If you don't mind traveling light, call for details.

From Europe

By Plane

If direct flights to Greece or Turkey are booked, your next cheapest option is to fly to London or another European location (e.g., Paris, Zurich, Frankfurt, Rome), and make way to the destination of your choice. In Europe, student/youth charters are still the least expensive way to fly. Budget fares are frequently available on high-volume flights between northern Europe and Greece but are usually offered only during the spring and summer months.

Budget agencies like Council Travel and Travel CUTS help you plan a travel itinerary before you go. If you're willing to take a risk in order to save money, wait until you're abroad to make further arrangements; see *Let's Go: Europe* for listings of student travel agencies in other European countries. London offers a veritable plethora of travel options and **STA Travel,** 74 & 86 Old Brompton Rd., London SW7 3LQ (tel. (071) 937 99 21 for European travel) or 17 E. 45th St., New York, NY 10017 (tel. (800) 777-0112 or (212) 986-9470) is a good place to begin your search. **Pilgrim Air,** 44 Goodge St., London W1P 2CE (tel. (071) 436 39 11), has good prices on London flights. If stopping off, be sure to check out London's **bucket shops.** These are travel agencies that allow travelers to buy unsold tickets at unofficially discounted prices (often over 50% off the regular flight). **Olympic Airways** (in England (081) 493 39 65 or (034) 558 11 91) offers a round-trip London-Athens fare of US$631, and a round-trip Paris-Athens fare of US$656. (Winter prices are 10-30% cheaper.) International flights also connect to airports in Crete, Rhodes, and Corfu. **Romanian Airlines** (Tarom) and **Pakistan Air** both offer low fares to İstanbul from the U.S. and major European cities. (Romanian has no offices in the U.S.) **Turkish Airlines' (THY)** fares are exorbitant, but a 60% student reduction brings them in line with the budget carriers (London-İstanbul round-trip US$442). THY also has regular service to Turkey from European countries and offers 50% discounts to ISIC holders and those under 22 on some international flights.

NOTE: If you have flown to Greece on a European charter flight, you are required to stay in Greece for your vacation (in other words, you can't take advantage of cheap fares to Greece in order to visit Turkey). Be certain to contact your agency for details.

By Train

Greece is served by a number of international train routes that connect Athens, Thessaloniki, and Larissa to most European cities. Count on at least a three-day journey from Trieste or Vienna to Athens. **Eurailpasses** are best for those travelers who want to see as much of Europe as possible; to make these passes pay off, you need to make a lot of stops. *The passes must be bought in the United States* or another non-European country as they are issued only outside of Europe. Passes include unlimited first-class travel and range in cost from US$460 for 15 days to US$1260 for three months. Children under 12 pay half-price (under 4 ride free). Those under 26 will want to purchase a **Eurail Youthpass** to get unlimited second-class travel. One month travel costs US$508, two months US$698. A group of three or more travelers can pay US$390 per person for the **Eurail Saverpass,** which allows for 15 consecutive days of unlimited first-class travel, provided the group travels together. (Children under 12 pay *full fare,* under 4 are free.) Two people traveling together can use a Eurail Saverpass as long as their traveling time falls between October and April. **Eurail Flexipasses** enable passengers to travel for a limited number of days while the pass is valid, at great savings. Five days travel in two months costs US$298, 10 days in two months costs US$496, and 15 days in two months costs US$676. Those under 26 can purchase the **Eurail Youth Flexipass,** which allows five days travel in two months for US$220, 10 days travel in two months for US$348, and 15 days travel in two months for US$474. All four types of passes offer free travel in Greece and 30% discounts on ferries from Brindisi to Patras on Adriatica Lines' or Hellenic Mediterranean Lines' ferries from Piraeus to Cyprus, Venice, Alexandria, and Turkey (Eurail passes are *not* good for inner-Greece ferries, however). Keep your validation slip and receipt of sale. For a free Eurail manual of train routes, ask your travel agent or write French Rail Inc., 610 Fifth Ave., New York, NY 10020 (tel. (212) 582-4813).

If you board a train that has no available compartment space for a long trip, consider getting off and waiting for the next one—three days in an aisle crowded with travelers and livestock can be a nightmare. *Couchettes* are the economy version of a full sleeping berth and come complete with blankets, sheets, and pillows. If you have any sort of railpass, couchettes are available at an extra charge of about US$11 per trip. Sleeping train riders are easy prey for thieves, so guard your goods. Request a top bunk when you buy your ticket; the awkward height may deter thieves. Put your valuables in your money belt and wear it while you sleep.

Turkey is accessible by rail from points in Europe and trains are among the cheapest transportation alternatives, but it certainly isn't the most convenient—Eurail is invalid in Turkey. The Turkish rail system is rivaled only by the Greek as Europe's most antiquated and least efficient. Rail service is provided from Venice, Munich, and Vienna.

By Bus

Bus travel is another inexpensive possibility. Amsterdam, Athens, İstanbul, London, and Munich are all centers for private bus lines providing long-distance tours across Europe. **Magic Bus** offers cheap, direct bus service between major cities in Europe, along with competitive air fares. Offices are located at 20 Filellinon St., Syntagma, Athens (tel. (01) 323 74 71); and 32 Tsimiski St., Thessaloniki (tel. (031) 28 32 80). Information on Magic Bus is available from cooperating offices in many other cities. **London Student Travel,** 52 Grosvenor Gardens, London SW1W OAG (tel. (071) 730 34 02) offers competitive rail, coach, and air fares all over the continent.

By Ferry

Ferry travel is a popular way to get to both Greece and Turkey. Reservations are recommended for many ferries, especially in the high season. Be warned, however, that *ferries run on very irregular schedules.* You should check in early, at *least* two hours in advance; late boarders may find their seats gone. If you sleep on deck, be sure to bring warm clothes and a sleeping bag. Bicycles travel free and motorcycles are transported for an additional charge (check each agency).

Some tips for traveling by ferry: avoid crossing from Italy to Greece during the last two weeks in July and the first two in August at all costs. From the third week in June until the second week in July, prices rise about 20%, and in mid-July they jump again—as much as 50%. Bring your own food to avoid high prices charged on board. Make sure you bring along toilet paper and a hand towel.

The major ports of departure for ferries between Greece and Italy are **Ancona** and **Brindisi,** on the southeastern coast of Italy. Boats travel primarily to Corfu (9hr., deck class in high-season 12,700-15,500dr, low-season 8150-8970dr), Igoumenitsa (11hr., same prices as Corfu), and Patras (19hr., deck class in high-season 15,500-16,300dr, low-season 8970-10,600dr). In addition to stops at Corfu, Igoumenitsa, and Patras, ferries also stop at Piraeus; Iraklion; Rhodes; Limassol; Cyprus; **Haifa,** Israel (from Piraeus high season 16,560-22,250dr); and **İzmir,** Turkey. Ferries also depart from **Bari,** Italy for other Mediterranean points.

Most lines offer **discounts.** Those 26 and under, and ISIC-holders 30 and under, can usually obtain student deck fares for 1000dr less than the regular price. Senior citizens may get a 10% discount, and children under 12 pay half-price (under 4 ride free). **Eurail** passholders may receive 30% off regular fares. Finally, there are group (usually 10-person minimum) reductions of approximately 10% on one-way and 20% on round-trip tickets. Regardless of the ticket, everyone pays the port tax (IT£11,000-18,000 in Brindisi, about 1000dr at Greek ports). Rates vary from company to company, so it pays to shop around. You can travel to Turkey by **boat** from points other than Greece, including Brindisi, Italy and Lattakia, Syria.

Travel Between Greece and Turkey

Note that the Greek government frowns on tourists taking advantage of cheaper fares to Greece for easy access to Turkey, and, depending on your sources, the information you receive on how to travel between the two countries may be confusing. Contrary to

what tourist authorities may lead you to believe, there is no law that prevents you from crossing the borders. Many travelers make one-day excursions, but you should check into regulations on longer trips. As noted earlier, if you fly to Greece on a European charter flight, you may not travel to Turkey.

Athens and İstanbul are connected by Euroways Eurolines bus and by train. If you have a railpass and are traveling from Greece to Turkey, take the train as far as Alexandroupolis, and ride the bus from there. Beware: the 38-hour ride from Athens will wear out even the most seasoned traveler. The quickest but most expensive option is an Olympic Airways **flight** to İstanbul or other points in Turkey.

If you decide to **hitch** between Turkey and Greece, try to make it between İstanbul in one ride from Alexandroupolis or Thessaloniki; there isn't much traffic, and you are not permitted to walk across the border. Make sure your driver's car license doesn't get stamped in your passport (but rather on some other, disposable piece of paper), or you'll need to produce the car to leave the country. The officials might suspect that you sold it on the black market. If you're bold enough to bring your own into Turkey, you can drive for three months without a *Carnet de Passage,* although the vehicle will be registered on your passport. If you plan to stay longer, you must apply for a *triptique* at the Turkish Touring and Automobile Club. (See Documents above.) We urge you to consider the risks inherent in hitchhiking. *Let's Go* does not recommend hitchhiking.

There is direct **ferry** service between Piraeus and İzmir, but it's cheaper to take a ferry from one of the islands. Travel agents in Athens and İstanbul can help you sort through options. From Samos, Greece, two boats travel daily in the summer from Samos Town to Kuşadası, Turkey, and nearby ruins at Ephesus (leaving at 8am and 5pm); three ferries per week also run between Pythagorion and Kuşadası. During the off-season, only half as many boats make the crossing. If traveling from Greece, you must deposit your passport with the travel agency the night before you sail, even if you don't plan to return. Authorities levy a newly imposed embarkation tax of 1500dr per person, and an US$8 port tax (paid on board) imposed during embarkation, in addition to the fare itself (6000dr, round-trip 1000dr). Try to pay in U.S. dollars, since the *drachma* suffers an outrageous exchange rate in Turkey (you will probably pay about US$2 more). Port taxes are charged only in Kuşadası, Antalya, İzmir, and İstanbul, so if you're planning to spend time elsewhere in Turkey, it may be worth your while to cross over at another point.

In the summer, Monday through Saturday, boats travel daily between Rhodes and Marmaris; in the off-season, service is reduced to four or five boats per week. Departure times are never fixed until the day before. To purchase tickets, get departure information, and deposit your passport (1 day in advance), go to **Triton Tours,** 25 Plastira St., Rhodes (tel. 306 57). (Open Mon.-Fri. 8am-2pm and 4-9pm, Sat. 9am-1:30pm and 4-8pm.) The trip (2hr.) costs 4000dr, round-trip 7000dr. In Turkey, tickets may be purchased from **Yeşil Marmaris Tur** (tel. 15 59) and **Engin Tur** (tel. 10 82).

You can hop the ferry to Çeşme from the island of Chios. It runs daily from July 1 to September 10, four times weekly from June 4-30 and September 11-Oct. 10, and once weekly for the rest of the year. The passage lasts 1½ hours and costs US$20, round-trip US$25. Leave your passport with the travel agent one day in advance.

Boats run daily between Lesvos and Ayvalık every day from May to October at 8:30am, and three times per week from November through April (1½hr., about 4000dr one-way). From **Patmos,** planned excursions go to Ephesus in Turkey (500dr round-trip, 1800dr Turkish port tax, 1500dr for a guided tour of the ruins).

From **Northern Cyprus,** the shortest crossing is from Girne (Kyrenia) to Taşucu (6hr.). There are two boats, the *Liberty* and the *Ertürk,* leaving on alternate days in the summer. Boats run less frequently in winter, on no set schedule. For information on hydrofoils, call 621 89 in Taşucu. There are also **flights** to İstanbul from Nicosia's Ercan Airport.

For information on getting to and from the **Republic of Cyprus,** please see the introduction to that fascinating country.

GREECE ΕΛΛΆΣ

US$1 = 175.0dr	100dr = US$0.57
CDN$1 = 146.93dr	100dr = CDN$0.68
UK£1 = 347.73dr	100dr = UK£0.29
IR£1 = 327.69	100dr = IR£0.31
AUS$1 = 125.04dr	100dr = AUS$0.80
NZ$1 = 94.67dr	100dr = NZ$1.06

Even before Odysseus made his epic voyage across the Mediterranean, Greece was a place for wanderers. Today, airplanes and ferries let the traveler see Greece without divine assistance, but if Odysseus were trying to navigate today, he would have a hard time finding his way home. Modern concrete structures dwarf the classical ruins, and in larger cities, the glare of electric light outshines the stars. Still, much of the land's enchantment would be familiar to him: the brilliance of turquoise waters and the silvery flash of olive leaves in the light, the rugged beaches and snug villages, the spirited nightlife.

After he had finished translating the *Odyssey*, Robert Fitzgerald remarked that his rendering of the Achaean world would have been very different had he not sipped retsina on the Ithakan shore or heard the crickets there. Something about the land itself defies translation. Whether the Greece you see is the oracular past or the lively present, you'll carry some of the "cradle of democracy" home with the traveler's standard baggage of stoicism and hedonism.

Once There

Tourist Offices

Tourism in Greece is managed by two nationwide organizations: the **Greek National Tourist Organization (GNTO)** and the **tourist police** *(touristiki astinomia)*. The GNTO can supply general information about sights and accommodations all over the country. Offices in the U.S. and other countries are listed under Useful Organizations; the main office is at 2 Amerikis St., Athens (tel. 322 31 11). Note that the GNTO is known as **EOT** in Greece. The tourist police deal with more local and immediate problems—where to find a room, what the bus schedule is, or what to do when you've lost your passport. They are open long hours and are always willing to help, although their English is often limited. Tourist information for Greece is available in English 24 hrs. by calling 171.

Nikis and **Filellinon Streets** in Athens are lined with agencies and organizations geared specifically towards budget and student travelers. We also list similar establishments in different cities in the Orientation and Practical Information section for each region.

Emergencies

In each regional section, under Orientation and Practical Information, we list police telephone numbers. We also list the telephone numbers for ambulances, medical emergency centers, local hospitals and clinics, and pharmacies. Emergency phone numbers, applicable throughout most of Greece and operating 24 hrs., include **police** (tel. 100) and **first aid** (tel. 166).

Business Hours

Most shops close on Sundays: and only restaurants, cafés, and bakeries remain open. During the week business hours vary, but most places close after 2pm for a siesta and

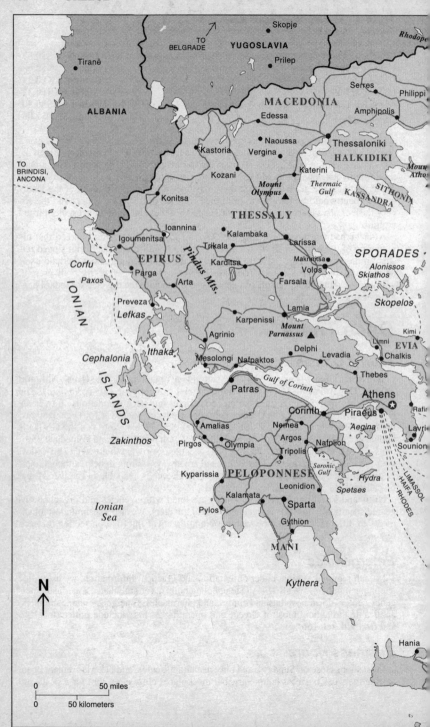

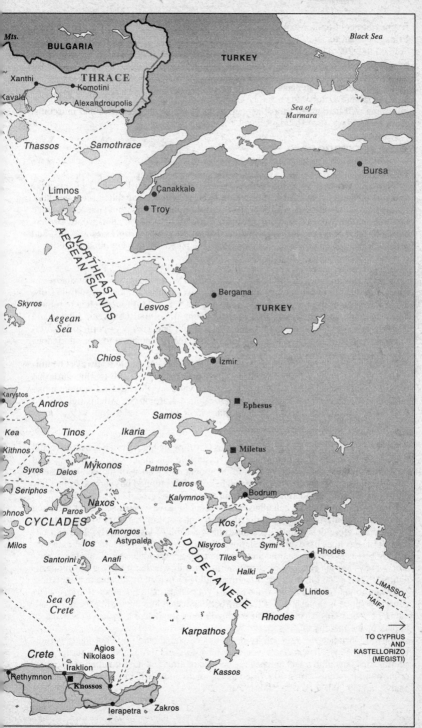

re-open at about 6pm. Most banks are open Monday through Thursday 8am to 2pm, Friday 7:45am to 2pm. Post offices and OTEs are open Monday through Saturday 7:30am to 2:30pm in small towns, and until 7:30pm or later in bigger cities. Shops and pharmacies are open Monday, Wednesday, and Saturday 8am to 2:30pm and Tuesday, Thursday, and Friday 8am to 1pm and 5 to 8:30pm. Food stores have slightly longer hours. Museums and archaeological sites close on Tuesdays, and have slightly shorter hours from mid-October to mid-May. On holidays, sights will often have Sunday opening hours. All banks and shops, as well as most archaeological sites and museums, close on holidays. (See Holidays below for dates.)

Transportation

Plane

Olympic Airways, 96 Syngrou Ave., 117 41 Athens (tel. (01) 92 92 111), serves many of the larger cities and islands within Greece. While flying might seem quickest, it may not be the most convenient or flexible option for travel within Greece; coverage in some remote areas is spotty at best. (For further flight information within Greece, check the regional Practical Information listings of airports, flight destinations, and prices, or pick up an Olympic Airways Timetable booklet at any Olympic office.)

Train

Greek trains are not quite as comfortable as the sleek, modern lines in northern Europe, and run only to major cities. Furthermore, service to some areas is painfully slow, and no lines go to the western coast. Trains are not very useful for traveling to remote areas or many archaeological sites, either. Trains travel daily between Athens and Thessaloniki (8hr.), continuing on to Alexandroupolis and Turkey or north to Yugoslavia and the rest of Europe. Lines also extend into the Peloponnese to Corinth, Patras, Olympia, and Kalamata.

Eurail passes are valid on Greek trains. In addition, the **Hellenic Railways Organization (OSE)** connects Athens to other major Greek cities. OSE sells touring cards that offer unlimited travel for 10, 20, or 30 days (also valid on OSE buses). For more information, write to Hellenic Railways Organization, 1 Karolou St., Athens (tel. 522 45 63). For schedules and prices in Greece, dial 145 or 147.

Bus

Spending time in Greece invariably means traveling by bus. Service is extensive and frequent in most areas, and fares are very reasonable. On major highways, buses tend to be more modern and efficient than in the mountainous areas of the Peloponnese or Northern Greece. The **OSE** (see By Train below) offers limited bus service from a few cities. Unless you are sticking close to train routes, **KTEL** should be sufficient.

Always ask an official when a bus is scheduled to leave (posted schedules are often out of date, and all services are curtailed significantly on Sun.), and try to arrive at least 10 minutes before departure (Greek buses have a habit of leaving early). In major cities, KTEL bus lines have different stations for different destinations. In villages, a café usually serves as the bus station, and you can only get schedules by asking the proprietor. Always ask the conductor before entering the bus whether it's going to your destination (the signs on the front are often misleading or outdated), and make clear where you want to get off. If the bus whizzes past your stop, stand up and yell *Stasis!* (The general practice is to push one of the few buttons which line the roof of the bus in advance of your stop.) If you're on the road, you must stand near a *Stasis* (ΣΤΑΣΙΣ) sign to pick up an intercity bus.

For long-distance rides, generally in Pullmans, you should buy your ticket beforehand in the office. (If you don't, you may have to stand throughout the journey.) For shorter trips, just grab a seat and pay the conductor after you have boarded. Some lines offer round-trip fares with a 20% discount. In towns and cities, local buses and trolleys charge around 30dr for a ride, 50dr in Athens.

Car

Driving might just be the ideal way to tour Greece. There are highways on the mainland, and ferries can take you island hopping if you pay a transport fee for the automobile. Small villages usually cater to cars only through the main road running through town.

Potential drivers should be comfortable with a standard stick shift, mountain dirt roads, reckless drivers (especially in Athens), and the Greek alphabet. Greek signs are placed about 100m before the transliterated versions, which are stuck right at the turnoffs.

Rentals with unlimited mileage and very limited insurance range from 25,000dr in the off-season to 35,000dr in the summer. Gasoline is 80dr per liter—about $2 per gallon. In a full day of touring (300km), Hertz's Subaru 600 (an economy hatchback) will eat up a full tank, translating into 17½ liters and about 2000dr. Agencies quote low daily rates, but these prices exclude the 20% tax and Collision Damage Waiver (CDW) insurance. Without CDW, the driver is responsible for the first 150,000dr worth of damage if theft or accident is not the driver's fault, and the full amount otherwise. CDW insurance (500dr per day) is strongly recommended.

Check the fine print with care. Some places quote lower rates but hit you with hidden charges—exorbitant refueling bills if you come back with less than a full tank, 1½-2½dr per kilometer drop-off or special charge, or 100km per day minimum mileage even if you never leave their driveway. Most companies will not permit driving the car outside Greece or ferrying it out of the country. Hertz and InterRent rent to drivers aged 21, but most other companies only rent to those 23 and older.

The cheapest and largest rental agencies are Just, InterRent, and Retca, with offices in Athens and other mainland cities, as well as on Crete and several of the islands. In Athens, look for **Just,** 43 Syngrou Ave. 11743 (tel. 923 85 66 or 932 91 04); **Inter-Rent,** 4 Singrou Ave. 11742 (tel. 921 57 88/9 or 923 34 52), with other offices in Rhodes, Corfu, and Rethymno; and **Retca,** 20 Kalisperi St. (tel. 921 43 73). Another inexpensive agency is **Royal Rent A Car,** 44 Amalias Ave., Athens (tel. 324 53 66). **Avis, Hertz, Europcar,** and **Budget** also operate all over Greece; their rates are steeper, but they offer reliable service. It is often cheaper to make arrangements with these companies while still in your home country.

Foreign drivers are required to have an **International Driver's License** and an **International Insurance Certificate** to drive in Greece (see *International Driver's License* above). The Automobile and Touring Club of Greece (ELPA), 2-4 Messogion St., Athens 11527 (tel. 779 74 01), provides tourists with assistance and information, and offers reciprocal membership to foreign auto club members. They also have a 24-hr. emergency road assistance service (tel. 104) and an information line (tel. 174, open Mon.-Fri. 7am-3pm).

Moped

Motorbiking is a popular way of touring Greece, especially the islands. Bikes are cheaper than cars and offer more freedom than buses, particularly if you wish to visit remote areas. Plenty of places offer scooters or mopeds for rent, but the quality of bikes, speed of service in case of breakdown, and prices for longer periods may vary drastically. Nearly all agencies are open to bargaining. Expect to pay 1500-2000dr per day for a 50cc scooter, the cheapest bike able to tackle steep mountain roads. 150cc and 200cc motorbikes cost 20% and 30% more, respectively, and usually require a Greek motorcycle license. Many agencies request your passport as a deposit, but it is probably wiser to just settle up in advance. If they have your passport and you have an accident or mechanical failure, they may refuse to return it until you pay for all repairs. Before renting, ask if the quoted price includes the 20% tax and insurance, or you'll be hit for several hundred unexpected *drachmae*.

Thumb

Be sure to fully consider the risks involved before you decide to hitch. Let's Go does not recommend hitching as a means of travel.

It's hard to generalize about hitching in Greece. Greeks are not eager to pick up foreigners and foreign cars are usually full of other travelers. Sparsely-populated areas simply have little or no traffic. Those who do choose to hitchhike write their destination on a sign in both Greek and English letters, and try to hitch from turn-offs rather than along long stretches of straight road.

Ferry

Every summer, visitors to the Greek islands envision themselves sunning leisurely on spacious ship decks while being smoothly whisked from isle to isle; every summer, these same visitors are disillusioned by bewildering schedules and crowded boats. Nevertheless, ferries are still the cheapest way to cross the Mediterranean.

Ferry travel is notoriously unreliable. Always confirm your departure times with the tourist or boat office. Don't bother planning an itinerary far in advance. Although boat connections between major islands are frequent during the summer months, departure times fluctuate from year to year. To get to smaller islands, you often have to change boats several times, and some islands are accessible only a few times per week. Direct connections are less expensive than longer routes (the more stops, the higher the price), but also tend to be less frequent.

Foot

Walking is a lost pleasure for many, but the beautiful landscape of Greece can help you rediscover it. *Let's Go* describes many hikes and trails under each town and city listing; the local residents and fellow travelers can suggest even more. Always make sure you have comfortable shoes and a proper map. Remember that hiking under the hot sun at a high altitude may be more strenuous than you expect. A good sunscreen, a hat, and plenty of water are essential. For more information, check out *Greece on Foot* ($10.95) published by **The Mountaineer Books.** Write to 1011 SW Klickitat Way, Seattle, WA 98134 (tel. (800) 553-4453).

Island Hopping

For many people, visiting Greece means island hopping. The islands are all different, but a few basic rules of thumb apply to almost all of them. As you arrive on the more popular islands, people with rooms to rent will greet your boat. These rooms are usually cheapest, but it is imperative that you make owners pinpoint the exact location of their houses. "Ten minutes away, near the beach," by their definitions can mean a 45-minute hike from the main town. Camping is plentiful on these islands, and although freelance camping is illegal, some choose to hunker down when there are no official campsites nearby. Those who freelance should always take their trash with them when they leave the site. Singles are few and far between at hotels or pensions, and in peak season, solo travelers will usually have to take a double room at the standard price. In pensions, bargaining is always worth a try; remember that room rates should decrease for stays of more than two or three nights, and dock hawks will generally respond with scorn when you indicate a one-night stay. In the off-season (Sept.-early June), the cost of accommodations drops by at least 20%. You might consult the tourist agencies (private businesses that feign officialdom) or the GNTO—each will help you find rooms, but they often fill "their" hotels first. Most of the islands have official tourist information offices, usually near the port and easily differentiated from the others.

Although frequent bus service links ports to beaches, sites, and major interior and coastline towns, renting a moped will give the adventurous explorer the most freedom and flexibility. You should have little trouble finding a rental shop (mopeds 2000-2500dr per day), but often the bikes are in poor condition. Another concern may be the condition of the roads, many of which are intended more for donkeys than wheels, so don't bust your ass.

Your island-hopping existence will hinge on the often unreliable boat schedules. Expect ferries to be late: just relax and enjoy the view. Hydrofoils may depart early. When you arrive on an island, immediately check the timetable, and plan for your next departure. (Some smaller islands receive infrequent ferry service.) The redeeming port police *(limenacheio)* have offices in every port that are open around the clock, with exhaustive, up-to-date information about every boat sailing to or from of the island. Ticket offices will usually give information only about boats for which they sell tickets. Consider convenience, not prices, when you plan, as ferry fares are regulated by law.

Ferry prices are reasonable, but costs can accrue quickly if you do a lot of island-hopping. Traveling on night ferries can save you the cost of accommodations while allowing you to spend more daylight hours at the beach. However, night ferries don't make the most comfortable accommodations, and they often deliver you to your beach before the sun has risen.

Keeping in Touch

Most Greek **post offices** are open Monday to Friday from 7:30am to 2:30pm, although services (such as mailing parcels) may close early; some larger offices keep longer hours. To register a letter, ask for *systemeno;* for express, *epeegon;* for air mail, just "air mail." A letter or postcard to the U.S. costs 120dr to mail and takes on the average nine to 11 days, sometimes longer from smaller villages.

Even if you have no fixed address while in Greece, you can receive mail through the Greek post office's **Poste Restante** (General Delivery) service. Mark the envelope "HOLD," and address it: "Jane Doe, c/o Poste Restante, Main Post Office, the address of the appropriate office, the postal code, and GREECE (in capital letters)." Write "Air Mail" on the side of the envelope and use a first class stamp. If you are expecting Poste Restante to arrive for you after you leave a town, arrange at the post office to have it forwarded to another Poste Restante address. American Express offices will hold mail for up to thirty days, but often charge a small fee if you aren't a cardholder or don't use their traveler's checks.

Long-distance and collect phone calls and telegrams should be placed at the **OTE** (the Greek Telephone Organization) offices. In small villages, offices are usually open Monday through Friday 7:30am to 3pm, in towns 7:30am to 10pm (shorter hours or closed on weekends), and in larger cities 24 hrs. If you visit one of the latter in the middle of the night, the door may be locked, but ring and they'll let you in. Long-distance calls and collect calls take a while to get through because lines are usually jammed. Either way, there is often a long line; try, if at all possible, to call early in the morning. There is no surcharge if you go to an OTE. For assistance, ask the attendant at the OTE.

To make **direct calls** to the U.S. or Canada, dial 001 and then the area code and number. If you plan on talking for a while, ask the other party to call right back, since rates from the U.S. are cheaper. To make **direct calls** from the U.S. to Greece, dial 011-3 and then the city code and the number. If you call the U.S. **collect,** you'll be charged the U.S. person-to-person rate; in most cases, you'll still save money over the expensive hotel surcharges. To call the U.S. collect, dial 008 00 13 11 (AT&T) or 008 00 12 20 52 (MCI). This method only works on international phones and not on ordinary pay phones, and will incur a charge of 10dr. To use a calling card, dial 008 00 13 11 (AT&T only). Remember the **time difference** when calling North America: subtract seven (Eastern Standard Time) to ten hours (Pacific) from the Greek time, depending on the U.S. time zone.

Accommodations

Relative to those in the U.S. and elsewhere in Europe, accommodations in Greece are still quite a bargain. In addition to the usual budget hotels and student hostels, most Greek towns have inexpensive rooms and houses to let, as well as some camping facilities. Be skeptical about offers to be driven to a pension or hotel. Let the driver show you the destination on a map; it may be miles out of town.

Although the warm, sunny climate may tempt you to sleep on the beach, beware: freelance camping is illegal in Greece. You must be on a legal camping area or you will face a fine. At peak season when camps are crowded the police will sometimes ignore sleeping-bagged bodies sprawled in the sand. Those who decide to freelance camp should make sure to clean up after themselves. Many beaches offer beach huts as well as designated camping sections. For a small fee, some hotels may let you stretch out on their rooftops.

Hostels

Greek youth hostels offer excellent alternative to hotels. Rooms are good and the cost is reasonable: 800dr per night (1200dr in Athens, Delphi, Nafplion, and Thessaloniki). At present, Greece has more than 25 youth hostels affiliated with **Hostelling International (HI),** formerly the **International Youth Hostel Federation (HI/IYHF).** For information on HI/IYHF membership, consult the Documents and Formalities section in the General Introduction.

Greek youth hostels generally have fewer restrictions than those in northern Europe. Most are open year-round and have midnight or 1am curfews (which are strictly enforced, and may leave you in the streets if you come back too late). In summer, they usually stay open from 6 to 10am and 1pm to midnight (shorter hours in winter). The large hostels offer breakfast for 400-500dr. Hostels often have a maximum stay of five days. It is advisable to book in advance in the summer at some of the more popular hostels in Athens, Thira, or Nafplion.

Hotels

The GNTO governs the construction and classification of all hotels. The classification awarded to each establishment is determined by the size, decor, and furnishings of the rooms and public areas, and the services provided by the staff. Rates vary according to classification and are enforced by the government. Proprietors are legally entitled, and therefore inclined, to charge 10% extra for stays of less than three nights, and 20% extra overall in high season (July 1-Sept. 15). In order to squeeze more *drachmae* out of you, they may only offer their most expensive rooms, compel you to buy breakfast, squeeze three people into a hostel-like triple and charge each for a single, or quote a price for a room that includes breakfast and private shower and then charge extra for both.

One note on Greek toilets: if a trash container is within reach of the toilet, this is where used toilet paper goes. Otherwise, the toilet is likely to become jammed (Greek plumbing is not a technological wonder). If worse comes to worst, the pages of your *Let's Go* can also serve as the toilet paper of the budget traveler.

If proprietors offer you a room that seems unreasonably expensive, stress that you don't want luxuries and they may tell you of a cheaper option. Late at night, in the off-season, or in a large town, it's a buyer's market, and owners will be more willing to lower prices or offer free showers. You can—and should—bargain. As a security deposit, most hotels will ask for your passport and return it when you leave. You can often leave your luggage in the reception area during the afternoon, though check-out is at 11am or noon.

The tourist police are on your side. If a hotel flagrantly violates the prices shown by law at the registration desk, or if you think that you've been exploited in any way, threaten to report the hotel to the tourist police; the threat alone will often resolve "misunderstandings."

Most D- and E-class hotels start at 2000dr for singles and 3000-3500dr for doubles (prices may be about 300dr less in the off-season). A hotel with no singles may still put you in a room by yourself. If you're going to haggle over the price, make sure you do it *before* you accept the room. More information is available from the **Hellenic Chamber of Hotels,** 24 Stadiou St., Athens (tel. 323 35 01 or 323 66 44).

Rooms to Let

Wherever there are tourists, you'll see lots of private homes with signs offering *dhomatia* (rooms to let). The owners of these houses often crowd around incoming boats or buses in order to solicit customers. If you don't see them, go to a café and ask where you can find rooms. Most of the rooms are cheap and perfectly dependable. There may not be locks, towels, or telephones, but there may be warm offers of coffee at night and friendly conversation. Then again, in the more touristed areas, there may be more locks than conversation. Prices here are especially variable, so make sure that you're paying no more than you would at a hotel. If in doubt, ask the tourist police: they will usually set you up with a room and conduct all the negotiations themselves. Most *dhomatia* operate only in the high season and they are always a good option for those arriving somewhere without previous reservations. If you're really strapped for money, consider asking proprietors to let you sleep on the roof. In many cases, they will charge a small fee for the privilege.

Traditional Settlements

Greece has a number of traditional villages and buildings which have been preserved and restored by the GNTO in an effort to maintain the country's architectural heritage. The restoration of a number of Greek villages promises to offer a taste of "small town" Greek life to visitors, and to improve the economy in these areas. Thus far, eight settlements have been converted into guesthouses: Oia on Santorini, Makrinitsa and Vizitsa on Mt. Pelion, Mesta on Chios, Psara Island, Fiskardo on Cephalonia, Kapetanakos in Areopolis, and Papigo-Zagohoria in Epirus. Doubles range from 2000-7000dr; the GNTO can make your reservations for you and provide most of the necessary information.

Camping

Camping is one of the easiest ways to escape the monotony of barren hotel rooms, hostel regulations, and other limitations of conventional lodgings. More importantly, it's one of the cheapest ways to spend the night.

In Greece, the GNTO is primarily responsible for campgrounds (see Useful Organizations and Publications above). **Tourist Guide of Greece,** 137 Patission St., Athens 11251 (tel. 864 16 88) also puts out a list of official camping sites in Greece. Most of the official GNTO campgrounds have good facilities, including drinking water, lavatories, and electricity. The Hellenic Touring Club also runs a number of campgrounds, most of which are less expensive than the GNTO campgrounds. In addition, Greece has many campgrounds run by private organizations.

The prices charged at campgrounds depend on the facilities; you will usually pay 350-400dr per person, plus 200-300dr per tent. GNTO campgrounds tend to be ritzier and more expensive (up to 2500dr in some places).

On many islands, campers simply take to the beaches. Freelance camping outside campgrounds is illegal, but during July and August, when hotels and pensions are booked solid, illegal camping becomes commonplace. Penalties run the gamut from a stern chastisement to a 1,000dr or higher fine.

The basics for camping include a sleeping bag, foam pad, and tent (or tarpaulin). Although some campgrounds rent tents for a small fee, you might not want to risk relying on them. Sleeping bags with synthetic fillers are cheaper, more durable, and more water-resistant than their down counterparts, although down is warmer and lighter. Modern tents are designed to be "self-supporting"; they have their own frames and suspension systems, can be set up quickly, and do not require staking, unlike the monstrosities you had to wrestle with for your merit badges. When you are out buying a tent, make certain that it has a rain fly and ample bug netting and weighs no more than 3½kg.

Other basics include a battery-operated lantern (never gas) for use inside the tent, and a simple plastic groundcloth to protect the tent floor. If you plan on roughing it in extremely primitive areas, water sacks and/or a solar shower may be necessary. Most campgrounds provide grills and allow you to gather firewood for cooking, but in case a campground prohibits wood fires, purchase a small campstove that runs on butane or white gas. They come in handy, especially for making coffee, but expect to pay $40-150. Carry waterproof matches; a spill in the lake can leave you without a fire, fondly remembering the central heating of home.

Life and Times

History

Ancient Greece

Archaeological evidence suggests that migratory tribes settled on Crete as early as 5000 BCE. At the beginning of the fourth millenium BCE, a westward migration of Neolithic farmers led to the creation of small communities throughout the Cyclades. As the mining and crafting of copper became lucrative early in the third millenium BCE, Cycladic communities grew and early centralized governments were created. The introduction of metalworking from the east during the **Bronze Age** (around 2900 BCE) enabled these governments to establish great cities and powerful navies. By the second millenium BCE, waves of invaders from the north matched weapon and wit in the Balkans at the fringes of Cycladic territory. These invaders subjugated the *Pelagosi, Leleges,* and *Cares* people, and are considered by modern scholars to be the forerunners of the "Aegeans."

Cycladic civilization survived, though, until the rise of the **Minoans** on the island of Crete. Minoan society, which lasted from 2500-1500 BCE, was named after its most famous king, Minos, whose sturdy wife Pasiphäe had given birth to the mythical Minotaur without resorting to artificial painkillers. The Minoans left Crete an archaeological treasure trove, the climax of which is the unforgettable grand palace at Knossos. Whimsical Minoan pottery, found all over Greece, and the lack of walls around Knossos indicate that Cretan hegemony was as much economic as military. In 1600 BCE, Minoans were quick to recover from a huge earthquake which damaged the palace at Knossos. However, in 1400 BCE, the Minoans were not so lucky—the capital of the vast Minoan bureaucracy was destroyed by a league of city-states from the mainland.

Soon, the more warlike **Mycenaean** civilization was established. Surviving from 1500-900 BCE, the Mycenaeans were responsible for the capture and destruction of Troy in 1184 BCE. The Mycenaean empire, as described in Homer's *Iliad* and *Odyssey,* consisted of several nominally independent kingdoms, including Sparta and Corinth, each owing allegiance to the King of Mycenae. The origins of Greek mythology as we know it can be traced to this period.

The mass migration of four Hellenic tribes to the Greek mainland, beginning as early as 1100 BCE, put an end to the Mycenaean empire. Around 900 BCE, after the **Dorian Invasions,** some scholars believe that the peoples of Mycenaean origin migrated southward. During this time period—referred to as the **Geometric Period** due to the simple, geometric shapes common to its pottery—the *polis,* or city-state, began to supplant the village as the basic political unit in Greece. The Olympic Games were begun in 776 BCE·and soon became an expression of political as well as athletic pride. From 750-550 BCE, political rivalries also spurred colonization: seafaring states like Corinth, Megara, and Miletus each established *poleis* as far away as Spain and the Black Sea.

Sparta and Athens, though, soon emerged as the most powerful of the Greek **city-states.** Sparta, insulated by mountains, developed an extremely militaristic culture. Children were separated from their parents almost immediately after birth in order to begin a life of constant military drill. The unhealthy were left to die. On the other hand, life really pampered Athenians, especially the wealthy. Philosophy, learning, and attempts to institute democracy were the order of the day. Although Athens and Sparta developed an intense rivalry, they united in defense against the huge Persian Army, winning decisive victories at Marathon (490 BCE), Salamis (480 BCE) and Plataea (479 BCE). For the time being, Greece was saved from foreign rule.

The apex of Classical Greek civilization—called by many the **Age of Pericles** after the Athenian ruler—lasted from about 480 to 323 BCE. Athens, at the helm of the Delian League, grew extremely wealthy as the Athenian navy made possible the extension of trade routes. Though the Delian League had originally been established to fight the Persians, Athens insisted on maintaining it after the Persian threat had subsided. By siphoning off tribute from their Delian allies, Athenians were able to finance magnificent theaters, temples, state buildings, and the arts. Playwrights like Sophocles and the boisterous Aristophanes entertained thousands. There were times when the city streets were supposedly graced with more marble statues than actual people.

Sparta, meanwhile, grew increasingly nervous about Athenian ambitions and worried that the bipolar balance of power would soon collapse. When trouble began brewing among allies, the vast network of both Athenian and Spartan ties eliminated the chances for either power to back down and the **Peloponnesian War** erupted. Lasting the 27 years, Sparta emerged victorious only after the Athenians squandered their navy in a hopeless attack on Syracuse. While the war and intermittent plagues devastated the physical dominance of Athens, though, the city's culture thrived well into the 4th century BCE. Artists such as Scopas and Praxiteles; scientists like Hippocrates; and philosophers such as Socrates, Plato, and Aristotle, all of whom lived during this time, are today still much admired for their brilliance.

In the midst of the Peloponnesian War, however, a new political force was gaining strength in Macedonia. Between 360 and 320 BCE, the Macedonians, under King Philip II, conquered many of the Greek cities. After establishing a powerful confederacy known as the **Hellenic League of Corinth** (in 338 BCE), Alexander the Great, King Philip's illustrious son, embarked on an historic expedition in 336 to crush the extensive empire of the Persians. In only 13 years, Alexander extended Hellenic rule and influence deep into Africa and as far east as India.

Following Alexander's sudden death, violent internal conflicts ravaged his empire. In 146 BCE, after a half century of skirmishes and political intrigue, **Rome** formally stepped in to plug the Greek power vacuum. But as fast as the Roman legions conquered Greece, Greek culture conquered Rome. By the middle of the first century CE, even Nero had a soft spot for Athens, though Alexandria and Antioch far surpassed Athens in reputation. Two centuries later, after the Christianization of the Roman Empire and the establishment of the Greek Empire, the focal point of Hellenic culture shifted from the Peloponnese to Byzantium, much to the chagrin of many mainlanders.

The fall of Constantinople (Byzantium had been renamed after emperor Constantine) to the Ottoman Empire in 1453 CE propelled Greece into the **Middle Ages,** when Turks ruled Greece for four hundred years.

Greek Independence

After numerous false starts, a revolutionary army composed of guerillas from the Peloponnese and Aegean Islands began battling the Turkish armies in early 1821, eventually to declare independence on March 25. Initially successful, the Greeks then suffered substantial setbacks due to an outbreak of rivalry between various factions and the intervention of Muhammad Ali (the Turkish sultan's pugnacious governor of Egypt). Spurred on by the romantic Lord Byron and public sympathy for the Greeks—archaeological treasures from the Classical Age were just then being unearthed—European governments intervened. In 1827, at the Battle of Navarino, the navies of Britain, France, and Russia decimated a joint Turkish-Egyptian fleet, releasing the Ottoman grip on Greece.

British, French, and Russian participation ensured the establishment of Greece as an independent state but cost the latter much of its autonomy. The foreign powers not only set Greece's borders, they controlled the country militarily and even chose the first ruler. After offering the Greek crown to a number of petty European monarchs, King Ludwig I of Bavaria finally accepted in the name of his young son, Otto I. Under the auspices of three Bavarian regents and a Bavarian bureaucracy, Otto I traveled to Greece and became king at the tender age of 17.

Modern History

King Otto I, although generally well-liked by the Greek population, began losing political control in the 1850s after he refused to permit democratic reforms. Otto was then forced to acquiesce to demands for a constitution and the formation of a national assembly. Greece's 27 appointed senators and technically constitutional monarchy were largely specious signs, though, and the situation kept deteriorating; Otto quietly abdicated in October, 1862. King George I of Denmark replaced Otto in 1863. His rule, for the most part, was moderate until he was ousted in 1909. A Republican government ruled until 1930, when the Greek army returned the old monarchy to power.

During **World War II,** the Greeks fought alongside the Allies once again. Greek resistance fighters, led by the communist-backed ELAS, held off the Germans for several months, dramatically bolstering the Allied war effort. In 1941, though, Greece fell to Germany and many Greek civilians were summarily executed. Among the victims were virtually the entire population of Greek Jews and gypsies. With the defeat of the Nazis came a sudden surge of communist sentiment. Only the intervention of British forces successfully quashed an attempted communist coup. In 1949, with substantial assistance from the United States, the Greek government thwarted another coup attempt and put an end to the civil war. In the aftermath, the U.S. augmented its aid to Greece under the Truman Doctrine of 1952. From 1952 to 1963, a coalition of conservative parties led by Constantine Karamanlis governed Greece. Political instability convinced junior military officers to launch a coup on April 21, 1967, initiating a military dictatorship. The *junta,* led by General Papadopoulos, was criticized for placing restrictions on free speech and for intimidating political opponents by means of torture and imprisonment.

The collapse of the dictatorship brought the return of Karamanlis, who had been living in self-imposed exile for several years. As the new prime minister, Karamanlis skillfully orchestrated parliamentary elections and organized a referendum to determine the fate of the government. After the monarchy was defeated by a two-thirds vote, a constitution was drawn up in 1975 which established free general elections and a 300-member parliament charged with appointing a ceremonial president. The leader of the majority party in parliament, of course, became prime minister. Greece, furthermore, worked to strengthen its memberships in NATO (having joined in 1952), the Council of Europe, and the European Economic Community.

Under the leadership of the popular Prime Minister Andreas Papandreou, the leftist Panhellenic Socialist Movement (PASOK) obtained landslide electoral victories in 1981 and 1985. But 1988 marked a radical change in government. In September, Papandreou underwent major heart surgery. While hospitalized, he attempted to run the country while bed-ridden, refusing to appoint any interim leader. This absence undermined his authority within PASOK. Upon returning to work, Papandreou found the embezzlement scandal involving George Koskotas, the chairman of the Bank of Crete, threatening to implicate a number of government officials for corruption and bribery. When Koskotas asserted allegations against Papandreou himself, the beleaguered Prime Minister eked out only 125 seats in the 300-seat parliament.

In the wake of the scandals, Tzannis Tzannetakis, a conservative, became Prime Minister-designate through a compromise decision of the Communist-rightist coalition. As part of the compromise, the opposing right-wing New Democracy (*Nea Demokratia*—ND) and the Communist Party of Greece (*Kommunistiko Komma Ellados*—KKE) forged a short-term alliance to oppose the incumbent socialist leadership. Then in 1990, following three general elections within a space of 10 months, **Constantine Mitsotakis** of the ND became Prime Minister. Although the ND was only able to obtain 47% of the total vote, the vagaries of Greek electoral law left the party with a slim majority in parliament.

Mitsotakis has attempted to lead Greece into the mainstream of European politics and solve some of the country's festering economic and diplomatic woes. Part of Mitsotakis' conservative economic agenda is the deregulation of the tourist industry. No longer given upper and lower limits by the government, accommodations and restaurants are free to charge as much or as little as they can get away with. How this will affect the budget traveler is not yet clear.

The question of **Macedonia** is the latest issue to inflame Greece. In April, 1992, a former province of Yugoslavia declared itself the independent Republic of Macedonia. Greeks felt an important part of their history and cultural identity usurped and were suitably outraged. Ancient Macedonia, home to Alexander the Great, was very probably a Hellenic civilization and certainly not a Slavic one. (Slavs did not move into the Balkan peninsula until the 6th century CE.) The slogan "Macedonia is Greece 3000 years" adorns everything from bumper stickers to ferry tickets. The European Community has withheld recognition of the Yugoslav province and Greek-Americans are lobbying Congress to do the same.

Art and Architecture

Ancient Greek art may be divided into a number of periods, roughly corresponding to the historical eras. The earliest Greek societies were warrior tribes, which developed the craft of metalwork during a period known as the **Bronze Age.** Many sculptures remain from this period, during which the Cycladic, Minoan, and Mycenaean civilizations emerged. Examples of Minoan pottery, many featuring whimsical and colorful sea creatures, are plentiful as well.

In the **Geometric Period** (900-700 BCE), artists developed new techniques and more expressive styles of sculpture and painting. Pottery decoration became more elaborate; jars were completely covered with bands of meanders, zigzags, and identically posed animals and people. Architects of the time created simple structures; and designed one-room temples with columned porches and raised altars. Examples of Geometric architecture are concentrated at Olympia.

The **Archaic Period** (700-480 BCE) marked the transition from the simplicity of the Geometric Period to the more elaborate and realistic forms of the Classical Period. The cylindrical Doric column and the fluted Ionic column were developed in this period. At the end of the 7th century large-scale standing figural sculptures appeared in sanctuaries. These *kouroi* (feminine, *kourai*)slowly evolved into more graceful, simplified figures in which the depiction of life and movement became prime concerns. Vase painting similarly became more concerned with a realistic portrayal of life. The rigid friezes of marching animals and people of the Geometric period were replaced with narrative scenes from mythology and, later still, with genre scenes. The black figure technique, in which the figures were glazed black and details incised into them, gave artists greater precision than before. At the end of the 6th century BCE, vase painters adopted the Attic red figure technique in which the figures were reserved against a black background and the details painted in with a fine brush, giving artists even greater freedom of expression.

The arts flourished during the **Classical Period** (480-323 BCE), as Athens reached the pinnacle of its cultural, military, and economic power under Pericles. Sculptors such as Praxiteles and Scopas developed the heroic nude form in which the human body is idealized to severe and somber beauty. The Praxiteles statue of Hermes holding the baby Dionysus and Paeonius's statue of Nike (Winged Victory) are both housed in the Olympia Museum. Architecture of the Classical period, like Athens's Parthenon, features greater spaciousness, fluidity, and grace than the massive temples of the Archaic Period.

The famous Corinthian column, a fluted column with a multi-leafed top, was first designed during the **Hellenistic Period** (323-first century BCE). The Monument of Lysicrates in Athens typifies this architectural design. Several amphitheaters were built at this time, most notably those at Epidavros and Argos. When the Romans controlled Greece, they adopted the Hellenistic style and introduced it to the rest of Europe.

In 395 CE, the Roman Empire split into the Western Empire and the Eastern, or Byzantine, Empire. The Greeks fell under the latter. As the Empire was Christianized under St. Constantine, Greek artists began to incorporate Christian symbols into their work. During the **Byzantine Period** (500-1200 CE), many churches were built and Christian iconography developed an elaborate repertoire of symbols. Figures of veneration generally appeared in symbolic postures, the most unusual of which is the *anapezousa,* or sleeping Christ, in which the Christ figure is depicted lying down with his eyes open, to express God's vigilance at all times. The most notable examples of Byzantine art include the monasteries built at Ossios Loukas, Daphni, Mt. Athos, and Meteora. The churches were built in a cruciform style: a narthex or small chamber added at one end, and an apse, or half dome, at the other. The transept, or crossing, of the two lengths of the church was capped by a domed ceiling. Byzantine artists created beautiful, ornate icons and mosaics to decorate their churches. A mosaic of Christ *Pantocrator* ("creator of all things") was almost always placed in the dome or apse.

With the liberation of Greece from the Turks in 1821, nationalist sentiment caused the government to subsidize Greek art. In 1838, the Polytechniou, Greece's first modern art school, was founded. Many artists since have gone abroad to study, and **modern Greek art** has followed the trends and styles of 19th- and 20th-century European art. Theophilos, Alexos Kontoglou, George Bouzianis, and Michael Tombros are among the most familiar modern Greek artists.

Greek **folk-art** continues to fascinate even the most casual onlooker. Handicrafts include pottery, weaving, metalwork, and woodwork. Today in many Greek villages you can see artisans at work, creating objects in much the same way their ancestors did centuries ago.

Literature

The earliest appearances of the Greek language are palace record tablets inscribed in duo-syllabic scripts called Linear Script A and B. These treasury records, somewhat uninspiring in content and thought to date from the end of the Bronze Age (about 1200 BCE), were often preserved, ironically, as they were baked hard in the fires that destroyed the palaces themselves. From the 11th to the 8th century BCE, the Greeks seem to have been illiterate for the most part, and it is not until the **Homeric** *Iliad* and *Odyssey* that written material appears. It remains in controversy whether the Homeric works were actually written by the blind bard; scholars agree that the work shows evidence of originating from an oral tradition, and it is possible that Homer or a group of poets worked on the actual hard copy. Hesiod, roughly Homer's contemporary, composed *Works and Days,* a farmer's-eye-view of life as well as the *Theogony,* the first systematic account in Greek of the creation of the world and the exploits of the gods. During the 7th century BCE, Archilochus of Paros began to write his anti-heroic, anti-Homeric elegies, including the often imitated fragment in which he expresses no shame at abandoning his shield in battle to save his own life. On the island of Lesbos, during the 5th century BCE, the gifted lyric poet Sappho and her contemporary, Alcaeus, sang of love and the beauty of nature. Pindar (518-438 BCE), acclaimed by the ancients as being the greatest of lyric poets, wrote Olympic odes, works commissioned by nobles to commemorate athletic victories.

Literature flourished in the **Classical Period.** Aeschylus, Sophocles, and Euripides developed ritualistic dramas and staged innovative tragedies, while Aristophanes produced raucous comedies (see Theater below). Orators like Gorgias practiced rhetoric and the sophists taught methods of philosophical dialogue. Herodotus, the so-called "Father of History," captured the monumental battles and personalities of the Greco-Persian conflict in the *Persian Wars,* while Thucydides's stylus immortalized the Athenian conflict with Sparta in his *Peloponnesian War.* Callimachus (c.305-c.240 BCE) wrote Alexandrian elegies, of which only fragments remain. His influence, however, was to be felt during the Alexandrian revival in Rome, when neoteric poets like Catullus took his caution *mega biblion, mega kakon* ("Long book, big bore") to heart. Callimachus was also the first poet to write in the vision genre, a poetic topos that holds an important place in the literature of the Middle Ages. His pupil, Apollonius of Rhodes, wrote the epic *Argonautica,* chronicling the legendary voyage of Jason and the Argonauts.

During the **Byzantine Era,** religious poetry flourished, though not necessarily to the exclusion of secular works. Photios, (c. 820-93 CE) who was twice appointed Patriarch of Constantinople, admired the so-called pagan works of Homer and encouraged their study. Photios himself wrote several important works, including the massive *Biblioteca,* a Byzantine cross between the *Encyclopedia Britannica* and *Reader's Digest.* Later, under the Franks (1204-1797), Greeks developed the pseudo-historical romance, including the *Life of Alexander;* and personal love poems, such as the *Erotopaegnia* (Love Games). Klephts ("Bandits") composed stirring folk ballads in the 16th century, when they weren't raiding Turkish installations. Byzantine heritage survived in revolt against Roman Catholic and Turkish propaganda, manifesting itself during the **Period of Religious Humanism** (1600-69).

The Ionian School (beginning with the revolution in 1821), saw the rise of Andreas Kalvos (1796-1869) and Dionysios Solomos (1798-1857). Kalvos's lyrical poetry, known for its powerful tributes to freedom, has earned him high esteem among modern poets. Solomos is often called the "national poet of Greece," and it was his *Hymn to Liberty* that, set to music, became the Greek national anthem. While George Seferis's poems evoke the legacy of Greek past, and the mystical and erotic works of Odysseus Elytis celebrate nature, Yiannis Ritsos blends revolutionary and mythological symbolism. During the second half of the 19th century, revolutionary hero John Makriyiannes (1797-1864) wrote his vivid narrative *Memoirs,* considered one of the masterpieces of Greek literature. The 20th century has seen the emergence of a great many poets, including Angelos Sikelianos, Constantine Cavafy, and Kostas Varnales. Cavafy in particular has a huge following; writers such as E.M. Forster and W.H. Auden were influenced by him. Also among modern greats are Kostas Karyotakes and the lyricist Nikos Karvounes, who was the first to translate Walt Whitman's works into Greek. The talented George Seferis won the Nobel Prize for his outstanding lyric poetry. Stratis Haviaris's work *When The Tree Sings,* depicts World War II through the eyes of a young boy. Perhaps the best known modern Greek author is Nikos Kazantzakis. His many works include *Odyssey,* a modern sequel to the Homeric epic. Two of his novels, *Zorba the Greek (1946),* and *The Last Temptation of Christ* (1951), were adapted for the screen.

Theater

The earliest forms of drama are said to have developed in the 5th century BCE from goat songs *(tragodoi)* related to the cult of the god Dionysus. Wealthy patrons would sponsor huge public festivals in his honor; contests were held in open-air theaters and choruses of masked men would sing and dance. According to legend, drama was born when young Thespis, an Athenian, stepped out of the chorus to give a brief soliloquy (hence all actors are known as *thespians).*

One of the great tragedians, **Aeschylus** (525-456 BCE) perfected this new art form by adding a second actor and having the two actors each play several characters. He wrote such famous works as the perplexing *Prometheus Bound,* and the *Oresteia,* a trilogy about Agamemnon's ill-fated return home from the Trojan war and its aftermath; **Sophocles** (496-406 BCE) created the famous *Oedipus* trilogy; and **Euripides** (485-406 BCE) wrote *Medea* and *The Bacchae.* "Old Comedy," a bawdy, slapstick medium, arose in the late 5th century. The greatest playwright of this genre was **Aristophanes** (450-385 BCE), who wrote *The Clouds, Lysistrata,* and *The Frogs.* Unfortunately, only 11 of his 40 plays are extant. **Menander,** the father of "New Comedy," wrote more mannered comedies, love stories (usually involving lovers star-crossed though cases of mistaken identity, kidnapping, etc.) with happy endings which became the theme and pattern of later writers like Shakespeare. Greek theater did not just end with the Classical era: particularly on Crete, drama has been and continues to be a vital art form.

The **Athens Festival,** held from June to September, features Classical drama at the **Theater of Herod Atticus** located below the Acropolis. The festival also includes concerts, opera, choruses, ballet, and modern dance. Ancient plays are staged from July to September at the **Epidavros Festival,** 78km from Athens. Surrounded by a wooded grove instead of a jagged cityscape, the 3rd-century BCE circular stage is famous for its remarkable acoustics. Don't worry about the language barrier; it won't detract from the ominous choreography of the chorus, which, in Aeschylus's time, made "boys die of fright and women have miscarriages." Tickets and programs for the theater series at both festivals are available two weeks in advance at the Athens Festival Box Office, 4 Stadiou St., inside the arcade (tel. 322 14 59 or 322 31 11, ext. 240). The same office sells tickets for a number of other smaller theaters and festivals. The **Philippi, Thassos,** and **Dodoni Festivals** all feature performances of classical drama in ancient theaters. The **Lycabettos Theater,** on Lycabettos Hill in Athens, hosts a variety of artistic events from mid-June to late August, and the **Lyric Theater,** known as the *Lyriki Skini,* presents operatic plays at the Olympia, 59 Akadimias St., Athens.

Music and Dance

Musical instruments date from the Bronze Age on Crete, reinforcing scholars' belief that early poetry was often sung or chanted. As drama evolved, choruses played a major role in Greek plays. Before the 5th century BCE, the Greeks had no system of musical notation, yet they managed to develop a theory of harmonics.

Throughout the Byzantine era, folk music and dances assumed regional traits: the South emphasized tragic and mourning dances, the North featured war and rural harvest dances, and religious and burial dances were performed on Crete.

Today, it is common to see a wide circle of locals and tourists, hands joined, dancing to the tunes of a trio of *bouzouki* players. The leader of the dance performs the fancy footwork, winding around a white handkerchief and twirling around in circles, sometimes daring a few backward somersaults. The more sprightly dancers will sometimes clutch a table between their teeth and cavort across the floor. Don't hesitate to join in; the dance steps are repetitive (and the tables are small)—you'll learn quickly. Just stamp your feet, yell *Opah,* and have fun. If you watch, ask the rate for crockery before you engage in the "traditional" custom of throwing dinner plates in appreciation of the dancers, or you'll be rewarded with a hefty bill for the broken dishes.

To see authentic Greek dancing, check out the **Dora Stratou Folk Dance Theatre,** which performs at the open air theater at Philopappus Theatre in Athens and on 8 Scholion St. in Athens at 10pm, from May through September. (For information, call 324 43 95; after 5:30pm call 921 46 50.) From June through October in the old city of Rhodes, the **Nelly Dimoglou Troupe** features dances from northern and central Greece and the Dodecanese. The Athens and Epidavros Festivals (see Theater above) also include dancing. Check the Entertainment listings in major cities for additional information.

Classical Mythology

Greek mythology is second only to the Bible in its influence on the Western imagination. Greek myths were passed from generation to generation, region to region, gradually embellished and interpreted to reflect local concerns. The anthropomorphic gods and goddesses lived as immortal beings with divine power, yet often descended to earth to intervene romantically, mischievously, or combatively in human affairs, sometimes disguised as animals or humans.

Traditionally, 14 major deities preside: Zeus, king of gods; his wife Hera, who watches over child-bearing and marriage; Poseidon, god of the sea; Hephaestus, god of smiths and fire; Aphrodite, goddess of love and beauty; Ares, god of war; Athena, goddess of wisdom; Apollo, god of light and music; Artemis, goddess of the hunt; Hermes, the messenger god and patron of thieves and tricksters; Hades, lord of death; Demeter, goddess of the harvest; Dionysus, god of wine; and Hestia, goddess of the hearth.

In addition to the 14 gods, many humans and minor deities figured prominently in Greek mythology. The three Fates—Ariadne, Clotho, and Lachesis—spun, measured, and snipped the threads of humans' lives; the Furies, also called *Eumenides,* or "kindly ones," punished evildoers; and the nine Muses brought inspiration to poets, artists, and musicians. Dryads and Naiads inhabited trees and streams; nymphs cavorted in the fields; Satyrs, or goat-men, frolicked with Maenads in the holy groves. Humans had their place in mythology as well, though not always willingly: the talented weaver Arachne, because she dared compete with Athena, was turned into a spider, thus bequeathing her name to taxonomy; Tantalus, for attempting to violate Hera, was condemned to stand in a pool in Tartarus, forever tormented by hunger and thirst and always surrounded by tantalizing food and water just beyond his grasp; and Europa was ravished by Zeus disguised as a bull.

The extramarital exploits of Zeus are even more infamous than those of less powerful but equally randy minor deities. The Don Juan of the Olympian sphere, Zeus was a sexual gymnast, ready and willing to bed down with (it seems) just about anyone, as long as his baleful wife Hera wasn't looking. The mortal loves of Zeus, however, were not always so willing: Danae, imprisoned in a tower by her father, was impregnated by Zeus in the form of a golden shower, and Ganymede, a handsome Trojan shepherd, was snatched up from earth to be the cup-bearer of the gods. Worse still for mortals, Hera, powerless to injure her husband directly, lavished her vengeance on the hapless object of his philandering affections: Io was turned into a cow and chased pitilessly by an enormous gadfly; Leto, pregnant with Artemis and Apollo, was forbidden to rest on solid ground until the itinerant island of Delos lent its tiny shore for her to give birth upon, and Callisto, who got off relatively easy for her dalliance with Zeus, was changed into a bear. Semele, one of the few willing consorts of Zeus, dissolved into ash when he appeared to her in his full Olympian brilliance. The overarching moral of any story involving Zeus and sex seems to be that mortals never win.

An accompanying book of mythology might be just the thing to enrich your Greek travels. Both Edith Hamilton and Bullfinch's *Mythology* are eminently readable. A principal source for our knowledge of mythology is Ovid's *Metamorphoses*. The first-century CE Roman poet recounts all the familiar myths, using the gods' Latin names (Jupiter for Zeus, Venus for Aphrodite, and so on).

Religion

The practice of worshipping the mythological gods and goddesses ended after the death of the Roman Emperor Julian. In the post-classical period, Greece saw the rise of cults associated with mysteries such as the Eleusinian and Orphic, in which participants enacted rituals associated with the afterlife. Unfortunately, since the participants swore to keep the rituals secret, almost all that is known of the mysteries is reported by disapproving Christian authors, whose descriptions of the pagan rituals are as sensational as modern tabloids.

Under the Byzantine Empire, Greece became a stronghold of Orthodox Christianity; religion flourished in monastic communities such as those at Mount Athos and Meteora. In 1054 CE, the Christian Church divided into the Roman Catholic and Eastern Orthodox Churches (orthodox meaning "right belief"). Orthodox missionaries spread Christianity to Slavic peoples in Russia, Serbia Romania and Bulgaria. The patriarch of Constantinople was recognized as the head of an Orthodox Christian "nation." After the Greek War of Independence, the Church of Greece delcared itself officially autocephalous. The Church of Greece is the national religion of Greece although freedom of religion is guaranteed by the constitution to the small enclaves of Muslims, Jews, and Catholics. The Church comprises the archbishop of Athens, 85 bishops in 77 dioceses, and 7500 parishes. The Patriarch of Constantinople, meanwhile, still has jurisdiction over Mt. Athos, the Dodecanese, and the Orthodox Church in the rest of Europe, the Americas, Australia, and East Asia.

Greek Orthodox priests are closely associated with their parishes and can marry, as most do (although higher clergy remain unmarried). The congregation remains silent during mass while a *psaltis* and a choir sing the liturgy, and icons are used as symbols in worship. Festive occasions in churches include weddings, baptisms, and celebrations on the name day of the patron saint.

Language

The language barrier that tourists find upon entering Greece tends to crumble quickly (though slower in the mountainous north and in the southern Peloponnese); many Greeks who work in facilities catering to tourists have picked up some English; tourist officials and travel agents are often fluent. Nevertheless, try to master some essential Greek phrases; locals will appreciate any efforts you make. Take along the Berlitz *Greek for Travelers,* or a comparable book that will provide key phrases in a quick-access format. As you learn, ask for help from someone who speaks the language.

Be conscious of Greek body language. To indicate a negative, Greeks lift their heads back abruptly while raising their eyebrows. To indicate the affirmative, they emphatically nod once. Note also that Greeks wave a hand up and down in a gesture that seems to mean "stay there;" it actually means "come." Be careful when waving goodbye; if you do so palm forward, the gesture may be interpreted as an insult.

Even if you don't know any spoken Greek, familiarity with the Greek alphabet is essential. Some road signs, street names, and certain bus timetables may be transliterated (spelled out phonetically in Roman characters), but many are not. Because Greek is an inflected language, words have different case forms which correspond to their different grammatical functions in sentences. You'll sometimes find three different words representing the same name; for example, Patra, Patras, and Patrai all refer to the same place. For a pronunciation guide and a list of useful phrases, consult the glossary at the back of the book.

Food and Wine

Food in Greece is healthy and scrumptious, when it's not food in grease. Most restaurants in Greece work from the same culinary palette, but create original masterpieces with subtle shadings and intricate designs of taste.

A Greek restaurant is known as a *taverna* or *estiatorio,* while a grill is a *psistaria.* Before ordering in any restaurant, check the prices, look around in the kitchen, and investigate other people's plates. If you don't know the word for what you want, point. Most places have few fixed-price dishes available at any one time, so make sure they have your dish before you sit down. Waiters will subtly ask you if you want salad, appetizers, the Brooklyn Bridge, so be careful not to wind up with mountains of food and a nosebleed bill. And don't be surprised if the waiter charges you extra for the tablecloth and bread. The price for a full meal without entertainment should be about 1500dr per person. Service is always included in the check, but it is customary and polite to leave whatever coins you receive as change.

Breakfast consists of bread, *tiropita* (cheese pie), or a pastry with *marmelada* (jam) or *meli* (honey), along with a cup of coffee. Lunch, the largest meal of the day, is eaten in the mid to late afternoon. The evening meal is a leisurely affair; served late at night relative to American standards, usually after 8 or 9pm, and as late as 11pm-1am during the summer in the larger cities. Main entrees include grilled *moskari* (veal), *arni* (lamb), or *kotopoulo* (chicken), served with *patates* (french fries), *rizi* (rice), or *fasolia* (beans). Popular Greek dishes include *mousaka* (chopped meat and eggplant mixed with a cheese and tomato paste), *pastitsio* (thick noodles covered with a rich cream sauce), *yemista* (stuffed tomatoes and peppers), and *dolmadhes* (stuffed grape leaves with rice and minced meat, called *youvrelakia* when covered with egg or lemon sauce). Fried zucchini, stuffed eggplant, *tzatziki* (cucumber and yogurt salad), and/or *horta* (greens—either beet or dandelion—served with oil and lemon) accompany meals at most *tavernas.* Don't be afraid to order these veggies as the main dish. Vegetarians might also try *spanakopita* (spinach-filled pastry) or *tyropitakia* (cheese pie in a similar flaky crust). Seafood is as readily available as you'd expect in a such an oceanocentric nation, but is often more expensive than you'd think. Don't leave without trying fresh octopus marinated in olive oil and oregano: "I laughed. I cried. It was better than squid."

You can hardly avoid *souvlaki,* a large skewer of steak, generally pork or lamb. A *souvlaki pita,* appropriately known as "the budget food of the masses," consists of a pita crammed full of skewered meats and fillings (only about 120dr). Contrary to the claims of American "Greek" restaurants, *gyros* is not standard fare in most regions of Greece. For a healthier staple available at any *taverna,* try a *choriatiki,* a "Greek" salad containing olives, tomatoes, onions, cucumbers, and topped with hefty chunks of feta cheese. (Ask for it *horees ladhi* if you don't want it swimming in olive oil.) Usually accompanied by a basket of bread and a glass of water, these salads make inexpensive and satisfying meals.

Visit an *agora* (market) to stock up on the fruit available all summer—the fresh figs *(seeka)* are delicious. After dinner, Greeks enjoy *karpouzi* (watermelon) or *piponi* (yellow melon). You should also try the freshly made yogurt *(yiaourti),* a thicker, fattier version of what most Americans are used to, with honey and melon mixed in. Or, sample some indigenous cheeses like *feta* (a semi-soft, salty white cheese made from goat's milk) and *kaseri,* a yellow semi-soft cheese.

Greek pastries are a delectable treat and can be bought at *zacharoplastia* shops. *Baklava,* the honey-rich, filo-dough pastry filled with chopped nuts, beats all the rest (usually 150dr); also try *galaktobouriko,* a custard-filled dough; *kareedhopita,* a walnut cake; *melomakarones,* honey-nut cookies; *kataïfi,* strands of dough wrapped around nuts and cinnamon; *koulouria,* shortbread cookies; or *kourabiethes,* powdered sugar-coated cookies. Remember that the word *pasta* in Greek means pastry, not a dish of noodles.

Greek coffee is the most popular beverage, though you may wonder why. Like Turkish coffee, it is exceedingly strong, sweet, and has a sludge-like consistency. Ask for *metrio* to get a cup with only half the sugar. *Sketo* or *pikro* will get a bitter, sugarless cup. Specify *me gala,* if you want it with milk, or *gliko,* for sweet. Greek coffee is usually served and tempered with a glass of water. American-style coffee (called *Nescafé),* usually instant, is also available. If you ask for *caffè frappe,* you'll get a tall glass of frothy iced coffee. For a real thirst-quencher, try *portokalada* (orange soda), or *limonada* (lemonade).

A favorite Greek snack combination is ouzo with *mezes,* tidbits of cheese, sausage, cakes, and octopus. *Ouzo* is a distilled spirit to which anise is added, giving it a licorice taste. Some people drink it as an aperitif, all afternoon long; others have it after dinner as a liqueur. Just make sure you're sipping, not gulping—this is strong stuff. Mixed with water, it's sweet but not overwhelming.

One of the great arts in Greece is wine-making, and every region has its own specialty. Vineyards dot the Greek countryside and many locals still make their own wine. Long ago, the Greeks discovered that when wine was stored in pitch pine-sealed goatskins, it developed a fresh, sappy flavor. After studious deduction, they discovered that adding pine resin in varying amounts during fermentation achieved the same result. The resulting wine became known as *retsina.* Resinated wines now come in three varieties: white, rosé, and red *(kokkineli).* White *retsina* is generally cheaper than beer. There are also a number of non-resinated wines, which tend to be over-sweet (like Nemea or Herakles). These include sweet *(gleeko),* and semi-sweet *(imigleko).* Try the white wines of the northern Peloponnese: Rotonda, Demestika, and Santa Helena are dry and quaffable. Greek wines can be classified in two basic groups: ordinary wines, which are one to three years old, and special wines, which are three to nine years old. Achaïa-Clauss and Cambas Vintners are consistently good wines. As an after-dinner aid to digestion, Greeks imbibe Metaxa brandy or *ouzo* shots.

A good place to taste various Greek wines is at a local wine festival, where you can drink all the wine you want for a flat admission fee. The biggest wine festival around Athens is located at Daphni (11km out of town) from mid-June to mid-September. To reach Daphni from Athens, take one of the Elefsina buses from Platia Eleftherias at the end of Evripides St. The wine festival in Alexandroupolis runs from early July to mid-August. On Crete, the festival in Rethymnon is held in July, while the one at the village of Dafnes (near Iraklion) runs in mid-July.

Holidays

The Greek penchant for celebrations is infectious, and visitors are welcomed and swept up in the festivities. Many towns honor their own patron saint with special festivals. During the festivities, the towns generally offer free *fasolia* (beans) and wine for revelers. Businesses shut down for the day, but there is usually music and dancing in front of the local church to occupy townspeople and visitors.

The following list of festivals includes holidays of the Greek Orthodox Church and traditional festivals celebrated in rural and agricultural areas. Note: the dates for some religious holidays change annually. Check dates with the GNTO. For additional information on festivals, artistic events, and religious fairs contact the GNTO, the regional tourist's information office, or the local police.

Jan. 6: Epiphany. Celebrated in the West as the day the Magi appeared in Bethlehem to greet the baby Jesus. In the Eastern church Epiphany is an important feast day recognized as the day Jesus was baptized by St. John and secondarily as the day of the marriage feast at Cana, when Christ miraculously fed the throngs of wedding guests with only a few loaves and fishes. In Greece, *kallikantzaroi* (goblins and spirits) appear between Christmas and Epiphany. Village bonfires scare them away. At Epiphany, waters are blessed and evil spirits leave the earth.

Jan. 8: Gynaecocracy (St. Domenica's Day/Midwife day). Women of child-bearing age bring gifts to the midwife. In the villages of Komotini, Xanthi, Kilkis, and Serres, women gather in the cafés and other social centers, while men look after the households; the men are allowed to join their wives in celebrations after dusk.

Feb. 23-March 16: Carnival. Three weeks of feasting and dancing before the Lenten fast. During the first week fattened pigs are slaughtered, during the second villagers feast on meat, and during the third they feast on cheese. The most notable celebrations occur in Patras and Cephalonia.

March 25: Greek Independence Day. Commemorates the 1821 struggle against the Turkish Ottoman Empire. Also a religious holiday, the Feast of the Annunciation, when the angel Gabriel told Mary of the Incarnation.

Good Friday. In rural areas, people carry lit candles in a procession through town to begin Easter weekend.

Easter. Celebrations on Easter Sunday typically include feasting on spit-roasted lamb and red-dyed hard-boiled eggs, followed by dancing in traditional costumes.

April 23: St. George's Day. Celebration in honor of the "Knight on the white horse" who, although associated with England and an apocryphal slain dragon, was born in Smyrna. Festivities include races, wrestling matches, and dances.

May 1: Labor Day. Also Feast of the Flowers.

May 21-23: Anastenaria. Also called **Feast of St. Constantine and St. Helena.** Celebrations include fire dancing and walking on burning charcoal. Celebrated in Agia Eleni, Thessaloniki, and Veria.

Late June-early July: Navy Week. At various coastal towns, fishers and sailors have festivals (including Plomari, Lesvos, and Volos). On Volos, a re-enactment of the journey of the Argonauts is staged.

Early-mid June: The Day of the Holy Spirit. This national religious holiday takes place 40-50 days after Easter and is celebrated differently in each region.

June 24: Feast of St. John the Baptist.

Aug.: Epirotika Festival, in Ioannina; **Olympus Festival,** in Katerini; **Hippokrateia Festival,** on Kos. All three feature artistic exhibits and performances.

Aug. 15: Feast of the Assumption of the Virgin Mary. Huge celebration throughout Greece, particularly on the island of Tinos, in honor of Mary's ascent to Heaven.

Aug. 25: Feast of St. Dionysius. Celebrations in honor of the patron saint of Zante.

Aug.-Sept.: Aeschilla Performances. Performances of classical drama at Eleusis.

Sept. 8: The Virgin's Birthday. In some villages an auction is held to determine who will carry the Virgin's Icon. The money is used to provide a village feast.

Sept. 14: Exaltation of the Cross. In villages, the altar cross is venerated and paraded through the town, while children sing hymns.

Oct. 26: Feast of St. Demetrius. Celebrated with particular enthusiasm in Salonika. The feast coincides with the opening of new wine, so there is heavy drinking.

Oct. 28: National Anniversary of Greek Independence.

Dec. 24-25: Christmas. As a part of the festivities, children traditionally make the rounds singing *kalanda* (Christmas carols).

Dec. 31-Jan. 1: New Year's and **The Feast of St. Basil.** Local sailors carry model ships around the island as they make their way to the town square. Children sing and people exchange gifts. The Greeks follow the Byzantine custom of slicing a *vassilopita* on New Year's Day. Lucky diners who get the coin in their slice will be blessed with good fortune through the following year.

ATHENS ΑΘΗΝΑ

Athens boggles the mind due less to its dimension in space (although it is both spectacular and appalling) than its dimension in time. Under the watchful eye of the ancient Acropolis, this city of three-million-plus slowly drags itself towards the hi-tech Age of Efficiency. Having weathered the millennia, the column-bounded temples attest to an undecipherable dictate of worship, confounding and far less obvious than that of the scattering of tattered Byzantine churches. Paradoxically, it is amidst the chaotic tangle of buses and taxis criss-crossing Athens's steaming heart that the foreign stranger is apt to feel most strange: here each passageway is a neon, postered, or repainted bombardment of Greek, forcing the non-reader into a dizzying illiteracy.

Athens is a pit, people will tell you. Get out quick and onto an island, they'll say. Don't listen to them. Athens is nothing less than the birthplace of Western civilization. There is a lot to do and see in this city. And if Athens is indeed congested, short of breath and graying in the temples, its firstborn, Western Civ, is no spring chicken either.

History

A competition between Poseidon and Athena decided the appellation of Athens. The gods of Olympus decreed that whoever gave the city the most useful gift would become its patron god. Poseidon mightily struck the rock of the Acropolis with his trident, and salt water came gushing forth. The populace was duly awestruck, but Athena's more practical gift, an olive tree growing from the same rock, won her the right to rule.

The legend dramatizes the fact: Athens became a town of note in the 16th century BCE when Athena became the Goddess Not To Mess With on the Acropolis. History reveals little until the 8th century when Athens became the artistic center of Greece, notable especially for its pottery. This coincides with Attica's unification under Athens. But the best was yet to come.

After dramatic victories over the Persians at Marathon and Salamis in the 5th century BCE, Athens enjoyed a 70-year Golden Age, reaching its apogee under the patronage of Pericles. Iktinos and Kallikrates designed the Parthenon; Aeschylus, Sophocles, and Euripides wrote masterpieces of tragic drama and Aristophanes his ribald comedies. Early historians, Herodotus in particular, challenged the assumption that gods and not human beings governed history. Hippocrates, with a similar confidence in human autonomy, developed the science of medicine.

The demise of Periclean Athens was heralded by the bloody and drawn-out campaigns of the Peloponnesian War (431-404 BCE) between Athens and Sparta. Political power in Greece then shifted north to the court of Philip of Macedon and his son Alexander the Great. In the late 5th and 4th centuries BCE, however, Athens continued to be a notable cultural center, producing three of the greatest western philosophers: Socrates, Plato, and Aristotle, as well as the great orator Demosthenes. By the 2nd century BCE, the ravenous Roman Empire had feasted on Athens and drained the city of its zest. By the time the Byzantine Empire split off from the foundering remains of the Roman Empire (285 CE), Athens was no more than a minor over-taxed backwater specializing in Neoplatonism. Still, the city remained the center of Greek education, adorned with elaborate institutes of learning, but both the status and the structures fell into ruin when Justinian banned the teaching of philosophy in 529.

Around 1000, Basil II, the Holy Roman Emperor, visited Athens. After praying to the Virgin Mary in the Parthenon, Basil ordered craftsmen to restore Athens to its former glory. Under successive conquerors—the Franks in 1205, the Catalans in 1311, and the Accajioli merchant family in 1387—Athens underwent a mini, and unfortunately inadequate, renaissance. Although many hailed the introduction of Muslim Ottoman rule in 1456 as a great deliverance, Athens remained in cultural hibernation until 1834, when it was proclaimed the capital of the new, independent Greece. Modern Athens, with its squares, wide boulevards, and somewhat more tranquil National Garden, is the fruition of plans drawn up by German architects under the direction of the Bavarian King Otto, who was awarded the newly created kingdom of Greece in the late 19th century.

The 20th century saw Athens grow unchecked in population and industry with the arrival of workers from destitute regions of Greece and beneficiaries of the Turkish-Greek exchange. In an attempt to counteract noise pollution, the transit authority now bans cars from a number of streets in the **Plaka** (historic district) and limits drivers' access to downtown on alternate days. Zeus's thunderbolt now shakes down acid rain; long time residents rue the infamous *nephos* (smog cloud) that settled in a most sinister fashion over their city.

Orientation and Practical Information

Coming from either airport, the bus will drop you off at **Syntagma (Constitution) Square.** The center of modern Athens, this bustling plaza is packed with overpriced outdoor cafés, luxury hotels, and flashy banks. A pale yellow Neoclassical building, formerly the royal palace and now home to the Greek Parliament, gazes over (and tries to ignore) the toe-nipping traffic of Syntagma. The square is a good spot to begin your tour of the city. Two **GNTO** offices, the **post office,** the **American Express office, transportation terminals,** and a number of **travel agencies** and **banks** surround the square. **Filellinon Street** and **Nikis Street,** parallel streets which head out from Syntagma toward the Plaka, contain most of the city's budget travel offices, cheap hotels, and dance clubs.

In front of the Parliament, facing Syntagma Sq., is the **Tomb of the Unknown Warrior.** The Zappeion, an exhibition hall, rests in the tranquil National Garden, bordering the south side of the Parliament. Continue east and you will come upon the heavily guarded President's House and the Athens Stadium (constructed in 1896 for the first modern Olympiad). Hadrian's Arch and the Olympeion stand just south of the Garden in full view of the city's crowning glory, the **Acropolis.** On the north side of Syntagma, the city's embassies, consulates, and premier hospital (Evangelismos) group on broad **Vassilissis Sofias.** The Goulandris, Benaki, Byzantine, and War Museums, and the National Gallery cluster a few blocks over on this avenue. The affluent and chic **Kolonaki** district is bordered by Vassilissis Sofias and lies in the shadow of Lycabettos Hill.

Northeast of Syntagma, **Omonia Square,** actually a circle, is the site of the city's central subway station from which trains run to Monastiraki (3min.) and Piraeus (20min.), among other destinations. Inexpensive shops for food, clothing, and jewelry abound, but with the influx of refugees in recent years, this area has become emotionally taxing and very unsafe for locals and visitors alike. Follow the example of the wind-swept runner who graces the water fountain in the center of the square: race to get out as quickly as possible. Two parallel avenues connect Syntagma Sq. to Omonia (Panepistimiou/Eleftherias Venizelou and Stadiou). The *panepistimio* (university) and library are on Panepistimiou St., half-way between Syntagma and Omonia. North on Patission St., which intersects the two avenues just before Omonia, is the **National Archaeological Museum.** The main train station, **Larissis,** on **Konstandinoupoleus St.** northeast of Omonia, can be reached from here by walking straight along Ipirou St., (about 30min.)

Just west of Syntagma (follow Ermou St. or Mitropoleas St.), Eolu St. and Athinas St., running between Omonia and the Acropolis, are lined with shops and department stores that spill their wares out onto the sidewalk. Along Athinas St., midway between Omonia and **Monastirake** (Athens's garment district), between Evripidou and Sofokleous St., is the indoor-outdoor food market. Here, the **Athens Flea Market,** the city's "new *agora*" (marketplace) surrounds the old one. South of here towards the Acropolis lies the **Plaka,** the oldest section of the city, now overgrown with shops, restaurants, and hotels. South of the Acropolis and neighboring Philopappus Hill (toward Athens's port, Piraeus) is the **Koukaki** section, a relatively calm residential area, and **Koukaki Square,** containing an open produce market as well as the Olympic Airways headquarters. **Leoforos Singrou** divides this area from the **Kinossargous** section. To get to

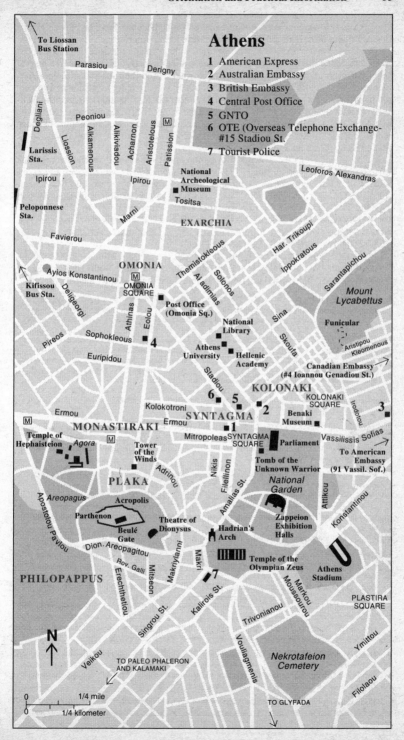

Athens

1 American Express
2 Australian Embassy
3 British Embassy
4 Central Post Office
5 GNTO
6 OTE (Overseas Telephone Exchange-#15 Stadiou St.
7 Tourist Police

To Liossan
Bus Station

Parasiou
Derigny

Degliani
Liossion
Peoniou
Alkamenous
Allikviadou
Acharnon
Aristotelous
Patission
M

Larissis
Sta.

Ipirou
Ipirou

National
Archeological
Museum

Peloponnese
Sta.

Marni
Tositsa

Favierou

EXARCHIA

Leoforos Alexandras

Ayios Konstantinou

OMONIA

Themistokleous
Har. Trikoupi
Ippokratous
Sarantapichou

Kifissou
Bus Sta.

Deligeorgi
M
OMONIA
SQUARE

Solonos
Al. adimas

Sina

Mount
Lycabettus

Funicular

Pireos
Sophokleous
Athinas
Eolou

Post Office
(Omonia Sq.)

National
Library

Aristipou
Kleomenous

Euripidou
4
Athens
University
Hellenic
Academy

Canadian Embassy
(#4 Ioannou Genadiou St.)

Stadiou
Skouta

KOLONAKI

Ermou
6
5
KOLONAKI
SQUARE
Irodotou

Kolokotroni
2
3

MONASTIRAKI
Ermou
SYNTAGMA
1
Benaki
Museum

M
Mitropoleas
SYNTAGMA
SQUARE
Vassilissis Sofias

Temple of
Hephaisteion
Agora
M
Tower
of the
Winds
Parliament

To American
Embassy
(91 Vassil. Sof.)

Adrinou
Nikis
Filellinon
Tomb of the
Unknown Warrior

PLAKA
Amalias St.
National
Garden
Attikou

Areopagus
Acropolis

Apostolou Pavlou
Parthenon
Beulé
Gate
Theatre of
Dionysus
Zappeion
Exhibition
Halls

Konstantinou

Dion. Areopagitou

PHILOPAPPUS
Rov. Galli
Mitseon
Erechtheiou
Makriyianni
Makri
Hadrian's
Arch

Temple of the
Olympian Zeus
7
Athens
Stadium

Markou
Moussourou

PLASTIRA
SQUARE

N
Singrou St.
Kalirois St.

Velkou

TO PALEO PHALERON
AND KALAMAKI

Trivonianou
Voullagmenis
Nekrotafeion
Cemetery

Ymittou
Filolaou

0   1/4 mile
0   1/4 kilometer

TO GLYFADA

Koukaki from Syntagma, walk down Amalias (which becomes Singrou beyond Hadrian's Arch) and turn right; for Kinossargous, turn left at Singrou.

The mapless tourist in Athens will experience the pain and pleasure of getting hopelessly lost. Make use of the two quality maps available at the GNTO; their free map of the city is clear and includes bus and trolley routes. And their magazine *Greece-Athens-Attica* has a more detailed street plan. Athenian geography mystifies newcomers and natives alike; when you do lose your bearings, ask for directions back to the well-lit Syntagma, where you can always catch a cab if necessary. Keep an eye out for the Acropolis: this age-old landmark provides a useful reference point. In contests between pedestrians and motorists, Athenian drivers will always take the right of way, so be alert crossing the street and join the crowd.

Several publications list general information about Athens and special events. Pick up a complimentary copy of the GNTO's *This Week in Athens,* which gives addresses, hours, and phone numbers for nightclubs, theaters, sights, museums, libraries, restaurants, airlines, churches, and more. News, as well as movie, exhibit, and restaurant listings appear daily in Athens's English-language newspaper, the *Athens News* (90dr). The *Weekly Greek News* (100dr) and *Greece's Weekly* (250dr) focus more on Greek politics, though they also contain international news. The monthly *Athenian* magazine (325dr) features stories about Greece and its culture.

In general, summer business hours throughout the city are Monday 1:30-8:30pm; Tuesday, Thursday, and Friday 8am-2pm and 5:30-8:30pm; and Wednesday and Saturday 8am-3pm. Summer officially runs from mid-June to mid-September.

Greek National Tourist Office (GNTO): Information desk in the **National Bank of Greece,** 2 Karageorgi Servias, Syntagma Sq. (tel. 322 25 45 or 323 41 30). Information sheets detailing transportation schedules and prices, embassy addresses and phone numbers, and museum hours and locations. Ask for the Athens city map. Open Mon.-Fri. 8am-2pm and 3:30-8pm, Sat. 9am-2pm; off-season Mon.-Fri. 8am-2pm and 3:30-6pm, Sat. 9am-2pm. A less harried office is 1 block away at 1 Ermou St. (tel. 325 26 67/68), inside the **General Bank of Greece.** Open Mon.-Fri. 8am-8pm, Sat. 8am-2pm. The GNTO at the **East Terminal** of the airport (tel. 969 95 00) is open Mon.-Fri. 8am-10pm, Sat. 10am-5pm; off-season Mon.-Fri. 9am-6pm, Sat. 10am-5pm. The head tourist office, which gathers the information for the other offices and usually has slightly more current listings, is at 2 Amerikis St. (tel. 322 31 11) near Syntagma. This office ordinarily does not deal with the public, but there is a Dept. of Information on the 5th floor in room #514. Open Mon.-Fri. 11:30am-2:30pm.

The Hellenic Chamber of Hotels: In the National Bank of Greece at the same service windows as the GNTO (tel. 323 71 93). Will answer your questions about accommodations and provide you with a list of D- and E-class hotels in Athens. Open Mon.-Fri. 8:30am-2pm, Sat. 9am-1pm. An early visit is a crowdless visit.

Budget Travel: For **ISIC/FIYTO** purchases, see Useful Organizations in the General Introduction. In Greece there are no student discounts for domestic travel; the discounts found here are for everyone. Most offices are on Nikis and Filellinon St., off Syntagma Sq. Shop around for the best prices but don't miss **Magic Bus,** 20 Filellinon St. (tel. 323 74 71/74), which offers cheap rail, air, boat, and long-distance bus tickets to almost anywhere. Extremely competent, English-speaking staff. Student discounts of 20-55% on international travel with ISIC or college ID. Open Mon.-Fri. 9am-5pm, Sat. 9am-1pm. **Sotiriou/Transalpino,** 28 Nikis St. (tel. 322 05 03), has half-price train tickets for those under 26 and cut-rate airfare. Open Mon.-Fri. 9am-6pm, Sat. 9am-1pm. **Grivas,** 25 Nikis St., (tel. 323 65 18/19) books a large selection of charter flights and student discount fares. Check out their prices posted on a large wooden board outside. Open Mon.-Fri. 9am-4pm, Sat. 9am-1pm. **Swift Travel,** 21 Nikis St. (tel. 322 16 23) and **KF Travel System,** 15A Xenofontas St. (tel. 323 54 72), offer similar deals. **USIT Youth Student Travel,** 1 Fillelinon St. (tel. 324 18 84) issues ISIC cards (1500dr) and caters to their holders. You can change plane reservations made with Council Travel here. Bus and train travel to far-away destinations is both lengthy and arduous; consider traveling by plane instead. Student international flights are particularly affordable. Spend the extra cash and you'll spare yourself the body cramps associated with narrow seats, long hours, sudden stops and winding roads.

Greek Youth Hostel Association: 4 Dragatsaniou St., 7th floor (tel. 323 41 07); the elevators are on your right by the guard as you enter the arcade. HI/IYHF cards are 2500dr; bring 2 photos (obtainable at Omonia Sq. or 18 Filellinon St.) and your passport. Most Greek youth hostels don't care and won't check whether you have a card. Open Mon.-Fri. 9am-2:30pm.

Embassies: U.S., 91 Vassilissis Sofias (tel. 721 29 51). Open Mon.-Fri. 8:30am-5pm. Visas can be obtained 8am-noon. Bring one picture. **Canadian,** 4 Ioannou Genadiou St. (tel. 723 95 11).

Open Mon.-Fri. 9am-1pm. **British,** 1 Ploutarchou St. (tel. 723 62 11), at Ypsilantou St. Open for visas Mon.-Fri. 8am-1:30pm. **Australian,** 37 D. Soutsou St. (tel. 644 73 03). Open Mon.-Fri. 9am-1pm. **New Zealand,** 15-17 An. Tsoha St. (tel. 641 03 11). Open Mon.-Fri. 9am-1pm. **Irish,** #7 Leoforos Vasileos (tel. 723 27 71). **French,** 7 Vassilissis Sofias (tel. 361 16 63). Enter at 2 Akadimis St. Open Mon.-Fri. 9-11am. Visas obtained at the consulate, 5-7 Vassilissis Konstantinou Ave. (tel. 729 01 51). **Italian,** 2 Sekeri St. (tel. 361 17 23). Visas obtained at the consulate, 19 Meandrou Michalakopoulou St. (tel. 723 90 45), near Vassilissis Sofias, 9am-11am. **Egyptian,** 3 Vassilissis Sofias (tel. 361 86 12); visa window on Zalokosta St. Bring 1 photo. Open Mon.-Fri. 9:30-noon. The Egyptian State Tourist Office is nearby at 10 Amerikis St. (tel. 360 69 06). **Turkish,** 8 Vassileos Gheorgiou B. St. (tel. 724 59 15). **Yugoslavian,** 106 Vassilissis Sofias (tel. 777 43 44); visas Mon.-Fri. 9-11:30am. Also at 25 Evrou St. (tel. 777 43 44). **Jordanian,** 30 P. Zervou St., Paleo Psihiko (tel. 647 41 61). More comprehensive listing of embassies available at the GNTO.

Currency Exchange: National Bank of Greece (tel. 322 27 30) in Syntagma, on the corner of Karageorgi Servias and Stadiou St. Open Mon.-Thurs. 8am-2pm and 3:30-6:30pm, Fri. 8am-1:30pm and 3-6:30pm, Sat. 9am-3pm, Sun. 9am-1pm. American Express and other banks change money, but most banks close at 2pm. East Terminal of the airport is open 24 hrs. Some hotels and hostels exchange currency, but their rates are usually not as good. Commission between 100-400dr, depending on the amount you change.

American Express: 2 Ermou St., P.O. Box 332, 1st floor, Syntagma Sq., back from the street, behind the McDonalds (tel. 324 49 75 or -76 or -77 or -78 or -79). Holds mail for 1 month; collects 400dr from those without Amex cards. Forwarding fee 500dr. Changes Amex checks with no commission, and cash for card-holders only. Summer hours (April-Oct.) are Mon.-Fri. 8:30am-5:30pm, Sat. 8:30am-1:30pm. Winter hours (Nov.-March) are Mon.-Fri. 8:30am-4pm, Sat. 8:30am-1:30pm. Another Amex office (tel. 722 02 01) is located at the Athens Hilton Hotel on Vassilissis Sophias Ave.

Central Post Office: 100 Eolou St., Omonia Sq. Poste Restante holds mail for 1 month at Omonia, on your right as you enter. **Postal Code:** 10200. **Another office** with Poste Restante is located in the subway station under the Omonia Sq. Will forward mail (100dr). Open Mon.-Fri. 7:30am-8pm, Sat. 7:30am-2pm. **Postal Code:** 10009. **Another office** in Syntagma Sq., on the corner of Mitreopolis. Open Mon.-Fri. 7:30am-8pm, Sat. 7:30am-2pm, Sun. 9am-1:30pm. **Postal Code:** 10300. For parcel post, walk through the arcade at 4 Stadiou St. and turn right. Open Mon.-Fri. 7:30am-3pm, for parcels abroad Mon.-Fri. 7:30am-2pm.

OTE (International Telephones): 15 Stadiou St. Open 24 hrs. Offices at Omonia Sq., at the end of Stadiou St.; and at 85/Patission/28 October St. are open daily 7am-11pm (Omonia closed Sun.). A fourth office at 50 Athinas St. is open Mon.-Fri. 7am-10pm. Make collect calls overseas at Patission, Stadiou, and Athinas offices. International collect calls (to countries other than the U.S.) take up to 1hr. to go through (2-3hr. on weekend), and you must wait there during that time. Come a couple hours before closing or you won't be able to place your collect call. For information on overseas calls, dial 162; for directory assistance in Athens call 131, outside Athens 132. You can make local calls at the OTE or at many of the street-side kiosks that have telephones on their side-window ledges (10dr). These are more reliable than the phone booths in the city (which are often empty). **Telephone Code:** 01.

Airports: East Terminal, for all foreign airlines and charters. Take the Express lines A and B double decker buses (yellow) from Syntagma or Omonia Sq. (every 20min. 6am-midnight, 160dr; every hr. midnight-6am, 200dr) or bus #121 from Vassilissis Olgas in front of the Zappeion (every 40min. 6:50am-10:50pm, 50dr). From airport to Athens: look to your left as you exit customs, take the blue, yellow, and white bus A or B to Leoforos Amalias, off Syntagma (every 20min. 6:20am-midnight, 160dr; and every hr. midnight-6am, 200dr). Purchase tickets at booths and stamp it yourself at the machine on board; drivers don't mess with money or stamping. **West Terminal,** for domestic and international Olympic Airways flights. Take bus #133 from Othonos on Syntagma (every 15min. 5:40am-midnight, 50dr) or bus #122 from Vassilissis Olgas in front of the Zappeion (every 15min. 5:30am-11:30pm, 50dr). Bus #167 from Akadimias and Sina St. runs late (at 12:30am, 1:15am, 2am, 3am, and 4am, 60dr). Or take the navy Olympic Airways bus from the corner of Amalias and Othonos (just off Syntagma; every 30min. 5:50am-8:20pm, 160dr). From the airport to Athens take city bus #133 leaving from the road outside the gates (every 20min.), or take the navy Olympic Airways bus to Singrou or Othonos St. in Syntagma (every 30min.). A taxi should cost 1000dr from either terminal.

Trains: Larissis Train Station, Degliani St., serves northern Greece. (Thessaloniki 2300dr, Volos 1680dr, Lamia 970dr.) Take trolley #1 to and from Syntagma. **Railway Station for the Peloponnese,** 3 Peloponnesou St. (tel. 513 16 01), behind Larissis, in a Victorian-style building with a silver roof. From Larissis, exit to your right and go over the bridge. Serves Patras (920dr) and elsewhere in the Peloponnese. For more information, call **Hellenic Railways (OSE)** (tel. 522 43 02) or **Railway Station for Northern Greece (Larissis)** (tel. 823 77 41).

Subway: One-line system. Fare 75dr. Free 5-8am. Be sure to hang on to your ticket stub until exiting or you may have to pay twice. Runs every 5min. 5am-midnight. Begins at Kifissia stop, just north of the city; stops at Attiki, Victoria, Omonia (midpoint), Thission, Monastirion, and Piraeus (on Rousvelt St.), among others.

Buses: Blue, comfortable, and bearing 3-digit numbers for trips within the city. Fare 75dr. Free 5-8am. Convenient for travel within the city, and the best (almost the only) option for daytrips outside Athens. Frequent service ends at midnight, but buses run every hr. on most routes throughout the night. **Kifissou St. Station** (Terminal A), 100 Kifissou St. (tel. 514 88 56), serves most of Greece including Northern Greece and the Peloponnese with the exception of Delphi and other destinations in Central Greece; take bus #51 from the corner of Zinonos and Menandrou near Omonia Sq. (every 10min. 5am-midnight, every 40min. midnight-4:40am). **Liossion St. Station** (Terminal B), 260 Liossion St. (tel. 831 70 59), serves Delphi, Evia, Lamia, and Larissa; take bus #24 from Leoforos Amalias in front of the entrance to the National Garden (every 15min. 5am-midnight). Also bus #24 to Athens from Liossion St. Note that the number of the bus may be either above the windshield or on a sticker in the windshield near the front door. Bus stops list the numbers of the buses they serve. Buy a ticket at a kiosk from a station vendor and stamp it yourself at the machine on board. Beware that bus strikes are frequent, but not all companies strike at once.

Trolleys: Yellow, crowded, and wearing 1-or 2-digit numbers. Fare 50dr. Trolleys no longer accept money. Buy a ticket (or book of 10) ahead of time at a kiosk. Frequent service and convenient for short hops within the city. From Syntagma, #1, 2, 4, 5, and 11 run to Omonia Sq. **Taxis:** 30dr plus 40dr per kilometer (minimum fare 240dr—cheap if you're still thinking in your home currency). Taxis are allowed to take in extra passengers if there's room. Get in the cab and *then* tell the driver where you're going—otherwise the driver might refuse if your destination is inconvenient. If you start at the airport or train station, make sure that your driver charges you only the allowed 40dr surcharge (and 20dr for each piece of luggage). You might also check that the driver is using a meter and not quoting outrageous prices.

Ferries: Most dock at **Piraeus.** From here they go to all Greek island groups except the Sporades (which leave from Agios Konstantinos) and the Ionian Islands (which leave from Patras in the Peloponnese). Some popular destinations from Piraeus: Santorini (10hr., 2444dr); Mykonos (6hr., 1935dr); Aegina (1½hr., 400dr); Paros (5-6hr., 1764dr); Rhodes (17hr., 3687dr). International departures to Haifa, Alexandria, and Limassol also leave from Piraeus. (**Port Authority of Piraeus** tel. 451 13 11.) From Athens to Piraeus, take the subway to the last stop, or bus #40 from Filellinon St. To reach Syntagma (in Athens) from Piraeus, walk left (facing inland) along the waterfront to Rousvelt St., take the subway to Monastiraki (75dr), turn right up Ermou St., and walk for 5min. Or take green bus #40 from Vassileos Konstandinou across from the Public Theater (every 10min., 75dr). Boats also leave from **Rafina**, a port suburb east of Athens, to: Andros, Tinos, Mykonos, Karystos. See also Piraeus and Rafina sections.

Hydrofoils (Flying Dolphins): Speed above water between islands and from some ports, serving the Argosaronic and Sporades groups, as well as Kea and Kithnos. Get a **Ceres Hydrofoil Joint Service** timetable from one of the 38 scattered offices; main office 8 Akti Themistokleous, Piraeus (Tel. (01) 428 00 11). The Athens office is on a second floor, two doors down from the National Bank on Karageori Servias St. on Syntagma Sq. (Tel. 324 22 81). Reservations are a good idea and must be paid 24 hrs. prior to departure.

> *Let's Go* urges you to consider seriously possible risks before you decide to hitchhike. The routes listed below and elsewhere in this book are not intended to recommend hitchhiking as a means of transport. *Let's Go* does not recommend hitchhiking.

Hitching: Should you decide to hitch, be forewarned that it's almost impossible from Athens. Hitchers have the most luck at the truck parks at the cargo wharves in Piraeus. Those headed to Northern Greece take the subway to the last stop (Kifissia), walk up to the town's central square, take the bus to Nea Kifissia, and walk to the National Rd. (Ethniki Odos). For the Peloponnese, they take bus #873 from Eleftheras Sq. to the National Rd.

Luggage Storage: At the airport 100m outside on your right as you exit baggage claim and customs. 130dr per piece per day. Open 24 hrs. Keep your ticket stub to reclaim; pay when you collect. After midnight you pay for an extra day. Several offices on Nikis and Filellinon Sts., including **Pacific Ltd.,** 24 Nikis St. (tel. 323 68 51 or 324 10 07). Daily 200dr per piece, weekly 500dr per piece, monthly 1500dr per piece. Open Mon.-Sat. 7am-8pm, Sun. 7am-2pm. Also, there is often free (or almost free) luggage storage for customers of many hotels and pensions; ask your hotel manager.

English Bookstores: Eleftheroudakis Book Store, 4 Nikis St. (tel. 322 93 88). The best. Open Mon.-Fri. 9am-8pm, Sat. 9am-3pm. **Pantelides Books,** 11 Amerikis St. Special section on social sciences. Open Mon., Wed., and Sat. 8am-3pm, Tues. and Thurs.-Fri. 8am-2:30pm and 5:30-8:30pm.

Libraries: American Library, 22 Massalias St., 4th floor (tel. 363 81 14), behind the university. Current issues of the *Herald Tribune* and American magazines. A/C. Open summer Mon. 11:30am-6:30pm, Thurs. 11:30am-4:30pm, Tues., Wed., Fri. 9:30am-2:30pm. The 7th floor houses the **American Union Greek Library** (tel. 362 98 86) and its large collection of English books on Greece. Open Mon. and Thurs. 10am-7pm, Tues.-Wed. and Fri. 9:30am-2:30pm. **The British Council Library,** Kolonaki Sq. (tel. 363 32 15), also has English reading material and sponsors cultural events. Open summer Mon.-Thurs. 9:30am-1:30pm; winter Mon.-Thurs. 5:30pm-8:30pm. **Blegan Library,** at the American School for Classical Studies, 54 Sovidas St. (tel. 723 63 13), has a good collection of books about Athens and Greece. Open Mon.-Fri. 8:30am-9:30pm.

Laundromats: 10 Angelou Geronta St., 1st floor, in Plaka. Wash 500dr, dry 300dr, soap 50dr. Open Mon.-Sat. 8:30am-8pm. Also at **9 Psaron St.** (tel. 522 28 59), off Karaiskaki Sq. near Larissis Station. Wash and dry 1000dr; free delivery to your hotel if they wash (full service) for you. Open Mon.-Fri. 8am-9pm, Sat. 8am-5pm, Sun. 8am-2pm. Also at **46 Didotou and Zoodochou Pigis St.,** near Exarchia Sq. (tel. 361 06 61). Take bus #025, 026, 230 or 813 to the Didotou stop. Wash 700dr, dry 100dr; or they'll do it all for you, 1000dr. English spoken. Open Mon.-Sat. 8am-9pm. The Greek word for laundry is *plintirio,* but most places have signs saying "Laundry" or *"Aytomata."*

Pharmacies: Indicated by a Byzantine-style red cross. Open Sat.-Sun. on a rotating basis; signs are posted in the windows of each to indicate the closest open pharmacy. You can also find out by phoning 166.

Emergencies: Tourist Police tel. 171. English spoken. **Athens Police:** tel. 100. Not likely to speak English.

Medical Emergency: Tel. 166. Most are open Mon. and Wed. 8am-2:30pm, Tues. and Thurs.-Fri. 8am-2pm and 5:30-8:30pm. English usually spoken. Free emergency medical care for tourists at many Athens hospitals, including **Evangelismos,** 45-47 Ipsilandou St. (tel. 722 00 01 or 722 01 01 or 722 15 01), opposite the Hilton.

Red Cross First Aid Center: #21, 3 Septemvriou St. (tel. 150 or 522 55 55). Three blocks north of Omonia Sq., on the left. Open 24 hrs. English spoken.

Accommodations and Camping

A night in a budget hotel in Athens usually includes mild ruckus and varying doses of grime, but the cost is low enough (no more than 2500dr per person) to make up for some of the discomfort. Since the rooms themselves are uniformly mediocre (except in the outlying districts), you should stay at a conveniently located hotel. If soaking up the sights and nightlife of the city is a priority, stay in the Plaka-Syntagma area: the region's proximity to the Acropolis, numerous eateries, shops, and streets made for strolling compensates, in part, for the noise and dust of the city. Be aware that Athens is notoriously noisy; cars and motorcycles speed through even the smallest of streets, and talk and music continue till the moon sets. Unless you're a heavy sleeper, the areas near the train station or south of the Acropolis are probably best. In any case, be sure to ask for a room that faces away from the street and remember, if you are planning to stay less than 3 nights, a hotel owner can legally add a 10% surcharge to your bill.

In July and August, when swarms of honey-seeking tourists buzz into this already bustling hive, prices may be 300-400dr higher than those quoted here. If you arrive late in the tourist season, venture beyond the Syntagma Sq. area, where there are many hotels on out-of-the-way streets. When hotels fill up, the management often allows guests to sleep on the roof for 1000dr per night. This option is not only cheaper, but also cooler, though you have to vacate early in the morning. Summer rain is rare in Athens, but an outdoor night can be chilly.

Many hotel hawkers meet trains at the station. Most distribute pamphlets with maps for decent places near the station, some of which are listed here. Others, however, have been known to lure tourists into fleabags miles from anywhere and then charge exorbitant rates. Have the hawker point out the place on a large map of the city and set a firm price, in writing if possible, *before* leaving the station. Men arriving by bus from the airport should be aware of "friendly bar-keepers" who may direct you to brothels rather than budget hotels. Do not sleep in the parks, even as a last resort. Besides being illegal, it is extremely unsafe.

Plaka-Syntagma Area

Most of the city's cheap hotels cluster in this central and rambunctious part of town. Syntagma, the Plaka, the Acropolis, the subway to Piraeus (from Monastirion station), and most of Athens's nightlife are all within easy walking distance. The following list is by no means exhaustive.

Festos, 18 Filellinon St. (tel. 323 24 55), 3 blocks down from Syntagma Sq. Noisy and popular. Students feast during Happy Hour on cut-rate drinks and inexpensive dishes in the funky bar. 24-hr. English-speaking reception. Check-out 9am. Curfew 2am. Roof 1000dr. Dorm bed 1500dr. Singles 1950dr. Doubles 3900dr. Triples 5400dr. Quads 7200dr. Hot showers 8-10am and 5-8pm. Free luggage storage for guests. Will hold luggage up to 3 mos. at 100dr per day per piece. Call ahead for summer reservations or arrive early.

Thisseos Inn, 10 Thisseos St. (tel. 324 59 60). Take Perikleous St. away from Syntagma. The 3rd right is Thisseos. On a small street with less noise than most in this district. TV in lobby. Kitchen for communal use. Hot showers mornings and evenings. Check-out noon. Curfew 1am. Dorm bed (4 to a room) 1500dr. Doubles 3500dr. Triples 4500dr.

George's Guest House, 46 Nikis St. (tel. 322 64 74). Several blocks down Nikis off Syntagma Sq. Spacious and cheery pink-and-green rooms make up for the dizzying spiral stairs. Dorm beds (4 to a room) 1500dr. Doubles 3500dr. Triples 4500dr. Laundry facilities 500dr.

Hotel Phaedra, 16 Herefondos St. (tel. 322 77 95 or 323 84 61). Across from the small, palm tree-filled park. Many rooms have balconies with great views of the Parthenon. Clean and comfy, but more expensive than most. Roof 1500dr. Singles 3000dr. Doubles 4800dr. Triples 6400dr.

Acropolis House, 6 Kodrou St. (tel. 322 23 44 or 322 62 41). Turn left off Mitropoleos onto Voulis and follow it to the end at the base of a small hill. A truly elegant hotel. Centrally located and thus noisy both morning and night. Check-out noon. Singles 4912dr, with bath 5133dr. Doubles 6650dr, with bath 6950dr. Breakfast 695dr. Luggage storage 50dr per day.

Hotel "Solonion", 11-13 Tsangari (tel. 322 00 08 or 322 30 80). 5 min. walk from Plaka or Syntagma in a less congested area. Take side street off 38 Amalias Ave., around the corner from State University of New York. Clean but dark. Singles 3000dr. Doubles 4000dr. Triples 5000dr.

Monastiraki/Thission Area

Near the central tourist market, the central food market, and the garment district, this neighborhood has an ever-increasing, never-ceasing noise problem. But it's also near the Acropolis and the subway, practically on top of the Agora archaeological site, and home to some good, clean bargains.

Hotel Ideal, 39 Eolou St. (tel. 321 31 95). Entrance on side street off shopping area closed to traffic. Victorian furniture adds a classy touch to the spacious rooms. Singles 2596dr. Doubles 4740dr. Triples 6208dr.

Pella Inn, 104 Ermou St. (tel. 325 05 98 or 321 22 29), a 10-min. walk down Ermou from Syntagma Sq. Two blocks from the Monastiraki subway station. Entrance on Karaiskaki St. Popular and lively, but in a noisy, grimy part of town. Most balconied rooms have a tremendous view of the Acropolis. Lounge and snack bar with eye-opening yellow and red furniture. Check-out 11am. Singles 5000dr. Doubles 6254dr. Triples 6500dr. Breakfast 700dr. Free luggage storage.

Hotel Hermion, 66 Ermou St. (tel. 321 27 53). Actually on an alley, a bit back from the street. Grim part of town, but building is clean and newly renovated. The bathrooms and showers sparkle. Singles 2200dr. Doubles from 3200-3600dr. Triples from 3900-4200dr. Continental (550dr) and English breakfast (650dr).

South of the Acropolis and North of the City

The accommodations listed below are in four relatively quiet residential areas south of the Acropolis. Farthest west, Koukaki and Veikou present you with a 15- to 20-min. uphill hike to Syntagma Sq. Ardistos, although somewhat closer, is practically devoid of public transportation services. Farthest east is Pangrati, almost a half hour from Syntagma, but easily accessible by trolley. Since these places are removed from the center of the city, food is cheaper. The youth hostel in Kipseli, north of central Athens, is also a good deal, though the distance may prove daunting both to your sight-seeing and your nightlife. If you take a cab, tell the driver the name of the district, then the street and hotel names. You can always point out your destination if you're carrying a map.

Youth Hostel #5 Pangrati, 75 Damareos St., Pangrati (tel. 751 95 30). No HI/IYHF card required. Take trolley #2, 11, or 12 from Syntagma. Or walk through the National Garden, down Eratosthenous St. to Plintira Sq., take Efthidou St. to Frinis St., and make a right on Damareos. Snack bar. Hostel guests get good rates for European Destination Buses at travel service nearby. Yiannis, the owner, speaks 6 languages. Roof 500dr. Dorm beds (5-6 to a room) 1200dr. Sheets 100dr. Hot showers. Breakfast 300-500dr. Laundry load 500dr.

Marble House Pension, 35 Zini St., Koukaki (tel. 923 40 58); take trolley #1 or 5 to Zini stop. Set back from the street, in a foliage-covered building on the left. Quiet residential neighborhood. Sparkling marble lobby; some rooms have balconies and private baths. Very cordial atmosphere. Clean rooms. Check-out noon. Singles 3000dr, with bath 4000dr. Doubles 5000dr, with bath 6000dr. Triples 6000dr, with bath 7000dr. Weekly and monthly rates as well. Breakfast 500dr. Free luggage storage.

Art Gallery Pension, 5 Erechthiou St., Veikou (tel. 923 83 76 or 923 19 33). Next to—you guessed it—an art gallery. The owner-architect, Yiannis, has converted his family's place into a pension with a balcony overlooking the quiet residential area. Spacious, clean rooms. Breakfast/bar area on the 4th floor is open daily 8:30am-midnight. Check-out noon. Singles 4900dr. Doubles 6000dr. Triples 7200dr. Quads 8400dr. Breakfast 400dr. Luggage storage 50dr per piece per day.

Pension Greca, 48 Singrou St., Veikou (tel. 921 52 62 or 923 32 29). Features congenial owners and a cozy lobby with TV and potted plants. Singles 3000dr. Doubles 6000dr. Triples 9000dr. Showers (7-11pm only) are hot and vigorous. Breakfast 1000dr. Luggage storage 200dr per day.

Joseph's House, 13 Markou Moussourou, Ardistos (tel. 923 12 04 or 922 11 60). In an old building with kitchen facilities, the establishment is cheap and quiet. No curfew. Check-out negotiable. Roof 500dr. Dorm beds 1000dr. Singles 1500dr with bath. Doubles 1500dr. Triples 3000dr. Solar-heated showers 100dr. Luggage storage.

Clare's House, 24 Sorvolou St., Ardistos (tel. 922 22 88 or 922 06 78). Take a taxi here (200dr) if you're luggage-laden, because it's a hike. Immaculate, comfortable, and modern. Some rooms have gorgeous stone balconies with flowers. Amiable staff speaks English. TV lounge, reading room, and laundry service (1000dr per load). Check-out noon. Singles 4000dr, suite with bath 4500dr. Doubles with bath 6500dr. Triples 7500dr. Breakfast included. Free luggage storage. Reservations advisable (postal code 11636, Athens).

HI/IYHF Athens Youth Hostel, 57 Kipselis St. at Agiou Meletiou, Kipseli (tel. 822 58 60). From Syntagma, take trolley #2, 4, or 9 and get off at Zakinthou. A long way from the town center, but cheap. Beds 1200dr.

Railway Station Area

This uninteresting and varyingly grim business and residential district is too far away from Syntagma for week-long stays, but ideal for a stopover because of its proximity to trains, buses, and (via the Victoria subway stop) Piraeus. Be careful getting around the Omonia Sq. area: carry your wallet in your front pocket and try to move in groups. Most places listed here are large, popular, lively, and generally cheaper than those farther south. Most hotels have bars that serve breakfast, snacks, and drinks. **Place Victoria** is quite alive at night, and not at all tourist-infested. The Athenians of this part of town take long peacock strolls around the area on their nightly *peripata,* or *voltes* (walks).

Athens Connection Hotel, 20 Ioulianou St. (tel. 882 83 34). A 2-min. walk from the Victoria subway stop, or take trolley #2, 3, 4, 5, 9, or 12 from Syntagma. An animated establishment with an interesting staff and some much-appreciated "extras": budget travel service and currency exchange. Excellent basement pub serves hearty continental breakfast (400dr). Fills quickly. Dorm beds 1000dr. Doubles 2500, with bath 3000dr. Check-out 11am. Free luggage storage.

Hostel Annabel, 28 Koumoundourou St. at Veranzerou (tel. 524 58 34). Friendly, helpful management. The cheery bar is a good place to meet other tourists. Travel services and information. Check-out 11am. Roof 600dr. Dorm bed (4-5 to a room) 1600dr. Doubles 3500-4000dr. Triples 5100dr. Hot showers 6am-noon and 6pm-midnight. Five scrumptious breakfast choices (300-500dr). Free luggage storage.

Athens Inn, 13 Victoros Ougo (tel. 524 69 06). From the station, bear right on Deligiani to Victoros Ougo. A family-run place in a relatively quiet neighborhood. Space-age Arabian Nights bar.

Dorm beds 1200dr. Singles 2000dr. Doubles 3000dr. Triples 4500dr. Quads 5200dr. Breakfast included. Free luggage storage.

Hotel Appia, 21 Menandrou St. (tel. 524 51 55 or 524 45 61). From Omonia Sq., walk down Tsaldari St. several blocks and turn left onto Menandrou St. Modern hotel with elevator and tidy, generic rooms. Bar (open 24 hrs.) and cafeteria. Check-out 11:30am. Singles 2000dr, with bath 2800dr. Doubles 3000dr, with bath 4000dr. Triples 3900dr. Quads 4500dr. Hot water 24 hrs. Breakfast 550dr. Free luggage storage.

Hotel Florida, 25 Menandrou St, (tel. 524 12 09). Take Tsaldari St. from Omonia and it's 3 blocks down on the left. Spartan furnishings and grim "views," but cheap. All rooms with baths. Singles 2500dr. Doubles 4000dr.

Hotel Rio, 13 Odisseos St., (tel. 522 70 75), a 5-min. walk from the railroad station. Take Diligiani St. to Karaiskaki Sq., and turn right. Newly renovated and quiet. Cheerful management. Bright bar. Telephones in rooms. Singles 2500dr. Doubles 3800dr. Triples 4800dr. Quads 5600dr. Breakfast 600dr. Free luggage storage.

Hotel Arta, 12 Nikitara St. (tel. 362 77 53). From Syntagma or Omonia, take Stadiou to Em. Benaki, turn left, and take the 3rd left on Nikitara. Modern hotel worth finding for the endearing non-English-speaking reception. Immaculate rooms with desks, telephones, and A.C. Singles 3000dr. Doubles 4500dr. Triples 5800dr. Breakfast with eggs 850dr.

Vienna Hotel, 20 Pireos St. (tel. 524 91 43). From Omonia, take Tsaldari St., which becomes Pireos. Pricier than the others in this area, but has commodious, clean rooms. Saloon open 24 hrs. Singles with bath 3000dr. Doubles with bath 5000dr. Breakfast 5000dr.

Hotel Hellas, 5 Third September St. (tel. 522 45 40 or 522 85 44), a block north of Omonia. Good upkeep and managed by a lovely couple. Sizable rooms with telephones. Singles with bath 2000dr. Doubles 3200dr. Triples 4500dr. **Pension Argo,** 25 Victoros Ougo St. (tel. 522 59 39). From the station, bear right on Deligiani to Victoros Ougo or take trolley #1, 3, or 5 from Syntagma. Quiet and clean. This scrubbed and tranquil pension provides self-service coin-op laundry, money exchange, and travel information. Check-out 11am. Singles 1500dr. Doubles 2800dr. Triples 3000dr. Quads 4000dr. Breakfast 400dr. Free baggage storage.

Athens House Hotel, 4 Aristotelous St. (tel. 524 05 39), 5th floor. Apartment converted into hotel. Tidy, snug rooms with balconies. Friendly, helpful proprietor. Money exchange. Single 2000dr. Doubles 3000dr. Triples 4000dr. Quad 5000dr. (Only 1 single and 1 quad.)

Athens proper has no **camping** facilities, and freelance camping is illegal. Nearby, however, are several campsites, including **Dionissioti Camping** (tel. 807 14 94), 18km north on the national road at Nea Kifissia, and **Acropolis Camping,** (tel. 807 52 53) 16km north at the Athens-Lamia crossing, also at Nea Kifissia. (430dr per adult, 220dr per child, 580dr per tent.) The sites at Daphni, Cape Sounion, and Voula are also accessible (see Near Athens). *This Week in Athens* lists campsites in the Athens area, while the GNTO distributes a booklet listing all of Greece's official campgrounds.

Food

Food in Athens is like food in the rest of Greece, only more so. Athens's culinary claim to fame is the cheap and plentiful street food. *Souvlaki* (150dr), either on a *kalamaki* (skewer), or wrapped in *pita,* is the Greek alternative to fast-food. A *tost,* a grilled sandwich of meat and cheese (175-300dr), is considered "strollable" as well. Locally brewed beer runs about 150dr per half-liter. *Tiropita* (hot cheese pie), and *spanakopita* (hot spinach pie) go for around 120dr. Ice cream is sold at almost every kiosk, and phallic yet tasty coconut treats go for 100dr or so, as do bags of nuts. Need a quick breakfast for a paltry few drachmae? Grab a donut-shaped, sesame-coated roll.

The best place to eat—and the place where the solicitors are in full force—is the Plaka. Although crowded, especially in peak season, outdoor *tavernas* and roof gardens make for terrific people-watching. When you eat in the Plaka, survey the streets and menus before you make your selection. You'll find a plethora of interesting places up and down Adrianou and Kidatheneon Sts. Once seated at the establishment of your choice, relax: Greek restaurants are not known for the speed of their service. Women should know that the Plaka is a popular spot for *kamakia* (literally, "harpoons") who enjoy making catcalls at women as they walk by. Keep walking. Most places in the Plaka serve early or all day, but outside these touristed quarters few restaurants open before 8pm. Many restaurants have signs in both Greek and Roman letters. If you spot a sign in English only, chances are that the establishment caters to tourists, and the food is more expensive than scrumptious.

Plaka/Syntagma

The following list includes simply a few of the inexpensive *tavernas* in the area. For a do-it-yourself meal, try the tiny **supermarket** at 52 Nikis St., or **Makrigiani's of Acropolis,** a big supermarket on Parthenonisos St. just up from the corner of Veikou St.

Theophilos's Tavern, 1 Vakhou St. (tel. 322 39 01). Walk down Kidathineon toward the Parthenon, turn left at Adrianou St., pass the circular monument of Lysikrates as you enter Vironos St., and turn right onto Vakhou. You might get serenaded or at least doted upon by the grandmother who has run the place for 50 years. Just be sure you agree firmly on the menu price before partaking. Try the *giouvetsi* (veal and rice, 750dr) or the *flogera* (appetizer plate, 600dr). Open Tues.-Sat. 8pm-1am.

To Gerani, corner of Tripodon and Epiharmou St., in the Plaka (tel. 324 76 05). Turn right on Kidathineon from Filellinon and follow it to Tripodon. Make a right and walk 2 blocks—it's on the left. Wonderful balcony. The waiters bring out trays of the day's delicacies and ask you to pick. Hors d'oeuvres (300dr) and flaming sausages (500dr). Open daily for lunch and dinner.

Tsekouras, 3 Tripodon, 30 seconds down from To Gerani. The tranquil garden, canopied by a fig tree, is filled with large wine casks. A relaxing restaurant, away from the hubbub of Kidathineon. *Souvlaki* 800dr, *dolmadhes* 500dr. Open Thurs.-Tues. 7pm-midnight.

O Kostis (sign in Greek, Ο ΚΟΣΤΕΣ), 18 Kidathineon St. (tel. 322 96 36), a few blocks below Filellinon on a small square. Great people-watching post: tables strategically bank one of the Plaka's main pedestrian thoroughfares. Reasonably priced, wonderful food. *Mousaka* 700dr, *keftedes* 500dr, stuffed tomatoes 400dr. Open daily noon-1am.

Eden Vegetarian Restaurant, 3 Flessa St (tel. 324 88 58). Turn off of Adrianou. Popular with both herbivores and omnivores. Tofu-meat in dishes like *mousaka* and lasagna (both 800dr). Greek salad 450dr. Outside terrace. Open daily noon-midnight.

To Xani, 138 Adrianou St. Delectable entrees from 470-2400dr. Fixed meals from 1200-1600dr. Beer 110dr. Open daily for dinner.

Tavern Barba-Stathis (ΜΠΑΜΠΑ ΣΤΑΘΕΣ), 19 Kidatheou St. The fresh flowers and primo location enhance the typical Plaka fare. Grilled specialties 900-1800dr. Entrees 550-950dr. Open daily for dinner.

Taverna Platanos, 4 Diogenous St. A hidden treasure. Take Minissikleous St. off Adrianou, go up the stairs and turn right. Tables clustered under a canopy heavy with grape vines. Vegetable dishes 320-550dr. Lamb with eggplant or okra 950dr. Open Mon.-Sat. 8am-4:30pm, 8pm-midnight.

Syntrivani, 5 Filellinon St. (tel. 322 55 68), 1 block from Syntagma Sq. Strategically located and very pleasant; the cool garden will make you forget the heat and noise outside. Breakfast of ham and eggs or omelette 350dr. Pork chops in wine sauce 1000dr. Spaghetti with meat 800dr. Open 7am-midnight.

Zonar's, 9 Panepistimiou, parallel to Stadiou St. off Syntagma Sq. An upscale pastry shop à la Paris. Mouth-watering treats around 360dr.

Michiko, 27 Kydathineon St. (tel. 322 09 80). Nirvana for some: eat sushi (prepared freshly at table, 1000-3600dr) in red Japanese garden with lanterns and delicately arching bridge. Miso soup 350dr. Open daily 12:30-2:30pm, 6:30pm-midnight.

For a change of pace, venture outside the Plaka. You may find better food, and you'll certainly find a different atmosphere.

Restaurant Gardenia (Γαρδενια), 31 Zini St., Koukaki. On the corner, a block before the Marble House Pension and near the Art Gallery Pension. Very cheap fare in a residential neighborhood. Sautéed eggplant only 350dr. Veal with potatoes 650dr. Open Mon.-Fri. noon-10pm, Sat.-Sun. noon-6pm.

Restaurant of Konstanoinos Athanasias Velly (ΚΟΝΣ ΑΘ ΒΕΛΛΕ), Varnava Sq., Plastira. Take trolley #2, 4, 11, or 12 to Plastira Sq. and walk 3 blocks up Proklou St. to Varnava Sq. In a small white house with flowers in front at the far right corner of the square. A real treat: small, authentic, delicious, and cheap. No English spoken; you'll have to point. Veal and potatoes 330dr, *keftedes* (Greek meatballs) 450dr. Open 8:30pm-1am.

Caravitis (ΚΑΡΑΒΙΤΕΣ) , 4 Pafsaniou St. (sign in Greek). From Syntagma, take trolley #2, 4, 11, or 12 to the Stadium, make your 3rd right, and go 2 blocks up the hill. A cool wine-cellar, where they make their own; large and very popular with locals. Try the flavorful *stamnaki*—cooked in a crock pot with wine and potatoes (830dr). Open daily 8:30pm-2am.

Taverna Kostoyiannis, 37 Zaimi St., 1 block behind the National Archaeological Museum. Enter through the kitchen—check out the variety of scrumptious dishes—and eat outside in the ivy-covered courtyard. Though tourist-tailored with a quadralingual menu and prices higher than most, the food is a taste sensation. Their specialty is beef cooked with bacon, mushrooms, and ham wrapped in a crêpe 1300dr. Tasty *mousaka* 850dr. Open Mon.-Sat. 8pm-2am.

O Giamas, 38 Zaimi St., behind the National Museum. All-Athenian clientele for friendly, cheap eats. Try the baked fish (250dr). Good alternative to the café in front of the museum. Open daily noon-2:30pm.

Golden Flower, 30 Nikis St. (tel. 323 01 13), in the Plaka, in the direction of Hadrian's Arch. Tired of Greek food? This is one of the cheaper Chinese/Japanese/Korean restaurants in the city. Sweet and sour shrimp 1600dr. Chow mein 1300dr. Open Mon.-Sat. noon-4pm and 7pm-midnight, Sun. 7pm-midnight. Take-away service noon-4pm, 7-11:30pm.

Sights

Acropolis

The **Acropolis**, or "high city," with its strategic position overlooking the Aegean Sea and Attic Plains, has served throughout history as both a military fortress and a religious center. Today, the hilltop's remarkable remnants grace grounds that are otherwise strewn with only rubble. While renovations go on, steel scaffolding clings to the ancient marble columns. Though the heady heights afford an expansive view of Athens and the Aegean, as you stand atop the city's main attraction, you may be a bit disappointed by the ungainly concrete creature prettied up by layers of awnings and television antennae.

In the 13th century BCE, wealthy landowners overthrew the monarchy in Athens who had ruled the city safely from their fortress in the Acropolis. The new rulers, the *Aristoi* (excellent ones) shifted the center of their government away from the Acropolis, ruling the *polis* (city state) from the lower foothills of the city. The Acropolis, far from being abandoned, was then used as a shrine to two aspects of the goddess Athena: Athena Polias, goddess of crops and fertility, and Athena Pallas, military guardian of the city. Following the Greek custom of putting money under the protection of a deity, the Acropolis also housed the city treasury.

In 507 BCE, the tyrannical *Aristoi* were overthrown and Athens began its successful experiment with democracy. Afterwards, in 490 BCE, Athenians began constructing a temple on the Acropolis. When the Persians sacked the temple ten years later, the Greeks threw the violated religious objects off the side of the Acropolis and buried the litter (now unearthed and displayed in the Acropolis Museum).

In response to the Persian threat, Aegean rulers formed the Delian league, an alliance among the area's cities. Pericles, to the indignation of many, appropriated part of the taxes and booty paid by the league to beautify Athens. Among his projects were the temples of the Acropolis, the Temple of Hephaestus in the *agora,* and the Temple of Poseidon at Sounion. These developments slowed during the long and gory Peloponnesian War (431-404 BCE), but by then Athenians were committed to Pericles's plans, and construction sputtered along throughout the war and after his death in 429 BCE. Four of the buildings erected then still stand today: the Parthenon, the Propylaea, the Temple of Athena Nike, and the Erechtheum. Their construction has had an unmatched influence on Western architecture.

Through the Hellenistic and Roman periods, the function of the Acropolis altered as often as its ownership changed hands. The Byzantines, for example, converted it into a

Christian place of worship. The Parthenon became the Church of St. Sophia ("Sophia," like "Athena," means wisdom). In 1205 CE, when Athens was liberated from the Byzantines by Frankish crusaders, the Acropolis once again became a fortress, serving as palace and headquarters for the Dukes de la Roche. The political situation settled down, and the Parthenon was then transformed into a Catholic Church (Notre Dame d'Athènes). In the 15th century, the Turks turned the Parthenon into a mosque and the Erechtheum into the lair of the Turkish commander's harem.

Tragedy befell the Acropolis during the Venetian seige in 1687 when a Turkish supply of gunpowder stored in the Parthenon was hit by a shell and exploded, destroying many of the original sculptures. In 1822, the Greeks finally regained the Acropolis. Apart from a six-year occupation by the Turks from 1827-1833 and the brief Nazi occupation during WWII, the Acropolis has been in Greek hands ever since.

The ramp that led to the Acropolis in classical times no longer exists. Today's visitors make the 10-minute climb to the ticket-window, enter through the crumbling **Beulé Gate** (added by the Romans and named after the French archaeologist who unearthed it), and continue through the **Propylaea,** the ancient entrance. Unfortunately, the site is not wheelchair-accessible. The marble can be slippery, so be careful if you are wearing shoes that have seen better days.

The Propylaea became famous for its ambitious multi-level design, although the entrance itself, begun by Mnesicles between 437 and 432 BCE, was never completed. In Roman times, the structure extended as far as 80m below the Beulé Gate. At the cliff's edge, the tiny **Temple of Athena Nike** was built during a respite from the Peloponnesian War, the so-called Peace of Nikias (421-415 BCE). Known as the "jewel of Greek architecture," this temple with eight miniature Ionic columns once housed a winged statue of the goddess. One day, in a paranoid frenzy, the Athenians feared that their deity (and peace) would flee the city, so they clipped Athena's wings. Below the temple are the remains of the 5m thick **Cyclopean wall,** which once surrounded the whole of the Acropolis, making this temple the only vantage point of the sea.

The **Erechtheum,** to the left of the Parthenon as you face it, was completed in 406 BCE, just prior to Athens's defeat by Sparta. Lighter than the Parthenon, the Erechtheum is a unique two-leveled structure that housed a number of cults, including those of Athena, Poseidon, and the snake-bodied hero Erechtheus. The eastern porch, with its six Ionic columns, was dedicated to Athena Polias and sheltered an olive wood statue of her. On the south side of the Erechtheum, facing the Parthenon, are the **Karyatids,** six columns sculpted in the shape of women. Considering the tons of marble they have supported for centuries, their expressions seem remarkably complacent. Their artful tunics that seem to flow into fluted columns towards the base, are plaster replicas. The originals were moved inside the Acropolis Museum in order to protect them from air pollution.

Looming over the hillside, the **Parthenon,** or "Virgin's apartment," keeps vigil over Athens and its world. The edifice, designed by the architects Iktinos and Kallikrates, was the first building completed under Pericles's plan to revive the city and once housed the legendary gold and ivory statue of Athena Parthenos sculpted by Phidias. The temple intentionally features many almost imperceptible irregularities; the Doric columns bulge in the middle and the stylobate (pedestal) of the building bows slightly upward in order to compensate for the optical illusion in which straight lines, viewed from a distance, appear to bend. Originally made entirely of marble save for a long-vanished wooden roof, the building's stone ruins attest to both the durability of the structure and the fleeting elegance of the classical age.

The metopes around the sides of the Parthenon portray various victories of the forces of order over disorder. On the far right of the south side, the only side which has not been defaced, the Lapiths battle the Centaurs (Centauromachy); on the east the Olympian gods triumph over the giants (Gigantomachy); the north depicts a still faintly visible victory of the Greeks over the Trojans; and on the west, one can vaguely make out the triumph of the Greeks over the Amazons (Amazonomachy). A better-preserved frieze in low-relief around the interior walls depicts the great Panathenaic procession in honor of Athena. Visit early in the morning to avoid the massive crowds and the broiling midday sun. Be forewarned that once you are there, a cold soft drink is hard to come by; instead, tourists flock to the water trough on the Parthenon's south side, a shady, refreshing spot. You can reach the entrance, which is on the west side of the Acropolis, from Dionission Areopagitou St. south of the Acropolis, or by walking up the hill from the Plaka. (Acropolis open Mon.-Fri. 8am-6:45pm, Sat.-Sun. 8:30am-2:45pm. Admission 1500dr, students 800dr with ISIC; free on Sun. and holidays.)

The **Acropolis Museum** (tel. 321 02 19), also on the site, contains a superb collection of sculpture from the area, including five of the Karyatids of the Erechtheum (the sixth is in the British Museum). Most of the treasures housed here date from the transition period from Archaic to Classical Greek art (550-400 BCE). You can trace this development in the faces of the statues, from the stylized, entranced faces and static poses of Archaic sculpture—seen in the famous *Moschophoros* (calf-bearer)—to the more familiar, naturalistic (though idealized), and free-moving figures of Classical art. Only a few pieces from the Parthenon are exhibited here—Lord Elgin helped himself to the rest, and they are now in the British Museum—but the collection is nonetheless impressive. (Museum open Mon. 12:30-7pm, Tues.-Fri. 8am-7pm, Sat.-Sun. 8:30am-3:30pm. Admission included in Acropolis ticket. Cameras with flash allowed, but no posing next to the objects.) From the southwest corner of the Acropolis, you can look down on the reconstructed **Odeon of Herodes Atticus,** a functioning theater dating from the Roman Period, c. 160 CE (see Entertainment below). Nearby are the ruins of the Classical Greek **Theater of Dionysus** (tel. 322 46 25, entrance on Dionissiou Aeropagitou St.), the **Asclepieion,** and the **Stoa of Eumenes II.** The Theater of Dionysus dates from the 4th century BCE and was part of the sanctuary of Dionyssos Eleftherefs. (Open daily 8:30am-2:30pm. Admission to all three 400dr, students 200dr.)

Near the Acropolis

Northwest

The **Athenian Agora,** at the foot of the Acropolis, was the administrative center and marketplace of Athens from the 6th century BCE through the late Roman Period (5th and 6th centuries CE). The decline of the Agora paralleled the decline of Athens, as barbarian attacks buffeted both the city and the square from 267 BCE to 580 CE. It was in the Agora and on the **Pnyx** (the low hill and meeting place of the assembly 1km to the south) that Athenian democracy was born and flourished. Socrates frequented the Agora, as did Aristotle, Demosthenes, Xenophon, and St. Paul. Plato says that Socrates's preliminary hearing was at the **Stoa Basileios** (Royal Promenade), which has been recently excavated and lies to the left as you cross the subway tracks upon leaving the Agora.

The sprawling archaeological site features three remarkable constructions. The **Temple of Hephaestus,** on a hill in the northwest corner, is the best-preserved classical temple in Greece. Built around 440 BCE, it is especially notable for its friezes which depict the labors of Hercules and the adventures of Theseus. The ruins of the **Odeon of Agrippa** (concert hall), built for the son-in-law of the Emperor Augustus, stand in the center of the Agora. In 150 CE the roof collapsed, and the odeon was rebuilt as a lecture hall at one-half its former size. The actors' dressing room was made into a porch, supported by colossal statues (the ruins of three of these statues remain to guard the site). To the south, the elongated **Stoa of Attalos,** a multi-purpose building for shops, shelter, and informal gatherings, was rebuilt with new materials in 1953-56 and houses the **Agora Museum** (tel. 321 01 85). The original structure, built in the 2nd century BCE, was given to Athens by Attalos II, King of Pergamon, in gratitude for the education he had received in the city. The museum contains a number of relics from the site and offers a cool sanctuary from the sweltering summer sun. (Agora and museum open Tues.-Sun. 8:30am-3pm. Admission to both 800dr, students 400dr.) There are several entrances to the Agora, including one at the edge of Monastiraki, one on Thissio Sq. and one on Adrianou St. You can reach the Acropolis from here by exiting the southern side of the Agora (follow the path uphill) and then turning right. The most commonly used gate is the one near the Acropolis entrance (turn right as you leave the Acropolis).

Northwest of the Agora, on the other side of the tracks at Thission Station, 148 Ermou St., is **Kerameikos.** This is the site of the 40m wide boulevard that ran from the Agora, through the Diplyon gate, and 1½km to the sanctuary of Akademos where Plato founded his Academy in the 4th century BCE. Public tombs for state leaders, famous authors, and battle victims were constructed along this road. Worshipers began the annual Panathenaean procession to the Acropolis at the Diplyon Gate, one of the two gates excavated at this site. The sacred road to Eleusis, traversed during the annual Eleusian processions, ran through the Sacred Gate, the second gate on the site. Family tombs adorn either side of the Sacred Road outside the gate. A **museum** on the site (tel. 346 35 52) exhibits finds from recent digs as well as an excellent pottery collection. (Site and museum open Tues.-Sun. 8:30am-3pm. Admission to both 400dr, students 200dr.)

East

The **Temple of Olympian Zeus** also deserves a visit. Fifteen majestic columns are all that remain of the largest temple ever built in Greece. Started in the 6th century BCE by the son of the tyrant Peisistratos, the temple was completed 600 years later by the Roman Emperor Hadrian. Nowadays, the Corinthian columns stand in the middle of downtown Athens, below the National Garden (Vas. Olgas and Amalias Ave.), withering from the city's chronic halitosis (tel. 922 63 30; open Tues.-Sun. 8:30am-3pm. Admission 400dr, students 200dr.) Next to the Temple is **Hadrian's Arch,** which was built in the 2nd century CE to mark the boundary between the ancient city of Theseus and the new city built by the Roman emperor Hadrian.

Museums

The **National Archaeological Museum,** 44 Patission St. (tel. 821 77 17), is well worth delaying your jaunt to the islands. Take bus #25 from Thission or Monastiraki to Syntagma and trolley #2, 4, 5, 11, or 12 from the uphill side of Syntagma or trolley #3 or 13 on the north side of Vassilissis Sofias. The collection contains an embarrassment of riches; pieces that would otherwise be the prizes of lesser collections seem almost unremarkable amidst the general magnificence. Expect to spend a long time here.

Among the museum's exhibits (all labeled in English as well as in Greek) are finds from Heinrich Schliemann's digs at Mycenae, including the golden "Mask of Agamemnon" (which is, in fact, the death mask of a king who lived at least three centuries earlier than the legendary Agamemnon) in room four. Also displayed are samples of Bronze Age jewelry, pottery, and other goldsmiths' art from Mycenae and other sites in the Peloponnese.

Don't leave without viewing the *kouroi*, or standing males (rooms 7, 8, 11, and 13). They are displayed chronologically, allowing you to see the evolution of this sculptural form. Minoan frescoes (also exhibited) intrigue casual museum-hoppers in addition to scholars and specialists; excavated from the town of Akrotiri on Santorini, these painted treasures were buried during a volcanic eruption around 1500 BCE. The frescoes present a unique glimpse of life in the Bronze Age. The comic mask of a slave from Diplyon, made during the 2nd century BCE, adds a note of hilarity to the exhibits—with a wide, toothless grin and crazy eyes, the face seems amused by the starkly stoic statues which surround it. Also worth viewing are the extensive coin and vase collections. (Museum open Mon. 12:30-7pm, Tues.-Fri. 8am-7pm, Sat.-Sun. and holidays 8am-7pm. Admission 1500dr, students 750dr; free on Sun. and holidays. Cameras without flash free, with flash 300dr. Coin collection open Tues.-Sun. 8am-2pm. Vase collection open Tues.-Sat. 8am-7pm, Sun. 8am-2pm.)

Opened in 1986, the **Goulandris Museum of Cycladic and Ancient Greek Art,** 4 Neophytou Douka St. (tel. 724 97 06), near Kolonaki, is another must-see. The collection is stunningly displayed in a modern air-conditioned building. Cycladic art is best known for its minimalist marble statues of female figures. The sculptures' beauty verifies that art, like seafaring and trade, was an important aspect of ancient Cycladic societies. Allow yourself to be lured to the bronze jewelry from Skyros as well as to the collection of Greek vases and statues from 2000 BCE to the 4th century CE. Another evocative exhibit displays simple Cycladic art and explores its influence on modern artists such as Picasso, Henry Moore, and Modigliani. (Open Mon.-Fri. 10am-4pm, Sat. 10am-3pm. Admission 200dr, students 100dr.)

The **Benaki Museum,** at the corner of Koumbari and Vassilissis Sofias (tel. 361 16 17), houses a diverse collection of treasures in a beautiful Neoclassical building which was once the residence of philanthropist Anthony Benaki. The museum displays Bronze Age Greek relics, Byzantine icons, gold jewelry of the 5th century BCE, textiles and costumes from the islands, and relics from the War of Independence. It also explores the influence of neighboring cultures on Greece by juxtaposing Islamic, Arabic, and Coptic artwork with the Greek. (Museum open Mon.-Sun. 8:30am-2pm. Admission 400dr, students 200dr, flash cameras 200dr.)

Inside an elegant Florentine building with serene courtyards, the **Byzantine Museum,** 22 Vassilissis Sofias (tel. 723 15 70), has an excellent and extensive collection of Christian art from the 4th through the 19th centuries. The collection includes early Byzantine sculptures, an icon collection that contains works from the entire Byzantine period, and a reconstructed Early Christian basilica. There are also a number of superb reliefs done in bronze, silver, and gold. One wing of the building features an array of well-preserved frescoes and mosaics. The exhibits are poorly labeled, however, so consider buying a catalog (600-800dr) before you visit. (Open Tues.-Sun. 8:30am-3pm. Admission 1000dr, students 500dr.)

Next door to the Byzantine Museum is the **War Museum** (tel. 729 05 43). This museum traces the history of Greek armaments from Neolithic eras, through the 5th-century BCE Persian invasion and the expeditions of Alexander the Great, to the submachine guns of the modern era. The primary emphasis is, however, on the worship of the modern Greek arsenal. (Open Tues.-Sat. 9am-2pm, Sun. 9:30am-2pm. Free.)

The **National Gallery** (Alexander Soutzos Museum) is set back from Vassilissis Sofias at 50 Vassileos Konstandiou (tel. 721 10 10). The museum exhibits Greek artists' works, supplemented by periodic international displays. The permanent collection includes some outstanding works by El Greco (the Greek). The drawings, black-and-white photographs, and sculpture gardens are also impressive. Consult *This Week in Athens* or call the museum for information. (Open Tues.-Sat. 9am-3pm, Sun. 10am-2pm. Admission 200dr.) At the **Theater Museum,** 50 Akadimias St. (tel. 362 94 30), behind the university, you can view costumes, models, photographic paraphernalia, and dressing rooms. (Open Mon.-Fri. 9am-3pm, Sun. 10am-1pm, Mon. 9am-3pm and 5-8pm. Admission 300dr.) In the Plaka, the **Greek Folk Art Museum,** 17 Kidathineon St. (tel. 321 30 18), exhibits *laiki techni* (popular art) from all over Greece, including embroidered textiles, costumes, and puppets. Ornamental ecclesiastical silver work and household pottery are also on exhibit. Don't miss the groovy wall paintings by folk artist Theophilos Hadzimichail. (Open Tues.-Sun. 10am-2pm. Admission 400dr, students 200dr, cameras 300dr.)

The **Jewish Museum,** 36 Leoforos Amalias, 3rd floor (tel. 323 15 77), is housed in a 19th-century building with a French flag in front, across from the Zappeion. An impressive collection of textiles, religious artifacts, and documents traces the historical roots of the Greek Jewish communities dating from the Hellenistic period. The museum also contains the reconstructed Synagogue of Patras. (Open Sun.-Fri. 9am-1pm. Free. Guided tour included.)

Byzantine sanctuaries, like their Classical counterparts, have been incorporated into the urban landscape. Traffic on Ermou St. must go around **Kapnikaria Church,** which has been stranded smack dab in the middle of the street, 1 block beyond Eolou St. Walking down Mitropoleos from Syntagma, you may also notice a tiny church on the corner of Pentelis St., around which a modern building has been constructed. Other Byzantine churches in Athens include the **Agia Apostrilli,** on Vrissakiou St., at the eastern edge of the Agora; **Metamorphosis,** in the Plaka near Pritaniou St.; **Agios Nikodimos,** on Filellinon St., a few blocks from Syntagma; and **Panayia Gorgoepikös,** next to the **Mitropoli Cathedral,** on Mitropoleos St. Peek in for a respite from the day's heat and your own mortality. Most of these churches are open in the morning and for services, and require proper dress: skirts for women, long pants for men, long-sleeved shirts required. Enter quietly.

Entertainment

Athens is far more than a mere conglomeration of ancient ruins, museums, and street-hawkers—the city offers dramatic vistas, charming byways, and cool foliage, as well as nightspots that will comfortably numb your already-aching feet. Long before recorded time, the Greeks invented the evening stroll *(volta)*. Today's place to ramble is along the romantic walkways of the Plaka under the shadow of the Acropolis. The streets, strung with white lights and replete with restaurants and cafés, are ideal for an evening's promenade. Today's bustling Plaka represents a rejuvenation of the historic area. In the past few years, the government has curbed the violence, prostitution, and general decay that once plagued this section of the city. Be sure to also venture uphill off the main drags through the shoulder-width streets of an anachronistic residential area

The chapel of St. Georgeon on top of rocky **Lycabettos Hill** offers a beautiful view of the city. You can burn off dinner by walking up, or take the funicular to the top—the station is a healthy hike at the end of Ploutarchou St. (Open Wed. and Sat.-Sun. 8:45am-12:15am, Thurs. 10:30am-12:15am, Mon.-Tues. and Fri. 9:30am-12:15am. 130dr, 220dr round-trip.) The café on top is disheartingly expensive, but the panorama of the city is stunning. Not as safe as it once was at night, the Acropolis, bathed in amber glow, offers a magical view of Athens. Up here, with the sprawling body of concrete a mere blur below, and the traffic no more than a low murmur, the breezes are decidedly refreshing and the aura of the city is inspiring. Afternoons are less crowded than evening.

The cool, pleasant **National Garden** (open sunrise to sunset) is a great escape from the noise, heat, and frantic pace of Athens. Walk along its tranquil paths and visit the duck pond and zoo. Women should avoid strolling alone: you're liable to be presented with an unsolicited view of Athenian genitalia. Every evening the cafés near the **Zappeion** (Exhibition Hall) present musicians, comedians, and acrobats on an outdoor stage. Standing is free; you can also get a table. The bar underneath the Aigli café opens at 11pm and requires a jacket and tie of men. The outdoor cinema in the Zappeion generally has a good selection of English-language films, showing at 9pm and 11pm for 800dr. *Cinema Paris,* on #22 Kidathineon, in the heart of the Plaka, shows recent films. Shows are at 8:50pm and 11:10pm for 900dr, but try to attend the late show since traffic noise and lingering dusk tend to mar the early one. Sit near the front to hear the already hushed film over the intruding *bouzouki* music. Check the *Athens News* for the complete addresses and schedules of all the Athens movie-houses. Most cost 500dr and are concentrated on Stadiou, Panepistimiou, and Patission St.

When you're passing through Syntagma Sq., don't miss the changing of the guard in front of the **Parliament** building. Every hour on the hour two sets of enormously tall *evzones* (guards) slowly wind up like toy soldiers, kick their heels about, and fall backwards into symmetrical little guard houses on either side of the **Tomb of the Unknown Warrior.** Unlike their English equivalents, *evzones* occasionally wink and even smile at tourists. Their jovial manner is as delightful as their curious attire—pom pom-laden clogs, short pleated skirts *(foustanela),* and pony-tail tasselled hats. Every Sunday at 10:45am, the ceremony occurs with the full troop of guards, a band, and even greater pomp than usual.

Athens's two principal markets attract everyone from bargain-hunters to inveterate browsers. The **Athens Flea Market,** adjacent to Monastiraki Sq., has a festive bazaar-like atmosphere and offers a potpourri of second-hand junk, costly antiques, and every-thing in between. The market is open daily (8am-2pm), and Sunday is the grand bazaar: the flea market overflows the square and Fillis Athinas St. A huge indoor-outdoor **food market** lines the sides of Athinas St. between Evripidou and Sofokleous St. It's open the same hours as regular food stores, but Athenian restaurateurs go early and purchase the choice meat and fish. You may be hassled a bit for buying only small amounts.

The **Athens Festival** runs annually from June until September, featuring classical theater groups performing in the **Odeon of Herodes Atticus.** Performances are also staged in Lycabettos Theater at the top of Lycabettos Hill, and in Epidavros (see

Peloponnese section). The Greek Orchestra plays during this festival, as do visiting groups, which have ranged from the Bolshoi to B.B. King; from the Alvin Ailey Dance Company to the Talking Heads (children under 6 not allowed). The **Festival Office** (tel. 322 14 59 or 322 31 11, ext. 240) is in the arcade at 4 Stadiou St.; a line forms by 9am so arrive early. Student tickets are generally cheap (500-1000dr depending on the show, student card required). (Open Mon.-Fri. 8:30am-2pm and 5-7pm, Sun. 10am-1pm.)

If you've had a bit (or a lot) to drink, the hokey **Sound and Light Show** on Pnyx Hill (opposite the Acropolis) can be quite entertaining, though you'll leave unsure whether the title refers to the program or the click and flash of cameras saving tourists thousands of words. (Tel. 322 14 59, after 2pm 922 62 10. April-Oct. daily in English at 9pm; in French Mon., Wed.-Thurs., Sat.-Sun. 10:10pm; German on Thurs.-Fri. at 10pm. Admission 800dr, students 400dr.) Nearby in Dora Stratou Theatre on Philopappou Hill, **Greek Dancers** kick and holler to live music on an open-air stage, celebrating traditions from all regions of the country. (Tel. 324 43 95 9am-1:30pm, from 7:30pm on 921 46 50. May-Sept. daily at 10:15pm with an additional show Wed. and Sun. at 8:15pm. Tickets 1000-1400dr.)

The **Wine Festival** in nearby Daphni (see Near Athens section) runs from the end of July to early September, nightly from 7:45pm-12:30am. (Tel. 32 27 944 for more information. Tickets 500dr, students 300dr.)

Athens proper boasts some wild nightlife, with or without the wine. At **Goa,** 6 Xenofontos St. (tel. 323 35 22), off Filellinon, the cheesy tropical atmosphere and funky music will keep you goan' all night. **Athens Down-Town,** 3 Souri St. (tel. 322 1334), off Syntagma, is up-stairs with a large dance floor in a charged atmosphere. The **Absolut,** 23 Filellinon (tel. 323 7197), is cozier, but still rocks. You can't see the **Oggi Music Pub,** but you'll hear it at 17 Filellinon; it fills before the rest. All three are open nightly 9pm-5am. Beer and *ouzo* 500dr, other drinks around 1000dr. No cover.

Merry wanderers of the night can venture to the posh Kolonaki district, on the way up to Lycabettos. Although the Gucci shoes in the chic shop windows might cost more than your whole vacation, a coffee or beer at any of the chit-chatty outdoor *tavernas* will not blow your budget. While in the area, dig **Jazz Club 1920,** 10 Ploutarchou St. (tel. 721 05 33), just up from the British Embassy. (Open nightly 10:15pm-1:15am for jazz, blues, latin, and rock. "Songs of the 50s" from 1:15-2:15am.)

Some Athenians party in the suburbs. A popular local hangout is the unique **Aerodromio** disco (known by most cab drivers) at the end of the International Airport runway, where the barstools are airplane seats. Also near the airport is the **Akrotiri** restaurant and nightclub, on Kosmas St. (tel. 98 11 124). Though the food is pricey, the dancing gets spicy after 11pm. In **Kifissia,** a posh residential area to the north of Athens, there are many hip *tavernas* and discos. Take the subway from Omonia to the last stop or bus #538 or 539 to Kaningos Sq. (off Akadimias, near Omonia Sq.). Here you'll find the **Divina,** 2 Argiropoulou (tel. 801 5884), where you can boogie in air-conditioned comfort. (Open Wed.-Sun. nights. First drink 800dr, second drink 600dr. No cover.) In **Glyfada,** south of Athens, you should stay near the shore since the center of town is packed with tacky bars. One excellent restaurant frequented by locals is **O Karachos** (O KAPAXO), 49 Theatrou Pavlo. Face the water and walk left along the shore about 200 yds. The tables are right on the shore and the fish is always fresh. After dinner, join the locals in front of the many gelato shops, sip iced coffee *(frappé)* in an outside *taverna,* or just wander among the herd of parked motorbikes corralled in the streets. Glyfada discos get crowded and stay open late. Take bus #121, 128, or 129 from the south side of the National Garden in the middle of Olga St. (30min.).

Near Athens: Attica ATTIKH

Piraeus

The natural harbor of Piraeus has been Athens's port since the early 5th century BCE, and its age is beginning to show. Themistocles first began fortifying Piraeus, then an island, as a base for the growing Athenian fleet. Around 450 BCE, Pericles added the Long Walls from Athens to Piraeus, bridging the land masses. Though the opening scene of Plato's *Republic* is set here, Piraeus offers little of cultural interest today; it serves primarily as the point of departure to most of the Greek isles. To get to Piraeus, take the subway (50dr) from Monastiraki or Omonia to the last stop, or take green bus #40 from Filellinon St., just off Syntagma. Get off at the Public Theater *(Demotikon Teatron),* and head right, toward the port. Either way, the trip takes about 20 minutes. Or do yourself a favor and take a cab (700dr, more than double at night). Long-distance trains for Patras and the Peloponnese leave daily from the station on Akti Kalimassiati. Long-distance trains for Northern Greece (Larissis) leave daily from the station on Ag. Dimitriou across the harbor.

Ferries ply the waters from Piraeus to all the Greek islands except the Sporades and Ionian groups. There is a small but invaluable map of Piraeus on the back of the Athens map available at the tourist office. The port area is shaped something like a horseshoe. Most of the ticketing agencies line **Akti Miaouli,** the lower left of the horseshoe and **Akti Possidonis,** the upper left side of the horseshoe. There are no student discounts on any kind of domestic travel in Greece, although international fares can be had for cut-rate prices. Agencies offering student services are to be found more in Athens proper on Filellenos St. and Nikis St. off Syntagma Sq. than at Pireaus. The larger ferries dock at Akti Miaouli; international ferries wait at the end toward the Customs House. Smaller ferries depart for the Saronic Gulf Islands from **Akti Posidonos,** around the corner, inland. **Hydrofoils** (Flying Dolphins) for the Aegean islands, Dodecanese, and Crete leave from **Provlis Tzelepi,** around the corner past the small ferries and toward the top of the horseshoe. Hydrofoils for Saronic Gulf islands leave from the opposite side of the peninsula, at **Zea,** the dock near **Platia Freatidas** (Freatidas Sq.). To get to Zea marina, walk away from the mainland down Akti Miaouli to Trikoupi St. Along the water and under the sidewalk is a **port police office,** a **post office** (open Mon.-Fri. 7:30am-2pm), and a **tourist office** (open Mon.-Fri. 7:30am-2pm, tel. 413 57 16). Commercial and personal boats dock in the harbor to the left. Turn right and follow the waterfront to reach the passenger carriers.

Back at the main port, the post office (tel. 41 24 202) is located on the corner of Tsamadou and Filonos St., two blocks inland from the principal waterfront street, Akti Miaoulis. (Open Mon.-Fri. 7:30am-8pm.) There is also a small post office in the subway station which is on the plaza at the end of Alpedou St. (open Mon.-Fri. 7:30am-2pm). The **OTE** is 1 block away at 19 Karaoli St. (Open 24 hrs.; collect calls 7am-9pm.) The **Commercial Bank of Greece** squats at a corner on Akti Poseidonas, across from the waterfront. (Open Mon.-Thurs. 8am-2pm, Fri. 8am-1:30pm.) There are other banks on the waterfront area where you can change money. Piraeus's **postal code** is 18501; the **telephone code** is 01.

Never sleep in the municipal park in Piraeus: especially with the influx of refugees in recent years, this area is a nightmare, even under the sun. **Hotel Santorini,** 6 H. Trikoupi St. (tel. 452 21 47), one block up from the far side of the harbor as you face the water, is a better option. The rooms are equipped with telephones and are cleaner than the marble reception area would lead you to believe. (Singles 3400dr. Doubles 4800dr. Triples 5760dr. Breakfast 590dr.) At **Hotel Galaxy,** 18 Sahtouri St. (tel. 451 05 79), behind Santorini on the next parallel street, you get what you pay for. (Singles 1350dr, with bath 1750dr. Doubles 2700dr, with bath 3500dr.) **Hotel Enos,** 14 Antistaseos St. (tel. 417 48 79), closest to the harbor, up from Platia Themis to Kleous, is in an old building with high molded ceilings. The rooms facing the street are considerably more spacious than those on the other side. Moderately clean. Reception is friendly. (Singles 1600dr. Doubles 2400dr. Triples 3300dr. Showers 300dr.) Inexpensive fast-food restaurants line the dock area like their food lines your stomach, all offering mediocre fare at uniform prices.

The prize possession of the **Archaeological Museum,** 31 Char. Trikoupi St. (tel. 452 16 98), is the ancient "Piraeus Kouros," a large hollow bronze statue with outstretched arms. (Open Tues.-Sun. 8:30am-3pm. Admission 200dr, students 100dr, camera permits 300dr extra.) Farther south at Zea, facing the harbor and underneath the sidewalk on Akti Themistokleous, is the **Maritime Museum** (tel. 451 68 22), which traces the history of the Greek navy using detailed models of ships. The courtyard is now the home port of torpedo tubes, naval weapons, and anchors. (Open Tues.-Sat. 8:30am-12:30pm. Admission 150dr, students free.)

Cape Sounion and the Apollo Coast

Sunium's marbled steep, where nothing save the
waves and I may hear our mutual murmurs sweep...
—Byron

The **Temple of Poseidon** (tel. (029) 23 93 63) at Cape Sounion stands on a promontory high above the coast. The sublime view of the Aegean makes a visit here a spiritual experience even for lapsed Poseidon worshippers. The original temple was constructed around 600 BCE, destroyed by the Persians in their 480 BCE temper-tantrum, and rebuilt by Pericles in 440 BCE. The 16 remaining Doric columns intimate a graceful symmetry of the original temple. Scattered remains of the **Temple of Athena Sounias,** the patron goddess of Athens, litter the lower hill. Sunrise is the ideal time to view the temples, but if you sleep in, try to visit before the early afternoon (when the tour buses funnel in), or around sunset (after they've drained out). Consider packing a lunch: the cafeteria near the temple is an ungodly expense for a budget traveler. (Site open Mon.-Sat. 9am-sunset, Sun. 10am-sunset. Admission 600dr, students 300dr. Last bus to Athens departs promptly at 9:30pm.)

To reach the ocean, follow one of the many paths from the inland side of the temple. For the agile and adventuresome, it is possible to negotiate the cliff on the ocean side. Chaotic with vacationing families, the beaches along the 70km Apollo Coast between Athens and Cape Sounion take on a crowded carnival atmosphere, especially on summer weekends. Most are owned by hotels, where admission is generally 100-150dr, but towns usually have free public beaches as well, and some seaside stretches along the bus route remain almost empty.

There are two campsites at Cape Sounion. Crowded but well maintained, **Camping Sounion Beach** (tel. 393 58) charges 680dr per person, 740dr per tent. Nearby **Camp Bacchus** (tel. 392 62) charges 700dr per person, 650dr per tent. Both lie about 5km past the Temple of Apollo toward Lavrio, along the inland bus route. Closer to Athens, along the coastal route, **Camping Varkiza** (tel. 897 36 13) charges 500dr per person plus 350dr per tent (take bus #115, 116, or 117 from Zappeion Station). Two buses travel the 70km road to Cape Sounion. One goes along the coast and stops at all points on the Apollo Coast, leaving every hour on the half-hour (6:30am-6:30pm) from the Mavromateon St. stop in the square opposite Areos Park in Athens; you can meet the bus 10 minutes later on Filellinon St., at Xenofondos St., but all the seats will probably be taken already (2hr., 800dr). The other bus, following a much less scenic inland route, leaves from Areos Park (6am-6pm every hour on the hour, 2¼hr., 750dr).

Accessible by the return inland bus, the bustling port of Lavrio hustles about 15km north of Cape Sounion. In 480 BCE, the Athenians used this region's rich silver deposits to fund their fleet—a good investment recouped when they defeated the Persians at Salamis. Ferries go from Lavrio to Kea (2½hr., 1955dr), Kithnos (4hr., 1645dr), Serifos, and Sifnos. For more info, call the Lavrio Port Authority (tel. (029) 22 52 49).

Kesariani

The purple heights of flowery Hymettus, a sacred
spring enclosed by soft green turf ...
—Ovid

Although it is only a short distance from central Athens, the **Monastery of Kesariani** (tel. 723 66 19) on Mt. Hymettus has preserved its serene beauty. The site is an excellent spot for a picnic lunch, a romantic walk in the surrounding woodlands, or simply a break from the noise and dirt of the metropolis. Originally, a temple to Zeus stood on the mountain, but in 500 BCE, a priestess named Saisara replaced it with one dedicated to Aphrodite, goddess of love and beauty. The present monastery, built in the 11th century, incorporates the floors and four Ionic columns of the earlier Classical temple. The frescoes were added in the 17th century by the painter Ioannis Ypatios. During the classical period, religious "mysteries" revealed themselves underneath the chapel in a huge hollow which later became monks' catacombs and a refuge from pirates. (Open Tues.-Sun. 8:30am-3pm. Admission 500dr, students 250dr.)

The mountain behind the Keseriani's monastery is crossed by hiking trails. On weekends, the grounds are crowded with Athenians so try to visit on a weekday. Bus #224 goes from Plaza Kaningos at the end of Akadimias St. (the farthest *stassis* up on the outside lane) to Kesariani; take it to the last stop (every 10-15min., 20min., 75dr). Follow the left-hand road uphill, and after crossing under the overpass, bear right at the fork and continue uphill; bear right again, and take the left-hand path (embedded with stones) to the monastery (35-min. walk).

Daphni

The **Monastery of Daphni** (tel. 581 15 58), built on the site of the ancient Temple of Daphnios Apollo and surrounded by a high fortified wall, is a peaceful retreat 10km west of Athens, along the Ancient Sacred Way. Cool breezes sweep the area, and the 11th-century structure is delightfully pock-marked with birds' nests. The monastery has served as both an army camp and a lunatic asylum, which may explain the pronounced scowl on Christ's face as he stares down from the masterful mosaic dome (Open daily 8am-3pm. Admission 500dr, students 250dr.)

An all-you-can-drink Bacchanalian **wine festival** (tel. 322 79 44) takes place on the grounds next to the monastery from the end of July until the beginning of September. (Festival grounds open daily 7:45pm-12:30am. Admission 300dr, students 150dr.) The food there is not for the frugal gourmet, though. **Camping Daphni** (tel. 581 15 63) is half-way down the road to the monastery. (Reception open 10am-7pm. Check-out 2pm. 800dr per person, 550dr for a small tent, 800dr for a large tent).

To reach Daphni from Athens, take bus #873 from Deligiori St. (every 30min. 6am-9:15pm, 25min., 75dr) or one of the Elefsina buses from Platia Eleftherias at the end of Evripidou St. (every 20min. 6am-9:15pm, 25min., 75dr). From Piraeus port, take #804, 805, or 845 (6am-11:30pm every 15min., 35min., 75dr). From the bus stop, cross the highway and go down the road toward the monastery. From Elefsina, it's a 15-minute bus ride (75dr). Cross through the plaza coming from the ruins—the bus stop is on your right across the road.

Elefsina (Eleusis)

After a visit to Daphni, continue down the Sacred Way to the ruins of the temple of **Eleusis,** site of the Eleusinian Mysteries, ancient prayer rituals that revealed the secrets of life and death. Here Demeter, goddess of the harvest, came to mourn the abduction of her daughter Persephone by Hades, god of the underworld. In her anguish and fury, Demeter halted the earth's production and consoled herself by suckling the son of King Celeus of Eleusis. She made the baby immortal by refusing him earthly food and dangling him over fire. In order to persuade Demeter to let the earth produce again, Zeus struck a bargain with Hades that would allow Persephone to return to earth, providing she hadn't swallowed any Stygian sustenance. But Persephone had eaten four pomegranate seeds, and was condemned to spend four months of every year underground. Demeter agreed to let the earth bloom upon reunion with Persephone, but gave Greece barren winter for the months she must spend apart from her daughter. She revealed herself to the Eleusinians and shared with them the mysteries of the underworld.

Historians believe the mysteries and the worship of Demeter were brought to Eleusis from the East or from Egypt in 1350 BCE. The sanctuary was closed by the Roman Emperor Theodosius (as part of his crusade against paganism) in the 4th century CE.

The small, six-room museum (tel. 554 60 19), in the yellow building near the entrance to the site, displays finds from Eleusis, all labeled in English. The headless statue of Demeter in the entrance hall and the enormous bust of a Caryatid of the temple are its most impressive pieces. (Site and museum open Tues.-Sun. 8:30am-3pm. Admission 400dr, students 200dr.) Buses #853 and 862 run every 20 minutes from **Platia Eleftherias** at the end of **Evripidou Street** (6am-9:15pm, 40min., 75dr) and from the bus stop in Daphni. Ask the bus driver to let you off at the second stop in Elefsina; go through the square and bear left to Eleusis.

Marathon

In 490 BCE, when the Athenians defeated the Persians at the bloody battle of Marathon, the messenger Pheidippides ran 42km (26 m.) to Athens to announce the victory, and then collapsed dead from exhaustion. Today this act (*sans* death) is commemorated in international marathons. Runners trace the original Hellenic route twice annually in April and September.

A mere 5km from the mundane town of Marathon stands the **Tomb of the Plataneans,** the ancient burial mound built as a tribute to the allies from the town of Platea, 6km from Thebes. The Athenians killed in the battle were cremated, and their ashes are in the **Marathon Tomb,** a larger burial mound 4km away on the road to Athens. Only the most avid historians will want to make the 45-minute trudge. (Tombs open June-Aug., Tues.-Sun. 8:30am-3pm.) The **museum** (tel. (0294) 551 55) at Marathon has the same hours as the tombs. (Admission 400dr, students 200dr).

Beautiful **Lake Marathon,** with its huge marble dam, lolls 8km past the town. Until World War II, the lake was Athens's sole source of water. At **Ramnous** 15km to the northeast are the ruins of the Temples of Nemesis, goddess of retribution, and Themis, goddess of custom, law, and justice. A **theater** (tel. (0294) 634 77) is located 300m from the water. (Open Tues.-Sun. 8:30am-3pm.)

On the coast near Marathon, **Schinias** to the north and **Timvos Marathonas** to the south are popular beaches. Thick pine trees speckle the long and sandy stretch at Schinias. Both beaches are too congested for comfort on the weekend, but they're relatively empty midweek. Many camp at Schinias since the trees offer good protection, but the mosquitoes are thirsty and mean. You will probably be more comfortable staying at **Marathon Camping** (tel. (0294) 555 87), located along the bus route to Marathon (650dr per person, 400dr per tent). From the campsite you can get a bus or walk to the beach, which overflows with outdoor cafés. The bus for Marathon leaves from Mavromateon St. by Areos Park in Athens (6am-10pm, every hr., 1hr., 480dr). Ask the driver to let you off in front of the sign for the museum ("Mouseion and Marathonas"). From there, follow the signs and don't despair: the museum is 2km farther (about a 30-min. walk) at the end of the paved road. To reach the Marathon Tomb or the nearby beach, walk 1½km back toward Athens. Lake Marathon, Amphiareion, and Ramnous are accessible by automobile only.

Rafina

Considerably less frenetic than bustling and dirty Piraeus, the petite port of Rafina is Attica's second most important ferry port. The town is south of Marathon along the coast and accessible by frequent buses from 29 Mavromateon St., by Aeros Park in Athens (5:45am-10:30pm every 45min., 1hr., 300dr). Boats sail to Karystos (2-3 per day, 2hr., 1320dr) and Marmari (3-4 per day, 1½hr., 755dr) in Evia, as well as to: Andros (2 per day, 2hr., 1500dr); Tinos (2 per day, 4hr., 2064dr); Mykonos (2 per day, 5hr., 2451dr); Syros (3 per week, 3½hr., 2064dr); Paros (1 per day, 2200dr); and Naxos (1 per day, 2256dr). It's more convenient to sail to Syros from Piraeus, but fares to Andros, Tinos, and Mykonos are 300-400dr cheaper from Rafina, and the voyage is only about half as long. You can also make the 15-hr. trip to Rhodes from Rafina with Strintzis Lines (Mon., Wed., Fri. at 2pm, 34,400dr).

The **port police** (tel. 228 88), in a small booth near the dock, have up-to-date information on all sailings, but don't speak English very well. To find English-speaking travel agents and to purchase ferry tickets, stop by one of the offices along the ramp leading up to the square. Karystos and Marmari tickets are sold at the Goutos Lines office (tel. 237 22 or 243 98).

Cheap food and accommodations are scarce in Rafina. If you must spend the night in order to catch an early ferry, turn left at the top of the ramp to get to **The Aktee Hotel,** 14 Bithynias St. (tel. 247 76), where every room has a balcony. (Curfew 2am. Singles 3000dr. Doubles 5000dr. Triples 6000dr. Shower 100dr.) **Hotel Corali** (tel. 224 77), in Plastira Square next to "The Humb" hamburger place, offers airy rooms. (Singles 3000dr. Doubles 5000dr. Triples 7000dr.) There is **camping** on the beach of **Kokkino Limanaki** at **Cococamp** (tel. 227 94), 1km from town. (660dr per person, 350-500dr per tent).

O Stanathis and **Ta Metepa,** right next door to each other just off Plastira Sq., serve food with similar prices. (Open daily for lunch and dinner. *Mousaka* 800dr. Veal with sauce 950dr.) Or shop at the **grocery store** across from the post office on the corner of Dmitrakon St.

The **post office** is on Eleftheriou Venizelou St. From the dock, go up the two ramp-like streets, and it's the second street on your right (open Mon.-Fri. 7:30am-2pm). The **OTE** is on Alexander Fleming St., across the street from Plastira Sq. (Open Mon.-Fri. 7:30am-3:10pm.) **Emborikes Bank** is in the square (open Mon.-Thurs. 8am-2pm, Fri. 8am-1:30pm). **Taxis** line up at the top of the ramp on the right as you cross the street (tel. 231 01). Many **pharmacies** are located on Agnostin Kurion St., between Plastira Sq. and the post office. Rafina's **postal code** is 19009; the **telephone code** is 0294.

Vravrona (Brauron)

Approximately 20km south of Rafina and 40km from Athens, Vravrona is the isolated setting for the 2000-year-old **Sanctuary of Artemis.** Although poorly maintained, the site contains the three remaining columns of the recently uncovered **Temple of Artemis** and the adjacent **Chapel of Agia Giorgiou,** decorated inside with decaying frescoes from the late 15th century. The **museum** (tel. (0299) 270 20) on the site displays finds from the sanctuaries. (Open Tues.-Sun. 8:30am-3pm. Admission 400dr, students 200dr.) There are no buses from Rafina to Vravrona. From Athens, take the orange bus from 14 Marromateon St., near Arcos Park (6am-6pm every 30min., 1hr., 340dr), then transfer to Vravrona (6:45am and 2pm, 150dr).

PELOPONNESE
ΠΕΛΟΠΟΝΝΗΣΟΣ

Ocean and mountains, olive groves and sandy beaches—the Peloponnese unites all that is quintessentially Greek. Its dusty, pink-blossomed roads wind their way to rocky coves, mountain peaks, and timeless ruins. Warm breezes waft the diverse redolence of the country. Separated from mainland Greece by the steep-walled Corinth Canal, this peninsula holds more than 3500 years of history. The pristine ancient theater at Epidavros, the haunting palace at Mycenae, the gargantuan stone blocks at Olympia, and the ruined Byzantine town of Mystra possess a ghostly communion with one another—these are the achievements of the once-undisputed leaders of the ancient world. Above all, the Peloponnese is for those who love to venture beyond quotidian towns and sites. The main attractions here are conveniently close to one another. Formidable ruins, ebullient ports, sequestered beaches, and serene mountain villages all lie within a few hours distance, a short bus trip away.

The easiest way to explore the Peloponnese is by car. Many of the most captivating locations are accessible only by dirt roads and buses are loath to make those trips. Trains scuttle across the popular northern route from Patras to Athens, servicing some western towns on the way south to Kalamata. As is the case throughout Greece, idiosyncracies in service and schedules should be no surprise. If you rent a moped, beware of the often treacherous drivers and driving conditions. But be wary of the other extreme, as well; the most prominent sites are plagued by frequent bus service and become unbearably crowded by midday. The Peloponnese's southern beach resorts and ports are becoming as popular in summer as the most touristed island coasts.

Before embarking on your adventure, remember to arm yourself with a good map of the entire Peloponnese. Freytag and Berndt publish a superb map (red-and-green cover); Sotiris Toumbis's *Peloponnisos* (red cover) is also good. A good archaeological guide to the region is *The Peloponnese* by E. Karpodini-Dimitriadi (1800dr), available at many kiosks, in bookstores, and at archaeological sites.

There are a number of places from which to enter and leave the Peloponnese. Patras in the northwest corner of the peninsula is a popular port of entry with ferry connections from Corfu and Italy's Brindisi, Bari, and Ancona. Boats for Crete and Piraeus leave from Gythion and Monemvassia in the south, stopping at the island of Kythera. During high season, hydrofoils run from Piraeus and the Saronic Gulf Islands to ports on the eastern Peloponnese. From Athens, you can enter through Corinth by bus, or through port towns on the Argolid by ferry.

Corinthia and Argolis
ΚΟΡΙΝΘΑ ΚΑΙ ΑΡΓΟΛΛΑ

Chronicled in the pages of ancient writers, Argos—a grotesque beast covered with 100 unblinking eyes—once stalked vast stretches of the northern Peloponnese, subduing unruly satyrs and rampaging bulls. Today, the quiet, dusty Argolid region would hardly suggest its tumultuous past if it weren't for the tourist-swarmed ruins of massive fortresses, temples, and theaters. In summer, try to visit the sites at Mycenae, Corinth, Tiryns, and Epidavros early in the day, before the myriad tour-groups arrive and the heat reaches its worst. The town of Napflion is a good place to base yourself as you visit the nearby ruins on daytrips.

Three different bus routes voyage through stunning terrain to Argolis and Corinthia. From Athens, after the last stretch of industrial outlets and gas stations, the road gives

Peloponnese

way to a bright blue sea on the left and precipitous cliffs on the right. From Porto Heli or Kosta, if you're coming from the Saronic Gulf Islands, the bus heads straight inland, following deserted, dust-blanketed asphalt roads that snake through dry mountain olive groves with no sea in sight. Finally, if you ride into the region from Arcadia (the central Peloponnese), you'll cross the rusty-green mountains that separate the upland Arcadian plain from the Argive.

New Corinth (Korinthos) ΚΟΡΙΝΘΟΣ

New Corinth is squat and square, facing the Gulf of Corinth just west of the Corinth Canal. Punished twice in a century by an angry Mother Nature with two devastating earthquakes in 1858 and 1928, the city now issues building permits for only the most shatterproof structures, proving the famous architectural axiom: the sturdier the structure, the drearier its exterior. With its seafront and tree-lined park in the center of town, Corinth is pleasant enough, but offers little besides a dispassionate nightlife and a few million homeless mosquitos with mammoth appetites.

Orientation and Practical Information

Buses leave Athens for New Corinth from the station at 100 Kifissou St. (6am-9:30pm every 30min., 1½hr., 1000dr). You can also take the train to Corinth from Athens (12 per day, 2hr., 470dr).

You'll find everything you need near the park. The main drag, **Ethnikis Anastasis Street** (sometimes labelled Vas. Konstantinou St. on maps), borders the park and runs to the sea. Parallel **Ermou Street** bounds the park on the other side. **Kolokotroni Street** runs along the eastern side and parallel to Ethnikis Anastasis. The station for buses to Athens and the vicinity lies at the corner of Ermou and Koliatsou right on the park. The other bus station, serving the rest of the Peloponnese, is 1 block past the park at Aratou and Ethnikis Anistasis. To reach the main park from the train station, walk half a block up Demokratias, turn right on Dimaskinou, then left on Ermou several blocks later.

Currency Exchange: National Bank, 7 Ethnikis Anastasis St., and **Commercial Bank,** 32 Ethnikis Anastasis St., off the corner of the park closest to the water. Many other banks are scattered around this area. Open Mon.-Thurs. 8am-2pm, Fri. 8am-1:30pm.

Post Office: On Adimantou St. which borders the park on the end farthest from the water. Open Mon.-Fri. 7:30am-2pm. **Postal Code:** 20100.

OTE: 32 Kolokotroni St. Open daily 6am-midnight; Mon.-Fri. 7am-midnight for collect calls. **Telephone Code:** 0741.

Train Station: Demokratias St. (tel. 225 22). To Athens via Isthmia (11 per day, 2 hr., 600dr). Two major train lines serve the Peloponnese: 1 along the northern coast from Corinth to Pirgos, and south to Kiparissia; the other south from Corinth to Tripolis and Kalamata. Almost all major coastal cities in the Peloponnese can be reached by train from Corinth. Trains to: Xilokastro (4 per day, 30min., 240dr); Patras (4 per day, 2hr., 750dr); Pirgos (2 per day, 4hr., 1310dr); Olympia (4 per day until 3:33pm, 4½hr., 1420dr); Argos (2 per day until 4:23pm, 1hr., 390dr); Tripolis (4 per day, 3hr., 690dr); Kalamata (4 per day, 5hr., 1310dr); Lefktro (910dr); Kiparissia via Tripolis or Patras (1640dr); and Kalavryta (5 per day until 5:05pm, 760dr). **Luggage storage** costs 200dr per piece. Trains from Athens to Patras may be full so be prepared to wait or take the bus.

Bus Station: Ermou and Koliatsou Station: Tel. 256 45 or 244 81. Buses run until 10:10pm. Buses to: Ancient Corinth (6am-9pm every hr., 20min., 140dr); Athens (5:30am-9:30pm every 30min., late afternoon and early evening service is more erratic, 1½hr., 1000dr); Loutraki (6am-7:30pm every 30min., 7:30-10:10pm less frequent service, 20min., 170dr), Isthmia (5 per day until 8pm, 20min., 140dr); and Nemea (7 per day until 9pm; 460dr to the ruins, 500dr to the town). **Ethnikis Anastasis and Aratou Station:** Tel. 244 03. The same bus travels to Mycenae (45min., 480dr), Argos (7am-9:30pm every hr., 1hr., 600dr), and Nafplion (1¼hr., 750dr); the bus leaves at 7:15am and every hr. from 8:30am-9:30pm. Note that the bus to Mycenae drops passengers at Fichtia, a 1½-km walk from the site (see Mycenae below). To catch a bus to Sparta and various other southern locations on the Peloponnese, you must take the Loutraki bus to the Corinth Canal and pick up the buses coming from Athens to: Sparta (7 per day); Kalamata (10 per day); Koroni; and Tripoli.

Taxis: Tel. 223 61, 248 44 or 269 00. Along the park side of Ethnikis Anistasis St.

Car Rental: Grig Lagos, 42 Ethnikis Anistassis St. (tel. 226 17), across the street from the moped rental place. 7500dr per day including 18% tax and 100km, 45dr each additional km. Open 8am-1pm and 5-9pm.

Moped Rental: Liberopoulos, 27 Ethnikis St. (tel. 729 37 or 218 47), past the park heading inland. Mopeds 2500-3500dr. Bicycles 1000dr. Open 8am-1:30pm and 5-8:30pm.

Laundromat: 49 Adimantou St. (tel. 222 47), across from OTE and 77 Koliatsou St. Walk through the park and head towards the water. Cheaper rates if you don't want clothes ironed, so specify.

Public Toilets: Across from the park on Ethnikis Anastasis St.

Pharmacy: 27 Ethnikis Anastasis St. (tel. 242 13). Open Mon. and Wed. 8am-2pm, Tues. and Thurs.-Fri. 8am-2pm and 5-9pm. Many others on Koliatsou St.

Hospital: Athinaion St. (tel. 257 11), inland past the train station as the road bears left.

Police: 51 Ermou St. (tel. 221 43), facing the park near the bus station. Open 24 hrs. Also an office of the **tourist police** (tel. 232 82; open daily 8am-2pm and 5-8pm.)

Accommodations and Camping

Most hotels in Corinth cluster near the waterfront and the railroad station. The accommodations here are comfortable and conveniently located near the ancient sites.

Hotel Belle-vue, Dimaskinou St. (tel. 220 88), along the waterfront. Take Ethnikis Anastasis to the waterfront, turn right on Ermou to the water, and turn left. Clean rooms with high ceilings and balconies overlooking the water. The owner Pete is eager to help travelers and can be found at either of his adjacent café/bars. Doubles 3000dr. Triples 4500dr.

Hotel Acti, 3 Ethnikis Anistasis St. (tel. 233 37). Around the corner from the Belle-vue with similar, if smaller, rooms. Singles 1800dr. Doubles 3500dr. Triples 4800dr.

Hotel Byron, 8 Demokratis St. (tel. 226 31), opposite the train station to the right. Spotless rooms with sinks and balconies. Clean hall toilet. Singles 1500dr. Doubles 2300dr. Showers 250dr.

Hotel Appollon, 18 Peirinis St. (tel. 225 87), diagonally across from the train station on the corner of Dimaskinou St. Clean rooms with wood paneling and a video game in the lobby. All rooms have a private bath. Doubles 4500dr.

Camping: Corinth Beach Campground (tel. 257 67 or 279 67), 3km west of town, near a beach. Take the bus to Ancient Corinth, and ask to get off at the campsite. 700dr per person, 400-400dr per tent. The **Blue Dolphin Campground** (tel. 25 76 67) is 3km from Ancient Corinth, right on the beach. 750dr per person, 500dr per tent.

Food

For a local favorite with delicious seafood, try **Taverna O Thodorakis** ("Ο ΘΟΔ-ΩΡΑΚΙΣ) on G. Seferis St., at the extreme right side of the waterfront (facing the water). (Whole fried *kalamari* 500dr. Open 12:30-5pm and 8:30pm-2am.) Another tasty option is **Taverna Anaxagoras,** under a bamboo canopy, at the opposite end of the waterfront. (Grilled meats 800-1000dr. Open 12:30-3pm and 8pm-midnight.) Fast food joints and pizza places crowd the waterfront. In the center of everything is the **Hambo** ("Club" sandwich with fries 500dr.) Evening meals are often serenaded by *bouzouki* acts performing on the stage outside. Various entertainments fill the summer weekends along the harbor front: music, dance, and car races. The most hopping bar in town is **Mordillo,** with dwarf palm trees and black lights. There's a well-stocked **supermarket** at 57 Adimantou St. near the bus stations.

Sights

If you spend the day in town rather than at the ruins, you may want to amble on out to the **Folklore Museum,** housed in a modern white building next to the waterfront at the end of Ermou St. (Open daily 8am-1pm. Free.) The **cinema** on Kolokotroni St. often shows English-language movies. The town **beaches** to the west are rocky, seaweed-strewn, and crowded. Don't waste your time wading when you can be inspecting the fascinating remains at ancient Corinth, just 7km away. The town is also convenient as a base for **daytrips** to the nearby ruins at Isthmia and Nemea.

Ancient Corinth

Once upon a time, somewhere out there, the gods contested for control of Corinth. Apollo and Poseidon, in the finest tradition of divine compromise, split the city between them, Poseidon settling for the isthmus, and Apollo the Acrocorinth. Upon another time, ancient Corinth was a powerful commercial center. While its harbors thrived, its hills rumbled with the clashes of countless conquerors. When Alexander the Great had the Peloponnese firmly under Macedonian rule, the Greeks met in Corinth to approve the new Hellenic League, comprising over 300,000 free men and 450,000 slaves. But after the Roman general Mummius trounced the city in 146 BCE, Corinth was left uninhabited for 100 years. Countless treasures looted from Corinth were sold on the open market in Rome.

Refounded as a Roman colony in 44 BCE by Julius Caesar, Corinth became renowned for its wild ways. Fat with the riches of trade, the Corinthians had time for indulgence. They worshiped Aphrodite with fervor, provoking the stern disapproval of the Apostle Paul, who futilely preached at Corinth with the hopes of reforming the city's decadent inhabitants.

The remains of the ancient city now stand on a plateau near the base of the towering **Acrocorinth,** just 7km from modern Corinth. Excavation of the city, still underway, has uncovered the ruins of the Roman settlement. The guidebook by Nikos Papahatzis (1200dr) is quite informative. Make the **museum** your first stop and overdose on its vast collection of sarcophagi (one still occupied), friezes of dancing maenads, and Roman mosaic floors. Outside in the courtyard stands an eerie line-up of headless statues. Off this courtyard, the **Asclepion Room** features votive offerings (usually a cast of the affected body part) from the sick to the god of medicine, and also houses terra-cotta figurines and pottery. To explore the entirety of the unrestricted site, turn off as you exit the museum. Before descending several steps, you will pass a garden of columns, each labeled by date. On the left presides the 6th century BCE **Temple of Apollo.** In the middle of the row of central shops, you'll see the **bema** on the right, a dais from which the Romans made general announcements and official proclamations. Ahead is the **Julian Basilica.** To the left a broad stone stair descends into the **forum.** At the right, on top of the steps, stands the Roman Fountain of Peirene, named for the woman who wept so profusely after Artemis killed her son that the resourceful gods transformed her into a fountain. Stick your head (or maybe more) into one of the six ornamented arches to see what remains of colorful frescoes and to hear the mysterious spring. hJust past the fountain, is **Perivolos of Apollo,** an open-air court surrounded by columns partially restored. Near the Perivolos is the **public latrine.** These latrines were only for men, the most outgoing of whom used to sit next to each other and chat. (Site and museum open daily 8am-7pm. Admission to both 1000dr, students 500dr; free on Sun. and holidays.)

Built on the lower of the Acrocorinth's twin peaks, the **fortress** has foundations dating back to ancient times. The upper summit originally held a **Temple to Aphrodite,** which was served by 1000 "sacred courtesans" who initiated free-wheeling disciples into the "mysteries of love." From atop this mountain on a clear day, you can see far enough to verify your mapmaker's rendition of the northeast Peloponnese and the Corinthian and Saronic Gulfs. Until about 20 years ago you could see all the way to the Acropolis of Athens. Pollution took care of that.

4km above, the Acrocorinth is open around the clock. People have been known to bring sleeping bags and spend the night (one ancient building on the grounds can provide semi-shelter). If you choose to do this, exercise caution, and never camp alone. You'll be on your own at the site, except for the **Acrocorinthos Restaurant** located just before the fortress. (Open daily 6am-10pm.) The ascent toward the entrance of the fortress can is navigable by car along a paved road which deteriorates into a rocky path. There is no bus service, but you can take a **taxi** from town (1000dr each way). If walking, make the arduous hike in the early morning or late afternoon to avoid the heat. **Buses** travel from Modern Corinth to Ancient Corinth at the mountain's base, on the hour, returning on the half-hour (140dr).

A small village flanks the ruins, and its main street runs in front of the site. To get to **Rooms Marinos** (tel. 312 09 or 311 80; call around 8:30pm), go right at the fork behind the bus stop (away from the entrance to the ruins), walk along Sisyphos St., and turn right, uphill, at the sign for Argos. Here Papa Spiros and Mama Elisabeth run a peerless, extended-family-style establishment with a huge yard and home-grown, home-cooked meals served with home-pressed wine. (Sparkling and newly renovated. Doubles 5783dr. Triples 6860dr. Private bath included. Suites for families available.) **O Tassos** is a delightful *taverna* on the road to modern Corinth (the best-we've-found *mousaka* 800dr) after the **post office** (post office open 7:30am-2pm with exchange). From July 1-3, Ancient Corinth celebrates Agiori Anargyroi, its most important summer festival, commemorating Saint Kosmos and Saint Damian, the physicians.

Near Corinth

Isthmia

Ancient Greek jocks used to gather in Isthmia and Nemea to compete in their renowned athletic contests, drink beer, and slap each other on the butt. Pindar preserves the memory of these games in his odes honoring the victors. Take the bus from Corinth heading toward **Isthmia,** and ask to be let out at the **museum,** a green building up the road from the bus stop and on the right. The carefully diagrammed exhibits present finds from the Temple of Poseidon and sites of the Isthmean games. Of particular interest are the glass *opus sectile* (mosaic panels) discovered at nearby Kenchreai which managed to survive the earthquake of 375 CE. The entrance to the ruins lies to the right of the museum. All that remains of the **Temple of Poseidon** is its despoiled foundation. The **theater** is below and farther to the right of the temple. **Cult caves,** where many enjoyed dinner and entertainment during the Archaic Period, lie above the theater.

The **Corinth Canal** began as Nero's pet project in 67 CE. The project died with him, but the French resumed work on the 6km waterway in 1881. To get a good view of the canal, walk toward its mouth from the Isthmia museum to the Dioriga *taverna,* next to a one-car ferry; then walk up the road that roughly parallels the waterway until you get to the bridge (2km). The canal's dramatically steep, razor-smooth sides, 30m apart, were cut into rock over 90m high. A footpath follows the water's western side. You can catch a bus coming from Loutraki back to Corinth at the canal bridge.

Nemea

Pausanias offered good advice in the 2nd century CE when he wrote: "Here is a temple of Nemean Zeus worth seeing although the roof has fallen in and the cult statue is missing." Were he to visit it today, he might be a bit peeved that the temple has dwindled to a mere three columns. The walkway takes you past a wall built around a glass-encased grave, complete with skeleton. Don't miss the well-preserved baths. The stadium, which has preserved its starting line and an entrance tunnel with fans' graffiti, is 500m down the road toward Corinth. The carefully organized museum on the site (tel. 074 62 27 39) has excellent explanatory notes in English, some artifacts, and several reconstructions of the site. (Museum and site open Tues.-Sat. 8:45am-3pm, Sun. 9:30am-2:30pm. Admission 500dr, students 300dr.) The ruins of Ancient Nemea are 4km distant from Modern Nemea, so if coming by bus from Corinth, ask to be let off at the ancient site (1hr., 460dr).

Loutraki

Loutraki rests across the crescent-shaped bay, a 20-minute bus ride from Corinth. Much of the bottled water you'll be clutching as you wander through the broiling landscape gushed from Loutraki's sweet wells. Loutraki hardly springs to mind as an ideal

Mediterranean vacation spot, but if you are visiting Corinth, you might want to stop by and tap the source of the town's allure. Take a stroll along the white stone boardwalk that flanks the body-blanketed beach, shadowed by the **Yerania Mountains** that rise abruptly above the small, verdant city.

Go west to **Lake Vouliagmene,** a tranquil cove that's perfect for camping. Buses connect Loutraki with Lake Vouliagmene at 10am, returning at 1am. You can also take a day's boat excursion with **Albona Cruises** (tel. 649 19; Tues. and Thurs. to Blue Lake at Vouliagmene 1900dr). Walk up Lekka St. and then stroll through the bushy park to the waterfront dock.

There are a few blessed exceptions to the high cost of living in Loutraki. One of these is the **Hotel Canada** (ΞΕΝΟΔΟΧΕΙΟΝ ΚΑΝΑΔΑΕ), 6 Yior. Lekka St. (tel. 280 11), with its large rooms and huge bathtubs. Follow El. Venizelou St. (which changes to Lekka St.) toward the mountains. (Singles 2800dr. Doubles 4500dr. Triples 6750.) Farther down toward the mountain (bear left) is the **Hotel Brettania** at 28 Yior Lekka St (tel. 223 49). The rooms and baths sparkle, and every floor has a refrigerator. (Singles 3300dr. Doubles 4400dr. Triples 5800dr.)

Cafeteria-style pizza and spaghetti are standard dining options here. Gorge yourself on an enormous plate of *kalamari* (400dr) at **Drosia,** 4 Alkidon St., parallel to the water and close to the bus station. The **bakery** on Lekka St., 1 block from the bank on the left, the **Zacharoplastia** at the corner of E. Venizelou and Kapodestrio, near the **taxi stand,** as well as the more expansive and expensive bakery next to the bus stop all offer volcanically sugared sweets. If you're going out at night, plan on taking a taxi—the trendiest Loutraki night-spots are 3-4km away from town. The **Aphroditi** (tel. 410 02) always draws crowds. Popular intown discos include the **Tropicana Disco** and the **Claxon,** both on El. Venizelos St.

To get to Loutraki from Isthmia, cross the canal bridge; the bus stop is next to a railroad station sign (120dr). Stay on the bus until the last stop, at a triangular road island (not to be confused with Muneer and Courtney's home state) across from the Hotel Mizithra. **Buses** from Corinth run every 30min. Buses (tel. 422 62) from Loutraki travel to: Athens (12 per day until 9pm, 1000dr); Corinth (every 30 min. 5:30am-10pm, 20min., 170dr); Perachora (nearly every hr. 5:30am-8pm., 20min., 140dr; and Vouliagmeni (July-Aug. only, at 10am, return 1pm, 45min., 500dr return).

From the bus station, walk down **El. Venizelou St.,** with the water to your left, and you'll reach the **post office** at #4 28th Octovriou St., 1 block down to the right. (Open Mon.-Fri. 7:30am-2pm.) The **OTE** is at 10 El. Venizelou. (Open Mon.-Fri. 7:30am-11pm, Sat.-Sun. 9am-2pm.) The **police** keep the peace across the street from the OTE (on the 2nd floor; tel. 630 00 or 222 58; **tourist police** Mon.-Fri. 8am-2pm). The **National Bank** is on 25th Martiou St.; where the road forks, bear left (open Mon.-Thurs. 8am-2pm, Fri. 8am-1:30pm). **Laundry Express** is Loutraki's beautiful launderette at 13 Agiou Ioannou St. (tel. 483 13; wash 700dr, dry 200). For moped rentals, make a right at the post office and turn at the second corner on the left to reach **Andreas** (tel. 438 12; Vespas 2500dr, bikes 800dr). Follow E. Venizelou St. (which changes to Lekka St.) toward the mountains. On the left, the densely congregated bushy green trees guard a public fountain that spouts Loutraki water; get in line to fill your bottle. **Public toilets** conveniently await at the end of this small park. For the **health center,** dial 634 44 or 266 66. Loutraki's **postal code** is 20300; the **telephone code** is 0744.

Xilokastro

In the traditional scurrying between Athens and the ferry drop-off in Patras, tourists usually ignore the windswept north coast of the Peloponnese. Thus, Greek vacationers alone enjoy this string of beach resorts lining the shore between Corinth and Patras. The expansive beach and ivory-tinted boardwalk of Xilokastro make for marvelous meandering. **Mt. Ziria** (2600m), the Peloponnese's second-highest peak, looms above the city.

The beach and most of the hotels are east of the square. From the *platia,* walk one block on Athomporto St. away from the water. On the right you'll see the **police station.** Ask here about the 3½-hour climb up Mt. Ziria. The **Hotel Periandos** (tel. 222

72) provides cozy rooms. Walk east along the waterfront, and turn inland after the Hotel Fadira. (Doubles 5500dr, negotiable.) The coast between Xilokastro and the town of Kiato to the east vaunts splendid beaches. The beach to Corinth is a continuing chain of campsites. Among them are **Camping Akrata** (tel. 313 78), **Camping Lemon Beach** (tel. (0696) 316 39), and **Kironeri** (tel. (0696) 314 05).

Buses (tel. 222 00 or 223 00) run to and from Athens (every hr. until 8:40pm, 1¼hr., 1600dr). If you are coming from Corinth, catch the bus at the canal or ask at the bus station about buses which stop at Xilokastro on their way to other destinations. The bus that runs along the new highway will drop you on the side of the road beside the speeding traffic (2km above the town), while local buses go directly into town. **Trains** from Kalamata, Patras, Corinth (7 per day, 1 hr., 175dr), and Athens stop here, but rail service is not as reliable as buses—expect delays. The train station (tel. 222 97) is on Dimitri Mousoura St.

From the bus station, walk 1 block down Leoforis Tsaldari St. (with the water on your left) to the **post office.** (Open Mon.-Fri. 7:30am-2pm.) The next block has a **drugstore,** and leads to the *platia* (main square), with banks and some good *souvlaki* joints. The **postal code** is 20400; the **telephone code** is 0743.

Mycenae (Mykenai) MYKHNAI

No city figured more prominently, or morbidly, in Greek mythology than Mycenae. Aeschylus immortalized the house of Atreus, rulers of the city, in his tragic *Oresteia* trilogy. Mycenae was allegedly founded by Perseus, the hero who duped Cerberus, the three-headed watchdog of the underworld, and slew Medusa, the snake-haired gorgon whose looks could kill. Eventually the Mycenaeans chose Atreus as their ruler. But out of hatred for his brother, Thyestes, Atreus murdered his nieces and nephews—Thyestes's sons and daughters—and served them to their father for dinner. This culinary faux-pas provoked the wrath of the gods—Thyestes pronounced a curse on Atreus and all his progeny. When Atreus's son Agamemnon returned after ten years at the Trojan War, he was met by his bitter wife Clytemnestra, her lover Aegisthus, and Aegisthus's lethal dagger. Agamemnon's son Orestes later avenged the murder of his father—by slaying his mother—but was thereafter haunted by the Furies, shadows of his anguished conscience on Zeus's payroll. According to Aeschylus, Athena finally pardoned Orestes and lifted the curse from the House of Atreus.

Mycenae's hazy origins, its interactions with other Near Eastern civilizations, and its decline have beguiled historians. The site was settled as early as 2700 BCE by tribes from the Cyclades who were colonizing the mainland. Clay tablets found at Pylos and Knossos preserve the Mycenaeans' bureaucratic account-keeping recorded in Linear B, an early form of Greek. Mycenae flourished financially after the fall of Knossos around 1400 BCE, and Mycenaean culture infiltrated Cyprus, Syria, and Sicily. Mycenae was probably destroyed by Dorian tribes from the north led by disgruntled rivals of the House of Atreus.

The well-preserved ruins of ancient Mycenae, which include an extensive fortress and remarkable treasures found in beehive tombs, are among the most celebrated archaeological discoveries in modern history. In summer, tourists stampede to the famed Lion's Gate and Tomb of Agamemnon. Visit early in the morning or late in the afternoon to avoid the democratic mobs. Although most travelers make Mycenae a daytrip from Athens, Argos, or Nafplion, you can spend the night in the adjacent modern village (alias "tourist strip"), 2km from the site.

The only direct **buses** to Mycenae are from Nafplion (3 per day, 1hr., 350dr) and Argos (6 per day, 30min., 250dr). Stops are in the town of Mycenae (up the street from the Iphigenia Restaurant) and at the site (a 20-min. uphill walk from the town). Alternatively, buses and **trains** (6 per day) run from Corinth to Fichtia, a 1½km walk from Mycenae Town. There is another bus stop by the intersection near the train station. Although the town has no banks, the **post office** at the site handles **currency exchange.** (Open Mon.-Fri. 9am-2pm.) Mycenae's **telephone code** is 0751.

Accommodations, Camping, and Food

Mycenae has few inexpensive accommodations. If the youth hostel and campgrounds aren't quite your thing, try *dhomatia;* look for signs on the sidestreets or below the town.

Youth Hostel (HI/IYHF) (tel. 662 85), on the roof above the Restaurant Iphigenia. HI/IYHF card required. Crowded sun-drenched rooms with foam mattresses. Only 20 beds, 10 for each sex. Water temperature varies. 800dr per person.

Belle Helene Hotel (tel. 662 55), on the main road. Also a bus stop. Clean, spacious rooms with carpeting. Some noise from the restaurant downstairs. Schliemann stayed here while excavating the site, and the register display on the wall claims that Virginia Woolf and Claude Debussy slept here as well. Doubles 4500dr. Singles negotiable.

Hotel Klitemnistra (tel. 664 51), on the main road, closest to the ruins. Clean rooms. Restaurant downstairs; hot water. Doubles 4000dr, triples 5000dr.

Camping: Mycenae has 2 decent campgrounds. The more luxurious is **Camping Atreus** (tel. 662 21), at the bottom of the hill on the side of town farther from the ruins. It offers a TV room, kitchen, cafeteria/bar, and rooms for the tentless, in case of rain. 500dr per person. 300dr per tent. Tent rental, 400dr. Hot showers included. In the middle of town, **Camping Mycenae** (tel. 662 47) is smaller, closer to the ruins, and fragrant from surrounding orange and lemon groves. There is also a bar/restaurant and a kitchen, where the gracious owner prepares homemade and inexpensive food. 450dr per person, 400dr per tent (tent rental is possible). Hot showers included.

Most of the restaurants in town prey on tourists willing to pay. Even groceries are expensive. Try the **Restaurant/Taverna Micinaiko,** next to the youth hostel—nice folks and tasty food. (Greek salad 500dr, chicken with tomato sauce 550dr.) The restaurant **Menelaos,** (tel. 552 24) next door gives students a 10% discount. **Aristidis O Dikeos** (tel. 662 52) across the street has a pleasant proprietor, lots of flowers on the porch, and cuisine including Greek salads (500dr) and *dolmadakia* (stuffed vine leaves, 650dr).

Ancient Mycenae

The excavated site of Mycenae extends over a large tract of rough terrain tucked between Mt. Agios Elias to the north and Mt. Zara to the south. The site is enclosed by monstrous walls 13m high and 7m thick called "Cyclopean" by the ancient Greeks because they believed that the stones in the walls could have been lifted by only the Cyclops, those one-eyed, foul-tempered giants with superhuman strength. Although modern historians scoff at monsters (and probably can't see Mr. Snuffleupagus either), they have no better explanations of how the massive stones were moved. While the city was settled as early as 2750 BCE, the bulk of the ruins standing today date from 1280 BCE, when the city was the center of the far-flung Mycenaean civilization.

Amateur archaeologist Heinrich Schliemann uncovered Mycenae in 1874, having located the site by following clues in the writings of Homer and later Greek tragedians who had placed the House of Atreus in the vicinity. Schliemann began digging just inside the citadel walls at the spot where several ancient authors indicated the royal graves would have been located. Discovering 15 skeletons "literally covered with gold and jewels," he believed he had unearthed Agamemnon and his followers. Less romantic archaeologists, however, have dated the tombs to four centuries before the Trojan War. One skull, sporting a golden death mask still referred to as "The Mask of Agamemnon," is now exhibited in the National Archaeological Museum in Athens.

Before visiting the site, consider obtaining a map and a flashlight. The book by S. E. Iakovidis, covering both Mycenae and Epidavros, includes a map of the site and is well worth the 1500dr. If you plan to go to many sites in the Peloponnese, or would like information on other ruins, buy the larger guide, *The Peloponnese,* by E. Karpodini-Dimitriadi (2000dr).

The bus will take you to the end of the asphalt road; on your right stand the ruins. Down the hill in the lower parking lot area is the largest of the beehive tombs, the so-called **Tomb of Agamemnon.** Two other *tholos* (beehive) tombs are on the right of the entrance booth, outside the walls. The gate and the **Cyclopean Walls** of the citadel date from the 13th century BCE. The imposing **Lion's Gate,** with two lionesses carved in relief above the lintel, is the portal into ancient Mycenae. The oldest example of monumental sculpture, these lions were symbols of the house of Atreus, and their heads (now missing) had eyes of precious gems. Schliemann found most of his artifacts (now exhibited in the Mycenaean Room of the Athens Museum) in **Grave Circle A.** These shaft graves have been dated to around the 16th century BCE, and were originally located outside the city walls.

The ruins on the hillside are the remnants of various homes, businesses, and shrines. The **palace** and the **royal apartments** are at the highest part of the citadel on the right. The open spaces here include guard rooms, private areas, and more extensive public rooms (note the pillar bases). To the left of the citadel sit the remaining stones of a Hellenistic **Temple of Athena.** At the far end of the city, between the palace and the **postern gate,** is the underground cistern used as refuge in times of siege. Use your flashlight to explore the cold, slimy passage, but be careful—the steps are worn and slippery.

Just outside the Lion's Gate are two of the excavated *tholos* tombs, used for noble burials. The one closer to the city was reputedly the **Tomb of Aegisthus** and the other the **Tomb of Clytemnestra.** (See Mycenae Introduction). If you follow the asphalt road 150m back toward the town of Mycenae you'll find the **Treasury of Atreus,** the largest and most impressive *tholos,* which Schliemann also unearthed. The **"Tomb of Agamemnon"** is reached through a 40m passage cut into the hillside. This famous tomb was found empty, but it is believed to have once held valuable goods that were spirited away by thieves long ago. Bring a flashlight. (Site open Mon.-Fri. 8am-7pm, Sat.-Sun. 8:30am-2:45pm. Admission to citadel and Tomb of Agamemnon 1000dr, students 500dr; free on Sun. Hang on to your ticket or you'll pay twice.)

Argos ΑΡΓΟΣ

Jean-Paul Sartre paints a rather bleak portrait of the ancient city of Argos in his play *The Flies.* Unfortunately, his portrayal still describes the modern city: Argos is indeed a chaotic and dusty metropolis. The chaos subsides for a brief spell in the afternoon, but even then the aesthetic appeal of the town scarcely improves. Luckily, frequent bus service to Nafplion makes it unnecessary to stay in Argos; a daytrip into the city is sufficient for a visit to its archaeological sites.

Orientation and Practical Information

The four streets that form the sides of the central square in Argos correspond roughly to the four points of the compass. Surrounding the large and beautiful **Church of San Petros,** they are the principal avenues of the city. Visible from the square is **Larissa Hill,** topped by the Venetian citadel of the same name. Larissa borders the city on the west. **Vassilios Georgiou B** is parallel to the citadel. Opposite this street on the east side is **Danaou Street.** The north edge is **Vassilios Konstantinou,** the south side **Olgas Street.**

Currency Exchange: National Bank, on the eastern side of the square, 1 block behind Danaou St. and the park. Open Mon.-Thurs. 8am-2pm, Fri. 8am-1:30pm. There are other banks around the square area.

Post Office: 16 Danaou St. (tel. 280 66), past the southern end of the square. Open Mon.-Fri. 7:30am-2pm. **Postal Code:** 21200.

OTE: 8 Nikitara St., north of the park. Open daily 7am-midnight. **Telephone Code:** 0751.

Trains: The train station (tel. 272 12) is about 1km south of the main square. To get to the main square from the station, take a right on Nafplion St. and then bear left on Vas. Sofias at the 5-way intersection. Four trains per day go to: Athens (3hr., 900dr); Corinth (1hr., 400dr); Tripolis (1hr., 550dr); Kalamata (3½hr., 1000dr); Mycenae (10min., 100dr); and Nemea (45min., 200dr).

Buses: There are 2 bus stations. A few doors down from the **Athinon Station,** on Vas. Georgiou B., near the corner of Vas. Olgas is the bus departure point. (Look for the Arcadia café.) Buses depart to: Athens (5:30am-8:30pm every hr., 2½hr., 1550dr); Nafplion (4:30am-9pm every ½hr.,

250dr); Nemea (2 per day, 1hr., 400dr); Mycenae (6 per day, 25min., 250dr); Galata (2 per day, 1200dr) and Prosimni (4 per day, 30min., 250dr). The **Arcadia-Laconia Station** is at 24 Pheithonos St. (tel. 272 40 or 235 15). Follow Vas. Olgas St., two streets past the museum, and turn left. Walk down several blocks, past the Agricultural Bank. Buses leave from here for: Tripolis (9 per day, last at 10:30pm, 1¼hr., 800dr); Sparta (8 per day, 2½hr., 1250dr); Olympia (change at Tripolis, 3 per day, 4½hr., 2000dr); Andritsena (10am, 3½hr., 1700dr); Gythion (4 per day, 1800dr); Monemvassia (1 per day, 2200dr); and Leonidio (3 per day, 950dr).

Hospital: Corinth St. (tel. 278 31), the road to Athens opposite St. Nicholas Church.

Police: 10 Agelou Bobou St. (tel. 272 22). From the northeast corner of the square follow Corinth St. and turn right on Agelou Bobou. Ask for someone who speaks English. Open 24 hrs.

Accommodations and Food

Argos has few overnight visitors, hence few accommodations. You'd probably be happier in Nafplion, or, if you want to camp, in Tolo or Mycenae. Argos lacks the charm and nightlife of Nafplion, and the sights can be seen in a half-day.

Hotel Apollon, 15 Korai St. (tel. 280 12). Take Nikitara off the square, turn left at the BP station, and then turn right immediately into the nearby alley—it's on the left. Signs indicate the way. Large, quiet, tidy rooms. Singles 2500dr. Doubles 4800dr.

Hotel Theoxenia, 31 Tsokri St. (tel. 273 70). Follow Vas. Konstantinou to the left (west) for about 150m until you see the arches on the left; it's just beyond. Closest of all to the Argos ruins and right across from the market place. Standard rooms. Singles 2100dr. Doubles 4000dr. Triples 4900dr.

Restaurants on the square or behind the bank offer standard, over-priced fare. If you're stuck, try **The Retro,** on the southwest corner near the bus stations (*mousaka* 650dr). You might want to stock up at the **supermarket** on Vas. Sofias St., off the northwest corner of the square, or try the **bakery** near the Arcadia-Laconia bus stop.

Sights

Archaeological evidence indicates that the plain of Argos has been inhabited since 3000 BCE. According to Homer, Argos was the kingdom of the hero Diomedes and claimed the allegiance of Mycenae's powerful king, Agamemnon. Invading Dorians captured Argos in the 12th century BCE, around the same time as the fall of Mycenae, and then used it as their base for controlling the Argolid Peninsula. Through the 7th century BCE, Argos remained the most powerful state in the Peloponnese, and even defeated its rival Sparta. But this was the last of its glories—by the 5th century BCE it was no match for the invincible Spartan war machine. In the famous battle of 494 BCE, Kleomenes and the Spartans nearly defeated Argos but failed to penetrate the city walls.

In medieval times, Franks, Venetians, and Turks captured and ruled Argos in turn. They each had a hand in the defensive structure of the **Fortress of Larissa,** a splendid architectural hodgepodge which also includes Classical and Byzantine elements. Getting to the fortress is a hike. You can walk along Vas. Konstantinou St. for one hour or climb the foot path from the ruins of the ancient theater (45min.).

Archaeologists had hoped to uncover a large part of the ancient city of Argos, but most of it lies underneath the modern town. The principal **excavations** have occurred on the city's western fringe; digs are currently going on there and in different areas throughout the town. To get to the site, walk past the post office to the end of the street and turn right onto Theatron St. The site is at the end of this street. A walk from the center of town takes 10-15 minutes. There is no admission fee.

With a seating capacity of 20,000, the ancient **theater** was the largest in the Greek world when it was built in the 4th century BCE. Though not as well preserved as its more famous counterpart in Epidavros, it is striking nonetheless. Next to the theater are the **Roman baths,** where segments of wall give a good impression of the original magnitude (and significance) of these ancient social centers. Some of the mosaic floors remain. You'll also find the **Roman Odeon** (indoor theater) here and the **agora,** with blue-and-white mosaics still in place. Past the Odeon are the remains of a smaller theater. (Site open Mon.-Sat. 8:30am-3pm, Sun. 8:30am-2:30pm. Free.)

There are a few other interesting, though less impressive, ruins in this area. To find them from the main site, walk north up Gounas St. (outside the gate). Turn left (west) at the intersection with Tsokri St. onto Karantza St., and continue out of town up the hill. At the top, you'll find a number of Mycenaean graves and the remains of the **Temple of Apollo and Athena,** encompassing various sanctuaries from antiquity to the Byzantine Period. To the right of the hill is **Aspis,** the main ancient citadel; Venetian Larissa stands proudly to the left. To reach this site from the main square, head west on Vas. Konstantinou, which becomes Tsokri St. The walk takes about 20 minutes.

Hera was the patron deity of the Argives and the temple of her cult, the **Argive Heraion,** is a short bus ride north of Argos. (Take the Prosimni bus; 250dr.) The complex contains, among other things, a pair of temples, a *stoa,* and baths. At **Prosimni,** several km northeast of Argos and past the Heraion, the archaeology aficionado will find a series of prehistoric graves. A few km east of Agias Trias lie the remains of the city of **Dendra,** where tombs yielded the completely preserved suit of bronze armor now on exhibit in the Nafplion museum.

The small but superb **museum,** west off the main square on Vas. Olgas St., contains a collection of Mycenaean and pre-Mycenaean pottery, some of which dates back as far as 3000 BCE. Among the exhibits are 5th-century Roman mosaics and an intriguing array of headless Roman figures displayed as if in conversation. The entrance hall and the second-floor gallery each contain "unpublished" Roman mosaics, in even better condition than those in the courtyard. (Open Tues.-Sun. 8:30am-3pm. Admission 300dr, students 200dr.)

Nafplion (Nauplio) ΝΑΥΠΛΙΟ

Nafplion's extensive fortifications may make it look a little paranoid. Its fortified acronauplia, fortress of Palamidi, and tiny Bourzi island guarding the bay create a tense atmosphere. But looks do deceive: Nafplion is really just a faded beach resort, with a picturesque and crumbling old town, some terrific waterfront *tavernas,* and a handful of ice-cream joints. Nafplion's plentiful bus connections make it the ideal base for exploring the ruins of the Argolid Peninsula.

Nafplion's history has suffered from chronic instability. Before the Venetians built it on swampland in the 15th century, the city (named for Poseidon's son Nauplius) consisted of the hilltop fortresses. The town passed from the Venetians to the Turks and back again. In 1821, it was headquarters for the revolutionary government, and then the capital (1829-1834), of newly independent Greece. John Kapodistrias, the first governor of Nafplion, was assassinated in St. Spyridon Church. (You can still gawk at the bullet hole.)

Orientation and Practical Information

The red "Peloponnisos" map has a good city plan of Nafplion and other cities of the Peloponnese (400dr). Pick it up at the tourist shop where the bus stops or at the shops above the dock. The bus terminal, on **Singrou Street,** sits near the base of the Palamidi fortress, which caps the hill to the right facing inland. To reach **Bouboulinas Street,** the waterfront promenade, just walk right (facing the bus station) down Singrou to the harbor. The area behind Bouboulinas and Singrou is the old part of town, with many shops and *tavernas.* If you arrive by water, Bouboulinas St. will be directly before you, across the parking lot and parallel to the dock.

There are three other principal streets, all of which run off Singrou Street parallel to Bouboulinas. Moving inland, the first is **Amalias,** a chief shopping street. The second, **Vassileos Konstandinou,** ends in **Syntagma Square** (Platia Syntagmatos), which has two good *tavernas,* the bookstore, the bank, the museum, and at night, scores of aspiring soccer stars. The third street is **Plapouta Street,** which becomes **Staikopoulou** in the vicinity of Syntagma Sq. Here you'll find more good restaurants. Across Singrou

St., Plapouta becomes **25th Martiou,** the largest avenue in town and the road toward
the tourist police. This side of Singrou St.—everything behind the statue of Kapodistrias—is the new part of town. A tiny pebble **beach** awaits you just a short walk down the
road between the Palamidi and the Acronafplion.

Currency Exchange: Banks on Syntagma Sq. and Amalias St. Charge 200-500dr commission.
Open Mon.-Thurs. 8am-2pm, Fri. 8am-1pm.

Post Office: on the corner of Sidiras Merarchias and Singrou St., 1 block from the bus station toward the harbor. Open Mon.-Fri. 7:30am-2pm. **Postal Code:** 21100.

OTE: 25th Martiou St. at Arvantias, in the yellow building 2 blocks in front of the bus station.
Open Mon.-Sat. 7am-midnight, Sun. 7:30am-midnight. **Telephone Code:** 0752.

Ferries: There are no regular ferries out of Nafplion or Tolo. The *Pegasus,* an expensive cruise
ship, offers day tours. A one-way ticket on the Spetses-Hydra cruise is 3000dr, leaving every Mon.
from Tolo. Consult **Bourtzi Tours** (tel. 226 91), next to the bus station. Open daily 9am-2pm and
5-9pm. Another option, probably more convenient, is the **hydrofoil** which operates in July and
August. Flying Dolphins leave for Piraeus Tues.-Sun. at 7:45am (4hr., 4980dr), stopping in: Tolo
(20min., 760dr); Porto Heli (50min., 2050dr); Spetses (1hr., 2060dr); Ermione (1½hr., 2130dr);
Hydra (2hr., 2390dr); Poros (2½hr., 2990dr); Methana (3hr., 3480dr); and Aegina (3hr., 3580dr).
From Porto Heli and Spetses you can make connections to Leonidio (2330dr); Monemvrassia
(3480dr); Kythera (7250dr); and Neapolis (7250dr). The helpful **G. Yannopoulos** travel agency,
83 Bouboulinas St. (tel. 274 56) at the waterfront, sells **Flying Dolphin** tickets. (Open Mon.-Sat.
8:30am-1pm and 5:30-8:30pm.) The office opens early to sell tickets for departing hydrofoils, and
reopens at 8:30am.

Bus Station: Singrou St. (tel. 273 23), off Pl. Kapodistrias. Buses go to: Athens (5am-8:30pm every hr., 3hr., 1750dr); Argos (6am-9:30pm every ½ hr.; 30min.; 220dr); Mycenae (3 per day, 1hr.,
350dr); Epidavros (3 per day, 40min., 370dr); Tolo (7am-8:30pm every hr., 30min., 220dr); Kranidi (4 per day, 2hr., 900dr); and Galatas (to Poros); (3 per day, 2hr., 950dr). Check the board for
information about Ligouri (6 per day), and Porto Heli and Ermione (3 per day, about 900dr.)

Taxis: Singrou St. (tel. 241 20 or 247 20) across from the bus station. The trick is to get a driver
who operates out of the destination you desire; they charge less if they're returning. Taxi to Palamidi fortress 500dr.

Moped and Bike Rental: Riki and Pete (tel. 245 47 or 280 94), on Navarino St., around the corner from the Rex Hotel on Bouboulinas St. Mopeds 3000dr per day, bikes 1000dr per day, 5000dr
per week.

English Bookstore: Odyssey (tel. 234 30), Syntagma Sq. Pick up all those *Penguin Classics* here
for light summer reading. Tour books, newspapers, magazines and dictionaries also available.
Open in summer Mon.-Sat. 9am-1pm, Sun. 5-9pm, Nov.-Feb. Mon.-Sat. 9am-1pm and 5-9pm.

Agricultural Work: Apricot orchards surround Nafplion and often hire foreign workers on the
sly. It's easier for men to find work, which often consists of loading boxes. Go to the **Soulis Ako-
stis** bar across from the Commercial Bank on Amalias. Ask fellow travelers or *taverna* owners for
tips on who is hiring this year.

Medical Emergency: Call the tourist police or visit **Nafplion Hospital** (tel. 273 09). Walk down
25th Martiou St. and turn left onto Kolokotroni St., which eventually becomes Asklipiou St.

Police: Praxitelous St. (tel. 277 76), a 15-min. hike along 25th Martiou St. from the bus station—
follow the signs. The location keeps most travelers away; if you show up, you'll get attention.
Open 24 hrs.

Town Hall (tel. 244 44), near the hydrofoil landing. Changes money and offers help. Open 9am-
1pm and 5-9pm.

Accommodations

Although prices have risen in the old part of town, it's still the cheapest district in
Nafplion. Check along the streets at the eastern end of town (below the Dioscuri Hotel)
for rooms-to-let. For **camping,** see Sights below. Some daring travelers flout the law
and sleep in Nafplion's more suburban parks.

Youth Hostel (HI/IYHF) (tel. 277 54), Neon Vyzantion St., at Argonafton, a 15-20 min. hike
from the bus stop. Renovated during the summer of 1989. Run by a friendly couple and their
daughter. Melodious Dimitrios will wake you at 8am as he strolls through the corridor playing

"Que Sera, Sera" on his accordion. HI/IYHF card usually required. Bedroom area closed 10am-5pm. Curfew 11pm. 800dr per person. Breakfast with fresh oranges, 350dr.

Hotel Amymoni (tel. 272 19), in the Ionian Bank building. Amalias St. dead-ends at this hotel—the entrance is on the right. Clean rooms and hall bathrooms. Singles 2000dr. Doubles 2800dr.

Hotel Epidavros, Ipsiladou St. (tel. 275 41), 1 block below Amalias and 4 blocks up from Boulinas. Clean and roomy. Doubles 3500dr, with private bath 4500dr. Triples 5100dr.

Hotel Argolis (tel. 277 21), in the new town, on the Argos road right before the turn-off for the youth hostel. Noisy but comfortable bedrooms. Doubles 4500dr. Triples 5200dr.

Hotel IRA (HPA in Greek), 9 Vas. Georgiou B St. (tel. 281 84), off Bouboulinas St. in the new part of town. Clean, airy rooms. Doubles 4000dr. Triples 4500dr.

Food and Entertainment

Nafplion's cuisine is cheap, if you go to the right places. Seafood, especially baby squid (about 800dr), is usually a good choice. *Souvlaki-pita* fanatics can enjoy a cheap lunch (150dr) at the stand by the bus station. Note that most restaurants' names are written only in Greek.

On the water: A reasonably priced place at the corner of Bouboulinas and Singrou St., on the edge of the new part of town is **Kanaris** (ΚΟΝΟΣ; open noon-midnight). Above the dock on Bouboulinas is a string of *tavernas;* the best is **Hundalas** at #63. The fish at **Kolios** (ΚΟΛΙΟΣ; tel. 276 75), is pricey but reputed to be some of Nafplion's best. Try an ice cream at **The Corner** or order a *caffè frappe* anywhere along Bouboulinas St. In the evenings on the dock, vendors open up enormous carts full of produce from the Phillipines: sugar cane, coconut, dried papaya, and pineapple.

Syntagma Square: Peaceful until the revelers arrive around 9pm. The traffic-free square has a number of outdoor *tavernas,* including an over-priced pizza place. **Ellas** has standard *taverna* food, **Noufara** is slightly more expensive. Both are respectable; neither is great. **Talazia** serves up delicious pastries and sweets. **To Sokaki** (ΤΟ ΣΟΚΑΚΙ) on the corner of Anti-stassis, is a popular hang-out. Try a coffee here or breakfast of yogurt with honey. The **bakeries** just off the square on Amalias and Staikopoulou are very good and inexpensive.

Plapouta-Staikopoulou Street: Most of the places along this street are small. The most popular and one of the best is **Kelari,** which has a charming garden out back. **O Nikolas** (Ο ΝΙΚΟΛΑΣ) has terrific fresh fish. Next door to the agreeable **Taverna Zorbas,** the **Pink Panther** has fancy fruits, yogurt, and ice cream. Look for the bright pink chairs.

Kapodistrias Square, next to the post office: Pines, palms, and Palamidi are all in full view from **Matsikas,** which stays open during siesta. Some dishes are expensive, but the food is among Nafplion's best. **Sidirasmerachios St.** has a strip of *tost, souvlaki,* "fast food," and breakfast places. The food and atmosphere are about the same in these establishments, which provide pleasant alternatives for lunch or dinner.

If you crave a livelier excitement than art and archaeology, take advantage of Nafplion's 70s-esque hotspots and dance the night away to popular rock or traditional Greek tunes. On the corner of Bouboulinas and Sofroni is **Sirena** (tel. 245 15), where you can learn the *syrtaki* nightly beginning at 9:30pm. For more up-to-date movements, try **Disco Idol,** on Singrou St. near the water, and boogie your bottoms beneath mirrors and glass. Locals frequent the **Disco Memory,** a few streets into the new town. Drink lightly, though: beer at most of these places goes for 500dr or more. For cheaper grog, hit the bars on Bouboulinas (beer 200-300dr). **KooKoo** is a hip spot where the DJ spins discs from a big red car. If your tail-feather has wilted, take a minicruise of the harbor (they run until 7pm), and tour around the Bourtzi. Small *caïques* leave from the end of the dock (500dr round-trip).

Sights

A stroll through the streets of Nafplion is more edifying than a slideshow in Architecture 101. Everywhere you look there are impressive examples of building styles from various periods jostling each other elbow to elbow. An amazing example is the 18th-century Palamidi fortress (ΠΑΛΑΜΕΔΕΙΟΝ), property first of Venice, then of Turkey, now of Greece. The 999 grueling steps that once provided the only access to the fort have been superseded by a 3km road. Taxis cost 450dr each way, but you can assault the road by foot. If you opt for the steps, bring water and climb in the morning when the hill blocks the sun. At the top, you can walk around the intricate, well-preserved walls. The views of the town, gulf, and much of the Argolid are spectacular. The lion steles that adorn some of the citadel's walls are Venetian. Years ago, there were eight working cisterns at the site—now you can tour the cool interiors of the two remaining underground reservoirs. The steps begin on Arvanitias St., across the park from the bus station. A snack bar on site opens at 9:30am. (Open Mon.-Fri. 8am-6:30pm, Sat.-Sun. 8:30am-2:45pm. Admission 400dr, students 200dr; free on Sun. Pay at the top.)

The walls of the **Acronafplion** were fortified by three succeeding generations of conquerors—Greeks, Franks, and Venetians. Approach the fortress either by the road near the back parking lot or by the tunnel that runs into the hill from Zigomala St., where you can take the Xenia Hotel elevator.

Ludwig I, King of Bavaria, had the huge **Bavarian Lion** carved out of a monstrous rock as a memorial after seeing many of his men die in an epidemic in 1833-34. Today, a small park sits in front of it. Instead of turning right onto Praxitelous St. to go to the tourist police, make a left onto Mikh. Iatrou St. and walk 200m.

Nafplion's **Folk Art Museum** (tel. 283 79), winner of the 1981 European Museum of the Year Award, comprehensively displays the styles and construction techniques of ancient, medieval, and 18th-century Greek clothing. (Enter on Ipsiladou St. off Sofroni.) The exhibits here are superb and include encyclopedic explanations in English. (Open Wed.-Mon. 10am-1pm, closed in Feb. Admission 400dr, students 200dr.) The **Military Museum** is 1 block above the Folk Art Museum. (Open Wed.-Mon. 9am-2:30pm. Free.) The **archaeological museum,** housed in a Venetian mansion on Syntagma Sq., has a small but esteemed collection of pottery, arranged by historical period, and a perfectly preserved Mycenaean suit of bronze armor. (Open Wed.-Mon. 9am-3pm. Free.) Across from the bus station, near the **statue of Kapodistrias,** there's a **playground** in a large peaceful park.

The tiny island of **Bourtzi,** just offshore and easily visible from Bouboulinas, was fortified at the end of the 14th century. *Caïques* run back and forth from the end of the dock between 9am and 1pm, and from 4pm to 7pm (30min., round-trip 400dr).

Near Nafplion

Several km south of town, crowded **Tolo** and **Asini** have sandy beaches. Rent windsurfers (1500dr), pedal boats (1600dr), and canoes (500dr) by the hour to cool off from the hot sands of Tolo Beach. Asini, 2km up the road from Tolo toward Nafplion, is cheaper and less crowded. If you've lost sleep over Homer's cryptic reference to Asini (we know we have), you can visit the **ruins,** 1km inland, where excavations have uncovered fortifications, chamber tombs, and pottery.

Karathona Beach (ΚΑΡΑΘΟΝΑ) is accessible from the road to Palamidi. Continue back rather than ascend the road to the fortress and it will curve down to this sedate, sandy beach. Some rascally scofflaws freelance camp here. In Tolo and Asini, however, prohibitions against sacking out on the sand are more strictly enforced. Coincidentally, there is an incredible concentration of developed **campgrounds** that welcome tent-toting tourists with open palms. A good deal is **Camping Star** (tel. 592 26), 2 blocks above the beach across from Europe Pizza, with relatively quiet sites, refrigerators, and indoor tables. (650dr per person 400dr per tent.) Nearby is **Camping Tolo** (tel. 591 33), right on the beach and main drag. (750dr per person, 600dr per tent. Warm showers. Refrigerator.) Further up towards Asini is **Lido Camping II** (tel. 593 56 or 595 56) which charges 600dr per person and 600-700dr per tent. The campsite also has a kitchen, hot showers, and a market. Near Asini Beach try the **Kastraki** campsite. It's more expensive but very comfortable and offers discounts on watersports equipment. Signs will also direct you to the nearby **Sunset** and **Tolo Plaz** sites, only slightly farther from the beach. After camping, **private rooms** are the cheapest accommodations. Unfortunately, owners like to rent for the long term (at least a week) during the high season. Look for signs on Bouboulina St. or pay a little extra for a hotel room. **Hotel Artemis,** (tel. 594 58 or 591 25) on Bouboulina St. is right on the beach. (Doubles with private bath and A/C 6000dr. Triples 7100dr.) The nearby **Hotel Spartacus** (tel. 595 21) might have inspired the slave revolt. (Bare doubles 5000dr.) You can reach both Tolo and Asini via bus from Nafplion (every hr., last bus returns at 8:30pm, 30min., 250dr). For Asini, ask the driver or the on-board assistant to let you know when to get off. Farther south, more campgrounds speckle the beaches of **Plaka, Kadia,** and **Iria.** For motorbike rental in Tolo try **Moto Rent** on the beach by the road to Nafplion. Mopeds 2500dr per day.

Just 4km northwest of Nafplion on the road to Argos lie the Mycenaean ruins of **Tiryns** (or Tirintha), birthplace of Hercules. The finest prehistoric site outside of Mycenae, Tiryns was nearly impregnable during ancient times. That is, until it was captured by the Argives and destroyed in the 5th century BCE. Although parts of the stronghold date as far back as 2600 BCE, most of what remains was built 1000 years later, during Mycenaean times. The massive walls that surround the site indicate the immensity of the original fortifications. Standing about 8m in height and width, the monstrous "Cyclopean" walls reach a width of almost 20m on the eastern and southern slopes of the ancient acropolis. Inside these formidable structures lurk vaulted galleries. The remnants of the palace at the top of the acropolis contained impressively decorated floors, but its frescoes are now on display in the National Archaeological Museum in Athens. One huge limestone block remains—the floor of the bathroom. The site is easily reached by the Argos **bus** from Nafplion (every 30min., 1000dr). (Open Mon.-Fri. 8am-7pm, Sat.-Sun. 8:30am-3pm. Admission 500dr, students 250dr.)

Epidavros ΕΠΙΔΑΥΡΟΣ

> *At Epidavros I felt a stillness so intense that for a*
> *fraction of a second I heard the great heart of the*
> *world beat and I understood the meaning of pain*
> *and sorrow.*
> —Henry Miller, The Colossus of Maroussi

While we might allow Henry Miller some hyperbole, the fact stands that the theater at Epidavros *is* acoustically impeccable. From the top of its graceful and perfectly preserved 55 tiers of seats, you can hear a *drachma* drop on stage. Nowadays, however, it's usually futile to listen for the heartbeat of the world—you won't hear it behind the din raised by eager tourists and bus-loads of schoolchildren singing hymns and folk songs. The theater is a grand structure, built in the early 4th century BCE to accommodate 6000 people. In the 2nd century BCE, additional tiers were added for a total capacity of about 14,000. Despite severe earthquakes that destroyed much of the sanctuary in 522 and 551 CE, the theater was miraculously saved; it is considered the best preserved of all Greek theaters. Note the restored Corinthian columns which support the entrances. Performances were staged here until the 4th century CE. A pine grove surrounding the theater hides it from the entrance path.

Whereas the other key sites in the Argolid (Mycenae, Nafplion, and Tiryns) were built as fortified cities, the small state of Epidavros was designed as a sanctuary for healing. Its ruins, the remains of hospital rooms and sick wards, attest to the blurred boundaries between medicine, magic, and religion common in antiquity. From its founding in the 6th century BCE, Epidavros was dedicated to gods of medicine—first Maleatas, then Apollo, and finally Apollo's son Asclepius. Although Asclepius was first revered as a hero, he was later worshiped as a god. His symbol is the sacred snake coiled around his leg.

The museum is on the way from the theater to the ruins. The first room includes painted decorations from the ruins and huge stones containing inscriptions of hymns to Apollo and Asclepius while other inscriptions describe cures and accounts of repairs to the temple. Prominently featured are a number of lamps, votive offerings, surgical instruments including dagger-like scalpels, and a stunning selection of original statues. The second room houses copies of statues and other offerings from the cured (the originals are in the National Archaeology Museum in Athens). You'll find sculpture fragments from the temples of Asclepius and Artemis, a reconstruction of the *tholos* floor in the third room, and a spectacular Corinthian column collection. (Site open Tues.-Fri. 8am-7pm, Sat.-Sun. 8:30am-3pm, and Mon. 1-7pm. Admission 1000dr, students 500dr; free on Sun. Hold onto your ticket stub for the museum.) For information, call (0753) 220 09, but the guards speak only a limited amount of English.

Among the excavated structures are the **xenon,** or *katagogeion* (guest house), which originally consisted of 160 rooms for housing worshipers and the sick. Although now merely a scattering of doorsills and column bases, the sheer size of the guest-house's layout is impressive. West of the guest-house are the **baths,** dating from the Hellenistic period, where the god Asclepius gave the afflicted instructions and cures in their sleep. The **gymnasium,** to the north, was a center for musical and athletic festivals held in his honor. The remains of a small theater, the **Roman Odeon,** rest next to the gymnasium. Nearby are the stadium and the ruins of the **tholos,** a round building of mysterious function. Next to the *tholos* is an active archaeological site where you can see museums in the making. A drawing of the original *tholos* is in the museum on the site. There is little left of the **Temple of Asclepius** except for some scraps of foundation. Be sure to consult the boards posted around the site, which is extensive and sometimes confusing.

Try to visit Epidavros on a Friday or Saturday night from late June to mid-August when the **National Theater of Greece** and visiting companies perform plays from the classical Greek canon (Euripides, Sophocles, Aristophanes, etc.). Performances are at 9pm, and tickets can be purchased at the theater four hours before showtime (tel. (0753) 220 26). You can also purchase tickets in advance in Athens at the Athens Festival Box Office, 4 Stadiou St. (tel. 322 14 59 or 322 31 11, ext. 240). In Nafplion, you can buy tickets at Olympic Airways, 2 Bouboulinas St. (tel. 274 56), or Bourtzi Tours (tel. 226 91), near the bus station, 4 Syngrou St. For performances by the National Theater of Greece, tickets are also available at the Athens Box Office of the National Theater (tel. 522 32 42), at the corner of Agiou Konstandinou and Menandrou St. Tickets cost 1500-2500dr, 600dr for students. The rule prohibiting children under six is strictly enforced. All performances are in Greek, so bring your favorite translation.

If you're not going to Epidavros for the theater, it's best to make the town a daytrip from Nafplion, Athens, or Corinth, since the town of Epidavros is small and has very few accommodations. Bypass the Xenia, the expensive hotel near the site, and head for cheaper lodgings in the long, thin tourist village of **Ligouri,** 4km from Epidavros. The rooms at **Hotel Asklipios,** (tel. (0753) 222 51) are dark and plain, but inexpensive. (Singles 2000dr. Doubles 3500dr.) The **Hotel Koronis** also has inexpensive rooms and groovy pink bathrooms with tubs. Both are on the main drag.

If you're in Ligouri long enough for a meal, visit the **Restaurant Oasis** (tel. 220 62), the first place on the road from Nafplion. Here the Greeks outnumber the tourists, and the owners imbue their service and food with the spirit of celebration. To get to Ligouri, take the bus from Nafplion (3 per day, 1hr., 350dr). Hitchhiking the 4km between the theater and Ligouri is also common. *Let's Go* does not recommend hitchhiking as a means of travel. A different **bus** from Nafplion will drop you near the two campgrounds at **Paleo Epidavros,** 15km from the site.

On nights of performances, additional **KTEL** buses make the round-trip to Epidavros, leaving Nafplion at 7:30pm (1500dr). Private chartered buses may actually be cheaper (try Bourtzi Tours at 1100dr round-trip); from Tolo, the fare runs about 2000dr round-trip. Taxis from Ligouri cost approximately 700dr one-way.

Elias and Achaïa (Northwestern Peloponnese)
ΗΛΑ ΚΑΙ ΑΧΑΙ

In the rural provinces of Elias and Achaïa, tomatoes ripen beneath a blazing sun as tourists redden to a similar hue. The area between Pirgos and Patras, the respective capitals of Elias and Achaïa, is a veggie farmer's dream, its fertile ground abundant with tassled corn stalks groping toward the sun. The soft golden sands here, rivals to beaches anywhere, lie mostly undisturbed, but some areas are being "remade" into resorts that cater to visitors from northern Europe. The northwest region of the Peloponnese is called Great Achaïa. Its main city, Patras, is a busy transport hub on the coast.

Patras ΠΑΤΡΑΣ

Mountains encircle the eastern and western edges of the bustling harbor of Patras. The older and more sedate streets encompassing the *kastro* look down on a homogenity of high-rises languishing under a shroud of smog. Every day thousands of people pass through this burbling city, the third largest in Greece, as they shuttle between destinations all over the Peloponnese, as well as ports in the Ionian islands and Italy.

Orientation and Practical Information

If you're coming from Athens by car, you can choose between the **New National Road,** an expressway running inland along the Gulf of Corinth, and the slower but more scenic **Old National Road,** which hugs the coast. Those coming to Patras from the north can take a ferry from **Antirio,** in central Greece, across to **Rio** on the Peloponnese (7am-11pm, 4 per hr.; 15min.; 55dr, 600dr per car), and then hop on bus #6 from Rio to the station, four blocks up the hill from the main bus station in Patras, at Kanakari and Aratou St. (½hr., 50dr).

If you're arriving by boat from Brindisi or any of the Ionian islands, turn right as you leave customs onto **Iroon Polytechniou Street** to get to the center of town. From the bus station to the train station, the road curves and its name changes to **Othonos Amalias Street.** Just past the train station is the large **Platia Trion Simahon,** with palm trees, cafés, kiosks, and a large floral clock.

Tourist Office: GNTO (tel. 65 33 68 or -69, or 65 33 60 or -61), right outside customs. Friendly multilingual staff gives free detailed maps, and help with accommodations. Check here for complete bus and boat timetables, since each company supplies information only for its own services, as well for the addresses of **consulates.** Open daily 7am-9:30pm.

Currency Exchange: National Bank of Greece, Platia Trion Simahon, on the waterfront, just past the train station. Open Mon.-Thurs. 8am-2pm and 6-8:30pm, Fri. 8am-1:30pm and 6-8:30pm, Sat.-Sun. 11am-1pm and 6-8:30pm. Also at customs daily 7-10am and 12-8pm, and at the **mobile post office** just outside (see below).

American Express: Handled by **Albatros Travel,** 48 Othonos Amalias St., (tel. 22 09 93 or 22 46 09). Full travel services. Holds mail for cardholders.

Post Office: Mezonos Enzieni St. (tel. 27 77 59). Walk 2 blocks towards the bus station from customs and make a left onto Zaïmi—it's 3 blocks up on the left. Open Mon.-Fri. 7:30am-8pm, Sat. 7:30am-2pm, Sun. 9am-1:30pm. Also a **mobile post office** just outside customs. Open Mon.-Sat. 8am-8pm, Sun. 9am-6pm. **Postal Code:** 26001.

OTE: At customs. Open daily 7:30am-6:30pm and 7:30-10:30pm. For collect international calls, go to the OTE at Platia Trion Simahon, 2nd floor. Open daily 8am-10pm. Also west of town at the corner of Gounari St., up from the waterfront, and Kanakari St. **Telephone Code:** 061.

Train Station: At Othonos Amalias St. (tel. 27 36 94), 5 blocks to the right down the waterfront from customs. To: Athens (1300dr) via Corinth (750dr); Kalamata (4 per day, 6hr., 1200dr); Kalavrita via Dialopto (5 per day, 630dr); and Pirgos (7 per day until 8:06pm, 2hr., 630dr), transfer here for Olympia. Expect many delays and few seats—especially on the trains to Athens. Even if you have a railpass, reserve a seat at the ticket window before taking a train. **Luggage storage** 200dr per day; closes at 8pm. Ask at "Dafni" Travel, 5 Othonos Amalias St. (tel. 427 029) for InterRail information.

Buses: KTEL (tel. 222 271 or 273 997), 3½ blocks to the right, down the waterfront from customs. To: Athens (every hr. until 9:30pm, 4hr., 2400dr); Killini (in summer only, 8am and 2:45pm, 1½hr., 850dr); Kalamata (2 per day, 4hr., 2700dr); Pirgos (10 per day, 1200dr); Tripoli (2 per day until 2pm, 4hr, 2050dr); Delphi via Itea (3 per day until 9pm, 1350dr); Ioannina (3 per day, 2800dr); and Thessaloniki (3 per day until 9pm, 5550dr); Kalavrita (4 per day until 3:30pm, 1000dr); and Egion (every hr. until 10:15pm, 460dr). Buses to Lefkas leave from the intersection of Favierou and Konstantinoupoleos St., several blocks up from customs. **OSE** buses leave from the train station for Athens and Methoni. Some ferry companies also run their own quick, air-conditioned buses to and from Athens (2500dr); check when you buy your ticket.

International Bookstore: Romios Librarie, just behind the bus station on Kapsali. Their small selection is the largest around. Also keep an eye on the street-side kiosks. Open daily 8am-9pm.

Laundromat: at Zaimi and Korinthou, up 4 blocks from the waterfront. Wash and dry 1000dr. Open Mon.-Sat. 9am-9pm.

Tourist Police: Tel. 22 09 02. New office at Patreos Korinthion St. These friendly men in blue offer the same services as the GNTO. Free, vague map. Open 24 hrs.

Hospital: Two open on alternate days. **Agios Andreas** (tel. 22 28 12) 3-4km up Gounari. **Rio Hospital of Patras University** (tel. 99 91 11), is 5km away. The **Red Cross Emergency Station** (tel. 150), at Karoloua and Ag. Dionissiou St., several blocks from customs, dispenses only minor first aid. For an ambulance, dial 166.

Ferries

From Patras, boats go to Cephalonia, Ithaki, and Corfu, in addition to Italy's Brindisi, Bari, and Ancona. Most boats depart at night; check-in is two hours before departure. For ferries to Brindisi or the Ionian Islands, show up at customs at the main terminal; ferries to Bari and Ancona leave from a pier 1km to the west. Ticket prices fluctuate tremendously. In general, expect a discount if you are under 26, a student, or on a railpass and going to Brindisi. In high season, it's a good idea to make telephone reservations with one of the travel agents.

Ferry Tickets: Most boat agencies are scattered along the ½km between customs and Platia Trion Simahon. For tickets to Brindisi, go to **Mertikas Travel,** 36 Iroon Polytechniou (tel. 42 87 50 or 42 36 97; fax 43 21 64), left from the port. You can get cheaper tickets to Brindisi here than in **Igoumenitsa** or **Corfu.** Deck fare with Eurailpass 3000dr. Everyone must pay a 1500dr port tax. Departures for Brindisi are at 5 and 10pm, in off-season only at 10pm (18hr.). Meritikas will send tickets abroad; customers pay upon travel in *drachmae.* (Open daily 9am-9pm.) All ferry tickets to Brindisi allow for a stop-over in Corfu (otherwise 10hr., 3500dr). **Tsimaras Travel,** 14 Orthonas Amalias St. (tel. 27 77 83 or 27 09 48), sells tickets for most agencies, and for ferries to Sami on Cephalonia (4hr., 1500dr) and Vathi on Ithaki (5hr., 2800dr). Some convenient agencies with comprehensive information and tickets include **Venardakis Brothers,** 38 Orthonos Amalias (tel. 27 78 57 or 22 44 39); **Manolopoulos,** 35 Othonos Amalias (tel. 22 36 21), 1 block before the train station; **Central Ticketing,** at the same address (tel. 27 44 51); **Achaia Travel,** 7 Kolokotroni (tel. 22 26 29); and **Happy Travel,** 25 Othonos Amalias (tel. 22 60 53). Most agencies open daily 8am-9pm. Check with agencies for updated schedules and special, seasonal tickets to Italy. You can also purchase tickets in Athens.

Accommodations and Camping

Cheap accommodations are threaded through the tangle of buildings on Agiou Andreou St., one block up and parallel to the waterfront.

HI/IYHF Youth Hostel, 68 Iroon Polytechniou St. (tel. 42 72 78). As you leave the ferry, turn left and walk 1½km. This small turn-of-the-century mansion sat empty for 40 years after it was used as a German officers' headquarters in World War II. It's a bit cramped (8 beds to a room), but distinguished by its convenient location and view of the harbor. No curfew. Check-out 10:30am. Roof 800dr. Bed 1100dr. Sheets 100dr. Breakfast 300dr. Metered telephone makes international calls.

Hotel Hellas, 14 Agiou Nikolaou (tel. 273 352). Commodious, clean rooms and a huge hall bathtub fill this ancient building. Singles 2000dr. Doubles 3000dr. Triples 4500dr.

Hotel Parthenon, 25 Ermou St. (tel. 27 34 21), off Agiou Andreou. Big rooms in an old building. Singles 1200dr. Doubles 1800dr. Triples 2200dr.

Camping: Kavouri Camping (tel. 42 21 45), 2km east of town, next to the Patras swimming pool. The beach is too polluted for swimming. Crowded, but cheap. Take bus #1 from in front of Agios Dionysios Church; walk up Norman St. 1 block and turn left. 500dr per person, 200dr per tent. **Rio Camping** (tel. 99 15 85), 8km east of Patras. 800dr per person, 800dr per tent. **Rio Mare** (tel. 99 22 63), near Rio Camping. 700dr per person, 500dr per tent. Simply Grande.

Food

Stop by the new **Europa center** (tel. 43 48 01), at the corner of Othonos Amalias and Karolou, east past the KTEL bus station. This pink establishment caters to all the needs of a traveler: tickets to Italy, tourist information, a café and restaurant, stores, a disco, and clean toilets. (Open daily 6am-3am.) There are also many decent fast-food places near Platia Trion Simahon. The best *souvlaki* grills are past Platia Georgiou along Korinthou St., west of town. A reasonably-priced **fruit stand** livens up the corner of Ermou and Agiou Angreou, and another sits under a canopy at the corner of Aratou and Korinthiou up a few blocks from the water. Bakeries rise up from on the corner of Karolou and Agiou Dionysiou, and at the youth hostel on Odos Kourou. Friendly, family-run restaurants wait to welcome near the **kastro.** Dried fruits and nuts, yogurt, and ice cream entice in the many little shops near the *platia* with the botanical clock.

Sights

The largest Orthodox cathedral in Greece, **Agios Andreas,** is dedicated to St. Andrew, who lived and died in Patras. As he felt himself unworthy to die on the same kind of cross as Jesus, St. Andrew was martyred by crucifixion on an X-shaped cross. A little over 10 years ago, the Catholic Church in Rome presented the Bishop of Patras with the disciple's head, which is enshrined in an ornate gold and silver reliquary in the church, in addition to magnificently colored frescoes, a tremendous wooden carved chandelier, and a Christ looking his most Greek. (Open to tourists 9am-dusk, except during services. Absolutely no shorts, bare shoulders, or plunging necklines allowed. Photography and videotaping are also prohibited.) To get here, follow the water all the way to the western end of town, about 1½km from the port.

The Venetian **kastro** and surrounding park dominate the city. This 13th-century fortress was built on the ruins of the ancient acropolis, which was once the site of the temple of the Panachaïan Athena. Parts of the walls are still intact, and the view from the surviving battlements is pacifying. To get here, follow Agiou Nikolaou St. inland from town; you'll see the daunting staircase up ahead. **Taxis** also make the trek here. Up from Platia Vas. Georgiou, the **Ancient Odeum** has been preserved; the Patras Festival brings a series of performances here. Take a deserved brake at Patras's **bumper-car rink,** Athinon and Agiou Sofias St., one block up and four blocks left from customs (300dr for 10min.). The **Patras Archaeological Museum,** 42 Mezonos (tel. 27 50 70), next to Platia Olgas at the corner of Mezonos St. and Aratou, exhibits vases and other artifacts. (Open Tues.-Sun. 8:30am-3pm.)

A scenic traipse will lead you to the **Achaïa Clauss winery,** 9km southeast of town. The winery's German founder, Baron von Clauss, was dazed with lust for a doomed woman named Daphne. Upon her death, he took his blackest grapes and made a sweet, dark wine in her honor, called *Mavrodaphne*—"Black Daphne." (Tours 7:30am-1pm and 4-7pm; off-season 10am-4:30pm. Free.) Take bus #7 (20 min., 75dr) from the intersection of Kolokotroni and Kalakari St.

The summer **Patras International Arts Festival** (festival office tel. 33 63 90) offers a volcano of events in the Ancient Odeum at the Patras *kastro* and at the castle at Rion.

The GNTO, tourist police, and the Festival Center Offices on the waterfront west of town will have more current information. The **carnival season** in Patras begins around January 17 every year, and lasts until Ash Wednesday (Feb. 24 in 1993). The locals talk about *karnivali* as that indescribable energy that sweeps through town. There are feasts and parties every night, with people of all ages dancing in the streets. Patras's bash is reputed to be the "best carnival in Greece."

Near Patras

A one-hour train ride east from Patras will take you to the town of **Diakofto**. From here, take the tiny rack-railway train and marvel at the glorious landscape (400dr). Midway to Kalavrita the train stops in Zachlorou and allows hikers and donkey-renters to climb to **Mega Spilaeou.** As the train ambles up the mountainous range, a whorling waterfall winds through the rocks alongside and under the train tracks. If you arrive hours before the next train, catch the **bus** to Kalavrita on the sidewalk just out in front of the pharmacy and hotel (800dr). The folks at the newspaper shop down the street have schedule information. The bus trip, winding through cherry orchards and tiny mountain villages, is stupefying. The village of **Kalavrita**, at the end of the line, is also a popular ski resort. From the train station, follow Agiou Alexiou St. straight up into the town—after four blocks you'll reach the **OTE** at the corner of Ag. Alexiou and Kommenou St. (Open Mon.-Sat. 7:30am-10pm.) The police (tel. 233 33) are three blocks beyond the OTE, off Ag. Alexiou at 7 Fotina St. (Open 24 hrs.) The main square is across from the large church a few blocks up from the train station. The **post office** is on the square (open Mon.-Fri. 7:30am-2pm). There's a **bank** on 25th Martiou, leading to the main square. The **Hotel Paradissos** (tel. 222 10) on Kallimani St. offers pleasant rooms with super-clean bathrooms. (Singles 2000dr. Doubles 5000dr. Triples 6000dr.) Down the street close to the main square, **Hotel Maria** (tel. 222 96) offers impressive rooms with private baths. (Singles 2500dr. Doubles 3500dr. Triples 4500dr.) Tidy rooms and breezy balconies can be found across the street at the **Hotel Magas Alexandris** (doubles 2800dr). The **bus station** is at the end of Kallimani St. The **postal code** is 25001; the **telephone code** is 0692.

The famous monastery of **Mega Spilaeon** is 9km away. The bus from Diakofto goes right past the monastery, 1km away, or you can be magically transported here by a town taxi (3000dr round-trip; the driver will wait 30min.). A monk will greet you and give you a guided tour through the museum and church. The extensive museum collection inclues an intricate 350-year-old cross and an icon of the Theotokos (Mother of God), said to have been made by St. Luke.

Five **trains** per day leave Kalavrita, stopping at Zachlorou, close to the monastery, on their way to Diakofto. Trains leave from here for Patras (last train at 6:45pm, 280dr) and Athens (last train at 7:41pm, 820dr).

Killini ΚΥΛΛΙΝΗΣ

Most travelers come to Killini simply to catch the ferries to Zakinthos and Cephalonia. If you're stuck here for any length of time, hunker down at Killini's broad, sandy beach. The few tourists who spend time here—mostly Greek, French, and Italian—neither spoil the town's uncommercial air nor rush its leisurely tempo.

Buses travel to Killini from Pirgos (6 per day until 2:35pm, 1hr., 760dr) and Patras (1 per day, 1½hr., 950dr). If you miss the bus from Patras, take the bus to Lehena (10 per day, 1½hr., 500dr); from there, buses continue to Killini (11:20am and 2:45pm, 20min., 70dr). Taxis also go from Lehena to Killini (1500dr). A daily bus to Athens leaves Killini at 9:30am. **Ferries** sail from Killini to Zakinthos (7 per day, 1½hr., 780dr), and Cephalonia (2 per day, 700dr). You can buy boat tickets on the dock. To get to Patras or Athens from Killini, take a bus from the dock.

The amble up toward town from the dock takes you to the **police** (tel. 922 02). The **tourist** and **port police** (tel. 922 11) are on the dock. (Open 24 hrs.) From the police station, walk a few blocks with the water on your left to reach the **OTE,** inside a tiny corner store. (Open daily in summer 8am-1pm and 3-10pm.) The **post office** is a few blocks farther down, on a side street leading inland. (Open 7:30am-2pm.) The **postal code** is 27068; the **telephone code** is 0623.

The cheapest rooms in Killini are in *dhomatia* along Glaretzas St., one block above the beach and parallel to the water. The **Glaretzas Hotel** (tel. 923 97) has light, fresh rooms with Scandinavian-revival decor. (Doubles with bath 5500dr.) Hardy backpackers have been known to freelance **camp** on the beach, even though it's illegal. Eat at the *psistaria* **O Choriatis** on Glaretzas St., an unassuming establishment asking only 500dr for spicy *yemista* (stuffed tomatoes).

Twenty km from Killini lounge the Frankish **Chlemoutsi Castle** and the mineral springs of **Loutra Killinis,** a well-manicured resort with a long beach. Getting to either place is difficult unless you have your own transportation or are willing to pay for a taxi (1000dr to the castle, 2500dr to Loutra) at the square with a fountain. At the square with the water fountain, buses leave for Loutra (8 per day, 100dr), and will let you off at either the turn-off to the castle, the mineral springs, or the excellent camping area, **Camping Killinis,** close to the sea with a market and hot showers (tel. 96 25 40; 1000dr per person, 400dr per tent). Three **buses** per day leave Loutra for the castle.

Pirgos ΠΥΡΓΟΣ

There's not an overabundance of activity in Pirgos, a sprawling commercial town on the western coast, but you're almost certain to pass through here on the way to Olympia, 21km to the east. Be warned that all of the hotels here are somewhat expensive. To get to the bus depot veer slightly left at the Hotel Olympos, then turn right at the supermarket on Manolopoulou St.; the chaotic bus station is on the left 50m ahead, and right next door **KTEL** offers free luggage storage. (This is a great idea for daytrips to Olympia.) **KTEL buses** (tel. 223 72 or 225 92) leave from Manolopolo St. for: Olympia (16 per day until 9pm, 45min., 260dr); Killini (6 per day until 2:35pm, 1hr., 700dr); Kiparissia (2 per day until 1:15pm, 1hr., 750dr); Kalamata (2 per day until 4:05pm, 2hr., 1400dr); Tripolis (3 per day until 5pm, 4hr., 1800dr); Athens (10 per day until 9:30pm, 5hr., 3500dr); Patras (10 per day until 8pm, 2hr., 1200dr); Andritsena (2 per day, 1½hr., 750dr); and Lehena (7 per day, 1hr.). There are no tourist offices in Pirgos. The **police,** though, may be of some assistance (tel. 236 85; open 24 hrs.). To reach them on Karkavitsa St., turn left just before the Hotel Olympos. The **OTE** is between the bus and train stations. (Open daily 7am-midnight.) The **post office** is on Kon. Kanari St., several blocks up the hill to the left of the OTE; ask for directions, because it's tough to find. (Open Mon.-Fri. 7:30am-2pm.) The **Commercial Bank** is on the street from the train station, 300m past the turn-off for the bus station. (Open Mon.-Thurs. 8am-2pm, Fri. 8am-1:30pm.) Pirgos's **postal code** is 27100; the **telephone code** is 0621.

Try the **Hotel Pantheon** (tel. 297 47), at 7 Themistokleous St. and Papaflessa St.; as you leave the train station and turn left, the street is your first right. (Doubles with bath 5700dr, negotiable.) For **English-language newspapers** and magazines, go to the shop at the corner of 28th Octovriou St. and the main square.

Olympia ΟΛΥΜΠΙΑ

When the ancient games were held in Olympia, crowds bivouacked in a huge tent city where vendors hawked souvenirs and performers entertained crowds with countless diversions. Little has changed over the centuries; only now in the modern Olympia, about ½km from the ancient ruins, hotels and tourist shops replace the tents. If you need a break from the heat, the shops, and the ancient rocks, an hour's walk takes you through pastures to the goat-trodden groves that have ringed Olympia for ages. To find them, turn right down a gravel road where the sign says "camping forbidden," on the way to the ancient site.

Orientation and Practical Information

Modern Olympia essentially consists of one long street, **Kondili Avenue.** About 500m past the tourist office across the river, you'll come to the archaeological site and the New Museum (see Ancient Olympia). On the other side of town, towards Pirgos, sports enthusiasts will find the **Museum of the Olympic Games,** a knockout. Located on Angerinou St., it is two blocks uphill from Kondili Ave. (Open Mon.-Sat. 8am-3:30pm, Sun. 9am-4:30pm. Admission 400dr.)

Most tourist shops open late (10:30am) and close late (10:30pm). Since the town caters solely to tourists, many restaurants and fast food places are open 24 hrs.

Tourist Office: Kondili Ave. (tel. 231 25), on the eastern side of town, towards the ruins. Helpful transportation information, an international telephone, and money exchange. Open in summer daily 9am-9pm.

Currency Exchange: National and **Commercial Banks** both on Kondili Ave. Open Mon.-Thurs. 8am-1pm, Fri. 8am-1:30pm.

Post Office: On an uphill side street, 1 block east of the tourist office. Open Mon.-Fri. 8am-2pm, Sat. 7:30am-2pm, Sun. 9am-1:30pm. **Postal Code:** 27065.

OTE: Kondili Ave., just past the post office. Open daily 9am-2pm and 5pm-10pm. **Telephone Code:** 0624.

Bus Station: The 2 bus stops (to Pirgos and to Tripolis) are clearly marked in front of the Hotel Hereon on Kondili Ave. To: Pirgos (13-17 per day, 10 on Sun., 45min., 250dr); and Tripolis (9:20am, 1:20pm, and 5:20pm, 4hr., 1500dr). Change at Pirgos for other points on the western Peloponnese. For Kalamata, change at Alfios (5 stops).

Bookstores: Galerie Orpheas, 1 block from the tourist police, carries a good selection of guide books and translations of Greek classics. Open 8am-11pm.

Hospital: Tel. 222 22. On the road to Camping Alpheios; follow the signs.

Police: 1 Em. Kountsa St. (tel. 225 50 or 221 00), ½ block from the tourist office.

Accommodations, Camping, and Food

If all you want is a cheap place to crash, head for the youth hostel. Otherwise, you can choose from dozens of inexpensive hotels, most of which offer private baths, balconies, and immaculate modern rooms. *Dhomatia* in Olympia all go for about the same price (singles 1500dr, doubles 2000dr), and the bulk of them line Spiliopoulou St., the road parallel to and one block up from Kondili Ave.

Youth Hostel (HI/IYHF), 18 Kondili Ave. (tel. 225 80). Narrow bunk beds line plain rooms. Curfew 11:45pm. Check-out 10am. HI/IYHF cards rarely requested. 800dr. Sheets 200dr. Hot showers 150dr. Luggage storage 200dr per day.

Hotel Hereon, Kondili Ave. (tel. 225 49), where the buses stop. Hostel-like atmosphere. Clean rooms. Singles 1500dr. Doubles 2500dr. Triples 3500dr. Prices negotiable.

Hotel Alexandros, 5 Spiliopoulou St. (tel. 225 36), parallel to and above Kondili Ave. Nice management and clean airy rooms. Doubles 3500dr. Triples with bath 4500dr.

Hotel Praxiteles, 7 Spiliopoulou St. (tel. 225 92). Next door to Alexandros. Unsullied rooms. Singles 2500dr. Doubles 3500dr. Triples with bath 4000dr.

Dhomatia: the **Spiliopoulon** family rents cheery rooms near the train station (walk out the door facing the tracks and turn right; tel. 229 16, about 1500dr per person). Look for the blue sign or inquire at the Ambrosia Restaurant. Mention *Let's Go* and get a 10% discount.

Camping: Camping Diana (tel. 223 14), just 200m uphill from Kondili Ave.—follow the signs. The most convenient. Shaded sites, sparkling facilities, electricity (hot showers 7-9am and 6-8pm), swimming pool, and a well-stocked store. Reception open 8am-10pm. 700dr per person, 500dr per tent, 10% reduction for students. If they're full, try **Camping Olympia** (tel. 227 45), 1km west on the main road to Pirgos (550dr per person, 450dr per tent), or **Camping Alphios,** (tel. 229 50), a 1km trek uphill from town, 4 blocks west of the tourist office—follow the signs from Tsoreka St. (550dr per person, 350dr per tent). Both sites have standard facilities.

Shop around for restaurants—most are overpriced tourist traps. In the center of town near the taxi stand, **Ambrosia** offers tasty, reasonably priced meals and a 10% discount from the menu to all *Let's Go* users. Continental breakfasts run about 400dr in Olympia, but the **Stronka** pastry shop, on the road to the Museum of the Olympic Games, serves an extraordinary *yoghurti meli* (yogurt with honey, 400dr). **Zorba's** is the only night spot.

Ancient Olympia

The legendary site between the Kladeo and Alpheos Rivers was less a city than an event. Here, the leaders of rival city states shed their protective armor and congregated in peace to enjoy the games and make offerings to the gods.

Olympia was always a place of worship. Initially, shrines were built here, first to the pre-Hellenic goddesses, then to the ancient god Kronos (meaning time), father of the little Zeusling, then to Zeus himself. In later years, the Olympiad celebrated men's physical form and athletic achievements. Women (except for the Priestess of Demeter) were not invited to participate in or attend the games; Pausanias, the Peloponnesian travel writer of the 2nd century CE, wrote of the cliff off of which women were hurled if they were caught entering the Olympic assembly.

In 776 BCE, young men from cities all over Greece (and later Rome) gathered in Olympia for the quadrennial festival of Olympian Zeus and the athletic competition that accompanied it. The games began as a simple footrace and wrestling match, but gradually expanded to a five-day extravaganza including six different kinds of races, boxing, no-holds-barred wrestling (*pankration*), regular wrestling, and the pentathlon (wrestling, discus toss, javelin throw, long jump, and 1 stadium-length race). The games themselves commanded respect; whereas Greek cities under normal circumstances perpetually battled each other, when the Olympic Truce was declared (for up to 3 months) to facilitate transit, warring subsided completely. The truce was violated only twice during the history of the games.

Only games officials were permitted in the sacred town of Olympia. The center of town was reserved for the **Altis,** a walled enclosure or sacred grove of Zeus. On the far east side were the **stadium** and the **echo stoa,** which was said to have had a seven-fold echo. Facilities for both administrators and participants comprised the remaining three sides of the Altis. Over the centuries, council houses, drug testing facilities, and treasuries were added to the site. In addition, victors often built monuments to the gods here; these once numbered 3000. Christian Emperor Theodosius I discontinued the games in 393 CE because he felt the festival was too intimately connected with the worship of Zeus. In 426 CE, his son Theodosius II called for the destruction of the "pagan sanctuary" of Olympia.

Today, the former site of the Olympics wallows in disappointing disarray. A guide and map are vital as the ruins are poorly marked or marked only in Greek and German. Two thorough guides are available at the site: the red *Olympia: Complete Guide* by Spyros Photinos (1000dr); and the blue *Guide to the Museum and Sanctuary* by A. and N. Yalonnis (1400dr). The thigh-high remains of the Gymnasium, dating from the 2nd century BCE, lie inside the main gate. To the left as you enter is the **Prytaneion,** with its sacred hearth. Past the Gymnasium stand the re-erected columns of the **Palaestra.** This building was the wrestling school, a place for athletes to practice and dress, and philosophers to ruminate. The next group of buildings include the **workshop of Phidias,** the famous artist (supposedly the creator of the ivory and gold statue of Athena for the Parthenon) who was commissioned to produce a sculpture for the site. His tools, terra-cotta molds, and a cup bearing his name turned up during excavations. Farther on is the huge **Leonidaion,** the former lodgings of all game officials.

The colossal **Temple of Zeus** dominated the entire complex. Parts of the original mosaic floor can still be seen on the temple base. The nave of the temple once housed Phidias's 13m statue of Zeus, reckoned by the Greeks to be one of the seven wonders of the ancient world. Emperor Theodosius ordered that the gold and ivory statue be brought to Constantinople, where a fire destroyed it in 475 CE.

On the northern edge of the Altis are the dignified remains of the **Temple of Hera** (7th century BCE), the oldest and best-preserved building on the site, and the oldest Doric temple in Greece. Originally built for both Zeus and Hera, it was devoted solely to the goddess when Zeus moved to separate quarters to the south. The temple testifies to the ancient worship of female deities, fecundity, and mother earth. To this day, the Olympic flame is lit here and borne to the site of the modern games by the necessary vehicles, then runners, school children, Hell's Angels, and anyone else wishing to join the panoply.

The archway on the east end of the Altis leads to the **stadium.** As originally constructed, the arena's artificial banks could accommodate some 40,000 spectators. The **judges' stand,** a paved area on the south side, is still in place, as are the starting and finishing lines. Beyond the stadium flows the Alpheos River, said to run underground all the way to Sicily, which Hercules once found handy when he had to clean the Aegean stables. (Site open Mon.-Fri. 8am-7pm, Sat.-Sun. 8:30am-3pm. Admission 1000dr, students 500dr.) Public bathrooms and water fountains are inside the site.

The gleaming **New Museum,** across the street from the site, displays two pediments from the destroyed Temple of Zeus, a huge head of Hera, and a statue of Hermes, supposedly the work of the 4th-century sculptor Praxiteles. (Open Mon. 12:30pm-7pm, Tues.-Fri. 8am-7pm, Sat.-Sun. 8:30am-3pm. Admission 1000dr, students 550dr. Cameras with flash, 500dr. Video cameras 1000dr.)

Arcadia (Central Peloponnese) ΑΡΚΑΔΙΑ

Poets since Theocritus have fancied Arcadia as the archetypal scene of pastoral pleasure and quietude. Gods, too, appreciated Arcadia—Pan and Bacchus chose this lush, mountain-ringed land as the site for their gleeful dances. Although today's rumble of buses and cargo have disrupted Arcadia's serenity, shepherds still roam the hills, meandering past the secluded monasteries and picturesque mountain villages.

Herodotus claims that the Arcadian people were the first settlers of the Peloponnese, and that their region figures prominently in Greek mythology. Arcadia was named for Arcas, one of Zeus's sons by Callisto. Lycaeon, Callisto's father, chopped Arcas into bite-sized pieces and served him to Zeus for dinner—just to see if Zeus would notice. Well, Zeus did notice, and promptly transmogrified the murderer into a wolf, disgorged Arcas, and revived the bits. The grown Arcas, to celebrate his reincarnation, embarked on a hunting expedition and encountered a bear: his mother Callisto whom the jealous Hera had blighted. The young man stood ready to kill Callisto when Zeus intervened. First he placed Callisto in the heavens as Ursa Major then Arcas as the constellation Ursa Minor (the Big and Little Dipper).

Doubtless, you will fare better following the region's two main routes to explore the area's countless remote villages. Traveling from the west, the road winds inland from Pirgos, continuing through Olympia on the way to Tripolis, the boisterous capital of Arcadia. From the east, meeting the border of the Argolid, the road passes through Tripolis and continues through the more tranquil surrounding orchards of Tegea to the south and Mantinea to the north.

Tripolis ΤΡΙΠΟΛΗ

Tripolis is the transportation hub of Arcadia, and a visit here includes all the thrills of a thriving Greek metropolis: suicidal drivers billow by at break neck speeds and the general brouhaha of the crowded streets underscores the city's chaotic air. Close to the ruins at Tegea and Mantinea, Tripolis is the departure point for some wonderful mountain villages. Since bus connections to out-lying villages often run only twice a day, you may have to stay here overnight. A plethora of wealthy Greeks living abroad return to their Arcadian homeland for the summer months and are willing to pay through the nose for the privilege of staying here; unfortunately, you'll have to as well.

Orientation and Practical Information

Most buses arrive at the Arcadias bus station in the big plaza, **Kolokotroni,** marked by the Arcadia Hotel. Five blocks down Georgion St., the unmarked street next to the Arcadia on the left leads to **Platia Agios Vasiliou,** an even bigger square marked by the Church of Agios Vasilios. The **bus station, OTE, police station, tourist office,** and **post office** are on sidestreets off Platia Agios Vasiliou. Buses to points south and to Patras leave from the KTEL Messinia café across from the train station. To get into the center of town from the train station, walk up Lagopati St. (directly in front of the station) and take a left on Benizelou St.; you'll arrive at Plateia Koloktroni. A dense and disorienting map hangs on the wall in the Galaxy Hotel on Plateia Agiou Vasiliou.

Tripolis Tourist Office: Tel. 23 93 92, in the town hall down Ethnikis Anistasis St. (Look for the flag.) This new office provides maps, books, and information on Arcadia. Open 7am-2:30pm.

Currency Exchange: National Bank, on Platia Agios Vasiliou. Open Mon.-Thurs. 8am-2pm, Fri. 8am-1:30pm. There are many other banks throughout the city.

Post Office: Plapouta St. Walk through the coffee shops in the corner of Platia Agios Vasiliou, next to the Galaxias Hotel. Open Mon.-Fri. 7:30am-2pm. **Postal Code:** 22100.

OTE: #29, 28 Oktovriou St. From Platia Agios Vasiliou, take Ethnikis Anistasis St. (on the right), and then bear left immediately on 28 Oktovriou St. Open 24 hrs. **Telephone Code:** 071.

Trains: The **train station** (tel. 22 24 02 or 22 52 24) is 1km west of Kolokotroni Plaza. Trains from Tripolis go northeast to Athens (5 per day, last at 5:44pm, 5hr., 1800dr), stopping in Corinth (2½hr., 600dr) and Argos (1½hr., 340dr); 5 trains per day go southwest to Kalamata (last at 1:48pm, 3hr., 600dr).

Buses: Arcadias Station (tel. 22 25 60 or 22 26 50) dispatches buses to: Athens (13 per day, 5am-8:45pm, 2hr., 1900dr); Dimitsana (at 12:45pm and 6:15pm, 1½hr., 850dr); Pirgos (3 per day, last at 6pm, 4hr., 1800dr); Andritsena (at 5:30am and 11:30am, 1hr., 900dr); and Megalopolis (8 per day from 4:45am-7:15pm, 30min., 420dr). Buses leave from the kiosk at Plateia Kolokotroni for Tegea and Mantinea (blue buses) every hr. 7am-9pm, or more frequently depending on demand (15min., 100dr). From the **KTEL Messinia and Laconia** bus depot across the street from the train station, you can take buses to: Kalamata (3 per day, 1050dr); Pylos (2 per day, 1650dr); and Sparta (9 per day, 700dr).

International Bookstore: Xartis, on Platia Agios Vasiliou, sells English newspapers and magazines. *Et in Arcadia Ego ...*

Hospital: Dial 23 85 42 for emergency or medical assistance. **Police:** Ethnikis Anistasis St. (tel. 22 24 11), off the right-hand side of Platia Agios Vasiliou across from the theater—go to the 2nd floor. Open 24 hrs.

Accommodations, Food and Entertainment

Tripolis is better suited for the numerous conventions in town than for budget travelers. **Hotel Ikinouria** (tel. 22 24 63) has small, dismal rooms and a closed shower, but it's the cheapest. (Singles 1800dr. Doubles 3500dr. Showers 200dr.) From Plateia Kolokotroni, walk down Ligouriou St. (also known as "Lavraki" or "the road to Sparta"); it's a block past the fruitstand/toilet paper merchant on the left. **Hotel Alex,** 26 Vas. Georgios (King George) St. (tel. 223 11), is close to the bus station but has only standard, more expensive rooms; try bargaining. (Singles 3000dr, with bath 3200dr. Doubles 4500dr, with bath 4700dr.) Camping near or around Tripolis is inconceivable. There are no official camp sites near the city and any unofficial camping is prohibited by the local authorities, and besides, gypsies have taken all the good sites. Conclusion: don't spend the night. Besides, nightlife here is unexciting: just a lot of expensive discos. The real entertainment in Tripolis during the summer is at the cultural events at Plateia Areos (400m from Plateia Agios Vasiliou) and at the nearby villages. Look for posters for dance groups, theatrical performances, and choirs. Also, keep an eye out for

"ΙΕΡΑ ΠΑΝΥΓΥΠΣ" (festival), advertising for festivals in small villages. You can find Greek-style parties in the *platias*.

Souvlaki fans rave about the restaurant located in the bus station. Sick of bus stations, you say? Try **To Konaki,** an agreeable restaurant off the main square on Petropoulou St. Clean, with attentive service and piquant *tzaziki* (200dr) or scrumptious *saganaki* (400dr). Opens for dinner around 9pm.

The new **Archaeological Museum** of Tripolis is on Evangelistrias St., in the yellow building with a riot of redolent blossoms in the garden. It's packed with decorated pottery from the Paleokastro *tholos* tombs. (Open Tues.-Sat. 7:30am-3pm, Sun. 9am-2:30pm. Free.)

Near Tripolis

For centuries in ancient times, the cities of **Tegea** and **Mantinea** maintained a fierce rivalry. The cities may be gone now, but the rivalry endures, as every day the ruins of these cities compete for tourists' attention. And the winner is...Tegea, with three times as much bus traffic than Mantinea. Mantinea's city walls, smack in the middle of a plain rather than in the usual position on top of a hill or mountain, are enough to amuse even the cynical tourist, but Tegea does have a bit more to offer.

To reach the ruins of Tegea, take a blue bus from the kiosk at Plateia Kolokotroni. The **museum** displays elaborately decorated marble thrones-of-honor, large sculpted heads of Hercules and Asclepios, and dramatic friezes of lions. (Open Tues.-Sun. 8:30am-3pm. Admission 300dr, students 200dr.) Outside the museum, a sign points toward the site of the 4th-century BCE **Temple of Athena Alea.** Unfortunately, in recent times, the neighborhood of modern Tegea has been encroaching on the remains of the huge building. The lived-in look is slowly replacing that of the divine.

Karitena ΚΑΡΙΤΑΙΝΑ

Karitena is a must-see on your swing through Arcadia. On the road between disgustingly grimy Megalopolis and sleepy Andritsena, this medieval village is the most picturesque village on the Peloponnese. There's a reason Karitena (pop. 250) is pictured on the 5000 *drachmae* bill. Built on a mountainside, the three- to five-story medieval houses built of mud, cement, and stone make for a post-card image that you'll never forget. Climb up to the 12th-century **Frankish castle** for a view of the peaks and the soaring valley of the Alfios River below. On the way down, visit the ruins of **Kolokotronis's House** on the hillside. To get to the castle, follow the Greek signs for "ΤΟΦΠΟΥΡΙΟΝ" from the square, and mount the treacherous steps. Bus connections to Karitena are infrequent, but once there many hitch a ride on the highway below. *Let's Go* does not recommend hitchhiking as a means of travel, and solo women should never hitchhike.

If you want to visit the 13th-century church of **Agios Nikolaos,** go to the main square and ask for George, who has the key to the church. Villagers still celebrate St. Nikolas Day (Dec. 6th), which remembers the series of laws passed during the Turkish occupation that made church attendance punishable by death. The medieval bridge hunched beneath the modern bridge on the main road below town is a Frankish remain.

The **post office** is downhill from the main square. (Open 7:30am-2:15pm.) The **police** (tel. 312 05) are located uphill and to the right of the square. There is no OTE, but the *kafeneion* (coffee shop) has a metered phone. The **public toilet** is on the main road, near the post office. Karitena's **postal code** is 27061; its **telephone code** is 0791.

For accommodations, try **Stamata Kondopoulo's** (tel. 312 62) small but fastidiously kept rooms across from the post office. (You'll see a sign. Singles 1800dr. Doubles 3500dr.) For rooms a little farther out of town, the modern **Hotel Karitena** (tel. 312 03; follow the signs) uphill from the square and to the right. The terrace provides fabulous views. (Singles 1800dr. Doubles 3500dr. Triples 4050dr.)

Buses traveling between Megalopolis and Andritsena stop in Karitena, except on Monday and Friday when they'll let you off below at the crossroads (it's a steep uphill hike to the town). Check in the café for up-to-date bus information. Buses travel to Andritsena (at 5:45am and 12:30pm, 40min., 350dr) and Megalopolis (at 9am and 3:30pm, 20min., 250dr).

Andritsena ΑΝΔΡΙΤΣΑΙΝΑ

Andritsena is falling apart and that's what makes it lovable. A haphazard tumble of red-roofed old houses and shops with faded, speckled façades sprawls endearingly along a mountainside. Crumbling balconies cast shadows across the tiny curving pathways of Andritsena's "streets." Needless to say, this is not a town vibrating with hordes of high-energized tourists or the roar of frequent buses. If you decide to stay overnight (infrequent bus connections might make your decision for you), mellow out with the villagers or languidly sip coffee in a café. Chances are you won't even notice that there isn't anything else to do. If you yearn passionately for touristy activity, visit the little **folk museum** with its collection of Andritsenian curiosities and an ingenious fly-catcher. (Open daily 11am-1pm and 5-6pm. Donation requested.) **Hotel Pan** (tel. 222 13), next to the Shell station, is the best option for blessed, coveted slumber (doubles 3800dr).

Andritsena is one and a half hours west of Megalopolis and the same distance east of Pirgos. Buses from Megalopolis (1¼hr., 650dr); Tripolis (3hr., 950dr); Argos (1450dr); Athens (6½hr., 27,501dr); and Karitena (300dr) lurch into mountains of red clay and green terraces. The **bus station** is at the Café Platinea, around the corner from the Shell station on the Pirgos side of town. Another bus station operates out of the Café Apollon in the main square. Departures to Pirgos (daily at 8am and 2pm, 750dr).

In town, the **police** (tel. 222 09 and 222 31) are at #11 on the Shell station side of the square. (Open 24 hrs.) The **post office** (open Mon.-Fri. 7:30am-2pm) and **banks** (open Mon.-Thurs. 8am-2pm, Fri. 8am-1:30pm) are next to the Shell station. The **OTE** is off the main street, near the church. (Open Mon.-Fri. 7:30am-3pm.) For the **clinic,** dial 222 10 or 222 11. Andritsena's **postal code** is 27061; the **telephone code** is 0626.

Near Andritsena: Vassae

> Like stranded ice when freshets die These shattered
> marbles tumbled lie; They trouble me. What so-
> lace?—Old in inexhaustion, Interred alive from
> storms of fortune, The quarries be!
> —Herman Melville, on seeing Vassae

Rising stately on the slopes of Mt. Kotilion, the **Temple of Epicurus Apollo** was built in tribute to Apollo, for he saved the people of Phygalia from a plague. Iktinos, the architect commissioned to build the monument in 420 BCE, later earned a fat fee by designing the Parthenon. The extant columns are thought to be the first of the Corinthian design.

Vassae remains sacred and solitary. The approach from Andritsena slithers up along cliffs for 14km, sneaking between smooth pinnacles of rock. At last, the temple appears, pillar fragments littering its ancient **agora.** Though grand, the temple is now veiled by a canopy and entombed by scaffolding to protect it from acid rain.   Those who hitchhike get to Vassae (there is no bus) by waiting at the turn-off just outside Andritsena on the road to Pirgos and sweating profusely. Some travelers wait around the center of town outside a café and flag down cars with foreign license plates. Others share a **taxi** from Andritsena (about 2000-2500dr, negotiable). Make it clear from the start that the rate is for the group; some drivers may try to charge by person. You may wish to walk back to town (it takes 3½hr. over the hills).

Dimitsana and Stemnitsa
ΔΗΜΗΤΣΑΝΑ ΚΑΙ ΣΤΕΜΝΙΤΣΑ

The Erimanthos, Menalo, and Oligirtos mountain ranges separate the ancient settlements of the western Peloponnese from the beach resorts of the east. Some have called this area of the central Peloponnese "the Switzerland of Greece": here the mountains are ancient and gnarled, and green vegetation clings to all but the highest summits. Tucked into the mountains west of Tripolis, the little villages of Dimitsana and Stemnitsa make good bases for hiking. Along the path of the Lousias River rest several silently inspiring monasteries. (When making these long treks, don't be fooled by Greece's daytime heat; mountain towns get unbelievably chilly after twilight.) **Buses** run from Tripolis to Dimitsana at 1:45pm and 6pm, (1½hr., 800dr.), returning at 8:30am, 2pm, and 4pm. Two buses daily also pass by on their way to and from Olympia and Pirgos in the western Peloponnese; you can catch them in the area near the post office at 7pm or at the café, 6km north at **Karkalou,** on the main highway. Ask at the police or in the cafés for details since not all buses stop in Dimitsana (if you don't speak Greek well, have them write out the times and specify Dimitsana or Karkaion).

In **Dimitsana** the bus will deposit you in front of a café next to the **post office.** (Open Mon.-Fri. 7:45am-2:15pm.) The **taxi** office is up the road a bit from the post office. (Taxi to Karkalou, about 700dr.) Nearby you'll find Platia Pesonton Labardopoulou St., the main road. A little further from the square is Nikolaou Makris St., off the main road toward the mountain. The helpful **police** are along this cobblestone path. There's not always anyone there who speaks English (tel. 312 05; open 24 hrs.). A little farther, at #110 and 112 Nikolaou Makris, are the **museum** and the **library** (open daily 8am-2pm). The town has been an educational center for more than 300 years; these two institutions commemorate its scholarly achievements.

Returning to the main road and continuing on you'll reach the **OTE,** 402 Labardopoulou St. (Open Mon.-Fri. 7:30am-3:10pm.) The **bank** is at #406 just past the OTE. (Open Mon.-Thurs. 8am-2pm, Fri. 8am-1:30pm.) The only lodging in town is the **Hotel Dimitsana,** 100m south of town on the main road. The rooms here don't live up to the Swiss chalet exterior, but all rooms have private baths. (Singles 3500dr. Doubles 4800dr. Breakfast 700dr. Be certain to specify "no breakfast" before accepting a room or they might charge you for one anyway.) Dimitsana's main square has a shop for groceries and a *souvlaki* restaurant. Dimitsana's **postal code** is 22007; its **telephone code** is 0795.

From Dimitsana, you can hike 11km along the main road through wonder-evoking scenery to **Stemnitsa.** Stemnitsa's brownstone and pinewood houses, set serenely on the steep mountainside, have been tastefully reconstructed. The village also has a gorgeous hotel on the main road, **Hotel Triokolonion** (tel. 812 97; singles 1800dr, with private bath 3600dr; doubles 3500dr, with private bath 7000dr). The **post office** is located behind the church in the main square (open 7:30am-2:30pm). The central square hosts a telephone booth, outdoor cafés and *tavernas.* Try **Kafe Psigoporio** for a sumptuous Greek salad (450dr).

From Stemnitsa, you can explore the mountains along narrow paths that crawl into the interior. Follow the main road out of town toward Megalopolis. On the left you'll see an arrow pointing to the small villages. Turn onto the concrete road for 20m and then up the stepped path on the right. The locals follow this route from their remote mountain settlements to bring goat milk and herbs to town. Donkeys bearing goods lumber down the rocks of the deeper mountain areas. Northeast from here is the Olympia-Tripolis highway at **Vitina** (15km east of Karkalou), where there are a fair number of rooms-to-let as well as an excess of woodwork shops. If you head west toward Olympia, stop in **Langadia,** which looks out over ravines and surging mountains. The village is constructed almost vertically; even the church graveyard is terraced. There's a **post office** at the eastern edge of town; the western edge holds the OTE. **Hotel Kentriko** is in Langadia's bustling center.

Messenia ΜΕΣΣΗΝΙΑ

Messenia is a land of abundance; olives, figs, and grapes spring up from the fertile soil as fast as the fortresses sprout to defend these riches. Most Messenians live around sprawling Kalamata, a convenient town from which to tour Mani's western coast. Even more alluring is the somnolent port town of Pylos, strategically located for bus, moped, and car travel to Koroni, Mehtoni, and the fantastic beaches of the south.

Kalamata ΚΑΛΑΜΑΤΑ

Kalamata, the second largest city in the Peloponnese after Patras, appears to be a flourishing port and popular beach resort. But when you look beyond the *agora* and the fish restaurants, you'll see the abandoned buildings crumpled from the shattering earthquake of 1986. Only a few sights still remain in Kalamata; the **kastro,** which crowns a hill above the old city, seems particularly indestructible. Built by the Franks in 1208, it was blown up by the Turks in 1685 and then restored by the Venetians a decade later. Now it houses an open-air theater, which hosts "Cultural Summer of Kalamata" in July and August with everything from jazz and rock to classical Greek drama. (Ticket prices depend on the event, and start at 500dr.) To get to the gates from Platia Martiou, walk up Ipapandis St. past the church on the right side, and take your first left. The remains of a Byzantine church molder at the far edge of the site: scamper up for asublime view. (Open 8am-dusk. Free.) At 221 Faron St., off the waterfront, Kalamata's **School of Fine Arts** exhibits work by Greek artists. (Open daily 9am-1pm and 6-10pm.) Kalamata also entertains two professional theaters and cinemas. Ask at the **tourist office,** 221 Faron St., for information on events in the new "Pantazoloulion Cultural Center" on Aristomenon St. The collections of Kalamata's **Benaki Museum** and **Folk Art Museum** have been moved to Sparta for safe-keeping until new earthquake-proof buildings are constructed.

The **beach** at Kalamata is crowded and littered, but improves as you proceed eastward. The water is supposedly the warmest in Greece. With large shady trees, cafés, a performance area, and a duck pond, the **Train Park** (at the end of Aristomenous St. on the waterfront end) extends up several blocks toward Platia Georgia. The main attraction is the simulated train station, life-size and open for exploration. At night either head to Platia Georgiou or to the real nightlife on the brimming waterfront. Kalamata's newest disco, **Palladium,** costs a fortune (cover 1200dr, includes one drink), but more moderately priced clubs surround it on the waterfront.

Orientation and Practical Information

Kalamata's busiest areas form an "L." The bus station and outdoor market are at the top of the "L." The vertical stem is formed by the main thoroughfare, **Aristomenous Street,** which runs through the vast **Platia Georgiou,** site of most of the city's amenities. At the corner of the "L" is the Levi's factory and the port; **Navarinou Street** runs along the waterfront to form the horizontal leg.

Kalamata is large and spread-out—the bus station is 3km from the beach—but has an efficient public transportation system. Bus #1 (70dr anywhere along the line) will take you everywhere you want to go. You can catch buses anywhere you see a blue *stassis* sign. They begin their route at Platia 23 Martiou. To get there, follow Artemidos St. three bridges from the bus station and three blocks to the left. Then cross the third bridge off Artemidos, turn right, and you'll be on **Aristomenous St.**

Messina Tourist Office: Run by the Municipality of Kalamata, 221 Farou St. (tel. 220 59 or 219 59). Open Mon.-Fri. 7am-2:30pm and 5:30-8:30pm. Look for the peach-colored building. They may have some printed information, or try **Mar-Nic Travel,** 147 Faron St. (tel. 240 00); ask for a map of Kalamata and the Peloponnese (300dr). **Tourist Police:** Tel. 231 87 and **Police** (tel. 100); both on Aristomenos St. #46. The tourist police are on the 2nd floor. Open daily 8am-2pm.

Port Police: Tel. 222 18. On the harbor past the Levi's factory.

Currency Exchange: National Bank of Greece, on Aristomenous St., off the northern end of Platia Georgiou and on the waterfront on Akrita St. Open Mon.-Thurs. 8am-2pm, Fri. 8am-1:30pm. Many banks throughout the city.

Post Office: 4 Iatropolou St., which cuts through the southern end of Platia Georgiou. Also on the waterfront at the port past the Levi's factory. Both are open Mon.-Fri. 7:30am-2pm. **Postal Code:** 24100.

OTE: Platia Georgiou, opposite the National Bank. Open 24 hrs. **Telephone Code:** 0721.

Flights: To Athens daily at 9pm (20min., 4000dr, ticket bought 21 days in advance 10% discount, children 5500dr). **Olympic Airways,** 17 Sideromikou Stathmou St. (tel. 223 76), just before train station. Open 7am-9pm. Runs a shuttle to the airport (180dr) leaving from its office 70min. before each flight.

Trains: Tel. 239 04. Station at the end of Sideromikou Stathmou St. (literally Railroad Station St.). Turn right on Frantzi St. at the end of Platia Georgiou, and walk a few blocks. Cheaper and slower than buses. To: Athens (6:55am-10:40pm 5 per day, 7hr., 1500dr) via Tripolis (2½hr., 640dr); Argos (4hr., 940dr); Corinth (5¼hr., 1250dr); Kyparissia (2hr., 450dr); Pirgos (3¼hr., 650dr); and Patras (5½hr., 1100dr). Train to Olympia is 820dr.

Buses: Tel. 228 51. Information 7am-2pm. To: Athens (10:30am-10:30pm, 8 buses per day, 5hr., 2750dr) via Megalopolis (650dr); Tripolis (950dr); Argos (1600dr); and Corinth (2650dr); Patras (daily 8:30am and 2pm, 4hr., 2750dr) via Pirgos (2hr., 1700dr); Sparta (daily 9:15am and 2:30pm, 750dr) via Artemisia (320dr); Mavromati (5:50am and 2pm, 330dr); and Koroni (Mon.-Fri. 5am-6:30pm 7 per day, Sat. 6:30am-6:30pm 5 per day, Sun. 6am-6:30pm, 7 per day, 1½hr., 520dr); the 5am, 1pm and 5:30pm buses continue to Methoni (1½hr., 750dr) and Finikoundas (2hr., 850dr). On Sun., only the 7pm bus connects to Methoni and Finikoundas. For Areopolis and Gythion, take the 5:15am, 7:30am, or 1pm bus to Itilo (2hr., 850dr), where you'll change buses immediately. The bus from Itilo goes to Areopolis (15min., 100dr) and then Gythion (another 30min.). There is also a 5:30pm bus to Itilo but with no connection to Areopolis until the next day. **City buses** depart from the bus depot near Platia 23 Martiou. Take the #1 here (100dr) for the waterfront or camping areas. A **taxi** to the campsites costs about 500dr.

Moped Rental: Bastakos Motor Bikes, 190 Faron St. (tel. 266 38). Mopeds 2500dr per day. Or **Moto World,** (tel. 813 83) on Bironos St. with Vespas for 2500dr per day. Both are near the waterfront.

Road Help: Dial 104 or call the auto club ΕΛΠΑ (Greece's equivalent of AAA) at 821 66.

Pharmacy: Many line Aristomenous St. Most open daily 8am-2pm, Tues. and Thurs.-Fri. also 5:30-9pm.

Hospital: Athinou St. (tel. 852 03). **First Aid** (tel. 255 55).

Accommodations, Camping, and Food

There are not many places to stay in Kalamata, but you shouldn't have trouble finding a room (as long as you aren't looking for the scarce singles).

Hotel Nevada, 9 Santa Rosa (tel. 824 29). Take bus #1 and get off as soon as it turns left along the water. The walls of these clean rooms are layered with a bizarre hodgepodge of posters. Tons, and we mean *tons*, of potted plants—you'll spot them a block away. Singles 2000dr. Doubles 3500dr. Triples 4000dr.

Hotel George, 5 Dagre St., (tel. 272 25). As you exit the train station, turn right—it's on your left. Perky rooms; convenient to the train and Platia Georgiou. Singles 2500dr. Doubles 4000dr. Triples 5000dr.

Avra, 10 Santa Rosa (tel. 827 59), across the street. Clean and comfortable rooms. Chirping birds in the lobby. Singles 2000dr. Doubles 4000dr. Triples 4600dr.

Camping: Camping Patista (tel. 295 25), 2km east along the water. Take bus #1 to the waterfront Mobil gas station and walk 100m. It's on the left, off a driveway. 350dr per person. 350dr per tent. The hotel here rents rooms for about 1500dr per person. Often have maintenance and fruitpicking work available to campers. More luxurious and farther east are **Camping Elite** (tel. 273 68; 450dr per person and tent) and **Camping Sea and Sun** (tel. 413 14; 600dr per person, 500dr per tent, hot showers included.) Take bus #1 (8am-10pm, every hr.).

Before leaving town, be sure to sample the famous Kalamata olives and figs. Stop by the mouth-watering collection of edibles at the **New Market,** just across the bridge from the bus station. The most entertaining and delicious sit-down meals can be found at the string of restaurants along the waterfront. Try **Psaropoula** for outstanding *kalamari* (625dr) and luscious dandelion greens (400dr). (Open 11am-3:30pm and 7pm-1am.)

Near Kalamata

If you're aching to see more antiquities, take the bus from Kalamata to **Mavromati** (Mon.-Sat.), where you'll find the well-preserved remains of ancient Messene (not to be confused with modern Messini) on Mt. Ithomi. The most striking part of the site is the 4th-century BCE walls, which epitomize the period's defensive architecture. An **agora, theater,** and **Temple to Artemis** also remain. If you continue up the road, you'll come to the fallen doorpost of the colossal **Arcadian Gate,** designed by Epaminondas, the architect of Megalopolis to the north. Also nearby is the 16th-century **Monastery of the Vourkano,** with some outstanding frescoes. The only difficulty with this trip is the timing. If you want more than 15 minutes at the site, you'll have to catch the morning bus and return on the post-Petralona leg of the afternoon bus. Hitching on these deserted roads is very difficult and not worth it.

The road from Koroni to Kalamata hugs the eastern coast of the Messenian peninsula. Between Harokopi and the coastal town of **Petalidio** is a long chain of sandy beaches. Petalidio hosts good beachside campgrounds. On the Messini side of Petalidio, **Petalidi Beach Camping** (tel. 311 54) rests on the water's edge (550dr per person, 400dr per tent). **Zervas Beach Camping** (tel. 310 09 or 312 23) is next door (500dr per person and per tent). Nearby is **Camping Velica** (tel. 247 89). On the Koroni side of Petalidi and across the street from the beach awaits **Camping Sun Beach** (tel. 312 00). *Dhomatia* signs materialize along most of the stretch between Kalamata and Koroni, near the small beaches. **Koroni** is a pleasant fishing village which also has its own *Kastro.* In the town center you'll find a **post office** (open 7:30am-2pm) and a **bank** (open Mon.-Thurs. 8am-2pm, Fri. 8:30am-1:30pm). Stop by one of the colorful *tavernas* which line the small harbor with vibrancy, or head straight for the sandy beach nearby (follow signs from the town center to "Hotel Panorama," then signs for "Zaga Beach"). Pleasant **Koroni Camping** (tel. (0725) 221 19) has watersports equipment.

From Kalamata to Areopolis

Just south of Kalamata, the bus to Areopolis winds through the spectacular Taygetus mountains, which soar to 2630m at their highest point. The alluring grey peaks of Mani loom behind olive-covered hillsides. The first major bus stop comes at the coastal village of **Kardamili.** The town is a popular beach resort, so there are many rooms to let, but call ahead in the summer (expect to pay 3000-4000dr for doubles). In the center of town the hospitable **Joan Stefansa** (tel. 732 42) rents spotless doubles with balconies, private baths, and a communal kitchen (4000dr). Look for the wooden sign above **Gelateria** (which serves delicious exotic ice cream). On the Kalamata side of town, you can find *dhomatia* near a white pebble beach euphoria by following the sign for "Camping Melitsina 1.5km." On the left hand side of the street, **Basileios Giannakeas** at Agias Paraskenis #18 (tel. 434 00) rents breezy rooms with hot showers, a communal kitchen, and a breakfast veranda (doubles 2200dr). Follow the blue signs to beachside **Camping Melitsina** (tel. 734 61; 500dr per person, 400dr per tent). On the other end of town, follow the red and white "rooms to let" signs right after the post office and a cobblestone path. Here you'll find **Olivia Koumanakou's** tidy pension with a communal kitchen (tel. 733 26. Doubles without bath 3200dr, with bath 4000dr). For meals, try **Taverna Kiki,** on the waterfront below the village. The food at this family-run restaurant is inspirational. There is a **supermarket** and **bakery** near the square. Kardamili's **police station** is on the main road across from the church; farther towards Itilo is the **post office** (open Mon.-Fri. 7:30am-2:30pm). Following the road from Kalamidi to Itilo you'll see several coves with pebble **beaches** opening onto the turquoise sea. The **telephone code** is 0721.

If you're bound for Areopolis, change buses in the village of **Itilo** immediately upon arrival—the bus leaves promptly. This peaceful town is riveted on the fully frescoed **Monastery of Dekoulo** and the 17th-century Turkish fortress poised on a neighboring hill. The entertainment quarter consists of two cafés off the small square and a reasonably priced restaurant. The bus continues 3km down to the magnificently situated **Neon Itilo.** At the heart of an enormous natural bay encircled by monumental barren mountains, the town's white pebble beach is ideal for swimming. Although it's illegal, many **freelance camp** along the right side of the cove (facing the water) or they stay at the **Hotel Itilo** (tel. 513 00). From Neon Itilo, the road winds uphill, affording a view of **Limani,** the old harbor of Areopolis, with its sprinkling of fishing boats on the shimmering water. The tiny port is home to the Mavromichaeli **Castle of Potrombei.** From here, buses continue to Areopolis. And by the way, the bad roads and reckless drivers make this ride almost as much fun as bus rides in Crete.

Pylos ΠΥΛΟΣ

Pylos's shady square and tile houses framed by bobbing flowers are typical enough for a port town. But the sharp rock face of Sfakteria Island is a peculiarity that gives Pylos a defiant appearance as well as a protected harbor. Also known as Navarino, the town is renowned for the eponymous 1827 sea battle which gave Greece its independence. As Turkish forces, reinforced by the Egyptian fleet, battered the coast, the English, French, and Russian fleets arrived at Navarino and saved the beleaguered Greeks.

The **police** (tel. 223 16) are located on the second floor of a building on the left side of the waterfront (facing the water). Continue around that turn to reach the **port police** (tel. 222 25). The **post office** (open Mon.-Fri. 8am-2:15pm) is on Nileos St., uphill to the left (facing the water) from the **bus station.** To get to the **OTE,** pass the post office and take your first left; it is on the right of the little square, 2 blocks uphill. (Open Mon.-Fri. 7:30am-3pm.) The national **bank** is also on the waterfront. (Open Mon.-Thurs. 8am-2pm, Fri. 8am-1:30pm.) The **hospital's** phone number is 223 15. Pylos's **postal code** is 24007; its **telephone code** is 0723.

Pylos is also an ideal base for visiting the southwest arm of the Peloponnese. Just 17km north lie the important, if meager, ruins of **Nestor's Palace** and the beach town of **Methoni** with its grand castle reclines 12km south of Pylos. For appealing beaches, go 6km north around **Yialova Beach** and the campground. **Buses** (tel. 222 30) leave regularly for Kalamata (Mon.-Sat. 6:35am-9pm 9 per day, Sun. 9am-9pm 6 per day, 1¼hr., 620dr); Athens (daily at 9am, 7hr., 3500dr); and Finikoundas (Mon.-Sat. 4 per day, 2 on Sun., 45min, 300dr), via Methoni (15min., 200dr). No buses travel directly to Koroni, but you can go to Finikoundas and take the 5pm bus from there to Koroni. Buses also leave for Kyparissia (Mon.-Sat. at 7am, 9am, 11am, and 1:35pm, Sun. at 11am, 2hr., 750dr), all stopping at Nestor's Palace (30min., 200dr) and Chora (35min., 220dr). The best way to see the southern peninsula, however, is to rent a moped and make a daytrip. Try **Venus Rent-A-Car** (tel. 223 93 or 223 12; open 8:30am-1pm and 6-8:30pm; 2000-4000dr per moped, insurance included.)

You will see many "rooms-to-rent" signs as the bus descends the hill. In general, expect to pay 2000-3500dr for singles, 3000-5600dr for doubles, and 3500-6000dr for triples. Try the clean and simple rooms of **Anna Panoskalsi** (tel. 229 53; doubles 3500dr). Go up a flight of stairs before the new Hotel Karalis, and follow the sign for rooms (about 50m left). Overlooking the harbor, the **Hotel Navarino** (tel. 222 91) is worth a try. To get there, follow the road along the waterfront to the left of the square (facing the water), past the police and port police. The blue walls and mustard-yellow floor may convince you that the interior decorators were Van Gogh Pro Painters. (Singles 2500dr. Doubles 4000dr.) **Navarino Beach Camping** (tel. 227 61) lies 6km north at Yialova Beach. (500dr per person, 400dr per tent. 900dr tent rental.) Though it is not legal, squatters camp on the wooded hill across from the expensive Castle Hotel. **Gre-**

gori's serves an extensive variety of delicious food in its garden: walk up the street from the Café Santarosa and bear right—the restaurant has a red sign. (Open 9am-3pm and 6pm-midnight.) For a reasonably-priced, tasty meal, try **To Diethnez** (ΔIEΘNEZ), to the left of the police station.

Fortresses guard both sides of Pylos's harbor. The southern one, **Neokastro**, is easily accessible from the town: walk up the road for Methoni and turn right at the sign. The well-preserved walls enclose a church (originally a mosque), a capacious citadel, a building flanked by detritus from the Battle of Navarino, and soon it will house a museum as well. (Open Tues.-Sun. 8:30am-3pm.) The **Paleokastro**, north of Pylos, is harder to reach. Drive to Petrochori and proceed south with caution—the road is poor. The overgrown castle is home to hundreds of slithering beasties.

Pylos's tiny **museum**, 1½ blocks up Fillelinon St. on the left side of the square, houses finds from Hellenistic and Mycenaean tombs. (Open Tues.-Sun. 8:30am-3pm. Admission 400dr, students 200dr; free on Sun.) To see **Sfakteria** up close, you can take a boat tour from the port. The hour jaunt around the island stops at various monuments to the allied sailors of the Battle of Navarino shows you a sunken Turkish ship. (1000dr per person). Boat captains often try to arrange groups for tours (usually about 10 people). Inquire at the small booth on the waterfront or at the neighboring coffee bar under the police station, where the captains often rest.

Near Pylos

While the *Odyssey* only vaguely mentions the location of the Palace of Nestor, and Homer describes three places called Pylos, the American archaeologists who dug at Pylos are confident that their excavations have uncovered the actual palace where Nestor, Odysseus's bud, met with Telemachus. Besides the thigh-high pieces of wall and a remarkably well-preserved ancient bathtub, though, the ruins are much ado about nothing. The University of Cincinnati's scholarly guide (500dr) is available at the entrance to the site. (Open Mon.-Sat. 8:45am-3pm, Sun. 9:30am-2:30pm. Admission 400dr, students 200dr; free on Sun.) Buses from Pylos and Kyranissia stop right outside the site.

The village of **Chora,** about 3km from Nestor's Palace, is quite forgettable except for its superb **archaeological museum,** which contains many finds from the Palace of Nestor along with other Messenian and Mycenaean artifacts. (Open Mon. and Wed.-Sat. 8:45am-3pm, Sun. 9:30am-2:30pm.) The museum lies 400m uphill from the square on Marinatou St. The **bus station** is on Carl Blegen St. (named after the site's excavator) St. 1 block to the right of the town square. Five buses travel to Pylos (Mon.-Sat. 6:20am-5:20pm, Sun. 9:15am-5:20pm, 35min.; 280dr).

In **Kyparissia,** a coastal town guarded by a mountain fortress, the train tracks end and only buses continue north or south; a stop here is almost inevitable. **Buses** leave for Athens via Argos and Corinth (daily at 8:45am and 3pm, 5hr., 3100dr); Patras (daily at 9:30am and 3pm, 2½hr., 2000dr); Chora (5 per day, 450dr); and Pylos (4 per day, 2hr., 750dr). **Trains** go to Kalamata (5 per day, 2hr., 540dr); and Athens (9 per day, 8hr., 2000dr); four of these go via Tripolis (2½hr., 500dr), and five go via Pirgos (1½hr., 500dr) and Patras (3½hr., 970dr). To get to Kyparissia's fortress, walk 1 block from the train station; at the five-way intersection take the second sharpest right.

Pension Trifolia, 25th Martiou St., just past the restaurants, charges 2000dr per person for humble but well-kept doubles and triples. For a night under the stars, follow the signs to the luxurious **Camping Chani** (tel. 233 30) downhill from town. There you'll find a minimarket, bar, and watersports equipment. (Site 500dr per person. 450dr per tent. Pedal boats 1000dr per hour. Canoes 500dr per hour.) **O Glaros Fish Tavern** on the main road serves such chewy delights as *kalamari* (550dr). Just off Kalanzakos Sq. are two restaurants which both claim to be the true **Nynio's Restaurant** cited in the French *Guide du Routard.* Decide for yourself which Nynio's is the authentic one, or leave *haute cuisine* behind and bite into a goopy piece of *baklava* from the nearby E APPAΔIA Bakery.

On the square, you will find a **bank** (open Mon.-Thurs. 8am-2pm, Fri. 8am-1:30pm) and the **post office** (open Mon.-Fri. 7:30am-2pm). The **OTE** is just off the uphill right corner (open Mon.-Fri. 7:30am-10pm, Sat.-Sun. 9am-2pm and 5-10pm). The **police** (tel. 226 00 or 220 39) are farther up the street. Kyparissia's **postal code** is 24500; its **telephone code** is 0761.

Methoni ΜΕΘΩΝΗ

With its hibiscus-lined streets and balconied tile houses, Methoni is just swell. Peer through the flowering trees at the spectacular 13th-century fortress along the beach and it will be easy to understand the allure and glorious romance of Methoni. Forever "the Camelot of Greece," Methoni was once offered by Agamemnon to Achilles to cheer the the sulking warrior. Cervantes was so taken with the place that he was able to churn out his romances even while imprisoned under Turkish guard.

The town's two main streets form a "Y" at the billiard hall where the Pylos-Finikoundas buses stop (ask inside for bus information). Shops are on the upper fork to the right; the beach and fortress are down to the left. The **police** (tel. 223 16 or 221 00) are on a side street off the left fork near the beach. Past the sign on the left fork, you'll find the **post office** (open Mon.-Fri. 7:30am-2pm) and the **OTE** (open Mon.-Fri. 7:30am-3:10pm). The **National Bank of Greece** is 40m down the right fork (open Mon.-Thurs. 8am-2pm, Fri. 8am-1:30pm). Buses go to Kalamata (Mon.-Sat. 4 per day, 1 on Sun., 1½hr., 700dr) via Pylos (15min., 200dr). Four buses per day travel to Finikoundas (30min., 150dr). Two doors down from the OTE, buses leave for Athens via Pylos, Kyparissia, Pirgos, and Patras. Ask at the police station or the billiard hall for information about Patras-Athens buses. The phone number of the **medical clinic** is 314 56. Methoni's **postal code** is 24006; the **telephone code** is 0723.

The **Hotel Iliodission** (ΕΛΙΟΔΥΣΙΟΝ; tel. 312 25), about 2 blocks up from the beach, has comfortable clean rooms in an old house next to the fortress moat. Ask for a balcony. (Singles 2500dr. Doubles 4000dr. Triples 4700dr.) **Camping Methoni** (tel. 312 28) is crowded, but beachside (400dr per person and per tent). On the fortress side of the beach, try the **Restaurant Rex,** under large, shady pine trees. *(Mousaka* 600dr. *Taramasalata,* for the fish-egg-lover in you, 250dr. Open 6:30am-4pm and 6pm-midnight.)

A visit to the southwest Peloponnese just wouldn't be the same without a trip to Methoni's **Venetian fortress,** a 13th-century minicity. The Bourzi, a small tower built by the Turks to fortify the shore even further, sits halfway around the wall over the sea. Venture into the fortified walls, cisterns, parapets, and vaulted passages if only to see the birds zipping to and fro above nests in the corners of the ceiling. (Fortress open daily 8am-7pm, Sun. 8am-6pm. Free.)

Conduct your own sea battle in the paddle boats you can rent from restaurants on the beach (1000dr per hr., windsurfers 2000dr per hr.). The beach at Methoni is quite crowded. There are closet-booths on the beach for changing.

Finikoundas ΦΙΝΙΚΟΥΝΤΑΣ

Halfway between Methoni and Koroni, Finikoundas has never had a need for a fortress. Rather than flaunt historical sites, this humble fishing village coaxes visitors to join the tranquil summer activities of basking in sunshine, swimming in a clear blue sea, and then watching the colorful *caïques* glide across the surface. For swimming, take the time to go to the significantly less-crowded cove beyond the rock jetty to the east. If you decide to stay, remember to change money in advance; Finikoundas still has neither a bank nor a post office. The **Supermarket Phoenix** (sign reads ΦOINIΞ) sells postage stamps and has an **OTE** (open daily 7am-1pm and 5-9pm). **Buses** to Kalamata stop across from the Hotel Filikounda (3 per day, 2hr., 950dr) via Methoni (½hr.) and Pylos (45min.). Buses also go to Kalamata via Harokopio (at 7:30am and 4:30pm, 1½hr., 950dr)

Look for *dhomatia* signs along the waterfront or on the road from Koroni as you enter town. Most restaurants either rent rooms or know people who do. **Moudakis Restaurant** (tel. 712 24), to the right of the KMoil gas station (facing the water), has doubles for 4500dr. Rooms on streets away from the water are slightly cheaper. Finikoundas also brandishes two campgrounds: **Camping Animos** (tel. 712 62) is 2km east of town (600dr per person and 500dr per tent). **Camping Anemomylos** (tel. 713 60) is 1km west.

Laconia ΛΑΚΩΝΙΑ

In the 10th century BCE, a tribe of Doric warriors from the north invaded the southwest Peloponnese, driving out its Mycenaean inhabitants, and summarily executing any stragglers who had the misfortune of getting in their way. The invaders set up camp in Sparta, and their Ancient Laconian qualities are still manifest throughout the area, especially in its barren central peninsula, Mani. Although Laconia boasts three of the most popular sites in the Peloponnese—Mani's Pirgos Dirou caves, Sparta's nearby Byzantine ruins of Mystra, and Monemvassia's "rock"—the untrammeled land in between remains suitably (you guessed it) laconic.

Sparta ΣΠΑΡΤΗ

> *Suppose the city of Sparta to be deserted and nothing left but the temples and the plain ground, distant ages would be very unwilling to believe that its power was equal to its fame.*
>
> *—Thucydides*

The Spartans are usually portrayed as the bad guys of the classical world—totalitarian war-mongers who insisted on pestering the democratic doves of civilized Athens. Sure, the Athenians were no angels, but here, at least, stereotypes hold true: Sparta's reputation for brutal, no-nonsense militarism is largely deserved. Around 700 BCE, after Sparta barely subdued a revolt of the Messenians, the leader Lycurgus instituted reforms that transformed Sparta body and soul, bone and sinew, into a war machine. For the next 350 years, it dominated the entire central Peloponnese with its invincible armies and austere discipline. Yet outside of war, Sparta contributed little to Greek history; no philosophy, poetry, underwater basket weaving, or architecture ever flourished here. Leery of further Athenian expansion and Pericles's attempts to dominate the Delian League, Sparta attacked its rival, beginning the 28-year Peloponnesian War. After triumphing in 404 BCE, it emerged the supreme military power in the Hellenic world. The Spartans reveled in their newfound power, not even bothering to build walls around their city. Ultimately, only the combined efforts of earthquakes, depopulation, and the united resistance of its neighbors broke Sparta's hegemony.

A young Spartan's training for the life of war began early—even before conception. Lycurgus believed that two fit parents produced stronger offspring, so he ordered all Spartan women to undergo the same rigorous physical training endured by men. Furthermore, newlyweds were only permitted an occasional tryst on the grounds that distance makes the heart grow fonder and that fond hearts produce more robust children.

If they weren't winnowed out as weak or deformed, boys began a severe regimen of training under the auspices of a Spartan citizen. The young were forced to walk barefoot to toughen their feet and wore only a simple piece of clothing in both summer and winter to inure them to drastic weather changes. The Spartan creed dictated that young men be guarded against temptations of all kind: strict laws, forbidding everything from drinking to pederasty, governed Spartans' actions. Moreover, young Spartans were given the plainest and simplest of foods for fear that rich delicacies would stunt their growth. (One visitor to Sparta, upon sampling the fare, reputedly quipped, "Now I know why they do not fear death.")

Modern Sparta hardly resembles a fascist bootcamp. Thucydides was not afraid to tell it like it is. With the nightly roar of mopeds and monotonous, modern architecture, the city is more like modern Athens. Although not the most exciting city in the Peloponnese, Sparta is a good base from which to trek through the ruins of neighboring Mystra.

Orientation and Practical Information

Sparta's two main streets, palm-lined **Paleologou** and **Lykourgou,** laced with orange and lime trees, intersect in the center of town. To get to the center from the bus station, walk left on Paleologou for 2 blocks. The town square is 1 block to the right of the intersection and all of the necessary amenities are nearby on these two streets. The ruins are on the northern edge of town, behind you at the end of Paleologou St. Sparta is laid out in an appropriately no-frills grid.

GNTO Tourist Office: (tel. 248 52) on the left side of the town hall in the square. Informative and friendly workers. Money exchange. Ask for a map of Laconia (400dr). **Currency Exchange:** National Bank, on the corner of Dioskouron and Paleologou St., 3 blocks down from the intersection. Open Mon.-Thurs. 8am-2pm, Fri. 8am-1:30pm. Other banks line Paleologou; take your pick.

Post Office: Past the OTE on Kleombrotou St., which is 1 block up from the intersection off Paleologou St. Open Mon.-Fri. 7:30am-2pm. **Postal Code:** 23100.

OTE: 11 Kleombrotou St. Open daily 7am-midnight. **Telephone Code:** 0731.

Bus Station: Vrasidou St. (tel. 264 41, little English spoken), off Paleologou, 2 blocks from the main intersection. All bus schedules are written in Greek: Buses run to Athens (9 per day, 5hr., 2500dr), stopping in Argos (2½hr., 1250dr) and Corinth (4hr., 1550dr). To Neapolis (Mon.-Sat. 4 per day, 2 on Sun., 4hr., 1300dr) and Monemvassia (Mon.-Sat. 2 per day, 1 on Sun., 2½hr., 950dr; change buses in Molai). To Pirgos Dirou and the caves (at 9am, 2¼hr., 950dr) via Areopolis (2 hr., 800dr; change buses in Gythion). To: Kalamata (at 9am and 2:30pm, 2hr., 390dr; change in Artemisia), Tripolis (7:50am-3pm, 4 per day, 1¼hr., 680dr), Gerolimenas (at noon, 3hr., 1100dr), and Gythion (5 per day, last at 9:30pm; 1hr.; 570dr). For buses to Mystra, there is a separate bus stop near the town square on the corner of Lykourgou and Agisilaos. From the main intersection, walk past the main square on Lykourgou; 2 blocks ahead is a sign marked **Mystra Bus Station.** A complete timetable is available at the main bus station. Frequent buses travel to Mystra (Mon.-Sat. 6:50am-8:40pm, 11 per day, Sun. 9am-8:40pm, 5 per day; 15min., 200dr).

Hospital: Tel. 286 71 or 286 72.

Police: 8 Hilonos St. (tel. 262 29). From the intersection, turn left on Lykourgou St. going away from the square—the police are on a sidestreet to the right just past the museum. Signs saying "tourist police" point the way.

Pharmacies: 4 on Paleologou St. and many more throughout the city.

Accommodations, Camping, and Food

The oft-used phrase "Spartan rooms" originated in this town. To get to most of the budget hotels from the bus station, turn left onto Paleologou, take the second right onto Lykourgou St., and continue past the large square on your left. Go up 3 blocks to reach the **Hotel Cyprus,** 66 Leonidou St. (tel. 265 90), just off Lykourgou, which offers refrigerator, maps, common area, bus schedules, free luggage storage, and cramped rooms, some with balconies and clotheslines. (Singles 1800dr. Doubles 3000dr. Triples 4000dr. Discounts for large groups. Open March 15-Nov. 15.) One block down, on the corner of Lykourgou and Agisilaos, is the **Hotel Anesis,** 60 Lykourgou St. (tel. 210 88), with lackluster but tidy rooms. (Singles 1800dr. Doubles 3000dr. Triples 3600dr.) On Paleologou, just past Lykourgou, is the **Hotel Panellinion** (tel. 280 31). The clean rooms have balconies for watching the ballyhoo on the streets below. (Singles 2500dr. Doubles 4000dr.) **Hotel Cecil** (tel. 249 80), 5 blocks north on the corner of Paleologou St. and Thermopilion St. The traffic roars audibly, but the rooms are unsullied. (Singles 2000dr. Doubles 3800dr. Hot showers.) About 3km away on the road to Mystra is **Camping Mystra** (tel. 227 24), which has a pool (650dr per person, 350dr per tent). Also near Mystra is the new **Camping Castle View** (tel. 993 03), with pool, wonderful modern showers and toilets, a minimarket, and amiable owners (600dr per person.

350dr per tent). To get to either campground, take the regular Mystra bus and ask the conductor to let you off at the appropriate camping site.

Sparta's few restaurants serve expensive fast food. For a Spartan meal under the fluorescent lights of **Dhiethnes,** (ΔΙΘΝΕΣ) head to the far right of the main square facing the row of cafés. (Spaghetti 650dr.) Downstairs on the corner of Lykourgou and Paleologou St., **Averof** (ΑΒΕΡΩΦ) serves similar meals. (Tasty chicken with potatoes 750dr.) A good *psistaria* (grill tavern) is across from the Hotel Cecil on Paleologou St. (Charbroiled chicken and fries 550dr.) Several blocks up from the post office, past Paleologou St., on Kleombrotou St., the sidewalks are crowded with fruit and vegetable stands. The **Imago,** a hip, artsy bar, is in the alley behind the town hall. (Open 8pm-1am).

For an evening excursion from Sparta, share a cab to the village of **Parolis,** 2km from Mystra. There you can sit in a *taverna* and watch the nearby waterfalls. If you have any strength left in your legs after clambering around the ruins of nearby Mystra, bop yourself 2½km on down the road toward Gythion to the **Aithrio Disco.**

Sights

In contrast to the other great cities of ancient Greece, little remains of ancient Sparta. The denizens' scorn for luxuries included a distaste for elaborate buildings. Modern visitors are apt to be disappointed if they expect to find a southern counterpart to the Parthenon. The ruins consist of the outlines of a theater (one of the largest of ancient Greece) and some fragments of the acropolis (1km from the main square at the northern edge of the modern city). At the north end of Paleologou St. stands an enormous **statue of Leonidas,** the famous warrior and king of the Spartans. A short walk east on the banks of the Eurotas River brings you to the **sanctuary of Artemis Orthia.** Spartan youths had to prove their courage here by unflinchingly enduring public floggings. A row of headless, grinning statues beckons you to enter the **local museum** through its park from Lykourgou St. (on the opposite side of Paleologou from the square). You'll see the spooky votive masks used in ritual dances at the sanctuary of Artemis Orthia and the famous head and shoulders of the statue of Leonidas (490-480 BCE). (Museum open Tues.-Sat. 8:30am-3pm, Sun. 9:30am-2:30pm. Admission 1000dr, students 500dr; free on Sun.) For modern art, visit the **John Coumantaros Museum,** 123 Paleologon St. (tel. 265 57, no English spoken). The permanent collection of 19th-century French and Dutch paintings is impressive. On the second floor, you'll find temporary exhibits of work by modern Greek artists.

Mystra ΜΥΣΤΡΑ

The extraordinary medieval ruins of Mystra stand 6km west of Sparta. Overflowing with Byzantine churches and castle ruins, this site is considered the landmark of Byzantium's final flourish. In the late 14th century, prospering from a lucrative silk industry, Mystra also became a humming intellectual center. Many free thinkers, unhappy with their repression under recalcitrant feudal lords and clergy, surged into town and set up schools. Philosophers and students wandered about the intricate network of paths that weaves the city together—and now renders sight-seeing a complicated affair. Try tracing a path around several key sites on the three tiers that correspond to the sectors for the commoners, the nobility, and the royalty (in ascending order, naturally). Fortunately, Mystra is one of the better-labeled sites in Greece. If you enter through the fortress gate, the complexity will be easier to handle.

Don't miss the **Metropolis of St. Demetrios** in the lower tier, with its sanctuary and museum of architectural fragments. Wander on to the two churches of the monastery of **Vrontokhion,** St. Theodori, and the frescoes of the **Aphentiko** (or Hodegetria). On the same tier is the **Pantanassa,** a convent with a beautifully ornamented façade and a multitude of frescoes. Finally, at the extreme left of the lower tier, the **Church of Perivleptos** is perhaps Mystra's most stunning relic—every inch of the church is bathed in exquisitely detailed painting. Climb up to the **kastro,** the fortress that was

Mystra's first building (the town developed downward), built by the crusader William Villehardouin in 1249 CE. The castle is closer than it looks—you can get there in about an hour walking from the main gate.

There are water fountains or taps just inside the entrance through the main gate, at the Metropolis and at Pantanassa, but it's a good idea to bring your own water along to combat Mystra's murderous heat. Also, wear tough shoes; many of the paths are rocky and slippery. You will enjoy Mystra more with a small guidebook—buy one at the entrance kiosk for 1000dr. Even a cursory inspection of the site requires at least three hours, including the long climb to the summit. (Site open Mon.-Fri. 8am-7pm, Sat.-Sun. 8:30am-3pm. Admission 1000dr, students 500dr; free on Sun.) In the summer, try to be at the site by 7:30am, since the sun becomes unbearable as early as 10am. If you arrive via bus from Sparta, don't get off until the last stop—the site is about 1½km beyond the town of Mystra. Follow the road around the bend after getting off. Aside from camp sites, accommodations at Mystra are pricey; you'd be better off going back to Sparta.

Gythion ΓΥΘΕΙΟ

Situated on the east coast of Mani and connected by ferry with Kythera and Crete, Gythion is a lively port town, and an ideal place to station oneself while touring the bleakly dramatic territory of Mani. A half-hour bus trip will bring you to Areopolis, the haunting fortified town which historically served as Mani's center. A concrete causeway connects Gythion to the tiny island of **Marathonisi,** where Paris and Helen consummated their ill-fated love.

Orientation and Practical Information

The bus will drop you on the waterfront, near the town's amenities and cheaper stores. Small **Mavromichaeli Square** is in the middle of the waterfront near the quay. The harbor road continues to the right, where it eventually meets the causeway to Marathonisi.

Currency Exchange: The Greek National Bank is just beyond the bus stop toward the water. Open Mon.-Thurs. 8am-2pm, Fri. 8am-1:30pm. There are other banks in this area. Farther down on the waterfront Theodore V. Rozaki's travel agency also changes money. Open Mon.-Sat. 9am-1pm and 5-10pm.

Post Office: Ermou St. Open Mon.-Fri. 7:30am-2pm. **Postal Code:** 23200.

OTE: At the corner of Herakles and Kapsali St. Open Mon.-Fri. 7:30am-9pm. **Telephone Code:** 0733.

Ferries: Depart from the quay to the right of Mavromichaeli Sq. The *F/B Ionian* leaves for Kythera (3hr., 740dr) and Crete (7hr., 2400dr) thrice weekly. It also travels once a week to Agia Pelagia on Kythera (2hr.), Neapolis (4hr., 1235dr), Monemvassia (5hr., 1625dr), and Piraeus (13hr., 2890dr).

Buses: (tel. 222 28) Along the north end of the waterfront. To Athens (5 per day, 2750dr) via Sparta (1hr., 570dr). To Kalamata via Sparta (at 7:30am and 12:15pm) or via Itilo (6am and 1pm). To Gerolimenas (at 1pm and 7:30pm, 2hr., 750dr) via Areopolis (½hr., 330dr), and Pirgos Dirou and the caves (1hr., returning at 12:45 and 5:30pm). To Monemvassia (at 8:45am, 2hr., 850dr). Buses also go to the campgrounds (including Meltemi, Gythion Beach, and Mani) south of town (at 6am, 10:15am, 1pm, and 7:30pm; 200dr).

Moped Rental: Moto Mani (tel. 228 53), on the waterfront near the causeway. Mopeds 2500dr per day; reduced prices for longer rentals and 100km allowance per day free. **Super Cycle Moto** along Gregoraki St. from the square before the church. Mopeds 2500dr per day.

Health Clinic: (tel. 220 01, or -02, or -03), along the right side of the waterfront.

Port Police: Tel. 222 62, at the right side of the waterfront, past Mavromichaeli Sq. For more coherent information and tickets, go to the **Theodore V. Rozakis Travel Agency** (tel. 222 29 or 222 07), on the waterfront near the square. Open Mon.-Sat. 9am-1pm and 5-10pm.

Police: Tel. 222 71 or 221 00, on the waterfront, 500m before the bus station.

Accommodations, Camping, and Food

You can bypass Gythion's expensive hotels by staying in *dhomatia* or at one of the four nearby campgrounds. **Xenia Karlafti's** (tel. 227 19) is in a house enclosed by a red railing, near the port police. The spacious rooms are clean and homey, and fill quickly. (Doubles 3500dr, with private bath 4500dr. Bed on the veranda 1500dr). Next to the OTE and near the bus station at Kapsali #22 you'll find newly remodeled rooms with groovy black balconies (doubles 3500dr). **Hotel Aktaion** (tel. 222 94), is centrally located on the waterfront between the bus station and the square. Some of the gloomy rooms in this old building have balconies with striking sea views. (Singles 2500dr. Doubles 4500dr. Triples 5300dr.) The most luxurious campgrounds are **Meltemi** (tel. 228 33; 600dr per person, 450dr per tent) and **Gytheio Beach Campgrounds** (tel. 225 22; 580dr per person, 350dr per tent). You can also try **Mani Beach** (tel. 234 50; 490dr per person, 350dr per tent) or the new **Kronos** campground (tel. 241 24; 650dr per person, 550dr per tent). The campgrounds are south of town and, except for Kronos, accessible by bus.

The restaurants along the waterfront and the grocery stores around the main square charge exorbitant prices. Grilled octopus is the comestible of choice here: if squeamishness deters you from partaking, at least watch it being prepared at restaurants. Locals are proud of **Kosta's,** a good non-tourist establishment across from the public beach near the bus station. (Chicken in tomato sauce 560dr.) **Supermarkets** are along Vassileos Georgiou St. As you walk along the waterfront toward the bus station, bear left at the fork for Vassileos Georgiou. There is a *laiki agora* (fruit and produce **market**) every Tuesday and Friday morning (4:30am— early enough for you?) between Herakles and Archaia Theatrou St. The **bakery** up from Super Cycle Moto to the right has delightful *tiropita* (120dr). This area also offers some cheap *souvlaki* joints. The small parks near the bus station or on the island a short walk away are perfect, cool spots for picnics.

Sights

The ancient **theater** of Gythion, tucked away in a corner, has endured the centuries remarkably well. Note the differences between the seats for dignitaries in front and the simpler seats further back. To get there, walk down Herakles St. from the bus station, go to Ermou St. and then right onto Archain Theatrou St. to its end. If you arrive in the early evening, you may be treated to a show—the local soldiers get their nightly pep talk here. **Paliatzoures** ("junk") **antique shop** (ΠΑΛΙΑ ΤΣΟΥΡΕΣ; tel. 229 44), on the waterfront next to the Hotel Pantheon, is the last of its kind in the entire Peloponnese, selling old Greek farming tools, household implements and even some "trade" tools from the Orthodox Church. (Open daily 11am-1pm and 7-10pm.) There is a small littered **public beach** on the left end of the waterfront, but the best beaches are south of Gythion on the coast between Mavrovouni and Skoutari. You may also want to go to the beach north of town where a large ship (an intercepted drug-runner from Cyprus) lies on shore abandoned. When traveling from Gythion to Areopolis, keep your eyes peeled for the Frankish **Castle of Pasava** on the right (about 10km down the road)—it is possible to tour these ruins. Farther along, closer to the coast, the **Castle of Kelefa** looks lugubriously out to sea.

Mani ΜΑΝΗ

Mani is a minimalist's dream. The sparsely settled territory stoically circles the immense cinnamon-brown Taygetus mountains, unaffected by the vibrancy of the neighboring sparkling sea. The plants and towering buildings add only muted greys and soft greens to the visionary landscape. Houses are like familial fortresses, with tiny look-out-post windows for watching the unfriendly outer-world. Mani reveals its surprising and simple beauty to the stubborn few; seemingly inscrutable and obscure, it is filled with treasures representative of the history and determination of its people.

The Mani broke off from Sparta during the Roman Period and, driven by the eternal impulse to alliterate, founded the League of Laconians. They resisted foreign rule ferociously, thereby gaining the name "Maniotes" (from the Greek *mania* or fury).

Even today, Mani's legacy of violence and repression remains, and the region contributes a disproportionate number of men to the armed forces. The region's first school was not founded until 1830, and the culture still disparages education: one hears stories of ambitious teenagers studying covertly in cavernous dungeons against their fathers' will. Mani's culture, which has traditionally preferred male offspring, remains adamantly patriarchal.

To see Mani properly, rent a moped in Areopolis or Gythion. If you opt for the bus, remember that any afternoon stop you make generally commits you to a night's stay. As usual, you can catch the bus anywhere along the way at signs marked *stassis,* but the bus runs only on the western side of the peninsula, south to Gerolimenas, sometimes continuing on to Vathia and Tsikalia. Despite all this, it's worth your while to visit the eastern coast, where the scenery is even more spectacular and the land less settled.

Areopolis

The town of Areopolis is most representative of Mani's architecture but least indicative of its spirit. In spring and autumn, this clifftop village attracts artists seeking inspiration from the scenery and the silence. Summer brings tourists to Areopolis in search of respite from the bustle of Gythion or a place to stay the night en route to the Glyfatha Lake Caves to the south. In Areopolis, one can just sit under the stars in contented reverie and listen to the occasional snorts of farm animals.

The **bus stop** is located on the corner of the square, near the restaurant "Nicolas." Three buses per day (tel. 512 29) make the trip from Kalamata to Itilo (2hr., about 840dr), with connections to Areopolis. Buses from Areopolis travel to Kalamata via Itilo (3 per day until 2:15pm, 700dr). Buses leave from Areopolis for Gythion (4 per day, 8am-6pm, 30min., 350dr), and for the Glyfatha Lake Caves near Pirgos Dirou (11am, returning at 1:30pm and 4pm; 200dr). Since the caves are one of the Peloponnese's greatest draws, many find hitching easy. *Let's Go* does not recommend hitchhiking as a means of travel. Buses also depart for Gerolimenas (at 2:15pm and 8pm, 30min., about 300dr, stopping in Pirgos Dirou). Buses continue on to Vathia (Mon., Wed., and Fri.) or to Tsikalia (Tues., Thurs., and Sat.).

The **police** (tel. 512 09) are down a little street off the square and opposite the bus station, but they speak very little English. Kapetan Matapan St., off the square, is home to the **post office** (open Mon.-Fri. 7:30am-2pm) and the **OTE** (open Mon.-Fri. 7:30am-3pm). To get to the **bank,** walk down Kapetan Matapan St. and turn right at the small church; it stands before the Hotel Mani. (Open Tues.-Thurs. 9am-noon.) The bus station will change traveler's checks for a hefty fee. The phone number of the **hospital** is 512 59. Areopolis's **postal code** is 23062; the **telephone code** is 0733.

If you spend the night here, definitely find a room in the old town and enjoy the old Mani atmosphere. On Kapetan Matapan St., a rooms-to-rent sign (tel. 513 01), hangs on the left behind a church. Downstairs, **George Versakos** has an impressive antique gun collection and a wonderful sense of humor. (Doubles 4000dr. Triples 5000dr.) If you don't mind a much bleaker room (snazzed up by lovely leopard furniture), George will rent you lodgings across the street. (Singles 2000dr. Doubles 4000dr). Unfortunately, Areopolis doesn't get much cheaper than this. In the square, the **Hotel Kouris** (tel. 513 40 or 513 07) has beautiful tidy rooms and spotless baths. (Doubles 5400dr. Triples 6000dr.)

For dinner, try the first restaurant on the far right of the town square. Delicious *spaghetti fournou* (baked spaghetti in tomato sauce, topped with a thick layer of cheese,

650dr). Good Greek coffee 100dr. Further down Kapetan Matapan St. are **supermarkets** and a **bakery.**

Pirgos Dirou and Glyfatha Lake Cave

With its subterranean river, the **Glyfatha Cave** (also known as Spilia Dirou or Pirgos Dirou), is one of the most splendid natural attractions in Greece. The boat ride through the cave is 1.2km and lasts about half an hour. Discovered in 1985, the cave is believed to be 70km long and may extend all the way to Sparta. Stalagmites and stalactites of vermillion, burnt sienna, and shiny white slice through the water, which is 30m deep in places and squiggling with eels; bats are among the other happy denizens of the caves. Don't miss "Poseidon's Foot," a formation that looks like a giant foot hanging in the air. If your guide speaks only Greek, buy the small book available in English from the store near the entrance. After the boat trip you can walk through more of the caves at your own pace. The caves are 4km away from the town, accessible by bus, and make for an easy trip from Gythion by moped. Many hitchhike, especially in summer when hordes of tourists accompany you. (Open June-Sept. 8am-6pm; off-season 8am-3pm. Astonishing admission 1500dr.) If too many tourists beat you there, you may not get in after 4pm. (For information, call 522 22 or -23.)

Continuing south along the road from Areopolis, you will soon reach the little village of **Pirgos Dirou.** Although far less interesting than Areopolis, the village is a good place if you want to be closer to the cave. It is also possible to walk here from Areopolis; just follow the signs at the other end of town from the road (about 5km). About ½km before Pirgos Dirou town **Yiannis Kolokouris** (tel. (0733) 522 04 or 522 40) rents petite, clean rooms above his restaurant. (Doubles 3800dr. Triples also available.) **To Panorama** (tel. 522 80) offers rooms closest to the caves (1km away). *Dhomatia* signs dot the road from town to the grottoes. In town, right at the turn-off to the caves, you'll find a **post office** (open Mon.-Fri. 7:30am-2pm) and **Baker's Supermarket,** farther along the road toward the caves (open 8am-10pm).

South of Pirgos Dirou

South of the caves, Mani sheds its tourist-brochure gloss. Here lies the Mani of bandits and blood feuds, where camouflaged tower houses peer warily from the rocky terrain. Byzantine barrel-vaulted churches complement the landscape with their striking simplicity. Plan at least one day to see Mani's western coast and to wander through the often unmarked side roads by moped or car. Refueling is often a problem. Because there are no gas stations in the south or east of Mani, be sure to ask about locations ahead of time. Just 2km from Pirgos Dirou, you will see a turn-off for **Harouda** and the church of **Taxiarchis** (another 2km away). This church, decorated with blue and green ceramic plates and intricately patterned masonry, is situated in a mesmerizingly calm olive grove; climb to the church terrace for the view. Parallel to the main road, a side street passes a series of hillside villages, including **Vamvaka** and **Mina,** each with tower houses and small churches. You can rejoin the main road by turning downhill at any of the extremely rocky junctures. Two sumptuous swimming caves are off the main road near **Mezapos,** which has a 12th-century church. Continuing south, you will eventually touch water at the craggy port of **Yerolimenas** ("old port") once called home by bloodthirsty pirates. You can stay at the **Hotel Akrotenaritis** (tel. 542 05), farther from town (doubles 2500dr, with bath 4500dr), or at the **Akrogiali** (tel. 542 04), on the far right of the harbor (doubles 3800dr, with bath 5000dr, A/C included). A few nice **beaches** lie beyond town, in the southeast. Two **buses** leave daily for Athens via Areopolis (about 300dr) and Gythion (6:45am and 5pm).

Buses continue to Vathia from Yerolimenas (Mon., Wed., and Fri.). Today, only 11 people live in **Vathia,** a photogenic medley of deserted towers, barren mountains, and huge crumbling fortresses. The GNTO is trying to revive the town by importing tourists to stay in the ten restored tower houses. Unfortunately, rows of concrete block buildings have sprung up as well.

Genial is the swimming cove that lies just before Vathia and enticing the three coves right before the turn-off to Porto Kagio. The main road suddenly winds down to **Porto Kagio** and its pebble beach. The beach isn't as nice as those you've already passed, but the town has a *taverna* to satisfy your pesky appetite. A path leads to the lighthouse at the end of Cape Matapan, the southernmost point on the continent after Gibraltar.

Mani's East Coast

To visit Mani's beautiful and less-touristed east coast, either head to Kotronas by cutting through the mountains on the road from Areopolis and then work south, or continue north from Matapan. If you opt for the latter, backtrack to Alika and take the road that leads to **Tsikkalia,** an eerie town with a tribe of empty tower houses and but a handful of residents. Next on the road is **Lagia,** a two-café town. After Lagia you can diverge from the main road to the fishing village of **Agios Kyprianos** with its small pebble beach and fish *taverna.* **Kokkala** ("bones" in Greek), on the main road, is something of a metropolis on this quiet coast. Kokkala holds a few *tavernas,* a minimarket, cafés, and the clean **Pension Kokkola** (tel. 583 07. Doubles with private bath 4000dr.) After Kokkala follows **Nifi,** with a small pebble beach, harbor, two cafés, and a *taverna.* Clean, standard rooms are available here above a restaurant on the main road (3000dr.) Turning off the main road past Flomochori and descending 3km will bring you to **Kotronas** (telephone code 0733), a cheerful port town with a small beach. Flowers deck the patio and rooms of the town's **pension** (tel. 532 09). This fishing village has a **post office** (open Mon.-Fri. 7:30am-2:15pm; currency exchange), as well as *tavernas,* cafés, and a supermarket.

Monemvassia ΜΟΝΕΜΒΑΣΙΑ

The ancient Byzantine city of Monemvassia soars out from a rocky island. Seen from the west, the island appears uninhabited, and from the mainland only a small *taverna* and gas station are perceptible; a short walk east along the sea, however, reveals sloping fortified walls and a staircase that climbs the sheer 350m promontory. At the mountain's summit is the **kastro** (citadel), fortified by the Venetians in the 16th century. The town, equally reinforced, rests below. Monemvassia was first conquered in 1248 CE by Guillaume de Villihardouin, and in the hands of the Franks it functioned as a stop-over for crusaders headed east. In later years it was captured by the Turks, the Pope, and finally the Venetians.

Today, one must pass through a small, covered gateway to enter Monemvassia's town. Visible immediately, a narrow, sinuous path lined with helical staircases serves as the "main street" and leads to shops and restaurants. Continue past the small strip of tourist traps to reach the **town square.** Once facing the ocean, the **Christos Elkomenos** (Christ in Chains) church is on the left. On your right is a church that underwent Turkish metamorphosis and is now a mosque. Follow the labyrinthine walkways and stairs to visit the island's myriad churches. The **Agia Sofia,** a Byzantine church modeled after the famous monastery at Daphni near Athens, presides on the edge of the ruins. Some of the original frescoes were restored 30 years ago.

Only a narrow causeway connects the island to the mainland and the modern town of Monemvassia, which is splattered with hotels, restaurants, and gift shops. Thus, the medieval village still retains its original character. Only its small main street is filled with souvenir shops, trendy cafés, and restaurants—serenity dominates elsewhere. This antique town, miraculously uncrowded, with its unsullied pebble beaches to the east and west on the mainland, could well be the cherry on top of your Peloponnesian sundae.

Orientation and Practical Information

In modern Monemvassia, 23rd Iouliou Street is the principal thoroughfare and runs along the waterfront straight up to the bridge that leads to the island. The **bus station** (tel. 610 00) is on this street. Buses for all destinations either connect or stop in Molai (no direct routes). Buses travel to Sparta (2½hr., 1150dr), Tripolis (3½hr., 1550dr), and Athens (6½-7hr., 3250dr) via Molai (½hr., 350dr). Buses leave Mon.-Fri. 7:15am, 8:30am, 11:30am, and 2:30pm; Sat.-Sun. 7:15am and 2:30pm. Daily buses connect from Molai to Gythion, leaving Monemvassia at 11:15am (1½hr., 850dr). Two or three **ferries** per week travel from Monemvassia to Piraeus. Ferries also go to Neapolis, Kythera, Gythion, and Crete. In the summer, hydrofoils go to Kythera (1hr., 3200dr) and Neapolis (Mon.-Thurs. at 12:55pm, Sat. at 11:45am). The **hydrofoil** also travels once a week to Piraeus (Zea; 4hr., 6050dr) with intermittent stops at the islands (Spetses, Hydra etc.). Schedules change frequently; check at the boat office (tel. 612 19), next to the Mobil station on the island side of the bridge.

In the modern town on Spartis St., off 23rd Iouliou St., you'll find the **National Bank** (open Mon.-Fri. 8:30am-1:30pm), and next door, the **post office** (open Mon.-Fri. 7:30am-2pm). Next to the post office is a **bakery** with tasty almond treats. On 28th Octovriou Street, which runs off 23rd Iouliou St. just past the bus station, you'll find the **police station** (tel. 612 10) in a house with a brown wooden door. The police have some *dhomatia* listings. The **OTE** (open Mon.-Fri. 7:30am-3:10pm), is uphill to the right; follow the signs. The helpful travel agency **Malvasia Travel** (tel. 614 97 and 614 32) is near the bus station on 23rd Iouliou St. (open 7am-2:30pm and 4-11pm). Ask manager Peter Derzolis for ferry information, money exchange, and moped rental (2500dr per day, plus gas) or bikes (1000dr per day.) Monemvassia's **postal code** is 23070; its **telephone code** is 0732.

Accommodations, Camping, and Food

There are three ways to stay in Monemvassia. The first option is in the medieval village on the island, but accommodations here are scarce and fail to meet even the loosest definitions of budget. A second, more affordable choice is to pitch a tent at **Camping Paradise** (tel. 611 23), 3½km along the water. (650dr per person, 450dr per tent.) Finally, "rooms to let" signs adorn many houses along 23rd Iouliou St., right on the water (doubles 3500-4500dr; triples 3800-5000). On Spartis St., near the bank and the post office, the **Hotel Akrogiali** (ΑΚΡΟΓΙΑΛΙ; tel. 613 60), wearing a sign bearing the owner's name, S. Sofos, is about the cheapest hotel in town. (Singles 2000dr. Doubles 3150dr.) The **Hotel Aktaion** (tel. 612 34), on 23rd Iouliou St. near the causeway, is more expensive, but you'll get clean, modern rooms with balconies, bug screens, and reading lamps. (Doubles 4500dr. Triples with bath 5700dr.)

For meals, try the **Kastro** at the island's base. On a windy day, you can watch waves batter the rocks. (Big portions. Pizza 800dr; Greek salad 600dr. Open noon-4pm and 7:30pm-midnight.) If you stay on the mainland, avoid the "tourist-strip" and grab some food at **Taverna Nikola,** on the main road (stuffed tomatoes, 500dr; chicken 600dr).

CENTRAL GREECE

Delphi ΔΕΛΦΟΙ

In order to discover the world's center, Zeus sent forth two eagles from opposite ends of the earth. They impaled each other with their beaks in the air over Delphi and fell to the ground where the *omphalos,* or navel stone, still marks the spot of the rendez-vous. Troubled or ambitious denizens of the ancient world journeyed to the Oracle of Apollo at Delphi. There, the *Pythia* provided them with pithy advice that was profound, but cryptic.

If modern Delphi is the center of anything, it's of the tour-bus circuit. Basically a one-oracle and two-street town, Delphi now caters to the tour groups that shuffle in daily. Visit in the morning or early evening, and, amidst the relative tranquility and silent ruins, awe your spirit with the site's ancient magic.

Practical Information

Buses leave Athens for Delphi from the station (tel. 823 17) at 260 Liossion St. (5 per day, 3hr., 1950dr). Take city bus #024 from Omonia Sq., or from Amalias Ave. (at the entrance to the National Garden) to the station (30min., 75dr), and buy your ticket at booth #1. In high season, badger the vendor into selling you a ticket an hour or so before the scheduled departure; otherwise, you'll get stuck in a ridiculously long line and may not get a seat at all. Also, note that often you must take the Amphissa bus, which stops at Delphi. A railpass will let you take the train to Levadia and the bus to Delphi from there (550dr). Coming from Patras, take the Thessaloniki bus to Itea (3 per day, 1600dr) and transfer (30min., 260dr).

Buses leave Delphi for Athens from 5:30am to 6pm (in summer 6 per day; fewer in off-season), stopping in Levadia (1¼hr., 550dr). A daily 2pm bus leaves Delphi for Thessaloniki (6hr., 4480dr.); you will have to transfer at the Amphissa stop. The same bus stops at Larissa. Of the three daily buses from Delphi to Patras, the 1pm bus makes a direct trip and rolls right onto the ferry (1600dr). Six buses per day leave for Itea (30min., 260dr), seven go to Amphissa (30min., 260dr), and six go to Arachova (20min., 150dr). You can make a connection to Galaxidi in Itea (30min., 150dr). For Thebes, take the Athens bus to Levadia and change for Thebes (500dr). Except for no service on Sunday, three buses per day make the 2½-hour trip to Lamia (1150dr), where you can change for Volos and Meteora. For help deciphering the many schedules, ask Mike at the **bus station/café** (tel. 828 80; open daily 7:30am-10pm); he speaks excellent English.

The tourist information office, 44 Pavlou St. (tel. 829 00), on the low road from the bus station, gives helpful tips about the area and can supply some hotel and camping rates (open Mon.-Sat. 8am-3pm). If the office is closed, check the front window for posted information about local businesses. On the second floor of 46 Apollonos St. on the left, just up the hill from the bus station, you'll find one of the most jovial **tourist police** offices in Greece (tel. 822 20 or 822 22; office open daily 8am-2pm, but someone's there all the time). On Pavlou St., the east-bound road below Apollonos, you'll find the **post office,** in the middle of the block on the right (tel. 823 76; open Mon.-Fri. 7:30am-2:30pm). You can change money here or at the **bank,** across the street and 30m farther down. (Open in summer Mon.-Thurs. 8am-2pm and 6-7:30pm, Fri. 8am-1:30pm and 6-7:30pm; in off-season Mon.-Thurs. 8am-2pm, Fri. 8am-1:30pm.) The **OTE** is on the same side of Pavlou St., at #10. (Open Mon.-Sat. 7:30am-3:10pm, Sun. 9am-2pm.) The **Red Cross** is at 57 Pavlou St. Delphi's **postal code** is 33054; the **telephone code** is 0265.

Accommodations, Food, and Entertainment

The **HI/IYHF youth hostel,** 29 Apollonos St. (tel. 822 68), at the crest of the hill, is a budget traveler's dream. The manager, a friendly New Zealander, provides clean rooms, hot showers, and excellent advice about exploring the region. The capacious hostel has unbeatable prices. (Hot water 6-8pm. Open March-Nov. Curfew 11pm. Check-out 10am. Two doubles 3500dr. Dorm beds in rooms of 4 or 6, 1000dr. Sheets and blanket 200dr.) Delphi offers many alternatives, all of which are charted on the town map hanging to the left of the café/bus station. Closest to the bus station the sparkling **Hotel Athina,** 51 Pavlou St., provides balconied rooms with breathtaking views of the Gulf of Corinth (tel. 822 39; singles 3000dr, doubles with excellent bathrooms 4000dr. Check-out 11am.). The pleasant **Hotel Pan,** 53 Pavlou St. (tel. 822 94), shares the same view, and features an airy breakfast room and storage facility. (Singles 2600dr. Doubles 3800dr. Triples 4600dr. All with bath.) The same friendly management presides over **Hotel Pythia,** 3 Pavlou St. (tel. 823 28), across and down the street where the views are slightly obstructed (same prices, all rooms include bath). If the open air calls you, try the pool-possessing **Delphi Campground** (tel. 823 63), 3km from Delphi (400dr per tent; 700dr per person; electricity 300dr), or **Apollo Camping** (tel. 827 62), 1km from Delphi (700dr per person. 300-400dr per tent. 300dr for electricity).

Adjacent to the hostel, **Taverna Vakhos,** 31 Apollonos St. (open 7am-11pm), has a terrace overlooking the mountains, the Gulf of Corinth, and scintillating sunsets. (Greek salad 400dr. *Mousaka* 600dr. Lamb or veal with potatoes 750dr.) The restaurant that doubles as the bus station, **Taverna Castri,** is also good, and **markets** can be found at 23 Pavlou (open daily 8am-2pm and 4-10pm) and at 23 Pavlou (open Mon.-Sat. 8am-10pm). For a cheap bite to take on a stroll, try the eats at **Quickly,** at the end of Pavlou St. just before the road to Athens *(gyros, souvlaki,* and other small treats only 150dr). For breakfast or an anytime treat, venture uphill off Apollonos St. past the left of the church and take your first left onto the wide Sugrou St., to the **bakery** (tel. 820 45) on the right. (Open 5am-10pm.) At nightfall, leering natives gather in front of the several **discos** and **pubs** on Pavlou St. while an older tour bus crowd strolls in and out of the many jewelry and gift shops open late into the evening.

Sights

Greece was first united not by the sword, but by the occult. The isolated city-states of ancient Greece were bound together in their worship of the gods, who expressed their wishes to humankind through oracles.

Politically, Delphi's was the supreme oracle: leaders throughout the Mediterranean sought its infallible advice. Whenever a Greek city won a battle, its leader would erect a dedicatory offering to the oracle. As a result, the entrance to the sanctuary was cluttered with monuments from all over Greece.

To the ancient Greeks, a temple's natural surroundings had to be as striking as the construction itself. Resting near the foot of Mt. Parnassos, the Oracle's site is flanked by a towering cliff on one side and the ominous 600m deep Pleistos ravine on the other. According to legend, a shepherd here found one of his charges bleating and shuddering, and shortly began to emulate the animal. All who subsequently visited the spot were similarly affected, and the ancient Greeks concluded that the gods had selected this secluded mountain ledge as the site for a divine oracle.

Another legend claims that Apollo slew the monster Python, which had presided over Delphi, and became sole lord of the city. But the snake, an earth-spirit, continued to speak to postulants through an intermediary, an elderly woman known as the *Pythia,* who was seen only by specially elected priests. She sat upon the *adyton,* the oracular tripod, directly over the *omphalos.* She inhaled the vapors wafting up from the chasm below, and then chanted in a state of delirium. The incoherent mutterings were "versified" by the watching priests, who would announce her prophesy to the waiting public. The Delphic Oracle remained important among Greeks from the 7th century BCE until after the Christianization of the Roman Empire.

The main body of structures, known as the **Pythian Sanctuary,** lies 400m east of town on the road to Athens (follow the highway and take the paved path on your left to the ruins and museum). To appreciate these treasures, consider purchasing the red, white, and black **map** of a first-century BCE reconstruction of the site, available in the shops in town, or at the kiosk across from the bus station, for 300dr. A **guidebook** should also help; Basil Petrakos's is good (1200dr), as is the one by Dr. Petros Thermelis from Delphi's museum (2000dr). The sights are labeled in English, French and some in German. The "Delphi" brochure (free from the GNTO) contains a small map of them.

The **Sanctuary of Pythian Apollo** dominates the site. The building burned in 548 BCE, and then in 373 BCE the reconstruction was shattered by an earthquake. What stands today are the remains of a second united effort at reconstruction. Here oracular priests would announce the *Pythia's* verdicts to their anxious audiences. The huge walls were once inscribed with famous maxims of Greek philosophers. (Site open Mon.-Fri. 7:30am-5:30pm, Sat.-Sun. 8:30am-2:45pm. In off-season Mon.-Fri. 7:30am-5:30pm. Admission 1000dr, students 500dr.) Be sure to visit Delphi's **Archaeological Museum** (tel. 823 12), located just before the Pythian Sanctuary along the path from town. It contains at least two indisputable masterpieces of ancient Greek art: the frieze of the Siphnian Treasury and the Charioteer of Delphi. (Open Mon. 11:30am-5:30pm, Tues.-Fri. 7:30am-5pm, Sat.-Sun. 8:30am-3pm; Admission 1000dr,students 500dr.)

Don't miss the unfenced ruins of the **Temple of Pronaia Athena,** about 180m past the main set of ruins as you head away from town. (Entrance on your right just past the sign saying you are exiting Delphi.) On your way, you'll pass the **Castelian Spring** on your left, where pilgrims cleansed themselves both physically and spiritually before calling upon the oracle. Unfortunately, wooden scaffolding covers the cliff here and the area is closed off (in 1992) because of falling rocks. To your right is the millenia-old **Gymnasium.** Enter at the small *taverna* just below the road. The three remaining Doric columns of the circular 4th-century **Tholos** at Athena's sanctuary are the most elegant and most photographed of Delphi's ruins. Although scholars have inferred from ancient texts that the *Tholos* was an important part of the Delphic complex, no one now knows exactly what function it served. Next to the *Tholos* lies the **Treasury of Marseilles;** this gift from the denizens of ancient France attests to the extent of the oracle's prestige. (Ruins open Mon.-Sat. 8am-7:30pm, Sun. 8am-7pm. Free.)

For practical if not oracular advice, ask the hostel manager to suggest a day-trip adventure. Always venture with someone else, bring plenty of water, and watch out for snakes. It is always wise to let someone know when and where you are traveling into the philosophic wilderness. Every summer, for a week, the European Cultural Center of Delphi presents a **Festival of Ancient Greek Drama** in the Delphi Stadium. Call them in Athens early in the season for information (tel. (01) 722 69 13 or -15).

Near Delphi

Levadia

In case you want a second opinion, the **Oracle of Trophonios** on a cliff overlooking Levadia (ancient Lebadea) attracted pilgrims on their way to Delphi. Pausanias describes an elaborate preliminary ritual in which the pilgrims would drink of both Lethe (forgetfulness) and Mnemosyne (remembrance) waters in order to forget everything before Levadia but remember distinctly the experience in its grove and the revelations the oracle offered. In the 14th century, Frankish Crusaders built a castle over the site of the oracle, now only a 15-minute walk from town. It remains the best-preserved medieval castle in the area.

From the bus station, turn right, and walk uphill to the square, and go right again onto Eleftheriou Venizelou St. At the end of the street make another right, and then left at the church. The stream you'll come to is where the oracle once stood; the castle ruins are 200m farther along.

If the grandeur of this spot or a scarcity of bus connections compels you to spend the night in Levadia, the **Hotel Xenodoheion/Erkinon** (ΧΕΝΟΔΟΧΙΕΟΝ ΕΡΚΥΝΑ; (tel.

(0201) 282 27)) on the first right off Venizelou, has rooms that are as cheap as they look. (Singles 1500dr. Doubles 3000dr.) You will probably prefer to push on to Delphi or Athens for the night; **buses** to Athens (and Thebes) leave every hour from 6am-3pm, and at 5pm and 8pm (2hr., 1100dr; to Thebes, 45min., 550dr). There are also daily buses to Distomo (11 per day, 45min., 400dr.) and to Ossios Loukas (1 per day at 1:30pm, 1hr., 550dr). There is no shortage of pharmacies, clothing stores, cafés, or *souvlaki* stands on the town's two principal streets, which head out to the east from the station. The **OTE** (open Mon.-Fri. 7am-midnight, Sat.-Sun. 8am-10pm) is located in Levadia's main square. To get there, turn left as you exit the station, take the first right onto the main street, and follow it past the park.

Arachova

Stacked onto the slopes below Mt. Parnassos, 10km east of Delphi, the village of Arachova revels in its own relaxed atmosphere. This is a perfect place to collapse after you've spent the day contending with the crowds at Delphi. A gaggle of grandparents sit in the town's central plaza, many wrapped in Arachova's intricate handwoven shawls. The area's culinary distinctions are its amber honey and *saganaki,* cheese dipped in flour and fried. Arachova's main incarnation, however, is a resort ski center. *Souvlaki* and souvenirs aren't hard to find in Arachova—the one main street is brimming with both. The sweaters, woven rugs, and coonskin-type hats that you'll find here befit the town's winter orientation.

Five **buses** per day run between Athens and Delphi, stopping in Arachova, while an additional eight make the run from Arachova to Delphi (150dr). Five buses per day go from Arachova to Itea (2hr., 550dr) and two continue from Itea to Galaxidi (¼hr., 150dr). If you want to go from Arachova to Athens via Levadia, walk east to the square with the fountain (read: trickle), or catch it at the station (6 per day). A pink and white "Celena" sign identifies the **bus station** (tel. 317 90), which doubles as a café and winter restaurant. Eleni, the heptilingual owner, will assist you with bus timetables and accomodations.

The **GNTO** (tel. 316 30 or 316 92) in the first of the town's three squares (coming from Delphi) on the west end, is there primarily for the ski season crowds. Next door, the **post office** also changes money. (Open Mon.-Fri. 7:30am-2pm.) Directly across the square from the post office is the **OTE**. (Open Mon.-Sat. 7:30am-3:10pm.) The **bank** is on the main street, 50m west of the bus station. (Open Mon.-Fri. 9am-2pm.) The **police** are located across from the bus station, on the second floor (tel. 311 33). Farther east, past the third square, you'll find a **pharmacy** (tel. 311 86). Arachova's **telephone code** is 0267.

On the east side of town, straight down the main road past the three squares, you'll find two adjacent hotels. The **Apollon** (tel. 314 27) and the **Parnassos** (tel. 313 07), owned by the same family and with identical prices, differ only in that the latter has a comfy wood-paneled lounge. (Singles 2800dr. Doubles 3700dr. Triples 4500dr. Breakfast 500dr.) Ask at the "Celena" bus station café for *dhomatia* around town. The closest **campground** is just west of Delphi (see Delphi section). The **Grill Room,** downstairs from the police station and across from the bus station, has matchless fare. Head east on the main road for **Taverna Karanthanassis** in the main square (one square to the east from the bus station), where lamb stew with potatoes is a mere 850dr.

Apollo and the Muses now share their abode with ski buffs on **Mt. Parnassos.** Parnassos (2700m) is one of the most accessible mountains. If you're interested in hiking up in summer, follow the road around to the northwest of Arachova to the **Mt. Parnasse Ski Center** (27km). From the ski center it's a steep 2km climb up to the summit, where vultures glower overhead. At the summit is an open, very small (1.5m x 1.5m) cabin where you can spend the night, but be prepared for the biting cold. The ski season on Mt. Parnassos runs roughly from December 15 to March 15. There are 14 lifts, and tickets average 1000dr per day; rentals are also about 1000dr per day. To stay in the area, try Delphi or Arachova, but you'll have to pay 4000dr for the round-trip cab, since the taxi lobby won't allow public buses to run to the ski center. (Taxi tel. 315 66.) Alternatively, you can make a daytrip from Athens (6am, 3hr., round-trip 2500dr). For information, contact the GNTO in Athens or call Delphi's information office (tel. 829 00).

Itea

A quiet escape from Delphi, this semi-industrial little town would offer nothing of interest if it were not for the beach and the long boardwalk waterfront lined with cafés and *tavernas*. Enjoy the view in the afternoon when the construction has silenced and the sun sparkles on the water. The beach east of town has outdoor showers and rows of graffitied benches for beachside reading. A cleaner and more solitary beach is **Kira Beach,** 2km from town. Walk or take a local bus from Delphi (every hr., 1hr., 270dr). If Itea's tranquility tempts you to stay longer, try the **Hotel Galini** (tel. 322 78 or 323 23) on the waterfront street, Akti Posidonos. (Singles with bath 4000dr. Doubles with bath 6000dr.) Or continue to walk, with the water on your right, down the street to **Hotel Akti,** (tel. 32 015 or 32 257) which is cheaper and fairly clean. (Singles 2500dr. Doubles 3850dr, with bath 4750dr. Triples 4600dr.) Moderate cuisine for moderate prices can be found all along the waterfront. The **post office** is along the beach near the bus stop (open Mon.-Fri. 7:30am-2pm). A **bank** is just around the corner: walk down the street away from the water and take the first right in front of the church (open Mon.-Thurs. 8am-2pm and Fri. 8am-1:30pm). Itea has the only **motorbike rental** shop in the Delphi area; inquire at the tourist shop Tsenos; it's past the post office about 100m to the left of the bus station (tel. 333 17; small bikes 2000-4000dr per day).

Frequent **buses** run from Delphi to Itea (6:20am-8pm 11 per day; in low-season 5 per day, 25min., 260dr). The last bus back to Delphi from Itea leaves at 5:45pm; a taxi may be a good option for later returns (tel. 322 00; 1200-2500dr according to the number of passengers).

Galaxidi

Galaxidi is 17km from Itea and the next noticeable town on the road to Amfissa. The name of this seafaring town, a coagulation of *gala* (milk) and *xidhi* (vinegar), reflects the bitter-sweet experiences of a seaman's wife. These days in Galaxidi, there's no need for wives to wring their hands—they can find the husbands floating their boats at one of the town's cafés. Years ago, the sailors took up shipbuilding—still the town's main industry—which gulped down all the surrounding trees. Early in this century, re-planting began and sentinels would guard the pine saplings with a shotgun. A wealthy town visited primarily by boaters, Galaxidi emulates life on the sea—a deep repose rippled with activity and the tide of visitors. The bus drops you off at one end of Nik. Mama, the main street in the town center that leads down to the waterfront and harbor. The cheapest place to stay is **Galaxidi Camping** (tel. 415 30), 2km from town. (Open late June-Oct. 500dr per person. 400dr per tent.) If you prefer freelance camping, there are plenty of beach spots, especially beyond the pine forest. In town, at the end of Nik. Mama, is **Hotel Poseidon** (tel. 414 26). (Singles 4000dr. Doubles 5000dr.) There are also *dhomatia* in town. Try just left of the bus stop at #35 in the Square (tel. 413 03 or 412 72; doubles with bath 4000dr), up the alley-like street perpendicular to Nik. Mama at the bus stop (doubles 3000dr), above Scorpios snack bar on your right just before you get to Poseidon (tel. 411 98; doubles with bath 4000dr), or ask at the bus station-*taverna*. Almost chic, the row of harbor restaurants caters to its seafaring clientele, but dining can be affordable. At the end of Nik. Mama on the water, **Restaurant Alekos** has tummy-tickling food, but make sure to order hot *(zesto)* in summer—otherwise they'll automatically serve it cold. Locals extol Alekos's *pastitsio* (800dr) and Greek salad (650 dr). On the same road farther back in town is the **Elida Souvlaki Shop** *(souvlaki* 130dr). For still cheaper belly-busters, the tempting array of cheeses at the **market** at 6 Nik. Mama is supreme.

For choice swimming, head to the forest side of the harbor (over the "bridge" as you walk down Nik. Mama past Restaurant Alekos), and walk all the way around. Small islands float offshore, and flooded caves overhang scant beaches. Rouse yourself from the beach to visit the nautical **Museum of Galaxidi** (tel. 410 86). Make a left off Nik. Mama opposite the Galaxidi Supermarket, walk two blocks and then turn right as you see the small church on your left. (Open Mon.-Tues. 9:30am-1:30pm, Wed.-Fri.

9:30am-2:30pm, 100dr.) The **Church of St. Nikolas,** near the museum, houses many fine mosaics. The 13th-century **Monastery of Transfiguration,** with sublime 1000-year-old wood carvings and an encompassing view of town, is 6km from Galaxidi (go preferably by car—hitching is reportedly pretty rough going all along this route, with few cars and plenty of heat.

Though Galaxidi appears to sleep in summer, it's livelier than a snail on a skillet come **Carnival** time in February. For the three to four days before Mardi Gras, the entire costumed town parties like crazy and dances around bonfires with indescribable exuberance. Definitely something to write home about, and—lucky for you—Galaxidi's **post office** is at the end of Nik. Mama (open Mon.-Fri. 7:30am-2pm). For indigestion and other mild post-party traumas, head to the **pharmacy** at 15 Nik. Mama. The ever-popular **OTE** is down the first right from the busstop off Nik. Mama (open Mon.-Fri. 7:30am-3:10pm). The **telephone code** is 0265.

Many travelers continue on from Galaxidi to **Navpaktos,** close to the mouth of the Gulf and to the ferry crossing for the Peloponnese at **Antiro.** The **bus** to Navpaktos runs out of Delphi (1350dr), and stops in Galaxidi (1¼hr. from Delphi, 45min. from Galaxidi, 1210dr). If you want to spend the night, stay at the **Aegli** (tel. 272 71; singles 1800dr, doubles 2500dr).

Thermopylae

Eighty km north of Delphi, the pass of Thermopylae once guarded the eastern flank of Athens against land attack from the north. King Leonidas and his 300 Spartans elected to remain here in 480 BCE—certain they would die—to ward off the Persians. Herodotus claimed that the heroic Leonidas held off Xerxes's army of over five million. The Athens-Volos highway traverses this once-strategic pass, and an imposing statue of a fierce Leonidas casting a spear stands guard at the site just before the turn-off to Lamia. The inscription reads, "O passerby, tell the Athenians that here, heeding their call, we remain." The large grave mound lies just opposite, and the famous therapeutic hot springs are nearby.

Distomo and Ossios Loukas
ΔΙΣΤΩΜΟ ΚΑΙ ΑΓΙΟΣ ΛΟΥΚΑΣ

Although off the beaten track and toilsome to reach, **Ossios Loukas** rewards you for your troubles. The inspiring halcyon atmosphere of this secluded spot will instill in you pangs of longing for the monkhood. This beautiful stone monastery 1700m above sea-level has splendid mosaics, as well as the occasional seraphic goat.

The main building in the complex, the **Church of St. Luke,** is dedicated to a local hermit, known for his powers of healing and prophesy, who managed to attain sainthood. According to locals, when Luke died in his cell in 953 CE, a myrrh tree sprouted from the cold cell floor. The large narthex providing entrance to the 10th-century church is adorned with Byzantine mosaics—most notably a faceless Doubting Thomas inserting his finger in Christ's wound. The surviving mosaics of premier pulchritude—the Nativity, Presentation at the Temple, and Baptism—are tucked into the squinches that support the dome. Although not as famous as the mosaics in the upper church, the 11th-century frescoes that cover most of the **crypt's** interior are every bit as beautiful; bring a flashlight to see them in their full glory. The oldest part of the monastery is the 10th-century **Church of St. Mary** adjoining the larger church. While Ossios Loukas has many indoor treasures, it is the robust flowers, twittering birds, and surrounding mountains outside the monastery which make the site most truly idyllic. (Tel. (0267) 227 97; open daily 8am-2pm and 4-7pm; in winter 8am-7pm; admission to the Church of St. Luke 600dr, students 300dr; monastery, crypt, and Church of St. Mary are free).

To allow for any transportation difficulties, it would be wise to give Ossios Loukas a full day. From Delphi, take one of the frequent Athens **buses** and ask the driver to let you off at the crossroads for **Distomo.** From there you can take a taxi for the 9km trip to the monastery. There is a bus from Distomo to Ossios Loukas but it arrives just around 2pm when the monastery closes for the afternoon, so you'll have to wait for it to re-open at 4pm. From Levadia, the bus to Distomo takes only 30 minutes (190dr). You can also take the bus to Kiriaki and tell them you are going to Ossios Loukas—they'll drop you off right at the turn-off (30min., 210dr). It's a 2½-km walk to the monastery from there. From the Liossion St. station in Athens, there is a daily bus to the monastery (10:30am, 3½hr., 1300dr.)

Getting out of Ossios Loukas is a lot easier than getting in; every tourist at the monastery is either going to Athens or Delphi, so many travelers mooch lifts from commericial tour buses (not private vehicles). If you find yourself stranded in Distomo, check into the salubrious **Koutiaris Hotel** (tel. (0267) 222 68), on the main square across from the church. (Singles 2800dr. Doubles 3800dr). The **American Hotel,** (tel. (0267) 220 79 or 220 80) up the road from the bus stop, is cheaper, if you don't mind the smell of mothballs. (Singles 2700dr. Doubles 4000dr. All rooms with private bath.) The only place to eat is a *souvlaki* joint called **Corner,** up the main road on the left. There are also several supermarkets in town. The **post office,** where you can change money, is down the hill near the bus stop (open Mon.-Fri. 7:30am-2pm). Call the **police** at 221 00, and for **medical emergency** (hospital) call 227 91. The **OTE** is a few buildings down the road (open Mon.-Fri. 7:30am-3pm).

Thebes ΘHBA

Thebes once ranked among the most powerful of the ancient Greek cities. Its importance was partly due to its location, which gave it control over the strategic routes connecting the Peloponnese and Attica with northern Greece. The fertile soil guaranteed Thebes's prosperity.

According to legend, Thebes was founded by Kadmos, following instructions he received from the Delphic Oracle. The town is most famous as the setting for the story of Oedipus. When Oedipus's father Laius, King of Thebes, learned from the oracle at Delphi that his son would some day kill him and marry the bereaved queen, he was duly perturbed. His solution was to abandon the infant Oedipus on a nearby mountain to die. For good measure, Laius had his son's feet nailed together to prevent escape. A shepherd, however, found the infant and gave him to the king and queen of Corinth, who raised him as their own. When he grew up and learned of his fate, Oedipus fled to Thebes, to avoid killing the King of Corinth, whom he thought was his true father. In a chance encounter on the way, he killed Laius, and then trotted on to Thebes and married Queen Jocasta, his mother. When the true story was revealed many years later, Jocasta committed suicide and Oedipus blinded himself.

Modern Thebes maintains none of its ancient complexity. Razed by Alexander the Great in the 4th century BCE, it has never recovered. It is a noisy, inelegant town, worth visiting only if you too fear you might kill one parent and marry the other. From the bus station, walk downhill on Epaminon St. and make the first right to the 13th-century Frankish tower and then a left down to the end of the road to see the museum's Mycenaean *larnakes* (clay coffins), adorned with paintings of funerary rites, mosaics, and reliefs. The guide book is particularly informative. (Open Tues.-Sun. 8:30am-3pm. Admission 400dr, students 200dr with cards.

Of slight interest are the scanty remains of the **House of Kadmos,** a Mycenaean palace dating from the 14th century BCE, visible from the street (opposite the Commercial Bank of Greece at 53 Pindari St.). Underneath the modern town of Thebes are an extensive Mycenaean palace and acropolis. Historians and archaeologists begrudge Thebes every new building, fearing construction may endanger what little remains of the great Mycenaean civilization.

If you are moved (or rather obliged) to spend the night in this tragic town, the **Hotel Niobi,** 63 Epaminon St. (tel. 298 88), up and across the street from the bus station, is your best bet. (Singles 3240dr, with bath 4320dr. Doubles 5400dr, with bath 6480dr.) Across the street, the more luxurious **Hotel Meletiou** (tel. 273 33 or 221 11) offers private baths. (Singles 4000dr. Doubles 44320dr.) In the evening the many *tavernas* that line the Epaminon and Pindari streets provide lively R&R for the neighboring military base. The **OTE** is just around the corner from the bus station (open Mon.-Fri. 8am-11pm, Sat. 7:30am-3:10pm). The **post office** is uphill on the left, one block from the hotels (open Mon.-Sat. 7:30am-2pm, Sun. 9am-1:30pm). Thebes's **postal code** is 32200; the **telephone code** is 0262.

Thebes is a bus juncture for Evia and the Sporades. **Buses** leave Thebes for Chalkis at 7:45am and 10am (500dr), but service is more frequent to and from Levadia (550dr) and the terminal at 260 Liossion St. in Athens (every hour on the hour, 900dr). Or to travel between Thebes and Chalkis, take the frequent Athens bus to the bus stop at Skimatari (30min.). There, walk across the street to catch the Athens-Chalkis bus which runs every half hour (10min.). For a **taxi,** call 297 88.

Agios Konstantinos

Come to this small resort town to take a ferry to the Sporades. The **ferry office,** Alkyon Travel (tel. (0235) 319 89 or 319 20), is located on a prominent corner of the waterfront. In high season, one or two ferries per day run to Skiathos (2240dr), Glossa (2200dr), Skopelos (2600dr), and Alonissos (2870dr). Flying Dolphin **hydrofoils** (tel. (0235) 316 14 or 318 74) run on a similar schedule, with higher prices: to Skiathos; Skopelos (5324dr); and Alonissos (5577dr). The office is to the left of Alkyon Travel. Just two doors down the street stands the **bank,** sandwiched between two cafés. (Open Mon.-Thurs. 8am-2pm, Fri. 8am-1:30pm.) The tall gray building behind Alkyon Travel on the waterfront road is the **OTE** (open Mon.-Fri. 7:30am-3:10pm); the **post office** and **currency exchange** are nearby (open Mon.-Fri. 7:30am-2pm). The **postal code** is 35006; the **telephone code** is 0235.

You can reach Agios Konstantinos by daily **bus** from Athens (2½hr., 2000dr), a bus from Halkida (2 per day, 1½hr., 1500dr), or by **ferry** from Aedipsos (6am-10pm, every 2hr., 1hr., 650dr). The ferry docks (for the ferries to the islands) are at Arkitsa, but frequent buses (marked *Lamia;* 100dr) run to Agios Konstantinos. The bus stop is several blocks up from the harbor.

Evia (Euboea) EYBOIA

Wrenched from the mainland by an ancient earthquake (or perhaps by Poseidon's trident), Evia kisses the coastline north of Athens. The second biggest island in Greece (after Crete), Evia was a major trading center and maritime power in ancient times. Although nowadays the local tourist committee likes to highlight Evia as a Greek island with frequent bus service from the mainland, it seems more a part of Central Greece—travelers may pass over the short wooden swingbridge at Chalkis and barely notice it. What is noticeable about Evia is its central mountain range: choked with chestnuts and pines, it is a paradise for hikers. Though several beaches are sprinkled around the coast of Evia, it has yet to be infested with swanky resorts. Few islanders speak English, but many speak German.

Bus transportation on Evia is generally reliable, but it often involves inconvenient transfers and indirect routes, so allow plenty of time to get from one place to another. If you plan to visit Marmari or Karystos on the lower coast, it is easier, faster, and cheaper to take a **ferry** from Rafina or Agia Marina than to take a bus from Chalkis. While the ferry from Rafina to Karystos takes only two hours (1-2 per day, 1318dr), the bus from Halkida to Karystos takes 4 hours (3 per day, 1500dr). Kimi, a hilltop town on the east side of Evia, is the gateway to Skyros and the other Sporades. The mountain and valley scope from the bus is spectacular, but the winding roads keep the rider vigilant and make for a very long ride.

Chalkis

The dingy and suffocating port capital of Evia, Chalkis (also called **Halkida**) is transportation central for the island, where visitors inevitably are marooned for a few hours. Although you probably won't want to spend much more time here, Chalkis does offer a few distractions for the idle tourist: a museum, a beach, and an interesting tidal current. The enigmatic Evia strait changes direction an average of eight times per day. According to local lore, Aristotle, in a fit of anguish, threw himself into these waters.

The **bus station** in the center of town, at the top of the road that crosses the bridge, is a more likely spot for the visitor to falter in despair. A **bus** from the Liossion Station in Athens runs to Chalkis (every 30min., 1½hr., 900dr). The **train** is cheaper (18 per day, 2hr., 450dr). Arrival by train leaves you on the mainland; just cross the bridge to the island and the busier section of Chalkis. About 5 blocks to the left of the bridge you'll find El. Venizelou Street, running uphill. If you get off at the bus depot, turn left and then right onto the wide, busy road; walk down one block to get to El. Venizelou St. The **hydrofoil** now leaves from the dock to the right of the bridge as you face the mainland. You can purchase tickets at the shack on the waterfront just in line with the dock (tel. 215 21 or 216 21). The English-speaking **tourist police** are located in the back of the police staion at 32 El. Venizelou (open Mon.-Fri. 8am-2pm), and will help tourists with questions (tel. 221 00). You can change money next door at the **bank.** (Open Mon.-Thurs. 8am-2pm, Fri. 8am-1:30pm.) The **post office** is on Karamourzouni St., the second left off El. Venizelou as you walk uphill from the water. (Open Mon.-Fri. 7:30am-10pm.) For **taxis,** dial 252 20. The **OTE** is located on Papiadaiou St.—walk up El. Venizelou four full blocks from the water (two blocks after the park with the fountain) and then make a left on Papaskiadaiou, continuing over for one block. (Open Mon.-Sat. 7am-midnight, Sun. 7am-10pm.) The **postal code** is 34100; the **telephone code** is 0221.

Hotels are conveniently located just to the left of the bridge, but the only affordable one is the **Iris Hotel** (tel. 222 46, no sign) in Plateia Gefyras, the plaza across from the bridge. (Singles 2000dr. Doubles 4000dr.) The Iris is next to the corner café on the left, just past the bridge from Attica. There are comely, expensive cafés all along the waterfront. You can find a quick and inexpensive meal at one of the many restaurants near the bus station. At the **Estiatopis Restaurant,** just across from the station's entrance, you can enjoy a whole roasted chicken *(kottopoolo)* for about 1400dr. *Souvlaki* and *gyros* havens are multitudinous on the road from the bridge to the station, and near the waterfront cafés. Chalkis's **Archaeological Museum,** across from the police station on Venizelou St., houses pottery and marble sculpture. (Open Tues.-Sun. 8:30am-3pm. Admission 400dr, students 200dr.)

Forty-two km from Chalkis, on the east side of the island, there is a winter ski center at Steni on spiffy Mt. Derfi (1150m). Take the bus from Chalkis to Steni (5 per day, 380dr.).

Southern Evia

The first settlement south of Chalkis is the modern resort town of **Eretria.** A shipping center and colonial power that rose to prominence in the 8th century BCE, Eretria continued to hold sway until the 4th century BCE. At that time, it joined the Athenian League, but revolted and was finally eclipsed by Athens, its puissant maritime rival. In the 3rd century BCE, the town became the center of the esteemed Eretrian School of Philosophy, founded by Menedemos, one of Plato's pupils. These days, intellectual endeavors are but trivial pursuits to the people here; Eretria is purely a vacation town.

Buses running from Athens to Kimi stop at the café in the center of Eretria (every 2hr., 2hr., 650dr) before continuing on to Kimi (1½hr., 600dr). It's easier to catch one of these than to go to Kimi via Chalkis. Buses travel from Chalkis to Eretria every hour (last bus at 8:15pm, 30min., 260dr). You can also reach Eretria by **ferry** from Skala Oropou on the mainland (every ½hr., 30min., 140dr). With your back to the bus depot, walk down the street to your right until you reach Archeou Teatrou St., the wide road lined with white-trunked trees. There is a town map on the left hand corner before you cross the street. Turn left and walk down one block to reach the **post office,** where you can change money. (Open Mon.-Fri. 7:30am-2pm.) Or turn right and walk one block in the direction of the water to reach the **OTE.** (Open Mon.-Fri. 7:30am-3:10pm.)

The best bargain in town is **Pension Theodorou** (tel. 624 79); take a right from the bus station on Apostoli St. to #6, a three-story building with balconies (just past the pharmacy and souvenir shops). It offers rooms with size and no sully. (Singles 1500dr. Doubles 2500dr.) **Pension Diamanto** (ΠΑΝΣΙΟΝ ΔΙΑΜΑΝΤΟ; tel 622 14), past Café Babylon at the end of Archeaou Teatrou St. as you walk towards the water, is the next best thing. (Singles 3000dr. Doubles 4500dr. Private bath included. Ask at Café Babylon.) For the rustic set, **Camping Eva** (tel. 610 81) is 4km from town on the road to Chalkis (500dr per person, 500-560dr per tent, 300dr per car).

Eretria does not lack places where you can indulge your gourmandise. **O Parlos,** across from the bike shop, is a good bet, serving up *tzatziki, gyros,* and *souvlaki* nightly from 7:30pm. If you're in town on Sunday, enjoy the fresh produce at the **market** which carnivalizes Teatrou St. The **Museum of Eretria** (tel. 622 06) houses artifacts from the ancient city and photos from the town's excavations. You can find it two blocks past the post office, at the end of Archeou Teatrou St. (Open Tues.-Sun. 8:30am-3pm. Admission 350dr, students 150dr.) To the right of the museum and across the road are the sparse remains of the city's ancient **theater** and the **Temple of Daphneos Apollo.**

Nine km south of Eretria is the more charming **Amarinthos,** with excellent piscatory pleasuredomes lining its luscious beach. Frequent buses from Chalkis pass through Eretia on their way to Amarinthos (400dr) and drop you off at the town square where you will find the **post office** which exchanges money (open Mon.-Fri. 7:30am-2pm) and the **OTE** (open Mon.-Fri. 7:30am-3:10pm).

There are no cheap pensions in Amarinthos, but ask around for one of the many **rooms to let.** Be clear that you mean room and not apartment. Visit the two small Byzantine churches of **Metamor Fossis** and **Kimissis Theotokou** one block back from the harbor. You can pick up another frequent daily **bus** in the square and head to Kimi (700dr).

Continuing south, you'll reach **Lepoura,** an indecisive hamlet that masks a fork in the road. One path heads to Kimi through, over, and around Southern Evia's most spectacular mountain scenery. The other path continues south, running inland along the island's spine toward Karystos.

The drowsy resort town of **Nea Stira** is 75km south of Chalkis on the west coast. Sprawled along a mile of the shore, and never more than two blocks deep, it lies on a calm bay protected by several islets. Sandy beaches flank both sides of the town. The hotels in town are expensive. Fortunately, it is possible to camp 10 minutes down the coast in either direction. About 2km along the beach (water on the left) is **Venus Beach,** replete with windsurfing and boating facilities. A **bus** connects Stira to Karystos (2 per day, 1¼hr., 440dr). **Ferries** run from Stira to **Agia Marina** on the Attic coast (7 per day, 45min., 430dr), where a bus connects to Athens (2hr.). You can walk from Agia Marina to the ruins of **Ramnous** (30-45min.). If you can catch a bus going up the hill to the crossroads, insist that the driver let you off at Ramnous.

Karystos

Surrounded by mountains and flanked by two long sandy beaches, Karystos, the largest town in Southern Evia, is a calm, clean, comfortable city. Pointed round straw umbrellas, like little headless hats, dot the sands that extend on either direction from the port.

The **bus** stops one block above the main square, next to the **National Bank.** (Open Mon.-Thurs. 8am-2pm, Fri. 8am-1:30pm.) To find the **police station** (tel. 222 52), turn into the small alley just past the bank and climb the stairs. The **OTE** is on the next cross-street beyond the square, across from the blue-domed **Church of St. Nicholas.** (Open daily 7:30am-3pm.) From the **OTE,** reach the **post office** by walking down the same street away from the church, and turning right after the playground; you'll see the round yellow sign. (Open Mon.-Fri. 7:30am-2pm.) **Taxis** (tel. 222 00) line up along the right-hand side of the square. The **postal code** is 34001; the **telephone code** is 0224. The tourist office can help you find rooms, or look for room-to-let signs at restaurants along the dock. Call jovial **George and Bill Kolobarus,** 42 Sahtouri St. (tel. 220 71), who offer cozy rooms in a homey atmosphere (doubles 3000dr; triples 4000dr; hot water and use of kitchen). The octopi lined up and drying in the sun give fair warning of the town's favorite food. The food and prices are peerless at **O Kavodoros,** 1 block inland on Parodos Sachtouri St., the alleyway a half-block right of the main square (fish 350dr, octopus 480dr; famous fried meatballs 600dr; open 7:30am-3:15pm and 6:30pm-midnight). Menu in Greek; friendly waiter in English. **Taverna Psistaria,** next to Hotel Als, prepares daily dinner specials on the spit. (Full meal about 850dr.) For good deep-dish pizza, try **Pizza Napoli,** one of the last restaurants on the main street. If you long for nostalgia and an incredible cheeseburger or homemade rice pudding (100dr), try **Jo Marie's Hamburgers,** four doors down and three steps up from the bank on Karystou St. (Sign in Greek; look for the round parlor chairs. Open daily for breakfast, lunch and dinner.) For cocktails-by-the-sea, head to the **Terrace et Phaedra,** one street inland on the left side of the waterfront as you face the water. Also popular with the night and daytime crowds are **Archipelagos, Milk Bar,** and **Nexus Pub** in a row on the far right side of the waterfront. From the last *taverna,* bear left along the water where the road splits. The dramatic view and heady sea air here may put you in the mood to linger, but if your toes start twitching, head to the **Barbados** disco (tel. 241 19), 3km from town towards the mountains. The 1300dr cover includes your first drink. It is safest and wisest to take some kind of wheels unless you're traveling in a big group. A cab will run you 500dr, maybe more after midnight.

If you want to inspect the interior of the coastal **Fort of Bourdzi,** which dates from the Crusades, ask at the tourist office. The fort is open for two morning hours Monday, Wednesday, Thursday, and Friday in July and August. Otherwise, peek into one of the big holes at the back of the fort and imagine life in the 1100s. If you're really lucky, you might catch a summer student theatrical production going on inside. The long, sandy beach of **Psili Ammos,** near the fort, is a good place to soak up the sun, or you can trek past the shipyard and enjoy the beach by the bars.

Twice daily **buses** from Karystos travel to: Halkida (4hr., 1500dr); Stira (1¼hr., 440dr); and the slightly crowded resort town of Marmari (30min., 200dr). Two **ferries** per day head to Rafina from Karystos (2hr., 1318dr) and Marmari (1½hr., 753dr). In Karystos, ferry tickets are sold at the tourist office (tel. 242 77) on the left of the square as you face the water (open daily 8am-3pm and 5-9pm).

If you have a free morning, explore the villages north of Karystos. Follow Aiolou St., 1 block east of the square, out of town; continue straight at the crossroads toward **Palaio Chora,** a village that dawdles among lemon and olive groves. Turn right at a sign saying "metamorphosis" and you'll find a shaded stone path leading up to an old church. For a more strenuous trek, turn right at the crossroads outside Karystos and go toward the village of **Mili.** The road ascends sharply and follows a clear stream to the village, where water flows from the mouths of three lions in a small roadside fountain. From Mili, a 20-minute hike up the hill on the left and across the stone bridge will bring you to **Kokkino Kastro** (the Red Castle), a 13th-century Venetian castle named for the blood that was spilled there during the war between the Greeks and the Turks.

For more extensive hiking, climb Evia's second-highest mountain, **Mt. Ochi** (1398m), located in the heart of the unspoiled southern area. Check out the stone refuge hut on the mountain, a three to four hour hike from Karystos. The refuge, made of unmortared stone blocks during the Pelasgian Period was, according to some, a temple to Hera; others claim it was a signal tower. The ruin is known as the "dragon's house," and since it is allegedly haunted, you will probably be the only mortal there.

Kimi

With an abundance of foliage and cool, tangy sea breezes, Kimi offers a refreshing respite from the parched Greek summer. Dubbed "the balcony of the Aegean" because of its perch 250m over the water, Kimi was once a major harbor renowned for its fishingfolk, figs, and wine. But 30 years ago, disease destroyed all the vineyards and the population dropped from 30,000 to 10,000. Although most buses stop at Kimi Beach (known as "Paralia Kimi"), some will go no farther than the bus depot in Kimi Town. To get to the beach/port from town, wait at the station or the stop by the post office on the main square. Buses navigate the 52 twisting turns to Paralia Kimi and back roughly every two hours (175dr). The 5km downhill walk affords glorious views, but beware of traffic on the hairpin turns. The cost of a **taxi** (tel. 236 66 in Kimi Town, 232 55 in Paralia Kimi) is roughly 700dr. If you are returning from Paralia Kimi to Chalkis or Athens, buses leave the port 10 minutes before their scheduled departure from Kimi Town.

To reach the main square of Kimi Town from the bus station, make a right as you exit the station and a left up the steep hill. The main street sprawls into a plaza around the town church (try to peek at the colorful and elaborate interior). Along this street you'll find the **bank** (open Mon.-Thurs. 8am-2pm, Fri. 8am-1:30pm), directly across from the church, and the **post office**, one block above the church (open Mon.-Fri. 7:30am-2pm). The **OTE** is one block below the church on the right. (Open Mon.-Fri. 7:30am-3:10pm.) The **police** (tel. 225 55) are located two blocks behind the church, at the corner where the road is intersected by another heading downhill; entrance to the yellow building is on the downhill side (open 24 hrs.). The road leading down to Paralia Kimi begins at the corner, just before the post office, also where the bus stops. The Georgios Papanicolaou **hospital/clinic** (tel. 223 22), which houses Kimi's **health center** (tel. 232 52/53), is located 3km from the station. To get there, head north from the station, make a right on the first main road, and follow it uphill until you reach the hospital. The **Folklore Museum** (tel. 220 11) is on the road descending to Paralia Kimi. They have an exhibit dedicated to Kimi's most famous son—Georgios Papanicolaou, discoverer and developer of the Pap smear. (Open daily 10am-1pm and 6-8:30pm, in low season Mon.-Sat. 10am-1pm and 4-6:30pm, Sun. 10am-1pm. Admission 200dr.) Kimi's **postal code** is 34003; its **telephone code** is 0222.

A small whitewashed seafarer's chapel and the ruins of a windmill are poised on the hill behind town. A climb to either affords tremendous views of Kimi and the sea. On the east side of the same mountain, 5km from Kimi, is the 700-year-old, majestically situated **Monastery of the Savior.** When pirates landed at Kimi in the late 18th and 19th centuries, signals calling for aid were sent from the **Venetian Castle** above the monastery and passed along to other castles.

July and August collude to create a scarcity of tourist accommodations in Kimi. In Kimi Town, cheap and comfortable lodgings are sometimes available at the **Kimi Hotel** (tel. 224 08), up the street and around the corner from the post office. (Doubles 3500dr. Triples 4600dr.) In Paralia Kimi, you'll find rooms showcasing cleanliness and comfort in **Roula Mutufariki's** home (tel. 226 12), the light-green trimmed house at the right end of the waterfront as you face the water. (Doubles 3000dr. Triples 3500dr.) Atop **Restaurant Balenti** at the center of the waterfront are beds with hot pink blankets so spiffy you could bounce a quarter on them (doubles with bath 6000dr) The luxurious **Hotel Beis** (tel. 226 04), at the other end of the waterfront, has bathrooms in every room. (Singles 3955dr. Doubles 6215dr. Triples 7400dr.)

Restaurants and cafés line the harbor at Paralia Kimi. On the south side of the waterfront, you'll find decent meals at **To Airaio** (chicken with vegetables 500dr.) For a quick and inexpensive meal in Kimi Town, go past the post office to **Pikantiki Restaurant** (spaghetti 450dr). Otherwise, you'll have to find sustenance at *souvlaki* or hot dog stands, or the **supermarket** (which has a good deli counter) down the main road past the OTE. You'll find fresh produce on the street behind the church.

Two agents in Paralia Kimi sell **ferry** tickets. To the left of the road descending from Kimi Town, next to the Sosco gas station, is the agent for the *Skiathos* (tel. 228 25). This ferry services: Skiathos (4½hr., 3398dr); Skopelos (4hr., 3050dr); Alonissos (3hr., 2870dr); and Volos (9hr., 5291dr). In July and August, the ferry runs four times per week, in off-season once or twice. The agent also has ferries to Limnos (7hr., 2234dr) and Kavala (14hr., 3441dr) once each week. The Flying Dolphin **hydrofoils** also make trips to Skiathos (6966dr), Skopelos (6286dr), Alonissos (5832dr), and Skyros (3010dr). To the right of the road descending from Kimi Town, in the blue and white striped building, is the agent for the *Anemoessa* (tel. 220 20 or 224 55; open 9am-1pm and 5-8:30pm; tickets sold on the dock 4-5pm). This vessel serves Skyros (2-3 per day, in off-season 1 per day, 2hr., 1312dr). **Buses** run to Kimi directly from 260 Liossion St. in Athens (6 per day, 3½hr., 1950dr) and from Chalkis (8 per day, 2¼hr., 1000dr). From

Karystos, take the bus to Lepoura for a magnificent tour of the mountainside (3 per day, 2½hr., 850dr) and transfer from Lepoura to Kimi (4 per day, 1hr., 480dr). For further information, call Kimi's **bus station** at 222 57 or 222 56. A 10-minute walk to the left (facing the water) from the ferry landing in Paralia Kimi brings you to a public beach where you can work on your island tan before traveling.

Northern Evia

Limni

According to legend, Zeus married Hera in Limni, but an infelicitous earthquake destroyed the wedding temple long ago. A lively port town, Limni is still a perfect venue for nuptials or any other get-away. Activity centers on the long waterfront stretch that curves into a smile as it grazes over bobbing moorings and into the bay. Adjacent to a solitudinous rocky beach and connected by bus and hydrofoil to surrounding towns, Limni makes a pleasant base for exploring Northern Evia. As tourists are few and transient, there are only two hotels, so call for reservations.

Buses run from Chalkis to Limni (4 per day, 2½hr., 1000dr). There is also bus service to Adepsos (25min., 260dr) with connections to Istea (30min., 260dr.) and on to Pefki (15min., 140dr). The **hydrofoil** runs from Chalkis to Limni (2 per day, 40min., 1850dr, round-trip 3130dr) and continues on to Aedipsos (25min., 1376dr). Others, also with return service, run from Agios Constantinos (1 per day, 50min., 1917dr) and the Sporades islands (Skiathos 4655dr, Skopelos 5989dr). All have extra connections in peak season.

If you arrive by bus, you will be dropped off at the center of the waterfront, next to the **bank.** (Open Mon.-Thurs. 8am-2pm, Fri. 8am-1:30pm.) The **post office** (open Mon.-Fri. 7:30am-2pm.) is in the little square just off the waterfront, just up the street from the bank. On the same street past the square on the left is the **hydrofoil agency** (tel. 312 54). To find the **OTE**, walk down to the far left of the waterfront and then follow the signs up the hill and to the right. (Open Mon.-Fri. 7:30am-3:10pm.) Limni's **postal code** is 34005; the **telephone code** is 0227.

The superlative English-speaking service will delight you at **Hotel Limni** (tel. summer: 317 48 or 313 16, winter: 313 78), at the far left end of the waterfront. The spacious clean rooms have private baths. (Open March-Nov. and Christmas, Dec.-Feb. weekends only. Singles 2650dr. Doubles 3900dr. Breakfast 400dr.) The **Plaza Hotel** (tel. 312 35), on the waterfront to the right of the bus stop, features charming rooms with a country decor. (Open year-round. Doubles 3724dr, with bath 4514dr.) Mr. and Mrs. Livaditis rent **apartments** on the beach, a mere 1½km from town. Call them or drop by their **Restaurant Pirofani** (tel. 316 40), at the right-hand of the waterfront. (5000dr per day. Kitchen and bath included.)

Nights are cool in Limni, but you may still wish to dine by the water. Go for a slow stroll (*volta*) before you choose something in a waterfront *taverna,* ouzerie or sweetshop. Notice the kicklines of severed octopus legs and other exotic catches hanging on racks by the tables that signal fresh seafood. **O Platanos,** to the left of the bus stop, serves good, standard fare and affordable fresh fish (2 small grilled fish, 800dr). You can watch the kebab broil as you munch on your own *souvlaki* at the **Ouzerie,** just past the puple-chaired **Gelateria** (tri-flavored cone, 150dr.) down left of the bus stop. If you're running out of *drachmae,* there's fresh food at unbeatable prices in the **Roussos Supermarket** along the water to the left of the bus stop (open Mon.-Sat. 8am-2pm, Tues. and Thurs. 5:30-8:30pm). After dinner, the outdoor **Video bar,** just past the market, rocks from 9pm to 4 or 5 in the morning. You can find clear-water bathing on a rocky beach just past the far right-hand end of the waterfront. Keep walking and you will find solitude under a plunging cliff.

Aedipsos

The village of Aedipsos, 30km north of Limni, is one of the biggest resorts in Evia. Praised by Herodotus, Aristotle, and Aristophanes for its healing sulphurous waters, Aedipsos attracts older tourists who suffer from arthritis and rheumatism, but is worth a day trip for anyone who wishes to enjoy the hot springs' relaxing vigor. Locals advise that you swim for 30 minutes at the most, as hours of bathing will leave you in a theraputic stupor. The bus will drop you off in a small square at Ermou St., from which you will be able to see the waterfront. The steaming golden waters are a short walk along the waterfront with the water on your right.

There are plenty of hotels in Aedipsos, but in the high season try the cheaper *dhomatia* along Ermou St. and in the town square. Residences are marked with official signs from the "Federation of Rooms to Let." The **tourist police** on the first floor of 3 Oceanidon St. (tel. 224 56) might be of some help. Facing the water, from the town square, take a right on Ermou St., then your first left. The **OTE** is hidden behind a black gate and a garden in the square (open Mon.-Fri. 7:30am-3:10pm). The **post office,** which exchanges money, is up the hill on the square (open Mon.-Fri. 7:30am-2pm). **Buses** run between Athens and Aedipsos (3 per day, 3¼hr., 1800dr) and between Aedipsos and Limni (30min., 250dr). **Hydrofoils** connect Aedipsos with Limni, Chalkis and the Sporades. The hydrofoil agent who doubles as a lotto distributor is located in the center of the waterfront (tel. 237 60 or 241 90).

Near Aedipsos

Seventeen km northeast of Aedipsos lies the sprawling town of **Orei** which guards the remains of the maritime acropolis of ancient Histiaea. On the way, you'll find only sand, solitude, breath-taking cliffs and fruit-speckled hills begging to be hiked. Continuing north by bus you'll have to make a connection in the town square of **Istiea,** a modern city, now the region's largest. In case you get stuck, you can find pleasant accommodations at the **Hotel Neon,** 7 Angeli Goviou (tel. (0226) 522 26), more cozy and quaint than it sounds. (Singles 1900dr. Doubles 3800dr.) From the main square, walk two blocks past the church to the small square with the bushy tree. The hotel is at your next right from there.

The rustic **Pefki,** 10km farther north, offers a camp ground and a popular expanse of beach. The bus drops you off in front of a kiosk along the beach. The many hotels along the stretch are expensive and fill quickly with tour groups, so call ahead. Try the bustling **Hotel Myrtia** (tel. (0226) 412 02 or 415 10), to the right from the bus stop as you face the water. (Doubles 5000dr.) Almost every roof along the beach shelters *dhomatia* which should be cheaper so just ask when you arrive. **Camping Pefki** (tel. (0226) 411 21) is just 1km outside of the town (500dr per person, small tent 500dr, large tent 700dr). The **bus** runs between Istiea and Pefki (15min., 140dr.) and there is **hydrofoil** service to the Sporades. Ask for hydrofoil information at the busstop kiosk or at the agent just down the street to the left, just off the waterfront (tel. 410 27 or 413 04).

NORTHERN GREECE

Northern Greece seldom finds its way onto postcards or promotional posters, but not for lack of beauty. Robust and without pretensions, Northern Greece waits to be discovered by the adventurous traveler. Here, unlike on the islands, no one caters to visitors or puts on a show: nobody whitewashes the buildings, translates the menus, or accepts American Express cards with a smile. Here, you're entering the Greek's Greece.

Northern Greece consists of four provinces. The largest is **Macedonia,** in the north-central part of the country. Thessaloniki, Greece's second largest city, sits in its center; the peninsulas of Halkidiki extend along its eastern edge; and the Kastorian Lakes mark its western edge. **Epirus** province hides sandy coves on its scenic coast and canyons amid rugged mountains, a few hours away from Ioannina. Crowned by Mt. Olympos, **Thessaly** stretches east to incredibly cool and verdant Mt. Pelion on the Aegean. **Thrace,** the least touristed of the four regions, sits in the northeast corner of the country, bordering Turkey.

Thessaly ΘΕΣΣΑΛΙΑ

Despite its industrialized urban centers, Thessaly manages to enchant the visitor with quiet villages and monasteries. To the west of the cultivated Thessalian plain, the monasteries of Meteora cling to towering pinnacles. The rocky crags of Mt. Olympos, throne of the pantheon of Greek gods, watch over Aegean beaches with stark majesty. To the southeast, traditional mountain hamlets on Mt. Pelion lie scattered among forests, apple orchards, and olive groves that reach out to the sea.

Volos ΒΟΛΟΣ

Jason and the Argonauts set sail from Volos on their quest for the Golden Fleece. Lucky for them, they got out before the arrival of the smog, noise, and dust that coat the modern port city. Apart from its **Archaeological Museum,** 1 Athonassaki St. (tel. 252 85), which displays findings from the latter part of the Paleolithic Era to the Roman period, Volos is attractive only as a base from which to explore Pelion and the Sporades Islands. (Museum open Tues.-Sun. 8:30am-3pm. Admission 400dr, students 200dr.) While you're biding time, waiting for the bus or ferry, stroll past the lively *tavernas* on the waterfront and through the orange tree-lined streets in the neighborhood surrounding the museum.

Practical Information

Greek National Tourist Organization (GNTO): On the waterfront in Riga Fereou Sq. (tel. 235 00 or 362 33). Eager to provide more information than you could possibly need. Hotel list posted after closing. Open Mon.-Fri. 7am-2:30pm and 6-8:30pm, Sat.-Sun. and holidays 5:30-8:30pm; Sept.-May 7am-2:30pm.

Tourist Police: 179 18th Octovriou St. (tel. 270 94). The street was recently renamed; locals still call it "Alexandras St." Provides assistance when the GNTO is closed. Open daily 7am-2:30pm, but bang on the door anytime.

Post Office: On P. Mela St., off Alexandras St. Open Mon.-Fri. 8am-10pm, Sat. 8am-2pm, Sun. and holidays 9am-1pm. **Postal Code:** 38001 or 38334.

OTE: Corner of Eleftheriou Venizilou and Sokratous St., across from the covered fruit and vegetable market. Open 24 hrs. **Telephone Code:** 0421. **Trains:** The **railroad station** (tel. 285 55 or 240 56) is 1 block west of tourist office. Must change in Larissa (12 per day, 1hr., 630dr) for Athens or Thessaloniki, except for one daily super-express train to Athens (4hr., 4500dr). Otherwise to: Athens (9 per day, 5hr., 2800dr); Thessaloniki (8 per day, 4hr., 1310dr); and Kalambaka (4 per day, 4hr., 910dr).

Ferries: 3 to 6 boats run each weekday to: Skiathos (3hr., 1742dr); Skopelos (4½hr., 2121dr); and Alonissos (5hr., 2384dr). Fewer ferries run on weekends. Flying Dolphin and Flying Eagle **hydrofoils** run with equal frequency at twice the price. Inquire at the agencies lining the waterfront.

Buses: The bus station (tel. 332 54) is located on Metamorfosseos (a 5-min. walk from the waterfront). Buses travel daily to: Athens (10 per day, 5hr., 3500dr); Thessaloniki (4 per day, 3¼hr., 2350dr); Larissa (9 per day, 1hr., 700dr); Portaria (10 per day, 45min., 150dr); Makrinitsa (10 per day, 50min., 190dr); Zagoria (2 per day, 2hr., 600dr); Horefto (2 per day, 2¼ hr., 650dr); Afissos (5 per day, 45min., 300dr); Platania (2 per day, 2hr., 850dr); Drakia (2 per day, 50min., 220dr); and Agios Ioannis (2 per day, 2 ½hr., 700dr).

Car Rental: Theofanidis Hellas, 137 Iasonos St. (tel. 323 60), 1 block parallel to the waterfront.

Accommodations, Food, and Entertainment

If you're stranded here late at night head for the downtown area near the waterfront where you'll find several unchic, but inexpensive hotels. **Hotel Iasson,** 1 P. Mela St. (tel. 260 75 or 243 47), has bare-bones, well-scrubbed rooms. Ask for one with a view of the harbor. (Singles 2500dr. Doubles 3600dr. Shared baths.) At the **Hotel Akropolis,** 47 Korai St. (tel. 259 84), the amiable manager rents spacious, clean doubles (3000dr) and singles for students at 2500dr with shared baths. The **Hotel Agra,** 5 Solones St. (tel. 253 70), half a block from the waterfront, offers singles and doubles with shared baths at 2500dr and 3000dr, respectively. Rooms with private baths are available. If you're willing to pay a bit more, the **Hotel Philippos,** 9 Solones St. (tel. 376 07), provides comfortable doubles with ceiling fans for 7800dr.

Cafés and *tavernas* drench the waterfront like oil on a Greek salad. After a hard day's work, many sailors look for *oktopodhi* (grilled octopus) or a less celebratory fish plate at the inexpensive **Ouzeri Nautilia,** 1 Argonafton, just before Riga Fereou Sq. (open daily 6am-2am). **Athenaiki Taverna** on Venizelou St. serves heaping portions of *mousaka* and other Greek staples (open daily 7am-11pm). During the day you can sit, sip a *caffè frappe* and people-watch under the bright blue umbrellas of the **Cappucino Bar** on Antonopolou St., just off bustling Ermou St. (open 8:30am-2:30pm and 7:30-11:30pm).

Between midnight and sunrise, the *tavernas* and *ouzeri* along the waterfront overflow with people slouched in chairs, absorbing alcohol. For an even more slothful form of entertainment, laze in one of the two movie theaters along the promenade (one is open-air with movies in English). In late July and August, Volos hosts a festival in Riga Fereou Park, featuring concerts, dances, and special exhibits.

Makrinitsa ΜΑΚΡΙΝΙΤΣΑ

Winding up the tortuous road from Volos to Makrinitsa, you'll transcend the noise and smog, but not the tacky souvenir stands. The stone houses and cobblestone streets of this ancient village clutch the hillside, which overlooks Volos and the Aegean. Hiking trails weave past sparkling mountain springs, goat-laden hills, and age-old monasteries.

Presiding over the town square, the diminutive **Agios Yiannis** monastery contains some nifty samples of wood carving. Walk 1km along the trail uphill from the parking lot to the austere **Agios Gerasimos,** with its clock tower and resident peacock, and continue on to the 17th-century **Monastery of Sourvias,** a pleasant half-hour stroll away.

The road from Volos to Makrinitsa ends at a large parking lot on the village's eastern end. About 150m from the lot is the town square. *Dhomatia* can be found uphill from the street that connects the lot and the main square. Lodgings usually fill in July and August, so call ahead. During high season, singles are more elusive than a summer shower. Try to pair up with an accommodating fellow traveler.

If you can afford to splurge, stay at a guesthouse. The GNTO has declared Makrinitsa a "traditional settlement," in an effort to preserve the old houses and prevent any new and unsightly construction. The organization has converted three villas into expensive guesthouses, but the best operation of this type remains in private hands: **Pension Diomidi** (tel. 994 30), uphill from the Galini Restaurant (look for the sign), with its beautiful rooms with whitewashed interiors, wood carvings, and flower-patterned patios. (Doubles 5000dr. Bath included. Triples and quads available. The **Hotel Achilles** (tel. 991 77), near the square, offers bright, modern rooms with expansive sea vistas. (Doubles 7500dr). The **Pilioritico Spiti** (tel. 991 94), also near the square, offers similar doubles for 6200dr.

The **Pantheon** (tel. 991 24), in the square, serves local specialties on a vast cliff-hanging terrace. Try *spetsophai*, a traditional Pelion stew of spicy *loukaniko* (sausage), green peppers, and eggplant (open daily 9am-midnight).

The tiny hamlet of **Portaria**, 2km away, re-enacts a traditional Greek wedding celebration for a week in mid-August. A pleasant spring swiggles in the town square. **Buses** leave regularly from the bus terminal in Volos for Makrinitsa (50min., 190dr) and Portaria (45min., 150dr). Those who hitch follow Venizelou St. out of Volos to the north; *Let's Go* does not recommend hitchhiking as a means of travel. Makrinitsa has paltry practical conveniences. To change money you must go to Portaria. There is no post office; the kiosk sells stamps, and letters must be left in the mailbox. Makrinitsa's **telephone code** is 0421.

Mount Pelion Peninsula ΟΡΟΣ ΠΗΛΙΟ

In mythology, the rugged Pelion Peninsula was home to those rascally centaurs—half-man, half-horse creatures—and to Chiron, their mentor. Legend proclaims that Chiron, a physician, chose Pelion as his stomping ground because it contained more than 1700 different medicinal herbs. The diversity of plant life in the region stems from its (relatively) cool, moist climate—a feature well appreciated by Greece's sun-singed tourists. Furthermore, Pelion's tortuous terrain has helped protect it from invasion; while the rest of Greece strained under Turkish rule, the peninsula was a hotbed of Greek nationalism. Those steep slopes now form a barrier to the modern tourist invasion, ensuring that Pelion's isolated beaches get far fewer visitors than they deserve.

There are two ways to explore the villages around Volos: either across the peninsula and along the road high above the Aegean coast, or along the coast of Pagassitikos Bay. The former is more agreeable, since the inland areas, Aegean coastline, and far ends of the peninsula are much more alluring and less crowded than the stretch along Pagassitikos Bay from Volos and Agria to Afissos. You won't find big hotels in this untouristed area, but smaller establishments and numerous *dhomatia* have filled the vacuum (doubles 3000dr). The peninsula's **telephone code** is 0426 for the eastern half, 0423 for the western.

Buses from Volos serve most of the 24 major villages 4-5 times per day (see Volos listings), but buses between the smaller towns are scarce. If you must hitchhike, do it in the morning hours, before mid-day siesta begins—you know we don't recommend you hitch. To explore the peninsula thoroughly in a short period of time, you might want to rent a car or a powerful motorbike in Volos (see Volos).

If you opt for the Aegean route, the first place of interest after Makrinitsa will be the ski town of **Chania,** 26km from Volos, where you can see both sides of the Pelion peninsula. The precipitous **ski slopes,** 2km off the main road, are served by chair lift and T-bar (open Jan. to mid-March). The **Youth Hostel Pan (HI/IYHF)** (tel. (0421) 242 90) serves as a sensible base for hikes in the hills and treks to the beach. (500dr per person. Open July-Aug.)

The road forks 14km east of Chania. Turn north for **Zagora,** the largest of the Pelion villages, with old vine-webbed stone homes and cheap rooms-to-let. Better yet, continue through the orchards of "the green" (the eastern part of the peninsula) to the fine sands hugging the Aegean at the town of **Horefto,** 8km from Zagora. On the far side of town, you'll find the sardinally packed **Seahorse Campground** (tel. (0426) 221 80; 600dr per person, 600dr per tent; open May-Sept.). A far better alternative is **Hariklia and Andy's** *dhomatia* (tel. 224 47), run by a warmhearted couple who offer sunny, spotless rooms with the Aegean as a front yard. (Doubles with shared bath 3200dr, with private bath 4500dr.) Their place is one of the first you'll come to on the waterfront street, next to the **Taka Mam,** Greek for "served immediately." (Open daily 11am-1am.)

Just 8km east of Horefto lies **Pouri,** "The Balcony of the Aegean," which at 400m offers a view all the way up to Halkidiki. For about 500dr, a local fisher will take you to one of the nearby sea caves. Two **buses** per day connect Volos with Zagora (2hr., 600dr), and Horefto (2¼hr., 650dr).

From Zagora, you can follow the right-hand fork through cherry and apple orchards into the picturesque hamlets of **Anilio** and **Makrirahi.** This stretch makes a great hike. Ten km from Makrirahi is the turn-off for **Agios Ioannis,** a beautiful but pricey beach resort. The **Hotel Anesis** (tel. 312 23) is typical of what you'll find here. (Singles 7000dr. Doubles 8500dr. Hot showers included.) On the far side of the footbridge, at the southern end of the beach, many freelance camp. **To Akrogiali** serves inexpensive regional specialties (open daily 8am-midnight).

The path over the footbridge and up the hill at the end of town leads to the secluded **Damouhari Cove,** with two small white pebble beaches, the remains of a Venetian castle, and an appealing olive grove (45-min. walk from town). **Buses** run to Agios Ioannis from Volos (2 per day, 2hr., 700dr). The road heads south, then forks to **Kissos,** the highest of the villages on the eastern slope, which harbors the 18th-century **Basilica of Agia Marina** and several *dhomatia.*

Stop by the hamlet of **Tsangarada,** 5km farther, to pay homage to the local landmark—a 1000-year-old plane tree with a 45m circumference. **Milopotamos,** an exceptional, but pint-sized beach near the cliffs is only 8km away. Morning **buses** come here regularly in July and August. Two *tavernas* serve the beach, and a few *dhomatia* rest 1km up the hill.

The alternative route from Volos along Pagassitikos Bay leads first to **Agria,** a resort town with schools of seafood *tavernas* where locals dine boisterously late into the night. Two campgrounds in the quiet olive groves around **Gatzea** make this part of the coast a satisfactory stopover. **Camping Hellas** (tel. (0423) 222 67) is crowded, but lies on a sandy beach. (700dr per person. 400dr per tent.) **Camping Marina** (tel. 222 77) is emptier and better-tended, with a rocky beach. (600dr per person. 500dr per tent.) Heading inland at Kala Nera, you'll come upon two rustic highland villages. From the cool plaza of the first, **Milies,** you can look down to the still blue bay below or visit the well-preserved frescoes in the **Church of the Taxiarches.** Skip the town museum (can you say "tourist shop"?), and try the *tyropsomo,* a local cheese bread. Three km north and uphill from Milies, the town of **Vizitsa** lies in sedate splendor with one café and a few rooms to let. The GNTO is restoring some of the mansions in this old village, but it remains more solitary than Makrinitsa. **Buses** run from Volos to Milies six times per day from 6am to 7:30pm (1hr., 340dr) and Vizitsa (1hr., 360dr).

Farther down the main road, 4½km after Kala Nera, a turn-off leads to **Afissos,** a popular beach resort, graced with Pelion-style pensions overlooking the water. There are two comparatively inexpensive hotels here. The **Hotel Rena** (tel. 334 39) offers doubles with sunny balconies for 6500dr, and the **Hotel Faros** (tel. 332 93) has about the same for 6000dr. **Buses** run from Volos to Afissos (5 per day, 45min., 300dr).

Trikala ΤΡΙΚΑΛΑ

Because Trikala (Ancient Trikki) is the major transport hub of the region, travelers to north central Greece may be unable to resist its pull. Fortunately, the twisting streets of the old city hold enough interesting sights to make stop-overs pleasant. The most conspicuous attraction is the restored **Fortress of Trikala,** with an elegant, turreted clock tower that's visible from the café district. Trikala is said to be the birthplace of the physician Asclepios, and the remains of an **Asclepion,** a prototypical hospital/faith-healing center, stands near the fortress. If you must, stay in one of the hotels in the bustling café district, 1 block upriver from the bus station and to the left. The **Hotel Palladion,** 7 Vyronos St. (tel. 280 91), 2 blocks upriver from the café district, flaunts lofty ceilings, parquet floors, and an English-speaking manager. (Singles 3000dr. Doubles 5000dr.)

The small 13th-century **Church of Porta Panayia** is reason enough to visit the town of **Pili,** at the base of a river valley 20km southwest of Trikala. An 800m walk upriver from the center over a long footbridge takes you to the small, beautiful churchyard protected by cypress trees and an empty moat. Request the key at the squat green-trimmed building on the hillside. Extremely well-preserved mosaics flank the altar with a serene imperturbability. As you get off the bus in Pili, you'll find the town's only hotel, **Hotel Babanara** (tel. 223 25). **Buses** to Pili leave from behind the Trikala station (12 per day, 30min., 350dr).

Regular **buses** connect Trikala to: Liossion St. Station in Athens (7 or 8 per day, 5½hr., 3600dr); Volos (4 per day, 3½hr., about 1500dr); Thessaloniki (6 per day, 3½hr., 2400dr); Kalambaka (at least 14 per day, 30min., 350dr); and Ioannina (2 per day, 3½hr., 1800dr). The **post office,** Sarafi St. (open Mon.-Fri. 7:30am-2pm), and the **OTE,** 25th Martiou St. (open 24 hrs.), are both in the neighborhood around Platia Polytechniou, just across the river from the hotels. The municipal **police station** (tel. 100) is at Kapodistrion and Asklipiou St. (Open 24 hrs.) Trikala's **postal code** is 42100; the **telephone code** is 0431.

Kalambaka ΚΑΛΑΜΒΑΚΑ

Once famous for its architecture, Kalambaka lost almost every building of importance to the occupying Nazis' brand of urban renewal. Today, the town caters to international visitors in the area to see Meteora, one of northern Greece's top tourist attractions (see below).

Kalambaka's foremost sight is the Byzantine **Church of the Dormition of the Virgin.** Follow the signs from Platia Riga Fereou, and after several blocks you'll see the graceful bell tower of the old church, haloed by a stork's nest. Built in the 11th century upon the ruins of a 5th-century basilica, the main structure was remodeled in 1573. Unfortunately, the interior frescoes, painted by the Cretan monk Neophytos, have been badly blackened by centuries of flickering candles and incense. Modest dress is strictly enforced. (Open daily 4:30-8pm. Admission 200dr.)

Buses travel from Kalambaka to Meteora (5 per day, 20min., 140dr.); Volos (4 per day, 3hr., 1950dr.); Ioannina (3 per day, 3½hr., 1550dr.) and Thessaloniki via Trikala (6 per day, 6hr., 2400dr.) Running north-south, with a *platia* (square) at each end, Trikalon Street bifurcates the town. From either *platia,* you can head uphill toward the stern cliffs. Private rooms abound in Kalambaka. About eight times out of ten, travelers arriving by bus or train will be approached by **Georgios Totis** (tel. 225 51 or 235 88), a local *dhomatia* magnate recognizable by his distinctive hat and sputtering motor bike. (The other two times, it's his wife who does the approaching.) The Totis family owns three buildings scattered about the city, filled with clean *dhomatia* of varying quality and size. (Singles 2000dr. Doubles 3200dr. Triples 4400dr.) The **Hotel Astoria,** 93 G. Kondili St. (tel. 222 13 or 235 57), across from the train station, has modern rooms with comfortable beds. (Singles 2000dr. Doubles 3000dr.) At the upper end of the central square, the **Hotel Aeolic Star** offers spotless rooms in a friendly atmosphere. (Singles with shared bath 2500dr. Doubles with shared bath 3500dr.) There are six **campgrounds** near Kalambaka, three of which are closer to Meteora in Kastraki (see Meteora).

The municipal **police,** 10 Hagipetrou St. (tel. 422 00), double as the **tourist police.** To get here from the bus station, walk one block uphill and take your first right. They are located about ten meters down on your left. (English not spoken.) The **OTE** (open Mon.-Fri. 7:30am-3:10 pm) and the **post office** (open Mon.-Fri. 7:30am-2:30pm) are diagonally across from each other on Ionninon St., which begins in the square and heads away from the cliffs. There are international **bookstores** on both main *platia,* but the one farthest from the bus station has the best selection of English-language books and foreign newspapers. The **Ionian Bank** is in Riga Ferou Sq. (open Mon.-Thurs.

8am-2pm, Fri. 8am-1:30pm). Kalambaka's **postal code** is 42200; the **telephone code** is 0432.

Take a seat at the outside tables of the **Panellina Cafe** in the Platia Riga Fereou and enjoy a fresh Greek salad (500dr) or try any beef dish—the region is known for its meat. For fresh produce, stop at any of the **markets** along G. Konkyli St. on the way toward the church.

Meteora ΜΕΤΕΩΡΑ

Jutting out of the Thessalian plain and towering over the surrounding countryside, the bizarre rock pillars of Meteora would make a fascinating tourist attraction all by themselves, even were they not host to a series of impregnable Byzantine monasteries. Meteora, meaning "suspended in the air" in Greek, could refer to the monasteries, or to the monks who only a century ago reached their lofty residences by riding up in a net at the end of a long rope. Today, the nets are obsolete as stairs connect the monasteries with the world below. Meteora is composed of 24 monasteries, of which five are still inhabited by religious orders. Although the site is one of northern Greece's most popular tourist attractions, the beauty and serenity of the monasteries transcend the sputtering tour buses.

History

In the 9th century, hermits and ascetics first began to occupy the pinnacles and crevices of Meteora. As religious persecution at the hands of foreign invaders increased in the 12th century, Christians flocked to take refuge on the summits of these impenetrable columns of rock. In 1356, the region's first official monastic community was founded. In the late Byzantine Period when the Turks ruled Greece, Meteora became one of the most stalwart bastions of the Christian faith, gradually growing into a powerful community of 24 monasteries, all embellished by the finest artists and artisans of the day. Ironically, the communities' wealth turned out to be their bane as well. Bitter quarrels over acquired riches led to neglect and consequent deterioration during the 16th century. Today, only a handful of the monasteries are still active: the Grand Meteoron, Varlaam, Agios Nikolaos, and Agios Triados among them. Agios Stephanos and Agia Barbara (Roussanou) now serve as convents.

The first ascetics scaled the sheer cliff faces by wedging timbers into the rock crevices, thereby constructing small platforms. After the monasteries were completed, visitors usually reached them by means of extremely long ladders. When these were pulled up, the summit became virtually inaccessible. People were also hoisted up over the sheer drop in free-swinging rope nets—the half-hour ascent doubtless fostered a most profound faith in God. Motorized winches have replaced monk-powered, rope-spool cranes, and today provisions, not pilgrims, are elevated. In 1922 steps were carved into the rocks and bridges built between the pillars.

The Monasteries

The Monastery of the Transfiguration (Metamorphosis), more commonly known as the **Grand Meteoron,** is the oldest and largest of the monasteries. Built on the most massive of the occupied stone columns, the complex looms about 500m above the Thessalian plain. Founded by Athanasius, a monk from Mt. Athos, the monastery rose in the hagio-hierarchy when the generous John Uresis, grandson of the Serbian prince Stephen, retired to its summit in 1388.

The Grand Meteoron's central feature is the 16th-century **Church of the Transfiguration,** with brilliant frescoes of the persecution of the Christians by the Romans within its narthex. Directly across is a chamber filled with carefully stacked skulls and bones, the remains of previous residents. (Grand Meteoron open Wed.-Mon.)

Just 300m down the road from the Grand Meteoron is the **Varlaam Monastery,** the second largest monastery on Meteora. Built in 1517, the monastery's crowning glory is the chapel's 16th-century frescoes, including a particularly disturbing depiction of the Apocalypse. (Open Sat.-Thurs.)

Visible from most of the valley, **Agia Barbara** (also called Roussanou) is the most spectacularly situated and frequently photographed monastery. Originally founded in the 14th century, Agia Barbara was abandoned in the early 1980s due to deterioration of its walls, which were built directly into the rock formation. Five years ago a small group of nuns moved in and, having worked to restore it, re-opened it to the public.

If you continue up the trail to its end, you'll eventually reach the road leading to the Agios Triados and Agios Stephanos monasteries. A short walk along the path brings you to two look-out points on the right which yield the broadest view of Meteora. Rides along this road to Agios Stephanos and Agios Triados are reportedly easy to come by.

The versatile **Agios Stephanos,** at the road's end, was founded as a hermitage, became a monastery in the 14th century, and is now a convent. Stephanos is cleaner, lighter, and more spacious than the massive Grand Meteoron and Varlaam. Of its two churches, only the more modern **Agios Charalambos,** built in 1798, is open to the public. Although relatively small, the museum here displays artifacts of intricate detail. (Open Tues.-Sun.)

The Monastery of **Agios Triados** (Holy Trinity) lies about 3km down the road toward the main intersection. Movie buffs will instantly recognize it as a setting of the James Bond flick *For Your Eyes Only.* Looming directly above Kalambaka, the soaring peak of Agios Triados gives a soul-searing view of the town 1320m below, and of the snow-capped Pirdos Mountains in the distance. The monk Dometius built the monastery in 1476, but the wall paintings were added 200 years later. Gardens punctuate areas between the wood and stone buildings. A 3km footpath from the right side of the entrance to Agios Triados leads to Kalambaka.

Back down the road, past the main intersection and only 2½km from Kastraki, rests the Monastery of **Agios Nikolaos,** also called **Anapafsa.** Built in 1388 and expanded in 1628, its highlight is the fresco work painted by the 16th-century Cretan master Theophanes. Visitors are admitted only in small groups, so wait in the entrance at the top of the steps for the door to open. (Open daily.)

Practical Information, Accommodations, and Camping

Two km from Kalambaka lies the hamlet of **Kastraki,** which is more restful and more traditional than Kalambaka, and closer to Meteora. The centrally located **Camping Vrachos** (tel. 222 93) has an algae-free pool. (600dr per person, 600dr per tent.) **Camping Meteora Garden** (tel. 227 27) lounges 3km out of Kastraki on the Ioannina-Kalambaka highway (600dr per person, 400dr per tent). The **Hotel Kastraki** (tel. 222 86) is conveniently located for daytrips to Meteora. (Doubles 3500dr.) *Dhomatia* are also available in town. Some hike toward Meteora to find secluded spots for freelance camping.

You'll need at least a full day to see the six visitable monasteries. Although their closing days are staggered, all six are open on Sunday, Wednesday, and Thursday. Open hours are always 9am-1pm and 3:30-6pm. Admission to each is 300dr. Modest dress is strictly enforced: men must wear long pants and women should have a long skirt or dress. Both men and women should cover their shoulders and men with long hair should wrap it in a tight bun at the nape. Some rather unflattering cover-ups are often available for rental at monastery entrances. Photography and video filming inside the monasteries is absolutely forbidden. **Buses** travel from the main square in Kalambaka to the Grand Meteoron (5 per day; in winter 1 per day; 20min; 140dr). Flag down the bus at any of the blue *stassis* signs along its route. You can savor the fantastic view during the 1½-hour walk. Bring a lunch and spend the morning at Grand Meteoron and Varlaam. Then take a path from the right-hand side of Varlaam and walk downhill until you reach the road to Agios Nikolaos. While the monasteries are closed for a siesta in early afternoon, ascend the road to Roussanou to view the surrounding countryside. In late afternoon, head to Agios Stephanos and Agios Triados. You can descend to Kalambaka by taxi (about 1000dr), or walk down a path starting beside Agios Triados.

Metsovo ΜΕΤΣΟΒΟ

Although officially designated a "traditional settlement" by the GNTO, **Metsovo** is to a traditional village as the Brady Bunch is to your family. All of the buildings have been spruced up and painted, and most of the original slate roofs replaced by maintenance-free tile. The subsistence-agriculture-and-petty-commerce economy has been replaced by a booming trade in postcards and hand-made wooden trinkets stamped with the word "Metsovo." Despite its pre-packaged commercialization, or perhaps because of it, this snug little mountain hamlet, perched just below the 1850m Katara Pass, is charming and delightful. The native Metsovians are descendants of the *Vlachi,* a people once believed to have migrated from Romania, but now thought to have been Greeks trained by the Romans to guard the Egnatia Highway connecting Constantinople with the Adriatic. The Vlachi language, so heavily influenced by Latin that it was used to communicate with the Italians during World War II, survives on the cobblestone streets of Metsovo. When you visit, bring a sweater—where it's hilly, it's chilly.

The **Tostitsa Museum,** housed in a beautiful stone and timber Epirot mansion on the left up the main road (look for the sign), displays intricate antique Vlachi handicrafts. Wait at the door until the guide appears (every 30min.) to take you through. (Open Fri.-Wed. 8:30am-1pm and 4-6:30pm. Admission 400dr.)

Gracing the central square is a statue of Michalis Tostitsa, a native who found fame and fortune in Romania and shared his luck (i.e., money) with fellow Greeks in Athens and Metsovo, building many stadiums and museums. Signs near the square lead to the **Agios Nikolaos Monastery** and its 14th-century chapel. Just minutes from the main road out of town toward the Katara Pass, you can hike over alpine meadows amid the Pindos Mountains. A small ski lift operates in winter right above the town (daily 9am-4pm).

On the evening of July 26, the **panigiria** (nameday festival) of Agia Paraskevi, the women and girls of Metsovo get decked out in traditional costumes and take turns leading each other in a two-step around the town square. On **panayia** (Aug. 15), they repeat the performance. Metsovo is also renowned for its goat's milk cheeses, concoctions pungent enough to burn blisters on your tongue.

From the little shed in the square, **buses** go to Ioannina (4 per day, 1500dr); Trikala via Kalambaka (4 per day, about 1500dr); and Thessaloniki (6 per day, about 2800 dr). The square also has two **banks** (open Mon.-Thurs. 8am-2pm, Fri. 8am-1:30pm). To reach the **OTE,** cut through the courtyard in front of the bank of Crete, then turn left and wind around to the right. The municipal **police** (tel. 411 83/89) are on the right past the courtyard. The police chief speaks English. Up the main road from the square is the **post office.** (Open Mon.-Fri. 7:30am-2:30pm.) Metsovo's **telophone code** is 0656.

Unblemished, inviting rooms fill the **Hotel Athens** (tel. 417 25), down the hill from the main square. (Doubles with private bath 5500dr.) The **Hotel Acropolis** is up near the highway. Climb the hill from the Acropolis to reach **To Spitiko,** with specialties such as *vrasto katsiki* (boiled goat, 750dr) and homemade *trahanas* (semolina soup, 300dr).

Epirus ΗΠΕΙΡΟΣ

If you came to Greece in search of idyllic, isolated settings, do your roaming in this region. Igoumenitsa may be your first stop on the Greek mainland (boats from Brindisi and Corfu stop here); why not begin exploring the country from here rather than heading straight for the mayhem of Athens? The craggy mountains—desolate and indistinct in summer, snow-capped in winter—dominate this hiker's utopia. Although the picturesque town and golden beaches of Parga see their share of tourists, the mountains and timeless villages of Zagoria near the Vicos-Aoos National Park remain undisturbed.

Igoumenitsa ΗΓΟΥΜΕΝΙΤΣΑ

Tourists don't go to Igoumenitsa; they merely go through it en route to somewhere else. Igoumenitsa is a transportation hub linking northern Greece, the Ionian Islands, and many foreign destinations. **Buses** leave for: Ioannina (10 per day, 2½hr., 1200dr); Thessaloniki (1 per day, 8hr., 4500dr); Athens (3 per day, 8½hr., 5450dr); Parga (2 per day, 1hr., 600dr); and Preveza (2 per day, 3hr., 1350dr). To reach the **bus station** (tel. 223 09), turn left from the Corfu port or right from the Italy port. Take El. Venizelou inland and make the second left onto Kyprou St. A right on the same street leads to De-marciou, the central square. **Ferries** steam to: Corfu (5am-10pm every hr., 2hr., 621dr), and Brindisi, Bari, Ancona, and Otranto in Italy. For the frequent Italian sailings, do some comparison shopping among the numerous waterfront agencies. Also, check on stopover charges for Corfu. Igoumenitsa's primary ferry agencies sell tickets for many of the shipping lines: **Jadrolinija** (tel. 228 71); **Adriatica** (tel. 229 52); **R-Line** (tel. 239 70); **Anek** (tel. 221 04); **Fragline** (tel. 221 58); and **Hellenic** (tel. 221 80). Desti-nations include: Brindisi (at least 1 per day, 10hr., deck passage 8000dr, students 7000dr); Ancona (at least 5 per week, 23hr., deck passage 12,800dr); and Otranto (6-7 per week, 10hr., deck passage, 9500dr, students 8000dr.) Most boats depart in the morning, so arrive early or plan to spend the night.

The staff of the **GNTO** (tel. 222 27), on the waterfront by the customs house, is knowledgeable and helpful. (Open daily 7am-2:30pm; Oct.-May Mon.-Fri. 7am-2:30pm). Don't expect any English to be spoken by the **tourist police** (tel. 222 22) or the **local police** (tel. 221 00), both in the police station. Three **banks** line the waterfront (open Mon.-Thurs. 8am-2pm, Fri. 8am-1:30pm). When they're closed you can ex-change money at most ferry agencies (open until about 9pm). The **OTE** (open daily 7am-8pm; Oct.-May Mon.-Fri. 7am-2:30pm) and the **post office** (open Mon.-Fri. 7:30am-2:30pm) are on Evangelistrias St., which runs inland, connecting the water-front to Kyprou St. The **hospital** (tel. (0664) 222 04) is 20km away in Filiates; for **emergencies** call 244 20. Igoumenitsa's **telephone code** is 0665.

The **Rhodos Hotel** (tel. 222 48), at #13 on the seaward side of the square offers dou-bles at 3000dr. A nearby campsite is **Kalami Beach Camping** (tel. 712 45 or 713 22), 12km south of town. Pick up **groceries** at the cluster of stores in the seaward corners of Demarciou Sq.

Parga ΠΑΡΓΑ

Parga is invigoratingly different from Preveza and Igoumenitsa, its bland coastal neighbors. Hunkered comfortably in an arc of mountains, the town is sheltered from the sea by a row of rocky islets. Compact and relatively uncrowded, Parga offers visi-tors an effervescent nightlife and friendly atmosphere. Lovers take note: the narrow streets, many whitewashed homes, and breathtaking views of the harbor create a sur-prisingly romantic ambience.

The **Venetian fortress** *(kastro),* the largest in the area, dominates the town. Con-structed by the Normans, the Venetians controlled it from 1401 to 1797. Today, howev-er, the structure stands as a mere shell beneath the shade of majestic pines. But in the afternoon heat it's a luscious locale for a picnic or a snooze. Follow the steps from the harbor up the hill, only five minutes from the water. (Open daily 7am-10pm. Free.) The subdued green floodlighting creates a tasteful backdrop for supper on the waterfront. Continue three minutes down and behind the castle to **Valtos Beach,** a voluptuous cres-cent of fine pebbles and clear water. All the beaches around Parga are steeply shelved—about 6m out from shore, the bottom plunges. The town beach is unimpres-sive compared to Valtos, although the islets, 100m off shore, are a rejuvinating swim or a relaxing pedalboat ride away.

A popular daytrip from Parga is the boat trek up the ancient **Styx** (the Acheron), the mythological waterway to the underworld, and on to **Necromanteion,** the Oracle of the Dead. The trip takes 45 minutes by boat from Parga to the mouth of the river; the boat then meanders for a half-hour up the river, between reeds and remarkably phlegmatic terrapins. Even more intriguing than the boat trip is a visit to Necromanteion, a 20-minute walk from the end of the boat's leg of the trip. The main subterranean chamber, cool and dimly lit, seems quite convincingly to be the threshold to another world. (Open 8am-3pm, but only feasibly accessible by the Acheron day trip. Admission 400dr.) The boat returns via **Lichnos Beach,** 3km south of Parga, for swimming and a late lunch at a *taverna.* (About 2000dr, lunch not included. Boats leave around 9am, return around 4pm.) For more information, inquire at the travel offices.

Parga has an elephantine herd of unofficial tourist offices: **Kanaris Travel** (tel. 314 90) and **Charitos Travel** (tel. 319 00), on the waterfront; **West Travel** (tel. 312 33) and **Parga Tours** (tel. 315 80), a ½ block inland; and **Ephira Travel** (tel. 314 39), 1 block inland. Each will help you find a room, rent a moped, or arrange a daytrip. (Open Mon.-Sat. 9am-1:30pm and 6-9:30pm.) **Excursion boats** visit Paxos and Antipaxos (daily, 3300dr roundtrip for a day-trip including both destinations or 2500dr roundtrip for just Paxos), Lefkas (1 per week, 6000dr) and Corfu Town (every Wed., 5000dr).

To reach the bus station from the port, head to the northwest corner of the waterfront (with the ocean behind you). Continue one block inland. Here you'll find the **National Bank of Greece.** (Open Mon.-Fri. 8am-2pm and 7-9pm.) Turn right and proceed up the street, passing the **OTE** (open Mon.-Sat. 7:30am-midnight and Sun. 9am-2pm and 5-10pm). About a two-minute walk up on Bagka St. you'll find the **bus station** (tel. 312 18), under the Snack Bar Pizza Grill sign. The **post office** (tel. 312 95; open Mon.-Fri. 7:30am-2pm) and **police station** (tel. 312 22) are also here. Parga's **postal code** is 48060; its **telephone code** is 0684. **Buses** conect Parga with Preveza (5 per day, 2hr., 1000dr); Ioannina (9 per day, 1500dr); Igoumenitsa (2 per day, 1hr., 600dr) and Athens (4 per day, 9½hr., 6000dr).

Although the number of tourists vacationing in Parga increases every year, the number of new *dhomatia* increases even faster. Check out the rooms extolled by folks who greet incoming buses, or try at the southern end of town and on top of the hill where few tourists venture. Most doubles go for about 5000dr. **Eugenia Azi** (tel. 319 71) offers clean, spacious *dhomatia* in her family's home on the corner directly across from the entrance to the *kastro.* It's a bit of a hike up here but the views are striking. (Doubles with shared bath 4000dr, with private bath 5800dr. Morning coffee included.) Another option is **Parga Camping** (tel. 311 61), 1km north along the road, complete with a private road to the beach, a market, a cheap restaurant, and spacious sites among the silver-leafed olive trees (about 500dr per person, open April-October.)

Head one block inland from the entrance to the Venetian fortress to the **Restaurant Panorama** (tel. 324 47; open 9am-midnight) and try the *mousaka* (700dr) or a feta cheese salad (600dr) while enjoying the spectacular view of the bay and beaches far below. Take a seat at the **Caravel Café** and have a *caffè frappe* before your ferry leaves, to the right as you head toward the ferry dock. The waterfront, sedate by day, becomes thronged with amblers during the nightly *volta* (promenade), around 10pm. Parga has an array of discos (most open 10pm-3am; no cover, but mandatory drink 800dr). Try the **Camaris,** following signs from the waterfront; or the **Rapeza,** 2 km from town.

Preveza ΠΡΕΒΕΖΑ

The dusty, rather shabby port of Preveza subsists at the entrance to Amvrakikos Bay, opposite Aktio. The town may be remembered by tourists solely for its bus station or harbor, since it is little more than a transit point between Parga or Lefkas and somewhere better. **Buses** leave for: Igoumenitsa (2 per day, 3hr., 1350dr); Parga (5 per day, 2hr., 1000dr); Ioannina (10 per day, 2hr., 1300dr); and Athens (4 per day, 6hr., 4100dr). The bus station, on Leoforos Irinis, is 1km from the harbor—walk to the end of Irinis and turn left. The ferry to Aktio leaves from the harbor (every 20min.-1hr. daily, at night every hr.; in winter every ½hr., 70dr). From Aktio the road south branches west to Lefkas, and east to Vonitsa and Patras.

Along the waterfront on **Eleftheriou Venizelou,** is a **tourist office** (tel. 272 77). Fluent in English, the affable, enthusiastic staff will give you a map of Preveza, accommodation listings, and just about anything else you need. (Open Mon.-Sat. 9am-2pm and 6-8:30pm, Sun. 9am-2pm; Oct. to mid-June Mon.-Fri. 7am-2:30pm.) In the same building, you'll find a **bank** (open Mon.-Thurs. 8am-2pm, Fri. 8am-1:30pm) and the **post office** (open Mon.-Fri. 7:30am-2:30pm for money orders, exchange, and parcels; in summer also Sat. 9am-1:30pm and Sun. 9am-12:30pm). The main thoroughfare one block from the waterfront, **Ethi Antistasis,** sports a collection of banks, bakeries, and minimarkets. Preveza's **postal code** is 48100; its **telephone code** is 0682.

The accommodations scene is limited, but so are the reasons for sleeping in Preveza. If you are compelled to slumber here, try **Hotel Urania,** (tel. 271 23), on Leoforio Irimis 17. Its small entryway is between a grocer and a hardware store. The Urania's un-attractive exterior belies cushy rooms with fine wicker furniture and balconies. (Singles 5000dr, doubles 7000dr, all rooms with private bath). As expensive and less impressive is the **Hotel Minos** (tel. 284 24 or 274 24, Doubles 6800dr). If you have a sleeping bag, skip town and head to **Monolith Camping** (tel. 223 47, open June-Sept.), a sandy beach about 10km outside of Preveza on the road to Igoumenitsa. The camp-grounds advertised in town are much farther away than the signs indicate. However, hitching to or from Preveza is feasible. Campsites include **Indian Village** (tel. 223 82 or 271 85, open May-Sept.), **Kalamitsi** (tel. 223 68, open all year), and **Kanali** (tel. 517 33, open May-Sept.). All campgrounds charge around 600dr per person and 600dr per tent. Cheap fast-food joints hound the main street, but for the best budget fare in town, pick up the ineluctably delectable *souvlaki* at the *photoleion* run by **K. Nikolos,** on Platia Tsaldari.

Near Preveza

Zaloggon (Zalongo), 27km north of Preveza and overlooking the village of Kamari-na, makes an interesting morning or afternoon trip. Though Zaloggon is somewhat in-accessible to the carless, you can take a bus to Kamarina from Parga (1hr.) or Preveza (½hr.), and walk the 4km up to Zaloggon. This mountaintop site figures tragically in modern Greek history. On December 18, 1803, 60 women from Souli threw their chil-dren off the cliff and then leapt themselves to avoid being taken as slaves by Ali Pasha and the Turks. A monument constructed to look like innumerable women linking arms and gazing into the distance, now stands at the cliff's edge.

The ruins of a prosperous Roman city built by Octavian Augustus in 31 BCE to com-memorate his naval victory over Antony and Cleopatra off the coast of nearby Actium lie at **Nikopolis**; the name "Nikopolis" comes from the Greek *nike* (victory) and *polis* (city). Although destroyed by the Vandals and Goths after Roman control waned, the city flourished anew under Byzantine rule. A 3km stretch of the Byzantine wall re-mains, along with the ruins of a theater and a few Roman temples converted into Byz-antine chapels. The site's renowned mosaics are presently covered, and, unfortunately, officials don't know when they will again be displayed. Nevertheless, the ruins are still worth a visit; brush the gravel away to uncover the mosaics on the floor. (Site and small museum open Tues.-Sun. 9am-3pm. Admission 400dr, students 200dr.)

Ioannina ΙΩΑΝΝΙΝΑ

Although tourists usually stop here only to change buses to or from Igoumenitsa, Io-annina (pronounced YAH-nee-nah), on the shore of Lake Pamvotis, merits a brief visit. Distinguished by the languorous island in its lake, the secluded alleyways of the walled Old Town, and its scandalous involvement with Ali Pasha, Ioannina elevates itself above a mere transport hub.

Ioannina, founded by Emperor Justinian in 527 CE, has suffered under a colorful succession of petty tyrants. Invaded by the Normans in 1082, conquered by the Turks in 1430, and finally taken by Greek armies in 1913, the town reaps most of its notoriety from the legacy of the brutal Turkish-Albanian tyrant Ali Pasha. Governor of the prov-ince of Epirus just before the Greek Revolution, Ali attempted to secede from the Otto-man empire and create an independent kingdom. He reportedly chained up his favorite mistress, Kira-Frosini, and his harem of sixteen women and threw them into the lake. In 1822 the irate Sultan belatedly assassinated him. The **Asian Aga Mosque,** a splendid 18th-century remnant of Turkey's 500-year ascendancy in the province, has been converted into a public museum. The mosque sits at the edge of the old town, reflecting on the lake next to Skilosofou St. (Open Tues.-Fri. 8:30am-3pm. Admission 400dr.)

The massive walls of the **Castle of Ioannina** were built near the time of the city's founding and reinforced in the 11th and 14th centuries. Today, they divide the ancient and modern parts of the city. After breaching the walls at the bottom of Aengrou St., you can wander through the traditionally styled houses of the Old Town. The clinking of the silversmith's hammer will follow you through the streets as you ramble towards Ali Pasha's tomb at the northern tip of the walls. From atop the lakefront wall, not surprisingly, you can catch the view of the lake.

The slowly gestating collection at the **Archaeological Museum** (tel. 914 87) includes minute stone tablets etched with political, romantic, and cosmological questions that Roman emperors asked of the oracle at Dodoni from the 6th to the 3rd century BCE. The museum is in a park off Averof St. below the clock tower. (Open Tues.-Sun. 8:30am-3pm. Admission 400dr.)

Arguably Ioannina's biggest attraction, the unnamed **island** lingers near the western shore of Lake Pamvotis. **Boats** leave every half-hour or so from 7:30am to 10:30pm (10min.). To reach the dock, walk straight down Averof Georgiou St. to the left of the walls. Seen as idyllic from Ioannina, the island's deceptive shores disappoint—all over the island, pungent, irridescent green foam clings to floating litter while dying fish struggle for air. Skip the perimeter path; instead, head inland to the tiny carless village where cunning, toothless chickens wander among whitewashed houses, elaborate gardens, the flustered Swedish chef, and tourist shops. In the island's pine-forested interior, winding paths lead to the gates of curiously silent monasteries. Ali Pasha once futilely sought refuge from the assailing Sultan's forces in the cellar of the church of St. Panteleimon in the **Agios Nikolaos** monastery. The **Ali Pasha Museum** on the site shows how he lived and where he died—shot through the floor of his apartments and then posthumously and ceremoniously beheaded on the second stone step from the top. Most unsavory. (Open daily 9am-10pm. Admission 100dr.)

About 5km northeast of Ioannina on the Metsovo highway is **Perama,** with its captivating caves. The 45-minute guided tour of the grottos takes you past astounding stalagmite and stalactite formations. (Open daily 8am-8pm; in off-season 8am-5pm. Admission 300dr.) Take bus #8 (60dr) from Platia Eleftheriou to the end of the line, then follow the signs.

Rooms in Ioannina are generally comfortable but sadly lacking in character. Motels cluster around the main bus station and in the roads off Averof St. The modern **Hotel Egnatia,** 20 Dagli-Aravadinou St. (tel. 256 67 or 248 86), one block from the main bus station, is pricey but very convenient if you're stranded here late at night and wish to catch an early morning bus. (Singles with bath 5000dr.) The **Hotel Metropolis** (tel. 255 07 or 262 07), at the corner of Averof and Kristali Streets, offers no-frills doubles with shared baths for 3500dr. Its neighbor, the **Hotel Tourist** at 18 Koletti St. (tel. 264 43 or 250 70), provides clean, simply furnished doubles with shared baths for 4000dr (with private baths for 5100dr). Along the shores of the lake, less than 1km from the city center (walk along A. Papandreou St.), you can pitch a tent at **Camping Limnopoula** (tel. 252 65 or 263 19; 600dr per person; open May-Oct.).

Several charmingly unpretentious and reasonably priced restaurants brim on Georgiou St. in the Old Town. **Restaurant HBH,** 4 Georgiou St. (tel. 731 55), has hunger-crushing daily lunch specials. Arrive before noon to avoid the line. Across the street, the **Restaurant Pantheon** (tel. 264 14), run by the affable English-speaking Saras Elias, has quick service and a varied menu (open 7am-midnight). Both establishments have entrees at 600-800dr. Located at the southern end of the central park (follow signs to the Archaeological Museum), **Restaurant Litharitsa** (tel. 200 43 or 230 85) offers a standard omelette-and-burger menu (600-1200dr) and a dramatic view of the lake and surrounding mountains from its terrace. This awe-inspiring setting makes the **Restaurant Litharitsia** a must-see for any visitor to Ioannina (open 6pm-1am). Go take in a beer and the view if nothing else. Evening action turns zesty along Averof St., where people sip *caffè frappe* in the cafeterias, while reckless young motorcyclists careen up and down with intent to cause grievous bodily harm.

Ioannina's **bus station** is between Zossimadon and Sina St. To reach the GNTO office, take the road to the left of the Agricultural Bank, go right at the grass triangle, and walk past Hotel Palladion to 28th Octovriou St. Turn left on this street, passing the **OTE** (open 6am-midnight; 6am-11pm in winter), the **police** (tel. 256 73), and the **post office** (open Mon.-Fri. 7:30am-8pm). Take a right at the main junction and the **GNTO** will be 200m along on the right in Botsari Sq. Pick up the free tourist booklet with its excellent town map. The staff will sometimes let you store luggage here. (Open Mon.-Fri. 7:30am-3pm and 5-8:30pm, Sat. 9am-2pm; Oct.-May Mon.-Fri. 7:30am-3pm, Sat. 9am-2pm.) Ioannina's main street runs northwest from the GNTO first as Demokratiou Sq., then as Averof St., then as Georgiou St., leading to the Old Town, castle, and port. Ioannina's **telephone code** is 0651.

Buses from the main terminal travel to: Athens (10 per day, 8hr., 4850dr); Igoumenitsa (10 per day, 2½hr., 1200dr); Thessaloniki via Larissa (5 per day, 7hr., 4050dr); Trikala (2 per day, 3½hr., 1800dr); and Metsovo (4 per day, 3hr.). Check the schedule, since bus routes change daily. The other station sends buses to Preveza (9 per day, 2hr., 1200dr) and Dodoni (3 per day, 150dr). To get there, continue on 28th Octovriou St. across Demokratiou Sq. and go about 4 blocks down Bizaniou St. Around the corner from the OTE at 6 A.G. Molaimido St., the local chapter of the **Hellenic Mountaineering Club** (tel. 221 38) is an excellent source of information on mountain trips. (Open Mon.-Fri. 7pm-9pm. See Vicos Gorge and Zagoria Villages.) About a five-minute walk along Napoleon Zerva St. from the GNTO at #86 you'll find a self-service **laundromat**. (Wash 600dr, dry 75dr per 10min.; open Mon.-Fri. 8:30am-3pm and 5:30-9:30pm, Sat. 8:30am-2:30pm.)

Vikos Gorge and Zagoria Villages
ΒΙΚΟΣ ΚΑΙ ΖΑΓΟΡΙΑΣ

This spectacular combination of dramatic scenery, Dali-esque rock formations and grey-stone villages inexplicably fails to attract more than a handful of adventurous travelers. From the 15th to the 17th century, the mountain villages of the Vikos area northeast of Ioannina formed a political and economic confederation recognized by the ruling Turks. A unique architecture and a fierce regional pride emerged from the confederation's prosperity. In 1973, the Vikos Gorge and the intersecting Aoos River and canyon were declared a national park. More recently, the GNTO labeled the Zagoria villages "traditional settlements," thus forbidding overly commercial development.

The area is small enough that you don't need a detailed topographical map. In Ioannina, drop by the Mountaineering Club and pick up the self-explanatory flyer *Vikos-Aoos National Park*. The club office has rough contour sketches of part of the area; you can photocopy these across the street. When you venture forth, keep in mind that these villages don't cater to tourists: bring some provisions and camping gear. There are no hotels (though you may be able to arrange a room with locals), and at best, a village might have a couple of small *tavernas*. Villagers are often kind, and amused that anyone would travel so far to romp through their backyards.

Since bus service is infrequent and hitching almost impossible, getting here without a car is difficult. The most frequent connections drop you off in Konitsa, near the northern end of the national park (5:15am-6:45pm, 7 per day, 750dr). Buses also travel to Monodendri, Papingo, Aristi, Kipi, and Tsepelovo, but the trips are infrequent (3-7 times per week), and the schedules are in a constant state of flux. Check the chalkboards in the Ioannina station for details.

The best place to start a journey through the gorge is at the hamlet **Monodendri**. Buses travel from Ioannina (1 per day, 1 hr., 600dr). Inquire at the restaurant for *dhomatia* (singles 2500-3000dr, breakfast inlcuded). Fill several canteens from the well in the town center (or bring bottled water) before setting off into the gorge— there's no more water until the Klima Spring, a 4½-hour hike from Papingo, and even that dries up in hot weather. Before you leave town, indulge in the something-to-write-home-about view of the Vikos Gorge from the unoccupied monastery **Agia Paraskevi,** atop a 300m high cliff about 800m beyond Monodendri.

Entering the gorge from Monodendri will put you at its southern end. A 4½-hour hike from here will bring you to **Vikos** village, located near **Aristi** and **Papingo.** Papingo gives you access to another gateway into the gorge. To get there, take the 5km road (not 2km, as the sign asserts) from Vikos. In the shadow of towering columns of rock, the stone-and-slate village of Papingo radiates the charm of traditional village life, despite the parade of backpackers who pass through here, another of the GNTO "traditional settlements." *Dhomatia* are your best bet for lodging (2500-3000dr per person), but the GNTO also operates an unabashedly expensive hotel in town. The hotel staff may be able to help you out in a pinch. The **mountaineering club** in the center of town is more helpful, but holds wildly erratic office-hours. Buses run from Ioannina to Papingo (2 per day on Mon. and Thurs.-Fri., 500dr). From there, they continue to the even smaller village of **Mikro Papingo,** site of the trail head and the welcoming pension, **Agnanti's Rooms** (tel. 411 23; doubles 5800dr).

From here, the trail wends its way up **Mount Astraka** (2436m) and through the five-to six-hour hike to the summit, **Gamila Park.** About half-way up you'll encounter the main hut, maintained by the mountaineering club in Papingo. Single travelers and small groups should sleep somewhere else—use of the hut costs 10,000dr for eight or fewer people, plus 1500dr for each additional person. From the hut, continue northeast over the **Koutsometros Range** into the **Aoos River Gorge. Mount Gamila** (2478m) looms on your right, and Konitsa is in sight far to the left, past the end of the gorge. The **Despina** and **Leonidos** refuges offer super vistas. From these, you can easily hike to the broad summit of Mt. Gamila.

Far below, **Konitsa** offers a convenient base to begin your trek in the opposite direction, with hotels, a choice of *tavernas,* and supermarkets for provisions. Leaving Konitsa, follow the road down to the bridge over the River Aoos. A one-hour hike along the footpath will take you up through the gorge to a monastery. Another four-hour hike will bring you to the Gamila shelter. In Konitsa's main square are the **bus station,** the **post office** (open Mon.-Fri. 7:30am-2pm), two **banks** (open Mon.-Thurs. 8am-2pm, Fri. 8am-1:30pm), and a couple of hotels. The **police** (tel. 222 02) are down the hill, on the main road. (Open 24 hrs.)

Dodoni ΔΩΔΟΝΙ

Ancient Dodoni is sheltered at the foot of a mountain 21km south of Ioannina. The site has been a religious center for almost 4000 years, playing host to successive waves of mother-earth worshipers, tree worshipers, Zeus worshipers, and garden-variety Christians. The first tribes of Hellenes occupied the area around 1900 BCE. Around 800 BCE, the site became an oracle dedicated to Zeus, who, while courting a nearby cypress tree, was believed to have resided here in the form of the roots of a giant oak. A temple was built sometime around 500 BCE, then destroyed along with the oak tree by the Romans in 167 BCE. The last vestiges of the old religion were further subverted by the Christians, who built a basilica on the site (its remains are still visible) in an attempt to diminish pagan influences by incorporating them into Christianity.

The central attraction at Dodoni is the restored 3rd-century **amphitheater** that originally seated 18,000 but was reconstructed during Roman times for gladiator games. In the first week of August, the theater hosts a festival of classical drama performed before a full house. The remnants of the oracles and the foundations of several buildings, including a temple to Aphrodite and a hall for pilgrims, are next to the theater. A small oak has been thoughtfully replanted in the middle of the ruins of the sanctuary of Zeus. (Open Tues.-Sat. 7:30am-7:30pm, Sun. 9am-6pm; off-season Tues.-Sat. 9am-5pm, Sun. 9am-3pm. Admission 400dr, students 200dr.) With permission, you can **camp** in the field by the theater, which has a toilet and running water.

The peaceful village of Dodoni, adjacent to the ruins, is frequented by **buses** from Bizanious St. in Ioannina (2 per day). The buses return almost immediately after they reach Dodoni, but it's not too difficult to sweet-talk your way onto one of the tourist buses heading back to Ioannina. A group could take a taxi (about 2500dr).

Macedonia ΜΑΚΕΔΟΝΙΑ

Once the stomping grounds of an infant Alexander the Great, Macedonia is the largest of the Greek provinces. Primary lines of transportation run to and from Thessaloniki, but you won't want to stay long in this noisy, modern city—the region's most interesting sights are in the countryside. Visit Mt. Athos (if you're male and it's reopened) for its austere spiritual vitality, see the intriguing excavations at Vergina and Pella, or tour the Lake District in all its vibrant natural splendor. Just don't confuse this part of Greece with that upstart chunk of the former Yugoslavia. (For more information on the struggle over the right to the name Macedonia, see the Modern History section in the Greece Introduction.)

Kastoria and the Lake District
ΚΑΣΤΟΡΙΑ ΚΑΙ ΠΕΡΙΦΕΡΕΙΑ ΤΗΣ ΛΙΜΝΗΣ

The districts of Kastoria, Florina, and Pela, tucked against the remote borders of the former Yugoslavia and Albania, are rarely visited by tourists. Despite the stunning natural setting and honestly traditional villages, most chatty shutterbugs and unwieldly tour mobs fail to make the trek. The dearth of tourists, though, has at least one drawback: English-speaking locals are as scarce as goats' wings.

The city of **Kastoria** (named after Kastor, one of a plethora of sons born to Zeus and discoverer of oil) originally rested securely on an island in Lake Kastoria. Around the 10th century CE, the townspeople began dumping garbage into the lake in order to build a causeway to the shore. Today, the bulk of the city is squeezed into this narrow ithmus, and the island proper is nearly deserted. Savor the beauty of the lake all you want, but don't even think about taking a dip; although the town recently stopped dumping raw sewage into the water, the biological clean-up process is still years away from completion. Along with its voluminous fur production (some 5000 garments per day), Kastoria is renowned for its churches—40 Byzantine and 36 post-Byzantine edifices scattered throughout the city—with elaborate masonry and exquisite decoration. In most of the churches, though, the saints' eyes have been gouged out. Greeks explain that occupying Turkish soldiers desecrated the images with their knives, while Turks claim that faithful pilgrims collected the eyes as talismans. Regardless, the tiny Byzantine **Panayia Koumblelidhiki,** in the center of town, and the **Church Mavriotissa,** about 3km outside, house particularly spectacular frescoes. To visit Mavriotissa, walk out of town past the hospital, and toward the island. The priest who lives there will conduct a tour (in Greek or German). To visit any other church, go to the **Byzantine Museum** (tel. 267 81), off Mitropoleos St., and ask for the genial gardener. He will provide keys and may even accompany you as a tour guide (usually available Tues.-Sun. 8:30am-2:30pm). The museum itself merits a visit for its extensive, ever-expanding collection of recently restored Byzantine icons. (Open Mon.-Fri. 8:30am-3pm. Admission 400dr, students 200dr.) The **Laographical Museum,** in the officially recognized "traditional area" of Oultso near the town center, occupies a charming, 590-year-old Kastorian house. (Open daily 9am-12:30pm and 2-6:30pm. Admission 100dr.)

A municipal **tourist office** (tel. 267 81) in the town hall, toward the island from the main bus station, has a handy, free map of the city's sights. The map is in Greek only, but the staff will be happy to translate the key. (Open Mon.-Fri. 8:30am-2:30pm and 6-7:30pm; off-season 7:30am-3pm.) There are no tourist police, but the amiable **municipal police** are relatively familiar with English. The **post office,** 19 Mitropolis St., also exchanges money. (Open daily 7:30am-2:15pm.) The **OTE** is up the hill at 33 Agion Athanasiou St. (Open daily 7am-midnight.) Kastoria's **main bus terminal** (tel. 224 55) is on the same street, by the lakeside. Buses run to Thessaloniki via Edessa (6 per day, 4½hr., 2500dr), Athens (2 per day, 6500dr), and Veria (1 per day, 1500dr). **Olympic Airways** flies from Athens to Kastoria and back (4-5 times per week, 11,900dr). The Olympic office on the waterfront (tel. 222 75 or 231 25) is open daily 8:30am-3pm. The **National Bank of Greece** is on the mainland at 11 Novembriou St. (Open Mon.-Thurs. 8am-2pm, Fri. 8am-1:30pm.) Kastoria's **postal code** is 52100; its **telephone code** is 0467.

Kastoria's **Hotel Akropolis,** 14 Gramou St. (tel. 225 37), 1 block behind the bus station, shows its age but remains thoroughly clean and comfortable. (Singles 3000dr. Doubles 4000dr. Tepid showers 200dr extra.) The only other cheap hotel in town is the **Hotel Palladion,** 40 Mitropolis St. (tel. 224 93), a get-what-you-pay-for operation. (Singles 1500dr. Doubles 2700dr. Triples 3500dr. Negotiable.) You can **camp** by Mavriotissa if you get permission from the priest and keep the grounds scrupulously clean.

Just 1km out of town stands **Mount Psalida,** where, legend has it, Alexander the Average resolved to become Alexander the Great by conquering the world. Locals say that if you look at the mountain just the right way, from just the right angle, in just the right light, you can see Awesome Al's profile gazing somberly skyward.

Between Kastoria and the Yugoslavian and Albanian borders lies the tranquil **Lake District,** an area of unspoiled wilderness, isolated villages, and swimmable lakes. **Florina,** accessible from Edessa and Thessaloniki, is a good base from which to explore the area. Trains run from Thessaloniki (5 per day, 4hr.; 5 buses per day, 3½hr.). From Edessa (4 trains per day, 2hr.; 4 buses per day). (Florina **bus station** tel. 224 30; **train station** tel. 224 07.) Florina has little to offer tourists apart from its location, a fragrant *agora,* and the **Hotel Ellenis** (tel. 226 71; doubles with bath 2800dr). The Alpine Club (tel. 223 54) can give you information on their large refuge near the village of **Pissoderi** on Mt. Verna. Florina's **telephone code** is 0385.

Northwest of Kastoria and 34km west of Florina, the **Great** and **Small Prespa Lakes** straddle the borders of Greece, Albania, and Yugoslavia. Twisting mountain roads north of Kastoria lead past hidden poppy fields, bear and fox lairs, and insular villages. The drive to **Psarades** takes you through a marshland aviary, with watchtowers and picnic tables alongside the Great Prespa Lake (the largest in the Balkans). Easiest to reach from Florina or Edessa is **Lake Vergokitida,** which borders the main highway to Edessa and Thessaloniki.

Edessa ΕΔΕΣΣΑ

Edessa's scenic waterfalls and temperate climate make it a favorite vacation spot for Greeks. Word has yet to leak out to the rest of the world, though, so foreign tourists are a real rarity. Perched securely on top of a steep, formerly fortified butte, the city was christened "Edessa" (meaning "the waters") by some astute observers from the occupying Bulgarian army. The town ends abruptly on the brink of a deep ravine, where the streams flowing under Edessa's arched stone bridges cascade into a gaping abyss, plummeting over 25m to the valley floor.

The **main bus station** is at the corner of Pavlou Mela and Filippou St.; turn left when Democrias becomes Egnatia near Hotel Pella. Buses run to Athens (3 per day, 8½hr., 5900dr), Thessaloniki (15 per day, 2hr., 1100dr), and Veria (5 per day, 1hr., 600dr). A second depot, marked by a bus sign, is located at a family-run sandwich shop and grill just up the block at Pavlou Mela and Egnatia (look for the letters KTEL painted on the window). From here, buses go to Kastoria (4 per day, 2hr., 1400dr) and Florina (5 per day, 2hr., 1000dr). The **train station** is at the end of 18th Octovriou St.—trains to Athens via Plati (7 per day, 8½hr., 3000dr), Florina (5 per day, 2hr., 600dr), and Thessaloniki via Veria and Naoussa (8 per day, 2hr., 640dr). Edessa's regular **police** force (tel. 233 33) has no tourist information and their English is limited. But if you're in dire need of information, turn left after 26 Democrias St., and look for the police cars at the corner of Filippou and Iroon Polytechniou. (Open 24 hrs.) Edessa's **post office** on Democrias St., one block from the *agora,* exchanges money for a piratical commission. (Open Mon.-Sat. 7:30am-2pm, Sun. 9am-1:30pm.) The **National Bank of Greece,** 1 Demikratou St., is surrounded by an iron fence on the corner of Arch. Penteleiminos. (Open Mon.-Thurs. 8am-2pm, Fri. 8am-1pm.) The **OTE** is the blue and white building directly behind the Hotel Olympion. (Open Mon.-Fri. 7am-midnight, Sat.-Sun. and holidays 7:40am-midnight.)

The **Hotel Olympion** (tel. 234 85) on Democrias St. (entrance is diagonally across from bus depot at Pavlou Mela and Egnatia), has polished rooms with shiny bathrooms. (Singles 1800dr. Negotiable.) **Hotel Pella,** 30 Egnatia St. (tel. 235 41), diagonally across from Olympion, keeps its marble and tile floors thoroughly scrubbed. (Singles with bath 3000dr. Doubles with bath 5000dr.) Edessa may well have the most outdoor tables per capita of any city in Greece. On warm summer nights, the avenue to the cataracts overflows with Greek vacationers eating supper, sipping *frappe,* and taking evening *voltas.* At the **Taverna Tsarouksaki** (ΤΣΑΡΟΥΞΑΚΙ), 32, 18th Octovriou St., harried waiters sprint to the outdoor tables with plates of succulent grilled veal. (Opens at 8pm.) The **Omonia** restaurant (tel. 254 59) on 20 Egnatia St. is a neghborhood eatery extemely popular with local families. Large portions o' food about 1200dr. Take-out available.

Edessa's largest waterfall, **Katarrakton,** foams in a lush tree-tufted park. Walk along Filippou St. from the main bus station to the train station, then walk toward town 2 blocks and turn left at the first river. Enthusiasts should continue down the path at the bottom of Katarrakton into the valley to see the three more sizable falls near the hydroelectric plant. The only other tourist attraction is a small **Archaeological Museum** in the Tsami Mosque on Stratou St. on the very edge of town.

Vergina ΒΕΡΓΙΝΑ

The discovery of the ancient ruins of Vergina, 13km southeast of Veria, in 1977 and 1978, was an archaeological watershed. The royal tombs and remains of a large palace date from 350 to 325 BCE. The identities of the deceased royalty remain disputed, but given the superb artistry of the magnificent treasures found in the tombs, some scholars believe that these could have belonged only to the royal Macedonian family of King Philip II, father of Alexander the Great. Although the dig has turned up some fabulous treasures, all the good stuff is on display at the Archaeological Museum in Thessaloniki. The scattered rubble that remains of mortality and mercy in Vergina makes little sense to the dilettante. As you proceed down the road leading out of the village, you will see a sign pointing to the left for "The Royal Tombs." "The Archaeological Site" is straight ahead. The tombs to the left are still being excavated, but 2km from the village lie the open ruins of the 3rd-century **Palace of Palatitsa** (tel. (031) 92 347). Look for the exquisite mosaic floor on the south wing of what remains of the palace. (Open Tues.-Sun. 8:30am-3pm. Admission 400dr, students 200dr.)

A short climb up from the site to your left takes you to a partially excavated **royal tomb.** Archaeologists found a gold chest within that contained the cremated remains of some royal personage, along with a great many works of art and pieces of jewelry. Buses run from Thessaloniki to Veria, 74km away (every ½hr., 2hr., 1000dr). From there, take the "Alexandria" bus and get off at Vergina (15min.).

Thessaloniki ΘΕΣΣΑΛΟΝΙΚΗ

Fashionable Thessaloniki encircles its harbor and waterfront promenade with assurance. The capital of Macedonia and second largest city in Greece, Thessaloniki is riddled with Byzantine churches, an excellent archaeological museum, and Roman ruins. Lefkos Pirgos (White Tower), the symbol of Thessaloniki, presides over the harbor like an oversized chess piece. About 15 blocks up from the waterfront, just to the north of Athinas St., wind the streets of the old town, the *kastro.*

On the crossroads of important trade routes, Thessaloniki has flourished since its founding in 315 BCE by Cassander, brother-in-law of Alexander the Great. Named for Cassander's wife, ancient Salonika prospered after the Roman conquest of Greece. Being the only port on Via Egnatia (the ancient east-west highway) no doubt helped. **Egnatia Street,** six blocks from the waterfront, still serves as the city's main avenue. Paul the Apostle, in the first century CE, wrote two epistles to disciples of the churches he founded here. While Athens was in the throes of a cultural slump, Thessaloniki usurped its position as the most important Greek city in the Byzantine Empire. After the 10th century, the missionary followers of the brothers Methodius and Cyril (inventors of the Cyrillic alphabet) exerted a considerable influence over Balkan culture from their headquarters here.

Orientation and Practical Information

Thessaloniki's gridded street plan simplifies transit. The three main streets—Nikis, Tsimiski, and Egnatia—run parallel to the waterfront. You will find the cheapest hotels on **Egnatia,** banks and the post office on **Tsimiski,** and nondescript office buildings on **Nikis.** The main shopping street is **Ermou,** between Tsimiski and Egnatia. **Aristotelous** intersects all three at right angles then form **Aristotelous Square** on the waterfront, where the tourist information center, train office, and airport bus terminal are located. The railway station is west of the square along Monastiriou St.; the main park, fairgrounds, and university are east of the downtown area.

Greek National Tourist Organization (GNTO): Off Aristotelous Sq. at #8 (tel. 26 31 12 or 27 18 88), 1 block from the water. Take any tram on Egnatia to Aristotelous Sq. Very helpful. Has city maps, hotel listings, and train, bus, and boat schedules. Ask about annual events, especially the **International Trade Fair,** the **Film and Song Festival,** both held each year in Sept., and the **Dimitria Cultural Festival** held in Oct. Open Mon.-Fri. 8am-8pm, Sat. 8am-2pm. Another office at the **airport** (tel. 42 50 11, ext. 215).

Tourist Police: 10 Egnatia St. (tel. 54 41 62). Less helpful than the GNTO.

Consulates: U.S., 59 Nikis St. (tel. 26 61 21), on the waterfront west of the Lefkos Pirgos. Men can pick up a form letter here requesting permission to enter Mt. Athos (women are forbidden there; see section on Mt. Athos for more info.). Open Mon.-Fri. 9am-noon. **Britain,** 8 Venizelou St. (tel. 27 80 06). Also for other Commonwealth countries. Open Mon.-Fri. 9am-2pm. **Bulgaria** (tel. 82 92 10); **Cyprus** (tel. 26 06 11); **Italy** (tel. 83 00 55); **Turkey** (tel. 20 99 64).

Ministry of Northern Greece: Platia Dikitiriou, #218 (tel. 26 43 21), on Ag. Dikitiriou St. north of Egnatia St. After obtaining form letters from the U.S. consulate, men wishing to visit Mt. Athos must obtain permits here. (See section on Mt. Athos.)

Currency Exchange: National Bank of Greece, 11 Tsimiski St. Open for exchange Mon.-Fri. 8am-2pm and 6-8pm, Sat. 8am-1:30pm, Sun 9:30am-12:30pm. Smaller banks charge slightly higher commission.

American Express: Northern Greece representative is located at **Doucas Tours,** 8 Venizelou St. (tel. 26 99 84, 26 99 87, or 22 41 00), on Platia Eleftheria. Services for card holders only. Holds mail. Open Mon.-Fri. 8:30am-2pm and 5:30-8:30pm, Sat. 8:30am-1:30pm.

Post Office: 45 Tsimiski St., midway between Agia Sophias St. and Aristotelous St. Open Mon.-Sat. 8:30am-8pm. **Postal Code:** 54101.

OTE: 27 Karolou Diehl St., at the corner of Ermou, 1 block east of Aristotelous. Open Mon.-Sat. 24 hrs. **Telephone Code:** 031.

Airport: (tel. 47 32 12) 16km out of town. Take bus #78 (75dr). Taxis to and from the airport average 1200 to 1400dr. **Olympic Airways Office,** 7 Nikis St. (tel. 23 02 40). Flights to Athens (6 per day, 13,700dr), Lemnos (1 per day, 10,200dr), Lesvos (one per day, 16,000dr), Crete (2 per week, 21,800dr), Rhodes (2 per week, 23,500dr), Ioannina (4 or 5 per week, 7400dr). Olympic Airlines flights also connect Thessaloniki with major European cities and Larnaca in Cyprus. Open Mon.-Fri. 7am-9pm, Sat.-Sun. 8am-4pm. Lufthansa, British Airways, and charter companies fly into Thessaloniki as well.

Train Stations: Main Terminal, (tel. 51 75 17), Monastiriou St., in the western part of the city. Take any bus heading down Egnatia St. (50dr). Trains to: Athens via Larissa, Levadia, and Thebes (3 or 4 per day, 8hr., 2860dr); Edessa (8 per day, 2hr., 640dr); Florina (5 per day, 4hr., 1100dr);

Alexandroupolis (5 per day, 8hr., 2500dr); İstanbul (2 per day, 23hr., about 9000dr); Sofia (2 per day, 9hr., 10,000dr). You can also catch trains from Athens headed for Czechoslovakia (one per day at 9am), Germany (one per day at 7:20am), Hungary, Poland, and parts of the former Soviet Union. Buy tickets at the station or at **State Railway Offices (OSE)**, 18 Aristotelous St. (tel. 27 63 82). Open Tues.-Fri. 8am-8:30pm, Mon. and Sat. 8am-3pm.

Buses: The privately run **KTEL** bus company operates out of stations scattered throughout the city, each generally servicing a different area. While printed schedules and price lists are virtually nonexistent, departure times are posted above ticket counters. The depot directly across from the railway station runs buses to Athens (9 per day, 7½hr., 5500dr). To the left of this terminal is a KTEL station with buses heading to Trikala (6 per day, 3½hr., 2400dr). Behind the Athens bus depot sits another KTEL station (tel. 52 72 65 or 52 82 81) with buses leaving daily at 10am for Preveza and Parga (5100dr). The nearby KTEL (tel. 52 21 61) on the corner of Anagenniseous St. and I. Venizelou has departures for Florina (6 per day, 3½hr. 1090dr). From **22 Anagenniseous St.**, a few blocks further towards the waterfront and away from the railway station, buses run to Edessa (every hour, 2hr., 1100dr) and Volos (4 per day, 3hr., 2350dr). From 2 N. Kazantzaki St. (tel. 52 21 62) buses leave for Kastoria (5 or 6 per day, 4hr., 2500dr). For transport to the Halkidiki peninsula take the #10 bus from Egnatia St. to the depot on the East side of town at **68 Karakassi St.** (tel. 92 44 44 or 92 44 45). See Halkidiki section for more info.

Magic Bus: 32 Tsimski St. (tel. 26 35 66, 28 32 68, or 28 32 80), 1 block from the tourist office. Buses leave for London at 11pm each Tues. and arrive at 8am on Fri. (25,000dr). Buses also run to destinations in Germany, Italy and Holland. Open Mon.-Fri. 9am-6pm, Sat. 9am-1pm.

Ferries: Departures every Sat. in summer for Lesvos (15hr., 4970dr), Limnos (8hr., 2970 dr) and Chios (18hr., 5020dr). Every Mon. and Fri. boats leave for Paros (5000dr), Santorini (5430dr) and Skiathos (2520d.). One ferry leaves each Wed. night for Iraklion (6210dr). Get tickets at **Nomikos Lines**, 8 Kountourioti St., to the right of the main port, (tel. 52 45 44 or 51 30 05). Open Mon.-Fri. 8:30am-2:30pm and 5-8:30pm. **Flying Dolphins hydrofoils** travel daily (Sept.-June 4 per week) to: Skiathos (3½hr.), Skopelos (4½hr.), and Alonissos (5hr.). Fares average about 6000dr. Buy hydrofoil tickets at **Crete Air Travel**, 1 Dragoumi St. (tel. 54 74 07 or 53 43 76), directly across from the main port. Open 8:30am-2:30pm and 5-8pm.

American Center and USIS Library: 34 Mitropoleos St. (tel. 27 07 47), off Aristotelous Sq. Open Mon.-Fri. 9am-1:30pm; Mon., Wed. and Thurs. also 5-8pm.

British Council Cultural Center: 9 Ethnikis Aminis St. (tel. 23 52 36). Open Mon.-Fri. 8am-2pm and Mon.-Thurs. 5:30-8:30pm.

Bookstore: Molcho Books, 10 Tsimiski St. (tel. 27 52 71), across from the National Bank. Extensive selections in English, French, and Serbo-Croatian. International newspapers available daily. Open Mon., Wed., and Sat. 8:30am-2:30pm, Tues. and Thurs.-Fri. 8:30am-2pm and 5-8:30pm.

Laundromats: Bianca, 3 L. Antoniadou St. (tel. 20 96 02). From the Arch of Galerius, go inland up the median boulevard, and turn right at the KousKous café. It's directly across from the small church. 1000dr per load (includes wash, dry, and soap). Open Mon.-Fri. 8am-2pm. **Mimoza 2** (tel. 24 00 53), located at 56 Olimbou St., north of Egnetia St., does dry cleaning and pressing.

Camping Equipment: Petridhis, 43 Vassiliou Irakliou. Open Mon.-Fri. 8:30am-1:30pm.

Hospital: Ippokration, 49 Konstantinoupoleos (tel. 83 00 34). This public hospital is supposedly the best in Thessaloniki. While finding a doctor in Northern Greece who's fluent in English can be quite difficult, you're most likely to find one here. Lower back surgery can be fun.

Medical Emergency: Red Cross First Aid Hospital, 6 Kountorioti St. (tel. 53 05 30), located at the entrance to the main port. Provides minor medical care in an unpampering fashion. Bring a Greek-English dictionary. Services are free.

Police Emergency: Tel. 100.

Accommodations and Camping

Hotels await you along the western end of Egnatia St., roughly between Vardari Sq. (500m east of the train station) and Dikastirion Sq.

Youth Hostel (HI/IYHF), 44 Alex. Svolou St. (also called Nikolaou St.), (tel. 22 59 46). Take tram #8, 10, 11, or 31 east on Egnatia and get off at the Arch of Galerius. Go toward the water and turn left 2 blocks later onto Svolou. Clean. On a noisy street. Communal facilities. Reception open 9-11am and 6-11pm. Lock-out 11am-6pm. Curfew 11pm. 1296dr per person. Showers (6-10pm only) 70dr.

YWCA (XEN in Greek), 11 Agias Sophias St. (tel. 27 61 44), between Tsimiski and Mitropoleos. Women only. Emphasis on the "C." Reception open Mon.-Fri. 7am-midnight, Sat. 7am-3pm and 7pm-midnight. Clean, high-ceilinged rooms. Dorm beds average1700dr, depending on number of beds per room. Cold showers included. Continental breakfast 150dr.

Atlantis, 14 Egnatia St. (tel. 54 01 31). Best deal in town. Sunny rooms facing a quiet street. Glittering shared bathrooms. Singles 2500dr. Doubles 3000dr. **Hotel Kastoria,** 24 Egnatia St. (tel. 53 62 80). Corner location means cacophony in stereo. Clean baths. Singles 3000dr. Doubles 4000dr. Shared baths.

Hotel Argo, 11 Egnatia St. (tel 51 97 70). Clean rooms and a convenient location. Singles 2500dr. Doubles 3000dr. Some private baths. **Hotel Atlas,** 40 Egnatia St. (tel. 53 70 46 or 51 00 38). The accommodating owner speaks English. Singles 3500dr. Doubles 4000dr. Triples 6000dr.

Hotel Tourist, 21 Metropoleos (tel. 27 63 35). Centrally located one block from Aristotelous Sq. 14-ft. ceilings, cavernous hallways, and an old-fashioned elevator make for a charming ambience. Singles 3800dr. Doubles 5700dr.

Camping: Take city bus #72 to **Agia Triada** for **Thermaikos Beach Campground** (tel. (0392) 513 52). **Asprovalta** (tel. (0397) 222 49) has similar prices. About 600dr per person, 800-900dr per tent.

Food and Entertainment

Inexpensive self-service foodlets and shops fleck the downtown area. Lively and full of bargains, the *agora* (marketplace) is bounded on four sides by Irakliou, Egnatia, Aristotelous, and Venizelou St. To stock up on fruits, vegetables, bread, and groceries, visit the bustling open-air markets of Vati Kioutou St. just off of Aristotelous. The restaurants along the seaside serve standard fare at comparable rates. On weekend evenings, mingle with the locals along the plaza **Dhimitrio Gounari.** Overdressed couples promenade from the waterfront to the Arch of Galerius. Others mellow out with a cup of Greek coffee in the park and at **Navarinou Square,** one block west of D. Gounari. Younger crowds celebrate along the waterfront and **Koromila St.,** one block inland of Nikis St. Lesbian and gay revelers head to **Shic,** 5 Layamargerita (off Morgendao St., between Nikis and Mitropoleos), and **Entasis,** 29 Koromila St.

Merrymakers frolic through the cobblestone streets of **Kastra**--old city—until the wee hours, when the *bouzouki* music and Greek dancing finally ceases. To get to the *Kastra,* take bus #22 or 23 from Eleftherias Sq. on the waterfront, or walk.

Ta Spata, (tel. 23 19 66), conveniently located at 28 Aristotelous, offers a wide selection of tasty and inexpensive entrées (around 800dr). Crowded with Greeks and tourists. Open 8am-1am.

Vlahos, 3 Nikiforev Foka, west of the Lefkos Pirgos, offers a view of the water *sans* touristy atmosphere. Casseroles served at lunch, grill at night. Open noon-4pm and 7pm-1am.

Canoniero, 130 Epta Pirgiou, is in Kastra, just outside the walls. Splendid view of Thessaloniki by night and even better pizza. Open daily 10am-3am.

New Ilisia, (tel. 536-996) 17 Leontos Sofou St., a neighborhood restaurant and grill located off of Egnatia St. serves traditional Greek food in an unpretentious setting. Entrées around 900dr. Open daily 6am-2am.

Rafaella (tel. 27 57 75), on the corner of Metropoleous and Kominon Sts. (just 1 block from Aristotelous Sq.), a trendy café with croissant sandwiches (350dr) and a fresh juice bar.

Olympion Palace, 77 L. Nikis (tel. 27 30 30), on the waterfront, a hip bar very popular with the young and beautiful people of Thessaloniki. This crowd could be the cast of a Greek *Beverly Hills 90210.*

Take bus #5 or 6 to the American-style dance clubs in **Kalamaria** (pronounced Kala-mar-YA), by the sea. Kalamaria is burdened with a surfeit of overpriced *caferia* and pizza houses. In summer, weekend nightlife centers in the suburb of **Nea Krinis.** Take bus #5 from Aristotelous Sq., or pick it up on Mitropoleos St. to get to the **Amusement Park** in Salminan. **Natali Cinema,** 3 Vassilissis Olgas (tel. 41 30 19), on the waterfront, just five minutes past the White Tower heading away from the city center, shows open-air English-language movies in summer. Two shows nightly at 9pm and 11pm. (Admission 900dr.)

Sights

If you have time for only one stop in the city, head to the superlative **Archaeological Museum** (tel. 83 05 38 or 83 10 37), which spotlights a collection of Macedonian treasures such as delicate gold foil crowns and wreaths, figurines and gold *larnakes* (burial caskets), which once contained the cremated royal family of Vergina. (Open Mon. 11am-5pm, Tues.-Fri. 8am-5pm, Sat.-Sun. 8:30am-3pm; in winter Mon. 10:30am-5pm, Tues.-Fri. 8am-5pm, Sun. 8:30am-3pm. Admission 1000dr. Take bus #3 from the railway station to Hanth Sq.) The **International Fairgrounds,** next to the museum, hold a variety of festivals in September and October (for information call 23 92 21). During these months, accommodations usually go the way of the dodo bird in Thessaloniki; if you're fortunate enough to find a place, expect a 20-30% hike in the room rate.

On the other side of the park on the waterfront looms the **Lefkos Pirgos** (White Tower), (tel. 26 78 32), all that remains of a Venetian seawall. Formerly known as the Bloody Tower because an elite corps of soldiers was massacred within it, the structure was painted white to obliterate the gruesome memories. The tower, which houses a fascinating museum featuring early Christian and Byzantine art, presents a slide show every hour. (Open Tues.-Fri. 12:30-7pm, Sat.-Sun. 8:30am-3pm; in off-season Tues.-Fri. 8am-5pm, Sun. 8:30am-3pm. Admission 500dr.) The more extensive ruins of the **Eptapirgion Walls,** erected during the reign of Theodosius the Great, stretch along the northern edge of the old city. Take bus #22 or 23 from Eleftherias Sq. on the waterfront. Eleftherias Sq. is also where buses #5, 33, and 39 leave for the traditional costumes in the **Ethnological and Popular Art (Folklore) Museum,** 68 Vas. Olgas St. (tel. 83 05 91). (Open Fri.-Wed. 9:30am-2pm. Free.)

The celebrated **Arch of Galerius,** the finest of Thessaloniki's ancient Greek and Roman ruins, stands at the end of Egnatia St., at the corner of Gounari St. (undergoing renovation and covered with scaffolding in 1992). Next to it and temporarily closed for reconstruction is the **Rotunda,** which started out as an emperor's mausoleum, but was rechristened by Constantine the Great as **Agios Georgios** (Church of St. George).

For further historical pursuits, head north of Dikastirion Sq. to the Roman ruins between Filippou and Olibou St. The ruins, which include a somewhat hyper-restored theater, are still being excavated. The crux of the remains of the **Palace of Galerius,** near Navarino Sq., is the well-preserved octagonal hall. The usual **Roman bath** remains lie next to the church of Agios Dimitrios at the corner of Agios Dimitrios and Aristotelous St. (Always open. Free.)

Over the centuries, most of the churches in this region were damaged or destroyed by recurring earthquakes. The few lucky survivors, such as **Agios Dimitrios,** (tel. 27 00 08; visiting hours Tues.-Sun. 9am-2:45pm), **Panagia Halkeon** (tel. 27 29 10; on the corner of Egnatia and Aristotelous St.), and **Agios Nikolaos Orfanos** (tel. 21 44 97; 20 Iradotou St.; visiting hours 9am-2:30pm) all feature brilliant mosaic work and superb frescoes from the late Byzantine era.

Another noteworthy example of Byzantine art in Thessaloniki is the splendid 9th-century mosaic of the Ascension in the dome of the **Agia Sophia** (tel. 27 05 23), in the park of the same name at the corner of Ermou and Agia Sophias St. The church, modeled after the Aya Sofia in İstanbul, is currently undergoing restoration, but the public is welcome to view the scaffolded debris. More mosaics decorate the **Panayia Ahiropiitos** (tel. 27 28 20), two blocks farther north at 56 Agia Sophias St. (Churches open approximately 8am-1pm and 5-8pm; closed for morning services Sun. and holidays.) You can also visit the beautiul **Old Synagogue** at 35 Sigrou St. (tel. 52 49 68). The temple is no longer in use, but the caretaker at the Jewish Community Center, 24 Tsimiski St, will let you in.

Near Thessaloniki

Atop Mt. Hortiatis, **Panorama's** name tells all—its dynamic view of Thessaloniki and the Aegean makes it an orchideous spot to linger over a *caffè frappe.* Because of the cool, nerve-massaging weather at the summit, the suburban village is a popular destination for summer excursions. Make the 10km trip by bus #57 or 58 from Dikastirion

Sq. (every ½hr.; 20min.). Bus #61 goes to the village of **Hortiatis,** perched on the side of the mountain 10km past Panorama.

During World War II, occupying Germans burned the village to the ground in retaliation for partisan sabotage. Perhaps not coincidentally, Panorama is one of the few villages in the region yet to be invaded by vociferous and gregarious German tourists. More often, the village is filled with quiet Greek visitors from Thessaloniki hoping to enjoy an evening meal above the smog and chaos down below.

In **Langadas,** 12km northeast of Thessaloniki, villagers celebrate the feast day of Sts. Constantine and Helen (nightly from May 20-23) by dancing barefoot across a bed of burning coals. This ritual is thought to have its roots in a form of worship practiced by an ancient Dionysiac orgiastic cult and since adapted to Christian beliefs. The Greek Church, worried that the 700 Club might do an exposé, refuses to authorize any service performed on this day. Regardless, the rite has become an annual tourist attraction. Festivities begin around 7pm, but try to arrive by 5:30pm to get a good seat. If you can't get to Langadas, you can catch the show on the ERT-TV news. The bus to Langadas (every ½hr.) leaves from the station at 17 Irini St., near Langada St., at the western end of Egnatia.

Perea, Agia Triada, and **Nea Mihaniona,** the beaches closest to the city, are as bikini-blessed as you would expect of beaches accessible by bus from Greece's second largest population center. From Dikastirion Sq., bus #72 (90dr) goes to Perea, Agia Triada, and to Nea Mihaniona (100dr, every 10min., 45min.). Agia Triada has **Epanomis** (tel. 413 78) one of the best GNTO campgrounds in northern Greece. Restaurants along the beach offer private rooms. The water is somewhat fetid; for less bacterial swimming, head to the Halkidiki peninsula.

Pella ΠΕΛΛΑ

For those with a flair for history and a vivid imagination, the ruins of ancient Pella, discovered by a farmer in 1957, prove a rewarding daytrip 38km west of Thessaloniki. Pella served as a port in ancient times, when the surrounding plain was covered with water fed from the Thermaïko Gulf. Around 400 BCE, King Archelaus opted to build his palace there, and it rapidly became a great cultural center and the largest city in Macedonia. Pella became the first capital of a united Greece during Philip II's reign; his son, Alexander the Great, shoved off from the city on his lifelong mission to unify the world under Macedonian rule. On the other side of the highway is the small but impressive **Pella Museum** (tel. (0382) 312 78 or 311 60), with the exquisite mosaics *Dionysus Riding a Panther* and *The Lion Hunt*. Through the skillful use of chiaroscuro and foreshortening, these mosaics are the earliest known which attempt to convey a sense of three-dimensionality. (Both the museum and ruins are open Tues.-Sat. 8:30am-3pm. Admission to both 400dr).

Buses to Pella run every hour from the 22 Anagenniseos depot near the railway station in Thessaloniki (8:30am-7:30pm, 45min., about 400dr). You are probably better off making a daytrip, since the nearest hotels are 12km away in the unattractive modern city of **Giannitsa.** Although there is no official campground, many freelance camp near the site. The nearby *taverna* provides food, rest rooms, and an outdoor sink. **Buses** to and from Thessaloniki (2-3 per hr.) pass the site, which is right on the main highway. To go between Pella and Vergina, change buses at Halkidona, about 3km east of Pella.

Mount Olympus ΟΠΟΣ ΟΛΥΜΠΟΣ

*The charm [of Olympus] does not lie in its natural
beauty; nor its physical magnitude; the beauty of
Olympus is spiritual, it is divine . . .*
　　　　　　　　　　　　　　—*Boissonade*

Rising from the coastal plain 90km southwest of Thessaloniki, Mt. Olympus so impressed the seafaring ancient Greeks that they exalted it as the lofty home of the gods. First climbed in 1913, Olympus has been harnessed by a network of well-maintained hiking trails that make the summit accessible to any mortal with stout legs and lungs. Hikes to the summit reward visitors with dizzying views of land and sea, seen through the high-altitude prism of ethereal blue skies and piercing sunlight.

Because storms bury Mt. Olympus in six or more feet of snow each winter, the unofficial climbing season lasts only from May to October. If you make the ascent between May and September, you'll need no special equipment besides sturdy shoes, sunglasses, a butch sunscreen, a hat, and water. If you plan on climbing the upper regions (especially when the summit is shrouded in clouds), you may need a waterproof windbreaker, an extra shirt, and gloves. Water purification tablets or tincture of iodine may also come in handy. You can rush through the climb in one long day, but plan on a two- or three-day trip to fully imbibe the wilderness. Consider staying overnight in one of the refuges; leave your pack in the village of Litohoro. You can also camp on the mountain. In either case bring warm clothes.

Litohoro

The gateway to Olympus is the small village of **Litohoro** (pronounced Li-TO-horo or Li-TO-hor-on), conveniently situated 5km from the Athens-Thessaloniki highway and accessible by both bus and train via Katerini, 22km away. Despite its proximity to an attraction of ungodly worldwide fame, the town is relatively free of souvenirs and other tourist accoutrements. **Buses** (tel. 812 71) travel from Litothoro to and from Thessaloniki via Katerini (9 per day, 2hr., 1080dr), Katerini (every 30min., 20min., 280dr), Larissa via Katerini (10 per day, around 1000dr), and Athens (3 per day, about 6hr., 4500dr). **Trains** (tel. 612 11) stop at the Litohoro station on the line between Thessaloniki and Volos (from Athens 7 per day, 7hr.), but since the station is close to the beach and several km from town, you must catch the Katerini-Litohoro bus on the main road 150m from the station (100dr).

Near the bus station in Litohoro, down the main street on your right, are the offices of Greece's two alpine clubs: the **EOS Greek Mountaineering Club** (tel. 819 44; open in summer only Mon.-Fri. 9am-noon and 6-8:30pm) and the **SEO Mountaineering Club of Greece** (tel. 823 00; open daily 9am-1pm and 6-9pm). SEO's main refuge is higher and offers a glorious view of the mountain, the valley and Thessaloniki (2760m; open July-Aug.), but EOS's Refuge A (open June-Sept.) is closer to the end of the road, and thus more accessible by car. Both refuges have running water. EOS owns three other refuges on Mt. Olympus that are locked on weekdays; keys are available at the EOS office. Both clubs provide maps and information about the mountain, maintain the soil of the trails and refuges, and organize emergency rescue helicopters and first-aid stations. Litohoro has a **health center** with emergency facilities (tel. 221 10 or 221 57).

The **tourist office** at 15 Ag. Nicolaou (tel. 812 50 or 812 63), is in the town hall, adjacent to the **police office** (tel. 811 11). The English-speaking staff can reserve a spot for you in one of the refuges, and give you maps and information on the trails. (Open daily 9am-2pm; Mon.-Sat. also 5-9pm.) For more detailed information, head to one of the alpine clubs up the street. Litohoro's **National Bank** (tel. 810 25) resides in the main square (open Mon.-Thurs. 8am-2pm, Fri. 8am-1:30pm) with the **post office** (open Mon.-Fri. 7:30am-2pm). The **OTE** is across from the playground on the main street (open Mon.-Sat. 7:30am-9pm, Sun. 9am-1pm). Litohoro's **postal code** is 60200; the **telephone code** is 0352.

Most youthful ramblers stay at the small **Youth Hostel (HI/IYHF)** (tel. 813 11 or 821 76), and all vie for the two shower/bathrooms at once. Follow signs 200m up the hill from the square. The hostel is closed each day from 2-6pm, has a checkout at 9am each morning and a curfew of 11pm. The reception is open 9am-2pm and 6-11pm. Guests having stayed a minimum of one night may leave their luggage here for 250dr. Lockout 11am-6pm, but guests can drop off their luggage (200dr). The proprietor sells topographical maps, provides information, and rents motorbikes (200dr per day), hiking shoes (400dr), day packs (300dr), mountain clothing (450dr) and bikes (600dr). Beds in dorm-type rooms go for 800dr per night (shower included). Private singles are available for 1500dr and doubles for 2500dr. The hostel is open year-round and phone reservations are accepted. The pleasant **Hotel Aphroditi** (tel. 814 15 or 830 71) is located on the road to the youth hostel. Many of the comfortable rooms offer stunning views of the Mount. (Singles 4000dr. Doubles 5000dr). Four **campgrounds** and countless freelance camping spots squeeze between the railroad and the beach, 5km out of town across the highway. **Do not freelance camp** on the north side of the road connecting the town and the highway; this is a training ground for the armored units of the Greek army.

The **Olympus Café** in the main square is popular with tourists and locals alike. (Entrées 500-600dr. Open noon-midnight.) Ignore the cars whizzing around the outdoor tables at **Taverna Pazari** (from the northwest corner of the main square, follow the road uphill 5min. and turn left) and enjoy *kalamari* or red snapper (both 700dr).

Trails to the Summits

Mount Olympus has eight peaks: Kalogeros (2701m), Toumba (2785m), Profitis Ilias (2786m), and Antonius (2815m), are dwarfed by the thrones of Skala (2866m), Skolio (2911m), Stefani (also called the Throne of Zeus, 2909m), and **Mytikas** (or the Pantheon, 2917m). There are two approaches to the peaks from Litohoro. To reach the beginning of both trails, take the road that winds upward just before the square in Litohoro. There is no bus service between the trails and the village, so it's best to find a group at the hostel to share a taxi (3500dr to Prionia). Those who hitch should start early, since most climbers drive up in the morning; Hiking alongside the Enipeas River from Litohoro to Prionia is another option; the 18km trail is good but rugged. It begins past the town cemetery and Restaurant Mili in the upper part of Litohoro. At the fork in the trail, follow the yellow diamond marker uphill on the left side of the **Mavrolungo Gorge.** This four-hour roller coaster of hills is exhausting, but remunerates with rib-shattering scenery. Note the cave where Agios Dionysios, Litohoro's patron saint, lived in the 16th century. You will also pass the charred shell of a monastery that gave refuge to Greek partisans during World War II until the Nazis found out and torched the place. If you decide not to hike through the gorge, walk to Prionia along the asphalt road (which becomes an unpaved path after 3km).

At **Diastavrosi,** just 14km from Litohoro, the first trail slopes up to the right of the road. This route offers impressive views of the Aegean, the Macedonian plain to the north, and the smog layer over Thessaloniki far below. You can find water in two places along this trail: the turn-off between Barba and Spilia (1½hr. from the trail head), marked on the trail, and at the spring at Strangos. It's a long haul (5-6hr.) from the start of the trail to the **SEO refuge,** "Giosos Apostolides," where you can seek shelter (1500dr). Ample blankets are provided and hot meals are served throughout the day. Bottles of water cost 150dr. At 2760m (only 157m from the summit of Olympus), the shelter is less frequented than its counterpart "A," below, and proffers a magnificent view of the Stefani peak at sunrise. Just as exhilarating is the lunar landscape overlooking the Plateau of the Muses, aptly named after the mythological sisters who inspired creativity. From here, the summit is a painless 1½hr. away.

The second, more frequented route is the unpaved road past Diastavrosi, another 4km from **Prionia,** where you can fill your canteens at a spring. The hike from Prionia (1½-2½hr.) winds through deciduous and evergreen forests to **Refuge A** (tel. 818 00), just below the tree line, at 2100m elevation. Guides may be hired for the rest of the climb for a steep 6000dr or more per day, depending on the size of the entourage and the duration of your climb. Rates go up 50% between December 15 and May 25, the dangerous season when guides are truly essential.

Mitikas is the highest (2917m) and most-climbed peak of Olympus. From Refuge A, take the path uphill and follow the red marks along rubble switchbacks and mountain meadows strewn with indigo wildflowers.

The last leg of the ascent to Mitikas is usually made by one of two routes. If you take the fork in the path at Refuge A, you'll see the peak **Skala** (2866m) to your left and the

SEO Refuge to your right. From Skala, there is a sinuous descent a bit before the ascent to Mitikas. This trail to Mitikas is justly considered the most dangerous part of the hike, prone to rock slides and avalanches. It's not a good idea to lug a large pack along this route unless it's jet-propelled. If you return to Skala, it's a relatively easy walk to **Skolio,** the second highest peak (2911m) and the best point for viewing the sheer western face of Olympus. From Refuge A, you can go directly to Skolio, taking the path left off that to Skala.

The great challenge on Olympus is **Stefani** (also known as *Thronos Dhios,* or "Throne of the Gods"). The turn-off for the ridge is very close to that for Mitikas and the first part of the scramble is very similar. Once you've reached the narrow ridge, however, you must snake your way along it, with a 300m void on either side of you.

Near Litohoro—Dion

Unknown to all but the most enlightened tour groups, the archaeological site at the city of **Dion** makes an excellent daytrip. Representing Philip II's early attempts at town planning, the area encompasses well-preserved mosaic floors and three ancient theaters (one classical, one Hellenistic, and one Roman). Archaeologists are currently busy excavating the latter two. During the annual International Festival of Olympus (July-Aug.), Dion's classical theater hosts performances of ancient Greek tragedies and comedies. The local **Zeus Museum and Archaeological Site** (tel. (0351) 532 06) displays the objects found during the excavations of Dion (dating from the 7th to 2nd century BCE). Of special note is the gold filigree laurel wreath of Apollo with its moveable leaves. (Open Mon. 11am-6pm, Tues.-Fri. 8am-6pm, Sat.-Sun. and holidays 8:30am-3pm; 400dr.) To get to Dion, take a bus from Katerini (Mon.-Sat. every hr., Sun. every 30min. until 11:30pm, 150dr).

Halkidiki ΧΑΛΚΙΔΙΚΗ

Three-pronged like Poseidon's trident, Halkidiki thrusts southward into the Aegean. On the eastern prong is the restricted region of Mount Athos, the largest enduring monastic community in Western society. The western side is **Kassandra,** a playground for sun disciples. Sandwiched between them is **Sithonia,** whose barren interior is ringed with gorgeous, if crowded, beaches.

Public transportation on Halkidiki does not have the tourist in mind. Frequent buses run between the 68 Karakassi St. station in Thessaloniki (tel. 92 44 44) and each of the three peninsulas, but hopping from peninsula to peninsula invariably involves watching the asphalt melt as you wait for connections.

In Halkidiki's northern interior, **Poligiros** hosts an archaeological museum, and **Arnea** is known for its wines and handwoven fabrics. Farther west and more difficult to reach is the celebrated cave at **Petralona,** where a neanderthal skull dating from 700,000 BCE was found sulking in a corner. Other items found in the cave include a female skull about 50,000 years old and enough bear and deer bones to suggest the cave was the site of some pretty outrageous feasting. These findings are all on display in an anthropological museum near the cave. To the west of the Halkidikian mainland and on the bays between the peninsulas are several crowded beaches. During July and August, at the height of the beach season, there's a greater chance of finding sun-stroke than sand, water, or peace.

Kassandra

Kassandra had been an important trading region from the 7th century BCE when Corinthians built a port, Potidaia, on the northeastern coast of the peninsula. Now, however, Kassandra is merely a favorite weekend getaway for Thessalonikians and a popular playground for European tourists. Long, sandy beaches and cornflower-blue waters, unfortunately, attract far more visitors than can be gracefully accommodated. The tourist build-up on the coastline has effectively nullified options for the budget traveler, but at least the outdoor freshwater showers on most of the popular beaches are free.

To get to Kassandra from Thessaloniki, take a **bus** to Kassandria and get off at Kalithea (10 per day, 2hr., 1150dr). Buses go to Paliouri on the southern tip (9 per day, 3hr., about 1400dr), and to Agia Paraskevi (4 per day, about 1400dr). Buses for Kassandria depart from **68 Karakassi St.** in Thessaloniki (tel. 92 44 44 or 92 44 45). **Kassandria,** the peninsula's administrative center and transport hub, has nothing to offer except an **OTE** (open Mon.-Fri. 7:30am-3pm), a **post office** (open 8am-2pm), and the **National Bank of Greece** (open Mon.-Thurs. 8am-2pm and Fri. 8:30am-1:30pm). All lie along a two-block stretch in the town center. Otherwise, Kassandria has no hotels, no beach, and little excitement. Kassandra region's **postal code** is 63077; its **telephone code** is 0374.

Lively **Kalithea** reverberates with the noise of the peninsula's largest tourist population. Once the site of a temple to Zeus Ammon, now high-rise temples to Mammon here open their doors to tourists for several thousand *drachmae* per night. Kalithea has branches of the main banks plus a privately owned **phone center.** (Open daily 9am-2pm and 5pm-midnight.) The bus station, in the town center on the road perpendicular to the main drag, is simply a sheltered bench with a posted schedule. You can rent motorcycles at **Motorent** (tel. 220 50), 50m north on the street behind the main road. A two-seater 150cc Vespa starts at a high-octane 3800dr a day. (Open daily, roughly 8:30am-9pm.) The **Ionian bank** (tel. 221 60) at the plaza handles currency exchange. (Open Mon.-Fri. 8:30am-1pm.) A rudimentary **post office** sits across the street from the main intersection. (Open daily 8:30am-1:30pm and 2-8pm.) Start your room search around the corner from the bus stop on the main street, but don't expect any bargains. The English-speaking staff at **Doucas Tours** (tel. 223 41 or 227 76), located just opposite the Athos, and at the Pallini hotels can also provide some assistance. Solo travelers will have to shell out the money for a double; singles in Kalithea are merely abstract concepts. A bit of a walk from the water, but clean and reliable, is the **Penzione Panorama** (tel. 232 66/67). The sparkling rooms have kitchens and dependable hot water (doubles 6000dr). To **camp,** walk past the Toroneon and turn down the dirt road to the left, which leads to a pine grove on the bluffs overlooking the water. Just toward the beach from the Kassandria junction, the cheapest restaurant on the ledge, **Fotis,** has a fantastic view (delicious *guvetsi,* veal with pasta, 800dr; open 7am-2am).

Sithonia ΣΙΘΩΝΙΑ

Although it withstood the tourist barrage longer than its western neighbor, Sithonia has recently been seduced by visitors sporting BMWs and fistfuls of *drachmae*. Its innocence lost, the area has wasted no time in plunging headlong into the sordid world of beachside villas and plastic souvenirs. On the more isolated beaches of the peninsula's southern extreme, however, a measure of tranquility persists. There are two rugged routes through Sithonia: west via Nea Marmaras, and east via Vourvourou. Travel is more flexible going west, since buses travel to Nea Marmaras (5 per day, 3hr., 1650dr), continuing around the peninsula to Sarti (5 per day, 3½hr., about 2000dr). Buses run directly to Vourvourou (3 per day, 3hr., about 1600dr). Another option is to take a bus to Agios Nikolaos at the neck of the peninsula (3 per day, 3hr., about 1600dr), and work your way down from there.

Before arriving at **Nea Marmaras** (also called Marmaras), you'll pass the beach at **Agios Ioannis,** a prime spot to stake a tent. Nea Marmaras is a small upscale vacation spot with stylish jewelry and trendy bars. Rooms here are expensive (doubles 4000-6000dr, singles virtually unheard of). Katerina Valsanidou or another of the helpful English-speaking staff at **Doucas Tours** (tel. (0375) 719 59), located at the bus stop, can recommend hotels and rooms. **Albatros Rooms To Let** (tel. 710 03 or 717 38), located on Themistokli St., has incredibly spacious, modern, clean rooms with kitchenettes, large balconies and comfortable beds. (Doubles a steal at 5000dr.) On the beach,

Camping Marmaras (tel. 719 01) is 1km back and clearly marked by road signs. (900dr per person, 1000dr per tent. Open June-Sept.) As long as you clean up after yourself, you can freelance camp in a pine grove 1km beyond, or right on the beach. The **tourist police** (tel. 711 11) are in an unmarked house on the first street parallel to the highway. Hours are posted on the door. (Open daily approximately 8:30am-2:30pm and 8:30-10pm. English not spoken.) To reach the **OTE** from the bus stop, walk to the left corner of the bottom of the square. Then hike up the steep street for about two minutes. (Open 7:30am-midnight). Nea Marmaras's **telephone code** is 0375. The town **post office** is in the town's second square, near the Restaurant Giorg #3. (Open 8am-2pm). Nea Marmaras enjoys an elite reputation largely due to the presence of the **Porto Carras** hotel complex situated just across the bay. This luxury resort is a jet set playground with fine restaurants, chic boutiques, an open-air cinema, and beautiful beaches. Even with doubles starting at 26,700dr, all rooms are fully booked in the summer. Porto Carras offers activities such as windsurfing, waterskiing, and even parasailing, all starting at 25000dr. We suggest body surfing. The **Christina Beauty Parlor** (tel. 918 81), located in the Porto Carras hotel, is a decadent establishment where an English translator sits and conveys every minor comment or intstruction to your Greek stylist. Cuts start at 3000dr. Ferries shuttle between Restaurant Giorg #3 and Restaurant Propondis in Marmaras to Porto Carras (every ½hr. 8:30am-11pm, 15min., 200dr). The 25-minute walk around the coast is free.

The best dinner option is **George's Paradise Fish Tavern** next to Doucas Tours, offering traditional Greek fare and seafood at moderate prices (open 9am-midnight). The **Cool Bar** (tel. 718 29) on the waterfront in the town's second square is, surprisingly enough, just that. Chic young Greeks converge here on summer nights. (Open 10am-3am). The bus around the peninsula to Sarti (5 per day, 1hr., 500dr) passes by the most deserted and desirable turf on Sithonia. After climbing the road 5km south of Porto Carras, you'll see a beach near **Agia Kiriaki,** complete with a small reef and an outlying island. It's a long, hard climb down from here.

Bus service connecting Sithonia to the Mt. Athos peninsula fails to exist. The road through Pirgadikia, Gomati, and Ierissos is unpaved and frequented by goat trucks; waits between hitches are long and just not worth it. To get to Mt. Athos by bus, start early in the morning and catch the bus to Thessaloniki as far as Agios Prodomos, although you'll probably have to change buses and wait several times and you might do just as well returning to Thessaloniki and departing from there. Buses pass through Agios Podromos on the way to Ouranoupolis. For Kassandra, take the Thessaloniki bus that passes through Nea Moudania (6 per day from Marmaras).

Mount Athos ΟΠΟΣ ΑΘΟΣ

> As of August 10, 1992 Mount Athos has closed its doors to all tourists as a protest against the Greek government's decision to tax the monasteries. It is hoped the closing will be temporary. Consult the Ministry of Northern Greece in Thessaloniki for updated information.

The monastaries on Mount Athos *(Agion Oros),* have been the standard-bearers of ascetisism for more than a millenium. Today, the easternmost peninsula of Halkidiki is an autonomous state comprised of 20 Eastern Orthodox monasteries, with some 1700 monks. As it is the most vigorous spiritual center of Orthodox Christianity, there are no tourists in Athos—only pilgrims. The monks of Mount Athos attempt daily to transcend the material pleasures of the outside world and lead a simple, spiritual life. Food, dress, and possessions at Athos are very modest.

The community on Mount Athos has been structured to varying degrees since 883 CE, when Basil I issued an imperial charter to Athos forbidding local military officials from interfering with the monks. An edict of the Emperor Constantine from 1060, enforced to this day, forbids women from so much as setting foot on the peninsula. The absence of foraging goats and livestock has helped to preserve the luxuriant forests and the dense foliage. Although this lush tangle of green heightens the mystical aura pervading Athos, it is also provides cover for snakes, bats, and other interesting animals. Only the jagged marble peak of Mt. Athos itself, soaring 2033m above the encircling waves of the Aegean, is exposed

History

According to legend, the Christian history of Mt. Athos began when the Virgin Mary, on a sea trip to visit her friend Lazarus in Cyprus, was thrown off course by a storm and led by divine sign to the Athonite coast. The peninsula, known then as *Akte,* was a notorious center of paganism, but the moment Mary's foot graced its soil, the false idols all smashed themselves to bits in frenzied proclamation of their own worthlessness. Mary then declared Athos her holy garden, forbidden to all other women for eternity, and blessed the land before sailing back to Jaffa.

Following centuries of occupation by Christian hermits and ascetics, the oldest monastery (Agia Lavra) was established in 963 CE by Athanasius, a rich man's son turned monk. Under the protection of Byzantine emperors, the building of monasteries flourished until, at its zenith in the 15th century, Mt. Athos harbored 40 monasteries and some 20,000 monks. When Constantinople fell to Turkish armies in 1453, the monastic community prudently surrendered, thus remaining unplundered and relatively autonomous. In 1926, a decree of the Greek government made Mt. Athos officially part of Greece while allowing it to retain an autonomous theocratic government. Due to gradual attrition and the diminishing influx of young novices, Mt. Athos's eminence slowly declined until the 1950s, when it became a prime target of greedy real estate and resort developers. In recent decades, however, *Agion Oros* has been miraculously rejuvenated, and hundreds of young men, inspired to take their vows, have donned the black robes and hat of Orthodox monasticism. Now over 1700 monks live alone in tiny hermitages or inhabit the 20 monasteries and other communities known as *sketes, kellia,* or *kalyvia.*

Athos contains an unsurpassed wealth of Paleologian and Late Byzantine art, manuscripts, and architecture. **Megisti Lavra** is a veritable warehouse of crucifixes inlaid with precious metal and stones. Its antique libraries contain over 42,000 tomes. Graceful frescoes and painted icons, including numerous masterpieces by great artists of the Cretan and Macedonian Schools, adorn the church interiors.

Any visit to Athos will be greatly enhanced by reading beforehand about the art, history, and legends of the individual monasteries. *Athos the Holy Mountain,* by Sydney Loch, a book with the same title by Philip Sherrard (1985), and *Mount Athos,* by Norwich, Sitwell, and Costa, are highly readable and informative.

Monasteries of the Mountain

At one time, there were nearly equal numbers of Greek and Slavic monks at Athos, but the Russian Revolution cut off the supply of funds and novices at its source, and today only three Slavic monasteries remain. The Russian **Panteleimon,** the Bulgarian **Zografou,** and the Serbian **Chilandari** serve as interesting contrasts to the monasteries on the rest of the peninsula. Although **Megisti Lavra** and **Iviron** are beautiful and well worth seeing, these two largest, oldest, and most frequently visited of the cloisters can be aptly referred to as the "museum monasteries." Try to visit some of the smaller and more remote monasteries such as **Koutloumousoiu** and **Xenophontos** as well; these lack the grandiose art that attracts the bevvies of tourists.

The most complete experience at Mt. Athos involves developing an understanding and appreciation of the monastic way of life. Always address monks by their title, *Pateras.* Although most monks are Greek, the Athos renaissance has drawn neophytes from the U.S., Canada, France, England, and elsewhere. Many young monks are university educated, and several speak English reasonably well. When you arrive at a monastery, ask the *Archontari* if it's possible to speak with one.

Life on Mt. Athos befuddles the non-ascetic. This theology is not a cold academic exercise, but a way of life. The scanty meals are entirely meatless and often eaten in near silence. Men cover their bodies completely at all times and male animals are castrated. Novices learn to pray with each breath: inhaling they recite, "Lord Jesus Christ," and exhaling "Have mercy on me, a sinner" until prayer becomes reflex and the disciple acquires the gift of the Holy Spirit. Most monasteries follow a time system that is different from the one now used worldwide: midnight is marked by the setting of the sun.

Climb Mt. Athos for a day or two of invigorating hiking crowned by an august view. The approach is by path from the community of **Agia Anna.** A five-hour climb will take you to the **Church of the Panayia,** dedicated to the Virgin Mary, which has beds for an overnight stay. The summit is another hour away. You might want to stay overnight at Panayia to watch the sun rise.

Practical Information

When visiting Mt. Athos, keep in mind that guests from "the outside world" inherently conflict with the spiritual goals of the monastic life. The monks, however, have an old tradition of requiring hospitality, so now's as good a time as ever to hone your awareness and sensitivity; it's essential to keep from disrupting the delicate atmosphere of holiness.

A special **entrance permit,** issued only to adult males, is required in order to visit Mt. Athos. To get this, you must first get a letter of recommendation from your embassy or consulate (tell them you are a student interested in theology, history, architecture, or Byzantine art); a letter from your university stating your academic interest in Mt. Athos could be helpful. Deliver this letter to the **Ministry of Northern Greece,** at room 218 Pl. Dikitirou, Thessaloniki (tel. (031) 27 00 92; open Mon.-Fri. 8am-2pm). A separate permit for photographing the art in the monasteries is required. Citizens of countries with consulates in Thessaloniki can conduct the entire process there (see Thessaloniki for consulate info); U.S. and British consulates can give you the form letter in very little time. If you rush from there to the Ministry then you might be given your permit on the same day. They might insist that underage visitors be accompanied by someone over 21, though the Ministry can waive this restriction. Because only 10 foreigners per day are admitted to Mt. Athos, the summer months are always booked well in advance. You can either wait for a cancellation or write a letter to the Ministry of Northern Greece at least a month in advance to secure a reservation. If you can show proof that you are Orthodox (baptism papers, a letter from your bishop, etc.), you may be allowed to be the day's eleventh visitor.

Permits allow only for a four-day stay and the date of arrival on your permit must be strictly observed. If you arrive a day late then you're out of luck and will be turned away. Extending your stay, however, may be possible if you speak with the authorities in Mt. Athos's capital of Karyes once you've arrived. You must remember to bring you passport or you will not be admitted. The GNTO office in Thessaloniki (tel. (031) 22 29 35) can give you more information.

Permit in hand, arrive in Halkidiki the night before your scheduled entry date into Athos. The standard approach to Athos is via Ouranopolis, by boat to Daphni, then by bus to the capital city of Karyes. **Buses** for Ouranopolis leave from Thessaloniki's KTEL/Halkidiki station (tel. 92 44 44), located at 68 Karakassi St. (7 per day, 3hr., 1650dr).

Ouranopolis is a crowded beach resort. Stay here overnight to catch the morning ferry to Daphni. Tickets may be purchased on board. Two inexpensive hotels in Ouranopolis are the no-frills **Hotel Akrogiali** (tel. 712 01), on the waterfront (singles 2500dr) and **Hotel Athos** (tel. 71368), above the supermarket one block from the bus stop. With sparkling clean modern baths, marble floors and spacious balconies, this is an affordable luxury. (Singles 3000dr. Doubles 5000dr.) The **postal code** is 63075. The **telephone code** is 0377.

Since you'll be doing a lot of hiking at Mt. Athos, arrange to leave your belongings behind in Ouranopolis (preferably at the place you've stayed), and just carry a daypack. Bring a water bottle and some snacks. If you're visiting during a fasting period, don't panic: guests are fed normal rations while the monks are purifying their souls and gastrointestinal tracts.

Two **ferries** serve the Mt. Athos peninsula: one from Ouranopolis to Daphni, and one, on the other side of the peninsula, from Ierissos to Monastery Iviron. In winter, the first bus from Thessaloniki to Ouranopolis (6am, 1150dr) arrives in time for the ferry (9:45am). In order to catch the early one, you must arrive the night before (last bus 6:30pm). The Ierissos ferry departs daily at noon in summer, and three times per week in off-season. Both trips take about two hours (560dr). The Ierissos ferry continues all the way to Monastery Megisti Lavras; if you're impatient or unable to walk, you can catch this ferry to go monastery-hopping once you have your final permit.

When you board the ferry you must hand over your passport and entrance permit. Your passport will be returned to you by the **Monastic Authorities** in the headquarters of the Athonite Holy Council. When you arrive in Daphni or Iviron head right for the bus which will take you up Athos's one paved, cliff-hanging road (built in 1963 for the monastery's millenial anniversary) to the capital city of Karyes a tiny hamlet built around a well-restored 10th-century church. The town also contains an **OTE** to the right of the Athonite Holy Council building, and two inexpensive hotels. When you arrive in Karyes, follow the crowd right to the Athonite Holy Council headquaters, climb the steep steps and wait to obtain the final permit *(Diamonitirion)* and claim your passport from the Monastic Authorities. This permit costs 800dr (students 500dr) which is used to reimburse the monasteries for the costs of their hospitality. This process may take some time and you'll be lucky to find an English-speaking person here, but be patient and before long you'll be on your way. Don't bother with the police; they're here to keep order, not assist tourists.

Remember that walking is an integral part of the Athos experience. Before you leave Karyes, pick up the *Mount Athos Touristic Map,* which includes a pamphlet offering general information (150dr). For greater detail about Mt. Athos, pick up one of the well-illustrated guidebooks (2000dr).

Accommodations and **food** in the monasteries are free, but you are entitled to a one-night stay only unless you receive permission for an extension from the *archontari* (guest-master). Generally, two meals are served daily. The gates close at sunset. You *must* reach the monastery before this or you may have to camp outside with the wolves. Allow plenty of time to get to the monasteries. Paths are narrow, overgrown with vegetation, and poorly marked; furthermore, the ones on the map might unexpectedly fork in four different directions or not exist at all. It's a good idea to keep to the roads or seaside paths and not to travel alone. Even if you are turned down for lodging at a monastery, you will be offered a cup of Greek coffee and *loukoumi* for your efforts.

Those without a permit can view the monasteries by boat. A day cruise from Thessaloniki costs 8000dr. Contact **Doucas Travel,** 8 Venizelou St., Thessaloniki (tel. (031) 26 99 84).

Kavala ΚΑΒΑΛΑ

The modern port city of Kavala (pronounced Ka-VAH-lah) stretches from the seaside up the slopes of Mt. Simvolo. Buried beneath it, the 3000 BCE city of Neapolis served as an equally important port city for the ancient Greeks. A few centuries later, Paul the Apostle came here to preach and christened the city Christoupolis. For some time afterwards, Kavala bore the brunt of Greco-Turkish conflict and Bulgarian occupation, but it has now reclaimed its role as a trading center.

Kavala is accessible by bus from Thessaloniki (2hr., 1900dr). Transit from the west is via two different routes: the scenic coastal road passes by **Lake Korona** and **Lake Volvi,** both unmarred by tourist trappings; the inland route passes through the city of **Serres** and its notable Byzantine church. There are also daily flights from Athens to Kavala (55min., 13,600dr).

Orientation and Practical Information

Kavala's charming old section, known as the **Panayia (Virgin Mary) District,** is the city's main draw. The old town sits east of the port on its own peninsula and is hemmed in by ancient walls. Just outside these walls is the main square **Platia Eleftherias,** from which Kavala's two major commercial streets, **Eleftheriou Venizelou** and **Erithrou Stavrou** extend westward.

Greek National Tourist Organization (GNTO): on the corner of Eleftheria Sq., 1 block inland from the main port (tel. 22 24 25, 22 87 62, or 23 16 53). One of the friendliest and best-informed tourist offices in northern Greece, this establishment has maps of the city, lists hotels, arranges for inexpensive accommodations, and helps with travel to Turkey, Bulgaria, and Yugoslavia. Open Mon.-Fri. 7am-7pm, Sat. 8am-1pm; Oct.-April Mon.-Fri. 7am-2:30pm, Sat. 8am-1pm.

National Bank of Greece: on the corner of Omonias and Paulo Mela St., 1 block north of the GNTO. Open Mon.-Fri. 8am-2pm.

Post Office: Main branch at K. Mitropoliteou St., on the corner of Erithrou Stavrou, 1 block north of the bus station. Will exchange currency. Open Mon.-Fri. 7:30am-8pm. Main branch **Postal Code:** 65110.

OTE: West of the main port at the corner of Ethnikis Andistassis and Averof St., across from the Thassos ferry. Open daily 7am-midnight. **Telephone Code:** 051.

Train Station: There is no train station in Kavala, but you can catch a bus to Drama (every 20min., 1hr., 600dr), and the 6pm train daily to: İstanbul (7hr., 5000dr). Otherwise, ride the bus to Xanthi (every ½ hr., 1 hr., 490dr) and hop on the 7:41pm train to İstanbul (5000dr).

Bus Station: at the corner of Filkis Eterias and K. Mitropolitou St., 1 block from Vassileos Pavlou St. and the waterfront, just around the corner from the OTE. Buses go to: Thessaloniki (every hr., 2hr., 2000dr); Philippi (every 20min., 20min., 200dr); Keramoti (every hr., 1hr., 600dr); and the beaches to the west (take bus to Iraklitsa, every hr., 190dr). For buses to Alexandroupolis, first go to Xanthi (every ½hr., 1hr., 700dr) and then Komotini (every hr., 1½hr., 600dr). From Komotini there are hourly buses to Alexandroupolis.

Ferries: Hydrofoils connect Kavala to Thassos's main port of Limenas (6 per day, 40min., 1050dr). Contact Mr. Gargalds at **Dolphin Hydrofoils** (tel. 22 20 05) for more information. **Nikos Miliades** (tel. 22 61 47), in the corner at the beginning of the main port, also runs ferries to Limnos (5 per week, 5hr., 2300dr), Lesvos (3 per week, 12hr., 6000dr), Samos (1 per week, 20hr., 5500dr), and Chios (3 per week, 16hr., 4300). Two ferries per week shuttle to Samothraki. Schedules are subject to change depending on demand. Contact **Arsinoi Travel,** 16 Karaoli Dimitriou (tel. 83 56 71) for further information.

Police Station: 119 Omonias St., 4 blocks north of the port (tel. 22 29 05). Provides information when the GNTO is closed. Open 24 hrs.

Accommodations and Camping

The outlook is bleak for the summer, especially Saturday nights; start searching early. **George Alvanos** is the only hostel in the old city; most others are cramped around Platia Eleftheria.

George Alvanos, 35 Anthemiou St. (tel. 22 84 12 or 22 17 81). A homey establishment with spotless bathrooms, and access to a kitchen. Proprietors speak only Greek. Doubles 3000dr. 10% discount with a copy of *Let's Go* from Oct.-May only. Call ahead; it fills quickly.

Hotel Panorama, 26 Venizilou St. (tel 22 42 05). Offers clean rooms, a professional staff, and a convenient location just one block from the waterfront. Singles 3000dr. Doubles 5000dr.

Camping: Camping Irini (tel. 22 97 85 or 22 97 76). Take the #2 bus east or walk 2km along the coast from the port. The campground closest to town. 1085dr per person. (You must have your own tent.) Small bungalows available for 1500dr per person.

Food and Entertainment

Panos Zafeira, 20 Karaoli Dimitriou St. (tel. 22 79 78), on the waterfront. *Mousaka* for 650dr. Open 9am-midnight.

Milano Spaghetti (tel. 83 85 08), across from the Thassos ferry dock and next to the OTE. A variety of Italian dishes for 900-1500dr. Open 9am-midnight.

Verona Pizza Grill (tel. 83 54 00), at the Thassos ferry dock and around the corner from the OTE. A great place to sip a cool *caffè frappe* and people watch. Open 10am-1am. If you're feeling homesick, catch a show at the **Apollo Cinema** (tel. 22 34 03) on Venizilou St., one block inland from the waterfront. American films are screened nightly at 8 and 10pm (800dr).

Sights

The sprawling, gray 13th-century **Byzantine Fortress** (tel. 83 86 02) dominates the city; marvel at its immense, turreted walls as you approach Kavala from the sea, or saunter atop them for a view of the city itself. (Free. Open daily 10am-7pm. The guard often gives mini-tours; tipping is polite.) During the **Eleftheria Festival** in the third week of June, Kavala's students celebrate Kavala's liberation from the Turks by performing traditional dances at the castle. Join in if you dare.

The 400-year-long Ottoman domination of northern Greece has left its mark on the city. The **Imaret,** reputedly the largest Muslim building in western Europe, has been converted into a trendy bistro. On the corner of Pavlidou and Mehmet Ali St. stands the **House of Muhammad Ali.** Born here in 1769, Ali was the self-appointed ruler of Egypt who reportedly floated like a butterfly but could sting like a bee. (Ring for the caretaker to visit. Free, but customary tip 100dr. Closed for renovations as of the summer of 1992.)

Even if you try, you can't overlook the colossal 16th-century **Kamares Aqueduct** at the northern edge of the old town, near Nikotsara Sq. Süleyman the Magnificent (1520-66) had the graceful, double-tiered structure built to transport water from the mountain springs above the city. On the other side of town, overlooking the water, the **Archaeological Museum** (tel. 22 23 35), on Erithrou Stavrou St. contains such treasures as polychrome busts of goddesses from Amphipolis, and a Hellenistic dolphin mosaic from Abdera. (Open Tues.-Sun. 8:30am-3pm. Admission 400dr, students 200dr.) Kavala also has a small **municipal museum** (tel. 22 27 06; open daily 8:30am-2:30pm; free).

Near Kavala

Several sandy **beaches** to the west of Kavala are accessible by inter-city bus. The closest is just outside the city of **Kalamitsa.** As you move farther along the coast to Batis, Iraklitsa, and Peramos, you'll find progressively more secluded beaches. At **Batis,** 3km outside of Kavala, is a **GNTO campground** which you might mistake for a parking lot (tel. 22 71 51; currency exchange; 800dr per person, tent, and sleeping bag; 50dr to swim). Every 30 minutes, blue bus #8 treks to Batis from Kavala. Hourly buses to Iraklitsa stop at Batis (100dr).

Philippi, about 15km north of Kavala, lies in ruins. Philip II of Macedonia founded the city to protect Thassian gold miners from Thracian attacks. Modestly enough, he named the city after himself—his son later followed suit in Egypt. Crucial battles of the Roman civil war dogged the city in 42 BCE, when Mark Antony's soldiers defeated the army of Brutus and Cassius (Julius Caesar's friendly assassins).

In 50 CE, missionaries Paul and Silas arrived to preach Christianity, and the first European Christian, Lydia, was baptized here. According to the Bible, after Paul was imprisoned for proselytizing (Acts 16:9-40), an earthquake struck the town, inspiring the rest of the townsfolk to follow in Lydia's footsteps. The **Cell of Paul,** the apostle's version of budget accommodations, can still be visited. A modern highway, following the same route as the ancient Via Egnatia, splits the archaeological site at Philippi, where you'll find a Roman basilica with splendid Corinthian capitals; the size of the hulking structure caused it to collapse before it was finished. Be sure to shut the door and take a peek at the Roman **latrines;** most of the 42 marble seats are still intact, but the lids have all been inexplicably left up. (Site open Tues.-Sun. 8:30am-3pm; admission 400dr. Call 51 64 70 for more information).

The entrance on the other side of the highway leads up to the **acropolis** and a theater from the Hellenistic Period. On summer weekends, classical drama is performed; these shows are worth attending even if it's all Greek to you. Ask at the theater or the Kavala GNTO for details. (Cheapest seats 500dr. Site open daily sunrise-sunset. Admission 200dr, students 100dr.) There is a somewhat disappointing **museum** nearby (tel. 51 62

51), with artifacts from Philippi, the neolithic Dikili-Tach settlement, and Sitagri. (Open Tues.-Sun. 8:30am-3pm; admission 400dr, students 200dr.)

A **bus** to Philippi leaves every 20 minutes (200dr). Tell the driver you're going to the archaeological site, and not the village. Otherwise, you'll end up in the boonies. The bus back to Kavala stops down the road from the site.

Thrace ΘΡΑΚΙ

The northernmost province of Greece, Thrace has for centuries served as the gateway between Turkey and Greece and thus as the meeting place for the diverse cultures of East and West. Ruled by the Ottomans until 1922, Thrace still bears evidence of Turkish influence in the small Turkish and Armenian communities scattered throughout the region. Today, the Evros River separates the Greek province from Thracian Turkey, once a united area. In general Thrace has become as Greek as the blue and white gate at its border. The complex political history of the region, once the home to mysterious and remote cults, seems to be mirrored in the chaotic landscape—a tangle of rivers, arable land, swamps, and lonely rolling hills.

Alexandroupolis ΑΛΕΧΑΝΔΡΟΥΠΟΛΗ

If you travel through Thrace, you will almost inevitably stop at the modern city of Alexandroupolis, which lies on the main west-to-east highway and is accessible by rail. Not surprisingly, this clean and modern port city is packed in the summer with overland travelers and Greek vacationers. Accommodations in July and August are scarce, so calculate your boat and train connections to avoid an overnight layover.

Boat and trains deposit passengers on the southeast part of Alexandroupolis's hub. The train station (tel. 263 95; open daily 5am-11pm) is at the southeast corner of the small roundabout, and the ferry docks are 500m west of the train station. From the train station, turn left and continue along the waterfront. Just before the lighthouse (built in 1880), you'll see Karatskaki St., perpendicular to the waterfront. To get to the **post office** (tel. 231 22), continue along the waterfront, past Karatsaki. (Poste Restante is at the branch near the corner of 14th Maiou St., 6 blocks north of the main boulevard; both offices open Mon.-Fri. 7am-3:30pm). Backtrack to Karatskaki and follow the inland road 1 block to reach the **police station,** 6 Karatskaki (tel. 264 18). Both the police (open 24 hrs.) and the **tourist police** (open daily 8am-3pm) work here. The **Municipal Tourist office** (tel. 249 98) rests on the main boulevard, Leoforos Demokratias (2 streets inland from the police), inside the city's theater on the ground floor. The English-speaking staff will provide information on inexpensive accommodations and travel (open Mon.-Fri. 8am-2:30pm). The **OTE,** is around the corner from the MTO, on the corner of Ioakim Kaviri and Venizelou St. (open daily 6am-midnight). The KTEL **bus station** (tel. 264 79) is half a block from the OTE on Venizilou St. Back on L. Demokratous St., a few blocks east of the buses, is the **National Bank of Greece** (open Mon.-Thurs. 8am-2pm, Fri. 8am-1:30pm). To get back to the railroad station and the port, follow the blue directional sign about 300m east of the bank. The **postal code** is 68100; the **telephone code** is 0551.

Trains chug slowly to Thessaloniki (5 per day, 8hr., 2500dr). KTEL **buses** will get you there via Kavala but you will have to switch buses first in Komotini and then in Xanthi (5hr., 2000dr). **Ferries** never go directly to Kavala; you must go via Samothraki, an easy daytrip away (1 per day, 2½hr., 1200dr). Ferries run twice a week from Samothraki to Kavala. (See ferry information for Samothraki.) You cannot buy tickets on board the ferry; get them at one of the ferry ticket offices or travel agencies clustered around the small square across from the ferry dock.

Accommodations, Camping, and Food

Inexpensive accommodations in this city are hard to come by. If you must stay a night, try the **Aktaion Hotel,** 74 D. Karaoli St. (tel. 280 78), across from the railroad station. (Singles 2500dr. Doubles 3500dr. Triples 4500dr. Sinks in rooms. Showers 400dr extra.) The kind owners will wake to let you in at any hour, and will make space for you even if all the rooms in town are full. Look for *dhomatia* signs along the street leading inland from the train station, or consult a local for directions.

If you have a tent, **Camping Alexandroupolis** (tel. 287 35) is conveniently located 3km northwest of Alexandroupolis, off L. Demokratias St. (600dr per person. 750dr per tent. 250dr per sleeping bag. Less in off-season.) You can take a bus from the train station (1 per hr., 70dr). The campground is on the beach, has clean facilities, and hosts the **Alexandroupolis Wine Festival** in July and August (for information, tel. 270 11). Freelance camping is legal unless GNTO signs indicate otherwise.

The only options for evening dining are the seaside cafés. During the day, the **Zolota** and the **Samothraki** (both just before the lighthouse) will help stave off starvation.

Pay your respects to the 18th-century icon of a particularly limber Christ—his legs form a heart—at the excellent Neoclassical **Ecclesiastic Art Museum,** next to the Cathedral of St. Nicholas, 2 blocks inland from the bank. (Open Mon.-Fri. 9am-noon or ask someone in the cathedral. Free.) Daily excursions to Feres, the Evros Delta, Kipi Soufli, Didimothio, Metaxaedes, and the hills of Dadia, depart from the KTEL office.

Transit East

Especially during summer, Alexandroupolis is not the ideal departure-point for travel to Turkey. The trains are nightmarishly hot, slow, and crowded; most buses to Turkey originate in Thessaloniki and are also steamy and tourist-laden by the time they reach Alexandroupolis. Ferries to Turkey at least offer a sea breeze. If you must, however, take a train (daily at 9:30pm, at least 6hr., 4040dr) or bus (9am and 10pm, 6hr., 4000dr) to **İstanbul.** Both depart from the train station, where you must buy your tickets. Those hitching from Alexandroupolis make a trilingual sign asking for a ride to take them across the border—you can't cross on foot. *Let's Go* does not recommend hitchhiking as a means of travel. Count on at least a one-hour wait in customs when going to and from Turkey.

CRETE KPHTH

In middle of the sable sea there lies An isle call'd
Crete, a ravisher of eyes, Fruitful, and mann'd with
many an infinite store; Where ninety cities crown
the famous shore, Mix'd with all-languag'd men.
　　　　　　　　　　　—Homer, Odyssey

Indeed, it seems Crete has an infinite store of mosques and monasteries, mountain villages, ragged gorges, dark grottoes and crystalline beaches. Greece's largest island embraces a remarkable variety of architecture and terrain. Crete's distinctive amalgam has produced a culture that remains unique even within Greece: Cretans have their own traditional folk dances, handicrafts, and costumes. The people here have their own mindset, too; first they are Cretans, then they are Greeks. Local artisans are known for pottery, leatherwear, and featherwork. A few islanders still don traditional garb—high black boots, pantaloons, and embroidered jackets. It is said of Crete that both its weather and its people are usually nice but are liable to get rough very quickly.

Crete's history combines mythological and historical trauma, glory, and mediocrity. Legend has it that this island was the birthplace of Zeus, and home of the Minotaur, the monstrous man-eating miscreation who dwelled at Knossos. Archaeologists claim that the island's golden days began when the Minoans arrived from Asia Minor around 2800 BCE, but the island was inhabited as far back as 6000 BCE (Neolithic Period). Arriving from Asia Minor, these earliest inhabitants dwelled in caves and open settlements. Among the artifacts found from this time are stone and bone tools and female figurines signifying a cult of the Mother Goddess. This period lasted until 3000 BCE, when the great **Minoan civilization** commenced on the island of Crete.

The Minoans, also from Asia Minor, established a rich civilization now known for its sophisticated art and embellished architecture. In 1700 BCE an earthquake devastated the entire island. The Minoans subsequently began rebuilding vast, elaborate villas and formidable palaces, which exemplify the intricate and expert work of this time. Following the reconstruction and revival, Crete entered its most glorious days. The buildings that we find standing today hail from this period. Prosperity, stemming from newly established trade with other countries, lasted until an unknown catastrophe, either invading Mycenaeans or more natural disasters (possibly the eruption of Thira), destroyed the island's cities once again in 1450 BCE.

After this second obliteration, Crete took on a less influential role in world affairs, but remained at the forefront in the world of art and culture. By the 8th century BCE, Dorians were occupying the island. At this time, arts were flourishing, especially jewelry-making, sculpting, and pottery. The period from the 5th century BCE to the Roman conquest in 67 BCE found the island in the throes of instability, with aristocratic families dominant and intercity warfare frequent. Crete, in the Medieval and Modern periods, has been ruled in succession by the Byzantine, Arab, Genoese, Venetian, and Turkish empires, and in 1898, Crete became an English protectorate. Finally, after the Balkan War of 1913, Crete joined the Republic of Greece.

Today, Crete appeals to beach-blanket bingo buffs, amateur archaeologists, and hardy hikers. Most of the appeal lies in the solitude that this island offers with its inland areas unsullied by development and its stretches of virgin shoreline.

For more background on Crete, read Adam Hopkins's witty and anecdotal history, *Crete: Its Past, Present and People;* Dilys Powell's melding of archaeology and modern Crete, *The Villa Ariadne;* or Michael Herzfeld's anthropological account of the Cretans, *History of the Past: A Cretan Town.*

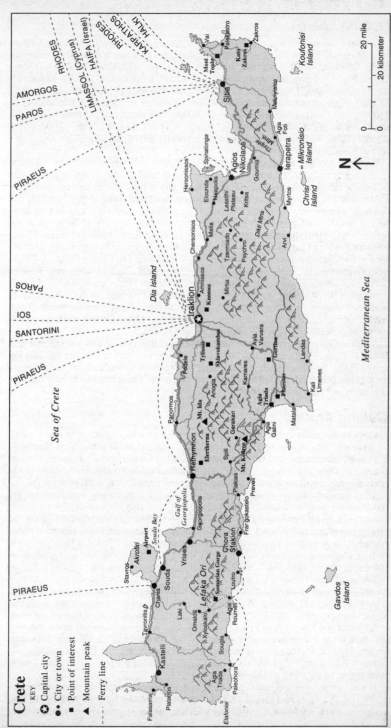

Getting There

Olympic Airways has cheap, fast—though often booked—flights to a few Cretan cities from within Greece. Most flights take less than an hour. You can fly to Iraklion from: Athens (at least 6 per day, 14,400dr; after 6pm 10,800dr); Mykonos (Mon., Thurs., Sat. 1 per day, 13,800dr); Paros (via Athens, 6 per day, 13,500dr); Rhodes (1 per day, 13,800dr); Thessaloniki (2 per week, 21,800dr); and Santorini (2 per week, 8200dr). Flights to Chania arrive from Athens (at least 3 per day, 12,100dr, after 6pm 9100dr); and Thessaloniki (every Tues., 21,800dr). You can also fly to Sitia from: Athens (2 per week, 16,900dr); Karpathos (Tues., 8200dr); Kassos (Tues., 6300dr); and Rhodes (Tues., 15,700dr). Most European airlines fly directly into the international airport in Iraklion.

Most travelers arrive in Crete by **ferry.** The island is well-served during the summer. Even slightly rough seas, however, put boats behind schedule. One good rule of thumb is that the larger a boat is and the more frequently it runs, the more dependable its schedule is. Prices listed are for deck-class accommodations. Boats depart regularly for Iraklion from Piraeus (7:00 and 7:30pm, 12hr., 3800dr), Santorini (mid-July to mid-Sept. 1 per day; off-season 3-5 per week, 5hr., 3100dr), Ios (July 15-Sept. 15, 3 per week, 10hr., 3100dr), and Paros and Naxos (July 15-Sept. 15, 3 per week, 12hr., 3480dr). Leaving Crete, you can make connections in Santorini to almost any other island in the Cyclades. Boats also run regularly from Piraeus to Chania (11hr., 3580dr); from Gythion on the Peloponnese to Kastelli (2 per week, 7hr., 3350dr); from Rhodes to Agios Nikolaos (2 per week, 12hr., 4010dr); and from Piraeus to Agios Nikolaos (2 per week, 13hr., 4310dr), via Milos, Folegandros, Santorini, and Anafi. The **hydrofoil** *Nearchos* connects Iraklion with the Cyclades. It runs to and from Santorini (3 per week, 2½hr.), Ios (3½hr.), Paros (4½hr.), and Mykonos (5hr.). Once a week, the *Nearchos* travels between Iraklion, Santorini, Ios, and Naxos.

Additionally, you can make **international ferry** connections to and from Cyprus and Israel. In Cyprus you can change boats for Egypt. From April to October, the *Vergina* leaves Haifa, Israel on Sundays and travels to Cyprus, Rhodes, Iraklion, and Piraeus; deck-class costs about 19,400dr between any two ports. Those heading to Italy must go to Piraeus and change boats there.

Getting Around

Crete is divided into four prefectures, each with its own capital—Chania (Hania), Rethymnon (Rethimno), Iraklion (Herakleion), and Agios Nikolaos. This chapter is broken into three sections: Western Crete, including Chania and Rethymnon; Central Crete, including Iraklion; and Eastern Crete, including Agios Nikolaos. Major transportation networks strangle the northern areas, and a number of roads connect the villages in the southeast and south central regions, but few connections thread through the towns on the southwest coast; to visit them, you must make use of the ferry service. Sometimes it is simpler to zigzag across the island than to travel directly along the south coast where rudimentary paths and erratic ferry boats are the only means of transportation. In general, maps in Crete indicate the width and condition (e.g. paved vs. dirt) of roads. Major transportation routes are generally smooth and well marked. A good map of the island, available at all GNTO offices, is invaluable.

Bus service is extensive, especially in touristed areas of the island. At least nine buses per day travel between each of the major north coast cities (west to east: Kastelli, Chania, Rethymnon, Iraklion, Agios Nikolaos, and Sitia). Each inter-city trip along this stretch costs roughly 1000dr and takes slightly over an hour. Most villages have daily service, but don't expect more than "market buses," which load up early in the morning and then bring people home after work. The bus schedules often make rural daytrips impossible, but it's easy to find budget accommodations even in Crete's smallest villages. A final warning: rumor has it that Cretan bus drivers are the craziest in Greece, with nerves of steel and no fear of death.

If you can procure some cash and three or four companions, a **car** is a great way to tour Crete. Agencies rent cars at Chania, Rethymnon, Malia, Iraklion, Agios Nikolaos, Ierapetra, and Sitia. Open jeep-type vehicles are fine for jostling down rough roads to deserted beaches, but insufferable under harsh winds and dust storms, and useless for locking up gear in cities. The bottom-of-the-line Fiat 127 or Suzuki Alto is a better alternative. In high season, rentals with unlimited mileage and insurance start at 7000-9000dr per day (There is an 18% VAT on all rentals). A Suzuki van is reputedly tippy, but comfortably sleeps two (10,000-12,000dr per day plus mileage and 18% VAT).

Motorbikes and small motorcycles simplify daytrips from the cities, but amplify the harshness of the wind on long, tortuous highways and rocky dirt roads—we're talking dust clouds that keep eyedrop companies in business. The 50cc automatic and semi-automatic models run about 2000dr per day plus tax and insurance. The 150-200cc models cost 20-30% more. "Insurance" provides only third-party liability coverage, and does not cover damage to you or your bike. Bargaining over rental rates often reduces the price 10-20%, and is even more effective with long-term rentals. If you intend to rent long-term, do so in Malia, Chania, or Sitia, where supply is great, prices are low, and supply-side economics is king. Try not to rent long-term in Iraklion, where prices are higher.

Few cars stop for hitchhikers in towns, but thumbers report rides can be found by walking a few kilometers out of town in the direction you're headed. As always, everyone should exercise caution and women should never hitch alone.

As is the case throughout Greece, accommodations are often difficult to find in July and August. If you really want a room, arrive early in the day to begin your search. Fortunately, many major cities have youth hostels, which rarely fill. The Greek government prohibits, but usually does nothing to stop freelance camping and it remains a popular option. In general, off-season rates for accommodations are about 20% less than the prices quoted here.

Central Crete

Iraklion (Heraklion) ΗΡΑΚΛΕΙΟ

If your ferry to Crete leaves you in Iraklion, take in the magnificent ruins at Knossos, the impressive archeological museum, and maybe even the tomb of Kazantzakis; but then take the first bus out—all that remains are most of the vices and few of the virtues of urban life. Iraklion, Crete's metropolis, and the fifth largest city in Greece, has festered with abandon in recent years as developers have crammed concrete hotels even within the old city's imposing Venetian walls. The tourist may tan, but the city rankles.

Iraklion's slick bars and discos save it from utter dreariness. If you're rambling through Crete in summer, you'll probably meet throngs of people headed for Iraklion to help with the mid-August grape harvest. Along with various other opportunities in bars and *tavernas,* the harvest enables you to earn a few *drachmae* to keep you on the road. Farmers from the surrounding area hire casual workers early in the morning (around 6am) at the Chania Gate. Arhanes, 20km south of Iraklion, is another popular work center.

Orientation and Practical Information

Head for café-laden Venizelou Square, in the center of town. Though Iraklion spreads for miles, almost everything important lies within the circle formed by Dikeosinis Avenue, Handakos Street, Duke Beaufort Avenue, and the waterfront. The city centers are **Venizelou Square,** where Handakos St. meets Dikeosinis and 25th Augustou Ave., and **Eleftherias Square,** at the intersection of Duke Beaufort and Dikeosinis Ave. in the east side of the old city.

Greek National Tourist Organization (GNTO): 1 Xanthoudidou St. (tel. 22 82 03 or 24 46 62), opposite the Archaeological Museum in Eleftherias Sq. City maps, lists of hotels, message-board for travelers, bus schedules, and some boat schedules (check times with the boat company). Open Mon.-Fri. 7:30am-2:30pm.

Tourist Police: 10 Dikeosinis St. (tel. 28 31 90), one block from 25th Augustou St. and Dikeosinis intersection. Open 7am-11pm. Provides general tourist information, very similar to GNTO.

Budget Travel: Hordes of travel agencies line 25th Augustou Ave. Head to this street and shop around. Two reliable agencies for budget air, boat, and bus tickets are **Prince Travel**, #30 25th Augustou Ave. (tel. 28 27 03), and **Kavi Club Student Travel**, 2 Papa Alexandrou St. (tel. 22 11 66 or 22 23 23), near the GNTO.

Currency Exchange: The banks on 25th Augustou Ave. are open Mon.-Thurs. 8am-2pm, Fri. 8am-1:30pm. **Gift shops** in Venizelou Sq. exchange after hours at slightly lower rates. Many **tourist agencies** exchange currency at bank rates and remain open until 9pm.

American Express Office: Located in **Adamis Tours**, #23 25th Augustou Ave. (tel. 22 32 03; fax 22 47 17). Handles client mail and arranges for cardholders to cash checks at local banks. Sells Amex traveler's checks to cardholders. Open May-Oct. 9am-4pm for financial transactions, 8:30am-8pm for authorizations.

Post Office: The main office is located in Daskalogiani Platia. There's a branch office in El Greco Park. Both are open Mon.-Sat. 8am-8pm, Sun. 9am-6pm. **Postal Code:** 71001.

OTE: 10 Minotavrou St. Follow the signs down Minotavrou near El Greco Park. Telephones, telegrams, and telex. Open daily 7am-11:30pm. Branch office in Eleftherias Sq. Open Mon.-Fri. 7:30am-3:10pm, Sat.-Sun. 9am-2pm. **Telephone Code:** 081.

Airlines: Olympic Airways (tel. 22 91 91), 42 Eleftherias Sq. Open daily 6am-10pm. Buses leave from here for the airport 75min. before each departure (50dr). The Stratones city bus #1 goes from Eleftherias Sq. to within 50m of the airport (6am-11pm every 20min., 105dr). For detailed information on flights, see Getting to Crete in the Crete Introduction.

Ferries: Boat offices on 25th Augustou Ave. Most open daily 9am-9pm. **Iraklion Port Authorities,** tel. 282 002. For detailed information, see Getting to Crete in the Crete Introduction.

Buses: There are several bus terminals, so match the station to your destination. **Terminal A** (tel. 28 26 37), between the old city walls and the harbor near the waterfront, serves: Agios Nikolaos (29 per day until 9pm, 1½hr., 900dr); Lassithi Plain (8:30am and 2:30pm, 2hr., 950dr); Hersonissou (6:30am-9pm every ½hr., 40min., 240dr); Malia (6:30am-9pm every ½hr., 1hr., 460dr); Sitia (5 per day until 5:30pm, 3½hr., 1900dr); Ierapetra (8 per day until 5:30pm, 2½hr., 1400dr); Archanes (12 per day until 8:30 pm, 9 on Sun., 30min., 260dr); Agia Pelagia (4 per day untl 5pm, 30min., 390dr); and Milatos (2 per day until 3pm, 1½hr., 700dr). **Terminal B** (tel. 25 59 65), just outside the Chania Gate of the old city walls, serves: Phaestos (9 per day until 5:30pm, 7 on Sun., until 5pm, 2hr., 800dr); Agia Galini (9 per day until 5:30pm, 6 on Sun. until 5pm, 2½hr., 900dr); Matala (7 per day until 4:30pm, 6 on Sun., 2hr., 1000dr); Lendas (at 8:45am and 1pm, Sun. at 8:45am, 3hr., 1000dr); Anoghia (6 per day until 4:30pm, Sun. at 8:30am and 2pm, 1hr., 540dr); and Fodele (Mon.-Fri. at 6:30am and 2:30pm, 1hr., 320dr). The **Chania/Rethymnon Terminal** (tel. 22 17 65) is near the waterfront. Walk down 25th Augustou Ave. to the waterfront, turn left, and look for the Xenia Hotel after a few blocks—it's at the top of the courtyard to your left. To Chania (28 per day until 8:30pm, 1800dr) and Rethymnon (28 per day until 8:30pm, 1½hr., 1050dr).

Car Rental: Rental car companies are scattered along 25th Augustou Ave. Shop around. Make the owners compete for your business by quoting prices from their neighbors. You won't make many friends, but you will save a couple thousand *drachmae*. For advance reservations, call **Budget Rent-a-Car** on 25th Augustou Ave. in Iraklion or their central office in Athens (tel. (01) 922 44 44) . Also, **CaRavel** at #56 25th Augustou Ave. (tel. 28 80 60) offers cars to anyone over 21 years of age (rather than the usual 23 year old requirement).

Motorbike Rental: Iraklion's rates are among the highest in Crete. Cheap rentals line Handakos St., El Greco Park, and 25th Augustou Ave., but prices fluctuate significantly. Be sure to ascertain if the quoted price includes the 20% tax and insurance. Also ask what the bike insurance covers. 50cc bikes 2500-3000dr per day, tax and third-party liability insurance included. **Nikos Rent-a-Vespa**, 16 Duke Beaufort Ave. (tel. 22 64 25). Open daily 8:30am-9pm. **Motor Tours,** 4 Agiou Titou St. (tel. 24 18 22), off Venizelou Sq., lets you return your bike to one of their 10 offices in Crete; but the convenience is most expensive (mopeds a whopping 3580dr per day). Because of the enormous competition, many prices are always negotiable. As always, shop around.

Luggage Storage: #48 25th Augustou Ave., opposite the National Bank. 300dr per day per piece. Open 7am-midnight. It's cheaper at the Chania/Rethymnon terminal (200dr per day). Unguarded, but next to ticket seller's desk. Open 7am-11pm.

Library: Vikelaia Municipal Library (tel. 28 07 07), in Venizelou Sq. Open Mon.-Fri. 9am-2pm, 6-9pm.

Bookstores: 6 Dedalou St. has a wide variety. Newsstands in Eleftherias Sq. sell foreign newspapers like the *International Herald Tribune* as well as paperbacks. Open 8am-10pm. The bookstore at the base of Chandakos St. near the water (tel. 28 96 05) has a huge selection of *Penguin* classics.

Laundromat: Laundry Express, 1 Sapfous St. (tel. 22 24 59). Wash 700dr. Dry 450dr. Soap 200dr.

Greek Alpine Club: Tel. 22 76 09. For information about hiking on Mt. Ida.

Iraklion Bicycling Club "Kastro:" 19 Averof St. (tel. 24 34 45), on the 3rd floor.

Public Toilets: El Greco Park. Open 7am-9pm, 30dr. Also in the public gardens near Eleftherias Sq.

Pharmacy: One pharmacy is always open 24 hrs.; its name and address is posted on the door of every pharmacy each morning. All pharmacies are prominently marked by a red cross.

Women's Clinic: Dr. John Baltzakis, 4 Koroneou St. (tel. 28 44 04).

Hospital: Venizelou St. (tel. 23 75 80), on the road to Knossos. Take bus #2 (20min.).

Police: 10 Dikeosinis Ave. (tel. 28 31 90). Less knowledgeable than the GNTO, but sometimes more willing to help. Open daily 7:30am-10pm.

Emergency: Tel. 100.

Accommodations and Camping

Iraklion has quite a few cheap hotels and hostels, most of which are on or near Handakos St., at the center of town. Others are on Evans and 1866 St., near the market. Daredevils who arrive at 2:30am take their rest next to the port in the grassy park around Kountouriotou Sq., or under the trees near Bus Terminal B—this is ill-advised, especially for women traveling alone. If you arrive late at night and decide to take a taxi, beware: taxi drivers often work on commission with larger hotels, so bear that in mind when considering their recommendations.

The **Rooms to Let Association** is not a great resource for finding a place to stay in Iraklion, but is a godsend for advance bookings in Hersonissos, Malia and other resorts of Eastern Crete. Good luck finding the small office at Plateia Kornarou, but a phone call should suffice (8:30am-2pm, tel. 22 92 52).

Youth Hostel (HI/IYHF), 5 Vironos St. (tel. 28 62 81), just off 25th Augustou Ave. Cleanish, cool, and quiet. 11:30pm curfew. 750dr per person. Luggage storage 100dr (non-guests 150dr). Open year-round. Hot water 5pm-11pm. Great café-bar on the roof. (Beer 200dr.)

Hotel Rea, Kalimeraki St. (tel. 22 36 38), off Handakos St., 2 blocks above the waterfront. Clean, airy rooms. Eat-off-the-floor spotless, with restful pastel decor. Hot showers included. Doubles 3500dr. Triples 4300dr. Dorm-like quads 5500dr.

Rent a Room Vergina, 32 Chortason St. (tel. 24 27 39), near Handakos. Clean, homey rooms. Washtubs and clotheslines. Small collection of English books. Doubles 3500dr. Triples 4200dr.

Hotel Hellas, 11 Kantanoleon St. (tel. 28 44 00), between the Morosini Fountain and the OTE. Relaxing garden and bar (open until 11pm). International phone. Singles 2800dr. Doubles 3500dr. Triples 4000dr.

Kretan Sun, #10 1866 St. (tel. 24 37 94). Bare, tidy rooms. Some are huge. Directly above the open air market, so it's very noisy in the mornings. Singles 2500dr. Doubles 3200dr. Triples 3600dr. Negotiable.

Camping: Camping Iraklion (tel. 28 63 80), 5km west of town. Take bus #6 from Eleftherias Sq. (every 20min. until 10pm). The tent pitches are on packed earth, and the nearby beach is sandy. Swimming pool. Washing and kitchen facilities available. 700dr per person, 300dr per tent. Open March-Oct.

Food

While in most other Cretan towns you can barely take two steps without tripping over the chairs of a café, in Iraklion, restaurants are as rare as good television. Around the Morosini Fountain, near El Greco Park, and in Eleftherias Sq., you'll find caches of overpriced cafés. Take a left off 1866 St., 1 block from Venizelou Sq., to reach tiny Theodosaki St. Though not the most elegant place in town to dine, it is certainly the most colorful, with 10 *tavernas* jammed side by side, and territorial rights hopelessly intermingled. The cheapest dishes go for about 650dr and the helpings are impressive indeed, but cement the price before you sit down.

During the day, the best show in town is the open-air **market** on 1866 St., which starts just off Venizelou Sq. Both sides of the narrow street are lined with stalls piled high with sweets, spices, fresh fruits, vegetables, cheeses, and meat. Full-time fly swatters at the butcher's ensure hygiene. The huge cauldrons of yogurt sold here far excel the filtered, pasteurized brands found elsewhere (700dr per kg). (Market open Mon.-Sat. 8am-8:30pm.)

Souvlaki joints abound on 25th Augustou Ave. **Thraka** is the most fun thanks to Plateia Kallergon, the loud and exciting owner from Thessaloniki. Try the *souvlaki* with bread crust (200dr).

> **Ta Psaria,** at the base of 25th Augustou Ave. Decent seafood at moderate prices. Mixed-fish grill 850dr. A great spaghetti special 600dr. Open 10am-midnight. **Tavern Rizes,** Handakos St., 1 block from the water. Cheap, tasty food (including pizza) in its intimate, covered flagstone courtyard. Open 6pm-midnight. **Pizzeria Napoli,** Eleftherias Sq. The best pizza in town. 20 varieties, most small pizzas under 600dr.

Sights

Iraklion's capital attraction is its superb **Archaeological Museum,** considered one of the finest in Greece. Exhibits are organized chronologically from the Neolithic period to Roman times. The museum's most outstanding feature is the **Hall of the Minoan Frescoes.** (Open Tues.-Sun. 8am-7pm, Mon. 12:30-7pm. Admission 1000dr, students 500dr; free on·Sun.)

Iraklion also has a **Historical Museum** (tel. 28 32 19), near the waterfront off Grevenon St., 2 blocks from the Xenia Hotel. Unlike the overcrowded Archaeological Museum, this museum is undeservedly undervisited. Its eclectic collection includes colorful frescoes, Turkish gravestones, finely woven tapestries, and photographs of the World War II German invasion. (Open Mon.-Fri. 9am-5pm., Sat. 9am-2pm. Admission 500dr; free on Sun)

Locals often visit the austere **Tomb of Kazantzakis** for its views of Iraklion, the sea, and the Mountain of Zeus to the east. To get there, either walk along the top of the Venetian Walls to Martinengo Bastion at the southern corner of the city, or go down Evans St. until you reach the walls and the bastion. Because of his heterodox beliefs, Kazantzakis, the author of *The Last Temptation of Christ,* was denied a place in a Christian cemetery and was buried here without the full rites of the Orthodox Church. His gravestone bears this inscription from one of his novels: "I hope for nothing. I fear nothing. I am free." True aficionados can visit the **Kazantzakis Museum,** in the nearby village of Varvari. The carefully presented exhibit includes many of the author's original manuscripts, as well as photographs and documentation of his theatrical productions. A slide show (in English) provides historical background. A bus from Station A takes you to Mirtia (22km from Iraklion), only a short walk from the museum. (Open Sat.-Mon. and Wed. 9am-1pm and 4-8pm, Tues. and Fri. 9am-1pm; off-season Sun. 10am-4pm. Admission 350dr.) Resist the last temptation to buy Kazantzakis t-shirts at the tomb or museum. The open-air market sells them for a mere 1200dr.

Several interesting churches hide in the modern maze of city streets. Built in 1735, the **Cathedral of Agios Minas** in Agia Ekaterinis Sq. features six icons by the Cretan master Damaskinos (open 24 hrs.). **St. Catherine's Church,** also in the square, served as the first Greek university after the fall of Constantinople in 1453, and now hosts an icon exhibit. (Open Mon., Wed., and Sat. 10:30am-1pm, Tues. and Thurs.-Fri. 10:30am-1pm and 5-7pm. Admission 250dr.) **St. Titus Church,** 25th Augustou Ave., is a Turkish mosque recently converted into a Christian church. The **Armenian Church** at 16 Kaloukarinou St. (tel. 24 43 37), dates back to 1666; its Israeli-born priest gives free tours of the grounds. **Agios Mattheos,** a 10-minute walk on Markopoulou St. from Agia Ekaterinis Sq., houses several excellent icons. Ask the priest behind the church to lend you the key.

As you caper about, take note of the various monuments built during the long Venetian occupation of the city. The most popular is the 17th-century circular **Morosini Fountain** in Venizelou Sq., graced with handsome marble lions. Several others deserve a visit: the reconstructed **Venetian Loggia,** Venizelou Sq.; the 13th-century **Basilica of St. Mark,** 25th Augustou Ave., now an exhibition hall; the **Venetian Arsenal,** off Kountouriotou Sq., near the waterfront; **Koules Fortress,** which guards the old harbor (open Mon.-Sat. 7am-6pm, Sun. 9am-2pm; admission 300dr, students 200dr); and the impressive 15th-century **Venetian walls** that encircle the city.

Entertainment

Locals are the first to point out that the "in" places change rapidly, so look and ask around. After a long, archaeological day, unwind in the **Bokras Bar,** which plays a variety of rock, jazz and Greek music (beer 300dr). Across the street is the small air-conditioned dance-bar **Tunnel,** a friendly though expensive place to begin dancing the night away (beer 500dr). If your wallet overfloweth, rock on the port region where expensive drinks and hefty cover charges await you. Check out **Disco Trapeza** ("bank"—locals say they are going to the bank to make their deposit). A great time, but pricy beer (600dr) and a cover charge (which includes your first drink) of 800-1500dr. You can also pass the evening at one of the many *ouzeries* along Vironos St. (*ouzo* 250-500dr).

Schedules for Iraklion's movie theaters are posted next to the tourist police office on Dikeosinis St. For an evening of free sociological entertainment, join the locals and tourists at Venizelou Sq., where Iraklion's annual **summer festival** (mid-June to mid-Sept.) combines Cretan and occidental cultural events such as concerts, theater, ballet, and folk dancing. Get a schedule from the GNTO, or call 28 22 21 or 24 29 77 for information.

Iraklion's harbor is unswimmable, but there are two public beaches nearby: a rather sullied one 4km west at **Lindo,** and a better one 8km east at **Amnissos.** Amnissos is also the site of the ancient port of Knossos. The famed Amnissos frescoes, now in Iraklion's Archaeological Museum, were found in a villa here. To reach Lindo, take bus #1, which leaves from in front of the Astoria Hotel in Eleftherias Sq., stopping at several overcrowded but clean and free hotel beaches. Bus #1 also goes to Amnissos (every 30min. until 8pm, 150dr). Bus #6 goes 8km west to Linoperamata, the best beach west of Iraklion.

Near Iraklion

Iraklion is an ideal base for exploring part of Central Crete. Many archaeological sites, including the great Minoan complex at Knossos and lesser Minoan finds at Malia, Tylissos, and Arhanes, are within a half-day's excursion from the city.

Knossos

Knossos is undoubtedly the most famous archaeological site in Crete, and few visitors escape the island without at least a token visit. According to myth, when King Minos of Crete refused to sacrifice a fine white bull to Poseidon, the sea-god drove both Minos's queen, Pasiphaë, and the bull mad with lust. Their torrid passion resulted in the Minotaur, who stalked through the labyrinth and required 14 well-cooked Athenian youths per year. Finally Theseus, Prince of Athens, entered that labyrinth. The hero slew the monster with the aid of Ariadne, Minos's daughter, and Daedalus, the master architect who designed the maze. Theseus had intended to take Ariadne back to Athens and marry her (at least that's what he said--the cad), but at the bidding of Dionysus, he abandoned her on the island of Naxos. When the volatile Minos discovered that Daedalus had helped Theseus escape, he imprisoned both the architect and his son, Icarus. Daedalus came up with a crafty means of escape: he built them both wings of feathers and wax and off they flew. The hubristic Icarus, however, soared too close to the sun. The wax melted, his feathers fell off, and he plunged to his death in the sea. Mary

Renault's novel *The King Must Die* gives a compelling account of the story, as does Ovid's *Metamorphoses*.

During the first millennium BCE, Cretans were ridiculed for imagining that they sprang from such illustrious forebears as the Minoans of Knossos. Time, however, has proven the Cretans right. Arthur Evans, one of Heinrich "Troy" Schliemann's British cronies, purchased the hill and spent the next 43 years and his entire fortune excavating it. His thorough work showed that from 1700 BCE to 1400 BCE, Knossos was indeed a great city that stood at the center of the first great European civilization.

Evans restored large portions of the palace to what he believed were their original configurations, based on internal evidence unearthed during the excavations. Walls, window casements, stairways, and columns were reconstructed in reinforced concrete, and copies of the magnificent frescoes were mounted in place of the originals (now in Iraklion's Archaeological Museum). In some cases these restorations prevented the walls from falling down as the excavations continued, but Evans's reconstruction crossed the boundaries of preservation and continued deep into the realm of interpretation. While purists feel that the complex at Knossos is an outrage, there is no question that the effect is impressive.

There is no point in suggesting a tour route of Knossos because you are bound to get lost in the maze-like site—this is, after all, the original labyrinth of Daedalus. However you choose to pick your way among the ruined walls and incomplete frescoes, you should not overlook the most impressive parts of the palace, the **King's and Queen's Rooms** and the **Throne Room.** An ingenious lighting and drainage system made the King's Room bright and airy without the aid of modern engineering. The Queen's Room, at the end of the corridor, is decorated with reproductions of the beautiful dolphin frescoes. Inside the Throne Room, a replica of the throne stands where the original was found.

A guidebook to this extensive, meagerly-labeled site will help immensely. The best and most comprehensive is J.D. Pendlebury's *Handbook to the Palace of Minos, Knossos, and its Dependencies,* with an introduction by Arthur Evans himself (600dr, on sale at the site only). Also informative are *Knossos and the Iraklion Museum,* by Costis Davaris (650dr) and *Knossos: The Minoan Civilization,* by Sosso Logadiou-Platonos (800dr). (Ruins (tel. 23 19 40) open Mon.-Fri. 8am-7pm and Sat.-Sun. 8:30am-3pm. Admission 1000dr, students 350dr; free on Sun.) Take bus #2, which stops along 25th Augustou Ave.—look for the signposts along the western side of the street. (7am-10:30pm every 10min., 20min., 150dr).

Tylissos, Anogia, and Fodele

Although Knossos is secure in its status as most popular site on Crete, it cannot lay claim to being the oldest. At **Tylissos,** 14km southwest of Iraklion, archaeologists have unearthed a Minoan city dating back to 2000 BCE. Unlike Knossos, the ruins at Tilissos remain relatively unchanged by modernity and modification. (Open daily 8:30am-3pm. Free.) Buses for Tylissos leave from Terminal B every 15 minutes (25min., 210dr). Halfway between Tylissos and Anogia are the remains of the Minoan villas at **Sklavokambos.**

Another 22km from Tylissos along the same road is the popular tourist destination of **Anogia,** a center for weaving and folkcraft. The craftsmanship of Anogia, however, has a bitter origin. During World War II, the villagers sheltered the British kidnappers of German General Kreipe; in reprisal, the Germans shot all the men of the village, leaving the widows to eke out their livelihoods with their domestic skills. Today, Anogia celebrates its renewed vigor with a traditional music and marriage festival on the day of The Assumption of Our Lady (Aug. 15). Call (0834) 312 07 for information. The best bet for budget accommodations is the **Psiloritis** (tel. (0834) 322 31).

It's a four-hour hike from the village through the gorgeous **Nida Plain** to the **Cave of Ideon Andron,** an ancient sanctuary dedicated to Zeus. Also accessible from Iraklion is **Fodele,** a village full of orange trees and famous as the home of El Greco. The celebrated Greek painter, born Domenikos Theotokopoulos, left Fodele at the age of 20 to study under Titian in Venice; from there he moved on to Toledo, Spain, where he spent most of his life and did his finest work. For information on buses to Anogia and Fodele, see the Iraklion bus section.

From Iraklion to Matala

If you flee Iraklion by way of the north coastal route east or west, you'll miss the best of Central Crete—the south, with its remarkable archaeological sites and beaches. From Iraklion, buses head south from Terminal B, first climbing into the mountains and then descending to the fertile **Messara Plain,** whose agricultural wealth supported Gortyn, the Roman capital of Crete, as well as the twin Minoan centers at Phaestos and Agia Triada. While these sites can be seen on a daytrip from Iraklion, you'd do better to continue south and spend the night in the coastal resorts of Matala or Agia Galini. One bus runs to Gortina, then Phaestos. From here, you can continue on to Matala or change buses for Agia Galini. It is possible to travel northwest to Rethymnon from Agia Galini and see far more than you would by traveling the north coast freeway from Iraklion.

Gortina ΓΟΡΤΗΝΑ

The first stop of historical interest on the road south, Gortina contains the ruins of the Greco-Roman city, Gortyn. In 67 BCE, when ancient Gortyn fell to the Romans, the city was designated the capital of the island. Most of the remaining ruins here are from the Roman occupation, including the **Roman Odeon** (music hall). One of the few remains from the Hellenistic city, the Law Code tablets, are the most important extant source of information regarding pre-Hellenistic Greek law. They are written in a Dorian dialect of Greek and date from about 450 BCE when the city thrived under Greek control. The stones were so handsomely cut that the Romans used them as building materials for the odeon.

The site of ancient **Gortyn,** en route to Phaestos, is on your right as you come from Iraklion. The first thing you'll see is the bird-inhabited 7th-century **Basilica of Saint Titus.** The odeon is behind the church. The site also has a hall with 14 sculpted figures, and a mammoth statue of a soldier. (Site open Mon.-Fri. 8am-7pm and Sat.-Sun 8:30am-3pm. Admission 400dr, students 200dr; free on Sun.) To get to Gortyn, take one of the many **buses** that go to Matala or Phaestos. See those towns for schedule details.

Phaestos and Agia Triada

Imperiously situated on a plateau with a magnificent view of the surrounding mountains and Messara Plain, the palace at **Phaestos** housed powerful Minoan royalty. At the turn of the century, Halbherr began excavations here, and unearthed two palaces. The first was destroyed by the earthquake that decimated Crete around 1700 BCE; the second was probably leveled in the mysterious catastrophe of 1450 BCE. Surprisingly enough, a final excavation in 1952 came upon traces of two even earlier palaces. Since the excavations, minor reconstruction work has been done on the walls, chambers, and cisterns.

Built according to the standard Minoan blueprint, the complex included a great central court, from which radiated the private royal quarters, servants' quarters, storerooms, and chambers for state occasions. The grand staircase is still intact. The room with the corrugated roofing to the extreme northeast is believed to be the **King's Chamber.** Separated from it by three stairs is the **Queen's Chamber.** The rich finds from Phaestos, including vases, jewelry, altars, and the famed Phaestos Disk (imprinted with as yet undeciphered symbols) are all on display in Iraklion's Archaeological Museum. Phaestos may be a disappointment to those not well-versed in Minoan archaeology because it is difficult to visualize what the palace must have looked like in its prime. The poor labeling of the site and the dry, poorly translated guidebook (750dr) only exacerbate the frustration. (Open Mon.-Sat. 8am-7pm. Admission 400dr, students 200dr; free on Sun.)

A 10-minute walk down the hill leads to nearby **Agios Ioannis** where you can find *dhomatia* (doubles 1700dr, hot showers included). While here, don't miss the tiny **Church of Agios Parlos,** in the cemetery on the road toward Matala. Parts of the church are thought to be pre-Christian and the restored frescoes date from the early 14th century CE. Buses from Phaestos trek to: Iraklion (9 per day, 6 on Sun., 2hr., 800dr); Matala (7 per day, 20min., 130dr); and Agia Galini (7 per day, 5 on Sun., 25min., 270dr).

Three kilometers from Phaestos is the smaller Minoan site of **Agia Triada.** The small Byzantine church of the same name at the southeast corner of the site is now overshadowed by the unearthed pagan structure. A kind of miniature version of the great Minoan palaces, Agia Triada may have been a summer home for the royal family. Although the site itself is not nearly as impressive as Phaestos, important discoveries here include frescoes, Linear A tablets, and the grand painted sarcophagus now in Iraklion's Archaeological Museum. The pleasantly untouristed site offers a view of the Libyan sea to the west and the Psiloretis and Ketilnos Mountains to the north. (Open Tues.-Sun. 9am-3pm. Admission 400dr, students 200d; free on Sun.)

To get to Agia Triada from Phaestos, follow the road to Matala, and take the right fork uphill 200m beyond the parking lot. Agia Triada is 3km past the fork, a 45-minute walk. Leave your bags at the guard booth at Phaestos while you visit either site.

Matala ΜΑΤΑΛΑ

Matala is no longer the hedonistic hippie haven of yesteryear. Today's visitors generally have more money to throw around than their flower generation predecessors. The soundtrack from *Zorba the Greek* now plays instead of *Janis Joplin's Greatest Hits.* But all is not lost; the influx of sun-worshipers has not only spawned a host of new pensions, it has enhanced Matala's cheerful informality as well. A few remnants of Matala's groovy past remain: you're still likely to hear strains of The Doors escaping from the fast food haunts, and camping, though no longer allowed in the caves, is still all the rage.

Orientation and Practical Information

Matala has three main streets: one on the waterfront, one behind it, and one that intersects both running all the way to Phaestos. On the first you will find cafés, restaurants, souvenir stands, and a covered market of sorts; on the second, the bus station, motorbike rental agencies, and stores. At Matala's main square, these two intersect the road to Phaestos, along which are hotels and pensions.

Matala Travel (tel. 423 85), in the main square, **exchanges money** at bank rates, dispenses tourist information, sells boat and excursion tickets, and swaps books. (Open 9am-11pm.) Several motorbike rental places also handle currency exchange at close to bank rates—try **Festos Rent-A-Car, Monzo Bikes** (both open 8am-8pm), and **Motor Manos** (tel. 423 59; open 8am-11pm). These shops also serve as informal tourist offices, and provide information on hotels and beaches. Monzo and Manos rent **mopeds** for 2500dr per day, with reduced prices for longer rentals. The **OTE,** in the beach parking lot, resembles a small prison. (Open Mon.-Sat. 8am-11pm, Sun. 9am-2pm and 4-9pm.) A **bookstore,** on the road to Phaestos, offers a good English-language selection. The **laundromat** across from the campground charges 700dr per wash, 400dr per dry. (Open daily 9am-1pm and 3-7pm.) The **post office** is near the covered market. (Open Mon.-Sat. 8:30am-7pm and Sun. 9:30am-5pm.) In summer, **buses** go to Iraklion (7 per day, 2hr., 1000dr), Phaestos (7 per day, 20min., 330dr), and Agia Galini (5 per day, change at Phaestos, 45min., 450dr). The town's **police station** (tel. 421 68) is behind the bakery on the second inland road. The **hospital** and **pharmacy** are in Mires, 17km to the northeast. In an emergency, call 233 12 and a doctor or dentist will drive to Matala. **Public toilets** are located in the main square next to Monza Bikes. Matala's **postal code** is 70200; the **telephone code** is 0892.

Accommodations, Camping, and Food

Matala has over a dozen hotels and pensions, but bargains are scarce; singles cost as much as doubles, and almost never drop below 3000dr in the summer. German and British developers have packed the town with tour groups. Many establishments no longer rent to the public. It may be a good idea to make Matala a day trip. Cheaper accommodations are available in Matala's surrounding villages, and hitching from the main road to Phaestos or Matala is easy. Don't try to sleep on the main beach or in the nearby caves; it's illegal and police do occasionally raid them.

Matala Camping, on your right as you enter the town center, is spacious, and has shower facilities. Be prepared—the water is cold and the clientele hails from both genders. (300dr per person, 300dr per tent, 300dr per car or motorcycle.) Other places in town fill quickly, so start searching early.

Rent Rooms Dimitris: A real treat—each room has a clean, private bath with hot water. Shady courtyard. Show Dimitris your *Let's Go* and he'll give you a discount. Doubles 3400dr. Triples 4000dr. Inquire at Matala Travel.

Pension Matala View (tel. 421 14). Turn right opposite the Zafira Hotel. Tidy, good-sized bedrooms. Singles 2500dr. Doubles 3400dr. Triples 4200dr.

Pension Jannis (tel. 423 02), a 10-minute walk past Tsirterakis on the road to Phaestos. Ask at the Xenophon Hotel. Well-tended little oasis, but the rooms don't live up to the setting—paper-thin walls and dusty stone floors. Singles 1600dr. Doubles 3100dr. Triples 4700dr.

The restaurants along the waterfront are hard to tell apart. One thing is sure—you pay for the view. Better food is further away from the mainstream hangouts. **Nassos,** near the waterfront by the covered market, offers stupendous *souvlaki-pitas* for 200dr. **Matala Burger,** in the main square, has terrific Greek salads for 450dr. There are a number of inexpensive minimarkets and bakeries in town as well.

Sights and Entertainment

Matala's main attraction is its three tiers of caves next to the beach. Hike along them to find a private one. You can sit in its cool dim interior and spy on the beach action below while reflecting on the cave's possible previous occupants: flower children, Nazis searching for British submarines, and long ago, Roman corpses.

Matala has more than its share of fine beaches. Past the crashing waves you can see the dim outline of Paximadia island. The hundreds of people crammed around you will also enjoy the view. For an equally good shore and more secluded caves, join the nude bathers on **Red Beach,** 20 minutes down the path behind the church. (Don't forget your birthday suit.) On the way, you'll pass numerous caves within easy climbing distance. The cliffs between Matala and Red Beach all offer spectacular views of the Mediterranean, and most paths take you back down to the beach. For a change of pace, rent a paddle boat on Matala beach and pedal to Red Beach (paddle boats 1000dr per hr., canoes 500dr per hr.).

Also secluded, with its own small community of freelance summer residents and a lone *taverna,* **Kommos Beach** is a 5km walk from Matala. The bus from Iraklion will let you off about ½km from the beach (bus schedule is posted by the station in Matala). The beach, 5km long and even sandier than Matala's, leads to the makeshift beach-town of **Kalamaki.** The dirt track from the Phaestos road precludes bus traffic, but mopeds can still make it to Kalamaki, where **Karandinos** (tel. (0892) 421 80) has a few doubles for 3500dr. A handful of mediocre restaurants and a small bar/disco provide Kalamaki's casual nightlife. Nightlife in Matala means drinking, dancing and lazy gazing at the ocean until the wee hours of the morning. Safe-bet bars on the waterfront include **Giorgos, Kahlua** and **Rock** (all three offer beer for 300dr).

Agia Galini ΑΓΑ ΓΑΛΗΝΗ

Agia Galini, a once-tranquil fishing village west of Matala on the southwest coast, is now about as Greek as Vegas. This flashy resort town is plastered with glitzy hotels, discos, and bars, and topped off with a beach paved with bodies.

Agia Galini is perched on a hill—no matter where you are, just head downhill and you'll reach the sea. The **post office** (open Mon.-Fri. 7:30am-2pm) is below the bus station, and the **OTE** (open daily 8am-3pm) is a little bit uphill. Several agents rent bikes, both in the upper and lower level of town; try **Biggis Bikes** (tel. 911 42), near the post office. (Automatic 50cc mopeds 1900dr. 125cc Vespa scooters 3300dr, insurance included. Open 8am-10pm.) Facing the harbor, turn left at Biggis and then turn right— you'll find yourself on Vassilios Ioannis Street, Agia Galini's main drag. **Candia Tours** (tel. 912 78; open daily 8:30am-2:30pm and 5-10pm), and a **bookstore** (open daily 9am-11pm) are both on this street. Agia Galini's **postal code** is 74056. Its **telephone code** is 0832.

The pensions along the upper tier of Agia Galini are generally cheaper than the hotels in the center of town. Overlooking the ocean, **Rent Rooms Michael** (tel. 913 15) is in a white, aqua-trimmed house at the top of the hill. (Singles 1800dr. Doubles 3800dr.) You'll find **Hotel Ariston** (tel. 912 85) at the end of Vassilios Ioannis St. All the rooms have balconies, some with ocean views. (Singles 2500dr. Doubles 3500dr. Private bath included.) Across the street is **Hotel Acteon** (tel. 912 08) whose soft mattresses bode badly for those with bad backs. Ask for the middle floor—it's high enough for a view of the water, but too low for the glorious panorama of the parking lot. In the morning you may be awakened by the cheerful tweeting of Mike the canary. (Doubles 3800dr. Triples 4000dr.) You can get to **Camping Agia Galini** by motor or by foot. The turn-off is 3km before town on the road from Iraklion. The grounds, 150m from the beachfront, have gravel tent sites shaded by olive and carob trees. Beware of the dogs. (Ample facilities, market, and bar. Open April-Nov. 500dr per person, 200dr per tent, 200dr per car.)

Agia Galini is smothered by restaurants, bars and discos. Their prices are virtually the same: 300dr for beer and too much for food. Agia Galini's specialty is the roof garden bar/restaurant; almost all roofs serve food and beer, but you probably won't find a filling meal for under 1200dr. Even *gyros* are expensive (250dr). Along the isolated secondary route from Iraklion to Agia Galini, the mountain village of **Kamares** offers a vantage point of Mt. Ida's twin peaks (2600m) and a base for exploring the **Kamares Cave,** sanctuary of the 19th-17th century BCE Minoan polychrome pottery which is now exhibited in Iraklion's Archaeological Museum. The strenuous four-hour hike is not always well-marked; look for orange-painted trail markers.

Buses travel to Iraklion (9 per day, 6 on Sun., 2½hr., 900dr), Rethymnon (6 per day, 1½hr., 750dr), and Phaestos (9 per day, 20min., 270dr). To get to Matala, change at Phaestos. For Plakias, change at Koxare.

Near Agia Galini

Spili is, at best, a pleasant day trip from Agia Galini. The main road from Agia Galini to Spili twists through fertile valleys, expansive mountain terrain, and melancholy hamlets. Spili is a striking village with cascading waters and shady trees. Benches in the *platia* (square) surround the town's centerpiece, a long Venetian fountain that spouts cool spring water from 19 carved lion heads. Unfortunately, legions will enjoy the refreshing water with you.

If you have a vehicle that can take a pounding, ride the mountain roads east from Spili to **Gerakari.** Very few maps show the unpaved route, but follow the mountains and you'll be fine (really). Just 2km southeast of Gerakari is a shady spot with running water, prime territory for freelance camping. Across the road are the ruins of a tiny, 11th-century Byzantine monastery, **Agios Yiannis Theologos,** with well-preserved frescoes inside. Consider approaching Gerakari from the eastern side; access from the secondary road that runs parallel to the Rethymnon-Agia Galini highway is much easier.

Western Crete

Rethymnon ΡΕΘΥΜΝΟ

The Turkish and Venetian influences that pervade the cities of northern Crete are best appreciated in the harbor town Rethymnon. Arabic inscriptions lace the walls of its narrow, arched streets, minarets highlight the old city's skyline, and an imposing Venetic fortress guards the harbor's western end. On any given day, even the most energetic travelers may inexplicably find themselves waking up just in time for the afternoon siesta, wandering aimlessly through sinuous streets at sunset, and lounging until the wee hours in a café by the ocean.

Orientation and Practical Information

To get to Arkadiou St. and the waterfront from the bus station, walk down Demokratias St. to the Venizelou monument, cross Kountouriotou St., and walk straight down Varda Kallergi St. You'll find everything you need in the rough triangle formed by **Arkadiou, Antistasseos,** and **Gerakari Street.**

Greek National Tourist Organization (GNTO): Down by the waterfront (tel. 291 48 or 241 43). The efficient staff will provide you with maps, bus and ferry schedules, museum hours, and a list of all-night pharmacies. They also suggest daytrips and publicize local events. Open Mon.-Fri. 9am-3:30pm.

Tourist Police: Iroon Polytechniou St. (tel. 281 56), just off the waterfront, 3 blocks south of the fortress. Similar services as the GNTO. Open Mon.-Fri. 7am-2:30pm.

Association of Rooms to Let: 2 Petichaki St. (tel. 295 03). The English-speaking staff on the second floor of Nileas Tours represents the association, which can hook you up with 1 of 7000 beds in the Rethymnon prefecture.

Post Office: Moatsou St., near the public gardens. Open Mon.-Sat. 7:30am-2pm, Sun. 9am-1:30pm. **Postal Code:** 74100.

OTE: 28 Kountouriotou St. Open daily 7am-midnight; Nov.-April 7am-11pm. **Telephone Code:** 0831.

Currency Exchange: Bank of Crete, at the intersection of Kountariotou and Varda Kallergi, near the bus station. Open Mon.-Thurs. 8am-2pm, Fri. 8am-1:30pm. Many banks are marked on the free GNTO map.

Bus Stations: (tel. 222 12), facing each other on opposite corners of Demokratias and Moatsou, 1 block inland from the Venizelou monument on Kountouriotou. To: Iraklion (28 per day until 8:30pm, 1½hr., 1000dr); Chania (29 per day until 10pm, 1hr., 950dr); Agia Galini (5 per day, Sat.-Sun 4 per day, 1½hr., 800dr); Plakias (5 per day, 1hr., 610dr); the Arkadi Monastery (4 per day, Sat.-Sun. 4 per day, 40min., 300dr).

Taxi: Tel. 223 16 or 250 00. Available 24 hrs.

Motorbike Rental: Motor Stavros, 14 Paleologou St. (tel. 228 58). Automatics 1800dr. Bikes 1000dr. Prices negotiable. **Fahrrad Rent-a-Vespa,** 15 Kountouriotou St., across from the OTE. 50cc bikes 2500dr. Other car rentals and motorbike shops centered around the Venizelou monument.

Library: 24 Tsouderon St. From the museum, walk right (facing the water) for 3 blocks on Arkadiou St., turn right on Tsouderon: it's next to the church Agias Varvaras. Some English books. Open Mon.-Tues and Thurs. 7:30am-2:30pm and 6:30-8pm, Wed., Fri. and Sat. 8am-2pm.

English Bookstore: International Press, Petichaki St. (tel. 249 37), near the water. Open Mon.-Sat. 8am-11pm, Sun. 8am-2pm. **Spontidaki Toula** (Sign in Greek, ΣΠΟΝΤΙΑΚΗ ΤΟΥΛΑ; tel. 203 07) 43 Touliou St. Buys and sells used books.

Laundromat: 45 Tombasi (tel. 220 11), next to the youth hostel. Wash 800dr. Dry 300dr. Open Mon.-Sat. 8:30am-3pm and 5-9pm.

Public Toilets: Next to the GNTO by the waterfront. Not too clean. Okay, quite dirty. Cold showers on the public beach.

Hospital: Trantalidou St. (tel. 278 14), in the southwest corner of town. Open 24 hrs.

Emergency: Tel. 100

Police: Tel. 252 47

Accommodations, Camping and Food

Arkadiou Street and the harbor, near the fortress and the Venetian port, are lined with hotels and rooms to let. Most are spacious, sparsely decorated, and expensive. The Rooms to Let Association headquarters on Petichaki St., a block from the harbor, will tell you what's available

Youth Hostel (HI/IYHF), 41 Tombasi St. (tel. 228 48). Friendly, relaxed, and crammed in summer. Breakfast in the morning and *ouzo* at night. No curfew. 800dr per person. HI/IYHF cards not necessary. Long lines for occasionally hot showers 8-10am and 5-8pm.

Olga's Pension, 57 Souliou St. (tel. 298 51), on a nicely restored street off Ethnikis Antistaseos. George, the jovial proprietor, keeps a continual garden party going. Homemade wine at the terrarium café 50dr. Roof 500dr. Singles 2500dr. Doubles 3000dr. Triples 4000dr. Quads 4500dr. Private bath included.

Vrisinas, 10 Chereti St. (tel. 260 92), off Arkadiou St., 1 block from the bus station, and before the youth hostel. Centrally located, but still tranquil. Top-notch rooms. Doubles 2000dr.

Hotel Paradisos, 35 Igoum Gavril St. (tel. 224 19). From the bus station, walk down to the Venizelou monument and turn left on Kountouriotou St., which becomes Igoum Gavril. Clean, quiet, nondescript rooms and an immaculate, spacious shower and bathtub. Singles 2500dr. Doubles 4000dr. Triples 4800dr.

Hotel Zania, 3 Pavlou Vlastou St. (tel. 281 69), off Arkadiou. Spotless, palatial rooms with soft beds. Gracious proprietors speak French. The building and some of the richly carved wood bedframes are 200 years old. Doubles 4000dr. Triples 5000dr. Hot showers included.

Hotel Achillo, 151 Arkadiou St. (tel. 225 81), left from the corner of Arkadiou and Varda Kallergi. High-ceilinged rooms, some with balconies. Large airy TV lounge with comfortable chairs. Attractively furnished except for the cheesy prints. Large, clean rooms. Singles 2500dr. Doubles 3500dr. Triples 4000dr. One huge quint 5000dr.

Barbara Dokimaki, 14 Plastira St. (tel. 223 19). All rooms with kitchen, bath, and fan. Roof 1000dr. Doubles 3500dr. Huge quint 6700dr.

Camping: Elizabeth Camping (tel. 286 94), 3km east of town at the beginning of the old road to Iraklion. Tent pitches on shaded grass. The staff will lend you camping and kitchen supplies. Self-service *taverna* 9am-11pm. 800dr per person, 600dr per tent, 500dr per car. Open May-Oct. **Arkadia Camping** (tel. 288 25), 500m beyond Elizabeth. Gravel pitches. Self-serve *taverna* 7am-11pm, and store 8am-9pm. Money exchange and motorbike rentals. 800dr per person, 600dr per tent, 400dr per car. Buses run from the Rethymnon station to both campsites (100dr). If you're arriving from Iraklion, ask the driver to let you off at one of the sites.

Rethymnon has plenty of *souvlaki-pita* (150dr) stands scattered throughout the city. There is also an open-air market on weekdays next to the park, between Moatsou and Kountouriotou St. There are many generic seafood restaurants lining the old harbor. For reliably tasty if overpriced meals, visit the restaurants on the old Venetian harbor. Locals hang at **Restaurant Samaria,** in the middle of the waterfront. **Restaurant Apostolaki** at 10 Kalinois Siganou (tel. 244 01), parallel to Koutourioutas away from the harbor, is the proverbial best deal in town (Greek salad 250dr, *tzatziki* 150dr, *mousaka* 550dr). For a special meal, seek out **Alana's,** 11 Salaminos (tel. 277 37); on a quiet side-street. The roomy courtyard, attentive service, and Venetian fountain create a romantic setting. (*Souvlaki* 900dr, stuffed tomatoes 750dr. Open daily noon-3pm and 6pm-2am.) If you have access to a car or feel like taking a walk, join the locals at **Zizi's Taverna,** 4km east of town in Platanes, on the old road to Iraklion.

Sights and Entertainment

Rethymnon has been occupied nearly continuously since the late Minoan period. At its cultural and economic apex in the 4th century BCE, it was overrun by Myceneans. During the Fourth Crusade, the Franks sold the island to the merchants of Venice for 520 pounds of silver. The latter considered Rethymnon crucial to their chain of trading outposts, and fortified the city. The Ottomans took the city in 1646, enlarging it and incorporating Turkish designs into the extant Venetian buildings. For enlightening background, read *Rethymnon: A Guide to the Town,* by A. Malagari and H. Stratidakis (900dr).

Rethymnon's **Archaeological Museum** is adjacent to the fortress. Once inside, you'll feel as though you've wandered into the storeroom of a dotard archaeologist: headless statues lean on walls behind rows of figurines, and Minoan sarcophagi lie next to cases of Roman coins. (Open Tues.-Sun. 8:30am-3pm. Admission 300dr, students 200dr.) The new **Historical and Folk Art Museum,** 28 Mesologiou St., on a back street near the fortress, displays Cretan crafts. (Open Mon.-Sat. 9am-1pm and 6-8pm. Admission 200dr, students 100dr.)

At some point during your visit to Rethymnon, make a pilgrimage to the colossal **Venetian Fortezza,** dating from around 1580. The walls of the enormous citadel are in excellent condition, but most of the buildings in the interior of the fortress were destroyed by the Turks in the 17th century, and even more bit the dust three centuries later during World War II. Rethymnon's **Renaissance Festival**, held in the fortress in July and August, is a must for Rethymnotes and tourists alike (400dr).

Rethymnon's Turkish legacy looms in the city's Islamic structures: the **Neratzes Minaret,** on Antistasseos St. (top open daily 11am-7:30pm; free); the **Nerdjes Mosque,** 1 block farther, which was formerly a Franciscan church; the **Kara Pasha Mosque,** on Arkadiou St., near Iroon Sq.; and the **Valides Minaret,** which presides over **Porta Megali** gate at the beginning of Antistasseos St. in 3 Martiou Sq. Ask at the GNTO for hours.

Rethymnon's annual **Wine Festival,** during the first week in August, is a crowded all-you-can-snozzle fest which costs only 500dr. (Bring your own carafe—souvenir glasses are expensive.) A local dance troupe performs early in the evening in traditional costumes, while later on it's a free-for-all.

Every odd year, an exhibition of Cretan handicrafts coincides roughly with the wine festival. The work is worth a look, but you won't pick up any bargains; you can usually find better prices at local artisans' shops in each major town. Rethymnon's own craft shops cluster around Arkadiou, Antistasseos, and Gerakari Street. The **Herb Shop,** 58 Souliou St., stocks folk remedies and herbs exclusive to Crete.

The bar scene at Rethymnon centers on Petichaki St. and Nearchou St. near the west end of the harbor. The happening **Rock Bar Café** (beer 500dr) on Petichaki St. and the **Fortezza Disco Bar** (tel. 21493) at 14 Nearchou St. (beer 500dr) bookend several Greek *bouzouki* places. On the other side of the beach, the outdoor **Dolphin Disco** sports a pool.

Near Rethymnon

In 1866, over 1000 Cretans took refuge from the Turks in the **Arkadi Monastery.** When hundreds of Turks besieged the monastery on November 9 of that year, the abbot ignited his handy store of gunpowder, blowing up the building to prevent its capture. Hundreds, maybe thousands, of Cretans and Turks died in the explosion, bringing worldwide attention to the Greek struggle for independence. The Arkadi Monastery is regarded as a symbol of freedom and independence throughout Greece. The anniversary of the battle is observed November 7-9 with solemn celebrations at Arkadi and in Rethymnon. (Monastery open daily 6am-8pm.)

The trip is worth taking to view the handsome stone buildings of the monastery. The roofless gunpowder room is at the far left corner of the courtyard, near the unused eastern entrance to the monastery. The historical museum on the right (southern) side of the courtyard contains war mementoes. (Open daily 9am-2pm and 3-8pm. Admission 250dr, students 150dr.) To the left as the bus enters the site is the octagonal **Sanctuary**

of the Heroes, a memorial to the victims of the blast. Inside are displayed the skulls of many Cretans who perished in front-line combat. Several tour companies offer expensive one-day excursions to the monastery, but you can easily go on your own: **Buses** make the round-trip from the Rethymnon bus station (Mon.-Fri. 4 per day, Sat.-Sun. 3 per day, 40min., 300dr).

If you take any bus about 10km west along the coastal highway, you'll pass one of Crete's sandy beaches, which extends all the way around the **Gulf of Georgiopolis.** The highway has taken away some of the beach's splendid solitude, but at the same time it has also added to it by running so close to the water that almost no hotels could be built. Although cars and motorbikes can pull over along the road, the nearest inexpensive accommodations are in the quiet coastal village of **Georgiopolis;** try the **Amfimalla Hotel** (tel. 224 70; singles 2500dr, doubles 3000dr; hot showers included) or the nearby **Hotel Penelope** (tel. 224 77; doubles 3000dr). There's a **campsite** on the shore just outside of town. Georgiopolis's **telephone code** is 0825.

The ruins of **Elevtherna,** including its curious Hellenistic bridge, are near the village of Prines, southeast of Rethymnon. At the **Late Minoan Cemetery** of Armeni, 8km south of Rethymnon, more than 150 rock-cut chamber tombs have been found, some containing clay larnax coffins with ax and horn decorations. The area is easily reached by the bus headed for Agia Galini.

Plakias

Metamorphosis from tiny fishing village to full-blown resort has seriously diminished Plakias's small-town atmosphere. A decade or so of rapid one-dimensional development has left Plakias with paddleboat rentals and *tavernas* galore, but no bank or doctor's office. Awkward imbalances aside, Plakias remains an affordable option if you're yearning for the cool breezes and wide, sandy beaches of Crete's southern coast.

Candia Tours (tel. 312 14), near the Lamon Hotel, provides general tourist information. If you need medical assistance, call the **Spili Hospital Clinic** (tel. 225 31; about 20min. by car). There is a tiny yellow **post office** where you can **exchange money** next to the row of *tavernas* near the quay (open Mon.-Sat. 8:30am-2pm, Sun. 9am-1pm). **Bus** information and **currency exchange** are available at **Hotel Livikon** (tel. 312 16). Buses to: Rethymnon (5 per day until 5pm, 610dr); Agia Galini (at 10am and 6:30pm, 650dr); and Chora Sfakion (at 10am, 435dr). For **moped rental,** Motoplakias (tel. 314 69) and Galaxie Bikes are on the main street, past Sofia's as you walk from the quay. (Mopeds 2000dr at both shops. Insurance included.) Plakias's **postal code** is 740 60; its **telephone code** is 0832.

You can live quite comfortably and very cheaply in this wave-lapped beach town. Most of the rooms to let are on the waterfront or on the few streets that run perpendicular to the beach. The **youth hostel** (tel. 313 06), all the way up the road from the beach, is friendly and *loud* (even the staff calls it the "party hostel"). The sound system blasts a staggering variety of music (from Janis Joplin to New Kids on The Block) throughout the day and into the night. The staff is happy to play guests' tapes too. (No curfew. Beds 1000dr. Open March-Dec.) In the west end near the quay and just past Smerna's Restaurant is **Rooms to Rent Stefanakis** (tel. 312 47), where doubles with bath, kitchen facilities, and seaside view are 3000dr; singles are only 1500dr. Approaching from the east, turn off the main road at the "Greek Art Maria" sign, and walk 50m. There rests **Pension Asteria** (tel. 313 12), with tranquil rooms on the garden side. (Singles 2500dr. Doubles 3500dr. Private bath included.) **Camping Plakias** (tel. 314 04), close to the beach, is a pleasant option with cold showers, clean facilities, and a supply store. The grove of trees which separates it from the rest of town lends the campsite an air of isolation, and thus some women might feel uncomfortable alone here (750dr per person. Tent free. Follow the signs from town). A swanky new campground should be ready by the summer of 1993. Sleeping on the beach at the far eastern end of Plakias beach or on Damnoni beach is usually a hassle-free, cost-free alternative.

The cheapest sustenance in town can be found at the three **supermarkets** on the main road, at the *souvlaki* and pastry stands, and at the bakeries right before the row of expensive waterfront restaurants. **Mitos Taverna,** near the youth hostel, is popular with the younger crowd, and serves the best Greek salads in Plakias (400dr). At **Restaurant Gorgones** (tel. 31469) on the beachfront, the friendly English-speaking waiters embody *filoxenia* (hospitality) Roast chicken 500dr, *kalamari* 500dr, beer 160dr. (Open from noon to 11pm daily.) **Café-Bar Swing**, on the waterfront, is a step up from the everyday cheesy café-bars that are endemic to Greece. Swing plays classical music in the morning, jazz in the afternoon, rock in the evening and 300dr Budweisers all the time.

Meltemi, a nightclub about 200m from the youth hostel, gets underway very late and winds down around 5am. The club attracts a younger crowd by giving hostel guests a discount. (Beer 300dr.) With blinding neon decor, the **Hexagon Club,** farther into town on the main strip, is the place for the hip and aloof. **Ostraco,** close to the quay, features a bar below, a dance floor above, and music from the 60s and 70s.

The surrounding villages offer cheaper rooms without the homogenized tourist throngs. Breezy **Myrthios,** a half-hour walk up the hill from Plakias, has an excellent mosquito-free **youth hostel** (tel. 312 02). Unlike its neighbor in Plakias, this hostel is peaceful and quiet. (Refrigerator and kitchen facilities. Beds in rooms or on the roof 1000dr. Hot showers available 8-10am and 5-8:30pm. Open year-round.) **Vasilonikol-idaki,** the *taverna* in the square, has good *tiropites* (cheese pies, 300dr), fresh lamb (800dr), and an international phone. (Open 7am-midnight.)

The fringe beach cove of **Damnoni,** to the east of Plakias, attracts a community of informal campers. There are two *tavernas* and cold public showers on the beach. Police make occasional attempts to disperse the campers, but pleasure seekers invariably return. The **Akti Damnoni** pension (tel. 312 58) has clean doubles with baths for 4200dr. (English breakfast 600dr. Open April-Oct.) To reach Damnoni, walk 1km on the road to Lefkogia or take the Rethymnon bus (5min.), and then take a right on the dirt road. The coves to the west and east make good beach hideaways.

Chania XANIA

Having survived World War II and endured occupation by the Minoans, Turks, Venetians, and Egyptians, Chania (pop. 70,000) today faces a new enemy: tourists. Fortunately, Chania's mountain and sea surroundings provide a natural buffer from the raucous tour buses and strident, tourist-laden motorbikes. Chania was the capital of Crete until 1971, when the title was passed to Iraklion. With its thriving nightlife and chaotic history, however, Chania is still regarded by many islanders as the spiritual capital of the island. Meander through the winding streets, an architectural pastiche of styles from the different occupations, absorb the folk music in streetside cafés, or while the day away gazing at the old Venetian Harbor. Despite the bustle, Chania offers escape from the heat and relentless activity of other Greek capitals.

Orientation and Practical Information

From the bus station, walk right on Kidonias St. for 2 blocks and turn left onto Platia 1866; going north, the road becomes Halidon St. and leads to the old **harbor,** the setting for much of Chania's nightlife. To lighten the load while you're looking for a room, leave your bags at the bus station (storage open from 6am to 8pm; 50dr per bag). If you arrive in Chania by way of ferry, your boat will dock in the nearby port of **Souda.** A bus from Souda will drop you off at Chania's Municipal Market (10min., 150dr). From there, walk 2 blocks west on Gianari St. and then right onto Halidon. Even with the maps provided at the GNTO and at the kiosks, finding your way around the city is no cinch. Street names change with alarming frequency—sometimes from block to block. Luckily, Chania isn't very big; you can't stay lost for long. Chania's business district is mostly contained within the area across from the market, around the intersection of **Gianari Street** and **Tzanakaki Street.**

Greek National Tourist Organization (GNTO): 4th floor of the Megaro Pantheon, Platia 1866 (tel. 264 26), above the Greek Agricultural Bank. Provides tourist information: plane, ferry and bus schedules, hotel, package tour and general information. Open Mon.-Fri. 7:30am-2:00pm.

Tourist Police: 44 Karaiskaki St. (tel. 244 77), near the central bus station. Provides maps and directions. Open daily 7:30am-8pm. **Association of Rooms to Let:** 18 Isodion St. (at Unikreta travel agency) (tel. 436 01), facing away from the waterfront, it's a block to the left of the center of the harbor. Open daily 8am-9pm.

Budget Travel Office: Interkreta, 9 Kanevaro St. (tel. 525 52 or 521 42), a few steps east of the waterfront. Student discounts on international air fare, ferry tickets and **Magic Bus** tickets for the mainland. Also has currency exchange. Open daily 9am-2:30pm and 5:30-9pm.

Currency Exchange: Credit Bank, 2 Kanevaro St. (tel. 576 44), off Halidon St. on the east side of the harbor. Open in summer Mon.-Thurs. 8am-2pm, Fri. 8am-1:30pm, Sat. 9am-1:30pm. Another branch at 106 Halidon St., near Platia 1866. Open Mon.-Thurs. 8am-2pm, Fri. 8am-1:30pm. **National Bank of Greece,** on Kidonias St., next to the bus station, and on Tzanakaki St., across from the market. Open Mon.-Thurs. 8am-2pm, Fri. 8am-1:30pm. **Gift shops** by the harbor will sometimes change money after hours at slightly lower rates. Cash advances on Visa charge cards obtainable at the **Ionian-Popular Bank** (tel. 255 08), on Gianari St. a block east of Halidori St. Open Mon.-Fri. 8am-7pm.

Post Office: 3 Tzanakaki St. Will exchange currency. Open Mon.-Fri. 7:30am-8pm. **Postal Code:** 73100.

OTE: 5 Tzanakaki St. Exceptionally efficient. Open daily 6am-midnight; off season 7am-11pm. Telex and telegram Mon.-Fri. only. **Telephone Code:** 0821.

Airport: Olympic Airways, 88 Tzanakaki St. (tel. 277 01), near the public garden. You can also get information on Olympic flights at Interkreta (see above under Budget Travel Office). Buses for the airport leave from the main office on Tzanakaki 1½hr. before each flight. Open daily 5:30am-8:30pm. For detailed information on flights, see Getting to Crete in the Crete Introduction above.

Buses: Central bus station, on the corner of Kidonias and Kelaidi St. (tel. 230 52 or 233 06). Bus schedules change constantly; go to Chania Tourist Information Office for an updated schedule. Buses go to Rethymnon (every ½hr. 5:30am-8pm, 1hr., 950dr); Iraklion (every ½hr. 5:30am-8pm, 3hr., 1900dr); Omalos (3 per day, 1hr., 650dr); Kastelli (15 per day, 6am-8:30pm, 1hr., 600dr); Paleochora (7 per day, 2hr., 1000dr); Chora Sfakion (or Sfakia) (4 per day, 2hr., 1000dr); Sougia (8:30am and 1:30pm, 2hr., 950dr); and Kalyves (4 per day, 25min., on the Vamos bus, 200dr). Regular buses also go to the seaside resorts west of Chania: Platanias (15min., 330dr); Maleme (30min., 160dr); and Kolimbari (45min., 330dr). Buses to Souda (150dr) leave Gianari St. in front of the market (every 15min., 6am-11pm). Other local buses (navy blue) leave Platia 1866 at the intersection of Sfakianaki and Kidonias St. The bus to Kalamaki (every 20min., 150dr) stops at Camping Chania. The buses are reliable and leave on time, but sometimes the signs indicating their destinations are wrong. Check when you board. For airport buses see above.

Ferries: ANEK Office, Venizelou Sq. (tel. 256 56), near the National Bank of Greece. The *Kriti* and the *Aptera* go between Piraeus and Souda (7pm, tourist-class 4900dr, deck-class (that's us) 3756dr). Bring food and warm clothing; the trip takes 11hr., and it's chilly at night.

Moped Rental: Cluster on Halidon St. Automatic mopeds at 2000dr per day; 90cc models at 3000dr, 125cc at 4000dr, and 250cc at 5000dr. Olympic Rent-a-Car at 74 Halidon St. (tel. 549-15), rents mopeds and offers a 10-20% discount for *Let's Go* users.

Foreign Bookstores: Pelekanakis, 98 Halidon St. (tel. 225 12); and **Kalaitzakis,** 27 Tsouderon St. (tel. 227 63). The bookshops in the harbor sell foreign newspapers.

Municipal Market: Walk down Halidon St. away from the harbor, then turn left on Tsouderon. Buses from Souda stop in front. Market open Mon.-Sat. 8am-2pm. Saffron only 200dr per package. Sat. morning fruit and vegetable market on Nik. Foka St.

Lost and Found: Immigration Police, 32 Sfakianaki St. (tel. 533 33).

Laundromat: 7 Episk. Dorotheu (tel. 498 69), a small alley east of Halidon St., behind the cathedral in Platia Metropolis. Warm and womb-like. Wash 600dr per load; including dryer 1000dr. Mon.-Sat. 8am-3pm. Also 18 Agia Deka (tel. 576 02), near the cathedral. Wash and dry, 600dr each. Open daily 8am-8pm.

Public Toilets: In the middle of Platia 1866. Look for faucets attached to the fountain to rinse out clothes. Other W.C.s located behind the harbor across from the Piraeus Hotel on Zambeliou St., on Kastelli Hill near the Rector's Palace and in the Municipal Gardens on Tzanakaki St.

Women's Clinic: Dr. Kapakis Manousos, 3 Nik. Foka St. (tel. 526 88). Open Mon.-Sat. 9am-2pm and 5:30-8:30pm.

Pharmacy: Athanassaki Artemis, 25 Haliclon St. (tel. 544 99). Open daily 8am-2pm and 5:30-9pm. Pharmacies are scattered throughout Chania; look for the "red cross" sign in front.

Hospital: At the corner of Dragoumi and Kapodistriou St. (tel. 272 31), in the eastern part of town. Out-patient clinic open Mon.-Sat. 12:30-2pm and 6-9pm, Sun. 8am-9pm. For **emergencies,** call 222 22.

Accommodations and Camping

In the old town, most of the inexpensive pensions overlook the harbor, a convenient but noisy area. Small hotels sprout from the beaches on the west coast, but expect to lay out the cash for the brown sand of **Nea Kydonia** and **Agia Marina.** Tourist officials and police are obliging with information, but don't give recommendations. Freelance camping on the eastern side doesn't seem to bother anyone, as long as you remember to clean up your ungainly garbage; no need to add to Chania's growing trash problem. Be wary of the eclectic bunch of locals who offer you rooms when you get off the bus from Souda. It is illegal for them to be at the bus station trying to entice customers. As in many other tourist towns, try the "Rooms to Let" Association. Tell them what you are looking for in a room and they will give you a list of addresses and phone numbers. These rooms to let are often cheaper than hotels.

Youth Hostel (HI/IYHF), 33 Drakonianou St. (tel. 535 65), on the southern outskirts of town. Walk or take the Agios Ioannis bus from Apokoronou St., near the market, and ask the driver to let you off at the youth hostel. The view of the valley is breathtaking, but no match for all the breath lost on the long hike from town. No curfew. 800dr per person. Open March-Nov.

Hotel Piraeus, 10 Zambelou St. (tel. 541 54), left off Halidon St. as you face the harbor. Very quiet on the street side, scenic on the harbor side. English-speaking management. Singles 2000dr. Doubles 3000dr. Triples 4500dr.

Meltemi Pension, 2 Angelou St. (tel. 401 92), at the very end of the west side of the harbor, next to the Naval Museum. This cozy townhouse has camera-ready vistas and a library of foreign books. Singles 2000dr. Doubles 2500dr.

Kydonia Pension, 15 Isodion St. (tel. 571 79), near the Cathedral Church. Friendly English-speaking management. No showers, but relatively clean. Doubles 3000dr. Triples 4000dr.

Hotel Fidias, 6 Sarpaki St. (tel. 524 94). From Halidon St., turn right at the cathedral on Athinagora St., which becomes Sarpaki St. With poster-coated walls and linoleum floors, the lodgings look like cleaner versions of freshman dorm rooms. Hot showers. Singles 2000dr, with bath 2200dr. Doubles 3000dr, with bath 3200dr. Dorm triples 1250dr per person.

Pension Kasteli, 39 Kanevaro St. (tel. 570 57), near the east end of the harbor. From the banana trees in the backyard to the free washing machine and maid service, Pension Kasteli is the Shangri-La of the budget traveler. Balconies available. Bar downstairs. Noisy at night. Singles 2000dr, with bath 2200dr. Doubles 3000dr, with bath 3300dr. Full breakfast 500dr. For small groups, the owner rents a nearby Venetian townhouse with a kitchen in each apartment.

Rooms for Rent No. 47, 47 Kandanolou (tel. 532 43), on Kastelli Hill. Turn left off Kanevaro as you come from the harbor. Hard to find. Balconies with stunning views of the open sea. Rooms with basins. Singles 1800dr. Doubles 2500dr.

Pension Teris, 47 Zambeliou St. (tel. 531 20). The walls are psychedelic pink, the showers are hot, and the price is right. Doubles 1500dr.

Camping: The camping sites are west of Chania proper, within walking distance of the beaches. **Camping Chania** (tel. 314 90), is about 2½km from town. Take the Kalamaki bus from Platia 1866 (100dr). Sites bordered by flowers and shaded by lush olive trees. *Taverna* and minimarket open daily. 600dr per person, under 12 300dr, 500dr per small tent. **Camping Agia Marina** (tel. 685 55). Take the Kastelli Bus. Snack bar and supermarket. 800dr per person, ages 4-10 400dr, 500dr per tent, cars 400dr. Hot showers available. Both sites open March-October.

Food and Entertainment

Most tourists, along with the many American sailors stationed in Souda, subsist on the homogenized "Greek" and imitation American cuisine offered at the *tavernas* lining the Venetian harbor (most are open 11am-midnight). Their prices are almost the same: Greek salad 500dr, pork chops 950dr, etc. Plenty of *souvlaki* stands offer gyro for 200dr. Try **Perasma Fast Food** (tel. 439 23) at the end of Halidon to the right for a perfectly spiced *gyro*. Leaving the harbor is a good idea for a real *taverna* atmosphere with live "Rembetiki" music, a passionately-sung music introduced by Greek refugees from Asia Minor. Most of these *tavernas* are somewhat overpriced but a must, especially for couples (most accept Visa, Mastercard and AmEx—you can pay for it later). **Seniramis Taverna** (tel. 460 78) offers home cooking with a decent band, a great atmosphere, and friendly English-speaking waiters. If your appetite is not that large, then one of the fast food places that offer pizza slices, croissants, and other pastries may be the answer. Another alternative is one of the café-bars at the Old Harbor which offer ham and cheese sandwiches, which Greeks simply call "toast" (350dr). **Remezzo Café Bar** (tel. 520 01) is one such place that plays easy listening music. Beware of the fancy ice cream sundaes—they are very expensive. Most of these café-bars open around 7:30am and offer breakfast. **Café Calypso** (tel. 468 93) on the Old Harbor, 100 meters to the left of Halidon St., offers omelettes for 450dr.

As the chimes of midnight approach, Chania rocks. Bars fill up around 11:30pm and around 1:00am the crowds move to the discos. Bars to visit during the first shift include: **Café-Bar Lissos** and **Remember Pub** on the Old Harbor, and **Fun-Pub** at 10 Kondilaki St. (tel. 280 73) off the waterfront; all three serve beer for 300dr and mixed drinks for 700dr. The later dance club shift gets more expensive, but the loud bass at the **Ariadni Club, Canale Club,** and **Club Street,** all on the waterfront, keeps hundreds dancing until the morning hours. The clubs close when the last patrons leave. Dry off your sweaty brow at the air-conditioned **Café Bar Point** at the center of the harbor on the second floor.

Sights

Kastelli Hill, the area north of Kanevaro St., is studded with Chania's history. Remnants of Ancient Kydonia's Bronze-Age prosperity are evident at the **Late Minoan House** (circa 1450 BCE), on the corner of Kandanoleu and Kanevaro St. Unfortunately, the entire site is fenced off. In the Middle Ages, the Venetian occupiers enriched the city's architecture, but much of their artistry was destroyed in World War II. All around old Chania you'll see the empty frames of Venetian houses, now open to the sky and intermingled with modern structures. Many relics are housed in the **Venetian Archival,** 35 Lithinon St., north of Kanevaro. With their mélange of Turkish and Venetian buildings, the waterfront alleys reflect the city's varied history. The old Chania Tourist Office at the harbor's eastern end inhabits a converted Turkish mosque that dates back to the arrival of the Turks in 1645. A **synagogue,** on the Kodilaki near Zambeliou St., is all that remains of the old Jewish quarter. Pass through several archways on Moshon St. to reach the **Venetian Chapel,** decorated with Latin inscriptions and Turkish graffiti. Young Greeks mellow out in the **Municipal Gardens,** once the property of a Turkish *muezzin* (prayer caller). Beyond the gardens to the east, turn left onto **Sfakianaki,** a 19th-century neighborhood where lurks the **Historical Museum and Archives,** 20 Sfakianaki St. (tel. 226 06).

The **Venetian Inner Harbor** is both a thriving social scene and an architectural relic that retains its original breakwater and Venetian arsenal. The Venetian **lighthouse** was restored by the Egyptians during their occupation of Crete in the late 1830s. Enter at the eastern end of the harbor. On the opposite side of the main harbor, the **Naval Museum** (tel. 264 37) exhibits Greek nautical pictures, models, pieces of boats, and seashells. (Open Tues., Thurs., and Sat. 10am-2pm. Admission 300dr, students 200dr.) The **Archaeological Museum** (tel. 203 34) on Halidon St. opposite the cathedral displays Cretan artifacts. Once a Venetian monastery, it more recently served as the Turkish Mosque of Yusuf Pasha. (Open Mon.-Fri. 8am-7pm, Sat., Sun. and holidays 8:30am-3pm. Admission 400dr, students 200dr.)

Chania will disappoint beach lovers. The harbor has been polluted by fishing boats, and the nearest swimming is in **Nea Chora** (20min. by foot to the west around the new harbor). Blue buses from Platia 1866 for Kalamaki or Galatus bring you to brown beaches speckled with pebbles. **St. Apostle's Beach,** via the Kalamaki bus, is popular for its wide sandy coves, sheltered by steep rock walls. On the Akrotiri Peninsula, try **Stavros** or the **Bay of Kalathas. Platanias,** 20 minutes away on the Kastelli or Chandris bus, has a pleasant but crowded beach with a lot of grown-up toys (jet skis and parasails among them).

Samaria Gorge ΦΑΡΑΓΓΙ ΣΑΜΑΡΙΑΣ

The most popular excursion from Chania, and a "must" on any trip to western Crete, is the five-hour hike down the formidable 18km Samaria Gorge, Europe's longest. Worn away by millions of years of river runoff, the White Mountains pass has managed to retain its allure despite being mobbed by visitors—as many as 2000 people per day scramble down the gorge in July and August. Bird watchers can glimpse the rare Bearded Vulture; horticulturalists can admire the wild flowers and shrubs which peek out from sheer rock walls; goat lovers (aren't we all?) can spot the nimble *agrimi,* a wild Cretan species in one of its few remaining natural habitats.

The 44km bus ride from Chania to **Xyloskalo,** where the trail begins, passes spectacular scenery—catch the early bus to see the vermillion sunrise. The road climbs through the Omalos Mountains, past the enchanting village of Laki, to an altitude of 1500m at the head of the gorge. Then the 18km trek begins: passing between cliff walls up to 300m high, the path, only 3m wide at some points, winds down along a river bed that runs nearly dry in the summer. Parts of the hike are shaded by clumps of pine trees, goats, or the towering walls of the gorge itself. The hike ends in the small town of Agia Roumeli on the southern coast. From there a boat sails to Loutro and Chora Sfakion, where you can catch a bus back to Chania. Experienced hikers and masochists can hike from Agia Roumeli to Chora Sfakion (10hr.) along one of the most outstanding coastlines in the country (see Southwest Coast). The bus to Chania from Chora Sfakion passes through the village of **Vrises,** where there are doubles to let (about 2800dr).

The downhill hike favored by most people (from Xyloskalo in the Omalos Plain to Agia Roumeli) takes from four to six hours. A less-traveled path next to the tourist pavilion ascends Mt. Gingilos to the west. Whichever route you choose, bring plenty of water and trail snacks, and wear good walking shoes. The Gorge is extremely dry and dusty in summer, and the stones on the path become quite slippery. Because of its altitude, the top of the gorge is often cold and rainy (though not as much in the summer), so bring appropriate clothing. If you get tired on the hike, don't worry: you can always take the donkey-taxi. (But at a staggering 6000dr for a ride, you'd do best to drag yourself home.) If you want to see only the dramatic tail of the gorge, start from Agia Roumeli. The path to the trail begins just behind Rooms Livikon. From the quay, walk straight to the rear of the village. Known as "Samaria the Lazy Way," the two-hour climb to the north takes you to the gorge's dramatic and narrow pass, the "Iron Gates." This should suit those travelers on the south coast without the time or inclination to take a bus to Xyloskalo. Walking all 18km uphill is not recommended unless you are prepared to do some pretty hefty work along the top half of the trail. If you hook up with an organized excursion you can leave your cumbersome pack in the tour bus and pick it up when the bus meets you in Chora Sfakion. Or leave your bags at the bus station for 200dr per day. The ferry from Agia Roumeli to Chora Stakion costs 850dr, and there is a 500dr entrance fee for the gorge.

The gorge is open from May through October; during the winter and spring, the river goes back to work cutting its trail through the rock. Flash floods in the winter have claimed many lives. During the other months, passage is officially allowed through the gorge between 6am and 3pm. For gorge information, call the **Chania Forest Service** (tel. 222 87).

Overpriced accommodations for the night before the hike are provided at the **Tourist Pavilion** (tel. 632 69) in Xyloskalo. Reservations for one of the 13 beds should be placed with the Chania GNTO. Five km north of Xyloskalo, **Omalos** has cheaper lodgings and food. Gorge yourself or stay at **Drakoulaki's Restaurant** (tel. (0821) 672 69. Doubles 2500dr. Triples 3300dr). On the plain of Omalos, take a left onto a dirt road for the 1½-hour trek to the minimalist **Kallergis refuge huts.** From there, hikers can make a day's climb to the summit of **Pakhnes** or **Mount Ida** (2456m), where Zeus, king of the gods, was raised from babyhood. Call the **Greek Alpine Club** (tel. 246 47) in Chania for more information.

Buses for Omalos and Xyloskalo leave Chania (at 7:30am, 8:30am, and 4:30pm, 1½hr., 650dr). When you ask to buy a ticket to Omalos, the ticket office at the bus station will sell you a round-trip ticket from Chania to Omalos and from Chora Sfakion to Chania (1000dr); if you don't plan to return to Chania by bus, via Chora Sfakion, ask explicitly for a one-way ticket. Since Agia Roumeli is connected by boat to Chora Sfakion, you can make the complete round-trip from Chania in one day, leaving on either of the morning buses. Taking the earliest bus will ensure cooler weather and less company for the hike. Alternatively, you can plan a leisurely hike and spend the night in one of the southern coastal towns.

A hot and dusty hike beyond the official exit from the gorge will bring you to **Agia Roumeli,** a seedy oasis for tired and thirsty hikers. Those 3km aren't entirely terrible, though—think of it as a goat photo-op. Finally you arrive in Agia Roumeli proper, a town with nothing to recommend it except the beach. The black pebbles are unbearably hot, but the water is refreshing after a long hike. The town itself exists mainly to sell food, favors (pick up an "I survived Samaria Gorge" T-shirt), and lodgings for exhausted, susceptible hikers. Sodas go for 200dr each. It's better to move on to Loutro or Chora Sfakion to the east, or Paleochora or Sougia to the west. If you do decide to stay, you can sleep at **Hotel Livikon,** on the inland end of town. (Singles 2000dr. Doubles 3000dr. Triples 4000dr. Private bath included.) For cheap sustenance, bypass the overpriced restaurants and head straight for the coast where you'll find a *souvlaki-pita* stand. In the evening, when the crowds leave town, the beach is a pleasant place to sleep, and many travelers camp around the wide river mouth, which is mostly dry in summer. Just remember, as you roll up your sleeping bag to leave, to take your trash with you, too.

You can take a boat from Agia Roumeli to one of the less crowded resorts along the southwest coast. Boats travel to Chora Sfakion (mid-June to Aug. 5 per day, last at 6pm, 1¼hr., 1000dr; sometimes boats extend service until 8:30pm if necessary). All of the boats stop in Loutro, except the last one (1hr., 600dr). Boats to Paleochora go once per day (Tues.-Sun. at 4pm, 2hr., 1000dr), stopping in Sougia (1hr., 700dr). This daily service begins May 1; before then, boats go to Paleochora three times per week (Tues. and Thurs. at 11am, Sat. at 5pm). Check all schedules with the tourist office. Buses from Chora Sfakion to Chania (1000dr) depart when each ferry from Agia Roumeli arrives. Don't dillydally, since the drivers take off as soon as their buses are full.

Near Chania

Although many intriguing villages and sights cluster around Chania, few others besides the Samaria Gorge are frequented. Northeast of town, the **Akrotiri Peninsula** hems in the sparkling Souda Bay and features three monasteries and several good beaches. Akrotiri is ideal for a daytrip by moped: distances are short and roads are passable. To reach the monasteries, follow signs for the airport and then signs for **Agia Triada** (Holy Trinity; not to be confused with the Minoan site of the same name). The monastery's pink buildings, crumbling since the 17th century, shelter a small collection of icons and manuscripts. Buses run from Chania to Agia Triada (250dr), leaving at 6:45am and 2pm, returning at 7:30am and 2:30pm.

The church of **Gouvernetou,** or Agios Ioannis, 4km north along the same road, was knocked down so many times that the caretakers finally installed an unbreakable copper dome to avoid the trouble of repairing it. Today, the building's 500-year-old fresco of Christ surrounded by saints and martyrs is set in the dome itself. Because Gouvernetou is less popular with tourists than its neighbor to the south, the monks are more inclined to explain the histories of the buildings and St. John. (Monasteries closed 2-5pm.) Dress appropriately: men must wear pants and women skirts or dresses.

A 30-minute walk from Gouvernetou leads to the ruins and cave of **Katholiko,** the first monastic settlement on Crete, built around 1200 CE. The monks at Gouvernetou will show you the well-marked footpath that continues past Katholiko to the sea. The

10-minute hike takes you down the mountainside and through a ravine. Mark the place where you leave the trail to enter the ravine; otherwise, you may have trouble finding the path again.

Most Greeks venture out to Akrotiri to visit the **Hill of the Prophet Ilias,** 7km from Chania. In 1897, Cretan fighters hoisted the Greek flag on this hill in defiance of Turkish forces. In addition to its fine view of Chania and the bay, the hill contains the grave of Eleftherios Venizelos (1864-1936), the Cretan revolutionary and statesman who served as Prime Minister of Greece for several administrations.

Your feet will cry out in thanks to the smooth sand at **Stavros,** 18km from Chania. (Buses at 7am, 10am, 1pm, 7pm, return at 7:30am, 10:30am, 1:30pm and 7:30pm, 180dr.) The film *Zorba the Greek* was set in this small, quiet cove. You can also pitch a tent behind the beach. There is another sandy beach, livelier than Stavros, at **Kalathos** (12km from Chania); the beach is near **Choraphakia,** also on the peninsula's western side.

Buses cruising along the new highway to Rethymnon pass a turn-off towards the water which leads to the growing village of **Kalyves.** Concrete skeletons of future hotels already loom ominously on the hillside next to the beach, but the sand and sea are still smooth and peaceful. If you walk along the rocks past the tiny marina, you may butt heads with a herd of bleating Cretan goats. The *platia* is packed with cafés, a *periptero* (kiosk), and some rooms for rent. Past the *platia* on the left is **Kalyves Travel,** which exchanges money and sells fishing harpoons. As you come into town, the **OTE** is on the right side (open Mon.-Fri. 7:30am-3:10pm) and the **post office** on the left, near the *platia* (open Mon.-Fri. 7:30am-2:15pm). Several small hotels operate around the *platia;* singles run 1800dr, doubles 2500dr. Buses to Varnos stop at Kalyves (250dr). The **postal code** of Kalyves is 73003; the **telephone code** is 0825.

The isolated coastal village of **Almirida** is tucked away 4km east of Kalyves. Archaeologists have uncovered the ruins of a basilica-style church with a large cruciform mosaic, dating from the 6th century. **Alekos Farm** (tel. 315 89) emerges just in time on the hot road inland from Almirida to Gavalohori. (Doubles 2900dr, with bath 3300dr. Triples without bath 3600dr.)

Green hills quickly turn steep and rocky to the south of Chania, becoming the **Lefka Ori** (White Mountains). The inland villages of **Alikianos** and **Vatolakos** offer shady alternatives to beach burnout. There are several small *tavernas* which will sell you inexpensive beer and soda. Since few foreigners visit this village, the locals will probably be thrilled to talk to you. The **postal code** for Mournies, Alikianos, and Vatolakos is 73005.

The fragrant 1km walk from Vatolakos to Alikianos takes you past flowering bushes and orange and lemon groves. To find Alikianos's OTE, turn right (with your back to Vatolakos) at the labeled light blue sign. (Open Mon.-Fri. 7:30am-3:10pm). Also on the central street are a few *tavernas,* a **Bank of Crete,** a **pharmacy,** and the **post office,** where you can change money. (Open Mon.-Fri. 7:30am-2pm.)

The town's sole architectural treasure, the 14th-century Agios Ioannis, stands unmarked, about 1km from Alikianos as you veer right for **Koufos.** The abandoned church, with its 15th-century frescoes amidst orange groves, makes a nice picnic spot.

The mountain village of **Skines,** on the road to Sougia from **Vatolakos,** overflows with blooming vines, roses, and sunflowers, while the adjacent countryside bursts with orange groves. Turn off here for Omalos, where the Samaria Gorge begins. Buses to Alikianos (230dr) and Vatolakos (250dr) leave Chania eight times per day, returning every ½-hour after departure. As always, check times in the off-season.

On the Omalos Rd., 15½km after the junction for Sougia, the road meets the tiny town of **Fournes.** Here the road forks: to the left, 6km down, several streams converge at the serene village of **Meskla,** where there are rooms above the local *taverna* (tel. 672 76; doubles 3000dr). Hikers will enjoy the one-hour climb up the hill from the churches to **Theriso.** From the right fork of the Omalos Rd., 25km from Chania, is the whitewashed mountain village of **Laki.** Minimalist is the word for the makeshift rooms and toilets at **Kokkinakis Café-Bar** (tel. 672 32; singles 1500dr; doubles 2500dr; triples 3300dr; hot showers included). For a day at the trendiest and most expensive beach around, join the pink-fried tourists at **Platanias.** This little city, expanding into a thriv-

ing resort area, succeeds admirably in the way of blaring signs and beachfront entertainment. You can rent jet skis (3000dr for 20min.), motor boats (3000-4000dr),
paddleboats (1000-1500dr), and canoes (500dr per hr). Waterski (2200dr for 10min.) or
parasail (6000dr for one flight) for even more thrills. The **Hotel Moon,** next to the
Bank of Crete at the east end of town, offers traditional rooms (with fridges). (Doubles
3800dr. Triples 4800dr.) **Stella's** (tel. 680 63), across from the Kantari Tavern at the
edge of town, supplies swanky new doubles with bath and kitchen for 4200dr. She also
has two-room suites (4500dr for three people, 5500dr for four). **Canada's Montreal
Rooms for Rent** doesn't offer discounts to Canadian citizens, but it wouldn't hurt to
flash the flag. Spiffy doubles 3125dr.

The **OTE** and **post office** (which also exchanges money) are both in the *platia.* For
nightlife, check out the **Porto Cali Disco** (tel. 613 35) at the end of town (as you travel
away from Chania). Open 9pm until everyone goes home. **Buses** leave Chania for Platanias (20min., 170dr), Maleme (25min., 200dr), and Kolimbari (35min., 300dr) every
30 minutes. **Bus tickets** can be purchased at the *periptero* (kiosk) nearby. Several buses
run to Chania daily (150dr); early-morning fare from Platanias to Omalos and Samaria
Gorge, 1500dr round-trip. **Kolimbari,** 6km west of Maleme, clings to the elbow of the
peninsula that encloses the gulf of Chania. The views are ravishing, but the beach is
painfully rocky. The town's **post office** (open Mon.-Fri. 7:30am-2:15pm), **OTE** (open
Mon.-Fri. 7:30am-3:10pm), and the **police station** (tel. 221 00) are all on the main
street, which also houses several *tavernas.* **Money** may be exchanged at the post office.
The **postal code** is 01824. For beach-front **rooms,** turn right after the police station at
the west end of town. Ask at **Vera's Grocery Store** (tel. 221 23) for secluded rooms
with bath. (Doubles 3000dr. Triples 4000dr.) **Kumentakis** (tel. 223 45), above the
OTE, has old-fashioned, clean rooms. (Doubles 3000dr. Triples 4000dr. Communal
kitchen included.) Kick off your flip-flops and watch the surf at **Spatha,** to the right
down a small alley as you enter town. (Beer 250dr. Open daily 8am-midnight.)

Just past the Kolimbari crossroads is the **Monastery of Gonias,** founded in 1618 by
Blaise, the Cypriot monk. The view off the back balcony is superb; bring some of those
postcards you've been meaning to write and relax here for a bit. In the 19th century, the
monastery was an important center of resistance against the Turks. Several cannon
balls lodged in its walls attest to the monastery's role; the monks have even peppered
their balcony with the detritus as decoration. Inside the monastery, there is also a small
museum with documents, vestments, and icons. Dress appropriately. (Church and museum closed 1-4pm.) Up the road about 100m from the monastery are pebbly coves
good for snorkeling. If you miss the last bus back to Chania (9pm) or to Kastelli
(8:30pm), don't worry: Kolimbari's main road is sprinkled with "Rooms for Rent"
signs. A double should run you 3000-3500dr. To get to the gulf towns, take the bus to
Kastelli or one of the frequent buses that go as far as Kolimbari.

Loutro and Surrounding Area

Between Agia Roumeli and Chora Sfakion, Loutro reclines contentedly in a tiny
cove which yawns open into the Libyan Sea, and holds the distinction of being the only
town in Crete where you cannot buy postcards of naked women. Surrounded by the
ocean on one side and austere mountains on the other, the prawn-sized village can be
reached only by boat. The beach here is rocky, but not entirely uncomfortable, and the
locals usually don't mind if you appropriate their docks for tanning exercises.

There are rooms to rent all along the cove and, since it takes about four minutes to
see all of Loutro, it's pretty easy to check them all out. On the western end of the cove,
Vangeli and Giorgo's, one of the best restaurants in Loutro, rents standard doubles for
3000dr and harbors the only phone in town. Next door is Loutro's creatively nameless
hotel, where you'll find spotless doubles for 2500dr (3000-3500dr with bath; discounts
for longer stays; inquire at the minimarket). East of the kiosk is **Manousodakis,** which
lets antiquated doubles with waterfront views and showers. On the opposite side of the
harbor, **Keramos** offers fancy doubles for 3800dr. Single-seat **canoes** can be rented in
the harbor (300dr per hr., 1500dr per day). **Maistrali,** next to the quay, is the scene of

tourist nightlife, but the pace is more mellow than manic. Christina serves home-con-cocted kahlua cocktails (600dr) and a delicious fresh fruit and yogurt dish (650dr). **Maria and Zambia's Loutro,** is another good restaurant (next to Maria's Minimart). Fishing boats run daily from Loutro to Sweetwater Beach. **Ferry** service connects Loutro with Chora Sfakion (4 per day, 450dr) and Agia Roumeli (3 per day, 850dr).

The path from Agia Roumeli to Loutro (6hr.) and onward to Chora Sfakion (8hr.) wanders along a spectacular strand of coastline and provides views of the Libyan Sea. To pick up the trail in Ag. Roumeli, walk east along the beach over the dry river bed and climb up to the path. After 4km you'll pass a small 16th-century church; the spring under the rocks can replenish your water supply. To continue the hike, stay above the church. A bit farther down the trail, the *taverna* at Liko, **Nikos's Small Paradise,** rents doubles (2700dr). Follow the steep path behind the *taverna;* **Finix** (or "Phoenix"), is about 20 minutes east. Sifis Atithakis and his family are the only permanent residents of this secluded cove and archaeological site (purportedly the spot of St. Paul's first visit to Crete). (Doubles 2600-3100dr. Single-seat canoe rental 300dr per hr.)

The walk from Ag. Roumeli to Loutro has its moments, but the plunge onward to Chora Sfakion is prolonged joy. Pick up the trail in Loutro behind the *taverna* marked "Anapoli-Beach-Chora Sfakion." Just outside town, the trail diverges: one path leads upward to Anapoli and along the coast to Chora Sfakion; the other passes through three coves to **Sweetwater Beach** (a nude beach—the clad are tolerated but pitied for their inhibitions), so named because several natural springs just below the pebble surface provide fresh drinking water. A fishing boat from Chora Sfakion sails to the beach dai-ly at 10:30am and 5pm, returning at 11am and 5:30pm. For a similarly exciting excur-sion from a different direction, hike from Anapoli to Loutro; a bus leaves Chora Sfakion to Anapoli daily at 4pm (250dr). For information about ferries between Chora Sfakion, Loutro, and Agia Roumeli, see Chora Sfakion and Frangokastello.

Chora Sfakion and Frangokastello

The scenic but stoic town of **Chora Sfakion** (or Sfakia) lacks the intimacy and friendliness of Loutro or Paleochora. Its pebbly cove and fishing fleet look tempting from afar, but once close you see that the beach is actually littered with bottles, discard-ed flip-flops, and wedges of half-eaten brie. Chora Sfakion's one strong point is that it is connected by bus to Chania and Rethymnon, and by boat to the entire southwest coast; the village thus serves as a good base from which to explore the region. Because Chora Sfakion lacks the dusty heat that pervades Agia Roumeli, it is an adequate rest-ing spot after the Samaria Gorge hike. (Better, though, to move on to one of the smaller beach towns and avoid the group tours that pile up along the promenade at night.) The **post office** (open Mon.-Sat. 7:30am-2pm) and **OTE** (open Mon.-Fri. 7:30am-3:10pm) both stand on the street behind the waterfront. The **supermarket** is on the same street; stock up here if you plan an extensive tour of more remote beaches. Fruit is a real bar-gain. The **police station** (tel. 912 05) is on the eastern corner of the waterfront near the **bus station** and a small travel office, **Sfakia Tours** (tel. 912 72; open daily 8am-10pm; mopeds 3000dr). The **hospital** (tel. 912 14) is on the road leading out of town above the harbor. The **Hotel Stavris** on the port **changes money** and also houses Sfakia's in-ternational phone. (Open 8am-8pm.) The **postal code** is 73001. The **telephone code** is 0825.

There are plenty of inexpensive accommodations here. **Hotel Xenia** has immaculate rooms. (Doubles 3000dr, with bath 3500dr. Triples 4000dr, with bath 4500dr.) **Lefka Ori** (tel. 912 09), right on the waterfront, rents doubles with small, dark bathrooms for 3000-3500dr. **Pension Sofia** (tel. 912 59) rents singles for 2100dr and doubles for 3100dr (private bath 500dr extra). **Hotel Stavris** (tel. 912 20), near the post office, is a good bet. All rooms come with private bath and balcony. (Singles 2500dr. Doubles 3000dr. Triples 4000dr.) The economically named **Rent Rooms,** on the east end of the back street, is large and cool, with a marble staircase and wrought-iron balconies. (Tri-ples with terrace, 4200dr. Open March-Nov.) **John Braos,** the market owner (tel. 912

06), rents doubles with a view of the harbor. Or head up the hill away from town and you'll find countless "rooms for rent" signs.

Boats from Chora Sfakion travel to Agia Roumeli (5 per day, 1¼hr., 850dr). Most of these routes stop in Loutro (400dr). These ferries run only from April to October; in winter, you can reach Loutro by foot or fishing boat. Always check boat schedules with the ticket office. (Chora Sfakion to Gavdos, Sat. and Sun. 9am, returning at 5pm, 1400dr.) **Caïques** to Sweetwater Beach run twice daily (1100dr). **Buses** from Chora Sfakion go to Plakias (3hr., 500dr) and then to Rethymnon (4hr., 650dr) to meet the ferry. At the same time, a bus leaves for Agia Galini (4hr., 675dr). A bus leaves at 4pm for Anapolis (45min., 300dr). To get to Iraklion from Chora Sfakion, change buses at Rethymnon. Buses to Chania leave at 7am, 11am, 4:30pm, and 6:30pm (900dr). If your ferry is late, don't worry—the buses wait until the boats arrive.

Frangokastello, 12km east of Chora Sfakion, has a sandy beach and an impressive fortress at the shoreline. In 1828 the Turks invaded the region, seizing the fort from the Sfakiates. An aura of enchantment surrounds the edifice. Legend has it that at sunset in mid-May, the Cretan army of Khatsimihalis can be seen dancing around the fort along the water's edge. For the curious who dare to spend a night, several *tavernas* rent doubles, though facilities are somewhat primitive. About 500m west of the castle, try **Koukounaraki Taverna and Pension** (tel. (0825) 920 92), across from the Blue Sky Disco. (Doubles 3300dr. Triples 3700dr. Bath included.) From the downstairs *taverna,* a small path leads to the beach where **Fata Morgana** (tel. 921 98) rents doubles (2500dr, with bath 3000dr). Discreet **camping** along the broad, clean stretch of sand is accepted, as is nude bathing. One **bus** per day runs to Frangokastello from Chania (at 2pm, 850dr), passing through Chora Sfakion and returning to Chania the following morning. The bus from Chora Sfakion to Plakias also passes through Frangokastello.

Paleochora

Once a refuge for the embattled rear guard of the 1960s counterculture, Paleochora has become a central attraction for some along Crete's southern coast. For a few devotees it is the only stop. Just 77km from Chania, Paleochora has all the elements of an idyllic retreat: a wide, sandy beach with a pine grove and excellent impromptu tent sites, one main street with necessities and *tavernas,* and a harbor lined with reasonably priced pensions. Locals claim that Paleochora's only fault is a powerful wind that occasionally plagues the summer.

Paleochora is on a small peninsula. Running north-south through the center of town is **Venizelou St.**, the town's main thoroughfare. It crosses **Kentekaki St.** which leads west to the beach and east to the harbor. Buses to and from Chania (3 per day, 2hr., 1000dr) stop at this intersection.

The **GNTO** (tel. 415 07) is located on Venizelou St., as is a **bank** (open Mon.-Thurs. 8am-2pm, Fri. 8am-1:30pm), and the **OTE** (open Mon.-Fri. 7:30am-3:10pm). Local and international calls can also be made from the kiosk on Venizelou St. The **post office** (open Mon.-Sat. 7:30am-2:15pm, Sun. 9am-1:30pm) is on the beach next to the Galaxy Café. The **Association of Rooms to Let** is based at Paleochora Travel on Venizelou St. (tel. 4121 23). The agents at **Interkreta Travel,** 4 Kontekaki St. (tel. 413 93) sell student air fares, Magic Bus and ferry tickets. **Paleochora Motorent,** around the corner from Interkreta, rents mopeds for 2000dr, and 125cc bikes for 4500dr (open 8:30am-9pm). The **pharmacy** is on Venizelou St. (tel. 414 98; open Mon.-Sat. 8:30am-1:30pm, 5:30-9pm). The **police station** (tel. 411 11) is on Kontekaki, near the quay. Paleochora's **postal code** is 73001; its **telephone code** is 0823.

Right on Venizelou St. is the well-maintained and cozy **Lissos Hotel** (tel. 412 66; refrigerator and washing facilities available; doubles 3500dr, with bath 3700dr). Tucked away, just west of Venizelou St. is **Manousakis,** Daskaloyiani 4 (tel. 414 15). **Village Restaurant** adjacent to the bus stop (tel. 410 51) serves a tasty *mousaka* for 600dr and the New Zealander that works there offers beautiful rooms on the outskirts of Paleochora at **Savas Rooms** (tel. 410 75. Singles 2500dr. Doubles 3500-4000dr. Triples 5000dr). **Rooms Oriental Bay** (tel. 410 76) is the most picturesque alternative: it's right on Rocky Beach as you enter the town (Singles 2500dr. Doubles 3800dr. Triples 4500dr). Downstairs you'll find the cheapest drinks in all Western Crete, and an inexpensive meal on the waterfront (beer 150dr; mixed drinks 300dr; delicious rabbit *stifado* 750dr). There are several markets in the center of the town, on Venizelou St. Taverns that line the road have similar menus at similar prices.

If you walk along the road closest to the harbor, towards Camping Paleochora, you'll find plenty of small hotels. **Camping Paleochora** (tel. 411 20), rests 1½km east of town. (Open March-Oct. 800dr per person. Hot showers and a *taverna.)* The campground is next to the open-air disco, the **Paleochora Club.** (Beer 300dr. Open 11pm-3am.) To reach the campground, walk north on Venizelou, away from the harbor, turn right opposite the Fina gas station, and take your second left on the last paved road before the beach. From there it's 1km to the site.

Six km inland and above Paleochora lies the peaceful town of **Azogizes,** with a lovely view of the promontory and the sea. Here you'll find the 13th-century caves of the 99 Holy Fathers and a museum which features relics of the Turkish occupation dating from 1770. Farther inland, the frescoed churches of Kakodiki date back to the 14th century. These mountain villages can be approached by taking the bus toward Chania. Boats run twice weekly (1950dr) to the nearly deserted island of **Gavdos,** the southernmost point of Europe.

You can make the difficult but satisfying journey to miraculous **Elafonissi,** a small uninhabited island at the southwest corner of Crete. No boats make the crossing, but at low tide the ocean is so shallow that you can wade out to the island. A recent influx of tourists has left this retreat strewn with litter, but the Greek authorities are increasing their efforts to keep it clean. Stock up on provisions ahead of time in Kefali and Vathi; the residents of nearby **Moni Chrisoskalitissis** can provide water and simple lodgings. Buses run from Kastelli to Vathi and as far as Chrisoskalitissis daily (9:30am and 2:30pm, 900dr). From there, a 5km hike leads to a pinkish-white beach. Alternatively, you can hook up with organized excursions leaving from Paleochora or Chania.

Kastelli (Kissamos) and West Coast
ΚΑΣΤΕΛΙ

Consider yourself lucky if your visit to Crete begins in the slow-paced merchant town of Kastelli. The fine fish *tavernas,* immaculate lodgings, and unspoiled landscapes more than compensate for the construction sites and commercialized streets. Kastelli is pleasantly spread out and hence never appears very crowded.

Kastelli is officially referred to as Kissamos to avoid confusion with the classical site of the same name at Pediada, but Cretans continue to use the old Venetian title. Strong summer winds cool down its northwest coast to sweater temperatures. Get to Kastelli via bus from Chania (12 per day, 600dr), or on the twice-weekly ferries from the Peloponnese, leaving Kythera (4hr., 2700dr) and Gythion (7hr.,3000dr).

The heart of Kastelli is **Platia Tzanakaki,** situated between the highway and the waterfront. In the *platia* is the bus station, a ferry ticket office, two hotels, and a local museum. To find the post office and the OTE, head east on the highway. The **post office,** where you can change money, is on the left. (Open Mon.-Fri. 7:30am-2pm.) The **OTE** is in a white building set back from the right hand side of the road, next to a kiosk (open Mon.-Fri. 7:30am-3:10pm). A small **hospital** lies just off the highway after the BP station. On **Skalidi Street,** running parallel to the highway, two streets closer to the water, you'll find food markets, ferry ticket offices, several **banks** (open Mon.-Thurs. 8am-2pm, Fri. 7:45am-3:30pm), and a **pharmacy** (open Tues.-Fri. 8am-10pm). You can catch a rather luxurious cab in the square: Kastelli's fleet consists entirely of silver Mercedes. Several agents let **motorbikes; Daratsianos** (tel. 229 65 and 234 40) is near the post office. Prices start at 1800dr. Kastelli's **postal code** is 73400; the **telephone code** is 0822.

Good clean beach-front rooms are easy to find here. **Kastanaki Rooms** on the beach front is the center for the **Association of Rooms to Let** in Kastelli (tel. 226 10). They'll find you singles for 2500-3000dr, doubles for 3500-4000dr and triples for 4500-5000dr. For sunbathing bliss on the best beach near Kastelli, try **Camping Mithimna** (tel. 314 44) at Drapanias, 5km east of Kastelli and a 1km walk from the road. (750dr per person. 650dr per tent.) To reach the campsite, just get on the bus to Chania and ask to get off at Drapanias (200dr).

The fish *tavernas* by the sea in Teloniou Sq. offer excellent meals and idyllic sunset views. **Makedonas** (tel. 221 84), in the center of town on the waterfront, offers refreshingly large portions at low prices *(mousaka* 600dr). Across the street on a cement pier on the water is **Papadakis** (delicious stuffed tomatoes 500dr). Both restaurants are open daily until midnight. **George Stimadorakis's Fish Restaurant,** nestled in a little harbor just west of the town line on your right as you leave Kastelli, has tasty fish soup (800dr).

In addition to the Chania route, **buses** head to Omalas, where you can hike the Samaria Gorge. Buses leave early in the morning and return from Chora Sfakion at 5pm (round-trip to the gorge, 2700dr). For Magic Bus tickets and rentals, go to the **General Tourist Agency,** on Skalidi St. (tel. 229 80) east of the *platia.* Student discounts on Magic Bus and boat tickets.

If you have a moped or the stamina for the 7km walk uphill and inland from Kastelli, consider the secluded mountain village of **Polirinia.** The road climbs through terraced hills and olive groves, ending at the base of the village. Just before you reach the town, a small paved path on the left leads to the ancient acropolis. At the top, shepherds and an army of sheep stand guard over ancient campfire circles, the **Church of the 99 Martyrs,** and the remnants of Byzantine and Venetian fortifications. Before setting back to Kastelli, relax at the **Restaurant Polirinia;** the veranda here, canopied with grapevines, offers a commanding view of the countryside. **Buses** also travel from Kastelli to Polirinia (Mon., Wed., and Fri. 7am and 2pm, returning 30min. later, 200dr).

West of Kastelli, the creeping onslaught of tourism recedes, leaving isolated villages and deserted beaches. Buses are infrequent and hitching requires patience (especially after mid-day, when goats are more common than cars). Motorbikes make good sense, but the hairpin turns and rocky roads down the far west coast and inland villages require finesse and caution.

The choice beach along the northwest coast, **Falassarna,** lies along the road from Kastelli, just north of Platanos. A paved (later dirt) road will lead you down to the beachfront hamlet of rooms and *tavernas.* Look for the rooms for rent signs on the right as you descend to the beach. **Stathis** (tel. 414 80) has new stucco rooms. (Doubles with bath 3800dr. Full breakfast 500dr per person. Call ahead in summer.) Next door, **Golden Sun** (tel. 414 85) has adequate but institutional rooms. (Doubles 2500dr.) Across the street, the **Sun Side Hotel,** offers a café and rooms to let (doubles 3500dr). The small sandy cove below the hotel is popular with campers, and has a fresh-water spring. North of the hotels and *tavernas* is the acropolis of a Hellenistic city. Along the dirt track to the site and rocky harbor, take a look at the mysterious stone throne. The long beach at the south end attracts serious sunbathers and peace-seeking campers. It's easy to get away from the crowd (which isn't that big to begin with) by taking a left as you face the ocean and walking down the beach for a few minutes. Local fishermen regularly clean their boats in the waters off the west coast. Some of this black goop reappears in clumps on the beach, and may reappear on you. Don't worry—it washes off easily. Scramble around the twisting rock formations, and rinse off in the warm turquoise water.

Two **buses** per day go from Kastelli to Falassarna (at 10am and 5pm, returning at 10:30am and 5:30pm, 45min., 330dr) and from Cohania to Falassarna (at 8:30am and 3:30pm, 700dr). You can also take a bus to Platanos and then walk another 5km along the road to the beach.

Solitude awaits 15km south of Falassarna at the secluded fishing and farming village of **Sfinari.** The beach here is narrow, rocky, and almost deserted. Tomato- and banana-growing greenhouses run all along the beach and down the coast. The seaside restaurant in this windy coastal town, **Diolinis** (open at 9am), has a symbiotic arrangement with foreign visitors: you can camp for free behind the *taverna* and use the toilets and showers, if you feed yourself at the restaurant or the small store in Sfinari. Diolinis is a five-minute walk down the beach to the left, out of sight from the road. Pleasant doubles are available at the **Fidias Restaurant** (tel. 225 89), at the turn-off for the beach (1200dr per person); you can try **Antonios Theodrakis** (tel. 221 53), who also runs a restaurant (doubles 2800dr). Both places are within a 20-minute walk from the beach. One **bus** for Sfinari leaves Kastelli Mon.-Fri. at 2pm (45 min., 400dr), and returns at 7am Mon.-Fri., and 3pm Sat.-Sun. and Tues.-Thurs. The bus trip—more fun than a Disney World ride—will take you along tortuous mountain roads ablaze with pink blossoms. From Sfinari, the road heads inland until it reaches **Kambos,** perched atop a mountain stream. Modest rooms are available as you come into town, but go around the bend until reaching **Lefteris Hartzoulakis** (tel. 414 45), who will drive you the 3km to the beach if you stay at his hotel/café. (Singles with precambrian stone floors 2600dr.)

Eastern Crete

The coastal highway east of Iraklion reveals dreamy beaches, cool blue waters, and an instant tourist industry. Vathiano Kambos, Kokkini Hani and Gournes all line the highway with beautiful hotels, rooms to let on overcrowded and soon-to-be-overcrowded beaches.

Hersonissos

This port town, 26km east of Iraklion, is wholly free of ancient sites, monasteries, or Cretan village culture. Over 40 bars, discos and nightclubs cluster in a 500m radius, and the beach is never far away. There is one main road in Limenas Hersonissou (usually referred to simply as Hersonissos), with perpendicular lanes that lead to the beach and upper parts of the town.

Orientation and Practical Information

Tourist Police: 4 Minoas St. (tel. 222 22, 221 00), in the police station. Some information on Hersonissos. Open daily 9am-2:30pm and 5pm-9pm.

Travel Office: Zakros Tours on Main St. (tel. 221 37). Open daily 9am-9pm. **Mareland Travel** at 13 Minoas St. (tel. 228 68), up the street from the police station. Open daily 9am-1:30pm, 4:30pm-9:30pm. Both provide all necessary tourist services.

Currency Exchange: There are several banks on Main St. that change money (8:30am-2pm). The tourist offices also exchange money.

Post Office: 2 Eleftherias St., perpendicular to Main St., next to a supermarket. Follow the signs. Open Mon.-Fri. 8:30am-2:30pm, and Saturdays during peak season. **Postal Code:** 70014.

OTE: Behind the town office ("Koinotiko Yrafio") on Eleftherias St., up the street from the post office. Open Mon.-Fri. 8am-2pm. During peak season open daily 8am-11pm. **Telephone Code:** 0897.

Buses: There are several bus stops in Hersonissos but no central bus station. Buses run in both directions (east and west) every 30min. Service to Iraklion (240dr), Malia (220dr), Agios Nikolaos (660dr), Sitia (760dr) and Ierapetra (1160dr).

Car and Motorbike Rental: There are several agencies on Main St. **George's Motor** (tel. 223 41) offers both motorbikes and cars at a 10% discount for *Let's Go* users. Open daily 8:30am-10:30pm.

Pharmacies: Several pharmacies on Main St., one of which is open 24 hrs. Consult the sign on the door of any of the pharmacies.

Hospital: next to Evangelistria Church near the waterfront (tel. 220 42). Open daily 9am-2pm and for emergencies.

Police: 4 Minoas St. (tel. 222 22, 221 00), same address as Tourist Police.

Emergency: tel. 100.

Accommodations

Hersonissos's digs can be expensive and hard to come by. Tour companies book a majority of the rooms for the entire season. Before arriving, consult Iraklion's Rooms to Let Association (see Iraklion).

Youth Hostel (HI/IYHF): Plaka-Drapanos (tel. 232 82). Cheap beds (800dr) and fun owners. No curfew.

Selena Pension, off Main St. Follow the signs. Immaculate rooms with bathroom. Doubles 3800dr.

Camping: Camping Hersonissos, Anisara (tel. 229 02), 500dr per person. **Camping Caravan,** Limenas, (tel. 220 25), 500dr. Right by Main St. Open March-Oct.

Food and Entertainment

The Hersonissos waterfront sports the usual assortment of restaurants serving "traditional Greek food." If bigger is better, the largest is **Acropolis Restaurant** at the center of the waterfront (mixed fish 950dr). The best deal is **Selena Restaurant**, beneath Selena Pension (Greek salad 300dr, *kalamari* 500dr).

Nightlife is what Hersonissos is all about. The bars and discos that line Main St. and the Paraliakos offer every kind of atmosphere, music, and drink imaginable. A few bars to start the evening are the **Black Cactus, Quarto,** and **Prince,** all on Main St. As the night progresses, hit the bars on Paraliakos and on the waterfront. Bars generally serve beer for 300dr. The dance floors of **Disco 99, Laluna,** or **On the Rox** should complete your evening of hedonism. During the day, most people wake up around noon and head to the beaches to rest up for another night out on the town.

Malia ΜΑΛΙΑ

Malia, 15km east of Hersonissos, shares that town's *raison d'être*. Package tours swarm the hotels, the shops sell primarily junk, and deep-fried sun-bathers saturate the beach. Oh, there are some Minoan sites here, too.

Orientation and Practical Information

Buses connect Malia with Iraklion via Hersonissus (every 30min., 1hr., 460dr); Agios Nikolaos (29 per day, 40min., 460dr); and Lassithi (8:45am, returning at 2pm, 1½hr., 800dr).

The main road from Iraklion should satisfy most practical needs, while the path down to the beach, with the discos and watering holes, panders to the primal. The **post office** lies just off the main street toward Iraklion, behind the church. (Open Mon.-Fri. 7:30am-2pm.) The **Bank of Crete** is on Beach Rd., the main road. (Open Mon.-Thurs. 8am-2pm, Fri. 8am-1:30pm.) All the luxury hotels and most travel agencies will change money after hours. The **OTE** is on the main road, about 300m from Malia's center toward Iraklion. (Open Mon.-Fri. 7:30am-3pm.) Dr. James Hodge (tel. 313 32) runs a **clinic** near the bank. (Open 8:30am-1pm and 5:30-8:30pm.) In an after-hours **emergency,** call 712 65. There's a **laundromat** next to the Malia Holidays Hotel. (Open 9am-8pm. Wash and dry 2600dr.) **Taxis** idle at the intersection of the main road and the beach path. Malia's **postal code** is 70002; its **telephone code** is 0897.

Finding reasonably priced rooms in Malia is a challenge. Your best bet is the **HI/IYHF Youth Hostel,** 200m past the OTE on the way to Iraklion. When you see the Mobil Station on the right, turn around and head back toward Iraklion; the hostel will be on your left. (No curfew, 800dr. Bring super-duper mosquito repellent.) If you'd rather stay closer to the beach, wait in the middle of town for one of the *dhomatia* to make you an offer you can't refuse. Unmarked private homes are your best bet. One such pension is **Rooms Nikos Fanourakis** (not to be confused with Hotel Fanourakis),

#2 Grevenon. Go up Beach Rd. and take a left where the road ends. Stuffy but clean doubles go for 2800dr, triples for 3600dr. **Pension Aspasia** (tel. 312 90), off 25th Martiou St., has cheap, but shabby rooms (doubles 3300dr; triples 4700dr). **Camping Sissi,** (tel. 713 61) is 12km to the east on an uncrowded stone beach with grassy tent-pitches. (500dr per person, tents 450dr, cars 300dr.)

Chowing down in Malia is cheap compared with the rest of Crete. Many places on the Paraliakos (Beach Rd.) serve an English breakfast for 300dr. All of the restaurants offer special combination dinners: salad, a main course (typically *mousaka,* lasagne, or chicken), and coffee or metaxa brandy for under 1000dr.

Sights and Entertainment

The **Minoan Palace** at Malia, one of the three great cities of Minoan Crete, lacks the labyrinthine architecture and magnificent interior decoration of Knossos and Phaestos, but is nonetheless imposing. First built around 1900 BCE, the palace was destroyed in 1650 BCE, rebuilt on an even more impressive scale, but then destroyed again around 1450 BCE. Notice the **Hall of Columns** on the north side of the large central courtyard, incomprehensibly named for the six columns supporting the roof. The *loggia,* the raised chamber on the west side, was used for state ceremonies.

West of the *loggia* are the palace's living quarters and archives. Northwest of the *loggia* and main site slumbers the **Hypostyle Crypt,** believed to have been a social center for Malia's intelligentsia. Follow the road to Agios Nikolaos 3km to the east and turn left toward the sea, or walk along the beach and then 1km through the fields. (Open Tues.-Sun. 8:30am-3pm. Admission 400dr, students 200dr.) You can freelance camp near the beach behind the site as long as you clean up after yourself.

Predictably, the Parakliakos is the center of Malia's nightlife. It's a zoo. Start the pub crawl at the **Picadilly Pub** with a cheap brew. Brits hang out in Malia's only all-night pub, **Gallia,** on the road to Iraklion, about 15 minutes past the Mobil Station. Also try **Cloud 9, George's Dancing Bar,** and the **London Pub. Flash Flash** is the flashiest of them all. **Cosmos** plays acid-house and hip-hop. **Aria** is the largest disco in Crete—enough said.

Lassithi Plateau ΚΑΜΠΟΣ ΛΑΣΣΗΘΗ

Bypassing much of the unsightly northern coastline, the inland route to Agios Nikolaos traverses the Lassithi Plateau, ringed by steep mountains. The plain is a rural area laden with whitewashed buildings, exhausted donkeys, and villagers husbanding their fields. The residents of the region have harnessed the plain's persistent breezes with thousands of wind-powered water pumps. In recent years, electric pumps have supplemented this form of irrigation, but windmills still bristle on the horizon.

In harvesting season (July-Aug.), wheat leans on church porches, lies stacked in the fields, and covers overburdened donkeys so that you can only see their heads. Unless you have access to wheels, or plan to visit only one town, Lassithi is not a good choice for a daytrip. You may find yourself stranded for hours in a town due to the infrequency of bus service.

If you're coming from Iraklion, take the coastal road 8km past Gournes, and then turn right on the road to Kastelli (not the one on the west coast). After about 6km the road forks right to Kastelli; stay left, heading toward **Potamies.** Stand akimbo and ogle the giant plane tree in the center of Potamies. It takes 12 men to wrap their arms around the trunk, but you have to get the villagers really drunk to do it. Bypassing Krassi, the main road winds around mountain ridges with tibia-fracturing panoramas. The road continues to climb among the abandoned stone windmills of the Seli Ambelou pass, finally descending into the Lassithi Plateau. No matter which route you take, bring a jacket—it's real nippy here.

Once you enter the plain, the first and only "major" town you pass through is **Tzermiado,** capital of the sub-province of Lassithi, with a few gift shops and three hotel-restaurants catering to day trippers. In the evening, Tzermiado returns to its own peaceful ways, with the male population—divided among its 10 or so cafés—drinking, arguing, and playing backgammon. On the road to Agios Nikolaos, past the **pharmacy** (open Tues., Thurs., Sat. 9am-2pm and 5:30-10pm; Wed., Fri., Sun. 9am-2pm), you'll find the **Hotel Kourites** (tel. 221 94; doubles 5000dr, triples 6000dr; breakfast and private bath included). The **Hotel Lassithi** is across the street (tel. 221 94; doubles 3800dr, triples 4800dr). The **Kronio Restaurant** offers daily vegetarian dishes. (Open 7:30am-11pm.) The **post office** (open Mon.-Fri. 7:30am-3pm) is next to the Kronio Restaurant. The **OTE** (open Mon.-Fri. 7:30am-3:10pm) is a few doors down from the Kronio, on the main street to the right. Tzermiado's **postal code** is 72052; the **telephone code** is 0844.

An insignificant zit compared to the speluncar wart of Dikteon Cave at Psychro, the **Kronion Cave** merits a quick side trip. Clear signs in Tzermiado will direct you to the grotto (2km away), the mythical home of Kronos and Rhea, parents of Zeus. The last kilometer is badly marked and manageable only on foot. Stay on the widest people path—don't stray onto the numerous goat paths, and don't forget a flashlight.

A right fork at the church 2km southeast of Tzermiado will take you to **Agios Konstantinos,** where rooms are available behind most of the shops (doubles 2500-3500dr). **Agios Georgios,** 2km farther down the same road, is home to a **folklore museum,** whose human models and stuffed fowl are more amusing than edifying. (Open April-Oct. 10am-4pm; admission 200dr.) The **Dias Hotel** (tel. 312 07) rents doubles for 4000dr (showers 200dr).

The village of **Psychro** caters to afternoon tourists but retains its rural charm. The only hotel in the village, the **Dikteon Andron** (no phone), charges 1800dr per person for small rooms with cot-like beds. Look for the sign near the church on the main road. One kilometer past Psychro is the **Dikteon Cave.** Legend has it that Zeus's father, Kronos, ate his newborn children here after hearing a prophecy that one of them would dethrone him. By the time Rhea gave birth to Zeus, she was stuck in a cave, and she handed Kronos a tasty, swaddled stone to eat in his place, and hid the baby. Zeus emerged to kill his father and free his five older brothers and sisters, who had luckily survived in Kronos's stomach. When archaeologists excavated the cave at the beginning of this century, they found hundreds of Minoan artifacts crammed into its ribbed stalactites. Many of these are displayed at Iraklion's Archaeological Museum.

Arthur Evans (of Knossos fame) excavated this spot and, in a wave of misguided enthusiasm, blew apart the entrance. Bring a flashlight: candles sold at the site create a great aura, but are of negligible use. If you get to the cave by 9:30am or after 3pm you should be able to explore it without the distraction of tour groups. The guides who hover around the base of the path seldom justify their fee (600dr). (Cave officially open 8am-6pm. Admission 200dr, students 100dr.)

Buses to Lassithi leave from: Iraklion via Tzermiado and Psychro (2-3 per day, 2hr., 950dr); Elounda and Agios Nikolaos (2 per day, 2hr., 750dr); and Malia (1 per day, 1½hr., 800dr).

Agios Nikolaos ΑΓΙΟΣ ΝΙΚΟΛΑΟΣ

The closest thing to indigenous culture in Agios Nikolaos is the early-morning fishermen mending their yellowing nets. With convenient beaches, pulsating nightlife, and twin waterfronts for primo people-watching, Agios Nikolaos is a choice destination for both one-stop holiday makers and aspiring souls eager to explore the entire eastern half of Crete. There are few bargains in Agios Nikolaos and its satellite beach towns, but for those hungry for nocturnal play, this place will seem like home. And if you wander the streets in the daytime, you'll find some of the friendliest people on Crete: Agios Nikolaos may be the "big city" of eastern Crete, but somehow this overgrown hamlet manages to retain the spirit and feel of a humble town.

Orientation and Practical Information

It's easy to get around Ag. Nikolaos—the center of town is actually a small peninsula, with beaches on three sides and most services, hotels, restaurants, and discos in the middle. If you've just gotten off the bus, walk to the end of the block (with your right side to the terminal), and take your first right. Follow **Venizelou St.** to the monument, where it leads into **Roussou Koundourou.** The street then heads downhill to the harbor, where the tourist information office rests to the left, across the bridge. When getting around the city, do your best not to confuse R. Koundourou, I. Koundourou, and S. Koundourou St.

Agios Nikolaos Tourist Information Office: 22 S. Koundourou St. (tel. 223 57), at the bridge between the lake and the port. Knowledgeable staff will arrange accommodations. Messages, currency exchange, bus and boat schedules, and a free brochure with town map and practical information. Open daily 8:30am-9:30pm.

Currency Exchange: National Bank of Greece (tel. 288 55) at the top of R. Koundourou St., near Venizelou Sq. Open for exchange Mon.-Thurs. 8am-2pm and 6-7:45pm, Fri. 8am-1:30pm, Sat. 9-11:45am. At night, you can change money at the tourist office or most hotels and travel agencies for close to the bank rate.

Post Office: #9 28th Octovriou St. (tel. 222 76). Open Mon.-Sat. 7:30am-2pm. **Postal Code:** 72100.

OTE: Tel. 280 99, corner of 25 Martiou and K. Sfakianaki St. 3 blocks east of the lake. Open 6am-midnight; Nov.-May 6am-10:30pm. **Telephone Code:** 0841.

Olympic Airways: 20 Plastira St. (tel. 220 33), overlooking the lake. Open Mon.-Sat. 8am-3:30pm. Closest airports are at Iraklion and Sitia.

Bus Station: Atlandithos Sq. (tel. 222 34), on the opposite side of town from the harbor. To: Iraklion (30 per day, 1½hr., 900dr); Malia (31 per day, 40min., 440dr); Lassithi (2 per day, 2hr., 750dr); Ierapetra (12 per day, 1hr., 480dr); Sitia (8 per day, 2hr., 1000dr); and Kritsa (15 per day, 15min., 150dr). Buses to Elounda (15 per day, 20min., 150dr) and Plaka (6 per day, 40min., 200dr) leave from the stop opposite the tourist office.

Ferries: Massaros, 29 R. Koundourou St. (tel. 222 67). Sells all tickets for departures from Ag. Nikolaos and most of Crete. Open 8:30am-2:30pm and 5-10pm. To: the Dodecanese, Amorgos, Paros, and Piraeus (Wed.); Kassos, Karpathos, Halki, and Rhodes (Sat.); Arafi, Santorini, Folegandros, Milos, Sikinos, and Piraeus (Sun.).

Taxi: Tel. 240 00. Taxis wait along the lake and in Venizelou Sq.

Car Rental: Economy Car Hire, 15 S. Koundourou St. (tel. 289 88); also an office at 5 K. Sfakianaki St. Fiat 127 7000dr, 100km and insurance included.

Motorbike Rental: Adonis, on S. Koundourou, near the Perikleous St. intersection, rents 50cc mopeds for 3000dr, 100ccs for 4000dr, insurance included. (Open daily 8am-8pm.) **Ferryman Café,** on the bridge, rents Yamaha automatics for 2800dr. There are lots of agencies—shop around and bargain.

English Bookstores: Next to Economy Cart Hire. Good selection of books and magazines to buy or swap.

Pharmacy: At the top of R. Koundourou St. Open daily 8:30am-2pm and 5-8:30pm.

Hospital: Paleologou St. (tel. 223 69), at the northern end of town. From the lake, walk up Paleologou St., 1 block past the museum.

Tourist Police: Tel. 223 21, at the foot of the stairs, on the southern corner of the lake on Paleologou St. Maps of the town, bus and boat schedules, and a list of accommodations. Open daily 7:30am-2pm; reduced hours in off-season.

Police: Tel. 223 38, on Latouse St., above the lake.

Emergency: Tel. 100.

Accommodations and Food

As a result of Ag. Nikolaos's popularity, many of the better hotels are booked months in advance by European tour groups, and the few cheap places in town have a slow turnover rate. Neighboring tourist beach resorts have been similarly affected. Even the youth hostel and pensions fill up occasionally. If you plan to stay in town, arrive early in the day or make reservations.

The Green House, 15 Modatsou St. (tel. 220 25). From the tourist office, find and turn left onto R. Koudourou, left again onto Iroon Polytechniou, and right onto Modatsou. Relax in the shady, tangled garden. If you're lucky, you'll get homemade Italian ice from the multilingual proprietors. Doubles 2850dr.

Argiro Pension, 1 Solonos St. (tel. 287 07). From the tourist office, walk up 25th Martiou and go left onto Manousogianaki. After 4 blocks, go right onto Solonos. Unsullied rooms in a huge, stately old house with a serene, jasmine-scented garden. Quiet, yet very close to town. Communal fridge. Doubles 3000dr, with bath 3500dr. Triples 3700dr, with bath 4000dr.

Christodoulakis Pension, 7 Stratigou Koraka St. (tel. 225 25). Next door to the youth hostel. Spotless rooms, excellent location, and friendly proprietors. Kitchen facilities. Doubles 2800dr. Triples 3000dr.

Pension Perla, 4 Salaminos St. (tel. 233 79). Big rooms, some with balconies and ocean views. Comfortable TV lounge. Singles 2200dr. Doubles 2500dr, with bath 3000dr. Triples 2500dr.

Food is dear in Ag. Nikolaos. Most restaurants lie in wait around the town's harbor, immediately west along the waterfront, or on the beach at the east end of town. Surprisingly, the restaurants without views of the sea cost as much as the waterfront spots. There are plenty of breezy eateries along the "bottomless" lake. If you don't mind slow service, go to **Stelio's,** at the bridge, for a dazzling harborside view and excellent *tzatziki* (200dr). Next door at the **Actaion,** fish dishes start at 1000dr. (Open 10am-11pm.) **Haris,** on the east side of the waterfront, is the least touristed of the best harbor restaurants. (Fried cheese 450dr. Open noon-3am.) For those craving more familiar cuisine, there are plenty of Chinese restaurants. For a cheap meal, visit the fast-food joints along 25th Martiou, R. Koundourou, and 28th Octovriou. Better than chow-chow but a far cry from Chao chow, **Ciao-Ciao Pizza,** #4 25th Martiou St., offers good pizza by the slice (250dr), mediocre wine by the glass (200dr), and a few places to sit by the counter. (Open noon-3am.)

Sights and Entertainment

The town's pole star, no doubt, is its scenic waterfront locale. The "bottomless" lake, **Xepatomeni** (actually 64m deep), is near the tourist office. Artemis and Athena, according to legend, bathed here. In 1867, the regional governor dug a canal linking the lake with the sea, creating a perpetual flushing mechanism. Today, cafés surround the shores and pleasure-boats line the dock. The town's three beaches are all within easy walking distance of the main harbor. You can sunbathe on the concrete piers which jut out from S. Koundarou St. Skip the municipal beach and head to one of the finer spots—catch an hourly bus headed to Ierapetra or Sitia and get off at **Almiros Beach,** 2km east of Agios Nikolaos. Local legend has it that fairies bathe in the fresh springs around Almiros. The sandy beach at **Kalo Chorio,** 10km farther along the same road, is less crowded, but dirtier and utterly devoid of the wee folk. Get off the bus at the Kavos Taverna.

For more cerebral pursuits, visit one of Ag. Nikolaos's two museums, or see if anything's playing at the theater on M. Sfakianaki St. The **Archaeological Museum** (tel. 249 42) houses a modest collection of Minoan artifacts from the Lassithi area; it's just outside the center of town, a few blocks down the road to Iraklion. (Open Tues.-Sun. 8:30am-3pm. Admission 300dr, students 150dr.) The **Folk Art Museum,** in the tourist office's building, vaunts a collection of weavings and fine embroidered clothes. (Open Sun.-Fri. 9:30am-1:30pm and 5-9pm. Admission 200dr; free on Sun.) For inexpensive clothes and local color in an otherwise tourist-oriented town, visit the weekly **market** on Ethnikis Antistaseos St., next to the lake. (Open Wed. 7am-noon.) The feast day of St. Nicholas (Dec. 6) is heartily celebrated by local residents. Around Easter, locals burn an effigy of Judas, encirled by hundreds of candles, in the harbor.

For nightlife, stroll around the harbor on I. Koundourou St., or walk up 25th Martiou St. The **Tequila Bar** and **Sorrento Bar** on the waterfront are good places to warm up before hitting the dance floors. (beer 300dr.) For a bit of "class," hit **Charlie Chan's** nightclub, further down on the waterfront (beer 400dr, mixed drinks 700dr).

Daytrips Near Agios Nikolaos

Although only 9km from the relatively upscale port of Ag. Nikolaos, the hilltop village of **Kritsa** seems worlds apart. Accomodations are scarce, but Kritsa offers a wonderful escape, if only for a daytrip. Every balcony and rooftop is trimmed with vines and ripening fruit; under their shade, women weave blankets and embroider blouses. Many of the homemade crafts are embarrassingly cheap. Be choosy when buying, however, as not every item is produced locally. The unloading buses of tourists are an unfortunate reminder of your proximity to Ag. Nikolaos, but the buses come only for a short time; nightfall returns serenity to the town.

The **post office** is above the *platia* to the right. (Open Mon.-Sat. 7:30am-2pm, Sun. 9am-1:30pm.) An **international phone** is in Koutoulakis Snack Bar in the square. (Open 7am-9pm.) **Buses** run hourly between Ag. Nikolaos and Kritsa (15 per day, 30min., 110dr). In summer, afternoon buses to Kritsa fill up quickly; arrive early. Kritsa's **postal code** is 72051; its **telephone code** is 0841.

One km before Kritsa on the road from Ag. Nikolaos, Crete's Byzantine treasure, the **Panagia Kera,** honors the Dormition of the Virgin. The interior of the domed church is adorned with a patchwork of smoky 14th-century paintings in the central nave, and 15th-century Byzantine frescoes in the adjoining wings. (Open Mon.-Sat. 9am-3pm, Sun. 9am-2pm. Admission 300dr, students 200dr; free on Sundays.) Manolis Borboudakis's small but invaluable guidebook to the church is sold at the gift shop next door (800dr). Just below town is the turn-off for the 3km dirt road to the classical ruins at **Lato,** where wind whistles down a staircase and through an 8th-century BCE temple with a sacrificial altar.

With an attractive port and plenty of nearby beaches, **Elounda** (10km north of Agios Nikolaos) swells with hotels, restaurants, and holiday villas. As with Krista, accomodations are hard to find, but a daytrip is recommended. Elounda's **post office** is in the main square. (Open Mon.-Sat. 7:30am-2pm, Sun. 9am-1:30pm.) The **OTE** is at the north end of the waterfront. (Open Mon.-Sat. 7:30am-2pm, Sun. 9am-1:30pm.) In the *platia,* **The Book Shop** (tel. 416 41) has an international phone, and a moderate selection of foreign newspapers and guide books. (Open daily 9am-11pm.) The **pharmacy** (tel. 413 08), is in Elounda Sq. (Open Mon.-Sat. 8:30am-1:30pm and 5-9:30pm, Sun. 8:30am-1:30pm.) The town **doctor** (tel. 415 63 or 414 68) is around the corner. You'll find the **National Bank of Greece** to the right of the main square. (Open Mon.-Thurs. 9am-noon, Fri. 9-11:30am.) The **police** (tel. 413 48) are based one block behind the main square to the left of the post office. You can rent motorbikes (1500dr per day) at **Elounda Travel and Rent-A-Car** (tel. 413 33), at the south end of the harbor; they also have Suzuki Altos (14,100dr for 3 days, unlimited mileage), and provide general tourist information. Fifteen **buses** per day roll by the remarkable sea and sand scenery between Agios Nikolaos and Elounda. Elounda's **postal code** is 72053; its **telephone code** is 0841. Restaurants are generally out of the budget traveler's range, but many supermarkets, bakeries, and pita stands are scattered along the waterfront.

Plaka, a fishing village with three desolate rock beaches, lies 5km beyond Elounda. Several *tavernas* have rooms to let; try **Maria's** (tel. 413 19), at the north end of town. (Open year-round. Doubles 4000dr. Triples 4500dr.) **Buses** run every other hour from Agios Nikolaos to Plaka, stopping in Elounda (200dr). Fishing boats from Plaka go to Spinalonga on demand (1000dr).

On the main road to Iraklion, a small turn-off leads to the beach communities of **Sisi** and **Milatos.** The tiny harbor of Sisi has several good *tavernas* and a swimming cove to the east. **Camping Sisi** (tel. 713 61) has a sea-water swimming pool and *taverna.* (500dr per person. Small tents 450dr. Cars 300dr.) The family-run **Arismaris,** on the main road from the harbor, serves inexpensive, traditional Cretan dishes. (Open 7pm-11pm.) Buses leave daily for Neapoli (at 7am), Milatos (at 9:45am and 4pm), and Iraklion (at 7am, 10:20am, and 4:20pm).

The ruins of the ancient Minoan town of **Gournia** are 19km south of Agios Nikolaos. On a hill just 50m from the highway, a maze of walls hems in an infinity of tiny cottages. The cobbled quarter was once the home of carpenters, smiths, and potters. The palace quarters overlook the *agora* to the south, and the well-constructed south wall was probably used as a platform for official declarations. The finds from Gournia are now housed in the Iraklion Museum. (Open Tues.-Sun. 8:30am-3pm. Free.) Just 3km farther lounges the seaside retreat of **Pahia Ammos,** a town with more garbage than sand. Several pensions offer doubles starting at 3700dr. Try the **Zeus** (tel. 932 89) in the center of the village. (Doubles 3900dr.)

Ierapetra ΙΕΡΑΠΕΤΡΑ

Ierapetra tries hard to be a resort town but hasn't quite mastered the complex technique. The drab restaurants blast music, and the shops sell leggings with "Ierapetra" written in bold letters down the side, yet with all these valiant efforts, the entire town still shuts down for siesta. Although most of the hotels are prefab monstrosities, Ierapetra's proximity to unspoiled beaches and villages means a slow but steady influx of the baked and bored.

Ierapetra's star attraction is its remote island, **Chrisi,** eight nautical miles away from the mainland. The one small ferry that goes there leaves at 10:15am and returns at 5pm. Free from residents, stores and crowds, Chrisi is a simple, magnificent showcase of nature. Most of Ierapetra's services are located on the streets running parallel to the waterfront. The **tourist office** (tel. 286 58), on the waterfront at the foot of Kostoula St., offers town maps, bus schedules, and numerous pamphlets, including a list of all the campgrounds in Greece and their facilities. (Open June-Sept., Mon.-Fri. 9am-9pm, Sat.-Sun. 9am-1pm and 4-8pm.) The **bus station** is on Lasthenous St. To get to the waterfront from there, head past the palm tree and you'll see signs for the beach. The **Ionian Bank,** on Venizelou Sq., changes currency (open Mon.-Thurs. 8am-2pm, Fri. 7:45am-1:30pm). In Kothri Sq., 5 blocks west of the bus station, you'll find the **post office,** 1 Stilianou Hota St. (Open Mon.-Sat. 7:30am-8pm.) The **OTE** is at 25 Koraka St., 3 blocks from the water. (Open Mon.-Sat. 7:30am-10pm, Sun. 9am-2pm and 5-10pm.) Opposite the OTE, **Panelinios Travel Agency** (tel. 287 10) sells ANEK-line boat tickets. (Open 7am-2pm and 6-9pm.) Motorized transportation in Ierapetra can be expensive to rent; for daytrips, try **Rena Motorbike Rental,** 18 Stilianou Hota St. (tel. 284 18; bikes 1500dr per day; open 8am-8pm). The **hospital** (tel. 222 52) and the **police** (tel. 225 60) are on the water near the tourist office. **Taxis** line up in Venizelou Sq. Ierapetra's **postal code** is 72200; its **telephone code** is 0842.

For accommodations, try **Cretan Villa,** 16 Lakerda St. (tel. 285 22), northeast of Venizelou Sq. The drab exterior of the 200-year-old building hides a cool, green garden surrounded by high-ceilinged rooms. (Doubles 3500dr. Triples 4500dr.) Nikos's **Rooms for Rent,** one block from the bus station at 27 Lasthenous, offers modern rooms with baths and huge balconies. (Singles 3000dr. Doubles 3800.) Two neighboring campgrounds, **Ierapetra** (tel. 613 51), and the new **Koutsounari** (tel. 612 13), 9km away on the coastal road to Sitia, both charge 500dr per person, 400dr per tent. Each has a restaurant, bar, and beach. Take the bus to Sitia via Makri Gialo (7 per day) and ask to be let off at the campgrounds.

Nearly all of Ierapetra's restaurants lie along the waterfront, offering generic fare at identical prices. Most of the town's shops and grocery stores are one block up from the waterfront on Kountourioti St (open 9am-2pm and 5pm-10pm). There are loads of historical sights in Ierapetra; unfortunately, you can't go into any of them. The 13th-century **Venetian Fortress,** slowly sinking into the sea, has been closed indefinitely. Locals will direct you to **Napoleon's House,** in the old town. According to tradition, the French commander spent the night there on June 26, 1798, en route to Egypt to battle the Mamluks. The restored **Venetian fortress** *(Kales)* standing at the extreme southern end of the old harbor, was begun sometime in the early 13th century. Also in the old town is a **mosque** and an **Ottoman fountain** built near the end of the 19th century. Ierapetra's **Archaeological Museum,** on the waterfront, has a small collection of Minoan and classical artifacts from the southern coast. (Open Tues.-Sun. 9am-3pm. Admission 400dr, students 200dr; free on Sun.)

Near Ierapetra

Several villages with swimming coves and pensions dot the bleak, rugged coastline of the Libyan Sea on either side of Ierapetra. The farther east you go, the more expensive it gets. The closest, cheapest hideaway is **Agia Fotia**, on a badly marked dirt road off the coastal route to Sitia. If you make the 18km trip east from Ierapetra by moped, beware of treacherous hairpin turns.

Rooms in Agia Fotia's only pension go for about 1500dr per person; ask at the restaurant. Many people freelance camp on the beach. Nearby **Gallini** has a restaurant and a pension. (Doubles 1700dr.) Farther east is the growing resort town of **Makrigiolas,** with a **bank.** The beaches here slope so gradually that you can wade out 50-100m before you even get your knees wet. A handful of pensions rent doubles for 3500-3900dr, depending on the length of your stay and the demand. About 3km from Makrgiolas, where the main road to Sitia turns away from the sea, a dirt road continues along the ocean for 13km to **Goudouras,** where the town's *taverna* fills campers' stomachs.

Some pleasant villages lie west of Ierapetra. Quiet and relatively untainted by tourism, **Myrtos** has a long beach with hot black sand. Buses stop at Myrtos from Ierapetra (7 per day) and from Iraklion via Viannos (2 per day). The town has inexpensive food, a few pensions (doubles start at 3000dr), and one hotel, the **Myrtos** (tel. 512 15; doubles with baths 3600dr). Three km east of Myrtos is the Early Bronze-Age settlement of **Fournou Korifhi,** which dates back to 2500 BCE.

The coast to the west of Myrtos leads to the pseudo-secluded village of **Arvi**, which, despite its inaccessibility, grows bloated with tourists during the summer. It offers a pleasant beach and a monastery, both of which can be reached on foot at the bottom of the gorge (20min.). Buses run from Ierapetra to Viannos, 10km from Arvi (2 per day, 1hr., 600dr); you can walk or hitch from there. Buses from the village of Amiras, near Viannos, journey there at 10am and 4:30pm. The **Alkion** restaurant rents clean doubles for 3900dr; the **Pension Gorgona** (tel. 312 11) has slightly nicer rooms at slightly lower prices. (Singles 3100dr. Doubles 3800dr. Triples 4300dr.) Both have superb views of the Libyan Sea. A word of caution—*don't* sleep on the beaches at Myrtos or Arvi; there have been reports of sexual harassment of both men and women.

Sitia ΣΗΤΕΙΑ

A scenic drive on coastal and mountain roads from Ag. Nikolaos leads to Sitia, an etherized port town. The wave of tourism that has engulfed the coast from Iraklion to Ag. Nikolaos slows to a trickle before Sitia, leaving visitors a fishing town we can call old-fashioned without losing our integrity. Use Sitia as your base for exploring Crete's eastern coast, including Vai, the Toplou Monastery, and Kato Zakros.

Orientation and Practical Information

To get to the center of the waterfront from the bus station, head for the sign for Vai and Kato Zakros, and bear left. Dimokritou and Venizelou intersect with the waterfront at the *platia,* where you will find a small palm tree traffic island, Sitia's restaurant strip, and several kiosks.

Tourist Police: 24 Mysonos St. (tel. 242 00).

Currency Exchange: National Bank of Greece, in Venizelou Sq. Open Mon.-Thurs. 8am-2pm, Fri. 8am-1:30pm. **Travel Agencies,** on the waterfront, are convenient during evenings and weekends.

Post Office: Main branch, 2 Ethnikis Antistasis St (tel. 222 83). From the bus station, walk south and follow the road around to the right. Open Mon.-Fri. 7:30am-2pm. Smaller office on Dimokritou St. (tel. 223 22), off the main square. Open Mon.-Fri. 7:30am-8pm, Sat. 7:30am-2pm, Sun. 9am-1:30pm. **Postal Code:** 72300.

OTE: 22 Sifis St. Go to the main square on the waterfront, turn inland at the National Bank, and walk uphill 2 blocks. Open Mon.-Sat. 7:30am-11pm, Sun. 8:30am-10:30pm. **Telephone Code:** 0843.

Olympic Airways: 56 Eleftheriou Venizelou St. (tel. 222 70), off the main square to the east. No buses go to the airport. Taxis cost 400dr for the 1km uphill ride. Flights to Kassos (1½hr., 6300dr) and Karpathos (1hr., 7000dr).

Buses: 4 Papanastasiou St. (tel. 222 72), on the east end of the waterfront. To: Agios Nikolaos (8 per day, 2hr., 700dr); Iraklion (7 per day, 3½hr., 1900dr); Ierapetra (6 per day, 1½hr., 900dr); Vai (7 per day, 1hr., 280dr); and Kato Zakros (2-3 per day, 1hr., 670dr).

Ferries: Spanoudakis Travel, (tel. 284 66 or 228 14), next to the main post office. Sells tickets for boats leaving Sitia and other Cretan ports. Likely to be helpful with practical information about Sitia, but not, paradoxically, with boat information. The *F/B Sifnos Express* comes through en route to: the Dodecanese islands, Amorgos, Paros, and Piraeus (Wed.); and Kassos, Karpathos, Halki, and Rhodes (Sat.).

Taxi: Tel. 228 93, in Venizelou Sq.

Car Rental: Sitia Rent-a-Car: 4-6 Itanou (tel. 237 70), near Petras toward the water. Fiat 127 7000dr per day, 20dr per km over 100km.

Motorbike Rental: Petras (tel. 248 49), next to the bus station. Vespa 80cc 2500dr. Open 8am-8pm.

Hospital: Tel. 243 11, at the corner of Arkadiou and Sifis St.

Police: 24 Mysonos St. (tel. 222 66).

Emergency: Tel. 100.

Accommodations and Food

Rooms are hard to find in Sitia only during July and August, and especially during the Sultana Festival at the end of August. The youth hostel is friendly and informal, but for more privacy, head for the two areas in Sitia where you'll find budget rooms—along the main road up to the hostel, and in the back streets at the west end of the waterfront, especially Kornarou and Kondilaki St.

Youth Hostel (HI/IYHF), 4 Therissou St. (tel. 226 93), ½km uphill from the bus station back toward Iraklion. The management provides a kitchen and an outdoor garden. Only 50 beds, but you're always welcome to sleep on the veranda or the floor. Reception open 9am-1:30pm and 4:30-9pm; if no one is around, find a bed and register later. Hot water all day. No curfew. Open year-round. 700dr per person.

Pension Artemis (tel. 225 64), on your left as you head toward the hostel, across from the post office. Pink-walled doubles, some with a view of the countryside, 3000dr.

Venus Rooms to Let, 60 Kondilaki St. (tel. 243 07). Walk uphill from the OTE and take your first right. Green courtyard, ambrosial rooms, and kitchen facilities. A real bargain. Tiny singles 1700dr. Doubles 2800dr.

Rooms to Rent Victoria (tel. 280 80), a 3-min. walk on the road to Ierapetra. Out of the way but worthwhile. Sparkling courtyard with lots of plants and even a tiny pond. Every room has a fridge. Singles 1800dr. Doubles 3000dr. Triples 3500dr.

Many of Sitia's restaurants specialize in fresh fish and lobster. **Zorba's Restaurant,** on the west side of the harbor, has a variety of dishes from 300dr. (Open 8am-2am.) Or just have another *gyro* or some more fast food. (*Gyro* 200dr, hamburger 300dr).

Sights and Entertainment

Life in Sitia centers around the waterfront. Much of the old quarter is terraced along the hillside on the western part of the city. The **fortress** at the hilltop affords a capital view of the town and the entire Bay of Sitia. The town's sandy **beach,** extending about 3km east of Sitia, is right next to the road. Its distant end is usually empty.

The **Archaeological Museum** (tel. 239 17), 100m past the bus station on the road to Ierapetra, houses a small collection from nearby sites. (Open Mon. and Wed.-Sat. 9am-

3pm, Sun. 9:30am-2:30pm.) The **Folklore Museum,** 10 Arkadiou St., displays at least one tool for any household chore imaginable. To get there, take Katzanzaki St. up from the waterfront near Zorba's, turn right on Arkadiou St., and walk 4 blocks uphill. (Open Mon.-Fri. 9:30am-3:30pm, Sat. 9:30am-1pm. Admission 100dr, 50dr for students.)

The region around Sitia begs to be explored. Those with an archaeological bent will be interested in the half-excavated ruins of **Praisos,** south of Sitia, which have yielded many fine small bronzes. You'll need your own means of transport or a taxi to get here.

During the third week of August, Sitia hosts the **Sultana Festival** which features unlimited wine, dancing, and music for about 800dr. Nightlife is not Sitia's strong point: catch up on sleep lost on the rest of Crete. **Kamalia's** beach-side bar is worth a visit for its waterfront atmosphere and good prices. (Beer 300dr; open 9pm-4am.)

Toplou Monastery

Constantly under seige by Turks and pirates from the 10th to the 19th century, Toplou's monks armed their monastery to the teeth. Their efforts went for naught in 1471, when the entire complex fell to the Turks who destroyed it. The rebuilt three-story structure now contains a number of relics, including the 2nd-century BCE inscription of a treaty between the Cretan cities of Itanos and Ierapetra and the province of Magnesia in Asia Minor, and elaborate icons by the 18th-century master Ioannis Kournaros. Dress appropriately (pants for men, long skirts for women), or the monks will lend you some drabby clothes.

Buses do not run to the monastery; you must get off the Vai bus 12km outside Sitia at the *Moni Toplou* turn-off, and walk the last 3km. If you're driving, follow the road east from Sitia along the coast and turn left at the junction onto the road marked Toplou.

Vai

Not long ago, tourists headed east to the sylvan palm beach at Vai for refuge from Sitia's crowds. Today, several buses roll into this outpost every day, depositing tourists eager to ponder Europe's only natural palm forest. Legend has it that the forest is the legacy of the Arabs who conquered Crete in the 9th century CE. Weird as this place is, it's hardly worth battling the mobs for your stamp-sized piece of beach. A restaurant and café service the beach, but there are no accommodations. (Park open 7am-9pm. Free.) Most travelers visit Vai via the crowded public bus from Sitia. Buses leave Sitia and stop at Paleokastro en route to Vai (6 per day, 1hr., Sitia-Vai 310dr, Paleokastro-Vai 180dr).

Although camping is forbidden in the park itself (and they mean it), many people unfurl sleeping bags in the cove to the south of the palm beach. The southern cove (on your right) is the more accessible, and the northern the less frequented. If neither sandy pyjamas or the possibility of arrest sound appealing, rent a room in the quiet town of **Paleokastro,** 8km back toward Sitia, The **Itanos** (tel. 225 08) on the main square in Paleokastro, rents doubles for 3400dr; the **Paleokastro,** 100m down the road to Sitia, charges 3600dr. Or just head back to Sitia.

Kato Zakros

The remains of the **Palace of Zakros** mark the site of the fourth great center of Minoan civilization. Excavations began in the early 1900s, but the late Minoan palace and township were not uncovered until 1962. Built on a plan similar to those at Knossos, Phaestos, and Malia, most of the palace was destroyed around 1450 BCE. Fortunately, the city of Zakros seems to have escaped the pillaging that devastated other major Minoan sites. As a result, archaeologists were able to recover the contents of the once sumptuous palace (on display in Iraklion's Archaeological Museum).

Kato Zakros (tel. 933 23) is worth the trip only if you have a genuine interest in Minoan history and architecture—it basically looks like a heap of rocks. (Open daily 8:30am-3pm. Admission 400dr, students 200dr.) What really makes the village worth a trip is the gorgeous beach and the interesting niches and nearby caves. Kato Zakros has three *tavernas* and a café-bar. The **Anexis Taverna** exchanges currency. While there is no public shower on the beach, the restaurants allow customers to use their toilets. **Buses** leave Sitia for Kato Zakros about twice daily.

CYCLADES ΚΥΚΛΑΔΕΣ

> *The isles of Greece, the isles of Greece! Where*
> *burning Sappho loved and sung, Where grew the*
> *arts of war and peace, Where Delos rose and Phoe-*
> *bus sprung...*
>
> —*Lord Byron, Don Juan*

Chances are that when people wax rhapsodic on *the* Greek Islands, they are referring to the Cyclades. Romantics picture the islands' gilded beaches deserted, lapped by cerulean seas and tinged by warm *ouzo* sunsets. Traditionalists imagine demure villages bound by winding cobblestone streets and whitewashed homes spotting the mountainsides. Hedonists drool in inebriated anticipation of moonlit revelry and celebration. The wonder of today's heavily touristed Cyclades is that they actually can be each of these dreams, provided you approach your visit with the right mix of ingenuity, perseverance, and durability of the liver.

Although each island has a distinct character, members of the Cyclades all share a complex past of cultural prodigiousness stifled by battles and conquest. Archaeological excavations suggest that the islands were inhabited as far back as 4500 BCE. Around 3000 BCE, islanders developed the Early Cycladic culture, which thrived for over 1000 years. These early Cycladeans had learned to cope with the temperamental sea and benefited from their skilled bronze smelting and from robust trading in obsidian. Minoans conquered the islands during the Middle Cycladic period (about 1900-1500 BCE), curbing this cultural boom. The time between the fall of Crete to the rise of the Mycenaeans makes up the Late Cycladic period.

In about 1000 BCE, Ionian Greeks from the mainland began populating the Aegean and occupied these islands. And until the Persian invasion in 501 BCE and full conquest eleven years later, various tyrants controlled the region. In 478 BCE, the Cyclades became members of the Delian League, under Athenian rule which was only minimally less rigid than that of the foreign invaders. After Athens's power waned, the Cyclades, a pawn in the struggles of Alexander the Great's successors, endured a series of conquests by the Macedonians and Egyptian Ptolemies (in the 3rd century BCE). Resulting from Roman occupation beginning in 146 BCE, these islands in fact prospered from the expanded trade markets now open to them. Foreign rule, including that by the Venetians (in the 13th century) and the Turks (in the 16th century), lasted until the Greek War of Independence in 1827.

To do as locals do, visit the islands in May, early June or sometime after September; only then do the jumbo crowds thin out, the prohibitive prices decrease, and life begin to approximate normality. But for nightlife, nothing compares to the Cyclades in summer. In July and August, the islands (practically international colonies) host an assortment of backpackers, hippies, package tourists, and the yacht-toting offspring of shipping tycoons. Homes are transformed into pensions, and sleepy villages resound with the rhythm of the night.

Huge car ferries, small excursion boats (the smallest and most sea-jostled), and fast but expensive Flying Dolphin hydrofoils serve the islands. During July and August, boat connections between the major islands of Syros, Paros, Naxos, and Ios are extremely frequent—at least one per day. In June and September, service slows down; in other months it is sporadic at best. For some of the northern Cyclades (Andros, Tinos), boats leave from Rafina rather than from Piraeus.

Although there is frequent summer service within the eastern Cycladic islands, it's a bit more difficult to reach the Western Cyclades, and if you plan on visiting another island group, you may have to make boat connections in Paros or Piraeus.

The Cyclades

Psara

TO THE
NORTHEAST
AEGEAN ISLANDS

Chios

TO
THESSALONIKI

Aegean Sea

EVIA

Karystos

*Strait of
Kafireos*

Bouros

TO RAFINA

← TO
ATHENS

TO PIRAEUS

Andros

Gavrion

Andros

Batsi

Tinos

Tinos

Korissia

Giaros

Ioulis

Kea

Mykonos

Mykonos

Airport

Kithnos

Syros

Merihas

Hermoupolis

Rheneia

Delos

Serifos

Chora

Livadi

Naxos

Koronida

Donoussa

Naxos

Makares

Antiparos

Filoti

Sifnos

Kamares

Strongili

Parikia

Aliko

Koufonisi

Platis Gialos

Paros

Keros

Ormos

Antimilos

Despotiko

Iraklia

Katapola

Kimolos

Schinoussa

Psathi

Amorgos

Airport

Poliegos

Sikinos

Ios

Adamas

Ios

Milos

TO THE
DODECANESE

Folegandros

N
↑

Santorini

Oia

Thirasia

Thira

Airport

Anafi

Akrotiri

Agios
Nikolaos

*Sea
of
Crete*

TO
CRETE
↓

0   20 miles

0   20 kilometers

Mykonos ΜΥΚΟΝΟΣ

Mykonos, whose primary appeal is a surfeit of glorious beaches, is dangerous for the budget traveler. But the peril is not due to a hefty pirate population as was the case until the 18th century. The Mykonos of today, of the summer months especially, is the strutting-ground of the chic-and-sleek, and temptations abound: shop windows scintillate with glints of gold and trendy restaurants lure with exotic menus and colorful interiors. Although still smothered by the rich-and-famous, Mykonos has blossomed into a perennial favorite of the backpacker. Mykonos is also lively with a large number of gay bars, clubs, and beaches. An atmosphere of controlled and invigorating mayhem prevails. Also of interest, despite its less lively population of arthritic statues, Delos, a small island full of archaeological finds, is a short, 30-minute boat ride away.

Mykonos is well-connected by **ferry.** Boats sail frequently to: Tinos (1-2 per day, 45min., 730dr); Paros (1-2 per day, 2hr., 990dr); Ios (1-2 per day, 4hr., 2020dr); Santorini (1-2 per day, 6½hr., 2140dr); Rafina (1-2 per day, 5hr., 2510dr); Syros (1 per day, 2½hr., 840dr); Naxos (1-2 per day, 2½hr., 880dr); Andros (1-2 per day, 3½hr., 1880dr); and Piraeus (2-3 per day, 6hr., 2750dr). Catamarans flit between Mykonos and Piraeus (5930dr).

Olympic Airways has **flights** to and from Athens (18 per day, ½hr., 9900dr). Catch the airport bus at South Station (5 per day, 20min.). The main office is perched uphill from the stop.

Mykonos Town

If you stay in Mykonos long enough, chances are that you will spend at least one drunken evening lost in Mykonos Town's maze of endless, winding alleys all lined with anonymously whitewashed buildings. These labyrinthine streets, closed to motor traffic, were initially created to disconcert and disorient pirates. Jammed with tourists from May to October, the town has successfully resisted huge hotel complexes. The fishing boats in the harbor, the basket-laden donkeys, and the pink pelicans roaming the streets seem to come right out of an overwrought musical. Depending on your degree of homesickness, you will either exult or grieve over the availability of cheeseburgers, milkshakes, fish and chips, Chinese food, and "English breakfasts." Don't come to Mykonos to experience Greece; come here instead to witness an unstoppable world of bacchanalian delight.

Orientation and Practical Information

Everything you need is in and around the waterfront. Boats dock at a pier near the town beach. Inland from the pier is the North Station bus stop; South Station is clear on the other side of town, through the maze. Two blocks from the beach is beach is **Taxi Square** (Mavroyenous Sq.), lined with cafés and shops. The pier for excursion boats is at the far right end of the waterfront (facing inland).

> **Currency Exchange: National Bank of Greece,** in the center of the waterfront. Open Mon.-Thurs. 8am-2pm, Fri. 8am-1:30pm; exchange window open Mon.-Fri. 6:30-8:30pm, Sat.-Sun. 10am-1pm and 5:30-8:30pm.

> **American Express:** Left of the bank inside Delia Travel Ltd. Full AmEx travel services for cardholders. Open daily 9am-9pm.

> **Post Office:** At the edge of the town beach, next to Olympic Airways. Currency exchange. Open Mon.-Fri. 7:30am-2pm. **Postal Code:** 84600.

> **OTE:** On the far left of the waterfront, uphill from the ferry dock. Open daily 7:30am-midnight. **Telephone Code:** 0289.

> **Olympic Airways:** Tel. 224 90 or 224 95. On the uphill side of the square at the South Station bus stop. Open Mon.-Fri. 7:30am-2:30pm. 5 buses per day leave to the airport from the stop. Schedule posted.

> **Motorbike Rentals:** Agencies surrounding both bus stops. 1300-3000dr per day. Jeeps 10,000-20,000dr per day.

Police: Tel. 224 82 for tourist matters, 227 16 for passport matters, 222 35 for general information. Follow "Bus to Plati Yialos" signs and turn left on Plateia Dim. Koutsi. English spoken. Open 24 hrs.

Medical Assistance: Tel. 239 94 or 239 96. 1km east of Mykonos Town. Take the bus to Anamara (90dr) or a taxi.

Port Police: Tel. 222 18, above the National Bank. Open 24 hrs.

Buses: Two stations. **"North Station,"** inland uphill from the ferry dock. Serves: beaches at St. Stephano (last return 2:15am), east to Elia (last return 7pm), Kalo Livadi (3 per day, last return 5:30pm), and Ano Mera continuing to Kalafati (last return 12:30am). **"South Station,"** uphill from the windmills at the opposite edge of town. Follow Matogiannis St. as it winds through chic and thin, take a left at Jimmy's Gyros, then a right at the top of the street and follow the signs from there. Serves beaches at Plati Yalos, Psarou (last return 1am), Ornos (every hr. 9am-1am), Al Yiannis (last return 1am), and the airport (5 per day). Schedules posted at both stops.

Laundromat: Tel 249 82. In the "Little Venice" section of town (behind the cluster of seaside churches—follow the signs), across from the Montparnasse bar. Open Mon.-Sat. 9am-10pm. Wash 1800dr. Dry 1200dr. Soap included.

Accommodations and Camping

Accommodations-hawking is an industry in Mykonos. The usual mob of "representatives" (sometimes dubbed dock hawks) at the port are armed with slick photo-montages of rooms. Beware of rooms "on the beach"—they are bound to be miles away. In addition, owners have formed island-wide associations; pushing past the hawkers and their shuttle vans, you can't miss the offices for hotels (tel. 295 40), rooms-to-let (tel. 246 80), camping, and the port police. (All offices open daily 8am-midnight, or at least when the ferries come in.) These offices provide information on availability, location, and prices, and will telephone *dhomatia* proprietors on your behalf. The following are official rooms-to-let prices for third class rooms (a government designation for cheap), but don't hesitate to bargain once you meet the owner: singles 2155dr, with bath 2835dr; doubles 3062dr, with bath 4306dr; and triples 4423dr, with bath 4563dr. There is another hotel office at the airport (tel. 247 60). Only same-day reservations can be made for hotels. In high season, empty rooms fill up faster than you can say ΥΠΟ-ΒΡΥΧΙΟ ΨΑΡΕΜΑ, so don't dillydally getting off the boat. **Angela's Rooms** (tel. 229 67), above Apollo's self-service in the back left corner of the Taxi Sq., rents noisy roof space "under the auspices of Orion." Freelance camping is illegal in Mykonos.

Prices for the hotels listed below are at the very least 20% lower in off-season. In high season, you'll probably have to spend at least one night camping or in a private room before you'll find a vacancy in one of the hotels.

Hotel Phillippi, 32 Kalogera St. (tel. 222 94). Go up Matoyanni St. and turn right onto Kalogera St. Friendly owners with a magnificent flower garden and spacious rooms. Open April 1-Oct. 30. Singles (not many) 4700dr. Doubles 7500dr. Triples 10,500dr. Showers included.

Hotel Maria, 18 Kalogera St. (tel. 242 13), at the end of the small alley with the bakery (which serves dynamite apple pies, 200dr). Beautiful, newly-renovated rooms run by the soccer champ President of the Mykonos Sports Club. Pricey, but worth it. (*Not* to be confused with the Marios Hotel or the other Maria below.) Doubles with bath 8000-10,000dr.

Rooms Chez Maria, 30 N. Kalogera St. (tel. 224 80) just past the Hotel Phillippi. Cheaper than most, but always full. Clean, traditionally decorated rooms. Open April-Oct. Doubles with bath 6000dr.

Apollon Hotel, (tel. 232 71 or 222 23), on the waterfront. The oldest hotel in Mykonos. Traditional house with balcony overlooking the harbor. Singles from 6208dr. Doubles 8465dr, with bath from 10,727dr. Triples 11,286dr. Open April-Oct.

Camping: Paradise Beach Camping (tel. 221 29 or 228 52). Spacious and clean. A self-sufficient community with restaurant, disco, minimarket, currency exchange, an international phone with a long line, newsstand, film processing, and even an aviary. 24-hr. check-in. Open April-Oct. **Mykonos Camping** at Paraga Beach (tel. 245 78). New with restaurant, bar, mini-market, hot water, cooking, and washing facilities. Both campsites 800dr per person, 400dr per tent. If you miss their vans, take the bus for Plati Yialos (140dr) and then a boat to the beach in front of the campsite entrance (250dr).

Look for rooms-to-rent signs at St. Stephanos Beach. If you'd prefer a hotel right on this beach, try the **Mina Hotel** (tel. 230 24); doubles with bath and breakfast go for a 7000dr. The **Panorama Hotel** (tel. 223 37) is also beachside. (Singles 3000dr. Doubles 6000dr. Bath included.) At Megali Ammos Beach, you can crash at the **Markos Beach Hotel** (tel. 228 11; doubles 5000dr, with bath 7000dr).

Food

On Mykonos, you may find yourself adrift in a sea of exotic menus and exorbitant prices. But fear not—inexpensive restaurants, though an endangered species, do still exist.

Ta Kiouria. In a cluster of restaurants inland from the excursion boat docks. Some interesting specials—lamb or veal, pasta, and tomatoes 950dr. Open 5pm-midnight.

La Scala, across from Ta Kiouria, with the pastel purple tablecloths. Serves big plates of Italian food for two. Pasta Roma 1400dr.

Niko's Taverna, opposite Ta Kiouria. A hoppin' place to get traditional Greek cuisine. *Mousaka* 800dr. Open daily noon-3pm and 6pm-midnight.

Paraportiani Taverna, opposite Niko's. Smaller portions but a tad more quiet and sedate. Stuffed tomatoes 700dr, lamb with okra 900dr. Open April-Oct. noon-midnight.

Taverna Antonini, in the lively, convenient Taxi Sq. Stuffed eggplant 600dr. Fried meatballs 800dr. Open daily noon-midnight.

Kounelas, 2 blocks north of Niko's; turn left at the Apollon Art Gallery. Decor humble; prices not. Good for the indecisive—only 1 entree: fresh grilled fish 1000dr. Open 7pm-midnight.

Alexi's, at the back of Taxi Sq., below the Piano Bar. Fast food with a smile. *Souvlaki-pita* 170dr, Hawaiian-style hamburger 300dr.

Andrea's Bakery, off Taxi Sq. Fruit pies and *spanakopita* (spinach pie) from 250dr. Open daily 6am-10pm.

The Donut Factory, at the intersection of Mitropoleos, Ipirou, and Enoplon Dinameon St., about 3 blocks down from the bus station. Delightful doughnuts, fresh fruit juices (350-500dr), apple fritters (300dr), and pizza slices oozing with cheese (400dr). Open daily 6am-2am. Some other nearby fast-food joints are **Snowball,** with scrumptious homemade ice-cream, and **Jimmy's Gyros,** with *gyros* (250dr).

Entertainment

There are too many bars and discos to fully list, so here are some of our favorites. Most places close at 3am. Few have cover charges, but drinks are so expensive you'll forget you got in free.

Scandinavian Bar, near Niko's Taverna and the waterfront. This perenially packed party complex sprawls over 2 buildings and a patio. Early evening mellowness becomes madness around midnight. *Everyone* will pass through. Open nightly 7:30pm-3am. Beer 400dr. Cocktails 800dr.

Windmill Disco, near Scandinavian Bar. Very popular spot in a refurbished windmill; go crazy by the indoor palm tree. Greek music 9-11pm, then the hackneyed sounds of disco. Beer 500dr, cocktails 1000dr. No cover, but 1 drink is mandatory.

City Disco Bar, between the Scandinavian Bar and the Windmill Disco. Catch the spectacular 2-man drag/strip show featuring everything from Tina Turner to Marilyn Monroe look-alikes nightly around 2am. Hasty Pudding look out. The 1000dr cover charge includes 1 drink. **Pierro's,** on Matogianni St. Mainly gay. Good dancing, loud music, and a crowd that spills out of the propeller-laden building into the square. Beer 700dr, cocktails 1200dr. Similar atmosphere upstairs at **Nepheli-Hollywood Bar** (beer 700dr), and **Icaros,** which opens around midnight.

Montparnasse, on Agios Ayarguros St. in the Little Venice district. Step into a Toulouse-Lautrec; sit by the bay window overlooking the water while you are serenaded with classical music. Peaceful and romantic. Wine 500dr. Cocktails 1000dr.

Oasis, inland from the Scandinavian Bar on Mitropoleos St. Amid stark-white streets reverberating with rock, this mood-lit refuge welcomes with verdant foliage, mellow music, and plenty of drinks. Beer/wine 500dr. Cocktails 1000dr.

The Yacht Club, near the port on the south side of the waterfront. Where the island goes for the party after the party. A motley mixture of music and people. Beer 300dr. Closes at 8am.

Sights

The prime daytime activities on Mykonos are shopping and perfecting that tan. While other parts of Greece boast exquisite handicrafts, here you will find designer clothes of international repute. **Galatis,** to the left of Taxi Sq. (facing town), has unique handwoven sweaters and outfits (from $50). Note the long list of signatures of famous people, like Jackie O., who shopped here. (Open April-Oct. daily 9am-10pm.) **O Liondis**, 55 Matogianni St., sells handmade leather sandals from 1800dr. **Vienoula's,** around the corner, carries handmade jackets and sweaters (colorful sweaters from 4500dr). Mykonos is also famous for its gold, silver, ceramics, and water colors. None of these goods are cheap by budget-travel standards; you might have to settle for a T-shirt.

To pretend that people come here to experience cultural enrichment or indigenous Greek life verges on the ridiculous. Nevertheless: the **Archaeological Museum,** on the waterfront between the ferry dock and the center of town, has a 7th-century BCE *pithos* (large earthenware vessel) with relief scenes from the Trojan War, and a bronze *kouros*. (Open Tues.-Sat. 9am-3pm, Sun. 9:30am-2:30pm. Admission 400dr, students 200dr.) The **Aegean Maritime Museum,** at Tria Pighadia, on the upper part of town, contains ship models, rare ancient coins with nautical subjects, and navigational instruments. (Open daily April-Oct. 10:30am-1pm and 6-9pm. Admission 200dr.) The **Folk Art Museum** is in the nearly 300-year-old house of a former sea-captain, at the northern edge of town inland from the excursion boat docks. The lovely collection is open at convenient hours for beach-goers. (Open April-Oct. Mon.-Sat. 5:30-8:30pm, Sun. 6:30-8:30pm. Free.) Next door is the **Paraportiani.** This cluster of convoluted white churches, probably the most famous of Mykonos's sights, sits below three stoic windmills.

You will inevitably find yourself on the beach. Nearest to town, excepting the unexceptional town beach, is **Megali Ammos,** a 1km walk past the windmills on the southwestern corner of the harbor. **St. Stephanos Beach** is unspectacular, but very convenient (buses from North Station inland from the ferry dock every ½hr. or every hr. 8:15am-2am, 10min., 120dr). Crowded **Psarou Beach** is also close to town. The nudist beaches full of gay men—though straight men and families are far from rare—are unquestionably the best on the island and can be reached by taking a bus (140dr) to **Plati Yialos** (not bad in its own right), and then taking a *caïque* from there. **Buses** leave every hour from 9am to midnight from South Station about 250m up the hill along the street that runs behind the windmills. (Look for painted signs pointing to "buses for Plati Yialos.") From Plati Yialos, *caïques* go to **Paradise Beach,** officially called Kalamopodi (200dr), and **Super Paradise Beach** (250dr). Paradise Beach can also be reached by the 7km strip of road connecting it to town. A large and more secluded nude beach is **Elia** (300dr). Or catch a sight-seeing boat ride for 1000dr. From the same bus stop, buses also run hourly to the beach at **Ornos.**

If you feel you can abandon the beaches and divorce yourself from tourists, visit **Ano Mera,** the island's only other village, 7km away. The main item of interest is its 18th-century **Tourliani** monastery, with an ornate 16th-century marble tower covered with folk carvings. Buses travel from North Station every two hours, 7am-midnight.

Delos ΔΛΟΣ

The sacred heart of the Cyclades, Delos holds the famous Sanctuary to Apollo, built to commemorate the birthplace of Apollo and his twin sister Artemis. After Zeus impregnated Leto, he cast her out, fearing his wife Hera's wrath. Leto searched desperately for a place to give birth and at last sighted this barren, rocky island bobbing in the sea. When she declared that the child would stay forever at his birthplace, casting light upon the light and riches all around the island, it stopped floating, and a reassured Leto decided to stay. Upon his birth, a grand radiance drenched the island and its name, A-delos (meaning invisible) was changed to Delos because it could now be so clearly seen. Immensely grateful, Hera promised to make the island the seat of Apollo's worship there. The presence of the sanctuary made Delos an eminent religious center. Thus Delos became the hub of all of the Cyclades, the "wheeling" islands that radiate around this tiny, somewhat geographically central island.

The mortal history of the island is less charmed. Colonized since practically forever, Delos had long been a religious and commercial center for the Cyclades when the Ionians dedicated it to the cult of Leto in the 10th century BCE. By the 7th century BCE, Delos had become the political and trade center of the Aegean League of Islands; three centuries of struggle for hegemony between the Delians and the Athenians ensued. During these years, the Athenians ordered at least two "purifications" of the island, the latter in 426 BCE, when they decreed that no one should give birth or die on its sacred grounds. Delians facing either exigency were removed by caïque to the nearby Rheneia. Following purification, the Athenians instituted the quadrennial Delian Games, in which they always dominated.

After Sparta's defeat of Athens in the Peloponnesian War (403 BCE), Delos enjoyed an independence characterized by wealth. Sweet prosperity soured, however, during the Roman occupation in the 2nd century BCE. The island subsequently became the slave-trading center of Greece, where the transfers of as many as 10,000 slaves occurred daily.

By the 2nd century CE, after successive sackings, the island was left virtually uninhabited apart from a few odd pirates. Today, its only residents are leaping lizards and members of the French School of Archaeology, which has been excavating ruins here since 1873.

A map to the sprawling site is highly recommended, whether you choose to follow the tour below, tag along with a guided tour, or improvise. For more background information, read the revelatory *Delos: Monuments and Museum,* by Photini Zaphiropolou, which includes a map (800dr, available at the entrance and at the museum or at tourist shops in Mykonos). If you visit Delos unprepared, you may feel overwhelmed by the multitude of ruins.

Occupying almost an entire square mile of this lilliputian island, the archaeological site is neatly quartered: the central part of the city, including the Sanctuary of Apollo and the Agora; the outlying parts of the ancient city; Mt. Kynthos; and the theater quarter. While it takes several days to explore the ruins completely, the tour suggested below would allow for an efficient, three-hour survey of the highlights. Most of your fellow passengers on the boat will follow a similar route when they disembark, so reverse the route if you want some privacy while you inspect the ruins. Remember to bring a water bottle; the cafeteria on site is pretty expensive.

From the dock, head straight to the **Agora of the Competaliasts,** where Roman guilds built their shrines. Nearby are several parallel **stoas,** the most impressive of which Philip of Macedon built. This line of altars, pillars, and statue bases (you can still see the statues' prints) forms the western border of the **Sacred Way.** Follow this road to the **Sanctuary of Apollo,** with its immense, partly hollow hexagonal pedestal that once sustained the weight of the 8m-tall marble statue of the god of light. The famous **Delian Lions,** a gift of the people of Naxos to the holy island, lie 50m to the north. In the 7th century BCE, nine marble lions were placed in a row on a terrace facing the sacred lake; only five remain here—a sixth, pirated by the Venetians, guards the entrance to the arsenal in Venice.

Proceed up the small crest left of the lions, to the creatively named **House of the Hill.** Because the building was dug deep into the earth, much remains of this archetypal Roman house. Downhill lies the **House of the Lake,** with a well-preserved mosaic decorating its atrium. The dessicated **Sacred Lake** will remind you of your own parched throat—you did remember your water bottle, didn't you? Next to the cafeteria, the **museum** contains an assortment of archaeological finds from the island; unfortunately the best sculpture from the site is in Athens. (Delos museum open Tues.-Sun. 8:30am-3pm.) From there, hike up the path on Mt. Kynthos (where Zeus watched the birth of Apollo) and you'll pass several temples to the Egyptian gods. The elegant bust in the **Temple of Isis** depicts the sun. At the top of the 120m hill, gape at the tremendous view of the ruins and islands. The **Grotto of Hercules** is on the way down. Its immense building-blocks seem to date it to Mycenaean times, though some experts suggest it is a Hellenistic imitation of such architecture.

At the base of the hill, go north to the **House of the Dolphins** and the **House of the Masks,** which contains the renowned mosaic *Dionysus Riding a Panther.* Continue on to the **ancient theater,** which has a rather sophisticated cistern (as cisterns go), **Dexamene,** with nine arched compartments. Try to explore, too, the **House of the Trident,** graced by a mosaic of a dolphin twisted around a trident (may be closed in 1993), the **House of Dionysus,** with another mosaic of Dionysus and a panther pal, and the **House of Cleopatra,** with its remaining columns. The famous statue of Cleopatra and Dioscourides is sequestered in the museum; a plaster copy will replace it on the site. (Ruins open Tues.-Sun. 8:30am-3pm, Sun. 9am-2pm. Admission 1000dr, students 500dr.)

If you visit Delos as a daytrip from Mykonos, you will be at the mercy of ferry timetables. Weather permitting, government boats for Delos depart from the pier near the tourist office in Mykonos Town every day except Mon. (departs 12:10pm or 2:15pm, returns 8:50pm or 10:10pm, 30min., 1160dr round-trip). The ride sometimes feels like a rusty roller coaster, so Dramamine might come in handy. A bigger, more stable boat also makes the trip (leaving at 10am, returning at 2pm, 2500dr round-trip, with guide 4500dr). Many ferry agencies in Mykonos make this journey, but if you really want to stay longer, hire an expensive excursion boat. There are also joint excursions to Delos and Mykonos from Naxos (3000dr), but they allot only 1½ hours for visiting the Delian ruins. It is illegal to stay overnight on Delos.

Tinos ΤΗΝΟΣ

Legend has it that Tinos in ancient times teemed with snakes. Heralding the isle's salvation, Poseidon sent a ferocious squad of storks to destroy the slithering serpents. Tinos is presently home to the most sacred relic of the Orthodox church—the Icon of the Annunciation, also known as the "Megalochari" ("Great Joy"). To the disbeliever, the 1822 discovery of the nearly 900-year-old icon, still in perfect condition, is dubious. To the faithful, the find is evidence of "the wonder-working power and presence of the Holy Virgin." In 1822, Sister Pelagia, a Tiniote nun, had a vision in which the Virgin Mary instructed her to find an icon buried at the site of an ancient church, destroyed in the 10th century by pirates. A year later, the icon was housed, amid great rejoicing, at the **Panayia Evangelistria,** wherein it still resides. The relic reputedly has curing powers and is almost entirely covered with gold, diamonds, and pearls left at the church by people wishing to thank the Holy Mother for their good health. The innumerable *ex-votos,* beautifully crafted plaques praising the Virgin for healing the body part depicted have won the church the title of "Lourdes of the Aegean."

The most devout pilgrims make the journey up Leoforos Megalochares—the wide road rising from the sea to the church—on their knees, to show their reverence. Others purchase and light offertory candles (100 to 1000dr as devotion swells from one to six feet). In a chapel below the marble entrance stairs flows the Well of Sanctification—a natural spring discovered during excavations—from which the faithful fill their jugs for drinking or carrying as talismans. On March 25 (the Annunciation of Mary) and August 15 (the Assumption), flocks of devout pilgrims arrive at the church. There are pilgrim lodgings and sinks for washing hands and knees after the crawl up, but on August 15, **Tinos Town** is so crowded that the near 30,000 visitors sleep *everywhere*— along the dock, on the sidewalks, and even in the church itself. No one will stop you here, but try to come modestly attired—long sleeves and pants or skirts, no bare shoulders. A free and piously-crafted English information booklet full of the entire history, colorful reports of miracles, and explanations of holidays, is available at the second floor to the right of the sanctum. (Open daily in summer 7am-6pm; off-season 7:30-10am and 1-5pm. Free.) Tinos is also famed for its art. After you visit the Panayia, drop by the church complex's art and archaeological museums, featuring works by native Tiniotes. (Open same hours as church. Free.)

It is primarily the sacred icon that attracts Tinos's visitors, about 80% of whom are Greek, but the island also offers 100 other churches, 15 natural beaches, a beautiful rustic interior, and a more authentic Greece than most of the other Cyclades.

Boats travel from Tinos to: Mykonos (3-4 per day, 40min., 730dr); Andros (2 per day, 2hr., 1265dr); Rafina (2 per day, 4hr., 2065dr); Piraeus (2 per day, 5½hr., 2695dr); and Syros (at least 1 per day, 40min., 640dr). The *Megalochari* sails four to seven times per week to Paros (3hr., 931dr), Ios (5hr., 2320dr), and Santorini (7hr., 2320dr). You can also take an excursion to Mykonos and Delos (daily at 9am, return 6pm, 2800dr). **Tinos Tours** (tel. 222 18 or 230 00) near the two statues on the waterfront, offers daily excursions around the island (1500dr, half-day and evening excursions 1000dr).

All boats dock in **Tinos Town.** Facing inland left, you can't miss **Leoforos Megalo-chares** leading up to the Neoclassical façade of the **Panayia Evangelistria.** On the right a few blocks up is the **OTE** (open Mon.-Fri. 7:30am-midnight, Sat.-Sun. 8am-1pm and 6-11pm). A smaller **OTE** is located at the harbor, in the white building by the water (open in summer Mon.-Sat. 8am-midnight, Sun. 9am-midnight). Running parallel to Leoforos Megalochares up to the church, **Evangelistrias Street** (nicknamed Bazaar St. by the locals) overflows with a colorful selection of religious trinkets. Continue from left to right, facing inland, take your fourth left and you'll find Lazarou Sohou St., and the **police** (tel. 221 00 or 222 55; open 24 hrs.). The **port police** (tel. 223 48; open 24 hrs.) are based in the center of the wharf (to the right of Megalochares and Evangelistrias facing inland.) The **National Bank of Greece** is on the waterfront, across from the bus depot (open Mon.-Thurs. 8am-2pm, Fri. 8am-1:30pm, Sat. 9am-1pm, and additionally in summer Mon.-Fri. 6-8:30pm, off-season closed for currency exchange Sat.). The **post office** is on the far right-hand end of the waterfront, behind the small square with the war monument (open Mon.-Fri. 7:30am-2pm). **Public toilets** are at the opposite end of the waterfront near Dolphin Sq., behind the Hotel Lito. Tinos has no official tourist office, but you can get information from one of the many English-speaking travel agents. Tucked into a row of *tavernas* next to Tinos Tours on the left-hand side of the waterfront is an English-language **bookstore** (open daily 9am-10:30pm). Tinos's **postal code** is 84200; it's **telephone code** is 0283.

For a **taxi**, dial 224 70. English **bus** schedules are posted on a mammoth placard to the left of the National Bank. Renting a **moped** is probably the best way to see Tinos, but be extremely careful on the narrow, gravel mountain roads. Both the yellow and red paths on the map are reportedly pretty bad: go with caution. Try **Vidalis,** 16 Zanaki Alavanou St. (tel. 234 00), leading off the right side of the waterfront (facing inland), or **Jason's** (tel. 225 83), just before Alavanou St., on the waterfront. (800dr-1800dr per day.)

Not a traditional part of the backpacker's archipelagian schedule, Tinos has plenty of accomodations, except at *panagieri* time (days of Eastern Orthodox celebration). Most hotels are expensive, but you'll be met by smiling faces with rooms-to-let when you get off the boat. (Doubles 2500-300dr depending on the set-up and your bargaining prowess.) To find the fine rooms of **Lucas Apergis** (tel. 239 64 or 232 31) take a left onto Zanaki Alavanou St. just before the post office, then the second left after the garden with the dry little-boy-fountain, and a final left at the top of the street, where you'll see signs. (Singles 1500-2000dr, doubles 3000dr, triples 4000dr.) **Stratis N. Keladitis** rents rooms up on Evangelistras St., and features fax service. (Doubles 2000dr.) On the far right side of the waterfront in a traditional house with green shutters and a balcony overlooking the harbor, marvelous **O Gianni's** offers airy rooms with the use of kitchen and laundry facilities, and a lovely flower-garden sitting area. (Singles 2000dr. Doubles 3629dr. Triples with bath 4926dr). A well-marked 10-minute walk to the right-hand side of town, well kept, verdant **Tinos Camping** (tel. 223 44) has kitchen and laundry facilities and a bar-restaurant-café. (750dr per person, 400dr per tent, 350dr per car. 2pm check-out. Gate secured with access for guests daily at 5:30pm).

The most reasonably priced food in Tinos Town can be found in one of the *tavernas* near Dolphin Sq., on the left side of the port (past the Hotel Lito). **Zygos** café and Greek/Italian restaurant, on the right as you walk from Dolphin Sq., serves delicious dishes under a verdant awning. For really cheap eats, hit the *souvlaki* and *gyros* joint at the base of Evangelistrias St. (*pita* sandwich 200dr). If you've got a sweet tooth, don't miss the walnut pie on your left (200dr). A cluster of happening bars hide from the Virgin behind Hotel Lito in Dolphin Sq. Check out dance club **Kalakathoumena** (ΚΑΛΑ ΚΑΘΟΥΜΕΝΑ) and **Remezzo** (open around 9pm and 11pm, respectively, both closing around 3am; beer 700dr). Beer is cheaper at the *tavernas*. Always full is **To Tzebarko** on the waterfront corner under Hotel Lito, defiantly facing the Holy Mother (beer 200dr).

Tinos's **Archaeological Museum,** across the street and uphill from the OTE, contains artifacts from Poseidon's sanctuary at Kionia, a first-century BCE sundial, and large, impressive vases from Xombourgo. (Open Tues.-Sat. 8:30am-3pm. Admission 400dr, students 200dr.) Buses (10:30am-5:30pm every ½hr., 10min., last return 5:40pm, 50dr) go to Kionia, where you can explore the ruins of the 4th-century BCE temple of Poseidon and Amphitrite, and then loll by the sea at either the steadily touristed **Tinos Beach** or **Stavros Beach,** both near the town. If you stay late at Stavros, partake of the nightlife at the locally-acclaimed **Homa Chroma** club. **Agios Fokas,** a closer and equally crowded beach, is a short walk east (on the opposite side) of Tinos Town.

To get to spectacular **Kardianis** beach, take the Pyrgos bus to Kardiani and travel down the winding road from the main road. Exploration of rustic Tinos will reward the adventurer with other secluded beaches and wonderful views of the fecund Tinos countryside. The 1000 dovecots freckling the landscape have become the symbol by which the island is identified. Built in medieval times, these small white buildings have intricate geometric lattice-work where birds roost. Stop by the picturesque town of **Pyrgos,** 33km northwest of Tinos Town. With an impressive marble quarry, Pyrgos has always been home to Tinos's artists and sculptors. If you really want peace and quiet, spend the night in a traditional house there. (Call Fotini at 314 65 or ask a local for directions.) Three km south of Pyrgos, Panormos Bay has a small beach and three *tavernas*. Buses travel to Pyrgos from Tinos Town (4 per day, 1hr., last return 5:45pm, 270dr). Be careful not to get stranded in the village—there are no night buses on Tinos and taxis are hard to find.

If you have wheels, investigate the delightful villages that encircle **Mount Exobourgo,** the precipitous site of the Venetian Fortress, **Xombourgo.** After withstanding 11 assaults, this 13th-century citadel, then the island's capital, fell to the Turks in 1715, and was the very last territorial gain of the Ottoman Empire. Climb the mountain from the east foothill (near the village of Messi), and indulge in the resplendent panorama.

Andros ΑΝΔΡΟΣ

Andros impresses with its mosaic countryside of multicolored, multitextured terrain: tiers of straw fields, ranges of imposing rock, stretches of low-lying green and purple growth are partitioned by a network of streams and stone walls, laying like a spider's web fallen on the face of the hillside. Winding above splendid scattered beaches, the hour drive from the ferry landing at **Gavrion** to the Chora (old city) of Andros is magnificent. The ruins sprinkled across the Andian hills memorialize the island's checkered history of Ionian, Spartan, Venetian, and Turkish oppression. Andros remains one of the most peaceful and least touristed of the Cyclades. Most accommodations are designed for longer term visits and family groups, but simple rooming arrangements and camping are available.

Ferries travel to and from Rafina to the port of Gavrion on Andros (2-3 per day, 2½hr., 1500dr). From Andros, the boats sail to Tinos (2 per day, 2hr., 1264dr) and Mykonos (1-2 per day, 2½hr., 1820dr).

Crowned with the three-domed Church of Saint Nikolas and replete with sunning and picnicking suppliers, the dusty port town of Gavrion has little else to offer the tourist. Stay here overnight to catch an early ferry or to best explore the smooth stretches of sand and empty turquoise coves along the coast between the port and the popular tourist beach town of Batsi. There is no official GNTO, but the ferry agents lined along the waterfront speak English and have island bus schedules posted inside their offices. Good maps are available at the many tourist shops (300dr). As you face the water, the

Agricultural Bank is on the corner at the left hand end of the waterfront façade. (Open for currency exchange Mon.-Thurs. 9am-1:30pm, Fri. 9am-1pm.) The **police** (tel. 712 20) are on a road parallel to the waterfront up the street from the bank (take a left; open 24 hrs.) The **OTE** is one block to the right of Hotel Galaxy (open Mon.-Fri. 7:30am-3:10pm, Sat.-Sun. 8am-1pm). The **post office** is two blocks farther on the waterfront in the same direction (open Mon.-Fri. 7:30am-2pm). A **pharmacy** is located in the right-center of the waterfront (tel. 229 58; open daily 8:30am-2pm and 5:30-10pm). Andros's **postal code** is 84501; the **telephone code** is 0282.

In Gavrion, **Eleni** offers not-so-stylish but sufficient doubles (3000dr) and triples (4000dr) with communal bath and kitchen. Inquire at the variety store one block down from the post office, under the gold Kodak sign. Up the small inland street, *dhomatia* are advertised at what seems to be a negotiable price (1000-3000dr). You'll see the "We speak English" sign; hope that "we" are in. At the center of the waterfront, the **Hotel Galaxy** (tel. 712 28), has shining rooms and smiling proprietors. (Singles 3000dr. Doubles 5000dr. Triples 6000dr. Private bath included.) **Camping Andros** (tel. 714 44) is very close to town and has some English-speaking staff; go to the left-hand side of the harbor (facing the water), walk up the road toward Batsi, and you'll see signs. Or take the bus and ask the driver to let you off at the road sign. It's 200m away. Cool off in the popular pool there. (500dr per person, 200dr per tent, 200dr per car.) In town, you can fix meals with goodies from the **supermarket** on the right end of the waterfront. If you're craving those *souvlaki pitas*, try **Souvlaki Express,** across from the bank in blue (*kalamaki pita*, 170dr). The **San Remo,** next to the post office, offers nightly Italian specials, and the **O Mourikis,** on the dirt path at the far left side of the waterfront, serves up cheap and tasty seafood specials (*kalamari* 750dr).

While in Gavrion, make the hour's hike north-west to see the **Agios Petros,** a stunning 19m tower dating from the Hellenistic period. To get to Andros Town, take one of the **buses** from the depot next to the ferry dock (7 per day until 7:30pm, last return at 9pm, 1hr., 500dr). The same bus passes through Batsi (from Gaviron 15min., 140dr; from Andros Town 45min., 400dr). A taxi to Andros Town costs 2500dr. You can rent a moped at **Takis Mopeds** (tel. 713 41), next to the supermarket at the left edge of the waterfront (2000dr per day), or at **George's Moto** at the right edge of the waterfront.

The road to Andros Town passes **Batsi,** a popular tourist beach. Look for "rooms-to-let" signs on the road leading out of town. Also en route to Andros Town are the ruins of the ancient capital, **Paleopolis,** where considerable remains of a theater and a stadium still stand. About 2km south of Palaiokastro is the **Bay of Korthion,** with some of the finest swimming spots on Andros. Just north of Korthion are the remnants of the **Castle of the Old Woman.** Many Venetians were slaughtered by the Turks at this site in the 16th century.

Andros Town is a sophisticated village with striking neoclassical architecture, three fine museums, and a festive main street that juts onto a blustery peninsula in the middle of the bay. The bus station is coupled with a friendly restaurant just to the right of the section of the town's main street that is closed off to traffic. A full schedule is posted in the outdoor waiting area. Follow the high blue domes of the church to find the town's center. At the far inland end of the main street the **police station** (tel. 223 00; open 24 hrs.) sits next to a playground. Towards the water, the **post office** resides on the right next to an open, airy *platia* alongside of which **taxis** (tel. 221 71) queue. Across from the central *platia* on the left is the **OTE** (open Mon.-Sat. 7:30am-10pm, Sun. 8am-1pm and 5-10pm). The **National Bank of Greece** is on the left farther down, on the way to the water (open Mon.-Thurs. 8am-2pm, Fri. 8am-1:30pm). There are several **pharmacies** along this route, and two magazine shops with a random assortment of English, French, and German-language books (open 9am-3pm and 5-10pm). **Aris Moped Rentals** (tel. 243 81; hourly mopeds 2000-2500dr) is located on the section of the main road open to traffic on the way to Gavrion. Andros Town's **postal code** is 84500; the **telephone code** is 0282.

At the end of the main road is a cheery square humming with cafés and *tavernas*. **Mitsaki's Taverna,** on the right, serves up indulgent views of the beach (stuffed eggplant 750dr, "God fish" 700dr). **Hotel Egli** (tel. 223 03 or 221 59) is conveniently located just off the main drag next to the towering, colorful church and palm garden.

(Singles 4300dr. Doubles 6500-8000dr. Breakfast included.) Ten minutes away, in the beach-side neighborhood behind the beach to the left of the town center (as you face the water), *dhomatia* abound. From the taxi line on the right side of the central *platia,* walk straight down two sets of stairs, follow the road over the little bridge to arrive just behind the crashing surf. In the third house on the left, **Firiou Efthimia** (tel. 229 21) has pleasant rooms with communal bath. (Singles 2654dr. Doubles 3600dr). Two doors down take a left to climb a wide stair slightly hidden by a bushy tree. Take a right at the top of the stairs and walk to the second house with a yellow canopy, where **Petros Stathakis** (tel. 229 05) offers huge, sparkling suites with kitchen and private bath. (Doubles 7000dr. Triples 8000dr.) Continue down the road to the big white balconied house and ring for information about rooms with private bath and refrigerators (tel. 226 04; singles 4000dr; doubles 6200dr). Back on the beach road, walk all the way past Irene's Villas. Several doors down, **George Katsiotis** has clean rooms complete with kitchen and bath. (Singles 5000dr. Doubles 6200dr. Triples 7800dr.)

Andros native Goulandris, a shipping tycoon and philanthropist, is responsible for the many high-quality museums in this small town. The modern, air-conditioned **Archaeological Museum** displays artifacts from sites on the island, as well as maps and exhibits detailing Andros's history. The *Hermes of Andros* statue from the Classical Period (4th-5th century BCE), reminiscent of Michelangelo's *David,* is the star of these collections. (Open Tues.-Sun. 8:30am-3pm. Admission 400dr, students 200dr.) The **Museum of Modern Art,** down the stairs below, has two wings, both with rotating exhibits. The new wing exhibits the development of 20th-century artists' work. (Open mid-June-mid-Sept. Wed.-Mon. 10am-2pm and 6-8pm. Admission 500dr, students 250dr). The old wing (tel. 226 50) features the work of a modern Greek artist (open year-round Wed.-Mon. 10am-2pm. Free.)

Syros ΣΥΡΟΣ

Hermoupolis

Spiritually sated, a Greek Orthodox church on one hill and a Catholic church on the other, Syros's capital reposes serenely on its natural harbor. Hermoupolis, "the city of Hermes" (god of commerce), was once the premier Greek port, but declined in the late 19th century with the advent of oil-fueled ships. Despite its fall as a major port, the city is still the shipping center and capital of the Cyclades. Elegant Miaouli Sq. and the 19th-century mansions in Dellagrazia evidence Hermoupolis's opulent past and explain its former nicknames—the "Manchester of Greece" and "little Milan." Most tourists visit the island only to make ferry connections to the more popular Cyclades. Hermoupolis's wide streets, tree-lined avenues, and comfortable plaza will tempt you; a prolonged visit here may well be the best antidote for the white-washed unreality of the other Cyclades.

From Syros, **ferries** sail to: Piraeus (2 per day, 4½hr., 2500dr); Tinos (1 per day, 40min., 670dr); Mykonos (1 per day, 1½hr., 812dr); Paros (1-2 per day, 1½hr., 812dr); Naxos (1-2 per day, 2½hr., 1418dr); and Rafina (1 per day, 4½hr., 1725dr). There is less frequent service to: Andros (2 per week, 3hr., 1305dr); Sifnos (1 per week, 5hr., 1415dr); Serifos (1 per week, 6hr., 1415dr); Ios (3 per week, 4hr., 1905dr); and Santorini (3 per week, 5 hr., 2360dr). The **catamaran** is faster and may be more convenient, but costs two or three times as much.

The bare necessities in Syros are located in **Maiouli Square** in **Hermoupolis,** 2 blocks up from the center of the harbor. Across from the town hall is the **post office.** (Open Mon.-Fri. 7:30am-2pm.) The **OTE** is on the right side of the square as you face the town hall. (Open daily 8am-midnight; off-season 7am-11pm.) The **National Bank** is on Kalomnopoulou St. in a palatial building 2 blocks to the right of Miaouli Sq. (facing inland). (Open Mon.-Thurs. 8am-2pm, Fri. 8am-1:30pm.) Located on the left side of the port (facing water), the **tourist office** (tel. 270 27) provides information on accommodations, and has boat timetables. (Open daily 11:30am-5:30pm.) The amiable **port police** (tel. 226 90), next door, provide up-to-date information about boat schedules. (Open 24 hrs.) The **tourist police** (tel. 226 20 or 226 10) speak English and are at 3 Timolegon Ambelas St. (Open 24 hrs.) The **city police** (tel. 235 55) keep the peace at 33 Eptanisou St., which runs parallel to the harbor road on the left side (facing inland). (Open 24 hrs.) **Taxis** can be found at 262 22 or at the stand on Miaouli Sq. **Buses** stop at the ferry dock and travel to Kini (10 per day) and Galissas (5 per day). A schedule in English is posted at the depot and printouts are available on the buses. For some beach-side reading, get English-language **books** at the two shops on the left side of the harbor (facing inland). Syros's **postal code** is 84100. The **telephone code** is 0281.

Hermoupolis has loads of cheap accommodations. Right at the ferry dock is a large map with rooms-to-let listed with phone numbers. The prices below are for high season, which lasts from mid-July through August. (Low season prices are about 30% lower.) Try **Hotel Athina,** 4 Antiparon St. (tel. 236 00 or 261 65), 2 blocks inland, up Evangelistra St. Rooms are spacious and the gigantic roof is great for sunning and laundry, and offers a panoramic harbor view. (Singles 1500dr. Doubles 3000dr. Triples 3600dr.) **Apollon Rooms to Let,** 8 Odysseus St. (tel. 221 58), off the inland street parallel to the harbor, is another delightful option. An evangelical arch of piebald stained glass and a singing bird greet you as you enter this old house with its high, frescoed ceilings and palatial sitting area. (Roof 700dr. Singles 31500dr. Doubles 3500dr. Triples 4900dr. Showers and kitchen facilities included.) Apollon's proprietors also rent **mopeds** at a 200dr discount if you stay in their rooms (call 263 66). For a chromophobe's nightmare of turquoise and crimson, climb the winding staircase to **Tony's Rooms to Let** at 3 Vocotopoulo St.. You'll see signs for it on the way to the bank. (Doubles 3000dr. Triples 3800dr.) Another possibility is **Kastro Rooms,** 12 Kalomnopoulou St. (tel. 280 64), off Evangelistrias St. and opposite the Evangelistrias Church and the National Bank. (Doubles 5800dr.)

For a traditional Greek dinner, try **Tempelis Taverna,** on Anastaseos St., below the Orthodox church on the right hill (facing inland). It's a hike, so you'll be starving by the time you arrive. From Miaouli, take Mantos Maupogenous St. (the long staircase behind the town hall just to the left of the clock tower) up to Diakon St. Make a left, then a right up Anastaseos St. The owner doesn't speak English, so scope out the food coming from the kitchen and point. Dine on tasty meatballs (550dr) or fried fish (690dr) or both. (Open for dinner only.) If your ferry arrives in Syros late at night and you're famished, head straight to **Elysee,** next to the tourist office. Chicken *souvlaki* (800dr). (Open 24 hrs.) For friendly, family-run service and all-around good food, go to **Maurikaki** (ΜΑΥΡΙΚΑΚΗ) on the left side of the harbor (facing inland). (Outstanding plate of black-eyed peas 300dr, Greek salad 500dr, take-away *gyros* 200dr; open daily 11:30am-2am). Mialou Sq. hums and strums with exciting nighttime activity. The **Piano Bar** to the left of Town Hall and the boisterous **Puramida** (ΠΥΡΑΜΙΔΑ) attract the local crowds. **Nefeli,** on the far right side of the waterfront (facing inland), has a DJ and bright, colored lights for late-night dancing.

During your stay, make the ascent to **Ano Syros,** the original medieval Venetian settlement which is still home to Syros's Catholics. Go up the steps behind Mialou Sq. or take the bus from the waterfront. The **Archaeological Museum,** just off Mialou Sq., to the left of the Town Hall under the campanile, has a small collection of Cycladic art. (Open Tues.-Sun. 8:30am-3pm. Free.)

Around the Island

Galissas, a village to the west of Hermoupolis, has a busy beach. You can camp on the gorgeous nudist **Armeos Beach** (climb past the chapel of Agia Pakou on the left side of the main beach). There are rooms-to-let all over the place. The helpful folks at the tourist office across from the bus stop offer discounts for students and youths. (Pleasant doubles 2400dr—regularly 3500dr). **Angela's Rooms to Let** (tel. 428 55), behind the mini-golf, has large, immaculate rooms surrounded by a spacious outdoor garden. (Doubles 5103dr. Triples 6237dr. Private bath included.) Angela also has fully stocked apartments which are suitable for up to four people (9000dr). The rooms at George's Restaurant (tel. 420 66) up the main inland street form the bus stop, are warmly decorated with homey weavings. (Doubles 5100dr. Triples 6000dr. Private bath included.) Also try **Tony's Rooms to Let** (tel. 424 82) at the end of the same street in the village. (Doubles 1500-2200dr. Triples 3200dr.) Nearby, clearly demarcated camping grounds **Yianna** (tel. 424 18) and **Two Hearts** (tel. 420 52) charge 700dr per person, 300dr per tent. The Two Hearts features a nightly barbeque (8pm-midnight), and also rents tents (500-700dr).

Galissas has most amenities imaginable—an inexpensive self-service restaurant on the beach, many *tavernas,* mini-golf, English-language books (at the Golden Corner, just before the beach), and even video games. At the **tourist office** (open daily 9:30am-11pm), you can make phone calls, change money, buy ferry tickets, or rent mopeds (2500dr) or cars (8800dr; third-party insurance included). **Galissas Tours** also offers boat excursions to the uninhabited Grammata, Lia, and Varvarousa beaches and to St. Stephano's Fisherman's Grotto (2000dr, with barbeque 4000dr).

All the music-filled *tavernas* lining the road to the beach advertise low prices (Greek salad 450dr, stuffed tomatoes 600dr), so take your pick. You can dance on the patio or in the air-conditioned building at the **Disco Aphrodite** across from Angela's (beer 400dr). Buses run to Galissas frequently from Hermoupolis. (6:45am-9pm, 20min., 160dr. The return trip, along a different route, takes a little longer; 7:05am-9:20pm, 50min., 200dr.) Farther south along the coast are the beaches at **Poseidonia, Finikas, Angathopes,** and **Komito,** all connected by bus to Hermoupolis. Komito offers free camping. The beach resort of **Vari** is most popular with family and package tour groups. Nearby is the tiny fishing village of Kini whose famous sunset melts all observers and certainly justifies the visit.

Paros ΠΑΡΟΣ

The geographical center of the islands, Paros is the place for those who want a taste of everything. To enjoy such variety, however, you'll have to skimp on quality. Paros's vast interior is less idyllic, its villages less picturesque, and its beaches not quite as luscious than those of nearby Naxos. Although the island's nightlife is lively, it is neither as raucous nor as chic as the parties on Ios and Mykonos. Yet the island's hamlets and beaches are easily accessible by motorbike or bus, and Paros is a convenient base for day excursions to other islands. Though it has quickly become one of the most touristed islands in the Cyclades, Paros's tranquil inland areas, hosting only Mt. Profitis Ilias (771m), a few villages, and some farmland, still provide refuge from the beachfront bonanzas.

In summer, pensions and *dhomatia* fill up before you can say "shitfaced Northern Europeans." If you can't find accommodations in any of the main coastal towns, don't panic. Try one of the small villages linked to the port town of Parikia by bus, Antiparos, or any of the island's secluded beaches. There are also several official campsites on the island, and unofficial camping is quite common, although still illegal. (To be safe, camp somewhere other than Parikia.)

Paros rivals Syros as the transportation hub of the Cyclades. **Boats** depart several times per day to all of the major nearby islands. A comprehensive schedule is posted in front of the tourist office to the left of the windmill. In summer, five to six boats per day leave for: Piraeus (5-6hr., 2510dr); Naxos (1hr., 853dr); Sifnos (2hr., 1520dr); Ios (2½hr., 1750dr); and Santorini (3½hr., 1885dr). One to two per day service: Rafina (5hr., 2230dr); Syros (1½hr., 810dr); Tinos (3hr., 960dr); and Mykonos (2hr., 960dr). Three to four per week run to: Amorgos (3hr., 1820dr); Ikaria (4hr., 1690dr); Crete (8hr., 3220dr); and Samos (6hr., 1885dr). Keep in mind that Paros and Syros are the only Cycladic islands that connect to the Dodecanese and the Northeast Aegean Islands. Twice per week, there are sailings to Sikinos (4hr., 1290dr), Folegandros (5hr., 1220dr), and Rhodes (16hr., 4000dr). There are also infrequent connections to Skyros (3440dr), Skiathos (4070dr), and Thessaloniki (5220dr). Tourist agencies sponsor excursions to Iraklion and Koufonisa (4500dr), Delos/Mykonos (5700dr), Santorini (6500dr), and Naxos (3200dr). Finally, **Olympic Airways** flies an 18-seater plane between Athens and Paros (10 per day, 10000dr). The Olympic Airways bus leaves for the airport before departures and awaits all arrivals; to be sure of the correct departure time, check the comprehensive schedule in their office (bus 150dr).

Parikia

Orientation and Practical Information

Parikia's waterfront is the island's commercial district. As you disembark from the ferry, most restaurants, hotels, and offices lie to the left (facing inland). Straight ahead, past the windmill and the tourist offices, is the *platia* (main square) behind which a white-washed labyrinth brims with shops and cafés. To the far right around the bend, a host of good bars and island's party district await you.

Tourist Information Center: Tel. 220 79, in the windmill by the dock. Boat and bus schedules, general information and maps of the island, and phone numbers for rooms-to-let. Currency exchange. Open daily 9am-11pm.

Currency Exchange: National Bank of Greece. From the windmill, head directly into the pedestrian square—it's at the far corner in the fortress-like building. Open Mon.-Thurs. 8am-2pm, Fri. 8am-1:30pm; for exchange also Mon.-Fri. 6-8pm, Sat. 9am-1pm.

Post Office: On the north side of the waterfront, 2 blocks past the bus stop. Open Mon.-Fri. 7:30am-2pm. **Postal Code:** 84400.

OTE: One block south of the windmill (its back borders the main square). Open Mon.-Sat. 7:30am-10pm, Sun. 8am-10pm. **Telephone Code:** 0284.

Flights: Olympic Airways: Tel. 219 00, on Propona St., the street bordered on its left by the garden with the small blue and white church which leads inland to the main church. Open daily 8am-3pm.

Bus Station: A few blocks to the left of the windmill. Complete schedule posted in front. Buses run 8am-9pm at least every hr. to: Naoussa (15min., 180dr); Lefkes (25min., 190dr); Piso Livadi (40min., 300dr); and Chryssi Akti (1hr., 380dr). Eight buses per day go to the Valley of the Butterflies (10min., 140dr) en route to Aliki and the airport (210dr).

Luggage Storage: Many line Propona St., heading back from the windmill. 300dr per piece, per day (not 24 hrs.).

Laundry Service: For full service, turn right before the bus stop. Wash and dry 1850dr. For self-service, take second right after the town beach starts. Wash, dry and soap for 1280dr. Both laundromats open Mon.-Sat. 9am-2:30pm and 5-9pm.

Public Toilets: Beside the small blue and white church north of the windmill. 20dr.

Medical Clinic: Tel. 225 00. Across the street from the toilets. Open daily 8:30am-1:30pm and 6-8pm.

Pharmacy: Tel. 222 23. Next to the laundromat. Open daily 8:30am-1:30pm and 5:30-8:30pm.

Port Police: Tel. 212 40, off the waterfront, past the bus station. Information about all sailings. Open 24 hrs.

Police: Tel. 212 21, across the square behind the OTE, on the 2nd floor above the travel agencies. Open 24 hrs. **English Bookstore: A. Tzougantous/S. Oragatis** tourist shop just past the bus stop behind the town beach has a small but respectable collection. Not the usual trash. Open daily 9am-11pm.

Accommodations and Camping

Most of the hotels and *dhomatia* rest just off the waterfront and in the old town, but a whole slew of new, fairly cheap pensions and rooms-to-let boarding houses have opened up behind the town beach. If you can get a good deal from the dock hawks, take it. In peak season (late July-Aug.), scarce cheap singles will cost around 2500dr, doubles 4000dr, and triples 6500dr. In the summer, arrive in Parikia early in the day, or you might have to go to Naoussa or Piso Livadi to find a room. The following are high season rates, which drop 30-50%.

John's Rooms (tel. 227 97), second right after the town beach starts. Plain but clean and spacious. Singles 3000dr. Doubles 6000dr. Triples 8000dr. **Rooms Mimikos** (tel. 214 37), around the corner from Agorakitou St. Follow the signs past the National Bank. Charming, clean rooms with balconies in a quiet neighborhood. Hot water. Doubles 4500dr. Triples 5500dr. **The Dina** (tel. 213 25), past the National Bank and at the very end of Market St. An upscale pension; quiet, immaculate, with a beautiful garden. Open May-Oct. Doubles 4100-6000dr. Private bath included. Many have balconies. Reservations by mail preferred.

Hotel Parko (tel. 222 13), just down from Olympic Airways, toward the waterfront. Spotless doubles 4600dr, with bath 6200dr. Triples 8300dr **Camping: Koula** (tel. 220 82), 400m north of town, and **Parasporos** (tel. 219 44), 2km south (take bus from port). **Krios Camping** (tel. 217 05), take the little boat to Krios Beach, across the harbor). All three 600dr per person, 250dr per tent.

Food

Cheap and cheesy restaurants infesting the street behind the town beach serve breakfast, lunch, and dinner and are popular with the tanning crowd. Greek plate specials, hearty and average, go for about 750dr. All are similar, so feast your eyes on the crowd and the eats when you choose where to dine.

Restaurant Posidon, behind the beach, set back from the street in a leafy garden. *Mousaka* and stuffed eggplant 730dr each. Open 8am-2am.

Restaurant 'Mondo', on the far left of the square, facing the windmill. Out of the cattle range, but outdoor seating provides fine people-watching vantage. Veal with eggplant 790dr. *Mousaka* 590dr. Open daily 10am-2am.

To Tamarisko, near Rooms Mimikos—follow the signs. Lush flower garden setting, but atmosphere doesn't come cheap. Meatballs 892dr, curried pork 1200dr. Open Tues.-Sun. 7pm-1am.

Corfu Leon, in a square on the far right side of the waterfront, close to the discos and bars. *Mousaka* 700dr, *kalamari* 600dr. Open 6am-11:30pm.

Nick's Hamburgers, turn right after Corfu Leon. Opened in 1977, the first hamburger joint in Paros. Nickburger 380dr. Bacon cheeseburger 580dr. 100% beef. Open 12:30pm-3am.

Pactia, down the alley from Nick's. Great, inexpensive fast food. Vegetable sandwiches 300-800dr. Open 10am-3am.

Sights

Anyone with a fondness for Byzantine architecture will be giddy with ecstasy over the **Panayia Ekatontapiliani** (the Church of Our Lady of 100 Gates), an imposing 6th-century edifice that houses three separate adjacent churches, cloisters, and a large peaceful courtyard. Supposedly, the church has 100 doors, but don't waste your time counting—only 10 are immediately obvious. The main structure is the mammoth **Church of the Assumption,** which houses three tremendous chandeliers. **Church of St. Nickolas** (the oldest of the three) flanks this central structure to the north as does the **baptistry** to the south. To reach the church, walk inland from the public garden with the little blue and white church. (Open daily 6am-noon and 5-9pm.)

Behind the church, next to the schoolyard is the **Archaeological Museum** which houses a 5th-century BCE statue of the Wingless Nike and a piece of the Parian Chronicle. (Open Tues.-Sat. 8:30am-3pm, Sun. 9am-2pm. Admission 400dr, students 200dr.)

Just 10km south of town is the cool, spring-fed **Valley of the Butterflies,** home to an enormous spawning swarm of brown-and-white striped butterflies. These winged wonders cover the foliage, blending into their surroundings until they expose their bright red underwings in flight. In June the butterflies' thoughts turn to love, and they wing their way to this lepidopterous metropolis to mate. You can visit here by taking the bus from Parikia that goes to Aliki (every 2hr., 10min., 140dr) and asking to be let off at the butterflies (in Greek *petaloudes)*. From there, follow the signs up the steep winding road 2km to the entrance. You can also take a tour from one of the various travel agents (750dr) leaving at 4, 5, and 7pm, or plod your way there via donkey (2½-3hr, 180dr). (Open Mon.-Sat. 9am-8pm, Sun. 9am-1pm and 4-8pm. Admission 200dr.)

Entertainment

Most of the nightspots are south of the windmill along the waterfront, on the far right end. You can down a few shots (250dr each) and dance to the loud, top-40 tunes at the dank **7 Muses Disco/Slammer Bar,** on the end of the waterfront before the entrance to a complex of "international" nightspots that cater to the English-speaking crowd: the **Viking Scandinavian Bar, The Londoner, The Koala Bar,** and **The Dubliner/Hard Rock Café Disco.** The Dubliner has a deli-bar and mini-market (canned Guinness 400dr); don't forget to buy water. At the **Irish Bar Stavros,** you can join the rambunctiousness embodied inside, or squanch pebbles between your toes in the sedate, bamboo-ceilinged garden. (Cocktails 500-600dr.) If you feel like hanging out on the main waterfront drag and sipping a cool cocktail, head for **Bolero's,** where all drinks are 600dr. Bohemians relax on pillows and catch the jazz and blues at the **Pirate Bar,** across from the Dina Hotel. (Cocktails 500dr.) Perched above the buildings, **Evinos** and its slightly more expensive neighbor **Pebbles Bar,** where jazz and classical music BamBam into the night, are great places to escape streetside din.

Naoussa

Naoussa is an alternative to Parikia for a home base on Paros. A natural harbor, cradled on both sides by long, sandy arms, Naoussa has been a popular port throughout history. Ancient Persians, Greeks, Romans, medieval Venetians, Saracens, Turks, and Russians have all anchored at the harbor. Owing to the magnificence of the beaches, brisk tourist trade has usurped parts of the town, but elsewhere, the fishing continues as always. Buses travel at least every hour to Naoussa from Parikia (7am-7pm, 15min., 180dr). On the way to Naoussa, these buses stop at the slightly sullied but still popular **Kolymbithres Beach.** From Naoussa, **buses** run to Santa Maria Beach (4 per day, 140dr). You can also catch a **boat** to: Santa Maria (every ½hr. 11am-5pm, 776dr); Laggeri (every ½hr. 10am-6:30pm, 500dr); and to the less secluded Kolymbithres and Monastri Beaches (every ½hr. 9:30am-6:30pm, 300dr and 362dr, respectively).

The tourist agencies in the walled square next to the bus stop help locate accommodations. Expect singles for 2000dr, doubles for 3500dr, and triples for 4500dr. They also organize excursions around Paros (2000dr) and to: Antiparos (daily, 800dr); Naxos (3200dr); Delos/Mykonos (6500dr); Santorini (5700dr); and Koufonisi and Iraklion (Mon., 4500dr). In addition they rent mopeds (1500-6000dr) and cars (8000-15,000dr). Contact English-fluent Katerina at **Simitzi Tours** (tel. 51 11 13 or 517 61) for friendly and helpful service. (Open daily 8:30am-midnight). To find the **post office,** walk away from the water, through the square. It's on the left, just after the church. (Open Mon.-Fri. 7:30am-2pm). The **police** sit on the left of the street running inland right from the post office (tel. 512 02; open 24 hrs.). The **OTE** is farther inland. Take a left at the end of the policemen's road. (Open Mon.-Fri.. 7:30am-3:10pm.) Around the corner from the post office is a **pharmacy** (tel. 517 04; open daily 8:30am-1pm and 5:30-9pm). To find the **National Bank** (open Mon.-Thurs. 8:30am-2pm, Fri. 8:30am-1:30pm) and the **public toilets,** walk towards the water from the bus stop to the small waterfront and take your third inland right. Both perch on the far right of a colorful inlet harbor, crowded with fishing boats, and inviting restaurants, and guarded by the remains of a Venetian castle on the far left. Inland Grammou St. covets two excellent **supermarkets** (open daily 8am-11:30pm) and several sophisticated clothing shops.

There is camping near the beach at **Camping Naoussa** (tel. 515 95/65; 500dr per person, 200dr per tent; their van meets boats at the port). There is no shortage of "Rooms to Let" signs in town. If you prefer a hotel, the cheapest average 5000dr per double. At that price, the **Naoussa Hotel** (tel. 512 07) offers balconied rooms overlooking the sea. Also try the cozy **Madaky** (tel. 514 75), near the main road (doubles 3500-4000dr), or the quieter **Stella** (tel. 513 17; doubles with bath 5869dr). To reach Stella's, take a left past the post office, then a sharp right after the pharmacy.

An excellent choice for cheap Greek fare, **Diamantes** is 1 block past the post office, behind the church at the red and white "grill" sign. (Swordfish *souvlaki* 850dr. Open 5:30pm-midnight.) Lounge in the roof garden at **Kavernis Creperie,** where jazz and incense hover in the background. (Behind the post office. Chicken and rice crêpe 1100dr; chocolate crêpe 550dr. Ice cream crêpe 750dr; open after 7:30pm.) Swat the mosquitoes at the outdoor **cinema** next to Diamantes. (Nightly 10pm; frequently English versions.) Then keep shaking at the discos advertised all over town—**Banana Moon, Apocalypse,** and many more. (Follow the signs leading under the main church.

Nightly 11pm-3am.) On the first Sunday in July, you can cruise around Naoussa's harbor and feast on free fresh fish and wine as you watch traditional dancing at the **Wine and Fish Festival.** On August 23, local festivities commemorate a naval victory over the Turks. Starting around September 10, foreigners can earn measly wages during the two-week grape harvest.

Around the Island

Cutting through the center of the island toward the east coast, you will reach **Marathi** (not to be confused with the Indian language), only 5km from Parikia. The marble quarries that made Paros famous in ancient times are located nearby. Still considered by many to be among the finest in the world, Parian marble is translucent up to 3mm thick, one-third the opacity of most other marble. The quarries are now idle and difficult to find as well.

Lefkes, 7km from Marathi, was the largest village on the island in the 19th century when Parians moved inland to escape the pirates swashbuckling off the coast. Now a quiet village of 400 inhabitants, its classic Cycladic architecture makes it the prettiest town in Paros's interior. Road meets sea at **Piso Livadi.** If you're not into Parikia's nightlife, Piso Livadi can be a fine place to while away your hours on Paros. The **tourist office** (tel. 411 35), home of the town's international phone, is directly across from the bus stop, and provides information on *dhomatia* (open 9am-10pm). The **Hotel Piso Livadi** (tel. 413 09) is just up from the bus stop. (Doubles 2000-4900dr.) **The Magia** (tel. 413 90), overlooking the town, on the hill between Piso Livadi and Logaras Beach, has doubles (3500dr), and in the summer rents cots on the roof and under a grapevine (500dr). **Londo's Hotel** (tel. 412 18), 100m up from Hotel Piso Livadi, offers clean, airy rooms (doubles with bath 4000-7000dr). **Captain Kafkis Camping** huddles nearby (tel. 414 79; 450dr per person, 100dr per tent). Follow the signs 1km back along the road towards Parikia.

About 3km south of the unimpressive Logaras Beach, ranges **Chryssi Akti,** the biggest and one of the best beaches on Paros. Recently, it has become a magnet for high-tech, expert windsurfing. You can rest your weary self at **Dara's Apartments** (tel. 412 24), beside **supermarket Xilaras.** (Two rooms, kitchen and bath for 8000dr.) Many also freelance camp on Chryssi Akti. Lovely **Dryos Beach,** the next beach south, is quieter and more isolated. Doubles in this area average 3000dr. Excursion boats sail from Piso Livadi to Naxos (2500dr), Delos, Tubis (4500dr), and Mykonos (2 per week, 3000dr round-trip), and to Santorini (2 per week, 6500dr). One-way tickets to Iraklion and Koufonisa cost 3500dr.

Another public bus runs to Pounda (every hr., 15min., 140dr) and Aliki (every 2hr., 40min., 210dr) on the west coast, where you will find even more pleasurable beaches. From Pounda, it is only a 15-minute boat ride to Antiparos (8:20am-8:20pm every hr., 260dr round-trip). Some beaches on the west coast are accessible by boat from Parikia (9am-6pm every 15min., 600dr). **Krios Beach,** the first stop, is a calm oasis; the next en route, **Martsella** occasionally gets a tired of convention and turns nudist, its sultry sands always inveigling. A 10-minute walk from Martsella, **Agios Fokas** is one of the most secluded of the western beaches. Boats also run to Santa Maria Beach (600dr).

Antiparos ΑΝΤΙΠΑΡΟΣ

Contrary to the development of the Hegelian dialectic, Paros and Antiparos will not be fusing in synthesis any time soon; although they were once, in fact, the same entity until an earthquake split them more than a millennium ago. Besides, Antiparos means "across Paros." According to local lore, the two isles are so close that, years ago, travelers would signal the ferryman on Paros by opening the door of a chapel on Antiparos. Fortunately, ferry service today is far more frequent and less antiquated. Antiparos, a popular daytrip, is a refuge for those unable to find accommodations on its larger neighbor. From Parikia, the trip takes 45 minutes (600dr round-trip, 1000dr with transport to and from the stalactite caves included); from Pounda, however, it takes a mere 15 minutes (8:20am-8:20pm every hr., round-trip 180dr).

Most of this small island is undeveloped—virtually all of its 700 inhabitants live in the town where the ferry docks, and there is no bus service to any other point on the island except the stalactite caves. At the harbor you'll find a sliver of sand alongside the dock, a few waterfront restaurants, and several hotels and pensions. Tourist shops, *tavernas,* a few bakeries, and more pensions line the street leading from the dock to the center of town where a cluster of funky pubs and bars has opened up. The center, up the road about 500m, has a wide-open plaza, with *kafenia* under its shady trees. Go through the stone archway to the right of the square to reach the **Kastro of Antiparos,** a village built in the 1440s by a nobleman named Lorentano.

The **tourist office** (tel. 613 90) on the the waterfront will assist with *dhomatia* (doubles around 3000dr, with bath 5000dr) and bus and boat schedules. It also has an international telephone and exchange facility. Next door you'll find the **National Bank** (open Mon.-Fri. 9:45am-1pm). The **post office** is on the left side of the street leading from the dock to the square (open Mon.-Fri. 7:30am-2pm). The **OTE,** which also sells stamps and maps of the island, is on the right side of the street which branches left at the main square (open daily 8am-noon and 5-9pm). The self-service **laundry** is on the same street as the post office, closer to the dock (open daily 10am-2pm and 5-9pm). On the left of the same street as the OTE, closer to the port, **Stelios** offers a superlative collection of English-language books—some second-hands are as little as 500dr (open June-Sept. daily 11am-5pm and 7:30pm-midnight). The number for the **police** in Antiparos is 612 02, for **first aid** 612 19. The **postal code** is 84007, and the **telephone code** is 0284.

Accommodations are easy to find on Antiparos. **Anargyros** (tel. 612 04), on the waterfront next to Morakis Travel Agency, is a pleasant hotel half-obscured by trees. (Singles 3000-5000dr. Doubles 3500-4000dr. Triples 4500-6000dr.) The **Mantalena,** to the right of the dock (facing inland), has clean rooms with private baths and balconies. (Singles 3000-7000dr.) **Camping Antiparos** (tel. 612 21) rests 800m northwest of town on Agios Yiannis Theologos Beach (500dr per person, 100dr per tent). **Psariliki,** a small beach with pebbles, sand, paddleboats, and canoes, is a 100m walk to the left of the docks.

Some excellent restaurants are the **Taverna Giorgios** (next to the bakery on the main road; dinner only) and the **Taverna Klimataria,** to the left off the main road, under blazing pink azalea bushes. With its throng of international rock 'n' roll houses and watering holes in the center of town, Antiparos follows the lead of its rip-roaring neighbors. The **Windmill** disco whirls on into the night inside the windmill.

An escape from the parched horsefly heat, the **stalactite caves** at the southern end of the island have been a tourist attraction since they were first discovered in the time of Alexander the Great—their floating stone staircase was once descended by the romantic heart of Byron. (Open daily 10am-4pm. Admission 350dr.) In the 18th century, Russian naval officers "donated" some of the stalactites to a St. Petersburg museum, while many of the remaining formations have been personalized by 19th-century knife-wielding tourists. Buses from Antiparos go directly to the caves every hour from 10:30am-2:30pm (round-trip 800dr). You could also take a boat there (round-trip 300dr), but the entrance is a hot 2km walk, or a 500dr donkey ride, from the water.

Naxos ΝΑΞΟΣ

Along with alluring interior villages and numerous tranquil beaches, Naxos has one of the most colorful of Cycladic histories; Carians, Cretans, Ionians, Athenians, Macedonians, Egyptians, Rhodians, Romans, Byzantines, Venetians, Martians, Turks, and Russians all ruled the island in succession. The island's strongest historical link to the past, however, is shrouded in myth. After Ariadne, the daughter of King Minos of Crete, saved Theseus from her father's labyrinth, the young prince fled with the princess to Naxos. After they had spent the night there, Theseus went to wash his hair and abandoned her. Ariadne wept at finding herself alone on the shore, but her despair was soon remedied. Along floated Dionysus who, on his way, had for himself quite an adventure. Captured by pirates, he immobilized the ship's sails with spontaneously growing vines and turned the mean-spirited buccaneers into serpents. Dionysus transformed himself into a mighty lion but it just wasn't the same without a sidekick to take the form of an iceberg. Arriving on Naxos, Dionysus took Ariadne's hand in marriage. When she died, the god put her bridal wreath among the stars where it still shines as the Corona Borealis.

Naxos might have even the most despairing soul seeing stars, so handsome are its rocky promontories, squat windmills, and demure villages tucked between rolling hills. This natural wealth has made Naxos one of the richest of the Cyclades, a fact which becomes apparent on a short walk through the town of Naxos (called Chora). Rather than a depressing dichotomy between islanders' small homes and luxury hotels full of mollycoddled tourists, in Naxos, the best belongs to its people. From Naxos, **ferries** travel to: Piraeus (7 per day, 7hr., 2500dr); Paros (4-6 per day, 1hr., 700dr); Ios (1-4 per day, 1½hr., 1400dr); Santorini (1-6 per day, 3hr., 1300dr); Mykonos (1-2 per day, 2hr., 1000dr); and Syros (1-5 per day, 2½hr., 500dr). There is less frequent service to Amorgos (5 per week, 3½hr., 1060dr), and Iraklion, Schinoussa, Koufinisia, and Donoussa (3 per week, 1½hr., 1600dr). Daily excursions go to Mykonos and Delos (9am-9pm, 3hr. on each island, 3000dr).

Naxos Town

As you wander through the tangled streets of old Naxos Town, you may feel as though you were lost in a painting. The ancient wooden porticoes and glimpses of the brilliant blue sea only enhance the charm; flowers and trellised plants engulf the old homes of the Venetian *Kastro,* and the vibrantly colorful markets whir with activity.

Orientation and Practical Information

All ferries dock in Naxos Town. Don't bother with maps; streets are poorly labeled and zigzag a lot. The arrows painted by hotels and restaurant owners are your best navigational guides. The old labyrinthine heart of the town swaddling the *Kastro* hides close to the ferry dock behind the waterfront veneer.

Tourist Information Center: Tel. 245 25 or 243 58, on west Paralia (waterfront), next to Creperie Bikini. If you need it, they have it: advice on rooms-to-let, free booking service for the island and everywhere in Greece, bus and ferry schedules, currency exchange, metered phone for collect and charge calls, used books, luggage storage (200dr), and safety deposit boxes (200dr). In case of *serious* emergency, ask for Despina (after midnight, call 229 93); she speaks fluent English and is very helpful. Open daily 8am-12:30pm; March 15-Oct. daily 8am-9:30pm. **Ciao Travel,** up from Theoharis's bike rental on a side street to the right (tel. 239 33) also has luggage storage (100dr) and accommodation and ticket information. Open daily 10am-4pm and 7-11pm.

Motorbike Rental: Theoharis, Neofitou St. (tel. 239 00), the first left after the tourist office. Theoharis is an English-fluent font of information. Mopeds 2300-2500dr. Yamaha 50cc 3000dr. Town bikes 1800dr, mountain bikes 2000dr. Helmets provided. 3rd party insurance included. Open daily 8am-2pm and 5-9pm.

Currency Exchange: National Bank of Greece. Walk down the waterfront with the water on your right; the bank is on the southern end of the Paralia. Open Mon.-Thurs. 8am-2pm, Fri. 8am-1:30pm. Many other places line the waterfront.

Post Office: Walk down the waterfront (water on your right), turn left after Hotel Hermes, then take your first right. Open Mon.-Fri. 7:30am-2pm. **Postal Code:** 84300.

OTE: Next to the Hotel Hermes and opposite the bank, at the southern end of the harbor. Open daily 7:30am-midnight; Oct.-May daily 7:30am-10pm. **Telephone Code:** 0285.

Buses: Buses stop directly in front of the ferry dock. Schedules posted, but double-check with the drivers or at the **bus office** up the street (left facing inland).The tourist office gives out a printed schedule. Arrive early, because buses are packed—especially the one from Chora to Appollonas via Filoti (4 per day, 2hr., 700dr). Buses also run frequently to Chalki (6 per day, ½hr., 210dr), and Apiranthos (4 per day, 1hr., 350dr). There is frequent service to west coast beaches, including Agios Prokopios and Agia Anna (every hr. 8am-midnight, 20min., 150dr and 200dr., respectively).

Bookstore: Naxos Popular Art Shop (sign in Greek), above a restaurant 50m south of the wharf. Buys and sells used books. Good selection and the best prices in the islands: 200-900dr per book. Open daily 9:30am-1:30pm and 6:30-11pm.

Laundromat: Pro Wash Laundry (tel. 220 90), just before the post office. Wash 800dr, dry 600dr. Also has international phone and luggage storage (150dr per piece). Mon.-Fri. 9am-10pm, Sat. 9am-7pm.

Public Toilets and Showers: Behind Toast Time on Nikodemos St. Turn left after Zas Travel. Toilets 50dr, showers 400dr. Open daily 9am-2pm and 4-11pm.

Pharmacy: several on the waterfront, open Sun.-Tues. and Thurs.-Fri. 8:30am-2pm and 5:30-9:30pm.

Health Center: (*Kendro Egias,* in Greek), on the edge of town on the road to the villages (tel. 233 33). Has 14 doctors (some English-speaking) and can access helicopter service to Athens in emergencies. Open 24 hrs.

Port Police: Nikodemos St. (tel. 223 00), just off the small square with the cafés, on the 2nd floor. Open 24 hrs.

Police: Tel. 221 00 or 232 80. Turn right off Neofitou St., and then first left, on the 2nd floor. Super jovial. Open 24 hrs.

Accommodations and Camping

Late July and August is peak season in Naxos, and most hotels fill to capacity. At other times of the year, expect to pay 20-50% less than the prices quoted. People who meet the boat charge about 2000dr for singles, 4000dr for doubles, and 5000dr for triples. A plethora of less expensive *dhomatia* can be found by pursuing the trail of rooms-to-let signs in old Naxos Town, where you will find the most charming of settings.

Eleni (tel. 240 42) has airy rooms in her white, brown-balconied house; take the first left before the post office and it's on the left. Doubles 3500dr. Triples 4300dr. Another good choice in the newer part of town is **Anna Legaki's** (tel. 228 37), across the street. Her rooms are smaller, but the hospitality makes up for it. Roof 1000dr. Singles 2000dr. Doubles 4000dr. Triples 4500dr. Breakfast included.

Hotel Dionyssos (tel. 223 31) in the old market section, near the Venetian Kastro. Look for painted red hands pointing there or the arrows to the Anixis next door. A little run-down, but still one of the best bargains in the Cyclades. Dorm beds in the basement 700dr. Roof 700dr. Singles 1500dr. Doubles 2000dr. Triples 3000dr. Cold showers only.

Naxos Camping (tel. 235 00/01), is about 1½km outside town on a dirt road off Agios Giorgios Beach. **Camping Apollon** (tel. 241 17/18), is farther down the road, between Prokopios and Agios Giorgos Beaches. Both campsites have self-service restaurants and laundry facilities. (600dr per person, 300dr per tent.) **Maragas Camping** (tel. 245 52) on Agia Anna Beach offers similar prices. Freelance camping is illegal on Naxos, though some take their chances on west coast beaches. To get to **Agios Giorgios,** walk past the post office, through the small square, and down the hill. The beach's hard-packed sand attracts crowds. A little beyond, the small dunes lining the cove provide a haven for high-performance windsurfers. A little farther along, the dunes give way again to open sand. **Agia Anna Beach,** about a half-hour walk south of Ag. Giorgios, is more scenic. Take the road to the Maragas campground from Ag. Giorgios or simply walk along the beach.

Food and Entertainment

The influence of tourism on Naxos is most easily discernible in the restaurants, many of which flaunt manicured interiors and menus in English and German. Picnicking is a down-to-earth alternative, especially since Naxos **markets** offer the best cheese, wine, fruit, and vegetables in the Cyclades. You'll find innumerable fruit stands in the *Kastro* and along the waterfront. **Mathiassos** supermarket is on the waterfront near the OTE (open Mon.-Tues., Thurs.-Fri. 8am-1:30pm and 6-9:30pm, Wed. and Sat. 8am-2:30pm). Try a locally produced wine; many are named after the villages in which they are made ("Glinado" and "Skeponi" are both super choices). Two famous local cheeses are "Naxos cheese," a type of *graviera*, and *anthotiro* cream cheese. You can find standard fare at the *tavernas* along **Nikodemos Street.** On the same street, you can buy delicious *tost* (about 140-390dr) at **Toast Time.** (Open 8am-3am.)

Manolis Garden Taverna, in the old town on Old Market St.—follow the signs. Pleasant outdoor garden setting. *Kalamari* 500dr. Delicious chicken *souvlaki* wrapped in bacon, 1000dr. Open May-Sept. daily 6pm-midnight.

Elli's, up from Theoharis's, on the water. A relaxing restaurant with a nice view. Vegetable soup 350dr. Crêpes 600-700dr. Open 6:30pm-1am.

Lucullus, on Old Market St. The oldest *taverna* in town, named after a luckless glutton who expired from overindulgence. Don't let it happen to you. Garden setting. Stuffed grape leaves 550dr. *Mousaka* 1050dr. Open nightly.

Panorama Restaurant, a 20-min. walk down Neofitou St. Very popular with the islanders, especially at sunset. Try the local barrel wine. Veal 600dr. Open year-round 8am-1am.

Rendez-Vous (Ραντεβου) on the waterfront. Hot, delicious, gooey *loukoumades* (honey doughnuts) 250dr, but only at night in July and Aug. Come early—they run out by 11pm. Home-made ice cream, luscious fruit tarts, and mile-high chocolate pistachio cakes, too. Open 6am-3am.

Naxos's nightlife isn't as frenetic as the other islands'. Up the street from Theoharis's, **Tony's (The Loft)** is an old favorite. Tucked under one of the arched streets in the Old Market district, **Diogenes** has a popular happy hour from 6-9pm (all cocktails 450dr). Loud music and colored lights seep out from **The Jam,** behind the OTE. **Mike's Bar,** across the street has mellower music. (Drinks 500-600dr.) For late-night dancing, try the **Ocean Club,** right behind the National Bank. There are also three discos along Ag. Georgios Beach. The liveliest is **Infinity Disco.**

Sights

While in Naxos Town, make sure to walk around the old **Venetian Kastro,** a series of mansions still inhabited by the descendants of the original Frankish and Venetian nobility. Up from the Hotel Pantheon "The Castle" and "The Loom" merit a visit to see their folk art merchandise. The excellent **museum,** where Nikos Kazantzakis, author of *Last Temptation of Christ* and *Zorba the Greek* once studied, is housed in one of the old *Kastro* buildings (follow the yellow signs through the labyrinth of streets). The museum contains many beautiful Cycladic artifacts, as well as vases, sculpture, jewels, and implements found in Mycenaean and Geometric chamber tombs. (Open Tues.-Sun. 8:30am-3pm. Admission 400dr, students 200dr; free on Sun. and holidays.)

From the waterfront, you can see the white chapel of *Myrditiotissa* floating serenely in the harbor on its man-made islet. Nearby is the **Palatia,** an intriguing marble archway on the hilltop near the port. According to myth, this was where Ariadne lost Theseus and found Dionysus; later, it was the site of Ariadne's palace. Excavation has debunked this delightful hypothesis—in fact, the archway, along with the platform and some columns, is merely detritus from yet another temple to Apollo. Today it makes an excellent spot for a banana liqueur and *baklava* picnic.

Around the Island

Those who leave having seen only Naxos Town and its environs will have missed the heart of Naxos. The ideal way to see the island is on foot. Villages are situated so that food and shelter are available at convenient intervals; many of these spots, at least in the interior, are connected by footpaths.

Mopeds are popular for excursions, but paved roads cover only a fraction of the island. This is not the place to *learn* how to use a moped; several people die each year on Naxos's rocky, tortuous roads. Many travelers opt instead to take the bus to Apollon, a small fishing village on the northern tip of the island (3 per day, 2hr., 700dr). Several of the villages along the way deserve closer attention than they can get from a bus window; if you're inclined, you can stop en route, and then catch a later bus or continue on foot.

The first hour of the ride, from Naxos Town to Chalki, takes you through cultivated mountainsides, rich with olive trees, churches, and wild flowers that erupt consistently each spring and summer. Before you reach Chalki, there's a turn-off for **Ano Sangri,** an isolated town of winding flagstone streets 1km west of the road. You can get off the bus at the turn-off and walk, or trek the entire way from Naxos Town (about 1½hr.).

At **Chalki,** a placid village surrounded by Venetian towers, begins the magnificent **Tragea**—a huge Arcadian olive grove of absolute stillness. Stop in at the **Panayia Protothonis,** the parish church of Chalki, right across from the bus stop. Restoration work there has uncovered wall paintings from the 11th through 13th centuries. If the church is closed, ask a local to find the priest who can admit you.

If you have a motorbike or car, an alternative route takes you from Naxos Town through Melanes to **Flerio,** where one of the magnificent **kouroi** of Naxos sleeps in a woman's garden. *Kouroi,* larger-than-life sculptures of male figures, were first made in Greece in the 7th century BCE under Egyptian influence. This one was probably abandoned in its marble quarry because it broke before completion. Its owner runs a small *kafeneion* in the garden. Farther along your drive north to Chalki, you'll pass through a trio of charming villages built in a river valley: **Kato Potamia; Mesi Potamia;** and **Ano Potamia.**

Soon after leaving Chalki you'll reach **Filoti,** an authentic village where the Tragea ends and the road climbs the flanks of Mt. Zas. These slopes offer superb views extending all the way to Poros and the sea beyond. In another 15 minutes you will enter the small town of **Apiranthos,** which houses the **Michael Bardani Museum** in a white building on the right side of the main street. The museum contains many remnants of Cycladic artifacts. (Open daily 8am-2pm, but hours are flexible—just ask for Giorgos, who can open the museum for you. Free.) The town also has a modest **Folk Art Museum** (sign in Greek) located in the main square. (Open daily 10am-1pm. Free.) Many homes in Apiranthos are 300-400 years old, and lie in the shadows of the two castles which dominate the town (closed to the public). The mountain views from the edges of the town are stunning, and the locals are cordial to the few tourists who venture this way. From Apiranthos through **Koronos** and **Koronida,** an hour's drive away, the road snakes through interior mountain ranges. The terraced landscape, laden with grapevines and fruit and olive trees, plunges dramatically into the valleys below.

A short walk from the harbor is one of the most famous **Kouroi** of Naxos. At 10½m long, this *kouros* is more massive, if less finely sculpted, than the one in Flerio, and is also incomplete. To reach it from the village, head back up the main road away from the beach and turn right at the small sign for "kouros;" from there, it's about a 20-minute trek.

On your return trip from Apollon to Chalki, you might want to get off the bus at Filoti (about 2km away) and walk through the Tragea. A footpath starts on the main road just outside Filoti, directly across from the sign for Kerami, and leads to **Agia Apostoloi,** a beautiful 10th-century Byzantine church, with 13th-century wall paintings. It is easy to get delightfully lost wandering among the scattered churches and tranquil scenery of the Tragea. Keep heading west to return to the main road.

The long sandy stretches at **Agios Prokopios, Agia Anna** and **Plaka** are crammed with crowds of sunbathers and poorly planned modern buildings, while farther south you will find quiet and unclaimed reaches of sand. The beaches at **Mikri Vigla, Kastraki, Aliko,** and **Pyrgaki** are also accessible by bus from Naxos Town. Here desert meets sea: scrub pines, prickly pear, and century plants grow on the dunes behind you, shooing you toward to the brisk sea.

Amorgos ΑΜΟΡΓΟΣ

Amorgos's cliff-side monastery, scattered churches, and pleasant beaches offer a respite from the throngs of tourists on other islands; however, following the filming of *The Big Blue* (1988) here, the island's popularity has greatly increased, especially with the French. Infrequent ferry connections somewhat preserve the peace of this easternmost of the Cyclades, but it sometimes seems as if the foreign passengers outnumber the Greeks. A daily **ferry** (692dr) connects Amorgos's two ports, the larger Katapola in the southwest and Egiali in the northeast. The road stretching along the island's spine is under construction, and the bus ride is somewhat treacherous (daily excursions depart 8am, return 6pm, 2000dr). Early morning ferries (usually 5-6am) leave Katapola daily for Naxos (5-7hr. depending on the boat—may be a rocky ride—1594dr); some stop at the small islands in between (Donoussa, Koufonissia, Keros, Shinoussa, and Iraklion, 932-1191dr). Ferries also head out to Piraeus (3 per week, 3063dr), via Naxos (1594dr), Paros (1784dr), and Syros (2050dr). In addition, liners pass through on their way to: Astipalea (1 per week, 1909dr); Mykonos (1 per week, 3hr., 1950dr); and Tinos (1 per week, 3½hr., 1950dr).

Katapola and Chora

Most ferries dock on the southwest side of the island at **Katapola,** the main port, where there is an **OTE** (open Mon.-Sat. 8am-midnight, Sun. 8am-1pm and 6-11pm). The ferry agencies of **Nicolas Sinodinos** (tel. 712 78) and **Nicolas Precas** (tel. 712 56) exchange money and sell stamps and maps (150-200dr) of the island. (Open daily 8am-1pm and 5-11pm.) The **port police** (tel. 712 59) are on the right on the way to the **pharmacy** off the main square where the ferry docks (pharmacy tel. 72 14 00; open Mon.-Fri. 9am-2pm and 6:30-9:30pm, Sat.-Sun. 10am-12:30pm and 6:30-9:30pm). **Public toilets** stink to high heaven but are conveniently located at the right-hand end (facing inland) of the rocky town beach. Just across the road you can rent a motorbike from a helpful English-speaker who gives good advice about exploring the island (open daily 9am-noon and 5-7pm; mountain bike 1500dr, motorbike 2000-3000dr). Amorgos's **postal code** is 84008; its **telephone code** is 0285.

Dock hawks offering *dhomatia* will swoop down even on the late-night ferry crowds. (Doubles range 3000-5000dr. Bargain for a roof, 800-1000dr.) Just off the waterfront, **Pension Amorgos** (tel. 710 13) offers spiffy, blue-trimmed rooms. (Doubles 4300dr, with bath 5800dr. Triples 5000, with bath 7000dr.) To find **Pension Anna** (tel. 712 18), a beautiful pension in a quiet, rose-trellised garden, go down the road leading back from the waterfront (to the left of Pension Amorgos, facing inland), and follow the sign leading to the right. (Doubles 3628dr, with bath 4500dr. Open April-Oct. Reservations preferred.) Also with an overflowing garden is **Dimitri's Place** (tel. 713 09). Head to the church behind the town beach, follow the signs to Minoa, and then to Dimitri's. (Doubles 2500-4000dr. Triples 4000-5000dr.) Pleasant **Amorgos Camping** is just a short walk out of town, near the top of the harbor; walk over the bridge from the port and back on the road past lounging mules and bulls. (400dr per person, 300dr per small tent, 400dr per large tent, 200dr for hot shower, motorbike 200dr, car 200dr.)

There are several excellent *tavernas* in town. Try **The Corner,** on the waterfront past the main square or friendly **Minos** back towards the sea (*mousaka* 750dr). **Akrogiali,** under the blue awning on the square, has huge Greek salads for 550dr.

Katapola literally means "below the town." In this case, "the town above" is **Chora,** also known as Amorgos. Chora, 6 winding km from the harbor along the island's only paved road, is a far more restful, though perhaps a slightly less convenient, base for your stay (buses 8am-midnight every hour, 70dr). Spectacular sights to explore include a 14th-century Venetian fortress and a row of retired windmills precariously perched on the mountain ledge above town. The **OTE** rests in the first of three traditional white houses with blue shutters at the entrance to town, near the bus stop (open Mon.-Fri. 7:30am-3:10pm). You *cannot* change money at the Agricultural Bank, but you can farther along the road at the **post office,** beyond the square at the opposite end of town. (Open Mon.-Fri. 7:30am-2pm.) **Pension Kastanis** (tel. 712 77) is located above the OTE (no sign, just go up and knock) and has comfortable rooms. (Doubles 3800dr, with bath 4800dr. Triples 5800dr.) Ask at any café in town for advice on rooms, but make sure you like the facilities and location before agreeing on a price (doubles start around 1800dr). There are a couple of friendly *tavernas* along the main street. **O. Kastanis** serves hearty fare and occasionally hosts live Greek music. (Open for lunch and dinner; *mousaka* 750dr.)

A 20-minute walk or five-minute bus ride from Chora down the east slope of the island towards the cove at **Agia Anna** brings you to the 1km path which accesses the remarkable 900-year-old **Chozoviotissa.** This Monastery of the Presentation of the Virgin is actually pressed into a tiny alcove on the sheer rock face. Be sure to observe the dress code: long pants for men, dresses or skirts for women, no bare shoulders. Contrary to the sign posted at the base of the 15-minute climb to the monastery, spare clothing is available at the entrance. If you arrive between sunrise and 2pm (additional summer hours 5-7pm), the monks will greet you with coffee or Naxion liqueur and sweets.

If sunny beaches tickle your fancy, head to the inlet of Egiali on the northern tip of Amorgos. Some inter-island ferries stop at the small harbor town of **Ormos** (5 days a week). A small boat to Ormos leaves from Katapoula every morning at 6am, returning at 5pm (200dr round-trip). The towns of **Potamos** and **Langada** on the hills above Ormos offer an abundance of whitewashed churches. The windswept village of **Tholarea,** inhabited by farmers and their donkeys, commands a ridge with a sweeping view of the island. To get there from Ormos, walk to the end of the beach and follow the stone path leading up the valley to the town (½hr.). You can quench your thirst at an old, sweet-water well along the way. A bus goes frequently from Chora to the jade waters at the cove of **Agia Anna.** Secluded beaches and coves, accessible only by dirt road, can be found at the southern tip of the island. To reach **Paradissia** beach, go by moped to Kalotaritissa and walk down the dirt path to the water.

Ios ΙΟΣ

You'll be hearing about Ios long before you arrive, and after one night here, you will be a believer. Ios is a dream come true for weary travelers, idle youths, and just about anyone who likes a sandy beach and inspired partying—there is ø to do here but sunbathe by day and party by night. Make the pilgrimage to this mecca of the young and wild only if you are prepared for hangovers, the occasional groping hand, and smooth conversationalists who eat your food outside the all-night fast-food stands. This place, in the words of Nigel Tufnell, goes to eleven.

The good life for tourists centers around three locations, each about 20 minutes apart along the island's paved road. The port is at one end of the road, and the village, the focus of nocturnal activity, is directly above on the hill. Pretty **Milopatos Beach** lies over the hill at the other side of the village. **Buses** run from port to village to beach and back again (daily 8-10am every ½hr., from 10am-midnight every 15min., 140dr).

Ferries from Piraeus, the other Cyclades islands, and Crete stop in Ios. Generally, 6-10 boats per day drop anchor in the late afternoon or early evening. There are frequent connections to: Piraeus (4 per day, 7-10hr., 3489dr); Naxos (3-4 per day, 2hr., 1650dr); Santorini (3-5 per day, 1¼hr., 919dr); and Paros (4-5 per day, 2½hr., 1868dr). One or two boats sail daily to Mykonos (2-5hr., 2114dr) and Tinos (6hr., 2432dr). Several times a week, boats travel to Syros (2359dr), Iraklion, Crete (2257dr), Thessaloniki (5817dr), Sifnos, Serifos, and Sikinos (851dr).

The port where the boat lets you off is not the heart of Dionysiac oblivion; it is a colorful, breezy harbor with restaurants both cheesy and pleasant, an abundance of ferry agents, an English-language book collection in its General Store (open daily 9am-11pm), and an overtaxed beach. To find the serious drinking, climb the steps on the right of the paved road, which lead to the village; the strenuous ascent assures that rooms along the stairs are among the last to fill up. Otherwise, simply join the rest of the visitors who cram themselves into the bus that shuffles between the ferry landing and the village (140dr). Bus service stops for the night at midnight. If you dock *very* late, after buses have stopped, and are feeling spry enough to head for the party, opt for the shorter, though more arduous, stairs rather than the main road into town (about 40min.) as the stairs are better lit and hold no whizzing moped or taxi surprises. You could always crash at the cute n' crowded **Camping Ios** (tel. 913 29), next to the port (1000dr per person, including cost of tent and shower).

The Village

Miraculously, Ios Village has not become as trashed as its visitors. If you arrive in the morning, you no doubt will peer skeptically at the cluster of whitewashed houses that look too innocuous to be Party Central. As you approach, however, the sheer density of bars with their storefront advertising gimmicks, the occasional dried sidewalk vomit, and the odd comatose carouser will be assurance enough that you got off the boat in the right place. Although budget travelers should thrive here, Ios veterans will admit that the attrition rate is quite high.

You can do most of your "serious" business within a 5-minute walk of the village bus stop. The **tourist information office** (tel. 910 28), behind the bus stop in Ios Town exchanges money, sells stamps, and has ferry schedules and information on Ios, but may only be open in August. (When open, daily 9am-3pm and 4:30-10pm.) Funky free maps and English information are available at most travel agencies in the village and at the port. Behind the tourist office are the friendly, English-speaking **police** (tel. 912 22; open 24 hrs.). Opposite the bus stop across the main road, the **bank** cowers in the shadow of the big church (open Mon.-Thurs. 8am-2pm, Fri. 8am-11:30pm). Follow the signs to the **post office** (open Mon.-Fri. 7:30am-2:15pm) and the **doctor** (open 10am-1pm and 6-10pm). For **emergency medical assistance,** call 912 27 or 911 97. The **OTE** is located up the main street from the church. (Open daily 8am-11pm.) Only 16 people can call out of Ios at any given moment. Collect calls to the U.S. and the Netherlands can be made all day, but to all other destinations only between 8am and noon. The **port police** (tel. 912 64) are at the far end of the harbor next to Camping Ios. If you aspire to see more of Ios than the beach and village, you can rent a moped (2300dr-2500dr) or a jeep (12,980dr), but motor travel is prohibited on bad roads as marked on the island map. Otherwise, public transportation should suffice. Two streets up in the densely packed village relaxes the town square, off of which you can find those oh-so-needed **public toilets.** The island's **postal code** is 84001; the **telephone code** is 0286.

Accommodations, Camping, and Food

Accommodations on Ios are very cheap (very rare singles 2400dr, doubles 3000-3500dr, triples 4500-6000dr.) but you may have to hunt around to find a room in peak season. A whole tribe of virtually identical, clean pensions cluster around the police station, behind the bus stop. *Dhomatia* huddle beneath the windmills. Since people sleep late here, most rooms open at midday.

Francesco's (tel. 912 23), above the village uphill from the bank. Spectacular conversation-starting view of the water. Recently renovated with popular bar. Come early or call for reservations. Doubles 3200dr, with bath 5000dr. Triples 4500dr, with bath 6000dr. Open March 20-Oct. 20.

Marko's Pension (tel. 910 60), behind the bus stop in the upper left of the cluster, under Hotel George Irene. Lively and clean. Doubles 4000dr. Triples 5500dr. Quads 6000dr. Bar serves breakfast until 3pm (with eggs 700dr) and hosts occasional BBQs. Hot water 24 hrs. 1-day laundry service. Open March 1-Nov. 1.

The Wind (tel. 911 39), behind the bus stop on the right before you turn for Marko's. A large and friendly pension among many. Doubles 4000dr. Triples 4500dr.

Petradi's (tel. 915 10), equidistant from the village and the beach on the main road. Every room has a balcony with a romantic ocean view. Quiet enough to actually sleep at night. Large, pleasant patio. Doubles 4000dr. Triples 600dr. Bath included.

Camping: Camping Ios (tel. 913 29), next to the port on the far left (facing the water). 1000dr per person, including cost of tent and hot shower. At Milopatos Beach, **Camping Stars** (tel. 413 02), near the bus stop (500dr per person). Both have showers, cooking, and laundry facilities, and will safeguard valuables. For freelance camping, head to **Koumbara Beach** or **Manganari Beach.**

There are many good, reasonably priced restaurants in Ios Village. For delicious Greek specialties, you absolutely can't beat **Pithari,** near the bank (*kalamari* with tomatoes over yellow rice, 750dr; open for lunch and dinner). On the village's central "road," **Saïni's** is also popular for Greek cuisine (veal with tomatoes 830dr; open for lunch and dinner). **Huggy Bears,** uphill from the OTE, serves international fare and draws a satisfied crowd for breakfast, lunch, dinner, and late-night drinks (omelettes 500dr, curry chicken 800dr, zodiac cocktails 500dr). The **Terrasini Pizzeria,** off the main drag uphill has a soothing roof garden (octopus salad 850dr, veggie pizza 1000dr; open 1pm-1am).

Entertainment

At night, each bar offers a different novelty to the amusement-seeking summer crowd. You can shoot pool or darts, watch rock and movie videos, or search for Homer's tomb. Most places offer happy hours from 10pm to midnight or 1am. Just after midnight, the crowds pack into the bars in the main square of the village and the real drinking begins. From there, follow the drunken mob to the ever-popular Irish bars and rattling discos along the main road. You won't have a problem finding the hot nightspots.

The Slammer Bar, off the main drag uphill from Cavo d'Oro. For the original Ios "slammer," a shot glass filled with tequila, Tia Maria, and Sprite slammed on the bar (350dr).

Disco 69, near the village square. The favorite in-town disco. Happy hour 8-11pm with drinks for 250dr (normally 400dr).

Satisfaction. Can't get no? Try this bohemian classic rock retreat. Fabulous liqueur milkshakes (300dr).

Dubliner, in the middle of it all. Wooden interior with pub-like charm. Jamming disco in rear. Don't dare the dreaded bottled Guinness (500dr). Alternative beers (even the Bud is better) 200-500dr.

Scorpion Disco, at the end of the line on the way to the beach. Outdoor dance emporium. Cocktails 600dr.

Beaches

With the exception of a solitary monastery and a modest pile of rubble at the northern tip of the island reputed to be Homer's tomb, the **beaches** are it on Ios. Most people head for **Milopatos Beach** on foot (about 25min. downhill) or by frequent bus service (7:30am-midnight, 140dr). The beach, like the town, is a bastion of bacchanalia. The outer reaches offer a modicum of privacy. The farther you go, the fewer clothes you'll see. Canoe, pedalboat, and windsurfer rentals line the beach.

There are prettier and less crowded beaches on Ios. The most popular of the outlying spots is the nude beach, **Manganari.** A boat leaves from the port at 10am, returning at 6:30pm (2000dr roundtrip). Other nudist beaches include **Koumbara** (a 2km walk from the port), and secluded **Psathi** (a 7km walk along donkey tracks) on the north coast.

Santorini (Thira) ΘHPA

Santorini is the diamond at the end of this string of pearls. Plunging cliffs, burning black-sand beaches, and deeply scarred hills make Santorini's landscape as dramatic as the volcanic cataclysm that created it; the island's whitewashed homes drip down the cliffside like honey. Even those with no interest in the island's intriguing past will find ample delights in its present: long stretches of beaches, tiny cliff-side towns, and spectacular landscapes forged by centuries of volcanic eruptions. The ridges slashing out of the Aegean, the black beaches stark against cobalt waters, and the boiling fields of pumice are unique among the Greek islands.

From about 2000 BCE to 1500 BCE, one of the most advanced societies in ancient Greece flourished on this volcanic isle (then called Thira). Then in 1500 BCE, a massive volcanic eruption buried every sign of civilization beneath millions of tons of lava and pumice. In the centuries since the catastrophe, fact and fiction have mingled, leading some to identify Santorini as Plato's lost continent of Atlantis. More serious historical speculation has convinced many scholars that the eruption of Santorini triggered a tidal wave large enough to account for the contemporaneous destruction of several Minoan sites in Crete.

In 1967, Professor Spyridos Marinatos, an advocate of the latter theory, resumed excavations on the Akrotiri site. The Greek School later unearthed a complete town, preserved virtually intact, like Pompeii, beneath layers of volcanic pumice. Its paved streets are lined with multi-story houses, with wood-framed doors and windows intact.

Modern Santorini is really only the eastern crescent of what was a circular island, originally called "Strongili." The explosion in 1500 BCE left a crust of volcanic ash overstretching the hollow center of the island. When the crust caved in, water filled the resulting *caldera* (basin) that is now Santorini's harbor. The two islands to the west, Thirasia and Aspronisi, appear to be separate, but are in fact a continuation of the rim of the original island. Approaching Santorini from the north, you will first see Thirasia, which has two small villages. Two extraterrestrial rock formations closer to Santorini, Nea Kameni and Palea Kameni, emerge from underwater. You can climb Nea Kameni, the larger of the two, which remains an active volcano. Be aware that there is a severe water shortage on Santorini: conserve. Fresh water accounts for most of the price of accommodations on the island.

Since Santorini is the final stop for many **ferries** in the Cyclades and also a stop for some Crete-bound ferries, it is accessible and thus densely crowded. Your boat will dock at one of the ports: **Athinios** is the most important and has buses to Thira (the main town) and to Perissa Beach. The easiest way to find a room is to bargain with the pension proprietors from all over the island who greet boats at Athinios. At the old port of **Thira,** you will be confronted by a 587-step footpath leading up the cliff to the town above (a difficult 20-min. climb). Hiring a mule for the trip costs about 900dr; the cable car on the left, which departs every 15 minutes from 7am to 8:45pm, is also 900dr. Boats occasionally dock at **Oia,** on the northern cape of the island. **Flights** from Athens to Santorini are reasonable, but difficult to reserve.

Thira Town

The center of activity on the island is the capital city of Thira (Fira). "Fira" in Greek means "door." Some speculate that the harbor below the town plunges into an abyss, having no bottom and leading to the door between heaven and hell. Perched on a cliff, the western edge of town provides stunning views of the harbor, Santorini's west coastline, and the neighboring islands and volcano. Thira's expensive cafés, trendy shops, and jewelry stores shimmer along the back streets. On the east side, the island's characteristic barrel-vaulted houses spread out on more secure footing, their quiet tree-arched streets trailing off into the surrounding countryside. Although the town is overrun with tourists in summer, nothing can destroy the pleasure of wandering among the narrow cobbled streets, inspecting the craft shops, and arriving at the western edge of town in time to watch the sun bathe the harbor in a deep magenta glow.

Orientation and Practical Information

You'll climb off the bus in **Theotokopoulou Square,** the town's hub. The narrow streets leading up behind Pelikan Tours go directly westward toward the cliff overlooking the harbor. Most of the restaurants and discos are located here. Both of the youth hostels are uphill off **25th Martiou,** the paved road leading to Oia (look for the competing signs). The road downhill past the square's newsstand leads to several moped dealers, bears left to the Olympic Airlines office, and continues for 2km to sprawling Karterados, where loads of cheaper accommodations have sprung up.

Travel Agencies: Dozens cluster around Theotokopoulou Sq. Most sell ferry tickets, exchange money, offer 20% student discounts, book rooms, and give excursions. Luggage storage 200-300dr per day. Open daily about 9am-11pm.

Currency Exchange: National Bank of Greece, off the square on Joseph Dekigala St. Open Mon.-Thurs. 8am-2pm, Fri. 7:45am-1:30pm. The **Agricultural Bank,** next door, and the **Commercial Bank,** in the square, also change cash. Most travel agencies exchange currency, but charge 2% commission.

American Express: c/o X-Ray Kilo Travel and Shipping Agency, Theotokopoulou Sq. (tel. 226 24). Full travel services. Open daily 8am-11pm; off-season Mon.-Sat. 9am-1pm and 5-7:30pm.

Post Office: 25th Martiou St., south of the square and just before the bus stop. Open Mon.-Fri. 8am-1:45pm. **Postal Code:** 84700.

OTE: In the new pink building up the stairs and to the right of the post office. Collect calls can be placed Mon.-Fri. only. If calling collect to places other than the U.S. or Holland, expect a 2-hr. wait. Open Mon.-Fri. 8am-2:30pm, Sat. 8am-2:30pm, Sun. 8am-1pm. **Telephone Code:** 0286.

Flights: Olympic Airways (tel. 224 93 or 227 93); go downhill from the bus station, make a left on the first paved road, and then a right. Flights to Athens, Iraklion, Mykonos, and Rhodes. Make reservations at least 1-2 weeks in advance. Arrive 2hr. before take-off for standby tickets (same price). Buses run from the Olympic Airways office to the airport in Monolithos (130dr). Office open daily 8am-6:30pm.

Buses: From Theotokopoulou Sq. to: Perissa (every 30min., 250dr); Kamari (every 30min., 200dr); Akrotiri (8:30am-11:30pm every hr., 240dr); and Oia (every hr., last at 12:30am, 240dr). Buses to the port leave 1½hr. before most departures (250dr).

Ferries: From Piraeus (10hr., 3488dr) daily to Paros, Naxos, Ios, and Santorini. Several boats per week from Piraeus to Santorini via Syros and Mykonos, or alternately Kithnos, Serifos, Sifnos, and Milos. Service reduced in off-season. Several per day from Santorini to: Piraeus (10hr., 3488dr); Paros (5hr., 2008dr); Naxos (4hr., 1834dr); Ios (1½hr., 918dr); and Mykonos (7hr., 2233dr). Several per week from Santorini to : Syros (6hr., 2479dr) and Milos, Sifnos, and Serifos (2008dr). Also to: Crete (8hr., 1933dr); Anafi (1373dr); Rhodes (4425dr); and Karpathos (3358dr). Hydrofoils to Paros, Naxos, Mykonos, and Crete take half as much time, but cost about twice as much as the ferry.

Moped and Car Rental: Mopeds 1500-3000dr. Fiats start at 9800dr, less in off-season. Many places are clustered downhill from Theotokopoulou Sq. Some travel agencies also rent cars.

International Bookstore: International Press, at the top of the plaza of chic shops between Theotokopoulou Sq. and the cliff (look for signs). International papers and magazines. Open daily 9am-midnight.

Laundromat: 25th Martiou St. (tel. 221 68), 150m north of the square. Wash 900-1100dr. Dry 600-900dr. Soap 200-300dr. Open daily 8am-11pm.

Public Toilets: 25th Martiou St., down and across the street from the bus depot.

Medical Emergency: Tel. 222 37, 231 24, or 231 25.

Tourist Police: 25th Martiou St. (tel. 226 49), north of the square. They handle lost and found.

Port Police: Tel. 222 39, 25th Martiou, 30m north of Theotokopoulou Sq.

Accommodations and Camping

Santorini certainly does not lack accommodations, but in summer the pensions and hotels are almost all booked by noon. If you arrive late, stay at one of the two youth hostels in Thira, one of the two at Perissa Beach, or at one in Oia (see Southern Santorini and Northern Santorini), and start hunting early the next morning. Though Thira is centrally located, there are good accommodations in private homes all over the island, so don't hesitate to branch out. The settlement of Karterados 2km south of Thira provides many options. Hawkers at the dock may falsely advertise these places as 700m from Thira city, so be clear about where you are going. Doubles in outlying towns run as low as 2500dr. Head for **Karterados, Messaria, Pirgos, Emborio,** or any of the small inland towns along the main bus routes.

In Thira, you'll be hard put to find doubles for under the standard rate of 4000-4500dr in peak season. Prices listed below are for peak season; rates decrease by about 20% in off-season. Naturalists often opt to **camp** at Perissa Beach or Kamari Beach (see Southern Santorini).

Youth Hostel (HI/IYHF), 25th Martiou St. (tel. 227 22), 400m north of town and to the right down the short slope past the police station; follow the signs. Friendly atmosphere and single-sex dorm rooms with bunk beds built into the hill make for cool refuge. Two annexes for large groups as well. Snack bar open 8am-noon and 6-10:30pm. English-language movies shown daily 9-11pm. Reception open 8am-1pm and 5-11pm. No curfew. Check-out 11am. 1000dr. Roof 800dr. Hot showers 5-9pm only. Breakfast 250dr. Dinner 400-600dr.

Kamares Hostel (tel. 231 42), on the ridge north of town to the left facing uphill. Follow the yellow signs along 25th Martiou St. Single-sex dorm rooms with bunk beds. Bunk beds on roof as well. Roof snack bar has a great view. (Open 8am-noon and 4:30pm-midnight.) Office open 8am-11pm. Check-out noon. No curfew. 1000dr. Roof with bunk beds 800dr. Hot showers 4-8pm only.

Villa Litsa (tel. 222 67), 25th Martiou St., north of the square. Large rooms with baths. Every 3 rooms share a kitchen. Doubles 6350dr. Triples 7450dr.

Villa Maria (tel. 221 68 or 220 92), next door and above the laundromat. Doubles 4000dr. Triples 7000dr.

Food and Entertainment

Escape from the tourists at **Nicholas Taverna,** on a side street a few blocks above Pelikan Travel. Although the menu is meager, this traditional *taverna,* frequented almost exclusively by locals, has tasty food at acceptable prices. (Open Mon.-Sat. noon-3:30pm and 7-11pm, Sun. 7-11pm.) The atmospheric **Restaurant Niki (NIKH),** overlooking the water, has inexpensive food, but disappointingly small portions. (Open daily 8am-2am.) For a touch of elegance, try **Barbara's Restaurant and Jazz Café,** below the Loucas Hotel, overlooking the ocean. Arrive around 8pm, order a bottle of wine from their private vineyard, and watch the sun set from a table on the balcony— one of Greece's greatest gastronomical experiences. Luscious chocolate-Bailey's-Metaxa mousse (690dr). (Open daily 6:30pm-2am, in off-season also open for lunch.) On the streets, *souvlaki, spanakopita* and crêpes are budget options. Santorini grapes produce some of Greece's best wine; be sure to sample some.

For a relaxed outdoor café, try **Canava** overlooking the water, with breakfast, cappuccino, and ice cream sodas amid Brahmsian lullabyes. (Open daily 8am-2am.) The **Kaktos Café,** past Nikolas Taverna, serves leisurely breakfasts, homemade pastries, and fresh fruit juices.

The hill behind the museum gives a spectacular view of Thira, the harbor, and the donkey path. In the evening, watch the sun set from one of the waterfront bars. Sprawling **Franco's,** with comfortable lounge chairs, is expensive, but worth it. Sip a *frullati* (600-900dr) while listening to Handel's *Messiah.* (Open 6pm-2am.) At the south end of the harbor, **Palia Kameni** offers comfy deck chairs, more classical music, and drinks (800-950dr). For a more social atmosphere, slip into the **Kira Thira Jazz Club,** a bohemian refuge with a funky Bosch-like wall mural, and instruments dangling from the ceiling (excellent sangria 500dr). Popular with the English-speaking crowds are the **Two Brothers,** across from Nikolas Taverna, one of the cheapest and most popular watering holes, and the sepulchral **Tithora Club** nearby (actually built in a 14th-century cave.) For some of the most intense, funkiest dancing in Greece, try **Casablanca/New Art** and **Enigma.** Most bars and discos stay open until at least 3am.

Thira's **Archaeological Museum,** near the cable cars, holds an impressive collection of vases, mostly from the site of ancient Thira. (Open Tues.-Sun. 8:30am-3pm. Admission 400dr, students 200dr.) The private **Museum Megaro,** near Kamares Hostel, has old maps, engravings, and photographs of Santorini and other islands. (Open daily 10:30am-1:30pm and 5-8pm. Admission 300dr, students 100dr.) A new museum will open soon with a collection of finds from Akrotiri. In September, Santorini hosts a small **classical music festival;** inquire at the Megaro Gyzi Museum.

Southern Santorini

Although roads are well paved here, and Santorini's bus service is excellent, the least painful (and least adventurous) way to travel around the island is to take an organized tour. The travel agents in Thira offer various half-day (about 1200dr) and full-day (about 3000dr) excursions. Kamari Tours is expensive, but has a good reputation, and can be booked from offices in Perissa and Kamari. Most agencies offer helpful student discounts.

You may want a tour in **Akrotiri,** where extensive excavations (still underway) will likely bewilder the novice. If you choose not to spend your *drachmae* on a tour, pick up one of the books on Akrotiri (600dr).

Professor Marinatos found the paved streets of Akrotiri lined with houses connected by a sophisticated central drainage system. Each house had at least one room lined with frescoes, some among the most magnificent found in Greece. Along with some pottery and stone vases unearthed at Akrotiri, the frescoes are on loan to the National Archaeological Museum in Athens pending completion of the new museum at Santorini.

Archaeologists found no bones in Akrotiri: the fate of the people remains a mystery. Since only heavy objects, and no valuable items, were found, a common theory is that everyone escaped before the eruption. Twelve buses per day run here, the last returning at 9:30pm. (Open Tues.-Sun. 8am-3pm. Admission 1000dr, students 500dr.)

Santorini's two most popular **beaches** are Kamari and Perissa in the south. **Perissa Beach** is the farther of the pair, but also the more touristed. Bring along a straw mat and sandals: the sun sizzles this black volcanic sand to scorching temperatures. The water here, as elsewhere on the island, is brisk and clear, but the rocks and seaweed on the bottom preclude snorkeling. The sociable **Perissa Youth Hostel,** 400m along the road leading out of town, has a snack bar and a minimarket. (Check-out 10:30am. No curfew. Roof 800dr. Mixed dorms 1000dr. Sheets 100dr. Hot showers 24 hrs. Breakfast 180dr.) Up and across the street, clean, fresh, and new **Youth Hostel Anna** has an outdoor sitting area and connects to a restaurant. (Check-out 11:30am. No curfew. Women's and mixed dorms 1000dr. Hot showers 9am-9pm.) Enormous **Perissa Camping** (tel. 813 43), right on the beach, has a minimarket, bar, and volleyball court. (Check-out 1pm. 750dr per person, 500dr per tent.) There are also several *dhomatia* in town. **Buses** from Thira travel to Perissa, stopping at the less crowded Perivolos Beach on the way (8am-midnight, every 20min., 250dr).

The boatman on the rocky shuttle between Perissa and Kamari Beaches serves a briny, anisette-tasting red wine for the ride (daily, every hr. 10am-6pm, 500dr). Smaller **Kamari Beach** is sea-to-shore umbrellas, but is slightly less polluted by tourist services and cigarette butts. A smaller selection of pensions and rooms-to-let line the breezy boardwalk. Doubles in private homes are about 3500dr in peak season. On the road back to town from the Yellow Donkey Disco, the **Hotel Golden Sun** (tel. 313 01) has clean rooms with balconies. (Doubles 4000dr, with bath 5000dr.) **Kamari Camping** (tel. 314 53) is about 1km up the main road from the beach. Ask the bus driver to let you off at the campsite; turn right at the church, and it's a 300m walk. (550dr per person, 300dr per tent.) You can catch a flick at the open-air cinema next door (daily 9:30pm, 650dr; occasional English showings). The nearby **Nikolas Taverna** serves traditional fare at good prices. 1km inland on the main road from Kamari, **Canava Roussos** (tel. 319 54 or 312 78) offers daily wine tasting (2-8pm, 400dr) and hosts a folklore festival with dancing, grape stomping, food, and juice of the vine (Thurs.-Sun. 8:30am-midnight, 4000dr). Get off the bus at Mesa Gonia just before Kamari. If walking from Kamari, bring water for the trek and to clear your palate between each swoosh.

Buses to Perissa stop in lofty **Pyrgos,** surrounded by medieval walls. A Venetian fortress from the 14th-16th centuries, the town then came under Turkish rule until 1828. The village's 25 blue and green domed churches dot the horizon. The **Profitias Ilias Monastery,** about an hour's hike up the mountain from Pyrgos, lugubriously shares its site with a radar station. On July 20, the monastery hosts the **Festival of St. Ilias.**

From Profitias Ilias, it's about an hour's hike to the ancient city of **Thira.** The ancient theater, church and forum of the island's old capital are still visible, though less spectacular than the Akrotiri excavations. (Open Tues.-Sun. 9am-3pm. Free.)

The southern end of the island has a few villages where you can spend the night. Cheerful, whitewashed **Emborio,** some 3km inland from Perissa, has frequent bus connections to the beach and to Thira. Rooms start at 2500dr.

Northern Santorini

With its pumice caves, time-worn churches, and winding streets, **Oia** (pronounced "ee-ya") is a fascinating mixture of devastation and renewal. The 1956 earthquake leveled this small town on the island's rocky northern point. Its present 600 inhabitants have carved new dwellings into the cliffside among shattered ruins of the old. A 20-minute climb down the 252 stone stairs at the end of Oia's main street, brings you to the rocky beach at **Amoudia,** with a few boats moored in its startlingly deep swimming lagoon. Gaze from the ruins of the Venetian castle above onto one of the most riveting views of the natural world. Be aware that many surfaces in Oia bear warnings not to step on them; obey them. Buses run from Thira to Oia (8:30am-12:30pm every hr., 240dr). A few ferries also dock at Oia before continuing to Thira; check where you buy your ticket prior to departure.

Accommodations in Oia have become pricier in recent years. The best option for the budget traveler is **Youth Hostel Oia** (tel. 714 65), a sparkling new hostel with a beautiful view of the sunset from its roof terrace. (Bar open all day. Hot water 24 hrs. Wheelchair accessible. Mixed dorms 1700dr. Roof 1500dr. Sheets 150dr. Breakfast 300-500dr.) The Youth Hostel is also available in the winter for seminars or retreats. (Contact **Karvounis Tours,** tel. (0286) 712 90; fax (0286) 712 91). The most tempting option is to rent a **cave house,** burrowed into the plunging cliff. Prices range from 6000 to 10,000dr per day (if you're lucky) for doubles; be sure you are satisfied with the cleanliness of the place before hunkering down. Ask at Karvounis Tours about cave houses in Oia, at **Kyma Travel** (tel. 713 37) about houses in Firikia, just inland of Oia, or search around on your own for the best bargain. Cushy, expensive *dhomatia* are the third option.

Chow will cost you. **Harmony's Bar,** next door to the Delfina Hotel, serves scrumptious breakfasts (500dr). Admire the view and relax over a leisurely lunch at **Café Lotza,** along the main road (open 9am-2am). For cheap fare, head to **Alexis Souvlaki,** across from the Delfini. For drinks, views, and live jazz piano nightly from 11pm, try **Melissa's** roof-top terrace (open 5pm-3am).

Thirasia and Surrounding Islands

Santorini's unspoiled junior partner Thirasia (population 300) is worthy of a detour. Built along the island's upper ridge, the villages of **Manolas** and **Potamos** have spine-tingling overlooks of Santorini's western coast. Thirassia has been virtually untouched by contemporary society, and a visit here will be a refreshing change from the usual Cycladic experience. The only way to reach Manolas is to climb the rocky stairs (about 30min.) or take a donkey (400dr). If you walk, do so when the sun is low—profuse perspiration characterizes the midday excursion. As you reach the top, you'll find a *taverna* on your left and a minimarket on the right. Farther down on the right is another *taverna,* with a breezy roof-terrace. Manolas has no hotels (and very few English-speakers), but you can ask a donkey-owner at the dock to direct you to someone with *dhomatia.*

Excursion boats to Thirasia leave Thira's harbor at 10am and usually include a round-trip tour of Akrotiri, the volcano, hot springs, Thirasia, and Oia, returning at 6pm (2000-3000dr; check for student discounts). Boats also leave from Amoudia in Oia for **St. Irene,** Thirasia's tiny port, at 11am, returning at 5:30pm (1100dr round-trip). Trips to the volcano and hot springs, as inexpensive as 1500dr round-trip, can be wonderfully convivial. Be forewarned that to get to the hot sulphur springs, you'll have to swim through cold water first; to get to the volcano's crater, you'll have to hike uphill for 30 minutes.

Western Cyclades ΔΥΤΙΚΕΣ ΚΥΚΛΑΔΕΣ

Having endured successive invasions by Athenians, Italians, and Turks, the islanders of the western Cyclades receive with stoic calm the friendlier expeditions of tourists. For years these islands have been the summer retreats of mainland Greeks who gobble up the limited supply of accommodations. In summer, rooms can be found only in the early morning, and then only with inextinguishable resolve. Camping is very popular, and amenities such as showers are often available. Also, nightlife is much tamer than in the eastern Cyclades. But these relaxing islands flaunt tranquil, sandy beaches, modest archaeological remains, and generally friendly locals.

Ferry connections to the western Cyclades are becoming more frequent, but can still be quite inconvenient. Daily ferries link Piraeus with Serifos (1527dr), Sifnos (1890dr), Milos (2081dr), and Kimolos (2081dr). These boats occasionally stop at Santorini, and each of the islands receives a boat from Piraeus bound for Ios and Santorini. There are also several daily connections from Paros to Sifnos. Boats sail from Lavrion daily to Kea (955dr) and Kithnos (1645dr).

Milos

For an island associated with such celebrated artistic achievement as the Venus de Milo, Thucydides's *Melian Dialogue,* and the *film-bête,* Milo & Otis, Milos at first glance underwhelms. Yet as you clamber around the island's archaeological sites, relax on its tranquil beaches, and trek through its volcanic landscapes, Milos will slowly captivate and inspire you. Years ago, however, Milos was dejected and desolate. After the island refused to join the Athenian League during the Peloponnesian War, Athens executed all the men and enslaved the women and children. The mineral-rich island eventually recovered, and later flourished as a mining and cosmopolitan center.

Practical Information, Accommodations, and Food

Ferries dock at Adamas, not the most picturesque spot the island has to offer, but a convenient base for your stay on Milos. One or two boats per day travel to Piraeus (5hr., 2825dr). Sunday through Thursday there are boats to: Serifos (2hr., 830dr); Sifnos (1½hr., 830dr); Ios (2hr., 1890dr); Santorini (3hr., 1890dr); and Crete (8hr., 2671dr). Once a week, a ferry goes to Rhodes (5822dr), and Paros (4hr., 1350dr). Olympic offers flights to and from Athens (2-3 per day, 7800dr).

Across from the dock, the extremely competent **tourist office** (tel. 224 45) will provide you with general information, and equip you with complete lists and maps of accommodations, both *dhomatia* and hotels: choose your venue and start knocking on doors. (Open 9am-midnight; Oct.-May 9am-1pm and 7-10pm.) A **public toilet** adjoins the tourist office. The **OTE** (open Mon.-Sat. 8am-midnight, Sun. and holidays 8am-1pm and 6-11pm), **post office** (open Mon.-Fri. 7:30am-2pm), **bank** (open Mon.-Thurs. 8am-2pm, Fri. 8am-1:30pm), and **port police** (tel. 221 00; open 24 hrs.) are all along the waterfront. **Olympic Airways** (tel. 223 80) is on 25th Martiou St., which runs off the square. (Open Mon.-Fri. 7:30am-2:30pm, Sat. 8am-1pm.) The **bus stop** (tel. 222 19) and **taxi stand** are in a bustling area on the waterfront. A complete bus schedule and a list of fixed taxi fares are posted. You can rent a **moped** from the dealer on the waterfront (1800-4700dr). Milos's **postal code** is 84801 in Adamas, 84800 elsewhere. The **telephone code** is 0287.

Even the cheapest accommodations in Adamas will appall the staunchly frugal wanderer. For clean, quiet rooms and a peaceful garden bar, stay at the **Semiaramis** (tel. 221 18), off 25th Martiou. (Doubles 4600dr, with private bath 5100dr. Triples 5500dr, with bath 6100dr. Breakfast 500dr.) There are a multitude of affordable rooms in private homes; use the tourist office list. (Singles 2000dr. Doubles 3500dr. Triples 5000dr.) There are no official campgrounds in Milos. The tourist office warns that camping is illegal except at shady **Boubarda Beach,** past the Hotel Venus off the dirt road over the hill. The 10-minute walk isn't too tricky, but watch out for bats. Many tidy backpackers also congregate at the town beach in Pollonia.

The servers at the two neighboring restaurants on the corner of the waterfront are understandably quick and harried with English-speaking customers in summer, but the food is superb: at **O Kinigos** you'll sit next to the speeding traffic. (Veal in clay bowl 750dr, broad beans 500dr. Open noon-3pm and 8pm-midnight.) Or at **O Flisvos** you can sit at an elevated table. (Beef with tomatoes 750dr, stuffed eggplant 600dr. Open noon-30m and 6pm-midnight.) For a more elegant dinner, ask for a table on the water at **Trapetseli's Restaurant,** a 5-minute walk on the road to Hivadolimni Beach. (Octopus salad 700dr.)

Around the Island

Six winding km from Adamas, the timeworn town of **Plaka** rests upon the mountains. The terrace of the **Church of Panayia I Korfiatissa** leans into a splendid view of verdant countryside, blue ocean, and red islets a mere God's-arm-length away. The town's **folk museum,** next door, has an eerie display of mannequins. (Open Tues.-Sat. 10am-1pm and 6-8pm, Sun. 10am-1pm. Admission 300dr, students 200dr.) Near the bus stop, on the road to Trypiti, the **Archaeological Museum** houses artifacts unearthed at Filakopi, including the mesmerizing "Lady of Filakopi." (Open Wed.-Sat. 8:45am-3pm, Sun. 9:30am-2:30pm. Admission 400dr, students 200dr.) From Adamas, buses run to Plaka and Trypiti (every hr. until 10:30pm, 100dr).

South of Plaka, outside the small town of **Trypiti,** are several more sights of hefty archaeological clout. The **catacombs,** hewn into the cliff face, constitute the oldest site of Christian worship in Greece. (Open Sun.-Tues. and Thurs.-Fri. 8:45am-3pm. Free.) Archaeological finds in the ancient city on the hillside above the catacombs represent three periods of Greek history. You can still see part of the stone wall built by the Dorians between 1100 and 800 BCE. A plaque marks the spot where the Venus de Milo was buried around 320 BCE; she now resides in the Louvre. Nearby, the well-preserved theater—dating from the Roman occupation—offers a riveting view of the ocean. **Pollonia,** to the northeast, is a quiet fishing town with a pleasant beach dotted with freelance campsites. Boats run between Pollonia and the tiny island of **Kimolos** (4 per day, 35min., 1500dr round-trip). Kimolos Town and the port of Psathi are perfect if you want to unwind for awhile. Few tourists venture here, so some travelers sleep peacefully on the beach. Buses run to Pollonia (10 per day, 200dr). Archaeology buffs will want to scramble among the ruins of **Filakopi,** 3km from Pollonia, where British excavations unearthed 3500-year-old frescoes of flying fish and lilies (now exhibited in the National Museum in Athens). About 6km west of Pollonia is Papafragas, where gangling rock formations surround a pool of clear blue water.

There are many nice beaches on Milos; most of them are in the eastern half of the island, inaccessible by bus. Rent a moped and head for beautiful **Firiplaka** (a 45-min. moped ride). Other beaches of repute are the adjoining **Paloehori** and **Kiriaki** (6 buses per day from Adamas, 120dr), or the more secluded **Plathiena.** Three daily buses from Adamas make the jaunt to the more densely populated **Hivadolimni Beach.** On the southern coast, **Provotas** (8km from Adamas) is an ideal spot for a swim. A daily boat travels to quiet **Embourio Beach;** ask for Captain Nicholas at the small pier in Adamas (900dr round trip). The excursion boat which travels around the island daily is an excellent way to see all the beaches, slivers of fishing villages, and the lava formations of **Glaronissia** and **Kleftiko** that are otherwise not accessible by road (boat departs at 9am, returns at 6pm; 2000dr).

Sifnos

Sifnos was once famous for its gold and silver. Legend has it that each year the islanders, in an effort to placate Apollo, would send a solid-gold dancer to Delphi. One year, the parsimonious locals decided to sneak in a gold-plated egg instead. As a result of this insult, Apollo decided to sink the Sifnian mines under the sea and curse the land with barrenness. Apparently, the god did not hold a grudge for long because today Sifnos is quite affluent, with olive grove-gorged hillsides plunging down to blustery rock caves and calm beaches. Although less known to foreigners, Sifnos is a favorite among Greeks. Tourism is more easygoing here than on most islands, but accommodations are still fairly limited, and simply not available in July and August. During the high season your best bet is a *dhomatia* from one of the island's affable residents, or a campsite. Or make reservations several months in advance.

Practical Information, Accommodations, and Food

Boats dock at **Kamares.** One or two **ferries** per day sail to: Piraeus (6hr., 2600dr); Paros (3hr., 1500dr); Milos (1½hr., 830dr); Serifos (45min., 730dr); Kithnos (2½hr., 1370dr); Sikinos (2½hr., 1261dr); and Folegandros (45min., 750dr). Three times per week, there are voyages to Ios (3hr., 1800), and Santorini (4hr., 1900dr). For more detailed information, contact the **port police** in Kamares (tel. 316 17; open 24 hrs.). You can catch a day's excursion to Milos, Serifos, or Folegandros for 2000dr.

The lack of accommodations on Sifnos can be downright discouraging: in general, hotels are crowded and expensive. The **tourist office** (tel. 319 77 or 318 04; open 1pm-11pm), on the waterfront can give you the scoop on *dhomatia* (doubles start around 4300dr in July and August, in low season 3100dr). Friendly **Maki's Camping** (500dr per person) lies just across the road from the beach in Komares, has fine facilities, and serves breakfast, snacks, and dinner with an ocean view. If you have your own tent, try calm, clean **Platy Yialos Camping** (500dr; tel. 317 86), with a restaurant and minimarket, set beautifully amid olive trees and stone walls, a 10-minute walk inland from the bus stop at Platy Yialos Beach. To get to the rustic, very basic **Farasolou Camping** (500dr per person), take the white stairs behind the bus stop at Faros to the top, turn right down the wide dirt road, and be greeted with a view of the island's secluded nude beach and the Monastery of Panayia Chrysopyi across the bay. All campsites are surrounded by dreamy mountains and none have hot water. Freelance camping is illegal; don't be surprised if the police oust your butt from the sand. Those arriving late at night still may dare to crash on the town beach at Kamares. **The Dionysos,** on the waterfront, offers hot showers (200dr). **Estiatorio O. Mpoulis** is one of the best waterfront *tavernas* (delicious lamb with lemon sauce 850dr; open 7am-midnight.) Almost every half-hour until 12:30am, **buses** leave Kamares for the main town of Apollonia (140dr), and then continue to other villages.

There are two bus stops in **Apollonia,** one for buses to and from Kamares (in the square), and another for buses to and from all other towns (around the corner, opposite the Hotel Anthoussa). The **tourist office** (tel. 321 90 or 311 45), up the street from the square, has detailed bus and boat information, exchanges money, and sells a small package with information about the island, and confusing but comprehensive bus and ferry information, for 400dr (open daily 9:30am-2:30pm and 5:30-9pm). The **pharmacy** is just opposite the tourist office. The **post office** (open Mon.-Fri. 7:30am-2pm), the **OTE** (open Mon.-Fri. 7:30am-10pm, Sat.-Sun. 8am-1pm and 5-10pm), and **bank** (Mon.-Thurs. 8am-2pm, Fri. 8am-1:30pm) are all in a row in the main square. The **police station** (tel. 312 10) is 1 block east of the square. (Open 8am-1:30pm and 6-10pm.) For **first aid,** call 313 15. The **postal code** is 84003; the **telephone code** is 0284.

During the summer, vacancies in Apollonia, the island's capital, are also rare. The **Hotel Sophia** (tel. 312 38), just off the square is peachy. (Singles 3500dr. Doubles 5000dr. Triples 6500dr. Private baths included.) The **Hotel Anthoussa** (tel. 314 31), above the pastry shop, has more luxurious accommodations with daily cleaning service. (Doubles 6500dr. Triples 8000dr.) You can find the cheapest rooms in Apollonia by asking at *tavernas* for rooms to let (doubles 3000-4000dr). Restaurants in Apollonia are excellent and not as expensive as their beautiful exteriors might suggest. The best *tavernas* lie down the path across from the police station. If you're hungry on Sunday, sample the hearty local specialty *revithia,* a chick-pea dish with olive oil and lemon cooked over a low fire all of Saturday night in the special ovens at Artemonos. (About 500dr at your friendly *taverna.* Go early: it'll be gone by 9:30pm.)

The **Museum of Popular Art** on the square in Apollonia features beautiful hand-woven laces and linens, traditional dress, a large sampling of local pottery—still a primary industry—and several curious paintings (open daily 10am-1pm and 6-10pm; admission 100dr). Travel in Sifnos is easy enough with the map, available at any kiosk (200dr). Explore the hillside towns adjacent to Apollonia. The quiet city of Artemonas, to the north, has many fine mansions built by refugees from Alexandria and boasts a magnificent view. A few km to the east, the enchanting **Kastro,** fitted like a skull-cap atop a rocky dome loosed from the mainland and heading out to sea, more than merits a visit. Climbing to the top of the island's fortified former capital through its twisted white-washed streets, you'll find a tiny **Archaeological Museum.** (Open Tues.-Sat. 9am-3pm, Sun. 10am-2pm; free.) The solitary seaside chapel is arresting. There are no hotels, but you can ask around for *dhomatia.* You can swim at the pebble beach to the right (facing the water) or walk left at the base of the hill to the monastery of **Panayia Poulati.** The smooth rock alcove below reputedly offers the best swimming on the island.

Casual **Faros,** to the south, has several popular beaches. **Fasolou,** farther east, the island's only nude beach, and the westernmost beach are tucked away beneath promontories. Continue west along the rocky hillside path past a dilapidated mine to reach a better beach at **Apokofto.** You can also reach Apokofto by getting off the bus to Platis Gialos at the Chrysopyi stop. At the far end of this bay, you will see the striking **Panayia Chrysopyi.** A bridge connects this 17th-century monastery's rocky islet to the mainland. Many people swim from the flat rocks at the end of the islet. The monastery has rooms to let (doubles 2500dr); make reservations about two months in advance (tel. 314 82). Forty days after Easter, the two-day festival of Analipsos is celebrated at Chrysopyi. Up the path from Chrysopyi, **Vasilis Restaurant** offers food with a view; roast chicken (650dr) or veal in a clay bowl (850dr). (Open 9am-midnight.)

Platis Yialos, the longest and most popular beach on the island, is accessible by an hourly bus from Apollonia. To admire precious icons and an inspiring view, ask the busdriver to let you off 3km before the normal stop at **Panayiatou Vounou.**

The town at Vathi has a lengthy beach coiling around a shallow bay, and a waterfront glazed with many pottery studios and shops. If you don't have time for a 3-hour hike from Plati Yialos, you can take a boat to Vathi from Kamares (departs 10am, 1pm, and 2pm, returns 4pm and 6pm, 1100dr round-trip). At Vathi, you can also stay in the rooms at the monastery of **Taxiarchi** (doubles 2500dr). Contact Panayiotis (tel. 318 91) one or two months in advance for reservations. If you're in Sifnos on July 12, go to Vathi for free *fava* (beans), wine, and live music at the **Festival of Taxiarchi.**

Kastro (140dr), Faros (140dr), and Plati Yialos (180dr) are easily reached from Apollonia by buses every hour or hour and a half. If you want to go directly to **Chrysopyi** and **Panayiatou Vaunou,** take the bus heading towards Platis Yialos and ask the driver to let you off at the Panayia: each is a 20-minute walk from the drop-off.

Serifos

As the daytime boat docks in the port town of Livadia, your first vision of Serifos is of chocolate-brown hills blasted by the searing sun, and the ghostly white capital (Chora) gripping a naked mountain peak in a stranglehold. Mythology claims that on this rocky isle, Perseus, the son of Zeus and Danae, turned King Polidectis and his servants into stone by showing them Medusa's head: hence the stark, still, barren terrain. Today, mostly Greek tourists, but also international sailors and backpackers, frolic along the island's fringes. With bus service running only between its port and capital, this mysterious island challenges the adventurer and keeps much to itself.

Orientation and Practical Information

All boats dock in friendly, ephemeral **Livadia.** Ferries travel daily to: Piraeus (4hr., 2170dr); Sifnos (45min., 710dr); Kithnos (1½hr., 1320dr); and Milos (2hr., 850dr). Two or three times per week, there are sailings to: Ios (5½hr., 1860dr); Santorini (6½hr., 1890dr); Sikinos (1860dr); and Folegandros (1077dr). The **port police** (tel. 514 70), on the street parallel to the waterfront road, at the right end of the harbor (facing inland), don't speak much English, but the friendly workers at the Milos Express office, at the back of the supermarket in the center of the waterfront, are a good source of information about ferries (tel. 512 41; open daily 9:30am-2pm and 5:30-11pm). Livadia's **OTE** is next to the port (open in summer Mon.-Sat. 8am-11pm and Sun. 8am-1pm and 6-11pm). Serifos's **telephone code** is 0281. For a **taxi,** dial 512 26 or 514 34.

In summer, arrive prepared to **camp.** Cool showers are available for freelance campers at the **Relax Café** (200dr, just over the hill to the left of the dock, facing inland). Freelance camping is tempting but illegal below on tree-lined Livadakia Beach, but **Corali Camping** (tel. 515 00), at the far end of the beach, is a 10-minute jaunt from the harbor; take the inland road to the right of the dock, follow it up, and turn to the left onto the long, winding way through the settlement behind Livadakia Beach. The campsite, decked with flowers, offers a bar, restaurant, international phone, minimarket, and laundry facilities. There are also several private rooms here (doubles 6500dr, triples 7500dr, bath and refrigerator included; camping 700dr per person, 800dr with tent; open May-Oct.). *Dhomatia* can be found on the street parallel to the waterfront road (doubles starting at 3500dr). **Captain George Rooms** (tel. 512 74) next door has doubles with bath for 5800dr. The **Cavo d'Oro** (tel. 511 60 or 512 13), also off the waterfront, is more posh. (Doubles 5700dr.)

For an adventure of a meal, saunter down to the very end of the town beach (all the way to the right facing inland) and look left for square tables and loose chickens, under the care of an enormous fragrant tree. The restaurant has no sign, but just ask for "Sklavani's" to get directions. Though preparations take a while, fresh vegetables and juicy fish come to those who wait. (Dinner served from 7pm at prices too low to mention here.) Nearer the dock, **Benny's Tavern** serves traditional Greek fare. (Octopus salad 850dr. Open for lunch and dinner.) You can get fresh fruit at the "Marinos" market on the waterfront. (Open daily 8am-2pm and 4:30-10pm.) Make the two-hour walk or take a moped or taxi past Livadakia Beach to the three adjoining beaches of **Koutalas, Ganema,** and **Vaya Beach.** The best beach on the island is at **Psili Ammos,** in the other direction, past the town beach. **Karavi,** just over the hill from Livadakia Beach, is a popular nudist beach.

Chora, the capital, high above Livadia on a mountain top, cultivates a deep, aesthetic alienation, tumbling down the hillside like a cubist's attempt at urban planning. Pick your way through the alleys and underpasses up to the crown of the ghostly quiet town. Three white churches rise out of the ruins of the old *kastro,* giving way to an eagle-eye view of the southeastern hills of the isle and the surrounding sea. The **Archaeological Museum** hunkers behind the beautiful and surprising Neoclassical town hall in the central *platia* (open daily 9am-2pm).

Buses from the center of the waterfront in Livadia (8am-11pm every 45min., 15min., 140dr) stop downhill in Chora near the **post office** (open Mon.-Fri. 7:30am-2pm). Change your money here or at a travel agent; there is no bank on Serifos. Taking the paved road uphill to the main square, you'll pass the **police** (tel. 513 00) and the **clinic** (tel. 511 78 or 517 88) on the left, and the **OTE** (open daily 8:30am-1pm) on the right. The second bus stop is at the top of the hill in a square burgeoning with quiet cafés. To find the only rooms-to-let in Chora, follow the high paved road from the bus stop away from town, past the windmills. On the right, you'll spot the palatial rooms with startling views. Definitely worth it if you can afford it: doubles 5700dr, triples 6800dr, bath included. The northern part of the island promises small traditional villages, scattered churches, several monasteries, and traces of ruins. But you will need a map, a moped, and excellent driving skills or else a very good pair of shoes, plenty of water, and a lot of time to explore. The **postal code** is 84005.

Kea (Tziá)

A small, fertile island, Kea is criss-crossed with gray stone fences that snake through the island's plentiful fruit orchards, archaeological remains, windmills, and sandy beaches. Vaunted in antiquity as the birthplace of the 5th- and 6th-century BCE poets Simonides and Bacchylides, Kea was also infamous for its classical counterpart to the suicide machine: citizens toasted their 70th birthdays with a cup of hemlock. Today's alternative, tastier and less fatal, is the island specialty *pasteli,* a sticky-sweet confection made with sesame seeds and the golden thyme honey that pours forth from the keen Kean hills. Only recently accessible from the rest of the Cyclades, Kea remains uncrowded. The island's proximity to Athens has made it a popular weekend getaway for the city's residents, so it is best to visit on weekdays, when accommodations are not so much in demand and beaches deserted.

Orientation and Practical Information

To include Kea in your archipelagic journey, take the **ferry** (2 per day, 1hr.), or the **hydrofoil** (2 per day, 1hr., 2000dr) from Kea's neighbor, Kynthos. To reach Kea from Athens, take the ferry from Lavrio (2 per day, 1½hr., 950dr) or the hydrofoil from Zea in Piraeus (2 per day, 1½hr., 3000dr). Though a ferry departure from Lavrio is the cheaper option, getting there entails a 1½-hour bus ride: take the bus from 14 Mavro Mateou St. (tel. 821 32 03; 650dr). For time table information from Athens, call 267 77, or visit the **tourist office** at Kynthos (open daily 10am-1:30pm and 5:30-8:30pm). For all hydrofoil trips, it is wise to make a reservation, which must be paid at least 24 hours before sailing; call (01) 428 00 01 or reserve a seat with any of the many Hydrofoil Joint Service agents on the islands. (In Athens, try **Karageorgi Servias** (tel. 324 22 81), Syntagma Sq. Open Mon.-Fri. 9am-4pm.) Boats dock in mellow **Korissia.** You will find nothing here of particular interest, but it serves well as a base for a visit. From the left of the dock a strip of gift shops and cafeterias stretches along the waterfront. Look for **Keos Travel** (tel. (0288) 210 12), a hydrofoil agency which serves also has a tourist information office: find out about accommodations, boats, and bus schedules. The tourist map of Kea, available at the many shops, aids in planning exploration and delights with island lore. The **police** (tel. 211 00) are located at the end of the strip just where the road curves to the left around the beach. The **OTE** (open Mon.-Fri. 7:30am-3:10pm) is a stucco white square alongside the tiny beach parking lot. Six km uphill from Korissia, the buildings of the island's capital, **Chora Ioulis,** glare fluorescent white from the dark-green, oak-covered landscape. To the left of the bus stop is the p... ... (Open Mon.-Fri. 7:30am-2pm.) To the right of the bus stop is the **pharma-** c... ...es., Thurs., Fri. 9am-1:30pm and 6-9pm, Wed., Sat., Sun. 9am-2pm; tel. ... The **bank,** which doubles as an old-world convenience store and first aid sta- ... ope... Mon.-Thurs. 8am-2pm, Fri. 8am-1:30pm), is located farther into town. ...'s pos **al code** is 84002; its **telephone code** is 0288.

Rooms to rent in Korissia lie along the waterfront where the boats dock and behind the town beach, but they fill quickly in July and August. Try the spotless **Pension Ko-rissia** (tel. 214 84) behind the beach, and relax on the breezy terrace under a canopy of grape vines. Doubles 5000dr, with bath 5800dr.) **Kostas** serves tasty food at moderate prices. (Open noon-4pm and 8pm-midnight.)Two small **supermarkets** and a bakery make Korissia the place to gather goodies for an isolated picnic. Nearby, at the site of ancient Korissia, the **Kea Kouros** was discovered in 1930, but now resides at the Na-tional Archaeological Museum in Athens.

The capital houses a small **Archaeological Museum** (open Tues.-Sun. 8:30am-3pm), but ancient Ioulis's glory is best suggested by the enormous **Lion of Kea,** em-bedded in rock about 1km east of Chora. If you decide to stay in Chora, go to the **Hotel Ioulis Keas** (tel. 221 77). All rooms have balconies with sweeping views of the island. (Doubles 4900dr, with bath 5100dr.)

Beaches with clear emerald waters lie north of Korissa; there is a single road that fol-lows the shore, along which many homes double as *dhomatia.* **Yialiskari,** 1km away, is a small, clean, sandy beach. **Vourkari,** 2km away, is a fishing town with colorful sail-boats anchored in its harbor. There are several picturesque and characteristically ex-pensive fish restaurants along its waterfront. The peninsula of **Agia Eirene,** across the bay, contains remnants of settlements which may seem modest to the layman, but actu-ally constitute one of the most important archaeological sites in the Cyclades. (Open Mon.-Sat. 9am-3pm.) The road cuts inland at a highway sign and continues 3km to the quiet bay of **Otzias.** If the 10 or 15 people on the expanse of the beach are too many for you, rent a paddle boat (1000dr per hour) and go find your own sandy shore in the bay. The 5.5km, uphill country path after Otzias leads to the **monastery** of Panagia Kastri-ani (tel. 313 48) where rooms for a pious overnight may be available. A popular beach lies south of Korissia at the site of another ancient city, **Poiessa.** The only official campground on the island, **Camping Poiessa** (tel. 222 32), complete with showers, *taverna,* first aid station, and primitive laundry and kitchen facilities, is located near the beach at Poiessa (500dr per person, 400dr per tent). Freelance camping on other beach-es is prohibited.

Ask at Keos Travel or at the police station for the season's bus schedule. Buses con-nect each town at least twice a day, and run to Voukari and Otzias from Korissa (80dr), and from Chora (250dr), and to Poiessa (220dr from Korissa, 160dr from Chora). It is worth traveling from Chora to Poiessa just for the spectacular view. You may opt to rent a moped at Korissa (around 4000dr per day).

Kea celebrates a fine arts festival called **Ta Simoneida** in honor of the island's great ancient poet, from August 1-15, which features gala dancing, theatrical presentations, sporting events, and a grand bazaar.

DODECANESE
ΔΩΔΕΚΑΝΗΣΑ

While a few of its isles still hear the bleating of goats and the calls of their shepherds, the Dodecanese archipelago has almost completely plunged into a Dantesque abyss of tourist overdevelopment. This motley conglomeration of islands has become increasingly popular as historians, hedonists, and altitude-buffs have each found a place in the sun here. The Dodecanese are comparatively far from mainland Greece and exceedingly close to Turkey (in many places less than 10km). This location explains a rather mottled history. During ancient times, the islands were influenced far more by developments in the cities of Asia Minor than by events in Athens or Sparta. The region flourished through Roman times, but during the decline of the Byzantine Empire, it fell prey to a succession of foreign occupations. Italian merchants controlled some of the islands during this period, but the dominant force was the Crusader Knights of the Order of St. John of Jerusalem, who settled here in the 14th and 15th centuries after being evicted from the Holy Land. They constructed tremendous fortresses in the name of Christianity, and managed to hold off the Turks until Süleyman the Magnificent invaded in 1512. The inhabitants of the Dodecanese formed secret schools to preserve their indigenous culture and to organize the revolutionary movement in the early 19th century. Still, they were not included in the new Greek nation for another 100 years.

In 1912, Italian forces fought the Turks near Libya, ousting them from the Dodecanese. The natives of these islands anticipated the new conquerors to be their Christian saviors; instead, the Italians attempted to force Catholicism and their language on the Greeks. Today, the most common reminders of the Italian occupation are the public buildings that they erected in major towns, and the archaeological excavations and restorations they conducted (the value of which has been vigorously debated). The Italians surrendered in 1943, but the persecution did not end. The Germans took control of the Dodecanese, and decimated the Jewish communities, most notably in Kos and Rhodes. After Germany's surrender in 1945 and the Allied takeover, the Dodecanese finally united with the rest of the Greek nation. Today, every time even the slightest incident jostles the tenuous relationship between Greece and Turkey, the reverberations are felt in the Dodecanese. Check your charter company's regulations for crossing between the two countries to be sure no restrictions apply.

Most of the Dodecanese (literally "12 islands") are arranged in a rough, curved line that follows the coast of Turkey, making it easy to hop from one to the next within the main row without backtracking or changing boats. The main island row, extending northwest from **Rhodes** to **Kos, Kalymnos, Leros,** and **Patmos,** is served by large ferries that run each way between Rhodes and Piraeus daily in summer, and every other day in off-season. The islands of **Karpathos, Halki, Symi, Tilos, Nisyros, Astypalea, Lipsi,** and **Kastelorizo** are slightly more difficult to reach, and are served either by excursion boats from Kos, Rhodes, Patmos, and Leros, or by the *Papadiamandis* and *Sifnos Express,* local Dodecanese ferries. The *Nissos Kalymnos,* another local ferry, shuttles twice a week to all the islands of the northern Dodecanese. In general, it is very easy to travel within the Dodecanese, but difficult to get to other island groups. Only a few boats connect the Dodecanese with the Cyclades, the Northeast Aegean Islands, and Crete. All schedules are extremely erratic: do not base *any* firm plans upon them. The trips to Karpathos and Kassos in particular are plagued by cancellations; the surrounding seas are the roughest in the Aegean, and very few boats run in the off-season. A line of speedy **hydrofoils** serves the main island chain and Symi, but fares are at least twice that of conventional ferries. In addition, the vessels run only in summer and even then only on calm seas; postponements and cancellations are to be expected in August. From Rhodes, you can sail south to Limassol in Cyprus, and to the coast of the Middle East. Ferries also ply the waters to Turkey (from Kos to Bodrum, and from Rhodes to Marmaris); remember that international restrictions may apply.

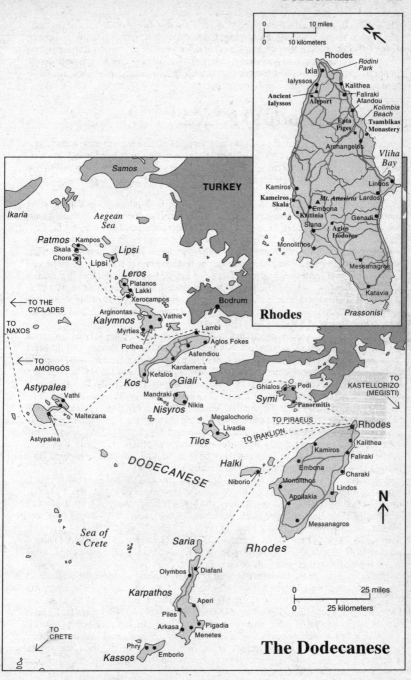

Rhodes

0   10 miles
0   10 kilometers

Rhodes
Rodini Park
Ixia
Ialyssos
Kalithea
Ancient Ialyssos
Airport
Faliraki
Afandou
Kolimbia Beach
Epta Piges
Tsambikas Monastery
Archangelos
Vliha Bay
Kamiros
Kameiros Skala
Mt. Attaviros Lardos
Lindos
Embona
Kritinia
Genadi
Siana
Agios Isodoros
Monolithos
Messanagros
Katavia
Prassonisi

The Dodecanese

Samos
Aegean Sea
TURKEY
Ikaria
Patmos Kampos
Skala
Chora
Lipsi
Lipsi
Leros
Platanos
Lakki
Xerocampos
Bodrum
TO THE CYCLADES
Arginontas
Myrties
Kalymnos
Vathis
Lambi
Aglos Fokes
TO NAXOS
Pothea
Asfendiou
Kardamena
Kefalos
TO AMORGÓS
Astypalea
Vathi
Kos
Giali
Mandraki
Nikia
Maltezana
Astypalea
Nisyros
Megalochorio
Livadia
Ghialos Pedi
Symi
TO KASTELLORIZO (MEGISTI)
Panormitis
Tilos
DODECANESE
TO PIRAEUS
TO IRAKLION
Rhodes
Halki
Kalithea
Kamiros
Faliraki
Niborio
Embona
Charaki
Monolithos
Lindos
Apollakia
Messanagros
Sea of Crete
Rhodes
Saria
Olymbos Diafani
Karpathos
Aperi
Piles
Pigadia
Arkasa
Menetes
TO CRETE
Phry
Emborio
Kassos

0   25 miles
0   25 kilometers

Kos, Rhodes, and Leros have airports, with daily **flights** from Athens and, in summer, flights connecting with each other, Crete, Mykonos, and Santorini. European charters also fly to both Rhodes and Kos. There are smaller airports on Karpathos and Kassos, with connections to Athens and to large islands nearby. Occasional student discounts of 25% on **Olympic Airways** flights with international connections can make them reasonably competitive with ferry fares.

Rhodes (Rodos) ΡΟΔΟΣ

According to myth, when the gods divided sections of the earth amongst themselves, Helios the sun-god, away on his daily journey across the sky, was overlooked. In an effort to avoid divine strife, Zeus agreed to give him any new land that happened to rise out of the sea. From his high vantage point, Helios spotted a ravishing, flower-strewn island and claimed it for himself.

Still a land of sun-worshippers, Rhodes today is the undisputed tourist capital of the Dodecanese. The resort towns have come to suffer from the maladies of unbridled tourism, but outside these areas, most of the island is uncrowded and celestial. Endless expanses of sandy beach stretch along the east coast, jagged cliffs skirt the west coast, and green mountainscapes fill the interior, where secluded villages continue centuries-old traditions. The island's classical past can be rediscovered at Kamiros, Ialyssos, and Lindos; medieval fortresses which rival those of France and Spain slumber in the cities of Rhodes, Lindos, and Monolithos. Although modern hotels dominate many cities' skylines, and burnished bronze tourists carom down all the major shopping streets and New Town beaches, you can find soothing strolls in the smaller villages and along the cobblestone streets of Rhodes City's Old Town.

Rhodes is the most accessible island in the Dodecanese. Regular **ferries** connect it with Piraeus, Crete, the Cyclades, the Northeast Aegean islands, Kavala, and the other Dodecanese islands. Boats bound for Rhodes leave daily at 3pm from Piraeus, stopping at the major Dodecanese islands: Patmos, Leros, Kalymnos, and Kos (17hr., 4021dr). Boats from Rhodes hot-propeller-it to Piraeus in 14 hours (noon daily Tues.-Sun. plus 6pm on Tues., Thurs., and Sun.). The local carriers of the Dodecanese transport network serve Crete (2149dr), the smaller islands in the vicinity (free-1800dr), Limnos (4350dr), Kavala (8070dr), and other islands in the Dodecanese. Connections with other island groups are nonexistent in the off-season, and are subject to long delays whenever the wind is strong. Daily **hydrofoil** service connects Rhodes with Kos (2hr., 7200dr). Excursion boats to Symi run daily (at 9am, returning to Rhodes at 6pm, 2hr.), leaving around 9am and arriving back in Rhodes around 6pm.

In summer, domestic **flights** to Rhodes are usually booked solid at least two weeks in advance. Flights from Rhodes go to: Athens (at least 5 per day, 1hr., day 19,000dr, night 14,900dr); Iraklion (daily, 40min., 14,800dr); Karpathos (at least 2 per day, 45min., 9800dr); Kassos (5 per week, 40min., 10,900dr); Kos (daily, 25min., 9400dr); Mykonos (daily, 1hr., 12,200dr); Paros (3 per week, 1hr., 15,800dr); Sitia (4 per week, 55min., 15,300dr); Thessaloniki (3 per week, 1½hr., 23,400dr); and Santorini (Thira; 4 per week, 1hr., 10,200dr). Departures are less frequent in the off-season, and, as always, schedules change with little or no notice.

Rhodes is also a center for **international travel** by sea and air. Most flights to northern Europe are group charters, but you may be able to snag an empty seat at a very reasonable price—ask at any one of the big charter offices. Boats travel to: Limassol, Cyprus (3 per week, 17hr., 10,600dr; off-season 1 per week, 10,800dr); Haifa, Israel (3 per week, 36hr., 19,900dr); and Alexandria, Egypt (in summer one per week, 15,740dr). Prices include port tax. Students receive a 20% discount on international ferry trips (except to Turkey). Inquire at the tourist offices or call the **Commercial Harbor** at 286 66 for information about arrivals and departures. Be sure to inquire about port taxes, which can be exorbitant.

Small boats leave Rhodes for **Marmaris** in Turkey at 5pm, and return at 8am the next day (daily Mon.-Sat., reduced service Oct.-April, 3hr., 6000dr, round-trip 10,800dr). **Triton Tours** (see Practical Information for the City of Rhodes) has information on the Marmaris trip. You must leave your passport at the office one day before departure. If you're traveling on a charter flight, be sure to check with the charter agency about making the visit, as you risk losing your return plane ticket if such transit is deemed illegal. If you have not yet purchased a return ticket, consult the appropriate consulate in Rhodes to confirm your flight status.

Buses serve the major coastal areas of the east and west quite extensively, but the farther you get from the city of Rhodes the fewer buses you'll find. The tourist office provides a free schedule. **Hitching** is unreliable in the southwest and inland. If you want to really make tracks, rent a motorbike in the city of Rhodes or in Faliraki (mopeds about 3000dr, motorbikes 3500dr). Prices vary greatly depending on the season. Off-season, mopeds go for 2000dr, but be prepared to pay as much as 4000dr in the peak season. Be sure to ask for proof that the bike is covered by third-party insurance. Making the circuit of the island in one day is impossible; the island's size is deceptive and roads in the south (especially the southwest, below Monolithos) are primitive. Allow several days at least. 1993 is a special year to be visiting Rhodes because it will be celebrating its 2400th anniversary. Numerous events, including recitals and plays, are being planned: consult the city tourist office.

City of Rhodes ΡΟΔΟΣ

During the 7th century BCE, the island of Rhodes began to flourish as a major trading center, led by the prosperous cities of Ialyssos, Lindos, and Kamiros. In 408 BCE, near the end of the long Peloponnesian Wars, the three city-states united and founded the city of Rhodes to serve as the island's capital. Determined to create a city which would reflect the prestige and prosperity of the new state, civic leaders hired Hippodamos from Miletus, the I.M. Pei of his day. From all accounts he performed well under pressure; with its exceptional harbor and fine architecture, Rhodes was considered one of the ancient world's most beautiful cities.

Always putting commerce ahead of politics, Rhodes flourished during the next centuries as a center of Hellenistic culture. Alliances with Rome during the Carthaginian Wars helped secure Rhodes's independence until, in 42 BCE, Cassius plundered Rhodes for backing his rivals. Rhodes fell to the Goths in 269 CE but 28 years later, the Byzantine Empire consummated its political and cultural control over the island. Over the centuries, Crusaders, Ottoman Turks, and Italians ruled in succession; Greece finally wrested control of the island away from the Germans after WWII.

Although Lindos is the one city on the island which has been continuously populated since ancient times, the city of Rhodes has always been the source of the island's vitality. Though dominated by the legacy of the Knights of St. John from 1309 to 1522, and unavoidably reminded of this by a vast impregnable fortress, Rhodes retains vestiges from each period of occupation.

Rhodes takes good care of its visitors. The New Town's hotels, bars and discos provide for the herds of tourists who roam bovinely aimless in this paved pasture. The main beach to the west of the city may well be the most crowded in Greece, and during the summer the tourists are packed thigh to sun-seeking thigh. If you go to Rhodes to view historical sights, the city amply rewards, but if you aim to find an isolated beach spot, you will fare far better elsewhere on the island.

You can pick up the *Rhodes Gazette,* a free monthly English newspaper, and the *Rhodes News* at the city tourist office. The *Gazette* publishes useful information about the city, including museum and site hours.

Orientation and Practical Information

The city is divided into two districts: the **New Town,** stretching to the north and west, and the **Old Town,** below it, encapsulated within the medieval fortress walls. There are three harbors. Most boat traffic uses the **Mandraki,** the New Town's waterfront. Larger ferries dock on the harbor's eastern side, yachts and excursion boats on the western side (where the most important services are located). International ferries, as well as some domestic ones, use the **Commercial Harbor** outside the Old Town, and **Acandia,** the harbor below it. Beaches are located north beyond the Mandraki and along the city's western coast. **Rimini Square,** beneath the fortress turrets at the junction between the Old and New Towns, encompasses the city's tourist office, both bus stations, and a taxi stand. To get here from the Mandraki, walk to the base of the vase-shaped Mandraki and head one block inland along the park on the New Town side. To get to **Symi Square,** which leads south to **Museum Square,** follow the city wall on the side of the park opposite Rimini Square back toward the water, and go through the gate into the Old Town. **Sokratous Street,** the major thoroughfare in the Old Town, runs east-west a few blocks south of Museum Square and is the yellow brick road for any search for lodgings. The tourist office's map is a great help.

City of Rhodes Tourist Organization: Rimini Sq. (tel. 359 45). Complete bus and boat handouts. Free map of city (detailed but microscopic). Accommodations service. Open Mon.-Sat. 8am-8pm, Sun. 9am-noon.

Greek National Tourist Organization (GNTO): At the corner of Makariou and Papagou St. (tel. 232 55 or 236 55), in the New Town. Walk up Papagou several blocks from Rimini Sq. Information a bit out-of-date. Open Mon.-Fri. 7:30am-3pm. Closed off-season.

Budget Travel: Triton Tours, 25 Plastira St. (tel. 306 57). Handles Egypt Air, Malev (Hungarian), and Olympic Air, as well as hydrofoil, ferry, and excursion boats to other islands and Marmaris, Turkey. Will refer you to relevant boat agencies. Open Mon.-Fri. 8am-2pm and 4-9pm, Sat. 9am-1:30pm and 4-8pm. Inquire at the municipal tourist information office about bus tours to the Temple of Apollo and various sites.

American Express: c/o Rhodos Tours Ltd., 23 Ammohostou St., P.O. Box 252, (tel. 210 10). Sells traveler's checks to cardholders and will cash their personal checks; holds mail. Open Mon.-Sat. 8:30am-9pm; off-season Mon.-Sat. 8:15am-1pm and 4:30-8:30pm. (Closes for lunch whenever hunger calls.)

Consulates: The Voice of America, just past Sgouru St. (tel. 247 31), southeast of the city. Equipped to handle consular matters, especially in an emergency. Open Mon.-Fri. 8am-4:30pm. A **British** Vice-Consul is available Mon.-Sat. 8am-2pm through Lloyd's Travel Bureau, #23 25th Martiou St. (tel. 272 47). The **Turkish** Consulate, 10 Iroon Polytechniou St. (tel. 233 62), helps people get to Turkey. Open Mon.-Fri. 8am-1pm.

Currency Exchange: Ionian and Popular Bank, 4 Symi Sq. (tel. 274 34), in the Old Town. Open Mon.-Fri. 8am-2pm, Sat. 8:30am-1pm. **National Bank of Greece,** Kyprou Sq. (tel. 270 31), in the New Town. Open Mon.-Thurs. 8am-2pm and 3:30-5:30pm, Fri. 8am-1:30pm and 5-8pm, Sat. 8am-2pm, Sun. 9am-noon. Many other banks in the New Town; few in the Old Town.

Post Office: Main branch on the Mandraki (tel. 222 12). Messages board. Open Mon.-Fri. 8am-8pm, Sat. 7:30am-1pm, Sun. 9am-2pm. (Poste Restante window takes a lengthy lunch hour.) Also a **mobile branch** (on wheels), in the Old Town on Orfeos, near the Palace of the Grand Masters. From Museum Sq., head down Ipoton. Open same hours. **Postal Code:** 85100.

OTE: 91 Amerikis St., at the corner of 25th Martiou St. in the New Town at Platela Orologou. Open daily 8am-midnight. Also an Old Town branch just off Museum Sq. Open daily 8am-10pm. **Telephone Code:** for the northern half of the island 0241, below Kolymbia on the east 0244, below Kalavarda on the west 0246.

Airlines: Olympic Airways, 9 Ierou Lohou St. (tel. 245 71), near the central OTE. Open Mon.-Fri. 8am-4pm. **British Airways** (tel. 277 56), adjacent to the Olympic Airways offices. Open daily 8am-8pm. The airport (tel. 929 81) is on the west coast, 17km from town, near the city of Paradisi; public buses run hourly (270dr). Arrive at least 1hr. before your scheduled departure.

Buses: East (to Lindos, Faliraki, Kalithea, Archangelos, Kolymbia and Afandou), served by KTEYL (tel. 277 06). **West** (to Paradisi (airport), Monolithos, Kamiros, Ialyssos and Koskinou), served by RODA (tel. 363 60). Stations on opposite sides of Papagou St., at Rimini Sq. Open daily 7am-8pm. City buses leave from in front of the New Market. Schedules at tourist offices.

Motorbike Rental: Butterfly, 75 Alexandrou Diakou St. (tel. 213 30), on the corner of Venizelou in the New Town. Mopeds 2500-3500dr per day, fuel and insurance included. Open daily 7:30am-7pm. Also a number of shops in both Old and New Towns; most open daily 8am-8pm. **Gas stations** open Mon.-Sat. 7am-7pm. For **road problems,** dial 104.

Bike Rental: 12 Evdimidou St., in the Old Town. 700dr per day. Cobblestones in the Old Town and maniacal drivers in the New Town make roads here generally unsafe for cyclists.

Taxis: Rimini Sq. (tel. 276 66). Radio taxis also (tel. 647 12 or 647 34).

Libraries: Catholic Academy Library: 7 Dragoumi St. (tel. 202 54), off Diakou in the New Town. English books on the island's history and a few novels. Open Mon.-Tues. and Thurs.-Fri. 9am-2:30pm, Wed. 9am-2:30pm and 5:30-8pm. The library in the **Municipal Cultural Centre,** Rodiaki Epavli-King's Garden (tel. 371 44), has an English section. Open Mon.-Fri. 8am-3pm and 5-8pm. The **Municipal Library** (tel. 244 48) is located at 1 Aristotelous St. in the Old Town.

Laundromat: #32 28th Octovriou St. (tel. 333 20), between Dragoumi and Fanouraki. Wash 600dr, dry 200dr for 20min., soap 100dr. Bring plenty of 50dr coins in case the owner isn't around or you want to practice your Galactic pinball wizardry. Open daily 7am-11pm.

Public Toilets: Strategic locations, including Rimini Sq., the new market, and in the Old Town at Orfeos St. and at Sokratous St.

Hospital: Erithrou Stavrou St. (tel. 222 22), off El. Venizelou. Open for emergencies 24 hrs. Visitors' clinic open daily 2-5pm.

Medical Emergency: Tel. 222 22.

Police: On Ethelondon Dodekanission St. (tel. 232 94), 1 block behind the post office. Lost and Found. Open 24 hrs. The **tourist police,** (tel. 274 23), located at Museum Square in the Old Town. The **port police** (tel. 286 66) are just to the left of the post office. Complete boat schedules.

Police Emergency: Tel. 100

Accommodations

Almost all of the town's inexpensive pensions are in the quiet, intriguing Old Town. Many places shut down during the off-season, but those that don't slash their prices. The city tourist office is a great starting place for advice on where to stay. Prices in Rhodes vary tremendously with the ebb and flow of tourists, so make sure to bargain.

Billy's Pension, 32 Pericleous St. (tel. 356 91). Jubilant and breezy rooms around a traditional Greek courtyard. Well-scrubbed mini-bathrooms. Doubles 3000dr. Dorm beds 1300dr.

Steve Kefalas's Pension, 60 Omirou St. (tel. 243 57). From the base of Sokratous, turn left onto Ag. Fanouriou, then right onto Omirou. Loud, welcoming, international atmosphere. French and English spoken. Beds 1500dr per person. Showers included.

Iliana Hotel, 1 Gavala St. (tel. 302 51). Follow the sign at Plateia Evneon and at the Palio Sintrivani. This traditional building offers spacious doubles (3500dr) and triples (4500dr) with private bathrooms. Hot water 24 hrs. Children under 10 stay free. Perfect for families.

Minos Pension, 5 Omirou (tel. 318 13). Worth the splurge for its luxurious new rooms and super views of the Old City and port. Doubles 3800dr.

Hotel and Pension Paris, 88 Agiou (Saint) Fanouribu St. (tel. 263 56). Turn left on Sokvatous and go up the street 150m. The hotel is beyond the budget traveler, but the pension is reasonable. (Singles 1500dr. Doubles 2500dr. Triples 3000dr.) Open all year round.

Food

Just because Rhodes is surrounded by sea doesn't mean the seafood is any cheaper here than it is anywhere else. **The Good-Time Seeking Hearts Restaurant**(ΟΙ ΜΕΡ-ΑΚΛΙΔΙΚΕΣ ΚΑΡΔΙΕΣ30 Agiou Fanouriou St. in Old Town has the cheapest grub and strangest name in town. (*Souvlaki* 140dr, Greek salad 350dr.) New Town is infested with fast food joints that have similar prices for most of their fare. (Ham and cheese sandwiches 200-250dr, hamburgers 300dr.) Unlike most in Greece, Rhodes's expensive restaurants generally accept major credit cards. Or give your wallet (and your colon) a break and hit the fruit and vegetable store or a supermarket.

Sights

Rhodes's most famous sight can no longer be seen. The **Colossus of Rhodes,** a 32m high bronze statue of Helios, patron deity of the island, was one of the seven wonders of the ancient world. Legend has it that boats passed between the mammoth statue's legs to enter Rhodes harbor. The colossus was erected in 290 BCE, but stood for only

65 years before an earthquake toppled it. More than 1000 years later, wily Arab traders ⁻old the remains of the statue for scrap. Today two bronze deer standing atop pillars mark the spot in Mandraki's harbor where the Colossus allegedly stood.

The Old Town—The Castello

One look at the Old City and it's clear that the Knights of St. John were building for keeps. Replacing Hellenistic structures (most of which had survived intact for centuries until the knights' arrival) with their own incredible array of medieval castles and fortresses, the knights left the most enduring mark on the city. The best place to begin exploring this quarter is at **Symi Square,** inside Liberty and Arsenal Gates, the main passages between the Old and New Towns and the waterfront. To the right with your back to the arch is the **Municipal Art Gallery,** which houses paintings by local artists. (Open Mon.-Sat. 8am-2pm, Wed. 8am-2pm and 5-8pm. Admission 250dr.) Behind the Temple stands the **Inn of Auvergne,** built in 1507, with a staircase attached to the façade in the Aegean style.

Walking past Symi Sq., you'll come upon **Argykastron Square,** with a relocated Byzantine fountain in the center. Set back on the right (west) of the square is the **Palace of Armeria,** built in the 14th century, now the **Archaeological Institute.** With its small windows and lumbering Gothic architecture, the whole structure looks like a fortress. Connected to the palace is the **Museum of Traditional Decorative Arts,** which houses Dodecanese costumes, carved sea chests, and ceramic plates. (Open Tues.-Sun. 8:30am-3pm. Admission 400dr, students 200dr.) By passing through a low archway, you'll reach **Museum Square.** On the left is the **Church of St. Mary,** a.k.a. the Church of the Virgin of the Castle. The Knights of St. John transformed this structure, originally an 11th-century Byzantine work, into a Gothic cathedral. Most of the rich interior frescoes were obliterated by the Turks as they transformed the building into the Enderoum Mosque. The Italians made the mosque into a church, which has since retired in schizophrenic dotage to a quiet existence as a museum featuring icons from all over the island. (Open Tues.-Sun. 8:30am-3pm. Admission 400dr, students 200dr.) The **Inn of the Tongue of England,** stands beyond the church. Built in 1919, the stately Inn is an exact copy of the original 1493 structure. Dominating the other side of the square with its beautiful halls and courtyards, the former **Hospital of the Knights** now houses the **Archaeological Museum.** Most of the island's archaeological treasures are located here. If you can peel your eyes away from the building's glorious interior, affix them to the small but exquisite *Aphrodite Bathing* from the first century BCE, the 4th century BCE Apollo, and the poignant collection of Classical and Hellenistic gravestones. (Open Tues.-Sun. 8:30am-3pm. Admission 600dr, students 300dr; free on Sun., as are most of Rhodes's museums.)

The wide cobblestone street (Ipotou St.) that slopes uphill next to the museum is the most ornate street in the Old Town. More than 500 years ago, this **Avenue of the Knights** was the main boulevard of the inner city, where most of the Knights lived. The Order of the Knights of St. John of Jerusalem consisted of seven different religious orders called "tongues," as each spoke a different language. Their Inns, now government offices, are not open to tourists. Because each tongue was responsible for guarding one segment of the city wall, parts of the wall are labeled "England" or "France" on the map. Though their order was officially dedicated to healing, the Knights were primarily warriors, and even these elegant residences bear resemblances to fortresses.

At the top of the street is a second archway that leads to Kleovoulou Sq., and to the right, the pride of the city, the **Palace of the Knights of St. John.** Also called the Palace of the Grand Masters, the complex has 300 rooms, moats, drawbridges, huge watch towers, and colossal battlements. The structure survived the tough Turkish siege of 1522, only to be devastated in 1856 by an explosion of 300-year-old ammunition left forgotten in a depot across the street. The Italians undertook the task of rebuilding the castle at the beginning of this century. Quixotically determined to outdo even the industrious Knights, they restored the citadel and embellished many of the floors with famous Hellenistic mosaics taken from the island of Kos.

In the early part of this century, the Italians used their palace as a seat of the Italian government, where notables such as Victor Emmanuel III and Mussolini were entertained. The interior decoration was completed only a few months before the start of World War II, however, so the Italians had little chance to savor the full fruits of their megalomaniacal effort. (Palace open Tues.-Sun. 8:30am-3pm. Admission 800dr, students 400dr.) On Tuesdays and Saturdays at 2:45pm, you can take a walk on the city walls (admission 800dr, students 400dr).

The Knights had complete control of the Old Town; any ancient remains are found mainly outside this area. Several blocks west of the southern end of the Old Town off Diagoridon, a **stadium,** a small **theater,** and the **Temple of Apollo** have all been partially reconstructed on the hill near Monte Smith. The stadium and theater are quite well preserved, but the temple, to put it graciously, is an irreparable ruin. You can see the few standing columns from the boat as you arrive or depart from Rhodes; they're just before the last stretch of modern hotels. (Open 24 hrs. Free.) The only other pre-Roman site, the sadly ruined 3rd-century BCE **Temple of Aphrodite,** is just inside the Old Town near Symi Sq., and is almost comically incongruous amid the modern traffic and medieval surroundings.

The Old Town—The Chora

To feel a different era of the city's history, turn right into Kleovoulou Sq. as you leave the palace. After passing under some arches, turn left onto Orfeos St., better known as the **Plane Tree Walk.** The large clock tower on the left marked the edges of the wall that separated the knights' quarters from the rest of the city. The set-up was identical during the Ottoman Era, but the boundaries changed: the Old Town as a whole became a ghetto of Turks and Jews, while the Christian Greeks lived outside its walls. Just 1 block from the clock tower stands the **Mosque of Süleyman.** The original mosque on this site was built immediately after Sultan Süleyman the Magnificent captured Rhodes in 1522. The present one, an early 19th-century construction, has red-painted plaster walls, a garden, and a stone minaret, thus a good landmark in the Old Town and the best-kept symbol of a time Rhodians would rather forget. (Closed for reconstruction as of the summer of 1992.)

Across the street from the mosque is the **Turkish library,** built in 1794 and full of 15th- and 16th-century Persian and Arabic manuscripts, including Qur'ans with extraordinarily intricate calligraphy. (Open capriciously Mon.-Sat. 9am-12pm. Free.) The other Turkish buildings and monuments in the Old Town are in various states of picturesque decay.

Leading downhill from the Mosque of Süleyman is the main shopping strip, **Sokratous Street.** Because fur can be imported to Rhodes duty free, outlets pelt all visitors here. Continuing east along Aristoteleous St. you'll reach **Platia Martyon Evreon** (Square of the Jewish Martyrs) in the heart of the old Jewish Quarter. In 1943, 2000 Jews were taken from this square to Nazi concentration camps; only 50 survived. A little way down Dosiadou St., where it becomes Symiou St., stands the **synagogue,** restored by the survivors after the war. Oriental rugs cover the stone mosaic floor, and "eternal lamps" hang in front of the curtained ark. Around the walk, plaques from foreign countries commemorate those lost in the war. To see the synagogue's interior, ask Lucia, who lives above it, contact the caretaker Mr. Soviano at 16 Polytechniou St. (tel. 273 44), or stop by the Jewish Community Office at 5 Polydoros (tel. 223 64). Services are held on Fridays at 5pm. Dress appropriately.

As you cross from the Old Town to the New Town at Eletherias Gate near Symi Sq., don't miss the small herd of deer kept in the city's moat. More than 800 years ago, deer were imported to alleviate a serious snake problem. Apparently, the deer got indescribable thrills by impaling the snakes with their hooves and antlers and Rhodians have been grateful ever since. Now indicative of a more general sense of protection, the statues of the deer in Mandraki's harbor have become the city's symbol.

The New Town and Mandraki

Italian architecture dominates in this modern business district. Massive Mussolini-inspired buildings of massive, multicolored stone preside over wide Eleftherias St. The Bank of Greece, the town hall, the post office, and the National Theater are the more imposing, dare we say fascist, structures on the far side of the street. Directly opposite, along the waterfront, is the majestic **Governor's Palace** and a cathedral built by the Italians in 1925. The cathedral replicates St. John's Church near the Grand Palace, which was leveled in the 1856 explosion.

Remnants of the Turkish presence persist at the **Mosque of Mourad Reis,** named after Süleyman's admiral who died while capturing Rhodes from the Knights of St. John in 1522. The small, domed building inside is his mausoleum.

The three old **windmills** of Rhodes (no longer functional) stand halfway along the harbor's long pier. The **Fortress of St. Nicholas,** at the end of the pier, was built in 1464 and guarded the harbor until the end of World War II. (The fortress is generally closed to the public.) Walk along the pier at Mandraki toward the mills, and you'll see many private yachts heading to Cyprus, Turkey, and elsewhere. An **aquarium** is located at the northern tip of the island. (Open daily 9am-9pm. Admission 300dr, students 150dr.)

Entertainment

The **Folk Dance Theater,** well signposted on Andronikou St. (tel. 290 85 or 201 57) in the Old Town, stages marginally hokey performances during the summer which feature dances and songs from northern and central Greece, as well as the Dodecanese. (Shows April-Oct. Sun.-Fri. at 9:15pm. Admission 1200dr, students 700dr, and well worth it.)

The evening **Sound and Light Shows** at the palace give an account of the Turkish siege of the city during the Crusader occupation. The entrance to the show is on Papagou St., across from the New Market. (English shows Mon.-Tues. at 9:15pm, Wed., Fri., and Sat. at 10:15pm, Thurs. at 11:15pm. Admission 600dr, students 300dr.) **St. Francis Church** (tel. 236 05), at the intersection of Dimokratias and Filellinon St., echoes with organ recitals Wednesday nights at 9pm. Once or twice a month, performances are given at the **ancient theater** near Monte Smith; check with the GNTO for details. The **National Theatre** (tel. 296 78), off the Mandraki next to the town hall, stages occasional winter productions. If your eyes are glazed with longing for the silver screen, take in a new flick or one of the classics with subtitles at the **Rodon,** near the National Theatre. (Shown daily at 8:30pm and 10:30pm, only 400dr.)

Supposedly, Rhodes has more bars per capita and per kilometer than London, Paris, New York, or Berlin. The New Town is definitely the buzz: most places heat up at 10pm and pump out the tunes until 3am. Crowds of young English tourists bestow upon the popular bars and clubs near Diakou and Venezelou St. a distinctly British flavor. Prices at the bars are virtually identical. (Beer 300-400dr, mixed drinks 600-700dr.) For a good time, call at **Tramp's, Inka's,** the **1960s Bar,** and the **Underground.** The Underground, due to its subterranean status, stays open later than the rest. For "distinct personality", stop in at **Symposium Garden** (from the top of Sokratous St. take a left and follow the signs). The relaxed outdoor garden atmosphere and ancient Rhodes flair make it a must. (Beer 400dr.) There are also several gay bars in Rhodes: **Bar Berlin,** 47 Orfanidou St. (tel 322 50), is in the farther group; **Valentino** (tel. 340 70) is on Sokratous St. in the Old Town. Discos in Rhodes City are almost as common as bars. The best disco in town is **La Scala,** but it's not designed for the budget traveler. The 2000dr cover charge (which includes your first drink) will set your head spinning, and the 800dr beers won't help either. But this place is chock full of fountains, tropical waterfalls, garden pools, and a light show straight out of Laser-Floyd. La Scala is one of a cluster of discos that lie toward the beach to the west outside of town. To get there from the Old Town, take Voriou Ipirou St. from near Amboise Gate—the clubs are just after the intersection with Kennedy St. A taxi back to the Old Town at night will run you 600dr. Try **Mike's,** on 17 Voriou Ipirou St., and note its outlandish decor. **Le Palais,** on the other side of the New Town on 25th Martiou St., draws a more mixed crowd.

Many people make an evening of **strolling** in the Old Town; the souvenir shops and clothing stores on Sokratous St. stay open until 9pm or so.

Eastern Rhodes

Excursion boats trace the length of beach-filled coast from Rhodes to Lindos, leaving at various times in the morning and returning in the afternoon. Many make several stops, often including Faliraki. Schedules and prices posted at their dock along the lower end of the Mandraki: Most (about 2500dr round-trip). The **Rhodes Diving Center** (tel. 336 54) offers full-day diving excursions that stop at Kalithea. (May-Oct., passengers 200dr, snorkelers 4000dr, certified divers 7000dr, inexperienced divers 7500dr.)

As you drive out of the city, the landscape slowly subsides into countryside. In between and served by any bus heading east from Rhodes, lies **Rodini Park,** a forested area with streams, trails, a restuarant, and some animals left from the time when Rodini was a zoo. Just 10km south of town is **Kalithea,** site of a deserted spa, and a pine park for freelance camping. Kalithea's thermal springs once bathed the bodies of leisure-class Europeans. Pebble mosaic walkways guide the visitor past chipped pink columns, and the dry central bath's roof has cut-out stars still showing traces of blue. During the day, you can use the shower on the park's beach. For food you'll have to make do with the meager snack-bar at the spa's beach cove, or go to nearby Koskinou (2km inland), Faliraki, or the city of Rhodes. In return for the use of the park, cops expect campers to clean up after themselves. Buses run every half-hour from 8am until 9pm (250dr).

Faliraki

The popular tourist resort of Faliraki is 5km further south from Kalithea. Its sandy beach and rocking nightlife have compelled many to call Faliraki Rhodes's Malia and Hersonissos (see Crete). **Buses** run between Rhodes City and Faliraki every half hour 6am-10pm for 300dr. Opposite the bus stop, a small white building houses the **post office** and **currency exchange** office (open daily 7:30am-2:30pm), as well as a **first aid** station (open Mon.-Sat. 9am-5pm). You can rent a car at the aptly named **Just Rent-a-Car** (tel. 861 32). (8000dr per day for economy models). The rental agency also provides travel services such as air and sea tickets.

There's an official **campsite** (tel. 855 16 and 853 58) off the main road ½km before Faliraki; ask the bus driver to let you off. Facilities include TV, disco-bar, market, and swimming pool. (600dr per person, 300dr per tent.) Otherwise, accomodations in Faliraki are hard to come by during the peak season because most establishments rent all their rooms to British tour package companies, but Faliraki makes for a great daytrip from Rhodes City. Food here isn't cheap, especially at the *tavernas* by the waterfront, but there are a couple of reasonable fast food joints on the main strip. The **Pie Shop** offers English pies, and along the main street (a street with no name) are many supermarkets.

During the day, the beach teems with sun bathers. Adjacent to Faliraki Bay Hotel on the north side of the beach you can enjoy **Mille's Windsurfing** (2000dr per hour). As night falls, the volume rises at all the bars on the main street. Relax at the **Palm Beach Bar,** or move on to **Champer's Pub,** the center of the action. All the bars in Faliraki serve beer for 300-400dr and the music quiets down around midnight. That's when everyone moves over to **Disco Set,** 200m off the main street. (Just follow the crowds, but pick up a free pass from one of the English tourists earlier in the evening to cover the 1000dr cover charge).

Eleven km farther south, just before Kolymbia, a road to the right leads to a partially dirt road 3km away, which continues to **Epta Piges** (Seven Springs). The nature walks in this area are wonderful, but most people trek no farther than the inexpensive restaurant next to the main stream. (Open 6am-7pm. Admission 200dr.) There's no direct bus service; ask any Lindos/Archangelos bus driver to let you off at the appropriate intersection. It's worth continuing inland past Epta Piges to visit the Byzantine **Church of Ágios Nikolaos Fountoucli,** 3km past Eleousa, which displays some extremely fine 13th- and 15th-century frescoes. One daily bus ventures to Eleousa, leaving at 1:20pm and returning at 6:20am the next morning. Villagers in Arthipoli, 4km away, rent rooms (doubles 3000-4000dr). Alternatively, take a moped; scarce traffic makes hitching difficult.

A worthwhile distraction if you're exploring via moped or car is the **Tsambikas Monastery,** a little Byzantine cloister atop Mt. Tsambikas. The asphalt ends at the Tsambikas Beach turn-off though the road ahead will take you most of the way there. You'll probably have to walk the last km. Both **Kolymbia** and **Tsambikas** beaches offer dethronged sands.

About 10km farther down the road from Tsambikas (15km south from Lindos), take the turn-off to **Charaki,** where you can swim next to a hill topped by the crumbling **Castle of Feracios,** built by the Knights of St. John. Quite a few rooms and several restaurants can be found along the beach. The Lindos bus will take you there.

Lindos

With its beautiful whitewashed houses clustered beneath a soaring castle-capped acropolis, Lindos is the most photogenic member of the Rhodos family. But it is perhaps the most spoiled as well. Vines and flowers overhang narrow streets, pebble mosaics carpet courtyards and doorways, and exhilarating views of the town, sea, and lovely beach lie quiescent at every corner. The town's charms, however, are no secret. In summer, the packed streets of Lindos make the city of Rhodes seem a ghost town—and the inflated prices match its demographics.

Buses run hourly between Rhodes and Lindos, leaving the former from Rimini Sq. (1hr., 650dr, last return to Rhodes at 6pm). **Excursion boats** from Rhodes depart at 10am and return at 6pm, sometimes stopping at other points on the coast (2000dr round-trip).

Orientation and Practical Information

Lindos is an entirely pedestrian city. All traffic stops at Eleftherias Sq. From there, the main avenue, **Acropolis Street,** leads through the eastern part of town and up to the well-signposted acropolis. The second main street, **Apostolous Pavlou,** runs perpendicular to Acropolis St., westward from the Church of the Assumption Madonna, whose stone belfry rises up in the middle of town. None of the other streets are named. Once you get into the loops and whirls of the alleys on the hillside, however, street names are irrelevant. Houses are distinguishable only by number (from 1 to about 700), and the numbers change periodically.

The **tourist office** (tel. 314 28), in Eleftherias Sq., helps with accommodations, maintains a currency exchange, and provides maps and transportation information. Their useless glossy brochure about Lindos costs 200dr. (Open 9am-10pm.) **Pallas Travel** (tel. 312 75), 100m east of the church, has an equally useless brochure for free. They also hold mail, arrange babysitting services, and offer various excursions. (Open daily 9-11am and 5-7pm.) The **National Bank** is on Apostolous Pavlou. (Open Mon.-Thurs. 9am-2pm, Fri.-Sat. 9am-2pm.) The **post office** (open Mon.-Fri. 8am-1:20pm), and **pharmacy** (open Mon.-Fri. 9:30am-2pm and 4:30-8pm, Sat.-Sun. 10am-1pm) are up the hill to the right of the donkey stand. Most of the town's other services are on or just off Acropolis St. The **OTE**, at 156, is up the stairs on the left behind Alexis Bar. (Open Mon.-Fri. 7:30am-3:10pm, Sat.-Sun. 9am-noon.) The woman with the washing machine at 456 Vas. Pavlou St. does laundry for travelers. Sheila Markiou, an American expatriate, runs a great **lending library** of over 7000 English books (100dr per day with a 1000dr deposit; used books 400-700dr). To get there, continue until 350, take the small side street on your left (opposite Yanni's), and follow the signs to 381. The **police** (tel. 312 23) are at 521 Vas. Pavlou. (Open Mon.-Fri. 8am-3pm; emergencies 24 hrs.) The **telephone code** for Lindos is 0244.

Accommodations, Camping, Food, and Entertainment

If you come in July or especially August, you'll want to make Lindos a daytrip; lodgings, even in the tiniest, most removed spots are hogged by European package tours. In the off-season, lodgings are easier to find and cost a fraction of the summer prices. Your best bet during the summer is to arrive early in the morning before the tour buses rumble in, and ask the tour companies' offices if they have any empty rooms. If you can find the few free agents in this permanent figurative diamond of alleyways, they will rent doubles for 5000-7000dr in high season. Singles do not exist. For a good place to start looking, take Acropolis Ave. past Palas Travel. The left fork will bring you to **Pension Elektra** (tel. 312 66), at 63, and a small sidestreet that leads to other houses with *dhomatia.* There is a Pyncheonesque network here—if one house is full, the owners will direct you to another. The pensions at 511 (tel. 312 69) and 506 (tel. 312 20) might have some empty rooms. In August, with the annual invasion of Italians, the accommodation situation gets desperate and prices go through the roof. **St. George's campground** (tel. 442 03) is only about 10km south, near the little town of Lardos; a free shuttle bus runs hourly to Lindos from the campground. The cheapest option is to camp on Lindos Beach, which has fresh-water showers—too bad it's illegal.

Eating without devastating outlay in Lindos poses a challenge: restaurant prices range from expensive to exorbitant. The only moderate alternatives are the *souvlaki-pita* bars or grocery stores on the two main streets. The air-conditioned **Café-Bar Poseidon,** just past the church at 173, is a small place with a more low-key atmosphere (beer 300dr). Poseidon also serves the best affordable snack in Lindos: a bowl of homemade yogurt with honey and fresh fruit—absolutely incredible (500dr). Lindos has a loud and fervent nightlife. Most people visit the town's bars until the music ends at midnight and then waggle down to the discos along the road on the other side of the main square. **Lindos By Night** (tel. 314 63), between the post office and the pharmacy, is cheapest (pints of beer 400dr; open daily 7pm-2am).

Sights

The premier attraction of Lindos, the ancient **acropolis,** stands in scaffolding at the top of the sheer cliffs, 125m above town. Impenetrable walls of a Crusader fortress further enclose the caged structure. Excavations of the site by the Danish Archaeological School in 1902-1912 yielded everything from 5000-year-old Neolithic tools to a plaque inscribed by a priest of Athena in 99 BCE listing the dignitaries who had visited Athena's Temple: Hercules, Helen of Troy, Menelaeus, Alexander the Great, and the King of Persia just begin the list. The winding path up to the acropolis is veiled in hundreds of lace tablecloths that village women sell; the cobwebbed pall makes for an interesting, if somewhat surreal, ascent. Right before the final incline, don't miss the fabulous *trireme,* or ancient Greek warship, carved into the cliffside as a symbol of Lindos's inextricable ties with the sea. The 13th-century **crusader castle** looms over the entrance to the site. As you leave the castle, make a U-turn to your left and you'll come to the imposing **Doric Stoa** (arcade) whose 13 restored columns dominate the entire level. The arcade, built around 200 BCE at the height of Rhodes's glory, originally consisted of 42 columns laid out in the shape of the Greek letter "Π." The large stone blocks arranged against the back wall originally served as bases for bronze statues which have long since been melted down for scrap.

At the top of the steps, the **Temple of the Lindian Athena** comes into view. According to myth, a temple was built here as early as 1510 BCE. All that remains today are parts of the temple built by the tyrant Cleoboulos in the 6th century BCE. Once a tremendously important religious site in the Mediterranean, it is now one of the few ancient Greek temples with inner walls still fairly intact, and colonnades on both sides. The donkey rides to the acropolis are a rip-off (600dr each way); the walk is not very strenuous. (Acropolis open daily 8am-6:30pm, Sat.-Sun. 8:30am-3pm. Admission 700dr, students 300d; free on Sun.)

The graceful stone bell tower projecting from the middle of town belongs to the **Church of the Assumption Madonna,** rebuilt by the Knights of St. John around 1489. Brightly colored 18th-century frescoes, retouched by the Italians in 1927, illuminate the interior. At the southwest foot of the acropolis are the remains of the **ancient theater.** The **Voukopion** is on the northern side of the rock face, visible from the donkey path. This cave, which the Dorians transformed into a sanctuary for Athena, is believed to date from the 9th century BCE and was supposedly used for special sacrifices that could be performed only outside the acropolis.

Lindos has one of the most crowded **beaches** on the island. At the center of Lindos beach, you can rent sailboards for 2000dr per hour. Water-skiing lessons relieve you of

2500dr in exchange for perfunctory instruction and about 10 minutes in the water. Check out the nifty paddleboats (1000dr per hour).

Western Rhodes ΔΥΤΙΚΗ ΡΟΔΟΣ ·

A string of high-rise hotels abuts the 8km stretch of sand west of Rhodes. The western end of this luxury hotel district is the town of modern **Ialyssos** (Trianda). The hotels were built in the late 60s and early 70s under Greece's military dictatorship and they look it. **Ancient Ialyssos,** 5km inland near the town of Filerimos, was in ages past one of the three great cities on the island, along with Lindos and Kamiros. The ruins are rather meager. Most impressive are the 4th-century BCE Doric fountain ornamented with four lion heads, the adjacent **monastery** and the **Church of Our Lady of Filerimos** (actually four conjoined chapels). Both the church and the monastery stand on the site of a 3rd-century BCE temple to Athena and Zeus Polias, and a renovated Byzantine church. On the stone floor just inside the doorway of the room to the left, rests a remnant of the original Byzantine structure: a fish (the symbol of Christ) carved into one of the red stones. The path past the chapel leads to the ruins of a **Byzantine castle.** (Site open Tues.-Sun. 8:30am-3pm. Admission 400dr, students 200dr; free on Sun.)

Unfortunately, there is no easily negotiable road to Filerimos. Taxis from Rimini Sq. will make the round-trip for about 2500dr. Aside from a motorbike, the only other alternative is the bus from Rhodes to modern Ialyssos (every ½hr., 200dr), but you'll have to take a taxi from there (about 1500dr). You can also walk the clearly marked 5km uphill.

Sandy cliffs inspect the rugged coast south of Filerimos. Nearby, two religious festivals take place on the road to Kamiros. At **Kremasti,** 12km outside of Rhodes, locals celebrate *Panayia* (the name-day of the Virgin Mary) for nine days beginning on August 14. The Monastery of Agios Soulas, 18km on the inland road at **Kalavarda,** puts on an especially grand name-day festival for its patron saint (July 28-29). In between, only tiny villages animate the sleepy coast, and the beaches are mediocre. In Kalavarda, the **telephone code** changes to 0246 for the southwest.

One interesting excursion, often done as a daytrip, is **Petaloudes,** a valley about 25km from the city. Also known as the **Valley of the Butterflies,** it is famous for its papilionaceous explosion of the creatures in July and August. On off-days, however, you'll find more befuddled tourists here than butterflies; and more lovey-dovey couples than singles: if you're alone you may get depressed. Nevertheless, the valley remains charming, with small waterfalls, pools, and wooden bridges. (Open daily from mid-June to the end of August only, 9am-6pm. Admission 200dr.) About 1km down the road is the 18th-century monastery of the **Panayia Kalopetra.** Buses from Rhodes travel here (5 per day until 1pm, returning at 1:50pm, 40min., 500dr). Petaloudes is accessible from the coastal road; 3km after Paradisi, take the turn-off to Kalamonas, and the valley is 9km farther.

Ancient Kamiros, 35km from the city of Rhodes, was a prosperous city surrounded by productive farmland in the 6th and 5th centuries BCE. Houses' stone walls, the reservoir cisterns, fallen pillars of temples and public places, and the main cobblestone street have lasted, providing a lifesize blueprint of a small ancient city. Though none of the individual ruins is outstanding, the site taken together with the sigh-evoking views of the Aegean and neighboring valleys is striking. (Site open Tues.-Sun. 8:30am-3pm. Admission 300dr, students 200dr; free on Sun.) Five buses per day make the trip from Rhodes, the last returning at 8:05pm (40min., 600dr). Some 15km beyond Ancient Kamiros, the hamlet of **Kamiros Skala** has a few houses, *tavernas,* and a boat launch. Boats leave here for Halki. (Inquire at the tourist office in Rhodes.) To get here, take the Monolithos bus (see below).

Beyond Kamiros Skala at Kritinia, there is a turn for **Embona,** a village famous for its dancing and traditional costumes. It is easily accessible by bus from Rhodes (6 per day, last return 10:05pm, 1½hr., 440dr). The Monolithos bus also passes through at around 7am and 7pm. In Embona a large group of squat, modern houses sits in conspicuous contrast to the lush farmland and forests, and the rocky slopes of Mt. Atavyros, the tallest mountain on the island (1215m). In spite of an uncomely mask, the town conducts a thriving tourist trade on summer evenings. Two restaurants offer traditional Greek dancing largely but not exclusively for tour groups from Rhodes. **Bake's Café** provides dinner and a show for 1700dr (dinner alone 1200dr). To get there, go left on the road behind the Church of the Holy Trinity (its tower is visible from the bus stop), and look for the café's sizable veranda. (Dances late Mar.-early Nov. Open 5am-midnight). Two pensions near the center of town offer inexpensive accommodations: both the dapper **Pension Panorama** (tel. 412 06; above the pharmacy near the statue of the angel), and the slightly shabbier **Pension Embona** (tel. 412 12) charge 1500dr per person. Running water is available only from 5:30pm to 8:30pm.

   South of Kamiros Skala, both coastal and mountain roads traverse high ridges, with intoxicating views of Alimnia and Tragousa and the other small islands off the coast on the way to Monolithos. A small **castle** on the cliffs by the sea rests near the quiet mountainside village of **Kritinia.** The inhabitants of **Siana,** 14km south, sell delicious honey (about 2000dr per kilo).

   Monolithos (literally "single rock,") on the island's southwest tip, is a tiny village, barely more than a collection of scattered houses. The **Castle of Monolithos,** 2km west, is well worth the trip. Though in ruins, the fortress keeps its dignity at the summit of a 160m rock pillar. You can walk around inside the castle and the small chapel of St. Panteleimon, but be mindful of the steep drop while the views knock you off your feet. (Open 24 hrs. Free.) To get here, follow the only western road out of town. You'll find few if any tourist conveniences in town, but the **Hotel Thomas** (tel. 612 91), several blocks from the center, has spotless rooms. (Singles 3000dr. Doubles 5000dr.) Despite its uninspired name, the **"Restaurant-Bar Greek Food,"** at the top of the road, serves decent entrees and refreshers (Greek salad 350dr). Two buses leave Rhodes daily for Monolithos, passing through Embona and Agios Isidoros. (Mon.-Fri. at 1:15pm and 3:15pm, returning at 6:30pm and 6:15am the next day, 2½hr., 850dr).

Southern Rhodes ΝΟΤΙΑ ΡΟΔΟΣ

   South of Lindos in the east and Monolithos in the west, the island assumes an entirely different essence. Here in farm and goatherding country, grassy yellow flatlands slope gradually into hills studded with low-lying shrubs. In the west, dunes buffer a long stretch of wave-battered beach, while in the east, numerous secluded coves pepper the coastline. One bus per day runs down the east coast to the extreme south, stopping at Lardos, Asklipios, Lachania, Katavia, and finally Messanagros (leaves at 3pm, returns next day at 6:30am, 2hr., 950dr). With few exceptions you'll find prices here unaffected by tourism.

   The beaches at the rotund **Lardos** (10km south of Lindos), **Kiotari** (18km south), and **Katavia** (24km south) are as somnolent as their towns. You can pitch a tent at **St. George's Campground** (tel. 442 03), 1km outside of Lardos, where roughing it entitles you to currency exchange, international telephones, a market, bars and a free hourly shuttle bus to Lindos. (Camping 500dr per person. Sometimes only uneconomical bungalows are available.) **Genadi,** 22km south of Lindos has rooms to let near the beach. The road on the southeast is ideal for motorbikes; southwest routes are unpaved.

   If isolation is what you're after, read Dostoevsky or take the bone-jolting dirt road (you may need a jeep) to the **lighthouse** at **Akro Prassonisi** on the absolute southern tip of the island. The couple living there rarely gets visitors in summer; during the winter they get none, as the sea covers the isthmus. The rustic **Skiadhi Monastery,** situated halfway up a hill on a steep alternate road between Apollakia and Messanagros, is an unsurpassed picture opportunity. Impress your family, friends, and goats. To get to the monastery from Apollakia, take the dirt road 4km in the direction of Katavia, then turn left onto the well-marked monastery turn-off (manageable on a motorbike). Follow the dirt road past pumpkin patches and wheat fields for several kilometers. Hitching will prove difficult as there is a paucity of traffic. Apollakia has a few cheap pensions and restaurants.

Karpathos ΚΑΡΠΑΘΟΣ

Karpathos is an invigorating change from the daily regimen of ruins and thronged island beaches. The seclusion of this long 42km island, anchored halfway between Rhodes and Crete, guarantees its serenity. Karpathos is more than just another island in the Dodecanese. This blessed plot's natural attractions are special and the Karpathians are a breed of their own, an embodiment of Greece's famed hospitality (*filoxenia*). Everybody greets you with a smile, and don't be surprised if some old man in a pick-up truck offers you a ride while you're waiting for the bus. (As always, sólo women should not hitchhike.) In the mountains, residents preserve traditional dress, ways, and even speech, but Karpathos Town (officially called Ta Pigadia) straddles the line between quaint and cosmopolitan. Since 1872, many Karpathians have been living in the U.S., and today a great many residents divide their time betwen the U.S. and Greece, infusing the island with American dollars. As a result, Karpathos has become one of the wealthiest islands in Greece. Because it's so far off the beaten ferry route, however, Karpathos remains inexpensive enough for the shrewd budget traveler.

As is the case with many small nations, war and conquest characterize Karpathos's history. Karpathians fought in the Peloponnesian War (on Sparta's side) in 431 BCE, and lost their independence to Rhodes in 400 BCE. In 42 BCE the island fell to Rome; in 395 CE Byzantium annexed it. A few centuries later, Karpathos was ruled by the Arabs followed by the Genoese pirate Moresco, the Venetians, and the Ottoman Turks in quick succession. Turkish rule ended only when the Italians conquered the island in World War I, and held it until the Germans relieved them in World War II. In 1948, after 654 years of foreign rule, Karpathos finally became part of Greece.

Infrequent ferries connect Karpathos with the rest of Greece. On Wednesdays, a ferry leaves Karpathos, bound for the other Dodecanese Islands, Amorgos, Paros, and Piraeus. Boats from Karpathos go to Rhodes every Saturday. Boats also chug to Kassos and Agios Nikolaos, on Crete (Fri. and Sat.). There are two nonstop **flights** per week to Athens (19,700dr), but you can go via Rhodes (daily, 35min., 8200dr). You can also fly to Kassos (2 per week, 2800dr) and to Sitia on Crete (4 per week, 9000dr). Additionally, many charter companies shuttle into Karpathos.

Ta Pigadia ΠΙΓΑΔΙΑ

Ta Pigadia, Karpathos's first city, means "the wells." Originally the new town was called Possi, for "Poseidon Polis," but many objected to the fact that "Possi" also means "drinking-bout." Today, the town is the island's administrative and transportation center. You'll find travel agencies and restaurants around the main *platia* of Ierou Polytechniou, along the waterfront, and up **Dimokratia Street,** which trails inland from the center of the harbor. Most other services are in the western half of town near **Platia 5 October.** You can get there by bearing left (inland) after the National Bank.

The **bus station** is one block up Dimokratia St. from the center of town. Most of the island's villages are serviced by buses (from 250-950dr); check the schedule at Karpathos Travel. **Taxis** (tel. 227 05) go to all of the island's villages, and are as cheap as the bus when split between four or more passengers. Taxi prices, regulated by the state, are posted in Karpathos Travel. On the same street as the post office, **Gatoulis Motorbikes** (tel. 227 47) rents excellent 50cc automatics (2500dr per day). (They also rent cars for 10,000dr per day plus tax. Open daily 7:30am-1pm and 5-10pm.)

Karpathos Travel (tel. 227 54 and 221 48), on Dimokratia St. between the bus station and the waterfront, has complete bus information and most boat schedules. Helpful Michael Maloftis will call for rooms, rent cars (27,000dr for 3 days, insurance and tax included), and **exchange currency.** (Open Mon.-Sat. 8am-1pm and 5-10pm, Sun. 9-11am.) Both Karpathos and **Possi Travel** (tel. 222 35, around the corner on the waterfront on Apodimon Karpathion St.) sell island maps for 200dr. (Open Mon.-Sat. 8am-1pm and 5-8:30pm, Sun. 9am-noon and 6-7:30pm.) The **National Bank** is across the street, to the left of Possi Travel. (Open Mon.-Thurs. 8am-2pm, Fri. 8am-1:30pm.)

To get to the **post office** from Platia 5 October, take the uphill road to the right of the kiosk. (Open Mon.-Fri. 7:30am-2pm). Next door you'll find the **police** (tel. 222 22;

open 24 hrs.) and **tourist police** (tel. 222 18; open 9am-midnight). They don't speak much English, but will valiantly try to help you. The **OTE** (open Mon.-Fri. 7:30am-midnight, Sat.-Sun. 9am-9pm), and the **Olympic Airways** office (tel. 221 50; open Mon.-Sat. 8am-2pm) are both in Platia 5 October. Karpathos's **postal code** is 85700; its **telephone code** is 0245.

There are three **pharmacies** in town. (Open 8am-1pm and 6-8pm.) In an emergency, call the **hospital** (tel. 222 28). Most of the town's several **minimarkets** are on the same road as Karpathos Travel. **John Pavlakos** (tel. 223 89), next to Possi Travel, has a small stock of writing supplies and guide books. (Open Mon.-Sat. 8:30am-1:30pm and 5:30-8:30pm.) You can swap books at the Porphyrous Hotel on Limiadis St.

Try the **Avra Hotel** (tel. 223 88), with small rooms and a small bath geared toward small people. (Singles 2800dr. Doubles 3800dr. Triples 4500dr with private bath.) From the waterfront, take the second right off Dimokratia St.—it's 1 block ahead on the right. The **Anesis Hotel** (tel. 221 00) is a block past the OTE. (Singles 1500dr. Doubles 3000dr. Triples 4000dr. Private bath included.) There are balconies with every room at **Harry's Rooms to Rent** (tel. 221 88), just up the hill and to the left from the Avra. (Singles 2500dr. Doubles 3800dr. Open April-Dec.) At **Sofia's** (tel. 221 54), you'll find attractive old tile floors and sweeping vistas; turn left (facing inland) at the bus stop intersection and walk south 200m. (Singles 2000dr. Doubles 3800dr. Triples 4300dr.) The **Blue Bay Hotel** (tel. 224 79), offers luxurious doubles in the off-season for 4000dr, breakfast included. Prices rise dramatically during peak season, but it may be worth a call. Freelance camping, though illegal, transpires mostly undisturbed on the town beach to the north.

Restaurants are scattered along the waterfront where Karpathians come for their nightly *volta* (stroll). To meet the demand of beachgoers, newer *tavernas* are poking up just north of town on Limiadis St. Most offer complete meals for a pricy 1300dr. **Burger Express** on the waterfront and the **7-Eleven Snack Bar** 600m down the road to Aperi provide the budget traveler a great alternative.

Nightlife converges around the waterfront's north end. **La Mirage,** a romantic spot hovering high above the harbor, plays live Greek music. (Beer 300dr). 200m from the Blue Bay Hotel is the disco **Highway** which rocks daily only during the peak season. Dance all you want, but keep an eye on your *drachmae:* drinks are expensive. (Beer 500dr.)

Southern Karpathos

The rest of southern Karpathos is known for its stone farmhouses, tiny isolated chapels, and tendon-tearing views over terraced hillsides to the sea. On August 6, the towns of Menetes, Aperi, and Othos hold lively church festivals with lots of eating, drinking, and dancing.

On a branch of the road south out of Ta Pigadia are the hillside towns of **Menetes** and **Arkasa.** Menetes's huge church seems to sprout out from the terraced houses below. Its marble pillars were salvaged from the ruins of an early Christian basilica. Ask at **Manolis Kafeneion** (tel. 223 80) for a key to the miniscule **folk art museum** (free). In Arkasa, the remains of five parallel cyclopean walls divide the peninsula southwest of town.

This beach town sports several *dhomatia.* The best, close to the sandy shore of Agios Nikolaos, is run by **Anna Diakomichali** (tel. 612 31); follow the road from Arkasa to Agios Nikolaos, and you'll see it across the street from the "Agios Nikolaos 0.3km" sign. (Singles 2700dr. Doubles 4000dr. Triples 5000dr. Breakfast and private bath included. Kitchen facilities available.) On the small beach cove, five minutes on foot from Anna's boarding house, freelance campers will find cold showers for bathing.

The island's only other paved road leads north and then west out of Ta Pigadia into lush hiking country. **Aperi** became the island's capital in medieval times when Arab raids forced the Karpathians to abandon their coastal town. Today it remains the island's bishopric, its spiritual capital. The church here contains the Panayia (Virgin Mary) icon revered throughout Karpathos. Legend has it that long ago a monk was chopping wood when blood suddenly spurted from one of the logs. The perplexed monk soon recognized the log as an icon of the Virgin Mary. The object disappeared several times, reappearing in an old church in Aperi. The monk understood that the Panayia wished to stay in that spot, and in 1886 a bishop's church was built there. (The church is open to visitors 8am-11am, when the church overseer is present.)

Two outstanding beaches are on the coast near Aperi. At **Ahata Beach,** a spring refreshes bathers and campers. And at **Kyra Panayia,** you can stay at **Vassili's Taverna** (tel. 313 00; doubles 4200dr; breakfast included). A boat stops at this quiet, secluded beach twice a week en route to Diafani. Inquire at Karpathos Travel.

Farther north on the coast, **Lefkos** is toilsome to reach, but with its fabulous beach, perfect for tuning out all distractions. A husky cave with pillars to support its ceiling is a 10-minute walk up the hill to the north. Buses travel three times per week to Lefkos and Mesochori. **Flisvos** (tel. 712 03), has clean beach doubles with bath and balcony (3800dr). Next door, 10 minutes on foot from the cave, **Nikos Pediaditis** (tel. 712 22) runs a small *taverna* and pension within a terrace trellised with geranium and oleanders. (Doubles 3500dr.) **Michalis,** above the beach-front pensions, serves delicious ichthyological inventions at any time of day or night. The irrepressible Michalis will give you tips on Lefkos and even take you in his boat to **Sokastro,** a fortified island with ancient underground chambers north of Frangolimionas Bay.

Amopi Beach, 8km south of Karpathos Town toward the airport, has clean golden sand, and the highest body count of any beach on Karpathos. At **Amopi Beach Rooms** (tel. 227 23), in the farthest cove to the north, doubles go for 1900dr. Two **buses** per day travel to the beach from Karpathos Town (20min., 60dr). For the illusion of seclusion, check out the several kilometers of relatively unpopulated beach that stretch southward below Amopi. If the fierce wind kicks up an infamous Amopi dust storm, move one cove south to the pebbly beach and enjoy the cooling breeze.

Northern Karpathos

No good roads connect the traditional north and commercial south of Karpathos. Whatever modernization might have struck this beautiful, arid region was stalled by the huge 1983 fire which devastated most of the Aleppo Pine Forests between Spoa and Olymbos. Daily **excursion boats** from Karpathos Town are the most reliable and scenic means of transport. Karpathos Travel offers excursions to Diafani (Tues. and Thurs.-Sun., 2hr. each way, 3000dr round-trip). Twice per week a boat journeys to the dazzling white beach of **Apela,** and to the island of **Saria** north of Karpathos (from Diafani 1200dr round-trip). Here you can visit **Palatia,** a deserted village halfway up the eastern coast with peculiar, cone-roofed houses built by Syrian pirates in the 7th-9th centuries. Don't get stranded here—the village is deserted and has no fresh water.

Diafani ("transparent") is sheer languor, but it's a good base for exploring Olymbos at leisure. There is no bank in Diafani, but the **Golden Beach Hotel** (tel. 512 15), at the center of the waterfront in Diafani, has boat schedules and tickets, currency exchange, and a restaurant. (Doubles 3800dr.) The **Mayflower Hotel** (tel. 512 28) next door has rooms for the same price and a restaurant serving standard Greek fare at standard Greek prices. One block back from the waterfront is the **Diafani Palace** with a quality restaurant (tel. 512 10; doubles and triples 2800dr). The **OTE,** merely a metered telephone, is in the house with the blue and green gate and the grape arbor on the street past Golden Beach. The **police station** (tel. 512 13) is in the center of town. (Open 24 hrs.) There's a **post box,** but the postman only rings twice per week. From Diafani, take the signposted half-hour walk north through the Pefka pine forest to **Vananda,** a terrific beach shingled with flat stones. Nearby, the **Minas Taverna** (tel. 512 88) lets rooms (1500dr per person), and a campsite offers shaded pitches (700dr per person).

"Traditional" does describe the lifestyle of **Olymbos,** but no single word can convey the thoroughness of its isolation and insularity. Ethnologists and linguists have lauded the region's preservation of its centuries-old customs; several words in the local dialect date to 1000 BCE. The radiant long-sleeved white shirts and flowered aprons worn by women vivify the gray, windswept village. Plaster-sculpted nymphs, angels, eagles, and Venetian lions decorate the outsides of traditional homes. Two working windmills overlook the cliffs on the west side of the village—here the women of Olymbos grind flour for bread, which they bake in huge stone ovens smoldering under the hillside. You can find the men playing backgammon or traditional musical instruments in the *kafenia* (coffeehouses).

Panayia (August 15) is, as in most parts of Greece, cause for a grand celebration. The festivities of the feast of Agios Giannis of *Vourgounda* (August 29), are even more intriguing. This feast is also an occasion for impromptu concerts of traditional music, featuring the *bouzouki* and an odd local instrument that resembles a bagpipe.

If you're willing to bound over a few stone walls, you can visit the oldest chapel on Karpathos, **Agia Anna,** one of two adjacent stone chapels easily visible from the town above. The frescoes inside Agia Anna are "aniconic," geometric paintings of birds and fish from the 13th or 14th century.

Pension Olymbos (tel. 512 52) is run by Anna and Nikos. (Singles 1200dr. Doubles 2800dr. Triples 3500dr.) If you're lucky, Nikos will serenade you with his *bouzouki* as you eat in their small restaurant. **Artemis Pension, Hotel Astro,** and **Posidon Pension** (tel. 512 64; doubles 3800dr, triples 4500dr), all have small bistros, comparably priced rooms, and terraces that peer over the village. One of the few men whom you'll see laboring in Olymbos is the cobbler **John Kanakis,** who crafts the red and tan leather boots that are standard footwear in the village. At 30,000dr per pair, though, these boots were made for balking.

To travel between Olymbos and Diafani, you can take a taxi (1000-1500dr for 5 people) or the small bus that leaves Diafani daily (when the boat from Diafani arrives) and Olymbos twice daily (20min., 600dr). The dusty one- to two-hour hike along a valley floor is another alternative, if you've got the time and energy.

Kassos ΚΑΣΟΣ

A trip to Kassos, taken with earnest imagination, is a lunar fantasy. Fierce winds stir the sea into a choppy froth, and pock-marked rocks litter the stark landscape. Moreover, Kassos is probably the least touristed island of the Dodecanese chain; you might be the only foreigner if you venture there. But the island is not as intimidating as it appears. Kassos has several sandy beaches, two intriguing caves, a few humble archaeological sites, and most of the island's 1200 inhabitants are Greek-Americans who only summer on Kassos. Their English is naturally quite good, and because they get few visitors, they are especially welcoming. If you're tired of the masses in Rhodes and Kos, isolated Kassos is the ideal retreat.

Ferries connect Kassos with Karpathos (2hr., 1000dr), Rhodes (9hr., 2500dr), and Agios Nikolaos on Crete (2435dr). Weather permitting, they run three times per week. Inquire at Karpathos Travel. Boats land at the port of **Phry** (pronounced FREE), the largest town on Kassos, but flying is a much more reliable and convenient way to travel to and from the island. There are **flights** to Karpathos (2 per week, 15min., 2800dr), Rhodes (6 per week, 40min., 9600dr), and Sitia on Crete (2 per week, 30min., 7400dr). A taxi from Phry to the airport costs 400dr, but you can easily walk the ½km west.

Several small villages share the valley with Phry and **Emborio** (the neighboring port town). A bus from Phry connects all of these (every 30min., 150dr). The bus stops at Kriti St., off Platia Iroon Kasou. For timetables and information about the island, go to **Kassos Maritime and Travel Agency,** Platia Iroon Kasou (tel. 413 23 or 414 95), right behind the church. (Open Mon.-Sat. 7:30am-1:30pm and 4:30-9:30pm, Sun. 9am-noon.) The **police station** is on the road to the airport (tel. 412 22; open 24 hrs.). The **post office** is off Platia Iroon Kasou. (Open Mon.-Fri. 7:30am-2:30pm.) Across the street you'll find the **Olympic Airways** office (tel. 415 55; open 7am-2pm). The **OTE** is several blocks inland. (Open Mon.-Fri. 7:30am-3:10pm.) The **hospital** (tel. 413 33) is on Kriti St., past the bus stop. (Open Mon.-Fri. 8am-2pm, and 6-8pm.) There is a **National Bank** representative (tel. 412 34) in the supermarket attached to the travel agency, and an **Ionian Bank** (tel. 412 33) representative in the supermarket next to the police station. (Currency exchange Mon.-Fri. 8am-1pm, sometimes later.)

Kassos has two C-class hotels, the **Anagennisis** on Platia Iroon Kasou (tel. 414 95), next to the travel agency, and the **Anesis** (tel. 413 32). (Doubles in both hotels 3400dr.)

A few locals have rooms to let. Try **Elias Koutlakis** (tel. 413 63) or **Nikitas Vrettos** (tel. 413 83). (Doubles at both pensions 2800-3100dr.) Sleeping on the town beach is illegal.

When you get off the boat, looking for somewhere to collapse after the rough journey, you'll probably stumble right into the **Panorama Restaurant** (tel. 413 19) by the dock. Along with **Milos** (tel. 415 80), next to the travel agency and overlooking the sea, the Panorama is the most popular eating establishment in town. There are several smaller *tavernas* inland and in Emborio. **Supermarkets** and a **bakery** sit one block inland from the travel agency.

Two caves lie within walking distance of Phry. The entrance to the cave of **Ellino Kamares,** 10 minutes from the village of Kathistres, is partially sealed by a Hellenic wall. Inside, inveterate spelunkers can clamber over slimy stones. On a footpath 1½km beyond Ellino Kamares, the cave of **Selai** bristles with stalactites and stalagmites. Kassos also has several beaches. Deserted **Ammoudia** is closest to Phry; unfortunately, garbage and black seaweed mar the fine sand. Occasionally, the travel agency runs boat excursions to **Armathea,** an island off the northwest coast of Kassos (950dr).

Agios Mammas Monastery overlooks the southeastern coast. The hike takes one hour by foot, but you can get a head start by taking the bus to Poli. Supposedly, the boulders you see from the monastery are the hulls of three ships, turned to stone by peeved monks.

On June 7, locals hold an all-night feast in remembrance of the 1824 Turkish slaughter of 7000 Kassiots. September 7 is a celebration of the Panayia on Kassos, and there is a party that evening at the church of **Panayia Ellerou** on the south coast.

Halki ΧΑΛΚΗ

If you're looking for a piece of the undiscovered country, away from the mobs that beseige the Aegean, Halki may be just the place. Even in the summer, there is a good chance that you will be one of just a smattering of tourists on this island. The *Sifnos Express* stops at Halki twice per week: once on the way to Rhodes (2hr., 1400dr) and the Cyclades, once on the way to Karpathos (5hr., 1650dr), Kassos, and Crete. Boats from the city of Rhodes are sometimes free (April-May and Sept.-Oct. Consult the GNTO.) A small boat also travels here from Kamiros Skala on the island of Rhodes (Mon.-Sat. at 2:30pm, Sun. around 6pm; returning Mon.-Sat. 7:30pm, Sun. 9am., 40min., 1500dr.)

In peaceful **Niborio,** box-shaped stone houses cluster around the clear waters of the harbor. In its heyday, this was an active fishing and sponge-diving community with several thousand inhabitants. Although the population is much smaller, villagers still fish for a living during most of the year. Uninhabited buildings squeezed below the orange roofs of freshly painted white houses are a reminder that many locals have moved to Florida to start an expatriate community.

Niborio has only a few *tavernas* and restaurants, a grocery store, a bakery, and a **post office** (open Mon.-Fri. 7:30-9am and 10am-2pm). There are no hotels, but some private homes rent rooms along the waterfront, so you shouldn't be troubled finding accommodations. (Singles 1500dr. Doubles and triples 1500dr per person.) A 10-minute walk from the village, **Pandemos Beach** has a modest stretch of sand on the other side of the small hill that rises above town. Follow the cobblestone street that starts behind the post office and winds its way up through the village.

If you take the road uphill towards the middle of the island, you will eventually reach **Chora** (4km from Niborio), a largely deserted village that thrived in the 18th and 19th centuries only, when pirates drove the islanders from the coast. You can climb to the **medieval castle** for a magnificent view of the entire southern coast.

Symi ΣΥΜΗ

With jagged peaks piercing the air like raw diamonds, the island of Symi is a small yet dramatic showpiece among the Dodecanese. The famous Panormitis Monastery rests secure and secluded at the island's southern end, while the historic port of Ghialos sits snugly near the northern tip. Monasteries were the only dwellings on these steep barren shores until rapid commercial growth in the 19th century led to the construction of the port at Ghialos. During this period, shipbuilding, sponge diving, fishing, and commercial trade flourished, while the Symiots received concessions from the Sultans. Ships made in Symi still have a reputation for being *yare*—easily handled and quick. Ghialos has been called "the loveliest port in Greece," and as you cruise into its titillatingly translucent water,.you'll see why. Islands dot the ocean corridor to the town, and pale pastel houses from the island's golden age ring the waterfront.

Excursion boats from Rhodes visit Ghialos and the Panormitis Monastery (5 per day, departure at 9am and return at 6pm, round-trip 2500-3500dr). You can also buy passage for individual segments of the journey (i.e. Ghialos to Panormitis 1000dr, Rhodes to Ghialos 1200dr). Every Thursday morning, the *Sifnos Express* stops in Symi on its way to Piraeus (19hr., 4500dr), making the following stops: Tilos (1000dr), Nissiros (1450dr), Kos (1400dr), Kalymnos (2000dr), Astipalea (2300dr), Amorgos (2480dr), and Paros (3650dr). Another ferry stops in Symi every Thursday afternoon on its way to Rhodes (40min., 1000dr), Halki (5hr., 1000dr), Karpathos (8hr., 2000dr), Kassos (11hr., 2550dr), Sitia (13hr., 3700dr), and Agios Nikolaos on Crete (18hr., 3950dr). The Greek government declared the port of Symi a historic site in 1971, and many neo-classical houses here date from the island's 19th-century glory days. As you walk around town, you'll see many abandoned buildings that attest to the depletion of the island's population from 20,000, at the peak of its sponge-fishing industry, to 2500. Symi is fighting its way back from this regress, but the island remains comparatively poor. Its economy hinges completely on the vagaries of tourism, and the entire island seems to anticipate the docking of excursion boats. The waterfront is unbearably crowded when these boats arrive. The evenings are more peaceful, as locals linger in the *tavernas* and drink; few tourists stay here overnight.

Practical Information, Accommodations, and Food

As you disembark at the Ghialos clock tower (on the right side of town facing inland), the **post office** is 50m down the quay, up the stone stairs on the right. (Open Mon.-Fri. 7am-2pm.) A **currency exchange** is in the small office several stores left of the clock. (Open daily 9am-2pm and 6-9pm.) If you go inland along the left-hand side of the park, and walk, veering right, 1 block past the Neraida restaurant, you'll find the **OTE.** (Open Mon.-Sat. 8am-3pm, Sun. 9am-2pm). Back along the waterfront, up where the harbor crooks, is the Ionian Bank in a large stone building with brown trim. (Open Mon.-Thurs. 8am-2pm and Fri. 8am-1:30pm.) Just behind it, **Symi Tours** (tel. 713 07) sells most boat tickets and arranges excursions around the island. (Open Mon.-Sat. 8am-3pm, Sun. 9am-2pm.) Ferry tickets are also available at **Nikos Psychas's Textile Shop.** To get there, go between Symi Tours and the bank, take a right, then an immediate left—you'll see the "shipping agency" sign. (Open 8am-1pm and 5pm-9pm, but expect capricious closings.) You can also buy tickets from a ticket-seller who comes to sit in the café closest to the clock-tower about 30 minutes before the boat comes in (ask any waterfront storekeeper when the boats come). Taxis congregate at **Oekonomou Square** on the waterfront about 200m beyond Symi Tours. A van going to Pedi, marked "The Symi Bus," leaves from the stop a short distance farther up (every ½hr., 100dr). Symi's **postal code** is 85600; its **telephone code** is 0241.

The **Hotel Glafkos** (tel. 713 58), the third building on the left side of the park (facing inland), proffers flower pots and an old-fashioned parlor. (Singles 1800dr. Doubles 3800dr. Triples 4500dr.) **Pension Agli** (tel. 713 92), off Oekonomou Sq., has small but tidy singles for 2500dr, doubles for 4000dr (negotiable); kitchen facilities and bathrooms are included, but make sure they show you how to turn on the electric water pump. There are a few rooms to let around the village—ask at a café. Waterfront restaurants are expensive, so the further you walk from the ferry landing the better. Check out the plaque above **Les Katerinettes Restaurant** even if you don't eat there: this is the house where the Italians signed the agreement surrendering the Dodecanese to the Allied Powers on May 8, 1945. **O Meraklis,** one block back from Symi Tours, specializes in excellent stuffed tomatoes for 500dr. For the brave, 200 grams of boiled brains *(myala vrasta)* 550dr. Two more fine options for dinner are **George's Restaurant,** and **Restaurant Panaroma,** both at the top of the steps to the upper part of the village. You can sit on a veranda overlooking the harbor below. Greek salad 400dr. *Kalamari* 700dr. Up the hill near George's, the **Jean and Tonic Pub** has mixed drinks for a reasonable 550dr. (Open 7:30pm-1am.)

Sights

You'll find few historical artifacts by the waterfront, so head uphill to **Chorio,** the section of town fortified against pirate raids. To get there, walk to Oekonomou Sq. and trudge up the 632 stairs (we counted), also known as *Kali Strata,* to the main road in Ghialos and Chorio. Follow the road at the top of the stairs and you'll see signs for the **museum,** which houses classical and Byzantine pieces, and island costumes and utensils. (Open Tues.-Sun. 10am-2pm. Free.) From here, signs lead through a maze of streets to the ruins of the old **castle.**

Nos Beach, a 10-minute walk from Ghialos (head north along the waterfront, past the shipyard), is miniscule, but the closest beach to the port; a small *taverna*/disco lingers nearby. **Emborio,** a mediocre beach, lies 45 minutes past Nos. The views along the way make the walk worthwhile. **Pedi,** a short distance by bus, boasts a beatific beach; you can stay at the Hotel Gallini (singles with private bath 2250dr). Symi's tiny coves shelter a few excellent beaches accessible only by boat (daily, 800dr) at **Agia Marina, Nanou,** and **Marathounda** on the eastern side of the island. Boats also go to **Sesklia Island** just south of Symi. You can walk around the whole island in a few hours, and still have time for its tranquil beaches (Tues., Wed., Fri., and Sun., round-trip 2500dr). Symi still cultivates its own spices (and many more grow wild in the hills). Prices here are cheaper than anywhere else in the Dodecanese.

Panormitis Monastery

The grand Monastery of the Archangel Michael the Panormitis, friend of travelers, looms at the center of a remarkable horseshoe-shaped harbor in the southern part of the island. The monastery was founded at the spot where a local woman chanced upon an icon of Michael. Although brought to Ghialos, the icon kept finding its way back to Panormitis. The palatial white buildings of the monastery, dominated by an elegant turn-of-the-century bell tower in the center, have been a popular stopover for Dodecanese sailors in years past. Within the monastery complex are a restaurant and small foodstore, a library, rooms to let, and a small museum featuring a bizarre collection of reliquaries and stuffed sea creatures (Museum open irregularly for tour-group visits 100dr). The small monastery church houses an exceptional wooden altar screen. The famous icon is known throughout the Dodecanese for its wish-granting powers, and tokens in the museum represent supplicants' wishes. Formerly monks' cells, the guest rooms in the complex are inexpensive (1000dr) and great for rest and contemplation. No reservations are necessary—there are plenty of beds—but bring your own bedding. Most of the other overnight visitors will be vacationing Greek families. Dress modestly.

No regular buses run to the monastery, but tour buses from Ghialos run about four times per week (1hr., 2500dr round-trip). All excursion boats from Rhodes stop here.

Nisyros ΝΙΣΡΟΣ

According to local legend, the volcanic island of Nisyros was created during a fight between Poseidon and the giant Polyvotis. Enraged, the sea god tore off a chunk of Kos with his spear and threw it on top of Polyvotis, who has been stuck that way ever since. Every once in a while, the giant grumbles and stirs, trying to free himself of his weighty cap; his most successful attempt was in 1522, when the mountain blew up to form the existing crater. The most recent, less violent, explosion was in 1873. Because the island is a volcano, there are no fresh springs; fresh water is imported from Kos and a few elderly locals still wash their clothes in salt water. Times grew hard in the aftermath of World War II, necessitating the emigration of three-quarters of Nisyros' population. Today, however, many are returning for at least part of the year with the bundles they made in business in New York. The result is that unlike other islands of comparable size whose main source of income is still sponge fishing and tourism, Nisyros is in vigorous financial health.

Efficient irrigation and cultivation have made the island green with olive, fig, and almond trees. Strict laws set by the island's historical commission maintain the architectural integrity of Nisyros. Because of these mandates, this quiet little island, in sharp contrast to the touristy abysses of Kos and Rhodes, still looks, smells, and feels uniformly authentic.

Practical Information, Accommodations, and Food

Tourists pack the small daytime excursion boats from Kos, lured perhaps by a vague hope that the dormant volcano will grumble and spit fire during their stay. Come nightfall, though, a traveler can find respite from pesky sightseers in Nisyros's undisturbed silence. Most of the 1200 permanent residents of the island live in the main port, **Mandraki,** where the narrow whitewashed streets and alleys wind beneath the Monastery of Panayia Spiliana. From the ferry dock, walk to the right to reach the town. Boats make excursions from both Kos Town and Kardamena daily in summer, and much less frequently in the off-season (about 1200dr one way). The *Papadiamantis* travels to Samos once a week via Kos, Kalymnos, Leros, and Patmos (16hr., 2000dr), and to Rhodes via Tilos (3 per week, 5-7hr., 1800dr). One or two ferries per week ride to Kos, Kalymnos, Tilos, and Piraeus. Ferry times change frequently, so always check with the **port police** for a current schedule (tel. 312 22); they're in the building in front of the ferry dock. (Officially open 24 hrs., but really only when boats arrive. Call the port police in Kos or Rhodes to get information when it's closed.) The **post office** (open Mon.-Fri. 7:30am-2pm) and the regular **police** (tel. 312 01; open 24 hrs., but sometimes you must knock loudly and shout) share the building with the port police. The **OTE** is in the center of the village on the main road (open Mon.-Fri. 9:30am-2pm). The **Enetikon Tourist Office** (tel. 314 65), a private agency near the port on the main road, organizes excursions, changes money, loans out novels, and is the best information source on the island. (Open daily 9:30am-1:30pm and 4:30-9:30pm. Fewer hours in off-season.) **I. H. Diakomihalis,** an agent of the National Bank of Greece, exchanges currency in his general store (on the main street past the square; open for banking Mon.-Fri. 10am-1pm). There is a **doctor** in Nisyros, who can be reached at 312 17, afternoons and evenings at 314 19. Nisyros's **telephone code** is 0242.

Finding rooms in Mandraki is generally not a problem, except during the holiday week of August 15. To the left of Mandraki's quay, **The Three Brothers Pension** (tel. 313 44) is run by a friendly family with a soft spot for animals. (One of the more eccentric brothers used to raise pigs in the basement.) All rooms have swineless private baths with hot water. (Singles 2500dr. Doubles 3500dr.) Across the street and inland, the **Romantzo Hotel** (tel. 313 40) has clean rooms. Wrap-around communal balconies and ocean views from most rooms. (Singles 2500dr. Doubles 4000dr.) They also rent **motorbikes** for 2500dr. The belly-sating site downstairs can cook up a fine dish of *kalamari* (550dr). **Pension H. Drostia,** on the main street, lets singles for 2000dr and doubles for 2500dr. Drostia's owner runs another pension, farther from the water and the action (doubles 2000dr). The waves lap right under your window at the **Pension Porfiris,** above the crafts shop next to Enetikon Travel on the main road. (Doubles 3000dr.) The **Irapanti Hotel** (tel. 314 85) uphill from the center of town, has new rooms for 4500dr. Many Mandrakians rent rooms for about 3000dr a double, but prices vary greatly according to tourist flow—ask around.

Most of Mandraki's *tavernas* serve earnest food, and all of their fish comes off the same boats. **Taverna Nissiros,** just off the main street, has some of the cheapest food in town. **Mike's Taverna** and **Cleanthis** are other local staples (full meals about 1000dr). The **Tassos Coffee-Bar** (tel. 313 86) and **Ladero's Place** never run out of that budget traveler's best friend—yogurt with honey. Mandraki's social center is a disappointing minimalist square strewn with a few forlorn chairs. Infrequent **buses** go from the harbor at Mandraki to Nikia, Emborio, and Pali.

Sights

The **volcano** is the biggest draw on Nisyros. Buses leave from the port at around 10:30am (ask the police or Enetikon Travel; bus 300dr round-trip). They'll take you to the edge of a crater in a valley, where you can wander among small holes that bubble and spew hot sulphur—you'll probably leave smelling like an antiquated egg. You can explore the rest of the island by moped, bus, taxi, or foot. The other towns are no more than 4km away. The roads are paved but narrow and littered with gravel. In Mandraki, the main street eventually leads to the small **Museum of Historical and Popular Folk Art.** (Open Tues.-Sun. 9am-2pm.) Across from the museum, with an icon over its door, rests the 700-year-old **Church of St. John.** The present frescoes were painted by Italians in the early 20th century, but you'll see 700-year-old Greek wall paintings in the circular frames. The **Monastery of Panayia Spiliani,** at the far end of town, 100 steps up from the quay, has a zesty view of the town. In the monastery is the 1000-year-old Chapel of Mary with its miracle-working icon. Above the monastery is the castle and the 3½m-thick city walls that the Knights of St. John of Jerusalem built. Every year from August 15-17, free food and entertainment flows forth at the huge religious festival.

A white 19th-century building containing the run-down but enduringly therapeutic spa of **Loutra** lies 1½km down the road. (Open late June-Sept.) The sulphurous spring water here, brewed by volcanic activity and packed with calcium and magnesium, is supposed to cure any number of ailments. You can take a bath and spend the night for 900dr per person, or just stop by for a salubrious immersion (baths 200dr). Visitors are usually required to see the doctor before bathing.

Three kilometers from Mandraki is the small fishing village of **Pali,** with three *tavernas,* a couple of supermarkets, and a motorbike rental. The **Hotel Hellenis** on your left as you enter town and the last *taverna* at the right edge of town (facing the water) both let doubles (2500dr). Go left at the turn-off for the volcano to reach the small, charming village of **Nikia,** hesitating at the rim of the great crater. A number of *tavernas,* a diminutive church, and the **Monastery of Agios Theodoros** rest like cold sores on the lip of the crater, 500m down from the town. Right before Nikia, the turn-off to **Avlaki** slithers its way down to a few forlorn abandoned buildings.

Easily accessible but oddly unattractive **beaches** extend along the shore past the Three Brothers at **Mira Mare,** and about 1km farther on the opposite side of the cove. **White Beach,** 3km out of Mandraki, past Pali, is the best on the island. The subdued, black pebble **Chochlaki Beach** lies on the other side of the monastery. Follow the shore through town and clamber over the rocky, pungent donkey path (wear shoes) by the sea's edge. The surf can be quite rough here.

Tilos ΤΗΛΟΣ

Tilos forces you to relax. At any given time, no more than 750 people dally on the island (and up to one-third of them may be tourists). There's really nothing to do here except explore beaches or hike to one of the seven castles scattered on the hills, but that seems to be enough to keep just about everybody on the island satisfied. Every July 25th, however, timid Tilos erupts into a three-day party. The food is free, the wine constant, and the Greek dancing absolutely berserk. Tourists and long-lost island emigrés pack the island for this memorable event. The festival happens mainly at the monastery but does migrate a bit: just follow the mobs.

Ferries only rarely make an appearance at Tilos. Boats travel from Tilos to: Rhodes (Tues., Wed., and Sat.); Samos (Mon.); Kalymnos (Fri.); and Piraeus (Thurs.). Excursion boats from Kos stop in Tilos once a week. For information on ferries or anything else, talk to Manos at the **Blue Sky Restaurant** or the **Tilos Travel Agency** (tel. 532 59) next door. (Open 9am-midnight.) He also rents **motorbikes** (3000dr per day), gives out maps, organizes excursions to remote beaches (3000dr including barbecue), and changes money. The only other place to change money on the island is the **post office** in the main square; you can make phone calls from the Blue Sky or the supermarket off the main square. (Open Mon.-Fri. 7:30am-2:30pm.) Rent **bicycles** at the Restaurant

Kostas (800dr per day) at the foot of the dock. Tilos's **postal code** is 85002; its **telephone code** is 0241.

It would take some innovative thinking to get lost in Livadia, the island's main town. From the ferry dock, walk along the water and a bit inland to get to the central square. The **Pension Castello** (tel. 532 92) uphill a bit from the square, has spic and span doubles for 3000dr. The **Pension Anna,** next door, is also exemplary. (Open June-Aug. Doubles 2400.) Three pensions neighbor one another on the beach. The **Stamatia Pension** (tel. 532 55) and the **Galini Pension** (tel. 532 80), both charge 3000dr for a double. Stamatia also offers singles for 2200dr. The **Hotel Levadia** (tel. 532 02), is the tallest building in town. (Doubles with private bath 3500dr.) Camp anywhere you like—no one will mind, as long as you clean up after yourself; you can use the public toilets on the road along the shore. Several *tavernas* populate Livadia. **The Blue Sky Taverna** has the best food, but is slightly more expensive than the others. (Open daily 9am-midnight.) Right on the beach, the **Restaurant Irini** is more reasonable than the hotel of the same name. (Entrees 650-900dr.; open daily 8am-4pm and 6pm-midnight.) **Sophia's Restaurant,** just down the beach, serves splendid morsels. (Open daily 9am-11:30pm.) The island's few backpackers generally kick back for a while at **Yannis's Bar,** past Sophia's on the beach (open pretty much all of the time).

Eight kilometers north of Livadia, near the tip of the island, hulks the capital of Tilos, **Megalochorio** (pop. 200, and aptly named "big town"). **Nikos Miliou** rents doubles with private showers for 3000dr; follow the road through town until it crumbles to dust. **Sevasti Ikonomou** runs the only restaurant in town and has decent rooms (tel. 532 36; doubles 3000dr). The ruins of a Venetian castle glare over much of the island. Continue up the main road to find the path. The hike is as hard as it looks, but making it to the top will give you not only a tremendous ego-boost, but also an id-numbing view. Eight kilometers farther (16km from Livadia), the **Monastery of San Panteliona** rests uneasily on a cliff. Although the monastery is now closed, it is possible to spend the night for free (ask at the Blue Sky).

Take a step to the left from Megalochorio to the wide, sandy **Erestos Beach.** The **Tropicana Taverna** has four freshly squeezed doubles with showers for 3000dr. (Breakfast 110dr.) The **Nausika Taverna** lets singles and doubles for 3000dr, triples for 3500dr. If you're camping, you can use the showers at either place for 100dr. Both *tavernas* are 100m from the beach. There is a general store 20 minutes up the road in Megalochorio. Dip to the right to reach **San Antonio,** which possesses a few houses, a small beach, and the **Hotel Australia** (tel. 532 96; decent doubles 4000dr). Two kilometers out of Livadia, on the road to Megalochorio, just past the turn-off to the OTE installation, you can see the ruins of the abandoned city of **Mikrochorio** ("small town")—the hill to the left. As recently as 1950 there were 1000 people living there, but the landlocked inhabitants relocated to the more convenient site of Livadia. Ask at the Blue Sky for directions to the secluded **Skafi Beach** and **Lethra Beach.** Tilos has one municipal bus which traverses the island 4 to 6 times per day in summer (200dr to Megalochario, 300dr to Erestos). Hitchhiking is reportedly unpredictable: few cars travel the roads but practically anyone will pick up riders—still, solo women should not hitchhike. Those hopping on a truck bearing a full load of travelers back to Livadia might be asked to pay a small fare (about 200dr).

Kos ΚΩΣ

Just as the pigs always snort out the truffles, so have the travel agents sniffed out the island of Kos. Ancient ruins, sandy beaches, and loud bars lure a motley assortment of visitors to this one-time paradise in July and August. If you're allergic to the tourist scene, suspend your trip to Kos until the off-season. Better still, somnambulate through the villages which sleep relatively undisturbed to the southwest of the main town.

A model for any liberal arts university's core curriculum, Kos has through the ages dabbled in the fields of medicine, literature, religion, politics, and piracy. Kos is known as the home of Hippocrates, father of medical science; the 2400-year-old oath is still taken by doctors. In ancient times, the island was respected both as a major trading power and as the sacred land of Asclepios, god of healing. The home of poets Theocritus and Philetas, it reached its prime as a literary center under the Ptolemies. At that time, its population neared 160,000 (compared to today's 20,000). Several hundred years later, Kos served as an episcopal seat under Byzantine rule. Before and after the fall of the Byzantine Empire, pirates and predatory naval forces from various nations repeatedly invaded the island. The Knights of St. John finally appropriated Kos in 1315, promptly transforming it into one of their invincible outposts. From then on, its history has been akin to that of the other Dodecanese islands.

Daily **ferries** travel to Rhodes (3am, 4hr., 2000dr) and Piraeus (daily 4pm; off-season Tues.-Wed. and Fri.-Sun., 4pm, 14hr., 3600dr) via Kalymnos, Leros, and Patmos. Twice a week, boats go to Rhodes via Nisyros, Tilos, and Symi. Every Tuesday, the notoriously tardy *Sifnos Express* makes its rounds to most of the Dodecanese Islands and Crete; Thursdays it returns and heads to Piraeus via Astypalea, Amorgos, and Paros. On Mondays, a ferry heads to Samos via all the northerly islands. Rhodes, Samos, and Patmos are also served regularly by **hydrofoil** (Rhodes 3800dr, round-trip 7000dr). The Municipal Tourist Organization can give you a rundown on the boat schedule, but be *sure* to check with the boat agency or the port police, as schedules often change without notice. Few direct boats go to Paros and the Cyclades—you may have to go first to Samos (3-4 boats weekly) and make a connection. More expensive excursion boats travel daily to Nisyros (8:30am), Kalymnos, and Rhodes. They go less frequently to Tilos (Tues.) and Symi (Thurs.). If you have not come to Greece on a charter flight, you can get to the Turkish port of Bodrum near the ancient site of Halicarnassus by Greek boat in the morning (3800dr, round-trip 6000dr), or by Turkish boat in the afternoon (about US$30, depending on the boat; be sure to bargain). You will also be required to pay a Turkish port tax (about US$9.70). Tickets are available at almost every travel agency in town or on the boat. **Olympic Airways** has flights to: Athens (3-4 per day, 45min., 15,800dr); Leros (2 per week, 15min., 5400dr); Samos (1-2 per week, 40min., 7500dr); Rhodes (daily, 25min., 9000dr); and Thessaloniki (1-2 per week, 45min., 26,100dr).

In Kos, the mode of transportation you choose will equal your destination multiplied by the amount of time and energy you are willing to expend. **Bicycles** (600dr per day) are the best way to see Kos, but you'll probably have to walk up a fair number of steep hills if you're headed to the southern end of the island or to one of the little villages in the mountains. A popular alternative is a **motorbike** (from 2000dr per day). You can rent both in the Kos Town area. **Motoway,** Vassileos Georgiou St. (tel. 212 09), along the water east of the castle, is reliable. In summer, about five convenient but often folkful **buses** per day (3 on Sun.) run between towns on the island (150-400dr, depending on where you go).

Kos Town

In Kos Town, minarets of Turkish mosques stand alongside grand Italian mansions and the massive walls of a Crusader fortress. Brilliantly colored flowers and date palms embellish the streets, squares, and ancient monuments. The town is an archaeological repository of Archaic, Classical, Hellenistic, and Roman ruins. Unfortunately, it's also one of the most expensive places in the Dodecanese. Package tour agents have made contracts with many of the cheapest pensions, leaving very few rooms for independent travelers. As in Rhodes, most of the tourists wallow only in or near the main town. Despite the crowds, the town is surprisingly clean, and most of the tacky souvenir and clothing stores are confined to the side streets.

Orientation and Practical Information

As your ferry pulls into the harbor of Kos Town, you will see only the colossal walls of the Castle of the Knights of St. John. Don't be alarmed; if you walk left from the harbor, the stately trees which frame the **Avenue of Palms** (also called Finikon Street) will assure you that you're not in Alcatraz. The street leads west to the beach that stretches along Vasileos Georgiou. Continue east to find the waterfront street **Akti Kountouitou,** where the tourist office and police are located. (Boats from Turkey dock directly across from the tourist office.) Four blocks to the left (facing the water), **Megalou Alexandrou Street** heads to **Paleologou Square,** to the ruins of ancient Kos Town, and eventually to the inland villages. If you continue walking along the waterfront, you will reach the dolphin statue and the popular **Lampi beach.** Kiosks around Kos Town sell good maps (250dr).

Municipal Tourist Organization (MTO): 7 Akti Kountouritou (tel. 287 24 or 244 60). On the waterfront at the corner of Vas. Pavlou. Boat and bus schedules, maps, information on hotels, and a refreshingly opinionated staff. Open April 15-Oct. daily 7:30am-9:30pm; off-season Mon.-Fri. 7:30am-3pm.

Currency Exchange: Banks open Mon.-Fri. 8:45am-1:30pm and 6-8pm, Sat. 9am-noon; off-season Mon.-Fri. 8am-1:30pm. You can use a Visa card to get money at the **Commercial Bank,** 25 Vas. Pavlou St., 1 block from the tourist office. The only other Dodecanese islands where you can get an advance on a Visa are Rhodes and Kalymnos. You can get money with a MasterCard at the **National Bank of Greece,** Riga Fereou St., near the tourist office. After banking hours, change money and cash traveler's checks at the **post office** or a travel agency along the waterfront. Agencies usually charge a 2% commission. Most are open Mon.-Sat. 9am-1pm and 6-8pm. Some open on Sun.

Post Office: 14 Venizelou St. (tel. 222 50), 2 blocks past the Eleftherias Sq. fruit market, turn left. Open Mon.-Fri. 7:30am-2:15pm, Sat. 8am-2:15pm, Sun. 9am-1:30pm; off-season Mon.-Fri. 7:30am-2:15pm. **Postal Code:** 85300.

OTE: Around the corner from the post office, at the corner of Vironos and Xanthou, 3 blocks inland and 2 blocks left from the tourist office. Open Mon.-Fri. 7:30am-11pm, Sat. 7:30am-2pm, Sun. 9:30am-2pm; off-season Mon.-Fri. 7:30am-10pm. **Telephone Code:** 0242.

Olympic Airways: 22 Vas. Pavlou St. (tel. 283 30), 4 blocks inland from the tourist office. The Kardamena and Kefalos buses stop at the airport. Taxis to the airport cost about 2500dr. Office open daily 8am-3:30pm.

Buses: Hourly buses to Agios Fokas and the Asclepion. Less frequent buses to Messaria stop next to the tourist office. Buses for other parts of the island stop at the square on Cleopatras St. (turn right past the Olympic Airways office on Vas. Pavlou). Schedules posted in square (tel. 222 92 for information).

Boat Agencies: All along the waterfront; hard to miss. Fares differ only by 100-200dr, so consider convenience, not prices. Ask the tourist office for advice.

Laundromats: 3 Themistokleus St. In the west end of town, 2 blocks from Akti Koundourioti on the waterfront. Wash 500dr, dry 300dr. Buy tokens at the shop next door. Open daily 8:30am-10pm. Also **Speed-o-clean** 124 Alikarnassan St., 2 blocks inland from the Pension Alexis. Wash and dry, 700dr. Open Mon.-Sat. 8:30am-8:30pm, Sun. 8:30am-6:30pm.

Public Toilets: Along the Avenue of Palms, behind the fortress walls. Fetid.

Hospital: 32 Hippocrates (Ippokratous) St. (tel. 223 00). There are several **pharmacies** down the street.

Police: Tel. 222 22. Vas. Georgiou St., in the Italianate building across from the castle. Some English spoken. Open 24 hrs.

Tourist Police: (tel. 282 27), next to the tourist office. Minimal English spoken.

Port Police: 7 Koundourioti (tel. 285 07). Next door and upstairs from the tourist office. Open 24 hrs.

Accommodations and Camping

During July and August, hotel and private room vacancies are exceedingly rare, so start your room search early. Many inexpensive places gravitate toward the right side of town (facing inland). Start at the MTO for a look at their rooms to let and hotel list. If your boat docks in the middle of the night (and Newton's Law of travel ease says it will), you might as well rent a room from one of the people who meet the boat. You may be tempted to camp on the beach or in the park along the Avenue of Palms. Don't: it's illegal, and police do patrol.

Pension Alexis, 9 Irodotou at Omirou St. (tel. 287 98). Take your first right off Megalou Alexandrou St. Friendly international ambience on the jasmine-vined patio. The proprietor Alexis is eager and helpful, and he won't ever turn you away. You'll get a place on the patio (1000dr) if need be. Doubles 4000dr. Triples 5000dr. Hot showers 24 hrs.

Xenon Australia, 39 Averof St. (tel. 236 50), behind the popular beach, in the north end of town. Clean and pleasant, but the bar-and-disco traffic on the street may be disturbing. Doubles 4000dr. Triples 4500dr. In summer, make reservations about 1 month in advance.

Pension Popi, 37 Averof St. (tel. 234 75), next to Xenon Australia. Generically tidy, but—like the Xenon Australia—plagued by nocturnal noisiness. Doubles 4000dr. Triples 4500dr.

Hotel Hara, Halkonos St. (tel. 225 00) near Arseniou St., 1 block inland from the water in the eastern part of town. Quiet neighborhood and charming rooms. Doubles with bath 5500dr.

Hotel Dodecanissos, 2 Alex. Ipsilantou St. (tel. 284 60 or 228 60), 1 block inland and 1 block right from the MTO. Sparkling and cheery. Singles 1800-2500dr. Doubles 5000dr, with bath. Triples 5800dr.

Kos Camping (tel. 239 10 and 232 75), in Psaldi, 2½km out of town. Inconvenient unless you've got a motorbike (which they rent) or you really want to avoid Kos Town. 700dr per person, 300dr per tent; in low season 500dr per person, 200dr per tent. Open April-Oct.

Food

Despite the high price of accommodations, Kos is not lacking in reasonably priced places to eat. There is, however, a dearth of quality control. You can always grab a *souvlaki-pita* for a mere 150-200dr. For authentic Greek food without the bombast of the tourists on the waterfront, head to **Stefanos's Café Ouzerie Torodon,** 11 Irodotou St., just past Pension Alexis (no sign, but you'll see the old men gathered around the outside tables). The kind elderly couple who run the restaurant speak no English, so point to what you want (huge Greek salad 250dr). To find the nearby **Taverna Barba George,** 21 Pindou St. (tel. 280 39), turn left from Irodotou onto Omirou St., and continue until the end of the road. Try the Greek specialty, *exokiko,* which waiter/cook/all-around-friendly-guy Nikos insists translates as "country-special on a spit." (Open daily noon-midnight.) **Hellas,** 7 Psaron St., 1 block from Stefanos, is a popular, reasonably priced restaurant (*mousaka* 600dr, *kalamari* 600dr). The **Olympada Restaurant,** Vas. Pavlou St. (tel. 23 03), behind the Olympic Airways office, also remains authentically Greek. (Various Greek specialties, around 800dr.) If you can't wring yourself from the waterfront, try **Romantica,** at the left end (facing inland) of the harbor (*calamari* 600dr). (Open daily 11am-11pm.) **Limnos,** next door, is also good (spaghetti 550dr, *pastitsio* 650dr; open daily 9am-4pm and 6pm-midnight). Breakfast is expensive, but on Averof St. to the north, a number of cafés offer better deals than those in the harbor area (eggs, bacon, potatoes, and coffee all for 500dr). The fruit and vegetable **market** near Eleftherias Sq. is in the big yellow building with bunches of grapes over the doors, 2 blocks inland from the MTO (open Mon.-Sat.).

Sights

Modern Kos lives very much in the present, but it does so under the myopic eye of the past. You can hardly walk a block without coming upon some structure of historical interest. Most sites are readily accessible, either in or near town.

The 15th-century **Castle of the Knights of St. John** was reinforced with elaborate double walls and inner moats during the following century in response to Turkish raids. You can explore in, on, and even under this jungle-gym of a fort. The Order of St. John on Kos was originally dedicated to nursing and healing the sick. The knights kept business flowing by spending more time engaged in warfare than social work. (Open in summer Tues.-Sun. 9am-3pm. Admission 300dr, students 200dr.)

Before you cross the bridge, between the Avenue of the Palms and the ruins of the agora, you'll see the **Plane Tree of Hippocrates,** allegedly the oldest tree in Europe. Hippocrates, the great physician of antiquity, reputedly taught his pupils and wrote many of his books under this aged tree's umbrage. A spring next to the tree leads into an ancient sarcophagus that the Turks used as a cistern for the nearby variegated **Hadji Hassan Mosque.** The Platanos Restaurant occupies one of the many fanciful mansions built in the vicinity during the Italian occupation of the island. Behind the tree, the monumental former **Town Hall,** originally the Italian Governor's Palace, currently houses the police, justice, and governmental offices. Other impressive Turkish structures are the **Defterdar Mosque** in Eleftherias Sq., and the **Mausoleum of Hadji Pasha,** on the corner of Ippokratous and Mitropoleos St. A few blocks away, on Diakou St., rests the abandoned **Synagogue of Kos,** in use until World War II. For a sample of Byzantine architecture, visit the city's **Greek Orthodox Cathedral** on the corner of Korai and Agios Nikolaou St.

The **Archaeological Museum** (down Nafklirou St. alongside the ruins of the ancient agora to Eleftherias Sq.) features the celebrated statue of Hippocrates found at the Odeon of Kos. A magnificent 2nd-century CE Roman mosaic in the central courtyard depicts Hippocrates and a colleague entertaining the god Asclepios. (Open in summer Tues.-Sun. 9am-3pm. Admission 300dr, students 200dr.)

The next field of ruins bounded by Nafklirou St, Hippocrates St., and the waterfront, is usually referred to as the **agora.** Here stand the remains of a **Temple of Aphrodite,** as well as the 2nd-century **Temple of Hercules.** (Agora open 24 hrs. Free.) The other expansive site, with structures dating from the 3rd century CE, is perhaps more impressive. Two short stairways descend to the ruins from Grigoriou St., which runs along the southern edge of town; any of the main roads intersect it about 1km from the sea. The site itself is bordered by two Roman roads—the **Cardo,** meaning "axis," which runs perpendicular to Grigoriou St., and the **Decumana,** meaning "broadest," which parallels Grigoriou and intersects Cardo to form a corner. An ancient gymnasium, a swimming pool from the Roman period, and an early Christian basilica built on the ruins of a Roman bath all loll nearby. At the end of the Decumana, the 3rd-century CE **House of Europa** contains a striking mosaic floor depicting her abduction by a bovine Zeus. (Open 24 hrs. Free.)

Down Grigoriou to the left (facing the Odeon), near Pavlou, stands the **Casa Romana,** uncovered by an Italian archaeologist in 1933. This 3rd-century CE structure concealed the ruins of an even more striking Hellenistic mansion two centuries older, with relics of man-eating creatures. (Open Tues.-Sun. 9am-3pm. Admission 300dr, students 200dr; free on Sun.) Across the street from the Casa Romana are the meager ruins of a **Temple of Dionysus.**

The town of Kos has a scanty, narrow and crowded strip of **beach,** running southeast of town. The more popular beach running north of town is far nicer, has watersport rentals, and is carpeted with prone, pinkening bodies. If you continue walking west about 4km, you will eventually reach **Lampi Beach,** a sandy and quiet point at the northernmost tip of the island. Several other splendorous beaches are a little farther from Kos Town. Shady, sandy **Tingaki,** 10km west of Kos, often attracts crowds. There are several pensions and various private rooms nearby (doubles around 3000dr). The police sometimes check for illegal freelance camping activity. Be prepared for "snug" bus rides to and from Kos (Mon.-Sat. 6 per day, Sun. 5 per day, 15min., 150dr).

In the other direction from Kos, **Agios Fokas** (8km) and **Thermi** (13km) are both accessible by a satisfactory road. Buses from next to the tourist office run here frequently (150dr). Thermi is the more pleasant town, with a café and, as the name suggests, a hot sulphur spring. If you swim here, take a short dip in the colder water around the point, or the sulphur will leave you smelling like a vintage egg.

Entertainment

At night, Kos Town is host to a romping party. The bar scene in Kos Town coagulates in two areas: near the Agora on Nafklirou St. in the south and by the beach in the north. On Plotairthou St., the **White Angel, Bar 33,** and **Music Hall** fight for breathing space. Along Nafklirou St., loud music and flashing disco lights inundate the Agora. Dance in the streets in front of the **Viva Pub.** In the north end, on Porfirov St., the **Mirage Pub** has a pleasant garden and serves a delicious house cocktail. All the bars in Kos Town stop playing music at midnight, while the discos rock until 4-5am. The discos on the beach both charge 1500dr cover, including one drink. The sprawling **Heaven Disco Club** has a crowded dance floor indoors and island bars by the bridges and pools in the backyard. Films flicker at the **Kendriko,** at 8 Agios Nikolou St., and the

Orpheus, in summer at 10 Vas. Georgiou St. (tel. 221 89), in off-season at 25th Martiou St. (tel. 229 50).

Asclepion

Most visitors make a pilgrimage of sorts to the Asclepion, an ancient sanctuary dedicated to the god of healing, 4km west of Kos Town. In the 5th century BCE, Hippocrates opened the world's first medical school here and encouraged the development of a precise and systematic science of medicine. Combining early priestly techniques with his own, Hippocrates made Kos the foremost medical center in ancient Greece.

Most of the ruins at Asclepion actually date from the 3rd century BCE. The complex was constructed on five different levels terraced into a hill with a goitrogenic view of Kos Town and the Aegean. Much remains of the ancient buildings, and if you can ignore the strident tour guides and the swarms of tourists, it's easy to envision the structures as they once stood. A forest of cypress and pine trees, held sacred in ancient times, adjoins the site. No one was allowed to give birth or to die in this area. The 2nd-century CE Roman baths lie inside the site. Stroll past the *natatio* (pool), the *tepidarium* (room of intermediate temperature), and finally the *caldarium* (sweating room).

The most interesting remains at Asclepion are in the three central terraced planes, called **andirons.** These contain the **School of Medicine,** various statues of deities, and a figure of the god Pan (half-goat, half-human). Climb the 30 steps up to the second andiron to see the best preserved remains of the Asclepion: the elegant, slender, white columns of the **Temple of Apollo** from the 2nd century BCE, and the 4th-century BCE **Minor Temple of Asclepios.** The 60-step climb to the third andiron leads to the forest-ensconced remains of the **Main Temple of Asclepios.**

Escape the droning tour guides with a packed lunch under the thick pines. Buses go to the Asclepion 11 times a day in the summer (100dr). The site is also easy to reach by bike or motorbike. (Follow the sign off the main road west and continue as straight as possible.) Taxis to the site should cost about 500dr. (Site open in summer Tues.-Sun. 8am-3pm. Admission 400dr, students 200dr; free on Sun.)

Central Kos

The traditional Kos lifestyle survives in the inland towns along the main road. The modern village of **Zipari** adjoins the ruins of the early **Christian Basilica of St. Paul,** 11km southwest of Kos Town. From there, a winding road (big fun on a moped) slowly makes its way through the green foothills of the Dikeos Mountains to **Asfendiou,** which consists of five small settlements, of which **Lagoudi** is the most beautiful. The best part of Asfendiou, however, may be the spaces between settlements—it's easy to hike for hours in the hilly woodlands and not encounter anyone. Buses from Kos go to Asfendiou-Zia (Mon.-Sat. 2 per day, 200dr).

Continuing south from Lagoudi, the road soon narrows to a mule path as the hills become even less cultivated. Traveling a mere 8km more, you'll come to the compact ruins of old Pyli—well-preserved 14th-century frescoes in a Byzantine church built within the walls of a Byzantine castle. Buses go to Pyli from Kos (Mon.-Sat. 4 per day, Sun. 2 per day, 200dr). All buses from Kos, except those to Tingaki, pass through Zipari, 6km down the hill from Evangelistria. From Pyli, a twisting, dusty road (rough on mopeds) climbs over the hills and descends into Kardamena.

One kilometer before Antimachia on the main road, to the left, is the turn-off for the **Castle of Antimachia.** Yet another legacy of the Knights of St. John, the fortress poises powerfully on an isolated hilltop. Mastihari and Kardamena are the two resorts of central Kos. Both offer grand beaches, streets with few cars, and places to eat fresh food, but the similarities end there. **Mastihari,** north of Antimachia, is quiet, cozy, and popular with families. Many pensions and rooms are available (singles around 2000dr, doubles 3500dr, flats 4000dr). Try **George Mavros's Café** (tel. 513 96), or anywhere else along the beach. Boats go twice per day from Mastihari to Kalymnos (700dr). Four buses per day (3 Sun.) leave Kos for Mastihari (45min., 290dr). **Kardamena,** 5km south of Antimachia, is a tacky tourist town filled with Europeans on package tours. It is difficult to find a room in this plastic village, but you won't want to stay long anyway. The **Community Tourist Office** (tel. 911 39) at the bus stop (which masquerades as a main square) can help you find accommodations. (Open in summer Mon.-Fri. 8am-2:30pm.) The **National Bank of Greece** is on the beach. (Open Mon.-Fri. 9am-1pm.) There is an **exchange office** behind the tourist office (open in summer daily 9am-2pm and 5:30-10pm); the travel agents lining the streets will also exchange money. The **OTE** is one block east of the main square where the bus stops. Various overpriced excursion boats also go to Nisyros, Patmos, and Kalymnos from Kardamena. Buses travel from Kos Town to Kardamena (5 per day, 3 on Sun., 35min., 300dr). **Hotel Paralia** (tel. 912 05), is 2 blocks to the right of the bus stop, around the corner from Kardamena Travel. Clean doubles with private bath go for 3300dr. The **Stelios family** (tel. 911 31), a few blocks west of the Paralia, in a yellow building with green trim, have decent doubles for 3000dr. Behind **Sebastion's Taverna,** 50m farther, doubles go for 3500dr. You can also try **Taverna Ta Delina,** next to the pharmacy on the road to Kos Town. (Spacious doubles with kitchenettes 3000-3500dr.)

Southern Kos

Rolling hills and ravines cover southern Kos. **Kefalos,** Kos's capital in ancient times and the only town of any real substance on the southern half of the island, is not corrupted by tourism but neither is it terribly interesting. The best beach in all of Kos, however, is just 5km before Kefalos on the main road. Beautiful and unspoiled (except for an overpriced restaurant), **Paradise Beach** reclines invitingly beneath a cliff. Many freelancers sack out on the peaceful beach (even though it's illegal). Just 2km before Kefalos, the road descends to sea level in **Agios Stefanos** to the north, where Club Med has appropriated an otherwise good beach and picturesque coastline.

In Agios Stefanos, the **Kritikos ("Zoi") Pension** (tel. 711 47) to the right just before the road levels out, has zealously cleaned doubles for 3000dr. About 200m farther, **Pension Agios Stefanos** (tel. 714 29) lets gorgeous doubles for 3000-3600dr. In Kamari, the **Hotel Maria** (tel. 713 08) rents bright doubles for 3500dr. Four **buses** per day (3 on Sun.) go from Kos to Kefalos (1hr., 350dr). There are also boat excursions to Paradise Beach from Kos Town.

Kalymnos ΚΑΛΥΜΝΟΣ

Kalymnos's primary claim to fame has always been its sponge-fishing industry. In years past, most of its menfolk would depart for five or six months to dive for sponges in the southern waters of the Libyan Sea, off the coast of North Africa—a unique solution to the problem of earning a living while living on a large, barren rock. Today, the industry has declined, but squishy amorphous lumps lurking in old warehouses, tourist kiosks, restaurant display-cases, and various odd corners, harken back to the island's days of glory as sponge-capital of the world. Kalymnos was the first island to revolt against Ottoman Turkey in the 1820 Greek War of Independence, and thereby absorbed a dollop of bravery to weight its already magnificent reputation.

Although Kalymnos receives a fair amount of tourists, especially on its western beaches, the island has managed to remain authentically Greek. Most of the development clings to the coast like a thirsty sponge, leaving the interior mysteriously barren. The rugged mountains, cascading into wide beaches and blue-green water, more than compensate for this island's scant ruins.

Ferries run every day at 5:30pm from Kalymnos to: Leros (1hr., 950dr); Patmos (2hr., 1350dr); and Piraeus (14hr., 3050dr). 8am boats travel south to Kos (2 per day, 1hr., 970dr) and Rhodes (1 per day, 6hr., 2530dr). Once a week, boats travel to Amorgos, Paros, Piraeus, Crete, and most of the Dodecanese islands. You can also travel to Kavala, Ikaria, and the Northeast Aegean islands from here. Schedules change frequently, so check with the port police. If you're feeling flush, ask about hydrofoils at the tourist office.

Daily excursions go from Pothea to **Pserimos,** a small island between Kalymnos and Kos with superior beaches and a few *tavernas* (1400dr round-trip). You can also take a trip to the **Caves of Kephalas,** accessible only by boat (2500dr round-trip; inquire at a travel agency in Pothea). Stalagmites and stalactites litter the caves where Zeus supposedly hid from his father before killing him.

Pothea

During the Italian occupation of Pothea at the beginning of the century, many feisty Potheans painted their houses blue, the national color of Greece, to irk their Italian rulers. Pink and green buildings have since infiltrated the neighborhoods and the original colors have greyed slightly, but this relatively large and bustling town (population 10,000) remains more colorfully piebald than its uniformly white Aegean counterparts. Pothea doesn't bother much with tourists; the people go about their daily business, race cars down narrow streets designed for donkeys, and let the foreigners fend for themselves. Most visitors quickly leave the main town for more alluring spots on the island.

Orientation and Practical Information

The main pier of Pothea runs parallel to **Eleftherias Street,** the waterfront promenade. The second most important avenue, **Venizelou Street,** intersects Eleftherias at the end of the harbor near the Agios Christos church. This narrow shop-filled street runs one way inland to **Kyprou Square** where you'll find the essentials: post office, OTE, taxis, and gasoline. Continuing on this road you'll reach the western part of the island. If you follow the harbor promenade all the way around past the police station, you'll join up with the road leading to Vathis. Most streets in Pothea remain unnamed, but it's easy enough to trace the landmarks.

Tourist Office: Eleftherias St. (tel. 231 40), 1 block from the customs house at the port. A small shack in the shadow of the Olympic Hotel, the office might easily be mistaken for an outhouse. Friendly, English-speaking staff will help you find a room and give you complete information on transportation and sights. Free maps of Pothea and Kalymnos. Open Mon.-Fri. 8am-1pm and 3-8pm.

Budget Travel: Blue Islands Travel (tel. 230 55 or 231 85), on the northwest corner of the harbor on the side of the Olympic Hotel opposite the tourist office. Helpful with bus and boat schedules. Will change money after banks close, and try to find you accommodations. Open Mon.-Fri. 8am-1pm and 3-8pm. **Kalymnos Tours** (tel. 283 29 or 220 36), on the waterfront before the tourist office, is also helpful. Both agencies open daily 8:30am-1pm and 5-8:30pm; in off-season open only Mon.-Fri.

Currency Exchange: National Bank of Greece and **Ionian and Popular Bank,** both on the waterfront. The National Bank advances cash on Mastercard; the Ionian Bank advances cash on Visa. Both open Mon.-Thurs. 8am-2pm, Fri. 8am-1:30pm.

Post Office: From Kyprou Sq., bear right and go 1 block inland. Open Mon.-Fri. 7:30am-2pm. Also has **currency exchange. Postal Code:** 85200.

OTE: Tel 295 99, just past the post office on the right. Open Mon.-Sat. 7:30am-midnight, Sun. 8:30am-11pm. Shorter hours in off-season. **Telephone Code:** 0243.

Buses: Buses leave every 15min. in summer for Massouri, Myrties, and Kantouni (100dr). On Mon., Wed., and Fri., 2 per day for Emborios (120dr). Three per day for Vathis (200dr). Buses to the west coast villages stop by the town hall (look for the blue dome). Buses to Vathis wait at the northeast corner of the waterfront.

Taxis: Kyprou Sq. (tel. 295 55). A slightly cheaper alternative is the **taxi-bus,** a taxi with 4-5 more passengers. Set rate per person, about twice as much as the bus. There are taxi-bus stands in each town and in Kyprou Sq., but you can flag one anywhere; they operate until 10pm.

Moped Rental: Several places on the waterfront. From 1500dr per day. Gas not included.

Port Police: In the yellow building across from the customs house (tel. 293 04), at the southwest corner of the waterfront. Updated ferry information. Open 24 hrs.

Police: Tel. 221 00, off Kyprou Sq. to the left of the street with the post office and OTE. Minimal English spoken.

Hospital: Tel. 288 51. 500m up the road towards Chorio.

Accommodations and Food

The easiest way to secure a room in Pothea is to strike a deal with one of the pension owners who await incoming boats. Otherwise, try the tourist office. To get to the hospitable **Greek House** (tel. 237 52), head inland from the waterfront at the National Bank, take the first left, follow the street, take a quick sprint to the right, and turn right at the wet sponge factories. Warm and welcoming hosts will greet you. (Singles 2000dr. Doubles 3000dr. Triples 4500dr.) From the Greek House, turn right past the moist sponge factories, and follow the signs to the Panorama Hotel for the pension of the ebullient **Katerina Smaliou** (tel. 221 86), just before the Panorama. (Bring a phrasebook or a Greek along.) The rooms are cooled with ceiling fans, and the terrace affords a smashing view of the city. (Doubles 2500dr.) Farther uphill and left toward the cross, you'll come to the homey **Travelo Pension** (tel. 280 41), owned by yet more friendly Kalymnosites Catrina and Stergos Platella. (Doubles 1300dr.) Back down and around the corner from the Greek House, **Mr. Christoforos Vythoulkas Pension** is noisy but cheap in the evening. (Small, drab singles 1800dr. Doubles 2000dr.) The **Patmos Pension** (tel. 227 50) next to the tourist office, has decent rooms upstairs (doubles 1800dr) and some cheaper rooms out back (doubles 1500dr). **Maria Tsoukala** (tel. 285 28) has doubles for 1500dr. From the Agios Christos Church, head inland, take the third left and look for "rooms to let" signs.

Most of the restaurants in Pothea are by the harbor, under the overbearing signs advertising traditional Greek food. The quality is decent but the price is a steep 1200-1400dr per person. Your best bet is among the *souvlaki/pita* shops by Christou Church. As you walk from the main waterfront roadway continue straight for **Serafino** (*souvlaki/gyro* 150dr) or take a left at Serafino for the fast food 30m up the street: the best cheeseburger in Kalymnos for 300dr.

Sights

There are not many things to see in Pothea. Two blocks inland from the left end of the harbor is the squidgy sponge factory of **Nikolas Gourlas,** where sponges are cleaned and chemically treated. Mr. Gourlas speaks English and will be happy to explain the absorbing process to you. (Sponge mementos from 500dr.) The original sponge factories stretch along the far east end of the harbor, on the road to Vathis. Follow the many signposts from Venizelou St. to the eclectic **municipal museum.** The most interesting feature of this former mansion is the sumptuously decorated parlor, which hints at the lifestyle of very wealthy Kalymosites at the turn of the century. (Open Tues.-Sun. 8am-2pm. Free.)

The hilltop **Monastery of Agios Pantes** overlooks the town. Visitors can enter at the gate on the right side; the first chapel on your left contains the bones of a canonized church official in an elaborate sarcophagus. Saints aside, the view from up here is heavenly; you can see all the way to Telendos Island and beyond. (Free.)

From the customs house, take the roads to the left to reach the beach at **Therma,** 2km away. Arthritic patients make pilgrimages to the sanitarium here to partake of its sulphur mineral baths. (You need a doctor's permission to bathe.) The main beach is crowded; a short walk around the bend leads to a quiet swimming spot. Farther west from Therma (backtrack toward Pothea and then head slightly north) is the tranquil beach at **Vlichadia** (6km from Pothea).

Western Coast

Kalymnos has two main roads: one runs northwest out of Pothea, the other northeast. A few km on the northwest road, a side road to the left leads up to a crumbling fortress of the Knights of St. John, also called the **Kastro Chrissocherias.** Hidden away in its remains are a number of little chapels, all open to view. Freshly painted sections of wall or floor indicate places where privateers dug holes to search for buried treasure. The **Pera Kastro,** a fortress from the Byzantine epoch, looms north of Chrissocherias across the valley. This structure, originally Byzantine, was enlarged and fortified by the

Knights. Nine tiny bright white churches are scattered throughout the ruins, maintained by elderly women from Chorio. Directly opposite, you can see the small village of **Argos,** once the ancient city of Argiens and now merely a suburb of Pothea. Both the Pera Kastro and Argos overlook the town of **Chorio,** once Kalymnos's capital but now little more than another of Pothea's tentacles.

A kilometer or so beyond Chorio, just after the road begins to descend into Panormos, a few white steps by the side of the road lead to the shell of the **Church of Christ of Jerusalem,** a Byzantine church built by the Emperor Arcadius to thank God for sparing him in a storm at sea. The stone blocks with carved inscriptions are from a 4th-century BCE temple to Apollo that stood on the same site. By incorporating and subordinating these architectural elements, the church was viewed as a symbolic victory over paganism. At Panormos, the road branches. One offshoot goes to **Kantouni,** where the beach is clogged with litter, shrieking children, and games of paddle ball. An antidote to this frenetic scene is the social atmosphere at the **Kantouni Beach Hotel/ Pool Bar.** Right on the waterfront, this relaxed pool bar is open to the public. Also on the waterfront, the **Rock and Blues Pub** and the **Domus Bar** effervesce late into the evening. Another road from Panormos leads, after 2km, to the sandy and less crowded beach of **Plati Gialos,** frequented by only the most devout of sun-worshipers. Stay at **Pension Plati Gialos** (tel. 220 14), perched on the cliff with a memorable view of the coastline. (Doubles 3500dr.) Both the grey-sand beach at **Myrties** 7km up the coast, and the pebbly one at **Massouri,** the next town up, can become alarmingly full. Both towns have just a few budget accommodations. Half a kilometer before Myrties, at a bend in the road, the **Pension Mikes** (tel. 473 18) has doubles (3500dr). Also try the **Rinio Pension** (tel. 227 26), about halfway between Myrties and Massouri. (Peaceful doubles 3400dr.) The best place to stay between Myrties and Massouri is **Niki's Pension** (tel. 47201). The sign on the main road leads you up stairs and over rough terrain to the most scenic rooms in Massouri (Doubles 3000dr, reservations a good idea.) Massouri, the center of the island's nightlife, entertains itself with a few excellent pubs: **Flamingo, No Name,** and **Smile.** Later in the evening everybody heads about 700m down the road towards Emborios to the huge, brand-new, outdoor **Look Disco** where they dance 'til they drop. (1000dr cover charge which includes your first drink.)

Myrties's finest attraction, a short boat ride (10min., 300dr) out of town, is the tiny, rocky islet of **Telendos,** severed from Kalymnos by an earthquake in 554 CE. A city occupied the faultline where the island cracked—traces of it have been found on the ocean floor, but the rift is invisible on the surface. The Roman ruins on Telendos are modest at best, but a few small, secluded beaches fringe the island. (Turn right from the ferry dock for most of the beaches; another beach awaits to the left of the dock.) Past the beaches to the right is the **Byzantine Monastery of St. Constantine.** (Dress modestly. Free.) Accommodations in Telendos fill only for a couple of weeks in August. Most pensions charge 3000dr for a double. **Uncle George's Pension** (tel. 475 02), near the docks, has a smile-inducing restaurant. (Doubles 2680dr.) **Demetrios Harinos** (no phone), just before the ruins, provides quiet, clean rooms. The rooms at the **Café Festaria** (tel. 474 01) are pretty much the same, but with spiffy bright-red shutters. Follow the signs to the left of the docks and back to the comfortable rooms let by **Mrs. Makarouna.** You can camp on the beach but be prepared for the wind. To the left of Uncle George's, **Ta Delina's** complements its fine Greek fare with live Greek music every Wednesday and Saturday night. Before leaving Myrties, take a look back at Telendos and notice the woman's profile along the left-hand side of the mountain. According to locals, she is looking forlornly out to sea, mourning her lost husband.

Back on Kalymnos, the emptiest beach stretches out at **Arginontas,** at the end of a long, narrow inlet. Both roads to and from the beach rise dramatically along cliffs that plunge into turquoise water. Though not the cleanest place on the island, **Vanzanelis's** (tel. 473 89), at Arginontas Beach, has a *taverna* and doubles for 2300dr. Two buses from Pothea venture this far (210dr). The last village on the western side, **Emborios,** remains quaint and unspoiled. **Harry's Restaurant,** (tel. 474 34) snozzles 20m from the beach, and provides good food and good beds. (Doubles 3000dr.) The **Restaurant Themis** (tel. 472 77), the white building with blue trim facing the beach, has nice doubles with a stately balcony (3500dr). A small boat makes an excursion from Myrties to Emborio daily at 10am (900dr round-trip).

Although most of Kalymnos supports only grass and a few diehard wildflowers, the valley at Vathis (6km northeast of Pothea) is a rich melange of mandarins, limes, and grapevines. The valley starts at the village of **Rina,** where the sea creates a kind of fjord. There is no beach here (you can swim off the pier), but the exquisite scenery and relative absence of tourists make sand an easy sacrifice. On the north side of the inlet is **Daskaleios,** a stalagmite cave you can swim to (persuade a local to point it out).

In Rina, stay at the **Hotel Galini** (tel. 312 41; singles 2000dr, doubles 3500dr; balcony and private bath included). The three *tavernas* on the tiny waterfront rent rooms, too.

Astypalea ΑΣΤΥΠΑΛΙΑ

Few tourists venture out to butterfly-shaped Astypalea, the westernmost of the Dodecanese islands—and they know not what they're missing. This quiet, unobtrusive island is one of the most savory secrets of the Dodecanese. Astypalea's colorful port, often strewn with fishing nets, harbors all the necessary services and is a charming base from which to visit the island's endless secluded coves and rugged hills.

Ferries arrive in Astypalea sporadically. The *Sifnos Express* passes through on Tuesdays and Thursdays. Boats from Piraeus and the Cyclades occasionally dock here (Thurs., Sat., and Sun.). On Tuesdays and Fridays, yet another ferry shuttles to Kalymnos (2hr., 1400dr) and Kos (3½hr., 1800dr). As always, ferry schedules change frequently; check with the port police. Be aware that ferries do not leave Astypalea every day, so you run the risk of being stuck here for two or three days.

All ferries land at the town of Astypalea, surrounded by tawny, sloping hills. The town itself is a hillside conglomeration of uninspiring cubical dwellings. The staff of the small **tourist office** (tel. 612 17) speaks no English (open Mon.-Fri. 8am-2:15pm). Just before the town's small beach, you'll find the **police** (tel. 612 07) and **port police** (tel. 612 08), sharing a building. (Both open daily 8am-7pm.) **Gournas Travel Agency** (tel. 613 34), on the waterfront amidst the cafés, organizes frequent excursions to otherwise inaccessible beaches, and arranges house rentals (3800-4500dr a night for two people; office open April-Oct. daily 9:30am-12:30pm and 6:30-9:30pm). The **OTE** (open daily 8am-11pm, in off season Mon.-Fri. 8am-3pm) and a **boat agency** (tel. 612 24), are at the foot of the Paradissos Hotel. The other boat agency in town is in the Vivamare Hotel. M. Karakosta, in the store underneath the Aegean hotel, is an agent of the **National Bank of Greece** (open Mon.-Fri. 8am-1pm). **Alexis,** just off the waterfront, rents **motorbikes** (2500dr). Astypalea's **postal code** is 85900; its **telephone code** is 0243.

On the waterfront, the **Paradissos Hotel** (tel. 612 24) has several stories of bare but spotless rooms (singles 2800dr, doubles 4800dr; bargain). Take a left up the hill before the beach for the **Hotel Aegean** (tel. 612 36; neat singles 2000dr, doubles 3500dr). The manager of the **Hotel de France** (tel. 612 45) just up the street from the Aegean, runs a bakery downstairs. He's up at 4am, so go to him if your boat arrives in the early morning. (Doubles 3500dr. Open June-Sept.) The **Hotel Vangelis** (tel. 612 81) overlooks the harbor from the far right (facing inland). (Doubles with great views 3500dr.) There are also some *dhomatia,* whose owners regularly greet incoming ferries. **Camping Astypalea** (tel. 613 38) is 2½km east of the town near Marmari; follow the signs or take a bus towards Maltezana. (500dr per person. 300dr per tent.)

Viki at **Viki's Taverna,** just up from the ferry landing, cooks up delectable victuals (open daily 8:30am-11pm; sometimes closed for *siesta).* **Galini's Restaurant,** up the hill towards the castle, is another local favorite.

At the top of the hill, a striking row of windmills leads to the **castle,** a ramshackle Byzantine structure shedding segments of walls and windows. From here you have a clear view of the island and its flock of tributary islets. The **post office/currency exchange** (tel. 612 23; open Mon.-Fri. 7:30am-2:15pm) and several **supermarkets** (open daily 9am-1pm and 5-9pm) are all in this older section of town. Astypalea's four bars, uphill from the square near the post office, compete for customers: the **Castro Bar** has Greek music; **La Luna** and **Laou Laou** have Western music; and with a little imagination, the **Kuiros Bar** can qualify as a disco. A 20-minute walk west (over the hill) from town will bring you to the sandy beach of **Livadia.** A jolly Aussie named Nikolas Kontaratos (tel. 612 69) rents doubles and triples (1500dr per person); his house is a five-minute walk inland from the beach on the main road. The **Tsaousi Pension** (tel. 614 84), two doors from the beach at the main road, has pleasant doubles (3500dr). There is a hefty number of other rooms to let. Buses leave four times daily (100dr). The pleasant beach is pestered with tents and children during July and August, but on the beach of **Tzanaki,** a 20-minute hike along the coast to the southwest, nude bathers do their thing in virtual solitude. The beach at **Agios Konstantinos,** one of the best on the island, is now served by a dirt road (1½-hr. hike from Livadia).

In the other direction from Astypalea Town, the quiet fishing villages of **Maltezana** and **Analipsi** occupy the narrow isthmus. Home to some largely intact Roman mosaics, peaceful Maltezana is accessible by bus (2 per day, 100dr). The narrow natural harbor at **Vathi** is subdivided into Exo Vathi (outside) and Esa Vathi (inside), and is visited twice per week by Gournas Travel boat excursions. In the winter when the winds are too strong for boats to dock at Astypalea, the ferries go to the bay at **Agios Andreas.** The lovely beach here is accessible by road. Another rocky road leads to the **Agios Ioannis Monastery,** majestically balanced atop a hill.

Leros ΛΕΡΟΣ

Local custom dictates that only women can inherit property on Leros and in fact they do own most of this woody and secluded island. Once the stalking grounds of Artemis, goddess of the hunt, this isle seems not to mind its lack of voluptuous beaches and paucity of intricate historical twists. Some people love Leros for its friendly people and the almost eerie absence of tourists. Others find it simply eerie. One local even claims the island's haunted. Do what thou wilt.

Ferries arrive at a number of ports. Larger boats dock in Lakki, while Agia Marina receives smaller vessels from Patmos and Lipsi. Boats of any magnitude, however, are liable to switch ports according to weather conditions. Small boats also leave from Xerocampos, on the southeastern part of the island, for Myrties on Kalymnos (7:30am, returning to Leros at 1pm, 45min., 900dr). The *Nissos Kalymnos* docks at Agia Marina and goes to: Lipsos (3-5 per week, 1hr., 940dr); Patmos (3-5 per week, 2hr., 940dr); Samos (3 per week, 4½hr., 1620dr); and Kalymnos (3 per week, 2hr., 970dr), continuing to Kos (3hr., 1330dr). Every night at midnight a ferry arrives in Lakki from Piraeus, for the Kalymnos-Kos-Rhodes route (7hr., 3010dr to Rhodes). There are also hydrofoils to Kalymnos (3 per week, ½hr., 1600dr), and Kos (3 per week, 1hr., 3100dr). Before leaving Leros, check with a travel agent to to confirm schedules and departure points. Schedules are fickle; a windy day can delay a boat for hours.

For the affluent, Olympic Airways (tel. 228 44 or 241 44) has **flights** to Athens daily (8am, on Mon., Wed., and Fri. also at 3:30pm, 15,100dr). A little puddle-jumper also goes to Kos (Tues., Thurs., and Sat. 2:15pm, 5400dr). There is an Olympic Airways office where the road from Platanos forks to Lakki and Pantheli (open Mon.-Sat. 8am-2:30pm). The airfield is on the north coast of Leros, 7km past Platanos.

Leros is best explored by bike (800dr per day) or **moped** (1500-3000dr per day). **John Komoulis** has rentals in all three towns (tel. 223 30 in Lakki, 230 14 in Platanos, 240 15 in Alinda). **Taxis** are a reasonable means of transport (tel. 230 70 in Platanos, 225 50 in Lakki, 233 40 in Agia Marina). Lakki to Platanos costs only 600dr. Leros's **postal code** is 85400; its **telephone code** is 0247.

Around the Island

The groping, centrally located capital of Leros, **Platanos** merges into two harbors: Agia Marina to the north and Pantheli to the south. Taxis and the mythical bus stop just below the main square, 1km uphill from both Ag. Marina and Pantheli. The **National**

Bank of Greece is in the square (open Mon.-Thurs. 8am-2pm, Fri. 8am-1:30pm). The **OTE** (open Mon.-Sat. 7:30am-3pm, Sun. 9am-2pm) and **post office** (open Mon.-Fri. 8am-2pm) are in the same building on Karami St., off the main square downhill towards Ag. Marina. **Letec** (tel. 234 96), **DRM** (tel. 243 03), and **Kastis** (tel. 225 00) **travel agencies** are sprinkled along the waterfront at Ag. Marina, near the intersection with Karami St. (All 3 open daily 9am-1pm and 5-9pm; off-season Mon.-Fri. 9am-1pm or closed completely.) Hopeful room-renters accost ferry passengers at the docks, offering the least strenuous option for accommodations. The **postal code** is 85400.

Leros is less popular with tourists than the neighboring islands; nevertheless finding accommodations here in July and August requires legwork. About 50m downhill from the post office, the **Venus Pension** (tel. 233 89), run by the hospitable Maravelia family, has clean and comfortable rooms (singles 2500dr, doubles 3500dr). The **Hotel Eleftheria** (tel. 235 50), near the taxi stop, has spacious doubles for 4000dr. From the main square in Platanos, a set of steep white-trimmed steps climbs 2km to the **kastro,** a Byzantine fortress. Share the view of the irregular coastline with the flock of birds and the Greek soldiers quartered in the castle.

Pantheli is a small waterfront village with a mediocre beach, but inexpensive accommodations, ideal spots to dine, and the only semblance of nightlife on Leros. About 50m to the left of the beach (facing the water), is **Pension Rosa** (tel. 227 98), with capacious waterfront doubles for 3000dr. A few doors down is the quaint **Pension Kavos** (tel. 232 47), sporting a kitchen, outdoor tables on a patio, and clean rooms. (Doubles 4000dr, with private bath.) Several restaurants line the waterfront, and many offer rooms to rent upstairs. (Doubles about 3000dr.) At the grapevine-trellised **Syrtaki,** you can feast on a yumlicious pizza (800-1200dr) or *mousaka* (600dr) to the merry sounds of the occasional *bouzouki* music extravaganza. Above the *taverna* are filthless, spacious rooms with private balconies and baths. (Doubles 3000dr. Triples 4000dr.) The popular **Kaliro's,** to the far right of the waterfront, serves up fresh seafood day and night (octopus 650dr). Dance until 3am at the well-advertised **Disco Diana** just up the road (drinks 900dr). **Nikola's Taverna** prepares cheap and traditional meals.

Sandy **Alinda Beach** is just a 3½km jaunt north of Platanos. **Pension Papa Fotis** (tel. 222 47) behind the Hotel Maleas Beach, offers pleasant, clean rooms with private baths. (Singles 2000dr. Doubles 3500dr.) The **Hotel Karina** (tel. 227 16) has a nice garden and similar singles for 2000dr and doubles for 3800dr.

The most popular haven on Leros is **Vromolithos Beach,** the next cave south from Pantheli. From here it's a mildly hilly 3km walk to **Lakki,** a detention center for political prisoners during the years of the Junta. At the foot of the ferry dock, a **tourist office** opens periodically. The main road in from Platanos abuts the waterfront at a small roundabout, where taxis stop. Near this intersection, there is a **National Bank of Greece** (open Mon.-Thurs. 8am-2pm, Fri. 8am-1:30pm). Two blocks from the waterfront is the **OTE** (open Mon.-Fri. 7:30am-3pm); the **post office** is nearby (open Mon.-Fri., 8am-2pm). The **port police** (tel. 222 24) hang out in a large building one block from the water; take the second left from the dock. In an emergency, call the **police** (tel. 222 22) or the **hospital** (tel. 232 51). Boats from Piraeus and Patmos habitually arrive in Lakki at 2 or 3am, in which case you will probably be neither willing nor able to leave the town (which otherwise would probably be your first impulse). Lakki supports a few hotels, of which the **Hotel Palace** (tel. 229 40), though a bit mysterious, is the cheapest. (Singles 2000dr. Doubles 3000dr.) The **Hotel Mira Mare** (tel. 220 53), one block inland and one block to the left from the roundabout, has much nicer rooms (doubles 3800dr).

Patmos ΠΑΤΜΟΣ

One of Greece's most sacred islands, Patmos exudes historical and religious significance. In ancient times, the people of Patmos worshipped Artemis, goddess of the hunt, who was said to have raised the island from the sea. Orestes built a grand temple to Artemis after finding refuge on Patmos from the Furies who were pursuing him for the murder of his mother, Clytemnestra.

When he was exiled from Ephesus, St. John established a Christian colony here and purportedly wrote the Book of Revelations in a grotto overlooking the main town. In the 4th century CE, when the Christian faith spread with the Byzantine Empire, a basilica replaced the razed Temple of Artemis. In the 11th century, the fortified Monastery of St. John was constructed on a hill that surveys the entire island. The monastery, protected by the Byzantines, then the Roman Pope, and finally the Turks, still stands today.

Until recent centuries, only monks inhabited the island, but news of its spectacular scenery, austere rocky mountains, and serene beaches soon spread. Now Patmos sustains a thriving tourist trade, but the sprawling monastery still bestows an encompassing tranquility upon the island.

Ferries from Patmos travel to Piraeus (daily at 8pm, 10hr., 3400dr); and along the Leros-Kalymnos-Kos-Rhodes route (daily at 10:30pm; off-season 3-4 per week, 900dr to Leros, 3200dr to Rhodes). To get to the Cyclades, you can take a boat to Ikaria (3 per week, 3hr., 1400dr), and then catch the ferry to Paros (4hr., 1400dr) or Samos (daily, 2½hr., 1610dr). Excursion boats travel to Lipsi every morning at 10am, returning to Patmos at 5pm (900dr, round-trip 1300dr). Ferries also head to Lipsi (5 per week, 1hr.) There is frequent **hydrofoil** service to Leros (1900dr), Kos (2900dr), and Rhodes (5800dr), but besides being expensive, hydrofoils are subject to cancellation in rough weather.

Skala

Built along a graceful arc of coastline, lively Skala gives only a hint of the diversity of the island's terrain. Patmos's port and main city, Skala was not developed until the 19th century, when fear of pirates subsided and people could live safely by the water. The main administrative buildings, which now house the post office and customs house, were constructed during the Italian occupation (1912-1943).

Orientation and Practical Information

Everything you'll need in Skala is within a block or two of the waterfront. Smaller ferries dock directly opposite the line of cafés and restaurants, while larger vessels park in front of the imposing Italian building that houses the port police and post office. The building borders the main square, where the banks are located. Skala is on a narrow part of the island, so if you walk away from the water, you'll be on the other side in 10-15 minutes.

Tourist Office: Around the corner from the post office, off the main square (tel. 316 66). Helpful with accommodations, maps, and bus schedules. Open year-round Mon.-Fri. 7:30am-2:30pm.

Travel Agencies: On the waterfront. **Astoria Shipping and Travel** (tel. 312 05/08). Information on private boats and ferries. Organizes guided tours of the monastery and the grotto (2 per week, 3hr., 900dr). Open daily 8am-9pm. **Apollon Tourist and Shipping Agency** (tel. 313 56 or 313 24). Information on boats and hydrofoils. Agents for Olympic Airways. Also has **currency exchange.** Open Mon.-Sat. 8am-9pm, Sun. 8am-2pm and 5-9pm; off-season Mon.-Sat. 8am-1pm and 5-8pm, Sun. 9am-1pm. Agencies have information on only those ferry lines for which they sell tickets. The port police or tourist office can give you more complete schedules.

Currency Exchange: National Bank of Greece in the square (tel. 311 23). Cash advances on Mastercard. Open Mon.-Thurs. 8am-2pm, Fri. 8am-1:30pm. Also at the **post office** and **Apollon Agency.**

Post Office: On the main square, next to the police (tel. 313 16). Open Mon.-Fri. 8am-2pm. **Postal Code:** 85500.

OTE: Follow the signs back and slightly to the left from the main square. Open Mon.-Fri. 7:30am-9pm, Sat. 7:30am-3:10pm, Sun. 9am-2pm. The café-bar at the boat dock has an international telephone. **Telephone Code:** 0247.

Bus Station: In front of the police station. Complete bus schedule posted. Buses run to Chora, Grikos, and Kampos.

Taxis: In the main square (tel. 312 25).

Moped Rental: On the waterfront. 1500-2500dr per day.

Public Toilets: Behind the medical clinic; use them if you can hold your breath longer than your bladder.

Hospital: Uphill toward Chora (tel. 312 11).

Police: Tel. 311 00 or 313 03. **Port Police:** In the large Italianate building by the main square (tel. 312 31). Friendly, with information on ferries. You can leave your pack in the arched doorway. Open 24 hrs.

Accommodations, Camping, and Food

In summer, Skala's few hotels are often full, but finding a room in one of the numerous pensions and private homes is usually easy. Even the boats arriving at 1am are greeted by a battalion of locals bearing rooms (singles 1500-2000dr, doubles 2800-4000dr). If your ferry arrives late, make arrangements with someone as you get off the boat. To seek rooms on your own, walk left from the ferry dock and right onto Vassileos Georgiou St. At your fifth left (past Pizza Zacharo), a warm-hearted family keeps up the **Pension Sofia** (tel. 315 01) and its immaculate rooms. Knock on the second floor or try the building to the right. (Singles 2000dr. Doubles 4000dr.) If you don't mind early morning farm noises, walk about 50m past Sofia's until you see the rooms-to-let sign across from a basketball court. **Maria Paschalidis** (tel. 321 52 or 313 47) runs this jubilant pension and offers spotless rooms off a garden. (Singles 2000dr. Doubles 3800dr.) Another option is **Liapis Kalliopi's Pension** (tel. 316 03), in the house with vines and bright orange flowers spilling over the sidewalk; turn left after Sofia's. (Singles 2000dr. Doubles 4000dr.) Diagonally across from her place, the **Metgoyiannakises** (tel. 310 09) rent a few rooms in their big house with the grapevine in the front. (Singles 2000dr. Spacious doubles 3800dr.) The **Hotel Rodon** (tel. 313 71), one block north and one block west of the square (take the little street next to the Pantelis Taverna) has corpulent, clean singles for 2000dr and doubles for 3800dr. Try the road leading from the left side of the square. The **Hotel Rex** (tel. 312 42), on the right side of the waterfront (facing the water), has old but spacious rooms. (Singles 1700dr, with bath 3000dr. Doubles with bath 3500dr. Triples with bath 4500dr.)

Two km northeast of Skala, the excellent **campsite** at Meloi (tel. 318 21) has a café and minimarket and is about 50m from a small and inviting nude beach. The restaurant across the road occasionally features *syrtaki* dancing. Follow the waterfront road to the left of the harbor, facing the water; you'll see signs. (700dr, showers included. Open April 15-Oct. 15.)

Several stupendous seafood restaurants line the waterfront. The snack bar at the back of the square sells fresh grilled octopus. **Avyerinos** (sign in Greek), on the road to the OTE, has excellent *souvlaki-pita* (200dr) and *tzatziki* (250dr). The **Platanos Taverna,** farther along the same road past the OTE, will leave a comfortable bulge in your stomach and your wallet. (Open daily noon-4pm and 6pm-midnight.) It's just to the right of the ferry landing (facing the water). For a change of pace, try **Skorpios Creperie,** on Vassileos Georgiou St. to the left of the ferry dock as you disembark; the French proprietor serves breakfast, dinner, and dessert crepes. (Open daily 9am-3pm and 7pm-midnight.) There are several small groceries around the square. If you're into loud funky music, drink at a table on the beach or dance indoors at the **Meltemi Bar** (tel. 313 64), at the left end of the waterfront when you face the water. (Beer 300dr, cocktails 550-750dr.) The **Café Arion,** right near the main square, has a good bar with mellow music (cocktails 700dr). Inside the Hotel Chris, on the left side of the waterfront (facing the water), skulks the island's only **disco.**

Chora

From any part of Patmos you can see the white houses of Chora and the majestic, gray walls of the nearby Monastery of St. John the Theologian. Roam Chora's labyrinthine streets, snug in the shelter of the monastery, and view the Patmos shoreline and the outlying archipelago.

Because of the convoluted layout of the town and the dearth of street names, it's impossible to give precise directions. Take care of business, such as exchanging currency, before arriving; a local telephone and mailbox at the bottom of the monastery hill are about the only links between Chora and the outside world.

In summer, **buses** travel to Chora from Skala (8-10 per day, 7:40am-9:30pm, 100dr). The bus lets you off at the top of the hill outside the town; this is also the point of departure for buses from Chora to Grikou. A taxi here from Skala costs about 550dr. If you decide to walk (4km and steep), the steps to Chora will be quicker and safer than the main road. The few rooms-for-rent in Chora are usually fully booked; check at the Skala tourist office before you go. You can also try Chora's one **pension,** right below the monastery. Walk past the pension and you'll reach the square surrounded by *tavernas:* **Vagelis** has a wide selection of inexpensive Greek dishes (*fasolia—* beans— 450dr), in the garden behind the restaurant. (Open daily 8am-2pm and 6pm-midnight.) The *taverna* also has a few rooms to rent. Nearby, **Markos Farmakakis** (tel. 321 14), has a couple of doubles in an old Greek house (3500dr).

Sights

The turreted walls and fortified gateway of the **Monastery of St. John the Theologian** look more like a fortress than a place of worship. But then again, this is no ordinary house of God. St. Christodoulos founded the monastery in 1088, nearly 1000 years after St. John's celebrated stay on the island. Pragmatics proved more important than aesthetics—the proximity of Muslim Turkey made the monastery a constant target of pirate raids, so it was only a matter of time before the memorial to St. John was transformed into a citadel with battlements and watch towers. There are 10 chapels in the monastery because church law forbade hearing mass twice daily in the same one.

As you enter the courtyard, notice the 17th-century frescoes to the left that portray stories from *The Miracles and Travels of St. John the Evangelist,* written by John's disciple Prochoros. To the right, a fresco portrays St. John's thaumaturgical duel with a local priest of Apollo named Kynops. When the saint threw Kynops into the water at Skala, the heathen was turned into stone. The rock is still in the harbor—ask any local to point out the unfortunate Kynops's corpse.

Continue to the **Chapel of the Virgin Mary,** swaddled in original 12th-century frescoes. In 1956, earth tremors revealed these frescoes underneath the 17th-century ones currently exhibited. The treasury safeguards jewels, icons, and ornamented stoles donated by Catherine the Great of Russia. The **Chapel of the Holy Christodoulos** guards the remains of the monastery's illustrious founder. Shortly after Christodoulos's death, many visitors attempted to appropriate his saintliness by carrying away his remains, so the monks built a marble sarcophagus and covered it with a heavy, silver reliquary. Ask to see the library. With over 2000 printed books and some 890 manuscripts, including a 6th-century copy of St. Mark's Gospel and an 8th-century Book of Job, the collection will invariably impress.

In the summer, try not to visit the monastery during midday when it becomes uncomfortably crammed with tourists and hollering tour guides. If you come in off-season, one of the monastery's 25 monks (there were once 1700) may volunteer to show you around. (Monastery open Mon. and Fri.-Sat. 8am-2pm, Tues. and Thurs. 8am-1pm and 4-6pm, Wed. 8am-2pm and 5:30-7pm, Sun. 8am-noon and 4-6pm. Dress appropriately. Free.)

Halfway up the hill on the winding road that connects Chora and Skala (2km from each) is a turn-off for another monastery, the **Apocalypsis,** a large, white complex of interconnected buildings. Most people come here to see the **Sacred Grotto of the Revelation,** adjacent to the Church of St. Anne. In this cave, St. John dictated the *Book of Revelation,* the last book of the New Testament, after hearing the voice of God proclaim to him "the things which are and the things which shall be hereafter" (Rev. 1:19). According to legend, when God spoke to St. John, he cleft the ceiling of the cave with a tripartite crack representing the Holy Trinity. Silver plating marks the spot where St. John presumably slept. (Apocalypsis open Mon. 8am-12pm, Tues. and Thurs. 3-6pm, Wed. 5:30-7pm, Sun. 8am-12pm and 3-6pm. Free.)

Around The Island

Grikos encompasses a comparatively empty sandy beach with watersport rentals, one luxury hotel, and a couple of restaurants. Only 5km southwest of Skala, and 5km west of Chora, the town is visited by seven **buses** daily from Skala and five per day from Chora (off-season 1 per day, 120dr). The **Vamvakos Hotel** (tel. 313 82 or 312 90) overlooks the southern and quieter end of the beach. (Doubles 3800dr.) If you camp, you'll have plenty of company on the extreme southern end of the beach. Motorbikers can continue 3km south to the essentially vacant beach of **Plaki,** where the road degenerates. Only 2km west from Plaki lies **Psili Ammos,** the best beach on the island. You can try hiking to it, but get directions first—the mountains are full of prickly shrubs, and the path is not well marked. A much easier route is by excursion boat from Skala (daily at 10am, returning at 4pm, 550dr).

Lipsi (Lipsos) ΛΕΙΨΟΙ

Some say Odysseus met the ravishing nymph Calypso on this tiny island—it's no wonder he chose to put off his homecoming for seven years. Today the island is no less alluring: 44 blue-domed churches are strewn along the mountainside, men on donkeys roam the streets, and visitors are welcomed to join the Greek dancing almost every Saturday and Sunday night in summer.

Excursion boats from Patmos visit Lipsi every morning at 10am, returning at 4pm (1hr., round-trip 1550dr). From Lipsi, the *Anna Express* makes excursions to: Leros (Fri.-Wed., 1hr., 960dr); the secluded beaches of Arki and Agathonsi; and the one-*taverna* island of Marathi (Thurs., 1300dr). The same boat also travels from Leros to Lipsi (Mon.-Wed. and Fri.-Sat.), and from Patmos to Lipsi (Sun., 1hr., round-trip 1300dr). The *Nissos Kalymnos* goes from Lipsi to Patmos (3-4 times per week, 900dr), to Samos (Sat., 1200dr), and along the Leros-Kalymnos-Kos route twice a week (Leros, 50dr; Kalymnos, 910dr; Kos, 1250dr). Most people coming from the other islands are daytrippers, so if you choose to stay the night, you'll find Lipsi empty and peaceful.

The terraced street to the right of the harbor leads up to the central square, where you'll find the new **tourist information office** (tel. 412 88) inside the **Ecclesiastical Popular Museum of Lipsi** (open Mon.-Fri. 9:30am-1:30pm and 4-8pm, Sat.-Sun. 10am-2pm). The **post office** is also in the square (open Mon.-Fri. 8am-2:30pm); the **OTE** is in the building diagonally opposite (open Mon.-Fri. 8am-1pm and 5-7pm). You can change money and buy ferry tickets at **Sveastos Supermarket,** one block behind the post office (open Mon.-Sat. 7am-9pm). On the waterfront, the post office and **Hotel Kalypso** (tel. 412 42) also exchange money. Try the fabulous **Studios Dream** (tel. 412 71), just past Lendou Beach. Every spacious double here has a small kitchenette, balcony, and bath (4500dr). There are many small *tavernas* along the waterfront which serve inexpensive fresh fish. Lipsi's **postal code** is 85001; its **telephone code** is 0247.

If you ask Lipsians about sights on their island, they shrug. Aside from the beaches, the inviting landscape and the chapels, there are few special attractions. You can camp and swim at the fine town beach, but it becomes congested in the afternoon when Lipsian children get out of school. **Plati Gialos** is indisputably Lipsi's most beautiful beach, with fine sand and calm turquoise water, waist-deep for most of the cove. Nude sunbathing and freelance camping are popular here. You can catch a ride with a local (look for the small trucks with signs for Plati Gialos; 600-800dr round-trip). Another lovely, less crowded beach is **Katzadia,** to the right of the town. **Chokla Kora** is a pleasant, pebbly beach behind the town; on the way there, visit the **Madonna of Charos Chapel.** On August 24, the church's festival day, the dried flowers in the chapel supposedly spring to life.

IONIAN ISLANDS
ΝΗΣΙΑ ΤΟΝ ΙΟΝΙΟΥ

For 400 years, while the rest of Greece was under Turkish rule, the Ionian islands remained relatively free. Their uninvited guests—the Venetians, British, French, and Russians—were milder than the Turks, and more concerned with commerce and construction. Nevertheless, these Wetern powers did leave their imprint. A British protectorate until 1864 and under Italian occupation during World War II, the islands are comparatively wealthy and retain an international flavor. The Ionians' new waves of colonizers are British holidaymakers, Italian villa-renters and ferry-hopping backpackers, none of whom diminish the grace and charm of the islands as they were when Homer described them.

Stretching from the Albanian coast to the southern tip of the Peloponnese, these islands present a disparate collection of landscapes. **Corfu** is green and plump and **Ithaki** nigh skeletal; robust **Cephalonia** variegates its contours and color from one ragged mountain to the next while **Zakinthos** is a dense jungle of vegetation. Lonely **Kythera,** unconnected to the rest of the Ionians by ferry or by association, challenges visitors with its barren, dramatic plateaus.

Ferries connect Corfu with Trieste, Bari, and Ancona in Italy. Both Corfu and Cephalonia have routes to Brindisi in Italy and to Patras on the Greek mainland. Between June and September, ferries travel several times per week to and from Italy and once daily to Patras. Expect to pay 7000-13,000dr for deck-class transport to Italy. Olympic Airways has **flights** from Athens to Cephalonia, Zakinthos, Corfu, and other points in Western Europe. Flights from Athens cost 15,900dr; regularly scheduled intra-European flights to Corfu cost an arm and a leg; in summer, look into nighttime charter flights from London (about £170-190) and Frankfurt. You can reach Zakinthos from Killini on the Peloponnese, and Lefkas by bus from Patras or Preveza. At least one ferry per day leaves Patras for Cephaloni and Ithaki, so moving among these islands, Paxos, and Corfu is easy. Check schedules with one of the harbor agencies or with the tourist police before planning any excursions.

Corfu (Kerkyra) ΚΕΡΚΥΡΑ

> pear follows pear, apple after apple grows, fig after
> fig ...
> —Homer

...and tourist follows tourist. Corfu, whose name comes from the Byzantine word *korufai* (breasts), and so inspired by the two rock fortresses which protected the population in medieval times, now suffers from a double-D onslaught of tourists. But even with its beaches overcrowded and its streets full of hopeful merchants, Corfu nonetheless remains the prettiest Greek island. Traditionally a favorite haunt of European royals and aristocrats, Corfu is the most eclectically international of the Ionians: only here do British palaces sit on an esplanade modeled after Rue de Rivoli in Paris and next to the shuttered alleyways of an ersatz Venice. Royalty ain't dumb: here is everything advantageous to life.

Planes fly into **Corfu Airport,** 2km from Corfu Town. Olympic Airways runs free buses from the airport. You may also catch bus #2 or 3 on the main road (100dr). A taxi ride takes only five minutes. (Before getting in, agree on a fare of around 1000dr.) Pick up a free copy of the *Corfu News,* filled with oodles of useful information, including transportation schedules.

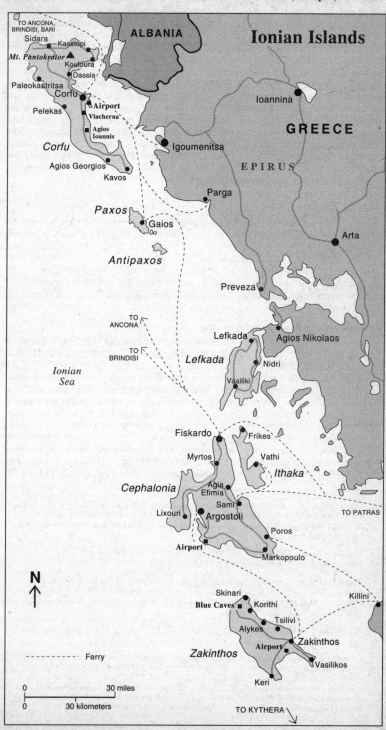

Buses run frequently between Corfu Town and major points on the island (fewer run in the afternoon and on Sun.), and all trips cost under 500dr. Schedules for the main KTEL line are posted on a billboard outside the new office behind Corfu Town's New Fortress, from which the green-and-cream KTEL buses leave. Other buses (blue ones), including those to Kontokali (youth hostel), leave from around Platia Sanrocco—schedules are printed on the signs. The most popular way to see the island is by **moped.** Rental places are everywhere; you shouldn't pay more than 2000dr per day. Make sure the brakes work. You're responsible for any damage to your vehicle, but the rental fee should include third-party liability and property damage insurance. As for **car rentals,** a Fiat Panda goes for 9000-10,000dr with 100km free, plus 20dr per additional km. Make sure quoted prices include the 20% tax. Third party insurance is usually included; full collision insurance costs about 1500dr per day. Despite the absence of traffic off the main roads, some people find hitching a feasible option. Roads are especially deserted during the afternoon **siesta** (2-5pm).

Corfu Town

Corfu Town is the logical base for touring the island; all ferries and most bus services originate here. At the New Port, a barrage of tourist officers greets arrivals, proffering scooters, ferry tickets, and rooms. Apart from this melée, Corfu's two fortresses hulk over the waterfront, still guarding the Old Town. Quieter and more dignified, the narrow lanes near the Spianada (esplanade) and near Sanrocco Sq. present a charming mix of Byzantine, Venetian, and Greek architecture. Despite the numerous souvenir shops and the preponderance of English-speaking tourists, the Old Town retains much of Corfu's traditionalism.

Orientation and Practical Information

Before long, you'll be cursing the Theotokis family. Four of Corfu's main streets are named after members of this clan; you may pass from N. Theotoki St. to M. Theotoki St. to G. Theotoki St. to I. Theotoki St. without even realizing it. Use a map and you'll be fine. On the north coast of town are the **New Port,** which services boats to Patras and the international ferries, and the **Old Port,** where boats leave for Paxos and Igoumenitsa. The New Fortress separates the two ports, behind which sits Corfu's long-distance bus station. The Old Fortress and the **Spianada,** a garden ringed by chic cafés, dominate the eastern shore. To get to the Spianada from the Old Port, follow Arseniou St. along the waterfront (with the water on your left). The Old Town, a befuddling maze of alleys, is at the point of the peninsula. From the New Port, walk left and away from the water on Napoleontos St. and turn left on I. Theotaki. This leads you past **Platia Sanrocco,** the city-bus terminus, and on to **Georgiou Theotoki St.** and the Old Town.

Tourist Police and Greek National Tourist Organization (GNTO): Tel. 302 65 or 375 20, on the northern end of the Spianada, in the Governor's house. Ask for the *Corfu News,* or the *What's on Corfu.* Very helpful and charming staff distributes free map and guide to the town and island. Open Mon.-Sat. 7am-2:30pm.

Municipal Tourist Offices: Tel. 585 09 or 426 01. Across from the new port and to the right. Look for the green "i" symbol. Open April-Oct. 8am-10pm.

Room-Finding Service: Tourist agencies along Arseniou St. from the Old Port to the Old Fortress and along Stratigou St. by the New Port can find you a room in a pension. Many operate without commission and have direct pipelines to cheap lodgings of which the tourist police are unaware. Most open 8:30am-1:30pm, 5:30-9pm.

British Vice Consul: 1 Menekratous (tel. 300 55 or 379 95), down the street from the post office. Open Mon.-Fri. 8am-2pm. Call 392 11 in an emergency.

Currency Exchange: Four banks on G. Theotoki St., near where it narrows and becomes Voulgareos. Open Mon.-Thurs. 8am-2pm, Fri. 8am-1:30pm. Some open in the afternoon in July-Aug., 4-6pm or 5:30-7:30pm, Sat. 8:30am-1pm. **Barclay's Bank,** Platia Sanrocco, open Mon.-Thurs. 8am-2pm, Fri. 8am-1:30pm; July-Aug. also Sat. 10:30am-12:30pm. Try the exchange window at the **airport** (open when planes arrive or depart). Though always obliging, tourist agencies near the Old Port and most hotels charge 10% commission.

American Express: c/o Greek Skies Travel, 20a Kapodistriou St., P.O. Box 24, (tel. 334 10 or 339 10) at the south end of the Spianada. Will hold mail and cash AmEx traveler's checks. Open Mon.-Fri. 8:30am-1:30pm and 5:30-8:30pm, Sat. 8:30am-1:30pm.

Post Office: 19 Alexandros Ave. Open Mon.-Fri. 8am-8pm for stamps and Poste Restante. **Postal Code:** 49100.

OTE: Main office, 9 Mantzarou St., off A. Theotoki St. Open daily 6am-midnight. Smaller offices at Kapodistriou St., on the Esplanade and in mobile white buildings at both Old and New ports. Open daily 8am-10pm. **Telephone Code:** 0661 for Corfu Town, 0662 for South Corfu, 0663 for North Corfu.

Olympic Airways: 20 Kapodistriou St. (tel. 386 94 or -95 or -96; airport 301 80), on the Spianada. Night flights to Athens (at 11:30pm, 45min., 12,000dr). Day flights at 7:30am are more expensive (15,900dr). Open Mon.-Fri. 1am-9pm and Sat.-Sun. 8am-2pm.

Ferries: Book early, especially to Italy; in high season, even deck-class sells out. Agents for the various shipping companies line Xen. Stratigou St., opposite the New Port. Prices vary little among agents, although occasional discounts are offered. Try **Adriatica,** 46 Xen. Stratigou (tel. 380 89) to Brindisi (daily at 9am, 8hr., 8000dr for a deck passage, students 7500dr), and Patras (daily at 7am, and Mon.-Sat. at 10pm, 10-11hr., about 3000dr for deck passage). **Mancan,** 38 Xen. Stratigou (tel. 245 03) sells tickets to Ancona (daily around 8am, 22hr., 12800dr). In addition, ferries leave for Piraeus (2 per week, 16hr., deck passage 6300dr), Bari in Italy (every 2 days, deck passage 7000dr), and numerous other destinations. When traveling to foreign ports be sure to find out if the port tax is included in the price of your ticket.

Buses: KTEL (long-distance), behind the New Fortress Sq. To: Paleokastritsa (13 per day, 45min., 280dr); Glyfada Beach (every hr., 45min., 200dr); Kavos (every hr., 550dr); Kassiopi (9 per day, 400dr); Athens (daily at 8:30am and 6:30pm, 5450dr); and Thessaloniki (daily at 7am, 5350dr). Full schedule posted on the station wall. Buy tickets for Corfu destinations on the bus, all others in the office. A good place to leave luggage. Open 5:30am-8pm.

City Buses: #10 from Platia Sanrocco to Achillion (6 per day), #6 to Benitses (7-8am and 9:30am-10:30pm every hr.), #7 to Dassia (every hour from 9am-11:30pm), #11 to Pelekas (10 per day). Schedule published in *Corfu News.* Buses much less frequent on Sundays.

Car Rental: Agencies along Xen. Stratigou all rent for around 8000dr per day. Hertz and Interrent/Europcar are more expensive. International car rental at **Greek Skies,** 20 Kapodistriou St. Reasonable replacement service for breakdowns at no extra charge. Minimum age 25. Full payment in advance or major credit card required.

Luggage Storage: Several places on Avrami St., directly across from the New Port. 200dr per day. Check access times before leaving your bags.

English Bookstores: Lycoudis, 63 Voulgareos St., 2 doors from the National Bank. The most comprehensive selection. Open Mon., Wed., and Sat. 8:30am-2pm, Tues. and Thurs.-Fri. 8:30am-1:30pm and 5:30-8:30pm.

Laundromats: I. Theotaki St. (tel. 353 04), near Platia Sanrocco. Wash 700dr, dry 300dr. Open 9am-9pm.

Public Toilets: On the harbor at the Old Port; on the Spianada near the bandstand; and in Platia Sanrocco.

Hospital: Corfu General Hospital, Polithroni Kostanda (tel. 458 11, -12, -13, -14, or -15, or 303 33; emergency room 254 00). For a list of foreign language-speaking doctors, call the Medical Association of Corfu at 396 15 or 460 23, or call the GNTO. For an ambulance call 394 03 or 166.

Emergency: Tel. 100.

Accommodations and Camping

Decent, reasonably priced rooms are available in Corfu, but a few cunning local proprietors find all kinds of loopholes in tourist police price regulations. Hotel managers sometimes fill their rooms with camp beds, which they then offer as dorms charging the price for singles. Singles are impossible to find so join forces with another traveler or bargain for a double. Hotels near the water fill up first, and the effectiveness of bargaining diminishes later in the day. Fortunately, prices drop about 100dr per person in off-season, and longer stays are often discounted at the small pensions. Be aware that some hotels may advertise that they are recommended by *Let's Go,* but if they're not listed below, we don't recommend them. Freelance camping is impossible and indubitably illegal.

Youth Hostel Kontokali (HI/IYHF) (tel. 912 02), 4½km north on the main road from the port on the edge of Kontokali Village. Take the #7 Dassia-Kontokali bus from Platia Sanrocco (every hr. until 11:30pm, 20min., 85dr). By taxi about 800dr. The cheapest place to stay on Corfu (800dr per person). No curfew. Inconveniently located for Corfu Town, but near a beach and an array of bars in Kontokali. Town restaurant, well-stocked minimarket, bar, and free swimming pool on the grounds. Management sometimes indifferent about HI/IYHF membership. Reception open 8am-noon and 5-8pm.

Hotel Cyprus, 13 Agion Pateron (tel. 300 32). Walking from the Esplanade to Platia Sanrocco, turn right after the National Bank on Voulgareous and follow the signs. Centrally located in the old town next to the enchanting ruins of a church, Hotel Cyprus offers tidy rooms with bedsheets you could eat off of. The best hotel for its price in Corfu Town. All rooms with shared bath. Singles 4000dr. Doubles 5000dr. Some triples available.

Hotel Constantinoupolis, 11 Zavitsanou St. (tel. 398 26), by the Old Port. Clean rooms, nice view, but noisy atmosphere. Doubles with shared bath 4600dr.

Hotel Crete, 43 N. Theotoki St. (tel. 386 91). Right in the middle of everything and hence a bit noisy. The Venetian architecture and wooden furniture combine to create a romantic ambience. Doubles 4000dr.

Camping: Corfu has several official campsites, and prices are strictly regulated by the local government. All campsites here should charge 600dr per person, 600dr per tent, and 550dr per car. Rates should be about 100dr less in the off-season. **Camping Kontokali** (tel. 912 02), by the HI/IYHF hostel, is the nearest to Corfu Town.

Food

The premier restaurant areas are at the two ends of **N. Theotoki Street,** near the Spianada and by the Old Port. Lunch is served outdoors until 3pm, dinner until 11pm. Because nearly all the restaurants in town are strictly regulated by the tourist police, the prices are fair but the cuisine monotonous. For cheap do-it-yourself fare, go to the open-air **market** on Dessila St., near the base of the New Fortress. Some stalls stay open all afternoon, but arrive around 7:30am for the best selection of goodies. The **Supermarket Spilias,** 13 Solomou St. near the bus station (open Tues. and Thurs.-Fri. 8am-1:30pm and 5:30-8:30pm, Mon., Wed., and Sat. 8:30am-1:45pm) and the **Supermarket Koskinas,** in Platia Sanrocco (open Mon.-Fri. 8am-2pm), have a more than adequate supply of edibles.

To Nautikon, 150 N. Theotoki (tel. 300 09), near the Old Port. As big and friendly as a Golden Retriever. Appetizing food, affordable prices, and 45 years of experience. The delicious *mousaka* (750dr) will impress even palates already tired of this ancient Greek standby. Open April-Oct. daily noon-midnight.

Pizza Pete, 19 Arseniou St. (tel. 223 01), on the waterfront halfway between the Spianada and the Old Port. New owners Takis and Yannis, former waiters of Pete's, carry on the nearly 30-year-old tradition of fine dining. Great grub (entrees 800-1400dr) and a great ocean view. Try the "Pete special" pizza. Open April-Oct. daily 10am-midnight.

Taka Taka, directly beneath the Hotel Cyprus, up the hill from the National Bank on Voulangeos St. *Souvlaki pita*—cheapest meal in town (180dr)—but you might need three. ½ liter of Heineken 200dr. Open daily 7pm-1am.

Restaurant Aegli, (tel. 319 49), on the Spianada. The outdoor tables are an ideal spot to dine on a warm summer's night. Try one of the large, fresh Greek salads (900dr).

Sights

Built by the Venetians in the late 14th century, the **Paleo Frouri** (Old Fortress), east of the Spianada, was once regarded as impregnable. In 1864, however, the British decided otherwise and blew it up before leaving Corfu to the Greeks. Much of the remains are now overgrown and barely accessible. When you cross the moat into the fortress walls, the constant din of Corfu slowly dissipates. A kitschy sound-and-light show accompanied by an opening act of folk dancing plays here nightly. (Fortress open 7am-7pm. Admission 200dr. Sound and light show May-Sept. Mon.-Fri. in English,

Sat. in Greek, Sun. in French, 9:30-10:15pm. Folk dancing May-Sept. Mon.-Sat. 9-9:30pm. Admission to both 600dr, students 400dr)

At the northern end of the Spianada stands the **Palace of St. Michael and St. George.** Unmistakably British, the palace was built as the residence of the Lord High Commissioner. Facing a cricket green where local clubs and visitors from abroad play matches in July, the building now houses the **Museum of Asiatic Art,** an extensive collection of Japanese, Chinese, and Indian wood carvings, silk screens, porcelain figures, and mosaics from the Byzantine basilica in Paleopolis. (Open Tues.-Sat. 8am-3pm, Sun. 9:30am-2:30pm. Admission 500dr, students 300dr.)

The **Archaeological Museum,** 5 Vraila St., on the waterfront south of the Spianada, contains relics of the island's Mycenaean and Classical past: an intimidating **Gorgon** sculpture glowers over the collection. (Open Tues.-Sun. 8:30am-3pm. Admission 400dr, students 200dr.)

Corfu's two most famous churches are the **Church of St. Jason and Sosipater,** and the **Church of St. Spiridon.** The former, named for the pair who brought Christianity to the island, is a 12th-century Byzantine structure located on the way to Mon Repos Beach (continue past the Archaeological Museum along the water front). It dazzles with an array of silver and gold ornaments, medieval paintings, and an impressive ceiling mural. The Church of St. Spiridon, named for the island's patron saint, was built in 1590. Although St. Spiridon had been dead since the 4th century CE, he is said to have appeared in 1716 and shattered the morale of the invading Turks. Following outbreaks of plague in the 17th century, residents of Corfu began parading the silver reliquary containing the remains of the saint around town every Palm Sunday and on the first Sunday of November. In the right light, you can still see his morale-annihilating grin beneath a black shroud behind the glass.

North of N. Theotoki near the Spianada is the **Ionian Bank Building,** with a museum of paper currency. (Open Mon.-Sat. 9am-1pm, Sun. 10am-noon. Free.) Behind the Old Port lies the old **Jewish Quarter** of town. The **synagogue,** on Velissariou St., served a growing Jewish community from its construction in 1537 until 1940, when 5000 Jews were gathered on the Spianada and sent to Auschwitz.

Entertainment

In the evening, parade up and down the Spianada and its adjacent park. But don't get too carried away—cafés along the Spianada charge three times more than cafés in less popular locations. Wander off the main catwalk into the streets of the Old Town. You'll catch the dulcet tones of Corfu's seven music schools practicing simultaneously. The **Pallas Cinema** on A. Theotoki St. near Platia San Rocco and the open air cinema on Marasli St. often screen English language films (about 350dr). The annual **Corfu Festival** in August and September features an international selection of ballet and orchestral music. Check at the tourist office for details.

The east coast of Corfu is awash with **nightclubs,** which cater mainly to the British package holiday-makers. South in Benitses and Kavos, the dancing can sometimes turn to fighting. There is less trouble at the resort towns of Gouvia, Dassia, and Ipsos north of Corfu Town, but here you might find yourself forgetting you are in Greece. In Corfu Town, the clubs start north of the city along the port road, and get more and more non-Greek as you approach the resorts.

Southern Corfu

Some 6km south of Corfu Town, the islet of **Vlacherna** connects to the main island via causeway: take bus #2 (Kanoni) from the Spianada and ask the driver to let you off near Vlacherna (every 30min. until 10pm, 150dr).

Nearby stands **Achilleion Palace,** 9km south of the port of Corfu in the village of **Gastouri.** Eccentric and ostentatious, it was commissioned by Empress Elizabeth of Austria as a summer residence in honor of Achilles and Thetis. Kaiser Wilhelm II of Germany whiled away his summers here, until World War I diverted his attention. The gardens are especially cinematic: the 1981 James Bond fantasia *For Your Eyes Only* was filmed here. On a clear day the view of Mt. Pantokrator in the distance is dazzles the eye. (Open Mon.-Sun. 8am-7pm. Admission 400dr.) The palace becomes a casino at night (tel. 562 10; open 8pm-3am). While in the area, do what most don't—visit the intriguing little traditional village of Gastouri. To get there, take bus #10 from Platia Sanrocco (6 per day, every 3hr., 30min.).

Farther south is the rowdy little tourist/fishing village of **Benitses,** where you can see the remains of a Roman bath house and a 3rd-century CE Roman villa. Bus #6 runs to Benitses from Platia Sanrocco (every hr., 30min., 180dr). At the lively waterfront bars and discos, you can shoot pool, watch videos, or simply cruise. At night, be forewarned that the brawling and dancing at some of the bars gets a little out of control. Most have happy hours and infamous all-you-can-drink specials. Benitses's beach is especially crowded. The **Shell Museum** offers hungover revelers a soothing way to pass the time (open Tues.-Sat. 10am-7pm).

Still farther south, **Agios Ioannis** has a less crowded beach. Take bus #11 from Platia Sanrocco (about every 2hr.). Pleasant but shallow, **Kavos Beach** lies at the southern tip of the island, 47km from Corfu Town (vaguely hourly buses from behind the New Fortress). Over on the southwest coast stretches the remote, sandy beach at **Agios Georgios** (2-3 buses per day from behind the New Fortress, 1hr., 380dr). The nearby **Vitalades Beach** is one of Corfu's few deserted spots.

Northern Corfu

The tourist industry has damaged the first 20km of the coastline north of Corfu Town. The resort towns of **Dassia, Ipsos,** and **Pirgi** consist of a long chain of hotels, discos, and boutiques. Official campsites are plentiful in this area: Dassia has **Karda Camping** (tel. 935 95); Ipsos offers **Ideal Camping** (tel. 932 43) and **Corfu Camping Ipsos** (tel 935 79), while Pirgi has **Paradissos Camping** (tel. 935 58). These campsites cost 600dr per person, 600dr per tent, and 550dr per car. All have markets on the premises, and hot showers are included. For nightlife, head to any of these towns; for less spoiled country, venture farther north.

The Kassiopi **bus** serves this whole coast, leaving from the KTEL station and stopping at every hamlet along the way (9 per day, 2 on Sun., 1¼hr., 400dr); unless you're a bus aficionado, renting a moped is best. Past Pirgi, the road begins to wind below steep cliffs. **Mt. Pantokrator,** on your left, towers 1000m above, and the cliffs on the right loom dramatic as Albania comes into view across the straits. After passing through Nissaki and Gimari, you'll eventually reach **Kouloura,** 28km north of Corfu, with its Venetian manor-house, pebbled beach, marina, and matchless *taverna*. The right fork to **Kalami** meanders down to a sandier beach where there are rooms to let (July-Aug. doubles up to 4500dr). The small white house of author Lawrence Durrell may still be seen. The walk to Kalami or Kouloura from the main road takes no more than 15 minutes.

Kassiopi is the next town, 36km north of Corfu and just 2km across the sea from the Albanian port of Agia Saranda. Greeks still like to warn you that if you swim too far into Albanian waters you might be shot on sight. The town, founded in 300 BCE by General Pyrrhus of Epirus, vaunts an incredible rock beach that stretches east along the coast for several kilometers. For a thrill, try parasailing (4000dr) or swashbuckle through the ruins of the 9th-century **fortress** which the Venetians destroyed in 1836, overlooking the rock beach and the **Panayia Kassiotropi Church.** The **Kassiopi Travel Service** (tel. 813 88), near the bus stop, can help you find rooms. Expect to pay 3500-4000dr for doubles in high season. The innkeepers here deplore one-night stays and often charge a premium for them. While eating in Kassiopi, remember that a waterfront location raises only price, not quality. From the bus stop, head inland for cheap if unremarkable galleries of gastronomy. For nightlife, try the **Just S.** disco near the bus stop. *Bouzouki* down at the **Kan Kan Bouzouki Club,** a 15-minute walk along the road back to Corfu (shows Wed. and Sat.-Sun.).

Northwest from Kassiopi on the main road, the beach resorts of **Rhoda Chanin** and **Sidari** provide excellent camping and sandy beaches enveloped by cliffs. A 5th century BCE temple has been found here as well. Try **Rhoda Beach Camping** (tel. (0663) 931 20) or just buy supplies at the market here, and freelance. Catch a sunset at **Perou-**

lades; the 3-km walk there takes you past farms and fruit trees. By the shore hides the surprisingly deserted **Sunset Restaurant.** The bus to Sidari leaves from behind the New Fortress (11 per day, 2 on Sun., 400dr). In Sidari, you can hire a motorboat for a daytrip to the tiny islands of **Othoni, Erikoussa,** and **Mathraki** (1hr., 1500dr), inhabited exclusively by fishers, farmers, and their crops. For more information, inquire at **Sellos Travel** (tel. 312 39).

To get even farther off the tourist trail, explore the mountain villages in the northern part of the island. A bus from Kassiopi occasionally runs to the village of **Loutses,** passing the little hamlet of **Perithia,** near Mt. Pantokrator. Moped travel allows you to revel in the rugged scenery, but gas stations in this area are few and far between. The station nearest Paleokastritsa is 15km back toward Corfu Town on the main road.

Western Corfu

Swimming here is like being trapped inside a kaleidoscope: crystalline water shifts from turquoise to aqua to blue to turquoise *ad infinitum.* A favorite with tourists, the **Paleokastritsa** ("Old Castle"), sits amid some of the loveliest scenery in Greece, with six small coves and sea caves jutting into the headlands. The 13th-century fort of **Angelokastro** sits above the town, while the natural balcony, **Bella Vista,** rests halfway up. Jutting out over the sea is the chaste white **Panayia Theotokos Monastery** with a quaint collection of Byzantine icons. (Open April-Oct. daily 7am-8pm. Dress appropriately. Expected donation 250dr.) Be sure to come as early as possible; by mid-morning it is a jangling mess of cameras and tour buses. **Buses** run to Paleokastritsa from behind the New Fortress (13 per day, 45min., 280dr). Travelers willing to hunt can find affordable lodgings: wander up the footpath to Lakones and comb the olive groves for inexpensive pensions. **International Camping** (tel. (0663) 412 04), 3km from town on the main road from Corfu, has a market and restaurant, but the sea is quite a distance. (Open mid-May to Oct.) **Le Pirate** offers good food for slightly less predatory prices than its neighbors. There is a **market** on your right as you come into town, about 300m before you hit the main beach.

South of Paleokastritsa, the swinging hilltop village of **Pelekas** is an excellent western base with a youthful atmosphere and a fine beach. Kaiser Wilhelm II used to watch the sun set over the Ionian Sea from a small hill outside of town. In town, **Jimmi's** and **Alexandros's** pensions offer rooms with little character for the same price. The street to the left of the church is lined with houses that rent doubles (about 3500dr). **Lina's Travel Service** (tel. 945 80) in town, rents mopeds (2000dr per day), exchanges money, and can help you find a room. (Open 8:30-11pm.)

The western exposure and elevation of Pelekas offer an ideal vantage for rejoicing with the sunsets over whitewashed villages in the hillsides. **Pelekas Beach,** a 30-minute downhill walk from town, attracts a large number of backpackers. The beach is popular with freelance campers, as accommodations are nonexistent and the police don't generally hassle sleepers. Don't attempt to make the harrowing, hairpin journey by moped—if you survive the dicey descent, you won't be able to make it back up. Bus #11 runs to Pelekas Town from Platia Sanrocco (10 per day, 30min.). **Glyfada Beach,** 5km up the coast from Pelekas Town, is served directly by the Glyfada bus from behind the New Fortress (every hr., 30min., 200dr), and as a result is far more touristed. Both beaches, crisply bracketed by scrubby cliffs, are remarkably shallow. Single women should watch out for smooth-talking Greek *kamakia* (literally, "harpoons") who cruise Glyfada, occasionally making a move.

A little north of Glyfada and accessible via dirt path off the main Pelekas road lie the isolated beaches of **Moni Myrtidon** and **Myrtiotissa,** extolled by Lawrence Durrell as the most beautiful beaches in the world. A section of sand at Myrtiotissa is the island's unofficial nudist beach. Everything here is very casual, although once in a while the local monks from the Monastery of Our Lady of the Myrtles complain to the police, who reluctantly bring offending nudists to court. Above these beaches in the olive trees is the small restaurant **Myrtiotissa.** You can camp here for free and use the bathroom if you buy breakfast (650dr) and clean your site when you're done camping.

Agios Gordios, with its sheer cliffs and impressive rock formations, is the setting for the **Pink Paradise,** also known as the Pink Palace (tel. (0661) 531 03 or 531 04). Run by the Greek George Grammenos, his charming sister Magda and their energetic crew of Brits, Yanks, Canucks, and Aussies, this establishment has attained legendary status among English-speaking travelers. This hotel/summer camp/frathouse/non-stop party includes thirteen buildings which often hold more than 700 people. Located on a fine sandy beach, you'll also find a pool-sized jacuzzi into which as many as 352 young bodies have been squeezed, daily volleyball tournaments, laundry services at 1800dr per load, a long distance phone service, an international money exchange, and a safety deposit service. Optional activities include parasailing, snorkeling, jet skiing and cliff diving (1500-3000dr). The free disco grooves all night. You'll either love the Palace or loathe it. (Rooms 3200dr per person or $17. Terrace cot 2500dr. Price includes two meals per day. Vegetarian options always available.)

Paxos (Paxi) ΠΑΞΟΙ

According to legend tiny Paxos, about 10km long and 3 wide, harbors 20 secrets. From the deserted village of Vasilatika to the hidden cavern of Ipapanti, which concealed the Greek submarine *Papanikolis* in World War II, the island hints at treasure ripe for discovery. But there are two secrets every visitor should know: first, the island's faucets offer only *glyfa* water, a mixture of rain and sea water that in times of drought is virtually indistinguishable from *eau de Mediterranean* (bottled drinking water is readily available); and second, in August, Paxos soaks up Italian tourists and its prices bloat accordingly. The island becomes what Greeks call *panakrivo*—super-expensive—and it may be impossible to find a room for under 7000dr if you can find one at all.

Paxos is so small that you can tour the whole island in a couple of hours. Two waterfront agencies in Gaios rent **Vespas** (3500dr per day). Test your brakes first, make sure you have a rear-view mirror, and diligently check the bike for damage so that you are not later charged for scratches or more serious wounds you did not inflict. Buses run from Gaios to diminutive **Lakka** (Mon.-Sat. 6 per day, 160dr), where you'll find some *dhomatia,* a wonderful beach, and a Byzantine church. A better way to see the island's offerings is by boat trip from Gaios. On the west coast are the **Mousmouli Cliffs** and the **Seven Sea Caves.** According to Homer, one of the caves, Ipapando, was Poseidon's home and was decorated à la Tammy Bakker's faucets with walls of glittering gold. (Boats leave daily at 10am, 2000dr). **Panayia,** an islet on the east coast, houses a religious shrine honoring the Virgin Mary; on the Feast of the Assumption (Aug. 15), visitors from other islands and the mainland make a pilgrimage. Many tourists view Paxos solely as a stopping-point on the way to **Antipaxos,** Paxos's little sister island (express boats leave hourly, breaking for siesta, from the main square in Gaios; round-trip 1000dr). With white, sandy beaches stroked by sumptuous waves, Antipaxos is the Caribbean island of the Ionians.

Most ferries to Paxos dock at the **New Port,** a 15-minute walk around the harbor from Gaios (with the water on the right). Building restrictions have prevented major hotel construction, but you should be able to find some *dhomatia.* Locals often wait at the dock to entice tourists into their homes. Agree on the price and length of stay prior to accepting the room—some proprietors will refuse accommodations if you only plan to spend one or two nights. Almost all rooms are doubles (7000dr in peak season; salty showers included), but resourceful travelers can usually find makeshift singles for less.

The family-run **Little Spiros's Restaurant,** by the stone tables just off the square, serves authentic Greek fare in lively, welcoming surroundings. Excellent fried squid 800dr. **Rex's Taverna,** 1 block from the waterfront, is another tempting choice (yogurt with honey 300dr, tangy *tzatziki* 350dr.) The main square at Gaios stays lively for most of the night. For concentrated excitement, trek out to the **Disco Phoenix,** just behind the concrete mixers of the New Port, or follow the left fork out of Gaios to **Disco Costello.**

Paxos is most easily reached by **ferry** from Parga on the mainland (2 per day, 1½hr., 1250dr) or Corfu to the north (daily, 3hr., 1758dr). Daytrips are available from Corfu or Parga and may be a good option in high season if you want to avoid the piratical room prices on Paxos. For more information, contact any of the waterfront travel agencies in Parga or Corfu Town. While on Paxos, you can get more details from **Paxos Holidays** (tel. (0662) 312 69 or 313 81),one block north of the main square in Gaios. They can help find you a room, apartment, or villa. You can **exchange money** here at National Bank rates. (Open May-Sept. 9:30am-1:30pm and 5:30-10pm.) The town **OTE** is located just next door. (Open Mon.-Sat. 7:30am-11pm and Sun. 9am-2pm, 5-10pm.) Paxos's **telephone code** is 0662.

Lefkas (Lefkada) ΛΕΥΚΑΔΑ

Separated from Greece by a 50m canal, Lefkas resembles mainland Greece shrunken and transmuted into a floating resort. Unfortunately, hyper-commercialization has marred many of the island's most beautiful settings. The hospitality of Lefkada's inhabitants swells the farther you travel away from the tourist-clogged northeastern edge of the island.

According to Thucydides, Lefkas (Greek for white rock) was part of the mainland until 427 BCE when inhabitants dug a canal. The modern bridge, which connects Lefkas to the mainland, has only recently replaced the archaic chain-operated ferry built by Emperor Augustus.

Ferries link Lefkas with Ithaka and Cephalonia to the south. One boat shuffles from Fiscardo on Cephanolia to Vasiliki on Lefkas (2 per day, 20min. 600dr); another sails from Frikes on Ithaki to Nidri on Lefkas (1 per day, 2hr., 693dr).

Lefkas Town (Lefkada)

Lefkas Town is situated directly across from the mainland. From the bus station on the waterfront (tel. 223 64), **buses** cross the canal to Athens (4 per day, 5½hr., 4100dr) and Aktion (4 per day, 250dr). To reach Preveza, take the ferry from Aktion across the mouth of Amvrakikos bay (every 30min., 10min., 70dr). To get from Preveza to Lefkas Town, take the ferry to Aktion, then a bus to Lefkas (4 per day, last bus 4:10pm). The 21km journey is difficult to hitch; taxis cost 4000-5000dr. The local island buses run to: Nidri (9 per day, 30min., 300dr), Agios Nikitas (5 per day, 20min., 200dr), Poros (2 per day, 45min., 500dr), and Vasiliki (4 per day, 1hr., 600dr). The excursion boat **Nidri Star** runs daily cruises visiting Cephalonia, Ithaki, and Skorpios (3000dr).

The first alleyway running inland from the harbor in Lefkas Town becomes **Dörpfeld Street,** the main street, lined with tourist services. (Wilhelm Dörpfeld was the archaeologist who unsuccessfully tried to identify Lefkas as Homer's Ithaka.) There is no GNTO, but many travel agents speak some English and can provide information about the island and the modes of transport available. For budget travel try **Lefkas Travel** (tel. 224 30) on Dörpfeld St., **Dana Travel** (tel. 246 50), **Melas Travel** (tel. 225 38 or 229 05), or the **tourist police** (tel. 223 46) on Dörpfeld St. The **Agricultural Bank** stands opposite the Hotel Patras off the same street, on Platia Antistasis. (Open Mon.-Thurs. 8am-2pm, Fri. 8am-1pm.) The **post office** is at 1 Stratigou Melas St. (open Mon.-Fri. 7am-3pm). For the **OTE,** turn right off Stratigou Melas to Pataneromenis St., head back toward the beginning of town, and look for the tower. (Open daily 6am-midnight.) The **postal code** is 31100; the **telephone code** is 0645.

The super-clean **Hotel Patras** (tel. 223 59), is next to the Agricultural Bank in the Platia Antistasis. (Singles 3300dr. Doubles 5500dr. Triples 6800dr. Shared baths. Hot showers 200dr. Open June 10-Sept. 10.) These rooms fill up quickly in high season. If you're stranded, ask at a travel company for a *dhomatia* (doubles average 5000-6000dr). The jolly owner makes for a right good time at the popular, expensive **Taverna Pyrofani.** Also try **Regentos,** right off the main square on Dimarxou Verrioti St., about 2 blocks down on the left. (Meals around 700dr; open daily 7:30pm-2am.) Frolic through the famous **Folklore Festival,** now in its 35th year, in the first and third weeks of August. (Details from Lefkas Travel, tickets about 500dr.)

Around the Island

While Lefkas Town has no sandy beaches, the northern half of the west coast offers miles of deserted white pebbles and clean water. Rent a moped (about 2500dr per day), and follow the signs for Kathisma. The best stretch lies north of **Agios Nikitas.** Buses leave from Lefkas Town for Ag. Nikitas (5 per day, 150dr). The road there also leads to the monastery **Moni Faneromenis,** which provides a sweeping view of the ocean. Follow the footpath through the woods for a pick-up game of basketball with the students at the monastery's school. Michael Jordan look out.

Nidri, a strip of garish tourist agencies and tacky cafés, ensnares unwary travelers solely because it is the last stop of the otherwise delightful Frikes-Nidri ferry. **Buses** from Nidri go to Lefkas (9 per day, 30min., 300dr). Rooms to let are scattered along the main and virtually only street, parallel to the waterfront. In July and August, when the entire island slumps under the burgeoning weight of tourists, rooms are always full, and prices inevitably high (doubles 5000-6000dr and up). The self-explanatory **Beautiful View** pension (tel. 923 61), along the main street to the left from the ferry, offers doubles for 5000dr (with shared baths) and will crowd beds onto their balcony for you when rooms are full (900dr, showers included). The **post office** (open Mon.-Fri. 7:30am-2:30pm) and **OTE** (open Mon.-Fri. 8:30am-12:30pm and 5:30-9:30pm) are on the main street, occasionally referred to as Center St. An additional, temporary OTE office opens in the summer (walk north on Center St.; open Mon.-Sat. 9:30am-1:10pm and 6-10pm, Sun. 9am-2pm). On the road from Nidri to Lefkas rests **Camping Episkopos** (tel. 230 43 or 713 88, 500dr per person, 400dr per tent). To escape the pervasive manufactured appeal of Nidri, climb the 5km to **Neochori** at dusk. Three km south is the tiny village of **Vliho,** accessible by bus from Lefkas (9 per day, 150dr), with a striking church (proper dress required) in an idyllic setting of wildflowers and cypress trees. **Vasiliki,** at the southern tip of Lefkas Island, crowds up against the waterfront and the slightly littered pebble beach. Smaller and currently less touristed than Nidri, Vasiliki is growing more and more popular with the young international watersports crowd. Touted as one of the finest windsurfing beaches in the world, Vasiliki is usually graced with consistent gentle winds in the morning, which rise to steady force-five gales in the afternoon for the pleasure of experts (and attention-starved poseurs). Try the **Vasiliki Club** (tel. 315 88), near the campground, for board rentals.

Vasiliki has a tiny **post office** and currency exchange (open Mon.-Fri. 8am-2pm). The rooms above the mini-market are clean and price includes kitchen use. (Doubles 2500dr.) **Camping Vasiliki Beach** (tel. 313 08 or 313 35), with a cafeteria, mini-market, and bar, proudly advertises its toilets as "superbly decorated" (700dr per person, tents available for 700dr).

At the southernmost tip of the island there is a **lighthouse** built on the site of the Temple of Lefkadas Apollo. Worshipers of Apollo exorcised evil with an annual sacrifice here. The victim, usually a criminal or a mentally ill person thought to be possessed, was thrown into the sea from the cliffs. Live birds were tied to the victim's arms and legs for popular amusement as well as for aerodynamic advantages. It was also from these 70m cliffs that the ancient poet Sappho leapt to her death when Phaon rejected her love. The cliff, called "Sappho's Leap," is known in Lefkas as *Kavos tis Kiras* (Cape of the Lady).

Cephalonia (Kefallonia) ΚΕΦΑΛΛΩΝΙΑ

Arid Cephalonia lacks the natural attractions of its fertile neighbors in the Ionian Sea. The west and east coasts are generally steep and rocky, and the inland areas are forbiddingly mountainous. When the Germans invaded in 1943, 9000 Italian soldiers occupying the island mutinied and resisted their Nazi "allies" for seven days. Only 33 Italians survived. In contrast to many of the other Ionian islands which have been home to vacationers since Roman times, Cephalonia, with its rugged countryside, has remained relatively touristless. Cephalonia's dandy sandy beaches along the south coast and unusual caverns near Sami are ideal for a stress-free vacation.

A flotilla of **ferries** links Cephalonia with other ports. From **Sami**, boats sail to: Ithaki (3 per day, 1¼hr., 321dr); Zakinthos (2 per day; 585dr); Patras (every day at 9am, about 1500dr); and Corfu (Fri., 5hr.). From **Agios Efimia**, service links Cephalonia with Astakos on the mainland (2 per day, 3½hr., about 900dr). From **Argostoli** boats shuttle back and forth to Killini on the mainland (2 per day, 1784dr). Ferries also leave **Fiskardo** for Ithaki (1 per day, 1¼hr., 693dr). Check current times with one of the many port travel agencies in Sami or Argostoli; the Marketou Travel/Strintzis Line office in Sami (tel. (0664) 220 55) is exceptionally helpful. **Olympic Airways** (tel. (0671) 288 08 or 288 81), 1 R. Vergoti St. in Argostoli, connects Argostoli with Athens (at least 2 flights per day, 11,600dr). **Buses** (tel. (0671) 233 64 or 222 76) link Argostoli, Sami, Fiskardo, Agia Efimia, Poros, and Skala (see Argostoli). The tourist office can provide you with a complete schedule. Cephalonia's **postal codes** are 28080 (Sami) and 28100 (Argostoli); **telephone codes** are 0674 (Sami), and 0671 (Argostoli).

Sami

A small town on a harbor surrounded by lush green hills, Sami stays quiet during the day, offering an ethereal small pebble beach. By night Sami waxes romantic to the glimmer of lighted ships in the harbor.

You can exchange money at the **bank** on Sami's waterfront (open Mon.-Fri. 8am-2pm) or at most of the travel agencies. The blue and white Hotel Kyma, 2 blocks from the ferry landing, dominates Sami's main square. I. Metaxa Street, which bears right as you face the hotel, leads to the **post office** (open Mon.-Fri. 7:30am-2pm). The **OTE** (open Mon.-Fri. 7:30am-10pm) is opposite the cathedral, near the **police station** (open 24 hrs.). There is no official tourist office, but the police may be able to answer your questions. The **Marketou Travel/Strinzis Line Office** in Sami (tel. (0674) 220 55) is also very helpful.

Accommodations in Sami cost up to 50% more in July and August. Try the **Hotel Kyma** (tel. 220 64) in the town square. Many of the clean rooms here offer spectacular views and cool breezes. (Singles with shared bath 3200dr. Doubles with private bath 6500dr.) The **Hotel Ionion** (tel. 220 35), near the cathedral, is comparable in price and quality. (Doubles 4200dr, with private bath 4800dr). The **Hotel Melissani** (tel. 224 64), several blocks back from the water on the left side of town as you face inland, offers singles (5000dr), doubles (6000dr), and spectacular views of the harbor and surrounding hills (free). The rooms above the **Riviera Restaurant** (tel. 222 46), on the waterfront, go quickly in summertime. (Doubles with private bath 5000dr.) **Caravomilos Beach Camping** (tel. 216 80) is just off the beach, 700m to your right while facing inland. The affable management offers laundry facilities, a mini-market, tennis and ping-pong. At night head to the **Disco Arocaria** (tel. 226 51; open midnight-3am), just 300m from the campground.

The caves of **Melissani** and **Drograti,** two sites near Sami, impress both troglodytes and surface dwellers. Melissani, the more impressive cave, can be reached by foot from Sami (30min.). Follow I. Metaxa and turn right at the sign for Agia Efimia, then follow the signs just past the village of Caravomilos. At the lake, guides punt about the two large caverns flooded with sparkling turquoise water and studded with lichen-covered stalactites. For best viewing, go when the sun is high, as the lake has no artificial lights. (Open until nightfall. Admission 400dr. A polite tip is expected.) To reach Drograti, 4km from Sami, head inland on the road to Argostoli and follow the signs. (Open until nightfall. Admission 200dr.) Just 10km north of Sami at the other end of the bay is the pretty harbor town of **Agia Efimia** (3 buses per day from Sami).

Argostoli

The capital of Cephalonia, Argostoli is a bustling town, whose palm tree-lined streets are regularly jammed with traffic. Argostoli hosts an international **singing festi-**

val in late August. On the night of August 15, the nearby village of **Omala** hosts a festival and a vigil in the saint's church. Due east of Argostoli is the monastery **Agios Gerasimos,** in which one lucky monk's preserved corpse lies in state; the town goes wild on the saint's namedays (Oct. 20 and Aug. 16). Contact the tourist office for more information. The town also has an excellent **Archaeological Museum** (tel. 283 00) that should reopen in 1993.

From the Archaeological Museum in the square (see below) turn left onto R. Vergote St. and continue 2 blocks to reach Cargialenios Library, which houses the **Historical and Folk Museum.** This museum is crammed with household belongings and knick-knacks from the 19th century. Argostoli's French coffee cups, English top hats, and antique dolls all create a picture of confident and careful luxury. Best of all are the photographs of Argostoli during the last century, including shots of the huge earthquake of 1953 and the ensuing reconstruction. (Open Mon.-Sat. 8:30am-2:30pm. Admission 400dr.)

The Venetian **Castle of St. George,** 9km southeast of Argostoli, rests on a hill overlooking the village of Travliata. Chug along the road to Skala and turn right when the road splits. A bus travels to the site (3 per day, 10min., 100dr). From the battlements you can view the very same panorama that inspired Lord Byron, a man dangerous to emulate. (Open Tues.-Sun. 8:30am-3pm. Free.) To swim at **Lassi,** one of the island's best sandy beaches, follow the road leading from the town to the airport. There are several options for exploring more of the island. Boats leave regularly for **Lixouri,** in the center of the western peninsula (every hr., 30min., 200dr). Once home to the satiric poet Lascaratos, Lixouri offers miles and miles of practically tourist-free coastline. You can rent **mopeds** at several places in Lixouri, and **buses** make it to most points on the peninsula.

A few beaches and interesting towns dot the island south of Argostoli. One of the best beaches is at **Ormos Lourda,** right in the middle of the south coast; closer to Argostoli is **Platis Gialos** (7 per day, 30min., 100dr). You can also visit one of Byron's hometowns—though his house no longer exists—at **Metaxata,** or see **Kourkoumela-ta,** a village completely restored by a Greek tycoon after the 1953 earthquake. While here, check out the comfortable **Hotel Kourkoumi,** (tel. 416 45), which offers doubles with private baths and breakfast for 4000dr. **Poros,** on the southeast coast, is like Argostoli but has a beach; *dhomatia* are everywhere. Buses run from Argostoli (5 per day, 1½hr., 500dr).

Accommodations are expensive in Argostoli. The **Hotel Parthenon** (tel. 222 46), a spiffy white building on a small side street left of the post office, offers sunny balconies and doubles for 4500dr (shared bath). The **Chara Hotel** (tel. 224 27), located a bit farther from the port on Devosetou St. (3½ blocks from the Gephra bridge) provides similar accommodations for 3600dr (shared bath). The **Hotel Allegro** (tel. 222 68) on Xoida St., 1½ blocks inland from the bus station, offers simple rooms and friendly managers. (Peak season doubles with shared baths 5000dr). The **Argostoli Beach Campground** (tel. 234 87), located just 1½ km from town, is another convenient option (open April-Oct.).

The restaurant **E. Kalafatis,** 144 Metaxa St., (tel. 226 27) 100m to your left on the waterfront as you leave the bus station, offers Greek salads at 600dr and omelettes at 350dr. Or try the **Diana,** (tel. 225 20) next door.

The **bus station** (tel. 222 76), a safe place to leave luggage, is on the waterfront. (Open 7am-8pm.) Buses head to: Fiskardo (2 per day, 600dr); Skala (3 per day, 460dr); Poros (5 per day, 500dr); Assos (1 per day, 460dr); Kourkoumelata (5 per day, 110dr); Agios Efimia (2 per day, 420dr); and Sami (5 per day, 300dr). Buses to Argostoli meet most of the **ferries** arriving in Sami (5 per day, 1hr.). The bus winds quixotically around hairpin turns, treating passengers to glorious mountain vistas, screaming engines, and high blood pressure.

The excellent **GNTO** office (tel. 222 48) at the port gives free maps and offers candid advice on accommodations, restaurants and beaches in the area. The office also has a list of rooms to let (open Mon.-Sat. 8am-10pm). Also pick up a copy of the *Kefalonian Tourist News*. To reach the **post office** (open Mon.-Fri. 7:30am-2pm), walk two blocks inland from the port to D. Konstantinou, the town's main street, and turn right.

Two blocks down, across from the church, is **Petratos,** stuffed with foreign newspapers and magazines. (Open Mon.-Sat. 8am-1pm and 5-9pm, Sun. 8am-noon.) Go one block farther and you'll hit the square and the **Argostolian Archaeological Museum.** Look behind the museum for the **Municipal Tourist Office** (tel. 228 47) with a cordial English-speaking staff and plenty of brochures. (Open March-Oct. daily 9am-1pm, 6-10pm.) On the uphill edge of the square you'll find the **OTE** (open 6am-midnight). Argostoli's **telephone code** is 0671. **Banks** are sprinkled along the waterfront and Konstantinou St. (open Mon.-Thurs. 8am-2pm, Fri. 8am-1:30pm). **Myrtos Rent-a-Car** (tel. 242 30) on the waterfront rents cars starting at 11,500dr per day. **CBR Travel and Tourism** (tel. 227 70) on Valianou St. near the main square rents Vespas for about 9000dr for 3 days. (open 8am-10pm). The **Olympic Airways** office is on 7 R. Vergoti St. (288 08 or 288 81). The **tourist police** at 52 Metaxa St. (tel. 222 00), to the right of the bus station, speak little English. (Open 24 hrs.)

Around the Island

Cliffs plunging into the sea adorn the coastal road north from Argostoli or Sami to the village of Fiskardo. The beaches of **Agia Kyriaki** and **Myrtos** are generally serene. Signposts on the main road after the hamlet of Divarata advertise Myrtos, but swim cautiously there: the undertow can be powerful and sudden. About 4km up the road rest the sweet-smelling gardens of **Assos,** joined by a narrow isthmus to an island with a Venetian prison-fortress. A daily bus from Argostoli departs at 2pm, returning the next day at 6:45am (460dr); the half-hour walk from the main road is a challenge. Around the bend from the Pension Geramia, across from the flaking pink church, is a small *dhomatia.* The bargainable singles (1000dr) and doubles (1500dr) are more quaint than comfortable, with stucco walls and a wooden barrel shower. More modern doubles go for 1600dr at the **Snack Bar Assos,** up the last street before the dock turns.

The road north ends at **Fiskardo,** the only town on the island left undamaged by the 1953 earthquake and thus the only remaining example of 18th- and 19th-century Cephalonian architecture. Once called Panoramos, the town was rather magnanimously renamed after Robert Guiscard, a Norman, who died here in 1085 while attempting to conquer the town. A ruined Norman church visible from the harbor is believed to antedate Robert by some 800 years. Alongside the dilapidated old Venetian lighthouse await pine-sheltered campsites. The **café** toward the bus stop rents rooms (doubles 2500dr). Inquire here about excursions to Ithaki. The **Panormos** is Fiskardo's only hotel (tel. 513 40; doubles 4000dr, showers included). The **Restaurant Fiskardo,** right along the harbor, serves the tasty local specialty *kreatopita* (meat pie). (Open noon-midnight.) In many respects, Fiskardo is unbeatable, with its beach ½km out of town on the road back to Argostoli, and flat rocks for sunbathing. Two **buses** per day arrive from both Sami and Argostoli.

On August 15, an unusual and spooky festival in the village of **Markopoulo** celebrates the Assumption of the Blessed Virgin Mary. Celebrants hold an all-night church liturgy. According to legend, during the service hundreds of small harmless snakes with black crosses on their heads appear and crawl all over the icons.

Ithaka (Ithaki) IΘAKH

The legendary home of Odysseus, Ithaki boasts an impressive reputation and a somewhat milder geography. Spare seaside villages and unspoiled coves encircle the mountains where Penelope waited faithfully for her husband. Ithaki offers little to do, but it's a wonderful place for doing little.

Getting here will be much easier for you than it was for Odysseus—the web of **ferries** around the Ionian islands enmeshes Ithaki. Boats run back and forth from Nidri on Lefkas (1 per day, 2½hr., 693dr); to Frikes on Ithaki; Agios Efimia on Cephalonia (1 per day, 1hr., 719dr); to Vathi on Ithaki; Astakos on the mainland (1 per day, 2hr., 798dr); and to Patras on the mainland (1 per day, 6hr., 2050dr). In addition, a ferry leaves Vathi on Ithaki every two days at 1am for Brindisi, Italy, stopping along the way in Corfu and Igoumenitsa (deck passage 14,000dr). Be sure to check boat schedules at your port of departure. **Vathi** (Greek for "deep") is the main port and the largest town on the island (population 2000). The town horseshoes around the edge of a long, natural harbor (the largest such harbor in all of Greece) and is almost completely circumscribed by mountains. The casual atmosphere here is a welcome change from the frenetic resortiness of neighboring Lefkas. In the evening, the town's cats, children, and scooters all carom around the main square with equal disregard for passersby. Shops and tourist services control the waterfront, at the far right-hand corner of the horseshoe as you face the town. There's no GNTO office here, but the tourist agencies can be of help. **Polyctor Tours** (tel. 331 20) is the most helpful (open daily 9am-10pm; in Sept.-June, Mon.-Sat. 9am-1pm and 5-8pm). The professional staff here can help you find a room. The average peak season room price in Vathi is around 6000-7000dr per night, although there are a few with shared baths starting as low as 3000dr. **Fanis Tours** (tel. 321 00), just around the corner from Polyctor Tours, also provides precise information. The **Ionian Lines** office (tel. 321 45), opposite the ferry landing, keeps somewhat irregular hours, but is open whenever boats come in. Nestled one block in from the corner of the harbor near Polyctor Tours is the **National Bank of Greece** (open Mon.-Fri. 8am-2pm). The **post office** is on the main square (open Mon.-Fri. 7:30am-2pm). The **OTE** sits on the water next to the chunky Hotel Mentor (open Mon.-Sat. 7:30am-3:10pm). Loads of **scooter-rental** places charge about 2500dr per day for a motorbike. Bargain furiously for any vehicle you rent, especially in the off-season, as no prices are fixed. The **bookstores** on either side of the bank sell English-language reading material ranging from Homer to *Beverly Hills 90210* fan magazines. Ithaki's **postal code** is 28300; its **telephone code** is 0674.

The recently renovated **Hotel Odysseus** (tel. 323 81), a two minute walk from the ferry landing with the harbor on your right offers doubles at 7000dr. If you wander up Odysseus St. you'll come across some cheaper rooms to let. An illegal, although usually tolerated, option is freelance **camping** on the beach under the eucalyptus trees. To save a few *drachmae* on food, continue about 1½km to the deserted side of the harbor opposite the ferry landing, where you'll find cheaper feederies. Try **Gregory's Taverna,** which serves fresh fish, pizza, Greek specialties, and local wines outdoors on the waterfront. (Open April-Oct. daily 8am-midnight.) You can also rent small motorboats in front of Gregory's for 7000dr. In the center of town, 1 block back from the water and across from the scooter rental place, is **Taverna To Trexantiri,** frequented by locals (stuffed tomatoes 700dr).

Vathi is not just another pretty face; a few of its sights are worthwhile. The **Vathi Archaeological Museum** is small but free (Open Mon.-Fri. 9am-2pm). Those with poetic imaginations will want to make the 45-minute climb up to the **Cave of the Nymphs,** where Odysseus hid the treasure the Phaeacians bestowed upon him. To get here, walk around the harbor with the water on your right, and then follow the signs. Peerless views of Vathi's cossetted position unfold as the climb proceeds. Bring a flashlight. (Admission 200dr.) It's a two-hour hike southeast to the Homeric **Arethousa Fountain** along a steep mountain path through pear orchards. In summer, the fountain is dry and, despite what the map says, there are no paths to the water. You can spend an afternoon sifting through the multicolored stones of the beach at **Piso Ateos Bay** about 5km from town. Ask at Polyctor Tours about the **Greek Theater Festival** (late August) and the popular **Music Festival** (early July) which take place in Vathi. Try to visit during local feasts for **saints' days:** July 17th is the feast of Agia Marina in the village of Exogi, and July 20th is Agios Ilias's feast in Kion. August 5th and 6th are the days of Agios Satiras in Stavros village; the biggest celebrations of the year on Ithaki takes place on August 14th in the village of Anogi and August 15th in Platrighia. In addition, there is a **Wine Festival** in Perahori on the last Sunday of July.

A trip away from Vathi will reward you with the charm of scenic, remote villages scattered across Ithaki's rocky coast. The island's one **bus** runs north from Vathi, passing successively through the villages of Lefki, Stavros, Platrithiai, Frikes, and Kioni. Leaving Vathi at 6am, 11am and 6pm, it arrives in Kioni one hour later (450dr). The stunning road skirts both sides of the isthmus, offering superlative views of the strait of Ithaki and Cephalonia on the west, and the voluptuous coastline on the east. Be prepared for bus drivers who blithely disregard both speed limits and the dearth of guard rails between the bus and the blotchy emerald water 300m below. Check the times of return buses before setting out; taxis from Kioni to Vathi cost around 3500dr.

Stavros merits a visit for its location, if not its lone sight. The village schoolmaster's wife has a key to a small museum at the alleged site of **Odysseus' Palace,** recommended for fanatical Homerists; a small tip is expected. **Frikes,** a half-hour walk from Stavros, rests snugly on a cove on the east coast; it takes about one minute to walk from one side of the village to the other. Relaxed and therapeutic, Frikes has a market, a couple of *tavernas,* and a branch of **Polyctor Tours** (tel. 317 71; open 9am-9:30pm). The latter sells tickets for the mellow little ferry that sails to Nidri (once per day at 11am). For a swim, walk along the coast road towards Kioni (past the memorial to the World War II Greek resistance operation against a German ship docked at Frikes). Beach-hoppers should sample the offerings of southeastern **Filiatro**—arguably the island's finest. A boat leaves Vathi for the beaches twice daily, returning in the afternoon (750dr round-trip).

Zakinthos ΖΑΚΥΝΘΟΣ

The sunniest of the Ionian Islands, Zakinthos draws droves to its enticing beaches which surround the florid lowlands of the east. Concealed by the long Vrachionas mountain ridge which hosts cliffs, caves, and a few locals, the western fringe is less explored. Pink blossoms carpet highlands and lowlands, linking the island's two faces.

Zakinthos Town

Tidy Zakinthos Town on the east coast of the island greets visitors with arcaded streets and whitewashed buildings. After an earthquake destroyed the town in 1953, locals revamped it, quickly restoring the city to its former polished state. In the high season tourists glut Zakinthos, but finding solitude off the trodden-down path is no vain dream. The island's interior will enmesh you in floral scents and pollen quite unbecoming to allergy sufferers.

Orientation and Practical Information

As you leave the ferry, you'll see the stately **Platia Solomou,** lined with palm trees and large buildings. Along the waterfront, **Lombardou Street** and the boardwalk beckon with an array of *gelateria* scattered among tourist gift stores. The first street parallel to Lombardou away from the water is **Filita Street,** home to the bus station; behind it are **Foskolou, Alex. Roma** (the main shopping street), and **Tertseti,** in that order. Behind Platia Solomou, **Vassileos Georgiou B'** leads quickly to **Platia Agiou Markou.**

Currency Exchange: National Bank of Greece, El. Venizelou St., near Platia Solomou, next to the town hall. The **Commercial Bank** lies behind the National Bank. The **Ionian Bank** is on Platia Agiou Markou. Banks open Mon.-Thurs. 8am-2pm, Fri. 8am-1:30pm. The **National Bank** will exchange your currency Sat. and Sun. 9am-1pm.

Post Office: On Tertseli and Skirou Gouskou St. Exchanges currency. Open Mon.-Fri. 7:30am-8pm, and Sat. 7:30am-2pm. **Postal Code:** 29100.

OTE: 2 Vassileos Georgiou B, between the two squares. Open daily 7am-midnight. **Telephone Code:** 0695.

Olympic Airways: 16 Alex. Roma St. (tel. 286 11 or 244 33). Open daily 8am-5:30pm. Flights from Athens (2 per day, 45min., 11,300dr; 1 per day off-season). The **airport** is 6km south near Laganas; Olympic Airways runs a **shuttle** there 70min. before scheduled departures (100dr).

Buses: (tel. 222 55 or 226 56), 42 Filita St. on the corner of Eleftheriou St. (6 blocks along the water from Solomou Sq., then 1 block back). Long-distance buses piggyback on the ferry to Patras (4 per day, 900dr) and then to Athens (3200dr). Schedules for local service posted outside the bus station. A more complete list is available at the information window here. Buses run to: Keri (2 per day, 220dr); Machairado (4 per day, 140dr); Vasiliko (2 per day, 160dr); Porto Rama and Geraka (2 per day, 180dr); Alykes, along the northern coast, (7 per day, 180dr); Tsilivi, 4km from town, (10 per day, 140dr); and Laganas (15 per day, 140dr). **Buses** run less frequently on Saturday and Sunday.

Ferries: Arrive at Zakinthos Town port from Killini on the Peloponnese (7 per day, off-season 5 per day, 1½hr., 770dr). Also from Korithi on the island's northern tip to Poros on Cephalonia (1 per day, 1½hr., 650dr). Tickets for both available at the **boat agencies** along the waterfront. For more information call the harbor master's office (tel. 224 17). Some agencies run a bus to the north of the island for the Cephalonia ferry (departing from Skinari and Agios Nikolaos).

Taxis: Vassileos Georgiou B' (tel. 286 55).

Moped Rental: All over the island. In Zakinthos Town, **Safari,** 6 Ethnikis Anistasis (tel. 235 43 or 281 54), just off Demokratias St. near Platia Solomou. Mopeds 1350dr with insurance, motorcycles about 1700dr. Open 8:30am-9pm.

Car Rental: Hertz (tel. 257 06 or 260 63), 38 Lomardou St. (on waterfront). Rentals starting from 3100dr per day and 45dr per km.

Library: Platia Solomou (tel. 281 28), across the street from the OTE. Open Mon.-Fri. 7:30am-2:30pm.

Laundromat: To Magiko, 71 Foskolou St. Dry cleaning, too. Open Mon. and Thurs.-Fri. 8am-1:30pm and 5:30-9pm, Tues.-Wed. and Sat. 8am-2pm.

Hospital: Tel. 225 15 or 225 14, above the city center.

Police: Lombardou and Fra Tzoulati St. (tel. 222 00 and 225 50), 5 blocks along the waterfront from Platia Solomou. Laid-back **tourist police** speak English, answer questions, and can help find accommodations. Open 8am to at least 10pm.

Accommodations and Food

Most people stay outside Zakinthos Town, nearer the beaches. Signs for rooms-to-let plaster every road on the island, and several excellent campgrounds dot the shore (see Around the Island). If you find a place outside town, don't worry—buses are frequent and taxis inexpensive on the main roads.

Rooms in Zakinthos Town are expensive and often hard to come by in July and August. The **Hotel Oasis** (tel. 222 87), located on Koutouli St., just four blocks north of the port police, offers small rooms and narrow beds. Run by a sweet motherly woman, rooms here are the cheapest you'll find. (Doubles 3000dr.) If you're stuck in town for a night you can also try the **Ionion Hotel,** 18 Alex. Roma (tel. 225 11), which offers clean doubles with big balconies (5000dr). For rooms to let just outside of town call **Mr. Fotis Giatras** (tel. 233 92) and speak slowly. Located 2km from a popular beach, Mr. Giatras offers doubles with shared baths and kitchenettes at 5800dr. Motorbikes are available for rental here (1200dr per day). Taxis to Mr. Giatras's place cost between 500 and 700dr.

The restaurants clustered in Platia Agiou Markou are a tad overpriced, but a *souvlaki-pita* or a *tiropita* will set you back a mere 100dr. At the corner of Rizospaston and Ignatiou, **To Tavernaki** serves wonderful veal with potatoes (880dr). There's a well-stocked **market** on Lombardou St. between the gas stations, and another 1 block back on Filita.

Sights

Zakinthos is famous for its **Church of Agios Dionysios** (named not for the Greek god, but in honor of St. Denis, the island's patron saint). Located about 10 blocks east on the waterfront, the church displays a silver chest which entombs the saint's relics. Dress code strictly enforced. In Platia Solomou, the **Byzantine Museum** (tel. 227 14), houses icons from the "Ionian School," a distinctive local hybrid of Byzantine and Renaissance styles. (Open Tues.-Sun. 8:30am-3pm. Admission 400dr, students 200dr; free on Sun.) Even more interesting is the **Museum of Solomos and Other Famous Zakynthians,** in Platia Agiou Markou. The tomb of Dionysios Solomos (1798-1857), the poet who wrote the lyrics of the Greek national anthem, occupies the ground floor. (Open daily 9am-2pm. Free.) On Platia Solomon, visit the **Church of Agios Nickolausto** to see a macabre icon of the saint.

Around the Island

The terrain and beaches on Zakinthos will easily lure you away from the port town. Seasoned visitors return year after year to the refreshingly quiet settlements. It's possible to see the entire island, including the otherwise inaccessible western cliffs, by boat. One leaves every morning from Zakinthos Town and circumnavigates the island in eight hours (5000dr). Other boats make excursions to the blue caves and the so-called "Smuggler's Wreck." Inquire at the tourist police. For more independent exploration, tour the island by moped (there's at least one rental place at each beach), or by bus. Hitchers find things difficult later in the day. Because the island is developing rapidly, many new roads won't appear on the available maps.

Your first impulse may be to whirligig down to the beaches at **Laganas** 10km south, but steer clear—they have been mangled by large hotels, souvenir stands, and mobs of tourists. If you must stay, try **Laganas Camping** (tel. 517 08 or 515 85; 500dr per person, 300dr per tent), which has a swimming pool. The white-sanded **Tsilivi Beach** remains one of the best beaches on the island, but unfortunately, it too has been discovered. **Tsilivi Camping,** also called Zante Camping has a cafeteria and mini-market (tel. 247 54). From Zakinthos Town, it's a bit of a walk to the beach along the asphalt road skirting the shore. **Planos,** just inland, has plenty of rooms to let. **Buses** run from Zakinthos Town to the beach (5 per day, 150dr).

Still-unscathed beaches carpet the peninsula extending out to the town of **Vasilikos,** 16km from Zakinthos Town, and are most plentiful near **Porto Roma.** Signs for rooms to let coat the road to Vasilikos, especially near **Agios Nikolaos Beach.** Just on the other side of Vasilikos, facing Laganas Bay, lies **Gerakas Beach.** Daily buses leave Zakinthos Town for Vasilikos (10:15am and 3:15pm, returning at 10:45am and 3:45pm, 180dr).

It is a five-minute walk from Gerakas to **Turtle Bay.** The turtles near Laganas Beach have been the subject of bitter controversy on Zakinthos and throughout Europe as ecologists petition to make Laganas Bay a marine park. Known by the Greeks as *kareta kareta,* these creatures have returned to the island for 90 million years to lay eggs. Two-hundred-pound females lumber ashore each night to deposit future generations in the softest sand in Greece. Developers, however, increasingly appropriate the beach for their own nest eggs and threaten the turtles' survival.

Alykes, 16km from Zakinthos Town, is a beach resort stuffed to the gills with package tours. There are a number of beaches in the area, so it's not hard to find a quasi-peaceful spot. The main beach has a water-sports center on its east end that rents sailboards, canoes and small paddle boats. Inquire for rooms on the main road across from the **Dionisios Restaurant** (tel. 614 19), about 1km from town. The rooms are spacious and clean, with private baths and kitchen facilities. (Doubles about 3000dr.) There is no dearth of bars, discos, and rooms to let in the general vicinity. The residents of the old, sprawling village of **Volimes,** the endpoint of the bus route, specialize in fine needlework. One km east up the hill in the upper part of the village (Ano Volimes), the **Women's Agricultural Tourist Cooperative** in the main square can find you a room with a local family. If the office is closed, inquire about *dhomatia* at the *panopoleion* (grocery store) opposite, or the **police** next door. Crumbling medieval bell towers and abandoned windmills dot the lower part of the village.

At the extreme northern tip of Zakinthos is the tiny village of **Korithi,** locally known as **Agios Nikolaos,** whence the ferry to Cephalonia departs. Special buses occasionally come out to meet the ferry (ask at the bus station in Zakinthos Town). Here you can embark on a visit to the beautiful **blue caves,** hewn by the sea into the side of the island and observable only from the water. A one-hour motorboat excursion costs around 1000dr per person; you can also rent canoes and other small craft on the tiny beach.

Kythera ΚΥΘΗΡΑ

> *Island of secret orgies none profess the august*
> *shade of Aphrodite plays like clouds of incense over*
> *your blue bays and weighs the heart with love and*
> *weariness.*
>
> —Baudelaire

Myth holds that Aphrodite sprang from the waters swashing the shores of Kythera. Appearing full-grown from the foamy waves, the radiant goddess of love clearly blessed her birthplace before ascending to lofty Olympus. Kythera, reclining beneath the Peloponnesian cities of Monemvassia, Neapoli, and Gythion, is an isolated and lovely spot. The land's tranquil mountainous landscape harbors a collection of evergreens and flowering shrubs, secluded villages, and sandy beaches. Although traditionally one of the Ionian islands, Kythera has slid under Piraeus's administration.

Despite the reluctance of the island's inhabitants, the GNTO recently decided to promote tourism on the island. Although most changes, like the addition of slick, new bilingual road signs, seem superficial, the persistently treacherous roads, scarce accommodations, and seclusion of the isle have not deterred the newfound tourists. For complete isolation, head to the nearby island of **Antikythera,** wired for electricity only five years ago.

Ferry service to Kythera is slowly settling into a reliable schedule. Nevertheless, many connections are still inconvenient, making it difficult to travel to and from the island. The ferry boat *Martha* leaves Neapolis for Kythera daily at 8am (additional trips Mon., Wed., Thurs., Fri. around 3:45pm, and Sun. 2:30pm; 3hr., about 6300dr). From Kythera, the *Martha* returns to Neapolis daily at 10am (also Mon.-Fri. at 5:30pm, and Sun. at 4:30pm). Boats travel to Gythion (Tues. and Sat. 10am). The *Ionian* travels from Gythion to Kythera (700dr) and Crete (Mon. at midnight, Wed., and Fri. at 11pm). From Kythera, the *Ionian* travels to Gythion (Mon. 7:45pm, Wed. and Fri. 7:40pm). There are trips to Piraeus (Tues., Thurs., and Sat). Information for both the *Martha* and the *Ionian* is available at the two boat agencies located next to each other at Agai Pelagia. There's also a boat agency in Kapsali on the left side of the waterfront. Ferry schedules are posted all over the island. The **port police** (tel. 312 22 in Kapsali; 332 80 in Agia Pelagia) can give you complete information about all sailings. **Flying Dolphin hydrofoils** whisk you from Piraeus to Kythera in mid-afternoon (while the ferry usually arrives at 2am or 3am). Dolphins leave from Monemvassia (Mon.-Thurs. 12:55pm, Sat. 11:45pm). To Piraeus (Mon.-Thurs. 2:05pm, Sat. 1pm, 5½hr., 6000dr) via Neapolis, Monemvassia, Spetses and Hydra. **Olympic Airways** flies to Athens (at 10:20am and 4:30pm, 35min., 7000dr). Get tickets at the travel agency in Kythera or at the giftshop in the Hotel Kythera at the dock in Agia Pelagia. The Olympic Airways office (tel. 333 62) is in the square in Potamos just past the OTE and post office. (Open Mon.-Sat. 8am-3pm and Sun. 8am-2pm.) A taxi from Kythera to the airport should cost 1500dr.

Ferries dock in Kythera at either the western port of **Agia Pelagia,** or the more attractive and lively southern port, **Kapsali.** The island's main road runs between these two towns, with smaller villages connected by subsidiary roads. Besides the port towns, this road passes through Potamos, Livadi and Kythera (Chora)—Kythera's larger inland towns. It's best to station yourself on the southern half of the island where you are closer to moped rentals (a must on this island), *dhomatia,* restaurants and shops. Kapsali has a hopping nightlife; Kythera has fabulous views and some of life's necessities (such as a bank); and the inland town of Livadi has the cheapest rooms. Uphill from Kapsali, just off the main road, is Kythera's capital, **Kythera** (or Chora), which sits beneath a well-preserved Venetian castle. This town's hues imbue the whole island—white houses with blue trim are tinged with a touch of custard yellow. In the town square, you'll find the **National Bank** (open Mon.-Thurs. 8am-2pm, Fri. 8am-1:30pm) and a helpful **travel agency** (tel. 313 90; open Mon.-Sat. 8am-1:30pm and 6-

9pm, Sun. 8am-1:30pm). The **post office** is on the road that leads downhill out of the square. (Open Mon.-Fri. 7:30am-2:30pm.) Across from the post office is a supermarket. Continuing down this road toward the castle, you'll reach the **police** (tel. 312 06)—if you're desperately roomless, they'll try to find a place. To find the **OTE,** go up the stairs next to the square's travel agent (look for the sign) and follow the path to the street behind the square. (Open Mon.-Fri. 7:30am-3:10pm.) Kythera's **postal code** is 80200; its **telephone code** is 0735.

Kythera Town has few budget accommodations, and most are booked weeks in advance, especially in August. Near the post office (look for the grey and blue sign), **Mr. Pizdio's** pension (ΠΙΖΔΙΟ; tel. 312 10) has doubles which share a stark bathroom. You'll find expensive, tastefully furnished rooms at **Pension Ketty** (KAITE; tel. 313 18). Look for the signs near the phone booth across from the bank. (Doubles 5000dr.) Near the bakery, **Mr. Lourandon** (tel. 311 06) lets clean doubles in the house with reddish shutters (starting at 3000dr). It may be easier to find somewhere to crash in Livadi.

Kapsali has a few rooms to rent and the added attraction of being right on the beach, near the ballyhoo of the partying crowds. Look for signs on the street behind the waterfront. **Mr. and Mrs. Megaloudi** (tel. 313 40) have pleasant doubles on the waterfront (4200dr with bath and refrigerator). Sheltered in a conifer forest, a beautiful **campground** (tel. 315 80) lies 300m from Kapsali up the road to Kythera (400dr per person plus 350dr per tent; open June 15-Sept. 15). Some of those arriving by ferry in the middle of the night freelance camp on the beach and head for the campground in the morning. Kapsali has an **OTE** located in **Mike's Bikes**. There is also a **post office** which operates out of the easily recognizable canary-yellow trailer parked in the street behind the waterfront (Open 8:30am-1:30pm. No packages).The small town of **Potamos,** 20km north of Kapsali on the main road, hosts a spectacular Sunday morning **market.** Kythera is renowned for its delightful honey; you can pick up a jar here for a sticky 1500-2000dr.

In general, blackboards near bus stops, supposedly marked with daily schedules, are conspicuously blank. One **bus** leaves Ag. Pelagia daily at 8am, and some ferry boats are met by buses. From Kythera Town a bus runs to the Potamos Sunday market at 7am. Hitching on this secluded island takes a great deal of patience or luck—probably not worth it. If you arrive with the car ferry, you have a better chance at a lift to Kapsali or Kythera Town (stand by the signs at the end of the quay). *Let's Go* does not recommend hitchhiking as a means of travel. The best way to see the island is by motorbike. Try **Mike's Bikes** (tel. 314 61 or 311 01), just off the waterfront in Kapsali; his bikes are considerably cheaper than the competition's. (Automatics 2000dr, with gears 2800dr; free gas.) With an outlet on the waterfront in Kapsali and one in the square at Kythera, the near-monopoly of **Panayiotis Rent** (tel. 310 04 or 314 61) is more convenient. Panayiotis has more expensive bikes and helpful maps (24-hr. rental 1-person automatic 2100dr, 2-person automatic 2900dr, motorbike with gears 3000dr). He also rents pedal boats (1000dr per hr.) windsurfers (1500dr per hr.) and canoes (500dr per hr.), which you can use to reach the otherwise inaccessible cove adjacent to the main beach at Kapsali (open 8:30am-6pm).

Most waterfront restaurants in Kapsali and Agia Pelagia are overpriced. For inexpensive Greek food with a twist, head inland and try **Toxotis Restaurant** in Livadi, one of the best on the island. For dessert, Livadi's bakery has delicious treats. In Kythera, try **Zorba's,** located on the main street, downhill from the square (chicken 600dr; open for dinner only). **Bananas** in Kapsali is a bar which tempts with terrific music, friendly owners, and a wacky crowd (drinks about 700dr). **Gone With the Wind,** the island's open-air dance club, is perched above Kapsali and presides over a fantastic view of the port. To get there turn off the main road between Kythera and Kapsali at the sign for Kalamos.

Sights

Kythera is very selective when it comes to exposing its secrets—only the bravest, most persevering travelers will uncover them. Start your exploration with a climb to the **kastro** in Chora. The summit, dabbled with the ruins of old churches and buildings, offers an intoxicating view of Kapsali's double harbor. The **museum,** with Mycenaean and Venetian finds, is just outside of town, past the turn-off into Chora as the road heads to Livadi. (Open Tues.-Fri. 8:45am-3pm, Sun. 9:30am-2:30pm. Free.) A visit to the cave of **Agia Sofia Milopotamou** takes most of an afternoon and would make Indiana Jones intensely envious. You'll have to bike down treacherous rocky roads, hike up a cliff, and crawl around in small clammy spaces while reciting poetry. Wear sturdy shoes—the passage is dark and slippery. A few feet from the entrance to the grotto are several beautiful frescoes. (Open July-Sept. Mon., Wed., and Sat. 4-8pm. Admission with tour 500dr; double-check times with the police; hours change often.) If you go to the square in Milopotamos at 4pm, the guide will lead you to the cave on the partially paved road in your car or motorbike. If you arrive later, follow the signs out of town leading to the cave. For a much smaller but more spiritual cave, go to **Feloti.** Take the first left onto a rough dirt road just past the turn-off to Chora. When you reach the coast, park your moped and follow the path to the left until you see a little white steeple poking out of the rock; just in front of it is the entrance to the cave. Many swim off the rocks near the cave or from the small pebble beach farther to the right.

Fryiammos beach is acclaimed as the superior beach on the island; its inaccessibility largely accounting for its excellence. Lying on the southeast coast, it is most easily reached by car or by motorcycle. It's also possible to walk from the road. Leave your moped at the fork in the road near Kalamos and proceed up the hill for a long hike; the left path leads to Fryiamnos. If you can't get there, try **Melidoni** on the southwest coast. When you are leaving Livadi, turn left at the fork, and continue on this road until you reach Drimona. Enter the town and follow signs to Agios Kosmas. Pass the church on the left and plunge down the treacherous, sandy road—be careful.

NORTHEAST AEGEAN ISLANDS
ΒΟΡΕΙΟΑΝΑΤΟΛΙΚΑ ΝΗΣΙΑ ΤΟΥ ΑΙΓΙΟΥ

The intricate, rocky coastlines of the Northeast Aegean Islands cradle thickly wooded mountains, cragged peaks, and isolated valleys where inhabitants seem cloistered in an earlier century. Though pirates and Ottomans no longer threaten, there remains on these islands a conspicuous Greek military presence: the islands' proximity to Turkey and the constant political tensions between those two countries explain the presence of guns and camoflage in the region (which may perturb single women traveling here). Less touristed than any other archipelago, these tranquil and alluring islands are a chance to experience true Greek culture.

Thassos ΘΑΣΟΣ

Thassos cut loose from the Delian League of Athens in the fall of 411 BCE. The Athenians recaptured the island in 389 BCE after making an alliance with the Cypriot King Euagoras and the Egyptian King Acoris, but Thassos maintained its veneer of wealth. During Roman times, builders from all over the world sought Thassosian marble, and Thassos's gold mines made it one of the wealthiest members of the Delian League. Thassos was the birthplace of Timoxenos, an athlete credited with some 1400 victories, and was the home of Hippocrates for three years. During medieval times, marauding pirates and Ottomans prompted the population to desert the city and hide out in the interior of the island. Controlled for a time by the Ottomans and, later, the Egyptians, the island was taken by the Greeks in 1912.

Thassos, while ranking as a popular tourist destination, still possesses fabulously untenanted stretches of beach. Nicknamed the "Green Island" for its foliage, Thassos suffered a devasting fire which destroyed half of its forest in 1985. Since then, the rich landscape has been marked by numerous fire prevention signs and mangy scrub.

Hydrofoils shuttle back and forth between Thassos's main port of Limenas and nearby Kavala (6 per day, 40min., 1050dr). Contact **Dolphin Hydrofoils** (tel. 22 20 05) for more information. To continue on to other islands of the Northeast Aegean, you must first return to Kavala for ferry connections.

Rent a moped for the day to explore both coast and inland areas thoroughly—pick a favorite spot, and return by bus with your pack for a longer stay. Limenas-Limenaria shuttle **buses** traverse the west coast (3 per day). Buses also run along the east coast (9 per day), with three going to Limenaria. You can travel to Limenaria via the western route (1hr.), or you can make a loop of the island (2½hr.). Ask at the tourist police or bus office for schedules. Because bus service is always erratic, leave several hours leeway if you want to catch the last boat off the island.

Limenas (Thassos Town)

Built atop the foundations of the ancient city, Limenas (also known as Thassos), is now the island's capital and tourist center. Accordingly, this lively port is more crowded and more expensive than the rest of the island. Stick around here for the nightlife, but not for scenery or quiet. The only street sign you'll ever see is that of 19th Octovriou St., the main way, 1 block parallel to the waterfront. Unless you don't mind wandering, you'll probably need to buy a street map, or get excellent directions.

Northeast Aegean Islands

Practical Information

The friendly **tourist police** (tel. 225 00; open 24 hrs.), in a gray marble building at the port, can give you a minimalist depiction of the town, a cubist map of the island, and an impressionist list of hotels. For inanimate help, the large blue sign across from the Mobil station lists the names and phone numbers of all hotels, pensions, and camp-grounds in the area. Continuing up the waterfront road toward the **old port** (now used only for small boats), you'll see the blue awning of **Thassos Tours** (tel. 225 46; open daily 9am-9pm). Here you'll get candid advice and honest deals on everything from ac-commodations to excursions. To the right of the ferry landing, next to the "Mobil" sign, is the **bus station** (tel. 221 62). Nine agencies rent **motorbikes**—best equipped is **Thassos Tours** (2000-6000dr per day). The **National Bank of Greece** is near the main square (open Mon.-Thurs. 8am-2pm, Fri. 8am-1:30pm). Diagonally across the square, past Gregory's Art, the road leads inland. Three blocks north and one block west is the **post office** (open Mon.-Fri. 7:30am-2pm). On the main street, behind the tourist police, you'll find the **OTE.** (Open Mon.-Sat. 7:30am-11pm, Sun. 7:30am-3pm.) A 24-hr. clinic (tel. 222 22) is nearby. Thassos' **postal code** is 64004; its **telephone code** is 0593.

Accommodations, Camping, and Food

Accommodations are a free-for-all on Thassos; prices may bear little relation to the official rates set by the government. The **Hotel Athanasia** (tel. 225 45), offers spa-cious, spic-n-span rooms. To get there from the ferry dock continue right along the wa-terfront about 100m. You'll see its sign just past the Hotel Xenia. (Singles 2500dr. Shared baths. Owners speak no English.) A stalwart few sleep on the town beach, but the festivities from the bars will keep you up. Instead, take the bus and alight at Skala Rahoni for **Camping Ioannidis,** (tel. 714 77 or 713 77), 13km west of Limenas on the road to Skala Prinos. (760dr per person. 860dr per tent.) There is more camping else-where on the island (see below). Just beyond the old harbor near the end of the beach, the popular **Restaurant Syrtaki** serves red snapper for only 430dr. (Open 9am-mid-night.)

Sights

In addition to impressive remains of walls and buildings dating from the 6th and 5th centuries BCE, the island flaunts a 4th-century BCE Greek **theater,** built on the re-mains of the acropolis of ancient Thassos. The ruins are easy to find: turn right behind the old port and continue to a three-pronged fork in the road beyond a recessed ruin—the middle path leads to the theater. Classical dramas are staged here each summer. (Buy tickets at the GNTO in Kavala or on the waterfront in Limenas, 500dr.) The ar-chaeological sites are free and always open. The **Thassos Museum** (tel. 221 80), near the old port, contains mosaic floors and sculptures found on the site, including a colos-sal 6th-century BCE marble statue of Apollo with a ram draped around his shoulders. (Open Tues.-Sun. 8:30am-3pm. Admission 400dr, students 200dr.)

East Coast

Eight buses per day travel from Limenas to Limenaria (600dr), stopping 10km south in the villages of **Panayia** and **Potamia** (150-200dr). Three km apart, both villages overlook Ormos Potamias, a gorgeous, sandy cove. The aromas of grilled goat meat and syrup-saturated walnuts will greet you as you approach Panayia. The town retains its traditions despite a minor tourist influx: even some of the international dancing clubs, located by the theater in the main square, echo with the clash of *mesethes* (dishes flung in Greek dancing). Potamia houses a small **Folk Museum,** tucked under the shadow of the town church. (Open Mon. and Wed.-Sun. 8:30am-3pm.) Both villages have *dhomatia;* Panayia also has an inexpensive hotel, the **Helvetia** (tel. 612 31), at the northern entrance into town.

The golden beach of **Chrisi Ammoudia** stretches endlessly 6km east of Panayia. There is plenty of room for camping here, but little privacy. Farther south, Potamia's beach is capacious, but less attractive. (Campers can use the water tap at the entrance to the olive grove, about 1km from the beach toward Potamia.) The twin coves of **Aliki,** (11km south of Kinira) hide the most tranquil beaches on the island. The northernmost, sheltered by foliage, is perfect for nude bathing. The southern beach cove, formed as sand shifted over a Roman marble quarry, shelters slabs of bleached white rock and crevices ideal for snorkeling. Towel off and trudge to the monastery of **Archaegelon,** where you'll find its simple whitewashed church with stone floors and colorful icons. (Cover-up clothing provided for visitors.)

Along the east coast of Thassos is a narrow road rambling past unexcavated ruins and beautiful coves. The rubble of several towers and light houses—set up to guard against pirates—may be found near Astiris.

West Coast

No longer the capital of the island as it was in Turkish times, **Limenaria** manages to maintain most of its charm. Even though daily buses haul in tourists from Limenas (600dr), finding a private room amidst Limenaria's quaint Turkish houses is no source of grief—*dhomatia* signs are all over. Exemplary beaches tumble at **Pefkari** and **Potos,** only 4km away. Seven buses per day run from Limenas to Potos (600dr). **Pefkari Camping** (tel. 511 90), 1km north of Potos, runs an outstanding campground.

Samothraki (Samothrace) ΣΑΜΟΘΡΑΚΗ

Samothraki first welcomed Greek colonists in the 7th century BCE. The island soon achieved fame as a religious center specializing in the worship of the *libiri,* twin gods who helped infertile women bear children. At the **Sanctuary of the Megaloi Theoi** (Great Gods) for example, Philip of Macedon met his wife Olympius. Thus Alexander, it is rumored, was conceived during a night of divine hanky-panky. Now home to fewer than 3000 people, the island, its barren beauty and village life unmarred, draws the occasional hardy adventurer. Fegari, the highest peak in the Aegean (1670m above sea level), rises out of this stony, oblong isle. According to Homer, it is from this summit that Poseidon cheered the Trojan War.

Today **ferries** connect Samothraki with Alexandroupolis (1 per day, 2½hr., 1200dr) and Kavala (2 per wk., 4hr., 2000dr). Contact **Arsinoi Shipping** (tel. 267 21 in Alexandroupolis, or 415 05 in Samothraki) for more information. Ferries arrive at Kamariotissa, at the western end of the island. Follow the road northeast along the coast to Paleopolis (5km) and Therma (also known as Loutra, 4km farther). About 6km down the inland road from the port, rests the island's capital, Samothraki (usually called Chora); Lakoma is 9km south. In summer, several different bus routes connect Paleopolis, Therma, Chora and Lakoma via Kamariotissa (120-300dr). Off-season, only two routes run daily.

Hike up the main street of the quiet hillside town of **Chora** and you'll come to the **OTE** (tel. 412 12) and the **post office** (tel. 412 44), both open Mon.-Fri. 7am-2:30pm, as well as the **National Bank** (Mon.-Fri. 8am-2pm). There is also a **National Bank** on the waterfront in Kamariotissa (tel. 415 70; open Mon.-Fri. 8am-2pm). The **tourist police** (tel. 413 03 or 412 03) are situated at the top of the hill in front of the ruins of the **kastro** (castle). Samothraki's **postal code** is 68002; its **telephone code** is 0551.

Except for the ruins and the accompanying hilltop panorama, there is little of interest in Chora. You can rent **motorbikes** to tour the island at a couple of places in Kamariotissa. The first is unnamed and just opposite the ferry dock. Look for its blue awning (tel. 415 11; open daily 9am-2pm and 5-10pm; 3000dr per day). The second agency, **Enoikiaseis** (tel. 415 49; open daily 10am-2pm and 5-8:30pm; 2500 per day) is located to your left behind the Skorpios Café as you come from the ferry dock.

Samothraki is a camper's delight. Tucker out at one of the many **campsites** along the northeast coastal road from Kamariotissa to Pirgoss Fonia or try haggling with the several **pension** owners on the island. A reliable bet is a **dhomatia** at Mrs. Karayiani's place (tel. 415 36), 2 blocks inland, a spotless establishment one block from the port. (Doubles 3500dr; private baths; little English spoken.) For service with a smile, try the *dhomatia* at Despina Remboutzias's place (tel. 412 70; doubles 2500dr). Mrs. Remboutzias and her Americanophile young daughter Rozalie speak English and are fine sources of information on Samothraki.

In **Therma,** visit the **thermal baths** (tel. 416 79; open 8am-10pm with extended hours in the summer; 210dr). Between Therma and Kamariotissa lies **Paleopolis** ("old city"), where you'll find the ruins of the *Megaloi Theoi*. Dedicated to Axieros (Demeter), the *libiri* beckoned by the fecund, and a mumbling hubbub of other deities as well, the Megaloi Theoi witnessed the initiations of both the Spartan King Lysander and the historian Herodotus. (Site open Tues.-Sun. 9am-3pm. Admission 400dr, students 200dr.) The worthwhile **Paleopolis Museum,** next to the ruins, houses local artifacts and a miniature copy of the *Nike of Samothrace* since the original is now at the Louvre. (Museum open Tues.-Sun. 9am-3pm. Admission 400dr, students 200dr; includes admission to the ruins. The island's best beach, **Pahia Ammos,** is a 5km walk south from here along the shore.

Limnos ΛΗΜΝΟΣ

It is said on Limnos that when one hapless chap made a dirty joke about Aphrodite's amorous habits, the goddess put a curse on the island causing all the women to kill the men. Only the king, helped by his daughter, escaped. Upon their arrival, the Argonauts found grieving widows and, shortly thereafter, the repopulation of the fair isle was underway.

Situated strategically as a potential "cork" for the Black Sea, and a buffer between Turkey and the rest of Greece, low, flat Limnos has a sizable Greek military presence. The military does not monopolize the island, however; with rolling countrysides and unspoiled coastlines, Limnos remains a popular vacation spot, especially with Germans.

In summer, **ferries** run from Kavala and Alexandroupolis (2 per week every other week, 5hr., 2316dr). Ferries also connect Limnos to Lesvos (2 per week, 7hr., 2295dr) and Thessaloniki (1 per week, 8hr., 3089dr). Despite the lines you may see drawn on your map, there is no direct ferry service to Samothraki. For further information, contact **The Travel and Shipping Agency** (tel. 224 60 or 235 60; open daily 7am-10pm) or the **Limnos Port Authority** (tel. 222 25), in the upstairs office in the beige building on the port road (open Mon.-Fri. 7:30am-3pm). **Flights** also service Limnos from Athens (3 or 4 per day), Lesvos (2 per week, 50min., 8500dr) and Thessaloniki (1 per day, 50min, 10,200dr). Limnos's airport is in the center of the island, 22km east of Myrina. The **Olympic Airways Office** (tel. 220 78) in Myrina is next to the post office on Garofalidi St.

Free of oversized hotels and unsightly resort complexes, the island's capital and primary port of **Myrina.** Turreted towers of a Genoese-Turkish fortress which peer out from behind the volcanic-rock formations overlooking the town and the harbor. For help finding accommodations and for general tourist information, contact Maria Liroudia (one of the few fluent English speakers in Myrina) at the **Town Administrative office** (*Eparheio*) (tel. 242 54), located on Dimokratias Rd. (open Mon.-Fri. 7am-2:30pm). From the ferry dock, head left up the main road through the center of town and cross the small footbridge. The *Eparheio* will be on the second floor of the office building on the right. The **tourist office** (tel. 241 10) is ½ block east of the Port Authority building, in the Municipal Office (the white building with a blue "M" on the front door). Here you might get help finding accommodations. (Open mid-July to mid-Aug. Mon.-Sat. 8am-10pm.)

In the square in the center of town you'll see the **National Bank of Greece** (open Mon.-Thurs. 8am-2pm and Fri. 8am-1:30pm) and the **OTE** (open Mon.-Fri. 7:30am-10:30pm and Fri. 8am-1:30pm). Past the square 1 block and around the corner to the right is Garofalidi St. (The street sign is partially painted over.) Here you will find the **post office** (open Mon.-Fri. 7:30am-2pm) and across the street, a self-service **laundry** (tel. 24 392; open daily 8:30am-2pm and 5-9:30pm). Farther down is the **Maroula Cinema** (tel. 224 75) which features films in English in its open-air roof-top theater during the summer, and indoors the rest of the year. Limnos' **postal code** is 84100; its **telephone code** is 0254.

When you arrive by ferry in July and August, locals muttering *dhomatia* will swarm around you. Bargain with them or stay at the **Hotel Aktaion** near the ferry landing; the shining rooms have sinks. (Singles 2493dr. Doubles 3600dr. Triples 4025dr.) If your wallet permits the comforts of an expansive room with a kitchenette and balcony, see Nick and Lucy at the **Apollo Pavilion** (tel. 237 12), a ½ block before the police station on Garofalidi St. (Doubles 6700dr. Triples 7700dr. Much less in the off-season.)

The legendary home of the smithy Hephaestus, Limnos is dotted with small clusters of stone houses with tile roofs, surrounded by checkerboard fields of hay, tobacco, and other crops. Explore the areas which lie beyond the port town; wherever you go, you're likely to be the only traveler. To rent **mopeds,** go to **Rent A Car** (tel. 249 01) on Garofalidi St., just past the post office. (Open daily 9am-1:30pm and 5:30-9pm; 3000dr per day.) **Petrides** (tel. 220 39), on the main shopping road past Garofalidi St., runs daily excursions from Myrina to several of the island's historical settlements, including the archaeological remains at **Poliochni.** There is no public transportation on Limnos, and few cars to pick up hitchers.

A few bungalows invite company about 2km southeast of Myrina, at the pristine beaches of **Plati** and **Thanos.** Follow the signs off the main road in Plati to **Gregory's** (tel. 227 15), where *bouzouki* playing and Greek dancing follow dinner (open July-Aug. 10am-1am).

Traveling north out of Myrina, you'll find the island's inveterate evening launch pad, **Avlonas Club** (tel. 23 885) just before the Myrina power station. Make a 180-degree turn onto the grey pebbled pathway lined with red and white spotted mushroom lights. This remote disco spins international music amidst the fauna-lined stream and hillside (open daily mid-June to Aug. 9:30pm-3am. Admission free). Just 8km north of Myrina is **Kaspaka,** where most of the old stone buildings still stand. **Agios Ioannis,** on the stony beach nearby, has a cheap restaurant with tables crammed underneath a rock canopy. **Poliochini** is considered to be the earliest neolithic city in the eastern Mediterranean, antedating even Troy I. During the early 1930s, excavations by Alessandro della Seta revealed the remains of a settlement here dating back to the 4th millennium BCE.

Lesvos (Lesbos) ΛΕΣΒΟΣ

Lesvos, once the home of the musician Terpander and the poet Arion, is most famous as the home of Sappho, the 7th-century BCE poet famous for her sensual lyricism. Until recently, the island, often called Mitilini after its principal city, abided unfettered by tourism. Most travelers to the sparsely populated isle stay for months at a time, exploring the many historical sites, and yawping at the tall pines, cornfields, and taffy-trunked olive trees that rise from the scruffy hillsides. The enchanting complement of these wonders is the traditional hospitality of the native Lesvians. Although Lesvos' major towns now host a growing number of foreign visitors, many villages remain untainted and tourism has not reached Cycladean proportions.

Legend has it that the population of Lesvos, Greece's third largest island, was once entirely female. The notion may owe its origin to the Athenian assembly's 428 BCE decision to punish the recalcitrant residents of Mitilini by executing all adult males on the island. After some debate, the decision was repealed. For hundreds of years, Mitilini flourished as an important center of Greek culture; its inhabitants would have been astonished to know that later generations were to consider 5th-century Athens to be the zenith of Greek civilization. The island was especially famed for its Philosophical Academy, where Epicurus and Aristotle taught.

Lesvos is connected to the Northeast Aegean and beyond by **ferry.** Frequency and departure times are regularly inconsistent; contact a local GNTO or the **Maritime Company of Lesvos,** 47 Pavlou Koudoutrioti St. in Mitilini (tel. 230 97 or 262 12), on the waterfront two blocks from the end of the pier, to confirm daily schedules. (Open daily 8am-4pm and 6-8pm.) Ferries travel to and from Piraeus (5 per week, 15hr., 3578dr), stopping at Chios in between (from Mitilini, 4hr., 2072dr). There is service to

Ayvalik, Turkey (3 per week, 1½hr., 6000dr). Ferries also head to Limnos (2 per week, 7hr, 2295dr), Kavala (2 per week, 3615dr), and Thessaloniki (every Sat., 15hr., 5210dr). **Flights** go to Athens (5-6 per day, 11,600dr), Limnos (3 per week, 8500dr), and Thessaloniki (2 per day, 16,000dr). Blue buses at the waterfront's local bus station serve the airport 8km south of Mitilini (300dr). You can also reach the airport by taking the Olympic Airways bus (300dr) from the main office, 44 Kavetsou Ave. (tel. 286 59, 286 60, or 228 20; open Mon.-Fri. 7am-8pm, Sat.-Sun. 8am-2pm). Check with any ticket agent for times and locations.

Mitilini and Environs

The central port city of Lesvos, Mitilini is busy, crowded, and encumbered with too many cars. Built like an amphitheatre on the Amali mountain, Mitilini impresses with several interesting sights, but not with the friendly character pervading smaller island port towns. The city bustles along the waterfront, **Pavlou Koundouriot,** and **Ermou Street,** which runs parallel 1 block inland. Lose yourself in the knotted streets of the neighborhood just above the waterfront, where a variety of traditional shops, flea markets, and produce stands conceal themselves. Here you can stock up on food and other necessities before vaulting into the island's interior. Absorb Mitilini's sights and sounds at a waterfront café as you watch the *volta* (evening promenade).

The **GNTO/tourist police** (tel. 227 76), in the faded mauve building at the end of the ferry dock (look for the sign), provides maps of Mitilini and Lesvos. (Open daily 7am-2:30pm and 6-9pm.) The **GNTO** at the airport provides the same service. **The Tourism and Travel Agency of the Union of Agricultural Cooperatives of Lesvos** (whew!), is at 5 Konstantinoupoleos Sq. (tel. 213 29), next to the inter-city bus station on Leoforos Eleftheriou Venizilou (open Mon.-Sat. 8am-1pm, 5-8pm). From the bus station's information office, it is the second building on the right (look for the CTTA sign). Mr. Panselinas and his co-worker Costas willingly assists visitors in finding rooms and stuff to do in and around Mitilini. Doubles in Mitilini start at about 3500dr in the off-season. Convenient but expensive, the **Hotel Erato** at 2 P. Vostani (tel. 411 60 or 411 03), located next to the Olympic Airways main office 3½ blocks from the inter-city bus station, offers clean rooms with balconies overlooking a park and the ocean. (Singles 3400dr. Doubles 5900dr. More in July and August.)

Several **banks** line Pavlou Koundouriot along the waterfront (open Mon.-Thurs. 8am-2pm and 8am-1pm). Many travel agencies also change money; be certain to check the rates (open daily 8am-10pm). The **mobile post office,** a yellow caravan on the waterfront, provides the same service (open in summer Mon.-Fri. 8am-8pm, Sat. 8am-2:15pm, Sun. 9am-1pm), as does the main **post office,** on Vournazon St. (tel. 288 23; open Mon.-Sat. 7:30am-2pm, Sun. 9am-1:30pm; parcels and money orders Mon.-Sat. 7:30am-2:30pm). Two doors up the road from the post office is the **OTE** (tel. 28 299; open daily 6am-midnight). The **hospital** (tel. 284 57) is southwest of the city on E. Vostani. The **port police** (tel. 288 88 or 286 47) are a few blocks south of the port on the waterfront. Mitilini's **postal code** is 81100; its **telephone code** is 0251.

The **inter-city bus station** (tel. 288 73) is adjacent to Agios Irinis Park, at the southern edge of the harbor. During the week buses leave for Molyvos (3 per day, 2hr., 900dr), Skala Eressos (3 per day in summer and 1 per day Oct.-mid-June, 3hr., 1300dr), and Plomari (5 per day, 1½hr., 600dr). Bus service on weekends, however, is minimal. To explore this large island your way, rent a moped. Spiros at **Lesvos Car and Motorcycles** (tel. 282 42 and 296 00), 47 Gudouriotou St., around the corner from the ferry dock, rents 50-600cc motorbikes for 3-7 days (9860 to 46,700dr). Hitchers and drivers should follow Zoodochos Pigis St. (an extension of Vournazon St.) out of town until it turns into the highway to Kalloni.

If you have a spare hour in Mitilini, visit the enormous Baroque **Church of St. Therapon,** on Ermou St., which towers above the daily catch at the fish market—sardines, octopi, and occasional small sharks. Behind the church, is the **Museum of Byzantine Art.** (Open Mon.-Sat. 9am-1pm. Admission 100dr.) From the ferry dock, all roads leading uphill will take you to the **kastro** (castle) (tel. 279 70). Surrounded by redolent pines above the town, the *kastro* protects its purview over Mitilini and across to Turkey. It was originally constructed by Emperor Justinian on the site of a Byzantine castle, but has since been repaired by the Genoese, the Turks, and the Greeks. The walls contain an interesting assortment of leftovers from each epoch, but are capped by a telephone conduit—the 20th century's incongrous contribution. (Open daily 7:30am-2:45pm. Admission 400dr.)

The GNTO **beach,** just north of the main pier beneath the Kastro, is pleasant and pebbly, and attracts hordes in the summer. (Open daily 8am-8pm. Admission 200dr, children 100dr.) **Neapolis Beach,** a 5km bus ride south, is also quite popular. For a peaceful, deserted stretch of sand, persevere and head 13km south of Mitilini to the beach at **Agios Ermogenis;** take the blue bus from the inter-city station marked "Loutra," then walk or take a taxi.

Only 4km south of Mitilini along the same route (El Venizelou), the tiny and unassuming village of **Varia** surprises wayfarers with the **Theophilos Museum** (tel. 416 44), named for and featuring the work of the famous neoprimitivist Greek painter Theofilos Hadzimichail (admission 100dr). Next door is the **Teriade Musée.** Teriade, a native of Lesvos, rose to fame as the foremost publisher of graphic art in Paris during much of the 20th century. The museum displays an excellent collection of Picasso, Miró, Leger, Chagall, and Matisse lithographs. (Open Tues.-Sun 9am-2pm and 5-8pm. Admission 250dr.) Buses to Varia depart from the waterfront depot five times per day (150dr).

Follow Naumahias Elis (running along the northern port of Mitilini) 4km north, then head 2km west to prance amid a well-preserved Roman aqueduct at **Moria.**

Northern Lesvos

> She who dons flowers attracts the merriful Graces:
> they turn back from a bare head.
>> —Sappho, No. 19

Molyvos (Mithimna), on Lesvos's northern tip, has successfully taken its cue from Sappho's verses: it is one of Lesvos's most alluring towns, and many visitors—mostly German and British—wisely choose to base themselves in this winding tangle of cobblestone alleys rather than in Mitilini. Red tile-topped stone homes are stacked into the hillside like huge steps, leading to the Genoese *castro*. The fortress is striking in the evening light; walk up during the day for a view of the coastline and a closer look at the wildflowers growing in the ruins. Descending from the fortress, take your first left and enter the small **church** with the brown gate; the soul-penetrating eye above the altar will disconcert even the most unrepentant hedonists. Complete your ablutions at the pebble beach of **Eftalou,** 5km north of town. Avoid the crowded beach in town.

Although the small **tourist office** (tel. 713 47) in Molyvos, just past the bus stop on Posseidonos St., keeps sporadic hours, it is usually open for several minutes after buses arrive. The woman in the office has a list of *dhomatia* available in town (most singles start at 3500dr, but there are a few to be had for 2500dr). If you're lucky, she will help you find a room. If the office is closed, walk up the cobblestone way on the opposite side of the street. This road is very steep, so see if you can leave your bags with someone at the bottom. If you come in the summer, you will soon be besieged by locals offering you *dhomatia*. Although this is a typical tourist row with overpriced restaurants and glitzy shops, the street's leafy grape vines and fragrant flowers form a soothing tunnel of cool air. In the summer, a large contingent of yoga practitioners converges here. The **OTE** (tel. 713 99) is at the bottom of the street (open Mon.-Fri. 7:30am-10pm, Sat.-Sun. 7:30am-3:10pm; off-season Mon.-Fri. 7:30am-3:10pm). The **National Bank** is farther along. (Open Mon.-Thurs. 8am-2pm, Fri. 8am-1:30pm and 6-8pm.) From there, follow the signs to the central **post office** (tel. 712 46; open Mon.-Fri. 7:30am-2:30pm) and the **police** (tel. 712 22). During the summer, there is also a **mobile post office** down on the main road, past the tourist office on the left. **Camping Mithyma** (tel. 711 69 or 710 79) is 1km east of town; follow the road to the right of the bus station. The campsite is comfortable, with hot water and a refrigerator, but quite a hike from town. Molyvos's **postal code** is 81108; its **telephone code** is 0253.

The rugged road north out of Molyvos will also take you to **Eftalou** (5km northeast), home to a long stretch of secluded **beaches,** many lying beneath towering rocky cliffs. To reach these beaches, walk through a small white building containing a **thermal bath** not much bigger than a jacuzzi (free). Walk fifteen minutes to the south of Molyvos along the coastal road for the tiny but breathtakingly beautiful **Avlaki Beach,** nestled in a secluded cove. Over the hill where the main road curves left you'll see a gate leading to a narrow dirt path. Hike down this steep, winding route to the beach and enter the gates of paradise.

Southern Lesvos

In 1841, after arson demolished the village of Megalochori, people resettled in the Turkish-inhabited region 12km south, now modern **Plomari.** From its first days, this southern coastal town has been a bizarre assemblage: it is at once a glitzy resort town (with discos, bright *tavernas* and hotels oozing package tour groups) and a traditional fishing village, with locals mending their nets on the pier and nailing octopi to telephone poles to dry in the sun. The overall effect, abetted by Plomari's large *ouzo* industry, is cheerful and relaxing. The local product is far better than the industrially produced bottled variety. Try a sample at the **Barbayanni Ouzo Factory,** (tel. 327 41), about 2km east toward Agios Isodoros (open Mon.-Sat. 8am-5pm) or during the annual **Ouzo Festival.** Throughout the summer, Plomari hosts several religious celebrations and cultural events, such as the **Festival of Benjamin** which commemorates the revolutionary leader of the 1821 war against the Turks (held during late June). In Plomari's main square, the **OTE** (tel. 323 99) and the **post office** (tel. 322 41) are both open Mon.-Fri. 8am-2pm. The **bank** is also in the square (open Mon.-Thurs. 8am-2pm, Fri. 8am-1:30pm). Plomari's **postal code** is 81200; its **telephone code** is 0252.

Manolis Stefanis at **Plomari Travel** on Lesviou St. (tel. 329 46) gushes information about everything from accommodations to excursions. To get to Plomari Travel from the Commercial Bank at the end of the square, turn right into **B. Lesviou Sq.,** and then take your first right up Lesviou St. Grab some Zs at **Mrs. Mayragani's** traditional home (tel. 323 29). Walk from B. Lesviou Sq., go over the second footbridge on your left, and follow the signs for the "traditional house." Newly renovated wood-paneled doubles cost 3000dr.

Beaches appear intermittently around Plomari. To reach rocky **Arnovdeli Beach,** turn onto Ag. Nikolaou Rd. and follow the signs; it's about a five-minute walk south of town. If you continue straight on Ag. Nikolaou, you'll come to **Agios Nikolaos,** a church sparkling with icons spanning 400 years. If you aren't into stone-infested coasts, the best and most popular beaches are at **Agios Isodoros,** 3km east of town along the main road.

Fifteen km north of Plomari, the village of **Agiassos,** on the slopes of Lesvos's Mt. Olympus, remains an active center for ceramic crafts. An Orthodox church here, even more exuberantly decorated than others, contains an icon of the Virgin Mary made by St. Lucas, originally destined for Constantinople in 330 CE. When the priest transporting it heard rumors of war there, he feared for the icon's safety and deposited it in the church. Every year on August 15, Agiassos hosts *Panayia,* the grand celebration in honor of the Virgin Mary, the church's patron.

Buses go to and from Mitilini and Plomari (Mon.-Fri. 6 per day; Sept-June, 3 per day; 600dr) and Agiassos (4 per day, 325dr). The road hugs the **Bay of Geras,** offering eye-dilating views of both the coast and the interior, and passes through the charming villages of **Paleokipos** and **Pappados.**

Western Lesvos

Determined sunbathers congregate at **Skala Eressos** (known as "Skala" to locals), located at the opposite end of Lesvos from Mitilini. Skala's 1½km **beach** recently won the EEC's "Blue Banner" award for cleanliness. Its eastern half is one of the few legal nude beaches on the island. Skala is hugely popular among families, nature lovers, and nudists. Its companion village of **Eressos,** (3½km inland), the poet Sappho's birthplace, is a popular gathering place for lesbian travelers during the summer. Both villages are unspoiled by hyper-tourism and have reputations as havens for carefree lifestyles.

To get to the west from Mitilini, you can take a bus (Mon.-Fri. 3 per day; Oct.-mid-June 1 per day; 3hr.; 1300dr). Renting a car or motorbike is even more convenient (if you can manage the 95km roller-coaster-like ride).

Lena Montzorou and and her amiable Canadian co-worker Linda at **Eressos Travel** (tel. 537 77, 530 76, or 530 77) are invaluable resources. The agency, located 1 block northwest of the main square, hosts a money exchange, a private kiosk for international and local telephone calls, excursion information, car and motorbike rental information, and accommodation arrangements (open daily 9am-10pm; April to mid-June 9am-1:30pm and 6-10pm). Ask here about the **Eressos House,** which has sparkling double rooms with private bathrooms and shared refrigerator (3000-5000dr). You could also ask around for *dhomatia* (singles about 2000dr) or sacrifice privacy and **camp** on the beach 6 blocks west of the town's center. Tassos Kokkas at **Exersis Travel** (tel. 530 44) also provides help in procuring rooms. There are **post offices** in Skala Eressos (off the main square; open daily 7:30am-2pm) and Eressos (tel. 53 227; open Mon.-Fri. 7:30am-2:30pm). The **OTE** (tel. 533 99; open Mon.-Fri. 7:30am-2:30pm) is located in Eressos along with the **police station** (tel. 532 22). Both **postal codes** are 81105; **telephone codes** are 0253.

Surrounded by new-fangled outdoor cafés and a serene view of the Aegean Sea, the stone-layered square of **Anthis and Evristhenous** is the local dwelling for Skala's young, international visitors. Restaurants with bamboo-covered wooden piers sit right at the beach and serve up elegant sunset views of **Sappho's Profile** along the western mountains. The **Gorgona** (open June-Oct. daily noon-4pm and 6pm-midnight) serves ample portions of authentic Greek cuisine at moderate prices. Adjacent to the Gorgona is the local hang-out, the **Sympathy Café and Pub** (open May-Oct. daily 10am-3am), with a rocky façade and billowing music. At the end of the walkway is the **Bennetts' International and Vegetarian Restaurant** (tel 536 24; open mid-April to mid-Oct. daily 9:30am-4pm and 6-11pm). Run by Max and Jackie Bennet, a British couple (Jackie's vegetarian, but Max likes meat), the restaurant has lots of meatless options. Prices are reasonable and you'll lick the platter clean. The cafe/bar **Filoxenia** (tel. 531 31), across the street from Eressos Travel, is a popular breakfast spot with a rooftop terrace (open daily 8am-3am).

The early Christian basilica of **Agios Andreas** 3 blocks north of the beach, has splendidly preserved 5th-century mosaics (open mid-June to Sept., 24 hrs.). Greek Orthodox services are held here on Sundays 7am-10pm. Behind the church is the **Skala Museum** (tel. 533 52), with displays of 5th- and 6th-century vases, sculptured tombstones, inscriptions in the Aiolian dialect, and an anchor of a Turkish frigate from the Greek War of Independence in 1821. (Open Tues.-Sun. 8:am-3pm. Free.) The uphill road leading east is the pilgrimage route for lesbian travelers going to the remains of **Sappho's Home** in Eressos. At dusk, the view from the hill of the area below is transplendent. The river, just west of Skala's center, gargles invitations to birdwatchers to see its collection of rare and exotic birds. (Peak birdwatching season here is early April-mid-June.) If impermeable deadwood intrigues you, visit the stumps at the **petrified forest** farther inland at **Antissa,** 15km inland from both Sigri and Eressos. Rent a car or moped in Skala Eressos or check at Eressos Travel about tours.

Chios ΧΙΟΣ

When the mythical hunter Orion drove all the wild beasts off Chios, the vegetation had a field day, pun intended. Grand pines, graceful mastic trees, and brown prickly shrubs speckle the valleys and coat the mountainsides. Since antiquity, Chios has cultivated and exported mastic (*masticha,* a gummy resin used in varnishes, cosmetic creams, chewing gum, floor waxes, and many color television sets). Roughly half of the annual crop was at one time sold to Iraq to be made into alcohol. Long a center of the Greek shipping industry (and a military base), Chios has only recently been opened to the tourist industry; hence, many locals avoid catering to foreigners. Only Chios Town is at all commercialized; its cluttered waterfront masks the mountainous interior and remote beaches.

Chios rose to fame as one of the seven alleged birthplaces of Homer, but gained greater renown for commerce and art in the 6th century BCE. The island's prime location has brought numerous invasions and catastrophes: the Genoese dominated Chios for 200 years. The Turks took control in 1566; a failed rebellion in 1822 resulted in the slaughter of over 25,000 Greeks. In 1881, a major earthquake brought more destruction. Foreign rule continued until 1912, when the Balkan Wars reunited Chios with the rest of Greece. The resilient island suffered again in 1981, when a huge fire destroyed one of its two forest regions in the north around Volissos, and in 1987 when another fire devastated part of the west.

Olympic Airways (tel. 224 14) flies to Athens (2-3 per day, 40min., 10,600dr), and has two or three additional flights per week to Lesvos (40min., 10,600dr), Samos (35min., 7800dr), and Mykonos (1hr., 12,500dr). Despite the expense and distance (the airport is 2km south of town), the air schedule is much more convenient than the ferry schedule, which seems specially designed to deprive passengers of sleep. **Ferries** run to and from: Piraeus (daily at 8pm, 10hr., 2850dr); Lesvos (daily at 4:30am, 4hr., 1800dr); and Samos (Mon., Wed., and Fri., 4-5 hr., 1385dr). Smaller boats also go to Inousses (Mon.-Sat. 2pm, returning 8am the next day, Sun. 9am, returning 5pm; 1hr.; round-trip 1800dr) and Psara (Tues., Thurs., Sat. 7am, returning at noon, 1200dr). Ferries also make excursions to Çeşme on the Turkish coast. (2 per day, off-season 2-4 per week, 7000dr, round-trip 9000dr. Port taxes included.) The price varies greatly. Once a week, a boat goes to Alexandroupolis and Kavala (17hr., 3800dr).

Chios Town

Bustling Chios Town is the center for all routes of travel around Chios, and the best starting point for your stay. The town spreads along the north-south waterfront. Buses, taxis, and most shops loiter around Vournakio near the middle of the waterfront.

Take your pick of information sources. Despite unfounded pretensions to officialdom, the **Hatzelenis "tourist office"** (tel. 267 43), the white building in the north corner of the *limani* (waterfront) can offer invaluable aid. They'll find you rooms anywhere on the island. (Open daily 7am-1:30pm and 5:30-9:30pm and whenever boats arrive, even the 4am boats from Piraeus.) If you're just off a night boat, you can also try the **tourist police,** 37 Neorion St. (tel. 265 55 or 259 14), on the north side of the harbor. To get to the official **tourist office,** 18 Kanari St. (tel. 242 17 or 203 24), turn off Prokymea St., which everyone refers to as the *limani,* onto Kanari, towards the square. Service here is amiable, attentive to detail, and chockablock with information ranging from lists of accommodations to the handy free booklet, *This Summer in Chios.* (Open Mon.-Fri. 7am-2:30pm.)

Chios Town's **OTE** (open daily 7am-11pm) faces the tourist office, in the vicinity of several **banks** (open Mon.-Thurs. 8am-2pm, Fri. 8am-1:30pm). The official tourist office and many travel agencies change money in the evenings. Immediately after the Olympic Airways waterfront office, Omirou St. leads to the **post office** (open daily 7am-2pm). **Buses** leave from both sides of Vournakio Sq., right off the public gardens. Blue buses head to Karfas, Karies, and Vrondados, all within 9km of Chios Town (hourly, 200dr; buy tickets at the bus stop). Green buses, on the left side, serve the rest of the island. Buses travel north to Marmaro and Nagos (6 per day), and south to Emberio (4-8 per day) via Pirgi (320dr) and Mesta (540dr). On Sundays, only one bus goes in either direction. One bus (Mon.-Sat. 1 per day) crosses the hills to Volissos. **Bolakis Rent-a-Bike** (tel. 201 24), behind the tourist office, has well-maintained **mopeds** (2500dr per day; open daily 7am-1pm and 5-8pm). **Taxis** stop at the main square. A hospital is 2km north of Chios towards Vrondtados (tel. 234 88). Chios' **postal code** is 82100; the **telephone code** is 0271.

Most of Chios Town's accommodations are converted Neoclassical mansions with creaky wooden staircases and high ceilings. Rooms almost make the endangered species list in high season; it's better to let a tourist agency call around for you. Rare singles start at 2000dr, doubles at 3800dr. **Rooms with a View** (still known to locals as "Stella's"), 7 Rodokanaki St. (tel. 203 64), is conveniently located just off the *limani,* and rents whitewashed rooms. Expect neither elegance nor peacockery. Don, the cheerful New Zealander who runs the place with his pooch Otto, is a font of information. (Bed in a quad room 1200dr. Singles 2000dr. Doubles 3800dr.) A few other cheap pensions can be found at the south end of the waterfront. **Pension Giannis,** 48 Livanou St. (tel. 274 33), helpfully signposted at the southern corner of the harbor, provides clean rooms off a garden. (Doubles 3400dr, with bath 4000dr.) The Hatzelenis office manages **Chios Rooms,** on the waterfront, past the turn-off to Pension Giannis. (Filth-free, high-ceilinged doubles 3500dr.) **Nikos' Rooms,** 72 Venizelou St. (tel. 247 30), 1 block inland from the water, has plain rooms in an uninspired modern building. (Singles 2500dr. Doubles 3500dr.) **Chios Camping** (tel. 741 11) on the beach at Agios Isidoros, 14km north of Chios Town, has its own rocky beach. A free bus shuttles to Chios Town and back twice a day; otherwise take a green bus going north and ask to be let off at the campsite. Because there are many small beaches scattered along the coast, unofficial camping, though illegal, is prevalent. **Agios Markelas,** near Volissos in the northwest, has a *taverna* and a few good shade trees. A small community of freelance campers often comes together at the secluded cove just north of Limenas.

Myriad vendors hawk their milk, cheese, meat, bread, and produce around Vounakio Sq. If you don't mind a longish stroll, the **Hotzas Taverna** (tel. 231 17), in a traditional house on 74 Stef Tsouris St., serves delicious and inexpensive fresh food. Follow Vamva St. inland from the waterfront to the Bank of Crete, turn left, bear right at the first fork, and keep walking. The homey **Two Brothers Taverna,** 36 Livanou St., 1 block inland from the waterfront near the Pension Giannis, delivers a great *pastistio* for 550dr. (Open daily noon-4pm and 8pm-midnight.)

For a nightcap, head out of town on Livanou St., past the grungy local beach; you will come to several discos packed with locals, tourists, and Greek soldiers catching a little R&R. A rule of thumb for judging the place's popularity is to count the number of motorcycles out front.

The town has several relics of its busy past, as well as an active shopping district centered on **Vournakio Square.** The walls of the **Byzantine Kastro,** a castle reconstructed by the Genoese, encloses the narrow streets of the **Old Town.** Inside the main gate off the square, stairs climb to a tiny and peaceful **Byzantine Museum.** (Open Tues.-Sun. 8:30am-1pm. Free.) The **Turkish Mosque,** on Vournakio Sq. (look for the stripe), has conveniently metamorphosed into a museum that displays various finds from the archaeological site at Emborio. (Open Tues.-Sun. 8:30am-1pm. Free.) The town's **Archaeological Museum,** on Porphyra St. four blocks inland on the far south of the waterfront, is at best only average. (Open Mon. and Wed.-Sat. 8:45am-3pm, Sun. 9:30am-2:30pm. Admission 200dr, students 100dr.) The popular sandful beach of **Karfas,** victim of Chios' latest burst of development, is only 6km south of Chios Town. The rocky beaches of **Vrondados** and **Daskalopetra,** 9km north of town, are also within easy striking distance. Take a blue bus from Vournako Sq. to any of these beaches.

Nea Moni and Anavatos

The impressive **Nea Moni** (New Monastery), built in the 11th century, sleeps peacefully inside the pine-covered mountains 16km west of Chios Town. Long ago, an icon of the Virgin Mary miraculously appeared to three hermits who promptly founded the monastery with the aid of an exiled emperor. Over the centuries, a less random group of people rebuilt and enlarged the monastery complex. Although rather run-down, it remains one of the most important Byzantine monuments in the world. Thousands of monks living here were killed in the 1822 Turkish massacre; the modest chapel to the left of the church still contains a chilling display of the victims' skulls and bones. Though an earthquake in 1881 destroyed much of the complex itself, most of it has been carefully restored and the interior is pleasingly chaotic. The 11th-century mosaics in the inner narthex are worth a look. Even their state of partial decrepitude can't hide the original artistry. (Open daily dawn-1pm and 4-8pm. Free.)

Fifteen km west of Nea Moni is **Anavatos,** staggeringly beautiful but tainted by tragedy. The women and children of the village's 400 families threw themselves off the precipitous cliffs of this "Greek Masada" after their attempt to withstand the Turkish invasion in 1822 failed.

A **bus** from Chios ventures to both sites once a week (Wed. 8am, returning 3pm, 300dr). If you miss it, you can take one of the more frequent buses to Karies (Mon.-Sat. at least 5 per day, 200dr), and walk the remaining 6km up the steep hillside to Nea Moni. Taxi drivers may agree to drive you to a site, wait half an hour, and bring you back. Assemble a group of fellow sightseers, since you'll pay by the carload. From Karies, a taxi-tour of Nea Moni costs about 1500dr, of Anavatos 4000dr-5000dr (bargain). The road is hilly but well-paved until Nea Moni, where it deteriorates into an uneven, rocky path, passable for cars and motorcycles, but very rough on mopeds.

Southern Chios

The southern half of the island, called *Mastichochoria,* is home to Chios's famous resin, produced by squat mastic trees. The main "mastic village" is **Pirgi,** 25km from Chios and high in the hills. The striking lace-like gray and white decorations on the housefronts, called *xysta,* are the town's trademark. Walk into town past the first seven or eight houses and you'll see the English-speaking Chios Headquarters of the **Women's Agricultural Tourist Collective** (tel. 724 96), which arranges rooms in private farmhouses here and in the other villages. (Office open Mon.-Sat. 8am-2:30pm; if closed, ask around for Mrs. Kyraki in the main square, a block to the right and a block up from the office. Singles 2150dr. Doubles 3800dr. Triples 4500dr.) *Dhomatia* are plentiful and a bit cheaper. Just northeast of the square is the 14th-century **Agioi Apostoloi** church, a resplendent replica of the Nea Moni; every inch of its walls and ceiling is bathed in frescoes and paintings. The caretaker must unlock the front gate for you. (Open Tues.-Thurs. and Sat.-Sun. 10am-2pm.) A mobile **National Bank** comes to Pirgi (Mon. and Thurs. 1-2pm). The **Commercial Bank** also drops by (Wed. and Fri, 10-11am). The closest **post office** is in Kalamoti.

One km back along the road to Chios and 5km south is the black pebble beach at **Emborio.** Jutting volcanic cliffs form a series of coves and a beach as striking as the postcard version. There is bus service to Emborio. Arrange to be dropped off at the harbor and follow the road to the right, facing the water, to reach the beach. Camping is not allowed here, and the beach gets patrolled frequently.

The anachronistic village of **Mesta** perseveres 10km west of Pirgi. The town seems one continuous building under its covered medieval streets. The stonework was built to defend the town from pirates, but nowadays it staves off only the scorching sun. Buses stop on the main road ouside the city walls. From here, follow the *kentro* signs to the main courtyard. The town's two **cafés** and one restaurant, all in the courtyard, serve specialties like *mesta* wine and stewed thistles. Usually in the square from 7am to 7pm, jovial Dimitris Pippides speaks flawless English, runs a tiny **GNTO tourist office** (tel. 763 19), and books tastefully restored rooms in old houses. Doubles are a steep 4081dr, but the medieval aura of the rooms might be worth it. There are a few *dhomatia* in town (doubles run about 4000dr). The **National Bank** occasionally comes to Mesta (Mon. and Thurs. noon-1pm) and so does the Commercial Bank (Fri. 9:30-10am). Six towers once punctuated the town's fortified walls. In 1850, the main tower was demolished to make room for the **Neos Taxiarchi,** the fourth-largest church in Greece, built entirely by volunteer laborers. This church, with its elaborate rich-blue interior, replaced the nearby **Paleos Taxiarchi,** which dates from 1200 CE. The caretaker must open both churches (ask around in the square for him); a polite tip is expected.

Northern Chios

Always the poorer region, the northern half of Chios, **Voriochora,** was left even more destitute by the 1981 fire, but the beaches and small villages survive, tranquil and inviting. Since few foreigners visit, it may be difficult to find a place to stay. To appreciate the rhythmic beauty of waves pounding a ragged hillside, travel by motorbike. About 5km outside of Chios town, just past Vrontados, the beach of **Daskalopetra** (teaching rock), is where Homer supposedly held class. After Daskalopetra, the main roads wind northwest along the coast past Marmaron to **Nagos** (30km away) with its gray stone beach. **Volissos** (40km west), Homer's legendary birthplace, is crowned by a Byzantine fort and girdled by stone houses. A few km south of Volissos, a long beach stretches out alongside the four-house village of **Limnia.** Green **buses** run to and from Kardamila (6 per day, 1 per day on Sun., 350dr) and Volissos (daily at 1pm, 450dr).

If you visit **Inousses,** the little islet northeast of Chios, you will probably be one of about 10 tourists on the island. The marvelous beaches here are completely deserted; during the afternoon siesta you can meander the charming streets of the town with only stray cats for company. Inousses will probably strike you as exceptionally posh—wealthy ship-owners are responsible for the private yachts, Mercedes, and luxurious villas that opulate the coastline. A ferry leaves Chios Town for Inousses at 2pm, returning at 9am the next morning (Mon.-Sat. 1hr., 1500dr). On Sundays, the boat leaves at 9am and returns from Inousses at 5pm. Less frequent *caïques* travel to the island as well.

Samos ΣAMOΣ

With its fertile, sultry landscape and enthralling architectural remains, Samos is perhaps the most beautiful and certainly the most touristed island of the Northeast Aegean. Although Samos is quieter than the most popular islands of the Cyclades and the Dodecanese, its asteroidal attractions—Samos Town, Pythagorion and Kokkari—are packed in July and August.

The wealthiest of the Aegean islands, Samos was home to many notable Greek architects, sculptors, poets, philosophers, and scientists, including Epicurus, the moral philosopher; Aesop, the author of fables; and Aristarchus, the astronomer who argued that the sun was the center of the universe nearly 1800 years before Copernicus. The island's most beloved native son is the ancient philosopher Pythagoras, whose visage has been adopted as the symbol of Samos.

Ferries run regularly between Samos Town and Piraeus in summer (1-3 per day, 12hr., 3100dr), stopping at Ikaria (2-3hr., 1200dr). Regular ferries travel to Chios (2 per week, 4hr., 1400dr); Patmos (4 per week, 1200dr); and Paros (4 per week, 2100dr). Excursion boats run to Patmos (4 per week, round-trip 5000dr). Boats also go less frequently to many other islands (such as Lesvos, Syros, and Mykonos), but prices and schedules vary widely. There are also twice-daily boats to Turkey (see below). Olympic Airways offers several daily **flights** to and from Athens (13,000dr). There are also bi-weekly flights to: Chios (7400dr); Lesvos (11,900dr); Mykonos (10,400dr); and Kos (6700dr). The **airport** on Samos (tel. 612 19), is 4km out of Pythagorion. A bus leaves 30 minutes before every flight from the **Olympic Airways** office (tel. 272 37) in Samos Town, one block to the right of the post office and OTE (facing inland). (Office open daily 6:30am-3:30pm; bus 250dr.)

Bus service on major routes around the island is sufficient, but considerably reduced on Sundays and in off-season. The main terminal is in Samos Town, and fares range up to 380dr. Buses travel to: Tsamadou (every hr.); Pythagorion (every hr., 250dr); Karlovassi (every 2hr., 380dr); Heraion (5 per day); Mitilini (4 per day); and Psili Ammos (3 per day). The best way to see the island, however, and the only way to get around the more mountainous and remote western end, is by **motorbike** (usually 2500dr per day). The main **taxi** stand (tel. 284 04) is at Pythagoras Sq. in Samos Town. Those who hitch out of Samos towards Pythagorion walk all the way around the waterfront (to their left facing the water), then head uphill past two or three hairpin turns.

Samos Town

On the northeastern end of the island, Samos Town is among the northgeast Aegean's more attractive ports, with wide white sidewalks, colorful fishing boats, and mountains silhouetted against the sky. While the waterfront is a snarl of tourist shops and cafés, the street one block inland holds mainly shops, and the residential lanes farther back are laced with garden terraces.

Practical Information, Accommodations, and Food

Samos Town unfurls from north to south around a crescent-shaped waterfront. **Pythagoras Square,** the center of activity in the middle of the waterfront, hosts banks, cafés and taxis. When you get off the boat, cartwheel down to **Samos Tours** (tel. 277 15), at the end of the ferry dock. The office is well-staffed and provides information on everything from museum hours to accommodations. Check boat schedules here before inquiring in the many ferry company offices on the waterfront, who withhold information about their rivals' excursions. (Open daily 6am-3pm, 5:30-11pm and usually whenever a boat arrives.) The **port police** (tel. 273 18) are to the left of Samos Tours. Almost all travel agencies along the waterfront (to the right of Samos Tours) offer assistance in finding rooms. The **tourist office** (tel. 285 30 or 285 82) is signposted from the waterfront, and is on a side-street one block before Pythagoras Sq. The staff here is helpful and can find accommodations. (Open July-Aug. Mon.-Sat. 9am-1pm and 6-8:30pm.) There is a **hospital** (tel. 274 07) to the left of the ferry dock (facing inland). The **post office** (tel. 273 04) is one block up from the waterfront behind the Hotel Xenia; turn up at the immense palm tree, and walk through the municipal gardens. (Open Mon.-Fri. 7:30am-2pm.) The **OTE** is to the right of the post office. (Open daily 7am-midnight.) The filthy public toilets lurk to the left of the entrance to the gardens. To get to the **bus terminal** (tel. 272 62), follow the waterfront past Pythagoras Sq. and the BP station, turn left at Europe Rent A Car onto Lekati St., and walk 1 block. The bus schedule is posted here as well as at the tourist office and Samos Tours. The **laundromat** is near Georgiou's Taverna. (Wash 600dr, dry 400dr, soap 100dr. Open daily 7am-11pm.) Samos's **postal code** is 83100; its **telephone code** is 0273.

Trying to find accommodations in Samos generally involves a mighty headache; there are not nearly enough rooms to go around. The **Pension Ionia,** 5 Manoli Kalomiri St. (tel. 287 82), consists of four buildings full of inexpensive and fairly attractive rooms. Turn right at the end of the ferry dock; before the Hotel Aiolis on the waterfront, take a left onto E. Stamatiadou St., and then the second left onto Manoli Kalomiri St. (Singles 1800dr. Doubles 3500dr. Hot showers 24 hrs.) Friendly Mr. Zavitsanov will give you a cot in the garden if all the rooms are full. Another delightful option is the **Pension Avli** (tel. 229 39); turn right from E. Stamatiadou St. onto Manoli Kalomiri St., and go up the stairs on Arios St. Set back in a cool, leafy, courtyard, this pension is a renovated 150-year-old building that was once a convent (doubles 3500dr, with bath 4000dr). The **Pension Kleopatra** (tel. 241 64), perches at the top of a long stairway overlooking the town (doubles 3200dr); from the Pension Avli, continue up the hill, scoot to the left, and climb the stairs. There are several pensions around the Ionian and the Avli. The **Hotel Artemis** (tel. 277 92) on Pythagoras Sq., has clean rooms and a few mattresses on the roof. (Roof 750dr. Doubles with bath 4000dr.)

The Dining Excellence trophy case in Samos Town is empty. **Georgiou's Taverna,** behind the Hotel Aeolis to the left of Pythagoras Sq. (facing inland) is a better deal than the tourist traps on the water. (Open daily 11am-11pm.) **Gregori's Taverna,** one block inland from the Olympic Airways office, serves tasty roast chicken. (Open daily 7pm-midnight.)

Sights

The **Byzantine Museum,** one block back from the ferry pier, behind the cathedral, holds a reliquary with a cast of St. George's footprint. (Open Tues.-Sun. 9am-1pm. Admission 100dr.) Finds from local digs have made their way to the recently re-opened **Archaeological Museum,** next to the post office. (Open Tues.-Sun. 8:30am-3pm. Admission 400dr, students 200dr.) Nearby, the lilliputian but lovely **municipal gardens** contain caged monkeys and birds, 200 varieties of flowers, and a little café from which to observe it all. (Free.)

Pythagorion

Boats from Patmos and points south arrive in Pythagorion, the former capital of Samos. Pythagorion, more expensive than Samos Town, is quieter and surrounded by the island's archaeological sites.

Fourteen km south of Samos Town, Pythagorion is served by hourly buses (250dr); in off-season five buses run per day. The **bus stop** is on the main street, which runs perpendicular to the waterfront. The **tourist office** (tel. 610 22) is halfway between the bus stop and the water (open April-Oct. Mon.-Fri. 9am-1pm and 6-9pm, Sat.-Sun. 10am-2pm.) On the same street, you'll find a **bank** (open Mon.-Fri. 8:30am-1pm), and the **post office** (open Mon.-Fri. 7:30am-2pm). Next door are the **tourist police** (tel. 611 00). The **OTE** (open Mon.-Fri. 8am-1pm and 5-9pm) is on the waterfront to the left of the intersection with the main street (facing inland). The **port police** (tel. 612 25) are at the other end of the waterfront.

Pensions in Pythagorion are always congested in summer (doubles 3500-4100dr). Most congregate on either side of the main street a block or two inland. The **Hotel Damo** (tel. 613 03) has doubles for 2500dr. Although it's illegal, some camp on the beaches at both the east and west ends of town; the one to the west is better and less crowded. But if you don't clean up after yourself, the *Let's Go* staff will hear about it and devise vengeful expressions of its bitter disappointment in you.

Sights

The ancient city of Pythagorion, known for a while as Samos, thrived during the second half of the 6th century BCE, under the reign of Polykrates the Tyrant. According to Herodotus, Polykrates undertook the three most daring engineering projects in the Hellenic world, all in and around Pythagorion. The most impressive is the **Tunnel of Eupalinos,** 1½km up the hill to the north of town, which diverted water from a natural spring to the city below. About 1.3km long, it is in remarkably good condition, though only about 50m is open for visitors to walk through. (Open Tues.-Wed., and Sat. 10am-1pm. Free.) Polykrates's second feat was the 40m deep **harbor mole** (rock pier) on which the modern pier now rests.

Polykrates's *magnum opus* stood 5km west of Pythagorion, toward Ireon. The goddess Hera had been worshipped on Samos for seven centuries when Polykrates decided to enormify her temple. Supported by 134 columns, the **Temple of Hera** (530 BCE) was 118m long and 58m wide, and one of the seven wonders of the ancient world. It was damaged by fire in 525 BCE and never completely reconstructed, perhaps because in 522 BCE Polykrates himself was damaged and never reconstructed. With the help of the map near the entrance (labeled in German), you can see how various incarnations of the temple were cantilevered atop each other. The map may also help you sort out the maze of foundations, walls, columns, and altars. (Open Tues.-Sun. 8:30am-3pm. Admission 300dr, students 200dr.)

There are two buses per day from Samos and Pythagorion to the site. An alternative is to stroll along the beach from Pythagorion; the Ireon is waterfront property with a back gate leading right onto the beach. If you can't enter via the gate, continue along the beach past two houses where a path brings you inland to the main road and main entrance. This inland path runs close to the route of the ancient **Iera Odos** (Sacred Way) from Pythagorion to the temple.

On the south side of town rests the **Castle of Lycurgus,** built during the beginning of the last century by Lycurgus, a native of Samos and a leader in the Greek War of Independence. The **Church of the Transfiguration,** built within the ruined walls, is a pale blue variation on classical Orthodox architecture and interior decoration.

Blocks of column, wall, and entablature are strewn throughout Pythagorion like Lincoln Logs after a floorquake, and the presentation in the small **Archaeological Museum** is no different. In fact, only a little over half of the collection fits into the building;

assorted ruins are scattered on the sidewalk in front. (Open Wed., Fri., and Sun. 9:30am-2pm. Free.)

Psili Ammos and **Poseidonion,** on the southern coast of the island, are great spots to cool off after a trek through the ruins. Directly across from the Turkish coast, these beaches afford spectacular views of the Straits of Mykale. You can reach either by excursion bus (10am, returning 5pm, 700dr), or by motorbike. Even more isolated are the beaches on the eastern end of the island from **Korveli** north to **Mourtia,** accessible only by bike or on foot.

Kokkari

Built on a peninsula 10km west of Samos Town, the village of Kokkari deserves a spot on your Samos itinerary. White pebble beaches and clear waters almost completely encompass the village. On the main road into Kokkari is a **Commercial Bank** (open Mon.-Fri. 9am-2pm). Farther down the road is an **OTE** in shack's clothing. (Open Mon.-Sat. 4-11pm, Sun. 6-11pm.) You can exchange money in the souvenir shops after hours. The **tourist office** (tel. 923 33) is down the road across from the OTE. (Open daily 9am-1pm and 5-10pm.) There are daily buses to Kokkari from Samos Town (200dr).

Over the past few years, tourists have begun to flock to Kokkari. There are still many reasonably priced *dhomatia* here (doubles start at 3500dr), but they fill quickly in peak-season. **Tsamadou Beach,** 2km west of Kokkari, has a café, a fresh water tap, and shady trees; freelance camping is illegal, but common.

North Coast

The northern coast of Samos, particularly the stretch between Kokkari and Karlovassi, has a few deserted pebble beaches tucked away in little coves that are occasionally whipped by strong winds. Most of the coast is easily accessible from the road to Karlovassi, and the drive or the bus ride is worthwhile for the scenery alone.

Lemonakia Beach, 1km west of Kokkari and next to Tsamadou, is the first habitable cove, and hence quite inhabited; the wide white beach just west of **Avlakia** is even more alluring. The 16th-century monastery, **Moni Vrontianis,** rests near the village of Vourliotes, 5km south of Avlakia. From here the coast continues relatively undisturbed.

Karlovassi, Samos's western port, is an unattractive city captured by mongo hotels and empty modern buildings. But since the bus stops here and many ferries dock here before continuing to Samos Town, you might use it as a base for excursions to western Samos. The best place to stay is the colorful unofficial **Krinonas Youth Hostel** (tel. 328 72), behind the huge Panayia Church (1200dr). The various "youth hostel," "pension," and "xenon pension" signs around town will all direct you here. The **OTE** (open Mon.-Fri. 7:30am-10pm), and the **post office** (open Mon.-Fri. 8am-2pm) are neighbors on Agios Nikolaos St., on the opposite side of the square from the hostel. If you head down toward the ocean (with the hostel on your left), you'll come to the popular beach of **Limani.**

Western Samos

Tourists have yet to explore much of Western Samos. Speckled with tiny villages and manicured agricultural fields, this area is best explored by moped, though bus service from Karlovassi is adequate (2 per day). The village of **Platanos,** planted 500m above the Aegean, offers an exquisite view of both sides of the island. **Mr. Menegas** runs a cheap foodlet and hotel right on the main square (tel. 332 29; doubles 3000dr).

Marathokampos, 7km southwest of Platanos, is uncrowded and probably the easiest place on the island to find rooms (doubles 3000dr). A couple of km west of this peaceful coastal hamlet stretches the spacious beach at **Votsalakia;** another km farther is an even better beach at **Psili Ammos.** Two buses per day serve these beaches from Karlovassi. From Psili Ammos, the unpaved road continues clockwise beneath **Mount Kerkis** (1440m), winding around the island's western end in a harrowing passage overlooking dramatic mountain vistas.

The road back to Pythagorion from the center of the island takes you through the quiet mountain villages of **Koutsi** and **Pyrgos.** There are rooms to let in these peaceful retreats, but no bank or OTE. Ten km after Pythagorion, the left fork in the road as you leave the village of Koumaradhi will bring you 3km to the **Monastery of Megali Panayia.** The monastery's idyllic setting on a thickly forested pine slope justifies a visit. (Open 8am-1pm and 5-9pm.)

Near Samos: Ephesus, Turkey

Many people come to Samos simply to make the short hop over to Kuşadası for the nearby ruins of Ephesus on the Turkish coast. The archaeological site is the most extensive and probably the most evocative remnant of ancient Hellenic civilization. Founded around 1100 BCE, Ephesus rapidly blossomed into the largest metropolis of Asia Minor. Most of what remains today dates from 300 to 400 CE. (See Ephesus in Turkey coverage.)

Ferries to Kuşadası, Turkey leave from Samos Town (daily at 8am and 5pm) and Pythagorion (3 per week). About half as many boats make the crossing in off-season. A boat ride to Kuşadası costs about 4600dr (8300dr round-trip). You'll have to pay a Turkish port tax of 1660dr or $9, payable in many currencies. If you stay overnight in Turkey and leave from Kuşadası, you'll have to pay the tax again. The overpriced tours of Ephesus are not worth it (3000dr or more). Remember to give the travel agent your passport the day before you intend to sail.

Ikaria ΙΚΑΡΙΑ

Legend has it that Daedalus fashioned wings for his son Icarus to use when escaping from Crete. Intoxicated with his newly acquired power, Icarus soared too close to the sun and melted his waxen wings. He plunged to his death near the coast of this island.

In the past, tourists generally bypassed Ikaria; most of its visitors were Greeks seeking solace in its radiated baths. Ikaria is split by a rocky, barren mountain chain, and its few villages cling to its leafy, fragrant coastline. Though the long, winding coastal road is manageable for cars and durable mopeds, the interior requires a sturdy jeep.

Getting here has become considerably safer since Icarus' time; the island is on the daily **ferry** line (off-season 3 per week) from Piraeus to Samos via Paros. Ikaria is a three-hour jaunt west from Samos Town (1100dr), two hours from Karlovassi on Samos (940dr), and nine hours from Piraeus (2400dr). Boats from Samos and Piraeus alternate stops at the island's two ports: Evdilos, on the northern coast of the island; and the larger Agios Kirikos, on the southern coast. From Agios Kirikos, boats also voyage to: Patmos (2 per week, 3hr, 1700dr); Paros (6 per week, 4 hr., 1100dr); and the islands of the Fourni Archipelago (see below). Boats also go to Naxos twice weekly. Dolihi Tours (see below) organizes excursions to Patmos (3500dr round-trip). Appropriately enough, Ikaria has no airport.

Orientation and Practical Information

Agios Kirikos, the island's main port, is primarily a fishing village, although the startling, overgrown metal sculpture of Icarus on the pier could scare away fish or any other creature. The rest of the scenery is more in keeping with the island's unassuming character: modest buildings line the shore, meek boats clutter the harbor, and terraced gardens slink up the steep slopes beyond town. The island's two **banks** are in the main square (open Mon.-Thurs. 8am-2pm, Fri. 8am-1:30pm), near several cafés and assorted ferry offices. **Dolihi Tours** (tel. 220 68 or 223 46), the only tourist agency of any kind in Ag. Kirikos, sells tickets and distributes tourist information. (Open daily 8am-1pm and 6-10pm; off-season Mon.-Fri. 8am-1pm.) The **port police** (tel. 222 07) and **tourist police** (tel. 222 22) share a building; climb the steps to the left of Dolihi Tours and continue down the road. There is a **hospital** nearby (tel. 223 30). About 100m up the street to the right of the National Bank is the **post office** (open Mon.-Fri. 7:30am-2:30pm), and the **OTE** (open Mon.-Sat. 7:30am-midnight, Sun. 8:30am-11:30pm). A few places on the waterfront, and in Evdilos and Armenistis rent **motorbikes** (2500dr per day). Ikaria's **postal code** is 83300; its **telephone code** is 0275.

Climb the stairs to the right of Dolihi's to reach **Hotel Akti** (tel. 220 64), a white-washed building with green shutters and an orange sign on the roof. (Small, crude singles 2000dr. Doubles 3800dr.) The **Pension Maria-Elena** (tel. 228 35) has spotless, tasteful doubles with bath (3800dr); follow the signs leading to the left (facing inland) from the foot of the ferry dock past the **Sine Rex**, the town's movie theater. The **Hotel Isabella** (tel. 228 39), on the main square atop the National Bank, has satisfactory rooms (doubles with bath 4000dr). The **T'Adelfia Taverna,** the town's only full-scale restaurant, favors fish dishes (entrees from 600dr, open from 9pm). **Taverna Klimateria,** 1 block inland, serves traditional Greek food *(mousaka,* 600dr). For a quick meal, go to the less expensive take-outs in the square on the waterfront.

There are a few rock beaches just west of the ferry dock, but if you continue past the tourist police to the east of town, you can clamber down to some pulchritudinous coves with sandy beaches and crystal blue water. From Ag. Kirikos, a bus and a boat leave every half-hour or so to the village of **Therma** (bus 100dr, but often doesn't run in the afternoons). Taxis also go to Therma (400dr). Many elderly people come to this hamlet because they believe that the radioactive waters cure rheumatism and arthritis. All **baths** are enclosed and cost about 500dr. (Most open daily 6am-1pm and 6-8pm.) **Apostolos Manolaros** (tel. 224 33) and his English-speaking granddaughter run boat tours around the island, excursions to Patmos and Fourni, and a room-finding service.

Heading north from Ag. Kirikos, the tiny road to **Evdilos** offers amazing views of the coast as it snakes along sheer cliffs, through the florid hill country. From the island's eastern heights you can see Samos, Patmos, and the Fourni Archipelago quite clearly, but taking pictures near the military base is forbidden. On the way to Evdilos, the road passes a few tiny villages and beaches. **Buses** to Evdilos (600dr), like most means of transportation on Ikaria, are unpredictable. The bus is scheduled to leave at 10am for Armenistis (via Evdilos) and at noon for Evdilos; it often departs earlier if it's full. Check with the bus driver in the main square at least half an hour beforehand. The bus returns from Armenistis at 3pm; it is often packed in summer and has been known to take more than two hours for the 58km journey. Taxis from Ag. Kirikos to Evdilos cost 4000dr, to Armenistis 5000dr.

Evdilos itself, the island's minor port town, is not particularly comely. Miniscule and withering, it still has a post office, an **OTE,** several restaurants, and rooms to let. Proprietors descend upon those stepping off the ferry from Piraeus. For silent euphoria, walk 500m west of town to reach the beaches near Kampos.

Armenistis, 58km from Ag. Kirikos, jealously guards the best beaches on the island. Most people sleep on the fine, white sand; rooms to let are plentiful, but often occupied in July and August. **Rooms O'Eligas** (tel. 414 45), run by a friendly American couple, has unsullied rooms and a patio overlooking rocks, surf, and snorkelers (open in summer only, doubles 3000dr). The **Gallini Pension,** uphill from the main road (follow the signs) has beautiful rooms. (Doubles with bath 4000dr. Triples with bath 4500dr.) The popular **Livadi Camping** (tel. 413 49), on the beach about 300m before town, charges 500dr per person. If the crowding at Armenistis overwhelms you, escape to the mountain villages of **Christos Rachon** (near the Monastery of Evangelistrias), **Frantato,** and Dafni.

Fourni Archipelago

Crunched between Ikaria and Samos, these small rocky islands outrank their neighbors for solitude and austere isolation. Most of the island's population spends the day fishing; once out of the villages, you'll find rocky shores all to yourself. **Fourni,** the largest island, has only two villages, **Fourni Village** (also called Kampos), and the smaller **Chrisso Milia.** Fourni Village has rooms and other travel services, but take care of the absolute necessities before coming. For information, contact the **port police** (tel. 512 07) or the **police,** (tel. 512 22). One of the island's two sandy beaches is in town; the other is a half-hour walk south along a cliff path. Pirates once preyed on the small island of **Thymaina,** on Fourni's opposite end, but rest assured that your visits to this tiny port, its **Monastery of St. John,** and its restaurants, will be nothing but settling.

Fourni Village can be reached by **caïque** (a.k.a. a skiff) from Ag. Kirikos in Ikaria (4 per week, 4000dr). Boat schedules are unpredictable, so confirm all plans with the driver. **Ferries** from Ikaria or Samos venture here occasionally (3 per week, 500dr from Ikaria, 900dr from Samos). Boats in Fourni might be available for travel within the archipelago. Dolihi Tours organizes daily excursions from Ikaria, leaving (weather permitting) at 9:30am and returning to Ag. Kirikos at 6pm (round-trip 1800dr).

SARONIC GULF ISLANDS
ΣΑΡΟΝΙΚΟΣ

Over the years, the shores of the Saronic Islands have sprouted houses as rife as weeds in a small yard. The narrow streets and walkways which barely divide the houses lead up to a mountainous interior speckled with ancient temples and tranquil monasteries. Most beaches on the islands are pebbly, but surrounded by hills, they are some of Greece's most scenic swimming spots.

Despite a familial resemblance, each island has a distinct personality. Spetses is the rowdy adolescent, Hydra the grown-up sophisticate, Poros the ageless drifter, and Aegina the fickle socialite. If you can visit with only a few of these characters, go to Spetses or Hydra for beauty in nature, and Poros or Aegina for the diversity and energy afforded by multitudes of tourists.

Unfortunately, the Saronic Gulf Islands are among the most expensive in Greece, and freelance camping is illegal. But if rooms are scarce, the tourist police tend to look the other way when people pitch their tents in secluded spots; just remember that your trash leaves with you. Because the islands, especially Aegina and Poros, are such a short distance from Athens, many Greeks weekend here, rendering the already crowded situation unbearable. Try to visit during the week and find a pension or private room.

Ferries charge about 900dr for passage between any two adjacent islands. The hydrofoil costs at least 350dr extra but cuts travel time in half, runs more frequently (in calm seas), and reaches places much farther away, including Nafplion, Tolo, Leonidio, Kiparissia, Monemvassia, Kythera, and Neapolis. Prices listed for ferries and hydrofoils drop 15% in the off-season. Schedules are posted in the port of each island, but be sure to confirm them at the ticket office or at a travel agency. The **Argosaronikos Line** (tel. 451 13 11) provides the main passenger service, while the **Flying Dolphins Line,** 8 Akti Themistokleus, Piraeus (tel. 452 71 07; in Aegina tel. 244 56 or 245 71) sends hydrofoils winging about.

Aegina ΑΙΓΙΝΑ

Aegina's mountainous terrain and many small, rocky coves amenable to swimming make the island attractive to visitors. Aegina is an easy daytrip for Athenians; on weekends, half the city makes its way there on the 1½-hour ferry ride from Piraeus. Aegina Town bears the scars of an expanding tourist industry, while Agia Marina, exploding with cafés, discos, and sunbathing Europeans, has a beachier, though even less Greek, aura about it. Luckily, the island is large enough to maintain places of refuge from the crowds.

"Chummy" is certainly the wrong word to describe the relations between Athens and Aegina in ancient times. The little island made up for its size with spunk and initiative, resisting Athenian encroachment at every turn. At pan-Hellenic games, Aegina's sprinters zoomed past their competitors, and the fleet-footed came to Aegina to train. The island produced the first Greek coins—the silver "tortoises"—which subsequently gained great financial leverage throughout the Greek world. With the onset of the Persian War in 491 BCE, the Aeginetans sided first with Xerxes's army, to the ire of the besieged Athenians. But then, at Salamis in 480 BCE—the greatest of all Greek sea battles—they returned to the Greek side and won the praise of the Delphic Oracle as the swiftest navy on the seas. Island life flourished and Aegina's inhabitants built the magnificent Temple of Aphaia within the next 30 years. But they suffered the misfortunes of having taken the wrong side in the Athenian-Spartan clash and were thoroughly tromped by Athens in 459 BCE. By 431 BCE, Athens had displaced the entire

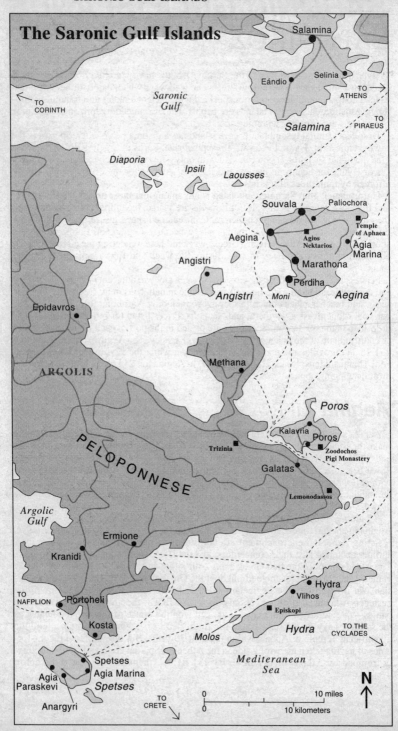

The Saronic Gulf Islands

Salamina

Eándio

Selinia

TO ATHENS

Saronic Gulf

TO CORINTH

TO PIRAEUS

Salamina

Diaporia

Ipsili

Laousses

Souvala

Paliochora

Temple of Aphaea

Aegina

Agios Nektarios

Agia Marina

Angistri

Marathona

Angistri

Perdiha

Moni

Aegina

Epidavros

Methana

ARGOLIS

Poros

Kalavria

Poros

Trizinia

Zoodochos Pigi Monastery

PELOPONNESE

Galatas

Lemonodassos

Argolic Gulf

Ermione

Kranidi

Hydra

TO NAFPLION

Portoheli

Vlihos

Episkopi

Kosta

Hydra

TO THE CYCLADES

Molos

Mediteranean Sea

Spetses

Agia Marina

Agia Paraskevi

Spetses

Anargyri

TO CRETE

N

0   10 miles
0   10 kilometers

Aeginetan population with Athenian colonists. Sparta restored the native population to the island in 405 BCE.

To get to Aegina from Athens, take green bus #40 from Filellinon St. and get off at the Public Theater (*Demotikon Theatron*) in Piraeus (½hr., 100dr). From there, you can see the pier where ferries leave for Aegina. Alternatively, take the subway (100dr) to the stop at Piraeus and walk the few blocks to the ferry from there.

Aegina Town

Most likely you will disembark in the port of **Aegina Town,** which serves as the central point of departure for buses around the island. If the ferry drops you at **Agia Marina,** walk uphill to the main road, turn left, and hop on the bus to Aegina Town (every hr., ½hr., 250dr). While there are some nice swimming spots nearby, Aegina Town does not have a great beach and thus avoids the effacing onslaughts of tourists.

Orientation and Practical Information

There are two main piers on the harbor. Hydrofoils leave from the smaller one, ferries from the larger one around the corner. The **tourist police** (tel. 221 00) have offices 2 blocks up Leonardou Lada St. (Open 24 hrs.) On the corner of Leonardou Lada St. and decorated by "Tourist Office" signs, **Tour Aegina/Leoussis Tours** (tel. 223 34) sells maps (350dr) and books. They can also help with finding a room. (Open daily 8am-9pm.) Both **banks** are on the waterfront to the right of the ferry landing. (Open Mon.-Thurs. 8am-2pm, Fri. 8am-1:30pm.) To the left of the ferry landing on Ethnegersias Sq. is the **post office** (tel. 223 98), which cashes traveler's checks. (Open Mon.-Fri. 7:30am-2pm.) The **OTE** is up Aiakou St. to the right; keep trudging up Aiakou when the street narrows into a walkway—the building has a monstrous satellite dish on its roof. (Open Mon.-Fri. 7:30am-3:10pm.) The **port police** are located on the pier. The **hospital** (tel. 22 20 90 or 222 51) on Nosokomiou St. above Aegina Town and beyond the OTE, has an English-speaking doctor. The **postal code** for Aegina is 18010; the **telephone code** is 0297.

From the **bus station** (tel. 224 12), in front of the post office, buses leave hourly from 6:15am-8:35pm for: Agia Marina (30min., 250dr), Perdika (20min., 150dr), and Souvala (30min., 200dr). Bicycles and motor-bikes are also available for rent from one of the many vendors. (Bikes 1000dr per day, 3500dr per week. Mopeds cost 2000-2500dr per day). **Lampados Rental,** near the police, rents medium mopeds for 9000dr for an entire week. Be careful: the island's roads are notorious for blind curves, absurdly fast drivers, and, hence, totaled motorbikes.

Ten **ferries** (tel. 223 28) per day keep Aegina well-connected to Piraeus (1½hr., 700dr). Six additional boats leave from Agia Marina for Piraeus (Mon.-Sat., 1½hr.). Passenger ferries for other Saronic Gulf destinations run as follows (complete information available from port police next to the hydrofoil ticket stand): 8 per day for Methana (45min., 600dr) and Poros (1½hr., 600dr). On Sunday, this ferry stops at Ermione. One per day to Hydra (2½hr., 850dr); Spetses (4hr., 1100dr); and Ermione (3hr., 1100dr). **Hydrofoils** (tel. 245 71) go 13 times a day to Piraeus (35min., 1000dr) and daily at 9:45am to: Methana (20min., 600dr); Poros (40min., 1040dr); Hydra (1¼hr., 1450dr); Ermione (2hr., 1750dr); and Porto Heli (2½hr., 2190dr). The schedules from Aegina are inconsistent, and the posted time-tables are rarely in English. You can make connections at Poros, Hydra, and Spetses to reach more locations on the Peloponnese.

Accommodations, Food, and Entertainment

The island fills up fast with family vacationers, so you may have trouble finding a place to stay. The high-season norm is 2500dr for singles, 4500dr for doubles. To find rooms, ask at the hotels or look for *dhomatia* ("rooms to let") signs in the back streets. Since the island has to ship in its entire water supply from Poros and Piraeus, expect to pay up to 300dr for a short shower.

Hotel Marmarinos (tel. 235 10 or 224 74), Leonardou Lada St., above the tourist police, has clean rooms, some with balconies. (Singles from 2500dr. Doubles 4500dr.) **Sklavenas Hostel,** 19 Kapothistries St. (tel. 223 27) has great roof-space and pleasant rooms. (Roof 1000dr. Doubles 3800dr.) Call 230 72 or 246 19 for information regarding *dhomatia* on #8 Agios Nikolau St. (Doubles with bath 4500dr.) Police sometimes tolerate freelance camping when the town is full, and sometimes not.

For traditional fish dishes in a no-nonsense restaurant behind the fish market on P. Irioti street, try **Psarotaverna Agora** (ΨΑΡΟΤΑΒΕΠΝΑ ΑΓΟΡΑ). A full meal at this popular restaurant costs about 1400dr. Other good choices are **To Maridari** and **Espaterion** on the waterfront. Behind the fish market and beyond the bank, fresh fruit dealers and food stands beckon.

At night, Agia Marina sublimes into a haze of club lights and a dissonant refrain of bar music. In Aegina Town, **Inoe (INOH)** disco offers dancing right above the beach. **Retro Music Bar** (tel. 224 37), next to the post office, caters to a mellow crowd. (Open 8pm-3am.) The outdoor **cinema,** up Aiakou St., often shows American films (500dr). Check the signs on the fence near the museum for more information about evening events.

Sights

Aegina Town's archaeological fame rests tenuously on the last half-column of the **Temple of Apollo,** a short walk out of town to the north. (Open Tues.-Sun. 8:30am-3pm. Admission 300dr, students 150dr.) The **archaeological museum** (tel. 226 37), within the temple grounds, has a small collection. Free with admission to temple.

Around the Island

Near Agia Marina, on the other side of the island, the 5th-century **Temple of Aphaia** claims to be the only surviving Hellenic temple with a second row of small superimposed columns in the interior sanctuary. Be still your beating heart. Even more striking is the view from the top of the hill. A short bus ride drops you off right at the temple. (Open Mon.-Fri. 8:15am-5pm, weekends and holidays 8:30am-3pm. Admission 400dr, students 200dr.) In Agia Marina, walk to the end of town with the water on your right and then straight up Kilokotroni St. until it becomes a wooded trail—this is the footpath to the Temple of Aphaia. At night, peacocks roam the quiet hills by the temple.

The pleasantly untouristed island of **Angistri** is a half-hour sail from Aegina Town (4 per day in summer, last return at 5pm, 350dr). The beach at **Skala** is the best place for swimming, although you might also want to explore **Milo** and **Limenario.** Try the **Angistri** (tel. 912 42) on the beach if you decide to stay.

On the road between Aegina and Agia Marina, in the middle of the island, is the village of **Paliochora,** where the islanders used to take refuge from invasions. Once "the town of 300 churches," only 28 of these remain, some with inspirational frescoes. Modest dress (no shorts) appreciated.

A westbound bus from Aegina Town will deposit you in Perdiha (150dr), a fishing village settled by a small population of artists and many more birds. From Perdiha travel to the tiny uninhabited island of **Moni.** Here brusque hills, a rock plateau, and sparkling blue water make the entire trip to the Saronic Gulf worthwhile. You can pitch a tent or unroll your sleeping bag, but be sure to bring provisions, including water, which is hard to find. Bring a garbage bag along so that trash will be hard to find here as well. A motorboat meets most buses coming from Aegina for the ride to Moni (about 200dr each way).

Poros ΠΟΡΟΣ

Only a sliver of water separates the sinewy hills of the mainland from this tiny isle. Poros, three hours from Piraeus, is actually two small, lush islands—Kalavria and Sphaeria—cut by a canal. Its name, meaning "passage," refers to the channel that is its border. The geographical conditions are comparable to those of the Bosphorus, and "Poros" is said to be a derivation from that name.

The arcane Kalavrian League, a seven-city council, met in Poros to ward off hostile naval powers and order the building of the Temple of Poseidon in the 6th century BCE.

Three hundred years later, the great orator Demosthenes, who improved his diction by speaking with marbles in his mouth, killed himself beside its columns. Poros had been sparsely populated for most of modern history until Greeks arrived from Turkey in the population exchange of the 1920s.

Poros Town occupies most of tiny Sphaeria, while woods extend over rugged Kalavria. Less crowded than Aegina, Poros still overflows with tourists on the weekends. Rather than spend all your time on the waterfront, you can find some serenity and spectacular views by climbing up the narrow passageways that lead to the top of Poros Town and the hills beyond.

Orientation and Practical Information

Ferries (3hr., 1200dr), hydrofoils (1hr., 2000dr), and hovercraft ferries (1hr., 1800dr) leave Piraeus for Poros several times per day. En route, the boats stop in **Methana** on a volcanic peninsula of the Peloponnese, known since antiquity for its curative springs. In Poros Town, hydrofoils dock at the main landing in the center of town, while car ferries dock either there or a dozen blocks to the left (facing inland) on the northwest side of town. Directly in front of the main ferry landing, **Family Tours,** 14 Troon St. (tel. 237 41; open daily 9am-10pm), sells maps of Poros for 300dr, as does nearby **Takis Travel** (tel. 220 48), located behind George's Café. Both agencies provide general information, change money, and locate overpriced rooms. Set back from the waterfront on Agiou Nikolaou St., 100m to the right of the main ferry landing, are the **tourist police** (tel. 224 62 or 222 56), who might help you find a room. (Open mid-June to Sept. Mon.-Fri. 8am-2:30pm; for emergencies, an officer is usually available 24 hrs.) The **bank** is #68, past the church, 175m from the main ferry landing. (Open Mon.-Thurs. 8am-2pm, Fri. 8am-1:30pm.) The **post office** occupies the first square to the right along the water (open Mon.-Fri. 7:30am-2pm). The **OTE** is centrally located at #30, off the alleyway on the wharf. (Open Mon.-Fri. 7:30am-3pm.) **Suzi's Launderette Service** (tel. 242 09) is next door. (Wash and dry 1150dr. Open daily 9:30am-1:30pm.) **Anita's Books,** 120m from the Canal gas station, swaps second-hand books in many languages. Rent bikes or mopeds from **Stelio's** (tel. 245 90) or **Kostas** (tel. 235 65). Both charge 800dr for bikes, 1500-2000dr for one-person mopeds, 2800dr for larger mopeds, and are open daily 9am-7:30pm. Stelio's also carries motorcycles for rent. In high-season, the earlybird gets the cycle. You can rent cheaper bikes across the water in Galatas at **Fotis Bikes** (Φοτισ) (see Sights). Poros's **postal code** is 18020; the **telephone code** is 0298.

The port police have a blackboard at the main ferry landing, showing the day's departures. From Poros, **ferries** run to Piraeus four times per day (3hr., 1100dr). All of these stop in Methana (45min., 450dr), Aegina (1½hr., 600dr) and Spetses (2½hr., 1100 dr). **Lela Tours** (tel. 244 39) has information and tickets (open daily 9:30am-4pm and 5-9:30pm), as do the **port police** (tel. 222 74), and **George's Café** (tel. 240 80), below Takis Tours. **Hydrofoils** serve Piraeus from Poros (Mon.-Sat. 7 times per day, Sun. 11 times; 1¼hr.; 2000dr). Information on additional destinations and hydrofoil tickets are available from the **Flying Dolphin office** (tel. 222 97), opposite the landing (open 6am-10pm), and on the landing itself before departure. There is a good map on the landing opposite Takis Tours.

Accommodations, Food, and Entertainment

Most of the low-priced pensions and rooms for rent in Poros are clean, but private baths and singles are extremely rare (doubles from 3800dr). Many of the better pensions and *dhomatia* flank the Hotel Latsis a dozen blocks to the left of the main pier. Two reputable places are **Nikos Douras** (tel. 226 33; doubles 4800dr) and **George Douras** (tel. 225 32). Rooms at both are spotless and comfortable. For Nikos, follow the blue "rooms" sign bearing the telephone number. People with rooms to rent will approach the ferries rather aggressively, and you should bargain aggressively in turn.

Poros Town has many of the best restaurants in the Saronic Gulf. For reasonably priced seafood and grilled meats, try **Caravella** (tel. 236 66; *kalamari* 700dr, chicken

600dr) or the neighboring **Lagoudera** (tel. 223 89; open noon-midnight). Both are on the wharf. In the square to the right of Takis, the atmospheric **Seven Brothers** (tel. 224 46) has large portions of well-prepared food (from 800dr; open noon-1am.) Another fraternal establishment, **Three Brothers** (tel. 223 36), opposite the museum 100m to the right, is the place to watch nightly Greek dances. For a good continental breakfast, including coffee with steamed milk, try **George's Café** (tel. 235 08), directly across from the hydrofoil/ferry boat landing (500dr). Several very good **grocery stores** lie to the right of the main landing. The coffee shops which line the harbor facing the Peloponnese sell reasonably priced breakfasts or Nescafé frappacinos. **Zorba's** (tel. 227 39) serves up tasty dishes and offers traditional dancing about ½km up the road to the left of the wharf (facing inland), across the canal. You can also find inexpensive *souvlaki* and chicken at the restaurant next to the **Diana movie theater** (#50 on the left-hand side of the port facing inland). The theater often shows American and British films (500dr). For more excitement, try the Greek dancing at **Kavos,** at the far right along the waterfront. **Corali,** a high-tech disco, is next door. Around the big bend, **Siroco,** the most popular disco, hosts a wonderful view of the Gulf.

Sights

In Poros Town itself, the **archaeological museum,** one block before the church along the water, is small but has some interesting inscriptions and photographs of the ruins at Troizen. (Open Mon.-Sat. 9am-3pm. Free.)

The main sight on Poros in general, the **Monastery of Zoodochos Pigis** (Virgin of the Life-Giving Spring), has an excellent vista and is situated in an overgrown glade 6km from Poros Town. Since early as 200 CE, monks have been quaffing the curative waters. Inside you'll find a spectacular altarpiece inlaid with gold illustrating scenes from the lives of Jesus and the Apostles, as well as of St. Barbara and St. Nikolas. Proper dress is required; men wearing shorts and women wearing pants are forbidden to enter. A few high-fashion skirt-like coverings are available at the door. (Open daily 6am-1pm and 3pm-sunset.) It's a scenic bus ride from the stop next to the main port in town (7am-11pm every 45min., 20min., 100dr). Along the route to the monastery is the little beach of **Askeli,** and an area of small restaurants and hotels.

Unless you're a Greek history maven, the main incentive to visit the knee-deep rubble of the 6th-century BCE **Temple of Poseidon** atop the mountain is the panoramic look at the Saronic Gulf. The Athenian statesman Demosthenes took sanctuary from his Macedonian enemies here. Ignoring the temple's tradition of sanctuary, the Macedonians graced him with only a few moments reprieve so he could write a farewell letter to his family. His captors mocked his cowardice as he sat trembling and chewing his pen. But the cagey orator had the last laugh—he died as they waited, having dipped the end of his quill in poison.

Boats run between the Peloponnese and the harbor of Poros (5min., 100dr). Take the *caïque* across the channel to **Galatas** on the Peloponnese for the sunny beaches of **Aliki** (the nicer but farther of the two) and **Plaka**, both quite a distance to the left as you walk along the shore. Aliki is a pleasant bike-ride from Galatas town center. Ride east towards Plaka beach and take a left on the dirt road 100m after Plaka. There is also a small aquasports center here. A 10-minute walk from both leads to the enormous fragrant lemon grove of **Lemonodassos,** with a waterfall. Although camping is officially forbidden in the area, tents do crop up behind Plaka and Aliki Beaches. Those who stay here exercise discretion (and often their walking shoes), since the tourist police are strict. Official camping can be found at **Camping Kyrangelo** (tel. 245 20), 1km northwest of Galatas.

Take advantage of the low bike rental prices at **Fotis Bikes** (tel. 244 09 or 246 76; bicycles 200dr per hr., 650dr per day), in Galatas, behind the harbor road to the right (facing inland). Most visitors to the island miss the surrounding Peloponnesian countryside and the best **cycling routes** around, which begin in Galatas going northwest away from the lemon groves. The terrain is flat and the fields range from cultivated flowers to apricot groves. You won't ever be far from a cold drink, especially if you pedal down the 3km turn-off by the carnation fields of **Trizinia,** the site of ancient

Troizen. (Buses run here from Galatas; call 224 80.) Back on the main road, it's 10km from Galatas to the turn-off for Nafplion. Before the bakery in Kaloni is a sign for the long, tranquil Agios Georgios Beach.

Neorion Beach is accessible by boat (60dr), foot, or bike. Take the road from the left of the pier about 3km and turn left at the Neorion sign over the little canal bridge. **Canali Beach** and its equally rocky neighbor lie just to the right of the canal bridge. The better beaches are farther from town.

Hydra (Idra) ΥΔΡΑ

Hydra at first seems to be merely a snazzy version of the typical Greek port town, with its dazzling white houses nestled quietly among steep rocky hills and a small but busy harbor. The uneasy knowledge that Hydra is unlike almost anywhere else you've been may come only gradually, as the absence of the horns and rumbles of cars sinks in. On the island you'll see donkeys, boats bearing the sign "Taxi," and steep roads and steps. The only automobile, however, is a lone garbage truck. It is no wonder that Hydra, "the well-watered," is now the lush island home of many Greek artists, some of whom display their work along the water. Others retreat to the backstreets where the only disturbance is the occasional bray of a cranky donkey. Visitors who seek a respite from the bustling town can take inexpensive boats from Hydra's port to far-off, peaceful beaches.

Orientation and Practical Information

For a daytrip, Hydra is accessible from Poros, Ermione, or Spetses. **Ferries** run to: Poros (1hr., 600dr); Methana (2hr., 840dr); Aegina (2½hr., 860dr); Piraeus (4hr., 1265dr); Ermione (1hr., 670dr); and Spetses (1½hr., 650dr). Friday through Sunday, the *Hydra* (ΥΔΡΑ) provides additional service. **Hydrofoils** serve Piraeus frequently (at least 9 per day, 2550dr). There are also frequent hydrofoil connections to: Poros (7 per day, 750dr); Methana (7 per day, 1500dr); and Aegina (3 per day, 2½hr., 950dr); Ermione and Spetses (5 per day, 40min., 1040dr); Porto Heli (6 per day, 45min., 1250dr); Leonidio (at 10am, 1hr., 1860dr); Kyparissia (1½hr., 2800dr); Monemvassia (2hr., 2300dr); Kythera (summer only, 5000dr); and Neapolis (about 5500dr). Tickets are sold by the **Flying Dolphin Ticket Office,** on Em. Tombaz St., 2nd floor (tel. 520 19), on the left corner of the harbor (facing inland). (Open 6am-8pm.) The **port police** (tel. 522 79) are located in the left hand corner of the harbor.

The **tourist police** (tel. 522 05) are along N. Votsi St. Walk along the wharf and turn left before the clock tower (a vital landmark on this island). The police (open 24 hrs.) provide a free guide, *This Summer in Hydra,* which has a map as well as some entertainment and sightseeing information. **Saronic Tours** (tel. 521 21) near the ferry and hydrofoil landing, also sells a map of Hydra (250dr). Opposite the tourist police is the **OTE** (open Mon.-Fri. 7:30am-3pm). The **post office** (tel. 522 62) is in the alley parallel to Economa St.—there are signs along the wharf. (Open Mon.-Fri. 7:30am-2pm.) The **National Bank of Greece** is right on the wharf (open Mon.-Thurs. 8am-2pm, Fri. 8am-1:30pm). Hydra's **telephone code** is 0298.

Accommodations, Food, and Entertainment

Hydra has the highest-priced accommodations in the Saronic Gulf. Singles are practically nonexistent and doubles cost at least 4500dr. Furthermore, it can be almost impossible to find a place here without reservations, especially on weekends in the summer. About the cheapest hotel in town is the **Sophia,** A. Miaouli St. (tel. 523 13), at the center of the wharf. (Doubles 4515dr. Triples 5420dr. Hot showers included.) You may find yourself tapping your foot to the loud Greek music that wafts up from the bar downstairs until 3am. The **Pension Agelika,** 42 Andreou Miaouli St. (tel. 523 60) has nice, expensive rooms on an attractive, calm street away from the port. (Doubles 6000dr. Breakfast included.) Making Hydra a day trip is the budget traveler's wisest move.

Food prices on Hydra vary quite a bit. The 200dr-a-hit *souvlaki* places coexist along-side more posh establishments. The juice café in the westernmost corner of the harbor is relatively affordable and serves enormous cheese *tost*. Make sure you know what you're paying before you order; also beware of price minimums. The **Restaurant Lulu,** straight up from the dock on the same road as Sophia's Hotel, is a bargain. (Salads 500-650dr; *mousaka* 500dr; veal dishes 750dr.) **Captain George's** has generous portions of the best fish around, but the price may stick in your throat like a bone. Sometimes the Captain provides live Greek music. Follow signs up the street from the hydrofoil office. (Chicken 650dr.) **Taverna Douskos,** (also known as Ee Kseree Eleeyah; sign in Greek: Η ΧΕΠΗ ΕΛΙΑ) is just around the corner, and **The Garden** is up the street from the hydrofoil office (follow signs). Both have a wide selection of reasonably priced food. Past the Flying Dolphin office on the left, the **bakery** can help hold you over with an immense selection of pastries, rolls, and tasty mini-pizzas. There's a produce **market** right by the post office.

The dance clubs all have over-priced cocktails (from 800-1000dr), but when you gotta dance, you gotta dance. Check out **Disco Kavos** or **Lagoudera**, both on the western edge of the harbor.

Sights

Hydra's arid land went untaxed for most of the Turkish occupation. With no natural resources and a growing refugee population from the Peloponnese, Balkans, and Turkey, Hydra's inhabitants turned to managing other areas' exports, and its merchant princes became shipping magnates. Hydriotes grew prosperous by dodging pirates and naval blockades during the late 18th and early 19th centuries, and emerged as effective financial and naval leaders in their country's revolt against the Turks in the 1820s. **Koundouriotis,** whose house is on a hill to the west of the harbor, was one of the many Hydriot leaders in the Greek War of Independence. To get to his house, walk up the narrow alley to the right of The Pirate Bar, which becomes Lignou St. The fourth alleyway on your right goes around the block where the house stands opposite a church. Visit the tourist police to make sure the house is open. The houses of **Votsis** and **Economou,** two Hydriotes who also contributed to the island's naval fame, are closer to the crest of the hill, right on Voulgari St. There are more houses and mansions; most are locked, but they're fun to find. The **art school,** 1 block up from the harbor's right corner, has occasional exhibits.

The Ecclesiastical Church, built in 1806, bears the large clock tower that dominates the wharf. Also of interest are the frescoes at the **Church of St. John** in the Platia Kamina. Around to the east of the harbor, set off by its winding, anchor-flanked white stairs, is the **Pilot School** of the Greek Merchant Marine, with intriguing paintings, models, and class pictures from the 1930s. (Open variably 8am-10pm. Free.)

A short hike (1hr.) trudges down A. Miaouli St. from the waterfront (the road takes you out of town) up the hill to the monastery of **Ilias,** and, on a lower peak overlooking the harbor, the nunnery of **Efpraxia.** (Both open 9am-5pm.) While the nuns at Efpraxia do beautiful embroidery work, Ilias is by far the prettier of the two monasteries and the home of two monks who may show you about. To return to the harbor, climb down the monastery steps and follow the steps and passageways down through the town. Another hike is to **Episkopi,** a deserted monastery at least an hour's walk west from Ilias along goat paths that take you through beautiful uninhabited countryside. The Greek word for footpath is *monopati;* use it when you ask for directions to return to town. Cut down to the north coast via the tiny village of **Vlihos.** The beach at Vlikos is a 40-minute walk from town along the coast. Some people discreetly pitch tents on the small deserted pebble beach here.

These are long and hilly walks, so bring water and go early. If you feel too hot to walk, take a swim. In general, the beaches on Hydra are rocky ledges a short walk west from town. When the water is calm, small *caïques* run regularly to pretty **Palamida** and neighboring beaches on the west side. **Mira Mare Beach,** at Mandraki, is easier to reach, either by a half-hour walk along the water from the east end of town, or by a 15-minute boat ride (200dr). This beach is less attractive than others, however, and dominated by a new watersports center. Don't take the water taxis; even their lowest fares are egregiously expensive.

On the trip between Hydra and Spetses, the boat and hydrofoil stop at the resort town of **Ermione** on the Peloponnese; get off here for daily bus connections to Epidavros or Nafplion. Stay on the boat if you're continuing to Spetses.

Spetses ΣΠΕΤΣΕΣ

Spetses, the "pine" island, looks like a piece of forest that floated away from the nearby Peloponnesian coast. Set in slender arcs of broad stone and pebbles, the beaches here are plenty enough to absorb their sun-starved clientele. Every drop of water, however, must be imported from the mainland; for this reason, the island was settled late and minimally. Those willing to risk a few scratches can descend from the single beaten path to the island's sweet-smelling interior. Spetses even boasts a famous native: Lascarina Bouboulina, a heroine who was captain of her own ship during the Revolution in 1821. Her little black book was supposedly as full as those of Catherine the Great and the mighty Zeus himself.

Practical Information

Restaurants and shops form a 2km line on either side of the port. The old harbor is eastward, beyond the town beach. The **tourist police** (tel. 731 00) are straight up from the dock on Botassi St. They provide an accommodations brochure and general information about the island. (Open 24 hrs.) The **port police** (tel. 722 45 or 720 05) post ferry and hydrofoil schedules and prices on the dock. The cobbled square directly behind the new harbor is called the **Daria**. The **post office** is near the police station. Follow the signs. (Open Mon.-Fri. 7:30am-2pm.) Two **banks** are open on the Daria, on the right side of the harbor (facing inland). (Open Mon.-Fri. 7:30am-2pm.) The **OTE** (tel. 721 99) is next door to the National Bank of Greece. (Open Mon.-Fri. 7:30am-11pm; Sat.-Sun. 9am-3pm and 6-9:30pm.) The newsstand to the left of the dock stocks maps of the island (400dr). Large maps are posted in several locations (e.g. on the dock, and in neighboring travel agents). For **first aid,** call 724 72. Spetses's **postal code** is 18050; its **telephone code** is 0298.

From Spetses, a **ferry** serves Piraeus daily at 2:30pm (Wed. and Sat. also 1:30pm, 5hr., 1500 dr). Boats also travel to: Ermione (½hr., 610dr); Hydra (1hr., 640dr); Poros (2hr., 830dr); Methana (2½hr., 850dr); and Aegina (3½hr., 1000dr). For tickets and information, go to Alasia Tours (tel. 738 32). New **Hovercraft ferries** speed from Piraeus to Spetses (2½hr., 2450dr). For information, contact the Supercats Marine Company (tel. (01) 325 36 40) in Piraeus. **Hydrofoils** go to Piraeus nine times per day in high season, but only about three times per day in off-season (2hr., 2770dr). The informative Flying Dolphin ticket office (tel. 731 41/2) is next door to Pine Island Tours, straight up from the dock in Daria Sq. Car ferries leave for Kostas five times per day, times are posted at the dock. **Catamarans** run from Spetses to Athens. For information, contact the port office of Pine Island Tourist Office in Spetses (tel. 724 64). To rent a motorbike, visit **Costas** (tel. 720 88), behind the Soleil bar, or **Mimi's** near the cleaners (mopeds average 1500-2500dr per day). At the **Spetses Hotel and Beach** and **Agii Anargiri,** you can parasail (5000dr) or rent water skis (3000dr per "go-around") and windsurfing boards (2000dr per hour); reductions for groups.

Accommodations, Food, and Entertainment

As elsewhere in the Saronic Gulf region, accommodations can be a serious hassle. **Takis Travel** (tel. 728 88), straight down to the left as you disembark, controls 80% of the rooms in town; that's 3500 beds, most of which are already booked by British package tours. Singles are virtually nonexistent, and doubles with clean communal facilities go for at least 4000dr. If you're traveling alone, you can try to find someone to share a room with, especially when the boats arrive. (Takis is open in summer daily 9am-2pm and 5-9pm.) Some noisy hotels line the docks; the **Saronikon** (tel. 737 41) has spiffy rooms which overlook the water. (Doubles 4500dr. Triples 5000dr.)

If you get to town early and want to find **dhomatia,** walk up past the tourist police following the signs for the Aporrito Bar. Two buildings past the bar, look for the white wall with a thin blue-lettered "Rooms to Let" sign painted over a tile of a boat. The family here (tel. 726 31) rents rooms with Victorian furniture and lace curtains. (Doubles 4000dr. Triples 5000dr.) Another home with rooms to rent is located behind the Anargyrios Mansion, 2 blocks up from the dock—look for dark green doors with a black hand-knocker or inquire at Pine Island Holidays Office, next to the Flying Dolphins ticket office. Huge rooms in an old building with antique furniture in the living room. (Hot water. About 1500dr per person.) You can also try any of the D- and E-class hotels from the tourist police pamphlet; they're often full, but may be able to refer you elsewhere.

Lirakis rooftop restaurant (tel. 722 88), just to the east of Takis, is one of the best on the island. Its portions and service only look expensive (chicken 700dr; omelettes 500dr). Also try **Stelios,** along the wharf past Takis, which has lamb dishes for 850dr. **Ta Tzakia** ("the fireplaces") offers *tzatziki* for 200dr. Try **To Roli** (το ρολι), in the clock square. The **Palm Tree Café,** on Botassi St. below the tourist police, serves an excellent full English breakfast, as does **To Rithion** (600dr). For authentic Greek coffee made over coals, stop by **To Kafeneio** (also known as "Argyris" το καφενιο), at the entrance to the port. (Coffee 100-150dr.) Don't miss *amigdalato,* the island confection. There are plenty of supermarkets and groceries in town.

At night, people on Spetses gather for drinks at **To Rithion,** the **Anchor II,** and the roof-top garden of **Hotel Soleil.** A short walk or hike along the water brings you to the quieter, more sophisticated **Old Harbor.** Stop at piano bar **Mourayo** for a terrific view of the harbor. On the other end of town, discos and bars across from the town beach blast dance music. Give in to the pulsating beat at **Delfinia,** several blocks west of the harbor (open 10pm-3am, cover 1000dr, drink included), or join in the ballyhoo at the **Rendez-Vous** (mixed drinks 800dr.) Most bars close at 3am. For a mellow evening, go to one of Spetses's two movie theaters. **Ciné Marina,** near the tourist police, often features English language films (700dr). The other cinema is in the Daria.

Sights

The **Anargyrios and Korgialenios College** (high school) is a 25-minute walk from town. John Fowles taught here from 1951-52 and memorialized both institution and island in his novel *The Magus.* For a beautiful walk, especially at dusk, go left past Takis and continue along the stone path between the water and the high, whitewashed stone walls to the old harbor, which is quieter and has fewer tourist shops than the new port. *Spetsai,* by Andrew Thomas, is a helpful book about the island's history, with suggestions for walks.

On the rise above the town is a **museum** in the crumbling mansion of Hadjiyanni Mexi, Spetses's first governor. It houses coins, costumes, ship models, weapons, and other memorabilia. Wooden window frames, doors, and chests set in the museum walls create the illusion of being on a 19th-century ship. To find the museum, follow Hadjiyianni Mexi St. through its several twists and turns until you see the signs. (Open Tues.-Sun. 8:30am-3pm. Free.) The house of Lascarina Bouboulina is next to the park near the Daria. A ship's captain in the Greek War of Independence, Mme. Bouboulina's heroic exploits are celebrated on Spetses in early September with a mock naval battle in which a small boat is blown up. The monastery of **Agios Nickolas** stands opposite a square of traditional Spetsiot-pebbled mosaics in the Old Harbor. Among its treasures is a plaque commemorating Napoleon's nephew, who was pickled in a barrel of rum stored in a monastic cell at Agios Nickolas from 1827-32.

A tour of the island, as you travel west from the harbor, will take you past the **beaches** at Spetses Hotel (which you can recognize by the rock-n-roll playing at their popular bar). The last 10km has a starker landscape with fewer beaches draping the shore. A couple of fancy mansions stand dignified in this stretch. The last beach before Spetses Town is the crowded, dirty, and ineptly-named **Paradise,** in pebbly Agia Marina. Be sure to watch out for sea urchins, which plague Spetes's beaches and vulnerable bare feet. The road past the tourist police leads to the island's main summit. The bumpy track takes you several km up into the hills through sweet-smelling pines to the panorama of the Peloponnese and its train of islands. There's a small chapel on the way with picnic tables. From here, trails of similar length descend to Vrelos, Anargyri, and Agriopetres.

Buses (380-450dr round trip) leave one to three times per day for Anargyri from the bus stop to the left of the harbor by the town beach. Be sure to buy a return ticket and keep your stub. Motorboats leave the harbor 9:30-11:30am, returning from the beaches at about 4pm. (600dr.) Anargyri is 40 minutes away. Sea taxis cost a fortune (5500dr for Anargyri). Since only registered cars are allowed on the island, overland transportation is provided by **horse-drawn carriage,** which will usually not travel farther than Kastelli Beach or Agia Marina. Spetses has two taxis. A car ferry runs back and forth between Spetses and the tiny town of **Kosta** on the Peloponnese (5 per day, 200dr); small boats make the same trip, but charge a bit more. The sea taxis cost a whopping 2000dr.

Kosta has the broadest sandy beach in the area. From there you can catch the bus to the immense resort of **Porto Heli** and its cemetery from the Classical period, or to **Kranidi** (200dr), where buses leave for Epidavros and Nafplion (4 buses per day until 5pm, some change in Ligouri, 680dr). From Kranidi, buses depart to Athens hourly (until 8pm); Argos (on the ½hr. until 10:30pm); Tolo (hourly until 8:30pm); Mycenae (4 daily until 5pm). The **bus stop** in Kosta is to the left of the boat landing, on the road between the hotel and the restaurant. **Camping Kosta** (tel. 515 71) charges 600dr per person 500dr per tent. Boats to Spetses often won't leave until they have enough people.

SPORADES ΣΠΟΡΑΔΕΣ

Lush islands of fragrant pines, luxurious beaches, and abundant fruit orchards, the Sporades ("the scattered ones") offer travelers a smorgasbord of earthly delights. Although word has gotten out about the Sporades, and the islands' fledgling tourist facilities are quickly maturing, this small archipelago remains relatively quiet and inexpensive.

Skiathos is the most popular of the Sporades. Daytime finds supine bronzed bodies blanketing the beaches, while at night the island's bars and discos overflow with cavorting, deep-fried tourists. Nearby **Skopelos** has thus far resisted overdevelopment, and many of its beaches remain quiet and uncongested. **Alonissos** remains far enough off the beaten track to provide a tranquil vacation and some of the finest sands in Greece, while **Skyros** has best maintained its traditional culture and the splendor of its beaches.

The jagged coasts and thickly forested interiors of the Sporades were first colonized by the Cretans, who cultivated olives and grapes on the scattered islands. The Athenians took over in the 5th century BCE, and developed more amiable ties with the Sporades than with the majority of the other island groups. Athena was, in fact, the most popular goddess in the islands' pantheon. The residue of ancient structures on these islands attests to the Roman presence there in the 2nd century BCE, and the Venetians' rule in the 13th century. The Venetians were forced out by the Turks, who controlled the islands until 1821, when the Sporades reembraced Greek rule.

In terms of transportation, you can think of these islands as a clique and a loner: Skiathos, Skopelos, and Alonissos—and Skyros. To reach the group from Athens, take the bus to **Agios Konstantinos** from the Liossion St. station (daily every hr. from 6:15am to 9:15pm, 2½hr., 2000dr) and then the ferry, which connects all three: Skiathos (3½hr., 2240dr); Skopelos (4½hr., 2600dr); and Alonissos (5hr., 2870dr). From the port of **Kimi,** on Evia (accessible by bus from 260 Liossion Station in Athens, 6 per day, 3½hr., 1950dr), ferry schedules are more sporadic, but at least two boats per week serve the group: Skiathos (4½hr., 3398dr); Skopelos (4hr., 3050dr); and Alonissos (3hr., 2870dr). Skyros can be reached by daily ferry from Kimi (3hr., 1312dr), or by hydrofoil from any of the other three Sporades (weekends only). **Alkyon Travel,** 98 Akadimias St., Athens (tel. 362 20 93), has information on getting to the Sporades. From the north, boats depart once or twice per day from **Volos.** From Skiathos, Skopelos, or Alonissos, a ferry departs once per week to Kimi, Agios Efstratros, Limnos, and Kavala. **Flying Dolphin hydrofoils** make daily trips connecting the islands with Volos (2-3 per day), Agios Konstantinos (1-2 per day), and Nea Moudania in the Halkidiki Peninsula (2 per week). Be sure to book ahead for weekend trips; shop around.

Skiathos ΣΚΙΑΘΟΣ

Sophisticated, cosmopolitan, and expensive, Skiathos is the place to ogle and be ogled in the Sporades. Whatever you've got, you can show it off here, bare-skinned on the sand or strategically clad on the street. Sophisticated, cosmopolitan, and expensive, Skiathos is the Mykonos of the Sporades. The main drag is lined with clothing boutiques, stylish jewelery shops, wheels of near-pornographic postcards and elaborate suntan lotion displays. Though traditional culture is obliterated; prices for food, accommodations, and entertainment high; the official camping facilities inconvenient; and freelance camping illegal, the island's rolling green countryside and 60-plus beaches lure a persistent and enthusiastic crowd.

From Athens, take the daily bus from the station at 260 Liossion St. (every hour from 6:15am to 7:15pm, and 9pm.; 2000dr; 2½hr.) to Agios Konstantinos, and then the **ferry** from there at noon or 1pm (2240dr). From Volos, one or two boats per day sail to Skiathos (3hr., 1750dr). Whether you begin your ferry trip in Agios Konstantinos or Volos, the ferry usually continues on to the islands of Skopelos and Alonissos. Ferries run

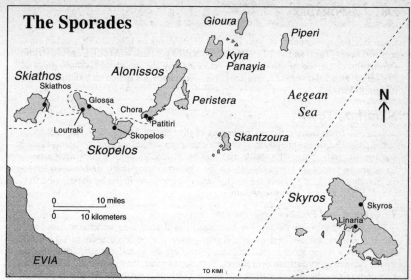

The Sporades

Gioura

Piperi

Kyra Panayia

Skiathos
Skiathos

Alonissos

Glossa
Chora
Loutraki
Patitiri
Skopelos

Peristera

Aegean Sea

N

Skantzoura

Skopelos

Skyros
Skyros
Linaria

0   10 miles
0   10 kilometers

EVIA

TO KIMI

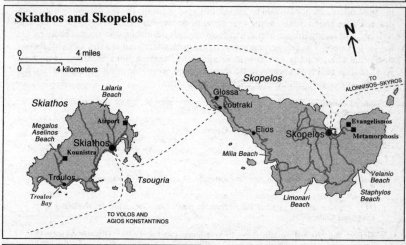

Skiathos and Skopelos

0   4 miles
0   4 kilometers

N

Skopelos

Lalaria Beach

Skiathos

Airport

Megalos Aselinos Beach

Skiathos
Kounistra

Troulos

Troulos Bay

Tsougria

Glossa
Loutraki

Elios

Milia Beach

Skopelos

TO ALONNISOS–SKYROS

Evangelismos
Metamorphosis

Velanio Beach

Limonari Beach

Staphylos Beach

TO VOLOS AND
AGIOS KONSTANTINOS

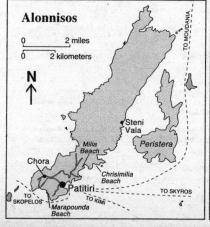

Alonnisos

0   2 miles
0   2 kilometers

N

TO MOUDANIA

Steni Vala

Peristera

Milia Beach

Chora

Chrisimilia Beach

Patitiri

TO SKOPELOS

TO KIMI

Marapounda Beach

TO SKYROS

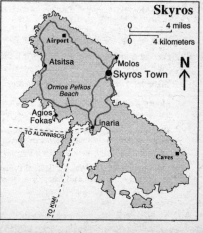

Skyros

0   4 miles
0   4 kilometers

N

Airport

Atsitsa

Ormos Pefkos Beach

Molos
Skyros Town

Agios Fokas

Linaria

TO ALONNISOS

Caves

TO KIMI

from Skiathos to Skopelos (1½hr., 790dr) and to Alonissos (2hr., 910dr), and in summer to Skyros (Tues. and Sat. 12:30am, 2750dr). To get back and forth from the **Pelion Peninsula,** catch one of the excursion boats leaving the mainland fishing village of Platania at either 8am or 9am, returning from Koukounaries Beach on Skiathos at 5pm (about 900dr).

Skiathos Town

Skiathos Town has weathered the impact of the foreign deluge far better than much of the coastline: on the cobblestone streets of the commercial section merchants pander and tourists ogle, but in the residential section, balconies burst with white gardenia blossoms and magenta bougainvillea. Grape vines overhang shady undisturbed terraces. Skiathos Town might be best known as *the* place to party in the Sporades—the slew of nightclubs rumba until at least 3am.

Orientation and Practical Information

When you disembark the ferry or hydrofoil, you'll see a long waterfront, lined with travel agencies, various rent-a-car and rent-a-bike dealers, and cushy *tavernas.* The **ferry agency** is one block inland from the left where the waterfront strip is intersected by the main drag **Papadiamandi Street.** Traveling inland, Papadiamandi is intersected by Pandra St. at the National Bank of Greece and further inland by Evangelistra St. at the **post office.** Parallel to and to the left of Papadiamandi, but not sprouting until Pandra, is Politechniou Street, home to a string of decent bars. On the far right of the waterfront, still facing inland, a road winds up towards the airport and several beaches. On the far left along a harbor perpendicular to the main waterfront is a row of small fishing boats that charter daily excursions. Frequent bus service links Skiathos Town with Koukanaries beach and points in between. A map, available at all kiosks (300dr), has the city on one side and the entire island on the other.

Tourist Police: Tel. 211 11, on the left side of Papadiamandi St., inland, past the OTE. English spoken. Open 24 hrs.

Currency Exchange: National Bank of Greece. Midway up Papadiamandi St., on the left side. Open Mon.-Thurs. 8am-2pm and 7-9pm, Fri. 8am-1:30pm and 7-9pm, Sun. 9am-noon. Lines are excruciatingly long and slow during July and Aug.; cash enough money to tide you over *before* you arrive in Skiathos.

Post Office: Papadiamandi St. at Evangelistria St. Open Mon.-Fri. 7:30am-2pm. **Postal Code:** 37002.

OTE: Papadiamandi St., 1 block inland from the post office. Open Mon.-Fri. 7:30am-3:10pm. **Telephone Code:** 0424.

Airport: Tel. 220 49. Five daily flights to/from Athens (50min., 9500dr). **Olympic Airways Office,** midway up Papadiamandi St. (tel. 222 00/29). Call 24 hrs. prior to take-off to confirm flight. Open Mon.-Fri. 8am-4pm. Take taxi to travel between airport and harbor (700dr).

Buses: From the bus stop shack at the far right end of the wharf (facing inland); every 30min. along the island's only road, ending at the pine grove of Koukounaries (7:15am-11:30pm, 200dr).

Ferries: Nomikos Lines (tel. 222 09/76). On the corner of Papadiamandi and the waterfront. Open daily 7:30am-11:30pm.

Taxis: Tel. 214 60, queue along the waterfront.

Moped Rental: Several shops along the waterfront and on Papadiamandi St. About 2000dr per day. Prices vary, so shop around and check inland dealers.

Hydrofoils: Flying Icarus at Nomikos Lines or **Flying Dolphins.** Main office at center of waterfront (tel. 220 18) or small agent across from the ferry office (tel. 229 86 Open daily 7:30am-10:30pm).

Laundromat: Pandra. Make a right off Papadiamandi at the National Bank. Wash 1200dr, dry 400dr. Iron 400dr. Open daily 8am-10pm. Detergent available at the grocery across the street (grocery open daily 8am-2pm and 5-10pm).

Pharmacy: Tel. 229 88, on the right side of Papadiamandi St. just past the post office. (Open daily 9am-1:30pm and 5:30-10pm.)

Medical Emergency and Hospital: Tel. 220 40 or 222 22, on the "Aeropolis" hill behind Skiathos Town.

Accommodations, Camping, and Food

Finding rooms in July and Aug., when most of Greece vacations, can be harder than the crust that forms on your clothes after a few weeks of travel. Usually visitors make reservations before they arrive. Since singles are almost impossible to come by in the high season, lone travelers should try to buddy up. *Dhomatia* are the best bet; some proprietors offer facilities such as a refrigerator and space on the roof to dry clothes. Warm and comfortable are the rooms of **Maria Papagiorgiou** (tel. 215 74), just off Grigoriou St., which runs parallel to Polytechniou St. (Take a left off Papadiamondi St. at Olympic Airways, onto Adreau Singrou, and then take your immediate right. Maria's is past the 1901 cornerstone and has bright green gates.) The rooms are spotless and there's a pleasant sitting area. (Singles 2500dr. Doubles 3000dr.) You'll find more restful rooms at **Hadula Tsourou** 17 Mitrop. Ananiou St. at the end of Pandra St. (Doubles 3000dr. Triples 4400dr.) Visit the friendly folk at **Australia House** (tel. 224 88), on the first left off Evangelistrias St., which offers rooms with private baths. (Singles 2500dr. Doubles 3500dr.) **Hotel Kastro** (tel. 226 23), down the alley on the right of Evangelistrias St. as you pass the Taverna Stavros, also offers rooms with private baths. (Singles 3000dr. Doubles 6000dr.)

Camping is feasible, though Skiathos' two campgrounds lie well out of town. **Aselinos Camping** (tel. 493 12), located near one of the town's nicest, least crowded beaches, offers a *taverna,* a palm canopy on the beach, and plenty of shady spots. Take the bus toward Koukounaries and ask the conductor for the correct stop. It's a 20-minute walk from there (500dr per person, 300-600dr per tent). **Camping Kolios** (tel. 492 49), closer to town and right on the bus line, is small and crowded, with shadeless, dusty sites. (600dr per person, 300-600dr per tent, 250dr car.)

Skiathos has a couple of good restaurants that don't charge extortionist prices. The best is **Taverna Stavros**, on Evangelistrias St. (take a right off Papadiamandi). The lamb dishes served with well-seasoned vegetables (1200dr) and *spaghetti Neapolitan* (650dr) are outstanding. The **Dionysus,** on Pandra St. off Papadiamandi as it slides into Mitrop. Ananiou St., serves delicious *dolmas* (400dr). The best-priced *gyros pitas* can be found on the left of Papadiamandi St. (230dr). The waterfront *tavernas* are pricy, but try the blue-and-white canopied **Zorba's,** which serves breakfast and tasty Greek specialties (*mousaka zorba* 700dr). For cheaper fare or beach-munchies, try the numerous fruit-peddlers and grocery stores: 50m up Papadiamandi St. at the "Souper Market" sign, you should find all you need for a do-it-yourself meal. (Open daily 7am-11:30am and 5-9:30pm.)

Entertainment

Nightlife here runs the gamut, from mellow waterfront *tavernas* to hellbent all-night discos. For more sophisticated decor, however, you'll pay up to a 1000dr cover charge which includes your first drink. Cruise along Polytechniou St., 1 block to the left of Papadiamandi as you face inland, and take your pick of clubs. The hubbub streets are full of hub and bub, but empty streets are really deserted, so navigate your booze cruise carefully. Most bars and discos close in winter. The following list includes merely an iota of the town's nightclubs.

La Piscine 600m down Evangelistrias St., but the funkorama of pink neon will light your way through the dark. A *Love Boat* style club, replete with swimming pool, piano, Gopher, and restaurant. Open daily for breakfast, swim, and booze 10am-6pm, nightly from 9pm. Cover 1000dr. Beer 500dr. Drinks 1000dr.

The BBCE Disco, 500m east of town along the waterfront, next to the rocking Music Bar. The most stylish disco/fashion show in town. Open nightly from 11pm, but rocks hardest from 3-6am. Cover 500dr.

Adagio Bar, Evangelistrias St., across from the Taverna Stavros. A leisurely atmosphere featuring classical music until midnight, when it gears up to jazz and light pop. Open nightly 8:30pm-2:30am.

Kentavros Bar, Mitrop. Ananiou St., a short jaunt inland from the waterfront. This groovy bar with space to boogie plays music ranging from Clapton to jazz. Open nightly from 9:30pm. Beer and wine 500dr. Drinks 1000dr.

Bourtzi Bar, on the small peninsula at the corner of the harbor. Secluded and romantic pirate-cove atmosphere. The sign says "Swim by day, stargaze by night." Open 24 hrs.

Around the Island

The northern part of Skiathos, accessible only by boat or by hiking paths has quiet beaches, secluded sandy coves, and relative peace. In contrast, the southern side, easily accessible by bus, car, or moped, is very crowded.

The island's one paved road (on the south side) runs from Skiathos Town to Koukounaries. Unsightly resort hotels dominate the beaches along the coast. **Buses** traveling this route leave from the harbor in Skiathos Town (7:15am-11:30pm every ½hr., 200dr to the end) and pass the beaches of **Mitikas, Nostos, Vromolimnos, Platanias,** and **Troulos.** The last bus back from Koukounaries to Skiathos Town leaves at midnight. The bus route and the road end at the pine grove beach of **Koukounaries,** where swaying branches shelter clear turquoise water and fine white sand. Water-skiing and wind surfing schools and sailboat, canoe, and pedal boat cartels all converge on these pristine shores, making the scene almost farcical. A short walk away is the putatively nude and conspicuously named **Banana Beach.** (Ripeness is all.) To get there from Koukounaries, take the paved road to the left of the bus stop, follow it to the bend, and make a right on the unpaved uphill road. At the top, take the worn path to the left of the skeletal concrete building, past the sheep and goats that munch in the shade of the olive grove. Here you'll also find Skiathos's **windsurfing school** (tel. 218 81). For relative peace 'n' quiet, take one of the treacherous paths through the brush and olive trees, continuing away from the Koukonories, to the less populated Eleni beach which also features watersport vehicles for hire.

Just east of Troulos, a road turns off for **Aselinos.** This road forks after 2km—the right branch leads uphill to **Panayia Kounistra,** a small monastery with a grape arbor and a *taverna* within its walls. Continuing past the monastery, you'll enjoy a fine view at the bend of the road: to the left is the beach of **Megalos** (big) **Aselinos;** to the right, **Micros** (small) **Aselinos.** The latter is the more secluded of the two, though neither is crowded, and both are only a quick scuttle from the end of the road. Megalos Aselinos has a campground, *taverna,* and rocks at both ends that make for fine snorkeling outings. You can reach it by car, troika, moped, rollerblades, inflatable armadillo, or just a long walk from Troulos. Getting to Aselinos Town is a bit easier—buses leave until 10pm from Aselinos Tours (tel. 210 95 or 493 94; on the waterfront) for the 20-minute, 200dr trip.

The rest of the northern coast is accessible only by boat. The most popular destination is **Lalaria Beach,** set in its own secluded pebbly cove, visible at one end through a natural stone arch. Near Lalaria are **Skotini Spilia** ("Dark Grotto"), striking **Glazia Spilia** ("Blue Grotto"), and **Chalkini Spilia** ("Copper Grotto").

East along the coast past Lalaria Beach, you come to the ruins of the medieval walled **kastro** (about a 2-hr. walk on a path from Skiathos Town). The Greeks built the kastro during the 16th century to take refuge from marauding pirates; when independence dawned last century, they abandoned this headland and began work on what has since blossomed into the present-day town of Skiathos. Two churches are all that remain of the ancient community: The **Church of the Nativity** is most intriguing, with fine icons and some frescoes. Daily excursion boats leave from the long strip at the far left side (facing inland) of Skiathos's harbor for Lalaria, a tour of the caves, and kastro (2000-3000dr round-trip). Buy a ticket on the boat; departure is around 10:30am, return 4pm.

For a full day of swimming, hop on one of the boats that leave regularly for the small island of **Tsougria** (10am-5pm every hr., 1000dr round-trip). Boats also leave the harbor each morning for a full-day excursion to Skopelos and Alonissos (2400dr round-trip).

Skopelos ΣΚΟΠΕΛΟΣ

The looming cliffs rising from the coastline gave the island its name: "steep rock from the sea." Complementing the ruggedness, acres of pine, olive, and plum trees blanket the hills. Originally a Cretan colony ruled by King Staphylos, strategic Skopelos has labored under the burden of occupation by Persians, Spartans, Athenians, Romans, Franks, Venetians, and Turks. It was conquered in 1538 by the Turkish admiral Khay El-Din Barbarossa (Red Beard), who massacred the entire population. It is still possible to catch a glimpse of women working in their traditional occupations of weaving and embroidery, and wearing their traditional costume, the *morko*—a silk shirt, short velvet jacket with flowing sleeves, and a kerchief, all finely hand-embroidered. It seems that Skopelos has kept the ravages of excessive tourism at bay: only the harbor area of Skopelos Town has been transformed.

Skopelos is the second island on the boat route after Skiathos. At least two boats per day put in from Volos and Agios Konstantinos. A daily bus from Athens runs to Agios Konstantinos every hour (6:15am-7:15pm, 2000dr); from there the ferry to Skopelos is 2600dr, from Volos 2120dr. **Boats** from Skopelos travel to Skiathos (1½hr., 784dr), and Alonissos (30min., 705dr). The ferry to Alonissos leaves in the evening and returns in the morning, so you'll have to spend two nights there to enjoy a full day. Alternatively, you can take an excursion boat from Skopelos (1hr., 2000dr). Note that some ferries from Volos, Agios Konstantinos, or Skiathos stop at the port of Loutraki for the city of Glossa before continuing on to Skopelos Town. **Hydrofoils** (Flying Dolphin or Nomikos Ferry Lines' Flying Icarus) fly from Skopelos to: Agios Konstantinos (3 per day, 2hr., 5324dr); Volos (3 per day, return 5 per day, 4230dr); Skiathos (8 per day, 45min., 1429dr); Alonissos (7 per day, 20min., 850dr); and Skyros (Tues., Thurs., Sat., Sun.; 2hr., 3433dr). Frequent **buses** along the island's main road link Skopelos Town with the towns of Glossa and Agnotas, and several beaches along the route. Mopeds can easily pass this route and most others on the island.

Skopelos Town

Except for the front line of tourist offices and *tavernas* curving around the horseshoe waterfront, Skopelos Town is a traditional delight. Tourists lose themselves in the complex cobblestone maze stacked up the hill side. The tightly packed architecture in Skopelos Town is a hodge-podge of Venetian, Byzantine, Turkish, Macedonian, and Neoclassical styles. The roofs here are made of overlapping slate tiles. Expensive to build and maintain, they are gradually being replaced by red ceramic tiles. For a view of this colorful settlement, climb to the top of the castle walls on the north side of town.

Orientation and Practical Information

Boats dock at the small jetty on the left tip of the horseshoe as you look seaward. Tourist agencies and scattered *tavernas* line the waterfront. Behind the crowded eateries, one block from the Commercial Bank, **Galatsaniou St.** darts upward, a fashionable path plump with tempting trinkets and tasty treats. On the right leg of the horseshoe, the lush pine hillside hides three monasteries.

Tourist Offices: Several on the waterfront, but most are only interested in selling their excursions or rooms. Shop around.

Currency Exchange: National Bank of Greece, on the left leg of the horseshoe waterfront. Open Mon.-Thurs. 8am-1pm and 6:30-8:30pm, Fri. 8am-1:30pm and 6:30-8:30pm. **Commercial Bank,** at the center of the waterfront. Open Mon.-Thurs. 8am-2pm, Fri. 8am-1:30pm. In summer also open daily 6-8pm and Sat. 10am-1pm.

Post Office: At the top of the horseshoe where the block of *tavernas* end and the bus stop area begins, take the first right inland, make a sharp left before you enter the small inland *platia,* then your first right, then your first left (then shake it all about and do the hokey-pokey). Open Mon.-Fri. 7:30am-2pm. **Postal Code:** 37003.

OTE: Take Galazano St. from the waterfront for 50m. Open Mon.-Fri. 7:30am-3:10pm. **Telephone Code:** 0424.

Buses: At the parking lot area behind the beach at the top of the waterfront horseshoe. From Skopelos Town to: Stafilos and Agnontas beaches (8 per day with 6 return, 140dr each way); Panosmos (11 per day with 8 return, 240dr); Milia beaches (11 per day with 8 return, 330dr); Elios swamp (7 per day with 7 return, 340dr); and Glossa Town (7 per day with 7 return, 480dr).

Taxis: Tel. 232 40, at the center of the waterfront amid the block of *tavernas*.

Moped Rental: Throughout town. A good one is **Nikos Bikes** (tel. 221 98). Make a left on the street heading diagonally away from the inland *platia*. 1800-2000dr per day. During July and Aug., supplies dwindle early in the day.

Laundromat: Tel. 226 02. Take the street heading to the center of town from the right-hand corner of the inland *platia*. On the left, down the stairs, advertised in yellow. Wash 1000-1500dr (soap included). Dry 800dr. Ironing services available. Open Mon.-Sat. 9:30am-1:30pm and 5:30-8:30pm, Sun. 9am-1pm.

Pharmacy: Tel. 222 52, 30m up Galatsaniou St. with short stairs and railing on the right. Open Mon.-Fri. 9am-1:30pm and 5-10pm.

Accommodations, Camping, Food, and Entertainment

If you don't get scooped up by islanders anxious to share their extra rooms for your extra *drachmae,* seek out the numerous *dhomatia* on the street behind the Commercial Bank, or on the road heading away from the water past the big hotels. You will also find many rooms to let in the maze of streets behind the Flying Dolphin agency; unroll a ball of string as you wander. Seventy-two steps run up the wide street to the left of Platanos restaurant, and you will find the home of kind, enthusiastic **Alexandra Karagiannis** on the right between the 67th and 72nd step. She has clean, spacious rooms with bathrooms, some with balconies (doubles 3000dr). Or if you take the first left off the same wide stair, then a right, then left, then right, say a prayer, you will find the clean rooms and studios of **Marigoula Triantaffilou** (tel. 224 45; singles 2000dr, doubles 3000dr). Because there are no campgrounds on the island, authorities have been known to tolerate freelance **camping** on any beach except the littered one in Skopelos Town. **Milia Beach,** with its shaded pine-needle beds, is one of the more appealing options.

The restaurants in town are fairly expensive, but **Ta Kymata,** at the end of the jetty right on the waterfront, has a busy family atmosphere and serves tasty fresh fish and *tzatziki* (200dr). For hefty pasta portions and tangy pizza, try **Aktaion** in the center of the waterfront (spaghetti dishes 500-900dr). For breakfast, **Platanos,** with the big *platanos* (tree), near the boat landing, features filtered coffee and serves an orgasmic yogurt special topped with fresh fruits, nuts, and honey (500-800dr). At night, perched in a perfect people-watching location, Platanos becomes a jazz and blues bar. Another **Platanos,** the *souvlaki* stand on the inland *platia* at the right side of the waterfront, sells take-out *gyros* (250dr) as well as tasty sit-down meals all day.

Shake it up at **Disco 52,** always the first disco to fill. Take the sharp left from the inland *platia* at the right side of town. (Open nightly from 11:30pm.) Next door, the **Labikos** has periodic beach parties. (Open nightly from 11pm.) For a different scene, try the **Skopelittsa,** closer to the center of town on the same street as the other two. Here you'll find a mixture of folk, pop, and traditional (live on weekends) Greek music. (Open nightly 11pm-3am.) Canopied by huge umbrellas, the more populated multi-level **Akro Bar** is one of the island's most popular sedentary hangouts. To get there, walk up Galatsanou St. 2 blocks past Alexander Restaurant and follow the steep steps to the top.

Around the Island

Three **monasteries** are buried in lofty seclusion on Mt. Palouki, which faces the town across the water. The town's main road splits just after the Amalia Hotel. Follow the left fork, which circles the harbor, ascends the mountain, and changes into a dirt road 600m past the Hotel Aegeon. At the next fork, two signs will point the way to the monasteries (30min. by foot from town). **Evangelismos,** clinging to the rocks across from Skopelos Town, dates from the 18th century, but its enormous gold-plated altar screen from Constantinople is 400 years older. Take the left-hand fork up the hot and winding mountain road (45min. to the monastery). It's best to start early in the morning before the heat and bugs intensify. (Monastery open daily 8am-1pm and 4-7pm.) If you are a dedicated monastophile or a masochistic hiker, descend back to the fork and climb to the **Monastery of Metamorphosis,** standing amid pines on a breezy knoll. The little chapel, set in a flowery courtyard, dates from the 16th century. (1½hr. walk from the fork, open daily 8am-1pm and 4-7pm.) **Propromou** is visible from Metamorphosis, on the next ridge. Once a monastery, this refuge is now a cloister, dedicated to St. John the Baptist and inhabited by nuns. (2-hr. walk from the fork, open daily 8am-1pm and 5-8pm.) All three monasteries provide bell-bottoms and long-sleeved smocks for men and women to meet the dress requirement and all are moped-accessible. Several tourist offices offer expensive excursions to the monasteries. (Wed. 10am-noon, 3000dr. Book in advance.)

Beaches line the coast south of Skopelos up to Loutraki. The main one, **Staphylos Beach,** is long and sandy, but crowded. Archaeologists discovered the tomb of the ancient Cretan general Staphylos on a hillside near here, as well as a gold-plated sword dating from the 15th century BCE (now in Athens). If you walk the length of the beach and clamber over the ridge at its eastern end, you'll reach **Velanio Beach,** which is more exciting than Staphylos. Because this is advertised as the one legal nude beach on Skopelos, it is considerably less crowded and less cluttered with plastic pails and their screaming, toddling owners. Along the paved road, the next place of interest is **Agnotas,** a pleasant harbor good for a seaside picnic. The beach is small, crowded, and too close to the boats, but from here you can catch the *caïque* every half-hour to **Limnonari Beach,** a long, uncrowded crescent of golden sand (250dr round-trip). **Panormos Beach** is crowded, but has several lively *tavernas.* Around the point to the north lies **Milia,** the prize beach of Skopelos. Adjacent pine groves make for great camping. The cliff-bound beach of **Sares** is accessible by boat from Skopelos Town. Small fishing boats leave from the dock approximately every half-hour (300dr). The bus runs from Skopelos Town to Staphylos, Agnotas, and Milia.

Following the road past Milia, you will come upon the **Elios** (literally "swamp"; needless to say, this eyesore is not accessible by moped). The peaceful and untouristed town of **Glossa** roosts on a high hill at the end of the road. A road runs from Glossa to **Loutraki,** where accommodations can be found at numerous *dhomatia.* If you continue around the coast there are some small, quiet, sheltered beaches.

For a superb hike, take the bus to Glossa, and walk the dirt track across the island to the **Monastery of Agios Ioannis,** clinging to a massive boulder above the ocean. (Take the main road east from Glossa and turn left on the first dirt road to Steki Taverna; after that it's clear sailing.) At the road's end, a steep path drops to the sea, and stone steps, cut in the escarpment, lead up to the monastery. You'll find a cistern of potable water in the rock. Allow at least four hours round-trip to visit Agios Ioannis, and bring at least a liter of water per person. The road is passable most of the way on motorbike.

Alonissos ΑΛΟΝΝΗΣΟΣ

True to its name, Alonissos is the most isolated and, with only 1700 inhabitants, the least populated of the Sporades. Its story is also one of the saddest in the tumultuous post-war history of Greece. In 1950, Alonissos's once lucrative vineyards were wiped out to the last grape by a virulent blight. Much of Alonissos's male population was forced to take up construction work in Athens. By 1965, just as the island had recovered some measure of prosperity through farming and fishing, an earthquake struck, shaking down both the harbor of Patitiri and the capital town of Alonissos on the hill above. The dictatorship then began a new housing development in the port town of Patitiri, and either inveigled or forced all but nine Alonissians to leave their town.

Alonissos is without doubt one of the friendliest and least touristed islands in Greece. The beaches are magnificent. The mountains and cliffs maintain a pristine, almost icy, emptiness. If the sedate, unruffled atmosphere here suits your style, you may be tempted to stay longer than you had planned.

Almost all **boats** to the Sporades, whether from Agios Konstantinos or from Volos, call at Alonissos. Ferries come from Athens via Agios Konstantinos (5½hr., 2870dr) and Volos (5hr., 2305dr). In addition, excursion boats travel here from Skiathos (2hr., 910dr), Skopelos (30min., 705dr), and Kimi (3hr., 2820dr). Flying Dolphins zip between Alonissos and Agios Konstantinos (2½hr., 5577dr) and Volos (2½hr., 4743dr), both with a 20% discount on a round-trip ticket, and Skopelos (15min., 850dr), Skiathos (1hr., 1811dr), Skyros (1hr., 3300dr), and Kimi (2½hr., 5832dr). All boats dock at **Patitiri,** for all intents and purposes the only town on the island. As your boat glides toward the port, you'll see whitewashed Old Alonissos clutching the slopes of the hill.

Patitiri

Patitiri, like its waterfront, is small and unassuming. **Pelasgon Avenue,** the main street, and parallel to it **Ikion Dolophon St.,** are quiet and simple. **Ikos Travel** (tel. 653 20 or 656 48/9), on the waterfront at the base of the jetty, is run by the amiable, English-speaking Mr. and Mrs. Athanassiou. Here you can find rooms, change money, buy Flying Dolphin tickets, or book excursion tours to other parts of the island. **Alonissos Travel** (tel. 651 88), just to the left, offers similar services (open 9am-10pm in July and August 8am-11pm). The similarly friendly English-speaking folks at **Nomikos Ferry Agency** (tel. 652 20 or 654 50), **Alkyon Ferry,** and **Flying Dolphin** offices are also nearby. The **National Bank of Greece** is on the corner of Ikion Dolophon St. and the waterfront. (Open daily 8am-10pm.) The **post office** is 100m up Ikion Dolophon St. (Open Mon.-Fri. 7:30am-2pm.) The **OTE,** on the right corner of the waterfront as you face inland, is in the tile-roofed building. (July-Aug. Mon.-Fri. 7:30am-3:10pm.) The Nomikos Ferry Agency also has an international phone. A **pharmacy** is located 50m up Ikion Dolophon St., on the left. (Open daily 9am-1pm and 6-8:30pm; off-season Mon.-Fri. same times.) **Orpheus Laundry** rests 150m up Pelasgon Ave., just before the gas station on the left. (Open Mon.-Fri. 9am-2pm, Sat. 9am-1pm. Wash 1300dr, dry 700dr.) Alonissos's **postal code** is 37005; its **telephone code** is 0424.

Taxis wait at the foot of the jetty on the waterfront (tel. 655 73 or 654 25). There are several moped rental agencies up Pelasgon Ave. and Ikion Dolophon St., so compare prices and makes (around 2000dr per day). The **bus** picks people up at the foot of the jetty and travels between Patitiri and Old Alonissos three or four times per day (250dr each way). Look for a timetable outside Ikos Travel.

You can ask for help with lodgings at Ikos Travel, or keep your eyes peeled for the many signs advertising *dhomatia* on the two inland streets perpendicular to the waterfront. Or ask at Boutique Mary, 20m up Pelagson Ave. on your right, for the **Dimakis Pension** (tel. 652 94; singles 1500dr, with bath 1900dr; doubles 2100dr, with bath 2650dr). There is an official campground, **Ikaros Camping** (tel. 652 58), on Steni Vala Beach. (500dr per person, 200-300dr per tent.) Covered with stones the size of baseballs, the town beach by the port is unsuitable for sleeping.

At the waterfront *tavernas,* you have the choice of dining under canvas or a canopy of leaves. Your sweet tooth will appreciate the decadent desserts at **Pub Dennis,** also on the waterfront. Bars start to warm up around 9 or 10pm and stay hot until 2 or 3 in the morning. The **Disco Rocks** lies on a peaceful, if distant, knoll south of town. Since it features only *bouzouki* dancing, however, disco purists disqualify it as a true "disco." Follow the road behind **Disco 4x4** after you've enjoyed the air conditioning and maybe won 4000dr in the Saturday night dance contest. It is advisable to travel swiftly by moped or in groups in order to ensure safety. **The Balcony** bar, set on a ledge overlooking the harbor (follow the signs throughout town) serves frozen peach juice (250dr) as refreshing as the view. (Open daily May-Sept. 9am-2am.)

Around the Island

Only the southern end of the island is inhabited, leaving the mountainous central and northern sections cloaked by pristine pine forests. Since the island's roads are unpaved and there is little public transportation, yer own two feets are the best means of transportation and exploration on Alonissos. The dirt roads are passable by motorbike as far north as Diasello, about three-fourths of the way to the northern tip. Motorbikes can be rented from both inland-leading streets of Patitiri (1700-2000dr per day—shop around). The tourist agencies sell good maps (300dr).

A trip to the island is not complete without a visit to **Old Alonissos.** Set high on the hill to ward off pirate attacks, this re-built "Chora" (Old Town) is a jewel among the craggy rock. Although you could never tell from the outside, Old Alonissos is an international village, chock-full of expatriates and the abodes of absentee home-owners. The island's only bus runs between the Chora and Patitiri several times daily (10min., 250dr each way). A schedule is posted on the sidewalk in front of Ikos Travel, where the bus picks you up. A **taxi** will take the trip for about 1600dr round-trip, which can be split by four people. Though steep, a walk to the town affords glorious views of the countryside once you've gotten out of the sprawling settlements neighboring Patitiri proper. To hike there, walk uphill on Pelasgon for 300m and make a left at the small blue sign for "Old Alonissos." Continue straight on the path, and make a right at the dried-up spring where malevolent horseflies lurk. Continue on for 10 minutes, cross the main road, and take the path into town. Make sure to bring at least a liter of water per person with you—the parching walk from Patitiri takes about an hour. On its hill, the town is quiet, breezy, and cool, with an awe-inspiring IMAX view. Old Alonissos's 12th-century **Christ Church** is one of the few churches in the Greek islands where men and women were segregated during services. To gain entrance, you'll have to speak to Papa Gregorias, the village priest and local legend. Women may feel more comfortable here in groups. While in the old town, stop at the **Paraport Taverna** at the end of the central street for a drink and equally intoxicating views. They serve good fare, as does **Palaia Alonissos,** which has excellent *kalamarakia* (fried squid).

A half-hour downhill walk south will take you to one of two beaches, **Marapounda** or **Vithisma,** sheltered beneath steep pine-clad slopes on the tip of the island. Alternatively, you can take an **excursion boat** from Patitiri (boats leave in the morning as they fill, 800dr round-trip). During the 4th century BCE, Alonissos was known as "Ikos," and Tsoukalia was the site of the island's pottery workshops. Many of the shards discovered at Tsoukalia are marked *Ikion:* "product of Ikos."

In the other direction, *caïques* (500dr) will bring you up the coast to **Milia** and **Chrisimilia**—considered by some to be the outstanding beaches of Alonissos—and **Kokkinokastro,** where the ancient acropolis of Ikos has been inundated by the sea. For an additional 400dr you can continue to **Steni Vala** or **Kalamakia,** or farther still to **Agios Dimitrios,** a long, sweeping, semi-circular beach out on a point. If you want to shop around before deciding, take the boat that circles the island, stopping at several beaches (1300dr). All of the main beaches have *tavernas* or café-snack bars.

For a negotiable 2000-3000dr per person, you'll find that Alonissos is the place from which to visit some of the smaller members of the Sporades by charter boat. The only inhabitants of lovely **Skantzoura,** to the east, are shepherds, their amiable sheep, and one lone monk. Another jaunt takes you to **Gioura,** home of the cyclops Polyphemos, where Odysseus and his crew nearly met their end. Several islands claim this distinction, but Gioura, with its large cavern complete with thousands of stalagmites, best fits the Homeric description (cavern is temporarily closed to tourists). The seaward view from atop the steep cliff mesmerizes. Gioura is home to herds of goats, who may or may not be descendants of those under whose broad bellies Odysseus and his crew crawled to safety from the prison of the Cyclops's cave. These brown beasts, with black crosses covering their spines and shoulderblades, have been a protected species in the national park of Gioura since 1930. **Kyra Panayia,** the largest of the small islands, has a charming monastery, and several fine snorkeling spots. **Psathoura,** a small island to the north of Alonissos, is home to a sunken city and the most powerful lighthouse in the Aegean. The distant island of **Piperi** is a wildlife sanctuary; waterfowl and a large abbey of monk seals make their homes there. Officials discourage visits to Piperi by nonspecialists, but you can ask at the GNTO in Athens for the requisite permit. Given this exception, excursion boats run to all the islands when the sea is calm enough.

Skyros ΣΚΥΡΟΣ

The terrain on Skyros, is rugged and serene. Rolling purple hills nibbled by goats, groves of fragrant pines, sandy beaches, and gnarled cliffs form the spectacular backdrop for daily life. Traditional culture is strong in Skyros; throughout the entanglement of sidestreets, women embroider and weave rugs, while men fashion sandals, ceramics, and intricately hand-carved wooden furniture.

Increasing tourism has not spoiled the island's charm—perhaps because most Skyrians seem uninterested in developing industrial-strength tourism here. Nevertheless, several *dhomatia* and small hotels have sprouted along the beach beneath Skyros Town and it is easy to find rooms in the town itself.

Gaggles of mythological geezers have been associated with Skyros. Legend has it that the Athenian king Theseus met his end when he was unceremoniously dumped off this cliff by Skyros's King Lykomedes, with whom he had hoped to find asylum. The warrior Achilles spent much of his youth here. To prevent his enlistment to fight in the Trojan War, his mama dressed him up as a girl. But when Achilles couldn't resist buying a sword from Odysseus, the well-worn traveler called the beskirted boy's bluff. Skyros was also the home of Atalanta, the princess who refused to marry anyone who could not defeat her in a foot-race. Her suitor Melanion (or Hippomenes), slowed her down and won the race by throwing three golden apples in her path.

To get to Skyros, first travel by **bus** from Athens to **Kimi** on Evia (6 per day, 3½hr., 1950dr). From June 15 through September 15, Lykomides line **ferries** from Kimi's port area, Paralia Kimi, travel to Skyros Mon.-Thurs. and Sat. at 11am and 5pm, 11am and 6pm Fri., and 11m and 7pm Sun., returning Mon.-Sat. at 8am and 2pm (2hr., 1320dr); a third boat operates according to demand. Olympic Airways has one **flight** each way daily (except Tues. and Thurs.) to Skyros from Athens (25min., 11,000dr). Twice per week a **hydrofoil** connects Skyros with the rest of the Sporades. There is no ferry between Skyros and the other Sporades.

Boats to Skyros dock at quiet **Linaria,** where a bus for Skyros Town and perhaps one for Molos on the beach, will be waiting (140dr). Be sure to hotfoot it on over to the bus so you don't get stuck. Ask the drivers their destinations, as buses may be marked somewhat counterintuitively (e.g., "Topikon" (the place), for the town and "Skyros" for the beach). A **taxi** ride to Skyros runs 1000dr.

There are rooms to let in tiny Linaria, and a peaceful beach on which many freelance camp. For most of your stay, however, you will probably want to base yourself in Skyros Town.

Skyros Town

Crowned by a Venetian *kastro,* Skyros Town spills down from the rocky summit into the sea. The town's unique architectural layout is a result of several pirate invasions—as a safety measure, homes were hewn into the cliffside. As you approach by bus, there is no sign of the the town until you actually enter it. Skyros Town's steep and narrow paths make for a *de facto* ban on cars

Orientation and Practical Information

The bus drops you off just outside of this maze-like town. Continue along the bus's aborted path to the town's central *platia* and you'll have found the main drag, **Agoras St.** Again, like the town, this strip of restaurants, travel agencies, and tourist shops is completely hidden until happened upon. Follow Agoras to its end on the opposite side of town and you will arrive at an open *platia,* overlooking Molos and the sea, in the center of which stands the bronze statue of the uncharacteristically nude English poet

Rupert Brooke. From this square a path leads down to Molos and the beach. Once downhill, the road will take you to a little church. Turn right and you will reach Molos Beach. Turn left and you will have a long inland walk to several hotels.

Tourist Office: No official GNTO, but **Skyros Travel** provides all necessary services. They organize bus trips around the island (1150-1300dr) as well as boat trips to the sea caves at Spiliés (3000dr), and the quiet bay off the port of Agia Fokas (2500dr). Helpful English speakers can also locate accommodations for you. Skyros Travel is an agent for **Olympic Airways.** Maps are available here. Open daily 8:30am-2:30pm and 6:30-11pm.

Currency Exchange: National Bank of Greece, up from the bus stop, on the left before the central *platia.* Open Mon.-Thurs. 8am-2pm, Fri. 8am-1:30pm. The **post office** also changes money and cashes traveler's checks.

Post Office: Make the first right as you walk from the bus stop to the cerebral *platia.* Open Mon.-Fri. 7:30am-2pm. **Postal Code:** 34007.

OTE: From the bus stop, turn left and continue straight—it stands 50m on the right, under the blue awning. Open Mon.-Fri. 7:30am-3:10pm. **Telephone Code:** 0222.

Airport: 10km from Skyros Town on the northern tip of the island. Accessible by foot or taxi. One flight daily to and from Athens (11,000dr).

Buses: From Linaria to Skyros Town, and then Skyros Town to the beach (140dr). Schedule depends on the inclinations of the bus driver, but there are usually connections every 3hr., when boats arrive, and 1hr. before each ferry departure.

Taxis: Tel. 916 66. Queue at central *platia.*

Motor Bike Rentals: There are several dealers in town. Follow the many signs on Agoras St. 1800-2500dr per day.

Pharmacy: Agoras St. (tel. 916 17), across from Skyros Travel.

Medical Center: Tel. 922 22.

Police: Tel. 912 74. Follow the street across from Skyros Travel to the end, then take a right. It's the white building with light-blue gates and trim. No English spoken, but officers will telephone an English-speaker to assist.

Accommodations and Camping

You can stay in Skyros Town or on the beach at Molos, 1km away. Buses run to both places (get off at the Xenia Hotel to be near both beach and town). Locals with rooms to let may greet the bus; if you'd prefer to look around on your own, wander the narrow streets of Skyros Town or comb through the streets behind the beach. There are plenty of *dhomatia* in Molos (doubles 3000-4000dr). In town, Skyrians chatting outside their homes will occasionally offer you a room. All households ask about 2000dr for a single and 3000dr for a double, some are willing to bargain.

One of the highlights of staying in Skyros is seeing the interior of a Skyrian home. Family heirlooms such as crockery, copperware, dolls, icons, portraits, and hand-carved furniture from all over the world embellish these beckoning homes. Initially, only aristocratic families possessed these precious items. By the late 19th century, though, members of the lower class began to decorate their homes as well; they purchased original objects from the upper class as they moved to Athens, and imitations from merchants and Skyrian ceramicists who copied the Italian and Dutch delftware. The ceilings of these homes are also an artistic *chef d'œvre*—reinforced with heavy cross-beams and thatched with local "bamboo."

Culture aside, if your primary goal in visiting Skyros is to soak up the sun, you may wish to stay a bit closer to the beach. **Manolis Balotis** (tel. 913 86), in the house with blue railings at the end of the steps leading to town, rents charming doubles (3000-6000dr). The **campground** (tel. 919 55) next door is in a pleasant, if dry, field. (700dr per person, 100dr per tent.) Camping on the beach itself is free of charge and hassles, except for the mosquitoes who lavish attention on each and every camper. Don't lure bugs and rodents to the site—take your trash with you when you leave. Other freelance camping options are available around Skyros (see Around the Island).

Molos, farther along the beach, is a veritable garden-of-plenty for the accommodations-seeker. In off-season, the following prices drop by up to 50%. **Restaurant Diethnes** (ΔΙΕΘΝΕΣ; tel. 911 88 or 911 85) offers doubles with private bath and use of kitchen facilities (3100dr). **Hotel Medusa** (ΜΕΔΟΥΣΑ; tel. 918 22) offers doubles and triples for 5000-6000dr. Next door, **Hotel Molos** (tel. 913 81) dispenses doubles for 3000dr, triples for 3500dr. **Pension Theodorou** (ΘΕΟΔΟΡΟΥ; tel. 911 62) boasts comfortable, new beds. (Doubles 3000dr. Triples 3400dr.) Make a right after the Theodorou to find **Paradise Pension** (tel. 912 20) and **Angela's Bungalows** (tel. 917 64 or 920 30). These clean, flower-bedecked lodgings offer doubles for 6500dr, triples for 7200dr. **Mr. Stamatis Maminis** (tel. 916 72) offers a few doubles (3000dr) just 20m from the water. To get there, go left at the fork where the right half branches off to the Paradise and Angela's, and follow around the bend to the right—it's the first house on the left. Call first.

Food and Entertainment

As always, avoid the tourist traps with outdoor tables and keep an eye peeled for the small *tavernas* which the locals frequent. Particularly cheap and authentic is **Kabanera,** tucked away in the maze of Skyros Town. Take a left at the end of the main road and then follow the signs to the "fish tavern" (ΨΑΡΟ-ΤΑΒΕΡΝΑ). (*Pastitsio* 600dr. Open for lunch and dinner.) For great *souvlaki,* go up Agoras St. to the "Chicken Souvlaki" sign on your left. (*Souvlaki* 110dr, chicken 900dr per kg.) Vegetarians will appreciate the **Sisyfos** on Agoras St., 50m past the bus stop (vegetarian specialties 600-800dr).

At the beach in Molos, try **Restaurant Akti** under the cornstalk awning. (*Mousaka* 538dr.) Farther up the beach is the **Taverna Marietas,** with fresh lobster and barrels of Skyrian *retsina* lining the walls. Skyros, with the rest of the Sporades, produces much of the pine resin that flavors *retsina* in the country's largest distilleries; its own brand of kegged *retsina* is among Greece's finest. Particularly good is *Kokkinelli* (rosé)—ask for it *apo to vareli* (from the barrel).

Most bars open at about 9 or 10pm and close at 2 or 3am, when everybody goes to objectify and be objectified at discos, which don't close until dawn. No one on Skyros is strict about hours—"whenever" is usually the answer to questions regarding closing time. **Agora,** 1 block from the bus stop, plays good loud music and has cheap drinks (cocktails 500dr). The **Renaissance Pub** on Agoras St., and the **Apocalypse** on the far side of the main square, are also popular with the young and carefree. At the end of the road to the right, **Kalypso** is a mellow little bar that never gets crowded.

The island's two discos are near the beach. **On the Rocks** has trees growing in the middle of its marble dance floor. The music here is Top-40, but after 2 or 3am, pop gives way to Greek tunes, and the local youths hit the floor. The dances show strong Anatolian influence, featuring some of the sleekest moves you'll ever see. Trot down the steps leading down from the Rupert Brooke statue and turn right at the sign. For a high-testosterone crowd, wend your way towards Molos, but go right where you'd make a left for the beach—you'll find **Skyropoula,** open to the sea. Both discos open nightly in July and August.

Sights

The sidestreets of the central part of the sprawling Skyrian town climb a steep rock wall to the **Monastery of St. George** and the ruins of a **Byzantine fortress.** Both sites afford spectacular views of the eastern coast of the island, from the craggy mountains to the shimmering Aegean Sea.

The *kastro* atop the town is generally believed to be of Venetian vintage, but evidence indicates that the Venetians cheated, simply renovating an earlier Byzantine fortification. The reclining marble lion set into the stone wall above the castle's entrance dates from the 4th century BCE, when Athenians taunted Skyrians with it as a symbol of Attic ascendancy. On the southeastern side of the castle peak lie the remains of an aqueduct whose main shaft was once used as a prison. To get there, make the steep hike up from Agoras St. As you climb to the fortress, you'll be surrounded by striking scenery, cooing doves, and scattering salamanders. Don't miss it. (*Kastro* open daily 7am-2pm and 6-9pm.)

If you follow Agoras St. to the tip of town, you'll find a plaza circumscribing the bronze statue of English poet Rupert Brooke, who died of fever here en route to Gallipoli during the disastrous Dardanelles campaign of World War I. The poet's tomb, constructed near a bay in southern Skyros, is the island's only modern claim to fame. On the right side of the statue, down the marble stairs (also leading to On The Rocks disco and the beach), is the **Archaeological Museum.** Check out the cult ceramic ring with two snakes devouring a series of ducks. Make way. All exhibits labeled in English. (Open Tues.-Sat. 8:30am-3pm, Sun. 9:30am-2:30pm. 400 dr; free on holidays.) Down the steps and behind the Brooke statue, the fascinating **Faltaits Museum** exhibits a superior folk-art collection. The building and its contents were given to the island by Manos Faltaits, a descendant of one of Skyros's 20 *archon* families, the island's governors from the 13th century until the 1820s. The display includes a superb collection of local embroidery, carved wooden furniture, pottery, costumes, and copperware, as well as rare books and relics from the island's yearly carnival. (Open daily 10am-1pm and 5:30-8pm. Guided tour in English. Donation requested.)

If you are on Skyros 40 days before Easter, you may witness the **Skyrian Carnival,** a part religious, part folk satire festival. A *geros* (an old man dressed in a goat mask and costume, clanging some 80 sheep bells attached to his waist) leads a *korela* (a young man dressed in Skyrian women's clothes but wearing a goat mask) and a *frangos* (a mocking figure dressed as a 17th-century European man with one large bell), on a wild raucous dance through the town to the Monastery of St. George. The ritual, commemorating a legendary land-use dispute between shepherds and farmers, is unique to Skyros.

The dark sand **beach** below the town stretches along the coast through the villages of Magazia and Molos, and continues around the point. Crowded and crawling with children in July and August, it's undeniably convenient: just a 15-minute walk down the stone steps from the Rupert Brooke statue. There you will find the **Skyros Windsurfing School** (rental 1500dr per hour, lessons 2500dr per hour or 6000dr for 5hr.). The regular public buses which run from Linaria to Skyros Town (see Practical Information above) also stop midway at the crowded **Ormos beach.** Ten minutes south of the town beach is the local nudist beach— ironically named *"Tu papa to huma"* ("the sands of the priest")—which is cleaner and less crowded than the town beach.

Around the Island

Skyros is about 5km wide at its narrowest point, and about 35km long, but most of the island is inaccessible. You can explore it by car, motorbike, or by one of the organized bus or boat trips (see Practical Information above). If you plan to rent a motorbike, a map is essential. Several roads have been paved recently, so travel has become easier and safer. Walking and hitching are also possible. *Let's Go* does not recommend hitching as a means of travel, and solo women should never hitchhike. Once home to a company of nymphs, **Nifi Beach,** on the south side of Skyros, is beautiful and deserted, with a natural spring spouting delicious water. The rest of the southern part of the island is rugged and barren, with small dirt paths leading to the beach. The most interesting sites here are accessible only by boat. The sea caves at **Spiliés** were once a pirate grotto, but one of the largest pirate centers in the Aegean was **Despot's Island.** During the Turkish occupation, merchant and war ships used this natural port as a shelter from storms; in World War I, the British commandeered it as a naval base.

In the wild barren interior of the southern region live the Skyrian *Pikermic*—ponies related to the Shetlands. In recent centuries, the population of Skyrian ponies grew very large, but starvation decimated the herds, and today only about 100 of the animals remain.

The northern part of the island, optimistically named *Meroi* (tame), is hilly, mildly cultivated, and covered with pine trees. Going north from Skyros Town, turn right for the beach at the little white chapel of **Agia Ekaterina.** If you continue straight and take a left on the road to the airport (marked with a highway sign), the road will take you high into the hills, and then dip down to cross a long valley. When you reach the top of the island, you'll come to a crossroad. Straight ahead lie two very pleasant beaches and the **airport.** The road continues around the west side of the island to the beach at **Kalogrias** and then the beautiful **Atsitsa Beach,** where rocks and pines are mirrored in the water. A *taverna* here lets rooms, and there's camping on the beach. The Atsitsa Center, a holistic health and fitness joint, is presently operating on the beach, so don't be surprised if mantras and a sense of peace emanate from the sands. A related enrichment center called the Skyros Center is in Skyros Town. For information on either, write: Skyros Center/Atsitsa, 1 Fawley Rd., London NW6 1SL, England.

Going inland from Skyros Town, bear right at the fork (rather than left to Linaria) to the walled Byzantine **Chapel of Agios Dimitrios,** with sections dating from pre-Christian times. From Dimitrios, head back toward town and take a right at the fork going south to the chapel of **Agios Antonios** or *Ta Kria Nera* (cold water), set in a magical garden with a spring and many varieties of trees. This road will bring you directly to Linaria. North from Linaria you can stop at **Kalogiros Beach,** where there are two *tavernas,* one of which lets rooms. Farther north, the beach at **Ormos Pefkos** may be the best on the island, if only for its lack of tourists.

CYPRUS ΚΥΠΡΟΣ

US$1 = C£0.43	C£1 = US$2.35
CDN$1 = C£0.36	C£1 = CDN$1.97
UK£1 = C£0.85	C£1 = UK£1.18
IR£1 = C£0.81	C£1 = IR£1.25
AUS$1 = C£0.31	C£1 = AUS$3.29
NZ$1 = C£0.23	C£1 = NZ$4.34

> **Note: Throughout this section, Cyprus pounds will be indicated by £.**

Cyprus is an island culturally and ethnically Hellenic, whose history is intimately bound up with that of both the Crusades and the Byzantine empire, and whose northern third is occupied by the Turkish army. A British crown colony until 1960, Cyprus is becoming increasingly popular with Arab tourists. You're excused if you feel a little disoriented here...

Cyprus, rising out of the Eastern Mediterranean snug between Anatolia and the Syrian coast, is rich with ancient mosaics, temples, remote monasteries, crusader castles, and warm, azure waters. Cyprus has understandably enchanted visitors from the the first Neolithic settlers and it continues to do so. As with other parts of the old British Empire, most residents speak and understand English. Most signs are in both English and Greek. Although Cyprus is about twice as expensive as Greece, a budget holiday here is not completely out of the question.

The unified island of Cyprus had been independent for 14 years when following a coup, Turkish forces to invade in 1974. In 1983, the northern third of Cyprus was declared a sovereign state. But only Turkey recognizes it as such, and since the island is peopled by both Greek and Turkish Cypriots, political and social tensions run high. The border between the two sectors is officially closed. Among Greek Cypriots at least, that northern portion of Cyprus is usually referred to simply as the "area illegally and temporarily occupied" by Turkey.

Getting There

The third largest island in the Mediterranean after Sicily and Sardinia, Cyprus lies 64km from Turkey, 160km from Israel and Lebanon, and 480km from the nearest Greek islands. The Republic of Cyprus is accessible by airplane or boat from points in Italy, Greece, and the Middle East. Seemingly thousands of boat agencies connect Limassol to almost every imaginable place. Among your possible destinations/points of origin are Larnaca; Rhodes; Piraeus; Iraklion, Crete; Haifa, Israel; and Port Said, Egypt. You can purchase ferry tickets at waterfront boat offices or from central offices such as:

Salamis Tours: 28th Octovriou Ave., P.O. Box 531, Limassol (tel. 05 15 55 55). In Piraeus, Afroessa Lines S.A., 1 Charilaou Trikoupi St. (tel. 418 37 77); in Rhodes, Red Sea Travel, 11-13 Amerikis St. (tel. 224 60).

Louis Tourist Agent, 63B Gladstone St., Limassol (05 16 31 61). To Egypt, among other places.

Vergina Lines, 3B Olympion St., Honey Court 7 (tel. 05 14 39 78). In Piraeus, inquire at **Stability Line,** 11 Sachtouri St. (tel. 413 23 92). In Iraklion, **Arabazouglon Travel,** #62 25th Augustou St. (tel. 22 66 97). In Port Said, **Mena Tours,** El-Gomboria St. (tel. 257 42).

The **Black Sea Shipping Company** (tel. 411 87 05) runs a monthly ferry from Odessa, Ukraine to Larnaca via Varna (Bulgaria), İstanbul, and Piraeus. In Greece, contact Transmed Shipping S.A., Akti Miaouli St. 85, Piraeus (tel. 413 14 02/03); in Egypt, Amon Shipping Agency, Adib St. 7, P.O. Box 60764, Alexandria; in Cyprus, Francoudi and Staphanou Ltd., New Port Rd., Limassol (tel. 37 03 35). For a vast account of all available agencies and departure points, ask for the Cyprus Tourist Organization's *In-*

Cyprus

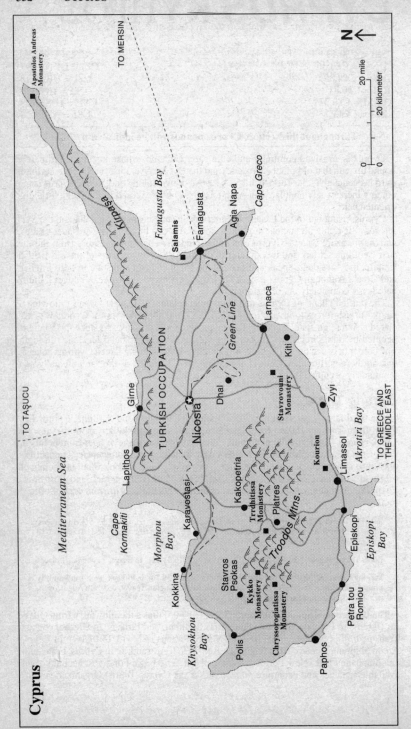

formation Paper Unit 2, available at tourist offices in Nicosia, Larnaca, Limassol, and Paphos.

By air, Cyprus is accessible from Greece as well as other European and Middle Eastern countries on **Olympic Airlines** (U.S. tel. (800) 223-1226), **Egypt Air** (U.S. tel. (718) 997-7700), **Cyprus Airways** (U.S. tel. (212) 714-2310), and other commercial lines. Flying to Athens from Cyprus is almost as cheap as taking the ferry (youth-fare £53 on either Olympic or Cyprus Airways). Deck passage to Piraeus runs about £46 for the two-night journey. International airports are in Larnaca and Paphos.

Northern Cyprus is accessible only from Turkey. For more information, on how to get there, see the sections on Northen Cyprus and the Mediterranean coast of Turkey.

Practical Information

A highway system serves much of Cyprus, but forays into the hinterland take grit and guts. Transportation is, for the most part, nonexistent in the evenings after 7pm. Service (shared) taxis run regularly Monday through Friday (until 4:30pm) between Limassol, Paphos, Larnaca, and Nicosia. Service taxis, most of which are converted Mercedes limousines, will pick you up and drop you off wherever you want in the city (£1.50-2.00 between the four major cities). Although they cost twice as much as the buses, their speed and frequency make them a good deal. When given a choice, take the front passenger seat in the taxis as drivers sometimes cram too many people into the back. Buses to the Troodos Mountains travel once daily from both Nicosia and Limassol. Paphos is not connected to Nicosia or Larnaca by public transportation; you must go there via Limassol. Bus service throughout Cyprus is less frequent in the winter, and hitching is popular, though as usual *Let's Go* does not recommend hitchhiking as a means of travel. Cypriots drive on the left side of the road, measure distances in kilometers, and require seat belts in front seats. All Cypriot rental cars have manual transmission, and rates are standardized: the cheapest small cars should cost no more than £15 per day, small motorbikes £3-5, larger motorcycles £7-8. You need a Cypriot motorcycle license to drive a bike. Some dealers turn a blind eye if you show them your country's license, but others might escort you to the police station where a temporary license plus appropriate photographs costs £5. Even though almost all dealers rent 50cc two-seaters, they officially can carry only passengers under 12. If two adults are riding a small bike, the police may stop and fine you.

Cyprus's extremely helpful and efficient **tourist information offices** provide free maps and invaluable information. There are offices in Limassol, Nicosia, Larnaca, Paphos, Agia Napa, and Platres. The main office is the **Cyprus Tourist Organization,** P.O. Box 4535, 18 Theodotou St., 2nd floor, Nicosia (tel. 02 44 33 74); in the U.S., 13 E. 40th St., New York, NY 10016 (tel. (212) 683-5280). Get a copy of the *Cyprus Hotels and Tourist Services Guide;* while it does not list all of the country's cheap hotels (since many are unofficial), it includes all government-regulated hotels and pensions. If you are quoted or charged a price higher than the one listed, you can register a complaint with the nearest tourist office, and you should get the appropriate reduction. The tourist offices can arrange accommodations for you, but you'll find better deals if you look on your own.

Most stores, offices, and banks close down for **siesta** at 1pm, and reopen from 4 to 7pm, except on Wednesdays and Saturdays. On Sundays, nearly all establishments—notably museums—reduce their hours or close entirely. Cyprus also closes down on the following **holidays:** New Year's Day; Epiphany (Jan. 6); Green Monday (Feb. 22); Cypriot National Day (April 1); Orthodox Good Friday; Orthodox Easter (Sat.-Mon.); Assumption Day (Aug. 15); Independence Day (Oct. 1); Christmas Eve; Christmas Day; and Boxing Day (Dec. 26). Two Greek national holidays, on March 25 and October 28, are also honored. During the 12 days between Christmas and Epiphany *(Phota),* werewolves supposedly haunt Cyprus. On the eve of their departure, women throw pancakes and sausages off the roofs of their homes. This ensures that the werewolves will shamble off sated and content, without causing any last-minute atrocities.

Cyprus hosts a few **festivals** every month, and more in August. *Panayifia* (the Dormition of the Virgin), is among the most important. A general list of the year's activities can be obtained by writing to the Cyprus Tourist Organization (see address above). Once in Cyprus, you can obtain a copy of *This Month's Principal Events* from any tourist information office.

Keeping in Touch

Post offices are open Mon.-Sat. from 7:30am to 1:30pm (1pm in the summer). Some branches have afternoon hours from 3:30-5:30pm (4-6pm in summer). *Poste Restante* is available only in Nicosia, Larnaca, Paphos, and Limassol at a cost of 5¢ per piece. In the summer of 1992 letters to Europe and the Middle East cost 19¢, to USA, Africa and the Far East 26¢, to Australia and New Zealand 31¢. Postcards cost 16¢, 18¢, and 23¢. All aerograms cost 16¢. Make sure your letter or card is affixed with the 1¢ refugee stamp—mail will go nowhere without it.

Cyprus has a fairly good **telephone company (CYTA).** Direct overseas calls can be made from nearly all public phones if you have enough 5, 10 or 20¢ pieces. To make a collect call, you must go to a CYTA office or a private phone. (Country codes are posted in the phone books.) It can take up to an hour for a collect call to go through. A more convenient method is to call overseas from a hotel's international phone and have the other party call you right back. To call Cyprus from the United States, dial 011, then 357, followed by the area code (without the zero) and finally the number. Hotels charge a 10% surcharge, but the convenience might be worth it. For **information** on unlisted numbers in Cyprus, dial 191; if the number is listed, call 192. For information on international calls, dial 194, and for the international operator, 198. To reach an international operator in the United States, dial 080-90-000 (MCI) or 080-90-010 (AT&T). For **ambulance, fire or police** call 190. For a list of all pharmacies call 192. All local numbers have six digits.

Accommodations and Food

Cheap, clean hotels are a conspicuous rarity. In general, prices for accommodations drop during the off-season to about 20% less than the rates quoted in this book. Nicosia, Troodos, Limassol, Paphos, and Larnaca all have **HI/IYHF youth hostels,** and Stavros tis Psokas has a loosely affiliated **forest station.** You don't need an HI/IYHF card. Although Cyprus has only a few formal campgrounds, you can sleep on beaches and in forests. Choose your site discreetly and leave it as clean as you found it. Be cautious if you do camp unofficially; women should be especially wary and never camp alone. In the Troodos area, try staying in the monasteries; they're free, but you should leave a donation.

Cypriot food has much in common with Greek, English, and Middle Eastern cuisine. Restaurants everywhere sell English-style cutlets and steaks. Try *meze,* a platter of about a dozen appetizers for two to four people which includes olives, tomatoes, and hummus, or try the *kleftiko,* lamb roasted in clay ovens over charcoal. Cypriot *kebab* is similar to Greek *souvlaki-pita,* but the sandwich is larger, the lamb drier, and the sauce absent. At 90¢-£1, one *kebab* makes a good meal. *Sheftalia* (grilled ground meat with onions) is also served in pita pockets. Try some *iranie* from a cart on the street; this Turkish drink made of yogurt laced with mint and salt will supposedly sober up even the most sloshed of beings. At festivals and streetfairs, Cypriots enjoy *soujoukko,* strips of jellied nuts (dipped in hot grape juice). Vegetarians will encounter difficulties eating in Cyprus: unless you like *trahana,* a soup made with yogurt and wheat, you'll eat Greek salad until you crumble into feta cheese.

History

Cyprus has been inhabited since Neolithic times, and first achieved importance at the onset of the Bronze Age because of its wealth of copper ore. Linguists are unsure whether *Kypros,* from which the word "copper," is derived, first referred to the island or the metal itself.

Cyprus, for most of its history, has been dominated by foreign powers. Around 1000 BCE, Iron Age Syrians came to Cyprus, followed a century later by Phoenicians from

Tyre. For the next several centuries, Cyprus was ruled by the Assyrians and eventually fell under Egyptian control. After the expansion of the Persian empire had ceased, Cyprus was overrun until Alexander the Great stopped by in 333 BCE. In 295 BCE, Ptolemy claimed Cyprus for Egypt following Alexander's death, but two centuries later, in 58 BCE, the island fell victim to Roman megalomania. In 36 BCE, Antony gave Cleopatra a heart-shaped box of chocolates and the deed to Cyprus. Through the early Dark Ages, ownership of the island passed from Rome to Byzantium, back to Rome, back to Byzantium, *ad infinitum.*

In 1191, Richard the Lionheart and his English fleet set sail for Jerusalem under the auspices of the Third Crusade. After being treated quite rudely in Cyprus, Richard quickly overran the island. He immediately sold the island to the Knights Templar to enrich is war chest. One year later, Cyprus passed into the hands of Guy de Lusignan, who had originally helped Richard take the island from the Byzantines.

The Lusignan Dynasty (1192-1489) suppressed Cypriot culture and Greek Orthodox Christianity. As setbacks in Palestine forced the Crusaders into full retreat, the Lusignans invited Crusader families to set up camp on the island. By the late 13th century, Cyprus had become the wealthiest island in the eastern Mediterranean. Yet in 1489 the Venetians forcibly annexed the island. They remodelled and strengthened Cypriot military defenses, but were still no match for the Ottoman Empire. In 1570, following a two-month siege, Nicosia surrendered, and Famagusta a year later.

The Ottomans taxed Cyprus heavily but allowed the Orthodox Church to flourish. As the Empire weakened in the 19th century, the British moved in. Following the Turkish defeat in World War I, Cyprus formally became a Crown Colony in 1925. Six years later, violent uprisings in the name of *enosis* (union with Greece) broke out, avalanching into violence and atrocities between ethnic Greeks and Turks. After years of instability and financial assistance from Britain, the Orthodox Church held a plebiscite in mid-January, 1950, in which 96% of the Greek Cypriots showed support for *enosis.* In 1954, when the United Nations vetoed the Greeks' appeal to grant Cyprus self-determination, General Grivas and the EOKA (National Organization of Cypriot Fighters) initiated a round of riots and guerilla warfare aimed at uniting Cyprus with Greece. At the same time, Rauf Denktaş founded a Turkish paramilitary organization to fight the EOKA. Tired of the fighting, the British withdrew. On August 16, 1960, Cyprus was granted independence, entered the U.N., and shortly thereafter, opted against union with Greece and joined the British Commonwealth.

Conflict undermined independent Cyprus almost from the start. Though Turks were guaranteed the vice-presidency and a certain percentage of parliamentary seats, they withdrew from the government when President Makarios (who was also the Greek Orthodox Archbishop) attempted to change the constitution. Makarios may have been known as favoring independence rather than *enosis,* but the economic boycott he propelled against Turkish Cypriots cleanly split the island along ethnic lines. Greek Cypriots proudly flew the Greek flag and adopted the Greek national anthem. Nicosia, meanwhile, became a divided city as Turkish and Greek "self-help" groups patrolled the borders of their neighborhorhoods.

Intermittent violence suddenly exploded into an international affair in 1974 when the Greek Cypriot National Guard, assisted by the military government in Greece, overthrew Archbishop Makarios III and replaced him with Nikos Sampson, a notorious EOKA gunman in favor of immediate *enosis.* Five days later, ostensibly moving to prevent the National Guard from attacking Turkish Cypriots, the Turkish army invaded Cyprus from the north, conquering 37% of the island. United Nations mediators established a peace-keeping force as both Greek and Turkish refugees flooded into their respective parent nations.

In November 1983, Turkish-occupied Cyprus proclaimed itself indpendent as the Turkish Republic of Northern Cyprus. Though only Turkey has gone so far as to recognize the new state, the TRNC has established trading relations with Britain, Europe, and several Arab states. Led by Rauf Denktaş, the TRNC lags far behind the Republic of Cyprus economically, but is generally supported by Turkish Cypriots who, in recent years, have been joined by thousands of settlers from mainland Turkey.

Travel to Northern Cyprus is almost completely prohibited from the Republic of Cyprus, though daytrips are sometimes allowed. U.N. negotiations continue, though many accuse the peace-keeping force of being so effective that there is little momentum to solve the problem. In the summer of 1991, President Bush visited Turkey and Greece in an attempt to begin negotiations for the resolution of this issue. And in 1992, the presidents of the Northern Cyprus and the Republic of Cyprus began negotiations.

Limassol ΛΕΜΕΣΟΣ

The port of entry for most passenger ferries that stop in Greek Cyprus, Limassol is not the most cordial introduction to this otherwise striking island. Rapid growth and a lack of urban planning have nurtured an endless row of hotels stretching east along the coast. The major arteries are lined by residential and commercial buildings and a new four-lane highway intensifies the sense of urban blight. Limassol is the industrial center of Cyprus, complete with a decaying downtown and dozens of ungainly merchant ships anchored offshore. Still, as the British and Arab tourists who fill the city's attractive palm tree-lined waterfront promenade can tell you, the town makes a good base for day trips in the area. Be forewarned, though, that the city shuts down almost completely on weekends, and you may find yourself wandering for hours in search of an open restaurant.

Orientation and Practical Information

Situated right in the middle of Cyprus' southern coast, Limassol is more or less equidistant from every other major city in Southern Cyprus (50-70km), and is the center for bus and taxi services.

The **new port,** where passenger boats arrive, is about 5km southwest of the town center. To your right as you enter the arrivals terminal is a **tourist desk,** where you can find excellent free maps of the city. Bus #1 runs between the port and downtown Limassol (every 20min., Sat. every hr., 35¢). After ships arrive, buses wait outside the customs building. Otherwise, the stop is right outside the port gates. To get to the port, you can catch bus #1 at the bus station near the Anexartisias St. market. A taxi to or from town should cost about £2-2.50. If you're headed directly for another major town, call the appropriate service taxi (see below), and you'll be picked up at the port at no extra charge.

Cyprus Tourism Organization Office: 15 Spiro Araouzos St. (tel. 36 27 56), on the waterfront 1 block east of the castle. The extremely capable and helpful staff can answer all questions, suggest daytrips, and provide maps, bus schedules, and general information for the entire island. Open Mon.-Thurs. 8:15am-1:30pm and 4-6:15pm, Fri. 8:15am-1:30pm; Sept.-May Mon.-Thurs. 8:15am-1:45pm and 3-5:30pm, Fri. 8:15am-1:45pm. A small office at the **port** (tel. 34 38 68) is open immediately following arrivals. Nearby office in **Dassoudi Beach,** 35 George I Potamos Yermassoyias (tel. 32 32 11), opposite the Park Beach Hotel. Same hours as the Limassol office.

Travel Agent: Amathous, 2 Syntagma Sq. (tel. 36 21 45), near the tourist office on the water. A large chain that sells most plane and boat tickets. Open Mon.-Fri. 8am-1pm and 4-6:30pm.

American Express: 130 Spiro Araouzos St. (tel. 36 20 45), in the offices of **A. L. Mantovani and Sons.** Open for AmEx transactions Mon.-Tues. and Thurs.-Fri. 9am-noon and 3:30-6:30pm.

Post Office: Main office, Gladstone St. (tel. 36 25 14), next to the central police station. Open Mon.-Fri. 7:30am-1pm and 4-6pm, Sat. 7:30am-12:30pm; Sept.-May Mon.-Fri. 7:30am-1:30pm and 3:30-5:30pm, Sat. 7:30am-1:30pm.

International Telephones (CYTA): At the corner of Markos Botsaris and Athinon St., in the convenience store next to the tourist office. (Open daily 7am-7:30pm). The phone takes 10¢ and 20¢ pieces. Guesthouses Ikaros and Excelsior and the Continental Hotel also have international phones. **Telephone Code:** 05.

Bus Stations: KEMEK terminal (tel. 36 32 41), corner of Irenis and Enossis St. Buses to Nicosia (9 per day, £1); Paphos (5 per day, £1); and Larnaca (5 per day, £1). Buses to Platres leave from Eleftherias St. (2 per day, £1).

City Buses: Andreas Themistokles St., near Anexartisias St. All municipal buses cost 35¢. Bus #1 goes to the new port, #6 and 25 go east along the coast. Most city buses don't run on Sunday.

Service Taxis: Karydas, 129 Spiro Araouzos St. (tel. 36 34 84). **Kypros/Akropolis,** 49 Spiro Araouzos St. (tel. 36 41 14). **Kyriakos,** 9 Pasteur St. (tel. 36 39 79). **Makris,** 166 Hellas St. (tel. 36 65 50). Karydas, Kypros/Akropolis, and Kyriakos run frequent taxis to Nicosia (£2). Akropolis and Makris run taxis to Larnaca (£1.70). All the companies except Akropolis go to Paphos (every hr., £1.70). Less frequent service Sept.-May. The taxis run only between 6am-4:30pm; plan accordingly or you might end up sleeping with the goats on a mountaintop.

Bike and Motorbike Rentals: Agencies cluster on the shore road, near the luxury hotels at the eastern edge of town. A motorcycle license is required to rent anything, but most agents will take you to the police station, where—if you've "forgotten" your license—you can be issued a temporary Cypriot license (£5 including necessary photos). Motorbikes £4.50 per day. If you plan to rent long term, you'll find lower rates in Polis.

Bookstores: Ioannides, 30 Athinon St. (tel. 36 66 04).

Laundromat: (tel. 36 82 93), Kaningos St. off Markarios Ave. near the Archaeological Museum. Leave laundry for same-day pick-up or do it here yourself. Wash £1.80, dry 75¢. Open Mon.-Tues. and Thurs.-Fri. 7:30am-1pm and 3-6:30pm.

Pharmacy: Call 192 for the current list of all-night pharmacies.

Hospital: Tel. 36 31 11. On Leondios St.

Police: Tel. 37 56 11, at Gladstone and Leondios St. next to the hospital.

Accommodations and Food

In Limassol, you get what you pay for: budget accommodations, clustered near the bus station, are cheap but of low quality. Sex-workers have been known to ply their trade in this area. Those traveling alone, particularly women, may not feel comfortable in many of these establishments and may want to stick to either the youth hostel or a starred hotel such as the Continental. As always, be sure to check the rates listed in the *Cyprus Guide to Hotels* (available free of charge at all Cyprus Tourism Organization Offices). If the price an establishment quotes you is higher, you should be sure to report it to the Cyprus Tourism Organization Office and you should have the difference refunded.

Youth Hostel (HI/IYHF), 120 Ankara (Angira) St. (tel. 36 37 49), a few blocks west of the castle. From the bus station, turn right onto Anexartis St., then right on Agios Andreas St., and walk all the way down until it becomes Ankara. If you've come off the ferry, take bus #1 to the bus station and walk from there. Not very clean, but the management makes an effort. No curfew. The door is always locked but they'll show you where the key is. Check-out 10am. Hot showers 35¢, cold showers 20¢, but expect to wait in line. Lights out at midnight. £1.50 per night, linen included. They also rent motorbikes, £4.50 per day.

Guest House Luxor, 101 Agios Andreas St. (tel. 36 22 65), on a pleasant pedestrian shopping street. Zingy, spacious rooms and a lovely outdoor garden. Singles £5.50. Doubles £12, with bath £13. Most major credit cards accepted.

Guest House Ikaros, 61 Eleftherias St. (tel. 35 43 48). Full of plants and unusual bric-a-brac. This place has definite character, if you don't mind clutter. They also have an international phone. Singles £3.50. Doubles £6. Triples £9. Showers included. Call for reservations in high season.

Guest House Stalis, 59 Eleftherias St. (tel. 36 81 97). Clean enough, with institutional beds and squat toilets. Bed in a 4-bed dorm £1.80. Singles £3.30. Doubles £5.60. Rents bikes (£1.70) and motorbikes (£5).

Guest House Excelsior, 35 Anexartisias St. (tel. 35 33 51). Tolerably clean. Uniquely decorated. Doubles £6. Showers included.

Guest House Hellas, 9 Zig Zag St. (tel. 36 38 41), facing Agios Andreas St. On a pleasant street of small shops and artisans' studios, with sculpturesque balconies. The rooms are decent, though bare. £2-3 per person, depending on your bargaining skills.

Continental Hotel, 137 Spirou Araouzou St. (tel. 36 25 30). A 1-star hotel. Pleasant and clean, with a run-down yet glamorous exterior. Singles £11.95. Doubles £19.60. Triples £22.75. Breakfast included. Air conditioning available at £2 per day.

Restaurant fare in Limassol is mediocre; many of the restaurants on the waterfront and in the town center cater to rich, undiscerning tourists: glossy, plastic-coated menus advertise boring food at startling prices. The **Windmill Café,** at the corner of Agios Andreas and Irenis St. has revitalizing sandwiches (£1), salads (£1.50), and A/C (free). Across the street from the castle is the appropriately named **Richard and Berengaria Café** *(kebab* and *sheftalia* 80¢ each). The **Popular Restaurant,** Kanaris St., near the city bus station, has tasty, filling meat dishes (£1.90). Nearby at the corner of Georgian Yenadiou St., **Anchos Theofanous** grills *kebab* on an outdoor patio. Unimpressive bars stretch down the coast to Dassoudi Beach.

Sights and Entertainment

The **Limassol Castle** is the only building of historical significance in Limassol proper. This 12th-century Frankish structure, where Richard married his Queen Berengaria in 1191, was destroyed by earthquakes and Genoese assaults; the only traces of the old Byzantine fort are in the western wall of the compact building. In the early 14th century, the Templar Knights fortified the castle's walls and covered the Gothic windows. Later, the Knights of St. John converted the great Western Hall into a Gothic church and the chapel into a series of prison cells. The Turks claimed the castle in 1570, and the capacious West Hall was used as a prison until 1940 under the British regime. The castle has finally retired to an unruffled existence as the **Cyprus Medieval Museum** (tel. 35 40 19; Mon.-Fri. 7:30am-5pm, Sat. 9am-5pm; off-season Mon.-Sat. 7:30am-5pm. Admission 50¢.) The **Archaeological Museum** (tel. 33 01 32), on the corner of Kaningos and Vyronos, contains an assortment of funerary *steles,* jewelry, statues, and terra-cotta figurines (once used as stand-ins for Bronze Age Cypriots who were always too hung over to do the temple thing on Sunday mornings). (Open Mon.-Sat. 7:30am-6pm, Sun. 10am-1pm; off-season Mon.-Sat. 7:30am-5pm, Sun. 10am-1pm. Admission 50¢.) On Byron St., closer to the sea, you'll find the town **zoo** and **public gardens.** The **folk art museum,** 253 Agios Andreas St. (tel. 36 23 03) rests 1 block east (left facing the water) of the intersection of Zenon and Agios Andreas. (Open Mon., Wed., and Fri. 8:30am-1pm and 4-6pm, Tues. and Thurs. 8:30am-1pm; off-season Mon., Wed., and Fri. 8:30am-1pm and 3-5pm, Tues., Thurs., and Sat. 8:30am-1pm. Admission 30¢.)

Wine-lovers should not miss the tour of the KEO factory on Franklin Roosevelt St. Since 1927, KEO has been Cyprus's premiere brewery/distillery. At the end of the half-hour tour, there's a free tasting with all the wine, beer, and chips you can possibly pack in at 10am. (Factory is 5min. from the castle—from Djelal Bayar, bear left onto Roosevelt. Free tours Mon.-Fri. 10am.) The recently opened **municipal art gallery** (tel. 34 32 12) is on 28th Octovriou St., east of the public gardens. (Open Mon.-Wed. and Fri. 8:30am-1pm and 4-6pm, Thurs. 8:30am-1pm; off-season Mon.-Wed. and Fri. 8:30am-12:30pm and 3-5:30pm, Thurs. and Sat. 8:30am-1pm. Admission 30¢.) You may also want to visit Limassol's **Reptile House** (tel. 37 27 70) at the Old Port, which showcases snakes, lizards, crocodiles, republicans, tortoises, and, oddly, monkeys. (Open daily 9am-7pm.) The city's long stone beach is no cause for spasms of ecstasy, but a new breakwater has recently made the area more pleasant for swimming. **Dassou-di Beach,** 3km east of town, is far better. Take bus #6, 13, or 25 from the market on Kanaris St. (every 15 min., 25¢). The ebullient **Ladies Smile Beach** at the new port is also quite popular. Take bus #1. At night the hip place to be is **Whisper's** nightclub on Nicosia Old Road (tel. 32 64 64).

At the end of June, thespians from all over the world arrive in Limassol for the **Shakespeare Festival.** A two-week **International Art Festival** is held in the zoo gardens during the first half of July. If you arrive in early September, you can drink yourself into divine euphoria at the **Wine-Fest.** During the **Carnival,** 50 days before Orthodox Easter (usually in Feb.), everyone roams the streets in search of a hidden yellow, glittering, precious gold coin. Contact the tourist office for details.

Near Limassol

The **Kolossi Castle,** a square-shaped, three-story structure about 9km west of Limassol, played a crucial role during the Crusades. Both the Templar Knights and the Knights of the Order of St. John made the castle their headquarters for a short while. When the latter order moved to Rhodes in 1310, Kolossi remained its richest overseas possession, garnering wealth from the surrounding vineyards. (Open 7:30am-sunset. Admission 50¢.) To reach Kolossi, take bus #16 from the urban bus station in Limassol (every 20min., 35¢).

Outside the British sovereign base of Akrotiri, the small resort town of **Pissouri,** frolics year-round with Her Majesty's military men. Built on a cliff with the standard enticing views, Pissouri hosts several bars and *tavernas*. The **Bunch of Grapes Inn** (tel. (052) 212 75) has a restaurant and rooms. (Singles £10. Doubles £15.)

Kourion

The remarkably well-preserved ruins of **Kourion** (Curium in Latin), 12km west of Limassol, lie within the British Sovereign Base Area, which includes all of the Akrotiri Peninsula. First settled during the Neolithic Period, Kourion was colonized by Achaeans from Argos in the Peloponnese during the 14th and 13th centuries BCE. It became famous for its sanctuary to Apollo (8th century BCE) and its stadium (2nd century CE), both located west of the main settlement. In the 4th century CE, Kourion was leveled by the same earthquake that destroyed several other Cypriot coastal cities. The city was rebuilt in the 5th century, only to be burned in the mid-7th century during an Arab raid.

Begin your tour at the impressive **theater,** with its oak-cleaving views of the Mediterranean. The theater is used for the Shakespeare Festival in June, occasional concerts and theatrical productions during the summer, and weekend theater in September. Limassol's tourist bureau can fill you in. The earliest structure on the site, a small theater built in the 2nd century BCE, was enlarged with limestone blocks in the first century CE. During Greek and Roman times, the theater was used for drama, but by the 3rd century CE, civilization had progressed and the odeum was transformed into an arena for bloody animal fights.

Across the dirt road from the basilica lie a group of ruins still under excavation. In the northern corner rests a large Hellenistic building and a water reservoir used until the 7th century CE. In the southwest corner lies a row of Corinthian columns, all that remains of the **Forum,** a market and meeting-place dating from the end of the 2nd century CE.

Farther northwest are the remains of the **House of Gladiators** and its mosaic gladiator pin-ups. Be careful not to fall into one of the nearby cisterns. If you do, call for help. The **House of Achilles** faces the highway at the end of the excavation site. The house is fenced off, but you can get the key at the ticket office, or climb in through the narrow path that follows the fence along the road. (Site open daily 7:30am-7:30pm; Oct.-May 7:30am-sunset. Admission 50¢.) Visit the nearby **Museum of Kourion** in Episkopi village for a clear explanation of the artifacts. (Open Mon.-Sat. 7:30am-1:30pm.)

The low walls of the **stadium** stand on the right side of the highway, 1km west up the hill. When built, the stands held 6000 people, but today, only a small section of the original seating remains. (Site open 24 hrs. Free.) About 1km farther lies the **Sanctuary of Apollo,** at one time second only to the Temple of Aphrodite (in old Paphos) as a center of religious worship on the island. Most of the present ruins date from 100 CE. (Sanctuary open daily 7:30am-7:30pm; in winter 7:30am-sunset. Admission 50¢.) **Buses** leave Limassol Castle bound for Kourion (6 per day, returning at 11:50am and 2:50pm and 4:50pm, 60¢). If you're mopeding to Kourion, go via Episkopi village. There are no signs for Kourion until you're within a couple of kilometers of the site, so bring a good map. Don't take the highway—the lanes keep changing and ending abruptly, and traffic is heavy. Without a helmet, it's suicidal.

Troodos Mountains ΤΡΟΟΔΟΣ

When summer heat descends, most tourists head to the coast. Should you prefer alternatives, find refuge in the serene mountain regions which are often 10-20 degrees cooler than the cities. In the Troodos mountain range, halfway between Nicosia and Limassol, tiny villages mingle with astounding Byzantine churches, while remote monasteries and forests of flat-topped pines ward off the summer heat. Hikers and campers in particular will find themselves sated here. What is usually a peaceful and rejuvenating natural experience in June and early July, however, can turn frustrating and costly in August when tourists and Cypriots mount; even the monasteries have been known to turn away visitors. The best time to visit in summer is midweek, when crowds are meager. From January to March, Mt. Olympus, the highest point in Cyprus (1951m), plays host to hundreds of skiers.

Public transportation to and from the area and between the villages runs very infrequently. One **bus** per day heads here from Nicosia and Limassol. The best way to get around is to rent some wheels. Some hitch, but we don't recommend it. The bohemian way to see this area is to leave your things in one of the coastal towns and travel around the area for a few days with only the map from the tourist office and a few essentials. In the mountains, only Platres has motorbike rentals. You can play it safe by renting in Limassol, Paphos, Polis, or Nicosia. Remember that the mountain roads are tortuous, bumpy, and sometimes steep. You could also rent a car in one of the major cities.

Platres

Platres will most likely be your first stop in the Troodos region, as it is the most accessible by public transportation. From Nicosia, KEMEK runs a **bus** via Kalopanayiotis, Moutoullas, Pedhoulas, and Prodromos. The bus leaves the Leonides St. station in Nicosia on weekdays at 12:15pm, returning from Platres at 5:30am (£1). A veritable fleet of buses runs from Limassol to Platres: Platres Bus Co. sends a bus from Eleftherias St. in Limassol. Gero-Demos has a bus that leaves from the KEMEK station and continues on to Prodromos and Pedhoulas (Mon.-Fri. at 1pm, returning the next morning, £1). In addition, **Karydas** service taxis in Platres (tel. 42 34 84) and in Limassol (tel. 36 34 84) leave for Platres most weekdays at about noon and return at 7pm (£1.50). Platres is divided into **pano** (upper) and **kato** (lower) sections; Kato Platres, 20 minutes downhill from Pano Platres, remains unharrowed by tourism. If you want to stay in Kato Platres, try the florid **Kapakioti** (tel. 212 02), where tidy doubles cost £12. Otherwise, all tourist facilities have formed a clique in Pano Platres: the **tourist office** is left of the parking lot in the main square. (Open Mon. and Wed.-Fri. 9am-3:30pm, Tues. and Sat. 9am-1pm.) The **post office** sits to the left of the tourist office. (Open Mon.-Fri. 8am-1:30pm and 4-6pm, Sat. 8am-1:30pm and 4-5pm; Oct.-May Mon.-Tues. and Thurs.-Fri. 8-10am and 3-5am, Wed. and Sat. 8-10am.) The **telephone office** is next to the post office (open Mon.-Sat. 9am-1pm and 4-6pm). The **Bank of Cyprus** is across from the Splendid Hotel. (Open Mon.-Tues. and Thurs.-Fri. 8:15am-12:30pm and 3:30-6pm; Wed. 8:15am-12:30pm.) The **hospital** (tel. 42 12 34) is just below Pano Platres and houses the **pharmacy.** The **police** (tel. 42 13 51) are across from the Splendid Hotel in a converted military chapel. Platres's **telephone code** is 05.

A comfortable place to stay in Platres is the **Pafsilypon Hotel** (tel. 42 17 38); past the Petit Palais, go right at the fork. The floors and beds are theatrically creaky, but Andreas, the helpful proprietor, makes sure they're spotless. Mystagogical mountain views off the back porch. (Singles £8.50, doubles £15, including English breakfast and coffee.) The **Spring Hotel** (tel. 42 13 30), just out of town toward Troodos, balances on the edge of a gorge overlooking a small waterfall. (Open May-Oct. Singles £12. Doubles £15. Breakfast included.) Next to the parking lot is conveniently located **Splendid Hotel** (tel. 42 14 25), which would be more aptly named the Kind of Nice Hotel. All rooms have balconies and showers, but not toilets. (Singles £16. Doubles £23.) Paul, the manager, also rents flats a few minutes out of town. (1-bedroom £22. 2-bedrooms £35.)

A large grocery store and fruit market is just past the Pafsilypon. Just north of Platres on the road to Troodos, **Psilo Dentro** (tall tree) serves sumptuous trout from its own fish farm (tel. 42 13 50). The urbane step out at **Andy's Disco** (tel. 42 11 22), near the main square. (No cover. Small beer 50¢. Open 10pm-2am.)

Troodos

Though just 8km north of Platres, **Troodos** is accessible by **bus** only from Constantza Bastion in Nicosia (Mon.-Fri. at noon, returning to Nicosia at 6am the next day, £1). Taxi fare from Platres is about £4 or you can try hiking it (at least 1hr.) Troodos Town is a graceless group of hotels, restaurants, and tourist facilities, including a **CYTA office** and a **post office,** which is open when the mayor is available.

About 400m from the center of town on the Trodos Kakopetria road squats the recently re-opened **HI/IYHF youth hostel** (tel. 42 16 49), offering clean and quiet rooms with communal kitchen facilities (£3). Another cheap place to stay is the **Troodos campground** (tel. 42 16 24), 2km north of the main square in a pine forest (£1.50 per tent, £1 per person). The campsite provides washing facilities, a minimarket, a small bar/restaurant, and a first aid station. The **Jubilee Hotel Bar** (tel. 42 16 47), just outside of town, is a favorite haunt of British expatriates.

Three guided **nature trails** originate in the Troodos area. The first is 8½km long and goes from the Troodos post office to Chromion, passing by various villages. A 3km trail leaves from the coffee shop in Troodos Sq. and finishes at a divine look-out point. Shorter but even more captivating is the 2km path that follows a stream from the Presidential Palace in Troodos and finishes at Kaledonia Falls near Platres. Noteworthy trees and plants are labeled along the way. The tourist office has a pamphlet outlining the trails, and information on horseback riding around Troodos (£5 per hr.).

Your last stop for both food and gas before ascending the mountains is at the **Diaryzos Café** (tel. (06) 43 23 35), in Mamonia, where you can spend the night. (Open 6am-11pm. Doubles £7.) Return to the asphalt road and head north until Mandria, where a 3km detour leads to the cordial lace and wine village of **Omodos.** Ask for a tour of the **folk museum** in the monastery, and the restored **wine press** *(linos).* You can buy a bottle of local, dry *krasi* (£1.70) or the fiery *tsipoura,* a Cypriot whiskey. Returning to Kato Platres, follow the signposts to the red-tiled village of **Phini** and revive. The **Pilavakion Museum** (tel. (05) 42 15 08) focuses on *pitharia* (large, red, ceramic jars), wine-making equipment, and the notable "Pithari Sauna" used in traditional Cypriot obstetrics to avoid post-pregnancy stretchmarks. (Open 9am-noon and 1-6pm.)

Picturesque **Kakopetria** (literally "bad stone"), on the main road from Nicosia to Troodos, is the most popular town in the northern part of the mountains. The local buzz is that the large rock perched on the hillside was supposed to bring good luck to newlyweds, until it rolled over one day and crushed a couple. The government is preserving the oldest section of the village, the shady, cobblestone roads and mudbrick houses overlooking a river. In the rest of the village, slick new pubs and "rustic" hotels cater to vacationers.

The **Bank of Cyprus** is in the main square (open Mon.-Fri. 8:30am-noon), near the **post office** (open Mon.-Fri. 7:30am-1:30pm, Sat. 7:30am-12:30pm). A **pharmacy** (tel. 20 20) is below the Rialto Hotel (open 9:30am-9pm), and the **doctor** (tel. 30 77) practices a few doors down. The **Rialto Hotel** (tel. (02) 92 24 38) offers singles for £11 and doubles for £19 (breakfast included). Clean rooms await you at the **Hekali** (tel. (02) 92 25 01; singles £12. Doubles £17. Breakfast included.) The **Kifissia Hotel** (tel. (02) 922 421) has calming views of the small river. (£7.50 per person. English breakfast included.) Kakopetria and its smaller neighbor **Galata** have five Byzantine churches between them; the most beautiful is **Agios Nikolaos tis Stegis,** about 4km southwest of Kakopetria on a dirt road. **Buses** to Kakopetria travel from Constantza Bastion in Nicosia (Mon.-Fri. at noon, 75¢).

After a walk through the **Old Village,** quaff a cold brew (90¢) at the **Village Pub.** (Open 10am-midnight.) There are several cheap *kebab* houses in the square, and the **Village Cellar,** in a tastefully restored house, is renowned for its *tatavas* (lamb and onions, £3) and fresh trout. (Open Fri.-Wed.)

Tourists can stay in many of the monasteries. Services are held daily at sunrise. Keep in mind that the Troodhitissa monastery officially closes its doors to overnight guests in summer, and Kykko prefers Cypriot tourists to foreigners, especially in high season. Get thee to the monasteries early; all beds are filled by noon. Donations are always welcome, and a few words of Greek and conservative attire go a long way with the monks.

Sixteen km northeast of Kakopetria, the tiny Byzantine church at **Asinou** *(Paniya Porviotissa)* stuns its visitors. The church and original frescoes date from the 12th century, but new frescoes were added and old ones restored after the church was vandalized by Turks in the 14th and 16th centuries. Today the church is used for religious purposes only twice a year on feast days of the Virgin, to whom it is dedicated. To visit the church, find the priest in the nearby village of Nikitare (ask in the village cafés). About 16km southeast of Kakopetria is the church of **Panayiatou Arakou,** another repository of elaborate 12th-century frescoes. South of the church is the comely vineyard village of **Agros,** with simple overnight accommodations (the only rooms in the vicinity). Try **Vlachos** (tel. (05) 521 330; singles £8, doubles £16.)

Forty hens, 15 cats, eight monks, one donkey, and a partridge in a pear tree make their home in the modern **Troodhitissa Monastery,** 5km from Platres on the Prodromos-Platres road. Dedicated to the Virgin Mary, the original monastery was built in 1250 specifically to house one of her miracle-working icons; the name Troodhitissa literally means "she who is resident of Mt. Troodos." During the chaos of the iconoclastic movement of the 8th century, a monk hid an icon of the Virgin Mary in Troodos, where a miraculous pillar of fire protected the icon. Over 100 years later, a sign revealed the site of the monastery, which still stands there today. (Open daily 6am-noon and 2-8pm; no overnight guests June 15-Sept. 15.)

Between Troodos and Prodromos soars **Mt. Olympus** (6401ft.), the highest peak on the island, now topped with monumental radar stations and observation towers. From January through March you can alternate sunbathing in Limassol with skiing on the north face of the mountain.

Prodromos

Ten km northwest of the town of Troodos, **Prodromos** is the second highest hill resort in the area (after Troodos). Take the road down the hill to the left for the **Alps Hotel** (tel. (02) 95 25 53; singles £9; doubles £11). The **Overhill** (tel. (02) 95 25 59) is larger (singles £9, doubles £11). You can relax at the nearby **Stephos Café** before heading on to **Kykko,** a village resort with a **Bank of Cyprus** and a **post office.** Just north of Prodromos is the small village of **Pedoulas,** with its Church of Archangel Michael and mural paintings dating from 1474. Up the street from the church is the **CYTA** (open Mon.-Sat. 9am-1pm and 4-6pm) and the **police** (tel. (02) 95 26 55), who will gruffly answer most tourist questions. Across the street is the miniscule **post office.** (Open Mon.-Sat. 9am-noon and 4pm-6pm.) Down the road, the **Capouralli Café** lets rooms. (£7 per person. Breakfast included.) Prodromos's **telephone code** is 0295.

Kykko Monastery, in the northwestern part of the mountains, 14km from Pedoulos, and 33km from Troodos enjoys more wealth and prestige than any other monastery on the island. The monastery was founded in the early 12th century when a hermit—after curing the Byzantine Emperor's daughter of an illness—was given the Apostle Luke's own Icon of the Virgin Mary. Though the monastery, fashioned of Koukou wood from the forest, has burned down numerous times, the celebrated icon has survived intact. Because the icon is considered too holy to be looked upon directly, it is completely ensconced in mother of pearl and silver casing. After entering the monastery's palatial courtyard, you may think you've wandered into a large luxury hotel by mistake; the rather banausic monastery, whose present buildings date from the early 19th century, boasts some 400 beds for visitors, a tourist pavilion, and shops. Recently, hotels have been complaining about business, so Kykko has officially restricted itself to taking in only Greek Orthodox pilgrims.

Kykko gained new fame this century as a communication and supply center during the Cypriot struggle and as the monastic home of Archbishop Makarios III. Only

1½km away were the headquarters of the first military leader of the struggle, "Dighenis" (General George Grivas). Makarios's tomb is just 2km further in the high hills west of the monastery. The site, guarded at all times by two Greek Cypriot soldiers, is partially open to the east. Makarios requested the opening so that on the day Cyprus was reunited, sunlight would enter his tomb and he could celebrate with his people. Just above the tomb is a path leading up to an icon of the Virgin, called the *throni* (small throne). The bushes alongside the path are laden with scraps of clothing placed there by sick children hoping to be cured. A supermarket, an extortionate tourist pavilion, and several sweet shops are nearer.

Nicosia (Lefkosia) ΛΕΥΚΩΣΙΑ

Landlocked Nicosia, the capital of the Republic of Cyprus, sits astride the Turkish Cypriot frontier (or "Green Line"). The presence of Greek Cypriot and Turkish border patrols, as well as a significant number of United Nations troops, serves as a constant reminder that violence and bitterness lie just below the surface. Many tourists bypass Nicosia for the sun and sand in other regions of Greek Cyprus, but a visit to this city is essential for anyone interested in Cyprus's political situation. Greek Cypriots call their city Lefkosia, but the use of Nicosia is common and inoffensive. The recent proliferation of museums and monuments reflects the town's eagerness to maintain both its spirit and cultural heritage. The city has also taken measures to restore old *Laiki Yitonia,* the pedestrian shopping district, whose cobblestone streets are now crammed full of shops and restaurants.

Built on the site of the ancient city of Ledra during the Roman occupation, Nicosia prospered until the invasions of Egyptian Mamlukes in 1426. When Egyptian strength waned, the Venetians took over (1489), and in 1567 built massive walls to ward off Turkish cannons. Monomaniacal, they razed all the buildings outside the walls that were in their line of fire, including the fabulous Lusignan abbey of St. Domenico. The fortifications were effective for a time, but three years later the Turks concentrated their effort, gained victory in seven weeks, and despoiled and presided over the city for the next several hundred years. The city prospered again only after the British takeover in 1878. When Cyprus achieved independence in 1960, Nicosia became its capital.

Orientation and Practical Information

The easiest way to orient yourself in Nicosia is to refer to the ominous Green Line running east-west at the north end of the city. This divider halves the **Old City** within its circular Venetian walls. When you walk down the streets slashed in half by the border, you'll come abruptly up against sheet metal barriers or white and blue painted dividers. At several points along the Green Line, and here and there throughout the city, signs forbid the taking of photos—they mean it. The southern (lower) part of Nicosia within the Walls (as the Old City is officially known) contains most of the budget accommodations, museums, and sights. From **Eleftherias Square,** Evagoras St. heads southwest into the **New City.** Intersecting Evagoras are Archbishop Makarios III Ave., Diagoras St., and Th. Dervis St., where the banks, embassies, and travel agencies are located. The New City is much busier than the old, and is the center of Nicosia's nightlife. Be sure to obtain one of the superb **maps** (free) from the tourist office.

Cyprus Tourist Organization: 35 Aristokypros St., *Laiki Yitonia* (tel. 44 42 64), within the city walls, in the Foll Neighborhood. Entering Eleftherias Sq., turn right and follow signs from the post office. Route maps, a complete list of village buses, and free copies of *Nicosia: This Month.* A two-hour-long combination bus and walking tour of Nicosia leaves here each Thursday at 10am. Sponsored by the Municipality of Nicosia, the tour is conducted in English and is free of charge. Open Mon. and Thurs. 9am-2:30pm and 4:30-6:30pm, Tues.-Wed. and Fri. 9am-2:30pm, Sat. 9am-1:30pm.

Embassies: U.S., at Dositheos and Therissos St. (tel. 46 51 51; fax. 45 95 71), near the Hilton Hotel, just off Archbishop Makarios III Ave. Take bus #16, 50, 55, or 58. Open Mon.-Fri. 8am-5pm. **British High Commission,** Alexander Pallis St. (tel. 47 31 31; fax 36 71 98), west of the old city. Open Mon., Wed. and Fri. 7:30am-1:30pm, Thurs. 7:30am-1:30pm and 4:30-6:30pm.

Australian High Commission, 4 Annis Comninis St. (tel. 47 30 01), at the corner of Stassinos Ave. Open in summer Mon.-Fri. 8am-3pm. **Canadian High Commission,** 4 Queen Frederica St., # 101 (tel. 45 98 30; fax 47 24 13). **Israel,** 4 I. Gryparis St. (tel. 44 51 95 or -96). Open Mon.-Fri. 8am-4pm. **Egypt,** 3 Egypt Ave. (tel. 46 51 44 or -45). Open Mon.-Fri. 8am-2pm. **Iran,** corner of Santa Rosa and Avlonos St. (tel. 45 00 20). Open Mon.-Sat. 8am-2pm. **Syria,** at Androcleous and Thoukidides St. (tel. 47 44 82). Visas in 24 hrs. or less; bring 2 photos. Visa department open Mon.-Fri. 8:30am-1:30pm. **U.N. Headquarters** (tel. 44 60 00), on the road to the Nicosia Airport.

Crossing to Northern Cyprus: The border is officially closed to everyone except diplomats. It is usually possible to make daytrips to Northern Cyprus, provided you return before nightfall; check at the tourist office, your embassy, the U.N. Headquarters, or the official checkpoint at the **Ledra Palace Hotel,** Markos Drakos Ave., just east of the city walls.

Currency Exchange: Bank of Cyprus, 86-88-90 Phaneromeni St. (tel. 46 40 64). Also a branch in *Laiki Yitonia* on Drakos St. (tel. 46 10 82).

American Express: 35-37 Evagoras Ave. (tel. 44 37 77), in the offices of **A.L. Mantovani and Sons.** They charge a 1-2% commission for cashing personal checks. Open Mon.-Fri. 8am-1pm and 3:30-6:30pm, Sat. 8am-12:30pm; off-season Mon.-Fri. 8am-1pm and 2:30-5:30pm, Sat. 8am-12:30pm. Check cashing service not available on Saturday.

Post Office: Main Office (tel. 30 32 31), Constantinos Paleologos Ave. just east of Eleftherias Sq., within the walls. Open Mon.-Fri. 7:30am-1pm, Sat. 7:30am-12:30pm, Mon.-Tues. and Thurs.-Fri. also 4-6pm; off-season Mon.-Tues. and Thurs.-Fri. 7:30am-1:30pm and 4-6pm, Wed. 7:30am-1:30pm, Sat. 7:30am-noon. Smaller offices on Dhigenis St., Palace St., and Loukis Akitas Ave.

Telephones (CYTA): Egypt Ave. (tel. 47 02 61). Open 7am-7:30pm. Dial 196 for telegrams. **Telephone Code:** 02.

Buses: KEMEK and **Kallenos Station,** 34 Leonides St. (tel. 46 39 89). To: Limassol (9 per day, £1); Larnaca (8 per day, 90¢); amd Platres (at 12:15pm, £1). **EMAN** bus stop, 50m east of the post office. To Agia Napa (1 per day, £1.50). No buses run on Sunday, and service is reduced in off-season.

City buses: Tel. 47 34 14. Leave from Solomos Sq., the first square to the west of Eleftherios. Run to city and suburban areas 5:30am-7pm. The tourist office has a complete list of routes.

Service Taxis: Makris (tel. 46 62 01); **Akropolis** (tel. 47 25 25); **Kypros** (tel. 46 48 11); and **Kyriakos** (tel. 44 41 14). All are on Stassinos Ave., which runs east along the city walls from Eleftherias Sq. **Karydas,** 8 Homer Ave. (tel. 46 22 69), is nearby. All run to Limassol (£2) and continue on to Paphos (additional £1.70); Makris, Akropolis, and Kyriakos lines also travel to Larnaca (£2.10).

Bookstores: Moufflon, 4 Sophoulis St., Chanteclair Bldg. Best place in Nicosia to buy guides on Cyprus. **The United States Information Service:** 33B Homer Ave. (tel. 47 31 43), around the corner from the museum, next to the Dept. of Antiquities. Current issues of the *New York Times* and other periodicals in a library with A/C. Open Mon.-Thurs. 9am-1pm and 4-6pm, Fri. 4-6pm; off-season Mon.-Fri. 9am-1pm and 2:30-5pm. Closed Aug.

British Council: 3 Museum Ave. (tel. 442 152), 2 doors down from the museum. Library with books, records, and tapes. Presents lectures, movies, and other cultural events. Open Mon.-Tues. and Fri. 7:30am-1:30pm, Wed. 7:30am-2pm, Thurs. 3-5:30pm, and Sat. 9am-noon; off-season afternoon hours are 3:30-5:30pm. Frequently has late hours.

Hospital: Tel. 45 11 11, between Hilon and Homer St., near the municipal gardens.

Police: Tel. 30 35 35.

Police Emergency: Tel. 199.

Accommodations and Food

Most of Nicosia's budget accommodations are located within the city walls and are at least tolerably clean. If you don't like the room you're shown, ask the proprietor to show you another one—degree of cleanliness and comfort tends to vary widely at most places.

Youth Hostel (HI/IYHF), 1 Hadjidaki St. (tel. 44 48 08 or 44 20 27), 700m from Eleftherias Sq. Clean with a communal kitchen and friendly atmosphere. Very popular with young folk from the Middle East. £3 per person. Sheets 50¢. Showers included.

Tony's Furnished Flats, 13 Solon St, *Laiki Yitonia* (tel. 46 67 52). Look for the sign on the 2nd floor. Conveniently located in the heart of the folk neighborhood just around the corner from the Cyprus Tourist Organization Office. Tidy rooms with fan and radio; some have a fridge and TV. Singles £7. Doubles £15. A/C £2. Breakfast included.

Sans Rival, 7C Solon St. (tel. 47 43 83), a few doors down from Tony's. Clean, but *sans* character. All rooms have a sink and fan, wooden floors and a balcony. Singles £6. Doubles £8.50. Breakfast 75¢.

Royal Hotel, 17 Euripides St. (tel. 46 32 45), on the corner of Euripides and Aeschylus. Clean; some rooms have private "showers" (a shower and drain sitting in the corner of the room). All rooms with fan. Singles £6. Doubles £9.

City Sunotel, 209 Ledra St. (tel. 46 31 13). A one star hotel. Singles £9. Doubles £16.

There is an abundance of dining options in Nicosia, but the best ones are hard to find. If you're not picky, the touristy restaurants around *Laiki Yitonia* serve Cypriot and continental cuisine in clean, cool surroundings with traditional music. Try the **Paphia Aphrodite Bar and Restaurant,** with fish *meze* for £4.75. The **Byzantine** (tel. 47 70 85), just one block from the Cyprus Tourist Organization Office, has wood-beamed ceilings, Byzantine arches, and a shaded courtyard. Try a Cyprus salad for £1.50. (Open for lunch until 5pm) For really authentic grub, try a light dinner at **Estiatorio,** 40 Arsinoes St., in the heart of the old city near the Green Line. You can buy your own provisions at the **municipal market** at Dhigenis Akritas and Kalipolis St. Every Wednesday, a colorful streetside **produce market** sets up shop along Constantinos Paleologos Ave., east of Eleftherias Sq. (Open 6am-1pm and 4-6pm.) The area east of the complex of museums within the old city has a number of restaurants where you can buy tasty, inexpensive Cypriot food for £2. Chickpea dishes usually go down smoothly, but the lamb's head is another story.

Sights

Sadly, many find the Green Line to be Nicosia's main attraction. The only spot along the border where you can take pictures is on Ledra St., where the military has erected something of a shrine to their lost country. For more morbid fun, visit the **Cyprus Museum** (tel. 30 21 89) and its collection of life-size terra-cotta models of tombs, complete with piles of bones, pottery, and other mysterious paraphernalia used in ancient religious and fertility rituals. (Open Mon.-Sat. 8:30am-1:30pm and 4-6pm, Sun. 10am-1pm; Oct.-May Mon.-Fri. 7:30am-2pm and 3-5pm, Sat. 7:30am-1pm and 3-5pm, Sun. 10am-1pm. Admission £1. Discounts for large groups.)

Nicosia's other important sights lie within the walls of the old city; four of them lie in a row on the right (east) side of the **Archbishop's Palace,** a gaudy and ostentatious modern structure with an overbearing statue of Archbishop Makarios that lights up at night. Located next to the palace is the **Byzantine Museum** (tel. 45 67 81), which houses one of the finest icon collections in all of Europe. (Open Mon.-Fri. 9:30am-1pm and 2-5pm, Sat. 9:30am-1pm; Oct.-April Mon.-Fri. 9am-1pm and 2-5pm, Sat. 9am-1pm. Admission 50¢.)

In front of the Byzantine Museum rests the 17th-century **St. John's Church,** adorned with 18th-century frescoes. In the same courtyard is the **Folk Art Museum** (tel. 46 32 05), housed in the old Archbishopric, a former 15th-century Gothic monastery. (Open Mon.-Fri. 8:30am-4pm and Sat. 8:30am-1pm. Admission 50¢.) For a more vivid interpretation of Cypriot culture, visit the neighboring **National Struggle Museum** (tel. 30 24 65). Founded in 1961 by the Greek Communal Chamber of Cyprus, the museum contains photographs, documents, and other relics from the struggle for *enosis* (union of Cyprus with Greece). (Open Mon.-Fri. 7:30am-1:30pm and 3-5pm, Sat. 7:30am-1:30pm; Sept.-May Mon.-Fri. 7:30am-2pm and 3-5pm, Sat. 7:30am-1pm. Admission 25¢.) Don't miss Nicosia's newest attraction, the **Levenis Municipal Museum** (tel. 45 17 75), located on Hippocratis St. in the *Laiki Yitonia.* The exhibit chronicles the history of Nicosia beginning with the modern city, and takes you back through time to 3000 BCE. (Open Tues.-Sun. 10am-4:30pm. Free.)

Down Koreas St. from the Archbishopric is another reminder of the Cypriot struggle for freedom, a marble monument depicting 14 Cypriots—each representing a period of the island's history—being released from jail by soldiers and overseen by a religious figure. Nearby, along the Venetian Walls at the end of Theseus St., is the recently restored **Famagusta Gate,** which served as the main entrance to the medieval city. Built in 1567, it now serves as a forum for plays, concerts, and lectures. Get a copy of *Nicosia: This Month* at the tourist office for a current schedule of events. (Open Mon.-Fri. 10am-1pm and 5-8pm, Sat. 10am-1pm; Sept.-May Mon.-Fri. 10am-1pm and 4-7pm, Sat. 10am-1pm.)

The **Konak Mansion,** known as **The House of Hadjigeorgiakis Kornesios** for short, 18 Patriarch Gregory St., is just around the corner from the Archbishopric complex. A famous Turkish dragoman—an interpreter for the Ottoman Turks and Greeks—lived in this luxurious, 18th-century structure. The dusty often take a dip in one of the only Turkish baths outside of Turkey: the historical **Omerye Hamam** is just in from the Podocataro Bastion; look for the nearby minaret. (Open 6am-2pm. Women on Wed. and Fri. only. Admission £2.) The colorful **botanical garden** is adjacent to the museum and behind the Garden Café (open daily 8am-10pm). The aviaries here showcase most of the island's indigenous species.

Paphos ΠΑΦΟΣ

When the Ptolemies, Greek kings of Egypt, conquered Cyprus, they made Paphos their capital. The city grew fabulously wealthy, developing into a center for commerce and pleasure. Paphos maintained its exalted position under Cato and the Roman conquerors, but a 4th-century earthquake ended its supremacy. The Cyprian capital, with the accompanying political and social prestige, moved to Salamis (now in the occupied area near Famagusta). Paphos remained a small village until the Turkish occupation rendered almost all of Cyprus's northern tourist areas inaccessible. Since 1974, Paphos has ballooned with luxury hotels and restaurants. Still, it remains a comfortable and manageable city, featuring archaeological discoveries, gorgeous mosaics, unmatched restaurants, and, in the surrounding countryside, superb beaches and isolated villages.

Orientation and Practical Information

The city of Paphos is divided into two sections: the upper **Ktima Paphos,** (also known as just "Paphos") centered around Kennedy Sq., and the lower **Kato Paphos,** about 1km to the south. Formed in the 8th century CE when the townspeople fled inland to evade Arab assaults from the sea, Ktima Paphos is now home to most of the city's shops, budget hotels, and services, while luxury hotels and holiday villas jam Kato Paphos, also the hub of Paphos's nightlife. Everything listed is in Ktima Paphos, unless otherwise noted.

Cyprus Tourist Organization: 3 Gladstone St. (tel. 23 28 41), across from Iris Travel. The helpful staff can provide every extant scrap of practical information on the region, including excellent free maps. Open Mon. and Thurs. 8:30am-1:15pm and 4-6:15pm, Tues.-Wed. and Fri.-Sat. 8:15am-1:30pm.

Budget Travel: Iris Travel, 10A Gladstone St. (tel. 23 75 85), opposite the tourist office. Airline tickets (student discounts), and special "Exalt" four-wheel trips (from £12) and excursions. They also rent cars (Suzuki 700 and Subaru £12 per day in summer), and apartments (from £3 per person). Open Mon.-Fri. 8am-1pm and 4-7pm, Sat. 8am-1pm; Oct.-May Mon.-Fri. 8am-1pm and 2-5:30pm.

Bank: Hellenic Bank, 86 Makarios Ave. (tel. 23 50 35). Open Mon.-Fri. 8:30am-noon and 4-7pm, Sat. 4:30-6:30pm. **Barclay's Bank,** Kennedy Sq. at Diogenis (next to the Paphos Palace Hotel). Open Mon.-Fri. 8:30am-noon and 4-7pm, Sat. 4-7pm.

Post Office: Nikodhimou Mylona St. (tel. 24 02 23), in the District Administration Bldg. Open Mon.-Sat. 7:30am-1pm and 4-6pm; Sept.-May Mon.-Tues. and Thurs.-Fri. 7:30am-1:30pm and 3:30-5:30pm, Wed. and Sat. 7:30am-12:30pm. The post offices in Kato Paphos are on Ag. Antoniou St., and on Leoforos Eliados.

Telephones (CYTA): Grivas Diogenes Ave. Open daily 7:30am-7:30pm, but may close early. **Telephone Code:** 06.

Airport: C.T.O., tel. 23 68 33. Opens when flights arrive. Exchange facilities. Private taxis from city center £4, from Kato Paphos £5.

Buses: municipal buses run between Ktima Paphos and Kato Paphos (31 per day, 14 on Sun.;30¢). Catch it in Ktima Paphos just up the road from the post office; in Kato Paphos, at any of the yellow benches lining the road to town. Buses also go to Coral Bay (20 per day, 40¢). Schedules in the tourist office. **Nea Amoroza Co.** (tel. 22 11 14) runs minibuses to Polis (12 per day, 85¢). A few go as far as Pomos. Minibuses leave from the easy-to-miss station on the west side of Pallikardi St. **KEMEK** (tel. 23 42 55) runs buses to Limassol from the Mitropolis Bldg. off Thermopylon St. (4 per day, £1). Change buses in Nicosia or Larnaca.

Service Taxis: Kyriakos, 19 Pallikaridi St. (tel. 23 31 81). **Karydas,** 29 E. Pallikaridi (tel. 23 24 59). **Kypros,** Archbishop Makarios III Ave. (tel. 23 23 76); in Kennedy Sq. **Makris,** (tel. 23 25 33) on Athens St., in the northern part of town. All companies go to Limassol (£1.60), Nicosia (£3.65), and Larnaca (£3.40).

Bike and Motorbike Rental: Most shops are in Kato Paphos. **Psomas Rentals** (tel. 23 55 61), at the intersection of Artemidos and Poseidonas St., across from the Paphos Beach Motel. **Max Rentals** (tel. 23 58 34). Bikes £1.50 per day, motorbikes £3-8 per day. Roadside service. Price includes 3rd-party insurance, but not gas. In Ktima Paphos, **Antonides,** at 38, 111, and 113 Pallikarides St. (tel. 23 33 01) rents one-seater automatics for £3.

Bookstore: Axel Bookshop, 62-64 Archbishop Makarios III Ave. (tel. 23 24 04). English-language books about Cyprus. Open Mon.-Sat. 8am-1pm and 4-7pm. Kiosks in Kennedy Sq. sell international newspapers and the English *Cyprus Mail,* and *Cyprus Weekly.*

Laundromat: Sun Rise (tel. 23 40 18), at Alkminis and Posidonos St. in Kato Paphos. Wash and dry £3. Free pick-up in town. Open Mon.-Sat. 9am-1pm and 4-7pm.

Women's Clinic: Dr. Efstathiou, 6 Giallourou (tel. 24 36 66), off Dallikarides St. English spoken.

Hospital: Neophytos Nicolaides St. (tel. 23 23 64). Free first aid. English spoken.

Police: Grivas Diogenes Ave. (tel. 23 23 52), in Kennedy Sq., opposite the now defunct Paphos Palace Hotel.

Police Emergency: Tel. 199.

Accommodations, Camping, and Food

Finding inexpensive accommodations in Paphos is a chore. Solo travelers should stick to the youth hostel; groups might try renting an apartment. The following are in Ktima Paphos, unless otherwise noted. Prices are higher, but the nightlife livelier, in Kato Paphos.

Youth Hostel (HI/IYHF), 37 Eleftherias Venizelou Ave. (tel. 23 25 88), on a quiet residential street northeast of the town center. From the KEMEK station, follow Athinas St. out of town and take a right on Canning St., just past the Esso station. When Athinas becomes Venizelou St., take another right and you'll see the hostel after you round the corner. Though a hike from town, the hostel is friendly, peaceful, and close to a few minimarkets and take-away joints. Call ahead if you plan to come in after 11pm. £2.50. Sheets 50¢. Breakfast 50¢-£1. Hot showers included. Open year-round. Moped rental £4 per day.

Lazaros Omirou, 25 Ayiou Kendia (tel. 23 29 09). As you walk down Makarios, go left at the Hellenic Bank. An old house with overstuffed chairs, antiques, and imposing art deco fireplaces. Free coffee and kitchen facilities. £5 per person. Apartments for 3 people (£110 per month).

Hotel Trianon, 99 Archbishop Makarios III Ave. (tel. 23 21 93). Institutional exterior in keeping with the older interior. Seedy except for the rather comfy TV lounge. Singles £5. Doubles £12.

Ambassador Apartments, across from the lovely but pricey Axiothea. 1 Maliotis St. (tel. 23 54 40). Fully furnished studios with kitchen, living room and bath £11. Quads with living room, bath and kitchenette £19. Free use of Axiotha Hotel facilities.

Kiniras Hotel, 91 Archbishop Makarios III Ave. (tel. 24 16 04). Expensive, but classy and clean. Singles £14.50. Doubles £26. A/C available at £2 per day. Price includes breakfast. Guests receive a 20% discount on car rentals.

Pelican Inn, Leoforos Apostolou Pavlou St., on the waterfront in Kato Paphos. Tidy rooms and accommodating management. All with private bath and balcony. Singles £13. Doubles £16. Breakfast included.

Othon, 3 Pnitagorou (tel. 23 43 03), near the Apollo Hotel in Kato Paphos. Fully furnished studios for two £14.

Pyramos Hotel, 4 Agios Anastasias St. (tel. 23 51 61), in Kato Paphos. Often booked full with British tour groups. Singles £14. Doubles £20.

Zenon Gardens Yeroskipou Camping (tel. 24 22 77), east of the tourist beach on the sea, 3km from Paphos Harbor. Minimarket, restaurant and communal kitchen. Limited shady pitches. £1.50 per pitch, £1 per person, £3.50 per small tent. Open March-Oct.

Most restaurants in Kato Paphos are geared to *drachma*-laden tourists. One frugal find, without much ambience, is **Yacinthus,** on Agia Napa St., next to the Kato Paphos post office. They serve delicious, large salads (tuna salad or Mexican salad) for £1. Also in Kato Paphos, with an eerie view of the harbor-side ruins, is **Hondros,** (tel. 23 42 56), 96 Pavlou St. Sit under the bamboo covered terrace beneath the grapevines and enjoy lamb *kleftiko* straight off the spit (£4.50), or a fresh shrimp salad (£2). (Open 11am-4pm and 7pm-midnight.) In Ktima Paphos, the best and most reasonable restaurant is **Trianon,** with a nice courtyard; hidden from the street on Archbishop Makarios III Ave. Or try **Feta's,** also called **Andreas Taverna,** on the corner of 25th Martiou and Andrea Ioannou St. by the roundabout. Authentic right down to the prices (lunch from £2). For breakfast, head to the **Axiothe Hotel,** where you can gorge yourself on their all-you-can-eat buffet (£2.50; open 7-9am). **Peggy's Miranda Café** in Kennedy Sq. serves up a tasty continental breakfast (£2). You can also swap books here. (Open Mon.-Tues. and Thurs.-Fri., 7:30am-5pm.) **Relax Take-Way** is a good spot—from the hostel, turn left onto Venizelou, and make your first right. A "portion" of fried chicken costs £2 and will last you for three meals. There are also grill houses throughout both Kato and Ktima Paphos that sell *souvlaki* (80¢).

Sights and Entertainment

Paphos possesses more interesting sights per square inch than any other city in Cyprus. (We measured and counted.)

Kato Paphos

The mosaic floors of the **House of Dionysus** are unquestionably the city's most dazzling ancient treasure. Discovered accidentally in 1962 by a farmer plowing his fields and soon thereafter excavated by a Polish expedition, the largely intact mosaics once covered 14 rooms of a expansive Roman villa. The floors depict scenes from mythology and daily life with vibrance, sensitivity, and subtle use of color and shading. All the colors are the stones' natural hues. The villa's pervasive wine theme has led some archaeologists to conclude that it belonged to a wealthy vineyard owner or wine merchant (or a drunkard). Even the abstract designs contain images of cups. Inscriptions here and there exhort "In Vino Veritas." (Open daily 7:30am-7:30pm; Oct.-May 7:30am-dusk. Admission £1.)

Farther towards the water rests the **House of Theseus,** dating from the 2nd to the 6th century CE. The ruins reveal a luxurious building complete with marble statues, a vast courtyard with marble columns, mosaic floors, and a bath complex. The two mosaics of Theseus and Achilles are accessible by walkways. On the road to the mosaics, you'll find the remnants of an *agora* beside the remains of a limestone Roman **odeon**—small, roofed semi-circular theater. Constructed in the 2nd century CE, the odeon accommodates 3000 spectators and is periodically used for performances. (Contact the tourist office for information.)

The cool, musty **Catacombs of Agia Solomoni,** along the road between Ktima and Kato Paphos, include a chapel with deteriorating Byzantine frescoes. Dedicated to St. Solomoni (Hannah), mother of seven children who were tortured to death for their faith during the persecution of the Jews in Palestine (168 BCE), the chapel supposedly sits on the site of the old synagogue of Paphos. Part of the deepest chamber is filled with extraordinarily lucent water, which you may fail to notice until you're drenched in it. A tree with thousands of handkerchiefs draped from its branches marks the entrance to the catacombs on A. Pavlos Ave.; the tree is said to cure the illnesses of those who tie a cloth to it. (Open 24 hrs. Free.) At **St. Paul's Pillar,** near the Chryssopolitissa Church, St. Paul was allegedly tied and whipped for preaching Christianity. Built in the late 7th century on a hill overlooking the harbor, the **Byzantine Castle** *(Saranda Kolones)* was intended to protect its inhabitants from Arab pirates. When an earthquake destroyed it in 1222, the Lusignans built the **Fort of Paphos** at the end of the pier. The fort was used and rebuilt by the Venetians and later the Turks. (Open Mon.-Fri. 7:30am-sunset. Admission 50¢.)

Ktima Paphos

The **Archaeological Museum** on Grivas Diogenes Ave. (tel. 2402 15), houses a fine array of Bronze Age pottery and tools, classical sculpture and statues, and artifacts from the House of Dionysus and the House of Theseus. (Open Mon.-Sat. 7:30am-1:30pm and 4-7pm, Sun. 10am-1pm; Oct.-May Mon.-Fri. 7:30am-2pm, Sat. 7:30am-2pm and 3-5pm, Sun. 10am-1pm. Admission 50¢.)

Don't miss the excellent **Ethnographical Museum,** 1 Exo Vrysi St. (tel. 23 20 10), just south of the town center in the 100-year old residence of the Eliades family. Admission (50¢) includes a guided tour in English conducted by the effervescent Mrs. Eliades. The garden vaunts a 3rd-century BCE Hellenistic tomb, Christian catacombs, and *kleftiko* ovens. (Open Mon.-Sat. 9am-1pm and 4-7pm, Sun. 10am-1am; Oct.-April Mon.-Sat. 9am-1pm and 3-5pm, Sun. 10am-1pm. Large groups admitted only on Sun. Admission 50¢.)

The **Byzantine Museum** #26 25th Martiou St. (tel. 324 66), houses icons and other religious relics from local monasteries and churches. (Open Mon.-Fri. 9am-12:30pm and 4-7pm, Sat. 9am-1pm; Oct.-May Mon.-Fri. 9am-1pm and 3-5pm, Sat. 9am-1pm. Admission 50¢.)

West of Ktima Paphos, a signposted road runs 1km to the Paleokastra, or **Tombs of the Kings**—a misnomer, since those interred in these hewn stone tombs were not royalty but merely local aristocracy. The larger tombs consist of an open court encircled by burial chambers, with Doric columns carved out of the underground rock and stairways leading down to the interiors. The tombs, dating from the Hellenistic and Roman periods, were also used as hideouts by early Christians fleeing persecution. To the north of the tombs within the circular asphalt road lies **Paleoeklisia** (literally "old church") with fragments of Byzantine frescoes. (Tombs and church open daily 7:30am-7:30pm; Oct.-May 7:30am-sunset. Admission £1.)

The two most popular beaches stretch out at **Yeroskipou** and **Coral Bay.** Yeroskipou is exclusively a tourist beach with showers and snack bars, while Coral Bay is sandier, marginally less crowded, and frequented by locals. Nightlife here is the peppiest in Western Cyprus. The **Rainbow** draws a sophisticated *kamaki* crew on the make for deep-fried women. (Drinks £1. Open 9pm-3am. Cover £3, includes 1 drink.) On the waterfront, the trendy **La Boîte Pub** attracts local artists from the nearby Lemba College of Art. (Drinks £2-2.50.) El numero uno de Cyprus for hot Latin rhythms is **Samba,** inland from Poseidonas St.

Near Paphos

Seventeen km southeast of Paphos, adjacent to the modern village of **Kouklia,** lie the ruins of the great **Temple of Aphrodite** and **Paleopaphos** (Old Paphos), once the capital of a kingdom encompassing nearly half of Cyprus. The temple itself was the religious center of the island and a destination for pilgrimages from all parts of the Roman world. Constructed in the 12th century BCE, it thrived until the 4th century CE, when the anti-pagan edicts of Emperor Theodosius—and a series of earthquakes—reduced it to inconspicuous rubble. The scant remains, merely piles of rocks, make little sense without a guide—buy *A Brief History and Description of Old Paphos,* a booklet published by the Cyprus Department of Antiquities and available at most museums (45¢). The modest **Archaeological Museum** at the site houses an unprepossessing collection of pottery and inscriptions. The **Epigraphical Museum** next door contains a variety of carved stones which represent aspects of life in the once-grand capital. (Museums and temple open daily 7:30am-7:30pm, Oct.-May 7:30am-dusk. Admission to ruins, city, and museums 50¢.)

Almost 9km north of Paphos, near Coral Bay Beach, you'll find the painted caves and buildings of the **Monastery of Agios Neophytos.** Here you'll find several striking icons, Byzantine frescoes, and vistas of the sea. About 100m from the monastery complex is a ravine with a winter stream and three contiguous rock caves carved out by Neophytos and covered with beautiful 12th-century frescoes. You can get here from the beach. Bring a flashlight. (Open 7:30am-sunset.)

Archbishop Makarios III was born in the mountain village of **Pano Panayia,** 38km northeast of Paphos, where he stayed until entering the Kykko Monastery. A monument to Cyprus's most revered figure stands in the town square, and the small house where Makarios was born has since been converted into a museum. (Open daily 9am-noon and 1-5pm. Free.) About 1km from Pano Panayia and 40km from Paphos is **Chryssorogiatissa Monastery**—perhaps the most picturesquely situated monastery in Cyprus. According to legend, Ignatius found one of three icons of the Virgin Mary, painted by St. Luke, on the beach at Paphos and the Virgin told him to build a monastery in her honor. He did, though the current structure dates from 1770. A fire destroyed much of the monastery's property in 1967, but its fine collection of 18th-century icons and frescoes is still intact. The monastery will usually house guests for free—ask the staff at the restaurant to translate for you or ask for details at the tourist office in Paphos. About 3km south stands the abandoned **Monastery of Agia Moni,** dating from the 17th and 19th centuries. Four buses per day (last at 4pm) run to Panayia from Pervola station, returning to Paphos the next morning at 6am and 7:15am (40¢).

North of Paphos, the lovely village of **Pegia** lies tucked in the hills about 11km from Paphos. To fully experience the road that runs along a mountain ridge between rolling hills and the sea, many rent motorbikes. Just past Pegia is the lovely beachside hamlet of Agios Georgios. The coastline around Agios Georgios is full of chalk formations that have formed fascinating underwater caves. Half of the four buildings here are hotels. **St. George Restaurant** (tel. (066) 210 75) lets new, clean doubles for £15; you can pitch a tent next to the restaurant for free. About 50m up the road toward Pegia is **Yeronisos Hotel and Restaurant** (tel. (066) 210 78), which is cluttered but comfortable. (Singles £10. Doubles £14. Breakfast included.) Down a dirt road from Agios Georgios is **Lara Beach,** one of the longest in Cyprus and a breeding ground for the endangered Mediterranean turtle. Aside from the area's lone restaurant, there is but vacuity, so unless your visit coincides with the boat excursion from Paphos, you should be all by your lonesome amongst the sand, trees, and turtles.

Polis and Environs

The minimalist name simply means "town." But the smooth sand, cheap food, and carefree mood which grace the small village of Polis have turned the town into a choice Cyprian spot for budget vacationers. Just 37km north of ritzy Paphos, Polis is easily accessible by minibus and taxi.

Polis boasts some stellar examples of traditional Cypriot mountain architecture—large rounded wooden doors and stone masonry. At the end of the windy main street is the *platia,* where several travel agencies offer advice and information. **Century 21** (tel. 32 16 58), the best equipped, rents mopeds (£4) and cars (£17.50), runs worthwhile excursions around the Akamas Peninsula, and exchanges money. (Open Mon.-Fri. 8am-1pm and 4-7pm, Sat. 8am-1pm.) Across from it is **Pegasus Video,** which rents mopeds for £4. Around the *platia* you'll find three **banks** (open Mon.-Fri. 8:30am-noon, and 4-7pm; off-season, Mon.-Fri. 8:30am-noon) and the **post office** (tel. 32 15 39; open Mon.-Sat. 8am-noon). **Kyriakos Taxi** (tel. 32 11 01) is also on the **platia.** The **police** (tel. 32 14 51) roost one block from the square in the direction of the beach. A **pharmacy** (tel. 32 12 53) is down the street from the post office. The well-staffed **hospital** (tel. 32 14 31) is on the way to the campsite. The **telephone code** for the area is 06.

Freelancers pitch their tents on bluffs above the shore to the west, and along the road to the Baths of Aphrodite. No one seems to squawk as long as the sites are kept clean. Several restaurants along this stretch provide free or almost-free camping and the use of facilities to customers. Carrying on the Polis tradition of abstruse names, **Campground** (tel. 32 15 26) lies 1km from the town center, in a fragrant eucalyptus grove by the sea (£1.50 per tent pitch, £1 per person. Open March-Oct.) The **Akamas Hotel** (tel. 3213 30), before the *platia,* has clean, breezy rooms and a quiet courtyard. (Singles £7. Doubles £9.) Also with a courtyard, the **Lemon Garden** (tel. 32 14 43), past the *platia* to the right, provides tasty meals and comfortable doubles with kitchen facilities (£5-6 per person). Look for inexpensive *dhomatia* down the hill from the Bank of Cyprus, or inquire at a *kafeneia.* You should be able to get a room for £5 per person. Rooms-to-let also line the road to the beach. On the right before the turn-off for the Vomos Taverna, **Mrs. Evlalia** (tel. 32 15 80) rents six bright, clean rooms, with access to a kitchen. (Doubles £5 per person.) **Vomos Taverna** serves *meze* by the beach. In town, **Arsinoe** (tel. 32 15 90), across from the church, is run by a fisherman's family and serves the daily catch. (Fish soup £2. Open 8am-1pm and 7pm-1am.) In the evenings, you can check out the beachside disco, or saunter over to **Brunnen,** before the Akamas Hotel and down some steps. Marios, a Famagustan refugee, has turned this dilapidated Turkish house into a sprawling, colorful garden bar. (Large beer 70¢. Wine 50¢. Breakfast served. Open 8am-1pm and 5pm-2am.)

Just 10km west of Polis are the **Baths of Aphrodite,** a pleasantly shady pool carved out of limestone by natural springs. Aphrodite came here to cleanse herself after her nocturnal exploits; today, mortals bathe in the thigh-deep waters, despite proscriptive signs. The pool of **Fontana Amorosa,** 5km away, can be reached by foot or with a sturdy off-road vehicle. The amorous pool was reportedly where Aphrodite married Akamas, the son of Theseus.

The road from Polis to the Baths of Aphrodite leads past several good beaches and some cheap lodgings. About 1km out of Polis, the friendly **Tamamouna** family (tel. 32 12 69) offers excellence all around. (Singles £5. Doubles £8.) Where the road turns to gravel, **CO-MA-NE** (tel. 210 42 or 213 10) rents fully furnished beachside apartments for £12. Inquire at their office in Polis's *platia.* The budding port of **Lachi,** 2km west of Polis, has a decent stretch of pebbles and several fish *tavernas* and hotels. Below the **Baths of Aphrodite tourist pavilion,** 1km west, is a long sandy beach. Just beyond it is **Ttakkas Bay,** a lovely cove that Cypriots consider the best beach on this part of the coast. The **Ttakkas Bay Restaurant,** above the beach, serves excellent fresh fish, and the oceanside view from its shady terrace is superb. (Fish *meze* £4. Open 9am-midnight.) The turn-off for the beach is marked by an effusive sign reading "Ttakkas Bay Restaurant Aphrodite Area Refugee."

The coastline and **beaches** east of Polis are just as lovely as those to the west. Between Polis and Kato Pirgos, about 65km to the east, there are no rooms to let, no seaside *tavernas,* and no freelance camping (but also no one to stop you from trying)—only sleepy farming villages and deserted stretches of sand. Touring the area is difficult without wheels. **Buses** from Paphos pass through Polis (2 per day, #1 from either town). Two buses from Kato Pirgos also pass through. Some minibuses from Paphos continue on to Pomos (95¢). Not many cars pass through, but those that do will probably stop. The second half of the journey is treacherous for mopeds; rent a car instead.

All of the coastline east of Polis is visible from the slender band of asphalt optimistically dubbed the "main road" just find a beach that suits your tastes and walk down to it. Some of the beaches close to Polis are littered with garbage, so head 5-10km out of town before breaking out the cocoa butter. The road runs west along the coast, through banana plantations and tobacco fields, to **Pomos,** a quiet village with a few *tavernas* and a nice pebble beach. A few miles beyond Pomos is the village of **Pahiammos** ("thick sand"). Between Pahiammos and Kato Pirgos, about 10km west, lies the village of **Kokkina** ("red"), a small enclave occupied by the Turks. To prevent an entrance into Turkish territory, the road to Kato Pirgos veers off into the parched mountains for a circuitous 25-km detour (45min. by car).

Larnaca ΛΑΡΝΑΚΗ

Quieter and cleaner than Limassol, sunny Larnaca (pop. 60,000) offers visitors a long beach bordered by numerous cafés and restaurants. While accommodations here may be a bit cheaper than in neighboring Agia Napa, they're every bit as hard to come by in the peak summer season. The modern city of Larnaca was built over the ruins of ancient Kition, making it one of the oldest continually inhabited cities in the world. In the north of town a segment of the ancient city walls and some Bronze Age temples remain.

Larnaca's main street, as far as tourists are concerned, is **Athens Avenue,** running along the waterfront. **King Paul Square,** off the northern end of Athens Ave., lodges much: the **bus station;** the **Cyprus Tourism Organization Office** (tel. 65 43 22; Mon.-Sat. 8:15am-1:30pm, Mon. and Thurs. also at 4-6:15pm; off-season Mon.-Sat. 8:15am-1:45pm, Mon. and Thurs. also at 3-5:30pm; airport branch open 24 hrs.); the **American Express** (tel. 520 24), in the office of **A.L. Mantovani and Sons** at 1 King Paul Sq. (open Mon.-Fri. 8am-1pm and 3:30-6:30pm, Sat. 9am-noon; off-season Mon.-Fri. 8am-12:45pm and 2:30-5:30pm, Sat. 9am-noon); and the **post office** (tel. 65 70 75; open Mon.-Fri. 7:30am-1pm and 4-6pm, Sat. 7:30am-noon; Oct.-April Fri. 7:30am-1:30pm and 3:30-5:30pm, Sat. 7:30am-noon). Another small office in St. Lazarus Sq. is open Mon.-Sat. 8am-12:30pm. The **police** are on Archbishop Makarios III Ave. (tel. 65 20 01), 1 block north of the tourist office.

To make an overseas collect call to countries other than the U.S., use the **telephones (CYTA)** on Armenkikis Ekkmesias St. near the Armenian church. Larnaca's **telephone code** is 04.

The **bus station** (tel. 65 48 90), is on the north end of Athens Ave. at Filiou Zannetou St. Buses venture forth to Nicosia (Mon.-Fri. 6am-4:45pm 11 per day; Sat. 9 per day until 2:45pm; 90¢) and Limassol (Mon.-Fri. 7 per day until 4:45pm; Sat. 6 per day until 2:45pm, £1). In summer **EMAN** buses to Agia Napa leave from the intersection of Athens Ave. and Vass. Pavlou at the Sun Hall Hotel (8:30am-6:30pm 18 per day, Sun. 4 per day, 75¢). On summer weekdays, bus #2 shuttles between the airport and the center of town (6:20am-6:50pm, 30¢). A more reliable airport bus runs hourly to Kiti Village from St. Lazarus Sq., passing within 300m of the airport. (Mon.-Sat. 6:30am-7pm, 30¢.) Taxis from the airport cost £2.50.

Makris (tel. 65 29 29; King Paul St., across from the Sun Hall Hotel), **Akropolis** (tel. 65 55 55; at the corner of Archbishop Makarios III Ave. and Afxentiou St., 2 blocks to the left of the tourist office), and **Kyriakos** (tel. 65 51 00; 2C Hermes (Ermou) St.) run **service taxis** to Limassol and Nicosia (in summer 6am-4:30pm about every 30min.), and will pick you up and drop you off anywhere in the city. A taxi to Nicosia costs £2.10, to Limassol £1.70. Alternatively, you could rent a moped or car from **Panipsos,** 25 Galileou St. (tel. 65 60 14), behind the waterfront. Another office in Agia Napa allows for convenient drop-off. (Small mopeds £4 per day. Subaru cars £13 per day with unlimited mileage and third party insurance. Bikes £1.50 per day.)

Because Larnaca attracts so few budget travelers, you'll have a hellish time finding a place to crash land here. The town's hotels and pensions fall into two equally repugnant groups—luxury hotels full of British package tourists, and dives. Fortunately, there is the **HI/IYHF Youth Hostel,** Nikolaou Rossou St. in St. Lazarus Sq. (No phone. For the central HI/IYHF office in Nicosia, dial 44 20 27.) In a converted Turkish mosque, this fairly clean hostel has a communal kitchen and friendly management. (£3. Sheets 50¢. HI/IYHF membership not required.) **Harry's Hotel,** 2 Thermopylon St. (tel. 65 44 53, near Marina Pier), is another inexpensive option. Popular with British tourists, Harry's offers doubles for £14 with breakfast included. Rooms fill up fast so call ahead. You can also try **Kitieos Court Larnaca** (tel. 62 80 80), 100m from the waterfront on the corner of 2 Kitieos and Cosma Lyssioti St. Furnished flats here go for £20-25 for two depending on your bargaining abilities. **Forest Beach Camping** (tel. 62 24 14), 8km northeast of Larnaca on the road to Agia Napa, offers a waterslide, supermarket, and restaurant. (£1 per person, £1 per pitch, free tents. Open April-Sept.) Take a taxi (£2.50), or catch the tourist beach bus from the Sun Mall Hotel.

Most of Larnaca's restaurants and bars are on the waterfront. **Megalos Pefkos,** at the southern end of the harbor, is relatively inexpensive (Swordfish £2.75; open Thrus.-Tues. 10am-11pm). Night owls can have a hoot at **Midnight Sun,** on the southern end of Athens Ave. (open 24 hrs.). There is a market adjacent to 180 Hermes St. (open Mon.-Tues. and Thurs.-Fri. 6:15am-1pm and 4-6pm, Wed. 6:15am-1pm, Sat. 5:45am-1pm). Then head to the hipper-than-hip **Cloud Nine** on the waterfront (open 10pm-3am; cover £4).

Larnaca's biggest tourist attraction is its town beach (a dismal mixture of packed dirt, cigarette butts, and ogling men), which manages to satisfy the vacationers who bake there every day, or escape to the water in canoes (£3 per hr.), pedalboats (£4 per hr.), windsurfers (£4 per hr.), waterskis (£4 per ride), paragliders (£12 per ride), or the ubiqui-popular banana boats (£3 per person). Beautiful, less crowded **beaches** are farther northeast on the way to Agia Napa. Tourist buses travel 8km up the coast and back, stopping at all the beaches along the way. Buses leave from the Sun Hall Hotel at the north end of Athens Ave. (in summer 7am-7pm every 30min., 30¢).

You can tour Larnaca's sights in one day. The ancient city of **Kition** is the most historically significant spot, although most of it now lies underneath Larnaca. First settled at the beginning of the 13th century BCE, and then abandoned at the end of the century, Kition was rebuilt in 1200 BCE by refugees from the Peloponnese who brought with them the thriving Mycenaean culture. The city was damaged in wars against the Phoenicians and Egyptians (4th century BCE), and finally leveled by earthquake and fire in 280 BCE. The ruins of the city reveal part of the ancient Cyclopean city wall, a large **Temple of Astarte,** goddess of fertility, and four smaller temples. To get to the ruins, follow Kimon St. inland to the Chryssopolitissa Church, cross in front of the church, and go straight on Sakellariou St. (Ruins open Mon.-Sat. 7:30am-1:30pm; Oct.-May Mon.-Fri. 7:30am-2pm, Sat. 7:30am-1pm. Admission 50¢.)

On the way to the remains of Kition, you'll pass Larnaca's **Archaeological Museum,** between Kimonos and Kilkis St. The small collection includes objects from Neolithic to Roman times. (Open Mon.-Sat. 7:30am-1:30pm; Oct.-March Mon.-Fri. 7:30am-2pm, Sat. 7:30am-1pm. Admission 50¢.) Next to Barclay's Bank, by the tourist office in King Paul's Sq., is the private **Museum of the Pierides Foundation,** in the former home of Demetrios Pierides (1811-1895), a collector of Cypriot artifacts. The museum boasts rare artifacts such as Bronze Age ceramic milk pots, *lefkara* lace from the time of Da Vinci, and old maps. The obviously-male terracotta figure is the largest Chalcolithic (3500-2500 BCE) piece yet found; it also performs lifelike renditions when water is poured into its gaping mouth. (Open Mon.-Sat. 9am-1pm. Admission 50¢.)

At the southern end of the port a small **medieval fortress** peers over the water's edge. Constructed by the Venetians in the 15th century and rebuilt by the Turks in 1622, the fort contains a small collection of finds and photographs from Kition and other excavations in the area. (Open Mon.-Sat. 7:30am-7:30pm; Sept.-May Mon.-Sat. 7:30am-5pm. Admission £1.) The first left north of the fortress leads to the **Church of St. Lazarus,** built over the saint's tomb. Jesus Christ reportedly resurrected Lazarus, four days dead, in Israel. The resuscitated Lazarus then came to Cyprus, became the island's first bishop, and lived in Kition another 30 years before dying again. Lazarus's remains were stolen from Constantinople, but reappeared later in Marseilles, France.

Near Larnaca

A bus bound for Kiti leaves St. Lazarus Sq. (7am-7pm every hr.; in winter until 5pm; 15min., 30¢), and travels west to the **Hala Sultan Tekke Mosque,** the fourth (or thereabouts) holiest Muslim pilgrimage site after Mecca, Medina, and Jerusalem. Also called the Tekke of Umm Haram, the mosque was constructed during the Arab invasion of Cyprus (647 CE) and then rebuilt in 1787, over the site where the Umm Haram (Muhammad's maternal aunt) fell off a mule and broke her neck. Three gargantuan stones—reputed to have been quarried in Mecca—surround her grave in the back of the mosque. The horizontal one supposedly hovered in the air for many centuries, until it lowered itself for fear of injuring the faithful. To be dropped at the turnoff, tell the bus driver you're going to "Tekke." From there, you'll have to walk along the paved road for 1km. The mosque lies next to the **Larnaca Salt Lake.** In winter, the lake is covered with pink flamingoes, but in the summer, the lake dries up and its flamingoes hop away. Legend claims that this body of water was created one day when St. Lazarus turned an old woman's vineyard into a barren salt lake as punishment for her lack of hospitality.

The same bus that goes to the mosque continues on to the village of **Kiti** (25min. from Larnaca), where you can visit the church of **Panayia Angeloktisti** ("built by the angels"). (Open daily 8am-4pm.)

Forty km from Larnaca and 9km off the main Nicosia-Limassol road is the **Stavrovouni Monastery.** According to tradition, the monastery was constructed by order of St. Helena in 327 BCE on a site called Olympus, which a pagan temple had formerly occupied. At the time, Helena, mother of the Roman Emperor Constantine, was returning from Palestine, where she had just happened to find the Holy Cross. She presented a fragment to the monastery, but to this day, no one has been able to locate the holy relic; the faithful believe that it performs miracles from a hiding place in the monastery. Despite the fact that their founder was female, the monks of Stavrovouni do not allow women into the monastery. (Open for male visitors Mon., Wed., Fri., and Sun.) There are no buses to Stavrovouni, but you can get to the pottery village of Kornos and then walk up to the peak. A private taxi will cost about £22.

Agia Napa ΑΓΙΑ ΝΑΠΑ

Fifteen years ago, Agia Napa was a quiet farming and fishing village. Most tourists went to Famagusta, 16km to the north, allowing Agia Napa's ruined monastery and white sandy beaches to lie peacefully vacant. But when the Turks occupied Famagusta in 1974, Greek Cyprus lost one of its major resorts, and Agia Napa was gussied up almost overnight into a tourist center replete with marble and brass glitz. Many refugees from Famagusta live in this area now.

The center of Agia Napa houses banks, many restaurants, and the **tourist office** (tel. 72 17 96), at the corner of Kyrou Nerou and Makarios Ave. (Open Tues.-Wed. and Fri.-Sat. 8:30am-1:30pm, Mon. and Thurs. 4-6pm; Sept.-May Mon.-Sat. 8:30am-1:30pm, 3-5:30pm.) Next to the tourist office is the **Hellenic Bank** and a **Cyprus Air** office. The **post office** is on Dionysiou Solomou St. (Open Mon.-Fri. 7:30am-1pm and 4-6pm, Sat. 7:30am-12:30pm.) Across from the tourist office is the 14th-century **Monastery of Agia Napa,** constructed after the discovery of a thaumaturgic icon of the Virgin Mary at the site. Following its Byzantine construction, the building was successively renovated by Venetians, French Crusaders, and 19th-century Cypriots. Every Sunday in summer at 8pm, locals perform Cypriot **folk dancing** in the square near the monastery. **Genesis No. 2**, just before the post office rents motorbikes for £14.50 for 3 days with insurance included. The **telephone code** for Agia Napa and surrounding area is 03.

Just about one in every two buildings in town is a luxury hotel full of European box-lunch tours, so inexpensive accommodations are elusive and nearly extinct in August. Call ahead if possible. Up the road and to the right of the tourist office, **Michael Antoniou's Jewelry Store** (tel. 72 10 78) lets doubles for £15 (including a communal kitchen). Farther away from the center, in the north of the town, **Xenis,** 34 Demokratias St. (tel. 72 10 86), has comparable furnishings, also with a kitchen. (Singles £12. Doubles £15.) Along the road to Paralimni, **Savvas Apt.** (tel. 72 11 87) rents very pleasant new rooms with kitchen facilities. (Studios £16. 2-bedroom flats £25.) On the west side of town, **Salmary** (tel. 72 12 06) has comfortable flats. (Studios £16.50. 2-bedroom flats £27.50.) The **campground** (tel. 72 19 46) also rents motorbikes for £3. (£2 per tent, £1 per person, £3 tent rental.) Three km from town, the campground is near the beautiful but crowded **Nissi Beach. Markos Tavern** is an inexpensive restaurant with tables in a courtyard out back. **Air Tours,** 18B Dionysos Solomou St. (tel. 221 33), rents bikes—50cc one- or two-seaters £3 per day. **Holiday Tours** (tel. 210 31), next to the tourist office, rents cars and runs excursions. **Raven's Rook,** above the Hellenic Bank and near the tourist office, serves meals in a pleasant rooftop garden (tuna salad £1.75, kebab £2.15). For nightlife, bam bam at the Flintstonely club **The Cave,** with pink and black decor. (Cover and first drink £4, beer £1.)

Deserted beaches wallow midway between Larnaca and Agia Napa, past the army base. Better yet, and closer to Agia Napa, are the beaches north and south of **Protaras** (10km from Agia Napa). On the Protaras public beach, next to the Flamingo Beach restaurant, is the private **Costas Camping,** with limited shady pitches and cold showers. If Costas isn't around, pitch your tent and pay when he returns. (£2 per person.) You might want to leave your things in Agia Napa, rent a motorbike, and scan the outskirts for a place to stay.

Close to Agia Anargyri and 8km east of Agia Napa is **Cape Greco**. You'll find no tourists here, no half-built concrete hotels, no *tavernas,* and no sand—just rocky coves cascading into the magnificent blue sea. The cape has remained undeveloped because of a military radar installation, giving James Bond aspirants the chance to enjoy swimming off the rocks beneath two realistic radar dishes. About 2km north of Paralimni, a stone's throw away from the green line, is the small village of **Dherinia;** there isn't much here, except **Taylor's** on Sotera Rd., an excellent restaurant that serves delicious, cheap fare. (Open noon-11pm.) Since you can't cross the border into occupied Famagusta (forgot your diplomatic passport again, didn't you?), the best alternative is to go to one of the several tourist viewpoints nearby to look at the "ghost" of the town; construction cranes still stand exactly as they did 15 years ago. Rumor has it that the Turkish government is considering repopulating the area with "settlers" from Turkey in order to rebuild Famagusta into a premier resort. International codes of propriety, however, will probably prevent this plan.

Buses make the 44km trip from the Sun Hall Hotel in Larnaca to the **EMAN station,** opposite the Leros Hotel in Agia Napa. (Mon.-Sat. 8:30am-6:30pm 10 per day; returning to Larnaca 6:30am-5pm; 75¢; arrive early to get a seat.) Buses also leave the Sun Hall Hotel in Larnaca for Paralimni via Protaras (Mon.-Fri. 6:30am-7pm, 9 per day 75¢). The buses return from Paralimni via Protaras twice a week (Mon. 8am-5:30pm 8 per day, Sat. 8am-2pm 6 per day, 75¢). Buses also run from Paralimni via Agia Napa to Proteras and back (Mon.-Sat. 9am-6pm 9 per day, 35¢). Eight buses go directly to Protaras (6:30am-10pm, returning 7am-11pm, 35¢).

Northern Cyprus

Northern Cyprus uses the Turkish *lira* as its currency. For currency information, see Turkey Introduction, p. 379)

If you talk to Cypriots living in the southern part of the island, they'll sadly admit that some of the most beautiful parts of their tiny homeland are in the northern 37% of Cyprus, occupied by the Turkish Army since the summer of 1974. Barbed wire, minefields, and 2000 peacekeeping troops partition the country. The government of the Republic of Cyprus considers the entrance into Northern Cyprus illegal. Tourists (excluding Greeks or those of Greek descent) are often allowed to cross the border in Nicosia, provided that they return on the same day by 6pm. To get the latest information on Cyprus's border policy, contact any Cyprus Tourist Organization office, the UN Headquarters in Nicosia, or the official checkpoint at the **Ledra Palace Hotel** (see Nicosia, p. 364).

The most sensible way to travel to Northern Cyprus is to go through Turkey. Over the past several years, tourism in the area has recovered: in 1988, Northern Cyprus earned some US$150 million from tourism. **Cyprus Turkish Airlines** and **İstanbul Airlines** have flights between İstanbul, Ankara, or Adana and Nicosia's Ercan Airport. There are also flights to and from Europe. However, the International Air Traffic Association (IATA) "does not recognize" the Ercan airport, as it operates unofficially and poses safety hazards, sharing air space with the airport in Larnaca. There is no public transportation from the airport, but sometimes people operate shared taxis to the major cities for about $2 per person. A taxi to Girne costs about $13 per car (maximum four people; rates are 40% higher between midnight and 6am). Panic not when you see your driver using the "wrong" side of the road: traffic here is on the left. You can take a **ferry** to Famagusta from the Mediterranean port of Mersin in Turkey. (Ferries leave Mersin Mon., Wed., and Fri. at 10pm, 10hr., $30, students 10% off.) Boats sail from Taşucu in Turkey to Girne (Kyrenia). (Sun.-Thurs. at midnight, returning Mon.-Fri. at 1pm, $13, students $10.) For faster, more costly travel, take a **hydrofoil.**

If you arrive by boat on the Turkish side of Cyprus, you cannot visit Greek Cyprus. U.N. resolutions have declared that Northern Cyprus remains part of the sovereign territory of the Republic of Cyprus, and Turkey is the only country that recognizes Turkish sovereignty in that region. Should you wish to visit Greece afterward, or to enter Greek Cyprus through Greece, you'll need a detachable visa. This visa can be obtained at any of the three Turkish Federated State of Cyprus consulates in Turkey: in Ankara at Incirli Sok. 20, Gaziosmanpaşa (tel. 437 60 31); in İstanbul at Büyükdere Cad. 99, Kuğu Is Hani, Kat. 5, Daire 9, Mecidiyeköy (tel. 275 29 90); and in Mersin at 71/1 Karadeniz Cad. (tel. 31 62 28). Most nationalities don't need a visa in advance. Despite your pleadings with customs officials to stamp a piece of paper instead of your passport so that you can continue on to Greece, chances are your passport will be stamped anyway. Be a pest and plan accordingly.

The territory has its own postal system, and Turkish Cypriot stamps must be used (rates a little better than in mainland Turkey). All mail going to Northern Cyprus should be suffixed with Mersin-10, Turkey. Northern Cyprus uses the Turkish *lira* as currency, but many people are eager to accept Cypriot pounds, pounds sterling, or U.S. dollars. Should you need consular help in Northern Cyprus, you're a bit out of luck. Since only Turkey recognizes this territory as sovereign, there is no U.S. or British Embassy in what most of the world considers "occupied territory." Cyprus public **phones** use the same tokens as Turkish public phones. However, phonecards (*telekarts*) cannot be used. **Post offices** keep shorter hours (Mon.-Fri. 8:30am-1pm and 2-5:30pm), so it is often hard to obtain tokens. To make an international call from Northern Cyprus, dial (00). The **telephone code** in Northern Cyprus is 905.

Northern Cyprus is sparsely populated. In villages that once housed thousands, only a few hundred residents abide and the emptiness is conspicuous and tangible. Beaches along the northern coast may be satisfactory, but are likely to be polluted; other areas in the countryside are sealed and used solely as training grounds for the Turkish Army.

Prices are higher in Northern Cyprus than in mainland Turkey. Furthermore, budget accommodations are difficult to find, public transportation rare, and the tourist offices of little help. Keep in mind that service hours are shorter (usually 8:30am-1pm), schedules are spotty and unreliable, and nothing save a few overpriced bars and restaurants is open after 9pm. Northern Cyprus used to be the shopping magnet for Turks, who would fly here with an empty suitcase under each arm to stock up on Western merchandise unavailable in Turkey. Now that the same goods are easily found in Turkey proper, the hundreds of little stores are today empty and hopelessly déclassé. In case you're interested, most shops here, unlike in Turkey, accept all major credit cards.

Northen Cyprus is small. It's a good idea to make one city your base and visit all the beaches and historical sites from there. Because of its relatively good public transportation and availability of budget accommodations, Girne (Kyrenia) is the most sensible choice. Sure, this introduction may be off-putting, but for amateur historians and travelers with a yearning for adventure, Northern Cyprus is still a land of intrigue and splendor.

Girne (Kyrenia)

Girne (Kyrenia) is a walled harbor town protected by a hulking medieval citadel. If you arrive here by ferry, your first impression of Northern Cyprus will be a stony, shadeless pier—**Yeni Turizm Limanı,** where all the tourist ferries arrive and depart. From here, there is no public transportation to the center of the city: walk or take a taxi

($2). The 30-minute walk will take you down the only road, Dr. Fazıl Küçük Bul., and then right onto Mersin Cad. Pass the cemetery, take a left onto Karakız Sok., and when you arrive at Akçiçek Hospital, take a right onto Mustafa Çağatay Cad., which will take you to **Belediye,** the center of town.

Practical Information

Tourist Office (tel. 521 45), by the sea, near the yacht harbor. From Belediye, go downhill on Hürriyet Cad., then take a right to Canbulat Sok., which will eventually lead you to the harbor. The English-speaking staff can provide you with good maps, but don't expect much else. (Open 7:30am-2pm and 3:30-6pm, Tues.-Fri. 7:30am-2pm; off-season Mon.-Fri. 8am-1pm and 2-7pm.)

Travel Agencies: There are several along Hürriyet Cad. They all sell ferry and plane tickets, and they usually rent cars and motorcycles as well. Nearly all the shops and banks exchange money. Rates fluctuate—check around for the best rates.

Post Office: on Mustafa Çağatay Cad. Take a left from the Belediye (municipality) building on Ecevit Cad. The post office offers all the services that Turkish PTTs offer, including *poste restante.*

Telephones: There are phone booths just outside the post office, as well as a couple on Belediye Square (open 24 hrs.). Tokens for public phones can be purchased in the new building across the street from the post office. Girne's **telephone code** is 081.

Buses: Municipal bus stations are so far from the cities that it is impossible to walk to and from them in the heat, and taxis to the station cost more than the bus fare. Use **Kombos** (tel. 523 17) on the square for service to Lefkoşa (Nicosia) for $1.50 and to Magosa (Famagusta) for $2. Buses run from 8am to 7pm. When you buy your ticket reserve a place for the trip back to Girne. Kombos also offers 24-hr. taxi service (to Magosa, $22; to Lefkoşa, $8; and to Ercan Airport, $13).

Bookstores: There are several on Hürriyet Cad., down the hill from Belediye, which sell foreign newspapers.

Medical Emergency: Tel. 522 26 or 522 24. Available 24 hrs.

Emergency: Tel. 521 25 or 520 14.

Accommodations and Food

Almost all of the budget accommodations in Girne are clustered in the area between Hürriyet Cad. and the yacht harbor. Make sure you set the price and the number of nights you're staying in advance or you might find yourself paying too much for too many nights. Furthermore, pensions with a sign reading "Aile Pansiyonu" usually serve Turkish families, and will not be very eager to host young foreigners, especially couples. The tourist office has the phone numbers of all the pensions, but not their addresses.

Zorlu Pansiyon, 3 Atilla Sok. (tel. 513 05). Going downhill from Hürriyet Cad., take the first right from the Castle. Spacious rooms with high ceilings. Neither particularly clean nor quiet, but its location is central and the management is helpful. $4.25 per bed.

Girne Pansiyon, 3 Canbolat Sok. (tel. 536 03), on the street parallel to Atilla Sok., down from Hürriyet Cad. Basic rooms and bargain-basement prices. $4.25 per bed.

Kangaru Pansiyon (no phone), Canbolat Sok. Rooms and prices like the others.

Eating cheap in Girne is not hard, but eating well is. The streets off of Hürriyet Cad. are full of little restaurants that serve the usual assortment of Turkish dishes. Full meals run about $4. In the bazaar right at the square there is the familiar choice of fast food items and drinks (burgers for about $1).

Sights

On the east side of the harbor is the daunting **Girne Castle,** built by the Byzantines in the 9th century CE in order to defend the city against the frequent Arab raids. The present form of the castle dates back to Venetian times. Housed within the castle is the **Shipwreck Museum,** which exhibits goods from the oldest commercial ship ever to have been recovered from the bottom of the sea, dating back to 300 BCE. Also on the waterfront is the **Museum of Folk Arts,** in a typical Cypriot house. (Open 7:30am-2pm and 3:30-6pm, Tues.-Fri. 7:30am-2pm; off-season Mon.-Fri. 8am-1pm and 2-7pm.) If you never tire of "exquisite examples of Ottoman architecture," visit the **Mosque of Cafer Paşa,** noted for its conical minaret. (Open to vistors 8am-5:30pm, except during prayer times.)

Nicosia

Nicosia (also called Lefkoşa) is the perfect city for those who miss the Berlin Wall. Here, the Green Line runs east-west, dividing into Greek and Turkish zones this lovely town chock-full of Gothic and Ottoman architecture. While southern Nicosia is filled with commemorations of the union of Cyprus with Greece, the northern sector vigorously asserts its Turkish character.

Except for a couple of pensions that mainly serve families, there are no budget accommodations in the city. You would be better off to make a day trip from Girne. The **post office** is on Atatürk Meydanı, at the center of the old city, and most of the banks and travel agencies are on Girne Cad., the avenue connecting İnönü Meydanı and Atatürk Meydanı. The **telephone code** is 020.

Within the city walls (built by the Venetians in 1570, ironically to protect the city from the Turks) is the **Mevlevi Tekke,** a 17th-century structure used by the dervishes of Mevlâna Celaleddini Rumi, founder of the Mevlevi Sufi religious order, famous for its devotional whirling dance. Today the building houses the **Turkish Museum.** Be sure to visit the **Selimiye Cami,** formerly a cathedral known as St. Sophia, built in French Gothic style from 1209-1326. Also of note are the **Library of Sultan Mehmet II** (1829), the **Arabahmet Mosque** (1845), and the **Venetian House,** a 15th century house which today houses the **Lapidary Museum.** Most sites charge less than $1 and are free with an ISIC.

Famagusta

Famagusta, also called Gazimağusa) was one of the most prosperous Mediterranean cities of the Middle Ages. The Lusignan kings, made holy by their wealth, built 365 houses of worship (collect 'em all). The 20th century saw the British fix up the port and start a railroad there. Today, Famagusta is worth a visit for the ancient ruins of **Salamis** to the north and the newer ruins of **Varosha** to the south. This complex of tourist resorts emptied out when the Turks came to town. It is now gaunt with ghost towns and skeletal vestiges of former prosperity.

As in Nicosia, anything of interest in Famagusta is within the city walls. The **tourist office** has the same hours and services as the one in Girne, and is just outside the city walls on Fevzi Çakmak Cad. (You may recall that the Girne office was nothing special.) The **post office** is at the southwestern corner of the city walls. **Köşk Yatıevi,** a pension on Canbulat Yolu, caters mainly to the wage workers in the city. It is fairly clean but not very comfortable. (Doubles $7.) Cleaner, but pricier, is **Hotel Altun Tabya** (tel. 653 63), featuring quite clean rooms and large, private bathrooms. (Singles $14. Doubles $21. Triples $28. Breakfast included.) Famagusta's **telephone code** is 036.

Lala Mustafa Pasa Mosque was constructed in 1298 as the St. Nicholas Cathedral. It was here that the crowning of kings of Cyprus as rulers of Jersualem took place. You can relax on the benches facing its slightly dilapidated exterior. Shakespeareans will feel once more well met in Cyprus when they gaze at the citadel by the waterfront, known as **Othello's Tower.** Legend has it that a governor of Cyprus killed his beautiful wife Desdemona here.

The ruins of **Salamis,** 7km north of Famagusta, include a gymnasium, theater and aqueduct from the Roman period, though archaeological evidence dates Salamis to the 11th century BCE or earlier. A taxi from Famagusta costs $6.

TURKEY

US$1 = 6913 Turkish Lira (TL)
CDN$1 = 5804TL
UK£1 = 13,736TL
IR£1 = 12,945
AUS$1 = 4939TL
NZ$1 = 3739TL

1000 Turkish Lira (TL) = US$0.14
1000TL = CDN$0.17
1000TL = UK£0.07
1000TL = IR£0.08
1000TL = AUS$0.20
1000TL = NZ$0.27

> **All prices are quoted in U.S. dollars because rampant inflation in Turkey tends to correspond roughly with the devaluation of the lira.**

Legendary birthplace of deities, gateway to the underworld river Acheron, and main forum of Süleyman and his Magnificence, Turkey is a modernizing nation with ancient sensibilities and idyllic, distinctive landscapes. While the gleam of the Mediterranean resorts contents beachgoers, the colorful animation of the cities magnetizes those of more a cosmopolitan frame of mind. Mountain ranges, crowned with snow, glisten over crops in Anatolia, and the surreal abandoned monolithlic settlements at Cappadocia at once defy description and the passage of time.

When Western ancients somewhat disdainfully dubbed the region that is now modern Turkey "Asia Minor," they didn't know what they were missing. Of course, tourism wasn't as prevalent in Roman times. Today, travelers all over the world are discovering that Turkey is a budget paradise replete with ancient ruins, modern amenities, gorgeous beaches, and that traveler's grail, affordable accommodations. Outside the touristed towns, the interest is genuine—cordial locals and low prices will enhance your appreciation of the land.

Once There

Shops in Turkey are generally open Monday through Saturday from 9am to 1pm and 2 to 7pm. Government offices are open Monday through Friday from 8:30am to 12:30pm and 1:30 to 5:30pm. Banks are open Monday through Friday from 8:30am to noon and 1:30 to 5pm. Food stores, open bazaars, and pharmacies have longer hours. During the summer, on the Aegean and Mediterranean coasts, government offices and other businesses close during the afternoons, and shops are open until 10pm.

Museums and archaeological sites in Turkey are generally open Tuesday through Sunday from 9am to 5pm. At some movies or concerts, students may receive discounts of up to 50%.

Official national **holidays** include New Year's Day (Jan. 1), National Independence Day and Children's Day (April 23), Atatürk's Commemoration and Youth and Sports Day (May 19), Victory Day (Aug. 30), and Republic Day (Oct. 29). Many establishments are closed during religious holidays, which fall on different dates each year (see Holidays below).

Tourist Services

Most major cities and resort areas have tourist offices and tourist police. Some English is usually spoken, and the staff can be very helpful. In places without an office, travel agents may provide similar services. Check in the regional sections for addresses and phone numbers.

If you encounter minor difficulties anywhere in Turkey, go to the nearest tourist office before you try the police. The tourist office can advise you whether it is necessary to turn to the authorities for help.

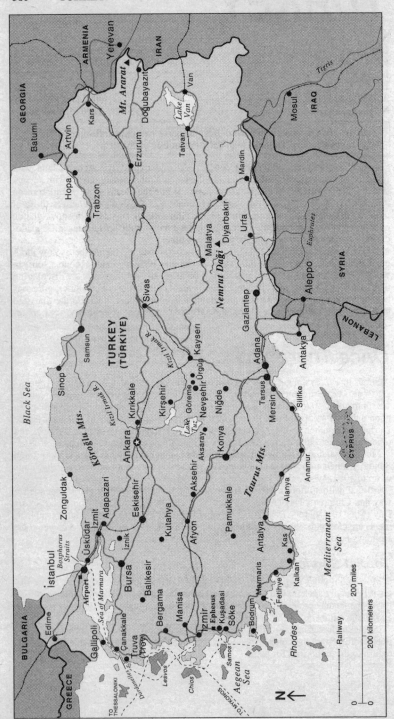

Emergencies

If you are in need of **medical care** in Turkey, the embassy or consulate can provide you with a list of English-speaking doctors, or you can find one in most major hospitals. For **emergency medical service dial 077**. İstanbul has several foreign hospitals, including:

American Hospital: Admiral Bristol Hastanesi, Nişantaş, Güzelbahçe Sok. (tel. 231 40 50).

German Hospital: Sıracevizler Cad., Taksim (tel. 243 81 00).

Keeping in Touch

Mail to or from North America can take anywhere from 13 to 17 days. **Post offices** (known as **PTT**) are easily recognized by their yellow signs. Large post offices in major urban areas are open Monday through Saturday from 8am to midnight, Sunday from 9am to 7pm. Major PTTs in İstanbul are open 24 hours a day. Smaller post offices share the same hours as other government offices (Mon.-Fri. 8:30am-12:30pm and 1:30-5:30pm). To send mail Poste Restante, write the person's name, "Poste Restante," and "Merkez Postanesi" (Turkish for main post office), followed by the town's name and postal code. Picking up letters costs a small fee: Be sure to check under both your first and last name, and have a form of identification handy. Also, specify *Uçak Ile* (airmail) when requesting stamps, and write it on your mail (or ask for aerogrammes). Postage to North America is 20¢ for postcards, 70¢ for letters; to Europe, 15¢ and 50¢, respectively; to Australia and New Zealand 20¢.

Turkey has a surprisingly good phone system. With few exceptions, even the smallest village is accessible by phone. When you make a local call (within the same area code), simply dial the number. Local numbers can have between two and seven digits. When making a long distance call within Turkey, first dial 9, wait for the tone to change to a lower pitch, then dial the area code and the number. Note that the area code and the number always have a total of eight digits. When making **direct international calls,** dial 9, wait for the tone, then dial 9 again followed by the country code and the number, without pausing. All calls cost less after 11pm, but post offices often disregard this (see below).

There are four kinds of public phones in Turkey. The omnipresent yellow public phones take tokens. To use them, unhook the receiver, wait for the little red light to shut off, stuff the tokens in the appropriate slots, and dial the number. There are three kinds of tokens: *küçük jeton* is the smallest and should be used for local calls; *orta jeton* is the medium token and is good for long distance calls within Turkey; and the *büyük jeton*—the big one—should be used for international calls. A big token is equal to three medium tokens and a medium token is worth six small tokens. (A small token is worth about 5¢).

To avoid finger cramps from frantically inserting tokens during international calls, buy a magnetic phone card (*telekart*). Magnetic phone cards are sold in all post offices in denominations of 20, 30, 60, or 100 small tokens. (Try to get them in big cities: small villages tend to run out of them quickly.) They are slightly more economical than tokens and a lot easier to use. Magnetic card public phones are abundant in big cities and resort areas, and they have on-screen instructions in English, French, and German. It takes about two 100-token phone cards to make a 10-minute call to the U.S.

Even more pleasant are the *kontörlü telefons*. These are phones in the post office where you make your call and at the end the officer tells you how much you owe. Note that there may be long lines for these phones, especially during the day. Try to use one late at night at one of the 24-hour PTTs. The same kind of phones are available at some hotels and restaurants, but they may charge you 20-500% more than what the call really costs.

Finally, there are phones at the post office from which you can make collect calls. You may have to wait two hours or more to make **international collect calls**, and often the post office official will tell you that it is impossible. To make a collect or calling card call, dial (9) 9800 111 77 for an MCI operator. For an AT&T operator dial (9)

9800 122 77. Don't forget the **time difference** when calling North America: subtract seven (Eastern Standard Time) to ten hours (Pacific), depending on the U.S. time zone.

Getting Around

Travel within Turkey is very inexpensive. **Turkish Airlines** has direct flights once or twice weekly from İstanbul to Trabzon, Van, Diyarbakır, Erzurum, İzmir, and Ankara. Prices for flights within Turkey average $80 one-way, but there is a fixed fare of $42 for those ages 12 to 24.

Frequent and cheap **buses** run between all sizeable cities. Private bus lines sometimes offer students a 10% discount (show an ISIC card). You will need to go from booth to booth to piece together a complete schedule; one company will not divulge the departure times of competitors. Exchanging your ticket can also be difficult. For long trips, there are always overnight buses; request a window seat in the middle of the bus, away from the driver's radio and behind the overhead window. Avoid the seats at the back of the bus: the assistant driver sleeps behind these seats and you may have to put up with his smelly feet for the whole night. The two seats in the very back of the bus recline. Every so often, an attendant comes around spritzing cologne to keep you smelling nice. If you're thirsty, say *"su lütfen;"* you'll be brought a bottle of cold water. For long trips, try the comfortable and quick **Varan Tours** buses. They're slightly more expensive but have bigger seats, air conditioning, bathrooms, and serve *çay* (tea). For frequent runs, you'll have to buy a seat an hour in advance or buy the ticket the day before.

Despite low fares (with a 10% student discount), **trains** within Turkey are no bargain. They are extremely slow and follow circuitous routes. First-class gets you a slightly more padded seat and a lot more room—most Turks travel second-class. *Couchettes* are also available. There are no train routes along the western coast. All-night train trips are preferable to all-night bus trips.

Extensive **shared taxi** *(dolmuş)* service follows fixed routes between small towns. These are usually vans or minibuses, though occasionally cars are in service as well. They leave as soon as they fill up *(dolma* means stuffed and they're not kidding), and are almost as cheap as buses. Best of all, you can get on and off anywhere you like.

Ferries do not service the western coast, but a **Turkish Maritime Lines** cruiseship sails from İstanbul to İzmir once weekly year-round, increasing to three times weekly from July through September. A boat also travels from İstanbul to Trabzon; another to Alanya stops at Datça, Marmaris, Kaş, and Alanya, returning via Antalya, Fethiye, Bodrum, Kuşadası, and İzmir. Still another boat enables transit from İstanbul to Bandırma. Bigger ports have ship offices; otherwise, just get on the boat and find the purser. The cost of the 11-day cruise buys you food and a bunk in a very crowded dormitory room, or a space on deck if you prefer. Students get 10% discounts on all fares.

English road signs make **driving** in Turkey somewhat easier. Archaeological and historical sites are indicated by yellow signposts. Turks drive on the right side of the road; the speed limit is 50kph (31mph) in cities and 99kph (61mph) on the highways. For some reason, official Turkish tourist literature warns against driving at night. If you try it, you may find out why. Gas is relatively cheap. Road rescue services are located along the major highways; the head office is in İstanbul (tel. 246 70 90 or 521 65 88). If you get into an accident, you must file a report with the police. You can rent cars in major Turkish cities. For details, see the local tourist authorities or travel agents.

Those who decide to **hitchhike** in Turkey generally catch rides with locals; when asked to pay for the ride, they usually offer half of what the trip would cost by bus. Hitchers in Turkey signal with a waving hand. *Let's Go* does not recommend hitchhiking as a means of transportation, and urges readers to consider the risks inherent in hitching. Women in particular should never hitch alone.

Accommodations

If you need help finding accommodations, consult the nearest tourist office. Like the GNTO in Greece, Turkish officials regulate hotels. See several places before deciding where to stay, as cleanliness varies. Make sure your hotel has water before paying. If traveling in winter, check for heating.

Inexpensive accommodations are usually plentiful. If the prices posted seem exorbitant, look disappointed and bargain politely. Budget accommodations average $3-7 per person on the Aegean coast, $2-3.50 in the east. In lieu of showers, many Turkish towns have a *hamam* (bathhouse), where you can take a steam bath for under $2.

Camping is a popular and cheap alternative, although many official campgrounds still aren't registered with the Ministry of·Culture and Tourism. Most places charge $1.50 per person. Official government campsites are open from April or May through October. Freelance camping is illegal but you may hear of those who do freelance. Women should never camp alone.

Always carry toilet paper with you, since most places don't have any; other toiletries, including tampons, are cheap and readily available, though they may be scarce in remote eastern towns.

Life and Times

History

Ancient Turkey

"Asia Minor" has always been a melting pot of Asian and Western cultures. During the third millenium BCE, an early Hittite nation flourished in Central Anatolia. Besides developing techniques for forging iron weapons, the Hittites sweet-talked their way into contemporary limelight, having spoken an Indo-European language considered by scholars to be closely related to modern European languages. During the 15th century BCE, the hegemony of the Hittite empire extended from Syria in the east to the Aegean coast in the west. Following the massive migration of Greek islanders and other peoples at the end of the second millenium BCE, the Hittite empire collapsed. Cyrus the Great extended the Persian empire along the coast of Asia Minor in the sixth century BCE, using the region as a launching pad for his, and his successor Xerxes's, forays into Greece.

Two centuries later Alexander the Great marched his army into Asia Minor and routed the Persians. Great metropoli sprang up and acquired extreme wealth after the second century BCE, when the coastline became the commercial and political core of the Roman province of Asia Minor. Following the creation of the Eastern Roman Empire in Byzantium (renamed "Constantinople"), Asia Minor flourished economically, emerged as the center of Greek Orthodox Christian culture, and oversaw a renewed and vigorous empire stretching from the Balkans through Greece to the Levant and Egypt.

The Turks began to migrate from their homeland in central Asia in the second half of the 8th century CE, moving westward and establishing independent states in eastern Iran, Afghanistan, and northern India. In the 11th century Seljuk Turks, originally inhabitants of Mongolia, began the most significant Turkish migration, inhabiting the Muslim lands of Iran, Iraq, and Syria, and settling on the plains of central Anatolia. Though Seljuk power was momentarily eclipsed by the pillaging Genghis Khan, the Seljuks were able to maintain their authority for a surprisingly lengthy period. The Byzantine ports along the coast began to lose much of their economic importance as land routes to Asia were monopolized by the various Seljuk fiefdoms springing up in the interior. Seljuk rule survived until the 14th century, at which time it crumbled and separate Turkish emirates picked up the many pieces. Claiming the northwestern corner of Anatolia was Osman, who in time united several fiefdoms to challenge and defeat the Greeks. From such humble origins grew perhaps the greatest empire in the history of civilization: the Osmanlı, or Ottoman.

The Ottoman Empire

From the beginning of the 14th century to the middle of the 15th, the Ottomans gradually gnawed away at the Byzantine Empire. In 1453, Constantinople, the target of the

Ottomans since the time of Osman, was finally captured. Renamed İstanbul, the city became the heart of a youthful and expanding Turkish Empire.

The Ottomans incorporated Greece and soon Cyprus into the Muslim/Turkish state apparatus, and penetrated the Balkans as far as Belgrade. Under Selim I (1512-1520), the Ottomans defeated the Mamluks at Maj Dabiq and Cairo, conquering Syria, Palestine, Egypt, and Arabia. In a feat of military and religious grandeur, the sultan became guardian of the three holy places of Islam: Mecca, Medina, and Jerusalem. Although all power in the empire was vested in a sultan accountable only to God, in reality, a number of different individuals ruled the territories of the empire. Under the sultans, professional governors (often competing heirs to the sultanate) were sent out to the provinces. Additionally, the sultans granted *timars,* or land grants, to gain the support of Turkish military chiefs. In accordance with Islamic law, other monotheistic communities paid the *jizya,* a special head tax, and were on the whole treated well. Orthodox Greek Christians, for example, fared far better under Muslim authority than they did under the Crusading Franks. Many Jews, upon their expulsion from Spain in 1492, settled in parts of the empire and took up trade. Despite the ruthless counters to occasional Greek rebellions and occasional abuses of minorities, the early days of the Ottoman Empire brought relative peace and prosperity.

As Ottoman expansion slowed, the military *timar* holders grew increasingly restless. Income from their estates had long been supplemented by booty from additional campaigns and conquests. Thus, in order to have a more loyal military, Sultan Murad I created the first corps of *janissaries* in the middle of the 14th century. Instead of merely collecting a head tax from Jewish and Christian subjects, the Ottomans took a certain quota of (mainly Christian) young boys from each province, forcibly converted them to Islam (contrary to the dictates of the Qur'an), and trained them for military or government service. After years of drills and classes, the *janissaries*—technically personal slaves of the sultan—would take exams at various levels in their training. Those who failed would be given positions in the lower echelons, those who passed would continue their studies. The few who passed all the way to the top would be assigned duties at the palace under the personal direction of the sultan; Sinan, the great architect (and a heck of a researcher), for example, was a *janissary. Janissaries* who rose high enough in the imperial service amassed immense personal power and often directly helped their villages and families in spite of separation since childhood.

When Süleyman the Magnificent became sultan (1520-66), the Ottoman Empire was already a daunting power spanning Europe and Asia. But under Süleyman, the empire enjoyed as much magnificence as its sultan; the expanse of the empire was doubled, stretching from the Balkans and Greece to the Black Sea, west to Iraq, and southward into Africa, court administration was centralized, and literature, architecture, and decorative arts flourished. Süleyman's military conquests earned him the title of Magnificent among the Europeans. (It was Süleyman who knocked on the gates of Vienna in 1529). A patron of legalese, Süleyman earned the title of *Kanuni,* the Lawgiver, for coalescing the *şeriat* (Islamic jursiprudence) with *fermans* (court decrees). The grandeur of the court was rivaled only by the enormity of the empire.

But subsequent centuries witnessed the long-playing Ottoman version of the Decline of an Empire. Süleyman's most influential wife, Roxelana, convinced the Sultan to name his less-than-magnificent son Selim as his successor. In order to spend more time carousing in the well-endowed imperial harem, upon taking power Selim turned virtually all matters of the state over to the Grand Vizier. During the period that followed (Selim, tipsier than a three dollar bill, had drowned in his tub in 1574), palace infighting was rife, and some scholars called the this the "rule of the women." The favorite wife or harem girl of the monomaniacal sultans vied for power. Mothers would order entire families strangled to ensure the throne for their own children. For example, Kösem, a concubine of Sultan Murad (1603-17), scarcely survived banishment to Beyazıt upon the sultan's untimely death, only to return triumphantly to the palace when her son Murad IV, and her other son Ibrahim, became sultans in rapid succession. Kösem even lived to see her grandson become sultan, but in 1652 she was strangled by order of her daughter-in-law.

Weakness at the top only encouraged abuses by those nearer the bottom. Religious and ethnic minorities, such as the Armenians, Kurds, Greeks, Cypriots, and Jews, were treated with marked harshness. Economic crises further eroded Ottoman control of the countryside. Following a period of devastating inflation caused by the Spanish discovery of American silver, the Ottomans became continually weaker in comparison to European powers. After a series of disastrous military entanglements with Peter the Great and the Venetians, the Ottomans signed the Treaty of Karlowitz on January 26, 1699, thus losing most of Transylvania and Hungary. For the first time, the Ottomans ceded a substantial chunk of territory hitherto considered an integral part of their empire.

End of an Empire

After the traumatic loss of Greece in 1832, life did not get any easier for the Ottoman Empire. Muhammad Ali, nominally the sultan's governor of Egypt, invaded the Levant. He would have captured İstanbul itself had it not been for the intervention of the European powers who unambiguously threatened to use force if necessary to preserve the fragile European balance of power. In the mid-19th century, after crushing conservative opposition including the *janissaries*, the Ottomans instituted a series of administrative reforms collectively known as the *tanzimat*. Besides providing *de jure* religious equality to all, the *tanzimat* attempted to regularize taxation and government conscription, and to establish the private ownership of land. Most peasants, however, were wary that the government's reforms were merely covers for more tax-raising schemes. So they registered their land in the name of wealthy shaykhs, whose great estates thus further accrued. As the Ottoman government became more and more indebted to British and French bankers, the Empire once full of vim and vigor limped in such decrepitude that it was commonly referred to as "the sick man of Europe."

The Ottoman Empire was at a loss to meet the demands of foreign powers. The British, after assuming a "protectorate" over Cyprus in 1878, began fearing that bondholders who had invested in Egypt would not be repaid, so they promptly marched armies into the Nile. Meanwhile, as the self-proclaimed protector of Greek Orthodox Christians everywhere, the Russians groped forth with more extensive claims against the Ottomans, occasionally liberating territory in the Crimea. Foreign missionary schools sprang up in the Ottoman Middle East; Arabs, ruled by Turks for more than five centuries, began to blame the Ottomans for the corruption of Islam and the recent impotence of the region. Indeed, the Arabs had never recognized the Turks as legitimate protectors of the faith in the first place.

With the advent of the telegraph and steamship, the Ottoman central government was able to reinforce its presence in the remote parts of the empire. As Britain and France with Russia for control of the strategic straits of Bosphorus, the sultans had the opportunity to dive headfirst into the intrigues of European *realpolitik*. Although unrest in the early 1870s prompted the granting of a constitution complete with elected parliament. Sultan Abdülhamid II (who ruled from 1876-1909) led a pan-Islamic counter-revolution and suspended all democratic reforms.

The 1908 coup of the "Young Turks," a secret organization which had busted out from the officer corps, ended Abdülhamid's hold on power. Welcomed at first by most of the ethnic populations, the triumvirate of military officials who controlled the empire soon began to implement a strident plan of Turkification. Traditionally, Islam had been the basis for Ottoman identity, and in accordance with Islamic law minorities had been allowed to open their own schools and keep their own customs. But the central government decreed that Turkish was to be the national language of the empire for non-Turkish-speaking Muslims and non-Muslims alike. At a time when nationalist aspirations were emerging throughout the empire, the Turks' belated attempt to suppress nationalist awareness managed only to further aggravate the situation.

The government of the Empire sided with the Axis powers in World War I. As British officers were leading an Arab revolt against the Turks (with the promise of then granting them independence), Turkish officials in the east began to systematically "solve" their ethnic problems. A three-year period witnessed the extermination of more than 1,500,000 Armenian civilians after Armenian forces sided with the Russian army in an attempt to win their own independence. Officials in the German government expressed dismay at the Turkish plan, but no real effort was made to interfere. Entire Armenian cities were "disinhabited" under the pretenses of a relocation of their inhabitants away from the Russian front to the "safer" environs of Mesopotamia. To this day, many Turks deny all responsibility for the slaughter, and Armenian activists exact their revenge on Turkish diplomats.

The Turkish Republic

The Ottomans, however, had breathed their last by siding with the Germans in World War I. After the Allies emerged victorious, Britain and France divided the Arab provinces, under the sanction and auspices of the nascent League of Nations. Plans for the division of Anatolia were drawn up, too, and Greece invaded in order to capture disputed territory. The latter two undertakings, regardless, were stifled by the rise of Mustafa Kemal, an Ottoman general who was able to reorganize his army in time to decisively defeat the Greeks. On October 29, 1923, Mustafa Kemal, dubbed Atatürk ("Father of the Turk"), was elected the first president of the newly-established Republic of Turkey. Atatürk turned his back on Ottoman tradition. Equating modernization with rapid westernization and secularization, Atatürk abolished the Caliphate, outlawed Muslim courts and the veiling of women, decreed that Turkish be written in Latin rather than Arabic script, and, for a time, ordered that the *adhan* (call to prayer) be recited in Turkish rather than classical Arabic. Naturally, these sweeping measures encountered extreme resistance from the religious establishment.

Since the rise of Mustafa Kemal, Turks have been determined in their program to become a part of Europe. The Republican People's Party program of 1931 proclaimed the six principles of the modern Turkish state: republicanism, populism, nationalism, statism, secularism, and revolution. Changes were introduced to "re-educate" the public about Turkish achievement, and the government began a systematic campaign to purge foreign-derived words from the Turkish language. Turkification triumphed over the competing systems of Ottomanism and pan-Islamism.

Shortly before WWII, the increasingly autocratic Kemal died and was replaced by his associate İsmet İnönü. Though Nazi Germany's early successes resulted in a popular clamor to join the war on the side of Germany to avenge the humiliation of WWI, the government remained neutral. At the end of the war, with the impending defeat of Germany, Turkey joined the Allies, the expansiyon of Soviet power into the south having become increasingly a more salient concern. When the Soviets demanded the sharing of control of the Straits and the ceding of large chunks of western Anatolia to Soviet Georgia, military and economic aid from the United States rambled off to Turkey.

WWII, however, led to the expansion of the Turkish military and nourished its ever-increasing role in politics. When a growing professional class demanded increased political participation, the Democrat Party (DP) broke off from the old Kemalist Republican People's Party (RPP). Throughout the 50s, the government, dominated mostly by the DP, continually rolled back censorship and allowed for further development of political rights. However, as the 50s progressed, economic conditions deteriorated almost as fast as relations between the RPP and the DP. When the DP threatened to outlaw the RPP, students participated in widespread demonstrations and the army stepped in and took control.

After the eradication of the DP, the military's ruling National Unity Committee promulgated a new constitution. Approved by voters in July, 1961, the constitution established a bicameral parliament which would elect the president jointly. Elections were held in October, and the army soon withdrew from politics. Many former DP members became influential in the new Justice Party (JP), which dominated elections after 1965. In 1970, after right-wing members of the JP split off and reconstituted the old Democratic Party, the army demanded the resignation of the government and assumed *de facto* control.

During the 1970s, the government was controlled by a coalition teaming the RPP with an emerging religious party. Tensions built, however, as economic conditions worsened and religious opposition to increased Westernization grew. Following the coup in Cyprus which overthrew President Makarios, public opinion in Turkey led to the army's invasion of northern Cyprus in July, 1974. Economic and arms embargoes soon followed; Turkey responded by closing foreign military installations. By the end of the 70s, tensions were relieved and most normal foreign relations resumed.

The military took power again in September, 1980, as the government's control over the interior of the country dissipated. The military dissolved all opposition parties and punished and tortured thousands of opposition leaders. By 1983, the military relinquished most of its hold on power and martial law ceased. Although Kurdish rebels in eastern Turkey still fight for an independent homeland and have benefited from renewed world attention to their plight after the Gulf War, the present government of Turkish President Turgut Özal remains firmly in control. Turkish assistance during the Gulf War against Iraq in 1991 proved economically debilitating and led to a spate of terrorist attacks against government installations and foreigners. But by cooperating with the United States, Özal raised his government's status, at least as seen by the U.S. and NATO. Boosted economic assistance from the West as well as the Gulf countries seems to have alleviated, for the moment, the threat of further crisis. Today, the prime minister at the time of the coup of 1980 is back on duty after the elections of 1992 and people are waiting for another military takeover, as the historically periodic occurrence of coups is late this time.

As the European Economic Community accelerates its drive toward unity, Turkey's role in the EEC remains undetermined. In 1987, Turkey applied for membership, but was in 1989 rejected on the grounds that the completion of a previously defined European market was necessary before any expansion could be considered. Furthermore, the Commission of the European Communities noted Turkey's less than stellar human rights record, high rate of inflation, and general swarthiness as objections to granting Turkey's membership. At the earliest, Turkey's application will be reconsidered in 1993. Snubbed by the West, Turkey has sought economic opportunity in the East, namely in the Muslim former Soviet republics of Kazakhastan, Tajikistan, and Uzbekistan.

Religion

Although there is no official state religion, over 98% of Turks are Muslim. Orthodox Christians of Greek, Armenian, and Syrian backgrounds, and Jews (mainly in İstanbul) comprise the remaining population. And while Atatürk set modern Turkey on a decidedly secular course, Islam plays a central role in the country's history and continues to enrich its contemporary society and culture. As such, a basic understanding of the religion, its meaning, and its practice is essential for any visit to Turkey.

The Arabic word *islam* means in its general sense "submission," and Islam the religion is the faithful submission to God's will. Islam has its roots in the revelations received from 610-22 CE by **Muhammad** (Mohammed in Turkish) who was informed by the Angel Gabriel of his prophetic calling. These revelations, received in Arabic, form the core of Islam, the **Qur'an** (recitation; *Kuran* in Turkish). Muslims believe the Arabic text to be perfect, immutable, and untranslatable—the words of God embodied in human language. Consequently, the Qur'an appears in Turkey and throughout the Muslim world—the majority of which is non-Arabic speaking—in Arabic. Muhammad is seen as the "seal of the prophets," the last of a chain of God's messengers which included Jewish and Christian figures such as Abraham, Moses, and Jesus, and the Qur'an incorporates many of the Biblical traditions associated with these prophets.

Muhammad slowly gathered followers to his evolving faith. Staunchly monotheistic, Islam was met with ample opposition in polytheist Arabia, leading to persecution in his native city of **Mecca** in Arabia. In 622, he and his followers fled to the nearby city of **Medina,** where he was welcomed as mediator of a long-standing blood feud. This **Hijrah** (flight, or emigration) marks the beginning of the Muslim community and indicates the beginning of the Muslim calendar. For the next eight years, Muhammad and his community initially defended themselves against raids and later battled the Meccans and neighboring nomadic tribes, until in 630 Mecca surrendered to the Muslims, making Muhammad the most powerful man in Arabia. After the surrender numerous Meccans converted to the new faith voluntarily. This established the pattern for *jihad* (struggle), a term often grossly misunderstood by non-Muslims. *Jihad* refers, first and foremost, to the spiritual struggle against one's own desires which are in conflict with the precepts of Islam. Another facet of *jihad* is the struggle to make one's own Muslim community as righteous as possible. A third sense of *jihad* is that of the struggle against outsiders who wish to harm one's Muslim community. It is this last idea of *jihad* which is most familiar to the West. War was intended to be waged only against non-Muslims in order to ensure that cities were ruled in accordance with Islam. A city was approached and given three choices: conversion to Islam, payment of the *jizya* (a special tax imposed on non-Muslims), or war. Individual conversions often followed because of the appeal of the Muslim message.

Islam continued to grow after the Prophet's death (632), flourishing in the "Age of Conquest." The first four caliphs (*halife* in Turkish), or successors to the Prophet, known as the Rightly Guided Caliphs, led wars against apostate nomadic tribes, and by the year 640 the Muslims had defeated the Byzantine and Persian empires. By 669-78, they had reached the walls of Constantinople. The fourth Caliph, Muhammad's nephew and son-in-law Ali, was the catalyst for the major split in the Muslim world; for the first time Muslims fought against Muslims. Ali slowly lost power, and was murdered in 661. The *Shi'at Ali* (Partisans of Ali or Shi'is) believe Ali as a blood relative of the Prophet to be the only legitimate successor to Muhammad, thus separating themselves from **Sunni** (orthodox) Islam. Contrary to popular Western perception, **Shi'ism** is not a creed of fanaticism or fundamentalism, but is Islam with a sharp focus on divinely chosen leaders (or *Imams*) who are blood descendants of the Prophet through Ali and his wife, the Prophet's daughter Fatima. The **Sufis** are a mystical movement within Islam, stressing the goal of unity with God. They are organized in orders, with a clear hierarchy from master to disciple. Sufi *shaykhs* (masters) are reputed to perform miracles, and their tombs are popular pilgrimage destinations.

Pillars of Islam

"Allahu akhbar. La ilaha il'Allah Muhammadun rasul Allah"—*"God is great. There is no god but God. And Muhammad is His prophet."* This beginning of the call to worship (the *ezan*) punctuates daily life in Muslim areas, sounding five times each day from the mosques. It expresses some of Islam's most important beliefs. The first line glorifies God, using the word for God in Arabic, *Allah*. Praise of God and the Prophet is a pious and meritorious action. These words are whispered into the ears of newborn babies, and are the last words uttered by dying Muslims. The next lines of the call form the **şahadet**, the testimony of faith. The *şahadet* is the first of the five pillars of Islam. It reflects the unity of God *(tawhid)*, which is Islam's strongest belief, and the special place of Muhammad as God's final Messenger.

Testifying to God's unity through the *şahadet* is only one of the **five pillars** of Islam to be an article of belief. The second pillar is prayer (*namaz*), recited five times per day following the example of the practice of Muhammad. Prayers, preceded by ablutions, begin with a declaration of intent and consist of a set cycle of prostrations. No designated person is necessary to lead prayers—they are often done wherever the Muslim happens to be at the time of prayer. On Fridays, congregational prayer is encouraged; this is the only distinguishing feature of the Muslim "sabbath."

The third pillar is **charity** (*zekât*, or purification). Although individual donations to worthy causes often substitute, *zekât* is technically an assessed tax on property given to a carefully regulated communal fund. However, in Pakistan and Saudi Arabia the government levies a *zekât* tax on all citizens.

It is believed that Muhammad received the Qur'an during the month of **Ramadan**. **Fasting** during this holy month is the fourth pillar. Not simply a month without eating, Ramadan is a time of daylight fasting and meditation, while nights are filled with feasting and revelry. During Ramadan (February 22-March 24 in 1993), offices and businesses not catering to tourists may be closed or keep shorter hours.

The last pillar, which is required only once in a lifetime, is **pilgrimage** (the *hac*). Every Muslim who can afford it and is physically able should journey to Mecca during the last month of the Muslim calendar.

Mosques

Any place where Muslims pray is a mosque *(cami)*. Beautiful buildings glorify God, and an Islamic ban on images, inspired by Islam's vehement opposition to idolatry of any kind, has led to an incredible ingenuity in geometric and calligraphic decoration. The direction facing Mecca, in which all prayer is spoken, is called the *qibla*. It is marked by a niche, the *mihrab*. The *imam* (leader of prayer, not to be confused with the Shi'i leaders) gives a sermon *(hutbe)* on Friday from the *minbar* (pulpit). In larger cities, you may also see a *türbe* (mausoleum) or *medrese* (Qur'anic school). There are no religious restrictions on non-Muslims entering mosques, but other restrictions may have been adopted for practical reasons in areas with mobs of tourists. Prayer is not a spectator sport, and visitors should stay away during times of worship and always wear modest dress. For information on the historical and architectural aspects of mosques, consult the Art and Architecture section below.

For more thorough introductions to Islam, try *An Introduction to Islam* by Frederick Denny, *Islam: The Straight Path* by John Esposito, or *Islam: An Introduction* by Annemarie Schimmel. A sampling of Islamic texts can be found in Kenneth Cragg and Marston Speight's *Islam from Within*. If you feel inspired enough to study the Qur'an, read Mohammad Marmaduke Pickthall's *Meaning of the Glorious Koran* or N.J. Dawood's *The Koran*.

Art and Architecture

Like Islam itself, Turkey is today confronted with its own bygone splendor. The significance of Atatürk's proclamation of the Republic in 1923 notwithstanding, Turkey's glory days were under the reign of the Ottoman Empire. The magnificence of the empire demanded an artistry and architecture to match. In particular, Sultan Süleyman—lawgiver, ruler of the empire, commander of the armed forces, guardian of Islam (in other words, the most magnificent of the magnificent)—introduced unprecedented imperial patronage of the arts, and an explosion in architecture and court artistry echoed the rapid expansiyon of the empire. Furthermore, the administrative centralization of the court and the empire that Süleyman achieved found prolific expression in the mosques, textiles, painted miniatures, and calligraphy of the 16th century.

Architecture was the crown jewel of the Ottoman Empire. Under Süleyman alone (1520-1566), over 80 major mosques and hundreds of other buildings were constructed by the empire. Most every sultan built and was subsequently buried in a mosque thus creating a topographical line of succession throughout İstanbul. The master architect Sinan served Süleyman and his sons from 1538 to 1588, during which time he created a unified style for all of İstanbul and for much of the empire. Recruited as a *janissary* and trained first as a carpenter, Sinan forged an architecture informed by early Islamic and Byzantine styles, but conforming to neither. The earliest influence for mosque architecture was the Prophet Muhammad's house in Medina. This hypostyle structure, featuring a pillared cloister around a courtyard, defined the only functional requirements of a mosque: the *qibla,* the wall of the mosque which faces Mecca, toward which Muslims face when praying; and an open space in which people can pray. As Islam requires Muslims to follow the example of the Prophet, his house became a model for many mosques, particularly in Arabia. Later, a Persian style characterized by four *iwan* (vaulted arches) emerged as a second architectural influence.

For Sinan, and for Ottoman architects who preceded him, the house of the Prophet indicated the structural considerations for a mosque, but the **Aya Sofiya** offered the greatest aesthetic challenge. Built by Byzantine Emperor Justinian between 532 and 537 CE as the Church of the Holy Wisdom, it was distinguished by a large dome buttressed by two half-domes, and was for 900 years Constantinople's cathedral. In both size and wealth, it was the world's greatest church. After the Ottoman conquest in 1453, the building was converted to a mosque. The half-domes were not part of traditional Islamic architecture, but more striking was the central dome, whose daunting height and girth had never before been achieved. So grand is the central dome that upon completion of the Aya Sofiya, Justinian is reported to have proclaimed, "O Solomon, I have surpassed thee!"

There is in Ottoman architecutre a progression toward the Aya Sofiya as court architects experimented with domes and half-domes. The **Üç Şerafeli** in Edirne (1438-47), for instance, has a central dome surrounded by four smaller domes; the **Fatih** in İstanbul (1463-70), has a central dome, three smaller domes, and a single half-dome. The **Bayezid II** in İstanbul has a central dome flanked by six small domes and two half-domes, while the **Şehzade** (1543-48), also in İstanbul, has four half-domes. Each mosque recalled the Aya Sofiya for its use of half-domes and the enormity of the central domes. It was Sinan who from 1568 to 1574 built the **Selimye Mosque** in Edirne, with a central dome supported on eight columns, with four axial half-domes and a single half-dome in front. Finally, the size of the central dome surpassed that of the Aya Sofiya, Sinan surpassed Justinian and Solomon both, and Ottoman architecture reached its logical apotheosis.

Court patronage of the arts often began within the court itself. The *nakkaşane,* imperial studios, developed the artistic vocabulary for the entire empire. Thus a style of illustrated manuscript designed in the *nakkaşane* would find expression not only in the court documents, but but in carpets, textiles, and paintings, and on the walls of mosques from Bosnia to Baghdad. The centrality of Süleyman's administration extended to every aspect of the court.

Ottoman decorative arts are more readily characterized by their nature motifs. While standard arabesques, inherited from earlier Islamic art, are common, the *nakkaşane* developed distinctly Ottoman styles as well. The naturalistic genre included realistic flowers, animals, while the *saz* ("reed") style, thought to have been inspired by Chinese sketches, features long and winding, piercing leaves wound around *hatayı,* abstract lotus blossoms. (They were painted with reed brushes.) Similar but unrelated is the *rumi* style, with split leaves, originating in Iran. While the Qur'an forbids the portrayal of living beings (a corollary of Islam's opposition to idolatry), the Ottomans did not follow this injunction strictly. Whereas in other Islamic societies non-figurative arts such as Qur'anic calligraphy flourished, in the Ottoman court more than calligraphy alone thrived.

Until the mid-1800s, calligraphy, miniatures, and decorations were the only formal examples of painting, while the celebrated İznik tiles and brightly colored *kilim* were the most familiar Turkish handcrafts. Music, dance, and theater have become more institutionalized in the past 150 years. In 1971, concern over the purity of Turkish culture prompted the government to establish the nation's Ministry of Culture. Today, several international arts and music festivals bring performers from all over the world to Ephesus, İstanbul, and other Turkish cities, while the tangibles of Turkish culture (crafted carpets, meerschaum pipes, and elaborately inlaid wood) continue to be prized alongside the grace and agelessness of the civilization.

Literature

Herbert Muller's *The Loom of History* traces the fascinating history of Asia Minor from prehistoric times to the 20th century. F.E. Peter's *The Harvest of Hellenism* discusses Turkey's Hellenistic heritage. Homer's *Iliad* is a classic traveling companion for these shores where the Trojan War took place. For years, verse was the only acceptable literary genre in the Middle East. Nâzım Hikmet's *Selected Poems* is one of the best Turkish collections. More contemporary authors include Cevat Şakir Kabaağaç, the famed fisher of Halicarnassus, and Yaşar Kemâl, whose *Memed, My Hawk,* and *The Wind from the Plains* have won him several nominations for the Nobel Prize. Aziz Nesin's humorous books have been translated into over 25 languages and garnered the Golden Palm Prize. Excellent books on modern Turkey are Bernard Lewis's *The Emergence of Modern Turkey* and Lord Kinross' *Atatürk: The Rebirth of a Nation.* For more scholarly works, try Steven Runcinan's *Byzantine Civilization* or Lord Kinross's *The Ottoman Centuries,* both histories of their respective periods. Mark Twain's *Innocents Abroad* offers curmudgeonly glimpses of the Turkish coast.

Language

Although you've probably never heard anything quite like Turkish, it is not difficult to master the basics. Once thought to be related to Finnish, Hungarian, and Mongolian, Turkish is today recognized as belonging to a distinct Turkic language group, along with Khirgiz, Kazakh, and Azerbaijani. In his effort to forge a secular Turkish identity, in 1928 Kemal Atatürk ordered the language written in the Latin alphabet rather than the Arabic script, an heirloom of the Ottoman Empire's Islamic heritage. Furthermore, Atatürk purged the language of many of its Arabic and Persian borrowings (the latter evidence of Persian literary influence). While these words continue to be replaced by new Turkish words, this linguistic cleansing is not absolute; Islamic terminology not-withstanding, words as common as "hello" *(merhaba)* are of Arabic and Persian origin.

English is common in major coastal resorts, although German is probably a more common second language. Buy a phrase book, such as the *Penguin Turkish Phrasebook* or *Harrap's Turkish Phrasebook.* **Langenscheidt** has an excellent Turkish-English pocket dictionary. Keep in mind that when Turks raise their chins and shut their eyes they mean "no," and when they wave a hand up and down, they mean "come." Placing the palm flat against the chest is a polite way of refusing an offer.

For a pronunciation guide and a list of useful phrases, consult the glossary at the back of this book.

Traditions

A popular pastime is visiting the Turkish *kahve* (coffeehouses), where people sit, sip coffee or tea, and play *tavla* (backgammon). In İstanbul you might still find men smoking *nargile* (hookahs).

It's definitely worth your while to visit to a **hamam** (Turkish bath) at least once while in Turkey. Because of the Islamic emphasis on cleanliness (pious Muslims perform ablutions before each of the day's five prayers), the baths have been a customary part of daily life since medieval times. Men and women use separate bath houses, or the same place on different days. Enter the bath house, deposit your clothes in a cubicle, don the provided *peştemal* (towel), and proceed to the sauna-like *göbek taşı* (large heated stone). As you sweat, an attendant will give you a rub-down. Following the massage, you can either bathe yourself (BYOSS&T—bring your own shampoo, soap, and towel, or pay to use theirs), or have an attendant bathe you. The *kese* (abrasive mitt) they use will deep-clean the pores of your pores. Men should never drop their *peştemal;* cleaning one's lower half is therefore tricky, but not impossible. Women seem less restricted by such standards of modesty. Afterwards, take a dip in the refreshing cooler pool. Be aware that heterosexual and homosexual assaults have been reported in *hamams:* visit the baths in groups.

Turkey retains a strong folk tradition. Turkish folk music is played mostly on traditional percussion and wind instruments. Each region has its own special folk dance, heroes, and traditional costumes. Some of the most popular dances include the *Kaşık Oyunu* (spoon dance), done from Konya to Silifke, with men and women in colorful garb beating wooden spoons; the *Kılıç Kalkan,* from Bursa, in which men dressed in Ottoman fighting gear act out battles; and the *Zeybek,* an Aegean dance performed to symbolize bravery and heroism. Traditional sports include *Yağlı Güreş* (grease wrestling), *cirit oyunu* (tossing javelins at competitors on horseback), and *deve güreşi* (camel wrestling).

Note that it is illegal to insult another person in Turkey. Conduct debate civilly or you may find yourself in jail. Even more serious than insulting another person is insulting modern Turkey's founder Atatürk. Turks take their nationalism and their national hero seriously, and expect visitors to pay equal respect.

Bargaining

Bargaining is one of the most useful arts to master in Turkey. It is best to make larger purchases in İstanbul or İzmir, where competition keeps prices low. Authentic Turkish carpets and other craftwork, however, should be purchased in other areas, since prices can be twice as high in İstanbul. Don't hesitate to haggle, especially when dealing with smaller establishments.

When shopping, take your time. Let the merchant know you've seen the competition—this will give you good bargaining leverage. Be persistent: decide how much you want to pay in the end and then don't budge. When you first offer a price (start with half the amount you are quoted) the proprietor will most likely make a face and act insulted. Remember that this a test of wills. Act shocked, try gaining their sympathy, or tell them you saw the same item around the corner for a much lower price. You should head for the door at least three or four times while bargaining; this technique works at hotels as well. The shopkeeper will probably call after you, demanding to know what you are willing to offer. Grab the chance to haggle again and stick to your last offered price.

Be aware of people who approach you as friends. After befriending you, they'll offer to take you to a shop with "the best prices." Every time you spend a *lira,* your new best friend earns a commission (up to 50%). This practice is known as *hanut.* A scam by any other name is still a scam.

American cigarettes (particularly Marlboros and Camels) are very popular and considered something of a status symbol. You may wish to carry several packs with you, as they provide a simple and appropriate way of reciprocating favors.

Food

Turkey is one of the few places left in the Mediterranean where eating very cheaply still entitles you to sample a great variety of dishes. In restaurants, it's customary to go to the back counter and look around before choosing, but do not insist on seeing the kitchen if the restaurateur demurs. Usually, you can't bargain in restaurants, except when ordering fish, because prices are fixed by municipalities. Streetside ice cream and drink vendors will usually overcharge tourists. Tap water in most larger cities is safe since it is heavily chlorinated. Food is often less than clean, but squeezing lemon juice over it aids digestion. If you develop a mild stomach ailment, yogurt may replace your body's natural bacteria content.

Contemporary Turkish cuisine finds its roots in Ottoman kitchens (as do the other foods from the Balkans to the Persian Gulf), in the nomadic traditions of the Turkish tribes of the Asian Steppes, and in the many civilizations that swept Asia Minor for thousands of years. An Assyrian cookbook found during recent excavations showed that similar dishes have been served for thousands of years. The most famous of these are *kebaps. Döner kebaps,* known as gyro in the U.S., are slices of lamb pressed against each other on a long skewer turning vertically over a charcoal fire and cut in thin slices. If you add yogurt, tomato sauce, and melted butter, it becomes the famous İskender *kebap* of Bursa. When small pieces of lamb are impaled on metal *şiş* (skewers), they become the famous—and ubiquitous—*şiş kebap.* Other variations on this original abound.

Other local favorites include the *zeytinyağli* dishes—literally dishes cooked with olive oil. Usually served cold, they can also be eaten as *meze. İmambayıldı,* a dish of eggplant and onions is popular, as is *ayşekadın fasulye,* green beans cooked in olive oil with tomatoes, onions, and a pinch of sugar.

One cannot talk about Turkish food without mentioning *dolma*—literally meaning "stuffed." Sometimes filled with meat and rice and served hot, sometimes without meat and cooked in olive oil and served cold, and sometimes using grape leaves rather than hollowed vegetables, these Turkish favorites will always leave you *dolma.*

A country surrounded by seas, Turkey naturally has its share of fish. The tastier (and unfortunately the most expensive) fishes are *kılıç* (swordfish) and *kalkan* (turbot). From any larger fish one can make a *buğulama* (steamed dish) that takes about an hour to cook, but is well worth the wait. The local fishes change from bay to bay, but the tastiest fish throughout Turkey are available in late August and September. For winter months, *hamsi,* a small fish from the Black Sea, is usually cheap and can be made into over forty dishes, including one dessert [blech]. In addition to the fishes, Turkey offers *kalamar* (squid), *karides* (shrimp), and *midye* (mussels). Especially good are fried *kalamar,* shrimp casserole, and *midye dolma.* Try also fried mussels and *ahtapot sal-atası* (octopus salad). Not surprisingly, the best catch is available at the most expensive restaurants, but some holes-in-the-wall will serve excellent fish at reasonable prices.

Be sure to try a *menemen,* a delicious loose omelette with tomatoes and onions. *Pide* is a distant Turkish relative of pizza—flat bread served with your choice of eggs, meat, tomatoes, cheese, or spices. Or try *köfte,* a spicy member of the meatball family—it comes either skewered and roasted or served in a tomato broth, with potatoes and veg-etables. For the brave there are *kokoreç*—grilled intestines with spices—and *işkembe çorbası,* tripe soup (very useful after a night of heavy drinking).

There is an endless array of confections—*baklava,* flaky pastry jammed with nuts and soaked in honey; *kadayıf,* a shredded-wheat dough filled with nuts and sugar; and *helva,* a sesame seed and honey loaf. Of course, there is always Turkish Delight *(lo-kum).* Most restaurants also serve some sort of fresh fruit or melon. *Tavuk göğsü* (chicken pudding) or *sütlaç* (rice pudding) are both excellent. For something new and exciting, try *künefe,* a cheesy dessert served hot. Make sure you order it at least half an hour before you want it. *Börek* is made of layers of thin pastry called *yufka* filled with anything from simple cheese and parsley to an elaborate mix of meat, vegetables, and spices.

It is difficult to spend a day in Turkey without pausing at a *çay* shop and ordering a glass of *çay* (a strong black tea). Tea will usually be offered at just about any shop you enter. Until recently heavily taxed and therefore difficult to procure, *kahve* (Turkish coffee), drunk so widely throughout Greece and the Middle East, is once again popular in its native Turkey. Bottled drinks include *meyve suyu* (fruit drink; try cherry or the ambrosial peach nectar); *meyveli gazoz* (a sweet Turkish soda); *ayran,* a mixture of yo-gurt and water; *su* (Turkish designer water); and *maden suyu* (carbonated mineral wa-ter, also known as *soda).* Coke, Pepsi, and other American soft drinks are also widely available. *Bira* (beer) is very popular: *Efes Pilsen* and *Tuborg* are the leading brands. The best domestic white wines are *Çankaya, Villa Doluca,* and *Kavaklıdere.* The best red wines are *Yakut* and *Kavaklıdere.* The cheapest wines are *Guzel Marmara* (found only in the İstanbul area) and *Buzbağı,* both with fragrant plastic corks. Finally, make sure to try *rakı,* the national liqueur, usually diluted with water and ice.

Holidays

There are numerous holidays and festivals in Turkey, both religious and secular. Is-lamic holidays are celebrated with mosque illuminations, prayer, and special food. Other festivals offer simple romp and rollick. Not surprisingly, travel can be difficult at these times as public services become more crowded and more scarce. On most nation-al holidays, banks and offices will be closed (exceptions are noted below). The largest holidays of the year, **Şeker Bayramı** and **Kurban Bayramı** (the only two religious holidays which are also public holidays), can create the biggest problems. Since people tend to combine these holidays with their yearly vacations, you are safer to avoid trav-eling the couple of days before and after these festivals. At these times accommoda-tions become impossible to find, traffic is jammed and dangerous, and prices are 30% higher, if not more. If you must travel, make sure you have bus or plane tickets and res-ervations at least three weeks in advance. If you plan accordingly, the frolic of festival will far outweigh any inconvenience it might engender.

The following list of festivals includes religious and secular holidays for 1993. Note that the dates of Islamic holidays are based on a lunar calendar, and so the dates given below may not be exact. Check with a local tourist office or the local police for more information or for region-specific festivals and events.

Jan.1: Yılbaşı, New Year's Day. Happy and festive, this is a public holiday.

Jan. 19: Miraç Kandili. Celebrates Muhammad's journey from Mecca to Jerusalem, whence he ascended to heaven.

Feb. 5: Berat Kandili. The eve of the month of Şaban, this celebrates the night that Muhammad's mission was revealed to him.

Feb. 22: first day of **Ramazan** (Ramadan in other parts of the world). During the month-long Islamic holiday, (ending March 24), pious Muslims abstain from eating, drinking, smoking, and sexual relations between dawn and sunset. Each day's fast is broken with an extravagant feast. While this is not a national holiday, only one or two restaurants may be open during the day in the smaller towns and inland, and in such areas it is inappropriate to eat or drink openly during the daytime: be discreet.

March 19: Kadir Gecesi (Night of Power). Celebrates the first night of revelation of the Qur'an to Muhammad.

March 24-26: Şeker Bayramı (Sugar Holiday). A three-day holiday celebrating the end of Ramazan. Family and friends exchange presents, and children enjoy oodles of sweets. Eating and drinking in public highly encouraged. Banks and holidays closed all three days.

April 23: Ulusal Egemenlik ve Çocuk Bayramı, National Sovereignty Day and Children's Day, a national holiday commemorating the first meeting of the Grand National Assembly in Ankara in 1920. An international children's festival is held in Ankara.

May 19: Gençlik ve Spor Günü, Youth and Sports Day; also Atatürk's birthday. A national holiday.

May 29: An İstanbul festival to celebrate Mehmet's conquest of the city from the Byzantines in 1453.

May 31-June3: Kurban Bayramı (Festival of Sacrifice). The most important holiday of the year, this four-day festival recalls Abraham's sacrificial offering of Ismael to God on Mt. Moriah (a Qur'anic variation of the Biblical story). When God saw Abraham's willingness to sacrifice his son out of devotion to Him, He had Abraham sacrifice a ram instead. 2½ million sheep are slaughtered each year in Turkey to commemorate the faith and piety of Abraham. A nation-wide feast. Banks and offices closed for up to a week.

First Week of June: International Festival. Classical and folk music in İzmir, Çesme, and Ephesus.

July 1: Denizcilik Günü, Navy Day. Although a national holiday, banks and offices are open.

Aug. 26: Armed Forces Day. Another national holiday on which banks and offices are open.

Aug. 30: Zafer Bayramı. A national holiday celebrating the Turkish victory over the invading Greek forces at Dumlupmar during Turkey's War of Independence in 1922.

Aug. 30: Mevlid-i Nebi. Celebrates the birth of Muhammad in 570 CE.

Oct.28-29: Cumhuriyet Bayramı. Turkey's largest civil holiday (and a public holiday), this commemorates Atatürk's proclamation of the Republic in 1923. Make like a politico and watch the ubiquitous parades.

Nov. 10: Marks the anniversary of Atatürk's death in 1938. At exactly 9:05am (the time of death), all of Turkey comes to a stop for a moment of national mourning. Horns are blown in mourning. A national holiday.

Climate

In the summer months, the Aegean and Mediterranean coasts are very hot, with average daily temperatures around 90°F (32°C). Beware of mosquitoes, particularly on the Mediterranean Coast, and *bring repellent.* The swimming season from Bodrum south, and all along the Mediterranean coast, lasts from early May well into October. On the Black Sea coast (İstanbul included), the swimming season is shorter, from June through early September, and fall brings considerable rainfall; winters aren't especially cold, but usually wet and miserable. As you move inland, the climate becomes more extreme. The area around Urfa usually exceeds 100°F (37.5°C) in the summer, while north of Van temperatures remain relatively cool because of the high altitude. In the winter, Urfa is temperate, while most of central and eastern Anatolia is bitterly cold, with heavy snowfalls.

NORTHWESTERN TURKEY

Istanbul

East meets west; rich meets poor; old meets new. You've heard it all before. These generalizations are the staple of the travel book industry, used to describe cities form Vienna to Little Rock. Welcome to the city that invented these clichés. Welcome to Byzantium, Constantinople, a crossroads, a melting pot. Call it what you will, you'll always find İstanbul a feast for the senses: grand mosques crouching atop red-roofed hills, *muezzins* who blare clarion calls-to-prayer, street vendors charring ears of corn on makeshift grills. Passersby snake their way through street merchants selling drill bits, cordless telephones, and tea sets. Seemingly oblivious to the constant stream of traffic and bargain-hunters, mustachioed Turks converse animatedly on doorsteps. Cracked-plaster buildings loom overhead, threatening to seal off the cobalt sky from the labyrinth of alleys below. Buses spew hot exhaust, coating tourists' legs with their piceous excrement, while young boys armed with rags and polish peddle shoeshines. Twisting streets lead unsuspecting wanderers to hole-in-the-wall shoemakers and subterranean teahouses. İstanbul's unbridled capitalism assaults you with every step you take. Yet the glorious remnants of the Byzantine and Ottoman empires preside over the dynamic, lurching circus of İstanbul. The city resounds with the cries of trinket hawkers and automobile horns, but the rhythm here is of the real İstanbul, a rhythm both seductive and mysterious, frenetic and stable, a rhythm unlike any other.

History

Archaeological findings suggest that the site of the modern city of İstanbul had been settled as early as the 13th century BCE. Evidence, though, is sparse and little is known about this early **Mycenaean settlement.** By the 11th century BCE the population had established various fishing villages here, one of which occupied the exact site of today's Topkapı Palace. But it was not until the arrival of Megarian colonists from Greece (Megara is near Corinth) on the Asian shore of the Bosphorus around 700 BCE that the city's history began.

Byzas, before embarking on his adventure, consulted the infallible Oracle at Delphi, who told him to settle "opposite the Land of the Blind." As Byzas and his crew sailed the Bosphorus, they spotted the Megarian settlement on the Asian shore at Chalcedon (now Kadıköy, one of the two centers of Asian İstanbul). A quick head turn to the left, though, and they knew where their new colony would lie. Overcome by the glory of the natural harbor of the Golden Horn on the European shore, they reasoned that the people at Chalcedon must have been blind to ignore this site. This set of colonists settled here in 667 BCE and Byzas's younger sister Ramona named the city **Byzantium.** During the following centuries, the city was primarily a pawn in the conflicts of innumerable other city-states and empires.

A power struggle within the Roman Empire at the beginning of the 4th century determined the city's fate for the next millenium. The retirement of Diocletian in 305 caused an intense struggle for power between **Constantine,** Emperor of the West and rival **Licinius,** Emperor of the East. Constantine pursued his nemesis to the city (then called **Augusta Antonina**) and on across the Bosphorus to Chrysopolis (Üsküdar) where he defeated Licinius in 324. Constantine consolidated his power here and declared Byzantium to be the "New Rome" and capital of his empire in 330. Subsequent to this official inauguration, though, the city came to be known as **Constantinople.**

HAREM

İstanbul

1 Aya Sofya
2 Topkapı Palace
3 Blue Mosque
4 Sirkeci Station
5 Yeni Camii
6 Süleymaniye Camii
7 Topkapı Bus Station
8 Hippodrome
9 Beyazıt Camii
10 Opera House
11 THY Air Terminal

Dolmabahçe Sarayı
Dolmabahçe Cad.
Cumhuriyet Cad.
Meclisi Cad.
Medusan Cad.
GALATASARAY Cad.
TAKSIM
Bosphorus Strait
İstiklal Cad.
Bahriye Cad.
KARAKÖY
Kemeraltı
Yüksek Kaldırım
Galata Br.
Atatürk Br.
Golden Horn
EMİNÖNÜ
Hamidiye Cad.
Ankara Cad.
Sirkeci İstasyon Cad.
Divan Yolu
SULTANAHMET
Kapalı Çarşı (Grand Bazaar)
İstanbul University
Süleymaniye Cad.
Yeniçeriler Cad.
AKSARAY
LÂLELI
KUMKAPI
Florya Sahil Yolu
FATİH CAMİİ
Atatürk Bulvarı
Fevzipaşa Cad.
Vatan Cad.
Millet Cad.
Topkapı Edirnekapı Cad.
Koca Mustafa Paşa Cad.
Florya Sahil Yolu
Yenişevre Yolu

TO AIRPORT

N

660 yards
600 meters
0
0

With Constantine came the espousal and spread of Christianity. The culmination of this influence is manifest in the edicts of the first and second Theodosii which established Christianity as the state religion (380) and forbade all pagan practices throughout the Empire (435). During the first half of the 5th century, **Theodosius II** supervised the construction of several significant structures: a new, better fortified set of walls around the city, and the original **Aya Sofya** which was later burned during riots.

The final triumph of Christianity over paganism came in 529 when the emperor **Justinian,** probably at the behest of his religiously ultraconservative wife, mandated the closing of all schools of pagan philosophy, including Platonic academies in Athens. This move closed the lid on the Roman Empire's casket and ushered in the **Byzantine Empire** which was really a continuation of the Roman, especially with regard to politics—only now Christian and Greek cultural influences were equally as salient. Under Justinian and his successor, Justin II, though, not all went swimmingly. A 532 insurrection, (the **Nika Revolt**) by factions in the Hippodrome very nearly achieved its goals, for Justinian was on the verge of abdicating and fleeing. It was far nobler, his wife convinced him, to stay and fight, and five days of bloodshed followed. Although victorious, Justinian faced a destroyed city; among the buildings in ruins was the Aya Sofya. Justinian had the city restored to twice its former majesty, and much of what allures us today is the product of this reconstruction. But frequent warring, a horrendous plague, and skyscraping taxes had devastated much of the population, and when **Heraclius** gained power, not just the city but the entire empire was in shambles.

Not one to be nonplussed by such trivialities as devastated empires, Heraclius set out to rebuild in 610. His successes commenced the heroic **Byzantine period.** Thanks to Heraclius, the empire regained Armenia, Syria, Egypt, Palestine, and Roman Mesopotamia, and regained its strength. This potency grew during the reign of **Basil II** whose rule from 976 to 1025 is said to be the most illustrious of the Byzantine Empire. Basil watched over a sort of second renaissance for the empire and meanwhile, defended against attacks by the Arabs and the Bulgars. For his treatment of the latter he earned the sobriquet "Bulgaroctonus" (Bulgar-slayer): to celebrate his final victory, Basil blinded all but 10 of the 10,000 survivors and these ten he had the mercy to leave with one functioning eye. This way, they could lead all the others home. Needless to say, the Bulgars never again saw the need to challenge Basil.

The empire was faced with plenty of other challenges, though, following Basil's death in 1025. The **Fourth Crusade** resulted in another devastation of the city in 1204. The Crusaders, attacking from the sea walls in the Golden Horn, plundered the city and maintained control for sixty years. Venice was the lucky recipient of much of the pillaged art, and subsequently, the West began to take a fresh interest in Greek civilization. Following Latin rule, internal crises of leadership and skirmishes with Turks, whose domain steadily encroached, seriously debilitated the Empire. When they weren't subverting rivals, the leaders were occupied with efforts to fend off Turkish attacks. The Byzantine decline was paired with the rise of a new power in western Asia Minor in the beginning of the 14th century. This was the conception of the Ottoman Empire.

By 1451 when **Mehmet II,** "the Conqueror" (Fatih), came to be leader of the Ottomans, the Byzantine emperor controlled little besides the coveted capital city; Anatolia and most of the Balkans were already in the hands of the Ottomans. Mehmet immediately began to orchestrate the siege of the city. A victory would not only secure the glory of the Ottoman Empire, but would cement Mehmet's control over the noble classes. So with this extra incentive, Mehmet spared no expense in his plans. His forces consummated work on two fortresses on the Bosphorus in 1452 in anticipation of the conquest. *Rumeli Hisar* and *Anadolu Hisar* (the Castles of Europe and of Asia respectively), stood on their corresponding sides of the Bosphorus and enabled the Ottomans to control the strategic strait. Even the Byzantine blockage of the Golden Horn did not foil Mehmet, who simply gathered all his boats at a cove and had them transported overland by rollers and slides to the other end of the gilded antler during the night; he soon had the unprepared Byzantine defenders in submission. He then began the bombardment of the Theodosian city walls as the final conquest of the enticing city. For this Mehmet would have only the very best. When his conventional cannons proved disappointingly inefficient, Mehmet purchased the largest cannon invented to that point. The city fell to the Ottomans in May 1453.

The conqueror Mehmet took to rebuilding and repopulating the city promptly, and transformed İstanbul into the exalted administrative, cultural, and commercial center of his burgeoning empire. The Ottoman Empire witnessed the development of this city into an architectural treasury, best known for its collection of grand mosques built by Süleyman the Magnificent. With the expansion of the Ottoman Empire to Eastern Europe, the Middle East, and North Africa, a motley assemblage of folks from around the world came to the "Paris of the East." By the 19th century a faded glory washed the city, but this glory was certainly still tangible; the opulent and celebrated *Orient Express,* the first international luxury train, connected Paris with İstanbul.

Ankara and not İstanbul served as the base for Atatürk's campaign for independence. Atatürk reasoned that the former capital was linked to too many imperial memories and dangerously vulnerable to attack by gunboats. On October 29, 1923, Ankara was officially declared capital of the Turkish Republic. Atatürk's modernization initiatives have somewhat dulled the colorful cultural zest of the city, but İstanbul still exudes its unique richness that is the product of 16 centuries of world prominence.

Orientation and Practical Information

İstanbul is the only city built on two continents: Asia and Europe. Waterways divide the city into three sections. The **Bosphorus Strait** (Boğaziçi) separates Asia Minor from Europe, distinguishing Asian İstanbul from European İstanbul. The Asian side, mostly residential, offers little for the tourist. Most historical sites, markets, mosques, and museums of the older quarters are situated on the southern bank of the **Golden Horn,** an estuary which splits the European half of the city. The more modern northern bank contains **İstiklâl Caddesi,** the main downtown shopping street, and **Cumhuriyet Caddesi,** with airline offices and expensive hotels, and leads into **Taksim Square,** the center of the northern bank. The northern and southern banks of the city were connected by the Galata Bridge, but a fire in 1992 destroyed the bridge. The bridge could take years to rebuild; in the meantime take a boat between Karaköy and Eminönü or the other bridges further back over the Horn. The **Sirkeci Train Station** lies just east of Eminönü. Budget travelers converge in **Sultanahmet,** the area around the Aya Sofya, south of and up the hill from Sirkeci. The main boulevard—leading west fom Sultanahmet towards the university, the Grand Bazaar, and Aksaray—changes its name from Divan Yolu to Yeniçeriler Cad. to Ordu Cad. (for no other reason, it seems, than to confuse innocent visitors). Shoppers and merchants cram themselves into the district between the **Grand Bazaar,** east of the university just north of Yeniçeriler Cad., and the less touristy **Egyptian Bazaar,** just southeast of Eminönü. The **Kumkapı** district, south of the university and Yeniçeriler Cad., makes wandering a lively undertaking. The tourist office will provide you with a free map; as long as you remain near landmarks you won't get lost.

If you come by plane, you'll arrive at either the international or the domestic terminal of **Atatürk Airport;** the two are connected by a free bus. There are a few campgrounds and one hotel nearby (see Londra Mocamp, Accommodations). To get into town, take the **Turkish Airlines bus** (tel. 243 33 99), which leaves from the Domestic Departures Building, stops in Aksaray and Bakirköy, and terminates its run at the THY Airlines Terminal in Şişhane. If you're going to Sultanahmet, you'll want to get off at Aksaray and take just about any city bus or spiffy new trolley along Ordu Cad. to the Aya Sofya in Sultanahmet. From the airport, the bus labeled "Havaş" runs every hour from 6am to 11pm, and after the arrival of late THY flights (30min., $2). Public bus #96 and *dolmuş* run into town until 9pm (25¢). The bus stop is on the highway in front of International Arrivals, beyond the parking lot. Taxis from the airport to Sultanahmet cost about $9-10 during the day and $14 at night. Don't try to bargain with the taxi drivers: they all have meters—or at least they should. Don't pay more than the meter shows, and make sure that the meter is on ("Gündüz Tarıfesı," or day rate), indicated by a light on the meter's front panel.

To get to Sultanahmet from the Sirkeci Train Station, take any bus or trolley going from Eminönü to Beyazıt. From the Haydarpaşa train station, take the ferry to Karaköy, or take a smaller ferry or a private boat to Eminönü, and take any bus or trolley going from Eminönü to Beyazıt. The Sultanahmet bus stop faces a large square with Aya Sofya on one side and the Blue Mosque on the other. From the **Topkapı bus station,** either take a taxi ($4) or walk through the Topkapı gate and catch city bus #84 to Sultanahmet.

Buses in İstanbul are convenient and cheap. Tickets (30¢, students 15¢) are sold in advance at kiosks marked "Plantonluk" and at larger bus stops (e.g. Eminönü, Karaköy, Taksim). The people hawking tickets at bus stops charge a 15¢ premium. (In a pinch, you can usually buy one from someone on the bus.) Buses marked "Tek Bilet" require one ticket; those marked "Çift Bilet" require two. Service begins at 6am and runs every two to five minutes on major routes, but buses are less frequent after dark, and stop around 11pm. The slowest routes pass through the commercial districts around İstiklâl Cad.—allow 30 minutes from Sultanahmet to Taksim. Read the wooden sign board at the side of the bus or ask the driver if that particular vehicle is headed for a specific quarter of town. The sign on a bus going to Sultanahmet will usually include Beyazıt if it's from the north, or Eminönü coming from the south or west. Buses suffer in İstanbul's ensnarled traffic, so if you're not going far, walk.

A **dolmuş** (shared taxi), either a minibus or a vintage Chevrolet or Buick with fins and buffed chrome (lots from '56), is faster than the bus and generally costs 25¢. *Dolmuş* run on fixed routes, usually between the main bus stops in each quarter (if you ask they'll let you off en route).

Hitchers to Asian Turkey or to Europe take bus #89 from Sultanahmet, Eminönü, or Aksaray to the Londra Mocamp. This and the mocamp outside of Ankara are two of the most popular places to snag a hitch into the Middle East. Hitching is slow and drivers expect to be paid the equivalent bus fare—it's not worth the trouble or the risk. Women should never hitch alone.

Some words of advice: İstanbul swarms with fast-talkers anxious to unburden naïve tourists of their money. There's no reason, however, to let a few swindlers ruin your impression of the Turkish people. A few things to watch out for: anyone who approaches you aggressively is probably trying to sell you something; truly friendly Turks are much less brash. Do not exchange money with random people on the street—they are most likely passing off fake bills. Make sure that taxi-drivers restart their meters when you get in the cab (night rates are in effect from midnight-6am). Most areas of İstanbul are relatively safe even at night, but some districts to avoid after sunset (especially alone) are: **Kasımpaşa,** northwest of Karaköy; the Galata tower; **Fatih,** west of the Süleymaniye Cami; and **Beyoğlu,** the area north of İstiklâl Cad. (a fashionable shopping area by day, but a seething red-light district by night).

Tourist Information Offices: In Sultanahmet, 31 Divan Yolu at the northern end of the **Hippodrome,** across from the Sultan Pub (tel. 518 18 02), open daily 9am-5pm; in Taksim, the Hilton Hotel Arcade (tel. 233 05 92), open Mon.-Sat. 9am-5pm; in the Karaköy Maritime Station (tel. 249 57 76), open daily 9am-5pm. Tourist offices supply superb country and city maps. Go early; these maps are more expensive and less available elsewhere in the country.

Budget Travel: There are many flavors, but the most palatable is **Gençtur,** 15 Yerebatan Cad., 2nd floor (tel. 520 52 74 or 520 52 75), right in the center of Sultanahmet. Very helpful. Sells ISICs, youth ID cards, distributes free maps, and provides a Poste Restante service (free; holds mail for 1yr.). Also organizes Turkish language classes and voluntary workcamps in villages. Open Mon.-Fri. 9am-5:30pm, Sat. 9am-1pm. **Seventur Travel Shop,** 2-C Alemdar Cad. (tel 512 41 83), next to the Aya Sofya, also sells ISICs and youth ID cards, lets you leave your luggage in the office while you look for a hotel, and provides a Poste Restante service (free; holds mail for 1yr.). This agency is authorized to issue plane and bus tickets. Be sure that your travel arrangements are complete and that your vehicle is authorized to enter all the nations you will cross en route. Other agencies in Sultanahmet may swindle travelers by selling bogus tickets. Seventur also provides a shuttle to the airport ($3, midnight-6am $4). Check the schedule in the office. Open daily 9am-6pm, Sat. 9am-1pm. For information on traveling to non-warring nations in the Middle East, check out the travel agencies on Ordu Cad. near the university.

Consulates: US., 147 Meşrutiyet Cad., Tepebaşı (tel. 251 36 02). **U.K.,** 34 N. Meşrutiyet Cad. (tel. 244 75 40). **Australia,** 58 Tepecik Yolu (tel. 257 70 50). **Bulgaria,** 44 Zincirilkuyu Cad., (tel.

169 04 78 or 169 22 16). **Canada,** 107 Büyükdere Cad., Gayrettepe (tel. 172 51 74). **Ireland,** 26/ A Cumhuriyet Cad., Pegasus Ezi (tel. 146 60 25). **Greece,** 32 Turnacıbaşı, Galatasaray (tel. 245 05096). **Jordan,** 63 Valikonaği Cad., Nişantaşı (tel. 230 12 21). **Lebanon,** Teşvikye Cad. (tel. 236 13 65). **Syria,** 3 Silâhtar Cad., Nişantaşı (tel. 248 27 35). **Russia** 443 İstiklâl Cad., Tünel (tel. 244 26 10). **Yugoslavia,** 96 Vali Konağı Cad., Nişantaşı (tel. 248 10 04).

Currency Exchange: Banks' exchange counters open Mon.-Fri. 8:30am-noon and 1:30-5pm. Most don't charge a commission. **Imar Bankası,** 9 Divan Yolu in Sultanahmet (tel. 522 73 09), is open Saturdays but charges a 5% commission. Open Mon.-Sat. 9am-5pm. The exchange booths at the **Yeşilköy Airport** and the **main post office** are open 24 hrs. The exchange booth at the **Sirkeci train station** is open daily 8am-9pm, but accepts only cash. The best rates are given by private exchange companies; they will also change *lira* back into dollars without any questions. Try **Çetin Döviz Hizmetleri,** 39 İstiklâl Cad. (tel. 252 64 28/9) at the Taksim end of İstiklâl Cad. facing the French Cultural Center. Open daily 8am-7:30pm. Remember to keep your receipts; some banks will not change *lira* back into dollars even with a receipt (see the General Introduction).

American Express: Türk Express, 91 Cumhuriyet Cad., 2nd Floor (tel. 241 02 48), up the hill from Taksim Sq., handles business related to American Express, including lost AmEx checks and credit cards. Open Mon.-Fri. 8:30am-noon and 1-5:30pm. Their office in the Hilton Hotel lobby, Cumhuriyet Cad. (tel 232 95 58), deals only with travel arrangements. Open daily 8:30am-8pm. For additional services, go to **Koç American Bank,** 233 Cumhuriyet Cad. Money wired here without a fee if you accept Turkish *lira;* 1% fee for other currencies. To get a cash advance on your American Express card, you must have a personal check or know your account number and the address of your bank. Open Mon.-Fri. 8:45am-12:30pm and 1:30-4:30pm (card-holder services until 4pm).

PTT: İstanbul has 113 post offices, with the main branch at 25 Yeni Postane Sokak, 2 blocks southwest of Sirkeci train station. Stamp, telephone and currency exchange, and telegram services open 24 hrs. Crowded around midday. All PTTs accept packages; if a customs officer is not present, you will be directed to the **Kadıköy, Beyazıt,** or **Tophane** (on Rıhtım Cad.) offices. Packages over 2kg can be mailed from the **packet service** on the back side of the main PTT. Open Mon.-Sat. 8:30am-12:30pm and 1:30-5pm. The branch just off the western end of Taksim Sq. on Cumhuriyet Cad. is efficient for mailing packages or making long-distance calls. Open Mon.-Fri. 8am-8pm, Sat. 8am-6pm.

Telephones: Payphones are scattered throughout the city, and a few even work. All İstanbul numbers have 7 digits; occasionally you encounter a 6-digit number, but these are prefixed by the single digit intra-city area code. The **area code** for the European side north of the Golden Horn (Taksim, etc.) is 2, for the European side south of the Horn (Sultanahmet, etc.) is 5, and for Asian İstanbul (Kadıköy) is 3. **International calls** can be made at payphones in the Taksim and Central PTTs. Look for the yellow phones marked *Uluslararası* or *Milletlerarası,* which means international. (Calls to the U.S. take 10 large *jetons* per minute—stuff them into the machine quickly and vigorously.) **Collect calls** can be made to only the U.S., Canada, England, Italy, Holland, Spain, Sweden, and Japan. İstanbul's **telephone code** (if you're calling from outside) is 1.

Airports: Atatürk Airport has a terminal for domestic flights and one for international flights, 5km apart and connected by regular bus service. For flight information call 573 04 33. Both terminals are 30min. from downtown. **Türk Hava Yolları** ("THY," or Turkish Airlines) offers a $45 reduction to ISIC holders on domestic flights and various discounts depending on the destination and season. Call 248 26 31 for information. **Pakistan Air, Yugoslavian Air,** and **Romanian Air** usually sell the cheapest tickets to and from Europe, though service can be very spotty.

Trains: Haydarpaşa Station, on the Asian side (tel. 348 80 20). Ferries between the station and Karaköy pier #7 run every 30min. (50¢, schedule posted on the pier). The pier is about halfway between the Galata Bridge and the Karaköy tourist office, where all tickets for Asia can be purchased in advance at the TCDD office upstairs. The office accepts couchette reservations for Ankara (should be done two days in advance if possible—see Ankara section for more details. Trains also go to Edirne (2 per day, $3). Europe-bound trains leave from **Sirkeci Station** (tel. 527 00 51), in Eminönü. To: Sophia (daily, 6:30pm, $36); Athens ($46); and Munich (daily, summer 11pm, winter 10:15pm, $130). 10% student discounts for those under 27.

Buses: All buses leave from the chaotic **Topkapı Bus Terminal,** just beyond the city walls on Millet Cad. (terminal doesn't appear on maps; don't confuse this with the palace in the middle of town). From Sultanahmet, take any bus with Topkapı written on the side panel (45min., longer at rush hour). All bus companies have offices at Topkapı, and many have offices in Sultanahmet as well. Only **Varan Tours** (tel. 251 74 74) is licensed to operate throughout Western Europe. These two and **Derya Turizm** are licensed for Greece. Most bus companies are authorized to go to Eastern Europe. Beware: unlicensed companies often offer substantial discounts for Western European destinations and then abandon their passengers in Eastern Europe. Expect delays, inefficiency, licensing problems, and/or border hassles with all carriers. Agencies downtown are clustered on

Hüdavendigâr Cad., behind the Sirkeci Railway Station in Sultanahmet, and on İzmar Cad., off Ordu Cad. to the left just before the Aksaray intersection. Frequent buses to: Ankara (8hr., $7-20); Bursa (4hr., $4-8.50); İzmir (9hr., $11-22); Bodrum (13hr., $15-30); and Trabzon (20hr., $13-18).

Ferries: Turkish Maritime Lines, on the waterfront at Karaköy (tel. 244 02 07), just west of the Haydarpaşa ferry terminal—it's the building with blue awnings marked "Denizcilik İşletmeleri." Ferries to İzmir and Trabzon and points between ($20-25, meals not included). Luxury cruises to Venice and Antalya also available. For these longer trips make reservations as soon as your plans allow. Frequent local ferries to: Kadıköy and Haydarpaşa from Karaköy (50¢); to the Princes' Islands, Eyüp, and the Black Sea (on the Bosphorus tour) from Eminönü ($2 round-trip to islands, $6 for Bosphorus tour); and Yalova from Kabatas (2½hr.). The faster but more expensive seabuses run to: Yalova from Kabatas (1hr., $6); the Princes' Islands (10 per day, 20min., round-trip $6); and Bostanci from Karaköy (20min., $1.50).

English Bookstores: Aypa Bookstore, 19 Mimar Mehmet Ağa Cad. (tel. 517 44 92, open daily 8am-8pm), accepts Visa and Mastercard. **İstanbul Kitaplığı,** 5 Kabusakal Cad. (tel. 517 67 82) up the street from Aypa has interesting books on İstanbul and Turkey and also publishes the bimonthly magazine *İstanbul, The Guide* ($3.50) which includes updated information on everything from sports to restaurants. **Elit Haşet Yayınulık,** 465 Istiklal Cad. (tel. 249 10 06, open Mon.-Sat. 8:30am-6:30pm), a 7-minute walk from Taksim Sq., has paperbacks, all major guide books, and wonderful art books.

Laundromat: Hobby Laundry, 6/1 Caferiye Sok., part of Yücelt Hostel building. 1kg wash and dry $1.40. Count your socks. Open daily 9am-8pm.

Hospitals: American Hospital, Admiral Bristol Hastanesi, Nişantaş, Güzelbahçe Sok. (tel. 231 40 50). **German Hospital,** Sıraselviler Cad., Taksim (tel. 243 81 00).

Police: Tel. 266 66 66. Might not speak English.

Tourist Police: In Sultanahmet, at the beginning of Yerebatan Cad. behind the obelisk in the park across from the information office (24-hr. hotline 527 45 03 or 528 53 69). Open daily 9am-6pm. Very helpful. If you lose your passport, first go to your consulate, then to the Tourist Police after obtaining a citizen certificate

Accommodations and Camping

İstanbul's budget accommodations are concentrated in the **Sultanahmet** district. The area's mesmeric setting amid major sights seems ideal, but here İstanbul's Turkish aura is diluted by droves of backpackers and legions of carpet and leather merchants.

Prices in Sultanahmet range from $2.15 for a rooftop to $15 for a single. Rates go up in July and August. If you're willing to spend a little more, look at third- and fourth-class hotels in the adjacent **Lâleli** and **Aksaray** districts. Today, these districts are crawling with Romanian and Bulgarian tourists. Also, prostitution is on the rise in these districts due to an influx of sex-workers from Romania and the former Soviet republics. But nice places do exist in the area. West of the **Grand Bazaar** and **İstanbul University,** these two quarters cater to large European tour groups. Although scenically inferior, the area suits travelers who seek quieter, classier rooms. Singles cost $10-15. Walk west from the university along Ordu Caddesi and turn right on Fethibey Caddesi, just after the Lâleli Cami.

✗   **Yücelt Hostel,** 6 Caferiye Cad. (tel. 513 61 50 or 513 61 51), on the street at the left of Aya Sofya when you face the gate of the Aya Sofya mosque. Sensitive, sensible management and a great place to meet travelers. Relatively large rooms, and very safe. The attached cafeteria is mediocre and overpriced. Dorm room $4.50. Doubles $6 per person. Triples $5.25 per person. Showers included (shower time 8-11am and 6:30-9pm). Reservations required.

More Hostels: There are four roughly equivalent and very pleasant alternatives to the Yücelt Hostel. All are within 2 blocks of one another. The **True Blue Hostel,** 2 Akbıyık Cad., 2 blocks down from the entrance of Topkapı Palace, is very basic, but comfortable, with a friendly young owner. Dorm beds (4-6 people) $3. Doubles $5. The **Sultan Tourist Hostel II,** 3 Cankurtaran Akbıyık Cad. (tel 516 92 60), on the same street as the True Blue, has a comfortable lounge and garden. Crowded and international. Free hot showers. Beds in triple and quad rooms $4 each. Doubles $12.

Hotel Anadolu, 3 Salkım Söğüt Sok. (tel. 512 10 35). Going up Yerebatan Cad., take the first left after the Yerebatan Cistern. Rudimentary, well-kept rooms. Impressive view of the Aya Sofya

✗ from some rooms. Pretty garden and terrace. Roof $3. Singles $7. Doubles $11. Triples and quads $6 per bed.

✗ **Hotel Elit,** 14 Salkim Söğü Sok. (tel. 512 75 66) across the street from the Hotel Anadolu. Affable management. Dorms $4.30. Especially comfortable doubles $15, with shower $21.

✗ **Hotel Ema,** 18 Salkim Söğü Sok. Next door to the Elit Hotel. Singles $10. Vast doubles $15, with private bath $21. Triples with bath $25. Breakfast included.

✗ **Hotel Holiday,** 10 Divanyolu Cad. (tel 522 42 81 or 526 17 65), across from the information office. Big lounge and happy-go-lucky terrace. Doubles with phone $13, with shower $15. Beautiful triples with shower $6.50 per person.

Hotel Yörük, 35 İncirli Çauuş Sok. (tel. 527 64 76). Taje Şeftali Sok. across from the information office, then take the first left. Ugly but clean rooms. A restaurant in the basement. Singles $7. Doubles with shower $11.

✗ **Hotel Tay,** 6 Tevkifhane Sok. (tel. 517 69 09). Take Tevkifhane Sok. across the little park between Aya Sofya and the Blue Mosque. Comfortable, very clean, with a café-bar on the terrace. Doubles with shared bathroom $17.

Alp Guest House, 4 Adliye Sok. (tel. 517 95 70 or 518 57 28). Near the Old Prison. A bit expensive, but worth every penny. A family-run guest house with a superb view of the sea from the terrace. Spacious, spotless rooms. The owner goes out of his way to help the customers. You may be invited to join the family for a true Turkish dinner if you say you want to try Turkish cuisine. A lot of professors stay here. All rooms with bath. Doubles $30-40. Garden breakfast included. Reservations required.

Yusuf Guest House, 3 Kutlugün Sok. (tel. 516 68 78), across from the Old Prison, farther towards the Topkapı Palace. Very clean rooms and efficient management in a pink building. All rooms with showers. Roof $3. Dorm beds $8. Singles $17. Doubles $19. Breakfast included. Reservations suggested.

Hotel La Mirajz, #28 Lâleli Fethibey Cad. (tel. 511 24 45). Walking west from the University on Ordu Cad., turn right off Lâleli Fethibey Cad. Building has brown and white stripes—the other hotel with the same name on the door is more expensive. Singles $12. Doubles $14-18. Hot showers and breakfast included.

Camping: Londra Mocamp (tel. 560 42 00), 1km from the airport, along the noisy and nerve-grating highway to İstanbul. Stay here only if you are marooned at the airport. Facilities include cafeteria, bar, pool, and showers. $2.30 per person, $1 per tent. Two-person bungalows $15. Much more pleasant are **Ataköy Mokamp** (tel. 539 60 00) and **Yeşilyurt Kamping** (tel. 574 42 30), on Sahil Yolu near the villages. Two people and a tent $7.50.

Food

If you like eating, you'll love İstanbul. From the sandwich stands in the streets to the elegant seafood restaurants on the Bosphorus, you can count on high quality, kaleidoscopic variety, and reasonable prices. While Sultanahmet may be the best place to stay, it's not the premier eating locale—you'll fare much better in the **Kumkapı** district, south of the Grand Bazaar, the **Sirkeci** district near the train station, or the **Tepebaşı** quarter, near the British consulate. For a quick stand-up lunch, the numerous *kebapçıs* or *köfteci* will easily fill you up for less than $3. Stop at a *büfe* (snack shop) for grilled cheese and a soft drink (less than $1). Even a complete meal at a cheaper *lokanta* shouldn't run you more than $3.50. And for a little more you can order grilled seafood in the towns of **Sarıyer** or **Rumeli Kavağı**—a scenic bus (#25 from Eminönü) or ferry ride north along the Bosphorus. Although eating out is economical, you should also experience one of the **open-air fruit markets.** Two markets are centrally located: one in Tepabaşı, and another in the Mısır (Egyptian) Bazaar, near the New Mosque and Eminönü.

Sultanahmet Area

The restaurants along **Divan Yolu** serve typical but slightly overpriced Turkish cuisine.

Sultanahmet Köftecisi, 12 Divan Yolu (tel. 511 83 26) at the end of Divan Yolu across from the tourist office, caters to a local crowd. Cheap cheap. *Köfte,* salad, bread, and drink $2.50. Open daily 11am-11pm.

Vitamin Restaurant, 16 Divan Yolu (tel. 526 50 86). A wide variety of humongous dishes, including *patlıcan dolması* (stuffed eggplant), *mercimek çorbası* (lentil soup), and *kebap*. Meals $3-6. Open daily 7am-midnight.

Pudding Shop, #6 Divan Yolu (tel. 522 29 70), known as "the beginning of the hippie trail," from which 1960s wayfarers journeyed east towards Nepal, Oz, and beyond. Don't leave İstanbul without visiting this "world-famous" attraction. The appeal to the Flower Children seems elusive in today's cafeteria-style atmosphere, but the proof is in the pudding; chicken ($2), *kebap* ($1.75), and beer ($1). Open daily 7am-midnight.

Elef Restaurant (tel. 512 38 34), on Gedikpaşa Cad. and **İstanbul Restaurant,** 24 Gedikpaşa Cad. (tel. 522 94 58), a ½ block down from Divan Yolu near the University and Grand Bazaar, serve cheap, hearty meals. Both open daily 6am-11pm.

Altu Kupa, 6 Yerebatan Cad. (tel. 519 47 70), on the street across from the tourist office. Clean restaurant, tasteful decoration, tasty dishes. There is also a bar. Drinks $1.50-$2. Full meal, including ½-bottle of wine, about $9.

Sirkeci Area

Numerous places to eat along the small pedestrian side streets make this area look like one giant restaurant. In summer, almost all have tables outside. Coming from the train station on Ankara Cad., turn left after you pass Muradiye Cad. Restaurants are especially thick along İbni Kemal Cad. and İbikemal Cad. People plop down on random chairs and eat whatever is served there. Sit only where you see a posted menu. More-than-you-can-eat meals run $2.50-6. Try **Konyalı,** close to the sea, on the left when going downhill. Cheap, and with a take-out option. (Open Mon.-Fri. 8:30am-6:30pm.)

Kumkapi Area

South of the Grand Bazaar, this quarter looks onto the Sea of Marmara and takes on a carnival atmosphere in summer. From the Grand Bazaar, cross Divan Yolu and walk down Tiyatro Cad. until you reach Büyük Kömürcü Sok; follow this scrawny street to the small square **Kumkapı Meydanı,** which is lined with scads of ichthyological eating exploratoria. Prices vary daily; it all depends on the catch, but some restaurants are definitely more expensive than others. Check the menu before sitting down. One commendable choice is the **Gölçek,** Ördekli Bakkal Sok. #1 (tel. 519 40 33), on the square. Don't miss the rooftop terrace which almost has a view of the Sea of Marmara. Try the delicious, rather spicy *Karides Güveç* (shrimp casserole) for $3, or ask the waiter about the catch-of-the-day. Full meals run $7-10, more if you're not careful.

Tepebasi Area

Tucked away in the heart of the new city, just north of İstiklâl Cad. on Sahne Sok., is **Çiçek Pasajı** ("Flower Passage"; not to be confused with the restaurant of the same name on İstiklâl Cad. itself). A plethora of restaurants cluster in this glorified alleyway. Once it was mostly the local crowd who patronized the Passage, but today tourists traipse with glee. This foreign onslaught notwithstanding, the Passage still plays host to Turkish folk musicians and serves up a lively, festive atmosphere, and a cheap and tasty meal to boot. The neighborhood around the Flower Passage is pretty seedy, so be sure not to wander too far from the center core of restaurants. Most of the nightclubs in this area are run by hustlers, eagerly awaiting tourists from whom they can siphon money.

Mahzen Restaurant, (tel. 249 03 29)on the main throughfare of the Passage. A great place to start the evening. *Midye dolması* (stuffed mussels) and beer $2.50. Open daily noon-midnight.

Kimene Restaurant, (tel. 244 12 66)also on the main thoroughfare. The bland, overlookable decor belies the upbeat atmosphere. When the *rakı* starts flowing, local musicians begin serenading restaurant patrons. *Kebap*, salad, and rakı $5. Open daily noon-midnight.

Behind Çiçek Pasayı, many small fish shops and vegetable sellers fill the streets. Get out at Çiçek Pasayı's back door, follow the little shops and take the first right: this is **Meyhaneler Sokağı,** literally "the street of pubs," with its twentysomething *meyhane*.

Krependeki İmroz (tel. 249 90 73), at the end of Meyhaneler Sok. A modest restaurant, but dear to the heart of İstanbul's gourmets and boozers. If you want to try *rakı*, the national drink, this is the place to do it. A full meal with *rakı* for $10, more if you want to eat fish.

Yeni Rejans Restaurant, #15 Ikuvi Geçidi (tel. 144 16 10), offers Russian food right in the middle of İstanbul. Walking north on İstiklâl Cad., turn left at #244, and go down a small alleyway— it's next to the Victoria Kebap Restaurant. Founded in 1930, this place is truly an anachronism. Under high ceilings, an elderly waiter clad in a green tuxedo silently shuttles among dimly lit tables. Russian dishes include *borscht* ($1.15) and *beef stroganoff* ($4). Try their home-distilled lemon vodka. Open daily noon-3pm and 7-10pm.

İstiklâl Caddesi

A century ago, İstiklâl Caddesi was İstanbul's most fashionable street, brimming with posh tea shops, smart office buildings, and embassies. Even today, although dusty and traffic-choked, it maintains some grandeur as well as some worthwhile eateries.

Duran Sandwiches, 9 İstiklâl Cad. (tel. 243 52 31), right at the Taksim end of İstiklâl Cad. An unbelievable variety of sandwiches. Bite-size with special toppings 40¢, full sandwiches $1.60.

Hacıbaba, 49 İstiklâl Cad. (tel. 244 18 86 or 245 43 77), a little bit down from Duran. Original decorations from 1921. Excellent Turkish dishes for connoisseurs. Use the side entrance from Meşelik Sok. Soups $1.30, hors d'oeuvres $1.60, main course $3-4. Open daily 11am-midnight.

Borsa Fastfood, 89 İstiklâl Cad., serves fast food versions of classical dishes as well as the usual fast food fare. Everything $1-2. Open daily 10am-10pm.

Hacı Abdullah, 19 Sakızağcı Cad. (tel. 244 85 61). From İstiklâl Cad. take a right from the Ağacamii (the only mosque in the area). Though heavily touristed, this remains a local favorite. Ask for the special of the day, and don't miss the marinated artichokes in June (smells like victory; $2). Full meals about $8. Major credit cards accepted. Open daily 11am-10pm.

Sights

İstanbul's incomparable array of world-famous churches, mosques, palaces, and museums can keep an ardent sightseer busy for weeks. Three or four days of leg-work, however, should be enough to acquaint you with the premier sights.

Aya Sofya, or the Church of the Holy Wisdom, was built by the Emperor Justinian between 532 and 537 CE. Upstart plebeians had destroyed the previous edition of the edifice during the Nika Revolt; Justinian undertook construction of a new and improved church in order to cement imperial authority. Converted to a mosque after the Ottoman invasion in 1453, in 1935 it came to rest as a museum. The architecture originally reflected the class structure of Church services. Only the Patriarch was allowed to enter through the center doors. The side galleries separated less perfect souls from the emperor. The Ottomans opened the side galleries, thereby eliminating an important class distinction. An elaborate marble square in the floor by the altar marks the spot where Byzantine emperors were once crowned. The upstairs galley contains several of the church's elaborate mosaics. (Open Tues.-Sun. 9:30am-7pm; Sept.-June Tues.-Sun. 9:30am-4:30pm. Gallery open Tues.-Sun. 9:30am-noon and 1-4:30pm. Admission $4, with ISIC $2.) (See also the Art and Architecture section in the Turkey Introduction).

Sultan Ahmet I built the **Blue Mosque** (the Mosque of Sultan Ahmet I) opposite the Aya Sofya in a brazen attempt to one-up Justinian. The mosque's formidable silhouette is unforgettable, and the interior, with its stunning blue İznik tiles, is especially powerful. In its day, the mosque was most famous for the controversy over its six minarets— religious leaders didn't want the sultan to match the number of minarets at Mecca. Always resourceful, Ahmet averted the crisis by providing the money and workers necessary to build a seventh minaret at Mecca. Inside the Blue Mosque, iron bars running across the domes ensure that the whole structure bends in earthquakes—it has withstood 20 so far. You may visit the mosque at any time between 9am and 5pm, except during prayers (as is the case with most mosques); modest dress required (as is the case with *all* mosques). English-speaking Turks often loiter around the entrance during the day, eager to give potentially instructive freelance tours. Agree on the fee before the tour ($4 for up to four people is reasonable). Or you can circumvent the tour with a guide book about the mosque ($5).

To your right as you leave the Blue Mosque are the **Carpet** and **Kilim Museums** with carpets and woven *kilim* (flat-woven mats) from all over the Muslim world (open Tues.-Sun. 9am-5pm). This is definitely worth visiting if you are at all interested in picking up a carpet or *kilim* of your own. Keep in mind though that the finer tapestries cost 50-100% more in İstanbul than in the Anatolian provinces. In any case, you will probably see enough rugs to fray your cultural fiber as eager multitudes of carpet sellers carouse on the way to the **Mosaic Museum.** Inauspiciously located in the gallery of shops below the mosque, the museum features a spectacular hunting mosaic dating from the 6th century, when the entire area was part of the Byzantine Imperial Palace. (Open Wed.-Mon. 9:30am-5pm. Admission $1.30.)

On the other side of the Blue Mosque is the ancient **Hippodrome,** where Byzantine emperors once presided over chariot races and circuses. The tranquility of the park today is misleading: long ago it was the site of violent uprisings and demonstrations. In 532 CE, 30,000 people were massacred here as Justinian's troops put an end to riots that had leveled much of Constantinople. In the Hippodrome stand the granite **Egyptian Obelisk,** the upper part of an obelisk from the 15th century BCE which was brought to Constantinople in 390 CE, and the repti-helical **Serpentine Column,** taken from the Temple of Apollo at Delphi. The coarse column of unknown origin at the end of the Hippodrome was coated with bronze plates until obstreperous members of the Fourth Crusade tore off the metal.

Across from the Hippodrome and next to İstanbul's legal administration buildings is the 16th-century **Ibrahim Paşa Palace.** The magnificent building houses a museum of Turkish and Islamic art featuring tiles, Qur'ans, and an especially fine collection of carpets. The courtyard fulfills its duty with a picturesque tea house. (Open Tues.-Sun. 10am-5pm. Admission Tues.-Fri. $2, Sat.-Sun. $1.)

Walking back to Divan Yolu along Klodfarer Cad., you'll pass a small park opposite the Klodfarer Hotel. Underneath lies the 4th-century **Binbirdirek Cistern.** Knock on the door of the shack to ask for a flashlight-guided tour (tip the guide about $1.30; don't let them charge you much more). This cistern is bigger but doesn't compare aesthetically to **Yerebatan Cistern,** by the Aya Sofya, which is İstanbul's most mammoth underground reservoir still in use. Wooden walks allow you to wander through the 336 columns, eerily reflected in the shallow water. Soft music and mood lighting complete the experience. Don't miss it (you'll kick yourself later if you do). Underground waterways originally connected the cistern to the Topkapı Palace—the passage was blocked to stop the traffic of stolen goods and abducted women. (Open daily 9am-5pm. Admission $4, 75¢ with ISIC.)

From the mid-15th century until the mid-19th century, the **Topkapı Sarayı** was the nerve center of the Ottoman Empire. The grandiose façade and the fabulous interior awe even the dispassionate visitor. Since the various museum collections housed in Topkapı are so extensive, it's best to punctuate your tours inside the palace with time spent sunning on the terraces or reposing in the rose gardens. The palace, built by Mehmed II and originally the site of the Ottoman government and the Empire's most exclusive schools, was also the home of the Sultan and his sizable entourage of wives, eunuchs, and servants. Don't be overwhelmed by the seemingly endless attractions: try to see the **First Court,** and its huge East Asian porcelain collection; the **Treasury,** which houses an inestimable wealth of diamonds, emeralds, gold, and jade, as well as a collection of important religious artifacts (including a lock of Muhammad's hair and the hand of John the Baptist); and the **Harem** with its lush rooms and magnificent İznik-tiled walls. The **Circumcision Chamber,** too, is beautifully decorated blue with İznik tiles. According to Turkish tradition, males were circumcized not at birth (as prescribed by Islam), but after they had come of age (an exceedingly unpleasant option). In some of the more rural parts of Turkey, mothers chastise their sons by threatening to call the dreaded "circumcizer." To see the Harem, you must take a guided tour (3 per day in English; open Wed.-Mon. 10am-4pm, $1.30). Mozart's opera *Abduction from the Seraglio* is performed in the palace seraglio every summer during the **İstanbul International Festival** ($15; call 260 45 33 or 260 90 72 for further information). (Palace grounds open Wed.-Mon. 9:30am-5pm. Admission $2.15. Often thronged so go early.) For a more scholarly and historical look at the Topkapı Palace, consult Gulru Necipoglu's *Architecture, Ceremonial, and Power: The Topkapı Palace in the Fifteenth and Sixteenth Ceunturies.*

West along Divan Yolu, the enormous **Grand Bazaar** (Kapalı Çarşı) is a great place to visit but you wouldn't want to buy here. Hawkers prey on tourists (even looking and smelling like you've been swashbuckling for months won't ward them off) and fake or faulty merchandise is widespread. The summer tourist invasion inflates prices as much as 300-400%. Beware of glassy, bright *kayseri*— these shoddy imitations of Persian carpets are worthless (see the city of Kayseri section, p. 471, for advice on picking up a real carpet). Few Turks are naïve enough to buy anything here.

The old part of the Bazaar is a jumble of shops selling hookahs, bright baubles, copper filigree shovels, Byzantine-style icons reposing on red velvet, ancient Turkish daggers (made in Taiwan), silver flintlock guns with mother-of-pearl handles, onyx, jade, and plastic miniatures, shoe-shine kits of polished wood and brass, Farsi texts, chess sets, and hand puppets, among other treasures. The gold is mostly 14-karat, and contrary to rumor, no cheaper elsewhere in Turkey. (Bazaar open Mon.-Sat. 9am-7pm.)

To the west and adjacent to the Grand Bazaar is the smaller **Sahaflar Çarşısı** (used book market). Old medical and technical books predominate. You'll also come across hand-illustrated manuscripts, paintings, and a variety of posters at near-reasonable prices. The market opens onto a shaded tea garden, bustling with Turks, tourists, and pigeons. If you're lucky, a long-haired bearded guy will be sitting under the tree in the tea garden. He is Avni Dede, a poet and vendor of unusual trinkets. He also loves to talk to tourists. Opposite is the gate to İstanbul University and **Beyazıt Mosque,** the oldest standing in İstanbul.

Trace the walls of the university, to the right, as closely as you can, and turn left when you reach the school's rear grounds. Here stands the **Süleymaniye,** a complex including a mosque, seven *medreses* (religious schools), and the *türbe* (tombs) of Süleyman and his wife Haseki Hürrem. Exalted as one of the grandest accomplishments of the Ottoman chief architect Sinan, the complex was intended as a center for Islamic higher education. Enter from the south, under an elegant colonnaded gallery, to see the regal stained-glass windows deftly sift the morning light. It is said that there are buried treasures in the minarets. To the east of the mosque is a majestic courtyard; to the west is a phantasmagoric graveyard where Süleyman and Haseki Hürrem rest peacefully in opulent *türbe* drenched in blue İznik tile and diamond. (Tombs theoretically open Wed.-Sun. 9:30am-4:30pm. You may have to get the caretaker to let you in.)

Walking back to the Golden Horn from Süleymaniye, you'll pass through the noisy agglomeration of the **market quarter.** In the middle of this quarter, only 200m from the Horn, is **Rüstem Paşa Mosque,** whose interior, almost entirely inlaid with the standard, captivating İznik tiles, compensates for a humble exterior. Walking towards the Galata Bridge, you'll come to the pigeon-packed **Yeni Cami,** with its radiant, soaring interior; this "new mosque" was built in the 17th century.

The **Mısır Çarşısı** (Egyptian Bazaar), built as part of the Yeni Cami complex, exudes authenticity—it caters more to the needs of locals—and is, therefore, an agreeable alternative to the Grand Bazaar. Don't miss the bazaar's open courtyard, a wonderful pocketful of umbrage lined with cafés and *kebapçı.*

İstanbul's other great museums are down the hill from Topkapı—enter the gate marked "Archaeological Museum." Inside you'll find the **Çinili Köşk** (Tiled Pavilion), once a petite pleasure palace, but today a museum. The **Museum of the Ancient Orient** (with English labels) has an interesting smorgasbord of Hittite, Babylonian, Sumerian, Assyrian, and Egyptian artifacts. Among them are a tablet on which part of the Hammurabi Code is inscribed along with even older laws, and another featuring a peace treaty between a Hittite ruler and the Egyptian Pharaoh Ramses II. The **Archaeological Museum** displays a sizable collection of early Greek, Hellenistic, and Roman marbles and bronzes, including a famous sarcophagus with carvings of Alexander the Great. (All three museums open daily May-Sept. 9am-5pm, except the Çinili Köşk, which is closed Mon. and Fri. Admission $3.) The park on the ramparts of the Topkapı Museum, overlooking the Bosphorus and the Golden Horn, offers necessary respite from İstanbul's sweltering streets. (Open until sunset. Free.)

A mandatory stop for Byzantine-art connoisseurs is the impeccably preserved **Kariye Cami,** a long way up Fevzipaşa Cad., near the Edirne Gate (accessible by *dolmuş,* bus #39 or 86 from Sultanahmet, or any bus in the direction "Edirnekapı"). Having undergone the transition from Byzantine church to mosque, and from mosque to museum, the building showcases superb 14th-century frescoes and mosaics. The insouciance, realism, and expressiveness of this strain of late Byzantine art influenced Giotto and other early Italian painters. (Open Wed.-Mon. 9:30am-4:30pm. Admission $2.50. Bushels of scholarship on Italian art available at bookstores everywhere around the Kariye Cami.) From here you can see the ruined **Theodosian Land Walls,** which stretch from the Golden Horn to the Sea of Marmara. The sole character ever to have surmounted these looming ramparts, a construction of the early 5th century CE, was Mehmet the Conqueror, in 1453 when the Ottomans captured Constantinople.

A full day of rollicking and surly chaos, namely of the Old City, may leave your head imploding and your skin caked with several flavors of dirt. Luckily, the calming area north of the Golden Horn on the European side is less frenetic. The **Galata Tower,** built by the Emperor Justinian in 528 CE and rebuilt in 1348 by the Genoese as a low-tech spy satellite for observing the old city, still serves its purpose today. The tower was also the take-off site for the first intercontinental flight, executed in a Da Vinci-style hang glider. The view mustn't be missed. (Open 10am-8pm. Admission 80¢, students 40¢.) After hours, the tower degenerates into a pricey nightclub. ($40 for dinner, show, and drink. $20 without dinner. Yeah, right.) Right along the Bosphorus, **Dolmabahçe Palace** was the home of sultans from the mid-19th century until the demise of the Ottoman Empire after World War I. Goose-stepping soldiers guard the royal dock and the memory of Atatürk, who died in the palace at 9:05 (all the clocks were halted at that moment). The chi-chi pseudo-French architecture exhibits the sultans' eclectic pretensions during the decline of their empire. (Open Tues.-Sun. 9:30am-4pm. Admission $4.) To get to Dolmabahçe from Sultanahmet, take bus T4. From Eminönü, take bus #25. Number of visitors per day is limited so go early.

After an extended day of sight-seeing, a **cruise** along the **Bosphorus** may foster the salvation of your frayed nerves and the rejuvenation of your spirits. Boats leave from pier #3 in Eminönü at 10:30am and 12:30pm, and return from the Black Sea in the evening ($6). No evening tours of the Bosphorus are available, but you could always ride a ferry to one of İstanbul's northern suburbs on either the European or Asian shore of the Bosphorus (60¢). Areas such as **Arnavutköy** and **Bebek** on the European side of the Bosphorus boast numerous seafood restaurants which offer piscatory pleasures at proper prices. Bus #25 runs along the shoreline of the Bosphorus, through Bebek and many other small communities to the town of **Sarıyer.**

Entertainment

İstanbul shuts down early—few places are open after midnight. Travelers and other nocturnal creatures congregate in the restaurants and bars at the foot of Divan Yolu Cad. The **Café Bodrum,** just off Divan Yolu at the foot of the Aya Sofya, draws a lively crowd. (Open daily 7:30pm-midnight. Beer $1.) Trek up to the **Çiçek Pasajı** (see Food above) to enjoy an evening of piquant food, potent drink, and traditional Turkish music. *Rakı,* a licorice-flavored spirit nicknamed "Lion's Milk," gushes freely in the many taverns of the "Flower Passage." A few rag-tag musicians and one or two gypsy dancers often perform in the courtyard. Alternatively, venture to Lâleli or Beyazıt and spend the evening at a Turkish tea house. **Ali Paşa's Bazaar,** a 16th century courtyard near the entrance to the Grand Bazaar on Divan Yolu Cad., is a great place to slurp a glass of delicious Turkish tea, meet some locals, and smoke a *nargile* (water pipe). Don't smoke dope in it though; Turkish anti-drug laws are taken very seriously (see Planning Your Trip: Safety and Security).

Whatever you've heard about the straight or gay **nightclubs** off İstiklâl Cad., north of the Horn, definitely *avoid* going. Most will vacuum you clean out of money with a tacky flash of neon and a twist of a swizzle stick. This area is also a popular hangout for thieves. The nightclubs north of Taksim Square along Cumhuriyet Cad. are a bit more respectable, but the choking price of your first drink may make you thunk yourself on the head for not having stayed at home. If you must swing in İstanbul, try **Hayal Bar** (tel. 244 25 58), near the Taksim side of İstaklal Cad., on Büyükparmakkapı Soq. (drinks $2-3). **Belly-dancing** may sound tantalizing, but the price will leave you belly-aching. Inquire at the tourist office if you're still interested—locations change frequently.

For a truly authentic **Turkish bath,** it is best to go to the nearby cities of Edirne and Bursa. However, İstanbul baths can provide a reprieve for the down and dirty. The much-publicized **Çağaloğlu Hamamı** (tel. 522 24 24) in Sultanahmet on Yerebatan Cad. is a celebration for the aesthetic epicurean but should be avoided if you are even minimally claustrophobic. Instead, try the **Mercan Örücüler Hamamı,** 32 Uzun Çarşı Cad., just outside the **Orücüler Kapısı** (Gate) of the Grand Bazaar (tel. 527 92 63). Although somewhat expensive (self-service bath $4, massage $4), the penetrating steam, immaculate chambers, and dearth of tourists make this a worthwhile deal. Before indulging in baths, female travelers should know that this Turkish tradition, like many others, is male-oriented: most *hamamı* have lesser facilities for women (no private changing rooms, fewer masseuses, etc.).

The **İstanbul Festival,** an international festival in its 21th year, unfurls with a flourish in June and July. In the past, performers have ranged from Konya's Whirling Dervishes to Joan Baez. Ask at the tourist office or call 260 45 33 or 260 90 72 for more information. The **Sound and Light Show** at the Blue Mosque is corny and soporific, but offers a gasply view of İstanbul's illuminated minarets and domes. (Daily at 9pm. In English every 4th night. Schedule posted at tourist office. Free.)

Near Istanbul

Eyüp, a popular Muslim pilgrimage site, houses the 15th-century tomb of the eponymous companion of Muhammad who died during an Arab siege of the city in the 7th century. The Golden Horn ferries ride the waves twice hourly from pier #6 in Eminönü, above the Galata Bridge (35min., 40¢). Islam has influenced many Turks in Eyüp. You may see nervous, regally costumed young boys brought here by their families; the trip is customary for İstanbul boys before circumcision. Climb the hill above the cemetery for a glimpse at the joyously protruding Golden Horn.

Another ferry line goes to the **Princes' Isles,** leaving from Eminönü or Beşiktaş on the northern side (hourly departures until 11pm, $2). The ferry stops at four of the nine islands of this minute suburban archipelago. Beauty soaks the scenery, overdevelopment takes a conspicuous leave of absence in towns, and best of all, cars are nowhere. You can tour an island by horse-drawn carriage; be sure to bargain over the fare. Some people prefer the quieter atmospheres of **Burgazada** and **Heybeliada,** but **Büyükada,** the largest and most picturesque of the islands, offers the best swimming (at Yörükali beach) in the İstanbul area (and this, sadly, is not all that great). In Heybeliada, take a horse-carriage to Değirmen for a picnic (fix the price beforehand).

Edirne

Though an easy *dolmuş* ride from the Greek and Bulgarian borders, Edirne is in many ways the consummate Turkish city. Without the tourists and hustle of İstanbul, the city still claims some of the finest examples of Ottoman architecture in the country. Wander down some of its cobblestone streets, lather up in an inexpensive *hamamı,* or visit what many consider the most beautiful mosque in the country.

The quiet city of today hides an eventful past. Named Hadrianopolis after the Roman Emperor Hadrian in the second century CE, the city witnessed the catastrophic defeat of the Roman army by the Goths 200 years later. The Ottomans pacified the city and made it the capital of their empire from 1363 until soon after the fall of Constantinople in 1453. In the Empire's final days, the city was occupied no less than four times as Bulgaria, Greece, Russia, and Turkey struggled for control of the Balkans. Today, Edirne assaulted by Romanian and Bulgarian "tourists" pillaging Levis and Sony Walkmans from the thousands of shops throughout the city.

Practical Information, Accommodations, and Food

Edirne throbs around **Hürriyet Square** at the intersection of Talatpaşa Cad., the main east-west thoroughfare, and Saraçlar Cad., the cobblestoned north-south avenue. Three imposing mosques crowd the center of town: the magnificent **Selimiye Cami** just uphill from the square, the **Üç Şerefeli Cami** (Mosque with Three Galleries), and the smaller **Eski Cami** (Old Mosque) poised between the main urban bus stop above and the *dolmuş* depot below. *Dolmuş* run regularly between this depot and the **bus station,** a few km from the center along the road to İstanbul (15¢). **Edirne Bırlık** bus company is the most reliable. Buses depart hourly to İstanbul (4hr., $6), and Keşan (2hr., $2.75). Buses also run to Bursa (2 per day) and Ankara (2 per day). Competition between bus companies sometimes reduces the fares to under $2. Two **train stations** serve Edirne, one on the road to İstanbul (tel. 114 12), and one in **Kapıkule,** within walking distance of the Bulgarian border. (To get to Kapıkule, take a *dolmuş* from behind Eski Cami ($1, every 10min.). Kapıkule is the last stop). Two trains per day travel to İstanbul ($5 and less efficient than the bus). One train per day travels to and from Europe (arriving from Munich early in the morning and leaving late at night). Buy your ticket at the Kapıkule station. The **Bulgarian Consulate** is located in two long blocks south-east of the Eski Cami on the road towards İstanbul. The consulate sometimes delivers visas in as little as one hour, depending on what side of the bed they got up on (transit visas $7 at consulate, $9 at border, although officers are known to extort extra money; open Mon.-Fri. 9am-noon. Prices change often and can be checked at the tourist office). Call 152 40 for the **tourist police.** The **tourist office,** 17 Talatpaşa Ca. (tel. (9181) 115 18) about 200m west of the Eski Cami gives out free maps (open daily 8:30am-6:30pm; Sept.-May Mon.-Sat. 8:30am-6:30pm). The staff is extremely helpful and friendly; these people are bored and would do anything for the rare tourist not from Romania or Bulgaria. They also cash American Express and Thomas Cook traveler's checks for a 1% commission. The **post office** at 17 Saraçlar Cad. has **telephones** and a 24-hr. **currency exchange.**

For a place to stay, try the hotels on Maarif Cad., off Hürriyet Sq., just down the street from the tourist office. The **Konak Hotel,** 6 Maarif Cad. (tel. 113 48), is a beautiful old wooden house built in the 1870s. It has rooms with sinks (Singles $4. Doubles $3.50 per person. Quads $3 per person. Hot baths $1.40, cold baths 70¢). The **Anıl Hotel,** 8 Maarif Cad. (tel. 217 82), has spacious rooms rooms and a talkative owner ($4 per person. Baths $1.15). The **Hotel Aksaray** (tel. 260 35), Maarif Cad., just down the street from the Anil Hotel, occupies a beautifully restored Ottoman house. It has large carpeted rooms with radios and phones. (Singles with sinks $6. Doubles $10, with bath $13. Triples $17.50). The Ministry of Culture has declared this hotel a historical site. Not convinced? Check out the ceiling decorations in rooms 101 and 103.

Fifi Camping, E5 İstanbul Cıkışı 9th km (tel. 115 54) sits on a green lawn without any big trees ($2 per person, tents $2). Take a *dolmuş* from the bus station, and ask to be let off at the campsite (50¢). Amenities include a tempting swimming pool and bus service to town (free for guests). Shower and electricity are included in the price. If you mention that you are a student, you may get an unofficial discount.

Edirne's restaurants are nothing special. **Saraçlar Caddesi,** with restaurants everywhere, offers the usual selection of Turkish grilled meat and stuffed vegetable dishes. Have a complete meal for less than $3. Fried liver is a local specialty, as is *badem ezmesi* (sweet almond paste) for dessert. The **Meshur Lâle Köfteçi,** Esat Paşa Cad. (tel. 118 28) just off Saraçlar Cad., nourishes a steady stream of hungry locals.

Sights

Edirne's mosques run the gamut of Islamic architectural styles. Coming into town, it's difficult to miss the distinctive silhouette of the **Selimiye Cami** built by the Ottoman architect Sinan (completed in 1579). This enormous mosque with its 71m minarets (the tallest in the Middle East) and 999 windows exemplifies symbolic geometric counterpoint. Behind the mosque, a museum features *fez* from the Whirling Dervishes, medieval armor, weaponry, and doldrums. (Open Tues.-Sun. 8:30am-noon and 1-5:30pm. Admission 30¢, free for ISIC holders). The **Üç Şerefeli Cami** (completed in

1447) and the understated **Eski Cami** (completed in 1415) each merit a short visit. The octagonal design of the Üç Şerefeli Cami marks an important transition towards the peculiarly Ottoman style of architecture. The coffee house behind the Üç Şerefeli Cami provides a quiet corner to sip your tea and relax. The **Beyazıt Cami** rests about 1km north of town; take a city bus from Eski Cami in the direction of "Yeni imaret" or "Yıldırım," or walk down the road which bears left past Üç Şerefeli Cami, marked by a yellow sign. The mosque was used in the 15th century as a sort of religious hospital where the Ottomans treated physical and psychological diseases with water, music, and prayers. Mosques can be visited during daylight hours, but avoid entering during services. Head scarves for women hang just inside the entrance to each mosque.

After ogling the mosques, visit Edirne's biggest bazaar, the **Ali Paşa Bazaar,** designed by Sinan, which runs along the top of Saraçlar Cad (Open 8:30am-7:30pm). The low prices, superior service, and inspiring architecture may beckon you to sprawl out in reverie at one of Edirne's Turkish baths. Try Sinan's 16th-century **Sokullu Hamamı,** beside Üçşerefeli Cami. (Open daily 6am-midnight for men, 9am-6pm for women; $1.75, with massage $5, but bargain.)

On the second or third weekend in June, Edirne hosts its annual **Kırkpınar Wrestling Tournament,** in which young, brawny men grease up and grapple. The tournament is said to have begun in the early Ottoman period, when two hulks vying for local supremacy wrestled in the fields outside the town. Both dropped dead in the cataclysmic juggernaut of their surging manhood (it was a stalemate). Every year since, a match has been held to commemorate this heroic event. Check for the exact dates at any tourist office. Tickets can be purchased in Edirne at the **Belediye** (town hall) across from the Eski Cami or at the Sarayiçi stadium north of the town's center where the events are held. (Tickets for Fri. preliminaries $1, Sat., $4, Sun. finals $10. 3-day pass, $12.50.) Beds are hard to come by during the Tournament: phone ahead. The tournament has inspired a vaguely obscene statue in the town center, as well as a room in the museum behind Selimye Cami displaying pictures of famous wrestlers, some of their personal belongings, and a history of oil wrestling.

Bursa

Osman, the founder of the Ottoman (Osmanlı) dynasty, besieged Bursa for nearly a decade, but entered the city only after his death: in 1326 his son, Orhan, interred Osman's body in the palace grounds. Bursa became the capital of the blooming empire, though Edirne usurped that distinction 75 years later. Today Bursa has a paradoxical identity as both an industrial center and a wealthy resort area. Money pumps into the city as steadily as the sulphurous waters flow into its thermal baths, and people here seem quite contented with this state of affairs. Modernity in Bursa moves at a pleasant pace. The deep green Uludağ Mountain, home of Turkey's leading ski resort, endows the city, settled at its base, with more color and animation. The greatest attractions here are the well-preserved Ottoman monuments scattered throughout the city and the myriad thermal baths in the **Çekirge** (Grasshopper) district. In 1991 Bursa won the "coveted" Eurocity prize for its fast and successful development.

Bursa is accessible by express ferry from Karaköy in İstanbul (Mon.-Fri. 5 per day, $3.50). On weekends the express ferry launches from Kartal on İstanbul's Asian coast. A slow ferry leads to Bursa from Kabataş near the Dolmabahçe Palace in İstanbul (8 per day, $2). Early ferries, leaving at 8:30 or 9am, beat the crowds. The ferries land in Yalova, where you can hop a *dolmuş* or bus to Bursa (every 30min., $1.25). The entire trip takes about 3½ hours. There is also seabus service to Yalova and Bostancı. uses to Bursa from İstanbul depart from Topkapı (hourly, 4 hr., $8.50-12 depending on the company). Kamıl Koç is more expensive than other companies, but it is safer and more reliable as well. Convenient bus routes connect Bursa to Ankara, İzmir, and other big cities. To get to the center of town, take a *dolmuş* marked "Heykel" from the bus station (30¢) and get off at Ulu Cami (Great Mosque). To get to the **main tourist office** go to the Ulu Cami side of Atatürk Caddesi, walk toward the *heykel* (a huge statue of Atatürk), pass the big fountain and go down the stairs on your left (tel. 21 23 59; open

June-Sept. daily 8:30am-noon and 4-7pm; Oct.-May Mon.-Fri. 8:30am-noon and 1-5pm). Their map is lousy, but they won't bite. A new tourist office has opened in the bus station, and it has the same hours. The **post office,** across the street from Ulu Cami, (open Mon.-Sat. 8:30am-noon and 1:30-5pm) has **currency exchange** and cashes traveler's checks. Bursa's phone codes are 24 and 25.

Accommodations, Camping, and Food

If you must stay in the noisy and distant area around the bus station, try the de-frilled **Otel Ozendim** (tel. 14 94 71) directly across from the depot at 135 Garaj Karşısı. (Singles $6.50. Doubles $6.70 per person. Triples $3.80 per person. Quads $3 per person. Hot showers $1.10.) The **Hotel Uğur,** #27 Tahtakale Cad. (tel. 21 19 89), has a central courtyard in traditional Turkish style, where time seems to pass slower. Though small, the rooms are zestfully clean, and the management is friendly. From the post office across the street from the fountain, take the third left off Atatürk Bul., go up 1 block, turn right and follow Tahtakale Cad. up the hill. The *muezzin's* call to prayer (five times a day) of the nearby mosque may prove disturbing. (Singles $2.60. Doubles $2 per person. Triples $1.65 per person. Quads $1.10 per person. No hot water, cold shower 60¢.) Down the street at #19, **Otel Deniz** (tel. 22 92 38) is more expensive, but graced with an unexpected decadence: hot showers on demand. (Singles $5. Doubles $7. Shower included.) The **Otel Bilgiç,** 30 Basak Cad., third right on Atatürk Bul. from the post office, is even more luxurious. Even the rooms without showers have toilets of their own. (Carpeted singles $9, with bath $13. Doubles $12, with bath $20. Hot water 4 hrs.) The **Hotel İpekçi,** Çancılar Cad. (tel. 21 19 35) is typical 1960s-Turkish-hotel: dark hallways and clean but spare rooms. (Singles with sinks $7.50, with shower $9.50. Doubles with sinks $11.50, with shower $13. Triples with sink $13, with shower $20.) From the information office, walk toward the *heykel,* take a left from Atatürk Cad. to Osmangazi Cad., then the third right to Çancılar Cad. On the top of Uludağ, **Millıpark Camping** (tel. 14 52 81) charges $3.50 per person, $2.50 per tent. (See Sights for directions to cable car.)

İskender kebap, an excellent Turkish dish made of ram with a rich sauce of tomatoes and butter, originated right here in Bursa. Naturally, several restaurants named "İskender Kebap" specialize in this dish; they cluster in the area between the Atatürk statue and the Green Mosque. **Kebabçı İskender,** one on 58 Atatürk Cad. after the tourist office when going towards the *heykel,* and another behind the *heykel,* is the originator and the most famous but it is overcrowded and expensive (tel. 21 10 76). For an excellent meal, try **Bursa 2** down the street from the tourist office, by the Orhan Gazi Mosque (*İskender kebap* $4, Visa and Mastercard accepted). Besides these famous joints, many small and cheaper restaurants are scattered throughout the area. Besides the big famous *İskender Kebapçıs,* all the prices in this area are about the same: $3.25 for a full meal. Locals highly recommend **Gumuş Kebapçı** on Gumuşçeken Cad., a block down from Atatürk Bul. **Rodop Izgara Salonu,** 93 Atatürk Cad., across from the Great Mosque (tel. 21 68 63), offers a full meal for $2. Picnickers can stock up in the market on Tahtakale near the budget hotels. Bursa's **Kültür Parkı** (take a *dolmuş* from Heykel, 30¢) harbors some decent restaurants and is a fountain of generally elusive alcoholic beverages (as well as concerts and plays).

Sights

Bursa's tourist route stretches from the Yeşil Cami in the east to Çekirge's thermal baths in the west. In spite of their names, the famous **Yeşil Cami** (Green Mosque) and **Yeşil Türbe** (Green Mausoleum) actually seem blue to many. Spangled inside and out in rich turquoise, cobalt blue, and occasionally green İznik tiles, the structures are truly sights to savor. Before the capital was moved to Edirne in 1402, the mosque served both religious and administrative functions for the Empire, as well as occasionally housing the sultan and his family. Across the way, finely carved wooden doors and small stained glass windows accentuate Yeşil Türbe's handsome turquoise interior. The large postcard stand nestled snugly in the tomb of Mehmet I and his children is a more recent enhancement. The **Turkish and Islamic Art Museum,** including the **Ethnographic Museum,** is nearby. (Mausoleums and museums open Tues.-Sun. 8am-noon and 1-5pm, Mon. 1-5pm. Admission for museum $1.30; students 30¢, but if you insist and there are not many people around, they let you in for free.)

Built in the Turkish style common before the conquest of Constantinople, the **Ulu Cami** (Great Mosque) diverges from the popular Aya Sofya designs of İstanbul. The rectangular layout and numerous supporting columns characterize the Seljuk style of architecture. Scholars believe the nearby intricately carved wooden *minbar* (pulpit) represents an astrological chart.

The mosque was built by Beyazıt to commemorate his victory in Nicopolis in 1396. It is said that Beyazıt had vowed to build 20 mosques if won the war but once victorious he built just the Ulu Cami with its 20 domes (a lousy trick to play on God). While the Ulu Cami was under construction, two builders, Hacivat and Karagöz, so entertained fellow workers with jokes, skits, and stories that progress on the temple became delayed. To speed things up, Mehmet I had the pair executed, then in a fit of remorse immortalized them, oddly enough, in puppet form. The Punch and Judy of Turkey, Hacivat and Karagöz can be seen on puppet stages throughout the country to this day. By the tomb of Hacivat and Karagöz, Şeyh Küşteri, a small theater, provides free shows nightly during the **Bursa Festival** in June and July. Also during the festival, international folk-dance troupes come to Bursa to perform. In June and September, you can witness the silk production for which Bursa is famous. The brilliantly dyed and patterned material, *ipek,* can be purchased in the **Kapalı Çarşı Bazaar** or **Koza Han** by the tourist office for $4-20 per square meter.

For more information on Karagöz, visit the **Karagöz Antique Shop** in Eski Aynalı Çarşı, down the hill from the tourist office (tel. 21 87 27). The shop is full of genuine handicrafts for all budgets. The owner, Şinasi Çelikkol, is full of Karagöz lore. He puts up little Karagöz shows in his shop and also provides guided tours to authentic Turkish villages, handicraft shops, and silk factories. He does not like to talk about money, but he expects you to pay or buy something in return for the entertainment. Talk to him in advance and learn about the prices. To go to the **Eski Kaplıca** bathing complex built by Justinian in the 6th century (tel. 35 30 00), take the Çekirge *dolmuş* and get off at Kervansaray Hotel (50¢). The Eski Kaplıca will be on the right when you face the hotel (open daily 7am-11pm. Men $4.20, women $3. Massage $3). After a long day of travel, ask for the "special washing": a hard massage with special gloves ($3). They'll show you all the dirt they get off of you afterwards. Just past the Kültür Parkı and down the hill to the right, a short *dolmuş* ride will take you to the **Yeni Kapıca** bathing complex built by Süleyman the Magnificent in 1555. Three adjacent baths (one per sex and one for families), fed by natural thermal springs, feature cavernous bathing pools. (Men $3 for 1st class bath, $2 for 2nd class; women $2. Open daily 6am-10pm.)

To reach the **Uludağ Mountain cable car** station, take a *dolmuş* marked "Teleferik" (30¢) from the Kafkaf pastry shop on Atatürk Cad., 2 blocks past the statue. The cable car runs every hour on the hour from 9am to 9pm to the mid-station ($1.75 round-trip), and every hour on the half hour from the mid-station to a small town perched 2000m up the mountain ($3.50 round-trip). Be prepared for a dose of chill, sudden changes of weather and exorbitant hotels. Terrific skiing lasts from late December until mid-March. The park provides beautiful trail and plenty of hiking opportunities (50¢ entrance fee). Beware of wolves, packs of wild dogs, and other terrifying creatures.

Iznik

"The history of İznik," as the tourist-office brochures aptly put it, "is very old." One of Alexander the Great's generals, Lysimachus, first named the city after his wife, Nicaea. The Romans later invaded (as was their wont) and built walls, theaters, and baths. Under the Byzantine empire, Nicaea hosted the First Ecumenical Council in 325 CE. Pressured by the Emperor Constantine, the assembly of bishops accepted the Nicaean Creed, which stated that God and Christ were one. Six more councils convened throughout Asia Minor to clear up debates. The last Council, called to resolve the issue of iconoclasm in 787 CE, returned to Nicaea and met in the Aya Sofya church. After brief flirtations with the Crusaders and the Seljuks, İznik fell under Ottoman rule in 1331 CE. A porcelain industry developed and thus began the production of the renowned İznik blue tiles.

For two months in the summer, tourists and vacationers fill the few lakeside motels and tea gardens of this otherwise drowsy town. The ruins here are in no way monumental, but the verdant hills and orchards, diversity of structures, and soothing waters of Lake İznik will certainly engage you for a day or two. İznik also makes a good daytrip from Bursa.

Practical Information, Accommodations, and Food

Buses and *dolmuş* make the bumpy trip to and from Bursa every half-hour or so during the day (1½hr., $1.40). There are also two or three buses per day to Ankara and İstanbul; *dolmuş* run to the ferry landing at Yalova ($1.40, or hop off the bus to İstanbul at Yalova, $1). With your back to the ticket offices at the bus station, walk three blocks to the right and then turn right onto Kılıçaslan Cad. to reach the **tourist office** (tel. 719 33; open Mon.-Fri. 8:30am-noon and 1-5:30pm). Kılıçaslan Cad. and Atatürk Cad. separate İznik into quarters and meet in the center at the Aya Sofya church. The lake is at the west end of town. The **telephone code** is 252.

The **İznik Pansiyon** (tel. 712 65) has a few comfortable rooms in a homey atmosphere. ($4 per bed, 3 beds per room. Hot showers and kitchen facilities included.) From the center of town, walk 500m toward the lake and turn right. The *pansiyon* is visible from the beach. Just across the street, the **Murat Pansiyon** (tel. 733 00) has triples for $16 (hot shower and kitchen facilities included). These *pansiyons* fill up quickly so call ahead. The **Babacan Otel** (tel. 712 11) on Kılıçaslan Cad. in the center of town has spacious doubles for $14, with a ping-pong table and the *bar amerikan* on the top floor. The **Tencan Aile Pansiyon** (tel. 714 41), 15km from İznik on the road to Bursa (catch a ride on a *dolmuş)* has triples and quads for $9-10. The **Nicaea Mocamp,** 200m to the left of Kılıçaslan Cad., has slightly overpriced bungalows on the beach for $9 (sleeps 3-4, no hot water). Some discreetly snooze in the open air on the bumpy beach; although the authorities may not bother you, the riff-raff probably will.

The *lokantası* (restaurants) along the lake occupy a glorious spot—and they charge for it. Try the viewless **Konak Lokantası, Kosk Lokantası,** or the **Ergun Lokantası:** all beneath the trees on Kılıçaslan Cad. in the center of town with interchangeable fare.

Sights

The **Aya Sofya** (Sancta Sophia) at the town's central intersection was built in the fourth century by the Byzantines, and converted into a mosque in 1331 by Osman, the founder of the Ottoman dynasty. Notable features include the mosaic floor and a mural of Mary and Jesus. (Open daily in the summer, 9am-6pm. Admission 70¢, 35¢ with ISIC.) The aging **Murat Hamamı** (Turkish bath) just south of the Aya Sofya, still offers baths. (Men only. Open daily 6:30am-1pm and 2-6:30pm. $2.) The **Yeşil Cami** (Green Mosque), close to the tourist office, was built by architect Haci Musa in 1378 CE. The green bricks that decorate the minaret were precursors of the celebrated İznik tiles. Murat I constructed the **Nilüfer Hatun İmareti,** across the street from the mosque, to honor his mother, the first Christian wife of an Ottoman sultan. The **museum** that now resides there briefly traces the history of İznik tile-making. In the winter, museum officials have the keys to: the Aya Sofya; a 4th-century underground **baptismal spring;** and a **catacomb,** intricately decorated with Byzantine murals, 4km out of town. (Taxi to catacomb $5. $2 donation expected at the museum.) Look for the Roman **obelisk** to the left of the catacomb. The **Roman Theater,** the several mosques around town, and the four major and 12 minor gates in the walls are all worth a visit, too.

İznik's *faïence* industry has not yet died. A modern-day tilemaker often lets visitors watch his work within a few blocks of the town center, at #26 behind a white wall punctuated with a blue İznik tile. Tiles and plates ($10 and up) are for sale in small shops along the main street (ask directions to the *firm,* or kiln).

AEGEAN COAST

With its incomparable collection of classical ruins and sinuous coastline that conceals a huddle of sublime beaches, the once tranquil Aegean Coast of Turkey is now frenetic with tourism. Carpet shops and discos are slowly choking out traditional Turkish bazaars and teahouses, transforming such resorts as Kuşadası and Bodrum into lollipopular tourist traps. The Aegean Coast's natural beauty and five millennia of history are captivating, but don't come here to observe an authentic Turkish community: you can only find that farther east, where fewer tourists venture.

Long ago, a tourism of sorts began here when the ancient Greeks established ports in the area. As Alexander the Great and subsequent Hellenic rulers pushed the empire eastward, those ports became the nerve centers of commerce along the major trade routes of the ancient world, burgeoning even as Greek civilization declined. Today, Hellenistic ruins, especially extensive at Pergamon, Ephesus, Aphrodisias, and Hierapolis, stand as weathered testaments to the coast's noble classical heritage.

Scholarship followed commerce to Asia Minor. Thriving trade necessitated exposure to Eastern cultures and languages. Western philosophy, mathematics, and science—particularly in the teachings of Heraclitus of Ephesus and in the works of Thales, Anaximander, Anaximenes, and Anaxagoras, all scholars in the Ionian school of Miletus—burst forth from the rocket of Hellenic civilization. The Apostle Paul's proselytizing mission sparked the pyrotechnic transmission of Christianity that culminated in Emperor Constantine's conversion in 323 CE, which then gave rise to the Holy Roman Empire. Islam has been the major religion here for the last 600 years, but a large Christian population survived until 1923 (when populations were exchanged). Christian pilgrims continue to converge here to visit the seven churches of Asia Minor, referred to in *Revelations:* Pergamon, Thyatira, Smyrna, Sardis, Philadelphia, Laodicea, and Ephesus.

The cross-over from Turkey to Greece, although somewhat problematic, is no great impediment to travel plans. No legal barriers prevent tourists from traveling from the Greek islands to Turkey, though travelers have reported complications and arbitrarily exorbitant port taxes. Charter-flight travelers to Greece who venture to Turkey should beware of the stringent minimum-stay penalties imposed by the Greek government. Consult the charter company, your travel agent, and the General Introduction portions of this volume before planning such excursions.

Çanakkale, Gelibolu (Gallipoli), and Truva (Troy)

Blessed with comfortable and inexpensive accommodations, **Çanakkale** is an easy base from which to explore Gelibolu and Truva. Buses arrive here every 1-2 hours from Bursa (5½hr., $6), Edirne (change at Keşan, 4hr., $7), İstanbul (5hr., $9), and İzmir (5hr., $7). From the bus station, take a left out the main doors, then your next right onto Demircioğlu Cad. (following the "ferribot" sign), and continue onto the docks. The town clocktower and the **tourist information office,** 67 İskele Meydanı (tel. (196) 111 87) will be on your left just before the land plunges into the sea. (Open Mon.-Fri. 8:30am-8pm, Sat.-Sun. 8:30am-noon and 1:30-8pm; off-season Mon.-Fri. 8:30am-noon and 1:30-5:30pm.) Since competition among establishments can be fierce here, it very well may be worth your effort to try striking a bargain; just name a price to start the bidding.

Most budget accommodations can be found in the area surrounding the clocktower. **Hotel Konak** (tel. 111 50), behind the clocktower to the left, has clean rooms, some with private bathrooms. (Singles $4, with shower $5. Doubles $7, with shower $9. Triples $9, with shower $11. Quads $11. For free hot showers, get the key from reception.) A little farther down, on the left, the **Hotel Efes** (tel. 132 56) offers colorful and airy singles for a mere $4, with private shower $5. Doubles $7, with private shower $8.50.) The **Çanakkale Öğrenci Yurdu,** on Atatürk Cad. (tel. (12906) 130 51), 20min. from the center of town, rents beds in a plain dormitory for 80¢ for students, $1.10 for teachers. (No joke. For students and teachers only—ID required.) From the bus station, hang a left and walk for 10-15 minutes—it's just past the archaeological museum. Ask for the "müdür" (director); it's best to call ahead and make sure they are not repairing the building (they do it every year).

You will find fresh seafood in restaurants along the quay. Try **Yeni Entellektüel Restaurant** for fresh *lüfer* ("learned" bluefish), salad, and a beer ($5). Cheaper restaurants lurk a block or two inland. **Yalova Liman Restaurant** sells fried mussels and beer for only $2. The rooftop terrace reveals an inspiring view of the Dardanelles. (Open daily noon-midnight.) The town has a smattering of jejune sights: an **archaeological museum** with artifacts from Troy (open Tues.-Sun. 8am-5pm; admission 70¢, 35¢ with ISIC), and a **fortress** with vintage World War I cannons to commemorate the Gelibolu battle.

The Aegean Coast's northernmost resort, Çanakkale faces the narrowest point of the Dardanelles. Across the Dardanelles on the European side lies the battlefield of **Gelibolu,** better known as Gallipoli, where in 1915-16, landing parties from Australia, New Zealand, and Great Britain suffered a brutal defeat to Turkish forces. This battle launched its hero, Atatürk, on a speed-of-light rise to his present status as Turkish demi-god. Each year thousands of Australians and New Zealanders make pilgrimages to war cemeteries here, where 22,000 Allied dead lie buried. To systematically explore the battlefields, you can take a guided tour, preferably from the **Troyanzac Travel Agency** (tel. (196) 158 47 or 158 49; not to be confused with the inferior Anzac House) to the right of the clocktower ($15). Bargain with Hüseyin, the theatrical guide. It is cheaper to take a tour than to shuttle around in taxis. (Leaves at 10am and 2pm, 4hr. If not enough people show, the tour is sometimes dropped.) Another option is take a ferry to Eceabat (hourly; in winter every 2hr., 50¢. Be careful not to take the smaller ferry to Kilitbahir; ask which one is going where.) In Eceabat you can hire a taxi (officially $23, but bargain) to tour the battlefields. Try to double up since price is per car, not per person. You could also take a *dolmuş* from Eceabat to the **Gabatepe Museum** (70¢). From there it's a 4km walk to **Anzac Cove,** and a 7km hike uphill to the **Lone Pine Monument.** The **Hotel Ece** (tel. (196) 412 10) in Eceabat has clean rooms. (Singles $5, with bath $6.40. Doubles $9, with bath $10.40.)

Truva, or Troy, is 32km south of Çanakkale. *Dolmuş* and minibuses leave frequently from the bridge (from the bus station, go left down Atatürk Cad.—it's a 5-10min. walk). The site slept forgotten until Heinrich Schliemann, a German-born American millionaire-turned-amateur archaeologist, decided to prove that the Homeric myths were not pure fiction. Staking out the most promising site along the coast, he hired local workers and began excavating. To the astonishment of the academic world, he proved his point and rocked the world of archaeology.

People raised on stories of the Trojan War should not expect imposing ruins; the city Homer wrote about tumbled down 3000 years ago. But the remaining Bronze Age fortifications, given their age, are remarkably well preserved. (The tacky wooden horse which assures you that you've reached Troy, however, is a new addition.) Nine distinct strata, each containing the remains of a city from a different period, have been identified and dubbed Troy I through Troy IX. Troy I dates from 3200 BCE. The city of Homer's *Iliad* is now believed to be Troy VI, *not,* ironically, Troy II, the city Schliemann excavated. (Open 8am-8pm; off season 8am-5pm. Admission $2.) In Tevfikiye, the village just outside the entrance to the ruins, the **Hotel Hisarlık** (tel. (1973) 19 92) rents decent rooms with a common balcony, but they ain't cheap: doubles with showers $21, triples with showers $26. For a bargain and a cultural experience, go to **Pansiyon Varol** (tel. (1973) 10 71) in the center of the village, which has homey doubles ($4.30 per bed including shower and breakfast) and a teahouse. You can also camp for free in the garden or terrace, then shower for $1. There are a few unattractive **campsites** on the road from Çanakkale.

Pergamon (Bergama)

Pergamon today is one of Turkey's most beautiful cities. On Pergamon's uneven cobblestone streets, 150-year-old Greek houses lean against thousand-year-old ruins. A charming river flows through the city in its deep green bed. The calm is divine. Add to this a colorful past and you've got a true Turkish delight.

Pergamon's long history of fame and wealth began when Piletarus, a regional commander, seized the treasury he had been entrusted to keep and set himself up as king. Its ruins, loping across over 30,000 acres, are located on two principal sites: the **Acropolis,** which looms majestic above the town, and the **Asclepion** (medical center), lying in the valley below. The most notable attraction is the mammoth **amphitheater,** capable of seating 10,000 spectators. Under the direction of Galen, the most famous physician in the Roman Empire, the Asclepion was well-known in the ancient world. Allegedly, no patient left here unhealed, though many were probably rushed out the back door in the throes of death. An impressive portion of the Asclepion remains, including a marble colonnade, a theater, and healing rooms. The ruins of a huge gymnasium, a Roman circus, several temples, and the lavishly frescoed **House of Attalus** also lie scattered about. Pergamon's most remarkable pieces, however, have been spirited to foreign quarters. In ancient times, only the library in Alexandria surpassed the library here of more than 200,000 volumes. When the Alexandrians attempted to eclipse the Pergamon book bonanza by limiting the flow of papyrus from the Nile, Pergamon scholars simply invented parchment from animal skin and read on in smug satisfaction. Yet the plot thickened—when the library's Egyptian rival went up in flames, Mark Antony plundered Pergamon's shelves and presented the pilfered collection to his beloved Cleopatra. Most of the **Altar of Zeus,** considered the cat's miâü of the Hellenistic era, graces Pergamon Museum—in East Berlin.

There are no buses to the ruins; take a taxi ($15 for full tour, $5 to the first site) or walk. To reach the Acropolis, follow the main road past the **Roman Basilica.** Turn left off the road and walk towards the first ruins, the Lower Agora. Here you'll find a footpath that winds among the ruins to the summit. The hike to the top of the Acropolis can be exhausting, especially on hot days. If too much *nargile* (water pipe) smoking has debilitated a better portion of your alveoli, you can take a taxi to the top (about $5 per carload). The Asclepion is on the other side of town, 2km past the tourist office, following the signs. (Do not take photos of the military base along the Asclepion; it is illegal, and armed soldiers take this law seriously.) The **Archaeological Museum** diplays artifacts from Pergamon as well as a collection of traditional Turkish crafts. (The Acropolis, Asclepion, museum, and basilica open daily 8:30am-7pm; Oct.-April daily 8:30am-5:30pm. Admission to Acropolis and Asclepion $1.40 each, 70¢ with ISIC.)

The ruins of Pergamon sit adjacent to the pleasant, modern city of **Bergama,** accessible by **buses** from Bursa (2 per day, 6½hr., $11), İzmir (every hour, 2hr., $2), and İstanbul (2 per day, 10hr. $16). Try to take a bus that trundles directly into Bergama; most buses from İzmir to Çanakkale drop you off at the turn-off 7km away. Frequent *dolmuş* service into town is available. Unfortunately, no streets in Bergama are marked and no folks seem to know what they're called. But there's really only one main street (sometimes called İzmir Caddesi), so problem scenarios are reduced. From the bus station, take a left onto the main road and walk two blocks for the **tourist office,** 54 İzmir Cad. (tel. 118 62; open Mon.-Fri. 8:30am-5:30pm). The center of town is to the right as you exit the bus station. The **post office,** on İzmir Cad., has a 24-hr. **currency exchange.** Bergama's **telephone code** is 541.

The most charming pension in Bergama is the **Pergamon Pension** (tel. 123 95), a 150-year-old Greek-style mansion with high ceilings, a cool garden, and an excellent source of gastro-fulfillment. All rooms have toilets. Heading from the bus station, pass the PTT and you'll see a fork; bear to the right—the pension is on the left. ($5 per person; breakfast $1.40.) Continue through the central square to find the clean and cordial **Pension Athena** (tel. 134 20) off to the left, in a restored Ottoman house ($6, breakfast included; for dinner, you can have two dishes, salad, and drink for $3.50.). Just up the main street from the bus station is the **Park Hotel** (tel. 112 46), popular with backpackers for its convenient location and unbesmirched rooms. (Singles $5. Doubles $7.50.) The **Nike Pansiyon,** in the vibrantly blue building across the bridge and up the hill from the Pension Athena (follow the signs from the main square) has a beautiful garden—almost a piece of heaven—warm, family atmosphere, a cute dog at the door, and grand, sunny rooms ($3.50 per person; free hot showers; breakfast $1.40; Visa, Mastercard, and Eurocard accepted). **Berksoy camping** (tel. 125 95) and **Karavan camping** (tel. 117 92) are 2km past the tourist office on the main road. **Samaşik Lokantası** on İzmir Cad. toward Pension Athena serves great food for great prices (full meals around $2.50). The resort town of **Foça** lies south of Bergama. Three buses per day connect it to İzmir.

Izmir

Of the original Hellenistic city-states along the Aegean coast of Asia Minor, only **Smyrna,** now Turkish **İzmir,** survived the catastrophes that befell the region. Smyrna first came into its own in the 9th century BCE and thrived before Lydians from Sardis destroyed the town in 600 BCE. In 334 BCE, Alexander the Great conquered and then refounded Smyrna atop Mt. Pagus, now called the Kadifekale ("Velvet Fortress"). During the Roman and Byzantine periods, the port of Smyrna grew prosperous and cosmopolitan. The diversion of the River Hermes prevented Smyrna's harbor from silting, thereby rescuing it from the landlocked fate of its neighbors. In 1535, Süleyman the Magnificent signed a treaty with France that brought booming trade to Smyrna. The constant influx of Christian and Jewish merchants during this time earned the city the name "Infidel Smyrna." After the Ottoman dynasty was reduced to slag in World War I, Greece, enticed by the vision of a born-again Byzantine Empire, attacked Turkey. The then little-known Mustafa Kemal, soon to be Kemal Atatürk, expelled the invaders with an impromptu army and regained the ashes of Smyrna in the final battle of the Turkish War of Independence on September 9, 1922.

From the fodder of Smyrna's past, İzmir has become Turkey's third largest city and second largest port (population 2 million). Reconstructed Western style with wide boulevards and plazas, İzmir may appear generic, but this prosperous, sprawling metropolis leads an existence of sprightly activity and vivid imagination. The tumult of modern buildings in İzmir's downtown is marked on northern and southern ends by monuments to the city's most prominent personages: Alexander's Kadifekale remains intact and menacing on the waterfront next to NATO headquarters, and an equestrian statue of Atatürk fearlessly leads a regiment of office buildings. The domes of small mosques, unexpected amidst tenements and towers, attest to the more traditional style of life that washes over the concrete. Although relatively untouristed and historically fascinating, İzmir offers visitors very little to do. The culture of this city which was not destroyed by the retreating Greek army in 1923 is still relatively inaccessible to the non-Turkish-speaking backpacker who will spend only a few days there. But if you want to experience an authentic Turkish town and don't have the time to travel east, İzmir is the place to go.

Orientation and Practical Information

İzmir's principal boulevards radiate from rotaries, called *meydanı*. **Cumhuriyet Meydanı,** on the waterfront, is the city's financial center, home to an overflow of banks, travel agencies, and consulates. An astounding number of budget hotels, and just as many cheap restaurants, huddle with several bus company offices and the **train station** around the 9 Eylül Meydanı center of the Basmane district. The **PTT,** on Cumhuriyet Meydanı, has full phone facilities (open Mon.-Sat. 8am-midnight). İzmir also has an **American Express** office, 2B Nato Arkası Talatpaşa Bulvarı (tel. 21 79 27); a **U.S. Consulate,** 92-93 Atatürk Cad. (tel. 83 13 69); a **British Consulate,** 49 St. 1442 (tel. 81 17 95); and a **tourist police** (tel. 21 14 76 or 22 34 61). There is a **tourist information and complaint office** in the bus station (open daily 8am-noon and 12:30-8pm). For **medical emergency,** call 077. For the **police,** dial 055. Izmir's phone code is 51.

Frequent buses travel to: İstanbul (9hr., $14); Bursa (6hr., $10); Çanakkale (6hr., $9); Bodrum (4hr., $7); Kuşadası (1hr., $4); Seljuk (1hr., $2); and Ankara (8½hr., $11); to name a few. Three ferries per week go to İstanbul (19hr., $20). The **currency exchange** booth at the bus station is open daily 8:30am-8pm. From the bus station, take a *dolmuş* marked "Cankaya-Mersinli" (40¢) or public bus #50 (buy tickets at kiosk) for Basmane. From the 9 Eylül Meydanı, walk west along Gazi Bulvarı and northwest along Gazi Ozmanpaşa Bulvarı for the main tourist office (tel. 84 21 47 or 89 92 78) and Cumhuriyet Meydanı. **Konak Square,** 10 blocks south of Cumhuriyet Meydanı along the coastal **Atatürk Caddesi,** is the center for metropolitan buses and *dolmuş.* For buses to Çeşme and other points west, go to the bus-lot at **Üçkuyular,** south-west of the center (to get to the lot, take trolleybus #1,2, or 3 from Konak (40¢) or a *dolmuş* marked "F. Altay" from Basmane).

Accommodations and Food

Look for hotels in the Basmane area: the small streets between Fevzipaşa Bulvarı and Anafartalar Caddesi are loaded with cheap hotels (not to mention starving artists and well-fed prostitutes). The **Otel Saray,** 635 Anafartalar Cad. (tel. 83 69 46), two blocks south and 500m west of 9 Eylül Mey. appears to be a transplanted Miami Beach resort hotel. Nice, airy rooms. (Singles $4. Doubles $7. Hot shower included.) The **Yıldız Palas Hotel,** #50, 1296 Sok. (tel. 25 15 18), one block north of Anafartalar Cad., is above the neighborhood standard, with small clean rooms. ($3.50 per person. Hot showers included.) **Bilen Palas Otel,** #68, 1369 Sok. (tel. 83 92 46), right off 9 Eylül Meydanı, is an aging but well-maintained building. ($3.50 per person. Showers $1.) **Otel Özcan,** 1368 Sok. #3 (tel. 83 50 52) has hotel pretensions such as a bellhop and a swish lobby to which you'll have to return every time you want the shower key. (Singles $5.25, with shower $7.50. Hot showers $1.50.)

Superb, inexpensive Turkish restaurants saturate Anafartalar Caddesi. **Şark Lokantası,** some four blocks toward the water beyond Otel Saray, is always jammed by locals at mealtimes. (Hefty meal of scrumptious food with complimentary cigarette, $1.25.) Open 7am-9pm. The jovial waiters at **Inci Lokantası** 51/A, 1369 Sok. (tel. 19 89 91) due west of 9 Eylül Meydanı, deal out *kebap* all evening long (open 10am-midnight, *kebap* $2). For Eastern Turkish cuisine, head to **Urfa Lokantası** across from the police station on Anafartalar Cad. Full, filling meals cost $2.50, and they're open 24 hours a day.

Sights

İzmir's **agora** was built in the 4th century BCE by Alexander, destroyed by an earthquake in 178 CE, and rebuilt by Emperor Marcus Aurelius soon thereafter. The mediocre remains are accessible from Anafartalar Cad. Walk south along 941 Sok. from the Otel Saray. (Open daily 8am-6pm; Oct.-May daily 9am-5:30pm. Admission 80¢.) Above the city at Mt. Pagos is the most enduring of Alexander's legacies, the **Kadifekale,** originally built in the 4th century BCE, but restored and altered numerous times by various conquerors (open 24 hrs.). Bus #33 from Konak ascends the mount for a flabbergasting panorama of the bay. If you stroll along Anafartalar Cad. from its beginning at the Basmane station, you'll pass remnants of a less westernized Turkey: *çay salonu* (teahouses), men smoking *nargile* (water pipes), children and vendors littering the air with their cries, and colorful streets that eventually explode into İzmir's full and authentic **bazaar.** (Open Mon.-Sat. 8:30am-7pm.) İzmir's **archaeological museum** holds a huge international import-export fair in Kültür Parkı (Cultural Park). İzmir's **International Festival** in late June and early July brings classical and folk music concerts to İzmir, Çeşme, and Ephesus.

Sardis (Sart)

Sardis was the capital of the Lydian kingdom, dominant over Aegean Ionia from 680-547 BCE. The Lydians embraced and embellished the Hellenic culture, giving the world dice, balls, and coin minting. The expression "rich as Croesus" refers to the Lydian King Croesus, once the wealthiest man in the world. When he consulted the oracle at Delphi, it prophesied that if Croesus crossed the river Halys, a powerful empire would be destroyed. Eager to fulfill the prophecy, Croesus promptly rushed his troops across the river and was there promptly trounced by the Persians.

You can visit Sardis easily from İzmir, or take an ambitious daytrip from Kuşadası (leave at 7am, return around 7pm). Take one of the frequent **buses** to **Salihli** and ask to be let off at Sardis, or Sart in modern parlance (every ½hr., 1½hr., $2.) Buses leave from the eastern end of the İzmir train station (away from the bus company booths), and drop you off on the highway amid a trickle of teahouses. (Sart may feel like the middle of nowhere, but don't worry—that's still a long way off.) Trains from İzmir to Sart take three hours. Most of the ancient city is on the left side of the highway, 100m from the bus stop.

The entrance to the ruins leads first to the **Marble Way,** lined by a row of **Byzantine shops.** From the end of the Marble Way, turn left to enter the **synagogue,** which has gripping mosaic floors. The imposing columns of the **gymnasium** shadow above a **swimming pool,** where fuming Lydians once chilled out. Go up the street that slips between two teahouses on the other side of the road, and follow it 1km uphill to the **Temple of Artemis.** Alexander the Great commissioned this temple, one of the largest in antiquity. Only a few columns remain, but their scrolled capitals are exquisite. Along the way to the temple, you'll pass an ancient Lydian gold refinery and a dome from a 12th-century Byzantine basilica built atop a 5th-century church. (Sites open sunrise-sunset. Admission 80¢ per site.)

Çesme

One hour west of İzmir chortles the popular seaside resort of Çeşme, once renowned for its abundant thermal springs, today prized for its proximity to the Greek island of Chios, and its access to the cornflower waters of the Aegean. Buses leave every half hour or so from the Üçkuyular bus-lot in İzmir (see İzmir), but beware of the weekend migration to the beaches. Even with buses heading back to İzmir as late as at 8:30pm (the last one), all later buses are often booked. You can reserve your seat at the bus station (see below). In Çeşme, the bus stops next to a private accomodations service. (In summer open daily 8am-10pm; note that the rooms they find for you are not the cheapest available.) From the bus stop, continue down the main road to the water for the main **tourist office,** 8 İskele Meydanı (tel. 266 53; open Mon.-Fri. 8:30am-8pm, Sat. 9am-5pm; Oct.-May Mon.-Fri. 8:30am-5:30pm). Continuing to the right along the shore you'll find the **PTT** (open 24 hrs.). For the **bus station,** walk about 300m in the opposite direction from the tourist office, and turn left before the small bridge. Çeşme's **telephone code** is 549.

Çeşme abounds with pensions that charge about $15 for doubles in high season; all prices are negotiable. Look for accommodations along Bağlar Sok., which runs diagonally inland south from the tourist office, and along Müftü Sok., which intersects it on the left. The bubbly manager of the **Adil Pansiyon** (tel. 274 47) speaks English faster than she can breathe. (Doubles with showers $14; kitchen available.) The **Işık Pansiyon** (tel. 263 05), behind the "Lunapark," is also cozy ($3.50 per person; free hot showers). The best beaches nearby are in Ilıca and Altınkum. In Çeşme, Beyalik Beach is a 10-minute walk from the center, and the Kerman Hotel has a bantam beach to the far right of the waterfront. *Dolmuş* travel around the peninsula until 8pm with routes to Ilıca (6km), Altınkum (10km), and south along the beach (5km). A few campsites dot the peninsula: the **Fener Mocamp** (tel. 280 94) in Çeşme (shadeless and noisy, but adequate) and the **Ve-Kamp** (tel. 714 68) in Paşalimanı, among others. Freelance camping is generally not allowed.

The **castle** across from the tourist office was originally built by Ottoman Sultan Beyazıt II to be used to spy on Chios, 11km away. It now houses a tiny museum. (Open daily 8:30am-noon and 1-5:30pm. Admission 70¢, 35¢ with ISIC.) In early July, Çeşme holds an annual international festival that showcases popular European actors and musicians; so are they all, all honorable men (and women). The performances are broadcast throughout Europe. Tickets start at $15.

The centrifugal force for nightlife in the area is **Ilıca.** Right on the Çeşme-Ilıca highway, **Disco 9** (tel. 328 87), fills up every night in summer, despite its steep cover charge ($7). If you yearn for languor, sip a beer in one of the many cafés lining Çeşme's harbor.

An hour's boat ride from Çeşme takes you to Chios. **Ertürk Ferryboat,** Cumhuriyet Meydanı 11/A (tel. 268 76), runs boats daily July-September 10, four days per week in June and the remainder of September, and one on Thursdays the remainder of the year. ($20 one way and same day return, $25 open round-trip.) **Seren Yachting** 13/B, Cumhuriyet Meydanı (tel. 279 88) has less frequent boats for the same price.

Kusadasi

Kuşadası is a saddening example of tourism run amok. When luxury cruise liners and day trippers from nearby Samos began adding Kuşsadası to their Greek island itineraries, the resourceful fisherfolk and farmers of this former somnolent town found ways to bait better business and nurture profit. Nowadays, English-style pubs advertising refuge from "stomach bugs" and clothiers hawking winter-weight fur and leather do exceedingly well. Kuşadası's popularity is deserved—this coastal town is one of the best places from which to visit the Aegean Basin's most luminous classical sites: Ephesus, Priene, Miletus, and Didyma. The town of Seljuk, 20km away and only 3km from Ephesus, offers quieter rooms that elate the frugal, but it lacks Kuşadası's nightlife and coastline.

Orientation and Practical Information

Most visitors to Kuşadası arrive by boat, a convenient method given that harbor master, duty-free shop, fish market, passport police, and customs are all in the port area. There is no way around paying the port tax, but it is cheapest in dollars ($9); in other currencies, most notably *drachmae,* there is a painful wallet drain of an additional $2.50. By bus, Kuşadası is a two-hour ride from İzmir. The bus station is about 2km east of the center and frequent *dolmuş* connect the two. The tourist office, 20km beyond the gangway, is conveniently positioned for those disembarking a cruise liner (they have excellent maps). Just beyond preside the turreted walls of an ancient Seljuk *kervansaray* (where itinerant merchants could spend a night with their goods protected). Now the **Kervansaray Hotel,** the structure's turrets make a good orientation point. Facing the Kervansaray, **Yalı Caddesi** runs right and uphill, passing through a grueling, covered luxury-goods bazaar. Continue up the hill to where **Aslanlar Caddesi** intersects; in both directions, you'll find many cheap pensions. Left of the Kervansaray Hotel is the broad pedestrian-only **Barbaros Hayrettin.** The PTT, travel agencies, and banks are also there. At the end of the street is a cubist medieval watchtower turned modern-day police station. Through the watchtower and along **Kahramanlar Caddesi,** you'll reach the major artery out of town and, within a kilometer, the bus station. **Atatürk Bulvarı,** parallel to the coastline, exists so that the denizens of Kuşadası have a place to cruise their mopeds and build their luxury hotels.

Perhaps the most practical information about Kuşadası is that if prices for anything are unlisted, you will most certainly be overcharged. Bargain on everything, from leather jackets to ice cream.

Tourist Office: On İskele Meydanı in the port (tel. 111 03). Listings of campgrounds, bus schedules, and the non-budget accommodations. Excellent maps. Will call and make reservations for you in town or elsewhere. Open daily 8am-7pm; Dec.-April Mon.-Fri. 8am-12:30pm and 1:30-5:30pm.

PTT: Halfway up Barbaros Hayrettin. Services open Mon.-Fri. 8:30am-noon and 1:30-5:30pm, Sat.-Sun. 9am-5pm. Stamps, telegraphs and long-distance **telephones** available 24 hrs. **Telephone Code:** 636.

Currency Exchange: Banks have booths by the waterfront. Open daily 8am-9pm. The PTT also exchanges cash daily 8am-11pm.

Budget Travel: Ekol Travel, Liman Çikmazi 3/1 (tel. 192 55; fax 126 44), in the bazaar at the end of the cruiseliner gangway. Cheap flights, ferry tickets, temporary baggage storage ($1 per day), accommodations referrals, transportation advice, message board, and emergency help. Will bend over backwards to assist you but also to sell you *something*. English spoken. Open Mon.-Sat. 9:30am-10pm, Sun. 1-9pm.

Buses: To: İzmir (every 30min., $1.85); Denizli (5 per day, $6); İstanbul (5 per day, $20); Pamukkale (6 per day, 4hr., $6.30); and Bodrum (15 per day, 3hr., $6). For Priene, Miletus, or Didyma, you must make connections in Söke.

Dolmuş: In the front half of the bus station. Every ½ hr. 7am-8pm to Ephesus, Seljuk, or Söke—tickets from the appropriate window. Less frequent runs to other neighboring villages, especially Davutlar and Güzelcamlı. *Dolmuş* run every 10min. or so from the bus station through town and to Kadinlar Plajı (Ladies' Beach).

Ferries: One-way ferry fares to Samos, Greece, are fixed by the government at at rate 25% higher on the Turkish side: $25, same day round-trip $30, open round-trip $45. Ekol Travel undercuts the official rate: $23, round-trip $30, open round-trip $43. Port taxes are included in the price of the ticket for the country in which it was bought. Turkish boats leave in summer daily at 8:30am, returning at 5pm; off-season, ferries run only when boats are filled to capacity (which is not often). From Greece, you are permitted to take only a Greek boat. For the morning ferry, you must purchase your ticket and leave your passport at a travel agency the night before.

Rentals: Toya-Sun Rent-A-Car, 60 Atatürk Bulvarı (tel. 33 44), offers cheap car rates: $20 per day, 20¢ per km. Also reasonable is **A.G. Tourism and Travel,** 60/4 Atatürk Bulvarı.

Bookstore: Kuydaş Kitabevi, 16 Kibris Cad. (tel. 118 28). Also on Bahar Sok., just off Barbaros Hayrettin. (Sign reads *Haşet.*) Sells newspapers, guidebooks, and stationery. The owner speaks perfect English. Open daily 7am-midnight.

Hospital (Hastahane): Atatürk Bulvarı (tel. 110 26), on the waterfront at the northern edge of town.

Police (Polis): In the watchtower (tel. 110 22). Headquarters, Hükümet Cad. (tel. 113 82). Tourists should go to the watchtower. English is spoken at the first station; at the second station they'll get a translator in an emergency.

Accommodations, Camping, and Food

While cheap compared to Greek rates, accommodations here are expensive by Turkish standards. Finding a room is rarely a problem, though women here should be careful in the cheapest places. Pensions cost the least, but are often full during high season. The high season rates listed here can often be haggled down. The cheaper pensions line Aslanlar Cad. and many of the small streets higher up.

Hülya Pension, 39 Mah. İleri Sok. (tel. 120 75). Straight down Beziryan Sok. Family atmosphere and a warm welcome. Clean and airy rooms, with showers $4 per person. Breakfast $1.20. Excellent more-than-you-can-eat-homemade-authentic-Turkish-dinner $3.

Hotel Rose (Salman's Pension), 7 Aslanlar Cad. Aydınlık Sok. (tel. 111 11). The owner Salman (a.k.a. Sammy) knows the needs of backpackers and handles problems well. Big, comfy rooms; nice lounge and bar; laundry service ($2 per kg). A home away from home for Australians and New Zealanders (Sammy's wife is Australian). Sammy tells you he's got the best deals on all sorts of goods and services. Just don't let him make you write to us. $4.30 per person. Triples can be had for $11.

Pansiyon Su, 13 Aslanlar Cad. (tel. 114 53). Walk up Yalı Cad. and make a left—it's one block down on the right side. Tiny spot-free rooms (especially singles). The lovely arboreal patio may be too noisy for some. $4.30 per person, solar-heated showers included. Breakfast $1.40.

Hotel Ada, 12 Aslanlar Cad. (tel. 195 59). All the comforts of a nice hotel. Big rooms with balconies and showers. Singles $7. Doubles $13. Triples $19. Quads $21. Breakfast $2.

Camping: Önder (tel. 124 13) and **Yat Camping** (tel. 113 33), 2km north of town on Atatürk Bulvarı. Take a Seljuk *dolmuş* or walk. Both have good facilities, but Önder is nicer. $1 per small tent, $2 per big tent. $1.50 per person (small, medium, or large). 3-person bungalows $8 at both campsites. (Both campsites are closed Nov.-April. If they're full, try **Mehtap Camping** (tel. 130 12; $2 per person).

There are countless small restaurants in Kuşadası and they differ only in the extent to which they'll overcharge. A good way to gauge is by the price of the ubiquitous *şiş kebap:* over $2.30 is a rip-off. There are many cheap but good slop stops along **Kahramanlar Caddesi** and its alley tributaries. Waterfront eating is expensive except for **Güvercınada Cafeteria** on Pigeon Island (not to be confused with the Ada Restaurant at the foot of the walkway). High on the rocks, it absorbs glorious sunsets and offers hot *lahmacun* (Turkish pizza) for $1. Lovely tea gardens flourish above.

Sights and Beaches

Connected by a slender causeway, Kuşadası's only substantial tourist attraction is the picturesque **Pigeon Island,** a tiny fortified islet on which cooing tourists have replaced the birds.

The Grand Bazaar and Barbaros Hayrettin are among the most expensive shopping infernos in the country. Nonetheless, as the merchants will never tire of reminding you, it doesn't cost anything to browse. Visitors are also often found imbibing the sun on the meager beaches that line the coast in either direction. The beach by the yacht harbor is crowded and dirty. A little better is **Kadınlar Plajı,** 3km beyond Pigeon Island (catch a *dolmuş*)--this, too, might induce mild depression. Vastly superior are sandy **Karovaplajı** (Long Beach) and **Yavansu plajı** (Silver Beach); take any *dolmuş* marked "Davutlar." Better yet, take a *dolmuş* marked "Güzelcamlı and Milli Park," to the National Park, just south of Kuşadası. The nicest of the three beaches here is probably the one at the end of the line for the *dolmuş.* Amble down to the far end of the beach and scale some rocks to find a strip of sand all to yourself.

Ephesus (Efes)

Dig no farther than Ephesus for your wholesale archaeological needs. And the findings here are not just your standard ancient heap but the remains of one of the most important cities of the Roman Empire. The ruins from the Roman and early Christian era are so extensive and well preserved that one need not struggle to imagine the daily interaction of the 250,000 people who lived here nearly two millennia ago.

Practical Information and Accommodations

Disregard the ominous signs at the travel agencies on Samos and in Kuşadası which insist that guided tours of Ephesus are "highly recommended." The tours are expensive (about $20 per day) and the guides tend to rush you through the 2000-acre site; visit on your own instead. Consider getting a good guidebook to Ephesus in one of Kuşadası's souvenir shops or at the entrance to the site ($7.50). Bring a water bottle with you—it gets toasty and the refreshment stands at the site overcharge shamelessly.

Getting to Ephesus needn't be a comedy of errors: from the Kuşadası bus station, take a *dolmuş* to Seljuk, and tell the driver you want to get off at Ephesus. From the Seljuk train station, take any *dolmuş* towards Kuşadası. Some hitch the 3km to the site, though lone women should never hitchhike, and *Let's Go* does not recommend hitchhiking for anyone as a safe means of travel. The main entrance, where you pay admission, is 1km away, but the actual ruins start close by the road to Seljuk. The *dolmuş* that return to Kuşadası are often full; go to Seljuk first if you want to be sure to get a seat. You should stop in Seljuk anyway to supplement your exploration of Ephesus with a visit to the impressive **Ephesus Museum** (see Seljuk).

The site at Ephesus is open daily from 8am to 7pm. Admission is $2, with ISIC $1. Next to the entrance are **toilets** (15¢), a **post office,** stands laden with orphaned guidebooks, and several overpriced restaurants with chewy Turkish ice cream (if it's really chewy, you can stretch it close to a meter). In the first or second week of May, the annual **Festival of Ephesus** presents drama, music, and folklore events in the ancient theater. For camping, try the ideally located **Tusan Motel and Camping** (tel. 10 60), at the foot of the access road. The motel is expensive, but camping costs just $1.40 per person and 70¢ per tent. Campers can use the motel's facilities, including the pool.

History

Unlike the many ancient ruins which rely on rubble to evoke their histories, Ephesus has a tangible allure which does justice to its illustrious past. As a strategic coastal gateway to the Eastern world, this Ionian refuge grew to be the second largest city in the Roman Empire, site of a Christian shrine, and one of the seven (or so) wonders of the ancient world.

The origins of Ephesus are shrouded in myth. Legend has it that the city was founded in a manner prescribed by the Delphic Oracle, which foretold that the appropriate site would be disclosed by a fish and a wild boar. The city's location had to be changed several times due to the continual recession of the harbor waters (and alas not due to the more boaring fish tales). Today, the ruins of the ancient port lie 10km inland from the coast.

Ephesians were reluctant to move, particularly because they sought to remain near the colossal **Temple of Artemis** (referred to as Diana by the Romans). Pausanias, pioneer budget traveler, deemed this stupendous structure the "most wondrous of the seven ancient wonders" and "the most beautiful work ever created by humankind." The first major structure to be built entirely of marble, and the largest edifice in the ancient Greek world, the Temple of Artemis was four times as big as the Parthenon in Athens. Remarkably, this massive monument was actually built twice. The temple was set afire during the reign of Mad King Hesostratos in 356 BCE on the night of the birth of Alexander the Great. According to legend, the arsonist Erostratus succeeded only because Artemis was absent, watching over Alexander's birth. Fittingly, Alexander himself reconstructed the temple to its original dimensions and aura. The offerings of hundreds of thousands of pilgrims each year enabled it to grow so wealthy that it became the world's first bank. Today, little remains of the magnificient structure (see Seljuk). Plundering Goths sacked the sanctuary in the 3rd century CE, to be followed by the Byzantines (you can see some of the original columns at the Aya Sofya in İstanbul), and more recently the voracious British School of Archaeology has grown corpulent on findings from this region of the world.

Ephesus reached its zenith after 129 BCE when the Romans established the province of Asia with Ephesus as its capital. Its inhabitants numbered more than 250,000, second in population only to Alexandria. The ruins that one sees today date primarily from this period. Saint Paul, recognizing the significance of such a metropolis, arrived in 50 CE and converted a small group of Ephesians to the new religion. (An inspired Paul recorded his divine exploits in the Biblical epistles to the Ephesians.) Some perceived this development of Christianity a threat to the glory of Cybele (mother goddess of Anatolia) and Artemis, and forced Paul and his followers to depart. The fledgling religion had taken root, however, and Ephesus became the center of Christianity in the Roman Empire.

Heraclitus of Ephesus, noting the ephemeral nature of life, once remarked that one can never step into the same river twice. If you do, you will surely drown in misfortune. This wisdom proved prescient and infallible. As the neighboring river Cayster emptied into the Aegean, it choked Ephesus's harbor with silt, transforming it into a marshy morass. By the 6th century CE, the recession of the sea had sealed the city's fate. The swamps became infested with malaria-carrying mosquitoes, which in turn triggered a tremendous epidemic that resulted in over 200,000 deaths.

Sights

If you don't take a guided tour, you'll approach the ruins from the road between Kuşadası and Seljuk; your first glimpse of the site will be of the outskirts of the ancient city. The most important of these remains is the **Vedius Gymnasium** to the left as you proceed down the road to the main entrance. On the west end of the gymnasium courtyard (the main entrance is at the north end of the site) are public lavatories and a source of potable but warm water. Farther on spread the contours of what must have been an enormous **stadium** (the seats were removed to build the Byzantine city walls). Just before the main entrance stand the ruins of the **Double Church** (Church of Councils) where the notorious Ecumenical Council of Churches met in 431 CE.

Once you pass through the main entrance, you probably won't be able to keep yourself from fervently charging to the center of the site and marveling straight down **Arcadian Street,** a magnificent, colonnaded marble avenue. Like the present-day tourist drag in Kuşadası, Arcadian was lined with shops and extended to the harbor, where visitors disembarked and trading ships docked with cargo from the Far East. The street eventually liquifies into a small marsh, but many of the original columns have survived.

Once at the far end of the avenue, turn around and drool over the dazzling view of the **Grand Theater.** With seating for 24,000 and remarkable acoustics, the theater dominates the entire site from an elevated setting, carved into the side of Mt. Pion. In ancient times, the Ephesians celebrated the Festival of Artemis every April; singing and dancing, the denizens marched 89 golden idols of the goddess to the Grand Theater.

Running before the theater is the slightly elevated **Marble Road,** which once led all the way to the Temple of Artemis. Peek down one of the small holes in the road for a glimpse of the scented sewage system. The **Commercial Agora,** the main plaza of the city, stretches nearby. In the center of the colonnaded square stood a huge horologium, a combination sundial and water clock. Marble Rd. leads past the agora to the **Library of Celsus.** Almost entirely reconstructed by Viennese archaeologists, its elaborately carved marble façade suggests the luxury of ancient Ephesus.

Across from the library at the corner of the Marble Rd. and Curetes St. are the vestiges of the **brothel** dedicated to the love-goddess Aphrodite. Romantic commerce took place by candlelight in the small, windowless side rooms. There is a secret passage from the library to the brothel. At the end of the brothel, farthest from the Grand Theater, is a sacred pump whose water supposedly made sterile women fertile. Here was found the forthright statue of Priapus, god of sacred fertility, and the Long Dong Silver of his day, now displayed in the Ephesus Museum in Seljuk.

Up the hill, the imposing ruins of the **Temple of Hadrian** dominate the left side of the road. Recent renovation blessed the intricately carved façade. The marble archway contains friezes depicting the mythical creation of the city of Ephesus; a bust of the goddess Cybele adorns the keystone. Beyond the temple and adjoining the rear of the brothel, rest the **Baths of Scholastikia.** Across the street from the Temple of Hadrian burrow the yet unearthed **Terrace Houses** that extend up the hill. They once housed the wealthiest and most prominent families of the city, who lavished the interiors with (superbly preserved) frescoes and mosaics. A visit here merits the extra entrance fee, though the attendant is not always there to collect it (80¢; closed noon-1:30pm).

Farther up the hill lie the ruins of the exquisite **Fountain of Trajan.** Various fragments found on this location have been piled piecemeal to reconstruct the original structure. The statue of the Emperor Trajan that stood before the fountain has been completely destroyed—except for the base, whose fascination factor is abysmally low.

If you make a left after the hill of Trajan's fountain, before the main road, you'll come to the site of the **Grotto of the Seven Sleepers.** According to Christian tradition, seven men fleeing persecution in the 3rd century CE hid in these caves. When they awoke, one of them went to buy bread and discovered that he and the group had been sleeping for 209 years. The story is more interesting than the site.

Seljuk

Seljuk's proximity to the ruins of Ephesus makes this quiet town a good base for exploration. The proliferation of pensions, carpet shops, and souvenir stands promises to spoil the tranquility of the town within a few years, but for now, Seljuk is a pleasant, slightly more Turkish alternative to Kuşadası. The village is also home to important attractions of its own: the **Ephesus Archaeological Museum,** the **Basilica of St. John,** and the **House of the Virgin Mary.** But Seljuk's most famous sight is also its least impressive—the scanty remains of the **Temple of Artemis** (on the road to Ephesus). For entertainment, on the second Sunday in January, Seljuk hosts a **camel-wrestling festival,** an all-day event in which two male camels are brought into the arena, and a female is placed between them. The males grapple for the female's honor and attention to the beat of the *davul* drum and the *zurna* flute. The fight ends when one camel has pinned the other, though it takes a score or more of brawny men to keep the camels from killing each other. Indeed, the lovely lumpies are not so much as bruised—camels are valuable property. The international **Seljuk-Efes Festival,** held in the first or second week of May, includes art displays, folk dancing, and musical performances. Performances range from Turkish classical to Santana.

Orientation and Practical Information

The main thoroughfare is the İzmir-Aydın road, or **Atatürk Caddesi** (not to be confused with the Atatürk Cad. in every other Turkish city). The road from Kuşadası and Ephesus, **Sahabettindede Caddesi,** intersects Atatürk Cad. The **bus station** from which the Kuşadası *dolmuş* runs is at the northwest corner of the crossroads. The **Tourist Information Office** (tel. 13 28), across the street at the southwest corner, provides free maps. (Open daily 8:30am-6:30pm; Oct.-April Mon.-Fri. 8:30am-5:30pm.) Just behind this office lies the Ephesus Museum, with sanity-restoring public bathrooms and a place to check your pack. The **hospital** (tel. 14 07) lies on the southeast corner of the intersection. With your back toward Ephesus, walk four blocks left on Atatürk Cad. to reach the center of town, a small square across from the ruins. Behind it, along **Cengiz Topal Caddesi** are the **PTT** (open 24 hrs.), the police, banks, restaurants, public baths, and the **train station** (tel. 10 06). There is an **English bookstore** at 1/2 Yokus Sok. (tel. 19 93) across Atatürk Cad. (open daily 6am-10pm). Seljuk's **telephone code** is 5451.

Accommodations and Food

Since the whole village goes into slumber mode after sunset, the main reason for staying in Seljuk is to arrive at the ruins bright-eyed and bushy-tailed early the next morning. For evening eventfulness, head to Kuşadası, only a short ride away.

Tuncay Pension, 3 İsabey Mah., Ay Sok. (tel. 12 60). Walking north from the bus stop, take the third left. Then the first right and right again. Large, hygenic rooms. Free service to Ephesus, hot water, laundry service ($2 per load), common kitchen. $3.50 per person in rooms with showers. Breakfast $1.60.

Pansiyon Öztürk (tel. 19 37), right by Tuncay Pension. Family-run, clean rooms with bathrooms. $2.85 per person. Breakfast $1.60.

Pansiyon Karahan, 9 I. Okul Sok. (tel. 25 75), second right after the bus stop heading north. Hotel luxury for pension prices. Big carpeted rooms. $4.30 per person.

Barim Pansiyon I, Muze Arkasi Sok. (tel. 19 23), behind the museum off Turgutreis Cad., is enriched with *kilim,* colorful artifacts, and nesting storks. The tiled tea garden in the rear hosts a family of rabbits. The rooms, however, are beast-free and clean. Popular with backpackers. $3.50 per person, with shower $4.30.

Australian Pension, 11 Durak Sok. (tel. 10 50), behind the museum (follow the signs). Ungrunged rooms and a pleasant courtyard. Owner lived in Australia for 20 years. Roof $2. Dorm rooms $3. Private rooms $3.50 per person.

Pansiyon Kirhan (tel. 22 57), behind the museum. An old Ottoman home with only three rooms to let. Lovely garden and very pretty. $3.50 per person.

Need to pamper yourself? Head to **Erdem Pansiyon** (tel. (5451) 14 30, ext. 69), 9km away in the village of Şirince. This pension is a 200-year old converted Greek home with fairytale rooms and a sublime stillness. Bed and huge breakfast buffet $20. Hardly cheap, but an unforgettable experience. Call at least a week ahead for reservations.

Along Cengiz Cad. are many super restaurants for dining al *fresco con* savings. **Bayrakli,** at the top of the street, serves a pastureful of salads for 60¢, and meat dishes for $1.70 (open 7am-midnight). Perhaps the nicest way to end the day in Seljuk is with a cup of *çay* on the square beyond Cengiz Topez Cad. Storks nesting on a ruined aqueduct stare at people playing backgammon and down those looking at storks.

Sights

Over a century's worth of excavations are tastefully arrayed in the **Ephesus Museum.** Its most famous pieces are statues of Artemis and Priapus. The rampant controversy persists as to whether the rotund body parts which cover Artemis are breasts or mountain oysters. They are, nonetheless, irrefutable fertility symbols. Also of note is a fine collection of ancient coins and glass. (Open daily 8:30am-6pm; Oct.-April Mon.-Fri. 8:30am-5:30pm. Admission 70¢, with ISIC 35¢.)

The 14th-century **İsabey Mosque** provides rare evidence that the Seljuks ventured this far west. A portion of the mosque is still used for worship, while the rest protects an impressive array of Ottoman tombstones. The four large granite columns that support the two domes come from the Harbor Baths at Ephesus. Some of the marble quarried to build the mosque was pillaged from the nearby remains of the Temple of Artemis. Farther up the hill stands the **Persecution Gate,** a colossus constructed in the 6th or 7th century CE.

Beyond the archway yawns the **Basilica of St. John,** superimposed on the tomb of St. John the Theologian. In the 6th century, Emperor Justinian decided to construct this massive basilica over the saint's grave in place of the original 2nd-century CE chapel. Initially, St. John's body was kept in a room underneath the capacious dome of the basilica; dust from this room was supposed to have supernatural healing powers. Whiff it up. Today four small marble columns surround the grave in the center of the site. (Open same hours as Ephesus Museum. Admission 70¢, with ISIC 35¢.)

The road that leads uphill to the right (facing the basilica) brings you to the **Seljuk Castle,** a Byzantine citadel with crenellated walls that suffuse the village skyline with a medieval aura. Don't collapse in disappointment, though, when from up close you see that what looked so impressive from town is really just a circular hall with a small, abandoned mosque in the center. (Open daily 7:30am-7pm, in winter 8am-5pm. Admission $1.10. Beware the overpriced restaurant.)

7km outside of Seljuk is **Meryemana,** or the **House of the Virgin Mary.** According to the Bible, the Virgin Mary lived in Ephesus in her dotage. As a consequence, Christian and Muslim pilgrims regularly congregate here. (While Muslims believe that Christ was a prophet and not the son of God, Mary is one of the most revered women in Islam.) In the early 19th century, a devout German nun who had never set eyes upon Ephesus supposedly saw the house of the Virgin in a vision. She wrote a book discussing the layout and location of the house in detail. After her death, excavations around Ephesus unearthed a 1st-century CE stone cottage that mirrored her description perfectly. A small chapel, recently built on the site, holds mass every Sunday at 9am. On August 15 the Archbishop of İzmir conducts mass here to commemorate the Assumption. If you visit Ephesus beforehand, exit through the back gate, where you will find taxis waiting. Besides tour package buses, which often include Ephesus in their itineraries, cabs are the only reliable way to visit the chapel ($13 per carload round-trip). Tours of Ephesus usually include this site.

Priene, Miletus, and Didim (Didyma)

Priene, Miletus, and Didyma lie in a tidy row south of Kuşadası, conveniently located to provide you with your recommended daily dose of ruins. Take some time and perch (securely) on the slopes of Mt. Mycale to view Priene, practice a soliloquy in the amphitheater of Miletus, and await a revelation from Apollo at Didyma. With an early start, a modicum of efficiency, and a blessing from Hermes, you can reach all three sites in a daytrip. But you may prefer to explore the ruins in two leisurely days, as the largest site, Miletus, deserves extra time. Less well preserved but interesting to mystery cult buffs are the ruins at Priene, the Delphi of the Ionian cities. The temple at Didyma deserves only a brief visit. It is possible to take a single-day organized tour of all three sites from Kuşadası (or more expensively from Bodrum) for about $20 per person. Check with the tourist office. Otherwise, visit all three sites from Kuşadası through a series of *dolmuş* rides.

For a daytrip, the best strategy is to get out to Didyma first and then work your way back north. Take a *dolmuş* from Kuşadası to **Söke.** Then pick up a second *dolmuş* to Didim (the Turkish name), where Didyma is located (get let off at the temple; otherwise the *dolmuş* will take you to the crowded beach 5km away). To get to Miletus from Didyma, you can easily catch a *dolmuş* or hitch a ride to **Akköy;** from there you must hitch or take a taxi the 7km north to Miletus. To get to Priene, either continue hitching north from Miletus or go back to Akköy; from there take one *dolmuş* to Söke, and another to the small town of Güllübahçe at the foot of the Priene ruins. While in Güllübahçe, visit the **Şelâle Restaurant,** where a waterfall from an ancient, moss-covered aqueduct cascades into a reflecting pool, within splashing distance of the tables. Taxis are usually waiting at every site. (All 3 open daily 8:30am-7:30pm; off-season 8:30am-5pm. The Miletus and Priene ruins are never fenced off. Admission to each 70¢, with ISIC 35¢.) Most of the eateries near the sites cater to tourists and are consequently a bit overpriced. Stock up on picnic supplies before you head off in the morning.

The small town of **Didim** offers some inexpensive pensions. The **Orakle Pansiyon** (tel. (6353) 15 85), overlooking the temple, is the cheapest (singles $4.20, doubles $7, triples $10.70), and has satisfactory rooms with a spectacular view of the temple. Just 3km south is **Altınkum,** a beautiful beach with a few sleeping options. Try **Petek** (tel. 10 85) or **Mıhçı** (tel. 10 11) **Pensions** along the beach to the left ($7 per person). For **camping** around Didim, try the fenced-off **Orman Bakanlığı,** the last campsite when going to Didim from Akköy. In **Güllübahçe,** near Priene, the **Pansiyon Priene** (tel. (6357) 12 49), 90m from the main square, boasts a charming garden, free laundry and ironing, common kitchen, and beautiful doubles ($15). There are a number of **campsites** ($3.50 per person some with restaurants) at Lake Bafa, east of Akköy.

Priene

Priene grew to prominence as a member of the Ionian Confederation of cities in the region of Smyrna (modern İzmir). The confederation controlled the Aegean coast after the decline of the Hittite empire, but Priene always lingered in the shadow of its neighboring economic rival, Miletus. The city's population never exceeded 5000; while its neigbors excelled in commerce, Priene devoted its resources to religion, art, and sport. The city's ruins, on a plateau before the sheer walls of Mt. Mycale, overlook the contortions of the River Meander. Despite the fairly dramatic setting, Priene remains humbled by its neighbors, as its ruins don't quite match up to the splendorous remains of Miletus and Didyma.

Dolmuş stop by a café; to reach the site from there, follow the road that struggles up the slope and forks off to the right of the road to Miletus and Didyma. First you'll encounter the massive ancient walls that circumscribe the ruined metropolis that was constructed upon the terraced slope of the mountain. The city's gridded street system is the oldest still in existence. From the main entrance, a path leads to what was once the main avenue of ancient Priene. The western side of the block (facing downhill) begins with the **Prytaneum,** the vaulted hearth of the city's sacred flame. Brought to Priene from Athens by the first settlers, the flame was extinguished only when the city was invaded, and rekindled from the flame of another temple upon liberation. After the Prytaneum is the unmistakable **Bouleterion,** or Senate House, a well-preserved and elegant square auditorium. The interior chamber was equipped with a huge marble altar on which sacrifices were offered both at the opening and closing of the sessions. Only the foundation of this altar remains.

More substantial congregations convened just up the hill at the handsome **theater.** The front row retains its five **thrones** of honor with their dignified bases carved in the shape of lions' paws. Farther along the upper terrace at the city's acme, the **Temple of Athena** transports you back to the heyday of Hellenistic architecture. Alexander the Great financed the project and Pytheos, the architect whose *chef d'œuvre* is the Mausoleum of Halicarnassus (one of the many seven wonders of the ancient world described in this book), designed the structure. The temple retains largely intact front steps and interior floors. Descend from the temple to visit the vast remains of the private houses of Priene, an unusual example of Ionian domestic architecture.

Heading back towards the entrance of the site, you'll pass through the spacious **agora,** where women were allowed only if accompanied by a man, either husband or slave. At the center, a public temple once hosted official ceremonies and sacrifices. Beyond the agora is the well-ruined 3rd-century BCE **Temple of Olympic Zeus.** Downhill on the lip of the plateau stand the **Stadium** and **Gymnasium,** with the names of many young athletes inscribed in the walls. On either side of the main hall were small rooms for bathing or exercise.

Miletus

Now landlocked by arid plains, Miletus once sat upon a slender tongue of land surrounded by four separate harbors. Envied for its prosperity and its strategic coastal location, the city was destroyed and resettled more than once. Miletus suffered the same fate as its Ionian confederates: the silting of its harbor and waters by neighboring rivers caused its decline. For centuries, Miletus was a hotbed of commercial and cultural development. In the 5th century BCE, the Milesian alphabet was adopted as the standard Greek script. Miletus later became the headquarters of the Ionian school of philosophers, which included Thales, Anaximander, and Anaximenes. The city's leadership, however, eventually faltered in 499 BCE, when Miletus headed an unsuccessful Ionian revolt against the Persian army. The Persians retaliated by wiping out the entire population of the city, massacring the men, and selling the women and children into slavery.

The site's main attraction is the **theater,** clearly visible from the Priene-Didyma highway. As well-preserved as my grandmother, the structure dates from Hellenistic times, though most of the visible portion is Roman work. The theater, which could seat 15,000, was originally positioned right at the water's edge. Notice the owners' names on some of the front row seats.

During all but the summer months, the remaining portions of Miletus are marshy wastelands. To the right of the theater as you enter the site is a Seljuk **Kervansaray** (perennially under restoration). Facing the theater, the footpath meandering to your right leads you to the mephistophelian **Faustina Baths** (behind the theater), erected by Faustina, wife of the Roman Emperor Marcus Aurelius. To the left of the baths are the **North** and **South Agoras.** Next to the baths is the **Delphinium,** or sanctuary of Apollo Delphinus. The temple was first constructed to honor Apollo, who transformed himself into a dolphin and led the Cretans to Miletus. All of the temple's priests were sailors. If nothing else, visit the abandoned 15th-century **İlyas Bey Cami,** the peculiar dome-shaped structure just beyond the baths. Weeds sprouting atop its tiled dome give it that very in-vogue huge-nest look. The family of storks who have made their home here appear extremely content with their modish abode. The interior offers refuge from the heat as well as an exquisitely decorated *mihrab.* About ½km before the main entrance stands a small **Archaeological Museum.** (Open daily 8:30am-6pm. Admission 70¢, with ISIC 35¢.)

Didim (Didyma)

Didyma takes about an hour to see. Ancient Didyma was the site of a sacred sanctuary dedicated to Apollo and of an oracle that brought in most of the city's fame and wealth. The first Didyma oracles date from about 600 BCE. About 100 years later, the sanctuary was destroyed by the Persians when they plundered Miletus. The temple lay deserted until Alexander the Great's arrival, which inspired the arid sacred spring to miraculously flow anew. The present sanctuary was begun during the second and first centuries BCE. Work continued until the second century CE, but the original plans, like those for Alexander's empire, proved too ambitious and were never completed.

The **sanctuary** at Didyma ranked as the third largest sacred structure in the ancient Hellenic world after its neighbors to the north, the Temple of Artemis at Ephesus and the Temple of Hera on Samos. Since virtually nothing remains of either of the latter two buildings, the sanctuary at Didyma stands alone as the best surviving example of such colossal temple architecture. It was built to last—many of its individual marble slabs weigh over a ton.

During the Roman period, the unfinished temple attracted pilgrims from all over ancient Greece. A church was constructed on the site in 385 CE after Emperor Theodosius I outlawed the solicitation of pagan oracles, and the priestesses fell silent. The sacred road that ran from Miletus to Didyma ended at the temple gates; the statues which once lined the final stretch were relocated to the British Museum in 1858 and have been replaced by souvenir shops which ineffectually strive to command the same regal presence.

Inside the main gate rests a bas-relief of a giant **Medusa head,** once part of an ornate frieze that girded the temple's exterior and now star of countless tourist brochures. The building's full magnitude is apparent only when you climb up the stairway to the main façade. Still, you are seeing only a fraction of the original: all that remains of the more than 100 magnificent columns are the bases and lower sections. To transport such immensely cumbersome chunks of marble, the Greeks constructed long shafts of stone leading to the temple site, lubricated them with soap, and then slid the building materials over the slippery surface, rejoicing all the while at the ease of their work and the silky feel of their skin.

In front of the temple trickles the spring that the priestesses supposedly tapped when receiving prophecies from Apollo. Climb the steps to enter the forecourt. Through the **Hall of Twelve Columns** is the **Hall of Two Columns,** where visitors waited to hear the pronouncements. From here, 22 steps lead down to the **audition,** where no visitors were permitted.

In the southeast corner of the courtyard are traces of another **sacred fountain,** as well as the foundations of a **naiskos,** a tiny temple that housed a venerated bronze statue of Apollo. The temple, which served as the site of the oracle, appears to have been erected in 300 BCE before the larger edifice was even begun.

Pamukkale (Hierapolis)

Whether as Pamukkale or ancient Hierapolis, this village has been drawing the weary and the curious to its thermal springs for over 23 centuries. The Turkish name—literally "cotton castle"—refers to the extraordinary surface of the snow-white cliffs, shaped over millennia by the accumulation of calcium deposited by mineral springs. Legend has it that the formations *are* actually solidified cotton (the area's principal crop) that was left out to dry by giants. Dripping slowly down the vast mountain side, the mineral-rich water foams and collects in bowls that terrace the decline, spilling over petrified cascades of stalactites into milky pools below. The ancient site of Hierapolis requires only a few hours to see in depth, enabling you to spend the rest of the day bathing in Pamukkale.

Practical Information

Most of the direct buses that run to Pamukkale leave from Seljuk and Kuşadası before 9am (5-6 per day, 4½hr.). Frequent *dolmuş* and minibuses run back and forth between Pamukkale and the bustling regional capital of Denizli, which has extensive service to all major Turkish cities. Less expensive and less comfortable—unless you get an overnight couchette—are the direct trains that travel from İzmir and İstanbul to Denizli. *Dolmuş* and minibuses to Pamukkale leave from directly in front of the Denizli bus station, about 100m south and across the street from the train station. Buses run twice hourly between İzmir and Denizli via Seljuk. From Pamukkale, there are infrequent direct buses to Bodrum (4-5hr., $7), İzmir (5hr., $6.50), Seljuk and Kuşadası (4-5hr., $4). The bus will drop you either in the central square of Pamukkale Köyü (the town near the foot of the cliffs), or near the bus-company offices just up a curving street. The tourist complex lies uphill from the train and has a **PTT** (open daily 8am-midnight) and a **first aid center,** which is behind the Roman Baths (now a museum). There is also a small **tourist information office** (tel. 10 77) at the end of the row of curio shops near the main site entrance. (Open daily 8:30am-6pm.) Pamukkale's **telephone code** is 6218.

As you stand in the central square of the town with your back to the tourist map/billboard, the road to the tourist complex starts off straight ahead and to the right, then curves around to the left past some bus-company offices and up the hill.

Accommodations, Camping, and Food

In Pamukkale, everyone and her proverbial brother will hound you with a room. The motels in the tourist complex are all expensive, but many relatively inexpensive pensions, often with small pools, crowd the village below. There are campsites in the village and at the Bel-Tes and Mis-Tur motels near the tourist complex. All charge about $2 per person. Many of the pensions in the village also allow camping on their property and use of their pools. All prices are negotiable as competition is intense.

Halley Pension (tel. 12 04), in the center of town directly across from the map/billboard. Quiet, sterile, recently renovated rooms, but warm management. Doubles with bath $6. Breakfast included. **Kervansaray Pension** (tel. 12 09). From the map/billboard, turn right and take a left after about 90m (you'll see the pension from here). Comfortable, carpeted rooms with phones. Small pool. $6 per person. Don't forget to sign their guest book.

Ziya Pension (tel. 11 95), 100m below the square, to the left and then down from the map/billboard. Spacious with high ceilings and a nice, semi-pastoral location. Decent restaurant and a pleasant terrace on the roof. $2-3 per person, with person $3.50 per person. Watch the pit toilets.

Hotel Türku (tel. 11 81). From the map/billboard, head straight and to the right, turn right, and then left (better yet, ask someone). Pool and terrace. Lovely wooden façade with epicurean rooms. Some exorbitant, so ask for one without shower or balcony. Bathrooms in every room. Singles $14. Doubles $17. Breakfast included.

Hotel Gül (tel. 12 89), continue past the Ziya Pension and turn left. Endearingly shabby with plants everywhere and a pool. Get a room with a view. Family atmosphere. $6 per person.

The town of Karahayıt, 4km north of Pamukkale and site of the Red Springs, has a few cheap pensions. Most rooms have private bathtubs (fed by the hot springs) that steam up the rooms. The camping facility at the Red Springs has swimming pools and reasonably clean bathrooms ($2 per person). **Ünal Restaurant** is the local favorite which serves gallivanting Turks tripe soup and other tasty items after a night's tippling. (Open daily 10am-2pm.) Most of the pensions are capped with roof-top restaurants that offer cheap, gobbleable food. **Restaurant Oba** is almost elegant and the *menemen* (spicy baked egg, tomato, and pepper) is only $1.

Sights

The warm baths at Pamukkale effervesce with oxygen bubbles like an seething glass of enthusiastic Perrier. There are two different series of terraces situated on either side of the main road down into the village. Elegant, shallow pools, located in front of the Tusan Motel (nearest the highway), gradually become deeper further down the slope. The deepest, most intricately shaped, and most popular terraces are directly behind the nameless restaurant-café facing the main parking lot. On weekends locals flock to bathe in the flat, fan-like pools. Near the entrance to the tourist complex, seek out a place away from the zealots in more crowded pools who attempt to submerge their entire bodies in the six inches of available spring water. Three large motels have sprouted up among the thermal springs and ancient ruins. The motels—demonstrating the awesome foresight characteristic of the Turkish tourist industry—have diverted the mineral-rich waters into their own pools, robbing the white cliffs of their calcium supply. Fortunately the government, responding to pressure from residents and environmental groups, recently decided to close the motels and restrict car access to the cliffs. Admission to the site is 45¢.

Between the motels soar the colossal vaulted archways of the **Hierapolis City Baths.** The visible portions of this first-century structure are all that remain of one of Asia Minor's greatest ancient tourist industries: hygienia. The springs of Hierapolis were particularly popular with vacationing Romans. After an earthquake leveled the spa in 17 CE, Hierapolis was promptly rebuilt, and it reached its heyday during the 2nd and 3rd centuries CE. The city bath's glossy marble interior has now been converted into a mediocre **Archaeological Museum.** (Open Tues.-Sun. 9am-5pm. Free.)

Carved into the side of the mountain, the monstrous **Grand Theater** dominates the vista of Hierapolis. Almost all of the seating area for 25,000 is intact, and the variety of ornately sculpted decorative elements adorning the façade and stage area are very well preserved. In front of the theater are the remains of the 3rd-century CE **Temple of Apollo.** Behind the temple stands the monumental fountain **Nymphaeum,** or Monumental Fountain. Nearby is the famous **Plutonium,** a pit that emits poisonous carbonic acid gas, a substance ancients believed could kill all living creatures except priests and pit-toilet-experienced backpackers. The Turks call it *Cin Deliği* (Devil's Hole). Further to the right lies a hot-water spring. If you continue on the footpath, you'll reach the 6th-century **Christian basilica.**

Down the road to Karahayıt is the north **city gate** on the right, and the ruins of a 5th-century Christian basilica dedicated to St. Philip, martyred here in 80 CE. Outside the gate is the **Necropolis,** with more than 1200 tombs and sarcophagi. People who wished to be buried here believed that proximity to the hot springs and vapor-emitting cracks would ease their trip to the Underworld (after, of course, trusting the same springs to relieve them of the need for such a trip). Among the tombs lies the **Martyrium,** an octagonal 5th-century edifice believed to have been erected upon the site where St. Philip was martyred in 80 CE.

Do not leave Pamukkale without a savory dip in the **sacred fountain** at the Pamukkale Motel (75m beyond the archaeological museum). Warm, fizzy waters bubble forth from the spring's source, now blocked off to prevent any more divers from disappearing into its depths. On the pool's floor rest remains of Roman columns, toppled by the same earthquake that opened the source. After a day's tramping through ruins, a bath here is sublime. (Open to the public daily 9am-9pm. $1.50 per hr.)

Aphrodisias

While the remnants of Aphrodisias have been scrutinized for decades, archaeologists believe that a great deal remains unexcavated. The highlights of the ruins excavated to date include a well preserved Roman stadium and *odeon,* as well as a temple, an *agora,* a palace, and some thermal baths. Although getting to Aphrodisias is a hassle because of the lack of major settlements nearby, the fairly expansive site is less overwhelming (and 100 times less crowded) than Ephesus, and the carefully preserved ruins make it worthwhile. Optimistic archaeologists believe Aphrodisias will outshine Ephesus within 50 years.

Ancient Greeks made pilgrimages here to pay their respects and ask Aphrodite for blesssings. The village evolved into a metropolis when King Attalos III bequeathed Pergamon to the hated Romans, spurring a massive exodus to this land of divine love and beauty. Aphrodisias gained fame for its sculpture; crafted from the fine white and bluish-gray marble of nearby quarries, the finest statues in the Roman Empire were often marked with an imprint from the celebrated Aphrodisian school. Aphrodisias was also an important think tank of Asia Minor. With the ascendancy of Christianity, temples were converted to churches and the city's name became Stavropolis ("City of the Cross").

The pinnacle of a visit to Aphrodisias is seeing the best-preserved ancient **stadium** ever excavated. Even the marble blocks that once marked the starting line for foot races are still in place in the central arena where the seating capacity was 30,000. The looming structure at the bottom of the hill is **Hadrian's Bath,** equipped with a sauna, frigidarium, and changing rooms. To the right, the **Temple of Aphrodite** marks the site of ancient venereal veneration. Although only a portion of its 40-column spiral-fluted Corinthian colonnade remains, the temple retains its elegance. Dating from the first century CE, the shrine originally housed a famous statue of Aphrodite, similar in appearance to the many-breasted Artemis of Ephesus. So far, only copies of the original have been unearthed. With its extraordinary blue marble stage, the **odeon,** just to the south, was the council chamber for the town's elected officials. The nine columns quivering nearby were resurrected as part of a building christened the **Bishop's Palace** by archaeologists owing to a large number of religious artifacts and statues unearthed on its premises. Some of the original marble floors remain intact. Among the highlights of the site's must-see museum are megastatues of Aphrodite and a satyr carrying the child Dionysus. (Museum and ruins open daily 9am-7pm. Admission to ruins and museum each $3, with ISIC $1.50.)

Transportation to Aphrodisias presents a challenge. The easiest way to see the ruins is to take a daytrip from Pamukkale. Pamukkale Turizm **buses** leave daily at 10am and return to Pamukkale at 5pm (2hr., $5, round-trip $8). The alternative is to take a bus or *dolmuş* from Denizli, Nazilli, or Kuşadası/Seljuk to the small town of Karacasu, and hitch from there; however, *Let's Go* does not recommend hitchhiking as a safe means of transportation. Buses on the Denizli-Muğle route pass through Tavas, 30km from Aphrodisias. From Tavas, it is possible to hitch, but very few cars pass along this road. Kuşadası travel agencies offer a hurried package day tour to Pamukkale and Aphrodisias ($40 per person). The **telephone code** for Aphrodisias is 6379.

The **Beydağ Pension** (tel. 14 90 or 16 13), overlooking the highway, has large private cabins for two ($6). Cross the highway from the turn-off to Aphrodisias and turn left on the dirt road up the hill. **Chez Mestan** (tel. 80 46 or 81 32), 300m down the highway, is très chic with comfortable rooms, free unlimited coffee, and an English-speaking, French-wed owner. (Doubles with showers $6.) The pensions all serve meals, but the best food around can be devoured at the **Anatolia Restaurant** (tel. 81 38), 3km away on the road to Karacasu. You can pet the owner's dog. (Open until November 15 daily 7am-8pm; free camping if you take your meals there.)

Bodrum

Esconced in the serpentine coastline of the Bodrum Peninsula—a heliophile's paradise brimming with beaches, secluded coves, and uninhabited islands—Bodrum is understandably the favorite retreat of many Turkish jet-setters, intellectuals, artists, and rich, jaded city-dwellers. But for all of Bodrum's fashionable sophistication, there really is not that much to see: the only noteworthy sights are the scanty remains of the mausoleum of Halicarnassus, yet another one of the seven wonders of the ancient world, and the solid crusader fortress (the *kale)* which guards the harbor. Still, Bodrum's glorious beaches, rip-roaring nightlife, and flocks of festive, extra-crispy tourists will surely keep you amused.

Bodrum was built upon the ancient city of Halicarnassus, a powerful port town and capital of ancient Caria. (The Carians were an Anatolian people who lived in this area around 1200 BCE, prior to the Greek invasion.) Halicarnassus was known for its succession of female rulers, who became leaders after the deaths of their fathers, husbands, or brothers. One such ruler was Artemesia I, who led a fleet against the Athenians in their war with Persia in 480 BCE; her story is related in the *Persian Wars* by Herodotus, another native of Halicarnassus. In 377 BCE, the famous Mausolus of Cairo came to power and made Halicarnassus his capital. Work on his tomb began during his reign, and was completed under his wife's direction after his death in 353 BCE. The tomb provided the inspiration for the modern word "mausoleum." Some 25 years after Mausolus, Alexander the Great razed Halicarnassus, and since then the city has been unable to recapture its former glory.

Until 1925, Bodrum was a small fishing village of less than 2000 people. Then, the British-educated Cevat Şakir Kabaağaç (known as "the fisherman of Halicarnassus") settled here in political exile and began to write short stories about Bodrum and the surrounding areas. He attracted a community of like-minded intellectuals, who thrived on the peninsula undisturbed until the early 70s, when, suddenly and inexplicably, Bodrum attracted the attention of tourists. Holiday villages filled the peninsula, the houses in Bodrum turned into pensions and bars. The early 80s saw thousands of British tourists looking for romance and sex (though not necessarily in that order) filling the city and made it the sex capital of Turkey. Somewhat diminished in stature today, Bodrum still has a thrilling nightlife and many opportunities to meet people of all sexes and orientations.

Orientation and Practical Information

Streets in Bodrum are often poorly marked. The city's most prominent and easily recognizable landmark is the centrally located fortress, the *kale* (literally "castle"), from which several main streets emanate. Some of the cheap pensions lie along the bank to the right of the *kale* as you face inland, right in the line of fire of zillion-decibel disco speakers. Breakwaters almost completely enclose the other port, which forms the older and more picturesque half of town. Ferries and most yacht cruises depart from this harbor.

The main thoroughfare along the waterfront starts from the castle and runs along the enclosed left harbor: it begins as **Karantina Caddesi,** becomes **Belediye Meydanı** after the mosque, changes to **Neyzen Tevfik Caddesi** along most of the harbor, and ends at the **Yat Limanı** (yacht harbor). Going right from the castle, Kasaphane Cad. becomes Kumbahçe Mahallesi, then changes to the main commercial drag of **Cumhuriyet Caddesi,** and ends by the Halikarnas Hotel as Paşa Tarlası. Extending inland from the castle towards the bus station, **Kale Caddesi** is Bodrum's main shopping strip; it becomes **Cevat Şâkir Caddesi,** which runs past the post office and the bus station, where all inter-city buses, taxis, and *dolmuş* depart.

Tourist Office: 12 Eylül Meydanı (tel. 110 91), at the foot of the castle. Accommodations listings and a lousy map. Slightly better maps available at the bookstore. They do have bus information. Open daily 8am-7:30pm; Nov.-March Mon.-Fri. 8am-noon and 1-5pm.

Travel Agents: Karya Tours, 6 Dr. Alim Bey Cad. (tel. 17 59 or 18 43), and at the ferryboat landing (tel. 119 14). Coordinate ferries to Kos and the Datça Peninsula, and daily excursion to Pamukkale ($27) and Ephesus ($27). Open daily 8am-9:30pm. Also excellent is **Flama Tour** (tel. 18 42), opposite the entrance to the yacht marina. They have ferry tickets, car rental, and give honest information.

PTT: Cevat Şâkir Cad., 4 blocks from the bus station as you walk towards the harbor. **Currency exchange** open 24 hrs. Another PTT at the ferry landing. International telephones also next to the castle. Open 24 hrs. In summer, expect to wait in line. **Telephone Code:** 614.

Bus Station: Cevat Şâkir Cad. Hourly buses to Marmaris (3hr., $3.75), and İzmir (6hr., $7). Frequent buses to İstanbul (10 per day, 14hr., $23), Ankara (6 per day, 14hr., $18), and Pamukkale (5 per day, 5hr., $10). Frequent *dolmuş* service (every 15min. in high season) to Gümbet, Bitez, Turgut Reis, Gümüşlük, and Gundoğan on the peninsula.

Ferries: Tickets sold through any travel agent. Boats to Kos leave at 9am and return at 5pm. (1 per day; Sept.-May 3 per week; 1½hr., $24, same day round trip $27, open round trip $40. Greek port-tax $8.25.) Ferry to Datça Peninsula, 8km from Datça and 80km from Marmaris (June-Aug. 2 per day; $10, with ISIC $9, same day round trip $14).

Bookstores: Recep E. Cingöz Gazeteler, Kale Cad. (tel. 26 30), behind Adilye Mosque. Wide selection of guidebooks, postcards, and newspapers. Open Mon.-Sat. 8am-9pm. You can find *Time* and *Newsweek* magazines near the Belediye Mosque. The **Bodrum Public Library:** *(Kütüphane),* 65 Cumhuriyet Cad., has a wide selection of English books and allows foreigners to check them out up to 1 week, with a passport as collateral. Open Mon.-Fri. 8am-noon and 1-5pm.

Hospital: Turgutreis Cad. (tel. 10 68), past the ruins of the mausoleum.

Police: 12 Eylül Meydanı (tel. 10 04), next to the tourist office at the foot of the castle.

Accommodations and Camping

Rooms become scarce during the summer. If you arrive in the evening in July or August without a reservation, do *not* plan on finding a room. Pensions are a better bet than hotels; there are hundreds of them and they're inexpensive—for Bodrum. The going rate for recent summers at most of the cheaper pensions has held firmly at about $6 per person. If you're traveling alone, it's a good idea to find a roommate, as pensions rarely have singles and are reluctant to let doubles to solo travelers. Often rooms are available in private homes called *ev pansiyons*. Look for signs that read "Oda Var" (literally "rooms exist") or "Boş Oda Var."

Yenilmez Pansiyon (tel. 125 20). Look for the sign along Neyzen Tevfik (the road along the left harbor) amid the offices of several car rental agencies. Quiet location with pleasant garden. Large, airy rooms. One of the best deals in town. $4.25 per person. Hot shower included.

Bahçeli Ağar Pansiyon, 4 Yat Limanı Sok. (tel. 16 48). Turn right at 190 Neyzen Tevfik Cad. across from the marina. This "family" pension is immaculate in every respect with capacious rooms, vine-canopied patio, and common kitchen. Singles $7. Doubles $10.

Polyanna Pension (tel. 115 28). Take a left to Ortanca Sok. from the Halikarnas Disco end of Cumhuriyet Cad. Very clean and tastefully decorated rooms with showers. Doubles $14-17. Triples $21-25. Breakfast included. Reservations recommended.

Fawlty Towers, 42 Cumhuriyet Cad. (tel. 115 44) is a bit more expensive, but it's worth the money. No Polly, no Manuel; the owner is nicer than Basil. Offers the comfort of a 3-star hotel. Huge rooms with comfortable beds and big bathrooms. Doubles $20-22. Triples $28. Breakfast included.

Camping: Bodrum's mostly grassless and shadeless campsites will probably persuade you to camp elsewhere. Turn right at Gerence Sok., 2 blocks from the center on Neyzen Tevfik Cad., and walk 200m for **Senlik Camping,** 30 Gerence Sok. (tel. 133 48). $1.50 per person with tent. Slightly nicer is **Uçar Kamping,** Dere Sok. (tel. 144 52), fenced off with barbed wire. $2 per person. They also offer sweltering bungalows named after characters from the television show *Dallas:* "Suelin," "Babi," "Pemelâ," and "Lusi." From the tourist office, follow Kale Cad. to Cevat Şâkir Cad., take the first right after the PTT, and follow Atatürk Cad. 450m to Dere Sok.

Food and Entertainment

Bodrum is not bashful about being an expensive resort. *Lira* are well spent on a fish meal as the port is famous throughout Turkey for its seafood, especially octopus and squid. For the cheapest provisions, stock up at the fruit and vegetable stands just down Cevat Şâkir Cad. from the bus station, or at the big **market** that comes periodically on the other side of the station. Along Cumhuriyet Cad., before the harbor, a number of *kebap* salons and stands offer fried mussels (70¢), and the usual *pide* and *şiş.*

Sokkalı Ali Doksan Restaurant, across from the PTT. Simple Turkish fare. Meat, salad, drink, and all the bread you can eat for $3. Open Mon.-Sat. 9am-9:30pm.

Orhan's No. 7, 7 Eski Banka Sok., off Kale Cad. in a vine-covered alley full of restaurants. Extraordinary seafood, especially octopus. Very popular with locals. Full meal with drinks $8. Open daily 8:30-11pm.

06 Lokanta, 156 Cumhuriyet Cad. Authentic Turkish food in a bustling atmosphere. From the tourist office, take a right on Cumhuriyet Cad. and follow it about 600m through the bazaar labyrinth. Open 24 hrs.

For nightlife in Bodrum, the **Halicarnassus Disco,** Z. Müren Cad. at the end of Cumhuriyet Cad., 1½km from the center, should be your destination (it's marked on the tourist map). Most budget travelers, however, balk at the $10 cover charge, allegedly necessary to recoup the $1.2 million plus poured into the building of this pseudo-Roman marble theater. (The stage is the dance floor.) The **Hadi Gari,** Cumhuriyet Cad., a bar with nominal dancing, is Bodrum locals' hangout of choice. Pleasant pubs suffice for just relaxing and listening to music. Most bars are visible from the street and full of tourists. Others, frequented by Turks who make their summer residence in Bodrum, are more discreet. If you can shoulder the $5 first-drink charge (later drinks $1.50), visit the **Mavi Bar,** near the end of Cumhuriyet Cad. This popular Turkish hangout features floor cushions, *kilim,* and musicians famous throughout Turkey. For a similar ambience without the high cost, try the back porch of the **Buona Sera Bar,** 75 Cumhuriyet Cad., which has a nice terrace garden. (Beer $1.50 *Rakı* $1.50. Officially open 24 hrs., although the place is deserted 8am-5pm.)

Sights

Rising from the azure waters of the harbor, the **Kale** epitomizes the squat austerity of the medieval fortress. It was constructed over of the ruins of the ancient acropolis by the Order of the Knights of St. John during the 15th and 16th centuries CE. The castle towers, built by knights of different nations, have been dubbed the English, German, French, and Italian towers after intense creative brainstorm. Nearby loom the stubby yet handsome **Harbor Tower** and the sinister-looking battlement christened the **Snake Tower.** Despite the castle's immense proportions and extensive fortifications, only 10 years after its completion in 1513 Sultan Süleyman the Magnificent overpowered the knights and forced them to retreat to Malta. The Order survives today as an international health organization. This well-preserved Crusader castle allows you to feel like a medieval knight for your fifteen minutes.

The castle houses Bodrum's **Museum of Underwater Archaeology,** a bizarre assortment of ancient shipwreck flotsam from sites along the surrounding Turkish coastline. The name is slightly more interesting than the museum itself, which consists mainly of some broken remnants back-lit for eerie effect. A Byzantine courtyard in the central courtyard of the castle houses the **Bronze Age Hall** which contains finds from a 1200 BCE shipwreck. Huge jars found on board date from 1600 BCE, and their artwork strongly suggests the existence of an ancient trade route between Crete and the Asia Minor coast. The museum also exhibits *cam* (glassware) recovered from a variety of ancient and medieval wrecks. (Castle open Tues.-Sun. 8am-7pm. Museum open Tues.-Sun. 8am-noon and 1-7pm. Admission to both $2, with ISIC $1.)

The ruins of ancient **Halicarnassus** are Bodrum's better known if less picturesque attraction. Most of the remains were either destroyed or buried underneath the modern town of Bodrum. The city walls are visible at points, as are the meager remains of the **theater** on Kibris Schitler Cad., on the main road uphill from and parallel to the left harbor. The most famous of the ruins, the once wondrous **mausoleum,** consisted of a rectangular foundation and stone pedestal upon which the sepulchral chamber rested, surrounded by 36 Ionic columns. The 50m-high mausoleum, covered with a pythonic pyramidal roof, was crowned by a statue of Mausolus driving a chariot drawn by four horses. To get to the mausoleum, turn onto Saray Sok. from Neyzen Teufik Cad. The mausoleum will be on your right at the end of the street. (Open Tues.-Sun. 8am-noon and 1-7pm. Admission 70¢, with ISIC 35¢.)

Near Bodrum

Bodrum's popularity among Turkish tourists stems largely from its location at the head of the enchanting **Bodrum Peninsula.** After a day of swimming and sunning, you can linger over dinner, or partake of Bodrum's rousing nightlife. A few of the beaches on the southern coast of the peninsula are accessible only by tour boats, which leave from the front of the castle daily between 9 and 11am, and return between 5 and 6pm. Itineraries for the tours vary widely (check the tour schedule at the dock). Some popular destinations are **Kara Island,** the village of **Akyarlar,** and the beaches at **Baradakçi, Çapa Tatil, Kargı Bay, Bağla,** and **Karaincir.** Boat tours cost $7 per person for the day, $11.50 with lunch. In summer, boats also leave daily from the castle to tranquil **Orak Island** (same prices). There are no cheap accommodations at these places. Day trips are your best bet.

Just 3km outside of Bodrum is **Gümbet Beach,** the most popular sunbathing spot in the area; unfortunately, it is crowded and chaotic. Pensions are expensive here, but **Zetaş Camping** (tel. 14 07) falls within budget range ($3 per person).

Because the beach at **Bitez** is narrow, seaside bars have built pontooned docks over the water, where you can order drinks while you sunbathe. The beach around the next large cove from Gümbet is peaceful but has no cheap accommodations. *Dolmuş* from the Bodrum bus station travel to both these beaches. The most accessible point on the west coast of the peninsula, **Turgut Reis,** is 18km away from Bodrum. It's a one-dimensional beach-eat-sleep tourist town, alluring to some because it has the widest beach on the peninsula. The stretch of coast, however, is usually crowded with sunbathers and beach chairs, and the town itself has none of the charm of the villages to the north. There are quite a number of pensions in Turgut Reis, but they all tend to fill quickly in July and August. They line the street parallel to the beach to the right of the bus stop as you face the sea. The **Ferah Pansiyon** (tel. (6142) 10 30) and the **Çeylen Pansiyon** (tel. (6142) 13 64) each charge $5 per person. From Turgut Reis, *dolmuş* run south along the coast to the crowded beaches at Akyarlar and Karaincir.

The most popular spot with elderly British and young French, **Gümüşlük,** a princely hamlet at the far western end of the peninsula, also makes an excellent daytrip from Bodrum. The Turkish name means "silvery," referring to the ancient silver mines that were discovered in the area. Near the beach lie the ruins of ancient **Mindos,** a 4th-century BCE Carian port impregnable even to Alexander the Great. The site consists of the impressive city wall, 3m thick, and a Roman basilica. The beach here is sandy and small. Gümüşlük's **telephone code** is 614.

Accommodations are scarce as groups usually reserve pensions and villas far in advance. The friendly **Anka Pansiyon** (no phone), on the main road about halfway between the village and the shore's developments, is new and has pleasant rooms; the 10-minute walk from the beach is the drawback. ($6 per person.) A little bit farther on the main road, **Pension Flower of '68,** is reasonably clean and run by neo-hippies. It has no phone and is therefore more immune to folks with foresight. Jam sessions every night: bring your instrument ($7 for rooms with bathrooms and kitchens. breakfast $1.40) **Mindos Pansiyon** (tel. 733 82) is not a pension at all, but a family home which sometimes lets out rooms. Call ahead with a Turkish friend (no English spoken; $7 per person). From the end-of-the-line *dolmuş* stop, go down to the water, turn right, and take another right up the past the Batı Restaurant; it's the unmarked building just above the mosque. For camping, try **Arriba Camping** (no phone, no reservations necessary), on the beach to the left of the *dolmuş* depot. You can also follow the sign for the main road. (Tent plus 2 people $4.30.) Nearby are several scrumptatious fish restaurants with delicious views of the water. Try the **Batı Restaurant,** where the main road meets the beach, which supremely entangles you in octopus and squid for under $4. (Beer 85¢.)

The northern end of the peninsula is less spoiled than the overpopulated southern coast. Its surroundings are beautiful, its beaches rocky, and its water deep. **Gölköy** and **Türkbükü** were once idyllic villages, now hives for Turkish tourists. A few old windmills dot **Yalıkavak,** at the northwest end of the peninsula, where many even smaller villages are scattered. Each of these towns has a few pensions. The best way to find a place to sleep is to walk the beach and look for pensions there. You can camp in Yalıkavak at **Yalı Camping** (tel. 441 42), across from Belediye beach at the harbor. The facilities are clean, and the owner Ahmet Günay is very helpful ($3.40 per person). In Gölköy, you can stay at **Ege Pansiyon** (tel. 771 34) to the right side of the beach (facing the water), past Hotel Daphis, left before Motel A ($7 per person). **Sugar Pension** (tel. 771 29/30) on the right end of the beach has clean but unspectacular rooms; second floor rooms are nicer ($6 per person). You can make phone calls from **Orhide Cafeteria** at Gağlayou Rest., where a full meal runs about $3. In Türkbükü, land of the overpriced restaurant and the way narrow beach, the cheapest place to sleep is **Genç Pansiyon,** (tel. 75012) which offers okey-dokey rooms with showers ($11 per person including breakfast and one meal). You can also camp on the pension grounds ($4.30 for a tent plus 2 people).

MEDITERRANEAN COAST

Extending from the edges of Greece to the Syrian border, Turkey's Mediterranean coast offers everything from lively resorts to remote expanses of untrodden sand. Pine forests and hidden coves and beaches garnish the rugged stretch between Fethiye and Antalya. Accommodations along the western segment of the Mediterranean coast are generally inexpensive, and excellent seafood eateries abound. Farther east, broad swatches of sand and concrete are dotted with castles and ruins, forming the tourist-saturated shoreline that the tourist propaganda has dubbed the "Turquoise Coast." While Antakya, screened by a mountain range, continues its centuries-old way of life, Mersin is commercialized and modern.

During the first and second millennia BCE, the area around Fethiye and Kaş formed the Kingdom of Lycia. The Lycians revelled in fancy burial rites and funerary monuments, and are not remembered for much else. Rock tombs are carved into cliff-sides all along the coast, while almost everywhere you look—in the middle of city streets, littered around the countryside, and even perched on off-shore islands—you'll see Lycian sarcophagi. Most significant of the Lycian cities that punctuate the coast are the ruins of **Xanthos** and **Patara.**

The best boat connection between the Greek islands and Turkey's Mediterranean shores is the ferry between Rhodes and Marmaris, which leaves daily in summer. Allow enough time to explore farther east, and west to the enchanting Datça Peninsula. Distances on maps are deceiving: beyond Fethiye, the road winds through mountain terrain and becomes as slow as it is scenic. Boats run regularly between Northern (Turkish-occupied) Cyprus and the ports of **Taşucu** and **Mersin.** Travel from these ports to the Republic of Cyprus (Greek Cyprus) is impossible. Antalya has an international airport with remarkably cheap domestic flights to major Turkish cities (to İstanbul $70, for students $43). Antalya also sees off speedy direct buses to İstanbul ($22). **Varan Tur** bus company is about 50% more expensive, but for such a lengthy trip, air-conditioning, comfortable seats, a bathroom, and continuous çay are well worth the extra money.

Marmaris

Although you may be disappointed when you first see Marmaris's overdeveloped shoreline and dirty beach, this stepping stone from the Dodecanese could be worse. At least here the tourists are mostly Turkish and the nightlife is hopping. If you can overlook the shops full of camera film and neon shorts, you'll see wooded mountains along the coast and on nearby islands, standing as a verdant backdrop to the harbor's deep blue water. If you look into the splendid distance for too long, you'll realize why most people come to Marmaris: to go somewhere else. Located at the intersection of Turkey's Aegean and only a short ferry ride from Rhodes, Marmaris makes a perfect point of departure.

Orientation and Practical Information

You're never more than 3 blocks from the sea in Marmaris—one flailing stretch of hotels, restaurants, and cafés hugging the shoreline. **Kordon Caddesi,** which eventually becomes **Atatürk Caddesi,** runs along the waterfront. The tourist office, castle, and boat marina are at the east end of the waterfront (to the left facing the water). From the bus station, cross the small footbridge over a channel of water and then follow along the coast to reach the tourist office, a handy landmark. Sometimes buses deposit passengers at the dusty *dolmuş* stop. From this stop, head to the water and turn left along the waterfront for 200m to find the tourist office.

Tourist Office: 2 İskele Meydanı on Kordon Cad. (tel. 110 35 or 172 77), across from the main ferry dock. They provide maps, suggest excursions, and can help locate rooms. You can leave your luggage here for an hour. English spoken. Open daily 8am-7:30pm, Sept.-April Mon.-Fri. 8am-5pm.

Bus Station: Follow the waterfront east (to the left facing the water) to the end, turn inland 1 block, cross the footbridge, and turn left. Buses to: İzmir (every hr., 5hr., $8); Datça (10 per day, 2hr., $3); Fethiye (10 per day, 3hr., $4.25); and Bodrum (10 per day, 3hr., $5).

PTT: Fevzipaşa Cad. Three blocks along the waterfront and 1 block inland from the tourist office. With **currency exchange.** Open 24 hrs. **Telephone Code:** 612.

Ferries: To Rhodes (Mon.-Sat. 9am; Nov.-April Mon., Thurs., Sat. 9am; $24, same-day round-trip $39). Passports must be given to the agency the night before departure. Tickets available at any travel agency; there are many along the waterfront. Private excursions must be arranged on the dock with the skipper.

Hospital: On Datça Rd. (tel. 110 29), near the *dolmuş* station, 1 block inland along Ulusal Egemenlik Bulvarı from the waterfront.

Police: Tel. 114 94. At the corner of Kordon and Fevzipaşa Cad., 3 blocks along the waterfront from the tourist office. No English spoken: they may ask the tourist office for a translator. The **passport police** (tel. 116 76) is directly opposite the tourist office at 2 Barbaros Cad.

Laundromat: Marina Laundry, behind the Amer Bar next to the boat marina. 5kg wash and dry $6. Open daily 8am-10pm. Note that many pensions have laundry service too.

Accommodations and Camping

Marmaris has quite a few resonably-priced pensions and hotels, most of which remain booked in July and August. Arrive early in the day to secure a room.

Interyouth Hostel, Iyiliktaş Merkii (tel. 164 32). From the *dolmuş* station, walk inland and take your first left; after 2 blocks, you will see it across the vacant lot. Clean and friendly. Cafeteria on the roof serves breakfast all day. Scanty baths. Free use of washing machine. Dorm beds $5. Single rooms or beds in a double $7. If the rooms are full, they'll give you a cot on the roof for $3.

Kordon Pansiyon, 8 Kemalpaşa Sok. (tel. 147 62). From the PTT, walk to the end of the block, turn left, and walk 1 more block. Halit's mission in life is to make his *pansiyon* a meeting point for backpackers from around the world. His bar, Images, helps the cause. $4. Flaunt your copy of *Let's Go* and get a 15% discount.

Maltepe Pansiyon (tel. 116 29), two blocks toward the sea from the hostel. Clean, airy rooms, a shady garden, free laundry service, and a common kitchen. Rooms with showers $4, roof $2.

Star Pansiyon, 28 Ismet Paşa Sok. (tel. 117 77). From the post office, walk 2 blocks inland and turn right. Quite clean, though cramped and a bit noisy. Some rooms have balconies. Singles $6. Doubles $9. Showers included.

There are several campsites in the area, most of them around the west side of the bay (to the right as you face the water). Every 5-10 minutes, the "İçmeler" *dolmuş* drives around the bay, and will stop at the campgrounds if you ask. **Berk Camping** (tel. 141 71) is right by the water ($3 per tent plus two people).

Food

Scrounge up your last filaments of willpower and resist the temptation to eat anything along the waterfront. Instead, search for sustenance on inland streets. At the **Marmaris Lokantası,** Fevzipaşa Cad., just inland from the post office, you'll get rushed service, and cheap, hearty meals. (Full meals $3.25; open 24 hrs.) Inexpensive meals are otherwise scarce in Marmaris, but most places serve *kebap* ($1.50-$2).

Sights

Marmaris itself has little to offer besides a large town beach and a **fortress,** built in 1522 by Süleyman the Magnificent as a military base for his successful campaign against the Crusaders of Rhodes. The alleyways hugging the castle-walk form the oldest and most picturesque section of the city. (Open Mon.-Fri. 8am-5pm. Admission

40¢, with ISIC 20¢.) Only 1½km away, **Günnücek National Park** features a small beach and picnic tables set against a forest fragrant with rare frankincense trees. Marvel myrrhthfully. To reach the park, follow the coastal road past the marina and out of town, across the small wooden footbridge.

The best **beaches** and scenery around Marmaris are accessible only by boat. Thick shrubbery, which covers the gray rocks along the coast, creates a striking contrast to the deep blue of the bay. Serving the bay, *dolmuş motorları* boats depart from the harbor along Kordon Cad. every morning for a variety of destinations. The drivers are casual about the itineraries, and destinations vary according to their moods. All-day tours cost about $7 per person. Most boats make the tour that stops at **Paradise Island Beach** and then the **Akvaryum,** the Turkish version of an aquarium. You're free to go diving when the boat anchors. The tour also visits some phosphorous caves, and then the **Turunç Beach,** across the bay from Marmaris; since electricity was installed in 1979, the beach has become popular with Turkish vacationers. Flanking Turunç to the north and south respectively are the **Gölenye Springs,** whose waters reputedly cure intestinal ailments, and the less crowded **Kumlu Beach,** near the scanty remains of an old fortress. Both are convenient by boat. Most of the mouth of the Bay of Marmaris is sealed off by the heavily wooded **Nimara Peninsula.** Along the far end of the peninsula are the fluorescent phosphorous caves near **Alkoya Point,** another favorite destination for Marmaris's excursion boats. Sandwiched between the peninsula and the mainland is the tiny uninhabited village of **Keçi,** which offers a good view of the surrounding coastline.

For a good daytrip, head to the fine sand beaches of **Kleopatras Island.** Take a bus going toward Muğla, get off at the Sedir turnoff, and walk or hitch the last 6km. From there, take a *dolmuş motorlarıı* to the island ($7 per boat).

Three *dolmuş* per day travel to **Bozburun,** an unspoiled town on a nearby peninsula peppered with ruins. Ask at the tourist office for details and a list of pensions.

Datça Peninsula

Jutting out from the coastline at Marmaris, the slim Datça Peninsula extends 120km into the sea, a short distance from the Greek island of Symi. This jagged spike of land, cleaved by indigo fjords, just becomes more idyllic the farther you go. A winding two-hour bus ride (not for those prone to motion sickness) drops you in the quiet town of **Datça,** a favorite vacation spot for Turks. Finding accommodations here from June to August can be tough unless you call a day or two ahead. Buses from Marmaris travel to Datça (10 per day, $3). You can also take a boat from Bodrum (in summer only, daily at 9am and 5pm, $10). Another boat returns to Bodrum from Datça at 9am. Tickets are available at most travel agencies in Bodrum. Buy tickets at the **Deniz Ticket Office,** right by the bus stop (open in summer daily 8am-midnight). The English-speaking staff at the **tourist office** (tel. 11 36 or 21 43) has a pamphlet on the city and can arrange a taxi to Knidos (round-trip $30; open daily 8am-7:30pm; Oct.-April Mon.-Sat. 8am-5pm). The **police** (tel. 17 92) also speak English. The **PTT** on the main road remains open until 11:30pm. For **currency exchange,** go to one of the several banks (open Mon.-Fri. 8am-5pm). Datça's **telephone code** is 6145.

Accommodations and Food

Bloodthirsty mosquitoes invade each evening—be sure that the pension you choose is well equipped with either repellent spray or pellets (ask for *kov* or *esem mat* in the local pharmacy). From the bus station, walk toward the harbor and make your first left for the **Huzur Pansiyon** (tel. 13 64), which has smirchless, breezy rooms. (Doubles $10, with shower $13.) Across the way, **Sadik Pension** (tel. 11 96) offers a family atmosphere and stunning views of the bay ($3-$3.50 per person). The **Umut Pansiyon** (tel. 11 17), above the Abdullah Carpet shop (follow the main road away from Marmaris as it curves around), offers respectable rooms for $9. The extremely well-run **Aktur Camping** (tel. (6146) 11 68), 30km east of Datça, is part of a vacation village with a beach, rooms to let, windsurfer rentals, and plenty of tourists. The campsite allows some privacy amid its pine trees ($2.70 per tent. $2.70 per person. Bungalows $13.50.) In Datça, **Ilica Camping** (tel. 14.00), on the beach beyond the harbor, has a restaurant and spartan two-person bungalows with private baths ($3.50 per person). Camping costs $2 per tent-plus-two-people. The animated owner, Feridun, might take you on a wild boar hunt for an afternoon of serenity. The boar, now roasted, reappears at the evening all-you-can-eat meal which also includes salad, wine, live Turkish music, and a belly dancer for $10. Backpackers freelance camp almost anywhere outside of town.

The self-proclaimed cheapest food in town is at **Deniz Lokantasy,** around the corner from the tourist office. Full meals a maximum of $3 (open daily 7am-4am—yes, 4am). For fabulous Turkish pastry, try **Nokta Pastanesi,** up the hill from the bus station toward the harbor (open daily 7am-midnight). There are a dozen restaurants at the harbor specializing in fish, all at similar prices (fish $10-20 per kg, *kalamari* $3.70, mussels $3.70).

Knidos

Once a wealthy port city and one of the original six cities of the Dorian League, **Knidos** was built in honor of Apollo. A pair of theaters and temples dedicated to Dionysus and Demeter languish above the east harbor. Outside this area are two remote medieval fortresses surrounded by the ancient necropolis of Knidos. At the tip of the peninsula, Knidos was one of the artistic and intellectual centers of the ancient Hellenic world. It was the home of Sostratos, the architect who designed the Pharos lighthouse at Alexandria (another of the seven wonders of the ancient world), and of the astronomer Eudoxos, who first calculated the circumference of the earth. The city was renowned in antiquity for its statue of Aphrodite, one of the first female nudes to be sculpted in ancient Greece. Sculpted by Praxiteles, the work scandalized Hellenic society, which until then had confined its art to the naked male form.

Because Knidos is a government-regulated archaeological zone, pensions and restaurants are forbidden to operate. There's a small café where you can get drinks and a snack, but it's overpriced, so stock up at Datça. Expensive boat tours leave for Knidos from Bodrum and Marmaris (ask at the tourist offices). From Datça you must take one of the boat tours that leave at 9am from the yacht harbor ($7 per person), or a taxi (daily at noon except Sun., 35km, tours $30 per carload, negotiable). *Dolmuş* also run for $7 per person if they can round up at least five people.

Caunos and Dalyan

The road from Marmaris to Fethiye passes by Lake Köyceğiz, an unspoiled treasure, connected to the sea by a river which passes a stretch of lush, green marsh. Along this river are the ruins of the ancient Carian harbor city of **Caunos,** where archaeologists are turning up new structures as fast as they can dig. Aside from the ruins, the area has an alluring landscape of tree-tufted mountains tumbling into swampy waters. The ruins are accessible only by boat from the nearby town of Dalyan. It's a 10-minute walk up the hill to the ruins. From the boat, look at the cliff above the river to glimpse the rock tombs, dating from the 4th century BCE.

As you come up the hill in Caunos, the precariously perched **Kale** (castle) inspects from above. From the base of the mountain, you can climb (though not easily) the lofty theater for a panorama of the ruins and the distant beach. Facing the theater, the ruins of the **basilica** are on your left, and the ancient harbor of Caunos holds the remains of several temples and a recently excavated fountain. Many people come to Dalyan with quixotic hopes of seeing the endangered Caretta Caretta (Loggerhead Turtle) which lays its eggs on nearby İztuzu Beach. It is *impossible* to see the turtle in Dalyan—the shy creatures appear only at night, when the beach is closed (open 8am-8pm daily). An overworked, underpaid band of environmentalists have struggled to prevent luxury hotels and creeping tourist development from destroying the turtles' last nesting ground in the Mediterranean. Don't try to visit the beach at night, don't hire speedboats (they destroy the reed beds), and don't litter or stick an umbrella into the beach.

Stretched along the reedy river, the village of **Dalyan** stays cool in summer, but also hosts the annual conventions of the Voracious Mosquitoes' Union. If you choose to stay, you should have no difficulty finding accommodations: there seem to be more pensions than inhabitants. Most of the pensions are to the left, down the road that follows the river. On the left-hand side, **Kristal Pansiyon** (tel. 12 63) has extremely genial management and spotless rooms ($3 per person, with shower $4). Farther along on the right is **Sahil Pansiyon** (tel. 11 87), a pleasant establishment with immaculate rooms (doubles $13, with shower $17; triples with shower $19). The **Albatross Pension** (tel. 10 70), close to the center of town, has a friendly, conservation-minded owner. ($3.75 per person, $5 with breakfast.) There are several campsites farther down the street. **Sapmaz Camping** (tel. 18 85) by the river, has hot water (tent plus 4 people $3). At the end of the road (a 10-min. walk) is **Gel-Gör Restaurant** (tel. 1078). Situated near the water, this romantic-yet-crowded restaurant serves a variety of superb dishes (*şiş kebap* $2). Ask the friendly staff about arranging a free boat ride to Caunos Beach. The brand new **Caretta Restaurant** is on the road between Sahil Pansiyon and Sapmaz Camping. Meals run about $3.50 at this riverside restaurant (open noon-2am). If you're looking for fish, try *kefal* (mullet), a both fresh- and salt-water species. Beware of chic (read: expensive) restaurants along the river.

There is a **conservation information office** in the center of Dalyan (open July-Sept. daily 9:30am-noon and 4-8:30pm). Stop in to say hello and see pictures of turtles. The **PTT** is in the tall white building in the center of town (open daily 7am-11pm). Dalyan's **telephone code** is 6116. *Dolmuş motorları* run to the ruins, İztaza Beach, and Köyceğiz Lake ($1.50 round trip). It is possible to cross the river by chartering a rowboat (40¢), or hiring a private boat ($10-20 for the day). Daily boat tours to the sights run about $4.

To get to Dalyan from either Marmaris or Fethiye, take a *dolmuş* or bus to Ortaca (2hr., $2.25), and then a *dolmuş* to Dalyan (15min., 40¢).

Fethiye

Most vacationers are in search of something more pristine and picturesque than a tumble of concrete buildings lining dusty streets. Thus most vacationers are not in search of the small, quotidian port of Fethiye. Aside from a few sights, there is little reason to stay here. Fethiye redeems itself by its proximity to Ölüdeniz, one of the Mediterranean's most captivating beaches, just 14 km away, and to a heap of interesting sights.

Telmessos, the ancient Lycian city founded on this site in the 4th century BCE, was known for its astrologists, mystagogues, palmreaders and oracles. In 1958, when an earthquake demolished its less ectoplasmic successor, Fethiye, miraculously, the thaumaturgical Necropolis of Telmessos survived.

Practical Information, Accommodations, and Food

From the bus station, head toward the water from **Çarşı Caddesi,** a street swamped with pension signs. Çarşı Cad. veers right into **Atatürk Caddesi,** the main avenue running parallel to the harbor. **Banks, pharmacies,** and most of the town's shops can be found on this street. The **tourist office** (tel. 115 27), on the waterfront at the large pier where cruise ships dock, has an accommodations service. You can leave your bags at the Tourism Association next door when looking for a room, but you can't leave them overnight. (Open daily 8am-noon and 1-7pm; Oct.-April Mon.-Fri. 8am-noon and 1-5pm.) The **police** (tel. 110 40), **PTT,** and **hospital** (tel. 140 17) are a few blocks east of the tourist office down Atatürk Cad. The **bus station** is about 1½km from the city center, just off Çarşı Cad. Buses depart to Kalkan and Kaş (12 per day, $4), and Marmaris (10 per day, $5). The *dolmuş* station to Ölüdeniz is behind the PTT. English-language newspapers are sold at **Net Imagine,** 18 Atatürk Cad., right before Yapıkredi Bank, and in the square by the *dolmuş* station. Fethiye's **telephone code** is 615.

Inexpensive pensions are what Fethiye is all about ($3-5 per person). They all seem to have "wellcome" and "24 hrs. hot water" signs, but they can be geographically divided into three categories. Those around the bus station are generally cheaper (singles $5, doubles $8), but often noisy and uncomfortable: avoid them unless catching an early morning bus. The best choice here is **Lale Pensione,** Cumhuriyet Mah. (tel. 31 33). Follow the signs on Carşı Cad, which lead you up Kale Sok. The owners are friendly, and a porch overlooks the water. ($4 per person. Doubles $5.75. Hot showers.) The second group of hotels is between Atatürk Cad. and Çarşı Cad. Heavily touristed, this area is close to the shops and nightlife, but tends to be noisy all day and *all* night. Try **Ulgen Pension,** Cumhuriyet Mah. (tel. 34 91). Follow the signs from the traffic circle (beneath the Terras Restaurant) or from Atatürk Cad. It's clean and friendly, although no English is spoken. Think of it as an opportunity to practice your Turkish. ($4 per person. Hot showers included.) The last group of hotels is situated on Atatürk Cad. Follow Atatürk Cad. with the sea on your right 300m from the tourist office. **Dereliğlu Pansiyon,** 41 Karagözler Feuzi Çakmak Cad. (tel. 159 83), is a spotless pension run by a very friendly young couple. (Singles with showers $5.50. Doubles with showers $10. Hot waters 24 hrs.—really.) The couple, Ömer and Gülag Şanlıgençler, may run another hotel in 1993, so ask for their new location at the tourist office. They offer a 10% discount to anyone with a *Let's Go* book. Ömer also organizes custom-made budget tours to all the sights surrounding Fethiye, Pamukkale and beyond. This is the perfect hotel for longer stays.

Rafet II, on the sea shore by the PTT, serves tasty—albeit small—portions. *Trança* (skewered fish) costs $5.40, and is a welcome variation on an old theme. (Open daily 8am-midnight.) **Pizza 74,** near the water, serves inexpensive *pide* ($1.15). If you absolutely must eat in the overtouristed area in the bazaar try **Mutfak** for quick service and a jovial atmosphere (full meal about $4). The best (and the cheapest) Turkish food in town is served in the modest-looking **Tuna Z,** 21 Eumhuriyet Mah. Tütün Soq. From the circle, take the first right open to car traffic, then the second street on the left. (Full meal including dessert about $3.)

Sights

The road from the north into Fethiye traverses dense pine forests and ascends steep hillsides thick with the ticking of crickets and the pungency of sap. This region, isolated from the rest of Asia Minor, insulated Lycian culture. Believed to be the descendants of the pre-Hittite Anatolian peoples, the Lycians remained independent until their quixotic stand against Cyrus' Persian armies in 545 BCE. The city of tombs that remains, the **Necropolis of Telmessos,** is the most significant vestige of Lycian culture. The façades of the cliff-hewn tombs resemble Greek temples down to the pediments, porticos, and cornices; the tombs themselves are thought to be replicas of Lycian homes. Connected to the road by several flights of steps just off Kaya Cad. (off Atatürk Cad.) is the **Tomb of Amyntas,** which is identified by a 4th-century BCE inscription on the left-hand column. If you climb the 150 steps to the tomb, you'll find a tiny chamber beyond the opening. You can enter the other tombs as well, though to reach them you must clamber around the rocks. From the necropolis you can see the remains of the **Fethiye Tower,** as well as several islands sprinkled about the Bay of Fethiye. The **Archaeological Museum** in town, 1 block down from the hospital toward the bus station, contains Lycian artifacts from neighboring digs. (Open June-Sept. daily 8am-7pm. Admission 75¢, 40¢ with student ID.) Be sure to see the stone inscribed with Aramaic, Greek, and Lycian characters.

Fethiye's main beach, **Çalis,** 5km to the north, is a relatively uncrowded crescent of sand extending over several km. From June through September, a municipal vehicle and *dolmuş* run every five minutes from behind the PTT (30¢). Boats run from here to the beaches on the off-shore isle of **Sövalye.** Twelve km farther lie the beaches of **Günlük Bay** and **Katrancı Bay,** both of which are even less inhabited than Çalis. Either beach can be reached by *dolmuş* or by any of the frequent buses to İzmir ($1; buses leave from behind the PTT). In recent years, campgrounds have given way to luxury hotels. You can still freelance camp at **Katrancı** in the picnic area, surrounded by pines and overlooking a rocky cove.

Near Fethiye

Excursion **boats** leave the harbor at Fethiye for a variety of destinations. Some jaunt to nearby beaches. The most popular daytrip is the so-called **Twelve Island Tour,** which hops among the 12 principal members of the archipelago scattered about the **Bay of Fethiye.** Several of the islands have small beaches, and the boats pause to allow time for swimming and exploration. (Leaves daily 9am-6pm, $10 including lunch if the boat is full, more if not.)

Other popular daytrips include tours to the historical sites of: Xanthos, Letoon, and Patara (see Near Kalkan; 2 per week, $23 per person); Dalyan and Caunos (3 per day, $20 per person); Kaş and Kekova (1 per week, $27 per person); and Tlos, Sakilient, and Ulupinar (1 per week, $20 per person). **Light Tour,** 4 Atatürk Cad., offers the best prices (tel. 38 11; open daily 8am-midnight). Tours leave more frequently from **Big Tur,** 18 Atatürk Cad. (tel. 134 56; open daily 8am-8pm), where you can also choose from a variety of cocktail cruises ($28 per person). For those who want to explore the region on their own, agencies rent motorbikes ($22 per day), mopeds ($13 per day), and bicycles ($9 per day). Be aware that insurance is unavailable, and many roads are treacherous.

Ölüdeniz

Posters of the partially enclosed lagoon at Ölüdeniz hang on the walls in almost every Turkish hotel or tourist office. Fourteen kilometers from Fethiye, the spot is a roasty blend of endless sandy beach and turquoise water. The usual seaside amalgam of ice cream stands, souvenir shops, and gaudy restaurants is absent. Instead, you'll find a string of self-sufficient campgrounds, replete with bungalows, hot showers, and cafeterias. Whatever distaste you have for campsites and tourists will fade if you walk along the beach at dawn or dusk, when the scenery is at its solitary best.

The hedonistic regimen requires all-day sunning and swimming (you can swim 9 months of the year), snarfing excellent food, and then dancing and drinking the night away at a campsite's free disco; **Moon Disco** and the discos at Derya, Deniz, and Sun Kamp start early and stay open until 2 or 3am. (Beer $1.)

Orientation and Practical Information

Even if you're coming from the east, you can easily reach Ölüdeniz from Fethiye. During the summer, *dolmuş* depart from Atatürk Cad. behind the PTT (7:30am-11:30pm, every 10-15min.). In off-season, *dolmuş* run less often, if at all, but you can always take a shared taxi from the parking lot across from the bus company offices (agree on a price before the ride). The *dolmuş* that takes you to Ölüdeniz will stop at a sandy beach. This is not Ölüdeniz—Ölüdeniz and most of the good (and cheap) hotels are further to your right as you face the water. To the left there are a string of bars, camping grounds, and restaurants. The large sandy beach is free but the sun umbrellas and chaise-lounges will cost $1.15 each. Those who choose to hitch (and you know *Let's Go* doesn't recommend it) must walk 2km to the main turn-off. There is no offical tourist information office but **Tourism Cooperative** (tel. 61 00), just to your left as you enter the lagoon, can help you find shelter.

The town has **grocery stores,** a **PTT** (50m to the right from the entrance to the lagoon; open daily 7am-11pm), and not much else. The phones at the PTT are almost always out of service, but there are phone booths scattered around town. You can change money at some of the larger campsites and at the grocery store behind Derya Camping and to the right. Take care of everything else in Fethiye. Ölüdeniz's **telephone code** is 6156.

Accommodations and Camping

If you stay in Ölüdeniz, you'll probably find yourself in a campsite along the beach. Some campsites have bungalowan buildings that are actually full-fledged motel rooms with furniture and private baths. Taxi drivers are frequently paid to drive prospective customers deep into a campsite, delivering them into the welcoming hands of the proprietors. Insist upon looking around before committing yourself and, of course, don't believe what the employees of one campground tell you about their neighbors. From the *dolmuş* stop walk to the right (facing the water) 200m to the fork in the road. The national park is on your left (see Sights), and on your right is the road to the campgrounds. Listed below are high-season prices; at other times rates will be much lower, and you should be able to bargain easily (up to a 20% reduction).

Ölüdeniz Camping (tel. 60 24), about 300m north from the exit road, past the municipal beach. Don't confuse this with Ölüdeniz Pension on the exit road or Deniz Camping (below). Distant from the center of activity, but set at the edge of the lagoon, with a small beach and grass. Camping $3, two-person bungalows $8.

Kum Tur Motel (tel. 60 26), south along the beach toward the dirt road. Friendly staff. Doubles with shower $11.50. Breakfast included.

Asmali Pension (tel. 60 13), near Ölüdeniz Camping. Comfortable safari tents jammed into a vegetable garden. $2 per person. Bedding included.

Deniz Camping (tel. 60 12), just south of the exit road. Usually crowded, but well-run, with clean bathrooms. Bungalows for two $12.50. Breakfast included.

Food

Eating inexpensively at Ölüdeniz is a task. Most people eat at the campground cafeterias, where the food is good but overpriced. **The Pirate's Inn,** 100m up the road to Fethiye from the beach, serves breakfast and delicious entrees for low prices. (*Kalamari* $3.50.) Though out of the way, the restaurant in the **Asmali Pension** has good Turkish food at reasonable rates. (Complete meal $5.) You can get good *pide* at Deniz Camping ($1.75). No bargain, but a good restaurant for seafood is at **Han Camping,** just south of the exit road (fish *şiş* $6). Your food options will be limited at the **Kum Tur Motel,** but whatever you order will be tasty (fish $2, *patlican* (eggplant) 80¢).

Sights

The primary attraction of Ölüdeniz is a sweep of patulous sand that plunges into sparkling turquoise waters. The tranquil circle of the **blue lagoon,** at the northwestern tip of the beach has the dubious distinction of being the filming site of the wholesome cinematic gem of the same name. Or so locals claim.

The area around the lagoon is now a national park that fills with Turkish families in the summer. It gets especially crowded on weekends. Picnic tables and a refreshment stand are nearby. (Admission 60¢, with ISIC 30¢. Potable water, showers, and restrooms available.) In the morning, before the heat, you can take the 20-minute walk; later in the day a *dolmuş* does the circuit. The coastline below the road is magnificent.

Kaya and Agia Nikola Island were thriving Greek Christian communities until they were dispersed by the local Muslim population. Two popular excursions from Ölüdeniz visit the remains of the villages. The larger of the pair is **Kaya,** 10km away and accessible only by a dirt road. The more popular destination, tiny **Agia Nikola Island,** has great swimming, a spine-tingling view of the coast, and the remains of a Byzantine basilica. Deniz, Derya, and Sun Camping all organize boat trips (full-day) for about $15, including breakfast and lunch. Boats leave daily from the lagoon sometime between 9:30am and noon, once 10-20 people have signed up for the trip. Also check the tours along the municipality beach: they offer the same kinds of tours for $3 less.

From Ölüdeniz to Kalkan

Just 85km from Ölüdeniz and 22km from Kalkan are the ruins of the ancient Lycian capital of **Xanthos**. Lycian rock tombs pepper this attractive site, perched above the Eşen (formerly Xanthos) River. Unwilling to surrender during a revolt against the Persians, the Lycians gathered their women, children, and valuables into Xanthos for a last stand. When all hope was lost they set the city on fire, and fought until their last soldier died. In the 2nd century BCE, the city fought just as desperately against Rhodes. Years later, the Romans fortified Xanthos in return for its peoples' support during the Roman invasion of Anatolia; most of the ruins in Xanthos date from this period. Check out the **Roman City Gate,** dedicated to Emperor Vespasian, and the **Roman Theater.** From the theater you can see the remains of the **Roman Acropolis** and a **Byzantine church.** Nearby are the **agora,** a **Byzantine basilica,** and a collection of rock tombs in the hillside. The **Xanthian Obelisk** near the agora bears an inscription which describes the Lycian-Athenian battles of the Peloponnesian Wars. At the end of the theater stands the 6th-century BCE Lycian **Tomb of the Harpies,** decorated with a plaster cast of the mythological winged creatures being summoned to destroy invading armies. The original frieze is in the British Museum. (Site open 24 hrs., but pitch dark after sunset. Free.)

To get to Xanthos, take any **bus** running between Fethiye and Kalkan or Kaş, get off at the village of Kınık, and follow the signs to the site (Fethiye-Kınık 1½ hr, $1.30.; Kalkan-Kınık 1hr., $1).

Ten kilometers southwest of Xanthos are the ancient ruins of **Letoon,** which date from the Roman and early Byzantine periods. Myth has it that Letoon, a Lycian religious sanctuary, was the place where the nymph Leto, mother of Zeus' children Artemis and Apollo, fled Hera's wrath. At the site there are three temples each to Leto, Apollo, and Artemis, a function-hall, and a pool. Scholars hope that an inscription found on the Leto Temple in Lycian, Greek, and Aramaic (now in the Fethiye Archaeological Museum) will prove as valuable in deciphering Lycian as the Rosetta Stone was in decoding hieroglyphics. There is no guard, and no information booth, and no lights: don't go after sunset.

Twenty km farther south (17km west of Kalkan) is the old Lycian port city of **Patara.** Choked with sand and brush, Patara's imposing, largely untouristed ruins lie isolated among a series of seaside hills. Until its harbor silted up, the city was the seat of the Roman governor to Lycia and the site of an oracle to Apollo. Given the size and unwieldiness of the site, most tourists are drawn instead to Patara's vast sandy beach, one of the finest in Turkey. On the right of the road to the beach, rests the **Mettius Modestus** triumphal arch, built in 100 CE. The **necropolis** with numerous sarcophagi surrounds the gate. Along the path from the gateway to the sea lie the ruins of Roman baths, a Christian basilica, the **Baths of Vespasian,** and a theater. At the beach opposite the road you can buy refreshments, but they are overpriced: you're better off bringing some munchies with you if you can. Farther back on the road are two restaurants (they, too, are overpriced), one with bathrooms and showers.

To get to Patara, take any bus going between Fethiye and Kalkan and get off at the turn-off ($1). From there it's 6km to the beach. Sometimes, *dolmuş* will take you as far as the pensions in the town. From town, you can walk or take a taxi (about $1.50) the last 1.5 km to the ruins and the beach. Minibuses go directly to the beach every morning around 10am from Kalkan and Kaş. From the beach, regular minibus service travels to surrounding cities (to Kalkan and Kaş 9 times per day until 6:30pm; to Fethiye 5 times per day until 5pm). Taxis from Kinik cost about $6. Apart from the ruins and nearby beach, the town of Patara consists of little more than pensions, restaurants, and stupid gift shops. There are two outstanding pensions: **St. Nikolas** (tel. (3215) 50 24; doubles $7, with breakfast $10; most with balconies, all with showers and toilets) and **Flower Pansiyon** (tel. 51 64; doubles with private shower $7.50). Patara has no official campsites, but ask about pitching a tent next to one of the restaurants in town. A large part of the beach is a sea turtle sanctuary; sleeping there is *strictly* forbidden.

So Rudolf and the elves may have been the fabrications of polar propaganda (sorry, it's time you knew anyway), but **Santa Claus** is as real as the tooth fairy. In fact, he actually grew up right here by the sunny Mediterranean. Born in Patara in the 4th century, St. Nikolaus was famous for his annual gift-giving expeditions. After Santa became Bishop of nearby Myra, he was martyred there. You can visit his birthplace, and then check out his church and grave at Myra near the village of Demre. The **Archaeological Museum** in Antalya houses St. Nick's relics—a few bits of bone that his 11th-century kidnappers dropped in their haste to get away.

Kalkan

Kalkan is the quintessential Turkish fishing village (minus, perhaps, the fishing). A graceful stone breakwater encloses its harbor, and austere stone houses with wooden balconies huddle by the water. The outside world has shown its appreciation by making the city a popular tourist stop, and Kalkan's narrow, winding streets are now crammed with clothing stores and ceramics boutiques. Advertisements hawking donkey rides and boat trips beckon visitors at every corner. Still, Kalkan's small size and tempting location—perched on steep hills overlooking the bay—make it a welcome change from the larger cities along the coast.

Kalkan is a haberdasher's fairyland. Tailors line the street to the left of the PTT and down to the water. If you stay a few days, you can get a pair of custom-made Turkish-style trousers (the baggy kind).

Kalkan proper does not have much of a beach—just a bunch of rocks on the left side of the harbor. Once you pass this by, however, the landscape improves. A short climb brings you to a smaller (and usually completely deserted) pebble beach. About 3km along the road to Kaş, beneath a small metal bridge, lies the lovely little sandy beach of **Kaputaş.** The best beaches, however, line the coast between Kalkan and Fethiye, especially around Patara.

Kalkan, on the main road between Fethiye and Kaş, is serviced by all buses running between the two ports (1½hr. from Fethiye, $2.15; 45min. from Kaş, $1.30). The highway between the two cities hugs the coast every inch of the way, revealing titillating glimpses of off-shore islands. Before you continue down the coast, be sure to do a little star-gazing here; according to Herodotus, nearby Halicarnassus is "where the moon and stars are observed nearest in the world." Buses stop at the top of the village on **Kalkan Cadessi.** The **PTT** is a ½ block down the street. (Open daily 7am-11pm.) Kalkan's **telephone code** is 32 15.

Rooms above the bus stop in Kalkan are generally less expensive than those in the center of town.

Pansiyon Muhil (tel. 11 47), up the hill from the bus stop, first right, and it is off the street on the left. Large, blue-tiled rooms with showers and toilets. Some with balconies. Romantic view from the terrace. Doubles $9. Breakfast $1.

Çelik Pansiyon, 9 Yalı Boyu (tel. 10 22), down the hill from the bus stop, to the left when the road forks. Spacious rooms with showers and toilets. Terrace overlooks the harbor. Doubles $12. Breakfast $1.75

Cengiz Pansiyon (tel. 11 96), across the alley from PTT. Good location, but with white walls and no views, Cengiz is quite like a Skinner box. Large and clean. Doubles $11, with showers $17.50.

Marjinal Inn, (tel. 13 19), Yalı Boyu Hah., 3 blocks down the hill from the bus station, then follow straight (not down the hill), and take a right. Not marginal at all. Friendly atmosphere and tastefully decorated rooms with sea view. Huge bathrooms with showers. Doubles $17.50, breakfast included.

Öz Pansiyon (tel. 13 06), down the hill, then first left past the bus stop. Happy rooms with toilets and showers. Discounts for *Let's Go* users, so proudly display your book. Doubles $7.

Many restaurants in Kalkan offer all-you-can-eat-in-one-trip buffets for the ravenous. Quality varies from place to place and night to night. You'll find one of the best deals at the **Köşk Restaurant,** which lays a sumptuous table of some 30 Turkish dishes for $3.50 per person and also serves dishes à la carte. Open daily 8am-1am. If you want to see and smell the sea as you feast, try one of the five restaurants grouped on the harbor by the only gas station in town. The prices are similar. (*Kalamari* $3.50, full meal about $6.) Pick and choose. **Belgin's Kitchen** is on the street going right from Köşk Restaurant. Belgin has created a truly authentic Turkish atmosphere here, complete with rugs, copper plate, floor tables, and live Turkish music. Full meals go for about $7. *Mantı* (a ravioli-like dish served with yogurt) is magically delicious.

Kas

The seductive village of Kaş, tucked away at the base of a rugged mountain and surrounded on three sides by the Mediterranean, casts an irresistible spell over its visitors. The gently winding road to town passes by glittering inlets dotted with deserted patches of pebble beach. Once you've set foot in town, inexpensive accommodations and genuine hospitality weave together to keep you in Kaş's comfortable web. An uninhabited peninsula curves around from one side of the town's harbor, creating a calm rock-lined lagoon ideal for swimming. You can sip *çay* by the soothing waterfront, explore the mountainous countryside strewn with ancient ruins, take a boat trip around the historic coast, groove to 60s rock in one of the many bars, or just seek out a secluded cove where you can swim and soak up the sun.

Practical Information

Most of the town's activity centers around the small harbor front along the main street, **Cumhuriyet Caddesi.** At its west end near the mosque, its name changes to **Hastane Caddesi.** Here it is intersected by **Elmali Caddesi,** which heads uphill to the bus station. At its east end near the statue of Atatürk, Cumhuriyet is intersected by **Çukurbağlı Caddesi,** which leads to the PTT. From the Atatürk statue, Hükümet Cad. goes above the harbor to the two local beaches. The street going up the hill behind the tourist office—the one with most of the souvenir shops—is **Uzun Çarşı Caddesi.**

Tourist Office: Cumhuriyet Cad. (tel. 12 38). English-speaking staff might refer you to pensions and allow you to leave your bags while you look for a room. Area maps must be purchased at bookstores. Open daily 8am-noon and 1-5:30pm; in off-season closed Sunday.

Travel Agencies: Nearly all agencies offer tours to Kekova ($7). Tour prices vary slightly, so shop around before you purchase your ticket. Beware of tour packages to other locations (Myra, etc.) that may cancel at the last minute due to insufficient interest. Any overland tour can also be done by local transport (*dolmuş* and bus) for a lot less money. Only **Saklikent Tours** boldly goes where no bus has gone before ($15-22). For all boat tours, try **Kaş Deniz Taşıyıcılar Koop.** (The Union of Boat Owners; tel. 16 66), on the pier. **Simena Tourism and Travel Agency,** 7 Uzun Çarşı (tel. 14 16), runs daily excursions. Purchase domestic airline or ferry tickets here; from the Atatürk statue, walk away from the water and make a right up the hill. Trips offered by local agencies to Kastelorizo are neither cheap nor worthwhile, since Greek law prohibits spending the night on a round-trip from Turkey.

PTT: Çukurbağı Cad. (tel. 14 36). Open daily 8am-11pm. Telegrams and international telephones open 24 hrs. **Telephone Code:** 3226.

Bus Station: At the end of Elmalı Cad. Buses to: Antalya (every hr., 4½ hr.); Fethiye (2 per hr., 2hr.); Marmaris (5 per day, 5hr.); and İzmir (5 per day, 10hr.).

Laundromat: The three down the street from Kısmet Pansiyon all charge $4 a load (wash and dry). Next day service.

Barber: By the marketplace on Emali Cad. The real reason to come here is the vigorous massage for $1.50, guaranteed to relieve traveling tensions (men only).

Hospital: Hastane Cad. (tel. 11 85), 500m past the mosque, just before the campground.

Police: Tel. 10 24. Continue uphill from the PTT and turn left.

Accommodations and Camping

The search for inexpensive accommodations in July and August will test your shopping and bargaining skills. Official prices stand at $4-6 for a single bed without shower, but will go about 20% higher in peak season. Bargaining here is a good idea.

Kısmet Pansiyon, 17 Ilkokul Sok. (tel. 18 88). Walk up Uzun Çarşı Cad. and take the first left. Clean rooms, some with harbor views. Doubles $9, with showers $12. Breakfast included.

Mini Pansiyon (tel. 10 38), next to Kısmet Pansiyon. Small but spotless rooms. The large rooftop lounge provides empowering breezes and views of the harbor and town. Doubles $9, with shower $12. Smaller rooms are cheaper. Breakfast $1.70.

Vizaron Pansiyon (no phone): Right across from the bus station. Clean, if somewhat noisy rooms with showers and toilets. Doubles $10, but bargain down a few dollars.

Yalı Pension, Hastane Cad. (tel. 11 32), 1 block up from the mosque. Look to the soothing sea from the deck at this homey but slightly noisy retreat. Doubles $11, with bath $15.

Hotel Turquoise (tel. 18 00), "in the narrow street behind the statue" (Askerlik Şubesi Yanı), this is not exactly the cheapest bed, but the service is worth more than they ask. Large, tastefully decorated rooms with huge bathrooms. Also telephone service and a wonderful terrace. Flash your *Let's Go* book and get a 10% discount. $9 per person, breakfast included.

Camping: Kaş Camping, Hastane Cad. (tel. 10 50), 30m past the amphitheater. Beautiful location, rocky and partly shaded, but mediocre facilities (mostly bungalows). The "beach" is a concrete slab, but there is good swimming from this point. Camping $4 for 2 people. Bungalows for 2 are $7.

Food

The fruit and vegetable **market** blooms midway between the bus station and the harbor. Another market is located one block above the mosque on Elmali Cad. The local government fixes prices on all food except fish, which can be quite expensive ($5-12). *Mercan* (red coralfish) and lagos are area specialties. *Dolma,* goulash, and other precooked dishes cost about $1.

For breakfast, try the **Noel Baba Pastanesi,** across from the harbor (coffee, freshly-squeezed orange juice, and pastry $2.25). If you can't choke down any more watery Nescafé, treat yourself to filtered coffee (75¢) and scrumptious pastries ($1) at the **Bar Papillion,** across from the PTT. (Open daily 8am-11pm.) Although the covered alley across from the harbor has five reasonably priced restaurants with varied menus including fresh fish, the crowds and overzealous maitre-d's can be claustrophobic and oppressive.

Picadilly Circus, on the way to the bus station on Elmalı St. The best sandwiches around, made on special bread (70¢-$1). Tasty hot dogs, too.

Çınar, down Çukurbağli Cad. from the PTT. Pleasant atmosphere but a little crowded. *Kebap* $1.75. Open daily 8am-midnight.

Mor Cafe, across the street from Kisman Pansiyon. A lovely couple will cook you up delicious homemade dishes for about $1 each. Make sure you try their fresh *baklava:*

Bilgin Restaurant, a little hut on the upper corner of the soccer field when you turn your back to the food shops. They only have 5 tables and are rarely visited by tourists. Their *pide* is the best in town. *Pide* with cheese 90¢, with meat $1.

Eriş Restaurant, 2 doors down from the tourist office. Fancier and pricier than other restaurants along the harbor. Delicious desserts. Meals from $5. Open daily 11am-midnight.

Sights and Entertainment

The two beaches of Kaş lie in coves surrounded by rocky cliffs and covered with smooth stones. If you survive the scramble over the stones and plunge in for a swim, you'll realize it was worth the effort. The entrance to **Küçük Çakil Plaji** (Little Pebble Beach) is at the top of the hill on Hükümet Cad., to your left as you face the harbor. Local youths romp and scream in this narrow inlet. More determined sunbathers and swimmers frequent **Büyük Çakil Plaji** (Big Pebble Beach), 15 minutes down the road. Rather than rent a mat on the water ($1.30), spread your towel on a smooth plateau amid the rocks to the left of the beach.

Beyond Kaş Camping on the other side of town, a more secluded swimming area shimmers in the calm waters of the penisula's inlet. Baked to bath water temperature and stocked with a myriad exotic fish, the peaceful lagoon is amenable to swimming or snorkeling. After the 20-minute walk from town, the road dips to meet the water at an ideal spot for off-shore swimming. Or climb down from the road and claim your own cove—but beware of the sea urchins lurking just off-shore and wear shoes. Farther along, the coast is virtually deserted except for an exaltation of butt-naked bathers, attracted by the extreme privacy of the area.

Kaş has several historic sights in or near the town. Most impressive is the **Hellenistic Theater,** just past the hospital on Hastane Cad. as you leave town. The only intact ancient structure in Kaş, the theater rests on a solitary, elevated perch, overlooking the sea and the Greek island Kastelorizo. Climb to the topmost level to admire the landscape and test the resonating acoustics. You can spend the night in the theater (bring a sleeping bag), but don't count on sleeping much: rowdy young folk crowd in after 3am, when most of the bars close, and sing and play guitar for most of the night (feel free to join in). Mosquitos abound and the sun rises early. If there were 'smores, it would be just like summer camp. Follow the footpath behind the theater about 50m to the 4th century BCE **necropolis.** Back in town, there's a free-standing **monumental tomb,** also from the 4th century BCE, up Uzun Çarçi Cad. behind the tourist office.

For good rock music and some dizzy dancing, try **Mavi Bar** on the harbor by Eriş Restaurant and close to the tourist office. (Beer $1.10. Tequila $2.) **Point Bar,** on the same street as the laundromats, offers much of the same. For that romantic evening, hit **Elit Bar** for live music and cozy atmosphere. (From the beginning of the pier take a right and pass between the tea houses on the shore.)

Kaş has many handicraft shops, leather merchants, and carpet sellers, as do all tourist towns, but one shop sets Kaş above the others: **Magic Orient,** 7 Cumhuriyet Medani (tel. 16 10). This carpet shop is unusual for its excellent prices and its forthright owner. He's known throughout town for his honesty.

Near Kas

The farming community of **Demre,** an hour's bus ride east of Kaş ($1.50) on the road to Antalya, sits on a smooth, fertile plain sandwiched between the mountains and the sea. The town itself is dusty and unattractive, but several interesting sites lie nearby; a long afternoon should take care of them. A short walk from the bus stop lies the **Tomb of St. Nikolas,** housed in a well-preserved 4th-century Byzantine basilica (follow signs for *Aya Nicola*). The saint is better known to Turks as Noel Baba, and to North Americans as Santa Claus. Remembered for his acts of charity, he came to be seen as a protector of sailors and children. In 1087, thieves plundered Santa's tomb, escaping to Bari, Italy with his bones and that funny red cap. Today, the burial chapel in the basilica houses his simple marble **sarcophagus,** located in a small niche immediately to your right as you enter. The entrance to the partially ruined basilica is covered with faded 4th-century frescoes of the saints. St. Nikolas is pictured on the wall above his sarcophagus. Each December 6, the saint's birthday is celebrated with a commemorative three-day festival and symposium. (Basilica open daily 8am-7pm. Admission $1.50, students 75¢.) In Demre, stay at **Noel Pansiyon** (tel. 23 04 or 22 67), which has clean, festive rooms and jolly management. (Doubles $6, with bath $7. Triples $9 with shower.)

The remains of ancient **Myra,** 2km inland from Demre, feature a spectacular collection of **Lycian rock tombs** carved into the cliffs above a Roman theater with impressive entrance galleries. Taxis gladly take you to the site for $1.50, but walking is easy. (Open 7:30am-7pm; in off-season 8am-5:30pm. Admission 70¢, students 35¢.) The only pension here is the clean, cramped, no-frills **Nomadic** (tel. 10 36), which you'll pass on your way to the ruins. (Singles $3. Doubles $6. Breakfast $1.50. No English spoken.) Right across from the ruins, you can pitch a tent at at **Myra Apa Restaurant**

Camping ($1 per person). Facilities are basic (toilets, showers), but clean. The restaurant serves full meals for around $3.50. At Demre's harbor, **Andriake** (Çayağzı), the sandy beach borders more Lycian and Roman ruins than your knowledge of Roman numerals can accommodate.

The main attraction around Kaş is **Kekova,** a partially submerged Lycian city about 2 hours east. On an excursion boat, you can visit some Byzantine ruins, Kekova, and two nearby fishing villages which flaunt a cliff honeycombed with Lycian tombs and a hill crowned with a half-ruined castle. Both towns are surrounded by a dozen or so huge Lycian sarcophagi, some actually leaning on the village homes. (Tours $7.) For lunch either stock up in the market or eat at one of the pricey restaurants on the tour itinerary.

The **Blue Caves,** home to the Mediterranean's only seal colony, are worth a visit, although you'll hardly see a seal nowadays. Try to swim in the phosphorescent water in the mornings, before the sea becomes rough. Nearby, 2km after Kalkan, is **Doves Cave,** which you can reach only by swimming. Opposite this grotto, the wide **Güvercinlik Cave** spouts a cold underwater stream.

You might also head north to the mountain village of **Gömbe,** famous for its trout and *kilim* farms. Choose your fish from one of the pools and watch it fry. Tours cost $15-20, but you'd do just as well taking a *dolmuş* ($1.15).

The coast east of Kaş has a great deal to offer. At **Finike,** the road leading inland to Elmalı and Korkuteli passes the Lycian site of **Limyra** (after 12km), where tombs stud the rock face above a Roman acropolis. The resort of **Kemer,** about 80km closer to Antalya, has long stretches of fine beach and some restaurants that will make you think you're in piscatory paradise.

Antalya

Poised between jagged mountains and the shimmying Mediterranean, Antalya is a rough but scenic four-and-a-half-hour bus ride from Kaş. Seen mainly as a base for exploring nearby beaches and Roman ruins, the city itself is surprisingly pleasant. While modern and prosperous, Antalya offers a taste of its past in the old town and around its quiet harbor. Here, crooked alleys and hidden courtyards provide a peaceful refuge from the crowds and concrete of the coast. Kâzım Özalp Cad. leads from the **bus station** to the harbor. From there, turn right onto Cumhuriyet Cad. to find the **Municipal Tourist Office** (tel. 47 05 41 or 47 05 42), below the Atatürk statue. The staff provides maps and information on accommodations and tours of nearby sites. (Open all year Mon.-Fri. 8am-noon and 1:30-5:30pm.) The **main tourist office** (tel. 11 17 47) is just west from here along Cumhuriyet Cad., in the white building set back from the street. (Open daily 8am-6:30pm; off-season 8am-5:30pm.) Next door is the **Turkish Airlines Office** (tel. 41 28 30 or 42 78 62; open Mon.-Fri. 8:30am-8pm, Sat.-Sun. 8:30am-5:30pm). Frequent flights from Antalya head to İstanbul ($70), İzmir ($60), and Ankara ($60), as well as to Munich and London. (60% student reduction on all international flights; youth (ages 12-24) price for all domestic flights $56). If you are going to İstanbul, consider the somewhat cheaper fares offered by İstanbul Air, a little farther down the street. The **airport** is 10km away. Buses marked "Havas" leave for it frequently from Cumhuriyet Cad., across from the Atatürk statue. On the corner of Anafartalar Cad. and Cumhuriyet Cad. stands **Selekler Çarşişi,** a mall with clothing stores and the **Ardıç Bookstore** (tel. 47 03 56, open Mon.-Fri. 8am-8:30pm). A block down Anafartalar on the left is the **PTT** (open 24 hrs.). Antalya's **telephone code** is 31. A full-service branch of **American Express** has its offices in the **Pamfilya Travel Agency** (tel. 42 14 02), near the water at the far end of 30 Ağustos Cad. They'll cash personal checks, replace lost cards or traveler's checks, and hold mail. (Open Mon.-Fri. 9am-noon and 2-6:30pm.) The **police** (tel. 43 10 61), based at the yacht harbor, speak English. For the **hospital** (Medical University), dial 45 08 00. The **government municipality** (tel. 48 36 61) can also help with complaints or problems.

If you're visiting Antalya for any length of time, be sure to stay in the old city, southeast of the yacht harbor, with twisting alleys and charming wood and plaster homes dating from Ottoman times. The 150 or so pensions and motels in the old city (called "Kaleiçi") can meet all taste and budget requirements. For a trouble-free stay try **Sabah Pansiyon,** 60 Hesapçı Sok. (tel. 47 53 45/46/47). To get there, take a left onto Hespaçı Sok. from Hadrian's Gate and follow the street: Sabah is 50m past the Broken Minaret (Kesik Minare). The friendly, English-speaking owner Ali is a professional tour guide and organizes tours to various locales. He also rents cars for $29 a day. Rooms range from quaint to luxurious (roof $2, singles $4.30-11, doubles $8.50-14, triples $13-17). Your copy of *Let's Go* gets you a 10% discount. **Garden Pansiyon** (tel. 47 90 30) is on the same street toward Hadrian's Gate, on your left when walking from the gate to the Broken Minaret (not to be confused with the other Garden Pansiyon across from the Broken Minaret). A lovely enclosed garden (of all things) with fruit trees and a chummy polyglot guitar-playing owner raise the hostel above average. ($3.35 per bed, $7.70 minimum. Reservations recommended.) **Adler Pansiyon,** 16 Civelek Sok. (tel. 41 78 18), in a beautiful Ottoman house at Barbaros Mah. and Ciuelek Sok., is located in the heart of the old city. From Hadrian's Gate, walk into the old city, veer left onto Hesapçi Sok., then take the second right. Adler is at the end of this alley. (Singles $5.75. Doubles $11.50.) Around the corner is **Aksoy Pansiyon,** 39 Kocatepe Sok. (tel. 42 65 49). The rooms are clean and tiny. (Doubles $3. Wow!) A row of cheap restaurants lines the busy alleyway at the intersection of Atatürk Cad. and Cumhuriyet Cad. From the bus station, walk to the main road, Kâzım Özalp Cad., and continue 1 block down to the left. In the center of the alley, **Kadir Usta'nin Döner Kebabi** has a leafy cornucopia of vegetable dishes. Full meals for $4.

Founded as Attaleia in the 2nd century BCE by King Attalos II of Pergamon, Antalya is still partially surrounded by walls built by the Greeks and later by the Byzantines and Seljuks. You can use the **Tower of Hıdırlık** (a 2nd century CE lighthouse), near the sea and the city park, and the now clockless **clock tower** as orientation points. A few blocks behind the clock tower stands **Hadrian's Gate,** built of marble in 130 CE to commemorate the visit of Emperor Hadrian. Nearby is the mosque of the **Kesik Minare** ("Broken Minaret"), which was transformed from a Byzantine church by the Seljuks. The structure was actually built as a Roman temple before it was converted into a three-nave basilica in the 4th century CE. To the left of the clock tower is the curious fluted minaret of **Yivli Minare Camil** (Alâeddin Mosque), also changed from a church to a mosque during the Seljuk regime. The **Archaeological Museum's** well-presented exhibits range from pre-historic times to the Turkish Republic, featuring finds from Perge, Aspendos, and Side, and an excellent collection of marble statues. Walk down Cumhuriyet Cad. away from town, where it becomes Kenan Evren Bul; you'll see the museum just before the road dips into the beach. (Open Tues.-Sun. 9am-6pm. Admission $1.40, students 70¢.)

Near Antalya

The closest beach to Antalya is **Konyaaltı,** just west of the Archaeological Museum. Though campgrounds are plentiful here, the area is quickly becoming an unsightly shanty town of campers. From any *dolmuş* stop in town, take a *dolmuş* marked "Konyaaltı Liman." Thirteen km to the east is the sandier and less crowded **Lara Beach.** *Dolmuş* leave every 15 to 20 minutes from the central *dolmuş* station on Ali Çetinkaya Cad. (actually the continuation of Cumhuriyet Cad. to the east) for *Lara Plajı* (20min.). Antalya is known for its spectacular **waterfalls** *(Düden).* The upper falls tumble 11km to the north, accessible by *dolmuş* (30min.); the smaller lower falls splash in the sea by Lara Beach.

About 34km northwest of Antalya, the ruins of **Termessos** sprawl atop a mountain in a dense woodland forest. Termessos's impregnable location spared it from destruction by Alexander the Great. The ruins include a **Stoa of Attalos,** a theater, a **Temple of Artemis,** and some tombs. Take a bus from the station to Korkuteli, get off at the sign for the ruins. Hitch or take a taxi ($4) the remaining 9km to Termessos.

From Antalya to Alanya

The former Roman province of **Pamphylia** stretches east of Antalya. A guidebook proves very helpful when visiting the extensive ruins: the local publication *Pamphylia: An Archaeological Guide* ($5), available in most souvenir shops, is more informative and better translated than most. You can take an organized tour of the sites from one of the travel agents (full daytrips start at $15), or rent a car in Antalya (around $33 per day with free mileage). Several travel agencies cluster along Cumhuriyet and Fevzi Çakmak Cad. All three principal sites near Antalya—Perge, Aspendos and Side—may be visited in one day, provided you start early. A hat, good shoes, sunscreen, and lots of water will repel malcontentedness.

From the extensive remains of ancient **Perge** (16km from Antalya), it is easy to imagine what life must have been like in this prosperous town of over 100,000 inhabitants. The city was supposedly founded by Greek heroes after the Trojan War, but the city did not earn its place in history until it prudently sided with that omnipresent boywonder Alexander the Great.

The stadium, which seated a gargamelian crowd of 12,000, has a wall at the far end meant to protect spectators during the wild beast fights that took place here. Against the opposite hill, an impressive **theater** features finely rendered reliefs of Dionysus. Entering through the **Roman gate,** you'll see a large **agora** (market place) to your right. Up ahead, two imposing **Hellenistic towers** mark the beginning of the long colonaded avenue leading to the **nymphaeum.** In ancient times, water flowed from here into a fountain that followed the entire length of the street. Don't miss the extensive remains of the **public baths,** to your left. (Site open daily 7:30am-7pm; off-season 8am-5:30pm. Stadium and theatre free; main site $1.40, students 70¢.) To get to Perge from Antalya, take a *dolmuş* to Aksu from the central *dolmuş* station, then walk 2km. Rather than cram all three sites into one day, it is best to visit on successive afternoons.

Founded by colonists from Argos, **Aspendos** (49km from Antalya) was built as a river port and naval base. The **theater,** with 15,000 seats, is one of the best preserved in the world—even the marble-tiled stage remains almost completely intact. During the Seljuk reign, it was converted into a palace and covered with green and blue tiles. On the opposite side of the ruined acropolis lie the impressive remains of the city **aqueducts** which once reached heights of 50m. (Site open daily 7:30am-7pm; in winter 8am-5:30pm. Admission $1.40, students 70¢.) To get to the turn-off from Antalya, take the Manavgat *dolmuş* 5km past the village of Serik; the ruins are another 4km from the turn-off. *Dolmuş* run infrequently, but taxis are available, and tractors are known to pick up hitchhikers.

Side has all the components of a classic vacation on the Mediterranean coast: substantial Hellenic ruins, a fine museum, a 1km stretch of sandy beach, and acres of tourists fresh off the bus. Greeks from Kimi colonized the ancient city of Side in the 7th century BCE. Most of the ruins, however, date from Roman times. After constant pillaging by pirates and Arab invaders in the 8th and 9th centuries, Side's exhausted inhabitants abandoned the city. The ancient site was first resettled in the 1890s by Turkish refugees from Crete. Side has become a favorite vacation spot for people from Ankara, so expect company.

Perhaps to torment sun-baked itinerants, the **tourist office** is placed about 1½km out of town on Manaugeat Rd. (you can take a *dolmuş* from the ancient theater). They provide free maps, accommodations listings, and will keep your bags while you look for a room. (Open daily 8am-7pm; winter Mon.-Fri. 8am-noon and 1:30-5:30pm.) Surprisingly, there is a full-service **American Express** office, 11 Cami Sok. (tel. 313 44), just past Özden Pansiyon. Side's **telephone code** is 321.

For comfortable lodgings with a lounge and flourishing garden make your way to the **Özden Side Pansiyon** (tel. 311 37; bungalows $9 per person). To get to **Caesar's Bar-Pansiyon,** Side's cheapest pension, follow the main drag and take a left at the Jungle bar. (Singles $5.50. Doubles $7. Triples $10.) Clean rooms open onto a lovely leafy terrace at the **Kale Pension** (tel. 12 66). Take the first left off the main drag, then the next left. (Doubles with shower $18 including breakfast; reservations suggested.) There are numerous campsites on the road from Manavgat to Side. About 200m to the east stretches the best beach in Side, where you can unfurl a sleeping bag on the sand or in one of the empty wooden shacks. The outdoor shower at the Nymfeum Disco is convenient.

You'll have no problem finding the well-marked ruins. The Hellenistic walls to the city are impressively large (1.7m wide, 10m high). When you enter Side, you'll see the **Nymphaeum** memorial fountain which once had a marble façade depicting punishments administered to those who committed sexual sins or sins against the gods. While most ancient theaters were hewn into the hillsides, the 2nd-century CE theater of Side was built on level ground using arches. It is also the largest in the area (seating 25,000 people) though not as well preserved as that of Aspendos. (Open daily 7:30am-7:30pm. Admission $1.40, students 70¢.) Other ruins include two **agoras.** The site is 1½km from the city and can be reached by following the beach to the west. The ancient Roman baths now house a delightful **Archaeological Museum.** (Open daily 8:30am-noon and 1-5:15pm; off-season Tues.-Sun. only. Admission $1.40, students 70¢.)

Several direct **buses** go daily to Side from Antalya and Alanya; otherwise take one running between Antalya and Alanya (about 1 per hr., $3), and get off at the turn-off near **Manavgat,** recognizable by its barber-pole minaret. From here it's an easy *dolmuş* ride to Side (3km). While you're in the area, visit the magnificent waterfalls at Manavgat. There's a fine beach at **Yeşilköy,** about 18km past Side towards Alanya, where the Alarahan River flows into the sea. If you're heading to Perge or Aspendos from Side, catch a minibus across from the entrance to the bus station and transfer at Manavgat.

Alanya

Alanya's 13th-century **Alâedden Castle** which rises from the sheer cliffs of a seaside promontory may be striking, but exactly what attracts so many German and Turkish tourists to the unappealing concrete resort at its base is an enigma. If you find yourself here, escape to the nearby beaches and caves of the peninsula or hike its rugged terrain. The town has more to offer at night, when throngs of tourists wander its narrow streets and flood the bars and discos along its waterfront. The *otogar* **(bus station)** is a 15-minute walk outside of town. Usually the bus will stop along the main coastal road after going to the *otogar;* tell the driver you want to go into Alanya just to be sure. Otherwise, minibuses to town from the bus station is 20¢. From the main coastal road, walk east and turn onto Güzelyali Cad., where the road forks (just before the "Alanya" sign). From here, it's a five-minute walk to the **tourist office,** staffed with cheery English speakers (tel. 112 40; open daily 8am-7pm; off-season 8am-5:30pm). Across the street, the small but well-organized **Museum of Alanya** houses a collection of very old coins, ceramics, carpets, and bronze statuettes. (Open Tues.-Sun. 8am-noon and 1:30-5:30pm. Admission $1.40.) You can buy **bus tickets** at bus offices along Atatürk Cad., opposite the Yeni Mosque in town. Minibuses will pick you up here 15 minutes before departure and take you to the bus terminal. The **PTT** (mail and phone services until 11:30pm; public phones 24 hrs.) is on Atatürk Cad., the main road leading from the bus station. Alanya's **telephone code** is 323.

The cheapest hotels are around Müftüler Cad. **Hotel Ankara Pala** (tel. 188 64) wins no prizes for aesthetics, but it's clean and safe ($2 per person, singles with showers $5). On the parallel avenue, Eski Hal Cad., is **Hotel Çınar** (tel. 200 63)—not very clean, but cheap cheap. Or try camping near the tourist office; ask them for the best sites for the time you are there. Prices are about $3 per tent and $1 per person. The restaurants along the water have atmosphere, but less expensive restaurants can be found in the crowded alleyways just before the beach. Forego atmosphere altogether and feast on half a chicken for $2 at the **Saray Lokantası,** at Müftüler Cad. (Open daily 6am-midnight.)

Alanya's historical sites are all concentrated on the peninsula. The present castle, consisting of three walls, was constructed by Seljuk Sultan Alâeddin Keykubat I after he procured Alanya from the Byzantines. The Mecdüddin cistern (reservoir) still delivers rainwater to houses within the inner castle. Facing the castle, the **Red Tower,** a five-story octagonal structure, was built in 1225 CE to protect Alanya's shipyard. (Open Tues.-Sun. 8am-noon and 1:30pm-5:30pm. Admission 80¢, students 40¢.)

Just north of the Red Tower is a dockyard where you'll find excursion **boats** which explore the caves and beaches around the peninsula. One hour tours take in most of the sights and run anywhere from $8 to $30 per person; travel agencies will overcharge you, but tours are among the most exciting activities in the otherwise staid Alanya. Beginning in the west by Damlataş Beach is the **Damlataş Cave,** which can also be reached by the road running along the beach. This cave is electrically lit and is famous for its curative effect on asthmatic patients. Accessible only by boat are **Kleopatra Beach,** the phosphorescent **Blue Caves, Lover's Cave,** and **Pirate's Cave.** Twenty km from Alanya, back towards Antalya, is **Incekum,** with a clean, clear sandy beach surrounded by a pine forest (camping and picnic facilities available). Take a *dolmuş* to Manavgat and ask to be let off at Incekum. From Alanya, buses run to Antalya every two hours ($2.80).

Five **buses** per day make the trip to Silifke (7hr., $7), via Anamur. The area east of Alanya is the beautiful ancient land of **Cilicia,** which Antony gave to Cleopatra as a token of his esteem. The Byzantines built many castles and forts here, but they were conquered by the Arabs and Seljuk Turks; the latter finally gained control of the region in 1077 CE.

Anamur

An ugly town of concrete houses, hotels, and bungalows, Anamur's charms lie below its skin. It is Anamur's quiet and serene atmosphere, its miles of sandy, open beaches, and its welcome dearth of tourist shops which invite relaxation and appreciation. Nearby, a seaside crusader castle and the Roman ruins of Anamurium provide the historical, aesthetic delights that the city itself lacks. The English-speaking staff at Anamur's **tourist office,** up the road from the bus station, can provide information and point you in the right direction for various sites and *dolmuş* routes. (Open all year daily 8:30am-noon and 1-5pm.) The **PTT** is just up the street from here. Anamur's **telephone code** is 7571.

Another one of Turkey's endless Atatürk statues stands in the center of town. To his right, *dolmuş* leave for the *kale* (castle) and for İskele Beach. Farther down the road to Atatürk's left is the *dolmuş* station for the Anamurium.

Since the actual town of Anamur is quite far from the sea, most people prefer to stay at İskele Beach, 3km away. The **Gündoğmuş Pansiyon** (tel. 23 36), just to the right of the *dolmuş* stop, offers tidy rooms and an affable staff. (Singles $4.40. Doubles $6. Triples $7. Quads $10. All rooms with showers.) Go farther down the same road and turn right at the army base to reach the **King Pansiyon,** (tel. 19 99; singles $6, doubles $10; all rooms with showers).

Camping is not too expensive ($3 per tent), but facilities are mediocre. Try the **Oba Mocamp** in the middle of the beach (tel. 56 19; bungalows $9 with shower and toilet) or **Dragon Camping** along the beach towards the east. Lodging gets tight in the high season, but in a pinch you can usually find rooms in the pensions near the *otogar* (doubles $6-8). For quiet dining on the sea, the restaurant in Oba Mocamp has adequate meals for about $3 (open daily 9am-1am). **Bak Gör Piknik,** a lovely restaurant just across from Oba Mocamp a little toward the *iskele* (the pier), serves mainly meat and chicken dishes, with full meals for $3.

Right at the water's edge, the **Kale** at Anamur was constructed by the Romans in the 3rd century CE, and reconstructed during the Crusades. Also on the beach, 12 km away, are the modest remains of **Anamurium,** an ancient Roman city originally built by the Phoenicians. *Dolmuş* drop people off at the turn-off to Anamurium. From there it's a 1km hike to the ruins.

Tasucu

The scenic road from Anamur to Taşucu is punctuated by pine forests and cliffs plunging onto sandy beaches. A deserted beach reclines between Anamur and Taşucu, right before Yanişli and after Sıphalı. Just 8km south of Taşucu in Boğsak is **Gürbü-zler Camping.** Sandless **Akçakıl Camping** is 6km closer to Taşucu (tel. 14 26; $3 per person, including tent, breakfast, and private facilities). There are no buses to Boğsak, so many hitchhike or take a taxi (about $2.50) from Taşucu.

Taşucu is the beach-front port for the larger city Silifke. Stay in this concrete tourist town only if you plan to catch a ferry to Northern Cyprus. In the harbor area are the **PTT** (open daily 8am-5pm) and four ferry boat offices, which sell tickets for the seven hour trip to Girne (Kyrenia). **Ertürk Feribot** (tel. 10 33; open 7am-9pm, and often later), on the waterfront, has boats to Girne (departure Sun.-Thurs. at midnight, return Mon.-Fri. at 1pm; tickets $13, students $10). **Devlet Deniz Yolları** (tel. 13 85 or 14 25) runs boats on the same schedule ($15, students $7), as do **Fergöu** (tel. 17 82 or 25 83; $15, students $6), and **İpekgolu** (tel. 32 57; tickets $15, students $11.50). Note that on Sundays Devlet Deniz Yolları runs boats to Girne from Alanya (not Taşucu), and on Saturday runs them from Girne to Alanya (not Taşucu). Add to your ticket price a $6.25 port tax from Taşucu and a $6 port tax when leaving Girne. Schedules change frequently; be sure to check ahead.

While waiting for the ferry, you can eat at the undistinguished restaurants on the left when facing the water. Full meals run about $5, while the restaurants right at the harbor are more expensive. To reach the sandy, crowded **beach** at Taşucu, walk east from the harbor. On the way, turn left at Tuğram Pension, then take a right, and you'll find the cluttered but hygenic **Sahil Pansiyon,** 9 Palmiye Sokak (tel. 10 52; $5 per person). Two more pensions sit right behind the harbor. They're no bargain, but both are clean and well-run. **Yuvam** (tel. 11 01) has carpeted rooms with refrigerators, and all rooms have showers. (Singles $8.50. Doubles $14.50. Triples $17. Add an extra 50% for an air-conditioned room.) **Fatih** (tel. 11 25 or 12 48) has rooms with telephones, bathrooms, showers, and excellent sea views. (Singles $9.25. Doubles $13. Triples $17.) Taşucu's **telephone code** is 7593.

Silifke

10km from Taşucu, Silifke is an overfed, unattractive town that could be painlessly bypassed unless you need its bus connections. From Silifke you can travel to Mersin (2hr., $1.45), Anamur (3½hr., $5), Antalya (9hr., $8.50), Alanya (7hr., $7), Marmaris ($15) and Bodrum ($15). **Buses** leave next to the tourist office for Mersin every 20 minutes, making stops at the beaches along the way (until 7pm; off-season 5pm).

See well-organized but unspectacular archaeological finds at **Museum of Silifke** which is 200m to the right, with your back to the bus station. (Open daily 8am-5pm. Admission 70¢, with ISIC 35¢.) Turn left downhill from the bus station to reach the hill with the city's ruins. Founded by Seleucus I, general of Alexander the Great and military head of Asia Minor and Syria, Silifke was originally named Seleucia. Before being captured by the Ottoman Turks in 1471, the town was successively controlled by the Isaurians, the Arabs, the Byzantines, the Armenians, and the Seljuks. **Silifke Castle,** which offers a hilltop view of the brown town, was constructed in the 12th century by the Armenians to defend themselves against the Seljuks (open 24 hrs.). A modern stone bridge built over the one constructed by Roman Emperor Vespasian and his sons crosses the Göksu River (Calycadnos of yore). The river is most famous for drowning German Emperor Frederick Barbarosa, leader of the Third Crusade, who expired while trying to cross it in 1190 and was never welcomed back.

The best place to stay in Silifke is the **Hotel Akdeniz,** 96 Menderes Cad. (tel. 112 85); walk 1km to the left from the bus station, past the 2nd century CE Temple of Jupiter. (Singles $3. Doubles $6. Hot showers $1.45. Bargain.) Though very clean, the **Otel Ünal,** 33 Ilhan Akgün Cad. (tel. 111 62), across the square from the tourist office, is an echo chamber for Silifke's noise. (Singles $3. Doubles $4. Triples $5. Quads $6.50. Add $1.30 for shower.) The **tourist office** (tel. 111 51), on the side of the river opposite the castle by Hotel Çadır, distributes maps, bus and accommodation information, and general information sheets. (English spoken. Open daily 8am-noon, and 1-5pm; off-season closed on weekends.) On the same side as the castle you'll find the **PTT.** (Open daily 8am-noon and 1-5pm; off-season closed on weekends. Mail and phone service daily until 11:30pm.) *Dolmuş* to Taşucu leave across the street from the PTT. Silifke's **telephone code** is 759. For **medical emergency,** dial 111 59. For the **police,** dial 110 97 (they may not speak English).

The underground **Church of Saint Thecla** lurks in the village of Meryemlik, 3km from Silifke. St. Thecla, a thaumaturgical spelunker, disappeared into the depths of this cave in Silifke to avoid persecution. After he converted to Christianity, Emperor Constantine constructed a basilica over the the site. Nearby is a rival basilica built by Emperor Zeno. Take the Taşucu *dolmuş* and get off at the small café where there is a sign for *Aya Takla;* then walk 1km to the church. (Open daily 8am-5:30pm; if closed, ask around for the *bekçi,* or guard.)

Thirty kilometers north of Silifke into the mountains are the ancient ruins of Olba-Diocaesarea and Ura at **Uzuncaburç.** To reach the site, take one of the infrequent *dolmuş* that depart across from the tourist office in Silifke. Ancient **Olba** ("happy city") became famous when Seleucus I constructed what is today the best-preserved **Temple of Zeus** in Asia Minor (built 295 BCE). For about 100 years, the city was ruled by priest-kings. When the Romans conquered Olba, they renamed it **Diocaesarea.** The site also includes a theater, an ancient fountain (still used today by locals), and a first-century BCE **Temple to Psyche,** of which only five Corinthian marble columns remain. On the way in, check out the 2nd- century BCE tombs that dot the rugged hills. In the Byzantine era of incorrigible church-loving, the temples were converted into churches, and still more churches were made from scratch. Three of these remain on the site. Three km to the east are the extensive ruins of **Ura,** including a 3rd-century aqueduct built by Emperor Septimius Severus. *Dolmuş* cost $1.45, but there is only one per day (at noon) from the main *dolmuş* stop at the center of Silifke. Taxis go, wait for you, and return for $21 (up to five people).

From Silifke to Mersin

The coast east of Silifke contains several modern boomtowns, each hosting hordes of Turkish tourists every weekend. The beach at **Susanoğlü,** 15 minutes from Silifke and copiously endowed with campsites, would be perfect if it weren't so crowded. Farther towards Mersin is **Narlıkuyu.** A subterranean river here dumps cold, fresh water into the sea, making the seawater almost potable; you can sometimes see animals lapping it up. Gracing the water's edge is a Roman bath which once contained a mosaic of the Three Graces. Today the largely intact mosaic can be seen at the mosaic museum of Narlıkuyu (open daily 8am-6:30pm; admission 60¢, with ISIC free).

The lovely caves of **Cennet ve Cehennem** (Heaven and Hell) are 2km from Narlıkuyu. The bus drivers have a nasty habit of dropping people 5km past the turn-off to the site; insist on having the bus stop at the Narlıkuyu Museum and walk the 2km uphill to the caves. The caves look paradisical, but the 450 steps leading down are infernal. Make sure you carry water down: you'll need it for the way back up. The site is actually composed of three caves: Heaven, Hell and the Wishing Well. Appropriately, the most impressive is called Heaven. Lying at the bottom of a deep gorge, the gaping entrance to the cave is marked by a 12th-century Armenian chapel which only adds to the general eeriness of the site. In ancient times the cave was thought to be an entrance to the underworld, and the subterranean river, roaring 125m below the surface, was identified with the River Styx and the beckoning gathering of angels. According to legend, the Heaven cave is where Mother Earth and Tartarus conceived Typhon, a grotesque, fire-breathing monster with serpents for arms and legs. Typhon came to challenge the gods but was defeated and imprisoned by Zeus in the nearby Hell grotto. The cave is actually a 120m pit, a guaranteed wonder-instiller for those with the courage to look into it. Up the road, the Wishing Well cave, bristling with stalagtite-stalag-mite formations, is now marred by graffiti. The descent into the wishing well is a 30m plunge down a rusty, winding staircase. The scraps of paper and rags in the trees around the caves are not just ugly, elevated litter: locals tie them to flora around the caves to ward off evil spirits. New, efficient lighting has eliminated the need for guides. But a flashlight is handy for a better look at the nooks and crannies. Unfortunately, there are no accommodations at the caves, so inquire in Narlıkuyu about private rooms ($7-10; for reservations, call Kerim Restaurant tel. (7596) 34 72).

The next town towards Mersin is the family-dominated **Akkum Beach.** You can pitch a tent for two on the beach for $3, but beware of the truculent bathrooms. **Rose Pansiyon,** across from the beach, has clean rooms and serves breakfast on the veranda overlooking the water (doubles $13, but bargain; breakfast and private bath included).

Just down the road from Akkum Beach is the resort town of **Korykos.** The Castle of Korykos stands on the beach opposite the ruins of **Kız Kalesi** (Maiden Castle), a sea castle situated on an islet offshore. According to legend, a king was told that his daugh-ter would die of a snake bite, so he imprisoned her in this castle out at sea. But some clwn, green in judgment, brought her a basket of figs with fig-colored snakes, and the prophecy came to pass. Now that the sea wall between the two castles has collapsed, the only way to get to the sea castle is to swim or take one of the small boats that shuttle back and forth. Although plentiful, accommodations here are all expensive and usually crowded, especially on weekends. At **Korykos (Kızkalesi) Cemre Pansiyon** (tel. (7584) 11 65), behind the castle, you'll find clean but very basic doubles ($12, but bar-gain). There is also a cheap restaurant which proffers full meals for $3. **Kız Kalesi Aile Playı** (tel. (7584) 10 36), right by the castle, has offers both rooms to let and camping area ($2.15 per tent, $1.05 per person; triples with shower and toilet $13). Farther to-ward Mersin, just past the town of **Kocahasanlı,** is the beautiful government-run **Er-demli Çamliği Campsite** with has the best facilities (including a pine-shaded picnic area and a supermarket) and the best prices between Mersin and Alanya. (Tel. (7585) 25 31; $1.65 per tent, $1 per person.)

Mersin

Mersin, sometimes called İçel, is Turkey's largest Mediterranean port and the gate-way to Northern Cyprus. This modern city is no place to dawdle, especially during the summer with its noise, heat, and hair-curling humidity. On the other hand, it has some of the friendliest and most helpful people on the coast. From the bus station it's a 10- to 15-minute walk into town; take a right along the main street as you leave the front of the station (the buses are in back), and turn left on Çakmak Cad. There is also a red minibus which shuttles into town (20¢). If you arrive by boat, walk west along Ismet Inönü Buluzri to reach the city center. The main **tourist office** (tel. 36 63 58) is at the harbor, just inland from the Turkish Maritime Lines Agency. The friendly multilingual crew can provide maps and suggestions for accommodations. (Open daily 8am-5pm; off-season 9am-noon and 1-5pm.) Another less helpful **tourist office** awaits at the bus station. (Open in summer only Mon.-Fri. 8am-noon and 1-5pm.) The **PTT** lies 1km west of the main tourist office. (Open 24 hrs.) The **train station,** 2 blocks in from the harbor near the hospital, services points east to Adana. Intercity **buses** leave from the station 2km north of the downtown area on Zeytinli Bahçe Cad. Municipal buses serve the length of the city along the waterfront, and run from the station to the waterfront. Mersin's **telephone code** is 74.

If the bus station is all you plan to see of Mersin, you can zonk out a block away (to the right when facing the station) at the hygienically pleasing, comfortable **Otel Murat 2,** Yeni Otogar Karşisi (tel. 32 46 81; singles $4; doubles $6). **Hotel Berlin,** 91 Yeni Mahalle 5C Soq. (tel. 33 71 62) is by the SSK Hospital and fire department. (From the main tourist office, take a *dolmuş* going to Kurdali, and ask to be let off at the hotel.) There are big, carpeted doubles, most rooms have basic bathrooms, and the lobby has a TV. (Singles with bath $6. Doubles $8, with bath $9.) The **Doğan Oteli,** 11 Büyük Hamam Sok. (tel. 32 17 50), though inexpensive and fairly clean, is dreary and hard to find. (Singles with shower $5. Doubles with shower $8.) It's in the labyrinth of shops 1 block inland from the Ulu Cami (Big Mosque).

Cheap food is abundant in Mersin. For the cheapest fish prices on the Turkish Mediterranean, visit any of the restaurants at the fish market around *Belediye,* the municipal government building. (*Mercan*—red coral fish—$1; beer 75¢.) For the royal treatment, go to **Doğan 99,** 10 Eski Taksi Alanı (tel. 31 20 91). To get there, go west one block from the intersection of Uray Cad. and Mastane Cad., then take a right. Ask for their special: a couple of *meze*s (appetizers) and salads, some bite-sized meat dishes, then the main course followed by *baklava* with ice cream and watermelon with crushed ice. (Open 11am-11pm, serving until 9:30pm. Complete, stuffing meals for about $6.)

Ferry tickets to Famagusta, Northern Cyprus can be purchased at the **Turkish Maritime Lines** office on the harbor. Ferries depart Monday, Wednesday, and Friday at 10pm (10hr., $30, students 10% off). For cheaper tickets, try **Ertürk** and **Fergün** companies, which run between Taşucu and Girne (see Taşucu section for details). They both have offices across from the main tourist office.

Keep in mind that because the governments of Greece and Greek Cyprus consider it illegal to enter Cyprus through occupied territory, you will not be admitted to either of these countries with Turkish Cypriot stamps in your passport. When you arrive in Northern Cyprus, you can request that officials stamp a separate sheet of paper that can be detached from your passport upon departure, but your pleas may go unheeded in the chaos that often accompanies arrival. Before you go, try to get someone to write you a short note in Turkish explaining what you want done. Policy concerning travel to Northern Cyprus changes frequently. For the latest information, you can call the **Consulate of Northern Cyprus,** 71/1 Karadeniz Apt. (tel. 31 62 28) on the west side of town—but the tourist office is friendlier and always has the updated information, so check with them first. In the summer of 1992, no visa was required, and the maximum stay allowed was 3 months. There was a $9 port tax, as well as a $5 port tax from Turkey.

East of Mersin is the city of **Tarsus,** supposedly established by Seth, son of Adam, but more famous as the birthplace of St. Paul. Most of the ancient city's ruins lie hidden beneath the modern metropolitan menagerie.

Antakya (Hatay)

In idyllic Antakya, which appears as Hatay on Turkish maps and schedules, few tourists are to be found, and a merciful breeze subdues the summer heat. The formidable mountain range that enlivens the ride into Antakya isolated the city from the rest of Turkey, and from the end of World War I until 1939, the area was actually part of Syria. If you're continuing on to Syria, this is probably the best starting point, though there is also bus transportation from Gaziantep.

As ancient Antioch, the city was one of the richest and most powerful in the Mediterranean. Seleucus, a general under Alexander the Great, founded the city and ruled over much of Asia from here. The population swelled to half a million and Antioch became famous for liberality and frivolity. During Roman rule, the Apostle Peter settled here and gathered the first Christian congregation in a grotto now outside of town. After a series of two earthquakes, the desperate denizens changed the city's name to Theopolis in hope that the powers that be would recognize their repentance. The city's importance, both strategic and commercial, made it a prime target for conquest. By the time the Turks got hold of it, Sassanians, Arabs, Byzantines, Crusaders, and Mameluks had all marauded through, and Antioch's glory had been reduced to ruins. A glance at the crumbling walls along the surrounding mountain ridge will give you an idea of the large size of the ancient city, compared to the population of 100,000 living here today.

From the bus station walk down the main street, **İstiklâl Cad.,** and cross over the bridge into the square with the Atatürk statue without which we would all be lost. The **Archaeological Museum** and the **PTT** (open 24 hrs.) keep Atatürk company. Walk about 5 minutes down Atatürk Cad. (to the statue's left) to reach the **tourist office** in the park on the opposite side of the circle. (Open daily 9am-noon and 1:30-6:30pm;

off-season open Mon.-Fri. 8:30am-noon and 1:30-5pm.) From the bus station, walk 2 blocks down İstiklâl Cad. toward the town center, and turn left into the parallel alley. Antakya's **telephone code** is 891.

Hotel Güney, 8 İstiklâl Sok. (tel. 117 78), has clean, basic rooms. (Singles with shower $6.50. Doubles with shower $12.) **Hotel Dinçkan,** next door at 14 İstiklâl Sok. (tel. 134 19), has dark, but pleasant rooms. (Singles with shower $5. Doubles with shower $8.) Farther into the town, off Hürriyet Cad., the decent **Hotel Saray** (tel. 246 89) offers good prices *sans* comfort, atmosphere, or hot water. (Singles $3. Doubles $5.) Both **Hotel Güney** and **Hotel Dinçkan** have good restaurants. **Restaurant Nuri,** 9 Hürriyet Cad., serves authentic food in front of their TV. English language books and newspapers can be found at **Ferah Koll. Şti.,** just past Restaurant Nuri.

Antakya's **Archaeological Museum** is world-renowned for its collection of Roman mosaics. Recovered from the nearby site of Daphne, these mosaics represent the late Roman style adopted by the Byzantines. (Open Mon. 1:30-5pm, Tues.-Sun. 8am-noon and 1:30-5pm. Admission $1.50, students 80¢.) **San Pierre Kilesi,** 2km from the center of town, is celebrated as the world's first church. Peter's original congregation coined the word Christianity to describe their new religion. The humble church in a small cave has no artwork apart from remnants of floor mosaics and a façade added by the Crusaders. To get there, walk down İstiklâl Cad. from the bus station and follow the signs to Reyhanli. (Open Tues.-Sun. 8am-noon and 1:30-5:30pm. Free.) The hillside near the church has been a holy spot since pagan times and is riddled with the remains of caves, tunnels, and parts of the city's defenses. A path zig-zags up from the church to the Hellenistic **fire altar** to Haron, god of earthquakes.

About 21km farther stand the 19th century BCE ruins of **Açscana,** capital of a small kingdom that was heavily influenced by the Hittites and Assyrians. Little remains of the palace and temple here except a few walls and some steps, but ruins this old are hard to find, so seize the moment. *Dolmuş* will drop you off 500m from the site. (Admission $1.) The inhabitants of Antakya frequently picnic around the water cascades at **Harbiye,** ancient Daphne, 7km south from the east side of the bridge. *(Dolmuş* run the route frequently.) Restaurants offer service at tables that stand in the chilly water; up the hill are several inexpensive pensions.

The most frequent connections are to Gaziantep and Mersin; buses also run to İstanbul and Ankara. If you have a Syrian visa already, you can take a bus directly to Aleppo (Halep in Turkish), 100km away ($7.50). You should apply ahead of time in İstanbul or Ankara, since it is theoretically not possible to get a visa at the border. If you are a British citizen, you'll have to wait 1-3 months for your visa. You are supposed to exchange $100 at the Syrian border, although you may be able to negotiate your way out of this; if you attempt the impossible and travel straight through Syria without spending the night, most of this money may be refunded. From Aleppo, you can change buses for other Syrian cities. Daily buses also run to Jordan (*Ürdün* in Turkish; $22.50), and Damascus ($10).

CENTRAL TURKEY

It's sometimes hard to avoid feeling the pervasive sense of isolation when traveling through the arid stretches of the Anatolian plateau. Jagged mountains along the coasts yield to vast terrains of rolling hills, some rich with vegetation, others chalk-white and barren. A few of the world's earliest settlements sprouted here, and Neolithic, Hittite, and Phrygian sites still splatter the area. In the 11th century, invading Seljuks from the Central Asian steppe made their capital in Konya, endowing it with a wealth of religious and historic architecture. Today, Ankara's broad avenues, bustling business sector, and fine universities and museums are a testament to the extensive modernization that Atatürk ushered in with the founding of the Turkish Republic in 1923. Not far off, the eerie rock formations of Cappadocia, sculpted into cities and churches, are one of Turkey's most spectacular sites and attract a lion's share of tourists. Few visitors stay long in either Konya or Ankara, though these cities are critical to the religious and political life of modern Turkey.

Ankara

When Atatürk moved the Turkish capital from İstanbul to its current, more central location in 1923, he gave the ancient city of Ankara a new lease on life. To a large extent the provincial Anatolian town is still there, perched majestically atop a number of dramatic hills which rise from the surrounding rolling plains. The new capital has grown up just to the south, with its main axis, **Atatürk Bulvarı,** vertically joining the two. At the pitched intersections of narrow, winding streets within the old citadel, wobbly round matrons wearing flower-print scarves still fill their water buckets from communal fountains. Meanwhile, the modern pedestrian streets of the Kızılay district teem with the European atmosphere of outdoor cafés. The weather can be windy and miserable much of the year, and the air choked with coal and diesel fumes anytime, but catch Ankara on a sunny summer day and you might well find it more lively and engaging than its poor reputation would suggest.

Orientation and Practical Information

Ulus, the most colorful district of the city, lies at Atatürk Bulvarı's northern end. The city's central districts, **Sıhhiye, Kızılay,** and **Bakanlıklar,** lie farther south along Atatürk. The Kızılay district is cleaner, more modern, and more western than Ulus. Bakanlıklar literally means ministries; most government buildings are found here. Ankara has a complex intracity **bus system.** The big red buses are municipal buses; they cost 40¢ and you must buy a ticket from the kiosks near major bus stops or, in a pinch, from another passenger. The big blue buses are a private company; they also cost 40¢ and you may pay on the bus. The ubiquitous minibuses *(dolmuş)* cost 50¢. No tickets are required. Buses run frequently along Atatürk Bulvarı. As usual in any Turkish town except İstanbul, the best way to find your way around is to ask a few friendly Turks.

The **bus station** is 500m south of the train station. To get from the train station to Ulus and its budget hotels, walk straight out along Cumhuriyet Bulvarı. (A park will be on your right and a soccer stadium will be on your left.) It's about a mile, so take a taxi if you've got a lot of baggage. Continue straight until you reach the equestrian statue of the elusive Atatürk, which stands at the center of Ulus, facing west. Continue east on Hısarparkı Cad. There are hotels off to either side.

Ankara serves as a transportation nucleus for travel east and south. Inter-city buses go everywhere often. Although it's quicker to travel between İstanbul and Ankara by bus (at least 2 per hr., 7-8hr., \$10-20), overnight trains may be more comfortable. The faster *Mavi Tren* departs from both Ankara and İstanbul at 11pm (9hr., \$11); *Anadolou Exspressi* departs at 9am and 9pm, (11hr., \$7, couchette \$9). The *Ankara Exspressi* contains only sleeping compartments; it departs at 10pm (11hr., about \$30 with couchette). Ankara is also connected by rail to İzmir, Konya, Cappadocia, Erzurum,

Trabzon, and other Turkish cities. Except for long hauls, you are better off traveling by bus.

Tourist Offices: One office at the airport. Main office at 121 Mustafa Kemal Bulvarı (tel. 488 70 07). From the bus or train stations, go under the train tracks to Tandoğan Square, then left on Mustafa Kemal Bulvarı. The office is on the ground floor of the Ministry of Tourism (Turizm Başkanlık), on your right. Keep on the boulevard for a mile; this will take you to Kızılay. Most employees speak only one foreign language, and often there is only one present at a time. Free city and country maps. Mon.-Fri. 8:30am-7:30pm, Sat.-Sun. 9am-5:30pm. Free **tourist information** telephone within Ankara: 980 04 70 90.

Embassies: All embassies in Ankara are south of Hürriyet Sq., along Atatürk Bulvarı. **U.S.,** 110 Atatürk Bulvarı (tel. 126 54 70). **Canada,** 75 Nenehatun Cad. (tel. 136 12 90). **U.K.,** 46a Şehit Ersan Cad. (tel. 127 43 10). **Australia,** 83 Nenehatun Cad. (tel. 136 12 40). Travelers from **New Zealand** should contact the British mission. **Bulgaria,** 124 Atatürk Bulvarı (tel. 126 74 55). **Greece,** 911 Zia Ul-Rahman Cad. (tel. 436 88 60). **Iran,** 10 Tahran Cad. (tel. 127 43 20). **Iraq,** 11 Turan Emeksiz Sok. (tel. 126 61 18). **Jordan,** 18 Dede Korkut Sok. (tel. 139 42 30). **Syria,** 7 Abdullah Cevdet Sok. (tel. 139 45 88). **Northern Cyprus,** 20 Incirli Sok. (tel. 137 95 38).

Currency Exchange: Vakif Bank offers the best rates, and charges no commission. There is one office on the north side of Ulus Sq., and two branches on Mustafa Kemal Bulvarı, in Maltepe.

American Express: 7 Cinnah Cad. (tel. 167 73 34). Cinnah Cad. branches off from Atatürk Bulvarı south of Bakanlikar. Take any bus marked "Kavaklidere" from across the Ulus post office. Provides emergency cash for cardholders and holds mail. Wired money not accepted. Open Mon.-Fri. 9am-6pm, Sat. 9am-1pm.

Post Office: PTT, on Atatürk Bulvarı in Ulus, 2 blocks south of the Atatürk statue. Open 24 hrs.; daily 9am-5pm for Poste Restante; 24 hr. currency exchange.

Telephones: At the post office. Open 24 hrs. Also at the bus and train stations. **Telephone Code:** 4.

Airport: Buses leave from the **Turkish Airlines** office (information tel. 312 49 10; reservations 312 62 00) at Hipodrum Cad. (next to the train station) and head to the airport, **Esenboğa,** 1½hr. before domestic and 2hr. before international departures ($1.50). Direct flights to: İstanbul (7am-10pm every hr., 1hr.); Adana, Diyarbakır, Erzurum, İzmir, and Trabzon (several each day, 1hr.); Malatya and Van (4 per week, 2¼hr.), Gaziantep (5 per week, 1hr.). Indirect flights to Antalya and Dalaman (1 per day, 3-4hr.) and Kayseri (1 per week, 3hr.). All domestic flights $62; students (14-24 yrs.) $38. Try to buy tickets 2 days in advance, because the flights fill up.

Bus Station: On Hippodrum Cad. Buses (usually at least one per hour) go to all Turkish cities of significant size: Konya (every hr., 3hr., $5); İstanbul (8hr., $7); İzmir (9hr., $7.50); Kuşadası (11hr., $10); Bodrum (13hr., $14); Adana (10hr., $8); Trabzon (11hr., $8); Bursa (6hr., $7); Sungurlu (2½hr., $3); Nevşehir (4hr., $4). Daily to the Iran border ($15), Baghdad ($30), and Aleppo, Syria. Lockers for storage 25¢.

Bookstores: ABCE Bookshop, 1 Selanik Cad. (tel. 134 38 42) Kızılay, 2 blocks north and ½ a block east of the main square. Good selection of English language books. The **American Association Library** (tel. 126 94 99), across from the Amex office, houses a comprehensive collection of English-language literature. Open Mon.-Fri. 11am-7pm, Sat. 10am-1pm. Closed July 31-Sept. 5.

Hospital: Hacettepe University Hospital, Hasircilar Cad. From the statue in Ulus, head south for about 2km, turn left onto Talat Paşa Cad. and climb the hill to Hasircilar Cad. Emergency health care.

Bath: Marmara Hamamı, 17 Denizciler Cad. in Ulus. Bath $2, massage $1.

Accommodations

Most of the less expensive hotels are to the west of **Ulus,** towards the citadel. Many have cheerless singles for $5 (without bath). The following places are clean, *reasonably* quiet, and generally less grim than most (and you wonder where Ankara gets its renown for mediocrity):

Otel Yavuz, 4 Konya Sok. (tel. 324 32 55), has some spacious rooms with sofas. Singles $6, with bath $11. Doubles with bath $12.

Otel Oba, 9 Posta Caddesi (tel. 312 41 28). Large, airy rooms. Singles $9, with bath $11. Doubles $13.

Hisar Oteli, 6 Hisarpark Caddessi (tel. 311 98 89). Front rooms offer a nice view of the old quarter; no private baths, but a Turkish bathhouse is attatched next door. Singles $6.

Otel Yakut, 19 Hilal Soq. (tel 312 51 58), on a small street between the Hacı Bayram mosque and the Roman baths; sunny, large, carpeted rooms. Singles $6, with bath $9. Doubles $14.

Otel Örnek, 22 Ada Sok. (tel. 324 36 21), on a side street near Roman baths; small, clean rooms. Singles without bath $5. Otel Yat and Otel Ersoy next door are similar.

Lale Palas, Telegraf Sok., near Hacı Bayram mosque. Singles with bath $6. Doubles with bath $14.

All hotels in the Ulus area fill up quickly, so if you arrive late you may get stuck at **Hitit Otel** up near the entrance to the citadel. (You can't miss the huge sign.) At $20 and up, their rooms are no bargain, but they do accept Visa and Mastercard and have a relaxing terrace restaurant. Some rooms have balconies, with excellent views.

In the Kızılay district, most hotels are most upscale and expensive. Your best bet here is the **Otel Ertan,** 70 Selanik Caddesi (tel. 118 40 84). They have decent rooms and a garden in front, very peaceful but close to the Kızılay nightlife, unlike the hotels in Ulus. Singles $11. Doubles $20. If you must stay at the bus station, Terminal Oteli has rooms starting at $9.

Food

Ulus, like all of Turkey, is full of cheap *kebapçıs*. They don't vary much in quality, price, or selection. Peer into a few and see what looks comfortable. If you're sick of kebab, try **Spaghetti House,** 65 Selanik Caddesi in Kızılay. There are a couple of tables outside, and spaghetti costs $2. From the Atatürk statue in Ulus, walk east on Hisarparkı Cad. and turn right just before Anafartalar Cad. to find Ankara's big **food market,** which sells everything from sugared almonds to live chickens. For beer, music, and a chance to hang out with university students, try **Café Melodi,** in the Batı Sineması building on Atatürk Bulvarı, one block north of Esat Cad. and three blocks south of Kızılay.

Sights

The **Anadolu Medeniyetleri Müzesi** (Museum of Anatolian Civilizations) grovels at the feet of the citadel dominating Ulus. The museum's setting is unique: a restored 15th-century Ottoman *han* and *bedesten* (covered bazaar), populated by canaries, houses a collection of astoundingly old artifacts which traces the history of Anatolia from the dawn of civilization. English-speaking guides and an illustrated catalogue of the museum are available. (Open daily 9am-5:20pm. Admission $2.75.) Take a taxi ($1-3) or walk up the hill east from the statue of Atatürk, on Hisarparkı Cad., and right onto Ipek Cad. Just up the hill from the museum, the town-within-a-town inside the wall of the **citadel** is a fascinating area for a stroll. The two towers of the citadel afford fine views of Ankara. Worth a brief look is the small, 12th-century **Alâeddin Mosque.** Merchants hawk Angora goat hair in the relatively sleepy **bazaar** you'll find on the way back down the hill.

Turks worship Atatürk, who was, as they never hesitate to point out, the founder of modern Turkey. The **Anıt Kabir,** Atatürk's mausoleum, and the attached museum of his personal effects faintly echo Lenin's tomb. The site occupies a large park on the west side of town (a 25-min. walk from Kızılay or southbound bus #63 on Atatürk Cad.; mausoleum open Tues.-Sun. 9am-noon and 1-5pm).

Other sights in Ankara include the **Temple of Augustus,** built in 25 BCE over the site of earlier temples to Cybele (an Anatolian fertility goddess) and to the Phrygian moon god; it was later converted into a Byzantine church. Nearby are the 15th-century **Hacı Bayram Mosque,** the old **Parliament,** and the **zoo.** The **Ethnographic Museum,** about half a mile south of Ulus on Atatürk Bul., has a collection of Turkish clothing and embroidery from the Seljuk period to the present while the neighboring **State Museum of Sculptures and Paintings** exhibits contemporary Turkish paintings.

(Both open Tues.-Sun. 8:30am-12:30pm and 1:30-5:30pm. Ethnographic Museum $1.50; State Museum free.)

Entertainment

When they roll up the sidewalks at dusk in Ulus, head south to Kızılay for the evening. For a peaceful walking tour, start up the tree-lined Yüksel pedestrian path a block south of Kızılay on the left. A lot of students hang out on the benches or amble about, some from Ankara University and others from the many private and professional schools in the area. To the right climbs café-laden Selanik Sokak. Strolling through the Gençlik Parkı, investigate the nice fountain or the many outdoor tea gardens. If you're heading to Eastern Turkey, Ankara might be your last chance to see a **film** in a language you understand: both the Kızılırmak (21 Kızılırmak Sok., just off Selanik) and the Metropol (around the corner at 7b Salonik) show American and European films, subtitled. Admission $2. Afterwards, you might try **Café Papillon,** a rock bar with shaded outdoor tables.

Near Ankara

The ruins of **Hattuşaş,** the once-glorious Hittite capital, sprawl about 200km from Ankara, 25km off the highway to Samsun. The first people to smelt iron, the Indo-European Hittites conquered Anatolia around 2200 BCE. United under a central authority at Hattuşaş, the Hittites vied with the Egyptians for control of the fertile lands and trade routes of Mesopotamia. The western Sea People razed Hattuşaş shortly after 1200 BCE, but archaeologists have unearthed enough of the ruins to provide a fair representation of the city. The road following the 6km wall that encircles Hattuşaş first passes by the **Bükük Mabed** (Great Temple) of the Weather God of Hatti and the Sun Goddess of Arinna. A drawbridge over two pools of water granted the only entrance to the original temple. The big green rock there was a wedding gift from the King of Egypt to his son-in-law, the King of the Hittites. Continuing up the hill and to the right, the road passes the **Aslanıkapı** (Lion's Gate; the original lions are now in the museum in Ankara) and the **Yerkapı** (Earth Gate). The two sphinxes from the Earth Gate are now in İstanbul and Berlin, and no longer overlook the 70m-long tunnel, built under the southern fortifications and used for surprise attacks. The figure carved in relief on the **Kralkapı** (King's Gate) just down the hill, is the Hittite war god. The **Büyük Kale** (Great Citadel) rounds out the tour. The small **museum** in the village of **Boğazkale,** 1km from the site, gives a sense of the area's history. (Open Tues.-Sun. 8:30am-12:30pm and 1:30pm-6pm. Admission to museum and ruins $2; to ruins alone $1.) Your admission ticket is also valid for **Yazılıkaya,** an open-air temple with 100 of the 1000 or so gods of the Hittite pantheon represented in bas-relief. Yazılıkaya lies 4km south of Hattuşaş along a well-marked road.

To get to Hattuşaş, take a bus to Sungurlu (2½hr., $4 from Ankara; frequent buses along the Ankara-Samsun route). The bus will drop you off either on the main highway or in the center of town. To get back to Ankara, flag a bus down on the highway. There are *dolmuşes* to Boğazkale that leave from the center of Sungurlu. (Ask someone other than a taxi driver.) Often local taxis function as *dolmuşes*. (Bargain with the driver; $3 is a good price.) Otherwise, a private taxi costs $10 for a one way ride to Boğazkale, $20-30 for a full tour of the ruins. Traffic on the road to Boğazkale is very light, so hitching may be a problem. Walking through the ruins takes about half a very sweaty day.

In Sungurlu, the **Hittit Motel** (tel. (1042) 14 09) has pretty rooms and a swimming pool. (Singles $15. Doubles $20.) In Boğazkale, **Başkent Pansiyon** has rooms from $10-12, and the **Aşıkoğlu Motel** (tel. (4554) 10 04) is conveniently located across from the museum. The restaurant is decent and the rooms are clean, but have no hot water. (Singles with bath $10. Doubles with bath $14.) There is a small **campsite** next to the motel.

Konya

Lying on a desolate plain high atop the Anatolian plateau, Konya has long been a center of culture and of Muslim faith. In recent years, the city has burgeoned into a commercial and financial center as well. Forlornly symbolic of its new identity, monuments from Konya's golden age stand marooned amidst a wide expanse of characterless buildings and wide, busy streets. In Roman times, St. Paul favored Konya (then called Iconium) with a visit, and sparked the city's transformation into a significant Christian center. In the 11th century, the Seljuks swept through Asia Minor, gaining a formidable reputation in the West and paving the way for later Ottoman conquests. They made their capital in Konya, replacing its churches with the greatest mosques of the era, most of which survive today. It was during this period that Celâleddin Rumi, known to his followers as Mevlâna (our master) came from his birthplace in Afghanistan and settled in Konya. After his death, some of his disciples founded a Sufi order which later became known for its "whirling dervishes." Today, Muslims often stop in Konya to visit Mevlâna's tomb before embarking on the pilgrimage to Mecca. Despite its rapid industrialization, Konya retains a very conservative Islamic character; you'll notice most of the older men wearing the traditional Muslim hats called *derviş*.

Most of Konya's sights are in the small city center; get a map from the **tourist office** (tel. 11 10 74), on Alaeddin Bulvarı, an extension of Mevlâna Cad., the main street in the city, next to the Mevlâna Tekke. (Open 8am-noon and 1:30-5:30pm.) The **PTT** (marked "Postane") sits on Alâedin Cad. (Open 24 hrs.) Konya's **telephone code** is 33.

Finding rooms in Konya is no problem. Many are clustered along the main drag. **Otel Çeşme,** 35 İstanbul Cad. (tel. 11 24 26), is well-kept and has rooms with private bathrooms. (Singles $9. Doubles $15.50.) Though not quite as nice, **Otel Mevlâna,** 1 Cengaver Sok. (tel. 11 98 24), has clean rooms and, in the summer, beds on the roof for only $3; coming from the station, turn right on İstanbul Cad. and follow the signs. The kilim-clad **Çatal Pansiyon** (tel. 11 49 81), is around the corner from the tourist office ($8.50 per bed). **Otel Konfor,** 51 Eski Garaj Cad. (tel. 11 31 03), is worth the walk for its new, smurfy rooms (doubles $10). **Başak Palas,** 3 Hükümet Alanı is clean and modern and serves a good breakfast (singles $11).

The local specialty is *firin kebap,* a chunk of oven-roasted lamb; try it at **Lokanta Şima Restaurant,** across and one block up Mevlâna Cad. from the tourist office, or the **Damak Restaurant,** across the alley from the Otel Mevlâna. Another restaurant with the same name at the end of the block has an outdoor garden. Across from Alaadin Tepesi, on the left as you walk from the city center, is the **Zafer Restaurant.** Treat yourself to *Saç Böreği,* a delicious cheese-stuffed bread.

You can spot the 13th-century **Mevlâna Tekke** by its enameled turquoise tower. Inside the complex, originally a type of monastery, are the *türbes* of Celâleddin and other dervishes, as well as a fascinating museum with prayer rugs, musical instruments, and elaborately decorated garments. The Whirling Dervishes wielded great political power from the Seljuk period until 1923, when Atatürk dissolved the order. The Turkish ruler reportedly believed that the Dervishes' monarchist and politically conservative beliefs were inconsistent with the reforms he sought to implement. Not long after his death, however, the government gave in, and now professional Dervishes are free to whirl once a year during a week-long festival held in Konya in mid-December (if that doesn't fit with your plans, you can see genuine dervish dances in İstanbul). The museum is open Mon. 8:30am-3pm, Tues.-Sun. 8:30am-5:30pm. (Admission $2, students $1.50.)

Konya's other major attractions are on or around **Alaadin Tepesi** (Alaadin Hill), several hundred meters up Hükümet Cad. Supposedly, this mound contains layers of civilizations stretching back to the Bronze Age. **Alaadin Cami,** near the hilltop, is an early 13th-century mosque in the Syrian Seljuk style. (The mosque was closed in summer 1992 and may not reopen by 1993.) Here, the Seljuks studied astrology in the reflection of the night sky off the pool in the main chamber. The **Karatay Medressi** now houses a collection of Seljuk ceramics and tiles (admission 75¢). The interior itself is a great example of Seljuk tilework. Several blocks south of the hill is the **Archaeological Museum,** an outstanding 3rd-century sarcophagus illustrating the labors of Hercules.

(Open Tues.-Sun. 8am-noon and 1:30-5pm. Admission $1.) Spend some time wandering in Konya's **bazaar** between the Aziziye Mosque and the PTT, or explore the older residential streets east of Mevlâna.

To get back to the bus station, over a mile north of the city center, take any *dolmuş* marked "Otogar." Buses run between Konya and Silifke (10 per day, 5hr., $4); Ankara (15 per day, 3hr., $4), and İzmir (15 per day, $7.50). Antalya is serviced by 3 buses (6½hr., $5.75), and there is frequent service to Aksaray (2½hr., $3) and to Nevşehir and Göreme (3hr., $4). Nighttime buses run to and from İstanbul. If you arrive at the bus station during the day, take a minibus marked "Mevlâna" to the center; at night, try a three-wheeled cart, a conveyance unique to Konya. Both leave from behind the station. After midnight, you'll have to take a taxi. You can buy bus tickets at bus company offices, which are located on side streets all along Alaadin Cad.

Near Konya

Every half-hour, a bus leaves from the municipal bus stop (on Alaadin Cad., across from the PTT) for isolated **Sille,** 8km away. Huddled in a small valley, the village faces a cliff into which numerous small rock dwellings have been carved. Sille also has a 4th-century church, **Aya Elena Kilisesi,** decorated by more recent frescoes. (Supposedly open daily 9am-4pm, but hours vary. Admission 50¢.)

The mountaintop site of **Karadağ,** approximately 160km southeast of Konya, is spotted with the crumbling ruins of several churches. The plethora of churches puzzles scholars, for there is no record of any sizable population here. There's no population now, either, which makes it difficult to reach. First take a bus to Karaman, then a *dolmuş* to Kilbasan; from there, you'll have to take a *dolmuş* ($15) to Karadağ. You might not make it back to Konya in the same day, in which case you can find accommodations in Karaman.

Çatalhöyük, (near the town of Çümra 50km south of Konya) is one of the world's oldest known settlements, dating back to the eighth millenium BCE. An advanced Neolithic community, Çatalhöyük vies with Jericho for the coveted title of "world's first city." Its famous cave drawings and artifacts have been moved to the Ankara museum and Holland; little remains on site but a few crumbling walls. The tour isn't worthwhile, but the guidebook on sale at Mevlâna is. Take a bus from the Eski Garage near Pira Paşa Mosque to Çümra (45min.), then take a taxi the remaining distance (entire journey about $10 round-trip).

Cappadocia

The peculiar grandeur of Cappadocia will lure you into this ancient province and keep your imagination roaming long after you've left. Volcanic formations shape a striking landscape of cone-shaped monoliths (fittingly called *peribaca,* meaning "fairy chimneys" in Turkish) clustered in valleys and along ridges. The region lies between three volcanoes—Hasan Dağı near Aksaray, Erciyes Dağı near Kyseri, and Melendiz Dağı near Niğde—which once deposited a thick layer of volcanic ash here, which subsequently hardened to form a soft rock called tufa, or tuff. The boulders protected the tuff immediately under them from erosion, leading to the creation of the bizarre structures. For at least 2000 years, until the Greek Christian inhabitants were expelled in 1923, people in this area carved houses, churches, and entire cities out of the same rock, uniting natural and man-made environments. The central area of the province is defined by the triangle formed by the city of Nevşehir and the smaller towns of Avanos and Ürgüp, about 300km southeast of Ankara.

Most visitors with only a day or two see the major sites of Derinkuyu and the Göreme Open-Air Museum. The region also contains farming villages, Byzantine chapels, and underground habitations that could occupy a visitor indefinitely. Of the several towns you can stay in, Göreme has a unique charm. Unfortunately, in the past few years tourism has grown here like a cancer. Ürgüp also makes a good base for visits to the area as it is larger and has better access to buses, taxi tours, rental cars and mopeds. Biking is an exhilarating way to tackle the area's rudimentary roads. Travel on cycle also allows you flexibility in visiting sites, which are sometimes quite a distance from one another. Though touristy in parts, Cappadocia is rather conservative; bikers may be the target of hurled rocks, and women should avoid wearing sleeveless shirts, short shorts, or miniskirts. Freelance camping in the rocks is strictly prohibited.

Aksaray and Ihlara

If you are approaching Cappadocia from the west, **Aksaray** is a likely destination. There are frequent buses to Nevşehir (every 1½hr, $2.50), but you really shouldn't miss the opportunity to visit what is up to now the least exploited attraction in the region: the **İhlara valley**, a true garden paradise hidden in a narrow gorge that the Melendiz River cuts through the treeless Cappodocian plateau. You won't even imagine it's there until you literally come up to the edge. Small surprise that for centuries thousands of Greek Christians found this valley an agreeable refuge for sedentary life while their nomadic Turkish neighbors grazed their flocks over the bleak, grassy plains above. Although the valley is still somewhat off the beaten track, it becomes more developed every year. Seven years ago there were no pensions and no public transport. Now there are three **buses** per day from Aksaray (8am, 3pm, and 6pm, 1hr, 75¢; return from İhlara at 7am, 2pm, and 4pm), and half a dozen places to stay. If you are coming on the bus from Nevşehir, be sure to take it all the way to Aksaray even though you will pass the turnoff for İhlara. The driver may think he's doing you a favor by dropping you off, but you'll still be 30km away with little passing traffic.

Coming 10km south from the turnoff, you'll pass the town of **Selime** beside huge rock cones similar to those at Göreme, pockmarked like Swiss cheese with the windows and doors of former troglodyte habitations. There are a couple of pensions here, but you'd be better off continuing to Belisırma or İhlara further along. At Belisırma, halfway alongside the valley, you'll find **Belisırma Valley Camping and Restaurant** (tel. (9) 48 23 12 00), a quality pension beautifully situated beside the river. They have modest rooms ($1.50-2.50), and a soothing shaded dining area by the water. This is a good stopping place for lunch if you are walking the length of the valley.

As you approach İhlara along the rim road, you will pass the brand new **Akar Pansiyon** on your right (tel. (9) 48 24 10 18; $6 per person with bath and private balcony, including breakfast). A little further on there is an intersection with a road leading to the "official" valley entrance on your left. On this road is the **Pansiyon Anatolia** (tel. (9) 48 24 11 28; $4.50 per person), and farther down the **Vadi Başı Eu Pansiyonu** (tel. (9) 48 24 11 22; $5 per person, including breakfast), where the family atmosphere is warm and genuine. Continuing into İhlara proper, you'll find the **İhlara River View Hotel** (tel. (9) 48 24 11 76; $4-6) in the town square. If you miss the bus and have to stay in Aksaray, you're better off staying at the **Pansiyon Ihlara** (tel. (9) 48 11 60 83), a block from the *otogar* (bus station), towards the main square. The pension at the bus station itself is pretty noisy. If you have some time to spend in Aksaray, visit the 12th century Seljuk **Ulu Cami** mosque, a few blocks past the main square. You can also make a short trip out to the village **Sultan Hanı,** which has an impressive Seljuk *han,* a traditional caravansary 40km away (buses every hour, 75¢), or stop there on your way in from Konya.

Nevsehir

Although Nevşehir is not especially interesting, it is the region's transportation hub. Don't let fast-talking travel agents at the bus station convince you to stay here if you have time to go on to Göreme or Ürgüp. Nevşehir is dusty and noisy and lacks the David Lynch-like weirdness of other locations in the valley. Most buses will drop you off here, though some stop in Ürgüp, Göreme, and Avanos as well. In addition to the Ankara bus (4hr., $3), a bus departs every morning for Konya (3hr., $3), Mersin and

Adana (4hr., $3.75). Overnight buses head to İzmir (13hr., $12), Pamukkale (10hr., $10), Antalya (10hr., $10) and İstanbul (12hr., $11.50). Frequent buses also leave for Keyseri (2hr., $2). Buses leave from the new bus station one km north of the center of town, with a luggage room, restaurant, and tourist office which provides free maps of Cappadocia. To get into town from the bus station, walk up the hill to the left.

If you are stuck in Nevşehir, first try the **İpek Palas Oteli,** 99 Atatürk Bul. (tel. 14 78), with a shiny marble lobby (singles $6, doubles $12). **Otel Nur,** 2 Belediye Cad. (tel. 14 44), has sparkling rooms, some with balconies (singles $6). To get there from the bus station, walk up to Atatürk Cad., the main street, and turn left. Or try one of the half dozen new hotels which line Atatürk Bul., to the left on the way to Göreme. The staff at the **tourist office** (tel. 36 59), on Atatürk Bul., proffers maps, brochures, and information about certified guides. (Open daily 8am-noon and 1:30-6pm; off-season Mon.-Fri. 9:30am-5:30pm.) There are two large *dolmuş* stations on Lâle Cad. near its intersection with Atatürk Cad. Coming down Atatürk, turn left on Lâle, and you'll find *dolmuş* for Göreme and Uçhisar (80¢). A right on Lâle will bring you to the *dolmuş* for Ürgüp, Avanos, Niğde, Aksaray, and the underground cities of Kaymaklı and Derinkuyu ($1-2). Municipal **buses,** cheaper than *dolmuş,* run nine times per day between Nevşehir and Ürgüp (check schedule at the tourist office). Alternatively you can hire a taxi ($30) or private car for the day. Nine-hour **guided tours** lollygag in Nevşehir, but less expensive ones are available in Göreme. The **restaurants** across from the bus station seem to be the best of Nevşehir's pantry of culinary concoctions. The 24-hr. **PTT** is on Atatürk Cad. Nevşehir's **telephone code** is 4851.

Kaymakli and Derinkuyu

In the villages of Kaymaklı and Derinkuyu, inauspicious passages lead to two of Cappadocia's most spectacular sites. Two stark but well-preserved underground cities, thought to be over 3000 years old, cower beneath the ground in an endless warren of tunnels, rooms, stairwells, and hallways. Throughout centuries of political uncertainty, Christians living in neighboring villages inhabited this labyrinthine tunnel system, some of which date to Hittite times. The size and complexity of Kaymaklı—five levels of elaborate passages burrowing down hundreds of meters—are mind-boggling, yet Derinkuyu is almost twice as big, with escape tunnels (now blocked) 5-6km long, and one passage believed to lead back to Kaymaklı. The cities are south of Nevşehir, on the road to Niğde; Kaymaklı is 20km away, Derinkuyu 29km. Derinkuyu, with eight levels excavated so far, is slightly more impressive with sizable public rooms and halls, good lighting and relatively easy access, but you might find the dark, narrow, often unmarked passages of Kaymaklı even more enthralling. In both cities, the tunnels were built low and tortuous to hamper the progress of invaders (and 20th-century tourists?). Though marked with arrows, the tunnels form a potentially confounding maze, and if you explore extensively you'll get lost at least once—just listen for other tourists. Both cities have unexplored tunnels which are out of bounds, and thus tempting, but be careful—there are stories about tourists who never made it back. Even during the hottest days it's dank in the tunnels, so bring a sweater. Buses run to and from Nevşehir run every half hour (75¢). (Both sites open daily 8:30am-6:30pm, in winter until 5pm. Admission $1.50, students 75¢.)

Göreme

Sequestered in a scenic valley, Göreme has maintained a distinctly Cappadocian appearance; some of its countless rock formations are still inhabited, and along narrow back streets a traditional way of life somehow continues, although perhaps not for much longer. Göreme's proximity to rock-hewn churches and the valley of Zelve, as well as its many fine and inexpensive pensions, make it a convenient base. Tourism has completely changed the face of Goreme: over sixty pensions have sprung up in the last few years. Prices for rooms without bath are standardized at around $4, so take your pick. If you want to experience cave-dwelling in hotel comfort, spend the night in the giant rock cone of the **Peri Pansiyon** (tel. 11 36), on the road to the Open-Air Museum; those on the lower level are cheaper, cooler, and windowless ($4 per person). Next door, **Paradise Pansiyon** (tel. 12 21) is equipped with a terrace perfect for sipping beer while watching the sun set ($4 per person). Go up the road opposite Rose Tours and you'll come to the endearing **Melek Pension** (tel. 14 63), set in a handsomely restored Ottoman house (dorms $2.50). Up the wide road near the mosque is another cluster of pensions. True hospitality, high-pressure showers, and airy rooms are the key to the success of the **Rock Valley Pension,** a good place to join informal excursions to some of the area's more inaccessible sites ($4). On the opposite side of town, **Halil Pansiyon** (tel. 10 30), is removed from legions of fellow travelers and has naturally cooled rooms carved into the rock ($4). **Arif Pansiyon** (tel. 13 61) has the best view, but it is quite a climb if you're loaded down with luggage ($3.50 per person). For clean rooms with bath (and character), the **Saksağar Motel** (tel. 48 57) is well worth the extra few dollars (singles $8). At **Göreme Dilek Camping** (tel. 13 96), across from Peri Pansiyon, the campsite, swimming pool and restaurant are nestled between unmistakably phallic rock edifices ($2 per tent).

The Rock Valley Pension has a decent restaurant ($3-5). For good *kebap* try the **Orient,** opposite the Saksağen Motel ($3). Up the hill a bit, and a bit more upscale, the **Atoman** restaurant has a terrace with a view ($5-15). And for a change of fare, drop in on Québecois Richard and Mario at the **Yöre Spaghetti Evi,** opposite the bus station ($3-5). The international backpacker crowd congregates here to swap stories and swill Tuborg (two-for-one drinks 5-7pm). Next door at **Sedef Restaurant,** the Bavarian bartender boasts a huge collection of classic rock cassettes. (He takes requests.) The **PTT** is in town. Göreme's **telephone code** is 4857.

The most impressive concentration of sights in the region is at the **Göreme Open-Air Museum,** 1km out of Göreme on the Ürgüp road (open 8am-6:30pm; admission $2, students $1.50). The churches here are the legacy of Cappadocian Christianity under the Byzantine Empire. In the 4th century, St. Basil founded one of the first Christian monasteries here, setting down religious tenets that greatly influenced the teachings of St. Benedict and subsequently the Western monastic movement. The monks of Cappadocia built most of the churches in Göreme between the 4th and 10th centuries, and inhabited the area until the formation of the modern Turkish Republic, when all Anatolian Greeks were relocated in an exchange for the Turks living in Greece. Be sure to visit the Apple Church and the Chapel of the Sandal in the hill right before the main entrance; both feature superb frescoes. At the museum, there is a **post office** in a trailer and a **bank** that charges no commission on traveler's checks. (Both open daily 9am-5pm.) The former residence of the Paşa of Göreme has recently been opened to the public, and its frescoed walls and ceilings restored to their 19th-century splendor. Take your first right on the road to the mosque; the domicile is above the Konak restaurant (free). **Guided tours** of Cappadocia's major sites are available from several agencies in town.

The valley is easily accessible by bike or moped, and rentals are available at reasonable prices. **Gör-Tur,** next to the bus station, rents mountain bikes ($3.50/2hr., $9/day) and motorbikes ($5/2hr plus gas, $11/day plus gas), as does **Hitchhiker Tour** across the street (bicycles $2/hr., motorcycles $9/hr.)

Be aware that there are no direct buses to Ürgüp: you must first backtrack to Nevşehir. It seems the two towns, Göreme and Ürgüp, are feuding over directorship of the historical site; thus no public transport between the two. Kayseri buses (6 per day, 80¢) go via Avaros. Long distance buses to the Mediterranean coast (6:15pm and 8pm) fill up quickly, so purchase tickets at least two days in advance. Same for the 7:15pm bus for İzmir.

Near Göreme

The road north from Göreme to Avanos leads past the church of St. John the Baptist, formerly a regional pilgrimage site, at **Çavuşin** (admission $1) to **Zelve Valley,** a city hewn into the pink rock: it had to be evacuated in the early 1950s because of landslides.

Though its frescoes don't compare with those at the Göreme Open-Air Museum (this was an ascetic, monastic community), its caverns are much more extensive. The best frescoes at the site are in the "Fish Church," in the valley on the left as you walk in. (Open daily 8am-6pm. Admission $1.50, students 80¢.) A few km farther, the landscape shifts from a Dr. Seussian dwelling to a more barren, inconspicuous setting. The potters of **Avanos** have been throwing the red, iron-rich Cappadocian clay since time began. Stop in at **Galip Körükçü's Cave-Studio** for a look at his stork-bearing bat and pots. Apart from being a master potter, he keeps an immense "hair collection" with more than 10,000 locks of hair from female visitors worldwide.

Just 3km southwest of Göreme, the village of **Üçhisar** was built at the foot of a craggy fortress. Sitting on a hill, the town commands a panoramic view of the entire Göreme Valley. Üçhisar has an inexpensive pension, the **Maison du Rêve** (tel. (4856) 11 99), on the opposite side of the castle from town—follow the signs. (Rooms $4 per person. Hot shower, breakfast, and sweet dreams included.) Admission to the fortress is $1.50. Üçhisar makes a pleasant hike from Göreme, but any bus or *dolmuş* traveling between Nevşehir and Göreme, or Nevşehir and Ürgüp, will drop you on the main road very close to Üçhisar.

Ürgüp

The town of Ürgüp, 20km east of Nevşehir, makes a pleasant base for exploring; the three main sights at Göreme and Zelve are easy daytrips. A bus runs every half hour to Nevşehir (40¢), where you must go before backtracking to Göreme. Most of the long-distance buses to and from Nevşehir also call here, and there are *dolmuş* and buses (7am-7pm on the hr., $1) to Kayseri for connections to the east. Daily buses go to: Mersin and Adana (6hr., $6.50); Alanya (9hr., $13); and Marmaris (15hr., $15). Ürgüp's telephone code is 4868.

The Ürgüp **tourist office** (tel. 10 59), on Kayseri Cad. inside the garden, provides maps of the region, *dolmuş* and bus schedules, and helps arrange tours. (Open daily 8:30am-8:30pm; Oct.-March Mon.-Fri. 8am-5pm.) Next door is a tiny **Archaeological Museum.** (Open daily 8:30am-6pm. Admission 50¢.) **Sarıhan Pansiyon,** 10 Güllüce Sok. (tel. 22 64), is a no-frills, family-run establishment ($2.50 per person). Walk 200m east from the bus station. **Seymen Pansiyon** (tel. 23 80), conveniently faces Atatürk's back in the center of town. Friendly atmosphere; comfortable rooms downstairs and a cool sitting room laden with local craftwork. ($4 per person. Breakfast included.) Circuitous stairways lead to clean rooms at **Hotel Yüksel** (tel. 23 81), in an attractive old Ottoman house tucked into a rock up the road to Nevşehir ($2.50 per person). Several tasty restaurants compete on Cumhuriyet Sq. near the center of town. Stuffed in the courtyard of an antique inn, the **Sofa Restaurant** serves delicious Turkish fare at fair prices, and has a beautiful courtyard to boot. *Saç Tava* (grilled meat and veggies) $2. (Open daily 7:30am-11:30pm.) For a healthy serving of cheese and meat pizza (75¢), try the **Cappadocia Restaurant.** Stock up at the Saturday market down Dumlupinar Sk. (sheep aplenty). Dance to Turkish and Western tunes in the dimly lit cave of the **Harem Old Rock Disco,** or try **Legend Disco & Cave Bar,** literally a hole in the wall.

Cappadocia's wine industry is centered in Ürgüp. The wineries marked on the tourist office map offer free tours and wine samples to visitors. The tourist agencies at Ürgüp organize a daily tour of the region (5 person minimum, $8 per person, $15 with a guide; entrance fees $7, students $3.50). The nine-hour tour is comprehensive, but a little rushed; you may find yourself too nerve-shot to appreciate anything by the latter half of the day. Consider taking a tour from Göreme instead. You can rent a moped at **Hepatu Rent a Motorcycle** (tel. 12 41; $10 per 4 hr., no insurance available). Go up from the bus station and turn right; it's in a small arcade on the left. Across the street, **İnce Tours** rents bikes ($10 per day), mopeds ($12 per day), and motorbikes ($25 per day).

Near Ürgüp

The village of **Ortahisar** coagulates around a tall castle hewn from volcanic rock. From the top of the fortress there's a tremendous view of the rock formations and river valleys (admission 50¢). If you hike around the area to the south of Ortahisar, you'll come across scores of abandoned rock dwellings and several rock churches, the best of which have frescoes from the 10th and 11th centuries, "modern" religious art by Cappadocian standards. Buses leave ürgüp for Ortahisar (7 per day until 6:15pm, 35¢).

You can easily walk or bike the 3km south of Ürgüp to **Mustafapaşa,** formerly the Greek town of Sinasas. Many of the houses carved into rock there are still inhabited. **Ayos Vasilios Church** was in use until the 1920s—you should be able to get a key from the tourist office in the village. The least visited of the Cappadocian valleys is Soğanlı, 47km south of Ürgüp. Unfortunately there is no public transportation, but the site is on the itinerary of several tours. Alternatively, you can get some people together and negotiate for a taxi.

Kayseri

This regional metropolis of half a million is set at the foot of the looming, snow-capped, extinct volcano Mt. Erciya. The city was in Roman times the capital of Cappadocia province, when it was called Caesarea. Today it offers a wealth of well-preserved Seljuk monuments, and is also the largest clearinghouse for rugs in Turkey. From the bus station, cross the boulevard and take a *dolmuş* towards the center of town. Get off just after you pass the gigantic fortress (*hisar*) on your right; the **tourist office** will be on your left across the street, beyond the **PTT.** Behind the fortress is the covered bazaar—not as fancy as the one in İstanbul, but far more authentic.

To return to the bus station from anywhere in town, take any *dolmuş* marked "Terminal." **Buses** run to: Ürgüp (every hour, 1½hr., $1); Ankara (19 per day, 3hr., $7); Adana (8 per day, $7); İstanbul (5 per day, 11hr., $16); Malatya (2 per day, 4hr., $5); Kahramanmaraş (2 per day, 5hr., $6); Van (2 per day, $16); Diyarbakır (daily, $13); İzmir (daily, $17); and Antalya (daily, $10). There are four flights a week between İstanbul and Kayseri airport.

The **Otel Berlin** on Maarif Cad. (tel. 31 52 46) is a good deal ($6, with bath $9), but takes a good deal of work to find. It's on a side street behind the bazaar: ask someone for directions. More than likely you will already have been accosted by an English-speaking rug dealer, so ask him. Or you can try **Otel Hunat** behind the tourist office ($3 per person without bath). For a truly delectable local specialty, go to the **Otağ Et Lokantası** by the bazaar entrance to the right of the fortress (tel. 12 56 17), and ask for their *hasanpaşa*—a baked dish of ground lamb topped with melted cheese. **İskender Lokanta** off the main square also comes highly recommended.

Kayseri has yet to face the full brunt of tourism, a fact many locals will point out to you as if it were an existential tragedy. As a result most of the monuments still don't charge admission. For a free view, scale the ramparts of the **hisar,** a fortress built by Justinian in the 500s and renovated by the Seljuks in 1224, although you do so at your own risk since there are no railings. Other attractions include the **Huant Hatun Cami** (mosque), built in 1228, and the **Huant Hatun Medrese,** built in 1237; next door is the ethnographic museum (admission 75¢). The **Gevherneshibe** was built in the 12th century and is allegedly the world's first hospital; now it is a medical museum. Behind the bazaar is the 12th century **Ulu Cami** (Great Mosque), a caravansary, and Turkish baths. You can also visit the **Sahibiye Medrese** (seminary), the **Hacı Kılıç Cami** and the **Korsunlu Cami** (Leaden Mosque), designed by the famous Ottoman architect Sinan in the 16th century. The **Archaeological Museum** three km from the center houses relics from the nearby Hittite site of Göktepe. Twenty km out of town is the "bird paradise" of Sultan Sazlığı, a park where you can see flamingos and other birds during the summer. A taxi will set you back about $30 for the round trip.

Buying Rugs

If you're planning to buy a rug or two while in Turkey, Kayseri is probably the best place to do it. You will be approached time and again by eager salesmen—don't be intimidated. Agree to take a look at the merchandise. Educate yourself. Look at the closeness of the weave (the tighter the better), and examine the colors: if they are too faded, the carpet has been in the sun too long, and if they run, the dye is of poor quality. Don't get defensive or feel pressured. All rug dealers are devious, but accept that with good humor. Buy when you're ready and sure. Kayseri is especially known for its silk rugs (not as fine as those from Hereke), but beware of mercerized-cotton imitations. Look around until you feel confident enough with your knowledge to make a purchase. In the end, there's only one rule for choosing a good rug: it should be the one you love the most.

EASTERN TURKEY

Perenially a border area, Eastern Turkey has witnessed the rise and fall of many empires. Everywhere are traces of its rich past: massive city walls, imposing fortresses, and endless ruins. From all of this, the region has taken on a unique but fractured character. Compared to its surrounding lands, Eastern Turkey's pace is far slower, the industrial age seems intangibly distant, and sheep bleat out the tourists in numbers. You'll find prices lower here, but tourist amenities—such as information offices and clean bathrooms—few and far between, and travel often difficult. Travel in the East is more of an adventure than that in the more European coastal areas of Turkey.

The beauty of this region lies in the harsh steppe lands and jagged peaks of the countryside. You will likely be entranced by the bewitching Armenian churches at Akdamar and Ani, the transfixing scenery of Kars and Hakkâri, the magical waters of Lake Van, the bizarre heads at Nemrut Dağı, and the exquisite palace at Doğubeyazıt.

Some caveats are in order for travel here. If anything, male tourists will tire of the excessive friendliness rather than malevolence. Women travelers, however, are frequently hassled by local males. Don't get discouraged—try to ignore amorous stares and other indignities. Dress modestly: long skirts, long-sleeved blouses, and head scarves are in order. Men should not wear shorts. If you dress discreetly, you may find yourself invited to weddings and family meals. You must buy toilet paper at a general store, since hotels rarely have it.

Weather here straddles every climatic extreme. Gaziantep, Urfa, Diyarbakır, and Mardin are hot as *cehennem*—hell—in summer: daytime temperatures often rise above 43°C (110°F). Conversely, in the winter of our discontent, deep snows periodically cut off much of the northeastern end of Turkey. In January, Kars experiences nighttime temperatures below -30°C (-22°F), and Hakkâri is virtually inaccessible from November through March. Locals often speak more German than English in Eastern Turkey, but most of the tourist offices have staff members who can speak some English. Still, sign language and bilingual dictionaries come in handy here. Just about every town large enough to stop in has a bank, but you should carry dollars and small denominations of traveler's checks just in case.

Less-than-sanitary restaurants and hotels can pose a major problem for the traveler in eastern Anatolia. Avoid the cheapest places at all times; your body will meet tiny creatures there the likes of which it has never encountered. Restaurants and hotels cheaper than those we recommend here are likely to be intolerably dirty. Avoid dishes made with ground meat, such as *köfte* (meatballs) and the suicidal *çiğ köfte* (raw meatballs). Lemon juice is not especially reliable as a disinfectant, and *eşki,* a potion concocted by some restaurants, is useless. If you want to avoid meat altogether, ask for dishes which are *et yok* (without meat). Don't try the tap water, especially in the southeast; drink only the nationally distributed bottled water, fruit juice, or soda. Traveler lore has it that *ayran,* a popular and refreshing drink made with yogurt and water, aids digestion and helps your body recover from the heat.

Transportation can also pose difficulties. Buses often leave only when they are full, and schedules change according to demand and road conditions. Overbooking often results in quarrels; luckily, hapless foreigners are often given priority in conflicts. If you get off a bus between two stops, it might be impossible to find another one later. Tourism in Eastern Turkey is extremely susceptible to the laws of supply and demand. Although the region is always relatively safe for travelers, its volatile neighbors may make people think twice about planning a trip here. When visitors are few, as they were in the summer of 1992, prices go way down but so does the amount of tours and other services available.

Kurds in Turkey

East of Adıyaman you'll encounter many Kurds, and their numbers grow as you approach the Iranian border. Published information about the Kurds is, however, virtually

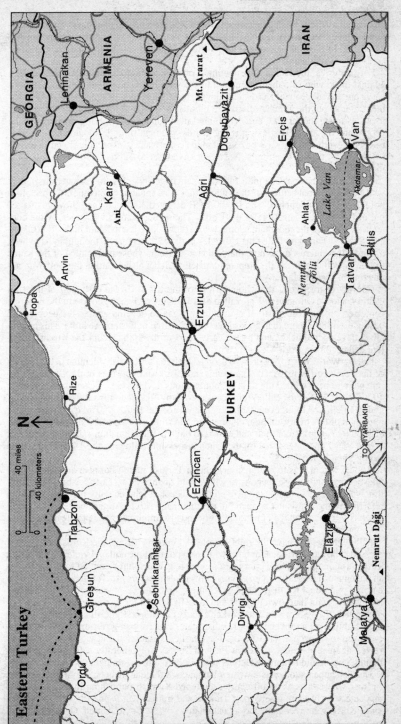

prohibited by the Turkish government. The Kurds are a people of about 20 million scattered throughout eastern Turkey, northern Syria and Iraq, and northern Iran into Afghanistan. In most of these areas they form the majority of the population, and some areas are entirely Kurdish.

For centuries, the Kurds have mounted raids from impenetrable mountain ranges against those who rule them. Centered in the wild Hakkâri region, they now fight to carve out an independent Kurdistan from the territory of five different nations. Government figures put the number of arrested dissidents at around 100 per year, but Hakkâri locals estimate that at least another 50 are killed annually in fighting between village people and the army. Tragic as it is, the Kurds' political struggle shouldn't affect your travels. Nevertheless, always be careful in the countryside—especially if you're traveling southeast of Van or at night. Never get any closer to Turkish military installations than you need to.

The Kurds, who speak an Indo-European language very close to Persian (Farsi), may well be the original settlers of the regions they now inhabit. Contemporary specialists hold that the **Kardouchoi,** who in 400 BCE defeated Xenophon and drove his forces out of Persia, were ancestors of the Kurds. The name "Kurds" was given by the conquering Arabs to the mountain people whom they converted to Islam in the 7th century CE. Salah al-Din, who foiled the Crusades in the 12th century, is thought to have been a Kurd. (It is interesting to note that Saddam Hussein, whose persecution of the Kurds in Iraq is well documented, compared himself to Salah al-Din during the Gulf War, neglecting his hero's ethnicity.)

Conflict characterizes the whole history of the Kurds. In the early part of the 16th century, a loose Ottoman rule prevailed over the Kurds. Over the course of the next two centuries, an inchoate sense of nationalism began to develop among the people, and during the 1880's more than 50 insurrections occurred in Eastern Anatolia. This nationalism developed quickly, and by the early years of the 20th century the Kurdish problem had become a worldwide concern.

During World War I, Woodrow Wilson addressed the Kurdish dilemma in the twelfth of his Fourteen Points. According to this, non-Turkish minorities of the Ottoman Empire were to be accorded the right to "autonomous devlopment." Several articles of the 1920 Treaty of Sevres called for "local autonomy for predominantly Kurdish areas" and even alluded to an eventual independence for the Kurds of Turkey. For all of the optimism of this treaty, though, nothing came to fruition. This problem was soon exacerbated by Atatürk's concentrated efforts to build a Turkish nation-state in the wake of World War I and intensified by the brutal repression following the 1925 insurrection led by Sheikh Naqshband.

Atatürk's goal was to establish not only a Turkish nation but also an identity. The question naturally arose then, as to who would qualify as a "Turk." A broader definition was adopted so as to capitalize on the concept of Islamic unity in Turkey. Thus in referring to the Kurds not as such but as "mountain Turks" Atatürk was able to simultaneously force an image of national unity and also minimalize the profile of the Kurdish population.

Although they do have the right to vote as Turkish citizens, the Kurds still live oppressed. The past two decades have witnessed political turmoil and violence in Eastern Turkey (including military intervention), much of which has stemmed from the Kurdish stalemate. The Turkish Government still takes measures to Turkicize the Kurds by curbing traditional Kurdish language, clothing, and cultural practices. Still, most Kurds adamantly retain their own identity and the will to fight for its preservation. Since August 1984, the PKK (Kurdish Worker's Party), a Marixst guerilla organization, has been fighting for an independent Kurdish state. The Turkish government has repeatedly vowed to stop these rebel Kurds. The conflict is continual, but violence is never directed against travelers. Cities in Eastern Turkey are generally safe, even at night, though you should remain as alert as you would in any unfamiliar city.

Kurdish appears today as a written language in three alphabets: the Arabic alphabet in Iraq, where there is an officially sanctioned Kurdish publishing industry; in Latin characters in Sweden, where most Turkish and Iranian Kurds publish; and in Cyrillic, since Kurds were recognized as a "nationality" by the Soviet Union. Generally hospitable to foreign travelers, Kurds are pleased if you can say a few words of Kurdish; however, such linguistic virtuosity won't impress local Turkish police, since the language is outlawed. A few helpful words are: *spahz dekem* (thank you); *merhaba* (hello; same as Turkish and Arabic); *begatirete* (goodbye, if you are leaving); *ogourbe* (goodbye, addressed to the person leaving); *héri* (yes); *na* (no); *keremka* (please); *návete çiye* (what is your name?); *véle* (come); and *heré* (go).

Armenians

The Armenians, an Indo-European people (they call themselves "Hai"), were the first nation to adopt Christianity, in 301 CE, several decades before the Roman empire. The Armenian alphabet was developed in 404 CE by a priest named Mesrop Mashtots. The Armenian Bagratid dynasty diplomatically weathered the Islamic conquests of the 7th century and flourished with increasing autonomy under Arab rule until the coming of the Seljuks, who sacked Ani in 1064. Caught between the Muslims and the Byzantines, many Armenians began migrating south to Cilicia on the Mediterranean coast of Asia Minor. By 1080 Prince Rupen felt strong enough to declare a new Armenian kingdom there—called "lesser Armenia" by historians—which endured for two centuries and played an important role in the Crusades.

Although Armenian territories served as battlegrounds between various Turkish, Persian, and eventually Russian empires, individual Armenians became highly successful, particularly in commerce, and were usually loyal subjects of each ruling power. Armenian merchant communities were established from Amsterdam to Calcutta. Under the Safavid empire in Persia, a large Armenian community grew in Esfahan in Iran, where remains to the present day. Much of the Armenians' present predicament, however, has its roots in the events of World War I, when, seeing a chance for independence from the Ottomans, many Armenians sided with the invading Russian armies, a traitorous act in the eyes of their Turkish and Kurdish Muslim neighbors. The results: a policy of extermination by the Ottomans under which 1.5 to 3 million Armenians were killed between 1915-1918; the founding of a small independent Armenian republic which was absorbed by the Soviet Union in 1920; and a bitter enmity between Turks and Armenians that endures today. Eastern Turkey today supports a few Armenian communities living in semi-secret; scattered populations live throughout the country. Diyarbakır has several active Armenian Christian churches; Armenians in İstanbul support two Armenian-language newspapers.

The Republic of Armenia declared its independence on September 23, 1991. The fledgling country of 3.3 million has been plagued with energy and food shortages as well as political upheavals. These problems are in large part due to the conflict in Nagorno-Karabakh, an Armenian enclave surrounded by the predominantly Muslim republic of Azerbaijan. Armenia is accessible from Turkey via either Kars or from Doğubayazıt. By 1993 the Armenian embassy in Washington should have begun issuing tourist visas. For updated information, contact the embassy at 122 C St. NW, Suite 360, Washington, DC 20001 (tel. (202) 628-5766).

Nemrut Dagi

One of the most impressive and long-lasting monuments to one man's ego is Nemrut Dağı (the 'g' is silent), a collection of huge statues of Antiochus Commagene (64-38 BCE) and his divine court perched atop a barren 6000 foot summit in East Central Turkey. The huge stone heads of travel guide and postcard fame have no match this side of Easter Island.

The Commagene Empire was founded in the first century BCE by Mithridates and was later ruled by his son Antiochus. The Commagenes allied themselves with Pompeii and then became a Roman buffer state of some wealth but marginal importance. Antiochus, however, was no believer in false modesty. He constructed huge statues in his likeness, which he sat next to images of Zeus, Apollo, and other deities. He capped off such hubris by piling tons of crushed rock behind the statues to create an artificial peak. Antiochus is believed to be buried beneath the rubble. Fairly hard to reach even today, the site was forgotten until "discovered" by a German engineer in 1881. (Admission $2, students $1. Admission to Arsemia, the site of the Commagene capital which you pass on the way, $1, students 50¢.)

Getting there can be a hassle, so be prepared. Until recently the standard base for visits to Nemrut Dağı was the ugly, unpleasant town of **Kahta**, 70km to the south. Since the new Atatürk Dam has flooded the former road across the Euphrates basin, Kahta is no longer on the through route to Urfa and Diyarbakır—so much the better. It makes more sense now to take a tour from **Adıyaman**, 30km to the west, although you wouldn't want to be stuck for long there either.

Dolmuş run between Adıyaman and Kahta (every ½hr., 80¢), and between Adıyaman and Urfa (every ½hr., 1½hr., $2.50). **Buses** run from Adıyaman to: Kayseri (6 per day, $11); Ankara (6 per day, $13); İstanbul (4 per day, $20); Adana (8 per day, $8); Mersin (8 per day, $8); Malatya (8 per day, $3.50); and daily to Diyarbakır, Antalya, İzmir, and Trabzon.

There is a private **tourist office** (open 24 hrs.) next to the Adıyaman bus station, which arranges day trips to Nemrut Dağı. In the summer of 1992 a dearth of tourists made for erratic tour schedules because they won't leave without a minimum of 6-10 people. This also meant that prices were low—$8 for a day tour. Hotel prices are similarly affected by the law of supply and demand. Although Adıyaman is sure to put Kahta out of business for Nemrut tours, the latter town still has the edge on hotels. The **Hotel Kommagene** (tel. 87 95 10 98), as you come into Kahta, has rooms without bath for $3, and tours for the same price as in Adıyaman ($8). But if you arrive too late in the day you may be stuck, so try Adıyaman first. If you have to spend the night there, the **Motel Beyazsaray** 1km east of the bus station on the main drag has decent rooms for $3-5 without bath (tel. 87 91 11 79).

You can avoid these dreary places altogether by booking a tour from farther off, in **Malatya** (a large market town) or **Urfa** (see below). This involves more money and a longer trip, but it may be worth it. In Malatya, people at the bus station can put you in touch with **"Ali Baba"** who arranges minibus tours for $20, including dinner and hotel at Nemrut Dağı. In Urfa, **Harran Tours,** across the street from the tourist office on Sarayönü Cad., arrranges tours according to demand. Be advised that nights on the mountain tend to be very cold and the restaurant is very basic, so bring a sweater or jacket and maybe even your own food.

If you stay in Malatya, try the **Merkez Oteli,** 16 PTT Cad. (tel. 421 55). To get there from the highway in front of the bus station, walk or minibus the 2km to the main street, İnönü Cad. (parallel to the highway), and veer left at the fork down PTT Cad. They have unsullied rooms and lukewarm showers (singles $3.50, doubles $5). Next door is the dark but reasonably clean **Çiçek Palas Otel** at 18 PTT Cad. (tel. 125 11; singles $3.50, doubles $5). More motels and pensions are scattered along the road up the mountain. When hunger calls, try **Şasak Lokantası** with its terrace and wide selection of dishes, on PTT Cad., just past its intersection with İnönü.

Urfa

A tourist brochure pronounces that Urfa (known to the Crusaders as Edessa, and renamed Şanlıurfa—"Glorious Urfa"—by Atatürk, although no one today uses either name) is famous for its "horses, lentils, and animal fat." The horses and lentils, among thousands of other things, can be found in the corridors of Urfa's bazaar; the animal fat you will find in abundance on your plate at any of the town's restaurants. Nevertheless, Urfa's exuberant tourist literature sells the city a little short. An age-old center of civilization, Urfa boasts a variety of religious and historical monuments, alongside a distinctive and vital culture. Since summer temperatures in Urfa can reach 50ºC (122ºF), you may want to do your sightseeing in the mornings or evenings and take the locals' cue at midday—either sip tea at one of the shady *kervansaray* in the market area or take a snooze.

The history of Urfa starts with the birth of Abraham in a cave at the foot of the citadel. Warned that Abraham would lead the populace away from the state religion, King Nemrut of Babylon had a huge fire built and made plans to cast Abraham into its flames. But as soon as Abraham was tossed in, the inferno turned into a pond of innocuous carp; their descendants still swim in it today. Bordered on one side by shady trees and the lovely 17th-century **Abdurrahman Mosque** and on the other by the 18th century **Rizvaniye Mosque** (also known as "Halil ar-Rahman"), the pool still has mythical dimensions to anyone wandering out of the indefatigable Urfan sun into its cool, tranquil aura. For some crazy fun, buy boiled chickpeas from nearby vendors and toss them to the hungry sacred fish as you sit in the shade by the pool. Nearby is a complex of holy sites, including the cave where Abraham was supposedly born, and the ornate Ottoman-style **Yeni Mosque** (New Mosque). Visitors to the cave traditionally lower the trusty bucket nearby into the well and take a swig for good luck—maybe not such a good idea microbially.

The **castle** and the ancient site opposite the present city suffered a tumultuous history as the frontier between Eastern and Western civilizations. The former city was conquered in succession by the Persians, Macedonians, Romans, Crusaders, Mongols, and Turks. A pair of monumental 3rd-century columns mark the summit of the ancient citadel. Take a stroll through the maze of the covered bazaar, and at dusk walk up to the citadel for a hyperbole-eliciting view of the city and the surrounding area. (Admission 80¢, students 40¢). There is also a **museum** (named, aptly enough, the Şanlıurfa Museum), featuring Hittite and Assyrian artifacts, two blocks north and two blocks west of the tourist office.

The **bus station** is about 1km out of town; to reach the center, head toward the castle and take a left through the middle of the cemetery. Frequent buses leave Urfa daily for: Diyarbakır (2½hr., $4); Mardin (2½hr., $4.50); Mersin (7hr., $7); and Ankara (11hr., $12). The **tourist office** (tel. 124 67) is on your right, 20m before the intersection with the town's main road, Sarayönü Cad. The staff can give you an accurate town plan and share information and photos about sites in the surrounding areas. (Office open May 15-Sept. 15 daily 8am-noon and 2-7pm.) Leaving daily at 10am and returning at about 11pm, the rather exhausting **Nemrut Tours** take in most of the Commagene sites along the way and include a swim in the Euphrates before reaching the mountain at sunset ($15.50, $13.50 if you stay behind in Kahta). Across the main streeet from the tourist office and a little to the left, a small side street leads to the **Hotel İstiklâl** (tel. 119 67) which offers rooms around a garden courtyard. (Dorms $2. Singles $4. Doubles $5.75, with A/C $11.50.) You may find a location between the bazaar and the castle considerably more interesting. The **Park Oteli,** 101 Göl Cad. (tel. 110 95), has an illuminated view of the religious complex from the terrace and a chummy staff, although the rooms are very basic. (Singles $2.50. Doubles $4.) Nearby, **Otel Şafak** (tel. 111 57) has the same set-up. (Singles $3.) Urfa is justifiably famous for its ice cream—have some anywhere marked "Dondurma." Or try it over *baklava*, the sweet, oozing specialty of **Çulouoğlu Baklavalari,** two blocks up Sarayönü Cad. from the tourist office (85¢). Heartier and healthier meals can be found just up the street at **Çiftlik Firinli Lokanta.** Outdoor restaurants in **Gölbaşı** (the park by the pools) proffer complete meals for $3. Head south of the tourist office along Sarayönü Cad. to reach the **PTT** (open 24 hrs.) and most of the sights. Urfa's **telephone code** is 8711.

Near Urfa

Mentioned in the Bible as a stopping place for Abraham, the ancient city of **Harran**, 40km south of Urfa, grew in importance during Assyrian rule, when it became associated with the moon god Sin. Now it is a curious town of beehive-shaped mud houses, inhabited by Arabs and Kurds. It makes an interesting half-day trip from Urfa (see Urfa section for tour information).

Diyarbakir

Perched on bluffs high above the Tigris River, the city of Diyarbakır rises menacingly above the Syrian plain. Its massive basalt walls, said to be the longest after the Great Wall of China, once protected the city from countless invasions. But like Urfa, Diyarbakır's location on the frontier made it vulnerable to conquest. The city's rich and extensive collection of sights is a testament to the many empires that have ruled here: the basalt walls are the work of the Romans, but were rebuilt and expanded upon by the Seljuks, who added fine carvings and inscriptions. Black stone alleyways and fortified architecture harken back to Diyarbakır's desert outpost days, but modernization has made considerable inroads. The churches here are more than timepieces: a small Christian community survives in Diyarbakır.

Near the center of town off İnönü Cad., the **Ulu Cami** (Great Mosque) is the oldest mosque in Anatolia and perhaps in all of Turkey. Built in 1091 on the site of an important Christian church, the present mosque has a rectangular layout and a square minaret. An agglomeration of styles, the building bears an uncanny resemblance to a modern train station. The **bazaar** is behind Ulu Cami. An Ottoman *caravanserai,* **Hasan Paşa Hanı,** now full of carpet shops, is across Gazi Cad. Turning down Melek Ahmet Cad., take your second left and you'll come to the 16th-century Behram Paşa Cami, with its exquisite black and white stone exterior. At the end of Melek Ahmet, turn left onto Turistik Cad. and go up the alley that you'll see just before the city wall meets the street. The "Marry Church" sign means you've found the Byzantine **Meryem Ana Kilisesi** (Church of the Virgin Mary), rebuilt several times since the 4th century. (Knock on the front gate to gain admission.) The writing on the walls and on some of the paintings is Aramaic, the language that Jesus supposedly spoke. You can also visit **Surp Giragos,** an Armenian church on Yenikapı Cad., as well as several other hard-to-find churches. (Half the fun is getting lost in the six-foot-wide cobblestone streets). The Tigris flows past the Bitlis Gate, near the ancient Byzantine citadel. Diyarbakır's **Archaeological Museum** is 300m north of the Atatürk statue and then right through the fairgrounds. (Open 8am-5:30pm except Mondays. Admission 80¢.) The home of 19th-century poet Zıya Gökalp, on Melek Ahmet Cad., has been converted to a museum as well. (Admission 20¢.) The signs posted past the city wall on the way to the bus station will lead you to the **public swimming pool,** infinitely valuable during the lethal summer heat of Diyarbakır. (Open daily 8am-6pm. Admission $2. Women should not go alone.)

To get to the **bus station,** get on a *dolmuş* marked "Garaj" outside the city gate. From the bus station, 3km northwest of town, buses head to: Ankara (5 per day, 9hr., $21); İstanbul (4 per day, 17hr., $30); Urfa (6 per day, 3hr., $4); Malatya (5 per day, 4hr., $9); Van (4 per day, 8hr., $12); Adana; and Konya (2 per day, 10hr., $20). *Dolmuş* and minibuses for Mardin leave from just below the PTT on Gazi Cad. The **tourist office** (tel. 121 73) is between the bus station and the old wall on Lise Cad. There you can pick up a map and a tourist brochure, both of which will prove invaluable as you make your way through this confusing city. (Open daily 8am-6:30pm.) The **THY office** (tel. 123 14 or 261 43) is on Kultun Sarayi Sok.—walk three blocks to your right as you come out of the tourist office, then turn left. Daily flights to Ankara (1hr., $65) connect to İstanbul (total 4hr., $75). A **PTT** and several **banks** are on **Gazi Caddesi.** Diyarbakır's **telephone code** is 831.

Inexpensive hotels and restaurants cluster around the **Dağ Kapi** area. In a passage on the left side of Gazi Cad. going into town, the **Hotel Bingöl** (tel. 118 97), has basic rooms with baths. (Singles $5. Doubles $6.) Several other inexpensive hotels dwell on İnönü Cad., which crosses Gazi Cad. between the old wall and Ulu Cami. The spotless **Safak Palas Oteli,** 3 İnönü Cad. (tel. 194 88), has an extremely amiable staff. Try to avoid staying on the sauna of a second floor. (Singles without bath $3. Doubles with bath $6.) Next door is the more dilapidated but still accommodating **Van Palas Oteli** (tel. 112 18). The fountain becomes a mini-swimming pool on hot summer nights, and the owner is a backgammon fanatic. (Outside beds $1. Singles $2.) **Şehrin Kebabçısı,** just inside the city gate on the left side of Gazi Cad. serves delicious *Adana kebap,* salad, and a glass of ice-cold *ayran* (yogurt drink) for an unbeatable $3. There are also several good *kebap* restaurants closer to the wall near the resplendent Atatürk statue on Kibris Cad. Some of the more retro eateries commemorate the zenith of North American culture with tunes from the 70s. Near the Şafak Palas, the **78 Kebap Salonu** serves a standard selection of eggplant dishes. Diyarbakır prides itself on its gigantic watermelons, which grow up to 50kg.

Near Diyarbakir

For a fascinating daytrip from Diyarbakır, visit the **Deyrulzafaran Monastery** via Mardin, a Kurdish city in a small chain of mountains 100km to the south. **Mardin,** one of the last bastions of Syrian Christianity, also boasts several Seljuk monuments: the 11th-century Ulu Cami and the Sultan Isa Madrese. But the big attraction is the monastery, 8km from Mardin, which housed the Syrian patriarch from the 4th century until 1922, when headquarters were moved to Damascus. Now only one monk and a handful of students reside here. The caretaker, who speaks only Turkish and Aramaic, will greet you at the gate and guide you through the chapel and a few other rooms. When you depart, show your appreciation with a *towdee* (Aramaic for "thank you"). *Dolmuş* to Mardin depart regularly from Diyarbakır's bus terminal and from the *dolmuş* station on Gazi Cad. ($1.50). From Mardin, you can take a taxi 8km to the monastery ($5 round-trip). The last bus to Diyarbakır leaves at 5pm, but there are a few cheap accommodations in Mardin if you get stuck. From the left of the bus station take a left down the main street to get to the **Hotel Kent,** 311 Kasım Tuğmaner Cami Yani, with immaculate rooms and views that would leave Lorraine speechless. (Singles $5.75. Doubles $7.75.) Farther down the street, the **Başak Oteli,** 360 #1 Cad. (tel. 162 46), is cheaper but not as clean. (Singles $2.25. Doubles $4.50.)

Lake Van and Environs

Lake Van's shifting waters form a gargantuan oasis in the arid altitudes of Eastern Turkey. Trapped by volcanic mountains, the lake sits 1720m above sea level and is surrounded by thickly cultivated fields, insouciant cow herds, and narrow gravel beaches. Rising from Lake Van's northern shore, Mount Süphan (4058m) and its snowy peak are dimly reflected in the water. If you're coming northward from the hot rocky hills, Lake Van will be a godsend, offering cool breezes, tremendous views, and free laundry—its strange sudsy water contains enough sodium carbonate to soaplessly clean your clothes. Although the lake is six times saltier than the Mediterranean and 12 times saltier than the Black Sea, the waters will not keep you effortlessly afloat. The modern city of **Van** lies 5km inland. Those coming by ferry can take a *dolmuş* into town. The main avenue in Van, **Cumhuriyet Caddesi,** runs north-south. Two other avenues, **İskele** and **Kâzım Karabekir,** cut Cumhuriyet Cad. perpendicularly on the northern and southern sides of the city.

From a stand one block north of the intersection of Cumhuriyet Cad. and İskele Cad., you can take a *dolmuş* 4km to the stunning **citadel** and **ancient city** (25¢). Located on the Rock of Van, the fortress was originally Urartian, but was later rebuilt by the Seljuks and Ottomans (admission 80¢). Much of the defensive work, several tombs, and a few inscriptions remain from the original inhabitants. The Urartians came from the northeastern steppes to fill the vacuum left by the declining Hittite Empire. Reaching their peak between 900 and 700 BCE, they then suffered numerous defeats at the hands of the Assyrians and the Scythians, finally yielding to the Medes in 590 BCE. The Armenians later occupied the region and made Van the capital of one of their several kingdoms. After the Armenians' unsuccessful revolt during World War I, the Ottomans destroyed the **Old City** of Van and its Armenian residents were either killed or fled. From the heights of the citadel you can view the town's ruins, now merely a series of small hills covered with grass and cattle. Two 16th-century mosques, abandoned and partially ruined, were all that was spared. Van's **museum,** one block east of Cumhuriyet Caddesi behind the Bayram Hotel, is worth a visit for its collection of Urartian pottery, jewelry, rock inscriptions, and Ottoman-era rugs and metalwork. (Open daily 8am-noon and 1:30-5:30pm. Admission 80¢.) There is also a rather grisly corner devoted to split Turkish skulls and other remnants of the 1915 Armenian uprising. This exhibit presents the Turkish side of the unfortunate story when some Armenians allied themselves with encroaching Russian armies in hopes of founding their own state.

The **tourist office** (tel. 120 18), is at 129 Cumhuriyet Caddesi, near the southern end, two blocks past the PTT. (Open daily 8am-6pm; off-season Mon.-Fri.) The **PTT** is centrally located on Cumhuriyet Cad. (Open 24 hrs.) Van's **telephone code** is 061.

Tuşba Travel Agency, on Posta Sokak off Kâzım Karabekir Cad., offers comprehensive tours of the area. For $18, they'll take you to Hoşap Castle, the Citadel of Çavuştepe, Akdamar Island, and Van Castle. A 14-hour-long tour visits Erciç, Adilcevaz, Ahlat, and Mt. Nemrut ($25). You can also rent a horse ($10 per hr., fuel extra).

The **bus station** is 5km outside of town, but Van Seyahat and Van Gölü offer free transportation to and from their offices near the tourist office. Buses run to: Diyarbakır (4 per day, 8hr., $9.50); Erzurum (4 per day, 7hr., $9.50); Ankara via Malatya (3 per day, 18hr., $10); İstanbul (2 per day, 24hr., $25); Hakkâri; and Ağrı. There are also buses to Doğubeyazıt via Ağrı. There are seven **flights** to Ankara per week (1½hr., $65), with connections to İstanbul ($80) and İzmir ($85). **Ferries** shuttle between Van and Tatvan at irregular hours (3 per day—maybe). Frequent buses also run between the two towns (2hr.. $4).

The best bet for a budget bed in Van is the **Hotel Çaldıran,** on Sihke Cad. near the Bes. Yol (five-way) intersection (tel. 127 18), offering comfortable rooms with bath. (Singles $6. Doubles $9.) Cheaper and simpler is the **Otel Kahraman** next to the tourist office ($3.50 per person, with shower). The **Hotel Tahran** (tel. 125 41), on the street behind the PTT and one block north, is slightly cramped but acceptable. Rooms have showers and share toilets. (Singles $4.50. Doubles $9.50.) Two blocks behind the PTT, the multi-fauceted **Kent Oteli** (tel. 125 19 or 124 04) offers hot water on tap and clean phone booths with beds. Ask for a room on the third or fourth floor; toilets on the lower floors are visited en masse. (Singles $5.30, with shower $7.60. Doubles $8, with shower $10.) **Hotel Aslan** (tel. 124 69 or 178 16) is a veritable blond beast of cleanliness. To get there, walk down the main street from the Atatürk statue, turn right at Şekerbank, and right again at the Otel Ipek. (Singles $4. Doubles $7.50.) Many inexpensive restaurants dot Kâzim Karabekir Cad. as you head west towards the lake. **Lokanta Sölen** offers good chicken *kebap* dinners for $2, and farther down about 500m on your left past the rug shops, **Cafe Milano** promises North American standards such as pizza and hamburgers ($3). Locals snack on a sour, fibrous root called *oskun,* sold in bunches on the sidewalk. If you're interested and you show it, they'll probably offer you a stalk for free.

Near Van

The 10th-century Armenian **Church of the Holy Cross** and its delicate friezes rest on the tiny island of **Akdamar,** 40km west of Van off the south coast of the lake. (Church admission $1.50.) The island itself is perfect for swimming, but if you venture beyond the main bathing area, beware of the four-foot water snakes that make the rocks their sinister cafeteria. Arrive in the morning for the boat to the island ($2). From Van, you can take a *dolmuş* from Sihke Cad. ($1.25). From the launch 45km west of Van, boats go wherever they're full ($1.50). The restaurant at the boat launch for Akdamar will let you **camp** on their grounds for $1. Almost 6km east (37km west of the city of Van) is the more serene **Cafer Camping,** with a restaurant. ($2.50 per tent. No showers.) Dreary, dust-choked **Tatvan,** across the lake from Van, is a necessary evil in the process of going to the ruins of **Ahlat** and the crater lake **Nemrut Gölü.** Ahlat, 38km north of Tatvan, was first populated by the Armenians and then by a succession of groups until it was abandoned under Ottoman rule in the 18th century. Today, a small village on the lakeshore has sprung up around ornately carved Seljuk and Ottoman tombs, the only remains of the old settlement. *Dolmuş* leave every hour at the stop down the side street from the PTT ($1). Just 28km to the north of Tatvan, another **Nemrut Dağı** (different from the one with the statues) rises 3000m into the sky, with a crater lake at 2400m. The crater is almost 7km in diameter, its north shore formed by stupendous cliffs hundreds of meters high. The view of Lake Van from the top is inspiring, and you can camp inside the crater next to the lake. Minibus trips leaving daily in July and August at 9am from the Hotel Üstün allow for a leisurely swim in the lake, and return at 3pm ($4). There should be three **boats** a day to Van (40¢—a bargain for a 4hr. trip), but they are unreliable since they wait for the train (3 per week to Ankara, 25hr.—not recommended!).

The **Hotel Üstün** is located at the bottom of the cross-street that runs from the town hall *(Belediye)* to the lake. ($6 per person, with bath $6.50.) Üstün's reception serves as an informal tourist office; the most helpful staff can give you information about Tatvan and its surroundings. Tatvan's budget hotels are no delight; if you're stuck here, the least dusty and noisy is the **Hotel Trabzon** (tel. 10 44; singles $4; on the street parallel to the main one). To quell your rumbling stomach, visit the **Aile Salonu** near the center of town on the main road (delicious *menemen,* a spicy omlette dish, is 75¢), or **Ak Restaurant** beside the PTT (complete meal $2).

Biltis, a historical town now known for its cigarette production (a vital industry in Turkey, as asthmatics will ascertain), is dramatically set in a narrow gorge 20km west of Tatvan on the Diyarbakır road. It used to be an Armenian town, and some houses still have Armenian writing on them. The Seljuk mosque, **Ulu Cami,** and an Ottoman one, the **Şerefiye Cami,** are worth seeing. There is a hilltop citadel from which you can look out over the entire town. Better to stay here than Tatvan. The best hotel by far is the centrally located **Hotel Hanedan,** whose stark exterior belies very comfortable rooms. (Singles $7. Doubles with bath $9.) **Hakkâri** lies 200km south of Van. Officials refuse to acknowledge it, but this mountain area is home to the Kurdish insurgency, which is comprised of 500-1000 guerillas who clash periodically with Turkish soldiers stationed at the military base here. Don't hike around or camp outside a settlement. If you stay in one of Hakkâri's two hotels, you shouldn't have any problems. In the summer of 1992, Hakkâri was said to be safe for travelers. On the way you might stop at the village of **Güzelsu,** dominated by the 17th-century Ottoman castle of **Hoşap,** which rests on a crag overlooking a river.

Erzurum

Given its location at a main Eastern Anatolian crossroads, you'll probably pass through Erzurum at some point. If you do, this wind-swept plateau town has a few things worth seeing. There are a number of Seljuk buildings, notably the **Çifte Minareli Medresse,** or Twin Minaret Seminary (1253), the **Ulu Cami** (1179) next to it, and the Byzantine hilltop castle around which the town spreads. The major Ottoman monuments are the **Yakutiye Medresse** (1310), a Mongol seminary, and the **Lala Mustafa-passa Cami** (1563). Erzurum is a major transportation hub for Eastern Turkey. The **bus station** *(otogar),* 3km northwest of the center, is also served by *dolmuş.* Buses go to Ankara (15hr., $13), Dogubeyazıt (4½hr., $6), Artvin (4hr., $6), Kars (3½hr., $4), Trabzon (6hr., $10), and Van (6hr., $11). To get to Yusufeli in the Tortum River valley, you must take a *dolmuş* from near the Atatürk Endüstri Meslek Lisesi northeast of the center (frequent *dolmuş,* 4hr., $5). Most of Erzurum's budget hotels are along Kazım Karabekir Cad. in the northeast part of town, just south of the train station. Try the **Hitit Otel** (tel. 112 04), with rooms ranging from $6-12.

Mount Ararat and Dogubeyazit

According to legends which date back to Babylonian times, it was on **Mt. Ararat's** jagged slopes that Noah's ark came to rest. Although on clear days it can be seen from Turkey, Armenia, and Iran, Mt. Ararat (5165m) is most often draped in clouds. The best time for mountain-viewing is dawn.

If you fancy climbing Mt. Ararat, you'll need permission from the authorities in Ankara. The best way to get a permit is to contact the Turkish embassy in your home country. Approval theoretically takes two months, but people sometimes wait up to a year. An escort is mandatory. If you are not an experienced climber, you should consider the more elaborate tours of the **Trek Travel Agency,** 53 Emniyet Cad. (tel. (0278) 19 81), which include food, horses, tents, an escort, a guide, *dolmuş,* and accommodations in town ($461). You don't have to be an expert climber to conquer the legendary mountain, but you must be in good shape. Write to the main office of Trek Travel, Aydele Cad. 10, Taksim, İstanbul, 80090 Turkey (tel. 154 67 06) for more information. They will also procure your permit in one month. Note that in 1992 no hiking was possible due to PKK (Kurdish Workers Party) fighting in the area.

Doğubeyazıt, at the foot of Mt. Ararat and the partially ruined palace of **Ishak Paşa** are worth a visit. An eccentric Ottoman feudal lord built the palace in the late 18th century; the Urartian fortress across the ravine offers a supreme view. The palace is a 5km trek uphill from town, but *dolmuş* go there until noon. The last *dolmuş* back to town is at 4pm (round-trip 30¢). (Palace open Tues.-Sun. 8am-5pm. Admission $1.)

In Doğubeyazıt, the **Hotel Erzurum** (tel. 10 80 or 16 75), near the end of town on the road to the palace, has commodious rooms and exceptionally amiable management. (Singles $3.50. Doubles $7.) The **Hotel Saruhan** (tel. 11 68), next door, is snug and tidy. (Singles $3.) Along the main street, 200m toward town from the Erzurum Hotel, the **Saray Restaurant** serves a variety of freshly prepared dishes ($1) in simple surroundings. (Open daily 4pm-11pm.) You'll find a **PTT** (open daily 7am-11pm) and a few banks in town. Doğubeyazıt's **telephone code** is 0278.

If you can't go directly to Doğubeyazıt from Kars or Van, or if you are coming from Erzurum, you must go through the wholly charmless town of Ağrı. A minor transport hub, Ağrı also has buses to Kars, Van, and Erzurum. Try not to get stuck here. **Visas to Iran,** though still difficult, are getting easier as the country loosens up under the leadership of Ali Hashemi Rafsanjani. Many nationalities (Canadians, British, and Australians) can obtain transit visas with little difficulty to allow overland travel to the Indian Subcontinent, and by 1993 even the U.S. may have reestablished diplomatic relations. *Dolmuş* to the Iranian border are $1.50 per person, taxis $10.

Kars and Ani

Many travelers feel literally disoriented in **Kars,** an Eastern Anatolian town guarded by Western Anatolian soldiers amidst Russian architecture; few travelers like it. The main reason for visiting Kars is to see the medieval Armenian capital of **Ani,** 45km away. Due to its proximity to the Armenian border, you must get permission to visit Ani from the Kars **tourist office,** Lise Cad. (tel. 123 00). The office is unmarked, on a hard-to-find back street, and the map they give out is grossly inaccurate—tourist beware! (Open daily 8am-5:30pm; off-season 8am-noon and 1:30-5:30pm.) Get a form from the tourist office (if you can find it; also, bring your passport), and take it to the police station, just opposite as you reach Faik Bey Cad, for approval. In the morning, you might find enough people in front of the tourist office to hire a minibus ($40; $4 each for 10 people) or taxi ($20) that will take you to Ani, wait there for two hours, and bring you back to Kars. A municipal bus runs to the site at 6am, returning from Ani at 3pm (20¢ each way); other trips between these hours are possible but unpredictable. The bus is a better bet if you want to stay for more than a couple of hours. If you find you have extra time in Kars, visit the captivating **Fethiye Cami,** once an Armenian church, or the small museum. (Open daily 8:30am-12:30pm and 1:30-5:30pm. Admission $1.) An **Ottoman bridge,** baths, and a 10th-century **Armenian church** hunker below the citadel. Russian buildings which remain from the Russian occupation of 1878-1920 line Ordu Cad. There is also a **museum**—well worth a visit—chronicling the history of the area from the Bronze Age on down. (Open 8am-5:30pm. Admission $6.) The **Ottoman citadel** that dominates the city is now part of a military compound and is strictly off limits.

Kars is connected to Trabzon, Ankara, Samsun, İstanbul, İzmir, Diyarbakır, and Konya by way of Erzurum (6 buses per day, 5hr., $6). **Buses** also run from Ağrı and Doğubeyazıt via Ağrı or the more scenic route through Iğdır. The spectacular nine-hour trip from Kars to Hopa, on the Black Sea coast, ends at Artvin (daily at 8am, $7.50). The bus from Ardahan to Artvin leaves only at 9am, requiring an overnight stay. If you are coming from Van, consider taking a tour that includes Ani and drops you off in Kars.

Kars is not celebrated for its hotels, and it is remarkably difficult to find specific establishments in the city's monotonous grid pattern, especially since Karsians have challenged themselves to change street names as often as possible. **Otel Karavansaray** on Fait Bey Cad. has fine rooms ($3 per person without bath). **Otel Lütfü,** 10 Karadağ Cad. (tel. 187 67), off Olgun Sok., may be the best budget hotel around. If you go through the arcade in the bus station, you'll see Lütfü signs. (Singles $4. Doubles $6.) Indulge in platefuls of traditional Turkish fare (only $1) at the simple **Imren Lokantası** 78 Kazım Paşa Cad., near the Hotel Asya. Try the Su Böreği, a Turkish version of quiche, at the **Ötogar Restaurant** (on the 2nd floor). The **Çobanoğlu Kahvesi,** near the Hotel Temel on Kerim Paşa Cad., often features improvisational *âşık* (Turkish string instrument) players; you can sit and listen from 8pm to midnight (75¢). The **PTT** is on Ordu Cad. (open 24 hrs.). Kars's **telephone code** is 021.

A great alternative to any hotel in Kars is the **Hotel Sartur** (tel. (0229) 13 32), in **Sarıkamış,** known as Turkey's best ski resort, 60km from Kars on the road to Erzurum. The hotel offers fine food and clean, comfortable rooms facing the famous pine forest of Sarıkamıç. All buses going to or coming from Erzurum visit Sarıkamıç. Hike 1½km up the hill or take a taxi ($1) to reach the hotel. (Singles with bath $6.50. Doubles with bath $8. Breakfast $1.) **Ani** was the site of the capital of Armenia during its "golden age" in the 10th and 11th centuries. The ruins at Ani are a sad reminder of the Armenians' fate. The site is unexcavated; most buildings are from the 10th and 11th centuries. Impressive double walls span the western side of the city, opening up only at the 13th-century double gate of **Alp Arslan Kapısı.** On the north side of the ruins near the wall, **St. Gregory Church** houses the finest frescoes in the area. The 10th-century **Cathedral of Ani's** high ceiling, blind arches, and elegant pillars compensate for the dearth of dome. Climb up the dark and dusty minaret of the **mosque** for a quenching view of the site and the river, which marks the Turkish-Armenian border. Taking photographs of any of the sites or of the empty fields just over the border is strictly forbidden. The nearby **Polatoğlu Church** is a unique example of Armenian architecture. Built in 1001 in honor of St. Gregory, the **Church of Gagik** represents a rare example of centrally planned design. (Open daily 8:30am-5:30pm. Admission $2.50.)

BLACK SEA COAST

Browsing through the tourist propaganda, you would think that Turkey had only two coasts, the Aegean and the Mediterranean. However, Turkey's longest and least visited coast skirts the Black Sea. Cool breezes from the north provide relief from the summer heat, and heavy rainfall nourishes this region's abundant forests and thickly cultivated farmland.

The isolation fostered by adjacent mountain ranges inhibited this coast's impact on the ancient world. Trading posts such as Sinop, Trabzon, and Amisus (now Samsun) did, however, become commercial cities; they first exported local products and later profited from the silk route trade when Arab invasions blocked the southern passage. Exemplary Byzantine structures remain around Trabzon. Elsewhere, you'll see an occasional Byzantine castle and several fine Seljuk and Ottoman mosques.

A highway follows the coastline so closely that you can't enjoy much privacy or quiet on most of the beaches. Most fishing villages have no accommodations since they see few visitors, but campgrounds are spaced about every 50km. Freelance camping is easy, though you may have to search a while to find an uncultivated piece of turf.

Amasya

Surrounded by mountains and castles, breezy and amiable Amasya is often considered part of the Black Sea region, even though it's not on the coast. This is due partly to its similar geography, mainly to its historical ties to the Black Sea. Amasya was the first capital of the Pontus kingdom that broke away from the Seleucids in the 3rd century BCE. The Pontic king, Mithradates the Great, conquered most of Asia Minor from his Black Sea base, and might have become another Alexander had his conquests not coincided with the rise of Rome; a generation later, Julius Caesar finished off the kingdom with his famous declaration, "I came, I saw, I conquered."

Buses run to: Ankara (every 30min., 5hr., $6); Boğazkale (every hr., 2hr., $2.50); and İstanbul (every hr., 11hr., $12). Several buses also run daily to Kayseri (8hr., $10), Malatya (9hr., $12), and Samsun (2½hr., $3). If you're lucky, your bus will drop you off in town, since the **bus station** is 3km away. If not, take a minibus into town from the green stand across from the station. Taxis to town are $1.50. The **PTT** is on the waterfront, to Atatürk's left. (Open daily 8am-midnight.) Amasya's **telephone code** is 3781.

In a courtyard on the river, the spacious **Konfor Palas Oteli** (tel. 12 60) rents clean rooms with lukewarm water, some with balconies overlooking the river. ($3 per person.) The **Hotel Aydın,** 86 Mustafa Kemal Cad. (tel. 24 63), charges only $2 per person, but darkness and noise thrive.

The bridge across the river traverses a century. The old town on the other side is filled with cobblestone streets and buttressed overhangs. Now a museum, the restored **Hazeranlar Konağı** allows you to peek at the furnishings of an Ottoman house. (Open Tues.-Sun. 8:30am-noon and 1:30-6pm. Admission 80¢.) Built for early Pontic kings, the **rock tombs** near the castle reach up to 8m in height and were originally ornamented with marble façades. If you return to Mustafa Kemal Cad. and take a right, you'll first pass **Beyazıt II Mosque,** a double-domed 15th-century Ottoman mosque with stained glass windows and geometric masonwork. Farther along is the small **Archaeological Museum.** (Open Tues.-Sun. 8:30am-noon and 12:30-6pm. Admission 80¢.) Continue farther along Mustafa Kemal Cad. to the **Gök Medrese,** a Seljuk religious school with a huge portal and some coffins.

Sinop

Sinop's location on the isthmus of a peninsula endows the city with two natural harbors, making it the largest ancient trade center on the Black Sea. Sinop was also the home of Diogenes the Cynic, a Hellenistic philosopher/historian who lived the ascetic life of a *Let's Go* traveler. When Alexander the Great asked him if he desired anything, Diogenes answered that he only wished the sovereign would move out of his light. Sinop's importance as a port city has declined since ancient times: it now supports an American military base and a small tourist industry. If you're on your way to or from eastern Turkey, you might stop by for a cup of *çay* and a view from its medieval walls.

Sinop is connected directly with İstanbul; from the east or south you must change buses in Samsun. From the **bus station,** head into town along Cumhuriyet Cad. and take a right at the large intersection and then right again at the harbor to reach the **tourist office** (tel. 19 96; open daily in summer 9am-8pm). One block inland is the clean but otherwise nondescript **Yilmaz Pension** (tel. 57 52; singles $2, doubles $3.75). The **Hotel Gülpalas** (tel. 17 37) is 50m into town from the bus station. (Singles $3. Doubles $7. Hot showers included.) You can swim in the water right by the tourist office. Sinop also has **camping** facilities on the southern shore, 2km away. The windswept, plant-strewn **Restaurant Uzun Mehmet** is by the tourist office. The **telephone code** is 3761.

Near the tourist office you can climb up the 3m thick walls of the Seljuk **castle** to sense the layout of the city. The **Archaeological Museum** is uphill on Atatürk Cad. and to the right. (Open daily 8am-5:30pm. Admission $1.) The courtyard full of *stelae* and mosaics is more interesting than the museum itself. The **Temple of Serapis** is here, too. The overgrown **Balatlar Church** is a 13th-century religious compound with a few surviving frescoes. From the upper end of Atatürk Cad., make a sharp right turn, and follow the street beside the taxi stand for ¾km. On the way from the bus station into town, you'll see the Seljuk **Alaadin Cami,** built in the Syrian style with several domes.

From Sinop to Trabzon

Yakakent, a fishing village with sandy beaches is the first stop east of Sinop. Next is **Bafra,** 100km from Sinop, a town famous for its tobacco. Check out the 13th century bath complex, the 15th century mosque and the *medresse* (seminary). **Samsun** is a large port city and a transportation hub for the coast. Linger not. From here there are **buses** to Amasya (every hr., 2½hr., $3), and frequent buses to: Ankara (7hr., $8); Trabzon (6hr., $8); Artvin (10hr., $11); Kayseri (9hr., $10); and İstanbul (12hr., $13). 100km east is the popular beach town of **Ünye,** which boasts an attractive 18th century town hall. Sleep at the **Çamile Motel** on the beach 4km west of town (tel. 37 31 13 33). (Doubles with bath $13.) Or camp at **Europa Camping** 1km further west ($2).

The port of **Giresun** was supposedly where the Romans first discovered cherries (spot the cognate), which are still an important regional product. **Fatsa,** which claims to have been a stopping point for Jason and the Argonauts, has a Byzantine church on a promontory overlooking the sea. The town of **Yalıköy** is famous for its sea snails, and **Ordu** holds a hazelnut festival in September (sea snails and hazelnuts—these are a few of our favorite things).

Between Fatsa and Ordu, black rock cliffs plunge into green water interspersed with the pleasant villages of **Bolaman, Yazılköy,** and **Caka.** Past Ordu until Tirebolu, the coastline reverts to sand. Twenty-six km west of Trabzon lies the fishing village of **Mersin** (not to be confused with the resort town on the Mediterranean coast). **Mersin Turistik Tesisleri** might let you camp for free near their private beach. Expect to stay up late though, since they often play blaring live music.

Trabzon

From its hilltop vantage point above the Black Sea, Trabzon has watched great empires come and go, preserving a little of each in its eclectic architecture and way of life. Founded by the ancient Greeks as the port of Trapezus, the city is best known as a trade emporium which attracted merchants from all over the world. Although it has lost much of its former glory, its cobblestone streets and important sights prepare the city as a prime port of call for a new trade: tourism. Though important in the Greek and Roman periods, Trabzon's heyday came when Alexis Comneni, fleeing Constantinople while the Crusaders sacked it in 1204, dubbed the city Trebizond and made it the capital of his empire. The dynasty that he founded became the longest in Greek history; its rulers lived in opulent Byzantine style off the profits of trade and nearby silver mines. The kingdom held out against the Turks until 1461, even longer than Constantinople, postponing its demise by diplomatically marrying off its daughters, reputedly the most beautiful women in the world. Now an industrial city of 1.4 million, Trabzon still retains some older sections and legendary historical sights from the Byzantine era. Unfortunately, the great palace itself was slowly quarried away over the last few centuries.

Trabzon is a great place to start or end a tour of Eastern Turkey. **Buses** run from the *otogar* three km east of the main square to: Artvin (4hr., $10); Erzurum (6hr., $9); Hopa (3hr., $5); Samsun (6hr., $10); Ankara (12hr., $18); İstanbul (20hr., $28); and Adana (16hr., $31). **Turkish Airlines** flies daily to Ankara (1hr., $70) and İstanbul (2-4hr., $80). Buses leave before departures from the THY office (tel. 134 46), west of the tourist office on the main square. A **Turkish Maritime Lines** ship traces the Black Sea Coast from İstanbul to Trabzon. It leaves İstanbul on Monday at 5:30pm, stops at Sinop and Samsun, and arrives at Trabzon at 3:30pm Wednesday. The return voyage leaves Trabzon at 7pm the same day and arrives in İstanbul on Friday at 11am. Purchase tickets in advance at the maritime office, next to the tourist office. (Office open Mon.-Fri. 8am-noon and 1-5pm. Armchair tickets $23. Rooms with bath $25-65.) The **tourist office** (tel. 146 59; open daily 8am-6:30pm) has maps and information about whitewater rafting trips on the Çorah River. The **PTT** is on a small pedestrian side street parallel to Maraş Cad. just after its intersection with Cumhuriyet Cad. (open 24 hrs.). Trabzon's **telephone code** is 031.

It is difficult to find a decent, quiet hotel in Trabzon. Most of the cheaper hotels, clustered around İskele Cad. off the main square, are no bargain for the cheerless, basic rooms they offer. Worse, since the opening of the Georgian border up the coast, Trabzon is swarming with Russian tourists and shoppers. They fill every hotel and are not shy about socializing well into the night. **Hotel Anil** (tel. 195 66) and the **Otel Ural** (tel. 114 14), both on Güzelhisar Cad., have rooms for $6-12. The **Otel Benli Palas** (tel. 110 22) has several rooms with great balconies, but they are often very noisy ($5-12). For a quiet place, you're going to have to shell out the big bucks, and the **Horon Oteli** north of the square (111 99) will gladly take them (singles $18) if they're not fully booked. For fresh, juicy Black Sea fish (just like mom used to make it, $2), try **Eyvan Lokanta** on the main square. If you're feeling homesick, **Tad Pizza and Burgers** on İskele Cad. isn't bad (pizza $2). **Cafe Kuğu** on the square is a popular breakfast spot.

The oldest extant Christian structure in Trabzon is the tiny 7th-century **St. Anne Church.** Head west from the square on K. Maraş Cad.—you'll find it behind a cluster of newsstands and trees on your left, just before the mosque. At the top of the hill behind the town is **Atatürk Köskü,** one of Atatürk's villas originally built at the turn of the century by a rich Greek. Though he stayed here only two nights in his life, the popular villa is now a museum fat with photographs and paintings of "Father Turk." (Open 8am-5:30pm. Admission 40¢.) To get there, take any bus marked "Atatürk Köskü" from the main square.

Romantically set in a rose and oleander garden overlooking the Black Sea, the lovely 13th-century **Aya Sofia** church was once part of a monastery. Now a museum, it features fine frescoes and carvings. (Open daily 8am-5:30pm. Admission 70¢, students 40¢.) From the lower end of the square, take a *dolmuş* marked *Ayasofia*. Within the walls of the old city is the **Ortahisar Cami,** formerly Panayia Chrisokefalos Church, the main basilica of medieval Trebizond. Although it is now covered with plaster, you can still see the basilica's layout and a few geometric mosaics.

Behind the town rises the hill of **Boztepe**. Check out what remains of the Panayia Theoskepastos convent, and 2.5km further back into the hills, the Armenian monastery at Kaymaklı with frescoes almost as impressive as those at Aya Sofia. Buses to the scenic town of **Akçaabat,** 14km west, leave from the main square. Dolmuşes to **Rize,** for hikes in the Kaçkar mountains, and to **Saykara,** on the alpine lake of Uzungol, leave from the waterfront station below town to the east. The most dramatic tourist attraction in the area, however, and one of the most fascinating Byzantine sites anywhere, is the **Sumel Monastery,** 47km southeast of Trabzon, set amongst lush forested mountains. Established in 385 CE, this cliffside monastery reached its zenith in the late Middle Ages, when it contained 72 rooms and an immense library. Monks lived here until the population-transfers between Greece and Turkey in 1923, and the monastery has been sadly neglected since, although restoration has recently been undertaken. Little remains except the frescoed main chapel. (Open daily 8am-6pm. Admission $2, students 15¢.) To get there you can either get a minibus tour from Ulusoy on Taksim Cad. (9 and 10am, $3.50 roundtrip; bus stops for lunch), or for more flexibility, you can share a taxi from the stand beside the tourist office on the main square ($6 per person).

East of Trabzon

This segment of coast is the Shangri-La of Turkey, if you can overlook the ugliness of the towns, with their ubiquitous half-built concrete black structures. Clouds shroud the cliffs that trace the shoreline, the air hangs moist, and vegetation sprouts at will (or at least on tea plantations). The best places for campers to find an uncultivated spot are along the beach by the highway or along riverbanks. Many locals spend their summers on plateaus and pastures called *yayla,* which are ideal for camping. If you follow the signs along the highway that point down dirt roads to small villages, you'll catch glimpses of handmade houses, local dress, and exquisite scenery.

Just 30km east of Trabzon is the fishing village of **Kalecik;** you can camp on the rock ledge on the opposite side of a Byzantine castle. A few km farther east, you'll pass the large towns of **Of** and **Sürmene;** both have accommodations. From Of you can get to the mountain lake of **Uzungöl** via **Çaykara,** but get an early start because *dolmuşes* are rare. There are cabins for rent at the lake. One km west of Of is another Byzantine castle, with a grassy spot nearby suitable for camping. About 30km away in the Hemşin Valley of the Kaçkar range bubbles the mountain resort of **Ayder,** renowned for its hot springs. Take a *dolmuş* from Pazar via Çamlihemşin to the mist-engulfed Ayder (2½hr., $1.50). It may be the only place you'll visit where you won't find an Atatürk statue gazing fondly down at you. Just behind the Hotel Saray sits the **Hotel Kaçkal,** with filthless rooms and cordial managment ($1.75). Over the bridge, the **Ayder Hilton** (no relation to the chain) has local flavor, good food, and hypnotizing views. (Singles $2.25. Doubles $4.50. The upper floors are less damp.) The hotels don't have showers—they assume that you will be taking a bath at the **hot springs.** (Open 4am-9am and 5-11pm for men; 9am-5pm for women. Admission 25¢.) Have *şiş-kebap* or *pirzola* (lamb-chops, $1.25) at the restaurant below Hotel Saray. The *Ayder muhlama* and *fondue* are both rich with the local cheese, butter, and eggs. From Ayder, you can hike towards **Mt. Kaçkar** (3937m) or trek around the surrounding villages. Guides are available in town, ($60 per day; up to six people per hike) but a map is all you really need.

The highway continues along the coast for about 60km, finally turning inland at **Hopa.** Near Hopa's bus station, the **Otel Kafkas,** 89 Cumhuriyet Cad. (tel. 10 40), is down the street to your right as you face the water. Buses stop here en route to Kars ($8.50). From Hopa, you can take a *dolmuş* to **Kemal Paşa,** a small town whose empty gravel beach, tea factory, and mysterious Byzantine church see few visitors. Hopa is 30km southwest of the Georgian border. The village of **Sarp** was cut in two when the border was drawn. Relatives can see each other by special permission, but they have to use the gate east of Kars. Sarp is accessible by taxi from Hopa ($10).

The situation at the **Georgian border** is constantly changing. In the summer of 1992, land crossing was only open to Turks and residents of Georgia—everyone else had to take the daily ferry from Trabzon to Batumi. By 1993, Georgia may have its own embassies but in the meantime the Russian consulate, slow as ever, is still handling Georgian visas. Local travel agents speed up the process to a one-hour fax exchange, providing tailor-made individual visas for anywhere you want to go in the former USSR, for a steep $120, worth it if you want to do some serious freelance traveling in what once was strictly Intourist-controlled territory. (Note that the price may go up or down, on the whim of the Russian consulate.) Try **Afacan Tour,** 7 İskele Cad. (tel. 21 58 04). **Karden Tour, Sarptur, Ulutur,** and **Kaçkar Tour,** all in Trabzon, are other possibilities.

Artvin

Clutching the slopes of a mountain south of Hopa, the vertical town of Artvin serves as a base for exploring the area's Georgian churches, or for whitewater rafting on the Çoruk River. Since all buses continue to Kars or Hopa, they can leave you at the foot of the city by the 15th-century castle. Some bus companies operate shuttles to run the 5km haul up to the city. If you miss the shuttle, you'll have to wait for the bus run by the municipality (30¢), or take a taxi. Surprisingly enough, the city centers around the statue of Atatürk in front of the *Vilâyet* (city hall).

One block down the hill, **Kültür Palas** (tel. 11 18) offers bathrooms and a view of the city and surrounding mountains. (Singles $2.50. Doubles $3.50.) The **Kaçkar Oteli** (tel. 33 97), right below the *Vilâyet* also has high quality bathrooms with hot water and clean towels. (Singles $4. Doubles $8.) Across from the Kaçkar Oteli, the **Genya Oteli** (tel. 11 92 36), offers cordial rooms and management. (Singles $3. Doubles $5.) These hotels are often full, so call ahead. Up the stairs next to the Artvin Express, the **Kibar** serves tasty Turkish pizzas for only 80¢. (Open 5am-11pm). For something heartier, try the appetizing specialties of the restaurant in the **Hotel Karahan** (tel. 18 00), down the main avenue. The adjacent bar is smoky but popular. The hotel also serves as a **tourist office,** and organizes rafting trips. The hotel entrance is not on the main street, but in back via a mosque. Various medieval Georgian churches are still scattered around Artvin, but none are easily accessible. To get to the **Church of Dolişhane,** take the *dolmuş* to Çavçat, walk 2km from the junction, and hike about 3km to the village of Hamamlıköy. For the churches of Işhan and Altipunk you must take a *dolmuş* to **Yusufeli** (1hr., $1). From there it's 10-15km by foot to each. A round-trip taxi to any of the three can cost a penance-inducing $20. Hotel Karahan runs a lodge at Yusufeli, mainly for rafting trips.

Artvin is close to many *yayla* ("summer pastures" in Turkish) that locals visit in summer or, in fact, use as summer pastures. The plateau of **Kafkanör,** 11km from Artvin, hosts an annual **Festival of Kafkanör** on the third weekend of June. Traditional dances and other performances take place, but the main events are **bull fights.** The bulls wrestle each other like the camels in western Anatolia. The winner's owner is rewarded and honored. The bull gets nothing but, of course, still revels in the simple pleasure of victory.

Buses operated by Artvin Ekspres and As Turism, both at the city center, run to Hopa (6-8 per day, 2hr., $2); Erzurum (5 per day, 4hr., $6); and Kars (4 per day, 7hr., $7), connecting to other cities. Frequent buses also run to Trabzon (4½hr. $6). The **PTT** is also at the center. (Open daily 7am-11pm.) Artvin's **telephone code** is 0581.

GLOSSARY

As most veteran travelers will tell you, it's wise to learn a few key phrases in the native tongue while traveling abroad. While fluency is neither necessary nor expected, a smidgen of Greek and a dollop of Turkish can make finding accomodations, buying carpets, and meeting local folks immensely easier and more rewarding. Both Greek and Turkish are difficult to master. If you're in a real squeeze, try to find someone of high-school age: English is a compulsory subject in Greek schools, and common in Turkish, so many younger Greeks and Turks speak a bit of English.

Greek

The table of the Greek alphabet (only 24 letters) below will help you decipher signs. The left column gives you the names of the letters in Greek, the middle column shows the printed lower case and capital letters, and the right column provides the approximate pronunciations of the letters.

alpha	α	A a as in car
beta	β	B v as in visionary
gamma	γ	Γ before vowels, y as in yet; otherwise ch as in the Scottish loch
delta	δ	Δ th as in the
epsilon	ε	E e as in dwell
zeta	ζ	Z z as in Zorba
eta	η	H ee as in beef
theta	θ	Θ th as in thermal
iota	ι	I ee as in preen
kappa	κ	K k as in kidskin
lambda	λ	Λ l as in Lola
mu	μ	M m as in mango
nu	ν	N n as in necromancer
ksi	ξ	Ξ x as in hex
omicron	o	O o as in rot
pi	π	Π p as in pine nut
rho	ρ	P r as in read on
sigma	σ	Σ before voiced consonants, z in Ziggley; otherwise s in sigh
tau	τ	T t as in tenpin bowling
upsilon	υ	Y ee as in scream
phi	φ	Φ f as in forte
xi	χ	X ch as in the Scottish loch
psi	ψ	Ψ ps as in drips
omega	ω	Ω o as in caught

In the phrases below, note that "dh" is pronounced like "th" in "the," and that "ch" is pronounced like "ch" in the Scottish "loch."

Greetings and Courtesies

Good morning	ΚΑΛΗΜΕΡΑ	kah-lee-ME-rah
Good evening	ΚΑΛΗΣΠΕΡΑ	kah-lee-SPE-rah
Good night	ΚΑΛΗΝΥΧΤΑ	kah-lee-NEE-chtah
yes	ΝΑΙ	NEH
no	ΟΧΙ	OH-chee
please/you're welcome	ΠΑΡΑΚΑΛΩ	pah-rah-kah-LO

489

thank you (very much)	ΕΥΧΑΠΙΣΤΩ	ef-chah-ree-STO (po-LEE)
excuse me	ΣΥΓΓΝΩΜΗ	seeg-NO-mee
hello (polite and plural form)	ΓΕΙΑ ΣΑΣ	YAH-sas
hello (familiar form)	ΓΕΙΑ ΣΟΥ	YAH-soo
OK	ΕΝΤΑΞΗ	en-DAHK-see
What is your name?	ΠΩΣ ΣΕ ΛΕΝΕ;	pos-se-LE-ne
My name is ...	ΜΕ ΛΕΝΕ	me-LE-ne ...
Mr./Sir	ΚΥΡΙΩΣ	kee-REE-os
Ms./Madam	ΚΥΡΙΑ	kee-REE-ah

Where?

Where is ... ?	ΠΟΥ ΕΙΝΑΙ	pou-EE-ne ... ?
I'm going to ...	ΠΗΓΑΙΝΩ ΓΙΑ	pee-YE-no yah ...
When do we leave?	ΤΙ ΩΡΑ ΦΕΥΓΟΜΕ	tee O-rah FEV-yo-me?
restaurant	ΕΣΤΙΑΤΟΡΙΟ	es-tee-ah-TO-ree-o
post office	ΤΑΧΥΔΡΟΜΙΟ	ta-chee-dhro-MEE-o
market	ΑΓΟΡΑ	ah-go-RAH
museum	ΜΟΥΣΕΙΟ	mou-SEE-o
pharmacy	ΦΑΡΜΑΚΕΙΟ	fahr-mah-KEE-o
bank	ΤΡΑΠΕΖΑ	TRAH-pe-zah
church	ΕΚΚΛΗΣΙΑ	e-klee-SEE-ah
hotel	ΞΕΝΟΔΟΧΕΙΟ	kse-no-dho-HEE-o
room	ΔΩΜΑΤΙΟ	dho-MAH-teeo
suitcase	ΒΑΛΙΤΣΑ	vah-LEE-tsah
airport	ΑΕΡΟΔΡΟΜΙΟ	ah-e-ro-DHRO-mee-o
airplane	ΑΕΡΟΠΛΑΝΟ	ah-e-ro-PLAH-no
bus	ΛΕΩΦΟΡΙΟ	le-o-fo-REE-o
train	ΤΡΑΙΝΟ	TRE-no
ferry	ΠΛΟΙΟ	PLEE-o
ticket	ΕΙΣΗΤΗΡΙΟ	ee-see-TEE-ree-o
doctor	ΠΑΤΡΟΣ	yah-TROS
right	ΔΕΞΙΑ	dhek-see-AH
left	ΑΡΙΣΤΕΡΑ	ah-rees-teh-RAH
here	ΕΔΩ	e-DHO
there	ΕΚΕΙ	e-KEE
closed	ΚΛΕΙΣΤΩ	klee-STO
open	ΑΝΟΙΧΤΟ	ah-nee-KTO

How Much?

How much?	ΠΟΣΟ ΚΑΝΕΙ	PO-so KAH-nee (PO-so ko-STEE-zee)
I need	ΧΡΕΙΑΖΟΜΑΙ	chree-AH-zo-me
I want	ΘΕΛΩ	THE-lo
I would like ...	ΘΑ ΗΘΕΛΑ	thah EE-the-lah ...
I will buy this one	ΘΑ ΑΛΟΠΑΣΩ ΑΥΤΟ ΕΔΩ	thah ah-go-RAH-so ahf-TO e-DHO
Do you have?	ΕΧΕΤΕ	E-che-te
Can I see a room?	ΜΠΟΡΡΩ ΝΑ ΔΩ ΕΝΑ ΔΩΜΑΤΙΟ	bo-RO nah-DHO E-nah dho-MAH-tee-o
bill	ΛΟΓΑΡΙΑΣΜΟ	lo-gahr-yah-SMO
newspaper	ΕΦΗΜΕΡΙΔΑ	e-fee-me-REE-dha
water	ΝΕΡΟ	ne-RO
good	ΚΑΛΟ	kah-LO
cheap	ΦΤΗΝΟ	ftee-NO
expensive	ΑΚΡΙΒΟ	ah-kree-VO

When?

What time is it?	ΤΙ ΩΡΑ ΕΙΝΑΙ	tee O-rah EE-ne?
first	ΠΡΩΤΟ	PRO-to
last	ΤΕΛΕΥΤΑΙΟ	teh-lef-TEH-o
one	ΕΝΑ	E-nah
two	ΔΥΟ	DHEE-o
three	ΤΡΙΑ	TREE-ah
four	ΤΕΣΣΕΡΑ	TES-ser-ah
five	ΠΕΝΤΕ	PEN-dhe
six	ΕΞΙ	E-ksee
seven	ΕΠΤΑ	ep-TAH
eight	ΟΧΤΩ	och-TO
nine	ΕΝΙΑ	en-YAH
ten	ΔΕΚΑ	DHE-kah
eleven	ΕΝΔΕΚΑ	EN-dhe-kah
twelve	ΔΩΔΕΚΑ	DHO-dhe-kah
morning	ΠΡΩΙ	pro-EE
evening	ΒΡΑΔΥ	VRAH-dhee
tonight	ΑΠΟΨΕ	ah-PO-pse
yesterday	ΧΘΕΣ	ech-THES
today	ΣΗΜΕΡΑ	SEE-me-rah
tomorrow	ΑΥΡΙΟ	AH-vree-o

Problems

Do you speak English?	ΜΙΛΑΣ ΑΓΓΛΙΚΑ;	mee-LAHS ahn-glee-KAH?
I don't speak Greek	ΔΕΝ ΜΙΛΑΩ ΕΛΛΗΝΙΚΑ	dhen mee-LAHO el-leen-ee-KAH
I don't understand	ΔΕΝ ΚΑΤΑΛΑΒΑΙΝΩ	dhen kah-tah-lah-VE-no
I am lost	ΕΧΩ ΧΑΘΕΙ	E-kho ha-THEE
I am ill	ΕΙΜΑΙ ΑΡΡΩΣΤΟΣ	EE-mah AH-ross-toss
Help!	ΒΟΗΘΕΙΑ	vo-EE-thee-ah

Turkish

Be aware that certain letters and combinations of letters in Turkish are pronounced differently than they are in English. Turkish is a phonetic language, with each sounds being clearly pronounced. Turkish is usually lightly accented on the last syllable; special vowels, consonants, and combinations include:

Turkish	English
c	"j" as in john
ç	"ch" as in church
ğ	lengthens the preceding vowel
ı	(no dot on the "i")"uh" as in her or bird
i	"e" as in me
j	"s" as in leisure
ö	"eu" rhymes with French deux
ş	"sh" as in ship
u	as in too
â	dipthong of ea, or faint ya
ü	"ew" as in dew
ay	"uy" as in buy
ey	"ey" as in obey
oy	"oy" as in boy
uy	"oo-ee" as in Louis

Greetings and Courtesies

good morning	*günaydın* (gun i-duhn)
good evening	*iyi akşamlar* (ee-ak-sham-LAR)
good night	*iyi geceler* (ee-geh-jeh-LEHR)
yes	*evet*
no	*hayır* (HIGH-er)
please	*lütfen* (LEWT-fen)
thank you (formal)	*teşekkürler* (tesh-ek-KEWR-ler)
thank you (informal)	*sağol* (SAA-al)
you're welcome	*bir şey değil* (bir-shay-DEE-eel)
pardon me	*affedersiniz* (af-feh-DEHR-see-neez)
hello	*merhaba* (MER-hah-bah)
good bye (said by a guest)	*allaha ısmarladık*
good bye (said by a host)	*güle güle* (gew-lay gew-lay)
beautiful, good	*güzel* (ge-ZEL)
okay	*pekiyi* (PEH-kee-yee); "okay" is widely understood; it is also the brand name of a Turkish condom.
What is your name?	*İsminiz nedir?* (ihs-min-niz NEH-dihr?)
My name is ...	*İsmim ...* (IHS-mim ...)
Mr./Sir	*Bay*
Ms/Madam	*Bayan*

Where?

Where is ... ?	*... nerede?*
I'm traveling to ...	*... ya seyahat ediyorum* (ya-say-yah-haht eh-dee-ohr-room)
How near is it?	*Ne kadar yakındır?* (NEH-kah-dahr yah-kuhn-dur?)
restaurant	*lokanta* (loh-KAN-tah)
post office	*postane* (post-AHN-eh)
museum	*müze* (MEW-zeh)
hotel	*otel* (oh-TEL)
room	*yer, oda* (yehr, OH-da)
toilet	*tuvalet* (too-vah-LET)
airport	*hava alanı* (hah-vah ah-LAHN-uh)
bus	*otobüs* (oh-toh-BOOS)
doctor	*doktor* (dohk-TOHR)
grocery	*bakkal* (bahk-KAHL)
pharmacy	*eczane* (ej-ZAHN-eh)
bank	*banka* (BAHN-kah)
police	*polis* (poh-LEES)
left, right	*sol, sağ* (sohl, saa)
passport	*pasaport* (pahs-ah-PORT)
train	*tren* (tren)
ticket	*bilet* (bih-LET)
here, there	*burada, orada* (BOOR-ah-dah, OHR-ah-dah)
closed, open	*kapalı, açık* (kah-pah-LUH, ah-CHUHK)

How Much?

How much is it?	*Kaç para?* (KACH pah-rah)
I want ...	*istiyorum* (ees-tee-YOH-room)
a double room	*iki kişilik* (ee-KEE kee-shee-leek OH-dah)
a twin-bedded room	*çift yataklı oda* (CHEEFT yah-tahk-LUH OH-dah)
I do not want	*yok* (YOKE)
cheap, expensive	*ucuz, pahalı* (oo-JOOz, pah-hah-LUH)
bill	*hesap* (hay-SAHP)
water	*su* (SOOH)

When?

What time is it?	*Saat kaç?* (sah-aht KAHCH)
yesterday	*dün* (dewn)
today	*bugün* (boo-GEWN)
tomorrow	*arm* (YAHR-un)

Numbers: *bir* (1), *iki* (2), *üç* (3), *dört* (4), *beó* (5), *altı* (6), *yedi* (7), *sekiz* (8), *dokuz* (9), *on* (10), *on bir* (11), *on iki* (12) etc., *yirmi* (20), *elli* (50) and *yüz* (100).

The days of the week: *Pazar* (Sun.), *Pazartesi* (Mon.), *Salı* (Tues.), *{it}çaróamba* (Wed.), *Peróembe* (Thurs.), *Cuma* (Fri.), and *Cumartesi* (Sat.).

Problems

I don't understand	*anlamadım* (ahn-LA-mah-dum)
Do you speak English?	*Ingilizçe biliyor musunuz* (in-gih-LEEZ-jeh bihl-ee-OHR moo-soo-nooz)
I don't speak Turkish	*Türkçe bilmiyorum* (TURK-cheh BIHL-mee-yohr-oom)
I'm lost!	*Yolumu kaybettim!* (yoh-loo-moo kay-bet-tim)
I am ill	*Hastaym* (has-tay-yim)
Help!	*İmdat!* (im-DAHT)

INDEX